1 MONTH OF
FREE
READING

at
www.ForgottenBooks.com

ISBN 978-0-331-18937-7
PIBN 11024759

PRACTICAL TREATISE

ON

BILLS OF EXCHANGE,

CHECKS ON BANKERS,

PROMISSORY NOTES,

BANKERS' CASH NOTES,

AND

BANK NOTES.

By JOSEPH CHITTY, Esq.

BARRISTER, OF THE MIDDLE TEMPLE.

THE SIXTH AMERICAN, FROM
THE SIXTH LONDON EDITION,

WITH NOTES

OF ALL THE RECENT DECISIONS AND STATUTES,

AND

AN APPENDIX OF PRECEDENTS.

TO WHICH ARE ADDED

THE CASES DECIDED

IN THE COURTS OF THE UNITED STATES

AND OF THE SEVERAL STATES.

BY A GENTLEMAN OF THE PHILADELPHIA BAR.

PHILADELPHIA:
PRINTED FOR H. C. CAREY & I. LEA,
AND SOLD BY THEIR AGENT, P. H. NICKLIN, LAW BOOKSELLER,
No. 175, CHESTNUT STREET.
1826.

TO

WILLIAM TIDD, Esq.

THIS TREATISE IS DEDICATED,

AS A

TESTIMONY OF RESPECT FOR HIS TALENTS,

AND AN

ACKNOWLEDGMENT OF THE

GREAT OBLIGATIONS WHICH HIS FRIENDSHIP

AND

HIS PROFESSIONAL INSTRUCTIONS,

HAVE CONFERRED ON

HIS PUPIL AND FRIEND,

THE AUTHOR.

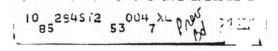

ERRATUM.

406 note (1) line 7, strike out " them "

ADVERTISEMENT

TO THE

SIXTH EDITION.

CONSIDERING the concise form of bills of exchange and promissory notes, it is singular that the law relating to them has of late become more complex and uncertain than formerly. Even since the publication of the fifth edition of this work in A. D. 1818, a great number of decisions have taken place upon new points, and important alterations have been introduced by a modern statute. The insertion of these in the present edition in the type of the last, would have rendered it inconveniently bulky, and therefore a smaller letter has been adopted. There is scarcely any part of the work in which some new decisions, altering the antecedent law, have not been introduced. Those relating to *special acceptances*, and particularly the celebrated case in the House of Lords of Rowe *v.* Young,(a) and the statute 1 & 2 Geo. 4. c. 78,(a) regulating acceptances, are fully noticed. The result of those decisions, and that enactment are, that where a bill, previous to the 1st August, 1821, has been accepted payable at a banker's or particular place, the same is a qualified acceptance, and it must be averred and proved, as well in an action against the acceptor, as against the drawer and indorsers, that it was presented there for payment; though the

---

(a) Rowe *v.* Young, 2 Brod. & Bing. 154. See a useful analysis of, and remarks on the points of this decision, and the operation of the statute 1 & 2 Geo. 4. c. 78, by Mr. Halcomb.

neglect to present on the precise day the bill fell due, or to give notice to the acceptor, would afford no defence in an action against him, unless he can show that he has really sustained loss by the laches of the holder.(a) But the acceptance of a bill since the 1st August, 1821, is to be deemed a general acceptance to all intents and purposes, unless the drawee express in his acceptance that he accepted the bill "payable at a banker's house or other place *only, and not otherwise or elsewhere*." And since that day no acceptance of an *inland* bill is to be sufficient to charge any person unless it be in writing on the bill, or one of its parts when drawn in sets.(b)

J. CHITTY.

MIDDLE TEMPLE,
1st January, 1822.

(a) Rhodes *v.* Gent, Mich. Term, 1821, K. B. *MS.* Parke moved for a new trial. Action drawer against acceptor, accepted before the 1st August, 1821, " payable, when due, at Messrs. P. & H., bankers," presented several days after it was due ; no proof by defendant of money in hands of bankers, nor of any prejudice arising from non-presentment at precise day. Parke contended, upon the authority of Rowe *v.* Young, that this being a special acceptance when due, the court would engraft the condition of presenting it *when due*, otherwise he might be obliged to keep money in his banker's hands an unlimited time ; but the court held that the mere omission to present the bill on the day when due would not discharge the defendant, it not being proved by him that he had sustained any prejudice. But the court added, it would have been otherwise if proof had been adduced by defendant of actual prejudice from the laches of the holder. (Since reported 5 Barn. & Ald. 244.)

(b) 1 & 2 Geo. 4. c. 78. s. 1 & 2.

PREFACE.

CONSIDERING the great circulation of bills of exchange and promissory notes in this kingdom, and the loss to which the parties are subject, if they neglect to observe the rules affecting these securities, together with the frequency of litigation respecting them, there is no branch of the Law so important to the merchant, as well as the lawyer, as that relating to these instruments. An intimate acquaintance with the commercial law in this respect, is particularly essential to the trader, who too frequently, for want of being sufficiently apprized of the rules affecting bills, &c loses the benefit of the security in his hands. It is also of the greatest importance to every professional man, because more ready and immediate advice is required from him in regard to bills and notes, than on almost any other point; and the pleader in particular is called upon, for the utmost expedition in advising and framing the legal proceedings. These considerations have induced the author to offer the following work to the public.

In order to facilitate reference to the particular parts of the treatise, it has been considered expedient, in addition to the General Index at the end of the work, here to give an Analytical Statement of the Contents.

The general division of the Work is into *two* Parts. In the *first*, is considered the *Right*, which may be acquired by a bill of exchange, check, or promissory note; and in the *second*, the *Remedies* to enforce payment of them.

The FIRST PART is divided into *eight chapters*. In the *first* chapter, the author has considered it useful, as tending to elucidate the peculiar properties of bills of exchange, (viz. their assignable quality, and that of their being *prima facie* valid, without proof of their being founded on any consideration,) concisely to state the doctrine relating to the assignment of *choses in action*, and the nesessity in general, for a contract, not under seal, being founded on a sufficient consideration; and he has then proceeded shortly to state the history, general nature, and use of foreign and inland bills, and of checks or drafts on bankers; the resemblance between bills, checks, and promissory notes, and how far the law, relating to each, is applicable to the other; postponing the consideration of promissory notes to the seventh chapter.

In the *second* chapter, the parties to a bill, &c. are stated; and *first*, is considered the capacity of the parties, or who may be concerned in making, or negotiating a bill of exchange; and in particular, how far a corporation, an infant, or a married woman, may be party thereto, and the effect of their incompetency, as to the liability of other parties to the bill. And *secondly*, the number and description of the parties, as drawer, drawee, acceptor, payee, indorser, indorsee, holder, and acceptor, or party paying supra protest; and the mode of becoming a party, as by agent, and who may be such, and how far he may bind his principal, or by the act of a partner and how far partners may bind each other.

In the *third* chapter the form in general, and the most essential requisites of bills, &c. are first stated; as that they be payable at all events, not dependent on any contingency, nor payable out of a particular fund; and that they be for the payment of money only, and not for the payment of money and the performance of some other act, nor in the alternative. These important points are fully considered, and the authorities are stated in the notes. The rules relating to the formation of bills of exchange, &c. and their more particular requisites, are next considered in their natural order, with reference to the parts of a foreign and inland bill, and check; the forms of which are for that purpose introduced. And 1st, The proper stamp, and the consequences of a mistake are considered. 2dly, The superscription of the place where the bill is made. 3dly, The date. 4thly, The superscription of the sum to be paid. 5thly, the insertion of the time of payment. 6thly, The request to pay. 7thly, and 8thly, The clauses to be inserted in foreign bills, drawn in several parts. 9thly, The person to whom payable, and of fictitious payees. 10thly, The insertion of the words, " or order, or bearer." 11thly, The sum to be paid. 12thly, of the words " value received."

Under the last head, it has been considered expedient fully to consider the points, *first*, as to the want or insufficiency of a consideration, and when it may constitute a defence to an action on a bill, &c. and *secondly*, are stated the leading decisions, as to the different descriptions of illegality of the consideration, or of the contract, and how far they may invalidate a bill, &c.; and *thirdly*, is shown what interest, &c. may be taken on discounting a bill.

Then are considered, 13thly, The insertion of the direction to place it to account. 14thly, Of the words, " per advice, &c." 15thly, The subscription of the drawer's name. 16thly, The address to the drawee. And 17thly and 18thly, The place where payment is to be made.

The rules, which govern in the construing, and giving effect to bills, &c.; the delivery of the bill to the payee, and effect thereof, and in general of the receipt of a bill, &c. on account of a pre-existing debt, and the consequences of the alteration of a bill, &c., and the liability of the drawer, are considered in the latter part of this chapter.

In the *fourth* chapter, the indorsement, transfer, and loss of bills, &c. are considered. And 1st, What bills are transferable. 2dly, Who may transfer a bill, and to whom it may be

CHITTY ON BILLS.   2

transferred. 3dly, the time when the tranfer may be made, whether before the bill is complete, or after it is due, or after payment. 4thly, The manner in which a transfer may be made, either by an indorsement in blank, in full, or restrictive, or by delivery. 5thly, the nature of the transfer, the right which it vests in the indorsee, &c. and the liability of the party assigning, whether by indorsement or delivery. And *lastly*, are stated the consequences of the loss of a bill, &c. and what conduct the holder should thereupon pursue, and whether he can sue the parties thereto at law, without producing the bill.

The *fifth* chapter contains *five Sections*. In section I. the presentment of a bill for acceptance; in section II. the nature of acceptances; in section III. non-acceptance, and the conduct which the holder should thereupon pursue; in section IV. protest for better security; and in section v. acceptances *supra protest* are considered.

Section I.—When a presentment for acceptance is necessary, at what time it should be made, and the mode of making it.

Section II.—1st. By whom an acceptance may be made. 2dly, At what time it may be made, and here some recent and very important decisions are collected showing that an acceptance cannot be made before a bill is drawn. 3dly, The form and effect of the different acceptances, whether in writing, or verbal, or absolute, conditional, partial or varying; and what amounts to an acceptance. 4thly, The liability of the acceptor, how far an acceptance is revocable, and how the acceptor's liability may be released or discharged. 5thly, The liability of a party promising to pay a bill.

Section III.—Non-acceptance, and the conduct which the holder must thereupon pursue. 1st, When notice of non-acceptance is necessary; and when the want of it is excusable. 2dly, Of the protest for non-acceptance and of notice, and how it should be given. 3dly, The time when the protest must be made, and the notice given. 4thly, By whom notice must be given. 5thly, To whom it must be given. 6thly, Of the liability of the parties to a bill on the dishonour of it by the drawee. 7thly, How the consequences of neglect to give notice may be waived.

Section IV.—Contains the points relative to the protest for better security.

In Section V.—The nature of an acceptance *supra protest* is considered, and *first*, by whom it may be made; *secondly*, the mode of making it; *thirdly*, the liability of such acceptor; and *lastly*, the nature of his right against the parties for whose honour he accepted the bill.

The *sixth* chapter contains four sections. In section *first*, presentment of a bill, &c. for payment; in section *second*, payment; in section *third*, the conduct to be pursued on non-payment; and in section *fourth*, payment *supra protest* are considered.

SECT. I. Presentment for payment; *first*, when it is necessary, and when the neglect is excusable; *secondly*, by and to whom, and where, the presentment should be made; *thirdly*, the time when a bill, check, or note, should be presented for payment, and herein in general of the mode of computing the time when a bill, &c. is due; of new and old style, or days of grace, of usances, of lunar and calendar months, of bills payable at sight, when due, when checks, bills, &c. payable on demand, or generally, should be presented for payment; and of the time of the day when the presentment should be made, and of leaving the bill on presentment for payment.

SECT. II. Of payment; *first*, by and to whom it may be made, and the consequences of the payment to a party having no interest in the bill, or *to* or *by* a bankrupt; *secondly*, within

xii PREFACE.

what time payment must be made; *thirdly*, how it should be made, and herein of payment by remittance of a bill, or by draft, and of giving up the bill to the acceptor, of the effect of giving time to the acceptor or prior indorser, and of receiving part payment from such parties, of the consequences of proving under a commission, and of compounding with the acceptor; *fourthly*, of the receipt for payment; *fifthly*, of the effect of payment, &c. and how far money paid by mistake may be recovered back.

SECT. III. Of the conduct which the holder should pursue on non-payment; which is in general governed by the same rules, as in the case of non-acceptance; and *first* when notice of non-payment is necessary; *secondly*, the form and mode of giving notice, by protest in the case of a foreign bill, and sometimes of an inland bill, and by notice of non-payment in all cases; *thirdly*, the time when protest must be made and notice given, and here some very important recent decisions are stated relating to the time when notice of non-payment is to be given, and whether the reasonableness thereof be a question of law, or of fact; *fourthly*, by whom notice of non-payment must be given; *fifthly*, to whom; *sixthly*, the liability of the different parties thereupon; *seventhly*, how the consequences of the neglect to give notice may be waived or done away; *eighthly*, of the effect of giving time, or receiving part, and of compounding.

SECT. IV. Of payment *supra protest* for the honour of the drawer, and indorsers, and of the right of the party making such payment.

In the *seventh* chapter of the present edition, checks on bankers are separately considered.

In the *eighth* chapter, the points relating to promissory notes, bankers' notes, and Bank of England notes are considered; and *first*, the origin and nature of *promissory notes*, the effect given to them by the 3d and 4th Ann. c. 9., their resemblance to bills of exchange, and how far the rules applicable to the one affect the other. The form and requisites of these notes, are governed in general by the same rules as those affecting bills, the stamps thereon, and the transfer thereof. *Secondly, bankers' cash notes* are considered, and the stamps thereon, and transfer thereof; and *lastly,* the nature of Bank notes, and the various points relating thereto.

————

The SECOND PART relates to the *remedies* or modes of inforcing payment of a bill, note, &c. and is divided into *seven chapters.*

In the *first* chapter is stated by, and against, whom an action of assumpsit may be supported.

In the *second* chapter, the requisites of the affidavit to hold to bail, and the arrest for a debt due on a bill, &c. the nature and parts of a declaration on a bill, &c. and the common counts applicable to the consideration thereof, and what are proper to be inserted, are considered; and in this chapter, as well as in the Appendix of precedents, with the Notes, the author has endeavoured to state all the points relating to the declaration.

The *third* chapter relates to the staying of proceedings on payment of debt and costs, to judgment by default, reference to the master to compute principal and interest due on the bill, &c. the writ of inquiry, and the defences and pleas in an action on a bill.

In the *fourth* chapter, the evidence in an action on a bill, &c. is fully considered. And *first,* what facts the plaintiff must prove, and *first,* the making of the bill, &c.: *secondly,* that the defendant became party thereto, as acceptor, drawer or indorser; *thirdly,* the plaintiff's interest in the bill, as payee, bearer, indorsee or acceptor *supra protest; fourthly,* the breach of the defendant's contract, as the default of acceptance or payment.

Secondly. The mode of proving these facts, and *first*, of the mode of proving the bill; *secondly*, how the defendant became party thereto; *thirdly*, the plaintiff's interest, and *lastly*, the non-acceptance or non-payment, and notice thereof to the defendant, and in general of the competency of *witnesses*. The evidence to be adduced by the defendant is also considered.

In the *fifth* chapter, the verdict and damages in an action on a bill, &c. are considered, and *first*, how much of the sum payable by the bill, &c. is recoverable when the defendant has not had value for the whole amount, or when the bill, &c. is payable by instalments; *secondly*, what interest; *thirdly*, what expenses, re-exchange, provision, &c. are recoverable.

The *sixth* chapter relates to the action of *debt*, on a bill, &c. and when sustainable.

In the *seventh* chapter the whole law relative to the effect of *bankruptcy* on the holder of a bill, &c. is fully considered.

In the APPENDIX are to be found a few of the forms of such affidavits, declarations on promissory notes, checks on bankers, and on inland and foreign bills, as usually occur in practice. Other forms will be found in the third volume of the Treatise on Pleading. The forms of notices and of judgments on bills, &c. on a reference to the master to compute principal and interest, a list of notaries' fees, the statutes relating to bills of exchange and promissory notes in general, and those relating to small bills and notes, and the stamps on bills and notes, &c. and relating to usury, and an interest table, are also inserted.

Considering the comparative simplicity of declarations on

bills of exchange and promissory notes, and the numberless
actions upon these securities, they are very often incorrect,
and nonsuits frequently occur, either from the insertion of
unnecessary allegations, or from the omission of second counts,
which it may be expedient to insert ; therefore, in this edition,
the appendix of forms has been considerably enlarged, and
notes to each part are given, pointing out what allegations are
necessary or advisable, together with the cases in which it
may be proper to insert more than one count on each bill, &c.

TEMPLE,
January, 1*st*, 1822.

ADVERTISEMENT

TO THE

PRESENT EDITION.

———

IN this Edition, all the notes to the former edition by Judge STORY, and Mr. *Ingraham* are retained, and the authorities down to the present time have been added by a Gentleman of the Philadelphia Bar.

PHILADELPHIA, }
January, 1826. }

NAMES

OF

CITED CASES.*

N. B. The page first referred to generally contains the longest report of the case.

CHITTY ON BILLS.   3

CHITTY ON BILLS. 4

TABLE

OF

AMERICAN AND OTHER CASES

IN THIS EDITION.

———

TABLE

of

AMERICAN AND OTHER CASES

IN THIS EDITION.

TABLE

OF

CONTENTS.

———◆———

PART I.

OF THE RIGHT ACQUIRED BY BILLS, &c.

CHITTY ON BILLS.   6

PART II.

A

TREATISE

ON

BILLS OF EXCHANGE, &c.

PART FIRST.

THE RIGHT ACQUIRED BY BILLS, &c.

CHAPTER I.

THE GENERAL NATURE, UTILITY, AND HISTORY OF BILLS OF EXCHANGE, &c.

A BILL of EXCHANGE is defined by Mr. Justice Blackstone to be an open letter of request, or an order from one person to another, desiring him to pay, on his account, a sum of money therein mentioned, to a third person.[a] It is consequently an assignment to a third person of a debt due to the person drawing the bill, from the person upon whom it is drawn. In other contracts and securities there are generally only two parties, or at most a third as a guarantee ; whereas, on account of the assignable quality of a bill of exchange, there may be, and usually are, many more parties, severally liable for the performance of the contract. The person who makes or draws the bill is termed the *drawer ;* he to whom it is addressed is, before acceptance, called the *drawee,* and afterwards, the *acceptor,* the person in whose favour it is drawn is termed the *payee,* and when he indorses the bill, the *indorser ;* and the person to whom he transfers it is called the *indorsee,* or *holder.*[b] Though this security is entitled to peculiar privileges, yet it is to be considered as a simple contract debt in the course of administration, which an executor or administrator cannot discharge until after satisfying debts by bond, without being guilty of a *devastavit.* And for the same reason a bill of exchange is considered as following the person of the debtor, and as *bona notabilia* where he resides at the time of the creditor's death, whereas a bond, or other specialty, is *bona notabilia,* wherever it may be at the time of such death.[c] And though a bond or bank note may

Definition: General nature and Utility.

---

[a] 2 Bla. Com. 466. Gibson v. Minet, 1 Hen. Bla. 586. Stock v. Mawson, 1 Bos. & Pul. 291. Walwyn v. St. Quintin, 1 Bos. & Pul. 654. Selw. Ni. Pri. 4th ed. 253. Bayl. on Bills, 3d ed. 1. Rex v. Box, 6 Taunt. 324.

[b] Bayl. 2.

[c] Yeomans v. Bradshaw, Carth. 378.

3 Salk 70 and 164. Comb. 392. S. C. Bac. Abr. tit. Executors, E. 2. Com. Dig Administrator, B. 4. The case of Yeomans v. Bradshaw, as reported in Carth. 373, was an action on a bill of exchange, brought by the plaintiff, as administratrix of her late husband, against the drawer; the bill was drawn in London.

B

General
nature and
Utility

be delivered in prospect of death, and be a good donation *mortis causâ*, bills of exchange, promissory notes, and checks on bankers, seem incapable of being the objects of such donation.[d] A bill of exchange also being merely a simple contract, it is affected by the statute of limitations, and must be sued for within six years after it is payable.[e] And being a *chose in action*, and a mere security for a debt, it is not to be considered as goods and chattels, and it therefore does not pass by a bequest of all the testator's "property" in a particular house, though bank notes would have passed, they being *quasi* cash;[f] and upon the same principle, a bank note or bill cannot be taken in execution, or as a distress for rent.[g] And the accepting of a bill or note, in satisfaction of a specialty debt or demand for rent, at most only suspends the remedy on the former security, and does not entirely defeat it.[h]

A bill of exchange is a security originally invented amongst merchants in different countries for the more easy and safe remittance of money from the one to the other, and has since been extended to commercial transactions in this kingdom.[i] The instance put by Mr. Justice Blackstone of the utility of the instrument, is this, "If A. live in Jamaica, and owe B. who lives in England, £1000. now if C. be going from England to Jamaica, he may advance B. this £1000. and take a bill of exchange, drawn by B. in England upon A. in Jamaica, and receive it when he comes thither: thus, B. receives his debt at any distance of place by transferring it to C., who carries over his money in paper credit, without the risk of robbery or loss." In the origin of bills of exchange, it is probable that their principal utility was the safe transfer of property from one place to another, but since the great increase of commerce, they have become the signs of valuable property, and equi-

The defendant craved oyer of the letters of administration, which were granted by the Bishop of Durham. Upon demurrer, it was insisted, that a bill of exchange was only a simple contract debt, and so followed the person of the debtor, wherever he might be, and that the right of granting administration belonged to the ordinary of the place where the debtor was at the time of the death of the intestate, and that the administration was void, and of which opinion were the court, and gave judgment for the defendant; and see the judgment of Holt, C. J. in the same case, 3 Salk. 70.

[d] Miller v. Miller, 3 P. W. 356. Ward v. Turner, 2 Ves. sen. 442. Tate v. Hilbert, 2 Ves. jun. 111. Lawson v. Lawson, 1 P. W. 441. 1 Roper on Leg. 2d ed. 3. Toller Executors, 3d ed. 234, 5, where see the exceptions. Miller v. Miller, 3 P. W. 356. A person, after having made his will and about an hour before his death, delivered to his wife two bank notes for 300l. each, and another note for 100l. (not being a cash note, or payable to bearer,) adding, that he had not sufficiently provided for her. On a bill filed in the name of the infant son, being the residuary legatee, against the widow and executors, for an account of the testator's personal estate, it was insisted, that the 600l. was in payment of a legacy given her by the testator in a codicil to

his will, and that, with regard to the other note for 100l., which was not payable to bearer, that was merely a *chose in action*, and consequently could not pass by a delivery thereof. Per Master of the Rolls, the gift of the 600l., contained in the bank notes, was a *donatio causâ mortis*, which operates as such, though made to a wife, for it is in nature of a legacy, though it need not be proved in the spiritual court as part of the testator's will. But as to the note for 100l., which was merely a *chose in action*, and must still be sued in the name of the executors, that cannot take effect as a *donatio causâ mortis*, inasmuch as no property could pass therein by the delivery. See also Ward v. Turner, 2 Ves. sen. 442. and Tate v. Hilbert, 2 Ves. jun. 120, in which it was held, that a check on a banker, delivered by J. S. on his death-bed, did not take effect as a *donatio causâ mortis.* But see 1 P. W. 441, and Toller's Law of Executors, 3d ed. 234, 5.

[e] Renew v. Axton, Carth. 3.
[f] Flemming v. Brook, 1 Sch. & Lef. 318. Stewart v. Marquis of Bute, 11 Ves. 662.
[g] Francis v. Nash, Cas. Temp. Hardw. 53. Knight v. Criddle, 9 East, 48.
[h] Curtis v. Rush, 2 Ves. & Bea. 446. Drake v. Mitchell, 3 East, 251. Harris v. Shipway, Bul. N. P. 182.
[i] 2 Bla Com. 466, 7.

General nature and Utility.

valent to specie, enlarging the capital stock of wealth in circulation, and thereby facilitating and increasing the trade and commerce of the country.[k] The trader whose capital may not be sufficient to enable him to pay ready money for the commodity which he purchases, on account of his not having the means of immediately obtaining payment of the debts due to him from others, and who might find a difficulty on his own individual security, to purchase goods, or obtain money for the purposes of his trade, by drawing a bill on one of his debtors payable at a future period, may obtain the goods on money on the credit of such bill ; the vendor of the goods, to whom the bill is handed as a security, may also, in his turn, obtain goods or money, in the way of his trade, on the credit of the bill, and the bill may have the same effect in different person's hands, to whom it may be transferred by indorsement or otherwise. This security is preferable to many others of a more formal nature, for each of the parties to a bill, by simply writing his name upon it, either as drawer, acceptor, or indorser, guarantees the due payment of it at maturity, and the consideration in respect of which he became a party to it can be rarely inquired into ; whereas, in the case of a formal guarantee, the Statute against Frauds[l] requires the consideration to be expressed, and other matters of form, which frequently render an intended guarantee wholly inoperative.[m] So with respect to interest, it is a better security than a bond, for when the principal and interest in a bond equal the amount of the penalty, the interest must thenceforth cease, for the obligor in a bond is not answerable in the whole beyond the amount of the penalty.[n] From the circumstance also of the exposure of the contract to the public eye, there is a stronger stimulus on every party to a bill, to take care that it be duly honoured ; whereas punctual payment of a guaranty or bond is not so frequent, and consequently less to be relied on in commerce, where certainty is so essential to the welfare of the merchant.

There are, however, some disadvantages accompanying this security, compared with others, and principally, that is in case of the dishonour of the bill by the person on whom it is drawn, the holder must immediately give notice of the non-payment to all the other parties, or he will lose the benefit of his security, whereas in the case of a guaranty, such nice and exact conduct on the part of the creditor is not in general requisite.[o] Again, in case of death, a bill of exchange being a simple contract, is not entitled to the same priority of payment out of the assets of the deceased as a bond ; nor is there the same expeditious or extensive mode of obtaining payment as in case of a bond, warrant of attorney, Statute Staple, or Statute Merchant.[p]

The pernicious effects of a fabricated credit, by the undue use of

[k] Per Eyre, C. J. Gibson v. Minet, 1 Hen. Bla.618.

[l] 29 Car. 2 ch. 3. s. 4.

[m] Wain v. Walter, 5 East, 10. In this case it was held, that an engagement in writing to pay the debt of a third person at an hour named, in consideration of the creditor suspending proceedings in an action till that time, but which consideration did not appear on the face of the written engagement, was void on that account ; but in Ex parte Minet, 14 Ves. 189, and in Ex parte Gardom, 12 Ves. 286. this

doctrine was denied ; and see La Morris v. Stacy, Holt N. P. C. 158, in notes.

[n] Hefford v. Alger, 1 Taunt. 220. Wild v. Clarkson, 6 T. R. 303. Ex parte Mills, 2 Ves. jun. 301. Clark v. Seaton, 6 Ves. 411. but observe, that in an action of debt on a judgment recovered on a bond, interest may be recovered in damages beyond the penalty of the bond, M'Clure v. Dunkin, 1 East, 436.

[o] Warrington v. Furbor, 8 East, 245. but see Philips v. Astling, 2 Taunt. 206. See these cases, post.

[p] 2 Saund. 70. a. and b. in notes.

General nature and Utility. accommodation bills of exchange, drawn out of the ordinary course of trade, have been too much felt to require any observation; the use of them, where there is no real demand subsisting between the different parties, is injurious to the public as well as to the parties concerned in the negotiation;ᵃ unless in cases where, from some sudden and unexpected event, a particular branch of commerce may be affected, and the trader unable to bring his commodities to a fair market in time to meet the payments for which he has to provide. In these cases, by the temporary assistance of friends, through the medium of bills of exchange, his credit may be saved, and he may be enabled to hold his goods till some fair opportunity of sale presents itself. The use of fictitious names to bills has not been unfrequent, but this practice is not only censurable, but in some cases punishable criminally.ʳ

Peculiar Properties of Bills, &c. The various advantages which commerce derives from the use of bills of exchange, have induced our courts of justice to allow them certain peculiar privileges in order to give full effect to their utility. These are, *first*, that although a bill of exchange is a *chose in action*, yet it may be *assigned* so as to vest the *legal* as well as equitable interest therein, in the indorsee or assignee, and to entitle him to sue thereon *in his own name*. And *secondly*, that although a bill of exchange, &c. is not a specialty, but merely a simple contract, yet a *sufficient consideration* is *implied* from the nature of the instrument, and its existence, in fact, is rarely necessary to be proved.ᵉ

The *first* of these privileges is of most essential importance in various points of view, and principally that a release by the drawer to the acceptor, or a set-off or cross demand due from the former to the latter, cannot affect the right of action of the payee or indorsee; because the *legal* and not the mere equitable interest is vested in such payee or indorsee, and the action is sustainable in his own name; whereas suits upon bonds, and most other *choses in action*, must be in the name of the original obligee; and though it be apparent that he sues merely as a trustee for another to whom he has assigned his interest, yet a release from him, or a set-off due from him to the obligor, may be an effectual bar to the action.ᵗ The *second* of these privileges is also of great importance. In general, an action cannot be supported upon a contract not under seal, without alleging in pleading, and proving on the trial, that the contract was made for a sufficient consideration; but in the case of bills of exchange, promissory notes, &c. a sufficient consideration is *presumed*, and the validity of the bill, &c. cannot in general be disputed on account of the want of sufficient consideration, when it is in the hands of a third person who has given value for it.

As it may tend to elucidate the properties of bills of exchange, and other negotiable instruments of that nature, we will shortly examine the doctrine relating to the assignment of *choses in action;* and the necessity in general for a sufficient consideration to give effect to a contract.

Doctrine as to the assignment of *choses in action.*ᵘ The first peculiar privilege of a Bill of Exchange is *its assignable quality*, and which is in direct opposition to a very ancient rule of law, the founders of which refused to sanction or give effect to the transfer

ᵃ Per Ld. Eldon, in Ex parte Wilson, 11 Ves. 411.
ʳ See post.
ᵉ Bishop v. Young, 2 Bos. & Pul. 79.

ᵗ Bauerman v. Radenius, 7 T. R. 663.
ᵘ As to the assignment of *choses in action* in general, see Master v. Miller, 4 T. R. 340. In Williamson v. Thompson, 16 Ves.

of any possibility, right, or any other *chose in action* (which is defined to be a right not reduced into possession,[x]) to a stranger; on the ground that such alienations tended to increase maintenance of litigation, and afforded means to powerful men to purchase rights of action, and thereby enable them to oppress indigent debtors, whose original creditors would not perhaps have sued them.[y] Our ancestors were so anxious to prevent alienation of *choses*, or rights in action, that we find it enacted by the 32 H. 8. c. 9. (which, it is said, was in affirmance of the common law,[z]) that no person should buy or sell, or by any means obtain any right or title to any manors, lands, tenements, or hereditaments, unless the person contracting to sell, or his ancestor, or they by whom he or they claim the same, had been in *possession* of the same, or of the reversion or remainder thereof, for the space of one year before the contract: and this statute was adjudged to extend to the assignment of a copyhold estate,[a] and of a chattel interest, as a lease for years, of land, whereof the grantor was not in possession.[b] At what time this doctrine, which, it is said, had relation originally only to *landed* estates,[c] was first adjudged to be equally applicable to the assignment of a mere *personal* chattel not in possession, it is not easy to decide: it seems, however, to have been so settled at a very early period of our history, as the works of our oldest text writers, and the reports contain numberless observations and cases on the subject. Lord Coke says,[d] that it is one of the maxims of the common law, that no right of action can be transferred, "because, under colour thereof, pretended titles might be granted to great men, whereby right might be trodden down, and the weak oppressed, which the common law forbiddeth." Accordingly we find, that judgment was arrested in an action on a bond conditioned for the performance of articles of agreement, which contained a covenant that the defendant should assign certain bonds to the plaintiff for his own use, on the ground that such condition and covenant amounted to maintenance.[e] And although it was decided, that the king, in respect of his prerogative, might transfer a right of action,[f] yet it was afterwards ruled, that his assignee had no such power.[g]

This doctrine, however strictly adhered to in our courts of law, was not adopted by our courts of *equity* :[h] for though it is said to have been decided on the 11th James 1.[i] that the assignee of a covenant could not sue in a court of equity to enforce performance, because it was against law to assign a covenant, yet that seems to be an insulated case; and no other authority is to be found, where a court of equity has refused to

Margin note: Doctrine as to the assignment of *choses in action.*

413. it was held, that the indorsement of an Indian Certificate did not pass the legal interest. In Glynn *v.* Baker, 13 East, 509. it was held, that an India Bond was not assignable, but this has been since altered by 51 Geo. 3. c. 64. which makes them assignable, and enables the assignee to sue in his own name.

[x] Termes de la ley, tit. Chose in Action. 2 Bla. Com. 442. In other words, " the interest in a contract, which, in case of non-performance, can only be reduced into *beneficial* possession by an action or suit."

[y] Co. Lit. 214. 265 a. n. 1. 232 b. n. 1. 2 Rol. Ab. 45, 6. Godb. 81. Termes de la ley, tit. Chose in Action. Scholey *v.* Daniel, 2 Bos. & Pul. 541.

[z] Partridge *v* Strange, Plowd. 88.

[a] Kite and Queinton's case, 4 Co. 26 a.
[b] Partridge *v.* Strange, Plowd. 88. As to a possibility in land, see Jones *v.* Roe, 3 T. R. 88. 1 Hen. Bla. 30. S. C. Cullen, 178.

[c] 2 Woodd. 388.

[d] Co. Lit. 214 a. See also Scholey v. Daniel, 2 Bos. & Pul. 541.
[e] Hodson *v.* Ingram, Aleyn. 60. *et vide* 2 Rol. Abr. 45, l. 40.
[f] Co. Lit. 232. b. n. 1. Breverton's case, 1 Dyer, 30. b. pl. 28. The King *v.* Wendham, Cro. Jac. 82.
[g] The King *v.* Twine, Cro. Jac. 180. Kingdom *v.* Jones, Skin. 6. 26.
[h] Per Buller, J. in Master *v.* Miller, 4 T. R. 310.
[i] 1 Rol. Abr. 376. l. b.

Doctrine as to the assignment of a *chose in action*, provided such assign-
as to the ment were made for a sufficient consideration.[k] A court of equity
assignment having it in its power to decree according to the justice of every case,
of *choses in* there could have been no danger of maintenance being increased by its
action. given effect to such assignments; we therefore find a great number of
cases where decrees have been made in favour of such assignees.[l]

In courts of *law*, the *equitable* interest of the assignee of a *chose in
action* seems to have been recognized as far back as the middle of the
last century, when we find it said by one of the judges,[m] "that if an
assignee of a *chose in action*, have an equity, that equity should be no
exile to the courts of common law." In another case also, the court
speak[n] of an assignment of an apprentice, or an assignment of a bond,
as things valid between the parties, and to which they must give their
sanction; and an assignment of a *chose in action* has always been deemed
a sufficient consideration for a promise,[o] although the debt assigned was
uncertain.[p] So, indeed it was decided, that where the obligee has assigned over a bond, and afterwards become a bankrupt, he might nevertheless bring an action on the bond;[q] and that in an action upon a bond
given to the plaintiff in trust for another, the defendant may set off a
debt due from the person beneficially interested, in like manner, as if
the action had been brought by the *cestui que trust*.[r] But though courts
of law have gone the length of taking notice of assignments of *chose in
action*, and of giving effect to them, yet in almost every case they have
adhered to the formal objection that the action should be brought in the
name of the assignor, and not in the name of the assignee; the consequence of which rule is, that the defendant may give in evidence a release, declaration, or admission of the plaintiff on the record, to defeat
the action, although it be evident such plaintiff is but a mere trustee for
a third person.[s] It has been observed, that the substance of the rule
being done away, there can be no use or convenience in preserving the
shadow of it; for where a third person is permitted to acquire the interest in a thing, whether he bring the action in his own name or in the
name of the assignor, does not seem to effect the question of maintenance.[t] However, in a late case,[u] Lord Kenyon expressed his determination not to sanction the assignment of a *chose in action*, so as to

[k] Vin. Abr. tit. Maintenance, B. 2 Rol.
Abr. 45, 46. Co. Lit. 232.

[l] Baldwin *v.* Rochford, 1 Wils. 229.
Wright *v.* Wright, 1 Ves. 411. 412. Peters
v. Soame, 2 Vern. 428. Baldwin *v.* Bil-
lingsley, id. 540. Crouch *v.* Martin, id.
595. Cole *v.* Jones, id. 692. Carteret
(Lord) *v.* Paschel, 3 P. W. 199; and it has
lately been decided, that an equitable assignment of a debt may be by parol as
well as by deed, Heath *v.* Hall, 4 Taunt.
326.

[m] In Kingdom *v.* Jones, 33 Car. 2. Skin.
6, 7. Sir T. Jones, 150. S. C.

[n] The King against the Parish of Aick-
less, 12 Mod. 554.

[o] 1 Rol. Abr. 29. Loder *v.* Cheslyn,
Sid. 212. Lewis *v.* Wallis, Sir. T. Jones,
222. Meredith *v.* Short, 1 Salk. 25. Banfill *v.* Leigh, 8 T. R. 571. Israel *v.* Douglass, 1 Hen. Bla. 239.

[p] Moulsdale *v.* Birchall, 2 Bla. Rep. 820.

[q] Winch *v.* Keeley, 1 T. R. 619. Carpenter *v.* Marnell, 3 Bos. & Paul. 40.

[r] Bottomley *v.* Brook, and Rudge *v.*
Birch, cited in 1 T. R. 621. and in 4 T. R.
841. *sed vid* Bauerman *v.* Radenius, 7 T.
R. 663. But the court refused to allow a
defendant to set off a bond debt of the
plaintiff assigned to him by a third person, to whom and for whose use it was
originally given, Wake *v.* Tinkler, 16 East.
36.

[s] Bauerman v. Radenius, 7 T. R. 663.
Banfill *v.* Leigh, 8 T. R. 571. Jones *v.*
Dunlop, id. 596. Offly *v.* Ward, 1 Lev.
235. Johnson *v.* Collings, 1 East, 104. *et
vide* Medlicot's case, Sel. Cas. 161.

[t] Per Buller, J. in Master *v.* Miller,
4 T. R. 310. *et vide* Winch *v.* Keeley.
1 T. R. 621. Israel *v.* Douglass, 1 Hen.
Bla. 239. and Banfill *v.* Leigh, 8 T. R.
571.

[u] Johnson *v.* Collings, 1 East, 104. Whitwell *v.* Bennett, 3 Bos. & Paul. 559.

allow the assignee to sue in his own name.(11)   The consequence of this
doctrine is, that if an instrument which is not assignable at law, so as to
pass the legal interest, be indorsed by the person to whom it is payable
to his agent to whom he is indebted generally, without any specific appropriation, the agent, in case of the death of the principal, will have no
legal or equitable interest in the instrument towards satisfaction of his
debt, but must restore it to the executor.[x]

Doctrine
as to the
assignment
of *choses in*
action.

Even at the earliest period of our history, the doctrine relating to the
assignment of *choses in action* was found to be too great a clog on commercial intercourse ; an exception was therefore soon allowed in favour
of mercantile transactions.   It was the observation of the learned and
elegant commentator on the English laws, that in the infancy of trade,
when the bulk of national wealth consisted of real property, our courts
did not often condescend to regulate personalty ; but, as the advantages
arising from commerce were gradually felt, they were anxious to encourage it by removing the restrictions by which the transfer of interests in
it was bound.   On this ground, the custom of merchants, whereby a
foreign bill of exchange is assignable by the payee to a third person, so
as to vest in him the *legal* as well as equitable interest therein, was recognised and supported by our courts of justice in the fourteenth century; and the custom of merchants, rendering an inland bill transferrable,
was established in the seventeenth century.   In short, our courts,
anxiously attending to the interests of the community, have, in favour

[x] Williamson *v.* Thompson, 16 Ves. 443.

---

(11) Courts of law now take notice of assignments of choses in action, and afford them
every protection not inconsistent with the principles and proceedings of tribunals acting
according to the course of the common law.   They endeavour in these respects to apply,
as far as may properly be done, the rules and doctrines recognised in Courts of Equity.
They will not therefore give effect to a release procured by the original debtor under a
covenous combination with the assignor in fraud of his assignee; nor permit the assignor
injuriously to interfere with the conduct of any suit commenced by the assignee to enforce the rights, which passed under the assignment.   *Welsh* v. *Manderville,* 1 Wheaton,
233.   See, as to the right of the United States to sue in their own name upon a bill indorsed to their agent, *Dugan* v. *United States,* 3 Wheaton, 172.   See also *Skelding et*
al. v. *Warren,* 15 Johns. 270.
   Upon these principles a release procured after a notice of the assignment has been held
to be a nullity.   *Andrews* v. *Beecher,* 1 John. Cas. 411.   *Littlefield* v. *Storey,* 3 John.
Rep. 426.   *Legh* v. *Legh,* 1 Bos. & Pull. 447.   *Raymond* v. *Squire,* 11 John. Rep. 47.
So a satisfaction of a judgment entered up by the assignor after the assignment has been
vacated.   *Wardell* v. *Eden,* 2 John. Cas. 121. 258.   8. C. 1 John. Rep. 531. *note.*   So
a dismissal of a suit or a retraxit entered up without the consent of the assignee will be no
bar to a subsequent suit.   *Welsh* v. *Mandeville, ut supra.*   And if the fact of the assignment be known to the court, it will not suffer the defendant, whose name is used, to
discontinue the suit without the agreement of the assignee.   *M'Cullum* v. *Coxe,* 1 Dall.
Rep. 139.
   There are many other cases in which the rights of the assignee have been recognised
and enforced in suits at law; but it is foreign to the purposes of this note to give them a
minute analysis.   The reader will receive further information on the subject by consulting
the subjoined cases.   *Perkins* v. *Parker,* 1 Mass. Rep. 117.   *Wakefield* v. *Martin,* 3
Mass. Rep. 558.   *Dix* v. *Cobb,* 4 Mass. Rep. 508.   *Dawes* v. *Boylston,* 9 Mass. Rep.
337.   *Crocker* v. *Whitney,* 10 Mass. Rep. 316.   *Wood* v. *Partridge,* 11 Mass. Rep.
488.   *Alner* v. *George,* 1 Camp. N. P. 392.   *Tuttle* v. *Beebee,* 8 John. Rep. 152.
Meghan v. *Mills,* 9 John. Rep. 64.   *Brisban* v. *Caines,* 10 John. Rep. 45.   *Inglis* v.
Inglis's Executors, 2 Dall. Rep. 45.   *Roussett* v. *The Insurance Company of North*
America, 1 Binn. 429.   *Woodbridge* v. *Perkins,* 3 Day's Rep. 564.   *Da Costa* v.
Shrewsbury, 1 Bay's Rep. 211.   *Administrators of Compty* v. *Aiken,* 2 Bay's Rep. 481.
Raymond v. *Squire,* 11 John. Rep. 488.   *Anderson* v. *Van Allen,* 12 John. Rep. 843.
Mowry v. *Todd,* 12 Mass. Rep. 281.   *Jones* v. *Witter,* 13 Mass. Rep. 304.   *Bowman*
v. *Wood,* 15 Mass. Rep. 534.   *Martin* v. *Hawkes,* 15 Johns. 405.

Doctrine of commerce, adopted a less technical mode of considering *personalty* than *reality*; and, in support of commercial transactions, have establish-ed the law merchant, which is a system founded on the rules of equity, and governed in all its parts by plain justice and good faith.[y]

Doctrine as to the assignment of choses in action.

Having thus endeavoured to point out the peculiar properties of a bill of exchange, in respect of its being assignable so as to give the holder a right of action in his own name, it will be proper to make a few obser-vations on the second privilege by which it is distinguished from other simple contracts, *that of its importing a consideration unless the contrary be shown.*[z]

Of the distinction between different contracts as to considera-tion, and which is presumed in the case of a bill of exchange, &c.

Contracts are of three descriptions. 1st. Matter of record. 2dly. Specialty. 3dly. Parol or simple contracts. The *first* of these, viz. the judgment of, or a recognizance acknowledged before a court of re-cord, on account of its being sanctioned by such a tribunal, cannot be impeached, or the propriety of it questioned, in any action on the judg-ment, but only by writ of error. Nor can there be any allegation in pleading against the validity of a record, though there may be against its operation. *Secondly. Specialties* rank next in point of estimation. These, on account of the deliberate mode in which they are supposed to be made and executed, have always been holden to bind the party making them, although they were executed without adequate conside-ration,[a] and consequently it is not incumbent on the plaintiff in an ac-tion upon a deed to state or prove upon what cause or for what conside-ration[b] it was made; and though the defendant may be at liberty to avail himself of the *illegality* in the consideration, it is incumbent on him to state it in pleading, and to establish it by evidence.[c] But the *third* description, namely, *parol or simple contracts*, which include as well unsealed written contracts as those which are merely verbal, are not in general entitled to such respect, because the law presumes that such contracts may have been made inadvertently, and without sufficient reflection,[d] and therefore, in general, they will not be enforced, unless the plaintiff can prove that they were made for a sufficient consideration.[e] It is otherwise, however, in the case of a bill of exchange,[f] it be-ing scarcely ever necessary for the *plaintiff* to prove that he gave a consi-deration for it; and the *defendant* is not at liberty to prove that he re-ceived no consideration, unless in an action brought against him by the person with whom he was immediately concerned in the negotiation of

When a considera-tion not es-sential to validity of a bill of ex-change, &c.

[y] Per Buller, J. in Master *v.* Miller. 4 T. R. 342.

[z] Per Lord Ellenborough, C. J. in Phil-liskirk *v.* Pluckwell, 2 M. & S. 395.

[a] See the argument in Sharington *v.* Strotton, Plowd. 308, where it is said, that deeds are received as a lien, final to the party making them, although he re-ceived no consideration; in respect of the deliberate mode in which they are suppo-sed to be made and executed, for 1st, the deed is *prepared and drawn*; then the *seal* is affixed; and lastly, the contracting party *delivers* it, which is the consummation of his resolution.

[b] Fellowes *v.* Taylor, 7 T. R. 477. Bunn *v.* Guy, 4 East, 200.

[c] Petrie *v.* Hanney, 3 T. R. 424.

[d] Fonbl. 329. 333. Sharington *v.* Strot-ton, Plowd. 308.

[e] See the case of Rann *v.* Huges, 7 T. R. 350, in which it was adjudged, that all contracts are by the law of England, dis-tinguished into agreements by specialty, and agreements by parol, and that there is not any such third class as contracts in writing; if they be merely written, and not specialties, they are *parol*, and a con-sideration must be proved. See also same case in 7 Bro. Parl. Cas. 550. Parker *v.* Baylis, 2 Bos. & Pul. 77. Johnson *v.* Col-lings, 1 East, 104. Sharington *v.* Strotton, Plowd. 308. Petrie *v.* Hanney, 3 T. R. 421.

[f] Simmonds *v.* Parminter, 1 Wils. 180.

the instrument,[g] or by a person who has given no value for it. In this respect, therefore, a bill of exchange, although it is not a specialty,[h] yet it carries with it the same presumption of a consideration as a bond, or other specialty, particularly when it is in the hands of a third person.[i] It is not, however, owing to the *form* of a bill of exchange, nor to the circumstance of its being in *writing*, that the law gives it this effect, but in order to strengthen and facilitate that commercial intercourse which is carried on through the medium of this species of security; for, notwithstanding a contract be in writing, it is essential to the validity of it, that it should in all cases be founded on a sufficient consideration, unless the writing, from its being of the highest solemnity, imports a consideration, or unless it be negotiable at law, and the interests of third persons are involved in its efficacy.(14)

When a consideration not essential to the validity of a bill of exchange, &c.

Having endeavoured to state two of the most peculiar properties of a bill of exchange, namely, its assignable quality, and its validity in the hands of a *bonâ fide* holder, though made without consideration, it may be proper to inquire concisely into the history, general nature, and use of these instruments.

The history, &c. of foreign bills.

Bills of exchange are foreign or inland. *Foreign*, when drawn by a person abroad upon another in England, or *vice versâ;* and *inland*, when both the drawer and the drawee reside within this kingdom.

It seems extremely doubtful at what period, or by whom, *foreign bills of exchange* were first invented. The elementary writers differ on the subject. It is said by Pothier,[k] that there is no vestige among the Romans of bills of exchange, or of any contract of exchange; for though it appears that Cicero directed one of his friends at Rome, who had money to receive at Athens, to cause it to be paid to his son at that place, and that friend accordingly wrote to one of his debtors at Athens,

[g] Guichard *v.* Roberts, 1 Bla. Rep. 445.
Lewis *v.* Cosgrave, 2 Taunt. 2.
[h] Yeomans *v.* Bradshaw, 3 Salk. 70.
ante, 2.
[i] Philliskirk *v.* Pluckwell, 2 M. & S. 96.
[k] Traites de Droit. Civil, tit. Traité du Contrat de Change, pl. 6.

(14.) The doctrines contained in this paragraph have been frequently recognised in the United States. In general, a written promise requires a consideration no less than a parol one. *Hosmer* v. *Hollenbeck*, 2 Day's Rep. 22. And a note made without consideration is a nude pact, and void as between the original parties to it. *Pearson* v. *Pearson*, 7 John. Rep. 26.—*Stockpole* v. *Arnold*, 11 Mass. Rep. 27. So if the consideration have totally failed. Dennison *v.* Bacon, 10 John. Rep. 198. *Tappen* v. *Van Wagenen*, 3 John. Rep. 465. *Fowler* v. *Shearer*, 7 Mass. Pep. 14. *Livingston* v. *Hastie*, 2 Caine's Rep. 247.
Every note within the statute imports a consideration unless the contrary appear on the face of the note itself. *Goshen Turnpike Company*, 9 John. Rep. 217. *Ten Eyck.* v. *Vanderpool*, 8 John. Rep. 120. And the words "value received" in a note not within the statute are *primâ facie* evidence of a consideration sufficient to cast on the defendant the burthen of proof of the want of a consideration. *Jerome* v. *Whitney*, 7 John. Rep. 321. *contra.*—*Lansing* v. *M'Killip*, 3 Cain. Rep. 286. The holder of a bill, check, or note, is *primâ facie* deemed the rightful owner of it, and need not prove a consideration given for it, unless where circumstances of suspicion attach to the transaction. *Cruger* v. *Armstrong*, 3 John. Cas. 5. *Conrey* v. *Warren*, 3 John. Cas. 259. 3 Wheaton 182. And an indorsement of a note is *primâ facie* evidence of being made for full value; and it is in general incumbent on the defendant to show the real consideration if it was an inadequate one. *Biddle* v. *Mandeville*, 5 Cranch's Rep. 322. The drawer of a Bill of Exchange may rebut the presumption of his liability, in case of non-payment by the drawee, by proving that between the payee and himself, there was no consideration, 1 Serg. & Rawle, 32.

CHITTY ON BILLS.   C

The histo-
ry, &c. of
foreign
bills.

and ordered him to pay a sum of money to Cicero's son, yet it is observed that this mode amounted to nothing more than a mere order, or mandate, and was not that species of pecuniary negotiation which is carried on through the medium of a bill of exchange; nor does it appear that the commerce of the Romans was carried on by means of this instrument; for we find by one of their laws,[1] that a person lending money to a merchant who navigated the seas, was under the necessity of sending one of his slaves to receive of his debtor the sum lent, when the debtor arrived at his destined port, which would certainly have been unnecessary, if commerce, through the medium of bills of exchange, had been in use with them. Most of our modern writers have asserted (probably on the authority of Montesquieu,[m]) that these instruments were invented and brought into general use by the Jews and Lombards when banished for their usury, in order, with the secrecy necessary to prevent confiscation, to draw their effects out of France and England, to those countries in which they had chosen, or been compelled to reside; but Mr. Justice Blackstone says,[n] this opinion is erroneous, because the Jews were banished out of Guienne in the year 1287, and out of England in the year 1290;[o] and in the year 1236, the use of paper credit was introduced in the Mogul empire in China.[p] Other authors have attributed the invention to the Florentines, when being driven out of their country by the faction of the Gebelings, they established themselves at Lyons and other towns.[q] On the whole, however, there is no certainty on the subject, though it seems clear, foreign bills were in use in the fourteenth century, as appears from a Venetian law of that period; and an inference drawn from the statute 5 Rich. 2. st. 1. 2.[r] warrants the conclusion, that foreign bills were introduced into this country previously in the year 1381.

[11]

The mode of transmitting money from one country to another by means of these instruments, being once discovered, the advantages derived from it soon induced merchants universally to adopt it; and from thence it very early grew into a custom, which seems to have been judicially sanctioned in this country at a very early period of our history, though no earlier decision relative to the custom can be found, than in Jas. I.[s] where it was adjudged, that an acceptance raised an *assumpsit* in law, for the breach of which an action on the case would lie. However, as our courts did not at first conceive it necessary to the encouragement of commerce, that this exception to the rule relative to *choses in action*, should be carried any further than to foreign bills drawn merely for the purposes of trade, we find that formerly they would only give effect to bills made between merchant strangers and English merchants,[t] however, it was soon extended to all traders, and finally, to all persons, whether traders or not.[u]

The histo-
ry, use, &c.
of *inland*
bills of exchange.

INLAND BILLS OF EXCHANGE, (which are so called because they are drawn and payable in this country,) according to Lord C. J. Holt's

[1] *De nautico fœnere.*
[m] Esp. L. 21. c. 16. n. 1.
[n] 2 Bla. Com. 467.
[o] 2 Carte. Hist. Engl. 203. 206.
[p] The only authority in support of this assertion is the 4 Mod. Un. Hist. 499.
[q] Poth. pl. 7.
[r] Claxton v. Swift, 2 Show. 411. 494.

[s] Martin v. Boure, Cro. Jac. 6. Oaste v. Taylor, Cro. Jac. 306. 1 Rol. Abr. 6. Hussey v. Jacob, Ld. Raym. 88.
[t] Oaste v. Taylor, Cro. Jac. 306, 7.
[u] Per Treby, C. J. in Bromwich v. Loyd, 2 Lutw. 1585. Sarsfield v. Witherly, 2 Vent 295. Comb. 45. 152. S. C. Cramlington v. Evans, 2 Vent. 310.

opinion, did not originate at a much earlier period than the reign of <sub-margin>The histo-ry, use, &c. of inland bills of exchange.</sub-margin> Charles the Second.[x] They were at first, like foreign bills, more restricted in their operation than they are at present ; for it was deemed essential to their validity, that a special custom for the drawing and accepting them should exist between the towns in which the drawer and acceptor lived ; or if they lived in the same town, that such a custom should exist therein.[y](16) At first also effect was only given to the custom when the parties were merchants, though afterwards extended, as in the case of foreign bills, to all persons, whether traders or not.[z] And even after the general custom had been established, and it had been adjudged, that all persons having capacity to contract, might make them, a distinction was taken with respect to form, between bills made payable to *order*, and bills made payable to *bearer ;* for it was once thought, that no action could be maintained on a bill payable to the *order* of a certain person, by that person himself, on the ground that he had only an authority to indorse ; and those payable to *bearer* were at first thought not to be negotiable in any case. These distinctions, however, have long been held to be without foundation ; and on the whole, as observed by Mr. Justice Blackstone,[a] although formerly foreign bills of exchange were more favourably regarded in the eye of the law than inland, as being thought of more public concern in the advancement of trade and commerce, yet now, by various judicial decisions, and by two statutes, the 9th and 10th W. 3. c. 17. and the 3d and 4th Anne, c. 9. inland bills stand nearly on the same footing as foreign; and what was the law and custom of merchants with regard to one, and taken notice of as such, is now by these statutes enacted with regard to the other.

Besides inland and foreign bills of exchange, there are two other descriptions of negotiable instruments for the payment of money, viz. promissory notes, and cheques on bankers, and which are transferrable so as to vest the legal right to receive the money in the holder.(17) Most of the rules applicable to bills of exchange, equally affect these instruments ; their peculiar qualities, and the law affecting them in particular, will hereafter be separately considered.

[x] Buller *v.* Crips, 6 Mod. 29. Anon-Hasdr. 485. Claxton *v.* Swift, 3 Mod. 86. Marius, 2.
[y] Buller *v.* Crips, 6 Mod. 29. Pinckney *v.* Hall, Ld. Raym. 175. Erskine *v.* Murray, id. 1542. Mannin *v.* Carey, Lutw. 279. Pearson *v.* Garrett, 4 Mod. 242.
[z] Bomwich *v.* Loyd, 2 Lutw. 1585. Sarsfield *v.* Whitherly, Carth. 82.
[a] 2 Bla. Com. 467.

(16.) A bill drawn in the United States upon any place within the United States, has been held in New York, to be an inland bill of exchange. *Miller* v. *Hackley*, 5 John. Rep. 375.

When a bill of exchange is drawn by one citizen of Kentucky, upon another citizen of that state, although payable in another state, the holder is not entitled upon payment to 10 per cent. damages. *Clay* v. *Hopkins*, 3 Marsh. 488. In *Lonsdale* v. *Brown*, *Circ. Co. U. S. Penn. Dist. Oct.* 1821. WASHINGTON J. held, that a bill drawn in one of the United States upon a person in another of the United States, is a foreign and not an inland bill of exchange ; and subject to all the law of evidence and damage of foreign bills. 1 Rep. Const. Ct. So. Ca. 100. Purd. Dig. 98.

(17.) Bank checks are considered as inland bills of exchange, and may be declared on as such. *Cruger* v. *Armstrong*, 3 John. Cas. 5. The rules, therefore, that are applicable to the one, are generally applicable to the other.

One possessed of a check, or order, for the payment of money to bearer, addressed to no particular person as drawee, can maintain no action against the person subscribing it, without showing that he came fairly by it, for a valuable consideration. *Ball* v. *Allen*, 15 Mass. Rep. 483.

CHAPTER II.

OF THE PARTIES TO A BILL OF EXCHANGE, &c.

IT is essential to the validity of every contract, that there be proper parties to it, and that those parties have capacity to contract. The parties to a contract are generally only two, namely, the person binding himself to perform some act, and the person in whose favour that act is to be performed : but in the case of bills of exchange, &c. on account of the assignable quality of each, there may be, and usually are, more than two parties. The *capacity* of the contracting parties, or, in other words, who may be concerned in the transaction, will be considered in the first part of this chapter The *number* of the parties, and the *mode by which they may become such*, will be treated of in the second part.

Sect 1. Of the *capaci-ty* of the contract-ing parties, and who may be parties to a bill.

All persons, if they have capacity to contract, and be not subject to any legal disability, may be parties to a bills of exchange.[a] In general, contracts with alien enemies are void ; but where two British subjects detained prisoners in France, one of them drew a bill in favour of the other on a third British subject, resident in England, and such payee indorsed the same in France to an alien enemy, it was held that the alien's right of action was only suspended during the war, and that on the return of peace he might recover the amount from the acceptor.[b]

It appears,[c] that in France, ecclesiastics were prohibited from being parties to a bill of exchange, or from carrying on commerce in any way, on the principle that such transactions were repugnant to the sanctity of their profession ; but in this country, although clergymen are prohibited by statute,[d] under penalties, from trading or farming ; yet the act of being a party to a bill would not constitute a trading within the statute ;[e] and if it did, as the act is merely prohibitory, the bill itself would not be void.[f]

[14]

---

[a] Therefore a bill drawn in war by an alien enemy abroad, on a British subject here, and indorsed during war to a British-born subject, spontaneously resident in the hostile country, cannot be enforced by the latter after peace restored. Willison v. Patterson, 7 Taunt. 439.

[b] Antonie v. Morshead, 6 Taunt. 237. 1 Marsh. 558. S. C.

[c] Poth. Traité de Change, pl. 27.

[d] 21 Hen. 8. c. 13. 43 G. 3. c. 84. s. 5.

[e] Hankey v. Jones, Cowp. 745. This was a case on an issue to try whether the defendant was a trader within the meaning of the bankrupt laws, and also the validity of the petitioning creditor's debt. The defendant, a clergyman, had drawn bills for the purpose of raising money for draining certain lands, &c. belonging to

him, and had allowed his banker a commission on paying his bills, also other persons for getting them discounted, and had also borrowed accommodation bills, in lieu of which he gave his own bills and notes to the same amount. The court held, that this was not a trading within the true intent and meaning of the bankrupt laws ; and Lord Mansfield said, " this case is merely a drawing by a person for the purpose of improving his own estate, and he pays discount on what he draws, and therefore there is no colour for saying he is within the description of the bankrupt laws."

[f] Ex parte Meymot, 1 Atk. 196. The petitioner applied to supersede a commission of bankrupt taken out against him, on, the ground, that being a clergymen,

It was once thought, that as the only reason why bills of exchange **Sect. 1. Of** were suffered to be assigned by one person to another, was, because **the** *capaci-* they were the means of increasing commerce, and facilitating the ends **ty of the** of it, no person who was not a merchant, or engaged in some trade, **parties.** could be a party to a bill.ᵍ It has, however, been long settled, that all persons, having capacity and understanding to contract in general, may be parties to these instruments;ʰ and as a person does not make himself a merchant, by drawing or accepting a bill of exchange, there- fore an attorney does not, by accepting a bill, lose his privilege from arrest and to be sued by bill.ⁱ

In general, a *corporation* can only contract by deed, under their cor- **Corpora-** porate seal ;ᵏ but the Bank of England have power to issue their pro- **tions.** missory notes,ˡ and notes and bills have been issued by other companies signed by their agent without objection.ᵐ A restraint, however, is im- posed by the legislature in regard to the mode in which corporations (ex- [**15**] cept the Bank and the East India Companyⁿ) may draw bills ; it having been enacted,ᵒ "That it shall not be lawful for any body politic or " corporate whatsoever, or for any other persons whatsoever, united, " or to be united in covenants, or partnership exceeding the number of " six persons, in England, to *borrow*, *owe*, or *take up* any sum or sums " of money, on their bills or notes payable at demand, or at any less " time than six months from the borrowing thereof, during the continu- " ance of the privilege of exclusive banking granted to the governor " and company of the Bank of England." But this statute does not preclude the members of a commercial firm, although exceeding six in number, from drawing bills at a shorter date than six months.ᵖ It

---

he was not liable to the bankrupt laws, the 21 Hen. 8. c. 13. s. 5. was cited in fa- vour of a petitioner. There was no dis- pute either as to the trading or act of bank- ruptcy. Per Lord Chancellor, " the sta- tute of 21 Hen. 8. is rather in the nature of a prohibition, and a prohibition will not ex- empt him from being a bankrupt, for if a man, with eyes open, will break the law, that does not make void the contract."

ᵍ Fairly *v.* Roch, Lutw. 891. Brom- wᵎch *v.* Loyd, Lutw. 1585.

ʰ Sarsfield *v.* Witherly, 2 Vent. 295. Comb. 152. Carth. 82. 1 Show. 125. S. C. Hodges *v.* Steward, 12 Mod. 36. 1 Salk. 125. S. C.

ⁱ Comerford *v.* Price, Dougl. 313. This was an action by original against defen- dant who was an attorney, as acceptor of a bill of exchange; defendant pleaded in abatement his privilege to be sued by bill, and the plaintiff demurred generally. The case was argued for the plaintiff. De- fendant's counsel was stopped by Lord Mansfield, who said, " This case is ex- tremely clear; a man does not make him- self a merchant by drawing or accepting a bill of exchange; if there are no cases, it is because the privilege cannot admit of a doubt." Same point ruled by Dam- pier, J. 6th May, Easter Term, 1815.

ᵏ Slark *v.* Highgate Archway Company, 5 Taunt. 794. Broughton *v.* The Man- chester Water Works Company, 3 B. & A. 3. The King *v.* The Inhabitants of Chip-

ping Norton, 5 East. 239. Bac. Ab. Cor- porations, E. 3. The King *v.* Bigg, 3 P. W. 432. 4. Yarborough *v.* Bank of Eng- land, 16 East. 11. 3 & 4 Anne, c. 9. s. 3. 1 Chitty on Pleading, 3d ed. 102.

ˡ 15 Geo. 2. c. 13. s. 5. 5 W. & M. c. 22. The King *v.* Bigg, 3 P. W. 432. 4. Bac. Abr. Corporations, E. 3.

ᵐ Edie v. East India Company, 2 Burr. 1216. Ryall *v.* Rolle, 1 Atk. 181. Wat- son's Law of Partnership, 1st ed. 53. Kyd. on Bills, 32. In Slark *v.* Highgate Arch. way Company, 5 Taunt. 792, which was an action of assumpsit upon their promis- sory note in the common form, and in- dorsed to the plaintiff; it seems to have been considered, that if a corporation is authorized to raise money on promissory notes for a particular purpose, evidence might be received to impeach the notes by showing they were issued for another purpose; and the court said, that assump- sit would not lie against a corporation, unless the act which authorized the making of promissory notes *eo nomine* by such cor- poration *ex vi termini*, impliedly empower- ed the corporation to make a promise.

ⁿ 33 Geo. 3. c. 52. s. 108, 9, 10.

ᵒ 6 Anne, c. 22. s. 9. 15 Geo. 2. c. 13. s. 5.

ᵖ Wigan *v.* Fowler and others, 1 Stark. N. P. C. 459. This was an action against seven defendants, co-partners, not bank- ers, on their promissory note for 1000*l.*, payable three months after date. It was

Sect. 1. Of the capacity of the contracting parties. has been recently determined, that a corporation not established for trading purposes, cannot be acceptors of a bill of exchange payable at a less period than six months from the date, because such a case falls within the provisions of the several acts passed for the protection of the Bank of England, and it was questioned whether any, except a trading corporation, can bind themselves as parties to a bill of exchange.q (23.)

Infants.

[16] With respect to the *competency* of the contracting parties in general, the law has wisely taken care of the interests of those who either have not judgment to contract, as in the case of *infants;* or who having judgment to contract, cannot in law have a fund or property to enable them to perform the contract, as in the case of a *feme covert;* and therefore it has, in general, rendered the contracts of infants voidable, and those of married women absolutely void. In general, all contracts made by infants, otherwise than for necessaries, which is a relative term depending on their station in life, are voidable by them ;r and a bond in a penalty, or for the payment of interest,s and bills of ex-

objected by the defendants, that the note was illegal, contrary to the above statute. At the trial, a verdict was found for the plaintiff, and upon motion to set it aside, Lord Ellenborough said, this objection, if it were available, would affect the holder's right of action in every case where it might be contended, that the number of the members of the firm, by which the bill was drawn, exceeded six. Such a decision would virtually incapacitate any number of persons exceeding six, from entering into a commercial partnership, to draw bills of exchange; and great inconvenience would result, since it would be incumbent on every person before he took a bill, to inquire whether the firm by which it was drawn consisted of more than six members. The statute must be construed *secundum subjectam materiam*, and it was the manifest object of the legislature in framing this act, to pro-

tect the Bank of England against rival banks. If a commercial partnership be made a mere colour for raising money by the issue of notes, I agree that the case would fall within the prohibition of the statute. Bayley, J. Admitting the case to be within the statute, the note would not be void, and the illegality would affect those only who knew the defect. The intention of the legislature was to protect the Bank of England against other banking companies, and the construction contended for might defeat their remedy in almost every instance in which they discounted bills. Mr. Justice Holroyd expressed the same opinion.

q Broughton and others v. The Company of Manchester and Salford Water Works, 3 B. & A. 1.

r Hands v Slaney, 8 T. R. 578.

s Fisher v Mowbray, 8 East. 330.

(23.) The same doctrine is asserted in respect to infants in the United States. They are not liable upon notes given by them, although carrying on trade as adults. *Van Winkle* v. *Ketcham*, 3 Caine, Rep. 323. A negotiable note given by an infant even for necessaries is void. *Swasey* v. *Adm.* of *Vanderhayden*, 10 John. Rep. 33. *Fenton* v. *White*, 1 Southard's Rep. 100. And the same evidence has been required of the confirmation of a voidable contract of an infant after full age, as of the execution of a new one. *Rogers* v. *Hurd*, 4 Day's Rep. 57. But if infancy be set up against a note executed in a foreign country, the party is bound to show that by the law of such country, such plea is a good defence. · *Thompson* v. *Ketcham*, 8 John. Rep. 189. A note made by an infant for a valuable consideration, but not for necessaries, in not confirmed by a clause in his will made after coming of age, directing all his just debts to be paid. *Smith* v. *Mayo*, 9 Mass. Rep. 62.

Banks and other commercial corporations may bind themselves by the acts of their authorized officers and agents without the corporate seal. *Hubner* v. *Bank*, U. S. 5 Wheat. 338. and it is now held in England that assumpsit will lie upon a bill of exchange against a trading corporation whose power of drawing and accepting bills is recognised by statute. *Murray* v. *East India Company*, 6 Barn. & Ald. 204.

The indorsement and delivery of a promissory note to a bank on its request is a sufficient consideration for an undertaking on the part of the bank to charge the indorser by notice: and if they neglect to do this, the holder may maintain an action against them and recover damages for the neglect. *Bank of Utica* v. *Smedes*, 3 Cowen. 668. in error. And a count for such neglect would be good as a count for misfeasance. Ibid.

change, in the course of trade, and not merely for necessaries, are clearly not binding upon them;[t] and though it has been considered, that a single bill or bond for the exact sum due, and not in a penalty given for necessaries, is obligatory upon an infant,[u] yet an indorsee of a bill or note cannot sue an infant upon either of those instruments, though given for such consideration, and it is as yet undecided, whether in any case, those instruments are available against infants, even between the original parties.[x] If one of two partners is an infant, the holder of a bill accepted by both partners may declare on it as accepted by the adult only in the name of both, and if the defendant plead in abatement that the other partner ought also to be sued, the plaintiff may

[17]

---

[t] Williams v. Harrison, Carth. 160. 3 Salk. 197. Sel Ca. 17. S. C. Williamson v. Watts, 1 Campb. 552. Com. Dig. Enfant, C. 2. In Williamson v. Harrison and others, the case was thus: In an action on the case brought by the plaintiff against the defendants, being merchants, according to the custom of merchants, upon a bill of exchange drawn by them and protested, R. Harrison, one of the defendants, pleaded infancy in bar, &c. And upon a demurrer to this plea, supposing that infancy was no bar to this action, founded on the custom of merchants, the court, without argument, over-ruled the demurrer, for they clearly held, that infancy was a good bar, notwithstanding the custom; for here the infant is a trader, and the bill of exchange was drawn in course of trade, and not for any necessaries; so judgment was entered, that the plaintiff *nil capiat, ber billam v.* R. Harrison, and Holt, Ch. Justice, cited a case, that where an infant keeps a common inn, yet an action on the case upon the custom of inns, will not lie against him, which is stronger than the principal case.

[u] Co. Lit. 172 a. n. 2. 1 Rol. Abr. 729. 1. 20. 1 Lev. 86. 8 East. 330. Trueman v. Hurst, 1 T. R. 41.

[x] It is laid down in Mr. J Bayley's Treatise on Bills, 19, "That an infant "cannot make himself responsible for "the payment of a bill or note, even "when it is given for necessaries," and in Williamson v. Watts, 1 Campb, 552, Sir James Mansfield appears to have considered, that an infant could not be liable as acceptor of a bill, although drawn on account of necessaries; the case was this: "Assumpsit on a bill of exchange. Plea, infancy. Replication, that the bill was accepted for necessaries, and issue thereupon. When the case was opened, Sir James Mansfield, C. J. said, this action certainly cannot be maintained. The defendant is allowed to be an infant; and did any one ever hear of an infant being liable as acceptor of a bill of exchange? The replication is nonsense, and ought to have been demurred to. As the point of law is so clear, I am strongly inclined to nonsuit the plaintiff; however, if I am required to hear the evidence, I will do so, and the defendant will find redress in the court above, should the

verdict be against her. It appeared, that the defendant was a woman of the town, and that the consideration for the acceptance, was the sale of silk stockings and other expensive articles of dress; whereupon Sir J. Mansfield directed a nonsuit. See also Selwyn's Ni. Pri. 4th ed. 287. But in the case of Trueman v. Hurst, 1 T. R. 40. and MSS. the court appear to have been of opinion, that a note given by an infant for necessaries is valid. From the manuscript of that case, it appears that the declaration was on a note, whereby the defendant acknowledged himself to be justly indebted to the plaintiff, in the sum of 10l., for board and lodgings, and for teaching and instructing the defendant in the business of hair-dressing, and did therefore promise to pay the same to the plaintiff on demand ; and after the common counts, there was an account stated. The defendant pleaded infancy to the whole declaration ; and the plaintiff replied, that the note was given for necessaries, and that the sum mentioned in the other counts were due for necessaries ; to which replication the defendant demurred; and it was argued for the defendant, that an infant cannot bind himself by a promissory note, even for necessaries; that there is a great difference between a single bill and a promissory note, because an action on the first, must be brought in the name of the person to whom it was given, in which case the consideration may be gone into, whereas a promissory note is negotiable. The court desired the counsel for the plaintiff to confine himself to the objection to the account stated, from which it has been observed, that it may be inferred, that they considered that the action on the note was sustainable, Bayley on Bills, 20, in notes.

In Kyd, on Bills, 29, it is urged, that if a single bill for necessaries be valid, there seems no reason why a bill or note for the same consideration should not be binding ; and a learned author has observed, that the circumstance of a single bill for necessaries being valid, seems to afford an argument from analogy, to show that a promissory note given by an infant for necessaries would be binding, if payable only to the person who supplied them, though he cannot be bound by his signature to a negotiable bill or note, as that not only

Sect. 1. Of the capacity of the contracting parties. reply his infancy, and it is no departure.[y] However, a person is liable as acceptor of a bill of exchange, which was drawn whilst he was an infant, but accepted after he came of age;[z] and as the contract of an infant is only voidable, and not absolutely void, he may, by a promise to pay the bill made, after he attains twenty-one, render it as operative against him as if he had been of age at the time it was made.[a] Such promise, however, must be express; and a bare acknowledgment of the debt is not a sufficient confirmation, nor will a promise to pay a part, or an actual payment of part, create any further liability.[b] An infant, however, may certainly sue on a bill in his favour.[c] Though where one of several persons who is an infant, has been suffered to appear as a partner with others, they are not obliged to join him in an action at their suit.[d]

Married women [18] A *married woman* cannot be a party to a bill of exchange, promissory note. or other contract, so as to charge herself to liability in a court of law, although she be living apart from her husband, and have a separate maintainance secured to her by deed;[e] and a *feme covert* sole trader in *London* is not liable to be sued as such in the courts at *Westminster.*[f] But sometimes a *feme covert* is chargeable in equity;[g] and where a married woman borrowed money, and gave her promissory note payable on demand, with interest, on a bill filed against the husband and wife, and trustees acting under a marriage settlement, it was decreed, that the debt should be paid out of the rents and profits of the estates, settled to her separate estate;[h] and the same point was recent-

---

primâ facie admits the debt and operates as an account stated, but if valid, would render him liable to an action at the suit of an indorsee, in which the amount of the original debt could not be disputed, 1 Campb. 553, notes. And it has been observed in Mr. Holt's Ni. Pri. Cas. 78, 9, that as a promissory note, by the stat. of Anne, may be indorsed over, it should seem, that an infant would not be bound by such security, at least not whilst it is in the hands of an indorsee, and in the hands of the person to whom it was originally made payable, it would probably be deemed to have no other qualities than a promissory note before the stat. of Anne, that of being merely *evidence* of a debt.

[y] Burgess v. Merrill, 4 Taunt. 468.
[z] Stevens v. Jackson, 4 Campb. 164.
[a] Taylor v. Croker, 4 Esp. Rep. 187.
[b] Dilk v. Keighley, 2 Esp. Rep. 481. Thupp v. Fielder, 2 Esp, Rep. 628.
[c] Warwick v. Bruce, 2 M. & S. 205. 6 Taunt. 118. Kyd, 30. Bac. Ab. Infants, I. 6.
[d] Glossop v. Coleman and others, 1 Stark. 25.
[e] Marshall v. Rutton, 8 T. R. 545.
[f] Beard v. Webb, 2 Bos. & Pul. 93.
[g] Vin. Abr. Baron and Feme, N. 3. pl. 4. 2 Ves. sen. 190. 2 P. Wms. 144. 2 New Rep. 163. Bac. Abr. Baron and Feme, K.
[h] Bullpin v. Clarke, 17 Ves. 366. This was a bill filed against Clarke and his wife, and the trustees under the marriage settlement, dated the 2d and 3d May, 1806, pre-

vious to the marriage and vesting several real estates and personal property in the trustees, for the sole and separate use of the wife; and the bill stated, that on the 4th October, 1806, the wife requested the plaintiff to lend her, 250l., *which she promised should be repaid to him, with interest, out of her separate property;* and the plaintiff knowing that she had such a separate property, accordingly advanced her that sum for her separate use; and she gave him her promissory note for the sum of 250l., with lawful interest, upon demand, dated the 4th of October, 1806. By a letter from the wife to the plaintiff, answer to an application for repayment, she acknowledged the debt, and promised to pay it out of her separate estate. The note and the letter were admitted by the answer. Sir Samuel Romilly, for the defendants, contended, that the promissory note was not the execution of a power; an appointment of any part of this settled property, and had no reference to it; constituting merely a debt for a simple contract, and that there was no authority establishing the right of a court of equity to apply the rents and profits of the separate estate of a married woman to the payment of a debt. The decree thereupon directed the trustees to receive the rents and profits of the several estates in the marriage settlement mentioned; that an account should be taken of what was due to the plaintiff for principal, interest, and costs, upon the note of the wife; and that the trustees should pay to him what should be found due in respect of

ly determined, where a *feme covert* lived separate from her husband, and had a separate maintainance, and accepted a biil of exchange;[1] so when her husband is in legal consideration dead, as where he is transported, banished, &c. she may contract so as to be liable at law.[k] And though it has been decided, that if a married woman give a promissory note, and after the death of her husband, promise to pay it in consideration of forbearance, such promise is void; yet if the wife had a separate estate secured to her at the time she gave the note, the promise may be enforced at law.[l] If a bill or promissory note be made to a [19] *feme sole*, and she afterwards marry, being possessed of the note, the property vests in the husband, and he alone can indorse the same;[m] and if such instrument be made payable to a *feme covert*, the legal interest vests in the husband, and he alone can indorse the same,[n] and though the wife might join with him in an action, yet It is. not necessary that she should do so, because by the act of marriage itself, the husband is virtually an indorsee.[o] And where a note was given by the defendant to a married woman, knowing her to be such, with intent that she should indorse it to the plaintiff, in payment of a debt, which she owed him in the course of carrying on a trade, in her own name, by the consent of her husband; yet it was held, that the property in the note vested in the husband, and that no interest passed by an indorsement in her name to the plaintiff.[p] But in another case, where on the note being presented for payment, the defendant promised to pay the indorsee of the wife, who passed and indorsed by a name different from her husband, and with his knowledge, the jury were directed to infer an authority to make such indorsement.[q]

Except in the instance of an indorsement by a *feme covert*, it seems, that although a bill, &c. be drawn, indorsed, or accepted, by a person, incapable of binding himself, it will nevertheless be valid against all

such principal, interest, and costs, out of such rents and profits; that they should account annually for the rents and profits, and pay to the plaintiff the balance which should from time to time be reported due, until the principal, interest, and costs, shall be fully paid.

[1] Stewart *v.* Lord Kirkwall and others, 3 Madd. 387.

[k] De Gaillon *v.* L'Aigle, 1 Bos .& Pul. 358, 9. Carrol *v.* Blencow, 4 Esp. 27.

[l] Lloyd. *v.* Lee, 1 Stra. 94. Lee *v.* Muggeridge, 5 Taunt. 36.

[m] Corner *v.* Martin, cited 3 Wils. 5.

[n] Philliskirk et Ux *v.* Pluckwell, 2 M. & S. 393.

[o] M'Neilage *v.* Holloway, 1 B. & A. 218. Arnold *v.* Revoult, 1 Brod. & B. 445.

[p] Barlow *v.* Bishop, 1 East, 432. 3 Esp. Rep. 266. S. C. Ann Parry was a married woman, carrying on trade in her own name with the consent of her husband, She became, in the course of such trade, indebted to the plaintiff, and to enable her to pay him, defendant, who knew that she was married, gave her a note, payable to her or order for the amount of the debt; she indorsed it in her own name to plaintiff, and he brought this action. Lord Kenyon, at the trial, thought it not maintainable, and saved the point, and after a rule for a nonsuit and

cause shown, said it was clear, that the delivery of the note to the wife vested the property in the husband; that as he permitted her to trade on her own account, and this was a transaction in the course of that trade, he was not prepared to say, that if she had indorsed the note in his name, that that would not have availed: and the jury might have presumed an authority from her husband for that purpose. But the indorsement being in her own name, it was quite impossible that it could pass away the interest of her husband by it. Rule absolute.

[q] Cotes *v.* Davis, 1 Campb. 485. Action by indorsee against maker of promissory note, payable to Mrs. Carter or order, and indorsed by her in her own name. The note, when due, with the indorsement thereon, was presented by a notary to defendant, who said it should be paid in a few days: defendant now offered to prove that Mrs. Carter was the wife of one Cole, who was still living. Lord Ellenborough said, the jury might presume, that her husband authorized her to indorse notes by the name in which she, herself, passed in the world, and that the defendant was estopped from contesting her authority for this indorsement. Verdict for plaintiff. See also Doe, ex dem. Leicester and another *v.* Biggs, 1 Taunt. 367.

Effect or other competent parties.[r] Therefore, if a husband indorse a note, by
incapacity which his wife promised to pay him a sum of money as between him
as to other and the indorsee, it is certainly good,[s] and as infancy is a personal privi-
parties. lege, of which the infant alone can avail himself; the drawer or accep-
[20] tor of a bill, cannot set up the infancy of the indorser as a defence to
the action,[t] and it is reported to have been decided, that where a bill
drawn and indorsed by an infant to a third person, who indorsed the
same to the plaintiff, had been misappropriated by the first indorsee, in
fraud of such drawers, and they had therefore demanded the bill from
the plaintiff, that circumstance afforded no defence in an action against
the acceptors, because it would materially injure the circulation of bills,
if such facts were to be inquired into.[u] (26)

Sect. 2. Of Bills of exchange differ from most other contracts in the circumstance
the number of there being frequently more than two parties to them: a bill has, in-
of the par- deed, previously to its being transferred, generally three parties, name-
ties, and ly, the person making it, who is called the *drawer*, the person to whom
mode by it is directed, who before acceptance is called the *drawee*, and after-
which they wards, the *acceptor*, and the person, in whose favour it is made, who is
may be- called the *payee*. It is not, however, necessary that there should be
come such. three parties to a bill; there are sometimes only two; as where a person
draws a bill on another, payable to his own order; and, indeed, a bill
will be valid where there is only one party to it, for a man may draw
on himself payable to his own order.[x] In such case it is said, that the
[21] instrument, in legal operation, is rather a note than a bill;[y] however,
in practice, it is usual to declare upon the instrument as if it were a
bill, not admitting the identity of the drawer and drawee,[z] and if accepted, the defendant may be charged in one count as the drawer, and
in another as acceptor, and in a third as the maker of a promissory

---

Poth. pl. 29. Haly v. Lane, 2 Atk.
182.
[s] Haly v. Lane, 2 Atk. 181.
[t] Haly v. Lane, 2 Atk. 182. and see the
general principle, Holt v. Clarencieux, 2
Stra. 937. Warwick v. Bruce, 2 M. & S.
205. 6 Taunt. 118. But in Jeune v. Ward,
2 Stark. 330, such a defence was permitted.
[s] Taylor v. Croker, 4 Esp. Rep. 187, sed
quære.
[x] Ex parte Parr, 18 Ves. 69. Per Lord
Eldon, " It is said by the counsel, that the
house at Liverpool was partner with the
other house at Demerara; but it has been
established above thirty years, that the same
persons may be both drawers and acceptors, as constituting different firms."
Starke v. Cheesman, Carth. 509. Christopher Cheesman, being in Virginia, drew a
bill on Christopher Cheesman in Ratcliffe,
London, which in truth, was upon himself,
and the plaintiff declared, that defendant
drew a bill payable after sight, and directed the same to Christopher Cheesman in
Ratcliffe, and then averred that the drawee
was not found, and thereupon the bill was
protested, and the defendant, as drawer,

became chargeable. The defendant suffered judgment by default, and moved in arrest of judgment; but made no objection,
on the ground that the bill was drawn by
the drawer upon himself, though other objections were taken, and the plaintiff had
judgment.
Dehers v. Harriot, 1 Show. 163. A.
drew a bill payable by himself in Dublin.
an action was afterwards brought thereon;
and no objection being taken on this account, plaintiff recovered.
Robinson v. Bland, Burr. 1077. The defendant being at Paris, drew a bill on himself in London; the consideration was partly for money lost at play in Paris, and partly money lent at the time and place of play,
and upon that ground, a case was reserved
for the opinion of the Court; but no objection was made that the defendant drew the
bill upon himself.
Jocelyn v. Laserre, Fort. 282. Per
Eyre, J. It is not necessary to have three
persons to make a good bill of exchange.
A man may draw a bill upon himself.
[y] Bayl. 21.
[z] See cases in note, ante, p. 20.

---

(26) Though a note given by an infant be void as against him, yet it will be good
against an indorser. *Ensign v. Woodhouse,* 4 Esp. Rep. *Davy's* Note (1.)

note. And an instrument in the common form of a bill of exchange, ex- Sect. 2. Of
cept that the word *at* is substituted for *to*, before the name of the drawees, the *number,*
may be declared on as a bill of exchange, and if refused acceptance, the parties.
the drawer may immediately be sued, or, as it seems, it might be declared on as a promissory note, after it is due.[a] So though husband
and wife are in legal consideration one person, and though a note given [22]
by a married woman to her husband is void, yet if he indorse it over to
a third person as between the husband and the indorsee, the note is
certainly good.[b] Various inconveniences, however, may arise from the
some person becoming a party to a bill or note in different capacities,
viz. as drawer, and also as second indorser, &c.[c]

[a] Shuttleworth *v.* Stevens, 1 Campb.
407. Declaration in common form, as
upon a bill of exchange, drawn by defendant on Messrs. John Morson and Co.
payable to John Jenkins, and indorsed
to him by the plaintiff. In support of the
action, a paper-writing of which the
following is a copy, was given in evidence :—

21st October, 1804.
Two Months after date, pay to the Order of John Jenkins 78*l.* : 11*s.* value received.

Tho. Stevens.

At Messrs. John Morson
and Co.

Lord Ellenborough held, that this was
properly declared on as a bill of exchange,
and that Messrs. Morson and Co. might
be considered as the drawees, although,
perhaps, it might have been treated as a
promissory note, at the option of the holder.

Allen *v.* Mawson, 4 Campb. 115. The
plaintiff declared, as indorsee, against
the defendant, as drawer of a bill of exchange, alleged to have been dishonoured
for non-acceptance. The instrument given
in evidence was in the following form :—

40*l.* Bradford, August, 2d. 1814.
Two Months after date, pay to Mr.
Lewis Alexander or Order, Forty Pounds,
value received.

George Mawson.

r Sir John Perring, Shaw,
Barber, and Co. Bankers,
London.

The word *at* was in very small letters,
enclosed in the hook of the following S.
This instrument was drawn in Yorkshire,
and being remitted to the plaintiff, who
was an attorney in London, he presented
it for acceptance to Perring and Co., and
as they refused to accept it, he immediately gave notice of its dishonour to the
defendant, and commenced an action
against him. The question was, whether
the plaintiff had a right to treat this instrument as a bill of exchange. Gibbs,
C. J., upon the authority of the above,

case, I should not have hesitated to decide, that in point of law this instrument
is a bill of exchange, had the word *at*
been distinctly written before the names
of the drawees ; but I shall leave it to the
Jury, whether the word " *at* " from the
manner in which it was written, was not
inserted for the purpose of deception, and
then the instrument is a bill of exchange
in point of fact. The *at* being struck out,
it is in the common form in which bills of
exchange are drawn. The defendant
says, " Two Months after date, pay to ;"
this is not a promise to pay ; but a request to third persons to pay. ¶ I cannot
receive evidence of the manner in which
such instruments are considered in Yorkshire. The defendant, in contemplation
of law, issued it in London, where the
plaintiff received it ; he took it to be a
bill of exchange, as almost any other
person in London would have done. I
can see no motive for drawing an instrument in this form, except to deceive the
public. If such instruments have been
common in the country, they ought not to
be continued or endured. The plaintiff
did well in immediately commencing the
action, when Perring and Co. refused to
accept the bill. The Jury found the insertion of the " *at* " to be fraudulent, and the
plaintiff recovered.

[b] Per Ld. Hardwicke, in Haly *v.* Lane,
2 Atk. 181.

[c] Mainwaring *v.* Newman, 2 Bos. & Pul.
120. Bishop *v.* Hayward, 4 T. R. 470.
Porthouse *v.* Parker and others, 1 Campb.
82. Ex parte Parr, 18 Ves. 65. Davison
v. Robertson, 3 Dow. 229, 230. As to
fictitious bills, see post.

Bishop *v.* Hayward, 4 T. R. 470, was a
declaration on a promissory note, stated
to have been made by one Collings, payable to plaintiff, or order, and afterwards
indorsed by him to defendant, who re-
indorsed it to plaintiff. The court, upon
motion, arrested the judgment ; and Per
Buller, J., the consequence of supporting
this judgment would be, that the plaintiff,
without having any real demand on defendant, might recover against him, by the
judgment of the court, without allowing
the defendant a possibility of defending
himself

Sect. 2. Of the *num-ber*, &c. of the parties.   It is by *transfer* of a bill of exchange from one person to another, when it is negotiable, that the parties may become numerous; in which case if the transfer be by indorsement, the person making it is called the *indorser;* the person in whose favour the transfer is made, the *indorsee;* and in all cases, the person in possession of the bill is called the *holder.*

The drawer, acceptor, indorser, and holder, are the principal, and *immediate* parties to the instrument; but besides them, a person may become a party to it in a *collateral* way;[d] as where the drawee refuses to accept, any third party, after protest for non-acceptance, may accept for the honour of the bill, generally, or of the drawer, or of any particular indorser, in which case the acceptance is called an acceptance *supra protest,* and the person making it is styled the acceptor for the *honour* of the person on whose account he comes forward; and he acquires certain rights, and subjects himself to nearly the same obligations, as if the bill had been directed to him. A person may also become party to the instrument by *paying it supra protest,* either for the *honour* of the drawer or indorsers. The right and obligations, attached to this collateral mode of becoming party to a bill, will be spoken of hereafter.

Mode of becoming a party.

[23]   With respect to the *mode of becoming party* to any one of these instruments, it is a general rule, that no person can be considered as a party to a bill, unless his name, or the name of the firm of which he is a partner, appear on some part of it;[e] however, a person may become drawer, indorser, or acceptor, not only by his own immediate act, but also by that of his *agent* or *partner.*

By act of agent.   It is a general rule of law, that whenever a person has a power, as owner, to do a thing, he may consequently, as incident to his right, do it by *attorney or agent.*[f] Hence it is clear, that a person may draw, accept, or indorse a bill by his agent, as well as by himself.[g] In these cases, he is said to draw, accept, and indorse by *procuration.*[h] As this agency is a mere *ministerial* office, infants, *feme coverts,* persons attainted, outlawed, excommunicated, aliens, and others, though incapable of contracting on their own account, so as to bind themselves, may be agents for these purposes.[i]

With respect to the *manner of their appointment,* it is said[k] that there ought to be a formal power of attorney; but this is by no means necessary; for the authority which an agent has, to draw, indorse, and accept bills, in the name of his principal, may be, and indeed most usually is, by parol.[l]

As to the *extent of the agent's authority,* if a person be appointed a *general* agent, as in the case of a factor for a merchant residing

[d] Poth. pl. 25, 26.
[e] Per Buller, J. in Fenn *v.* Harrison, 3 T. R. 760. Siffkin *v.* Walker and another, 2 Campb. 308. Emly *v.* Lye and another, 15 East, 7. 11.
[f] Combe's case, 9 Co. 75. b. Kyd. 32.
[g] Molloy. b. 2. c. 10. a. 27. Ward *v.* Evans, Ld. Raym. 930. 6 Mod. 36. S. C. —— *v.* Harrison, 12 Mod. 346. Anonymous, id. 564. Usher *v.* Dauncey and

another, 4 Campb. 97. *et vide* 3 & 4 Anne, c. 9. a. 1.
[h] Beawes, pl. 83. Kyd, 33.
[i] Co. Lit. 52. a.
[k] Beawes, pl. 86. Marius, 2d edition, p. 104.
[l] Per Lord Eldon, in Davison *v.* Robertson, 3 Bow Rep. 229. Porthouse *v.* Parker, 1 Campb. 82. and per Holt, C. J. in Anonymous, 12 Mod. 564. Harrison *r.*

abroad, the principal is bound by all his acts; but an agent, constituted **By act of** so for a particular purpose, and under a *limited* and *circumscribed power*, **agent.** cannot bind the principal by any act exceeding his authority.ᵐ Therefore, where A. desired B. to get a bill discounted for him, but declared that he would not indorse, it was decided,ⁿ that no representation of B. could bind A. as an indorser, though it was insisted, that what B. had done, was within the scope of his employment, which was to raise money on the bill, and that a subsequent promise to pay was inoperative. It appearing, however on a second trial, that A. did not declare that he would not indorse it, it was adjudged, that as he had authorized B. to get the bill discounted, without restraining his authority, as to the mode of doing it, he was bound by his acts.ᵒ

Upon the question what is a *general* authority, it has been decided, [**24**] that a person signing his name on a blank stamped piece of paper, and delivering it to I. S. authorizes I. S. to insert any sum which the amount of the stamp will warrant.ᵖ(32) It has also been held,�q that a letter of

---

¹ckson, 7 T. R. 209. The king v. Bigg, 4 T. Wms. 432. Bac. Abr. Corporations, L. 3. Bayl. 226. Payley Prin & Agent, 117 and see 3 & 4 Anne, c. 9.
ᵐ Per Buller, J. in Fenn v. Harrison, 3 T. R. 757. . East India Company v. Hensey, 1 Esp. Rep. 111.
ⁿ *Dissenté* Kenyon, C. J.
ᵒ Fenn v. Harrison, 3 T. R. 757. 4 T. R. 177. The defendants employed F. H. to get a bill discounted, but said that they would not indorse it; F. H. employed his brother J. H. and said he would indemnify him if he would indorse it. J. H. indorsed it, and the plaintiffs discounted it. The bill being dishonoured, the plaintiffs applied to the defendants, who proceed to take it up, but did not, and this action for money had and received, and money paid, was brought against them. Lord Kenyon told the jury, that if they thought that J. H. had made himself considerable as the agent of the defendants, it was sufficient consideration for their promise. A verdict was found for the plaintiffs, and on a rule nisi for a new trial and cause shown, Lord Kenyon inclined to think the verdict right, because, though the agent had exceeded his authority, he thought the principal bound by what he did, but the other Judges differed, because F. H. was a particular agent only, and the rule was made absolute. On the next trial it did not appear that the defendants had told F. H. that they would *not indorse* the bill, a verdict was had for the plaintiffs; and on a rule nisi

for a new trial, and cause shown, the whole court thought the verdict right; because, as F. H. was not restrained as to the mode of getting the bill discounted, the defendants were bound by his acts; but Buller and Grose, Justices, said, that if the facts had been the same, they should have continued of their former opinion. Rule discharged. See observations on this case, Bayl. 168, 9. Payley Prin. & Agent, 124, 5. 138. 146. See also Helyear v. Hawke, 5 Esp. 75. Alexander v. Gibson, 2 Campb. 555.
ᵖ Collis v. Emmet, 1 Hen. Bla. 313. Emmet signed his name on a blank paper, stamped with a shilling bill stamp (the highest stamp then in force for bills,) and delivered it to Livesay and Co. that they might draw such bill thereon as they should please; they drew one for 1551l. at three months date, which was duly transferred to Collis and Co., and Collis and Co. sued Emmet thereon. A special verdict was found, principally with a view to another point, and the court held Emmet answerable, and the plaintiffs had judgment.
Russel v. Langstaffe, Dougl. 496, 514. The defendant, to accomodate one Galley, indorsed his name on five copper-plate checks, made in the form of promissory notes, but in blanks, without any sums, dates, or times of payment being mentioned therein, and delivered them to Galley; Galley filled them up as he thought fit, and the plaintiff discounted them ; the plaintiff knew the notes were blank at the time of the indorsement; Galley not paying them

---

(32) A blank indorsement on a blank piece of paper, with intent to give a person a credit, is, in effect, a letter of credit; and if a promissory note be afterwards written on the paper, it binds the indorser. *Violett* v. *Patton*, 5 Cranch. Rep. 142. Where the defendants left their names indorsed in blank on papers, with their clerk, for the purpose of having notes of a certain description written thereon, and third person obtained these papers by false pretences, and wrote notes thereon, signed by himself as promissor to the indorser, and passed them to a third person, who had no notice of the facts, the defendants were held as indorsers. *Putnam* v. *Sullivan*, 4 Mass. Rep. 45.

By act of attorney, given by an executor to A. B. authorizing him to transact the
agent. affairs of the testator, in the name of the executor, as executor, and to
pay, discharge, and satisfy all debts due from the testator, conveys to
A. B. a sufficient authority to accept a bill of exchange in the name of
the executor, drawn by a creditor for the amount of a debt due from
the testator, and thereby to make the executor personally liable, on the
ground that an authority of this nature necessarily includes all inter-
[25] mediate powers, that is to say, all the means necessary to be used in
order to effect the accomplishment of the object of the principal, namely, the paying, satisfying, and discharging the testator's debts. But in
another case[r] which was upon the same letter of attorney, the court,
after consulting with the Judges of C. P., determined that the executor
was not personally liable, and that a power of attorney, given by an
executrix, to act for her as an executrix, does not authorize the attorney to accept bills to charge her in her own right, though for debts due
from her testator. So in a late case it was decided, that where one
gives a power of attorney to another, to demand and receive all moneys
due to him, on any account whatsoever, and to use all means for the
recovery thereof, and to appoint attorneys for the purpose of bringing
actions, and to revoke the same, "and to do all other business;" the
latter words must be understood with reference to the former, as meaning all business appertaining thereto; and although the attorney may receive moneys due to the principal in *auter droit*, yet he cannot under
this power indorse a bill for him, which comes to his hands.[s] It has
also been held, that a power of attorney to receive all salaries and money, with all the principal's authority to recover, compound, and discharge, and to give releases and appoint substitutes, does not authorize
the attorney to negotiate bills received in payment, nor to indorse them
in his own name ; nor can evidence of a usage at the navy office, to
pay bills, indorsed by the attorney in his own name, and negotiated by
him, under such a power, be received to enlarge the operation of the
power.[t]

An authority may also be *implied* and inferred from prior conduct of
the principal, for a special authority is not necessary to constitute a
power to draw, indorse, or accept by procuration, but the law may
infer an authority from the general nature of certain acts permitted to
be done, and usual employ is evidence of a general authority;[u] and
therefore, if a person has, upon a former occasion, in the principal's
absence, usually accepted bills for him, and the latter on his return,
approved thereof, he would be bound in a similar situation on a second
absence from home;[x] and if a drawee of a bill has previously paid

when they became due, plaintiff brought
this action. Hotham, B., before whom the
cause was tried, was of opinion, that as
the notes were incomplete when the defendant indorsed them, no subsequent act of
Galley could make them otherwise, because
that would alter the effect of the defendant's
indorsement, and he accordingly directed a
verdict for the defendant ; but upon application for a new trial and cause shown,
Lord Mansfield said, " Nothing is so clear
as that the indorsement on a blank note is
a letter of credit for an indefinite sum; the
defendant said, ' trust Galley to any amount
and I will be his surety;' it does not lie in
his mouth to say the indorsements were not

regular." See also Snaith *v.* Mingay, 1 M
& S. 87. Crutchley *v.* Mann, 5 Taunt. 529.
1 Marsh. 29. S. C. Crutchley *v.* Clarence,
2 M. & S. 90.

[q] Howard *v.* Baillie, 2 Hen. Bla. 618.

[r] Gardner *v.* Baillie, 6 T. R. 591. Kilgour *v.* Finlyson, 1 Hen. Bla. 156.

[s] Hay *v.* Goldsmid, 2 Smith's Rep. 79.
80

[t] Hog *v.* Snaith and others, 1 Taunt
347.

[u] Per Lord Eldon, in Davison *v.* Robertson, 3 Dow, 229. Malynes, B. 3. c.
5. s. 6. page 264. Bayl. 226.

[x] Beawes, pl. 86. Mar. 2d ed. 135.

several bills accepted in his name by a third person with whom he By act of agent.
had connexions in trade, he would be liable to an indorsee, though
such bill has been accepted without his authority;[?] and it has been
held, that if a person usually subscribes an instrument with the name [26]
of another, proof of his having done so in many instances is sufficient
to charge him whose name is subscribed, without producing any power
of attorney.[a] And we have seen, that where a married woman is permitted by her husband to carry on trade on her own account, and in her
own name indorses a bill or note, received in the course of such trade,
an authority may be presumed from the husband.[a] It has also been
decided, that a subsequent assent will make the act of an agent binding on the principal;[b] (35) and though a promise alone to pay a bill
indorsed by an agent would not support an action if the indorsement
were contrary to authority, yet if the authority is doubtful, such a promise is decisive.[c] A general authority to an agent is supposed to con-

[?] Barber v. Gingell, 3 Esp. N. P. C. 60.
In an action against the defendant, as acceptor of a bill, he proved that the acceptance was forged by Taylor, the drawer;
in answer to which it was proved that the
defendant had been connected in business
with Taylor, and that he had paid several
bills drawn as the present by Taylor, and
to which Taylor, (as it was supposed) had
written the acceptances in the defendants's
name. And Lord Kenyon held, that this
was an answer to the case of forgery set
up by the defendant, for though he might
not have accepted the bill, he had adopted
the acceptance, and thereby made himself
liable to pay the bill. Verdict for plaintiff.

[a] Neal v. Erving, 1 Esp. Rep. 61.
Haughton v. Ewbank, 4 Campb. 188.

[a] Cotes v. Davis, 1 Campb. 485. Barlow
v. Bishop, 1 East, 434. Anderson v. Sanderson, 2 Stark. 204.

[b] Ward v. Evans, Lord Raym. 930. 2
Salk. 442. S. C. Boulton v. Hillesden,
Comb. 450. 12 Mod. 564. Bayl. 226.
Payley, 124. 126, 7. 211. accord. Fenn v.
Harrison, 3 T. R. 757. Howard v. Bail-
lie, 2 Hen. Bla. 618. semb contra, and see
post, 30, 31, 32, in notes.

[c] Fenn v. Harrison, 4 T. R. 177. Payley, 124, 5.

(35) A person's acting as clerk to a merchant does not authorize him to sign notes in
the name of his master. Terry v. Fargo, 10 John. Rep. 114. But the clerk of a firm
may sign notes, accept bills, &c., in consequence of an authority given by one partner,
for each has full power to this effect. Tillier v. Whitehead, 1 Dall. Rep. 269.

An authority to sign a note may be by parol, or by letter, or by verbal directions, or
may be implied from certain relations proved to exist between the actual maker of the
note, and him for whom he undertakes to act. Long v. Colburn, 11 Mass. Rep. 97.
See Osborne v. Maxey, 15 Mass. Rep. 39.

If an agent act without proper authority, or exceed his authority, and the principal
ratify his acts, or acquiesce in them, or adopt them, he is bound in the same way as if
the agent had an original authority. Towle v. Stevenson, 1 John. Cas. 110. Cushman
v. Loker, 2 Mass. Rep. 106. Armstrong v. Gilchrist, 2 John Cas. 424. Codwise v.
Hecker, 1 Caine's Rep. 526. Banorgee v. Hovey, 5 Mass. Rep. 11. Van Reimsdyk v.
Kane, 1 Gas. Rep. 630.—Affirmed in Supreme Court of the United States, and reported in 9 Cranch, 155. Long v. Colburn. Conn. et al. v. Penn. et al. 1 Peters' Rep.
456.

If an agent act beyond his authority, he will be responsible personally to third persons. Dusenberry v. Ellis, 8 John. Cas. 70. Therefore if he sign a note for his principal without authority, he will be personally bound, and the name of his principal will be
rejected as surplusage. Ibid. Or a special action on the case would at all events lie
against him. Long v. Colburn.—But a mere stranger cannot disaffirm the contract of an
agent upon the ground that he has exceeded his authority. Jackson v. Van Dalfsen, 5
John. Rep. 43. If an agent compromise a demand of his principal, and take therefor
a negotiable note indorsed specially to himself, the note becomes the property of the
agent, and not of the principal; and the agent is responsible to the principal for the
amount, whether secured by him or not. Floyd v. Day, 8 Mass. Rep. 403.

A bill drawn by a general agent is binding upon the principal, although the former
misapply the money. Hoe v. Oxley, 1 Wash. Rep. 23.

A special authority must be strictly pursued. Therefore if an agent be authorized to
sign a note payable at six months, and he sign a note payable at a shorter time, the principal is not bound. Batty v. Carswell, 2 John. Rep. 48. See also Munn v. The Commission Company, 15 John. Rep. 44.

By act oftinue until its determination is generally known, and therefore, after
agent.the discharge of a clerk or agent usually employed to draw, accept, or
indorse bills or notes, the employer will be bound by his signature, made
after the determination of his authority, until the discharge be generally known.[d] When, therefore, the authority of such an agent has been
determined, or he has been discharged from his employ, and there is
reason to apprehend that he will attempt to circulate bills in the name
of his employer, it is advisable for the latter to give notice of the determination of the authority in the Gazette, and also to all his correspondents individually, notice in the Gazette not being in general sufficient
to affect a former customer, unless he has had express notice thereof.[e]
As the authority of an agent is not coupled with an interest, he cannot
delegate it so as to enable another person to act for his principal;[f] if
however, an express authority be given for that purpose he may exercise it.[g]

[27]   When a person has authority, as agent, to draw, accept, or indorse
a bill for his principal, he should either write the name of his principal,
or state in writing, that he draws, &c. as agent,(36) or expressly quali-

[d] Beawes, pl. 231. Molloy, B. 2. c. 10.
s. 27. page 107. Payley, 123, 4. 136. Bayl.
226. Anonymous v. Harrison, 12 Mod.
346. A servant had power to draw bills
of exchange in his master's name, and afterwards is turned out of his service. Holt,
C. J. If he draw a bill in so little time after, that the world cannot take notice of
his being out of service, or if he were a
long time out of his service, but that kept
so secret that the world cannot take notice
of it, the bill, in those cases, shall bind the
master.

Monk v. Clayton, Molloy, 282. cited in
Nickson v. Broham, 10 Mod. 110. A servant of Sir Robert Clayton, who had been
used to receive and pay money, took up
200 guineas after he had quitted the service, and the lender recovered against Sir
R. Clayton, by the direction of Keeling,
C. J. which was approved by the whole
court on a motion for a new trial.
[e] See post, 34, 5, cases of Partners.
[f] Combe's case, 9 Co. 75. 1 Rol. Abr.
330.
[g] Palliser v. Ord. Bunb. 166.

(36.) Where a person intends to make a contract as agent it should appear on the face
of the contract that he acts as agent, and he should sign in the name of his principal.
Stackpole v. Arnold, 11 Mass. Rep. 27. *Arpidson v. Ladd*, 12 Mass. Rep. 173. For
where an agent drew a bill of exchange in his own name on a commercial house, in
which his principal was a partner, and in the bill ordered the contents, when paid, to be
charged to his principal, and the bill was protested for non-acceptance, he was held personally liable to the payees, as drawer, notwithstanding they were privy to his instructions, and knew that he acted solely as an agent. *Mayhew, &c. v. Prince*, 11 Mass.
Rep. 54. See *Meyer v. Barker*, 6 Binn. 228.
And it is not sufficient to protect a party, to describe himself as agent, in the contract,
if the language of the contract import a personal responsibility. Therefore if a person
sign a note " as guardian" he will be held personally liable to payment. *Thatcher v.
Dismore*, 5 Mass. Rep. 299. *Forster v. Fuller*, 6 Mass. Rep. 58. And although it
may be said that as an administrator cannot by his promise bind the estate of the intestate, so neither can the guardian bind the person or estate of his ward, and therefore,
unless the guardian were personally liable, the payee would be without remedy ; yet the
principle of these cases is, that the description of the trust was not meant to exclude that
personal liability, which the language otherwise imported. And a similar construction
has been adopted where the party has been described as attorney or agent in the instrument.
A note subscribed " Pro A. B.—C. D." is the note of A. B. and not of C. D. if the
latter had authority to make it. *Long v. Colburn*, 11 Mass. Rep. 97. A note promising to pay A. B. " agent of the P. H. manufacturing company," for value received of
the company, is a good note to A. personally. *Buffum v. Chadwick*, 8 Mass. Rep.
103.—Post 52.
An agent and partner in a joint concern was authorized to take up money on the credit of the whole concern, and draw bills on a house in Amsterdam for payment, and he
took up money and drew a bill directing the amount to be *charged to the account of all
the parties*, but signed the bill *in his own name only ;* it was held that at least, *in equi-*

the act, by stipulating, in writing on the bill, that he is not to be By act of agent.
personally liable ; for otherwise the act will not in general be binding
the principal,[i] though in some cases an informal mode of executing
authority will not vitiate.[j] And if a person draw, indorse, or accept in his own name, without stating that he acts as agent,[k] he will be [28]
personally liable, unless in the case of an agent contracting on the behalf of government.[l](37)

Wilks v. Back, 2 East, 142. Barlow
v. ..., 1 East, 434. 3 Esp. Rep. 266.
v. White v. Cuyler. 6 T. R. 176.
...'s case, 9 Co. 75. Frontin v
... 2 Stra. 705. Com. Dig. Attorney,
41 Beawes, pl. 83, 4, 5, 6, 7.

... v. Davis, 1 Campb. 485, 486.
... v. Rumsey, 1 Campb. 384.

Thomas v. Bishop, 2 Stra. 955. Rep-
... Hardw. 3 S. C. Le Fevre v.
... 5 Taunt. 749. 1 Marsh. 318. S. C.
... v. Harden, 2 Marsh. 454. and Holt
N P. 342. S. C. Appleton v. Binks,
... 118. De Gaillon v. L'Aigle, 1 Bos.
P. 363. Macbeath v. Haldimand,
1 T. R 181. Poth. pl. 118. 3 B. & A. 47.
... v. Bishop, 2 Stra. 955. Ca.
..., Hardw. 1 S. C. The plaintiff
... of a bill of exchange, drawn
... Scotland upon the defendant, in
... words :—" At thirty days sight pay
... N. or order, 200l., value received of
... and place the same to account of
... York Building's Company, as per ad-
... from Charles Mildmay ; to Mr. Hum-
... Bishop, cashier of the York Build-
... Company at their house in Win-
... Street, London. Accepted per
d... " The bill not having been
... action was brought against defen-
... his acceptance ; at the trial he
... that the letter of advice was ad-
... d to the Company ; and that the
... ng been brought to their house,
... int was ordered to accept it, which
... in the same manner as he had ac-
... other bills. Page, J. directed the
... to find for the plaintiff, which they
... accordingly. On motion for a new
... the court held the direction right ;
... the bill on the face of imported to
... drawn on the defendant, and it was
... d by him generally, and not as ser-
... to the Company, to whose account
... no right to charge it until actual
... d by himself. And this being an
... by an indorsee, it would be of

dangerous consequence to trade to admit
evidence arising from extrinsic circumstances, as the letter of advice And this
differed widely from the case of a bill addressed to the master, and underwritten
by the servant ; where, undoubtedly, the
servant would not be liable, but his acceptance would be considered as the act
of the master. A bill of exchange is a
contract by the custom of merchants, and
the whole of that contract must appear
in writing. In this case there was nothing
in writing to bind the Company, nor could
any action be maintained against them
upon the bill ; for the addition of cashier
to defendant's name was only to denote
the person with certainty ; the direction
to whose account to place it was for the
use of the drawee only." Judgment for
the plaintiff.

Le Fevre v. Lloyd, 5 Taunt. 749.—1
Marsh. 318. S. C. If a broker, who being
employed to sell goods, procures a purchaser, and himself draws a bill on him
for the amount payable to the principal,
and which is accepted by the purchaser,
but dishonoured, the broker, as drawer, is
liable to be sued on the bill by such
payee ; and by the court, " The broker,
by giving this bill, put an end to all doubt
as to the buyer's responsibility. The vendors, upon receiving it, in consequence of
the good opinion of the defendant, dismiss
from their minds all care about the solvency of the purchaser."

Goupy v. Harden, 2 Marsh. 454. Holt
C. N. P. 342. S. C. Bills are drawn by a
house in London on a house in Lisbon, and
indorsed to A. in London. A. indorses
them without any qualification, to B. at
Paris. Held, that A. was bound to B. by
this indorsement, and could not offer evidence to show that he was acting merely
as B's. agent.

[j] Macbeath v. Haldimand, 1 T. R. 172.
Unwin v. Wolseley, id. 674. Myrtle v.
Beaver, 1 East, 135. Rice v. Chute, id.
579. 1 Gow. 117.

... payee was entitled to recover on non-payment from *all* the partners. *Van
... v. Kane*, 1 Gall. Rep. 630. S. C. 9 Cranch, 155.
(37) A like exception in favour of public agents has been repeatedly recognised in
United States. *Hodgson* v. *Dexter*, 1 Cranch. 363. *Jones* v. *Le Tombe*, 3 Dal. 384.
... v *Austin*, 1 Mass. Rep. 208. *Sheffield* v *Watson*, 3 Caine's Rep. 69. *Free-
... Otis*, 9 Mass. Rep. 272.
An agent who makes a contract on behalf of his principal whose name he discloses
... time to the person with whom he contracts, is not personally liable, and there is
... ference in this respect between an agent for government and an individual. *Rath-*

By act of agent.

With respect to the duty and liability of agents in relation to bills and notes, it has been well observed, that an agent employed in negotiating bills of exchange is bound ; first, to endeavour to procure acceptance; secondly, on refusal, to protest for non-acceptance ; thirdly, to advise the remitter of the receipt, acceptance, or protesting ; and fourthly, to advise any third person that is concerned ; and all this without any delay.[m] Losses occasioned by the fraud or failure of third persons, to whom an agent has given credit, pursuant to the regular and accustomed practice of trade, are not chargeable upon him.[n] And therefore, where the receiver of Lord Plymouth's estate took bills in the country of persons who at the time were reputed to be of credit and substance, in order to return the rents in London ; the bills were dishonoured and the money lost, and yet the steward was held to be excused ;[o] and if a trustee appoint rents to be paid to a banker at that time in credit, and the banker afterwards breaks, the trustee is not answerable. And it has been observed, that none of these cases are on account of necessity, but because the person acted in the usual method of business.[p] So, in an action for money had and received, the facts were, that the plaintiff had engaged the defendant,·as his agent, to receive money due to him from his customers, directing him to remit by the post, a bill for these and other sums due to him ; a bill was accordingly remitted to him by the post, but the letter was suppressed, and the money upon the bill received at the banker's by some unknown person, and was not recovered. Lord Kenyon said, " had no direction been given about the mode of remittance, still, this being done in the usual way of transacting business of this nature, I should have held the defendant clearly discharged from the money received as agent. It was so determined in Chancery forty years ago.[q] However, it may be collected from a case recently decided in Chancery, that if an agent place his principal's money to his own account with his general banker, without any mark by which it may be specified as belonging to the trust, and the banker fail, the agent will not be excused, because he cannot so deal with his principal's money, as that if the banker's solvency continue, he may be in a condition to treat it as his own, and if insolvency happen he may escape by considering it as belonging to his principal.[r] And a loss occasioned by any unauthorized disposal or adventure of the principal's money, and not prescribed by the usage of business, though intended for his benefit, is chargeable to the agent ;[s] and therefore where A. in London, consigned goods to the firm of B. and C. at Hamburgh, for sale, upon a *del credere* commission, and B. in London, made advances to A. to be repaid out of the proceeds, and B. and C., with the proceeds, purchase bills for A., which they transmitted to B. in London, specially indorsed to him, and these bills, whilst they were in B's. hands, were dishonoured, it was held that B. and C. must bear the

[29]

[m] Beawes, 431. Payley, 4 & 5. 34.
[n] Russell v. Hankey, 6 T. R. 12. Payley, 37, 8.
[o] Knight v. Lord Plymouth, 3 Atk. 480.
[p] Ex parte Parsons, Ambl. 219 : and see 1 Br. Ch. R. 452. 3 Ves. 566. 6 Ves. 226, 266. 5 Ves. 331, 839 ; and see Warwick. v. Noakes, Peake Rep. 68.
[q] Warwick v. Noakes, Peake Ni. Pri Cas. 68.
[r] Wren v. Kirton, 11 Ves. 382.
[s] Payley, 39.

less.[1] On the other hand, in general, whatever profit an agent may **By act of agent.** derive from dealing with bills, the property of his principal, belongs to his principal, and therefore where the master of a ship in a foreign port, from the state of the exchange, received a premium for a bill drawn upon England on account of the ship, it was held, that this belonged to his owner, although there may have been a usage for masters of ships to appropriate such premiums to their own use.[u] Where a person holds bills, as agent for another, and a third person sues him for the same, he may, by resorting to a court of equity, compel the two claimants to litigate the claim, without involving him in the expense of resisting two suits; and a bill of interpleader has been sustained upon bills of exchange, received by the plaintiff as agent, to procure payment for his principal in Scotland, to whom they had been remitted, against an order for goods, pursued in an action of trover by such principal, and also by attachment in Scotland by a creditor of the principal.[x]

With respect to a person becoming party to a bill, *by the act of his partner*, it is observable, that although in general one joint-tenant, or person jointly interested with another, in real or personal property, is not capable, by himself, of doing any act which may tend to prejudice the other; yet by the custom of merchants, long established as law, if one partner draw, accept, or indorse a bill or note, in the name, or as on the behalf of the firm, such act will render all the partners liable to a *bona fide* holder, although the other partners were ignorant of the transactions, and were even intentionally defrauded by their partner,[a] by entering into the partnership each party reposes confidence in the [30] other, and constitutes him his general agent as to all the partnership concerns, and it would be a great impediment to commerce, if in the ordinary transactions of their trade it were necessary that the actual consent of each partner should be obtained, or that it should be ascertained that the transaction was really for the benefit of the firm; hence the act of one, when it has the appearance of being on behalf of the firm, is considered as the act of the rest, and whenever a bill is drawn, accepted, or indorsed, by one of several partners, as on behalf of the firm, during the existence of the partnership, and it gets into the hands of a *bona fide* holder, the partners are liable to him, though in truth the partner only negotiated the bill for his own peculiar benefit, without

By act of partner.

[t] Lucas and others v. Groning and others, Mark. 391.
[u] Loplock v. Blackburn, 3 Campb. 48. Thompson v. Havelock, 1 Campb. 527. Story on Prin. & Agent, 41. 1 Ves. 83. Law of Apprentices, 67, 8, 9.
[x] Stevenson v. Anderson, 2 Ves. & Bea.

[a] Ray v. Ward, 1 Lev. 234. Tooker's ca. 2 Co. 67. Lingan v. Payn, Bridgm. 24. Bac. Ab. Joint-tenant, H. 3.
[b] See the older cases, Pinckney v. Hall, 1 Salk. 126. Lord Raym. 175. S. C. Carvick v. Jarves, Lord Raym. 1484. —— Mayfield, 1 Salk. 292. Anon. Sty. 370. Harrison v. Jackson, 7 T. R. 207. Anon. Mod. 345. Lane v. Williams, 2 Vern. 3 Ld. 292. S. C. Bac. Ab. Merchant, Vin Ab. Partners, A. Watson, 195; and the more recent cases, Sheriff v. Wilson, 1 East, 48. Swan v. Steele, 7 East, 210.

Ridley v. Taylor, 13 East, 175. Ex parte Bonhonus, 8 Ves. 542. Ex parte Gardom, 15 Ves. 286; and see Bayl. 55. 74, 5. Selw. N. P. 289. But the implied authority of a partner does not enable him to execute *deeds* in the name of the firm, Ball v. Dunsterville, 4 T. R. 313. Harrison v. Jackson, 7 T. R. 207. Holt C. N. P. 143. And the decisions are contradictory upon the question, whether one partner can give a *guarantee* for the debt of a third person, so as to bind the other without his authority, Ex parte Gardom, 15 Ves. 286. acc. Duncan v. Lowndes and another, 3 Campb. 478 contra. An executor who, after the death of one of several partners, continues to receive his share for the benefit of infants, is liable on a bill issued by the firm, although his name does not appear in the firm, Wightman v. Townroe and another, 1 M. & S. 412.

By act of the consent of his co-partners,[a] and as one partner is bound by the pro-partner.

[a] *Admitted* in Sheriff v. Wilkes, 1 East, 48. *Decided* in Swan v. Steele, 7 East, 210. 3 Smith's Rep. 199. S. C. Ridley v. Taylor, 13 East, 175. Barker v. Charlton, Peake, 80. Lane v. Williams, 2 Vern. 277. Arden v. Sharpe, 2 Esp. Rep. 524. Wells v. Masterman, 2 Esp. Rep. 731. Jacaud v. French, 12 East, 322, 3 ; and see Bayl. 55. 74, 5. In the case of Swan & al. v. Steele, 7 East, 210. the facts were these : A., B., and C. traded under the firm of A. and B. in the cotton business, C. not being known to the world as a partner ; and A. and B. traded as partners alone, under the same firm in the business of grocers ; in which latter business they became indebted to D. and gave him their acceptance, which not being able to take up when due, they, in order to provide for it, indorsed in the common firm of A. and B. a bill of exchange to D. which they had received in the cotton business, in which C. was interested ; but such indorsement was unknown to C., of whom D., the indorsee, had no knowledge at the time ; and it was decided that such indorsement in the firm common in both partnerships of a bill received by A. and B. in the cotton business, bound C. their secret partner in that business, and that consequently C. was liable to be sued by D. on such indorsement, the latter not knowing of the misapplication of the partnership fund at the time. Lord Ellenborough, C. J. said, " It would be a strange and novel doctrine to hold it necessary for a person receiving a bill of exchange indorsed by one of several partners, to apply to each of the other partners, to know whether he assented to such indorsement, or otherwise that it should be void ; there is no doubt, that in the absence of all fraud on the part of the indorsee, such indorsement would bind all the partners. There may be partnerships where none of the existing partners have their names in the firm ; third persons may not know who they are ; and yet they are all bound by the acts of any of the partners in the name or firm of the partnership. The distinction is well settled, that if a creditor of one of the partners collude with him to take payment or security for his individual debt out of the partnership funds, knowing at the time that it is without the consent of the other partner, it is fraudulent and void ; but if it be taken *bona fide* without such knowledge at the time, no subsequently acquired knowledge of the misconduct of the partner in giving such security can disaffirm the act ; if the interests of the plaintiffs in the bill were once well vested, no subsequent knowledge that such indorsement was made without the consent of one of the partners, will divest it; and it would be highly inconvenient that it

should; because, if the plaintiffs had been apprized at the time that the partner who indorsed the bill had no authority to do so, they might have obtained some other security for their demand."

In Ex parte Bonbonous, 8 Ves. 542. the Lord Chancellor Eldon said, " This petition is presented here upon a principle which it is very difficult to maintain; that if a partner for his own accommodation, pledges the partnership, as the money comes to the account of the single partner only, the partnership is not bound. I cannot accede to that; I agree, if it is manifest to the persons advancing money that it is upon the separate account, and so that it is against good faith that he should pledge the partnership, then they should snow, that he had authority to bind the partnership. But if it is in the ordinary course of commercial transactions, as upon discount, it would be monstrous to hold that a man borrowing money upon a bill of exchange, pledging the partnership without any knowledge in the bankers that it is a separate transaction, merely because that money is all carried into the books of the individual, therefore the partnership should not be bound. No case has gone that length. It was doubted, whether Hope v. Cust was not carried too far, yet that does not reach this transaction, nor Sheriff v. Wilkes, as to which I agree with Lord Kenyon, that as partners, whether they expressly provide against it in their articles, (as they generally do, though unnecessarily,) or not, do not act with good faith, when pledging the partnership property for the debt of the individual, so it is a fraud in the person taking that pledge for his separate debt. The question of fact, whether this was fair matter of discount, or, being an antecedent, separate, debt of Rogers, the discount was obtained merely for the purpose of paying that debt, by the application of the partnership funds, which question is brought forward by the affidavits, though not by the petition, must lead to farther examination. If the partners are privy, and silent, permitting him to go on dealing in this way, without giving notice, the question will be, whether subsequent approbation is not for this purpose equivalent to previous consent. In Fordyce's case, Lord Thurlow and the Judges had a great deal of conversation upon the law : and they doubted upon the danger of placing every man with whom the paper of a partnership is pledged, at the mercy of one of the partners, with reference to the account he may afterwards give of the transaction. There is no doubt, now the law has taken this course, that if under the circumstances the party taking the paper can be considered as being advertised in the nature of the transaction, that

By act of partner.

...e of his co-partner to provide for a bill, after such a promise, the .n cannot, though deceived by their partner, sue the acceptor;[b] and :.s rule prevails, although by the terms of the partnership deed, the ...tners were prohibited from circulating any bills or notes, if the bolder were ignorant of that circumstance at the time he received the ...ae : though on proof of such restrictive clause, and that the bill was .-ued by one partner without the concurrence, and in fraud of the ...ers. the holder must prove that he gave value for it;[c] and though at ...s the executor of a deceased partner cannot be sued, yet in equity the amount of a bill or note issued in the name of the firm, though in :aud of the deceased partner, will be recoverable from such executor .v a *bona fide* holder.[d] But with respect to a person who, at the time : received the instrument from the partner, knew, or had reason to ...pect, that he negotiated it for his individual benefit, and without their concurrence, he cannot avail himself of the security as binding ..i the firm.[e] It has been considered, that a bill being given for an

[32]

... was not intended to be a partnership ... eeding, as if it was for an antecedent '... *prima facie*, it will not bind them; ... t will, if you can show previous au-: .rity, or subsequent approbation; a ...ong case of subsequent approbation :.ng an inference of previous positive ...ority. In many cases of partnership, ... ifferent private concerns, it is fre-...ly necessary for the salvation of the ...nership that the private demand of ... partner should be satisfied at the ...ancet : for the ruin of one partner ...ld spread to the others; who would ...ther let him liberate himself by dealing ...h the firm. The nature of the subse-...ent transactions therefore must be looked ... as well as that at the time."
[b] Richmond v. Heapy and another, I Stark 202. 4 Campb. 207. S. C. San-...ds v. Marsh, 2 B. & A. 673. Rapp . Latham and Parry, id. 795.
[c] Grant v. Hawkes and another, K. B. ...nall, 4th June, 1817. Action against ...eral defendants as partners in the ...ly Company, and as acceptors of a ... at the suit of the plaintiff as indorsee ... defendants having proved that by the ...es of the company, the members ...re prohibited from circulating any bills ...tes, Lord Ellenborough said, " An ...rsee may recover on a bill against ...ers in a concern, though the drawing ...ccepting were contrary to agreement ...ween them: and by one of the partners ...id of the rest; but then the indorsee ... show that he gave value." Scarlett ... Reader for plaintiff. Topping, Jervis, ...nyatt, Gurney, Gazelee, Peake, &c. ... defendants. Bellamy, attorney for ...atiff. Anstice, for one of defendants.
Lane v. Williams and others, 2 Vern. 2.. 292. Newberry and Williams, the ...fendant's late husband, were partners, Newberry issued the note in the name of ... firm in their shop, and received the ...ney from the plaintiff, but which money ...as not brought into the trade. Williams ...ed, and afterwards Newberry, the plain-

tiff, first filed a bill against the executors of Newberry, but there being a deficiency of assets he filed the present bill to have satisfaction out of the estate of Williams; and *per cur.* The money being paid at the shop, the note of one partner binds both; and though at law the note stands good only against the executor of the surviving partner, who was Newberry, who received the money, and signed the note, yet proper in equity to follow the estate of Williams for satisfaction; and decreed it accordingly.
[e] Sheriff v. Wilkes, 1 East, 48. Arden v. Sharp, 2 Esp. Rep. 524. Wells v. Masterman, 2 Eas. Rep. 731. admitted by Lord Ellenborough, in Swan v. Steele, 7 East, 213. Ex parte Bonbonus, 8 Ves. 542. 544. Ridley v. Taylor, 13 East, 175. Henderson v. Wild, 2 Campb. 561. Hope v. Cust, 1 East, 53. Watson, 197. Green v. Deakin, 2 Stark. 347. Sheriff v. Wilkes, 1 East, 48. In October 1795, Bishop and Wilkes, who were then partners, became indebted to the plaintiffs for goods sold and delivered. Robson became a partner with Bishop and Wilkes, in April 1796, and continued so till the 8th of November following, when the partnership was dissolved. On the 5th November, 1796, the plaintiffs drew on the partnership for the amount of their demand against Bishop and Wilkes, and Bishop accepted the bill in the partnership firm. The plaintiffs now sued the three partners on this acceptance. Bishop and Robson were outlawed, and Wilkes pleaded the general issue A verdict was found for the plaintiffs, subject to the opinion of the court. Lord Kenyon said, he did not know how the case came to be reserved, as he had repeatedly decided the same question at the Sittings, the propriety of which decisions had not been canvassed. He said, the consideration of the bill was goods sold to Bishop and Wilkes only, when Robson was not a partner. Then the plaintiffs knowing this draw the bill on the three partners, and know-

By act of antecedent debt due from one of the partners, raises a presumption
partner. that the creditor knew that the bill was given without the concurrence
of the other partners,[f] and that the taking the instrument from one of
the partners in his own hand-writing, without consulting the others,
raises a presumption that there is not any concurrence of the firm;[g]
and where the plaintiff had, previously to the formation of a partnership, advanced a sum of money to one of the intended partners, to
enable him to become one of the firm, it was held, that the plaintiff
could not recover on a bill afterwards drawn by such party in the
name of the firm, in payment of such advance; and that the other
partners might defend the action without giving any notice of the intention to dispute the consideration.[h] But as a partner may in his
individual capacity have a claim upon the firm, in respect of which he
might draw, accept, or indorse a bill in its name, the mere circumstance of the party to whom he delivers it, knowing that he was using
it, for his private benefit, does not afford sufficient evidence of collusion to invalidate the transaction.[i] A strong case of subsequent ap-

---

ingly take an acceptance from one of
them to bind the other two, one of
whom, Robson, had no concern with the
matter, and was no debtor of theirs, no
assent or knowledge on his part being
found; the transaction is fraudulent on
the face of it. The other Judges concurred. Postea to defendant.

Arden v. Sharp and Gilson, 2 Esp. Rep.
523. Plaintiff indorsee of a bill of exchange against defendants as indorsers;
the plaintiff proved that defendant Gilson came to him on the 1st March, and
brought the bill in question, and requested him to get it discounted for him,
but wished the business to be kept secret
from his partner Mr. Sharp, to which
plaintiff assented and took the bill; the
indorsement of Sharp and Gilson was
proved to be the hand-writing of Gilson.
Lord Kenyon. "The party in this case
who brings the action, was himself the
person who took the bill with the indorsement by the one partner only, and
was informed that the transaction was to
be concealed from the other, he cannot
sue the partnership; the transaction indicates that the money was for that partner's own use, and not raised on the partnership account, therefore shall not be
allowed to resort to the security of the
partnership, to whom in the original transaction he neither looked nor trusted."
Plaintiff nonsuited.

Hope v. Cust, B. R., M. 1774, cited by
Lawrence, J. in 1 East, 53. and see ante,
32, in notes. Fordyce traded on his separate account as well as in partnership
with others, and being indebted to Hope
on his separate account, gave him a
general guarantee in the partnership
name for his own debt. Lord Mansfield
left it to the jury, whether the taking of
a guarantee were, in respect to the
partners, a fair transaction, or covinous;
with sufficient notice to the plaintiff, of
the injustice and breach of trust Fordyce
was guilty of in giving. The jury found

for the defendant. In Ex parte Bonbonus, 8 Ves. 544. the Lord Chancellor,
after mentioning the above case, said,
that if under the circumstances the party
taking the paper can be considered as
being advertised of the nature of the
transaction, that it was not intended to
be a partnership proceeding, as if it was
for an *antecedent debt primâ facie* it will
not bind them, but it will if you can show
previous authority or subsequent approbation, a strong case of subsequent approbation raising an inference of previous positive authority.

[f] Ex parte Bonbonus, 8 Ves. 544. Hope
v. Cust, cited in 1 East, 53. S. C. 1 Mont.
622.

[g] Hope v. Cust, 1 East, 53. ante, 32, in
notes.

[h] Green v. Deakin and others, 2 Stark.
347.

[i] Ex parte Bonbonus, 8 Ves. 542. 544.
Henderson v. Wild, 2 Campb, 561, 2.
Ridley v. Taylor, 13 East, 175. In the
last case it was held, that if one partner
draw or indorse a bill in the partnership
firm, it will *primâ facia bind the firm*, although passed by the one partner to a
separate creditor, in discharge of *his own
debt;* unless there be *evidence of covin*
between such separate debtor and creditor, or at least of the *want of authority*,
either express or to be implied, in the
debtor partner, to give the joint security
of the firm for his separate debt. But it
was held that no sufficient circumstance
appeared in that case, to raise any presumption adverse to the separate creditor, for taking such joint security, in
a case where the bill appeared to have
been drawn in the name of the firm, to
their own order, eighteen days before
the delivery of it to the separate creditor, and to have been accepted and indorsed before such delivery, and to have
been drawn for a larger amount than the
particular debt; and where, though the
indorsement was in fact made by the

By act of partner.

...bation **by all the partners, raises an inference of their previous** ...ority having been given to the particular partner to sign the part- nership name to a bill, or to negotiate it, and will subject the partners ...i liability in a transaction, where they would not have been charge- ...be without such subsequent assent.[k]

Even in transactions in which all the partners are interested, the ...thority of one partner to bind the other, by signing bills of ex- ...ange, or promissory notes, in their joint names, is only implied, ...and may be rebutted by express previous notice to the party taking the ...security from one of them, that the other would not be liable for it.[l] And though where A. was partner in a firm trading under a particular [**35**] name in one branch of business, and some of the partners in that firm carried on another line of business in the same name, and issued a bill in the name of the firm, merely on account of transactions concerning the latter business, in which A. had no concern, yet it was held that he was liable to a *bonâ fide* holder,[m] yet where persons are partners only

---

...l of the debtor partner, yet it did ...t appear that the fact was known to ...the separate creditor at the time ; and ...s too in a case where direct evi- ...nce might have been given of covin, ...want of authority, if it existed. For ...the action being brought by the separate ...ditor against the acceptor, either of ...the partners might have been called as a ...ness by the defendant, to disprove ...the authority of the debtor partner, to ...ve the joint security; for though if the ...parate creditor recovered against the ...acceptor, he would have his remedy over ...against the firm; yet the innocent partner ...ld have his remedy over against the ...and the bankruptcy of the debtor ...partner in the mean time does not vary ...the question of competency. And Lord ...llenborough, C. J. said, " *Prima facie* ...partner is bound by the indorsement ...another in the partnership firm ; but ...the presumption may be cut down, by ...wing collusion : but the difficulty of ...case is, that we have not the facts ...ficiently before us to show that collu- ...n. If this were distinctly the case of ...pledging by one partner of a partner- ...ship security, for his own separate debt, ...without the authority of the other part- ...ner, or if there existed in this case evi- ...ent covin between one partner, and the ...holder of the partnership security, upon ...which the action is brought, in order to ...charge the other partner without his ...knowledge or consent, either express or ...implied, for the private advantage of the ...parties to such covinous agreement, we ...should have no hesitation to pronounce a ...bill, drawn and indorsed under such cir- ...cumstances, void in the hands of the ...covinous holders, upon the principal laid ...down in the case of Sheriff and another ...v Wilkes and others, 1 East, 48 ; but ...upon the facts stated, such does not dis- ...tinctly appear to us to be the case ; nor ...does it appear that there was any such ...crassa *negligentia* on the part of the plain-

tiffs, in not inquiring whether Ewbank, the one partner with whom they dealt, was authorized to dispose of this security (which had originally been partnership pro- perty) as his own, as to render this trans- action on that account fraudulent, and therefore void."

[k] See the cases, 1 Mont. 622. Watson, 202. ante, 32, in notes; and Sandilands v. Marsh. 2 B. & A. 673.

[l] Lord Galway v. Matthew and another, 10 East, 264. ——— v. Layfield, 1 Salk. 291. Minnit v. Whitny, 16 Vin. Abr. 244. Bayl. 57. 225. Lord Galway v Matthew and Smithson, 10 East, 264. The de- fendants and Whitehouse (since deceased) were in partnership as brewers. Mat- thew applied to the plaintiff to lend his acceptance for 200l., to enable him to pay excise duties due from the house, and promised in return to give the note of the firm, payable four days before the acceptance. The plaintiff gave his ac- ceptance, and Matthew drew the note, and signed it for himself, and partners. He then got the acceptance discounted, and applied 180l. in payment of part- nership debts, reserving enough to him- self. The plaintiff, after Whitehouse's death, was obliged to take up his ac- ceptance, and now sued the defendants on the note. Matthew suffered judg- ment by default, and Smithson proved that the plaintiff, before he took the note, had received notice of an adver- tisement by him, warning persons not to trust Matthew on his account, and that he would be no longer liable for drafts drawn by the other partners on the part- nership account. And Lord Ellenbo- rough held, that the plaintiff having taken the note after such warning could not re- cover, and therefore nonsuited him, and on motion to set aside the nonsuit, the court refused the rule.

[m] Swan v. Steele and another, 7 East, 210. Baker v. Charlton. Peake, 80. ante, 30, note[a].

By act of partner. in a *particular* and single transaction, and not *general* partners, they are not liable even to a *bona fide* holder, on a bill issued by one of them in relation to a different concern.[a]

An *act of bankruptcy* committed by one of several partners, however secret, *ipso facto* determines his power to make use of the name of the firm, and no person can derive any benefit or right of action against the firm, upon any bill or note negotiated by the party, after such his act of bankruptcy.[o] And after the *dissolution of a partnership by agreement* [86] duly notified in the Gazette, one of the persons who composed the firm cannot put the partnership name on any negotiable security, even though it existed prior to the dissolution, or were for the purpose of liquidating the partnership debts, notwithstanding such partner may have had authority to settle the partnership affairs.[p] And after notice of the dissolution of a partnership published in the Gazette, and sent round to the customers of the firm, if one of the partners, who carries on the business under the old firm, draws, accepts, or indorses bills in the name of that firm, the other partners need not apply for an injunction against his doing so, for they are not liable upon such bills, given to a person ignorant of the dissolution of the partnership.[q] And though it has been held that notice in the Gazette is not sufficient against persons who were customers of the firm, during the existence of the partnership, and that a particular notice should be given to each; it appears to be clearly established, that notice in the Gazette is at all events sufficient against all persons who have not previously had transactions with the firm.[r] And where after the actual dissolution of

---

[a] Williams *v.* Thomas, Hunter and Latham, 6 Esp. Rep. 18. Messrs. Leake and List drew a bill for 1500*l.* in favour of plaintiff, for goods furnished the ship Cecelia, in which the defendants were charged as acceptors. Defendants proved that the acceptance was made by the defendant Latham on his own account. The defendants were partners in the ship Cecelia, of which defendant Thomas was Captain, and had guaranteed Leake and List to secure to them the money for the outfit Per Lord Ellenborough, Leake and List could give no better title to the holder than they had themselves ; they could not draw for a general account, but for the account of the ship only ; they could not bind Thomas by drawing a bill upon him, and the other defendants, for an account unconnected with the ship. Plaintiff nonsuited.[a]

[o] Thomason and others *v.* Frere and others, 10 East, 418. Thomason, Underhill, and Guest, were partners in trade at Birmingham, and being indebted to the defendants to the amount of 1800*l.*, and creditors upon Gamble and Co. for 1450*l.*, Underhill and Guest, on the 11th of October, 1807, without the knowledge of Thomason, who was then abroad, indorsed to the defendants a bill drawn by Thomason, Underhill, and Guest, upon and accepted by the agents of Gamble and Co. for this 1450*l* Underhill and Guest had on the 7th October, 1807, committed acts of bankruptcy, upon

which separate commission issued on the 19th. The bill for 1450*l.* became due on the 6th December, and was then paid. And to recover this money, the present action was brought by Thomason and the assignees of Underhill and Guest. The house of Thomason, Underhill, and Guest, was still indebted to the defendants beyond the amount of the sum now sought to be recovered. The plaintiffs were nonsuited by Grose, J. But on a rule *nisi* for a new trial, the court (Ld. Ellenborough *absente*) held, that the indorsement having been made after an act of bankruptcy, though before the issuing of the commission, and though for the purpose of paying a partnership debt, was invalid, and they inclined to think that this action being brought to recover the money received on the bill, which had been thus wrongfully indorsed, the defendants had no right to set off their demand upon the firm against this claim by Thomason and the assignees. Rule absolute. And see Ramsbottom *v.* Lewis, 1 Campb. 279

[F] Kilgour *v.* Tinlyson, 1 Hen. Bla. 155 Abel *v.* Sutton, 3 Esp. Rep. 108. Watson, 209. Henderson and another *v.* Wild, 2 Campb. 561 Wrightson and another *v.* Pullan and another, 1 Stark. 375.

[q] Newsome *v.* Coles, 2 Campb. 617. and Wrightson and another *v.* Pullan and another, 1 Stark. 375

[r] Gorham *v.* Thompson, Peake, 42. Graham *v.* Hope, id 154. Fox *v.* Hanbury, Cowp. 449. Godfrey *v.* Macauley.

a partnership duly notified in the Gazette, one of the parties accepted ^{By act of partner.} a bill in the name of the partnership firm, drawn after the dissolution, but dated before it, it was held that an indorsee who took the bill without notice of the dissolution, could not inforce the bill against the other members of the firm, and a distinction was taken by the court between such case, and the case of goods supplied after the dissolution of the partnership, but without notice, by a person who had been in the habit of supplying goods to the firm.[*] However, in a more recent case, where after the dissolution of partnership between A. and B. and the advertisement of it in the Gazette, A. accepted a bill bearing date previous to the dissolution, for the accommodation of a third person, who indorsed it for value, it was held that B. who permitted his name to remain over the shop in the Poultry as a member of the firm till after the dissolution of the partnership, and notice of it, and indorsement of the bill, was liable as partner to a *bona fide* holder.[t] An alteration in the printed checks is sufficient notice of a change in the firm of a banking-house to customers who have used the new checks.[u] And a dormant partner whose name has never been announced, may withdraw from the concern without making the dissolution of partner-[37] ship publicly known.[x] However, an admission made by one partner, after the dissolution, relative to a previous partnership transaction, will affect the firm.[y] (48)

The *death* of a party is in general a revocation of all express and implied authorities given by him, and dissolves the partnership, though it were for a term of years, unless there be an express stipulation to the contrary;[z] but where A. being member of a partnership consisting of several individuals drew a bill of exchange in blank in the partnership firm, payable to their order, and having likewise indorsed it in the partnership firm, delivered it to a clerk to be filled up for the use of the partnership, as the exigencies of business might require, according to a course of dealing in other instances; and after A's. death, and the surviving partners had assumed a new firm, the clerk filled up the bill, inserting a date prior to A's. death, and sent it into circulation; it was held that the surviving partners were liable as drawers of the bill to a *bona fide* indorsee for value, although no part of the value came to their hands.[a]

Wherever the law is silent, as to the extent of the above custom, it should seem that evidence of the usage of merchants is admissible,

---

1 Esp. Rep. 371.   Peake, Rep. 155.
1 Siderf. 127.   Leeson v. Holt and others,
1 Stark. 186.   Jenkins and another v. Blizard and another, 1 Stark, 418.   1 Mont.
on Partn. 105, 6.   Wright v. Pulham, M.
T 1816. M. S.; but see Williams v. Keats,
2 Stark. 291.
  [s] Wrightson and another v. Pullan and another, 1 Stark. 375.
  [t] Williams and another v. Keats and another, 2 Stark. 290.
  [u] Barfoot and another v. Goodhall and another, 3 Campb. 147.

[x] Evans v. Drummond, 4 Esp. 89.
[y] Wood v. Braddick, 1 Taunt, 104.
Halliday v. Ward, 3 Campb. 32.
[z] Gillespie v. Hamilton, 3 Madd. 251.
[a] Usher and another v. William Dauncey and another, 4 Campb. 97. Lord Ellenborough said, that this case came within the principle of Russel v. Langstaff, Dougl. 513. that the power must be considered to emanate from the partnership, not from the individual partner; and that therefore after his death, the bill might still be filled up so as to bind the survivors.

---

(48) Notice in the Gazette of the dissolution of a partnership, is sufficient to all persons who have had no previous dealings with the firm. *Lansing* v. *Gaine*, 2 Johns. Rep. 300. Post. 52. *note.*

By act of but not otherwise;[b] and therefore where two persons, who were not
partner. general partners, drew a bill on A. B. payable to their order, and
separately signed it, not in the name of any supposed firm, and only
one of them indorsed it with his own name, in an action at the suit
of an indorsee against A. B. the acceptor, Lord Mansfield, on a new
trial, admitted evidence to prove, that by the universal usage, and understanding of all the merchants and bankers in London, the indorsement was bad, because not signed by both the payees; and accordingly
the defendant had a verdict; notwithstanding it was insisted, that the
validity of the indorsement was a question of law, and although the
court of King's Bench, on the motion for a new trial, had previously
declared their opinion in the same cause, that when a bill goes out into
the world, the persons to whom it is negotiated, are to collect the state
and relation of the parties from the bill itself; and that if they appear
on the bill as partners, it would be of less public detriment to subject
[38] them to the inconvenience of being treated as such, than to permit them
to deny that they are so; and that persons, by making a bill payable to
their order, render themselves partners as to that transaction.[c] (1)

If a factor of an incorporate company, draw a bill on such company,
and one member accept it, the acceptance will not bind the company, because it is a private act of the party, and not a public act of
the company. And on the same principle, if several persons, each in
his individual capacity, employ one factor, and he draw a bill on all
of them, and one accept it, the acceptance will not bind the rest.[d]

Sometimes an *express* authority is given by several partners to one,
to act for all of them, in which case the person authorized acts as agent
as well as partner, and his power and authority being express, he must
be guided by it. An express authority given to one partner, after the
dissolution of the partnership, to receive all debts owing to, and to pay
those due from the partnership, on its dissolution, does not authorize
him to indorse a bill of exchange in the name of the partnership, though
drawn by him in that name, and accepted by a debtor of the partnership after the dissolution.[e] (2)

[b] Edie v. East India Company, 2 Burr.   [d] Bul. N. P. 270. Mar. 2d edit. 16.
1216. 1221. 1 Bla. Rep. 295. S. C. See   Beawes, pl. 228. Molloy, b. 2. c. 10. s.
Phillips on Evid. 2d edit. 434, 5, 6. Holt,   18.
C. N. P. 98, 9. in notes.
[c] Carwick v. Vickery, Dougl. 653. sed.   [e] Kilgour v. Finlyson, 1 Hen. Bla. 155.
quaere.   Abel v. Sutton, 3 Esp. Rep. 108.

---

(1) If the directors of a turnpike company become the drawer and indorsers of a note,
on which money is borrowed for the use of the company, and applied to the payment of
its debts, they are, in the absence of any special agreement, mutually responsible for
contribution in case of loss, if payment be made by one, whether, by compulsion or
voluntarily, Slaymaker v. Gundackers, Executors, 10 Serg. & Rawle. 75.
    If two persons indorse a note in virtue of a mutual understanding with each other, to
lend their names for the accommodation of the maker, evidence may be left to the jury
of such mutual understanding or agreement. Love v. Wall, 1 Hawks, 313.
    One joint indorser who has paid the whole amount of a note negotiated at bank, can-
not recover from another joint indorser his contribution, without proving the insolvency
of the drawer. Pearson v. Duckham 3 Litt. 386.
    (2) One partner may act for the whole by procuration Williamson v, Johnson, 1 Barn. &
Cress. 146. and the declaration stating a bill of exchange indorsed by certain persons
trading under the firm of H. & F. by procuration of J. D. it was held that this allegation
was supported by evidence of J. D's. handwriting, and that he being a managing partner in a firm which carried on all business of buying and selling, under the designation of

From this liability of partners to answer for the acts of each other, it By act of partner. necessary, that after the dissolution of their connexion, they should, order to avoid the consequences of any one of the partners making, indorsing, or accepting a bill in their names, give notice in the Gazette of the dissolution of partnership; and even this notice, as has been before observed, is not sufficient against persons who were customers during the partnership, unless they have actual notice of the dissolution: and the partners should therefore give notice of the dissolution to their individual correspondents.ᶜ Where one of several partners refuses to concur in signing notice of dissolution, to be inserted in the Gazette, or pending the partnership, has improperly issued bills in the name of the firm, it is advisable to file a bill. to prevent him from signing. or negotiating securities in the name of the firm, and praying a dissolution.ᵉ

With respect to the mode in which a bill should be drawn, accepted, [39] or indorsed, by or on the behalf of several persons, it has been laid down, that whenever a person draws, accepts, or indorses a bill for himself and partner, he should always express that he does so "for himself and partner," or subscribe *both the names* or the *name of the firm*, and that otherwise it will not bind the partner.ᵇ But it has been recently determined, that where a bill is drawn upon a firm, and accepted by one partner only in his name, it will bind the firm.ⁱ And where A., B., and C., being in partnership, A. drew a promissory note, by which he promised individually to pay the money, and signed the same with his own name only, but prefixing to his signature "for A., B., and Co." this was held to bind the firm.ᵏ It is said, however, that if a bill be directed unto two or more persons in these terms. "To Mr. Robert A., and Mr. J. B., Merchants, in London;" in this case, both A. and B. ought to accept the bill, and that if one refuse, the bill

ᶜ Gorham v. Thompson, Peake, C. N. P. 42. Graham v. Hope, ib. 150. Fox v. Hanbury, Cowp. 449. Godfrey v. Macrey, 1 Esp. Rep. 371. 1 Mont. Partn. 115. 6. Ante, 36; but see Wrightson v. Pulfian, 1 Stark. 375. Ante, 36.

ᵉ Master v. Kirton, 3 Ves. 74. Ex parte Noakes, 1 Mont. on Partn. 93. Ryan v. Macmarth, 3 Bro. Ch. Ca. 15. Newsome v. Coles, 2 Campb. 619. Lawson v. Morgan, 1 Price Rep. 303.

ᵇ Pinckney v. Hall, 1 Salk, 126. Lord Raym. 175. S. C. Carwick v. Vickery, Dougl. 653. Smith v. Jarves, Ld. Raym. 1484. The King v. Wilkinson, 7 T. R. 156. Meux v. Humphrey, 8 T. R. 25. Lepin v. Bayley, id. 325. Watson, 214.

ⁱ Mason v. Rumsey, 1 Campb. 384. A bill was drawn on "Messrs, Rumsey and Co." and T. R. Rumsey, jun. wrote upon it. "Accepted, T. Rumsey, sen." The present action was defended by T. Rumsey, jun. who contended, that even if he were a partner (which he denied) this acceptance would not bind him. It was

contended, that if a bill be drawn upon a firm, it must be accepted in the name of the firm, or by one partner for himself and his co-partners, otherwise the holder might protest the bill, as the mere signature of a single partner was binding only upon himself. Lord Ellenborough. There is no foundation for the doctrine contended for; this acceptance does not prove the partnership; but if the defendants were partners, they are both bound by it. For this purpose, it would have been enough if the word "accepted" had been written on the bill, and the effect cannot be altered by adding "T. Rumsey, sen." If a bill of exchange is drawn upon a firm, and accepted by one of the partners, he must be understood to exercise his power to bind his co-partners, and to accept the bill according to the terms in which it is drawn. The plaintiff had a verdict.

ᵏ Ld. Galway v. Matthews and another, 1 Campb. 403. 10 East, 264. S. C. but not same point. Bayl. 24.

H. and Co. was in the habit of indorsing bills in the manner above stated although there was no such person as F. in the firm of H. and Co. and no direct proof that J. D's. partners were privy to these transactions. Ibid.

By act of must be protested for want of acceptance.[1] So, if a promissory note
partner. appear on the face of it to be the separate note of A. only, it cannot
be declared on as the joint note of A. and B. though given to secure
a debt for which both were liable.[m] And when one of two partners
drew bills of exchange in his own name, and got them discounted, and
applied the proceeds to the partnership account, it was held, that the
party advancing the money, has no remedy against the partnership,
either upon the bills so drawn by the single partner, or for money had
and received through the medium of such bills,[n] though, in a subsequent case, in appearing that all the partners had caused such bills to
[40] be issued for the purpose of raising money for the firm, they were held
liable to be sued by the persons who discounted the bills for the money
as lent, and for interest.[o](52)

---

[1] Marius, 16; and see Carwick v. Vickery, Dougl. 653. Bayl, 55.

[m] Siffkin v. Walker and another, 2
Camp 308. Emly v. Lye and another, 15
East, 7.

[n] Emly v. Lye and another, 15 East, 7.

[o] Denton v. Rodie and another, 3 Camp.
493. Per Lord Ellenborough, "I think
this case is distinguishable from Emly v.
Lye. Here I conceive the partner in
America had authority from the two
others to raise money for the use of the
firm, and money was accordingly raised
from the plaintiffs upon these bills, in
pursuance of such authority. The transaction is a loan rather than a discount.
I. B. Clough was sent out to America to
manage the business of the house there,
and to procure homeward investments;
the shipments from this country did not

form an adequate fund for that purpose.
He says himself, that he had a carte
blanche as to the means he should adopt;
he accordingly raises money, for which he
gives, as a security, bills of exchange,
drawn in his own name, upon the house.
They know and recognize this mode of
dealing ; they regularly accept and pay
the bills so drawn, till the time of their
failure ; therefore, although I cannot say
they are jointly liable upon the unaccepted
bills, I think they are jointly indebted to
the same amount, as for money lent, or
money had and received." It was then
suggested, that the plaintiffs, upon this
supposition, could not claim interest; but
Lord Ellenborough thought, that from
the course of dealing, the plaintiffs were
entitled to interest, although they did not
recover upon the written securities. Verdict accordingly.

---

(52) A note given by one partner for his own private debt in the name of the firm,
but without the consent of the other partners, is not binding upon the partnership in the
hands of the payee. Livingston v. Hastie, 2 Caines' Rep. 246. Livingston v. Roosevelt,
4 John. Rep. 251. Dubois v. Roosevelt, 4 John. Rep. 262. note. Lansing v. Gaine, 2
John. Rep. 300. Brown v. Duncanson and Ray. 4 Har. and M'Hen. Rep., 350. Neither will a person who has become a surety or indorser upon such note upon the supposition that it was a partnership transaction, and bound all the partners, be liable under
such circumstances; to an indorsee who is cousant of the facts, Livingston v. Hastie,
But such note will be good, and bind all parties in the hands of a bona fide holder without notice. Livingston v. Hastie, Livingston v. Roosevelt.
   If after a dissolution of the partnership one partner issue notes in the partnership name,
these notes bind the partner who signed them, but not the other partners; for his power
to bind the partnership ceased with it, Lansing v. Gaine. Jones's Case, Overton's Rep.
455. And if such notes be ante-dated so as to appear dated within the term of the partnership, this does not vary the rule, since they bind only from the actual delivery, Ibid.
One partner, after a dissolution, cannot indorse notes or bills given before to the firm,
though he is authorised to settle the partnership concerns. Sanford v. Mickles, 4 John.
Rep. 224. This doctrine, however, only applies in cases where the dissolution of the
partnership has been duly notified, or is known to the party taking the notes. Ibid.
And for this purpose notice in the public newspapers of the dissolution is sufficient as to
all persons who have had no previous dealings with the firm. Ibid. Mowatt v. Howland, 3 Day's Rep. 353. But it seems that to persons who have previously dealt with
the firm, mere notice in the newspapers is not sufficient; but actual knowledge should be
brought home either by express or constructive notice of the dissolution, Ketcham v.
Clark, 6 John. Rep. 144.
   If after a dissolution of a partnership one partner sign a note in the name of the firm,
if such transaction be ratified subsequently by the other partners, it binds the partnership. And a part payment of such note by the other partner will be deemed a sufficient
adoption and ratification of the act. Eaton v. Taylor, 10 Mass. Rep. 54.

Where there is a limited and special partnership, and persons deal with it knowingly By act of as such, they are bound by the terms of it, and cannot make the partners liable, unless partner. upon the transactions of such special partnership. *Ensign* v. *Wands*, 1 John Cas. 171. Therefore, where one partner in such special concern gives a note for a debt not due from the concern, it does not bind the firm, although executed in their name, unless the other partner consent. *Lensing* v. *Gaine. Livingston* v. *Roosevelt.* And it seems that publication in the newspapers of the nature of such partnership at the time of its commencement, is constructive notice to all those who may afterwards deal with the partnership, or take their securities. *Livingston* v. *Roosevelt.*

There seems to be a difference of opinion among the courts of the United States, whether the acknowledgment of a debt by one partner after a dissolution of the partnership, binds the other partners. In *South Carolina* it has been adjudged in the affirmative, on the ground that it is not the nature of a new contract, but the recognition of an old one. *Simpson* v. *Geddes*, 2 Bay's Rep. 533. But the contrary has been held in *New York. Hackley* v. *Patrick*, 3 John. Rep. 536. But it is admitted, that in such case the acknowledgment of one partner is sufficient to take the debt out of the Statute of Limitations. *Smith* v. *Ludlow*, 6 John. Rep. 267. See 1 Barn. and Ald. Rep. 463. *Johnson* v. *Beardslee*, 15 John. Rep. 4.

It has been held in Connecticut in a suit on a partnership note, that it is no defence to one partner that he executed the note in the partnership name after the suit was instituted, and ante-dated it with a view to reserve to the defendants in preference to other creditors, the property attached without the knowledge of the other partners. *Minturn, &c.* v. *Berber, &c.* 1 Day's Rep. 136. The precise ground of this decision does not appear; but it may be inferred, that the court were of opinion that one partner might lawfully by such act create a lien upon the partnership property in favour of any creditor of the firm.

A. and B. being co-partners in trade, B. make a promissory note payable to C. or order, subscribes the name of the firm, and writes the name of C. as indorser, without his leave or knowledge, and with intent to defraud any future holder of the note: he delivered it thus indorsed to a broker, who sold it to the plaintiff. It did not appear that A. was knowing to the making of fraudulent indorsement of the note. The plaintiff recovered the amount of the note in an action against A and B. for money had and received *Boardman* v. *Gore*, *et al.* 15 Mas. Rep. 331. See also, *Manufacturers and Mechanics' Bank* v. *Gore*, *et al.* 15 Mas. Rep. 75.

If a promissory note beginning " I promise to pay," be signed by one member of a firm for himself and his partners, the party signing is severally liable to be paid upon the note. *Hall* v. *Smith*. 1 Barn. &. Cressw. 406.

CHAPTER III.

OF THE FORM AND REQUISITES OF BILLS, &c.—THE CONSIDERATION FOR WHICH MADE OR TRANSFERRED—CONSTRUCTION OF THEM—CONSEQUENCE OF ALTERATION IN THEM—AND OF THE DRAWER'S LIABILITY.

The form of bills of exchange, &c. in general. THOUGH a bill of exchange, check, promissory note, &c, must be in writing,[a] there is in general no particular *form*, or set of words, necessary to be adopted, any more than in the case of a bond or other deed.[b] And indeed our courts considering the general utility of these instruments, and how much they tend to the extension of credit, and consequent advancement of trade and commerce, have uniformly gone further in giving effect to them as instruments, than they have where a question has arisen on the formation of a deed.

[42] Thus an order or promise to deliver money, or a promise that I. S. shall receive money, or a promise to be accountable or responsible for it, will be a sufficient bill or note ;[c] and where a note was in these words, "borrowed of I. S. £50, which I promise *never* to pay," the word "never" was rejected, and the holder recovered ;[d] and in a late case it was decided, that an instrument in the common form of a bill of exchange, except that the word "*at*" was substituted for "*to*," before

[a] Thomas v. Bishop, Rep. Temp. Hardw. 2.
[b] Com. Dig. tit. Obligation, B. 1, 2. Bac. Ab. tit. Obligation, B. ——— v. Ormston, 10 Mod. 287. Dawkes v. Lord de Loraine, 3 Wils. 213. Morris v. Lee, Ld. Raym. 1397. 1 Stra. 629. 8 Mod. 364. S. C. Chadwick v. Allen, 2 Stra. 706. Rast. Ent. 238. Ruff v. Webb, 1 Esp. Rep. 129. Colehan v. Cooke, Willes, 396. Bayl. 3.
Morris v. Lee, Ld. Raym. 1396. 1 Stra. 629. 8 Mod. 362. S. C. Plaintiff sued as indorsee of a note in these words, "I promise to account with T. S. or order for fifty pounds, value received by me ;" and after verdict for plaintiff, it was insisted in arrest of judgment, that this was not a negotiable note: *sed per cur.* "There are no precise words necessary to be used in a note or bill. Deliver such a sum of money, makes a good bill ; by receiving the value, the defendant became a debtor, and when he promises to be accountable to A. or order, it is the same thing as a promise to pay A., and it would be an odd construction to expound the word 'accountable' to give an account, when there may be several indorsees." Judgment for plaintiff.

Chadwick v. Allen, 2 Stra. 706. A note was in these words : "I do acknowledge that Sir Andrew Chadwick has delivered me all the bonds and notes, for which 400l. were paid him on account of Colonel Synge, and that Sir Andrew delivered me Major Graham's receipt and bill on me for 10l., which 10l. and 15l. 5s. balance, due to Sir Andrew, I am still indebted and do promise to pay," and upon demurrer to the declaration, the court held it a note within the statute.
Cashborne v. Dutton, Scacc. M. 1 Geo. 2. MS. Sel. Ni. Pri. 363 Where the note set forth in the declaration was, "I do acknowledge myself to be indebted to A. in L——, to be paid on demand, for value received." On demurrer to the declaration, the court, after solemn argument, held, that this was a good note within the statute, the words "to be paid," amounting to a promise to pay, observing that the same words in a lease would amount to a covenant to pay rent.
[c] See cases in last note.
[d] Cited by Lord Mansfield in Russell v. Langstaff, B. R., M. 21 Geo. 3. and in Peach v. Kay, Sittings after Trin. Term, 1781. and per Lord Hardw. 2 Atk. 32. Bayl. 5.

the name of the drawee, may be declared on as a bill of exchange, or **The form** as a promissory note at the option of the holders ;[e] and we have seen, **of bills of** that an instrument that appears. on common observation, to be a bill of **exchange,** exchange, may be treated as such, although words be introduced into **&c.** it for the purpose of deception, which might make it a promissory note.[f](55) It is however advisable to draw bills, &c. according to the forms hereafter given. And in the case of bills and notes, for the payment of less than £5, certain forms must be observed.[g] for it is provided that all negotiable bills or notes made in England for less than twenty shillings, shall be void,[h] and all negotiable bills or notes made in England (excepting Bank of England notes and notes payable to the. bearer on demand) for the payment of twenty shillings and less than £5, should be void, unless they specify the name and place of abode of the person to whom or to whose order they are made payable, and be attested by one subscribing witnesss, and bear date at or before the time when they are issued, and be made payable within twenty-one days after the date, and be in the form prescribed by the act.[i]

There are *two principal qualities* essential to the validity of a bill or **Their ge-** note, *first*, that it be *payable at all events*, not dependent on any con **neral re-** tingency, nor payable out of a particular fund ; and *secondly*, that it be **quisites.** for the *payment of money only*, and not for the payment of money, and performance of some other act, or in the alternative ; for it would perplex commercial transactions, if paper securities of this nature, encumbered with conditions and contingencies were circulated, and if the persons to whom they were offered in negotiation, were obliged to inquire when these uncertain events would probably be reduced to a certainty.[k]

First. An order or promise to pay money, provided the terms mentioned in certain letters, shall be complied with,[l] or provided that I. S.

[e] Shuttleworth v. Stephen, 1 Campb. 407. Ante, 21.
[f] Allen v. Mawson, 4 Campb. 115. Ante, 21.
[g] 17 Geo. 3. c. 30. s. 1. See the statute in the Appendix.
[h] 48 Geo. 3. c. 88.
[i] 17 Geo. 3. c. 30. s. 1. made perpetual by 27 Geo. 3. c. 16. See post, Appendix.
[k] Per Kenyon, C. J. in Carlos v. Fancourt, 5 T. R. 485. Dawkes v. Lord de Loraine, 3 Wils. 213. 2 Bla. Rep. 782. S. C. Roberts v. Peake, 1 Burr. 325.

[l] Kingston v. Long, B. R., M. 25 Geo. 3. The plaintiff brought an action as indorsee against the defendant as acceptor, upon an order importing to be payable, " provided the terms mentioned in certain letters written by the drawer were complied with," and the court held clearly, that the plaintiff could not recover, though the acceptance admitted a compliance with the terms, for the order was no bill until after such compliance, and if it were not a bill when drawn, it could not afterwards become one. Bayl. 9.

(55) These requisites apply only to a bill or note in its original formation, for it seems that an acceptance may be to pay upon a contingency, or in bills, &c. and not in money. See post.

The doctrine that a bill payable out of a particular fund, is not negotiable according to the custom of merchants, has been recognised in Kentucky. *Mershon* v. *Withers*, 1 Bibb's R. 502.

A bill of exchange must not be made payable out of a particular fund, but if the fund is certain and is described only as a mean by which the drawee is to be indemnified, the bill is good. *Bank of Kentucky* v. *Sanders*, 3 Marsh. 184.

The word " *note* " is sometimes considered as a general term, comprehending both bills of exchange and promissory notes, and was held to embrace the former, when used in an assignment for the benefit of creditors. *Da Costa* v. *Guieu*, 7 Serg. & Rawle, 402.

shall not be surrendered to prison within the limited time," or provided I. S. shall not pay the money by a particular day,' or provided I. S. shall leave me sufficient, or I shall otherwise be able to pay it,' or when I. S. shall marry, or if the maker should be married within two months,' or to pay a sailor wages if he do his duty as an able seaman,' is no bill or note on account of the contingency upon which the payment depends.

So, if by the terms of the instrument, the payment is to depend upon the sufficiency of a particular fund, the bill or note will be invalid; thus an order to pay money out of the drawer's growing subsistence,' or out of the fifth payment when it should become due, and it should be allowed by the drawer,' or out of money when received,' [44] or an order to pay the amount of a note and interest out of the purchase-money of the drawer's house,' or an order or promise to pay out of the drawer's money that should arise from his reversion, when sold, is no

" Smith *v.* Boehm, 3 Lord Raym. 67. cited Lord Raym. 1362. 1396: Action by the plaintiff as payee of the note, against the makers, upon a promise to pay the plaintiff, or order, oh demand, the sum of 71*l.* 12*s.* 10*d.* or surrender the body of Samuel Boehm in an action brought against him by Smith. Verdict for the plaintiff, and judgment; and on error brought in the King's Bench, the court held that this was not a note within the statute, because the money was not absolutely payable, but depended upon the contingency whether the defendants should surrender Samuel Boehm to prison, and the judgment was reversed.

" Appleby *v.* Biddulph, cited 8 Mod., 363. 4 Vin. Abr. 240, pl. 16. An action was brought on this note, " I promise to pay T. M. 50*l.* if my brother doth not pay it within six weeks," and after verdict for the plaintiff, the court arrested judgment, because the maker was only to pay it upon a contingency.

° Roberts *v.* Peake, Burr. 323. The plaintiff, as indorsee of a note, sued one of the makers; the instrument was in these words; " we promise to pay A. B. 116*l.* 11*s.* value received, on the death of George Henshaw, provided he leaves either of us sufficient to pay that said sum, or if we otherwise shall be able to pay it;" and upon a case reserved, the court held it was not a negotiable note, because it was payable eventually and conditionally only, and not absolutely and at all events, and a nonsuit was entered; and see Ex parte Tootell, 4 Ves. 372.

* Beardsley *v.* Baldwin, Stra. 1151. A note to pay money within so many days after the defendant should marry, was held not to be a negotiable note; and in Pearson *v.* Garrett, Comb. 277, and 4 Mod. 242; an action having been brought upon a note, by which the defendant promised to pay the plaintiff sixty guineas, if he (the plaintiff) should be married within two months, the court inclined against the

note, because it was to pay money on a mere contingency.

9 Alves *v.* Hodgson, 7 T. R. 242.

' Jocelyn *v.* Laserre, Fort. 281. 10 Mod. 294. 316. Evans drew upon Jocelyn, and required him to pay Laserre 7*l.* per month out of Evans's growing subsistence. Laserre sued Jocelyn, and had judgment, but upon a writ of error, that judgment was reversed, because this draft was not a good bill of exchange, inasmuch as it would not have been payable had Evans died, or had his subsistence been taken away.

' Haydock *v.* Linch, Lord Raym. 1563. Rogers drew upon Linch, and requested him to pay Haydock 14*l.* 3*s.* out of the fifth payment when it should become due, and it should be allowed by Rogers. Linch accepted the draft, and Haydock sued him, but the court, upon demurrer to the declaration, held this was no bill of exchange, and gave judgment for the defendant.

' Dawkes *v.* Lord de Loraine, 2 Bla. Rep. 782. 3 Wils. 207. A draft was in these words, " 8 Jan. 1768. Seven weeks after date, pay to Mrs. Dawkes 32*l.* 17*s.* out of W. Steward's money, as soon as you shall have received it, for your humble servant, De Loraine. To Timothy Brecknock, Esq." Brecknock accepted the bill, but it not being paid, Mrs. D. brought an action against Lord de Loraine, who pleaded that Brecknock had not received W. Steward's money; and upon demurrer to his plea, insisted that this was not a bill of exchange. The court, after argument, held the objection good, because it was payable out of a particular fund, and on an event which was future and contingent, viz. the receipt of W. Steward's money, whereas a bill ought to be subject to no event or contingency, except the failure of the general personal credit of the persons drawing or negotiating it.

" Yates *v.* Grove, 1 Ves. jun. 280. 1.

bill or note.[a] So an order to pay a sum of money out of the rents or Their general requisites. other money in the hands of the person to whom it is addressed, is no bill, because he may not have rent or other money in his hands sufficient to discharge it.[b] So a promise to pay on the sale or produce, immediately when sold, of the White Hart Inn, St. Albans, and the goods, &c. is no note, although it be averred in the declaration upon such promise, that the White Hart Inn, goods, &c. were sold before the action was commenced.[c] So an order from the owner of a ship to the freighter, to pay money on account of freight, is no bill, because the quantum due [45] on the freight may be open to litigation,[d] but such an order from the freighter is, because it is an admission that so much at least is due.[e] So an instrument by which the party promises to pay the sum of £65, and also such other sum as, by reference to his books, he owed to another with interest, cannot be considered as a promissory note even as to the £65, and cannot be given in evidence under the count upon an account stated, without an agreement stamp;[f] however, a verbal agreement, qualifying the liability to pay the bill, will not vitiate.[g]

Secondly, the bill or note must be for the payment of money only, and not for the payment of money and performance of some other act,

[a] Carlos v. Fancourt, in error from the C. P. 5 T. R. 482. Assumpsit upon a promissory note, whereby Carlos, in the life-time of defendant's wife, promised to pay Fancourt's wife the sum of 10*l.* "*out of his money that should arise from his reversion of 43l. when sold.*" The defendant suffered judgment by default, and brought a writ of error, and the court held that this note could not be declared upon as a negotiable security under the stat. 3 & 4 Ann. c. 9. the object of which statute was to put promissory notes on the same footing with bills of exchange in every respect, and they must stand or fall by the same rules by which bills of exchange were governed; and unless they carried their own validity on the face of them, they were not negotiable, and on that ground bills of exchange which were only payable on a contingency, were not negotiable, because it did not appear on the face of them whether or not they would ever be paid. The same rule that governed bills of exchange in this respect must govern promissory notes, and therefore reversed the judgment. Hill v. Halford, infra, note [e], and post, p. 45, note.

[b] Jenney v. Herle, Lord Raym. 1861. 8 Mod. 265. Stra 591. Herle sued Jenney upon a bill drawn by him upon Pratt: and payable to Herle as follows: "Sir you are to pay Mr. Herle 1945*l.* out of the money in your hands, belonging to the proprietors of the Devonshire Mines, being part of the consideration money for the purchase of the manor of West Buckland." Herle had judgment in the Common Pleas: but upon a writ of error, the court of King's Bench held, that this was no bill of exchange, because it was only payable out of a particular fund, supposed to be in Pratt's CHITTY ON BILLS.

hands, and the judgment was accordingly reversed.

[c] Hill v. Halford and another, in error, 2 Bos. & Pul. 413. The defendants in error sued Hill, as maker of a note, thereby promising to pay them 190*l.* *on the sale or produce, immediately when sold,* of the White Hart Inn, St. Alban's, Herts, and the goods, &c. value received. The declaration averred a sale of the inn and goods before the commencement of the action. After judgment in K. B. by default, writ of inquiry executed, and general damage recovered. Hill brought a writ of error in the Exchequer Chamber, and the court held that this promise could not be declared on as a note, and therefore reversed the judgment.

[d] Banbury v. Lissett, Stra. 1211. Gibson drew on the defendant in favour of the plaintiff, "on account of the freight of the Galley Veale, Edward Champion, and this order shall be your sufficient discharge for the same." This action was brought against the defendants as acceptors, and they contended, that it was not a bill of exchange, because it was only payable out of a particular fund; and Lee, C. J. was of that opinion.

[e] Pierson v. Dunlop, Cowp. 571. M'Lintot freighted a ship, of which Nicholl was captain, and Pierson owner, and being unable to pay the freight, drew upon Dunlop and Co. in favour of Nicholl, on account of freight. Pierson afterwards sued Dunlop and Co. as acceptors, and though other objections were taken, yet it was never insisted that this was payable out of a particular fund.

[f] Smith v. Nightingale, 2 Stark. 375. As to the stamp, see Firbank v. Bell, 1 B. & A. 36.

[g] Campbell v. Hodgson, 1 Gow, 74.

G

or in the alternative. Thus, if an instrument be to deliver up horses and a wharf, and pay money on a particular day,[e] or to pay a sum of money, or surrender to I. S to prison,[f] or to pay money in good East India Bonds,[g] it is not a bill or note.

If the bill, note, &c. be insufficient in its formation in either of these respects, it will not become valid by any subsequent occurrence rendering the payment no longer contingent;[h] and the instrument will not be negotiable, not can it be declared upon as a bill, even between the original parties;[i] (1) and though it may in some cases be declared upon as **[46]** an agreement, yet it cannot be produced in evidence, unless stamped as such;[k] and even if it be stamped, the consideration on which it was founded must be proved. So, though the instrument may, on the face of it, be absolute, yet if by a memorandum on the back of it, the payment is rendered conditional, it cannot be declared upon as a bill or note between the same parties. And therefore, where upon an instrument in the common form of a joint and several promissory note, signed by three persons, there was an indorsement written at the time of signing it, stating that the note was taken as a security for all balances to the amount of the sum within specified, which one of the three might happen to owe to the payee, and that the note should be in force for six months, and that no money should be liable to be called for sooner in any case; it was decided, in an action against one of the sureties, that the payee could not declare upon this instrument as a promissory note, payable either on demand, or at six months after date.[l]

[e] Martin *v.* Chauntry, Stra. 1271. On error from the court of Common Pleas, the court of King's Bench held, that a note to deliver up horses and a wharf, and pay money at a particular day, was not a note within the statute, and reversed the judgment in favour of the original plaintiff.

[f] Smith *v.* Boehm, Gilb. Cases L. & E. 93. cited also in Lord Raym. 1362. 1396. and see 3 Lord Raym. 67. Error on judgment in C. P. upon a note to pay 72*l.* upon demand for value received, or render the body of A. B. &c. to the Fleet, before such a day. The court held such note to be contingent and invalid.

[g] Anon. Bull. Ni. Pri. 272. a written promise to pay 300*l.* to B. or order, in three good East India Bonds, was held not to be a note within the statute.

[h] Hill *v.* Halford, 2 Bos. & Pul. 413. Ante, p. 44. Colehan *v.* Cooke, Willes, 399. post p. 48. Kingston *v.* Long, ante, 42. Selw. N. P. 367, n. 71. acc. Lewis *v.* Orde, 1 Gilb. Ev. by Loft, 179. *semb. contra.*

[i] Carlos *v.* Fancourt, 5 T. R. 485.—Mainwaring *v.* Newman, 2 Bos. & Pul. 123 Alves *v.* Hodgson, 7 T. R. 243. Bayley on Bills, 8.

[k] Mainwaring *v.* Newman, 2 Bos. & Pul. 125 Kyd, on Bills, 58. Leeds *v.* Lancashire, 2 Campb. 207. Smith *v.* Nightingale, 2 Stark. 375. Ante, 45. Firbank *v.* Bell, 1 B. & A. 36. Butts *v.* Swan, 2 Taunt. & B. 78.

[l] Leeds *v.* Lancashire, 2 Campb. 205. The defendant, Marriott and Ball, gave a joint and several promissory note to the plaintiffs for 200*l.* No time for payment was mentioned in the note. On the back was written, "The within note is taken for security of all such balances as James Marriott may happen to owe to Thomas Leeds and Co. not extending farther than the within sum of 200*l.*, but this note to be in force for six months, and no money liable to be called for sooner in any case." This memorandum was written before the note was signed by the defendant or Ball. It appeared in an action upon this note, that, in the course of mercantile dealings, Marriott had become indebted to the plaintiffs, and that on their refusing to deal with him any longer without some guarantee, the above instrument, which the makers represented to be a note, was given. It was impressed with a promissory note stamp. Lord Ellenborough. As between the original parties this instrument is only an agreement, and not a note; in the hands of a *bona fide* holder, who received it as a promissory note, it might possibly be considered as such. The plaintiffs were nonsuited.

(1) On a draught payable out of a particular fund of money in the drawer's hands belonging to the payee, the payee may maintain an action against the drawer in case of the drawee refusing acceptance *Joliffe* v. *Higgins*, 6 Munf. 9.

And when it appears by any part of the instrument, that the money was not payable immediately, and that the payment was to depend on an uncertain event, it will not operate as a bill of exchange or a promissory note, but as a special agreement, and must be stamped as such; and therefore it was recently decided, that an instrument acknowledging the receipt of a bill of exchange which had two months to run, and promising to pay the amount with interest, is a special agreement, and not a promissory note, being in effect a special undertaking to repay the amount of the bills if honoured at maturity."

So, where an instrument, purporting on the face of it to be a promis- [47] sory note for the payment of money absolutely before it was signed, was indorsed with a memorandum. that if any dispute should arise between Lady W. and the plaintiff, respecting the sale of the timber for which the note was given, it should be void; it was held, that the indorsement was part of the note, and the payment being only conditional, the instrument was not a note within the statute." So, if there be a written stipulation to renew even on a separate paper, it should seem that it will qualify the liability, though it will not vitiate the instrument itself." But where an indorsement appeared merely to import the will or desire of the payee, that the maker should be indulged as to the time or manner of payment, and the original undertaking was positive, it was held, that such indorsement did not affect the validity of the note, or afford any defence." And if the instrument on the face of it, purport to be an absolute engagement to pay money at a certain time, no *parol* evidence of an agreement at the time, to renew or give indulgence will be admissible to defeat the action on the bill or note." And where a

---

* Williamson v. Bennett, 2 Campb. 417. The defendants were sued on the following instrument, which was stamped as and declared upon as a promissory note:—" Borrowed and received of J. and J. Williamson (the plaintiffs,) the sum of 200l., in three drafts, by W. and B. Williamson, dated as under, payable to us, W. Bennett and S. M. (the defendants) on J. and J. Williamson,) which we promise to pay unto the said J. and J. Williamson, with interest. As witness this 26th day of August, 1802."

August 21st. 1 draft at 2 months *L*120
1 ditto   -   30
1 ditto   -   50
                  ————
                  *L*200

Signed by the defendants.

Lord Ellenborough held, that this was not a promissory note; and said, there can be no doubt that the money was not payable immediately, and that it was not to be paid at all unless the drafts were honoured. The plaintiffs were nonsuited.

* Hartley v. Wilkinson and another, 4 M. & S. 26. 4 Campb. 127. S. C.
* Bowerbank v. Monteiro, 4 Taunt. 844. Steel v. Bradfield, id. 227.
* Stone v. Metcalf, gent. one, &c. Sit.

after Trin. 1815, MS. and 4 Campb. 217. 1 Stark. 53.

* Hoare and others v. Graham, 3 Camp. 57. Indorsee against the payees of a promissory note. The defendants gave in evidence that they had indorsed the note by way of collateral security for certain advances made by the plaintiff to Messrs. Grill and Son, and the verbal condition of the defendant's indorsement was, that the note should be renewed when it became due, to which the plaintiffs acceded, but that they afterwards demanded payment instead of calling for a renewal.

Lord Ellenborough. I do not think I can admit evidence of this sort; what is to become of bills of exchange and promissory notes if they may be cut down by a secret agreement that they shall not be put in suit? The parol condition is quite inconsistent with the written instrument. I will receive evidence that the note was indorsed to the plaintiffs as a trust, but the condition for a renewal entirely contradicts the instrument which the defendants have signed; such an agreement rests in confidence and honour only, and is not an obligation of law. There may, after a bill is drawn, be a binding promise for a valuable consideration to renew it, when due, but if the promise is cotemporaneous with the drawing of the bill, the law will not en-

premissory note on the face of it purported to be payable on demand, it was held, that parol evidence is not admissible to show that at the time of making it, it was agreed that it should not be payable till after the decease of the testator.[r]

But if the *event on which the instrument is to become payable, must inevitably happen some time or other*, it has been decided to be of no importance how long the payment may be in suspence.[s] Therefore if a bill be drawn, payable six weeks after the death of the drawer's father,[t] or payable to an infant, when he shall come of age, specifying the day when that event will happen, it will be valid and negotiable.[u](62)

force it. This would be incorporating with a written contract an incongruous parol condition, which is contrary to first principles. The plaintiff, therefore, had a verdict. The same point was decided in Campbell *v.* Hodgson, 1 Gow. Rep. 74. See this case cited by Gibbs, C. J. in Bowerbank *v.* Monteiro, 4 Taunt. 846. See 1 Taunt. 347. Skin. 54. Phil. on evid. 2d edit. 483. and see 1 M. & S. 21.

Dukes *v.* Dow, Sittings after Easter Term, 1817, *coram* Gibbs, C. J. Payee *v.* Maker of a note for 13*l.* : 8*s.* : 10*d.* payable nine months after date. Defence and proof that defendant, at time of giving the note, was charged in execution for a debt, and it was agreed between plaintiff and defendant, that the latter should be discharged on giving the note, and the plaintiff verbally agreed, at the time it was given, that if it was not convenient to the defendant to pay the note at maturity, the plaintiff would give him time, but had commenced this action contrary to such engagement. Gibbs, C. J. held, that such a parol contract collateral to the instrument, could not be admitted in evidence to annul the very terms of the written contract, and defeat its obligation.

Rawson and another *v.* Walker, 1 Stark. 361. Action on a promissory note for 66*l.*, payable on demand. Lord Ellenborough refused to receive parol evidence inconsistent with the terms of the note; that it was agreed between the plaintiff and defendant, that the defendant should not be called on to pay till a final dividend of a bankrupt's estate should be made.

[r] Woodbridge *v.* Spooner, 3 B. & A. 228. Chitty's Rep. 661. S. C.

[s] Colehan *v.* Cooke, Willes, 396. S.— Stra. 1217. S. C. Goss *v.* Nelson, 1 Burr. 226.

[t] Colehan *v.* Cooke, Willes, 396. Stra. 1217. S. C. On a writ of error from the Common Pleas, on a note whereby defendant promised to pay A. or order 150*l.*, six weeks after the death of his father. The court held this to be a negotiable note within the statute, and that the distance of time of payment was no objection, as the event on which it was payable, the death of the defendant's father must happen : and see Ex parte Mitford, 1 Bro. C. C. 398 ; but see Ex parte Barker, 9 Ves. 110.

[u] Goss *v.* Nelson, 1 Burr. 226. Action on a note payable to an infant, "when he (the infant,) shall come of age, to wit, 12th June, 1750," and it was objected, in arrest of judgment, that it was uncertain whether the money would ever have been payable, because the infant might have died under twenty-one, but the court held it a good note, because it was payable at all events on the 12th June, 1750, though the infant should have died before that time, and see 2 Bla. Com. 513.

(62) A promissory note payable to A. or order, at a day certain, " or when he (the promisee) completes the building according to contract," is payable absolutely at a day certain, and therefore good within the statute, and negotiable. *Stevens* v. *Blunt*, 7 Mass. Rep. 240.

A note, promising to pay a sum to the president, directors and company of a turnpike road, for five shares of the capital stock of said company, in such manner and proportion, and at such time place as the president, directors, and company should from time to time require, 'as been held in effect payable on demand and therefore a cash note within the statut[e] *President, &c. of the Goshen Turnpike* v. *Hurtin*, 9 John. Rep. 217. But a different opinion seems to have been asserted in the *President, &c. of the Union Turnpike Road* v. *Jenkins*, 1 Caine's Rep. 381.

A note for a certain sum payable to A. or order, " in foreign bills," (meaning thereby bills of country banks) has been held in Massachusetts not to be a good promissory note within the statute, and consequently not negotiable. *Jones* v. *Fales*, 4 Mass. Rep.

There are also decisions, that if the event on which the payment is Their general requisites. to depend, be of public notoriety, and relating to trade, and there be a moral certainty of its taking place, the bill, &c. will be valid.[1] On this ground the bills of exchange, called *Billæ nundinales* were formerly always holden to be good, because though the fairs on which the payment of them depended, were not always holden at a certain time, yet it was certain that they would be holden.[7] So it has been reported to have been decided, that if a bill or note be payable two months after a certain ship be paid off,[8] or be payable on the receipt on the payee's wages, due to him from a certain ship, it is valid;[9] but this latter decision seems questionable.[b]

[49   ]

The statement of a particular fund, in a bill of exchange, will not vitiate it, if it be inserted merely as a direction to the drawee how to reimburse himself; and therefore, a bill requesting the drawee, one month after date, to pay the plaintiff, or his order, a certain sum of money " as my quarterly half-pay, to be due from the 24th June to the 27th September next by advance," was decided to be a valid bill,[c] be-

---

[1] Coleban v. Cooke, Willes, 398. Andrews v. Franklin, 1 Stra. 24. Evans v. Underwood, 1 Wils. 262. Dawkes v. De Loraine, 3 Wils. 213. 2 Bla. Rep. 782. S. C. Lewis v. Orde, Gilb. Ev. 172. Hill v. Halford, 2 Bos. & Pul. 414., 5 ante, p. 44, note, and p. 45, note, *sed vide* Kyd. 58.

[7] Per Willes, C. J. in delivering judgment in Coleban v. Cooke, Willes, 394.

[8] Andrews v. Franklin, 1 Stra. 24. A note, payable two months after a certain ship should be paid off, was objected to, as depending upon a contingencey which might never happen ; but *per cur.* the paying off the ship is a thing of a public nature, and this is negotiable as a promissory note. Bayl 3d edit. 15. See also Selw. N. P. 4th edit. 367.

[9] Evans v. Underwood, 1 Wils. 262.— This was an action brought by an indorsee against the maker, upon a note payable on the receipt of the payee's wages from his majesty's ship the Suffolk; the court thought this case like that of Andrews v. Franklin, and after looking into that case, ARE SAID to have given judgment for the plaintiff. Upon this case there is a note in Bayley on Bills, 3d edit. 15, as follows :—" Quære tamen, because it was uncertain, though the wages might be paid, whether the maker would receive them." See also Lewis v.

Orde, 1 Gilb. on Evid. by Loft, 178.— Selw. N. P. 4th edit. 367, note 71.

[b] In Selw. N. P. 4th edit. 367, note 71. there is a note upon this point, and in the conclusion is stated the case of Beardesley v. Baldwin, E. 15 Geo. 2. B. R. MSS. in which the court said, that as to Andrews v. Franklin, if it ever was determined, which they could not find, it must have been decided on the certainty observed in the return of ships, and must be looked upon as an event in itself not contingent. *Sed quære.*

[c] M'Leod v. Snee, Stra. 762. Lord Raym. 1481. 11 Mod. 400. 1 Barn. 12. S. C. Error on a judgment, given against M'Leod, on a bill of exchange drawn by J. S. on the 25th May, 1724, upon M'Leod, and directed him, one month after the date, to pay A. B. or order 9l. : 10s. as his quarter's half-pay from 24th June, 1724, to 25th September following. The court were of opinion that this was a good bill of exchange, for it was *not* payable out of a particular fund, nor upon a contingency, and was made payable at all events ; and was drawn upon the general credit of the drawer, not out of the half-pay, for it is payable as soon as the quarter began for the half-pay mentioned in the bill, which was not to be due for three months after.

---

213. But in *New York*, a note payable to A. or bearer, in " York state bills or specie," has been held a negotiable note within the statute. upon the ground that the bills mentioned meant bank paper, which in conformity with common usage and understanding, is regarded as cash ; and therefore that the note meant the same as if payable in lawful current money of the state. *Keith* v. *Jones*, 9 John. Rep. 120.

A promissory note payable at a particular place, " in the bank notes current in the city of New York," is a negotiable note within the statute. *Judah* v. *Harris*, 19 Johns. 144. But in *M'Cormick* v. *Trotter*, 10 Serg. & Rawle, 94 it was held, that a note promising to pay A. B. or order five hundred dollars in notes of the chartered banks of Pennsylvania is not a negotiable note on which the indorsee can sue in his own name.

Their ge-
neral re-
quisites.

[50]

cause it would be payable, though the half-pay might never become due: and an order from the *freighter* of a ship, to pay money on account of freight, is sufficient, because it is an admission that so much at least is due;[d] though we have seen that an order from the *owner* of a ship, to the freighter, to pay money on account of freight, is not valid.[e] Nor will a bill be vitiated by the insertion of words, pointing out the consideration of the acceptance: as, for instance, "value received, out of the premises in Rosemary-lane;"[f] or "being a portion of a value as under deposited in security for payment hereof,[g] or on account of wine had of the drawer. (64) A note also, whereby the maker promised to pay to A. B. £8. "so much being to be due from me to C. D. my landlady at Lady-day next, who is indebted in that sum to A. B." was, on the same principle, held not to be conditional.[i](64)

---

[d] Pierson v. Dunlop, Cowp. 571. vide ante, 45.

[e] Baubury v. Lissett, Stra. 1112. vide ante, 45.

[f] Burchell, administrator, &c. v. Slocock, Lord Raym. 1545. Action on a promissory note, whereby the defendant promised to pay to A. B. 101l. : 12s. in three months after the date of the said note value received, out of premises in Rosemary-lane, late in the possession of G. H.
The court, upon demurrer, held this to be a promissory note within the statute, and gave judgment for the plaintiff.

[g] Haussoullier v. Hartsinck and others,

7 T. R. 733. Payee against the maker of a promissory note, whereby the defendant promised to pay ——, or bearer, 25l., being a portion of a value as under deposited, in security for the payment thereof. Upon a special case being reserved, the court said they were clearly of opinion, that though as between the original parties to the transaction, the payment of the notes was to be carried to a particular account, the defendants were liable on these notes, which were payable at all events. See also Lord Raym. 1545.

[h] Buller v. Crips. 6 Mod. 29. Mod. Ent. 812.

[i] Anonymous, Select Cases 80.

---

(64) So where a note was made payable to A. or order, and on the back of it an indorsement was written, that it was to be delivered to A. in consideration of a judgment against C. to be assigned to the maker, it was held a good promissory note within the statute, and that the indorsement only operated as a notice to any purchaser of the consideration of the note. *Sanders* v. *Bacon*, 8 John. Rep. 485.

(64) In *Massachusetts* the statute of 3 & 4 Ann. ch 9. was never enacted but in practice the provisions of the first section were early adopted, and the form of declaring on negotiable notes resulting from that statute was extended to notes not negotiable. It may therefore be considered as the common law of that state, that all cash notes are negotiable, and that all notes for merchandize may be sued by the promisee against the promisor, and when indorsed by the indorsee against his indorser, who may declare in the same manner as they might if the note were negotiable. *Jones* v. *Fales*, 4 Mass. Rep. 245. and *Eaton* v. *Fallensbee*, Sup. Court, Essex, June Term. 1779, MSS. Whether this doctrine applies also to notes and bills payable out of particular funds, does not seem to have been decided. But even admitting that a bill payable out of a particular fund, could not be declared on within the statute; yet if the drawee accept to pay it, when the funds come into his hands, this binds him to the payment when he receives the funds, and the payee may on his refusal recover the amount in an action for money had and received, *Stevens* v. *Hill*, 5 Espin. Rep. 247. stated *post*, 253, and see *Scarborough* v. *Girgar*, 1 Bay's Rep. 368. *Mêshon* v. *Withers*, 1 Bibbs Rep. 503. *Mowry* v. *Todd*, 12 Mass. Rep. 281. A writing was made thus——"good for——dollars on demand. A. B." In an action thereon it was holden to import no promise to the holder, without evidence to show that it was actually given to him or some subsisting connexion shown from which that fact might be inferred. *Brown* v. *Gilman*, 13 Mass. Rep. 158.

A written promise to pay the bearer a sum of money, "provided the ship —— arrives at a European port free from capture and condemnation by the British," was held not to be a negotiable note within the statute of 3 & 4 Ann. *Coolidge* v. *Ruggles*, 15 Mass. Rep. 387.

In *New York*, a like usage in relation to notes not within the statute, has not prevailed; consequently, a note for a sum payable in lands at a specific price per acre, cannot be declared on even between the original parties as a promissory note, but the conside-

Besides these principal qualities which bills of exchange must possess, *Their* there are certain other matters proper to be attended to in the formation *parts* and of them : these are, 1*st*, that in certain cases the instrument be pro- *particular* perly stamped. 2*dly*, that it be properly dated. 3*dly*, that the time of *requisites.* payment be clearly expressed. 4*thly*, that it contain an order, or, at least, a request, to pay. 5*thly*, that in the case of a foreign bill drawn in sets, each set contains a proviso that it shall only be payable in case the others are not paid. 6*thly*, that it be clearly expressed to whom the bill is payable. 7*thly*, that where the instrument is intended to be ne- gotiated, there be words inserted, giving the power of transfer. 8*thly*, that the money to be paid be distinctly and intelligibly expressed, and in certain cases, that it be above a certain amount. 9*thly*, that in certain cases, value received be inserted. 10*thly*, that under particular cir- cumstances, a bill state whether it is to be paid with or without further advice. 11*thly*, that the drawer's name be clearly signed. 12*thly*, that the bill be properly addressed to the drawee. And *lastly*, that where the bill is to be paid at a certain place, that place be properly described. The better mode of considering each of these matters, will be by pre- senting the reader with the usual forms of a foreign and inland bill of exchange, and of a check, and then considering the various parts of each in their natural order.

FORM OF A FOREIGN BILL. [51]

No.

2°   8   4

London, 1*st January*, 1718.   *Exchange for* 10,000 *Livres Tournoises.*

      5   6

1 | *At two usances* (or " *at* ... *after sight*," *or* " *at* ... *after date*,") *pay* Stamp.|

——   7   8

     this my first Bill of Exchange (*second and third of the same tenor and date*

          9   10   11

not paid,) *to Messrs.* ———, *or order* (" *or bearer*") *Ten Thousand Livres Tournoises*,

          12   13   14

value received of them, and place the same to account, or per advice from

    16   17   15

To Mr. ———, *in Paris,* }   *JAMES OATLAND.*

        18   }

payable at ———

* The Figures refer to the parts of the observations in the following pages of this chapter.

ration must be specially set forth and proved, as in other declarations in assumpsit. *Smith* v. *Smith*, 2 John. Rep. 225. And even the terms "value received" in a note not within the statute, have been held not of themselves to imply a consideration, but a consideration must be specially averred and proved. *Lansing* v. *M'Killip*, 3 Caine's Rep. 286. However this doctrine has been over-ruled, and it is now held that these terms were *primâ facie* evidence of a consideration in such a note, and sufficient to cast the burthen of proof of the contrary on the defendant. *Jerome* v. *Whitney*, 7 John. Rep. 321. *Jackson* v. *Alexander*, 3 John. Rep. 484. And therefore such a note would be good evidence to support the money counts. Ibid. and *Smith* v. *Smith*. But if no consideration appear on the face of a note, not negotiable within the statute, and so terms implying value received, it cánnot be given in evidence under the money counts. *Sexton* v. *Johnson*, 10 John. Rep. 418.

FORM OF AN INLAND BILL.

4
100*l.*

2   3
London, 1st January, 1798.

1
Stamp.

5
Two Months after date (or " at sight," or " on demand, or " at . . . days
6   9   10   11
after sight,") pay Mr. ———, or order, One Hundred Pounds, for value

12
received.

16
To *Mr.* ———, *Merchant,*
17   18
Bristol, payable at ———,

15
SAMUEL SKINNER.

FORM OF A BILL UNDER FIVE POUNDS.

As directed by Stat. 17 Geo. III. c. 30. Schedule No. 2.

[Here insert the place, day, month, and year, when and where made.]
Twenty-one days after date, pay to A. B. of ———, *or his order, the sum*
of ———, *value received by*

C. D.

To *E. F. of* ———,
Witness G. H. ———,

FORM OF A CHECK.

(2)   (3-5)
London, 5th October, 1798.

1

(16-17)
Messrs.
(6) (9)   (10)   (11)
Pay A. B. or bearer, Twenty Pounds.

(4)
L. 20 0 0

(15)
J. K.

1st, Stamp duty.
[52]

(1)—Before the statute of the 22 Geo. 3. c. 33, there was no *stamp duty* imposed on bills of exchange, &c. and they were in all cases made on plain unstamped paper, and. indeed, were expressly exempted from any stamp duty, by the 5th W. & M. c. 21. s. 5; but by the first-mentioned statute, certain duties were imposed in almost all cases upon these instruments. This and two subsequent statutes (23 Geo. 3. c. 49. and 24 Geo. 3. s. 1. c. 7,) were repealed by the 31 Geo. 3. c. 25. whereby certain duties were imposed. and which were increased by the 37 Geo. 3. c. 90, and which continued in force until the 10th October, 1804, from which day until the 11th October, 1808, the 44 Geo. 3. c. 98, regulated the *amount of the duty* on bills, notes, &c.; from that day until the 28th September, 1815, the duties on bills and notes were regulated by the 48 Geo. 3. c. 149. and from the last-mentioned period to the present time (1821,) the regulating statute is the 55 Geo. 3. c. 184.

Provisions of the stamp act, 55 Geo. 3. c. 184.

By this act, with respect to *inland bills* of exchange, whether negotiable or not, a distinction is made in the amount of the stamp between bills and notes payable at a time not exceeding two months or sixty days after date, and those exceeding that time, and a penalty of

52

£100 is imposed on any person post dating, or issuing any bill or note ^{1st, Stamp}
so post dated, so as to avoid the higher duty.^k It is also provided, that ^{duty.}
all drafts or orders for the payment of money by a bill or promissory
note, or for the delivery of any such bill or note in payment or satisfaction of any money, shall be liable to the like stamp duty as a bill
or note. There are other provisions in the act, which will be found in
the Appendix.

A *foreign* bill drawn in, but payable out of Great Britain, if drawn
singly and not in a set, is liable to the same duty as an inland bill of
the same amount and tenor. But foreign bills drawn in Great Britain,
in sets, are subject to a stamp duty, progressively increasing according
to the amount for every bill of each set.^l It is also provided, that
promissory notes made *out of Great Britain*, shall not be negotiated or
paid in Great Britain, unless the same shall have paid the duty on promissory notes of the like tenor and value in Great Britain, with an exception of notes made and payable only in Ireland.^m

Exemptions from these stamp duties are made in favour of *bills* or
bank post bills, issued by the Bank of England, and of all bills, orders,
remittance bills, and remittance certificates, drawn by commissioned officers, masters, and surgeons of the navy, or by any commissioner of the
navy, and other bills drawn by or upon persons in certain public employ-[53]
ments, and also in favour of drafts or orders for the payment of money to
the bearer on demand, and drawn upon any banker or person acting as a
banker, residing or transacting the business of a banker, within ten miles
of the place where such draft or order shall be issued, provided such
place shall be specified in such draft or order, and the same shall bear
date on or before the day on which the same shall be issued, and provided
the same do not direct the payment to be made by bills or promissory
notes.

With respect to *promissory notes*, a distinction is made in the amount
of the duty, between those which are payable at a time exceeding two
months after date, or sixty days after sight, and those payable at a longer
period, and also between those intended to be re-issued after payment,
and those which cannot be so circulated,ⁿ and notes for the payment of
money by instalments, are subject to the same duty as on a promissory
note payable in less than two months after date, for a sum equal to the
whole amount of the money to be paid, and negotiable instruments in the
form of promissory notes, and for the payment of less than £20, upon
a contingency, whether available or not, are, nevertheless, liable to the
stamp duty.^o

Exemptions are introduced in favour of notes of the governor and company of the Bank of England, and of notes payable upon a contingency,
and exceeding £20, but it is nevertheless provided that the latter shall be
liable to the duty which may attach thereon as agreements or otherwise.

The penalty of £50 is imposed upon any person who shall make,
sign, or issue, or cause to be made, signed, or issued, or shall accept or
pay, or cause or permit to be accepted or paid, any bill of exchange,
draft or order, or promissory note for the payment of money liable to

^k Sect. 12. See clause, post, App.
^l 55 Geo. 3. c. 184. Schedule 1.
^m Id. sect. 20.
ⁿ 55 Geo. 3. c. 184. Schedule 1. tit. Pro-
missory note.
^o Ib. Ibid.

CHITTY ON BILLS.   H

1st, Stamp duty. — any of the duties imposed by the act, without the same being duly stamped.[p] *Penalties* are also imposed upon persons drawing, receiving, or paying any post dated or other unstamped draft on a banker, not made conformably to the act.[q] *Regulations* are then made relative to re-issuable notes, and for the licenses to bankers drawing and issuing such notes;[r] and it is provided, that all the powers, regulations, and penalties contained in and imposed by the several acts of parliament relating to the duties thereby repealed, and the several acts of parliament relating to any prior duties of the same kind or description, shall be of full force and effect relative to the duties thereby granted.[s] Hence [54] therefore most of the decisions on the former acts, are applicable to the existing stamp duties on bills and notes.

Decisions on the statutes relative to stamps. — With respect to *foreign* bills, it is clear that the legislature did not mean to extend the stamp duties, imposed by these acts to such foreign bills as are made abroad, where the use of them could not be enforced; and it may be collected from the language of the acts, that the duty is only imposed on bills drawn in Great Britain.[t] And where a bill was drawn in Ireland, and blanks left for the date, sum, time when payable, and the name of the drawee, and transmitted to England, where it was completed and negotiated, it was held, that this was to be considered as a bill of exchange, from the time of signing and indorsing it in Ireland, and that an English stamp was not necessary.[u] So where a bill of exchange was drawn in Jamaica, upon a stamp of that island, with a blank for the payee's name, and transmitted to England, where a bona fide holder filled in his own name as payee, it was considered, that no English stamp was necessary;[x] but if a bill be drawn in England, though dated at some foreign place, such bill cannot be enforced here without an English stamp.[y]

With respect to the amount of the sum payable, it was recently made a question, whether a stamp for the exact amount of £50 was sufficient for a bill for that sum, with all legal interest, it was contended, that the stamp was insufficient, because the bill was to carry interest from the date, and therefore a larger sum was payable upon it than £50; but it is reported, that Lord Ellenborough inclined to think the stamp sufficient, as there was no interest due when the bill was drawn, and it was then a security for the sum of £50, and no more; and as there is always interest to be recovered, if the bill be not paid the day it becomes due. The case afterwards came before the court, when it was decided upon another point, and no opinion was given as to the sufficiency of the stamp.[s] In a subsequent case, where a promissory note for £30, and interest, from the date was, payable three months after date, and was impressed only with a 2s. 6d. stamp. On the trial before Holroyd, J. at the Sittings at Westminster, after Michaelmas Term, 1820, it was objected, that as the £30 with the interest for three months, secured by the note, exceeded £30, and the note was payable at a time exceeding two months, or sixty days, a 3s. 6d. stamp was necessary; but the learned Judge over-ruled the objection, and afterwards, on motion for a new trial, the whole court discharged the rule, saying that the addition of interest ought not to be [55] taken into calculation, for otherwise a bond for £1000, and interest,

p Id ibid. sect 11.
q Id. sect. 13.
r Id. sect. 14. to sect. 28.
s Id. sect. 8.
t 55 Geo. 3. c. 184. Crutchley v. Mann, 1 Marsh. 29.

s Snaith v. Mingay, 1 M. & S. 87.
x Crutchley v. Mann, 5 Taunt. 529. 1 Marsh. 29. S. C.
y Jordaine v. Lashbrook, 7 T. R. 601. Abraham v. Dubois, 4 Camp. 269.
s Israel v. Benjamin, 8 Camp. 40.

would require a stamp for a larger sum than £1000, which would be contrary to practice and principle.[a]

Decisions on the statutes relative to stamps.

It has been holden, that a bill payable at sight, is not to be considered as a bill payable on demand, so as to be exempt from duty, under the stamp act, 23 Geo. 3. c. 49. s. 4. in favour of bills payable on demand.[b]

Where a promissory note for £400 was drawn on 7th July, 1818, *payable two months after sight*, it was held, that as such two months exceeded sixty days sight, it required a stamp of eight shillings and sixpence, though a six shilling stamp would have sufficed if it had been payable at two months after, *date*, or sixty days after sight.[c]

Upon the exempting clause in the former acts, in favour of checks on bankers, it has been holden, that the person on whom the check is drawn, must be *bona fide* a banker,[d] and that a draft on a banker, post dated, and delivered before the day of the date, though not intended to be used till that day, must be stamped, or will be void.[e]

It was provided by the statute 31 Geo. 3. c. 25. s. 19. (to which 55 Geo. 3. c. 184. s. 7. refer) that unless the paper on which a bill or note be written, be stamped with the proper duty, or a higher duty, it shall not be pleaded or given in evidence in any court, or admitted to be good, useful, or available, in law or equity; and that it shall not be lawful for the commissioners, or their officers, to stamp any bill or note after it is made; and though, upon this statute, it has been held, that if the commissioners exceed their authority, and do stamp the bill or note after it has been made, no defence can be established, to an action founded on the bill or note, on that ground. because it would be injurious to paper credit, if it were necessary for an indorsee to ascertain, [56] before he takes a bill, whether or not it was stamped previously to its having been made;[f] yet, according to more recent decisions it should seem, that, at least, if the instrument be in the hands of the party, in whose favour it was originally made, a subsequent stamping would not render it available against such positive enactment.[g]

[a] Pruessing v. Ing, Hil. T. 1821, K. B. and 4 B. &. A. 204.

[b] l'Anson v. Thomas, B. R. Trin. 24 Geo. 3. Bayl. 42. In an action on an inland bill, the question was, whether it was included under an exception in the stamp act of 23 Geo. 3. c. 49. s. 4. in favour of bills payable on demand, and the court held it was not; and Buller, J. mentioned a case before Willes, C. J. in London, in which a jury of merchants was of opinion, that the usual days of grace were to be allowed on bills payable at sight. See also Dehers v. Harriot, 1 Show. 164.

[c] Sturdy v. Henderson, *coram* Abbott, C. J. Sittings at Guildhall, after Easter Term, 1821, and on motion for a new trial.

[d] Castleman v. Ray, 2 Bos. & Paul. 388. Action for money had and received: defendant pleaded set-off as to part, and produced the following paper, unstamped, in evidence, to support his plea:

Mr. Castleman,
Please to pay the bearer L——, his receipt will be your discharge from
                                        T. M.
Standgate, 3d Sept. 1790.
Mr. Castleman, Bricklayer,
        Camberwell.   Paid by R. Ray,
                                for C. Castleman.

The defendant objected to this paper being received in evidence, as not falling within section 4. of 23 Geo. 3. c. 49, Castleman not being a banker; and Chambre, J. before whom the cause was tried, being of that opinion, a verdict was found for the plaintiff, and the court, upon motion, refused a rule for a new trial. See also Ruff v. Webb, 1 Esp. Rep. 129.

[e] Allen v. Keeves, 1 East. 435. Whitwell v. Bennet, 3 Bos. & Paul. 559.

[f] Wright v Riley, Peake Rep. 178.

[g] Roderick v. Hovil, 3 Campb. 103. Rapp v. Allnut, id. 106. in notis.

Decisions on the statutes relative to stamps.

It being found that the above statute frequently defeated the claims of the holder of bills, the legislature passed a *temporary act*,[b] whereby the commissioners of His Majesty's stamp duties, on proof by the holder that no fraud on the revenue was intended, were authorized to stamp bills, &c. after they were drawn, on payment of a certain penalty; but as the power of commissioners under this act has long since expired,[i] and as bills and notes are excepted in the 43 Geo. 3. c. 127. s. 5. and 44 Geo. 3. c. 98. s. 24. the holder of a bill has no civil remedy thereon, if it be either *unstamped*, or bear a stamp of an *inferior* value to that required by the acts, or be of a different denomination.[k]

An authority, however, was given to the commissioners by 37 Geo. 3. c. 136. s. 4. to stamp bills, checks, and notes, with the additional stamp duty imposed by 37 Geo. 3. c. 90. at any time before the 1st November, 1797, without any penalty, and the following section (which appears to be still in force[l]) provides, that any bill, &c. made after the passing of the 37 Geo. 3. c. 136, and liable to any stamp duty under 31 Geo. 3. c. 25. and which shall be stamped with a stamp of a different denomination from that required by that act, may, if the stamp be of *equal* or *superior* value to the stamp required, be stamped with the proper stamp, on payment of the proper duty, and 40s. if the bill be not due, or £10. if due; and the commissioners are thereupon to give a receipt for the duty and penalty so paid, on the back of the bill, and such bill, will be valid in any court. Previously to this act, a bill stamped with an improper stamp was valid, provided it was a stamp required under 31 Geo. 3. c. 25. and was of the same or greater value than the proper one;[m] but

[57] where in an action on a note by an indorsee, the stamp appeared to be a 7s. *deed* stamp, Lord Kenyon said the note could not be received in evidence, and the plaintiff was accordingly nonsuited.[n]

Previously to the enactment in the 43 Geo. 3. c. 127. it was held, that a promissory note for £25 5s. written upon a 9d. stamp (being the stamp imposed by 31 Geo. 3. c. 25. on notes not exceeding £50, but which at the time of the making of the note had ceased to be the proper stamp, on any note whatever) instead of an 8d. stamp, (being that required by 37 Geo. 3. c. 90.) on notes not exceeding £30.) was void;[o] but it is afterwards held, that a promissory note for £45. which by law required a stamp of 1s. 6d. composed of three different sums, applicable to three different funds, under three acts of parliament, being written on a 2s. stamp, composed of three different sums, *applicable to the same funds*, though in *larger* proportions to each than

---

[b] 34 Geo. 3. c. 32.

[i] Bayl. 26. in notes. Phil. Evid. 3d ed. 459, n. [o].

[k] In criminal prosecutions, the want of a proper stamp is not in general an available objection. See the cases, I Chitty Crim. Law, 582 to 584. Phillips on Evid. 3d ed. 454 to 458. And as to the instances in which an unstamped bill or note may be given in evidence, see 3 Bos. & Pul. 316. Peake Rep. 75. 15 East, 449. 455. Phillips Law of Evid. 3d ed. 403. 454. In Gregory v. Frazer, 3 Campb. 454, it was held, that although a promissory note, without a stamp, cannot be received in evidence as a security, or to prove the loan of money, it may be looked at with a

view to ascertain a collateral fact; and therefore, in this case, the action being for money lent, and the defence was, that the defendant had been made drunk by the plaintiff, and induced to sign the note, without any consideration, Lord Ellenborough held, that the note might be looked at by the Jury as a co-temporary writing, to prove or disprove the fraud imputed to the plaintiff.

[l] Chamberlain v. Porter, 1 New. Rep. 30.

[m] 31 Geo. 3. c. 25. s. 19. Chamberlain v. Porter, 1 New. Rep. 34.

[n] Manning v. Livie, *cor.* Lord Kenyon, Sittings after M. T. 1796. Bayl. 37. n. (a.)

[o] Farr v. Price, 1 East. 55. see observations in Bayley, 37.

was required, such note is good.[r] To obviate the objection on account Decisions
of a larger stamp being imposed than was necessary, it was enacted by on the statutes relative to stamps.
the 43 Geo, 8. c. 127. s. 6. that every instrument, matter, or thing,
stamped with a stamp of *greater* value than required by law, shall be
valid, provided such stamp shall be of the denomination required by law
for such instrument. &c. and by the recent act 55 Geo. 3. c. 184. s. 10.
it is provided, that all instruments upon which any stamp duty shall have
been used, of an improper denomination or rate of duty, but of equal or
greater value in the whole with the proper stamp, shall be valid, except .
where the stamp used on such instrument shall have been specifically appropriated to any other instrument, by having its name on the face.

Under the former acts, qualifying the right to re-issue bills after payment, it had been determined that after a bill has been returned to, and
paid by the drawer, he may, without a fresh stamp, indorse the bill t /er
to a new party, who may in his own name sue the acceptor, because the
prohibition against re-issuing after payment imports only a payment by
the acceptor.[q]

If a bill or note be made in any part of the King's dominions, as in
Jamaica, where by the law of such place a stamp is required, such instrument cannot be recovered upon in any court here, unless properly
stamped, according to the law of the place where the same was made;[r]
but our courts do not regard the Revenue Laws of a foreign independent
State.[s](75)

When a bill of exchange or promissory note is not properly stamped, [58]
it has been held, that a neglect to present it for acceptance or for payment, will not discharge the drawer or indorser from liability to pay the
original debt, in respect of which it was indorsed or delivered to the
holder;[t] and if there be any such original debt, between the holder and

[p] Taylor v. Hague, 2 East, 414.
[q] Callow v. Lawrence, 3 M. &. S. 95.
[r] Alves v. Hodson, 7 T. R. 241. 2 Esp.
Rep. 528. S. C. Clegg v. Levy, 3 Campb.
166.
[s] Roach v. Edie, 6 T. R. 425. Boucher
v. Lawrence, Rep. Temp. Hardw. 198.

Holman v. Johnson, Cowp. 343. Clugas
v. Penaluna, 4 T. R. 467. Park on Ins.
7th edit. 390. Marsh. on Ins. 1st edit. 51,
55. per Grose, J. in Ogden v. Folliott, 3 T.
R. 735. in which this point is discussed.
[t] Wilson v. Vysar, 4 Taunt. 288. Action for goods sold, defence, payment. A

(75) It seems that the courts of one country do not take notice of the stamp acts of another country, so far as to enforce a violation of them by denying effect to written contracts made in a country, and not stamped according to its laws. Therefore where a
note was executed in *France* by a person resident there, payable at *New York* to another person resident there, as agent of a third person resident in *France*, and by the
laws of *France* existing at the time all notes for the payment of money were required
to be stamped, without which no note could be recovered in that country, it was held
that a suit could be maintained thereon in the courts of *New York*, notwithstanding the
note was not stamped. The Court said, that they did not sit to enforce the revenue
laws of other countries; nor to take notice of a violation of them; and if it were otherwise, it might be said that the parties in that case never contemplated exacting payment
of that note in *France. Trustees of Randall* v. *Van Rensselaer*, 1 John. Rep. 94.
A note not duly stamped according to the act of congress of 6th July, 1797, cannot
be read in evidence in an action brought upon it since the repeal of that act, unless the
holder has complied with the provisions of the repealing act of the 5th of April, 1802,
by paying a stamp duty of ten dollars. *Edeck* v. *Ranuer*, 2 Johns. Rep. 423.
A promissory note made in *Scotland* is negotiable in *England* and an action may be
maintained upon it by the indorsee against the maker. *Milne* v. *Graham*, 1 Barn. &
Cressw. 192.

Decisions on the statutes relative to stamps. such drawer or indorser, the holder, though he cannot recover upon such instrument, may nevertheless sustain his action for such original debt;[x] and if any banker pay any bill, draft, or order, insufficiently stamped, he is not to be allowed the payment in account.[1] But where there is no privity between the plaintiff and the defendant, as in the case of a remote indorsee and the acceptor, the former will have no remedy against the latter, if the stamp be defective, and not remediable by the above provisions, and a court of equity will not in general afford him relief.[y] But where a party had entered into an express agreement, to give a valid note, and had given one upon an improper stamp, a court of equity enforced the delivery of a valid note;[z] and if a defendant in an action at law, pay money into court, upon the whole declaration, he is precluded from objecting to the sufficiency of the stamp on which the bill was drawn.[a]

2dly, Place where made.

[59]

(2)—It is proper, in all cases, to superscribe the name of the place where the bill is really made, and when the maker is not a person well known in the commercial world, it is advisable for him to mention the number of his house. and the street in which he resides, in order that the holder may be the better enabled to find him out, in case his responsibility is doubted, or in case acceptance, or payment should be refused by the drawee. According to the form in the schedule contained in the 17 Geo. 3. c. 30. in certain cases where bills are under £5, it is absolutely necessary to insert the name of the place where they are made; and if this be omitted in a check on a banker it will not be exempt from the stamp duties imposed by the 55 Geo. 3. c. 184. and the prior acts.

3dly, Date.

(3)—As the *time, when a bill is to become due*, is generally regulated by the time when it was made, the *date* of the instrument ought to be clearly expressed,[b] and although it is the common practice, to write the date in figures, yet, in order to prevent intentional, or accidental alteration, which may invalidate the instrument, even in the hands of an in-

bill drawn by H. on B. and accepted by the latter, and indorsed by defendant to plaintiff, for such goods. It was not presented for payment when due, and in consequence of the laches, payment was refused by the drawer and the defendant. To rebut this defence, the plaintiff proved that the bill was drawn on a stamp of inferior value to that received by the statute and therefore could not be given in evidence for the defendant, it was then proved, that if it had been presented at maturity, it would have been paid; but the court held, that as the bill was not properly stamped, they could not consider it as payment. Ruff v. Webb, 1 Esp. Rep. 129. Assumpsit, for work and labour, and it was decided, that a draft in these words, "Mr. R. will much oblige Mr. W. by paying to I. R. or order 20l. on his account," was a bill of exchange, and could not be given in evidence without a stamp, and also that such draft, although taken without objection by the party at the time, was not any discharge of the subsisting debt. But in Swears v. Wells, 1 Esp. Rep. 317.

Where a creditor had agreed to take part of his debt in hand, and a note for the remainder at a future day, but which note was by mistake given upon a wrong stamp. it was held; that having taken the money to be paid in hand, be was compellable to wait till the time when such security would become due, unless in the mean time the party had refused to give a note properly stamped, and see Chamberlain v. Delarive, 2 Wils. 353.

[x] See the cases in the last note, and Brown v. Watts, 1 Taunt. 353. Alves v. Hodson, 7 T. R. 243. and Tyte v. Jones, cited 1 East. 58, n. (a.) Puckford v. Maxwell, 6 T. R. 22. White v. Wilson, 2 Bos. & Pul. 118. Wilson v. Kennedy, 1 Esp. Rep. 245. Wade v. Beazeley, 4 Esp. 7.

[x] 55 Geo. 3. c. 184. s. 13.
[y] Toulmin v. Price, 5 Ves. 240.
[z] Aylett v. Bennet, 1 Anstr. 45. 2 Bridg. 538.
[a] Israel v. Benjamin, 3 Campb. 40.
[b] Beawes, pl. 3. Mar. 2d ed. 91. Pardessus, Cours de Droit Commercial, 1 tom. 348.

nocent holder,[c] it may be advisable to write the date at full length in words, and it has been recently enacted, that it shall not be lawful for any banker or other person to issue any promissory note for the payment of money to the bearer on demand, liable to any of the duties imposed by the act, with the date printed therein, under a penalty of £50.[d] There is no legal objection to a bill being dated on a Sunday ;[e] and the date of a bill or note is *prima facie* evidence of its having been made on the day of the date.[f] A date, however, is not, in general, essential to the validity of a bill, for where a bill has date, the time, if necessary to be inquired into, will be computed from the day it was issued;[g] and if a bill of exchange be made payable two months after date, and no date be expressed, the court will intend it to be payable two months after the day on which it was made.[h] A check, if post dated and not stamped, we have seen is invalid ;[i] and though it has been decided that a bill of exchange may be post dated ;[k] yet we have seen that this cannot be done so as to postpone the payment for more than two months or sixty days from the time it is issued, unless the increased duty be paid.[l] By the statute 17 Geo. 3. c. 30, however, it is enacted, that all bills of exchange, or drafts in writing, being negotiable or transferrable for the payment of twenty shillings, or any sum of money above that sum, and less than five pounds, or on which twenty shillings, or above that sum, and less than five pounds, shall remain undischarged, shall bear date before or at the time of drawing or issuing thereof, and not on any day subsequent thereto. (78)

(4)—There is no necessity for the *superscription of the sum* for which the bill is payable, provided it be mentioned in the body of the bill ; but the superscription will aid an omission in the body ;[m] and it is the

3dly, Date.

[60]

4thly, Sum payable.

---

[c] Master *v.* Miller, 4 T. R. 320.
[d] 55 Geo. 3. c. 184. s. 18
[e] Drury *v.* De Fontaine, 1 Taunt. 131.
[f] Taylor *v.* Kinlock, 1 Stark. 175. The date upon a promissory note made by a bankrupt, of a time antecedent to an act of bankruptcy, is *primâ facie* evidence to show that the note existed before the act of bankruptcy was committed, so as to establish a petitioning creditor's debt in an action by the assignees.

[g] Armit *v.* Breame, 2 Ld. Raym. 1076. 1082. An award which directed the removal of some scaffolds within 58 days from the date of the award, had no date, an objection being taken upon this ground, the court said the time was to be computed from the delivery. See also 2 Show. 422. Goddard's Case, 2 Co. 5. (a.) Sel. Nl. Pri. 283. Bac. Ab. Leases, l. 1. Com. Dig. Fait, B. 3.

[h] De la Courtier *v.* Bellamy, 2 Show. 422. Case on a foreign bill of exchange, payable at double usance from the date, and it was alleged that the party beyond the sea drew the bill on a certain day, and that the same was presented to and accepted by the defendant. Exception, that the date of the bill was not set forth. The court said that they would intend the date of the bill from the drawing of it. See also Hague *v.* French, 3 Bos. & Pul. 173. S. P.

[i] Ante, 55, n.
[k] Pasmore *v.* North, 13 East. 517.
[l] Ante, 52, and 55 Geo. 3. c. 184. s. 12.

[m] Elliot's case, 2 East's P. C. 951. on an indictment for forging the following note:

No. 17. 73.
I promise to pay Mr. I. C. or bearer, on demand, the sum of fifty

London, 20 June, 1795.
L Fifty   For Governor and Company
                   of the Bank of England.
Entered C. *Blewart.*   *Thos. Thompson.*

---

(78) Notes made or first delivered after the time they bear date are valid only from the day of delivery, and are to be considered as drawn on that day. *Lansing* v. *Gaine,* &c. 2 John. Rep. 300.

And if a statute has made notes of a particular description illegal if issued after a particular time, it is competent for the maker to prove that a note was ante-dated to evade the statute. *Bayley* v. *Taber,* 5 Mass. Rep. 286.

A note may for honest purposes be dated as of a day antecedent to that on which it was really made. *Richter* v. *Selin,* 8 Serg. & Rawle. 425.

4thly. Sum payable. advice of Beawes, [n] that the sum payable be expressed so distinctly both in words and figures, that no exception can be taken to the instrument; and it is now the usual mode, to subscribe the sum payable, in figures at the head of the instrument, and in words in the body of it. In drawing a check on a banker, the sum is generally subscribed.

5thly, Time, and place of payment. (5)—By a French ordinance, it was required, that bills of exchange made in that country, should express *the time when they were to be paid*, or otherwise they would be invalid;[o] but there being no positive regulation affecting bills in this country, they would be valid although no time be mentioned in them, and would operate, as in the case of a check on a banker, as payable on demand.[p] It is advisable, however, in all cases, to express the time of payment as clearly and intelligibly as possible,[q] and it is therefore usual to write it in words, particularly as they are less subject to alteration than figures; and where a bill is drawn in one country using one style, and payable in a country using another, it is said that the drawer sometimes makes the date both according to the old and new style.[r]

[61] With respect to the *time when payment* is to be made, it depends entirely on the agreement of the parties, and there is limitation in point of law, though the payment must not be contingent.[s] But by the 17th Geo. 3. c. 30. negotiable bills and drafts under £5, of the description above-mentioned, must be payable within twenty-one days after the day of the date thereof. The operation of this act is suspended with respect to drafts payable to bearer on demand, by the statute 37 Geo. 3. c. 32. and other subsequent acts. Foreign bills are frequently drawn payable at usance or usances, but they, like inland bills, may be drawn payable at sight, or at days, weeks, months, or years, after sight or date, or on demand : bills, however, are very seldom drawn payable on demand ; but usually, when it is intended they should be payable immediately, are drawn payable at sight. If drawn at sight, the drawer of a foreign bill should express that it is payable according to the course of exchange at the time of making it;[t] for otherwise, it seems, that the drawee must pay according to the exchange of the day when he has sight of the bill. Checks on bankers very seldom express any time when they are to be paid, and consequently, as will be seen hereafter, are demandable immediately they are delivered to the payee or bearer.(80)

The forgery being proved, it was urged for the defendants, that this was not a note for fifty pounds, as the word "pounds" was not inserted, and judgment was respited for the opinion of the Judges, who all agreed that the L Fifty in the margin, removed every doubt, and showed that the fifty in the body of the note was intended for pounds.

[n] Beawes, tit. Bills of Exchange, pl. 3. Marius, 189.

[o] Poth. pl. 32. Pardessus droit Commercial, 1 tom. 352.
[p] Boehm v. Sterling, 7 T. R. 427.
[q] Beawes, pl. 3.
[r] Kyd. 8. Mar. 91. Bayl. 113.
[s] If a bill of exchange be made payable at never so distant a day, if it be a day that must come, it is no objection to the bill. Per Willes, C. J. in Colehan v. Cooke, Willes, 396.
[t] "En especes au cours de ce jour." Poth. pl. 174.

(80) The time of payment is part of a contract, and if no time of payment be expressed on a note the law adjudges it payable immediately ; and parol evidence is inadmissible to show a different time of payment. *Thompson* v. *Ketcham*, 8 John. Rep. 189. So to show a note payable in 1810, was so made by mistake for 1811. *Fitzhugh* v. *Runyon*, 8 John. Rep. 375.

With respect to the time when a bill drawn payable in either of these ways becomes due, the reader is referred to that part of the work which treats of the presentment for payment.

If it be intended that the bill shall be payable at a particular place, the drawer should so frame the bill which he may do either in the body of the bill, or in the direction to the drawee, as by the words, "payable in London."

(6)—It is said by Beawes, in his Lex Merc.[x] that payment of a bill should be *ordered* and commanded ; it is sufficient, however, if it be requested ;[y] and according to Marius, the direction to pay the money need not be contained in the body of the bill, or even on the same side of the paper, but this form is not recommended.[z]

(7, 8)—Inland bills, checks, and notes, consist only of one part, but foreign bills, in general, consist of *several parts*, in order that the bearer having lost one, may receive his money on the other ;[a] but if the drawer only give one bill, he will, if it should be lost, be obliged to give another of the same date, to the loser.[b] The several parts of a foreign bill are called a *set ;* each part contains a condition, that it shall be paid, *provided the others remain unpaid ;* in other respects all are of the same tenor. This condition should be inserted in each part, and should, in each, mention every other part of the set, for if a person, intending to make a set of three parts should omit the condition in the first, and make the second with a condition, mentioning the first only, and in the third alone take notice of the other two, he might, perhaps, in some cases be obliged to pay each ; for it would be no defence to an action by a *bona fide* holder on the second, that he had paid the third, nor to an action on the first, that he had paid either of the others.[c] But an omission is not, perhaps, material, which upon the face of the condition must necessarily have arisen from a mistake, as if in the enumeration of the several parts, one of the intermediate parts were to be omitted, for instance, "pay this my first of exchange, second and

---

[x] As to this point, see 2 Brod. & Bingh. 165, and post. Hodge v. Fillis, 3 Campb. 463. Post. This was action by the indorsee against the acceptors of a bill of exchange, drawn in the following form :—

"Cork,
"12th April, 1818.
"L2,314 : 15s: 11d.
"At two months date of this our first of exchange, (second and third of the same tenor, and date not paid) pay to our order, L2,314 : 15s: 11d. and charge the same to account as advised.
"W. & A. Maxwell.
"To Messrs. Fillis & Co."
"Plymouth."
"Payable in London."

The bill was accepted by the defendants, payable at Sir John Perring and Co. Bankers, London.
The plaintiffs failed to aver in their declaration, the presentment of the bill for

payment at a London banker's, which the defendants, on the trial, contended was a material omission.

Lord Ellenborough expressed himself to be of the same opinion, but as the plaintiffs' counsel on the trial, proved a promise by defendants to pay the *bill after it become due ;* Lord Ellenborough held, that that circumstance dispensed with direct evidence of a presentment for payment at the bankers, and therefore the plaintiffs had a verdict.

[z] Pl. 3.
[y] Morris v. Lee, Ld. Raym. 1397.— Brown v. Harraden, 4 T. R. 149. Ruff v. Webb, 1 Esp. Rep. 129.
[a] Mar. 11. Brown v. Harraden, 4 T. R. 149. and see Gray v. Milner, 8 Moore, 90. Post.
[b] Poth. pl. 39. Bayl. 18. 180.
[b] Poth. pl. 39.
[c] Davison v. Robertson, 3 Dow. 218. 228. Bayl 19. Beawes, 430. Poth. pl. 111.

7thly & 8thly, Of several parts. **& fourth not paid.**[d]**"** Each of the parts, when drawn in Great Britain, must be stamped.[e] Where a bill consists of several parts, each ought to be delivered to the payee, unless one be forwarded to the drawee for acceptance, otherwise there may be difficulties in negotiating the bill, or obtaining payment.[f] The forgery of an indorsement of the payee on one of the parts, will not pass any interest, even to a *bona fide* holder, and the real payee may sustain an action on the other part.[g]

9thly, To whom payable. [63] (9)—A bill of exchange and promissory note must specify *to whom it is to be paid,* for it is said that otherwise it will be merely, waste paper;[h] and therefore it has been recently decided, that a note payable to A. *or* to B. and C. is not a valid promissory note, and cannot be sued upon as such by one of the payees;[i] but Pothier[k] observes, that if the drawer have omitted to mention any person to whom the bill is to be paid, declaring in the bill, however, from whom he has received the value, it is but reasonable to construe the instrument to be payable to that person. And it is now settled, that if a bill of exchange be drawn and negotiated, and a blank left for the name of the payee, a *bona fide* holder may fill it up with his own name, and recover against the drawer.[l] But in an action against the acceptor, the holder must prove an authority from the drawer for inserting his name as payee.[m] Care also should be taken that the name be properly spelled, though, if there be a mistake, parol evidence is admissible to show who was intended.[n] Where there are two persons of the same name, it is advisable to describe the payee in such a manner that no mistake can arise;[o] and if there be father and son of the same names, and it be intended to be payable to the son, he must be so described, because, if the Christian and surname only be stated, it will be intended for the father until the contrary appear.[p]

[d] Bayl. 19.
[e] Ante, 52, 53.
[f] Bayl. 19.
[g] Cheap *v.* Harley, cited in 3 T. R. 127. upon this point, see Smith *v.* Mercer, 6 Taunt. 80.
[h] Per Eyre, C. B. Gibson *v.* Minet, 1 Hen. Bla. 608.
[i] Blanckenhagen *v.* Blundell, 2 B. & A. 417.
[k] Pl. 31.
[l] Cruchley *v.* Clarence, 2 M. & S. 90. An action against the defendant as drawer of a bill of exchange, the bill had been drawn on one Henry Mann, and a blank left for the name of the payee; the bill had been negotiated by one Vashon, and indorsed to the plaintiff, who filled up the blank with his own name, and upon the trial, a verdict was found for the plaintiff; the court afterwards refused to set aside the verdict, and observed, that as the defendant had chosen to send the bill into the world in this form, the world ought not to be deceived by his acts, and that by leaving the blank, he undertook to be answerable for it when filled up in the shape of a bill; see also Usher *v.* Dauncey, 4 Camp. 97. and see Powell *v.* Duff, 3 Campb. 182. The issuing of a bill with a blank for the payee's name was expressly prohibited in France, see post, p. 64. n.
[m] Crutchley *v.* Mann, 1 Marsh. 31.—5

Taunt. 529. S. C. This was an action on a bill of exchange drawn by one A. C. in Jamaica, upon the defendant in London, with the name of the payee left in blank; the drawer delivered it to the person from whom the plaintiff received it, and plaintiff inserted his own name as payee. The bill was not accepted, but the plaintiff produced a letter from the defendant, which he contended amounted to an acceptance. The Chief Justice left the case to the jury, who found for the plaintiff, reserving two points for the opinion of the court; first, as to the stamp, and secondly, whether there was sufficient evidence that the plaintiff had authority to insert his name, or that the bill was that to which the letter alluded. A rule nisi having been obtained, and cause shown, the court held, that the plaintiff ought to have proved that he was authorised to insert his name as payee; if he were to recover, as the case then stood, they did not know how the defendant could charge the drawer with the value of the bill, as he might say it was not the instrument which he delivered to the person from whom the plaintiff received it; see the preceding note.
[n] Beawes, pl. 3. Willis *v.* Barrett, 3 Stark. 29.
[o] Mead *v.* Young, 4 T. R. 28.
[p] Sweeting *v.* Fowler and another, 1 Stark. 106.

However, a misdescription of the character of the payee will not vitiate, provided it can, from the whole instrument, be collected who was the party intended.[q] Bills under £5 are, by the statute 17 Geo. 3. c. 30. to express the names and places of abode of the *persons* respectively to whom or to whose order the same shall be payable.

9thly, To whom payable.

[64]

A bill may be drawn payable to bearer, and in such case it will be transferrable by delivery;[r] and a bill or note payable to J. S. or bearer, is, in legal effect, payable to the bearer, and J. S. is a mere cypher.[s] In France, bills of this description were at first forbidden, but by a subsequent law they were established.[t] In that country, it appears that it was formerly usual to make bills payable to a person whose name was left in blank, in order that the holder of the bill, when he was desirous of not being known, might fill it up with any name he chose; but as these bills were employed as a cloak for usury and fraud, they were afterwards prohibited.[u] These bills seem to have been in the nature of those payable to a *fictitious payee*, the validity of which has been so frequently and fully discussed of late in our courts of justice; the result of which discussion seem to be, that a bill payable to a fictitious person or his order, is in effect, a bill payable to bearer, and may be declared on as such against all the parties, knowing that the payee was a fictitious person.[x] The use of these fictitious names has been

[q] The King v. Box, 6 Taunt. 325.
[r] Grant v. Vaughan, 3 Burr. 1526.—Bayl. 15.
[s] Id. ibid.
[t] Poth. pl. 231.
[u] Arrets de Reglements de la Cour du 7 Juin. 1611, et du Mars, 1624. and see Pardessus droit Commercial, 1 tom. 858.
[x] Ex parte The Royal Burgh of Scotland, 19 Ves. 311, 12. 2 Rose Bank. Cas. 201. Almost all the modern cases upon this question arose out of the bankruptcy of Livesay and Co. and Gibson and Co. who negotiated bills with fictitious names upon them, to the amount of nearly a *million sterling a year* The first case was Tatlock v. Harris, 2 T. R. 174. in which the court of K. B. held, that the *bona fide* holder for a valuable consideration of a bill drawn payable to a fictitious person, and indorsed in that name by the drawer, might recover the amount of it in an action against the acceptor, for money paid or money had and received; upon the idea, that there was an appropriation of so much money to be paid to the person who should become the holder of the bill. In Vere v. Lewis, 3 T. R. 182, decided the same day, the court held, there was no occasion to prove that the defendant had received any value for the bill, as the mere circumstance of his acceptance was sufficient evidence of this; and three of the Judges thought the plaintiff might recover on a count which stated that the bill was drawn payable to *bearer*. Minet v. Gibson, 3 T. R. 481, put this point directly in issue, and the unanimous opinion of the court was, that where the circumstance of the payee being a fictitious person, is known to the acceptor,

the bill is, in effect, payable to bearer. Soon after, the court of C. P. laid down the same doctrine in Collis v. Emmet, 1 Hen. Bla. 413. The decision was acquiesced in; but Minet v. Gibson was carried up to the House of Lords, 1 Hen. Bla. 569. The opinions of the Judges being then given, Eyre, C. B. (p. 598.) and Heath, J. (p. 619.) were for reversing the judgment of the court below, and Lord Thurlow C. coincided with them (p. 625.) but the other Judges thinking otherwise, judgment was affirmed. Parl. Cas. 8vo. ii. 48. The last case upon the subject reported is Gibson v. Hunter, 2 Hen. Bla. 187, 288. which came before the House of Peers upon a demurrer to evidence; and in which it was held, that in an action on a bill of this sort against the acceptor, to show that he was aware of the payee being fictitious, evidence is admissible of the circumstances under which he had accepted other bills payable to fictitious persons. *Vide* also Tufts's case, Leach Cro. Law, 172. but in Bennett v. Farnell, (1 Campb. Ni. Pri. 130.) Lord Ellenborough, C. J. held, that a bill of exchange made payable to a fictitious person or his order, is neither in effect payable to the order of the drawer, nor to bearer, *but is completely void;* though if *money* paid by the holder of such a bill as the consideration for its being indorsed to him, *actually* gets into the hands of the acceptor, it may be recovered back as money had and received. However, from a subsequent observation (1 Campb. 180 c.) it appears that the last case is to be taken with this qualification "unless it can be shown that the circumstance of the payee being a fictitious person was

9thly, To highly censured, and the person fraudulently indorsing the fictitious name
whom pay-on the bill, to give it currency, would be guilty of forgery.[y]
able.

As it is not necessary or essential to the validity of a bill of exchange
that there should be three parties to it, a bill may be drawn payable to
the drawer himself,[z] though in such case it is said to be more in the
nature of a promissory note. A bill may also be payable to one for
the use of another;[a] when drawn payable to a married woman, it is
payable to the husband, and transferrable only in his name.[b]

10thly,Pay-   (10)—As the commercial advantage to be derived from the *negoti-*
able to or-*able quality* of bills of exchange, was the only reason why our courts
der.
allowed in their favour an exception to the rule relative to the assign-
[66]
ment of *choses in action*, it was once thought, that unless they possessed
that quality, they would have no greater effect than that of being mere
evidence of a contract.[c] But it is now well established, that it
is not essential to the validity of a bill, as an instrument, that it be
transferrable from one person to another.[d] (86) If, however, it be in-

known to the acceptor." A new trial
was refused in this case, because no such
evidence had been offered at Nisi Prius,
and Lord Ellenborough said, he conceived
himself bound by Minet v. Gibson, and
the other cases upon this subject, which
had been carried up to the House of
Lords (though by no means disposed to
give them any extension,) and that if it
had appeared that the defendant knew
the payee to be a fictitious person, he
should have directed the jury to find
for the plaintiff. See also Ex parte Allen,
Co. B. L. 184. Ex parte Clarke, 3 Bro.
238. Parl. Cas. 8vo. 9th vol. 235. 255.
Cullen, 96. 1 Mont. B. L. 145.—Bayl. 22
to 24. Selw. N. P. 4th ed. 303.
[y] The King v. Edward Tuft, Leach
Cro. Law, 172. The King v. Taylor, id.
257, and note a. Tatloch v. Harris, 3 T.
R. 174. Vere v. Lewis, id. 182.—Minet
v. Gibson, id. 482. Collis v. Emmett, 1
Hen. Bla. 313. Gibson v. Minet, id. ibid.
569. 2 East's P. C. 957.
Rex v. Edward Tuft, Leach Cro. Law,
172. The prisoner was indicted for forging an indorsement on a bill of exchange,
and found guilty, but the Judge before
whom he was tried, submitted the case
to the consideration of the Judges, upon
the following statement:—The bill was
drawn payable to Messrs R. & M. and
indorsed by them generally, and became
the property of one W. W. from whom it
had been stolen; the prisoner, for the purpose of getting it discounted, indorsed on
it the name of John Williams.

The Judges were unanimously of opinion that this was a forgery, for, although
the fictitious signature was not necessary
to his obtaining the money, yet it was a
fraud both on the owner of the bill and
the person who discounted it, and referred to Rex v. Locket, where it was
holden, that the forging a name, either
real or fictitious, with an intent to defraud, was forgery; but see The King v.
Inhabitants of Burton-upon-Trent, 3 M.
& S. 528, where Lord Ellenborough said,
if a party sign an instrument in a name
assumed by him for other purposes, a
considerable time before, such signature
will not amount to a forgery, but otherwise, if he assume a name by which he
had never been known before, for the
purposes of fraud.

[z] Butler v. Crips, 1 Salk. 130. and
——— v. Ormston, 10 Mod. 286. Bayl.
22. Ante, 20.
[a] Evans v. Cramlington, Carth. 5.—
1 Ventr. 307. Skin. 264. S. C. Smith v.
Kendal, 6 T. R. 123. Marchington v.
Vernon, 1 Bos. & Pul. 101, note c.
[b] Ante, 19.
[c] Dawkes v. Lord de Loraine, 3 Wils.
211.
[d] Smith v. Kendall, 6 T. R. 123, 4. The
King v. Box, 6 Taunt. 328. Smallwood v.
Rolfe, Sel. Ca. 18. Bayl. 16. Smith v.
Kendall, Executor, &c. 6 T. R. 123. 1 Esp.
Rep. 231. S. C. Assumpsit for money
paid, &c. On the trial the following note
was given in evidence: "Three months

(86) The same principle has been recognized in the United States, *Downing* v. *Back-
enstoes*, 3 Caines' Rep. 137. *Goshen Turnpike Co.* v. *Hurtin*, 9 John. Rep. 217.
As between indorser and indorsee a note not negotiable is, in *Massachusetts*, treated
exactly as if negotiable. *Jones* v. *Fales*, 4 Mass. Rep. 245.
If the payee of a note payable to himself or bearer indorse it, he will be liable as indorser. *Bush* v. *Adm. of Reeves*, 3 John. Rep. 439.
And it has been held that the contract made by indorsement extends to all future in-

tended to be negotiable, care must be taken that the operative words of transfer, commonly used in bills, be inserted therein;[e] though if they be omitted by mistake,[f] it seems that if the bill was originally intended to be negotiable, the words "*or order*," may be inserted at any time without a fresh stamp.[f] The modes of making a bill transferrable, are by drawing it either payable to *A. B.* or *order*, or to *A. B.* or *bearer*, or to the drawer's own order, or to *bearer* generally. The use, operation, and effect of each of these forms of words, will be pointed out hereafter, in that part of the work which treats of the *transfer* of bills and checks.

10thly, Payable to order.

(11)—The *sum* for which the bill is drawn, should be clearly expressed in the body of it, and, as it has been before observed, it may be advisable to write it in figures at the head, and in words at length in the body of the bill, in order the better to prevent alteration.[g] But even in an indictment for forgery, an omission in the body of the bill has been aided by the superscription.[h] Care should be taken that the stamp be appropriated to the sum. If the sum in the superscription of the bill be different from that in the body of it, the sum mentioned in the body will be taken, *prima facie*, to be the sum payable.[i] The sum must be fixed and certain, and not contingent.[k] When there has been a contract by a third person, to guarantee a bill for a given sum, the bill should be drawn accordingly, for if it be drawn for a larger sum, the guarantee will not be liable even to the amount of the sum he engaged to secure.[l] With respect to foreign bills, there is no restriction as to the amount of the sum for which they may be made payable; but it is otherwise with regard to inland bills, and drafts, which are forbidden to be drawn for any sum under twenty shillings, by the statute 15 Geo. 3. c. 51. under the penalty of £20.

11thly, Sum payable.

[67]

(12)—It appears, that in France, it was not only essential to the validity of a bill, that it should express whether or not value had been received, but likewise the nature of the consideration which constituted the value;[m] but in this country it is otherwise, for *value received* is implied in every bill and indorsement, as much as if expressed *in totidem*

12thly, Of the words value received.

---

after date, I promise to pay to Mr. Smith carrier, 40*l.*, value received, in trust for Mrs. E. Thompson, as witness my hand, L. Askea, 25th June, 1787." The defendant objected that this was not a promissory note, within the statute, not being payable either to order or bearer. A verdict was taken for the defendant, with leave for plaintiff to move to set it aside and enter a verdict for him. Upon motion being made and cause shown, the court held, that a note payable to B., without adding " or to his order, or to bearer," was a legal note within the act of parliament. S. P. Burchell *v.* Slocock, Lord Raym. 1545. Moore *v.* Paine, Rep. Temp. Hardw. 288; and see the Entries,

Ewers *v.* Benchin, 1 Lutw. 231, 2. Manning *v.* Cary, id. 274. Clift 916.
[e] Beawes, pl. 3. Selw. N. P. 303, n. 16. Hill *v.* Lewis, Salk. 133.
[f] Kershaw *v.* Cox, 3 Esp. Rep. 246. Knill *v* Williams, 10 East, 435 437. Cole *v.* Parkin, 12 East, 471. Post, alteration.
[g] Poth. pl. 35. 99. Master *v* Miller, 4 T. R. 323 Ante, 60.
[h] Elliot's case, 2 East P. C. 951. Ante, 60, note.
[i] Beawes, pl. 193. Mar. 2d. ed. 138, 9. Elliot's case, 2 East P. C. 951. Ante, 60
[k] Smith *v.* Nightingale, 2 Stark. 375. Ante, 45.
[l] Phillips *v.* Astling, 2 Taunt. 206.
[m] Poth. pl. 8. 34.

---

dorsees, even where the notes are not originally negotiable; and an action lies in favour of an indorsee against a remote indorser. *Codwise* v. *Gleason*, 3 Day's Rep 12.

A bank note payable to *W. Pitt*, or bearer, is in effect payable to the bearer; as between any *bona fide* holder, and the Bank, such holder is to be deemed the Bearer to whom the Bank is originally liable. *Bullard* v. *Bell*, 1 Mason's Rep. 252.

12thly, Of *verbis ;* and though there are some old cases on the question, wheth-
the words er *indebitatus assumpsit* would lie on a bill of exchange, in which it
value re- appears there was a distinction made between a bill importing to have
ceived. been given for value received, and one not containing those words, and
it was holden, that in the first case the drawer was chargeable at common law, but in the latter on the custom only; yet it is now settled,
that there is no such distinction, and that a bill need not contain the
above words. However, to entitle the holder of an inland bill or
note, for the payment of £20, or upwards, to recover interest and
damages against the drawer and indorser, in default of acceptance, or
payment, it should contain the words, value received. And if a bill
or note contain those words, an action of debt may be sustained by the
payee, against the maker of each. These are distinctions which render
it advisable in all cases, to insert these words. It is said to have been
decided, that to aid a variance, the words may be inserted at the time
of the trial. (88) It has been considered, that when a bill of exchange
is in this form, " Pay to F. G. B. or order, £315, value received," and
was subscribed by the drawer, it may be alleged in pleading to be a bill
of exchange for value received by the drawer from the payee. But in a
[68] subsequent case, where a bill was drawn by I. S., payable to his own
order, " value received," it was held that this must mean value received by the drawee, and it was alleged in the declaration to be for value
received by the said I. S., it was adjudged to be a fatal variance, though
the plaintiff was permitted to recover on the account stated.

Of the It may be proper under this head to take a concise view of the *con-*
considera- *sideration on which a bill of exchange may be originally founded, or*
tion neces-
sary.

Per Lord Ellenborough, in Grant *v.* Da
Costa, 3 M. & S. 352. White *v.* Ledwick,
B. R., H. 25 Geo. 3. Bayl. 16, note b. A
declaration on a bill of exchange demurred
to, because it was not stated to have been
given for value received, but the court said
it was a settled point that it was not necessary, and gave judgment for the plaintiff.
Claxton *v.* Swift, 2 Show. 496, 7. Mack-
leod *v.* Snee, Ld. Raym. 1481. Josceline
v. Lassere, Fortes. 282. Jenney *v.* Hearle,
8 Mod. 267. Eveskyn *v.* Merry, 1 Barn.
88. Death *v.* Serwonters, Lutw. 889. *acc.*
Dawkes *v.* Lord de Loraine, 3 Wils. 212.
Banbury *v.* Lisset, 2 Stra. 1212. *semb. contra.* 2 Bla. Com. 468.

Hodges *v.* Steward, Skin. 346. Anonymous, 12 Mod. 345.

Beawes, pl. 233. Cramlington *v.*
Evans, 1 Show. 5. Vin. Ab. tit. Bills of
Exchange, G. 2.

Same cases as supra, note.

9 & 10 Wm. 3. c. 17. 3 & 4 Ann. c. 9.
s. 4 See Appendix.

Bishop *v.* Young, 2 Bos. & Pul. 78. 81.

Bul. Ni. Pri. 275. *sed quære.*

Grant *v.* Da Costa, 3 M. & S. 351.
Per Lord Ellenborough. It appears to
me that value received is capable of two
interpretations, but the more natural one
is, that the party who draws the bill
should inform the drawee of a fact which
he does not know, than one of which he
must be well aware. The words, " value
received," are not at all material, they
might be wholly omitted in the declaration, and there are several cases to that
effect. The meaning of them here is, that
the drawer informs the drawee that he
draws upon him in favour of the payee,
because he has received value of such
payee. To tell him that he draws upon
him because he the drawee has value in
his hands, is to tell him nothing, therefore
the first is the more probable interpretation. And per Bayley, J. the object of
inserting the words " value received," is
to show that it is not an accommodation
bill, but made on a valuable consideration
given for it by the payee.

Highmore *v.* Primrose, 5 M. & S. 65.

---

(88) Where the terms for " value received" are inserted in a declaration on a note,
whether they are material to be proved, depends on this consideration, whether they are
descriptive of the note itself or only an averment of the consideration of the indorsement or assignment of the instrument. If the *former*, and the words are set in the
note, the variance is fatal; if the latter, then as the proof of a value is not material, the averment need not be proved. *Wilson* v. *Codman's* Ex. 3 Cranch, Rep. 198.
Russell v. *Ball*, &c.. 2 John. Rep. 50. *Saxton* v. *Johnson*, 10 John. Rep. 418.

which may pass between the indorser and indorsee, &c. on the transfer Of the con-
of it ; and in making this inquiry, it will be advisable to consider, when sideration
the validity of the bill will be affected by necessary.

1st. The *want* of consideration.

2dly. The *illegality* of it.

It has already been observed,[y] that in general, a contract not under
seal, will be invalid, unless it be founded on a valuable consideration ;[z]
and that it is incumbent on the plaintiff, to state such consideration in
his declaration, and to prove it on the trial, before he can call on the
defendant for his defence. But in the case of bills of exchange, or
promissory notes, it is not necessary for the plaintiff to state any consideration in his declaration, or to prove it in the first instance on the
trial ;[a] unless where he brings an action as bearer of a bill transferrable
by delivery, and then only under suspicious circumstances, as where it
has been made under duress, or lost, and the holder cannot give a reasonable account how he came by it, and has had due notice before the
trial of the action, to prove the consideration which he gave for the instrument.[b](89) And whenever the holder has given full value for the bill,

---

[y] Ante, 2, 10.

[z] As to the distinction between *good*
and *valuable* considerations, see 2 Bla.
Com. 444. 297.

[a] Crawley *v.* Crowther, 2 Freem. 257.
Per Lord Chancellor. It is now held,
and the practice is so, that if a man gives
a note for money, payable on demand, he
need not prove any consideration ; and see
Trials per Pais, 301. Meredith *v.* Short,
1 Salk. 25. 2 Ld. Raym. 760. S. C. 2 Bla.
Com. 446. Selw. N. P. 4th edit. 804.

[b] Duncan *v.* Scott, 1 Campb. Rep 100.
Indorsee against the drawer of a bill. It
appeared that the defendant gave the bill
while under duress abroad, and under a
threat of personal violence and confiscation of his property, and that it was given
without consideration. Lord Ellenborough held, that the defendant, not having been a free agent when he drew the
bill, it was incumbent on the plaintiff to
give some evidence of consideration, and
no such evidence being given, the plaintiff
was nonsuited.

Grant *v.* Vaughan, 3 Burr. 1516. 1527.
This was an action on a note payable to
bearer, which had been lost, and came to
plaintiff's hands for a valuable considera-

tion. Lord Mansfield said, it is but just
and reasonable, that if the bearer brings
the action, he ought to entitle himself to
it on a valuable consideration, and strictly
to prove his coming by it *bonâ fide;* and
see Hinton's case, 2 Show. 235.

King *v.* Milson, 2 Campb. Rep. 5. Per
Lord Ellenborough. It would greatly impair the credit and impede the circulation
of negotiable instruments, if persons
holding them could, without strong evidence of fraud, be compelled, by any
prior holder, to disclose the manner in
which they received them See also Sir
John Lawson *v.* Weston, 4 Esp. N. P. C.
56. Rees *v.* Marquess of Headfort, 2
Campb. Rep. 574 S. P.

Pattison *v.* Hardacre, 4 Taunt. 114, in
which it was decided, that where a bill
had been lost, or fraudulently or feloniously obtained from the defendant, the
holder, who sued, must prove that he
came to the bill upon good consideration,
but that the defendant would not be permitted to object to the want of such
proof, unless he had given the plaintiff
reasonable previous notice, that the plaintiff might come to trial prepared to prove
his consideration.

---

(89) The doctrine, that where a bill has been lost, or fraudulently, or feloniously obtained from the defendant, the holder who sues, must prove that he came to the bill upon
a good consideration, seems entirely settled in England; but in a recent case it has received a very material qualification, viz. that the defendant will not be permitted to object
to the want of such proof, unless he has given the plaintiff reasonable previous notice of
the defence, so that the plaintiff may come to trial prepared to prove the consideration
given by him for the bill. *Patterson v. Hardacre,* 4 Taunt. Rep. 114.

And the general principles upon this subject seem as fully admitted in the United
States. It seems, indeed, at one time to have been doubted, whether the want of consideration could be set up even in an action between the original parties to a note; and it

Want of consideration, when material. before it was due, the defendant will not be at liberty to show that he had received none, although the plaintiff knew that circumstance at the time he became the holder, unless he also knew that the party, from whom he received it, was acting fraudulently.[c]

---

[*] Collins v. Martin, 1 Bos. & Paul. 651. Per Eyre, C. J. No evidence of want of consideration, or other ground, to impeach the apparent value received, was ever admitted in a case between an acceptor or drawer, and a third person holding the bill for value, and the rule is so strict that it will be presumed that he does hold for value until the contrary appear; the *onus probandi* lies on the defendant. If it can be proved that the holder gave no value for the bill, then indeed he is in privity with the first holder, and will be affected by every thing which would affect such first holder. This all proceeds upon the *argumentum ad hominem*, it is saying you have the title, but you shall not be heard in a court of justice, to enforce it against good faith and conscience. For the purpose of ren-

---

was then said, that all the cases cited were cases in which there was, not a *want*, but a *failure* of consideration. *Livingston* v. *Hastie*, 2 Canies' Rep. 246. and see also the opinion of *Livingston*, J. in *Baker* v. *Arnold*, 3 Caines' Rep. 279. But it is now held that there is no difference in this respect between a want and a failure of consideration; and that each may be set up as a defence not only between the original parties, but also against a holder claiming by indorsement after the note has become due, or taking it with a knowledge of fraud or other equitable circumstances, entitling the maker to avail himself of the defence. *Pearson* v. *Pearson*, 7 John. Rep. 26. *Store* v. *Wadley*, 3 John. Rep. 124. *Ten Eyck* v. *Vanderpool*, 8 John. Rep. 120. *Denniston* v. *Bacon*, 10 John. Rep. 198. *Woodhull* v. *Holmes*, 10 John. Rep. 231. *Frisbee* v. *Hoffnagle*, 11 John. Rep. 50. *Thatcher* v. *Dinsmore*, 5 Mass. Rep. 299. *Warner* v. *Lynch*, 5 John. Rep. 239. *Bacon* v. *Arnold*, 8 Caines' Rep. 279. *Tappan* v. *Von Wagenen*, 3 John. Rep. 465. *Bayley* v. *Faber*, 6 Mass. Rep. 451. And the want of consideration may in like manner be set up in an action by a second indorsee against his immediate indorser. *Herrick* v. *Carman*, 10 John. Rep. 224. But that a note was made for the accommodation of the maker, and without consideration, is no defence in an action by a *bona fide* holder for a valuable consideration against an indorser, although he had knowledge of the fact at the time he took the bill. *Brown* v. *Mott*, 7 John. Rep. 361. Nor if the action were against an acceptor for the accommodation of the drawer, would the like defence avail —Ibid; nor, as it should seem, even if the holder took the bill after it was due. Ibid. But if the indorser of a promissory note prove that it was put into circulation fraudulently, he may call upon the holder to show what he gave for it, and how it came into his hands. And the indorser is entitled to give such proof, in order to require such explanation from the holder. *Holme* v. *Karsper*, 5 Bin. Rep. 469. See also *Ball* v. *Allen*, 15 Mass. 433. See also *Braman* v. *Hess*, 13 John. Rep. 52, and *Olmstead* v. *Stewart*, 13 John. Rep. 238.

For further cases as to the effect of the indorsement of a bill after it becomes due, see the notes to Chap. IV.—see iii p. 160, *et seq.*

A promissory note whereby A. " as administrator of P. B. deceased, promised to pay" the plaintiff a certain sum, " for value received by J. B. and heirs, on demand, with lawful interest until paid," has, on demurrer to the declaration, been held void for want of a sufficient consideration. *Ten Eyck* v. *Vanderpool*, 8 John. Rep. 120. And a note made in aid of a fund for the support of a minister of a parish has also been adjudged void for want of consideration. *Rontelle* v. *Cowden*, 9 Mass. Rep. 254.

The consideration of a promissory note, may be inquired into as between the original parties, and if these is no consideration for the promise, it is *nudum pactum* and cannot be enforced by an action. *Schoonmaker* v. *Rose*, 17 Johns. 301.

When a promissory note is assigned for a valuable consideration, and in the course of business, the assignee cannot be affected by any transactions between the assignor and the parties to such note, to which the assignee is not privy, and evidence to that effect is not relevant. But such evidence is relevant if it shows that the assignee was a trustee or had notice of the transactions, or did not receive the note in the usual course of business. *Harrisburgh Bank* v. *Meyer*, 6 Serg. & Rawle, 537.

It has been lately decided in Pennsylvania, that although by an act of assembly passed in the year 1715, the indorsee of a promissory note is to recover " the money mentioned in such note, or so much thereof as shall appear to be due at the time of assignment ;" yet if the note be expressly made payable, " without defalcation" and be transferred to an indorsee for a valuable consideration and in the course of business, the maker cannot set up failure of consideration, in a suit by the indorsee. *Lewis* v. *Reeder*, 9 Serg. & Rawle, 193.

And though when a bill of exchange has been given for a particular *Want of consideration, whea material.* purpose, and that be known to the party taking it, then he cannot apply it to a different purpose; where a bill is given under no such restriction,' but merely for the accommodation of the drawer or payee, and sent into the world, it is no answer to an action brought on such bill, that the defendant accepted it for the accommodation of the drawer, and that that fact was known to the holder; and in such case the latter, if he gave a *bona fide* consideration for it, is entitled to recover the amount, though he had full knowledge of the transaction.[d] Though where he has once returned the bill as useless, it has been held, that he cannot, by afterwards obtaining possession of it, acquire a right of action against the acceptor.[e](1)

Between the drawer and the acceptor, the drawer and the payee and his agent, and the indorsee and his immediate indorser, fraud, or the total want of consideration, may be questioned.[f] And though we have

dering bills of exchange negotiable, the right of property in them passes with the bills. Every holder, with the bills, takes the property, and his title is stamped upon the bills themselves. The property and the possession are inseparable. This was necessary to make them negotiable, and in this respect they differ essentially from goods, in which the property and possession may be in different persons. Morris v. Lee, K. B., Hil. 26 Geo. 3. In an action by the indorsee against the maker of a note thirteen years old, the defendant obtained a rule *nisi*, to set aside a judgment by default, on an affidavit by a third person, that he believed the defendant was swindled out of the note; an affidavit was made on the other side, that the plaintiff took the note *bona fide*, and gave a valuable consideration for it, and the court held, that however improperly it might have been obtained, a third person who took it fairly, and gave a consideration for it, was entitled to recover, and discharged the rule; see this case cited in Anonymous, 1 Com. Rep. 43 ; and Bayl. 233.

Haly v. Lane, 2 Atk. 182. "Where there is a negotiable note, and it comes into the hands of a third or fourth indorsee, though some of the former indorsees might not pay a valuable consideration, yet if the last indorsee gave money for it, it is a good note as to him, unless there should be some fraud or equity against him appearing in the case." See also per Buller, J. in Lickbarrow v. Mason, 2 T. R. 71. Poth. pl. 118. 121. Selw. N. P. 4th edit. 304.

[d] Per Lord Eldon, in Smith v. Knox,

3 Esp. Rep. 47; and see Charles v. Marsden, 1 Taunt 224 ; and Popplewell v. Wilson, 1 Stra. 264.

[e] Cartwright v. Williams, 2 Stark. 340 ; and see Jones v. Hilbert, 2 Stark. 304.

[f] Jefferies v. Austen, Stra. 647. In an action by the payee of a note against the maker, Eyre, C. J., allowed the defendant to prove that it was given as a reward, in case the plaintiff procured the defendant to be restored to an office, and the defendant was not restored, and on this proof the defendant had a verdict.

Solomon v. Turner, Bart. 1 Stark. 51. If a promissory note be given as the stipulated price of a picture, the maker cannot give the inadequacy of the consideration in evidence, with a view to diminish the damages, but may prove such circumstance as indicatory of fraud, in order to defeat the contract altogether; and see Ledger v. Ewer, Peake, 216. Fleming v. Simpson, 1 Campb. 40.

Richmond v. Heapy, 1 Stark. 202. If one of three partners undertake to provide for a bill of exchange drawn by the firm, upon and accepted by the defendant, the latter may, in an action at the suit of the three partners, give in evidence such undertaking as a defence to the action.

Jackson v. Warwick, 7 T. R. 121. The defendant's son was apprenticed by indenture to the plaintiff, and the defendant gave the plaintiff a note for 10l. as an apprentice fee ; but this premium was not mentioned in the indentures, nor were they stamped pursuant to 8 Ann. c. 9. The son remained part of his time

---

(1) Where *A.* made a note payable to the defendant or order, which was indorsed by the defendant for the purpose of being discounted at bank, for the accommodation of *A.*, who, on its being refused at the bank, negotiated it to a third person at a discount with a knowledge of the circumstances, it was held that this did not amount to a fraud, which could affect the rights of the holder against the parties to it. *Powell v. Waters*, 17 Johns 176.

Want of consideration, when material. seen that a parol agreement to renew a bill, affords no defence to an action ;ᶜ yet if a bill or check be given on a verbal condition, which the drawer finds is to be broken or eluded, he has a right to stop the payment, and may defend an action thereon.ʰ

[71]   In those cases also in which a defendant would be at liberty to insist upon a total want of consideration, he may show that the consideration does not extend to all the money payable by the bill or note, and the plaintiff shall only recover for the residue ;ⁱ and therefore an acceptor of a bill may, in defence to an action against him by the payee, show that he accepted it for value as to a part, and as an accommodation to the plaintiff as to the rest.ᵏ

But the money as to which the consideration fails, must be of a *specific liquidated* amount ; for, where a partial failure of consideration arises from unliquidated damages, sustained by the breach of a subsisting contract, the performance of which was the consideration of the bill or note, such breach of contract cannot be investigated in an action on the bill or note; but the plaintiff will be entitled to a verdict for the

and then absconded. In an action on the note, and the failure of consideration (the apprenticeship) being relied on as a defence, it was contended that the avoiding the indentures could not collaterally affect the note, and that at all events the consideration had not wholly failed, inasmuch as the plaintiff had maintained the apprentice during his stay. Lawrence, J. however, thought that the consideration was entire, and had wholly failed; he allowed a verdict to be taken for the plaintiff, with liberty to the defendant to move to enter a nonsuit. The court concurred in opinion with Lawrence, J. and directed a nonsuit to be entered; see Grant *v.* Welchman, 16 East, 207.

ᵍ Ante, 47, 8.

ʰ Wienholt *v.* Spitter, 3 Campb. 376.

ⁱ Bayl. 234, 5. Barber *v.* Backhouse, Peake, 61. In an action on a bill of exchange by the payee, the defendant paid part of the money into court, and it appeared upon the trial, that there was no consideration for the other part; Law, however, urged that the payment of the money into court admitted the bill was good for part, and if it was good for part it was good *in toto;* but Lord Kenyon declared himself clearly of a contrary opinion, upon which the jury found for the defendant, and this case being afterwards mentioned by Lord Kenyon in the course of argument, Law said he was perfectly satisfied with the decision.

Ledger *v.* Ewer, Peake, 216. In an action by the payee of a bill against the acceptor, the consideration appeared to

be, that the plaintiff had taken the defendant into partnership ; but on the defendant's friend's advice he broke off the connexion ; there was evidence of fraud on the plaintiff's part in drawing the defendant into the engagement, which Lord Kenyon left to the jury ; but he told them, if they were against the defendant on the evidence of fraud, they should take into consideration the damages the plaintiff had really sustained by the non-performance of the contract, and were not obliged to find the whole amount of the bill. The jury, however, found for the defendant.

Wiffen *v.* Roberts, 1 Esp. Rep. 261. This was an action by the indorsee against the drawer of a bill of exchange accepted by one Yates. The defence set up was, that the bill ,was an accommodation one, and that the defendant had not paid full value for it. Lord Kenyon said, that where a bill of exchange is given for money really due from the drawee to the drawer, or is drawn in the regular course of business, in such case the indorsee, though he has not given the indorser the full amount of the bill, yet may recover the whole, and be holder of the overplus above the sum really paid to the use of the indorser ; but where the bill is an accommodation one, and that known to the indorsee, and he pays but part of the amount, in such case he can only recover the sum he had actually paid on the bill. The plaintiff was nonsuited on another ground.(93)

ᵏ Darnell *v.* Williams, 2 Stark. 166.

(93) The case of *Wiffen v. Roberts* seems incidentally recognised as law in *Brown v. Mott*, 7 John. Rep. 361.

whole amount of the bill, leaving the defendant to his cross action ;[1] *Want* of . and where a promissory note was given as a part of the consideration *considera-* of an indenture of apprenticeship for less than seven years, by being an- *tion, when* tedated, and the apprentice was discharged by a magistrate after two material. years, on account of the master having enticed him to commit felony, it [72] was held that these circumstances did not enable the maker of the note to resist payment of any part of the money payable, particularly as the apprentice fee was to have been paid in the first instance, and it was only in ease of the defendant, that the note was taken for part of it, payable at a distant day.[a]

Where, however, such contract has been rescinded *in toto* when entire, or in part when it may be divided, it will be competent to the defendant, in an action on the bill or note, brought by the one contract-ing party against the other, to prove that the contract has been thus wholly or partly rescinded, and thus prove a total or partial failure of consideration.[a]

It does not appear to have been decided, whether a promissory note or check, given by the maker to the payee as a *gift*, and without con-sideration, can be enforced between these parties.[a] In the case of

[1] Bayl. 236, 7. Moggeridge v. Jones, 14 East, 486. 3 Campb. 38. S. C. Drawer against the acceptor of a bill. The plain-tiff agreed to let a house to the defendant for twenty-one years, and in considera-tion of 500l., to be paid by three bills to be drawn by the plaintiff, and accepted by the defendant, agreed to execute a lease for that term. The bill in question, and two others, were drawn and accept-ed accordingly, and the defendant was immediately let into possession; but the plaintiff refused to execute the lease. It was urged therefore, that the considera-tion had failed. But Lord Ellenborough, and afterwards the court, on a motion for a new trial held, that this was no defence to the action; that the defendant was bound to pay the bills, and might have his remedy on the agreement for non-ex-ecution of the lease. Vide Broom v. Da-vis, cited 7 East's Rep. 400. And Basten v. Butter, 7 East's Rep. 479, and the cases therein cited. Morgan v. Richardson, 1 Campb. 100. To an action by the drawer against the acceptor of a bill drawn payable to the drawer's order, the defence was, that the bill had been accepted for the price of some hams, and that they had proved so bad as to be almost unmarketable. The sum for which they were actually sold was paid into court. Lord Ellenborough held, that this partial failure of consideration was no defence to this action; but that the defendant must take his remedy by action. See also 7 East, 482, note a. 3 Smith's Rep. 487, notes, S. P. Fleming v. Simpson, 1 Campb. 40. From Tye v. Gwynne, 2 Campb. 346, it appears that this case was afterwards brought before the King's Bench, and the court ap-

proved of the direction of the Chief Jus-tice. And see Solomon v. Turner, 1 Sark. 57. Tye v. Gwynne, 2 Campb. 346. This was an action on a bill of exchange by the drawer against the acceptor, and the same point arose as in the last case, with the exception that no money was paid into court, Lord Ellenborough said he should adhere to the judgment of the court in Morgan v Richardson, vide last case.

[m] Grant v. Welchman, 16 East, 207.

[n] Bayl. 236. Lewis v. Cosgrave, 2 Taunt. 2. This was an action on a bank-er's check drawn by the defendant, and given to the plaintiff for the price of a horse, sold by the plaintiff to the defen-dant, and warranted sound : the horse was in fact unsound, and that was relied on as a defence. The defendant proved that he had sent back the horse, but the plain-tiff refused to take it : he however sent it again, and left it in the plaintiff's stable without his knowledge. Heath, J. told the jury, that as the plaintiff had refused to receive back the horse, the contract for the sale was not rescinded, and that the defendant was therefore bound to pay the check and had his re-medy by action, for the deceit. They found a verdict for the plaintiff; but on a rule nisi for a new trial, and cause shown, the court, on the ground of there being clear evidence of fraud, made the rule ab-solute. See Weston v. Downes, Dougl. 23. Power v. Wells, Cowp. 818. Towers v. Barrett, 1 T. R. 133. [o] The general opinion appears to be that such a bill or note cannot be en-forced. In Nash v. Brown, Sittings at

Want of consideration, when material. *Tate* v. *Hilbert*,[p] it was held, that an absolute gift to take effect immediately, cannot be considered as *donatio mortis causa;* therefore such gift of a common check on a banker payable to bearer, and of the parties' own promissory note, was not *donatio mortis causa*, or an appointment or disposition in nature of it; and was not capable of any greater effect in equity than at law; it was therefore ordered, that the bill, as to the check, should be dismissed without prejudice to any action; and as to the note, it being doubted whether an action would lie against the executor for want of consideration, the court offered to retain the bill, if an account was necessary. In the same case it was also decided, that where a banker's check is given, and is paid away for valuable consideration, or to a creditor, the executor is liable; and if the person to whom it is given receives it, before the banker has notice of the death of the drawer, it cannot be recalled. If a bill, &c. have been fraudulently obtained, a court of equity will relieve, and detain the bill.[q](1)

[74] *Illegality of consideration, when it vitiates.* Whenever the defendant is at liberty to insist on the want of consideration as a defence, he may also insist that the consideration, or a part

Westminster, Trin. 1817, a bill of exchange was accepted by the defendant as a present to the payee, who indorsed it to the plaintiff for a small sum advanced to him. And Lord Ellenborough held, that the plaintiff was only entitled to recover so much as he had actually advanced on the bill. Formerly, such a bill or note seems to have been considered to be available. Williamson and Ux *v.* Losh, Executor, MS. Ashurst, J. Paper Books, 19th vol, 54. Mich. Term, 16 Geo. 3. cited 7 T. R. 351. This was an action of assumpsit against the defendant, as executor of John Losh, deceased, upon the following promissory note: "I, John Losh, for the love and affection that I have for Jane Tiffin, my wife's sister's daughter, do promise that my executors, administrators, or assigns, shall pay to her the sum of 100*l.* of money, one year after my decease, and a caldron, and a clock, a wainscot chest, and a bed and bed-clothes, seven pudder dishes: as witness my hand, this 16th day of February, 1763. Witnessed by us, A. B., C. D." Jane Tiffin afterwards intermarried with the plaintiff. Upon the trial, a verdict was found for the plaintiff, and a case reserved. The defendant admitted he had proved the will, and had assets sufficient to cover the damages, but contended that there was no consideration in point of law, and that the note could not be recovered upon, and that, as the testator was not bound, the executor was not. The court held, that the instrument being in writing, and attested by witnesses, the objection of *nudum pactum* did not lie, and ordered the postea to the plaintiff. This case was afterwards observed upon by Lord Chief Baron Skynner, in delivering the opinion of the Judges in Rann *v.* Hughes, 7 T. R. 351, when he intimated, that, so far as this case went on the doctrine of *nudum pactum*, it was erroneous.

Seton *v.* Seton, 2 Bro. Ch. Ca. 610. The mother of the plaintiff made a promissory note for 9,500*l.* and delivered it to a trustee, as a provision for a child, of which she was then pregnant; she afterwards filed her bill to have the note delivered up; the child, who was then born, together with the trustee, filed their cross bill, to have the agreement entered into by the note carried into execution. Upon general demurrer to the bill for want of equity, the court held it was not sufficiently *nudum pactum*, to allow the demurrer.

A moral, or even an honourable obligation, would be sufficient to give effect to a note. Lee *v.* Muggeridge, 5 Taunt. 36. Gibb *v.* Merrill, 3 Taunt. 311.

[p] Tate *v.* Hilbert, 2 Ves. jun. 111. 4 Bro. Ch. Rep. by Belt. 286. S. C.

[q] The Bishop of Winchester *v.* Fournier, 2 Ves. sen. 445. *et post.*

---

(1) If an order not amounting to a bill of exchange is accepted by the drawee, without consideration, he is not bound, it being *nudum pactum*. *Atkinson* v. *Manks*, 1 Cowen, 692.

In an action brought by the assignee in the name of the payee of a note not negotiable against the maker, it is competent for the defendant to give in evidence that the assignment was made without consideration, and that he had paid the amount to the payee, although he had notice of the assignment previous to the payment. *Dunning* v. *Hayward*, 1 Green. 366.

thereof, was *illegal*.[a] A contract is always legal, if it be not repug- *Illegality* nant to the revealed *Law of God*, to the *general policy of the Common of consider-* *Law*, or to some *Legislative Provision*. The principles on which ille- *ation,when it vitiates.* gality in a *contract* vitiates it, are pointed out in *Lightfoot* v. *Tenant*.[b] *Illegal considerations* have been considered as distinguishable into three heads—1. The doing an act *malum in se*, or *malum prohibitum*.— 2dly. The *omission* of the performance of some legal duty.—And 3dly. A stipulation encouraging such crime or omission.[c] But the distinction between *malum in se*, and *malum prohibitum*, has recently been denied.[d] Illegal considerations may be either those void at common law, or those void by statute.

First. Considerations *illegal* at *common law* are those which are pre- At common judicial to the *community at large*, or those which affect the person or law. interest of an *individual*. Those of the former description, are, 1*st*, any contract made with an alien enemy; and if a bill be drawn upon any such transaction,[e] it will not be available after a restoration of peace. 2*dly*, stipulations in *general restraint of trade*, as if a party engage not to carry on a trade in any part of England; but if the restraint be qualified, so as only to preclude the party from trading in a particular place, or within a certain distance, as, for instance, ten miles, and the breach of the stipulation tend apparently to the detriment of the party in whose favour it was made, and a consideration was given by such party, the contract will not be impeached either at law or in equity.[f] 3*dly*, A stipulation repugnant to the *Custom* and *Excise* laws of this country, as *smuggling*, &c.[g] 4*thly*, Dropping a *criminal prosecution*, or suppressing evidence, or soliciting a pardon, or compounding a felony, misdemeanour, or other public crime, unless it be with leave of the court.[h] 5*thly*, The recommendation to, or purchase of, an office [75] under government.[b] (96) 6*thly*, Every *illegal wager*, repugnant to the

[a] Guichard v. Roberts, 1 Bla. Rep. 445. Scott v. Gillmore, 3 Taunt. 226. Bayl. 237.

[b] 1 Bos. & Pul. 554, 5. 1 Foubl. 345; and see a learned note in Holt, C. N. P. 107.

[c] 1 Bla. Com. 57, 8. Co. Lit. 206. b. n. 1. Mitchell v. Reynolds, 1 P. W. 189. Lloyd v. Johnson, 1 Bos. & Pul. 340, 1. Lightfoot v. Tenant, id. 556.

[d] Aubert v. Maze, 2 Bos. & Pul. 375. Sedgwick on Bla. Com. 54. *Sed vide* Witham v. Lee, 4 Esp. Rep. 264.

[e] Willison v. Pattison and others, 7 Taunt. 439. Ante, 13; but see the exception, as to British prisoners in a foreign country, in Antoine v. Morshead, 1 Marsh. 458. 6 Taunt. 237. S. C. Ante, 13; and as to the effect of a subsequent promise to pay, Duhammel v. Pickering, 2 Stark. 90.

[f] Hunlock v. Blacklowe, 2 Saund. 156. n. 1. Mitchell v. Reynolds, 1 P. W. 190.

10 Mod. 134. S. C. Co. Lit. 206. b. n. 1. Davis v. Mason, 3 T. R. 118. 1 Powell on Contracts, 167.

[g] Biggs v. Lawrence, 3 T. R. 454. Vandyck v. Hewitt, 1 East, 97. Lightfoot v. Tenant, 1 Bos. & Pul. 551. Guichard v. Roberts, 1 Bla. Rep. 445. Johnston v. Sutton, 1 Dougl. 254. 1 Marsh, on Ins c. 5. Holt. C. N. P. 107. n. See Hodgson v. Temple, 5 Taunt. 181.

[h] Wallace v. Hardacre, 1 Campb. N. P. 42. Poole v. Bonsfield, id. 55. Nerot v. Wallace, 3 T. R. 16. Dragge v. Ibberson, 2 Esp. Rep. 643. Fallows v. Taylor, 7 T. R. 475. Edgcombe v. Rodd, 5 East, 294. Johnson v. Ogilby, 3 P. W. 279. Collins v. Blantein, 2 Wils. 349. Norman v. Cole, 3 Esp. Rep. 253. 1 Leon, 180. Beall v. Wingfield, 11 East, 46. Brett v. Close, 16 East, 293.

[b] Harrington v. Du Chatel, Bro. C. C. 114. Bayl on Bills, 122.

(96) A note given to a Sheriff on an arrest in lieu of a bail bond is void, as contrary to the statute respecting Sheriff's bonds. *Strong* v. *Tompkins*, 8 John. Rep. 98. A note given by an insolvent to his creditor to induce him to sign his petition under the insolvent law, with a blank in it for the date to be filled up after his discharge, is void, as against the general policy of the law. Nor can such note be revived by a subsequent promise to pay it. *Pyne* v. *Eden*, 3 Caines' Rep. 213. So a note given to a creditor to

Illegality of consideration, when it vitiates. principles of general policy, as a wager between voters on the event of an election,[c] upon the event of a war,[d] or concerning the produce of any particular branch of the revenue, &c. as of the hop duties;[e] and cricket, a horse-race, or a foot-race, against time, is a game, within the statute 9 Ann. c. 14. s. 1.[f] *7thly.* In *general restraint of marriage.*[g] *8thly, Procuration of marriage.*[h] *9thly, Future illicit cohabition;* but past cohabition is a legal consideration.[i] So a promissory note given to *indemnify a parish against a bastard child,* is illegal as being contrary to the general policy of the law, as well as the letter of the 6 Geo. 2. c. 31.[k] But the release by an Excise officer, of a person apprehended for penalties under the Excise Laws, will be a sufficient consideration for a note, the commissioners having approved of his taking it,[l] and this, although he had no previous authority.[m] So any stipulation *prejudicial to the feelings or interests of a third person,* and made without his concurrence, as a wager as to the sex of a third person,[n] or contrary to the benevolent intent of others,[o] as a secret stipulation, before a composition deed is signed, that one of the creditors shall have a larger dividend, or a better security, than the rest, is void.[p] Such a note cannot be sued upon, though the composition

[76]

---

[c] Allen v Hearn, 1 T. R. 26. Beeley v. Wingfield, 11 East, 46. Pilkington v. Green, 2 Bos. & Pul. 151.

[d] Lacaussade v. White, 7 T. R. 535. Allen v. Hearne, 1 T. R. 57.

[e] Atherford v. Beard, 2 T. R. 610. Shirley v. Sankey, 2 Bos. & Pul. 130.

[f] Jeffreys v. Walter, 1 Wils. 220. Lynall v. Longbotham, 2 Wils. 36.

[g] Hartley v. Rice, 10 East, 22, qualified. Gibson v. Dickie, 3 M. & S. 463. Lowe v. Peers, Burr. 2225.

[h] Co. Litt. 206 b; and see note [b], supra.

[i] Ex parte Mumford, 15 Ves. 289. Gibson v. Dickie, 3 M. & S 463. Walker v. Perkins, Burr. 1568. Marchioness of Annandale v. Harris, 2 P. W. 432. Turner v. Vaughan, 2 Wils. 339. Hill v Spencer, Amb. 641. Ex parte Cottrell, 2 Cowp. 732. Wightwick v. Banks, Forrest, 153.

[k] Cole v Gower, 6 East, 110.

[l] Pilkington v. Green, 2 Bos. & Pul. 151. Beeley v. Wingfield, 11 East, 46.

[m] Sugars v. Brinkworth, 4 Campb 46. This was an action against the maker of a promissory note. The note was given by the defendant for the amount of penalties, of which he had been convicted

before magistrates, under the Excise laws, to prevent an execution issuing against his goods. On the part of the defendant, it was contended, that there was no legal consideration for the note, as it was the plaintiff's duty to have levied the amount of the penalties, and not to have taken any security Lord Ellenborough. The defendant gave the promissory note at two months, in redemption of his goods, which were liable to be instantly sold for what they could fetch. This surely was sufficient consideration. I do not think any previous consent by the commissioners of Excise, or the magistrates, was necessary for the arrangement. Verdict for plaintiff. *Vide* Pilkington v. Green, 2 Bos. & Pul. 152. S. P.

[n] Da Costa v. Jones, Cowp. 729. Harvey v, Gibbons, 2 Lev. 161. Eastbrook v. Scott, 3 Ves. 456. Ditchburn v. Goldsmith, 4 Campb. 152. Gilbert v. Sykes, 16 East, 150.

[o] Jackson v. Duchaire, 3 T. R. 551.

[p] Cockshott v. Bennet, 2 T. R. 763. Leicester v. Rose, 4 East, 372. Spurrett v. Spiller, 4 Atk. 105. Jackson v. Lomas, 4 T. R. 166. Cooling v. Noyes, 6 T. R. 263. Bryant v. Christie, 1 Stark. 329. Bayl. 280.

---

induce him to withdraw his opposition to the debtor's discharge under an insolvent law is void. *Wiggin* v. *Bush,* 12 John. Rep. 306. See also on the point of illegal considerations, *Little* v. *Obrien,* 9 Mass. Rep. 423. *Jones* v. *Caswell,* 3 John. Cas. 29.

There seems to be some difference of opinion in the United States in respect to wagers. In *Massachusetts* the courts have held wager policies void at common law, upon the general ground that all wagers are injurious to public morals. *Amory* v. *Gilman,* 2 Mass. Rep, 1. In *New York,* however, actions on wagers are held to be maintainable at common law, *Bunn* v. *Riker,* 4 John. Rep. 426. *Campbell* v. *Richardson,* 10 John. Rep. 406. But wagers against principles of public policy are universally held void; as wagers upon the event of a public election. Ibid. *Mount* v. *Waite,* 7 John. Rep. 434. *Lansing* v. *Lansing,* 8 John Rep. 454. *M'Cullum* v. *Gourlay,* 8 John. Rep. 147.

with the creditors be not effected.ᵠ But after a composition deed has *Illegality of consideration, when it vitiates.*
actually been signed by all the creditors, a bill or note, affording a better
security to one of them, has been deemed valid.ʳ At common law, a
wager is legal, if it be not an incitement to a breach of the peace, or
to immorality, or if it do not affect the feelings or interest of a third
person, or expose him to ridicule, or libel him, or if it be not against
sound policy, or merely to try a point of law.ˢ

Secondly, Some considerations, as well as contracts, are declared to *By statute, Usury.*
be *invalid by statute,* as *usury,* by the 12 Ann. stat. 2. c. 16,ᵗ which
has two distinct provisions; first, avoiding all bonds, contracts, and assurances, for the payment of any money to be lent, &c. whereupon or
whereby there shall be reserved or taken above £5 *per cent.;* and secondly, subjecting the party taking above £5 *per cent.* to an action for
treble the sum lent, or forborne, &c. Thus it is enacted, "That no
person or persons whatsoever, upon any contract, take directly or indirectly, for loan, of any moneys, wares, merchandize, or other commodities whatsoever, above the value of £5, for the forbearance of
£100, for a year, and so after that rate for a greater or lesser sum, or
for a longer or shorter time; and that all bonds, contracts, and assurances whatsoever, made for payment of any principal, or money to
be lent, or covenanted to be performed upon or for any usury, whereupon or whereby there shall be reserved or taken above the rate of £5
in the hundred as aforesaid, shall be utterly void; and that all and
every person or persons whatsoever, which shall, upon any contract,
take, accept, and receive, by way or means of any corrupt bargain,
loan, exchange, chevizance, shift, or interest, of any wares, merchandizes, or other thing or things whatsoever, or by any deceitful way or
means, or by any covin, engine, or deceitful conveyance, for the forbearing or giving day of payment, for one whole year, of and for their
money, or other thing above the sum of £5, for the forbearing of £100
for a year, and so after that rate for a greater or lesser sum, or for a
longer or shorter term, shall forfeit and lose, for every such offence, the
treble value of the moneys, wares, merchandizes, and other, things, so
lent, bargained, exchanged, or shifted." Upon this statute it has been
determined, that the security is void, though, on the face of it, it may
appear legal, if their be any other illegal private stipulation between
the original parties, for matter, dehors the security, may, in all cases, [77]
be shown in pleading, if it be illegal;ᵘ and usury, in a small part of the
consideration, renders a bill invalid.ˣ It is not usury, though improper, for an acceptor to discount his own acceptance at a premium;ʸ and
a *bona fide* sale of a bill for a less sum than the amount of the bill, is
not usurious,ᶻ but if the sale be a mere colour for a loan at unlawful interest, it will be usurious; and therefore if the drawer of a bill, accepted by the drawee, and made payable to his own order, and indorsed by
him, gets his known agent to procure cash for it, who does so by allow-

ᵠ Wells v. Guling, 1 Brod. & Bing. 447.
ʳ Feise v. Randall, 6 T. R. 146, Bayl. 230, 1.
ˢ Good v. Elliot, 8 T. R. 693. Henkin v. Guerss, 12 East, 247. Gilbert v. Sykes, 16 East, 150.
ᵗ See the observations on this statute, Holt, C. N. P. 250.

ᵘ Petrie v. Hannay, 3 T. R. 424. Fisher v. Beasly, Dougl. 235.
ˣ Harrison v. Harrison, 1 Marsh. 342. 5 Taunt. 780. S. C.
ʸ Barclay v. Walmsley, 4 East, 55.
ᶻ Ex parte Lee, 1 P. W. 782, 3. The King v. Ridge, 4 Price, 56.

Illegality of consideration, when it vitiates. ing more than the legal discount to be taken, it is void, on account of usury in the hands of the discounters.[a] Where a check is given on a usurious transaction, it cannot be deemed an advance of money, unless specially agreed to be taken as cash, until it has been actually paid.[b] But a clause in a bill or note payable by instalments, and including interest, that the whole shall become due on one default, without providing for a rebate of interest, is not usurious.[c]

Before the late statute, usury affected the validity of the bill or note, although it were in the hands of a *bona fide* holder;[d] and a bill drawn in consequence of a usurious agreement for discounting it, was void in the hands of such holder, although the drawer was not privy to such agreement.[e] A second security given to a *bona fide* holder of a bill, ignorant at the time when he took it of the previous usury,[f] and a bill taken for what was fairly due,[g] were however considered to be valid ; [78] and after suffering judgment by default, or confessing a judgment in favour of a *bona fide* holder, was too late to object to the legality of the consideration.[h] By the late act 58 Geo 3. c. 93. (passed to June, 1818,) it was provided ; that no bill or note drawn or made after the passing of that act, shall be void on account of usury in the hands of an indorsee for valuable consideration, unless he, at the time he discounted or paid the consideration, had actual notice of such usury.[i] (100)

---

[a] The King v Ridge, 4 Price, 56.
[b] Brooke v. Middleton, 1 Campb. 445. Borrodaile v. Middleton, 2 Campb. 53. As to the principle on which the law of usury proceeds, see Molloy v. Irwin, 1 Sch. & Lef. 312. Drew v. Power, id. 195.
[c] Wells v. Guling, 1 Brod. & Bing. 447.
[d] Lowe v. Waller, Dougl. 735. Cuthbert v. Hanley, 8 T. R. 390. Ferrall v. Shaen, 1 Saund. 295. Parr v. Eliason, 1 East, 92. Bayl. 237, 8. Lowe v. Waller, Dougl. 708. 736. The defendant was acceptor of a bill which he gave to Harris and Stratton upon a usurious contract; Harris and Stratton indorsed it to the plaintiff for a valuable consideration, and the plaintiff had no notice of the usury. Upon a case reserved, the question was, whether the usury between Harris and Stratton, and the defendant, was a defence against an indorsee, who took the bill *bona fide*, and paid a valuable consideration for it; and after time taken to consider, the court held it was; and though Lord Mansfield had a wish that the law should turn out in favour of the plaintiff, the court found the words of

the act too strong, and could not get over the case of Bowyer v. Bampton, Stra. 1155, which see, post, 78, note. But see the observations of Gibbs, C. J. in Jones v. Davison, Holt, C. N. P. 256, where a doubt is suggested as to the propriety of this doctrine. However it was confirmed in the case of Lowes v. Mazzaredo, 1 Stark. 385. See post, 81, note.
[e] Ackland v. Pearce, 2 Campb. 599. Young v. Wright, 1 Campb. 139.
[f] Cuthbert v. Haley, 8 T. R. 390. George v. Stanley, 4 Taunt. 683, which see, post, 79, note. But if such holder knew of the usury at the time he took the renewed security, this was holden equally void. Chapman v. Black, 2 B. & A. 588.
[g] Barnes v. Hedley, 2 Taunt. 184. which over-rules 1 Campb. 167. But a fresh bill or note for the illegal interest will be as invalid as the former. Preston v. Jackson, 2 Stark. 237.
[h] Shepherd v. Charter, 5 T. R. 275. George v Stanley, 4 Taunt. 683. See post, 79, note, post, p. 83.
[i] See the statute, post, Appendix.

---

(100) A contract usurious in its inception cannot be afterwards rendered valid, even in the hands of a *bona fide* indorsee without notice of the usury. *Wilkie* v. *Roosevelt*, 3 John. Ca. 206. *Payne* v. *Trezevant*, 1 Bay's Rep. 23. Though a usurious note be void in the hands of a *bona fide* holder, yet a new security given to such holder for the usurious note is good. *Stewart* v. *Eden*, 2 Caines' Rep. 150. *Chadbourne* v. *Watts*, 10 Mass. Rep. 121. *Kilburn* v. *Bradley*, 3 Day's Rep. 268. *Jackson* v. *Henry*, 10 John. Rep. 185. And a judgment in the hands of a *bona fide* assignee, it seems, is not affected by usury in the original transaction. *Wardwell* v. *Eden*, 2 John. Cas. 268. S.

A gaming consideration is declared illegal by the statute 16 Car. 2. *Illegality* c. 7. and 9 Ann. c. 14.[k] The first statute avoids all securities, wheth- *of consideration, when* er *written* or *verbal*, given to secure any sum of money exceeding £100 *it vitiates.* lost at play: but the 9 Ann. only avoids *written* contracts, and an action of assumpsit will lie to recover money won at play, not amounting to £10.[l] By the 9 Ann. c. 14. s. 1. it is enacted, "that all notes, bills, bonds, judgments, mortgages, or other securities or conveyances whatsoever, given, granted, drawn, or entered into, or executed by any person or persons whatsoever, where the whole or any part of the consideration of such conveyances or securities, shall be, for any money or other valuable thing whatsoever, won by gaming or playing at cards, dice-tables, tennis bowls, or other game or games whatsoever, or by betting on the sides or hands of such as do game at any of the games aforesaid, or for the reimbursing or repaying any money knowingly lent or advanced for such gaming or betting as aforesaid, or lent or advanced at the time and place of such play, to any person or persons so gaming or betting as aforesaid, or that shall, during such play, so play or bett, shall be utterly void, frustrate, and of none effect, to all intents and purposes whatsoever, any statute, law, or usage, to the contrary thereof, in anywise notwithstanding." Under these statutes, a bill of exchange, or promissory note given for a gambling debt is void, even in the hands of a *bona fide* holder.[m] But as in the case of usury, a renewed security given for a gambling debt will be valid in the hands of a *bona fide* holder.[n] [79] But in an action against the drawer of a bill it is no defence that the

[k] 1 Pow. 207. Bac. Ab. tit. Gaming. Wilmot's notes, 194. Edward v. Dick, 4 B. & A. 212.

[l] Bulling v. Frost, 1 Esp. Rep. 235.

[m] Bowyer v. Bampton, 2 Stra. 1155. Several notes given by Bampton to Church, for money lent to game with, were indorsed by Church to the plaintiff, for a full and valuable consideration, and the plaintiff had no knowledge that any part of the consideration, from Church to Bampton was money lent for gaming; and after two arguments upon a case reserved, the court held that the plaintiff could not maintain the action, for it would be making the notes of use to the lender if he could pay his debts with them, and it would tend to evade the act, on account of the difficulty of proving notice on an indorsee, and the plaintiff would not be without remedy, for he might sue Church

upon his indorsement; and see Bayl. 237. Wilmot's notes, 194.

[n] George v. Stanley, 4 Taunt. 683. The defendant gave the bills in question for the amount of a gaming debt, which, when due, he renewed with the plaintiff the holder, and when the last mentioned bills became due, executed a warrant of attorney, and confessed a judgment for the amount, whereon execution being levied, a rule *nisi* was obtained to have the money restored and the warrant of attorney cancelled, but upon cause being shown, the court held the defendant ought to have availed himself of this ground of defence when he was applied to for the payment of the first bills, *and discharged the rule*, but permitted him to try an issue whether the plaintiff were implicated.

C. 1 John. Rep. 531. *note.*—A security originally valid cannot be invalidated by a subsequent usurious transaction between the original parties or privies. Bush v. Livingston, 2 Caines' Cas. in Err., 66.; and no usurious transactions between intermediate parties can affect the title to a note in the hands of a *bona fide* holder, Foltz v. May, 1 Bay's Rep. 486.

It is not within the scope of these notes to state the general doctrine as to what constitutes usury. But the learned reader will find valuable information as to the doctrine of usury upon discount of notes in the following cases: Atkinson v. Scott's Ex. 1 Bay's Rep. 307. Churchhill v. Suter, 4 Mass. Rep. 156. Portland Bank v. Storer, 7 Mass. Rep. 433. Jones v. Hake, 2 John. Cas. 60. Wilkie v. Roosevelt, Payne v. Trexevant, Musgrove v. Gibbs, 1 Dall. Rep. 216. Wycoff v. Longhead, 2 Dall. Rep. 92. Northampton Bank v. Allen, 10 Mass. Rep. 84. Thompson v. Thompson, 8 Mass. Rep. 135. Munn v. The Commission Company, 15 John. Rep. 44. Bennet v. Smith & Phelps. 15 John. Rep. 355.

Illegality of consideration, when it vitiates. bill was accepted for a gaming debt, if it be indorsed over by the drawer for a valuable consideration to a third person by whom the action was brought.[o]

A *horse-race* for a plate under £50, is illegal,[p] but a deposit of £25 a side is sufficient.[q] So *gaming in the lottery* is illegal ;[r] and a *stock-jobbing* transaction is declared void by the statute 7 Geo. 2. c. 8. ;[s] and a bill of exchange, given in respect of such a transaction, is invalid in the hands of a person who receives it after it is due, or with notice of the circumstances.[t] Promissory notes were given by a stock broker for the balance of an account of money advanced to him, to be employed in stock-jobbing transactions, against the statute 7 Geo. 2. c. 8. part of the consideration consisting of the profits on these transactions, proof under his bankruptcy was restrained to the residue, viz. the money received, which he had applied to his own use.[u] So a *gaming policy on ships or lives,* or other events, without being interested therein, is invalid.[x]

Other contracts declared void by statute. Trading *against the laws of the East India Company,*[y] or the *Russia Company*[z] is also illegal. And the sale of an office,[a] or of a *vote,* or *bribery at an election* is invalid.[b] So a *Simoniacal contract* ;[c] a stipulation to a *Sheriff,* in consideration of *ease and favour* ;[d] a contract in consideration of *signing a bankrupt's certificate* ;[e] an *illegal insurance* in the lottery ;[f] and a contract to ransom any British ship or goods captured by an enemy are declared unlawful.[g]

[80]

Besides these and many other cases of contracts and securities, expressly declared by statute to be void, there are other cases in which the legislature have prohibited a transaction, and a bill or note having been given to carry into effect such prohibited contract, the instrument has been held void. Thus a bill of exchange, part of the consideration for which was spirituous liquor, sold in quantities of less than twenty shillings value is wholly void, though the other part of the consideration was money lent, because such sale of spirit is contrary to the statute

[o] Edwards v. Dick, 4 B. & A. 212.
[p] 13 G. 2. c 19. 18. G. 2. c. 34. Whaley v. Pajot, 2 Bos. & Pul. 51. Robson v. Hall, Peake's Ca. Ni. Pri. 127. Johnson v. Bunn, 4 T. R. 1, a wager of above 10l. on horse race is illegal, though the race be legal. 2 Bla. R. 708. 2 Stra. 1159. 2 Wils. 309. 2 Campb. 438, 9.
[q] Bidmead v. Gale, 4 Burr. 2432.
[r] Deey v. Shee, 2 T. R. 617. Seddons v. Stratford, Peake's Ca. Ni. Pri. 215.
[s] Faikney v. Reynous, 4 Burr. 2069, Saunders v. Kentish, 8 T. R. 162. Tate v. Wellings, 3 T. R. 531.
[t] Brown v. Turner, 7 T. R. 630. Aubert v. Maze, 2 Bos. & Pul. 374. Steers v. Lashley, 6 T. R. 61.
[u] Ex parte Bulmer, 13 Ves. 313.
[x] 19 Geo. 2. c. 37. Kent v. Bird, Cowp. 583. Roebuck v. Hammerton, id. 737. 14 Geo. 3. c. 48. Nantes v. Thompson, 2 East, 385.
[y] Lightfoot v. Tenant, 1 Bos. & Pul. 551.
[z] Grose v. La Page, 1 Holt C. N. P. 105.

[a] 5 Ed. 6. c. 16. Blanchford v. Preston, 8 T. R. 93. Parsons v. Thompson, 1 Hen. Bla. 322. Layng v. Paine, Willes, 571. Com. Dig. "Officer," K. 1. Bac. Ab. "Officer," F. Stackpole v. Earle, 2 Wils. 133.
[b] 2 Geo. 2. c. 24. Anonymous, Loft. 552. Sulston v. Norton, 3 Burr. 1235. The King v. Pitt. 1 Bla. Rep. 380. Allen v. Hearn, 1 T. R. 56.
[c] 31 Eliz. c. 6. Totteridge v. Mackally, Sir W. Jones, 341. Co. Lit. 208. b. Layng v. Paine, Willes, 575. n. a. Bac. Ab. "Simony."
[d] 23 Hen. 6. c. 9. Rogers v. Reeves, 1 T. R. 418. Samuel v. Evans, 2 T. R. 569. Sell. Prac. 129. to 137. 1 Pow. 173.
[e] 5 Geo. 2. c. 30. s. 11. Smith v. Bromley, Dougl. 626. Cockshott v. Bennet. 2 T. R. 763. Nerot v. Wallace, 3 T. R. 17. Summer v. Brady, 1 Hen. Bla. 647.
[f] Wyat v. Bulmer, 2 Esp. Rep. 538.
[g] Statute 45 Geo. 3. c. 72. Webb v. Brooke, 3 Taunt. 6.

24 Geo. 2. c. 46.[b] And for the same reason no action can be support- *Illegality* ed by the plaintiff on a note given to him by the defendant as an ap- *of consider-* prentice fee, if it appear, that the indenture executed was void by the *ation,when* *it vitiates.* statute 8 Anne, c. 9. for want of insertion of such premium therein, and a proper stamp in respect to the same, although the plaintiff did, in fact, maintain the apprentice for some time, and until he absconded.[i] But it is no objection to an action on a promissory note, that it was given as part of the consideration of an indenture of apprenticeship for less than seven years, by being antedated, such indenture being by the statute of Elizabeth, only voidable and not void.[k]

Where a third person, having given value for a bill, knew at the time he became the holder, that it was originally founded on an illegal transaction,[l] or where a person became holder of such a bill after it became due, he cannot recover on it. [m] However, a person, who at the request of the holder of a bill indorses it, and is obliged to pay the contents to a *bona fide* holder, may recover the money paid, from any person whose name is on it.[n]

In those cases in which the legislature has declared that the *illegality* of the contract, or consideration, shall make the bill or note void (as where it is made in consideration of signing a bankrupt's certificate,[o] or for money lost by gaming, &c.[p] or, before the last act, for [81] money lent on a usurious contract,[q] for a ransom of a ship captured,[r] or made, indorsed, &c. in France during the war, contrary to the 34 Geo. 3. c. 9. s. 4.[s]) the defendant may insist on such illegality, though the plaintiff, or some party between him and the defendant, took the bill *bona fide*, and gave a valuable consideration for it. And the innocent holder can, in such case, only resort to the party from whom he received the bill, &c. (104) and then he cannot recover upon the same, but only on the original consideration;[t] and before the late act, it was decided, that a bill of exchange was void in the hands of a *bona fide* indorsee, if it were drawn in consequence of a usurious agreement for discounting it, although the drawer, to whose order it was payable, was not privy to such agreement.[u] And it has been recently decided, that

[b] Scott v. Gillmore, 3 Taunt. 226 ; but see Spencer v. Smith, 3 Campb. 9.
[i] Jackson v. Warwick, 7 T. R. 121.
[k] Grant v. Welchman, 16 East 207.
[l] Steers v. Lashley, 6 T. R. 61. 1 Esp. Rep. 166. S. C. Wyat v. Blumer, 2 Esp. Rep. 588. Brown v. Turner, id. 631. 7 T. R. 630. S. C. Feise v. Randall, 6 T. R. 146.
[m] Brown v. Turner, 7 T. R. 630.
[n] Seddons v. Stratford, Peake's Ni. Pri. R. 315. Petrie v. Hannay, 3 T. R. 424. Aubert v. Maze, 2 Bos. & Pul. 371.
[o] 5 Geo. 2. c. 20. s. 11. Smith v. Bromley, Dougl. 696. Sumner v. Brady, 1 H. Bla. 647. Bayl. 237. Ante, 80, n.
[p] 9 Anne, c. 14. s. 1. Bowyer v. Bamp-

ton, Stra. 1155. Bul. Ni. Pri. 274. Hussey v. Jacob, Carth. 356. Bayl. 237.— Ante, 78, n.
[q] 12 Anne, st. 2. c. 16. Lowe v. Waller, Dougl. 736. Cuthbert v. Haley, 8 T. R. 392. Parr v. Eliason, 1 East, 92. 94. Chapman v. Black, 2 B. & A. 588. Bayl. 237. Ante, 76, but see 58 Geo. 3. c. 93.
[r] 45 Geo. 3. c. 72. s. 16, 17. Webb v. Brooke, 3 Taunt. 6. Ante, 80.
[s] Bendelack v. Morier, 2 H. Bla. 338.
[t] Id. ibid. Bower v. Bampton, Stra. 1155. Wyat v. Bulmer, 2 Esp. Rep. 538, 539. Witham v. Lee, 4 Esp. Rep. 264. and see ante, 77, n.
[u] Acland v. Pearce, 2 Campb. 599.—and see ante, 77, n.

(104) On this point see *Payne* v. *Trezevant*, 2 Bay's Rep. 23. *Wiggin* v. *Bush*, 12 John. Rep. 306.
A bill of exchange expressed to be collateral to a ransom bill, is a contract upon which an action may be sustained at Common Law, the plaintiff and payee being an alien friend. *Maisonnaire* v. *Keating*, 2 Gallison, 325.

Illegality of consideration, when it vitiates. if the payee of. a bill of exchange, indorse it upon a usarious contract made at the time of such indorsement, a *bona fide* holder cannot afterwards recover upon it, against the accepter, because such holder must claim title through such first indorser.[x]

But unless it has been so expressly declared by the legislature, illegality of consideration will be no defence in an action at the suit of a *bona fide* holder, without notice of the illegality,[y] unless he obtained the bill after it became due.[z] Thus in an action by the indorsee against [82] the maker of a promissory note, the defence insisted on was, that the note had been given for hits against the defendant in a lottery insurance: Lord Kenyon, Chief Justice, thought the plaintiff was entitled to recover, observing, that the innocent indorsee of a gaming note, or note given on a usurious contract, could not recover, but that in no other case could the innocent indorsee be deprived of his remedy on the note; and that a contrary determination would shake paper credit to the foundation.[a] And a broker receiving an exorbitant brokerage on the discount of a bill, will not affect its validity in the hands of a *bona fide* holder.[b]

In general, a *subsequent* illegal contract or consideration of any description, taking place in a second indorsement or transfer of a bill, and not in its inception, nor in a transfer through which the holder must make title, will not invalidate the same, in the hands of a *bona fide* holder.[c] Where a new security in taken in lieu of another, void in respect of usury, &c. it will be equally invalid in the hands of the party to the first illegal transaction, but not if in the hands of a *bona fide* holder.[d] And a security given by the borrower to a person not privy to

[x] Lowes and another *v.* Mazzeredo and others, 1 Stark. 385. This was an action by the plaintiffs as indorsees, against the defendants as acceptors of a bill of exchange; the bill was drawn by one G. Lowes, and indorsed to Sir M. B., and by him to Ambrose, and then to the plaintiffs. The defence was usury in the *first* indorsement, and which was proved. Lord Ellenborough was of opinion, that the plaintiffs were not entitled to recover upon the bill, since they were obliged to claim through an indorsement, which had been vitiated by usury; but, upon the counsel for the plaintiffs insisting on the case of Parr *v.* Eliason, 1 East, 92, his Lordship permitted the plaintiffs to take a verdict, subject to a motion to enter a nonsuit. A rule *nisi* having been obtained, and cause shown, the court were of opinion, that the case of Parr *v.* Eliason was distinguishable from this, and might be supported upon other grounds; and that the indorsement was entirely avoided by the statute of Usury, and could not be dismissed for one purpose and retained for another, and that after the case of Lowe *v.* Waller, (ante, 77.) had been acted upon so long, its foundation could not now be inquired into.

[y] Wyat *v.* Bulmer, 2 Esp. Rep. 538.—Brown *v.* Turner, 7 T. R. 630. Le Franc *v.* Dalbiac, Sel. Ca. 71.

[z] Brown *v.* Turner, 7 T. R. 630.

[a] Winstanley *v.* Bowden, Middlesex, Sittings after Mich. Term, 41 Geo. 3. B. R. 1 Selw. 2d edit. 402. Id. 4th edit. 370.

[b] Dignall *v.* Wigley, 11 East, 43.—2 Campb. 33. S. C. Jones *v.* Davison, Holt C. N. P. 256.

[c] Lowes *v.* Mazzeredo, 1 Stark. 385.—Parr *v.* Eliason, 1 East, 92. 3 Esp. Rep. 210. S. C. Cuthbert *v.* Haley, 3 T. R. 391. 3 Esp. Rep. 22. S C. Daniel *v.* Carteny, 1 Esp. Rep. 274. Turner *v.* Holme, 4 Esp. 11. Ferrall *v.* Shaen, 1 Saund. 294, 5. n. 1. What is considered usury in making the bill, see Young *v.* Wright, Campb. N. P. 141 see also 1 Holt C. N. P. 270. Parr *v.* Eliason, 1 East, 92. A bill was drawn in favour of the plaintiff, he indorsed it to Persent and Bodeker, upon a usurious consideration, and they indorsed it over; it was afterwards indorsed back to the assignees of P. and B who had become bankrupts for a debt due to their estate, upon which the plaintiff brought trover to recover back the bill. Lord Kenyon directed a nonsuit, and after a rule *nisi* for a new trial, the court held, that as the bill was originally good, and as the indorsement by Persent and Bodeker was unimpeached, their indorsee had a good right to the bill, and that right was transferred to the defendant. (Rule discharged.) Vide also 1 Esp. Rep. 274. S. P.

[d] Cuthbert *v.* Haley, 3 T. R. 390. Pick-

the usurious transaction, and to whom the lender is indebted in so much *Illegality* money, shall not be avoided by the usury; as where W. was indebted *of consider-* to A. in £100, for the forbearance of which he agreed to pay more than *it vitiates.* legal interest, and A. being indebted to E. in £100, W. and A. joined in a bond to E. in payment of his debt, and it was held not usury.[e] And though it has been held otherwise at Nisi Prius, it has recently been decided, that after usurious securities for a loan have been destroyed by mutual consent, and there is a fresh contract by the borrower to repay the principal and legal interest, such fresh contract is valid.[f] **[83]** By suffering judgment by default, the defendant loses the opportunity of objecting to the sufficiency or illegality of the consideration.[g](106) So a warrant of attorney given to the holder of a renewed bill, will not be set aside unless it be shown that he was privy to the usurious transaction, though the person resisting the payment, may be permitted to try in an issue whether the party were implicated.[h]

The receiving a bill or note upon a usurious contract, but given for a previous legal subsisting debt, will not extinguish such debt, although the security itself will be void;[i] but where there was usury in the making the bill, or where the holder has himself been a party to the usury, he cannot sue at law, or prove under a commission of bankruptcy, even for the amount of principal and lawful interest,[k] and though it has been decided that if deeds or property have been deposited as a collateral security, the party guilty of the usury may retain the same until he has been paid such principal and interest ; it has recently been settled, that a court of law will set aside a judgment founded on a usurious security, without compelling the defendant to repay the principal and interest.[l]

The taking of discount in advance on the loan of money secured by *Interest.* bond, even before the statute of Anne, was considered usurious, and we find it laid down, that an agreement that the interest on the principal should be retained at the time of the loan, or paid before the expiration of the year, amounts to usury ; because the borrower would not have the use of the sum upon which the interest was taken for the whole year;[m] but an exception to this general rule has been allowed in the discounting of bills of exchange negotiated in the ordinary course of trade, the usual mode of doing which is to take interest upon the whole amount of the bill, at the time the money is advanced, until the time

ering *s.* Banks, Forr, Rep. 72 Harrison
[e] Hannel, 1 Marsh. 349. 5 Taunt. 780.
Parr *n.* Elisson, 3 Esp. Rep 210. 1 East,
92. 8. C Witham *v.* Lee, 4 Esp. Rep
264. See Barnes *v.* Headley, 1 Campb.
Ni. Pri. 187. over-ruled in 2 Taunt. 184.
Holt C. N. P. 270.
[e] Ellis *v.* Warnes, Cro. Jac. 32. Yelv.
47. Moore, 752. 2 Anders. 121.
[f] Barnes *v.* Headley, 1 Campb. 187.—Id.
2 Taunt. 184.
[g] Shepherd *v.* Charter, 4 T. R. 275.—
George *v.* Stanley, 4 Taunt. 683. Anne,
79. note.
[h] George *s.* Stanley, 4 Taunt. 683.

[i] Phillips *v.* Cockayne, 3 Campb. 119.
1 Saund. 295, n. 1.
[k] Benfield *v.* Solomon, 9 Ves. 84. Fitzroy *v.* Gwillim, 1 T. R. 153. Hindle *v.*
O'Brien, 1 Taunt. 413. *Sed vide* Roberts
v. Goff, 4 B. & A. 92. The statute enacts,
that the contract shall be void, and it
would militate against the policy of the
enactment, if any effect were given to
the contract by allowing the lender to retain deeds.
[l] Roberts *v.* Goff, 4 B. & A. 92.
[m] Barnes *v.* Worledge, Nay, 41. Cro.
Jac. 25. Yelv. 31. Moor. 644. 8. C.—
Grime's case, 1 Bulst. 20. and Per Popham, J. in Dalton's case, Noy, 171.

(106) On this point, see *Stewart* v. *Eden*, 2 Caine's Rep. 150.

Illegality when the bill will become due, and such transaction on a bill of ex-
of consider- change in the way of trade, for the accommodation of the party de-
ation,when sirous of raising money is not usurious, though more than five *per cent.*
it vitiates be in effect taken upon the money actually advanced ; for were it otherwise, every banker in London, who takes at the rate of five pounds *per*
[84] *cent.* for discounting bills, would be guilty of usury ; for, if upon discounting a £100 bill at five *per cent.* he should be construed to lend
only £95, then at the end of the time he would receive five pounds
interest for the loan of £95 principal, which is above the legal rate. [a]
In such cases it has been considered, that the additional sum is in the
nature of a compensation for the trouble to which the lender is exposed,
and unless that indulgence were allowed, it might not be worth while
for any merchant to discount a bill.[o] But if a bill or note be for a
large sum, and made or drawn at a period of two or three years, it
seems to have been considered, that the length of the date of the bill
will afford a presumption that the discount is intended as a cover for a
usurious bargain ; and in the case of a bill of exchange drawn for £5000,
and payable three years after date, upon which £750 was retained for
discount ; such transaction was holden to be usurious, as the sum
which was taken for interest was not then due, and the bill was given
to secure a much larger sum than legal interest on the sum which would
have been due at the end of three years, provided the bill had not
been given.[p]

Commis- Bankers who discount a bill or note payable at another place may,
sion. in addition to the legal interest or discount of five pounds *per cent.*,
lawfully take a customary and reasonable sum for remitting the bill or
note for payment, and other necessary and incidental expenses ; for if
they were allowed only five *per cent.* upon the whole transaction, they
might, in consequence of the expenses they incur in their establishment,
obtain less remuneration on the discount than other individuals.[q] And
the right to receive this additional remuneration does not appear to be
confined to cases where the bill is payable at a different place to that
where the banker resides, but extends to bills payable in the same
[85] place;[r] and though it has been considered that the case of bankers is
dissimilar to that of other persons, on account of the nature of their
business, and of the peculiar expense attending it,[s] yet it seems that a
merchant or other person may, under circumstances, legally receive a

[a] Per Eyre, C. J and Blackstone, J.
in Lloyd *v.* Williams, Bla. Rep. 792.—3
Wils. 256. S. C.
[o] Per Lord Alvanley, C. J. in delivering judgment in Marsh *v.* Martindale, 3
Bos. & Pul. 158. 1 Holt C. N. P. 262,
263.
[p] See Marsh *v.* Martindale, 3 Bos. &
Pul. 154. and the judgment of Lord Alvanley, p. 160, 1.
[q] Winch, qui tam *v.* Fenn, cited by
Buller, J. in Auriol *v.* Thomas, 2 T. R.
52. Ex parte Jones 17 Ves. 332. 1 Rose
Rep. 29. Benson *v.* Parry, cited in
Baynes *v.* Fry, 15 Ves. 120. 1 Holt C. N.
P. 263.
Winch, qui tam *v.* Fenn. This was an
action for usury against the defendant,
who was a country banker living at Sudbury. It appeared on the trial that the

custom was to discount bills in London,
for their correspondents at Sudbury, reserving five shillings *per cent.* on the gross
sum (beyond the legal discount,) without
any reference as to the time which the
bill had to run. The jury found a verdict for the defendant under the direction
of the Judge ; and Buller, J. in Auriol *v.*
Thomas, 2 T. R. 52, referring to the
above case, said, " It is now clearly settled, that the party is entitled to take not
only five pounds *per cent.* for legal interest,
but also a reasonable sum for remitting
and other necessary incidental expenses.
Vide also Ex parte Jones, in the matter of
Allen, 1 Rose Rep. 29. S. P. and 17 Ves.
332. S. C.
[r] Masterman *v.* Cowrie, 3 Campb. 492.
[s] Per Eyre C. J. Hammet *v.* Yea, 1 Bos
& Pul. 152.

commission on discounting bills; as where he has considerable trouble *Illegality* in keeping accounts for the party so charged.[t] *of consideration, when it vitiates.*

With respect to the *amount* of the commission which a banker may charge either for discounting, receiving, accepting, or paying bills, there appears to be no settled rule; but it is a question to be left to the jury upon the evidence, whether the charge is reasonable, and commensurate with the trouble and expenses incidental to the transaction; if it exceed a fair remuneration, and be mixed with an advance of money, then the transaction will be usurious.[u] The usual commission on discounting bills sanctioned by the decisions, is five shillings *per cent.*;[x] but there is no rule of law, that it shall not exceed that rate;[y] and in the case of a very large and complicated account, the commission of one-half *per cent.* was allowed.[z] But where a party charged seven and sixpence *per cent.* for commission on discounting a bill, without proving that he had been put to expense, or any considerable degree of trouble in the transaction, it was deemed usurious.[a]

Bankers cannot charge interest upon interest, without an express con- *Compound* tract for that purpose; and it has even been supposed, that they cannot *interest,&c.* legally make rests in their accounts, so as to charge interest upon prior interest and commission, but this seems unreasonable; and unless the rests in the account be made too frequently, and out of the ordinary course of business, and for the mere purpose of obtaining compound interest, such rests seem perfectly legal.[b] So also an agent who has advanced money for his principal in effecting insurances, and other [86] mercantile business, is entitled to charge interest, and at the end of every year to make a rest, and add the interest then due to the principal;[c] but where bankers seek to recover interest upon moneys advanced to a customer, it is not sufficient to show that it was the general custom of their houses to charge interest calculated upon half-yearly rests, without also showing that such customer knew that such was the practice.[d]

---

[t] Per Lord Alvanley, C. J. in Marsh *v.* Martindal, 3 Bos. & Pul. 158.

[u] Carstairs *v.* Stein, 4 M. & S. 195.—Palmer *v.* Baker, 1 M. & S. 56. Harris *v.* Boston, 2 Campb. 348. Masterman *v.* Cowrie, 3 Campb. 492.

[x] Winch *v.* Fenn, ante, 84, n.; but see the cases Ex parte Jones, 17 Ves. 332. 1 Rose, 29, where one-eighth *per cent.* was allowed upon discounts.

[y] Per Lord Ellenborough, Carstairs *v.* Stein, 4 M. & S. 199.

[z] Id. ibid.

[a] Brooke *v.* Middleton, 1 Campb. 448.

[b] Caliot *v.* Walker, 2 Anst. Rep. 495. The defendants in this case acted as bankers, and at the end of every quarter struck a balance, in which was included the principal money advanced by them, all interest then due upon it, and a commission of five shillings for every 100*l.* advanced. This balance was, at the end of every quarter, converted into principal, and carried interest. This the plaintiff contended to be usury.

The court declared themselves strongly of opinion that this case was not usurious. The statute allows interest, not merely of 5*l. per cent.* for a year, but after the rate of 5*l. per cent.* half-yearly payments of interest, or the discounting bills at the beginning of the time when they have to run, have both been argued to be usurious, as being a greater profit than 5*l. per cent.* for a year; but both these cases have been held to be legal, because they are after the rate of 5*l. per cent.* So here, the payment of interest quarterly is not illegal, and the custom of the place and practice of the parties being to strike a balance at those periods, brings it to the case of a fresh agreement, at the beginning of each quarter, to lend the sum then due. So the commission claimed may be a fair value for the trouble of the defendants, and unless it appeared to be a mere colour for usury, we should be very unwilling to decide against the general custom of the place.

[c] Bruce *v.* Hunter, 3 Campb. 467.

[d] Moore and others *v.* Voughton, 1 Stark. 487.

Illegality of consideration, when it vitiates. In all cases where bankers make any charge by way of commission for extra trouble or expense they may be put to, in transacting the business of a party, it is advisable to detach the charges for the trouble of keeping the accounts from the charge of interest for forbearance; and if a banker undertake to conduct any transaction not in his ordinary mode of business, and stipulate for a certain charge to be made by him in consideration of such extra trouble and expense, independently "of all costs, charges, damages, and expenses that he may be put to by means of the premises," it is not usurious; for trouble is not necessarily to be intended as a colourable reservation of further interest beyond the legal interest, but as a compensation for trouble not comprehended within the words "costs, charges, damages, and expenses."[e]

[87]   The party discounting a bill should pay the amount, less the interest in cash, or if he give a bill or draft in exchange, he should allow a rebate of interest for the time the latter has to run; for, if he were to impose upon the party applying for the discount of such draft or bill, without allowing interest thereon, the transaction would be usurious.[f]

[e] Palmer and Wilkins v. Baker, 1 M. & S. 57. The plaintiffs in this case were bankers, and had been put into possession of certain timber of I. H. and brought an action of trover against the defendant, who was sheriff of Worchestershire, to recover the value of part of the timber taken by him in execution, at the suit of a creditor of I. H. The cause was tried at the assizes at Worcester, and the plaintiffs had a verdict, subject to a question of law, upon the construction of a deed made between I. H. and the plaintiffs, which recited an agreement between I. H. and one I. L. for the purchase of growing timber, for 4800l. which timber was to be paid for by I. H. part on the execution of the agreement, and the rest by bankers' acceptances at different dates. The indenture further recited, that I. H. being indebted to the plaintiffs in 1424l., for the balance of an account between them, that he had agreed to assign the said agreement, and all his interest under it, to the plaintiffs, they undertaking to fulfil the agreement, with respect to the making the several payments at the times and in manner therein mentioned, upon the trust, in the first place, out of the proceeds which might from time to time arise from the sale of the timber, to retain and repay themselves the purchase-money, as aforesaid, then the said 1424l., owing to them from I. H. upon his account stated, together with the interest thereof, at five *per cent.* up to the time of payment, and also the further sum of 200l., as and for a reasonable profit and compensation for the trouble they would be at in the present business, and also all costs, charges, damages, and expenses which they should or might expend, be put to, or be liable for, on account of the premises, or in any wise relating thereto. A rule *nisi* for setting aside the verdict, was obtained, upon the ground that the covenant for payment of 200l. (besides the money advanced by them, and interest thereon, and all costs, charges, damages, and expenses,) by way of compensation for trouble, was usurious upon the face of it, and therefore void, and upon cause shown, the court were of opinion, that upon looking to the trusts of the deed, there appeared a considerable share of trouble imposed upon the persons who were to carry the trust into effect, which entitled them to compensation, and that to a considerable amount beyond the interest reserved; and although special provision was made for reimbursing them all costs, charges, damages, and expenses which they might be put unto, yet that was to be confined to expenses incurred by them in cutting down and felling the timber, but that there might be other sources of expense incurred by them, which would not properly fall under either of those heads, and that, under the special circumstances of the case, the 200l. was not more than their trouble might require in getting back their principal and interest, and discharged the rule.

[f] Matthews, qui tam v. Griffiths, Peake, 200. and see also Hammett v. Yea, 1 Bos. & Pul. 144. Per Eyre, C. J. Maddock v. Hammett, 7 T. R. 185.

Matthews, qui tam v. Griffiths and others, Peake's Ni. Pri. Ca. 200. This was an action on the statute against usury. The defendants were bankers at Portsmouth, and Mrs. S. residing there, drew a bill for 600l., on her agent in London, payable to the defendants or order, thirty days after date, which the defendants discounted by given her their note for 600l., payable in London, at three days after sight; for this the defendants received a discount at five *per cent.* calculating on the thirty days the bill had to run, but making no deduction on account of the three days grace which the bankers took thereon; it appeared that the

But where A. being a banker in the country, discounted bills at four *Illegality of consideration, when it vitiates.* months for B., and took the whole interest for the time they had to run, and B. on being asked how he would have the money, directed part to be carried to his account, and part to be paid in cash, and the residue by bills on London, some at three, others at seven, and others at thirty days sight, it was decided not to be a usurious transaction so as to induce the court to grant a new trial, it appearing to have been entirely optional on the part of the holder to receive the amount of the bill which was discounted in cash or bills.*

Where a party is *compelled* to take goods in discounting a bill of exchange, a presumption arises that the transaction is usurious, and to rebut this presumption, evidence must be given of the value of the goods by the person who supplied the goods, and sues on the bill.¹ **[88]** But where in discounting a bill, a proposal is made that goods shall be taken, although such proposal originate with the plaintiff, yet if the other party readily accede to it, thinking that he shall make a profit by the transaction, the presumption is, that the goods are fairly charged, and it lies upon the defendant to prove the contrary if he would impeach the plaintiff's title to the bill upon the ground of usury.¹

money to be received for the draft was intended to be remitted to London, but the defendants gave their note at three days sight, without asking any questions as to the mode in which she would be paid the money.

Lord Kenyon said he was clearly of opinion, that this was an usurious contract, whether the person discounting the bill, chose to receive a note or money. If Mrs. S. chose to have a note payable in town, the defendant should not have taken interest for the time that note had to run, but should compute his interest from the time it was payable. See also *Floyer v. Edwards*, Cowp. 112.

‡ *Hammett v. Yea*, 1 Bos. &. Pul. 144. 152.

ʰ *Davis v. Hardacre*, 2 Campb. 375. Indorsee against the drawer of a bill of exchange, defence usury; it appeared that the defendant had made application to the plaintiff to discount a bill of exchange drawn by him. Plaintiff consented, in consideration of his taking in part a landscape in imitation of Poussin, to be valued at 150l. The defendant offered to prove that the plaintiff had purchased the picture for a less sum than 150l., and which was its full value. Lord Ellenborough, before whom the cause was tried, said, "where a party is compelled to take goods in discounting a bill of exchange, I think a presumption arises that the transaction is usurious. To rebut this presumption, evidence should be given of the value of the goods by the person who sues on the bill. In the present case I must require such evidence to be adduced; and I wish it may be understood, that in similar cases, this is the rule by which I shall be governed.

for the future. When a man goes to get a bill discounted, his object is to procure cash, not to encumber himself with goods. Therefore, if goods are forced upon him, I must have proof that they were estimated at a sum for which he could render them available upon a re-sale, not at what might possibly be a fair price to charge to a purchaser who stood in need of them." *Jones v. Davison*, Holt C. N. P. 256. S. C. See also *Pratt v. Wiley*, 1 Esp. 40. 1 Esp. 11.

ⁱ *Coombe v. Miles*, 2 Campb. 553.— Defendant was acceptor of a bill of exchange drawn by Plimpton and Co. and by them indorsed to plaintiff. The defence was, that plaintiff had been guilty of usury in the discounting the bill, in obliging Plimpton to take a quantity of ready-made waistcoats at a given price. Plimpton agreed to take the waistcoats, *as he thought he could make a profit on them.* It was contended for the defendant, on the authority of *Davis v. Hardacre*, (last note) that the plaintiff was bound to show the waistcoats were of the value charged. Lord Ellenborough said, where circumstances of strong suspicion appear, I think it is fair to call upon the person who gives goods in discounting a bill of exchange, to show that they were of the real value at which they were charged; but here, although the proposal to take the waistcoats originated with the plaintiff, the other party readily acceded to it, and said he thought he should make a profit by it. Upon this evidence, therefore, we must presume that the goods were charged beneath their true value, and it lies on the defendant to prove to the contrary, if he would impeach the plaintiff's title to the bill on the ground of usury. Verdict for plaintiff.

CHITTY ON BILLS. **M**

Illegality of consideration,when it vitiates. The charge of commission, with reference to bills, is not confined to a transaction of discount ; for an agent may charge a reasonable commission beyond legal interest, for his trouble in procuring the acceptance and payment of bills.[k] So bankers and others may sustain a similar charge for accepting and paying bills, being provided with funds for such purpose before they became due, in which case, as there would be no advance of money, the transaction could in no point of view be deemed usurious ; but if an advance of money by such acceptors be in contemplation, it would then be a question of fact for a jury, whether the commission was a shift to obtain more than legal in-

[89] terest for the forbearance, or a compensation for the trouble and expense incurred in accepting and paying the bills.[l] But if the acceptor of a bill, at the request of the holder, discount such bill, and receive more than five *per cent.* for the time it has to run, this transaction, however improper, will not constitute usury, it being a mere anticipation of payment by the party primarily liable on the bill, and not a transaction of loan or forbearance sufficient to bring it within the terms of the statute against usury.[m]

So where a person, in order to get his acceptances negotiated, agrees with a broker to allow him to retain exorbitant brokerage, as ten *per cent.* out of the money received, upon getting them discounted, the broker himself not being the party to discount them; a bill accepted and negotiated upon such agreement is not therefore void.[n]

13th, The direction to place it to account It is said by Marius, that if the drawer of a bill is himself to be the debtor, then he inserts in the bill these words :—" and put it to my account ;" but if the drawee, or person to whom it is directed, be debtor to the drawer, that he inserts the following words ;—" and put it to *your* account ;" and that sometimes, where a third person is debtor to the drawee, it is expressed in the bill thus:—" and pay it to the account of *A. B.*"[o] It is, however, perfectly unnecessary to insert in a bill any of these words.

14th, Of the words, " as per advice." (14)—The propriety of inserting the words, " *as per advice,*" depends on the question whether or not the person on whom the bill is drawn is to expect further direction from the drawer. Bills are sometimes made payable " *as per advice ;*" at other times, " without further advice ;"[n] and generally without any of these words. In the former case, the drawee may not, but in the latter he may, pay before he has received advice.

15th,Drawer's name. (15)—To give effect to the bill, &c. the *drawer's name* must either be subscribed, or inserted in the body of it ;[q] and it must be written either

---

[k] Baynes v. Fry, 15 Ves. 120.
[l] Masterman v. Cawrie, 3 Campb. 483. Kent v. Lowen, 1 Campb. 178. Hanner v. Borton, 2 Campb. 348. See cases 1 Taunt. 511. 1 Holt C. N. P. 266.
[m] Barclay v. Walmsley, 4 East, 55.— 5 Esp. 11. S. C. but see Pothier Traite de l'Usure, part 2. sect. 5. num. 128.
[n] Dagnall v. Wigley, 11 East, 43. Ex parte Heason, 1 Madd. 112.
[o] Mar. p. 27. Com. Dig. tit. Merchant, F. 5. Thomas v. Bishop, Rep. Temp. Hardw. 1, 2, 3.
[p] Poth. pl. 36. 169.

[q] Beawes, pl. 3. Elliott v. Cooper, Ld. Raym. 1376. 1 Stra. 609. 8 Mod. 307. S. C. Erskine v. Murray, Ld. Raym. 1542. Taylor v. Dobbins, 1 Stra. 399. Bayl. 16, 17.
Elliott v. Cowper, Stra. 609. Ld. Raym. 1376. 8Mod. 307. It was objected on demurrer to a declaration on a note, that it alleged only, that the defendant made it, but did not state that he signed it; but, *by the court,* if he did not either write or sign it, he did not make it, for making implies signing, and making is alleged. Judgment for plaintiff.

by the person purporting to be the drawer, or by some person autho- 15th, Draw-
rized by him. ₵ If drawn and signed by an agent, it is usual to sign it er's name.
as follows:—" *A. B.* per procuration *C. D.*" and if he do not express
for whom he signs, he may be personally liable. ᵃ If signed by one
person for himself and partners, it is usual and advisable to subscribe
the name of the firm, or at least to sign it as follows:—" *A. B.* for
A. B. and Company," or to the effect;ᵇ but it is sufficient if it purport
in any way to have been signed on behalf of the firm. ᵉ If a bill purport to be drawn in the name of a firm as consisting of several persons,
in an action by the indorsee against the acceptor, the declaration may
aver in the plural, that certain persons using that firm, drew the bill,
although, in point of fact, the bill were drawn by a single person using
the name of that firm;ˣ and where money was deposited in the Bank of
England, in the names of three assignees, it was ordered by the Chancellor to be paid to the checks of the two.ʸ

It is not usual, nor indeed prudent, for the drawer of a bill or check
to sign his name before it is filled up in every respect; for if a person
sign his name upon blank paper, stamped with a bill stamp, and deliver
it to another to draw above the signature, he will be liable to pay to a
bona fide holder, any sum warranted by the stamp. ᶻ

(16)—A bill of exchange being in its nature an open letter of request 16th, Di-
from the maker to a third person, should regularly be properly *addressed* rection to
to that person. ᵃ But if a bill be drawn payable to the order of the the drawee.
drawer at a particular place, without being addressed to any person, [91]
and a party afterwards accepts it, the want of the address of the bill
to any particular party by name, is cured. ᵇ The address of the bill,
it is said, is usually made by the Italians and Dutch on the back of the
bill, but the French and the English uniformly subscribe the direction
in the form to which this paragraph refers; and this latter mode is recommended as preferable to the other, because, as the paper on which
a bill is usually written is but small, if the direction were on the back
of it, there would be very little room left for indorsements, which frequently are very numerous; nor would there be any space on which to

---

Erskine *v.* Murray, Ld. Raym. 1542.
In an action on a bill, it was alleged,
that the plaintiff made his bill in writing,
and thereby required the defendant to
pay. It was objected on error, that it
did not appear that the plaintiff signed
the bill; but it was answered that the
allegation that he made it, and required
the defendant to pay, implied that his
name was in it, (otherwise he could not
request,) and that he or somebody wrote
it for him. Judgment for the plaintiff was
affirmed.
Taylor *v.* Dobbins, 1 Stra. 399. The
declaration upon a note stated that the
defendant wrote it with his own hand,
but did not allege that he signed it, and
an exception was taken upon that ground.
Sed per cur. If the defendant wrote it,
his subscription to it was unnecessary;
it is sufficient if his name appeared in any
part. I "J. S. promise to pay," is as
good as "I promise to pay," subscribed
J. S. See also Saunderson *v.* Jackson,
2 Bos. & Pul. 238.

ˣ Ante, 23, 4. Bayl. 17.
ᵇ Thomas *v.* Bishop, Stra. 955. Ante,
27, n.
ᶜ Smith *v.* Jarves, Lord Raym. 1414.
The declaration upon a note drawn by
Jarves and Bailey, stated, that Jarves
for himself and partner, made his note
in writing with his own had subscribed,
whereby he promised for himself and
partner to pay. It was objected on demurrer, that it was not charged that
Jarves had signed the note for himself
and Bailey, but the Court held, the statement showed that Jarves did sign for himself and Bailey, and gave the plaintiff
judgment.
ᵃ Ante, 39.
ˣ Bass v. Clive, 4 Campb. 78. 4 M. &
S. 13. S. C.
ʸ Ex parte Hunter, and another, 2 Rose,
363.
ᶻ Collis *v.* Emett, 1 Hen. Bla. 313.—
Ante, 24, n.
ᵃ Poth. pl. 35. Beawes, pl. 3. Mar. 143.
ᵇ Gray *v* Milner, 3 Moore, 90.

16th, Di-write the receipt for payment.° A bill directed to A., or in his absence
rection to to B., and beginning "pray, gentlemen, pay, &c." being accepted only
the drawee. by A., may be declared upon without noticing B.ᵈ If a bill be intended to be accepted by two or more persons, it should be addressed accordingly, for where a bill was drawn upon one person, and was accepted by him and another, it was decided that only the first party was
liable as acceptor.ᵉ

17th, 18th,   (17, 18)—It is said that the *place where the payment is to be made*
Place of should be fully expressed in the subscription or body of the bill;ᶠ and,
payment. that if a bill be drawn upon a person not resident at the place where
the drawer intends the bill to be payable, the place where the drawee
resides, as well as the place where payment is to be made, should be
mentioned in the subscription.ᵍ In general, however, the drawer merely states the address of the drawee, without pointing out the place of
payment.

When it is intended that the bill should be payable at a particular
place, it is advisable to insert such place in the body of the bill, as
" Two months after date pay to my order in London," &c. but it will
suffice to insert such direction in the address to the drawee, as " To
Messrs. A. and B., Plymouth, payable in London." In these cases the
place of payment forms part of the contract; and in pleading, the bill
must be described accordingly;ʰ and though in the case of a note, where
[92] the place of payment was merely inserted as a memorandum at the bottom, and not in the body, it was decided that this formed no part of the
contract, and need not be stated in the declaration.ⁱ We shall hereafter find, that if a place be stated in any part of the note or bill, with
intent to qualify the contract, is must be so described in pleading.ᵏ

In general, no witness is essential to the validity of a bill of exchange
or promissory note;ˡ but in the case of bills drawn for a less sum than
five pounds, a witness is necessary,ᵐ and in other cases, if there be a
subscribing witness, the instrument must be proved by subpœnaing
him.

BILLS OF EXCHANGE, like every other contract, are to be construed

---

ᶜ Mar. 44. Com. Dig. tit. Merchant, F. 5.

ᵈ Anonymous, 12 Mod. 447.

ᵉ Jackson v. Hudson, 2 Campb. 447.

ᶠ Mar. 107, 8.

ᵍ Beawes, pl. 3.

ʰ Hodge v. Fillis and another, 3 Campb. 463. This was an action by the indorsee of a bill of exchange, drawn by Messrs. W. and A. Maxwell, at Cork, upon the de-fendants, and directed to them as follows : " To Messrs. Fillis and Co. Plymouth, pay-able in London." The bill was accepted by the defendants, payable at Sir John Per-ring's and Co. bankers, London. The plaintiff proved the hand-writing of the acceptors and indorsers. It was contend-ed for the defendant, that the plaintiff could not upon this evidence be entitled to a verdict, as there could be no doubt that where a particular place of payment is denoted both by drawers and acceptors, it becomes a term of the contract between the parties, and an averment that the bill was presented for payment there, could not possibly be rejected as irrelevant. Lord Ellenborough, before whom the cause was tried, expressed himself to be of this opin-ion. The plaintiff had a verdict on another ground.

ⁱ Price v. Mithell, 4 Campb. 200.—Exon v. Russel, 4 M. & S. 505.

ᵏ Poet, and Hardy v. Woodroofe, 2 Stark. 819.

ˡ Marius, 14.

ᵐ Ante, 51. 17 Geo. 3. c. 30. sect. 1 ; and post, Appendix.

in such a manner as, if possible, to give effect to the intention of the contracting parties; and, indeed, our courts, sensible how peculiarly conducive the negotiability of these instruments is to the ease and increase of trade, adopt a still more liberal mode of construing them than any other instrument.[a]

How bills, &c. are construed and given effect to.

It has been observed by a celebrated writer on moral philosophy,[b] that "every contract should be construed and enforced according to the sense in which the person making it apprehended the person, in whose favour it was made, understood it; which mode of interpretation will exclude evasion, in cases in which the popular meaning of a phrase, and the strict grammatical signification of words differ, or in general whenever the contracting party attempts to make his escape through some ambiguity in the expression which he used." These observations are applicable to the mode of construing a bill of exchange; thus, in a case before Lord Macclesfield, where a man for a past consideration gave a person a promissory note, in the beginning of which it was mentioned to be given for " twenty pounds borrowed and received," but at the latter end were the words, "which I promise *never* to pay;" it was decided that the payee might recover on it, because the person making the note had intentionally excited expectations which he ought to satisfy;[c] so if a bill be drawn payable to the *order* of a fictitious person, it may *ut res magis valeat quam pereat* be recovered upon against all the parties privy to the transaction, as a bill payable to *bearer*, on the principle, that as they gave currency to the instrument, which they knew could never be paid to the order of the fictitious payee, the law will presume they intended that the formality of indorsement should be waived.[d] Effect is also to be given to the intention of the parties according to the law of the country where the contract is made, and in which it is to be performed, and not according to the law of the country into which either or all of them may remove;[e] for what is not an obligation in one place, cannot, by the laws of another country, become such in another place;[e] and therefore where the defendant gave the plaintiff in a foreign country, where both were resident, a bill of exchange drawn by the defendant upon a person in England, which bill was afterwards protested here for non-acceptance, and the defendant afterwards, while still resident abroad, became bankrupt there, and obtained a certificate of discharge by the law of that state, it was held, that such certificate was a bar to an action here, upon an implied assumpsit to pay the amount of the bill in consequence of such non-acceptance in England.[f] The time of payment, is, however, in general to be calculated according to the laws of the country where the bill is made payable;[g] thus upon a bill drawn at a place using one style, and payable at a place using the other, if the time is to be reckoned from the date, it shall be computed according to the style of the place at which it is drawn, otherwise according to the style of the place where

[93]

[a] Hotham v. East India Company, Dougl. 277.

[b] Paley, 126. Anderson v. Pitcher, 2 Bos. & Pul. 168.

[?] Cited in Simpson v. Vaughan, 2 Atk. 32.

[d] Gibson v. Minet, 1 Hen. Bla. 586. Ante, 64, 5. Ex parte Bank of Scotland, 19 Ves. 311, 2.

[e] Burrows v. Jemino, 2 Stra. 733. Sel. Ca. 144. S. C. Potter v. Brown, 5 East, 130.

[e] Melan v. DeFitzjames, 1Bos. & Pul.141. Talleyland v. Boulanger, 3 Vcs. 447. Gienar v. Meyer, 2 Hen. Bla. 603. Mostyn v. Fabrigas, Cowp. 174. Robinson r. Bland, Burr. 1077. Folliott v. Ogden, 1 Hen. Bla. 123. Alves v. Hodson, 7 T. R. 242. Da Costa v. Cole, Skin. 272. Potter v. Brown, 5 East, 130. Johnson v. Machielyne, 3 Campb. 44.

[f] Potter v. Brown, 5 East, 124.

[g] Beawes, pl. 251. Mar. 142.

Construc-it is payable, and in the former case, the date must be reduced or
tion of bills, carried forward to the style of the place where the bill is payable, and
&c. the time reckoned from thence.[x] It has been observed,[y] that this is
contrary to the reason and the nature of the thing; yet, other writers
entertain a different opinion; and it is said, that a bill of exchange is
considered in this respect as having been made at the place where it is
payable, according to the maxim, *contraxisse unusquisque in eo loco intel-
ligitur in quo ut solveret se obligavit*, and that consequently the contract
should be construed and regulated according to the laws and usage of
that place to which the contracting parties have understood themselves
subject, following the other rule, *in contractibus veniunt ea quæ sunt
moris et consuetudinis in regione in quâ contrahitur.*[z] It further ap-
[94] pears, that although the *form* of the remedy must depend on the laws
of the country in which the creditor proceeds, it will, in respect of the
extent of it, be subject to the same regulations and restrictions as if it
had been pursued in the country where the contract was made; and
therefore if a man in a foreign country enter into a contract to be there
performed, the fulfilment of which cannot in that country be enforced
by arrest, he cannot in this country be holden to bail. (121)

[x] See Bayl. 112, 118. Mar. 75, 89 to 92.
101 to 108.

[y] Kyd. 8.

[z] Poth. pl. 155. Bayl. 68.

[a] Melan v. De Fitzjames, 1 Bos. & Pul.
141. Pedder v. Mac Master, 8 T. R.
609. Potter v. Brown, 5 East, 124; but
see Imlay v. Ellefsen, 2 East, 255. Tidd,
6th ed. 218.

---

(121) Many cases have occurred in the courts of the United States, which have drawn
in question the operation of the *lex loci contractus*. The rule is well settled, that the law
of a place where a contract is made, is to govern as to the nature, validity, and construction of such contract; and that being valid in such place, it is to be considered equally
valid, and to be enforced every where, with the exception of cases in which the contract is immoral or unjust, or in which the enforcing it in a state would be injurious to
the rights, the interest, or the convenience of such state, or its citizens. This doctrine is
explicitly avowed in *Huberus de Conflictu Legum*, and has become incorporated into
the code of national law in all civilized countries. *Pearsall* v. *Dwight*, 2 Mass. Rep.
84. *Lodge* v. *Phelps*, 1 John. Cas. 139. *Smith* v. *Smith*, 2 John. Rep. 235. *Ruggles*
v. *Keeler*, 3 John. Rep. 268. *Thompson* v. *Ketcham*, 4 John. Rep. 285. 8 John. Rep.
188. *Van Rough* v. *Van Arsdaln*, 3 Caines' Rep. 154. *Warder* v. *Arell*, 2 Wash.
Rep. 282. and the cases cited in *Van Reimsdyk* v. *Kane*, 1 Gallis. Rep. 371. 375. It
seems to follow, that if a contract be void by the law of the place where it is made, it
is void every where; and that a discharge of a contract in the place where it is made,
shall be of equal avail in every other place. *Van Schaick* v. *Edwards*, 2 John. Cas.
355. *Baker* v. *Wheaton*, 5 Mass. Rep. 509. *Thompson* v. *Ketcham*. *Smith* v.
Smith.; and the cases cited in 1 Gallis. Rep. 371. 371. A discharge, therefore, under
the insolvent or bankrupt law of a state, (supposing it to be conditional) is a good discharge of a contract made there, in every other state where a suit may be brought to
recover on such contract. *James* v. *Allen*, 1 Dall. Rep. 188. *Miller* v. *Hall*, 1 Dall.
Rep. 229. But it seems to have been held that this doctrine only applies where both of
the parties are citizens of, or individuals in, the state at the time when the contract was
made. *Harris* v. *Mandeville*, 2 Dall. Rep. 256. *Proctor* v. *Moore*, 1 Mass. Rep. 198.
Baker v. *Wheaton*, *Smith* v. *Smith*. But see *Hicks* v. *Brown*, 12 John. Rep. 142. And
such a discharge will not be valid against a suit upon a contract made, or to be executed
in another state, whether it be a foreign state, or the state where the suit is brought.
Van Rough v. *Van Arsdaln*, 3 Caines' Rep. 154. *Smith* v. *Smith*, *Thompson* v.
Ketcham, 4 John. Rep. 285. 8 John. Rep. 189. *Van Reimsdyk* v. *Kane*. *Shieffelin* v.
Wheaton, 1 Gallis. Rep. 441. However, in *Connecticut* a discharge under the insolvent
laws of that state, has been held a good discharge of a contract entered into another state
with the citizens of another state. *Barber* v. *Minturn*, 1 Day's Rep. 136.
As to the form of the action or remedy by which a contract is to be enforced, a different rule prevails, for the recovery must be sought, and the remedy pursued according to
the *lex fori*, not the *lex loci contractus*. *Dixon's Ex.* v. *Ramsay's Ex.* 3 Cranch Rep.
324. *Nash* v. *Tupper*, 1 Caines' Rep. 402. *Ruggles* v. *Keeler*, 3 John. Rep. 268.
Pearsall v. *Dwight*, 2 Mass. Rep. 84. *Smith* v. *Spinola*, 2 John. Rep. 198.; and the
cases cited 1 Gallis. Rep. 371. 376. *Bird* v. *Caritat*, 2 John. Rep. 342. *Sicard* v. *Whale*,

Construc-
tion of bills,
&c.

It has been observed by a celebrated writer on the law of nations,[b] that it is the first general maxim of interpretation, "that it is not allowable to interpret what has no need of interpretation;" and that when a deed is worded in clear and precise terms, when its meaning is evident, and leads to no absurd conclusion, there can be no reason for refusing to admit the meaning which such a deed *naturally* presents; to go elsewhere in search of conjectures, in order to restrict or extend it, is but an attempt to elude it, and if this dangerous method were once admitted, every deed might be rendered useless. It seems that on similar principles, our counts, notwithstanding their anxiety to give effect to the intentions of the contracting parties, have laid down as a general rule, that all latitude of construction must submit to this restriction, namely, that the *words and language* of the deed bear the sense which is attempted to be put upon them.[c]   However, in the case of bills,

[b] Vattel, 224 ; et vide Powell on Contracts, tit. Construction.
[c] Anderson *v.* Pitcher, 2 Bos. & Pul.
168. Hotham *v.* East India Company, Dougl. 277. Burnet *v.* Kensington, 7 R. R. 214.

---

11 John. Rep. 194. Therefore the statute of limitations of the state where the contract is made, has been held to be no bar to an action in another state, for it is only a modification of the remedy. *Pearsall* v. *Dwight, Ruggles* v *Keeler*. But the statute of limitations of the state where the suit is brought is a good bar. *Nash* v. *Tupper, Ruggles* v. *Keeley, Hubbell* v. *Cowdrey*, 5 John. Rep. 132.; and if a note be negotiable by the law of the place, where the suit is brought, but not by that of the place where it was made, an action may be maintained by the indorsee in his own name. *Lodge* v. *Phelps*, 1 John. Cas. 139. S. C. 2 Caines' Cas. in Err. 821. And a discharge under an insolvent law of a state which simply protects the debtor from arrest or imprisonment is no bar to a suit in another state, for it is held to be limited to the person only, without discharging the debt, and local in its effects. *White* v. *Canfield*, 7 John. Rep. 117.

Whether a state can, since the constitution of the United States, pass an insolvent act, which shall discharge the obligation of a contract, has been finally settled. Mr. Justice Washington, in the circuit court of the United States in Pennsylvania, in a very learned and elaborate opinion maintained the negative. *Golden* v *Prince*, April term, 1814, 5 Hall's Law Journal, 502. and the question being brought before the supreme court, it was decided that a state may pass a bankrupt law, provided such law *does not impair the obligation of a contract*, and provided there be no act of Congress in force to establish a uniform system of bankruptcy conflicting with such law. *Sturgis* v. *Crowninshield*, 4 Wheaton, 122. *M'Millan* v. *M'Neill*, 4 Wheaton, 209.

It has been held that a tender of payment of bills of credit, which would be good by the law of the place where the contract was made, would be a good bar in every other state, where a suit should be brought. *Warder* v. *Arell*, 2 Wash. 282. And it seems to have been thought that a stay of execution upon a foreign judgment, by the law of the place where the judgment was recovered, would be so far recognized here, as to exempt the party from arrest for the debt, and if arrested would entitle him to a discharge on common bail. *Conframp* v. *Burel*, 4 Dall. Rep. 419. and see *Melan* v. *Fitzjames*, 1 Bos. & Pul. 138. But the contrary seems asserted by Lord *Ellenborough* in *Imlay* v. *Ellesfen*, 2 East's Rep. 455. and see *Sicard* v. *Whale*, 11 John. Rep. 194.

And as the law of the place where the contract is made, regulates the rights and duties of the parties, if a bill be drawn and indorsed in a place, by a person resident there, he is answerable upon such indorsement only so far as the laws of that country bind him upon a bill so drawn and indorsed. *Powers* v. *Lynch*, 3 Mass. Rep. 77. See also *Hicks* v. *Brown*, 12 John. Rep. 142. And upon a bill drawn payable in a foreign country, whether payment in the current money of that country be good or not, depends upon the intention of the parties, and their reference in the contract to the *lex loci*. *Seabright* v. *Calbraith*, 4 Dall. Rep. 325. For where it appears that the performance of the contract in the contemplation of the parties, has relation to the laws of another country, the contract must be interpreted according to those laws. *Powers* v. *Lynch*. *Hicks* v. *Brown*.

The indorsement of a bill is deemed a new substantive contract; and therefore the indorser will be liable to damages on non-payment of a bill, according to the law of the place where the indorsement was made. *Semb. Slacum* v. *Pomeroy*, 6 Cranch, 221.

For other cases respecting the operation of the *lex loci*, see *Van Schaick* v. *Edwards*, 2 John. Cas. 355. *Harrison* v. *Sterry*, 5 Cranch, 289. *Ludlow* v. *Van Renssellaer*, 1 John. Rep. 94. *Winthrop* v. *Pepont*, 1 Bay's Rep. 468. *Green* v. *Sarmiento*, 1 Peters' Rep. 74.

and other negotiable instrument, our courts have relaxed this rule, and
therefore in the case just alluded to, where an action was brought by an
indorsee of a bill of exchange against the acceptor, and he could not
prove an indorsement by the payee, evidence was admitted to prove that
the payee was a fictitious person, and consequently could not indorse
it ; and it was adjudged, that as the drawer and acceptor knew of each
fact, the bill should against them operate as a bill payable originally to
bearer, and that the holder might recover thereon as such.[4] The courts
have always in mercantile affairs endeavoured to adapt the rules of law
to the course and method of trade and commerce, in order to promote
it, and when new cases have arisen on the mercantile law, they consult
traders and merchants as to their usage in regard to bills.[*](122)

---

[4] Gibson *v.* Minet, 1 Hen. Bla. 569 ;   linson, Willes, 561. Barnes, 164. S. C. ;
and see ante, 64, 5. note   but see 1 Holt C. N. P. page, 99, in
[*] Per Willes, C. J. in Stone *v.* Raw- notes.

---

(122) It may be well to collect in this place a number of cases in which a legal construction has been put upon written contracts, which do not properly fall under any
other head.

A note as follows, " Due the bearer hereof, 8*l.* 18*s.* 10*d.* which I promise to pay to
A. T. or order, on demand," is a note payable to A. T. or order, and not to the bearer,
and therefore cannot be transferred but by indorsement. *Cook* v. *Fellows,* 1 John.
Rep 143.

Where a person adds at the bottom of a note of another, that he acknowledges himself to be holden as a surety for the note, he is in law deemed an original joint promissor.
Hunt v. *Adams,* 6 Mass. Rep. 519.   *Leonard* v. *Vredenburgh,* 8 John. 29.

If a person write his name on the back of a note in blank, as guarantor, and authorize
another person to write a guaranty over his name, it is good and may be filled up accordingly. *Ulen* v *Kittredge,* 7 Mass. Rep. 233.   *Moies* v. *Bird,* 11 Mass. Rep. 436.

If a note be made payable to A. or order, and a person who had previously intended
to have become indorser thereon, write on the back of the note, " for value received, I
undertake to pay the money within mentioned to A. ;" he will be held as an original promissor. *White* v. *Howland,* 9 Mass. Rep. 314.   *Leonard* v. *Vredenburgh, Bailey* v.
Freeman, 11 John Rep 221.

The payee of an accommodation note not negotiable, indorsed it in blank to a creditor
of the maker, intending thereby to become security for the debt of the maker to the creditor ; it was held that the creditor might lawfully write over the indorsement " for value
received, I undertake to pay the money within mentioned to A. (the creditor ;") and so
hold the payee as an original promissor. *Joscelyn* v. *Ames,* 3 Mass. Rep 274.

And if a note be payable to the creditor only, and another person indorse his name in
blank on the note as security for the payment, he may be treated as an original promissor. *Moies* v. *Bird.*

If a bill be drawn in *England on a firm in Boston,* payable to the drawer himself or
order, and be accepted by one of the firm then in *England, payable in London,* it is a
foreign bill of exchange, and on non-payment it is to be governed by the law of *Massachusetts* as to damages. *Grimshaw* v. *Bender,* 6 Mass. Rep. 157.

Where a note dated the 15th of *July,* was payable immediately with interest from the
first day of *June,* it was held to mean the first day of the preceding *June. Whitney* v.
Crosby, 3 Caines' Rep. 89.

Where the payee of a note payable to himself or order, indorsed on it, " I guarantee
the payment of this note within six months," and signed his name thereto, such a signature was held to operate a transfer of the note to every subsequent holder, even supposing that the guaranty should be construed a mere contract between the payee and his
immediate indorsee. *Upham* v. *Prince,* 12 Mass. Rep. 14.   But see *Tyler* v. *Binney,*
7 Mass. Rep. 479.

Such a guaranty by a third person, made at the time of the execution of the note is
an original collateral undertaking, and is sustained by the original consideration in the
note. *Leonard* v *Vredenburgh,* 8 John. Rep. 29.   *Bailey* v. *Freeman,* 11 John.
Rep. 221.

Where the payee of a note payable to himself or order, indorsed on it upon a transfer, " I guarantee the payment of the within note in eighteen months, if it cannot be
collected before that time ;" the guaranty was construed not to mean to give an unlimited currency to the note, and no person other than an original party to the guaranty could
maintain an action thereon. *Tyler* v. *Binney,* 7 Mass. Rep. 479.

A BILL OF EXCHANGE, &c. in general, is delivered by the drawer Delivery of a bill to the payee; and effect there- of. to the payee, and where it consists of several parts, as is usual in the case of foreign bills, each ought to be delivered to the person in whose favour it is made, unless one part be forwarded to the drawee for ac- ceptance, and in that case the rest must be so delivered; were it other- wise, difficulties might arise in negotiating a bill, or obtaining payment of it,[r] though a delivery is not essential to vest the legal interest in the payee.[s]

In general one contract not under seal cannot be extinguished by another similar contract,[h] and a mere promise to give time for the pay- ment of a pre-existing debt, is not binding.[i] But a person by taking a bill of exchange or promissory note, in satisfaction of a former debt, or of a debt created at the time, is precluded from afterwards waiving it, and suing the person who gave it him, for the original debt before the bill is due; for the taking of the bill amounts to an agreement to give the person delivering it credit for the length of time it has to run.[k] And even on behalf of the crown an extent in aid cannot be issued against a person from whom the principal debtor has taken a bill which is not due.[l] But where an action having been brought against the ac-

[f] Ante, 62, 3. Bayl. 19.

[g] Smith v. M'Clure, 5 East, 477. The plaintiff declared on a bill payable to his own order, and averred that he delivered it to the defendant, to whom it was ad- dressed, and who accepted it according to the usage and custom, &c. and by reason of the premises, &c. the defendant became liable to pay. The defendant de- murred specially, and assigned as cause, that it was not alleged that the defend- ant re-delivered the bill to the plaintiff. Per curiam, the acceptance of the bill, which was admitted by the demurrer, and must be taken to be a perfect accept- ance vested a right in the drawer to sue upon it, and if, after such an acceptance, the acceptor improperly detained the bill in his hands, the drawer might neverthe- less sue him on it, and give him notice to produce the bill, and on his default, give parol evidence of it.

[h] Story v. Atkins, Ld. Raym. 1430.— Scott v. Surman, Willes, 406. Taylor v. Wasteneys, 2 Stra. 1218.

[i] De Symons v. Minchwick, 1 Esp. Rep. 430.

[k] Stedman v. Gooch, 1 Esp. 3. As- sumpsit for goods sold; defence that plaintiff had taken three promissory notes of Finlay; it appeared that these notes had been returned to the defendant be- fore they were payable, and it was in- sisted, that the plaintiff having taken them in discharge of her debt for goods sold could not maintain an action on her original debt until an actual default in the payment of these notes, as the notes might be paid when they became due, nor should the plaintiff be allowed to judge of the probable or improbable ability of the party to pay at a future day.

Lord Kenyon said, that the law was clear, and that if in payment of a debt, the creditor is content to take a bill or note payable at a future day, he cannot legally commence an action on his origi- nal debt, until such bill or note becomes payable, or default is made in the pay- ment; but that if such bill or note is of no value, as if, for example, drawn on a person who has no effects of the drawer's in his hands, and who therefore refuses it, in such case he may consider it as waste paper, and resort to his original de- mand, and sue the debtor on it.

[l] The King v. Dawson, Wightw. 32. It was pleaded to an inquisition founded on an extent in aid, that the defendant had accepted a bill drawn upon him by J. C. (the original debtor) and which did not become due until after the inquisition was taken; the replication stated, that the bill was dishonoured, and that the original debtor to the crown, had been obliged to take it up; upon demurrer, that as the inquisition was executed be- fore the bill became due, the bill could not, at that time, have been taken up by the said J. C. The court held, that as on the day of taking the inquisition, no action could have been maintained by

If a person indorse his name in blank on a negotiable note, but not at the time when the note was made, he not being a party to the note, and the same not having been in- dorsed by the payee; such indorser cannot be held as a joint promisor, nor will such indorsement be evidence in itself of any contract between him and the holder of the note. Birchard v. Bartlett, 14 Mass. 279.

CHITTY ON BILLS. N

ceptor of a bill of exchange, it was agreed between the parties, that the defendant should pay the costs, renew the bill, and give a warrant of attorney to secure the debt, and the defendant gave the warrant of attorney and renewed the bill, but did not pay the costs, it was held, that the plaintiff might bring a fresh action on the first bill, while the second was outstanding in the hands of an indorsee. And if the person delivering the bill knew that it was of no value, the holder, on discovering the fraud, will not be precluded from immediately suing such party on his original liability. We have already seen what conduct the holder may pursue, when a bill or note given in payment of a debt, is upon a wrong stamp. Where one of three joint covenantors gave a bill of exchange for part of a debt secured by the covenant, on which bill judgment was recovered, it was held, that such judgment was no bar to an action of covenant against the three, such bill, though stated to have been given for the payment and in satisfaction of the debt, not being averred to have been accepted as satisfaction nor to have produced it in fact. And the taking a bill or note does not prejudice a prior specialty security, so as to preclude the party taking them from recovering interest payable on the specialty. And it has been held, that a vendor does not waive his lien on the estate sold, by taking the promissory note or acceptance of the vendee, and receiving its amount by discount. Bills, in lieu of which other bills were given, if permitted to remain with the holder, may be sued upon in case the latter bills are not paid.

[97] When an account for goods sold is settled, and the defendant gives a bill of exchange for the amount which remains unpaid, it has been holden, that the defendant cannot, in an action on the consideration of such bill, go into evidence to impeach the charges in the first account which has been settled, the giving of the bill being conclusive evidence of the same being due.

J. C. against the defendant upon this bill of exchange, the interest in the bill at that time being in his indorsee, there was, in fact, at that time, no right of action against any person.

Norris v. Aylett, 2 Campb. 329. Per Lord Ellenborough. There was to be no extinguishment of the bill, (until amongst other things) the costs were paid. If they had been paid this might have brought it within the case of Kearslake v. Morgan, but the agreement remaining unperformed on the part of the defendant, the plaintiff reserved to himself the power of rendering the bill available ; this is like accord without satisfaction. Verdict for the plaintiff, on his delivering up the substituted bill to the defendant.

Stedman v. Gooch, 1 Esp. Rep. 5.—Anonymous, 12 Mod. 517. Puckford v. Maxwell, 6 T. R. 52. Owenson v. Morse, 7 T. B. 64. Bishop v. Shilleto, 2 B. & A. 329, note a.

Ante, 58.

Drake v. Mitchel, 3 East, 251.

Curtis v. Rush, 2 Ves. & B. 416.

Ex parte Loaring, 2 Rose, 79. Grant v. Mills, 2 Ves. & B. 306.

Ex parte Barclay, 7 Ves. 597. Barclay was indorsee and holder of two bills drawn by Kemp to Barclay; these bills were dishonoured, and Clay drew two

other bills upon Sampson for the amount of the former bills, interest, and charges, and the former bills were permitted to remain with Barclay, one of the two last bills was paid by Sampson. Upon petition by Barclay to be allowed to prove these bills under a commission of bankrupt against Kemp, it was objected on the ground that the two latter bills were accepted in discharge of them. Lord Chancellor. If the two bills are dishonoured, and two others given " in lieu" of them, but the former allowed to stay in the hands of the holder, that fact will give a construction to the words " in lieu," and the meaning will be only in case they are paid. See also Bishop v. Rowe, 3 M. & S. 363.

Knox v. Whalley, 1 Esp. Rep. 159.—(Sed quære Trueman v. Hurst, 1 T. R. 40. Chandler v. Dorsett, Finch Rep. 431. Vin. Ab. Partner, E. 2.) The defendant was indebted to the plaintiff 74l., for clothes, &c. and gave him a bill of exchange for 84l., and received the difference. The bill being dishonoured, plaintiff brought his action on the bill and for a further sum for clothes furnished since the bill was given. At the trial the defendant was proceeding to impeach the plaintiff's charges contained in the first bill, which was objected to by the counsel

The effect of taking a bill of exchange or promissory note in satisfaction of a precedent debt, is, that the creditor cannot proceed in an action for such debt, without showing that he has used due diligence to obtain acceptance or payment;[u] and also showing if the defendant was a party thereto, or delivered it to the plaintiff, that the defendant had due notice of the dishonour;[x] and it is a good plea in an action for the original debt, that the defendant delivered a bill or note in payment, or for or on account of such debt, and compels the plaintiff to reply that the bill or note has been dishonoured;[y] and in an action for the original demand, if it appear in evidence that a negotiable bill or note was given, [98] the plaintiff cannot recover without producing the instrument, or proving that it was destroyed, or showing that it was on a wrong stamp.[z] It suffices, however, for the plaintiff, when the bill was received in satisfaction from a third person, and the original debtor, the defendant, was no party to it to prove the due presentment for acceptance or pay-

for the plaintiff. Lord Kenyon ruled, that up to the time of the giving the bill of exchange, all matters must be considered as closed, and that the giving the bill must, to that effect, be taken as conclusive evidence of the sum due at that time.

[u] Smith v. Wilson, Andr. 187. This was a special case for the opinion of the court. It appeared that the defendant being indebted to the plaintiff for goods sold, and money paid, had in part payment, indorsed to him a note for 100l., drawn by Jones, and payable to defendant or order; and at the foot of an account stated between the parties, plaintiff wrote, "received the contents, when the above mentioned bill is paid." Plaintiff indorsed over the note which became due, 28th, March 1735. Jones carried on business, and continued his payments till the 13th May following; one question therefore was, whether the plaintiff, by receiving this note, and not applying for the money due thereon, had lost his original debt? The court held, that where a note is taken for a precedent debt, it must be intended to be taken by way of payment, upon this condition, that the note is paid in a reasonable time, but if the person accepting it, doth not endeavour to procure such payment, and the money is lost by his default, it is but reasonable that he should bear the loss, see Ward v. Evans, 2 Ld. Raym. 928, 9, 30. Chamberlain v. Delarive, 2 Wils. 353.

Hebden v. Hartsink and another, 4 Esp. Ni. Pri. 46. Assumpsit by the plaintiff for wages as a clerk to the defendant. Pleas of non-assumpsit and a set-off. To prove payment of 140l., in part discharge of the plaintiff's demand, the defendants gave in evidence that they had given him bills of the house to that amount. It was contended for the plaintiff, that before this could be deemed a discharge to that amount, the defendants should prove the bills to have been paid. Lord Kenyon said, it was not necessary; that where a party took bills in payment of a debt, he would presume the money was received, unless the contrary was shown.

[x] 4 Ann. c. 9. s. 7. Bridges v. Berry, 3 Taunt. 130. but see Bishop v. Rowe, 3 M. & S. 362.

[y] Kearslake v. Morgan, 5 T. R. 513. Assumpsit for goods sold and delivered, and for money lent. The defendant pleaded the general issue, and that as to 4l. 14s. 6d. one W. P. made his promissory note for 10l., payable to the defendant or order, at a time which elapsed before the commencement of the suit, and that the defendant, before the note became due, indorsed it to the plaintiff, for and on account of the said sum of 4l. 14s. 6d. and of the sum of 5l. 5s. 6d. paid by the plaintiff to the defendant, and that the defendant accepted the note, for and on account of those sums; to this plea there was a general demurrer, and it was urged, that the plea ought to have alleged that the note was received in satisfaction of the debt; but the court on argument, held the plea good, and advised the plaintiff to withdraw his demurrer and reply, which he did.

[z] Dangerfield v. Wilby, 4 Esp. Ni. Pri. Ca. 159. The declaration contained a count upon a note made by the defendant payable to the plaintiff, and the money counts. At the trial the note was stated to be lost, but no evidence of the fact was offered. It was proved however, that on the money being demanded, the defendant had apologized for not having paid the money on account of the note. This was the whole of the plaintiff's case, and he contended that the note was only evidence of the consideration (which was stated to have been money lent) and that he might abandon the note, and go for the consideration. But Lord Ellenborough said, that as the note, for any thing that appeared in evidence was in existence it might be still in circulation, so that the defendant might be subjected twice to the payment of the same demand, without therefore proving the note lost, the plaintiff was not entitled to recover. Nonsuit.

Effect of delivery of bill to payee.

ment and the dishonour, without showing that he gave notice thereof to the drawer of such bill, unless the defendant can prove that he sustained some actual loss for want of such notice ;[a] and if the defendant admit the refusal of the drawee to accept the bill, although he request the creditor to present it again for acceptance, this will be unnecessary, and the creditor may recover his original demand without further proof of the dishonour of the bill.[b] We shall hereafter see that in general when the holder has been guilty of *neglect*, either in presenting a bill for acceptance, when necessary, or for payment, or in giving notice of non-acceptance, or of non-payment, or by giving time to the acceptor, this conduct will render the original delivery of the bill equivalent to a payment of the debt, and discharge such debtor from all liability.[c]

In general when the bill is dishonoured, and the holder uses due diligence, not only the parties to the bill are liable to be sued thereon, but the first liability on the original consideration revives.[d] Therefore [99] where A. sold goods to B. for which the latter was to pay in a bill at three months, and B. gave A. a check on his bankers, who were also bankers of A. requiring them to pay A. on demand in a bill at three months, and A. paid the check into the bankers and took no bill from them, *but the amount was transferred in the banker's books from B's. account to A's. with the knowledge of both*, and the bankers failed before the check became due, it was holden that A. could not recover the value of the goods against B., as A., instead of taking bills from his bankers, agreed to leave the check with them, it was as if he had discounted it with them and then deposited the money ;[e] but where the amount was not so transferred to A's. account, it was holden that B. was still liable for the goods.[f] And where A., wishing to send goods to B.

---

[a] Bishop v. Rowe, 3 M. & S. 362. Swingend v. Bowes, 5 M. & S. 65. Post; but see Bridges v. Berry, 3 Taunt. 130.

[b] Hicklin v. Hardy, 7 Taunt. 812.

[c] 4 Ann. c. 9. s. 7. Smith v. Wilson, Andr. 187. Chamberlain v. Delarive, 2 Wils. 353. Ward v. Evans, 2 Ld. Raym. 930.

[d] Smith v. Wilson, Andr. 187. Popley v. Ashley, 6 Mod. 147. Ward v. Evans, 2 Ld. Raym. 928. Hickling v. Hardy, 7 Taunt. 312. Bishop v. Rowe, 3 M. & S. 362. Tempest v. Ord, 1 Madd. 89. The manager of a colliery paying a creditor on the colliery with a bill which was not paid, the colliery remains liable to the payment of the original debt. Per the Vice Chancellor: The justice of the case, independent of authorities is clear. Crowther has supplied goods, and received a bill, which turns out to be mere waste-paper, and ought not therefore to be considered as a payment. Where a bill of exchange is given in payment of a debt, and the bill is not paid, the creditor, unless he has purchased the bill out and out, has a right to resort to his original cause of action. So if before a bill becomes due, it is dishonoured, the creditor may resort to his original debt.

Ward v. Evans, Ld. Raym. 928. A banker's note was paid to plaintiff's servant at noon, and presented for payment the next morning, at which time the bank-

er stopped payment. On a case reserved, the court held it was presented in time, and judgment was given for the plaintiff on the original consideration.

Puckford v. Maxwell, 6 T. R. 52. The defendant having been arrested by the plaintiff for 80l., gave a draft for 45l., and promised in a few days to settle the remainder, on which the plaintiff consented to his being discharged out of custody The draft was dishonoured, and the defendant was again arrested upon the same affidavit. On a rule to show cause why he should not be discharged out of custody, it was urged, that the draft having been accepted as part payment, could not be treated as a nullity. But per Lord Kenyon, in cases of this kind, if the bill which is given in payment, do not turn out to be productive, it is not that which it purports to be, and which the party receiving it expects it to be, and therefore he may consider it as a nullity, and act as if no such bill had been given. These questions have frequently arisen at nisi prius, where they have always been determined in the same way. Rule discharged.

[e] Bolton v. Richard, 6 T. R. 139 Vernon v. Boverie, 2 Show. 296. Ex parte Blackburne, 10 Ves. 204. 6

[f] Brown v. Kewley, 2 Bos. & Pul. 518. Ex parte Dickson, in the matter of Parker, a bankrupt, cited 6 T. R. 142. Dickson sold sugars to Parker, for which the latter was to pay him in one month by a good bill

at X., employed C. to carry and deliver them to B. and engaged to pay Effect of delivery of bill to payee. C. for the freight, and C., on delivering them according to the order, took a bill of exchange from B. drawn on A. which bill was never paid, it was holden that A. was liable to pay the amount of the freight to C. notwithstanding the bill of exchange.[s] And where a person, in payment of goods, gives an order on his banker to pay the amount in bills, [100] and the vendor takes bills for the amount, he will not lose his remedy against his original debtor, unless he be guilty of laches.[h] And it has been decided, that the circumstance of the manager of a colliery paying a creditor on the colliery, with a bill, which is not paid, the colliery remains liable to the payment of the original debt.[i]

In Ex parte Blackburne,[k] the Chancellor said, "I take it to be now clearly settled, that if there is an antecedent debt, and a bill is taken, without taking an indorsement, which bill turns out to be bad, the demand for the antecedent debt may be resorted to. It has been held, that if there is no antecedent debt, and A. carries a bill to B. to be discounted, and B. does not take A's. name upon the bill, if it is dishonoured there is no demand ; for there was no relation between the parties, except that transaction; and the circumstance of not taking the name upon the bill, is evidence of a purchase of it. In a sale of goods, the law implies a contract that those goods shall be paid for. It is competent to the party to agree that the payment shall be by a particular bill. In this instance it would be extremely difficult to persuade a jury under the direction of a judge, to say, "an agreement to pay by bills was satisfied by giving bill, whether good or bad." (130)

at two months. Parker gave Dickson a check on his bankers at Liverpool, requesting them to pay him in a bill at three months; the Liverpool bankers drew upon his agents in London, in favour of Dickson for the amount, but before the last bill became due, Parker and the banker became bankrupt. The Chancellor ordered that Dickson should prove the bill under the commission against the bankers and their agents, and claim the rest under Parker's commission.

[s] Tapley v. Martens, 8 T R. 451. This was an action of debt on charter-party from London to Ancona Plaintiff delivered his cargo to the consignor of defendant, and applied to him for the payment of the freight. Plaintiff took a bill of exchange drawn by the consignee on defendant, which was not paid, in consequence of the consignee becoming insolvent. It was urged on the part of the defendant, that the plaintiff had given personal credit to the consignee by taking the bill in question, the defendant having furnished the consignee with money for that purpose. The court held, that the plaintiff neither having taken the bill for his accommodation, nor having been guilty of any laches in enforcing the payment, that the bill could not be considered as payment of the plaintiff's demand, and that the defendant was liable for the amount under the charter-party. See also Wyatt v. Hertford, 3 East. 147. Marsh v. Pedder and others, 4 Campb. 257. 1 Holt, C. N. P. 72. Everett v. Collins, 2 Campb. 515. S. P.

[h] Ex parte Dickson, cited in 6 T. R. 142, 3. Ante, 99. Ex parte Blackburne, 10 Ves 204 acc. Bolton v, Rickard, 1 Esp. Rep 106 semb. contra.

[i] Tempest v. Ord, 1 Madd. 89 Ante, 98.
[k] 10 Ves. 206. S. P. Tempest v. Ord. 1 Madd. 89.

(130) The rules laid down in respect to the operation of payments by bills and notes are in general recognised in the United States ; but with some seeming diversity arising from local usages. In New York a bill of exchange or promissory note, either of the debtor or any other person, is not payment of any precedent debt, unless it be so expressly agreed. Murray v. Governeur, 2 John. Cas. 438. Herring v. Sanger, 3 John. Cas. 71. Tobey v. Barber, 5 John. Rep. 68. Schermerhorn v. Loomis, 7 John. Rep. 311. Johnson v. Weed, 9 John. Rep. 310. Putnam v. Lewis, 8 John. Rep. 389. Wetherby v. Mann, 11 John. Rep. 513. Arnold v. Camp, 12 John. Rep. 409. Neither is a receipt for a note, as cash, evidence that it was taken as an absolute payment. Tobey v. Barber. The receipt of a note is merely a suspension of the right of action on the original consideration, during the time allowed for the payment of it. Tobey v. Barber. The creditor is not obliged to sue upon such note ; he may return it when dishon-

If a bill of exchange or promissory note be *altered*, without the consent of the parties, in any *material* part, as in the date, sum, or time

---

oured, and resort to his original demand. It therefore only postpones the time of payment of the old debt until a default be made in the payment of the note. Ibid. Yet the acceptance of a *negotiable* note on account of a prior debt, is so far evidence *prima facie* of satisfaction, that no recovery can be had on such prior debt without producing the note at the trial and cancelling it, or showing that it has been lost without having been indorsed. *Holmes* v. *De Camp*, 1 John. Rep. 34. *Angel* v. *Felton*, 8 John. Rep. 149. *Cummings* v. *Hackley*, 8 John. Rep. 202. *Pintard* v. *Tackington*, 10 John Rep. 104. *Smith* v. *Lockwood*, 10 John. Rep. 366. And if the creditor part with the note or bill, or if it be the note or acceptance of a third person, and the creditor be guilty of laches in not presenting it for payment in due time, it will discharge the debtor from the original debt. *Tobey* v. *Barber*. And the same rules apply to a check given in payment of a pre-existing debt, for unless it be paid by the drawee, resort may be had by the holder to his original debt. *The people* v. *Howell*, 4 John. Rep. 296. And if upon a sale of goods the notes of a third person payable at a future day, are upon a fradulent misrepresentation agreed to be received as an absolute payment at the risk of the vendor, the vendor may *immediately* bring an action for the goods sold ; for the fraud will avoid the transaction. *Wilson* v. *Force*, 6 John. Rep. 110. If there be an agreement to accept notes in payment of goods sold, and before delivery, of the goods the notes turn out to be bad, the party is not bound to receive them unless he agreed to receive them at all events, and to run the risk of their being paid. *Roget* v. *Merritt*, 2 Caines' Rep. 117. And if a party receive in payment for goods sold, counterfeit bank notes, or other notes which prove of no value, it is not a payment, although the debtor paid them *bona fide* supposing them to be valid, unless the vendor took upon himself expressly, the risk of forgery. *Markle* v. *Hatfield*, 2 John. Rep. 455. And see *Ellis* v. *Wild*, 6 Mass. Rep. 321. *Breed* v *Cook* & *Caldwell*, 15 John. Rep. 241.

In the Supreme Court of the United States it has been held that no action can be maintained for goods sold by a person who has received a negotiable note as conditional payment and has passed that note away. *Harris* v. *Johnson*, 3 Cranch. Rep. 311.; and that a note without a special contract, does not of itself discharge the original cause of action, unless by express agreement it is received as payment. *Semb. Sheehy* v. *Mandeville*, 6 Cranch. 253.; and that where a note has been received as conditional payment, it will be a discharge of the debt, unless it be proved that due diligence has been used to receive the money, and that it cannot be obtained. *Clark* v. *Young*, 1 Cranch, 191.

In *Massachusetts*, a note of the debtor, *not negotiable*, is not deemed a payment of a pre-existing debt. *Greenwood* v. *Curtis*, 4 Mass. R. 93 *Maneely* v. *M'Gee*, 6 Mass. R. 143. But it has long been settled as law in that state that a *negotiable* note, given in consideration of a simple contract debt, is a discharge of such debt; and that the law will presume that a negotiable note is agreed by the parties to be payment of such contract. This presumption however may be encountered by proving an express agreement that the note should be received as collateral security. *Thacher* v. *Dinsmore*, 5 Mass. Rep. 299. *Maneely* v. *M'Gee*, *Chapman* v. *Durant*, 10 Mass. Rep. 47. If the note of a third person be taken in payment of a debt, it operates as a complete discharge of the debt. *Wiseman* v. *Lyman*, 7 Mass. Rep. 286. However, where an order was drawn on a third person in favour of the vendor in part payment of the cargo of a vessel, and payable *on the return of the vessel from her voyage*, it was held no payment of the original demand, although upon the giving of the order and receiving payment of the residue of the sum, the vendor had signed a receipt in full. The court did not think that there was sufficient proof that the vendor was to depend in all events for the payment of this sum upon the vessel's return; but that this event was probably to fix the length of credit. *Tucker* v. *Maxwell*, 11 Mass. Rep. 143. And if A. sells goods to B. and agrees to receive certain notes in payment, and it be afterwards discovered that the notes are forgeries, though unknown to the parties at the time, no action lies against B. for the price of the goods. *Aliter* if payment by the notes was not part of the original stipulation, but an accommodation to the vendee. *Ellis* v *Wild*, 6 Mass. Rep. 321. See 1 Peters' Rep. 266.

If bills are received on account of a debt, and protested for nonpayment, and in an account rendered, the drawer is charged with the usual damages, this amounts to an election to consider the bill as payment. *Watts* v. *Willing*, 2 Dall. Rep. 100. See also *Chapman* v. *Steinmetz*, 1 Dall. Rep. 161. And if in such a case, the creditor return the bill and request a remittance on account of the debt, this amounts to an extinguishment and waiver of the bill; and, if it be one of a set, to an extinguishment of all of them. *Ingraham* v. *Gibbs*, 2 Dall Rep. 134.

A note given by a debtor to the agent of his creditor for goods sold in order to obtain a discount thereon, and afterwards given up through misrepresentation of the drawer, is

when payable, such alteration will, at *common law*, and independently Effect of the altera-tion of a bill, &c. of the stamp acts, render the bill or note wholly invalid, as against any party not consenting to such alteration ; and this although it be in the hands of an innocent holder. Thus, an alteration in the date of a bill of exchange after it has been accepted and indorsed, without the acceptor's or indorser's consent, will discharge them from liability, even though such alteration were made by a stranger ;[1] and where a bill of exchange had been accepted generally, and the drawer without the consent of the acceptor added the words, "payable at Mr. B'.s Chiswell Street," it was held that this was a material alteration, and that the acceptor was thereby discharged ;[m] and where an alteration is made with a fraudulent intent, it will amount to forgery ;[n] and if there be no privity between the holder and the party sued, the former cannot recover even for the consideration of the bill.[o]

[101]

But if an alteration be made in any part of a bill which is *not ma-*

[1] Master *v.* Miller, 4 T. R. 320. 5 T. R. 367. 2 Hen. Bla. 141. Anstr. 225. S. C. Com Dig. Fait. F. 1. Powell *v.* Divett, 15 East, 29.

Master *v.* Miller, 4 T. R. 320. 2 Hen. Bla. 141. S. C. In an action by indorsees against the acceptor of a bill payable three months after date, to Wilkinson and Cooke, the declaration had one count on the bill, as dated the 20th March, and another as dated the 26th March. The jury found a special verdict, stating that the bill was drawn and dated the 26th, that it was accepted, and that afterwards and whilst it remained in the hands of Wilkinson and Cooke, the date was altered from the 26th to the 20th March, without the defendant's knowledge, and by some person unknown to the jury. That after such alteration it was indorsed for a valuable consideration by Wilkinson and Cooke, to the plaintiff's. After two arguments, Lord Kenyon, Ashurst, and Grose, Justices, held, that the alteration, although by a stranger, vacated the bill. Buller, J. differed, but on error, the whole court was so clear that it was vacated, that they would not bear a second argument, and judgment for the defendant was affirmed. See Henfree *v.* Bromley, 6 East, Rep. 309.

[m] Cowie *v.* Halsale, 4 B. & A. 197 ; but see 2 Geo. 4. c. 78.

[n] The King *v.* Treble, 2 Taunt. 329. This was an indictment against the defendant for forgery, with intent to defraud Messrs. Kelliway. It appeared that Messrs. Kelliway, who were bankers in the country, made their re-issuable notes payable at Sir M. Bloxam and Co. bankers, London ; upon the failure of Bloxam and Co. Messrs. K. appointed Messrs. Ramsbottom and Co. their agents, and caused the words "Ramsbottom and Co." to be engraved on small slips of

paper, with which they covered the words Sir M. Bloxam and Co. and fastened them on their notes with gum-water. It also appeared that a parcel of notes which had been sent by Messrs. Bloxam and Co. to Messrs. K. by the coach, had been stolen, and that the defendant had caused similar slips of paper to be pasted over divers of the stolen notes, containg the words "Ramsbottom and Co." and negotiated them, but it did not appear that either Messrs. Ramsbottom and Co. or Messrs. K. had paid any of the notes so altered. It was objected for the defendant, this alteration did not amount to forgery, and the prisoner was respited until the opinion of the twelve Judges could be had. After argument, the Judges were of opinion, that the act done by the prisoner was a false making in a circumstance material to the value of the note, and its facility of transfer, by making it payable at a solvent instead of an insolvent house ; and see 4 Bla. Com. 247, 249. Master *v.* Miller, 4 T. R. 325. 330.

[o] Long *v.* Moore, Sittings after Hil. Term, 1790, cited 8 Esp. 155, in notes. Assumpsit by the indorsee of a bill against an acceptor ; after the acceptance, the word, "date" was inserted in place of "sight," in which form it had originally been drawn. The acceptor being thereby discharged, the plaintiff wanted to go on the common counts, and offered in evidence another bill, drawn by the same drawer on the defendant, for the same amount, but not accepted. Lord Kenyon ruled, that it could not be done ; nor could the plaintiff recover at all against the acceptor (the defendant) for he was liable only by virtue of the instrument : which being vitiated, his liability was at an end.

no extinguishment of the original debt, *Lewis* v. *Manly*, 2 Yeates Rep. 200. *Suckley* v. *Furse*, 15 John. Rep. 338.

Effect of *terial*, or be made merely for the purpose of *correcting a mistake*, and
the altera- in furtherance of the *original* intention of the parties, such alteration,
tion of a though made after the bill is complete, will not invalidate it either with
bill, &c. regard to the stamp-laws or otherwise.[p] Thus, before the late decision,
and where an acceptance engaging to pay at a particular place, was considered as not qualifying the contract, if after a bill has been accepted
generally, the acceptor wrote upon it the place where he wished it to
be presented for payment when due, it was held, that such addition
would not render the bill void.[q] So the insertion of the words " or
order" in a note intended to be negotiable, but which had been omitted
by mistake, will not render it inoperative against any of the parties.[r]
So where a person who was indebted to another, had agreed to give him
a bill of exchange in payment, which was to be drawn by him and accepted by a third person, and sent a promissory note drawn by himself, and
indorsed by the person who was to have been the acceptor, it was held
that such promissory note might, before it was circulated, be altered into
a bill of exchange, according to the original agreement of the parties,
such alteration being considered as a mere correction of a mistake ;[s] and

[p] Sanderson v. Symonds, 1 Brod. &
Bingh. 426.
[q] Trapp v. Spearman, 3 Esp. Rep. 57.
In an action on a bill by an indorsee
against the acceptor, the defence was, that
the bill had been altered by the insertion
of the words " when due, at the Cross
Keys, Blackfriars Road." But Lord Kenyon said, that the alteration was immaterial, and the plaintiff had a verdict ; and see
2 Geo. 4. c. 78.
  Marson v. Petit, 1 Campb. 82. Indorsee against the acceptor of a bill, after
acceptance, the drawer, without the consent of the defendant, wrote under his
name the words " Prescott and Co."
Lord Ellenborough held it immaterial, as
it did not alter the responsibility of the acceptor. See observations on this case in
Tidmarsh v. Grover, 1 M. & S. 735. and
French v. Nicholson, 1 Marsh, 72. and see
Jacobs, v. Hart, 2 Stark. 45.
[r] Kershaw v. Cox, 3 Esp. 246, recognised in Knill, v. Williams, 10 East, 435,
7. and 12 East, 475, and Bathe v. Taylor,
15 East, 517, and see Robinson v. Tou-
rays, 1 M. & S. 217. In an action on a
bill it appeared, that the defendant, who
was the payee, had indorsed the bill to
one K. by whom it was indorsed to the
plaintiffs ; that they, on discovering the
words " or order" had been omitted, returned it the day after it was drawn, and
the drawer, with the consent of the defendant, then inserted those words. Le
Blanc, J. held, that no new stamp was necessary, that this was not a new instrument, as in Bowman v. Nicholl, but
merely a correction of a mistake, and in
furtherance of the original intention of
the parties, and the plaintiff had a verdict. A new trial was afterwards moved
for, but the court refused a rule. In
Knill v. Williams, 10 East, 437, Le
Blanc, J. said, that Kershaw v. Cox, could
only be supported on the ground that the

alteration was merely the correction of a
mistake, for the alteration was a very material one. And see Coles v. Parkin, 12
East, 471.
[s] Webber v. Robert Maddocks, 3
Campb. 1. Indorsee against the acceptor
of a bill of exchange. It appeared that
Samuel and Robert Maddocks, being indebted to the plaintiff in the sum of 110l.,
they agreed to give him a bill of exchange
at four months for this amount, to be
drawn by Samuel and accepted by Robert. Instead of a bill of exchange they
sent him a promissory note in the following form :

                          London, 10th Dec. 1810.
  Four months after date, I promise to pay
to my own order, one hundred and ten
pounds, value received.
                               S. *Maddocks.*
Indorsed, S. *Maddocks.*
           R. *Maddocks.*
  The plaintiff was dissatisfied with the
security in this form, and returned it
that it might be altered into a bill of exchange, according to the agreement. The
words " I promise to," were immediately
struck out, a direction to R. Maddocks
was subjoined, and he wrote his name as
acceptor of the bill. It was then delivered
back to the plaintiff.
  For the defendant it was insisted that the
instrument was completely vitiated by this
alteration.
  Lord Ellenborough. I think the stamp
impressed upon this paper is sufficient to
render the instrument available in its present form. It cannot be considered as
having been negotiated as a promissory
note. It never was issued to third persons.
It remained in the hands, and under the dominion of the original parties. Every thing
continued in *fieri* till after the alteration.
The stamp was not occupied till then.
Webber instantly rejected it as a promissory note. The alteration only fulfilled the

at the request of the drawer, a bill may, before acceptance, be altered, and postponed as to the date, without vitiating it, or rendering a new stamp necessary.[t]

Where, however, the drawer of a bill of exchange, which was accepted, payable at the house of a banker, who had become insolvent, erased the name of that banker, and substituted the name of a solvent banker, without the consent of the acceptor, such alteration was considered so material, as at common law to invalidate the bill against him, though in the hands of an indorsee for a valuable consideration, who was ignorant of the circumstances, upon the ground that it caused the bill to carry with it the appearance of solvency, by being directed to a solvent house instead of an insolvent one, and thereby held out a false colour to the holder, and likewise varied the contract of the acceptor by superadding an order upon another house to pay the bill.[u]

Any material alteration made in a bill of exchange or promissory note after it has been once perfected, even with the consent of the parties, except in the before-mentioned cases, will render it absolutely void, it having been enacted, that there shall be no alteration in a stamped instrument after it has been used for one purpose;[x] and every alteration of a bill or note after it is once complete, is considered as a fresh drawing or making, and the circumstance of the bill or note not having been negotiated, will not afford any exception.[y] And even where a bill which had been accepted for the accommodation of the drawer, was altered by him as to the time of payment, with the consent of the acceptor, and before it was actually negotiated, such alteration was held to render the bill absolutely void.[z]

[104]

So where the date of a bill of exchange was altered by the payee at the request of the acceptor, such alteration was considered to render the bill wholly void, and to preclude the payee from maintaining any action thereon even against such acceptor.[a] And if a bill be altered in the

terms of the agreement, and may be treated as the correction of a mistake. The plaintiff recovered.

[t] Peacock v. Murrell, 2 Stark. 558.

[u] Tidmarsh v. Grover, 1 M. & S. 735. and Rex v. Treble, ante, 101, n.

[x] See 1 Ann, stat. 2. c. 22. s. 2 and 3. to which the subsequent acts refer; per Le Blanc, J. in Bathe v. Taylor, 15 Last, 416.

[y] Bowman v. Nicholl, 5 T. R. 537. A bill was dated 2d September, and payable twenty-one days after date; while it was in the hands of the drawer, it was altered with the consent of the acceptor to fifty-one days; on the 30th September it was again altered to twenty-one days; but the date was brought forward to 14th September, after which it was negotiated, and an action brought against the acceptor. Lord Kenyon said, that every alteration in an instrument requiring a stamp, made a new stamp necessary, and nonsuited the plaintiff. Upon a rule nisi for a new trial, it was urged that there was a distinction between an alteration made after the negotiation of a bill, and an alteration made before, and in the latter case, the whole might

be considered as one transaction, but the court said, that as the operation of the bill as it originally stood was quite spent when the last alteration was made, that alteration made it a new and distinct transaction between the parties, and therefore there should have been a new stamp, and the nonsuit was confirmed.

Bathe v. Taylor, 15 East, 412. It was held, that a bill drawn on the 1st of August, at two months, by A. on B. payable to the order of the drawer, and accepted and redelivered by B. as a security for a debt, and kept by A. for twenty days, could not be altered in its legal effect by bringing forward the date to the 21st, without a new stamp, though with the consent of the acceptor, and before indorsement and delivery to a third person.

[z] Calvert v. Roberts, 3 Campb. 343. Bathe v. Taylor, 15 East, 412. See also Prince v. Nicholson, 1 Marsh. 72, n. (c.)

[a] Walton v. Hastings, 4 Campb. 223. 1 Stark. 215. S. C. Payee against the acceptor of a bill of exchange. The bill was drawn by one Brooks on the defendant, payable to the order of the plaintiff, dated 5th July; when the bill was presented for

Effect of the alteration of a bill, &c. date by the drawee after it is drawn and indorsed, but before it is accepted, such alteration will invalidate the bill, and discharge the drawer and indorsers from liability, though it be in the hands of a *bona fide* holder, who is ignorant of the circumstances.[b] And after a promissory note has been made by one person, the name of another cannot be added thereto as surety, unless by indorsement.[c] So also where A. and

[105] B. having exchanged their acceptances, it was held that the delivery of the respective bills for acceptance, and the re-delivery of the same by the acceptors to the respective drawers, was a negotiation of the bills, and that such bills could not, after they had been so exchanged for a valuable consideration (as the exchange of acceptances is) for twenty days be post-dated, although during all that time each had remained in the hands of the original drawer.[d] And even the subsequent insertion of the nature of the consideration of the bill will render it void.[e]

But where the drawee of a bill of exchange payable at three months after date, requested the drawer that it might be altered to four months, to which the latter consented, and which was done whilst in his hands, and before it was negotiated or accepted, it was held that such altera-

---

acceptance, defendant requested that the date on the bill might be altered to the 10th, to which plaintiff agreed, but did not inform Brooks. The plaintiff contended, that as the alteration was made before acceptance, the defendant was liable as acceptor, although the drawer might be discharged. Lord Ellenborough. Upon the stamp laws, I think the bill is void. It was an existing valid instrument before the alteration. It was negotiated when delivered by Brooks to the plaintiff. The plaintiff, as payee, had acquired an absolute interest in it, and might have maintained an action upon it against the drawer. It did not remain in *fieri* till the acceptance. As to the drawer, it was before then a perfect instrument, nor was there any mistake to be rectified. When drawn on the 5th of July, it corresponded with the intentions both of the drawer and payee. Here, when the date was altered, a new bill was drawn, and that could not be done without a new stamp.

[b] Outhwaite and another v. Huntley, 4 Campb. 179. Indorsee against the indorser of a bill, payable to the order of the drawers. It appeared that after the bill had been drawn and indorsed, it was left for acceptance with the drawees, who altered the date (from the 5th to the 15th March) without the consent of the drawers, and then accepted it. It was contended for the plaintiffs, that this alteration did not vitiate the bill, for it was not perfect till acceptance. Lord Ellenborough said, that before acceptance the bill of exchange was a perfect instrument, on which the drawers might have been sued; any material alteration of it in that state, therefore, rendered it void. Besides, consent would not justify the alteration, with a view to the stamp laws after the bill had been negotiated.

[c] Clark v. Blackstock, Holt C. N. P. 474. A promissory note signed by A. and subsequently by B. whilst in the hands of the payee as surety for A. unless such signature of B. is in virtue of a previous agreement at the time of making the note, it will be void without an additional stamp.

[d] Cardwell v. Martin, 9 East, 190. 1 Campb. 79. S. C. On the 3d of June, 1807, the defendant and Giles and Co. exchanged acceptances; on the 23d, before either of the bills had been passed away, they altered the dates to the 23d; the bills were payable at certain periods after date; Lord Ellenborough thought a new stamp necessary, and nonsuited the plaintiff, with liberty to move to set aside the nonsuit: on motion accordingly, the whole court thought that the exchange of acceptances was a negotiation of each bill, and that the subsequent alteration rendered a new stamp necessary. Rule refused. Note.— Each bill way payable to the drawer's order, and the plaintiff was a *bona fide* indorsee. 9 East, 357. 6 East, 312.

[e] Knill v. Williams, 10 East, 431. This was an action on a note by which nine montes after date, the defendant promised to pay the plaintiff or order, 100l. value received, *for the good will of the lease and trade of Mr. F. Knill, deceased.* It appeared at the trial before Le Blanc, J. at Hereford, that the words in italics were added by the consent of both parties, on the day after the note had been signed and delivered to the plaintiff, without any new stamp being impressed upon it, upon this the plaintiff was nonsuited; and upon a rule *nisi* to set aside the nonsuit, the whole court held that the alteration was material, and therefore discharged the rule.

tion did not invalidate the bill, it not having been a complete instrument prior to the alteration.[f]

If upon a bill being presented for acceptance, the payee alters it as to the time of payment, and accepts it so altered, he vacates the bill as against the drawer and indorsers; but if the holder acquiesces in such alteration and acceptance, it is a good bill as between him and the acceptor; and keeping the bill and presenting it for payment at the deferred period, is proof of such acquiescence; and the holder cannot afterwards maintain an action on the case against the acceptor, for thereby destroying the bill.[g] The effect of an alteration in the acceptance of a bill will be hereafter considered. It is proper to observe, that alterations and erasures will frequently give the transaction the [106] appearance of fraud;[h] and in an action by the indorsee against the acceptor of a bill, the date of which appeared to have been altered by such acceptor, the plaintiff was required to prove that such alteration was made before the indorsement of the bill by the drawer, but proof that it was in the hands of the latter after the acceptance will *primâ facie* suffice.[i](136)

---

[f] Kennerly v. Nash, 1 Stark. 452. Jacobs, v. Hart, 2 Stark. 45.

[g] Paton v. Winter, 1 Taunt. 420. See 6 East, 309. The drawee altered the time of payment of a bill from one month to two and accepted it; the holder kept it two months and then presented it for payment. The court held that this was an acquiescence in the alteration, and directed a nonsuit to be entered in an action on the case brought by the holder against the acceptor, for having mutilated the bill.

[h] Singleton v. Butler, 2 Bos. & Pul. 283.

[i] Johnson v. The Duke of Marlborough, 2 Stark. 313. Bul. N. P. 255.

---

(136) Any alteration, whether material or not, in an instrument under seal, made by the party to whom it is given, will avoid it, unless made by the consent of the party who executed it. But this consent may as well be implied from the nature of the alteration as be expressed. In a simple contract, which is merely evidence of a promise, an immaterial alteration, however made, not at all affecting the terms of the promise, seems not to be within the same principle of deeds, which, from the alteration, may not be the deeds of the parties ; while a similar alteration in a written simple contract might leave it complete evidence of the same contract. Indeed the assent of the party signing such contract, that the omission of a word by a clerical mistake which the law will supply, might be cured by inserting such word, ought to be presumed, to protect him from the imputation of intentional fraud. And in a simple contract an addition by the unnecessary supplying of a word, which the law would supply, is not an alteration in matter or form which would destroy the contract. *Per Curiam, Hunt v. Adams, 6 Mass. Rep.* 519. See *Griffith v. Cox,* Overton's Rep. 210.

If an acceptance of a bill be cancelled by mistake, it does not avoid the acceptance, and all parties to the bill are bound in the same manner as if the act had not been done. *Nevins et al v. De Grand,* 15 Mass. Rep.

An alteration of the date of a promissory note by the payee whereby the time of payment is *retarded,* and afterwards discounted with innocent persons by the payee on indorsing it, avoids the note. *Bank of U. S. v. Russell & Boone,* 3 Yeates' Rep. 391. See 3 Cranch, 37.

The law will not presume that an alteration apparent on the face of a note was made after its execution. *Cumberland Bank v. Hall,* 1 Halsted. 215. But whether the alteration, was made after or before the execution of the note, seems to be a question for the jury. *Ibid.*

An alteration of the date of a promissory note without consent, vitiates it in the hands of an innocent indorsee. *Stephens v. Graham,* 7 Serg. & Rawle, 505.

Where after a note was made and indorsed, the maker, without the knowledge or consent of the indorser, (both of whom resided in *Albany,* where the note was made,) added in the margin " payable at the Bank of *America;*" (which is in the city of *New York,*) and payment was accordingly demanded at that bank, and due notice of non-payment was sent by mail to the indorser at *Albany,* it was held that the addition of the place of payment was an immaterial alteration, and that the demand and notice was suf-

Liability of the drawer. Upon delivery of the bill to the payee or indorsee the *liability of the drawer* becomes complete. The act of drawing a bill, implies an undertaking from the drawer to the payee, and to every subsequent holder fairly entitled to the possession, that the person on whom he draws is capable of binding himself by his acceptance ; that he is to be found at the place where he is described to reside, if that description be mentioned in the bill ; that if the bill be duly presented to him, he will accept in writing on the bill itself, according to its tenor ; and that he will pay it when it becomes due if presented in proper time for that purpose. This engagement is in all its parts absolute and *irrevocable,* and therefore where A. in England drew a bill of exchange on B. in a foreign country, who, by the laws of that country was prohibited from paying it, although it was urged that the undertaking of the drawer did not extend to the case of a prohibition to accept or pay the bill, imposed by the law of a foreign country in which the drawee resided, yet it was ruled in an action against the drawer, that this was no defence, it not being necessary for the holder to inquire for what reason the bill was not paid.[k] But if the payment or acceptance be prohibited by the law of *this* country, it is otherwise.[l] The drawer will also be

[107] equally liable, whether he draw the bill on his own account or as agent of a third person.[m] And we have also seen, that a person signing his

[k] Mellish v. Simeon, 2 Hen. Bla. 378. Poth. pl. 58. Tooting v. Hubbard, 3 Bos. & Pul. 291.
Mellish v. Simeon, 2 Hen. Bla. 378. A bill drawn in London upon Paris, and negotiated through Holland ; before it became due, the French government prohibited the payment of any bill drawn in England, in consequence of which, it was dishonoured and sent back through the different hands by which it had before been negotiated to London ; the re-exchange between Paris and Holland raised the bill from 603l. 19s. 10d. to 905l. 13s. 9d. and the re-exchange between Holland and London, to 913l. 4s. 3d. which the plaintiff, the payee, paid ; and upon an action by him against the drawer, Eyre, C. J. left it to the jury, whether the defendant was liable for the re-exchange occasioned by returning the bill through Hol-

land, and they found that he was. An application was made for a new trial, upon the ground that the defendant was not liable for the re-exchange, because there was no default in him, the payment being prohibited by the government of France. But the court held it immaterial why the bill was not paid ; that as it was not paid, he was liable to all the consequences, of which the re-exchange was one, and the rule was refused.
[l] Pollard v. Herries, 3 Bos. & Pul. 340. Lord Alvanley, C. J. It cannot be disputed, that whatever be the nature of the contract into which a subject of this country enters, he is excused from the performance of it if the laws of his country interpose and forbid the performance.
[m] Le Feuvre v. Lloyd, 5 Taunt. 749. 1 Marsh. 318. S. C. Ante, 27, note.

ficient to charge the indorser. *Bank of America* v. *Woodworth,* 18 Johns. 315. But this judgment was afterwards reversed on error. 18 Johns. 391.
Three persons joined as drawer, acceptor, and first indorser in making an accommodation bill, and it was afterwards issued for value to J. S. Previously to its being so issued its date had been altered; it was held that the acceptor having assented to the alteration when he was informed of it, it was no answer to an action on the bill against him, that the bill had been so altered without the consent of the drawer and first indorser, and that a fresh stamp was not necessary in consequence of such alteration, the bill having been altered before it was issued in point of law. *Downes* v. *Richardson,* 5 Barn. & Ald. 674. See post, 184.
If the obligee of a sealed bill procure persons not present at the execution, to add their names as witnesses, without the knowledge of the obligor ; this is such an alteration as avoids the instrument. But if they did it by mistake, supposing that they were witnessing an assignment then made by the obligee, the bill is good. *Marshall* v. *Gougler,* 10 Serg & Rawle, 164.
If a person draw a note leaving a blank for the name of the payee, and authorise a person to obtain the money from the payee and insert his name, the note is valid, if the directions are complied with. *Stahl* v. *Berger, Ib.* 170.

name on a blank paper stamped with a bill stamp, will be liable to pay Liability of the drawer. to a *bona fide* holder any sum inserted in the bill, and warranted by the stamp.[a]

On failure of the performance of this engagement, the drawer of a bill will *immediately*, and before the time specified in the bill for payment, be liable to an action,[o] not only for the principal sum, but also in certain cases for interest, re-exchange, and costs, as a consequence of the bill not being honoured.[p] Besides this obligation to the payee and the holder, the drawer is also bound to indemnify the acceptor, if he accepted for his accommodation for any loss he may sustain in consequence of his acceptance.[q] These obligations, though absolute and irrevocable, may be discharged by the laches or neglect of the holder, or by other means which will be spoken of hereafter. If a bill be drawn abroad on a person in this country, and the latter refuse acceptance or payment, the drawer will, if discharged by the foreign law, be discharged in this country.[r] Where an annuity was granted in consideration of a bill accepted, which was dishonoured by the acceptor, but paid by the drawer on notice, it was held that this was not such a non-payment of the bill as to vacate the annuity, though the bill was accepted for the accommodation of the drawer, who undertook to furnish assets, but neglected to do so.

[a] Usher and others *v.* Dauncey and others, 4 Campb. 97. Ante, 24, note, and 90.

[o] Bright *v.* Purrier, Bul. Ni. Pri. 269. A foreign bill payable 120 days after sight, was presented for acceptance, but acceptance being refused, the holder brought an action immediately against the drawer; the defendant objected that he was not liable till the expiration of the 120 days, and offered to call witnesses to prove that such was the custom of merchants; but Lord Mansfield said, the law was clearly otherwise, and refused to hear the evidence; so the plaintiff recovered. Milford *v.* Mayor, Dougl. 54. Indorser

against the drawer of a bill, which the drawee had refused to accept. On a rule to show cause why the defendant should not be discharged, the ground stated was that the bill was not due. *Per curiam.* It is settled that if a bill of exchange is not accepted, an action on the bill will lie immediately against the drawer, because his undertaking that the drawee shall give him credit, is not performed.

[p] Mellish *v.* Simeon, 6 Hen. Bla. 369. Ante, p 106, n. Poth. pl. 6.

[q] Poth. pl. 97, 8, 9.

[r] Cook *v.* Tower, 1 Taunt. 372. Potter *v.* Brown, 5 East, 131.

CHAPTER IV.

OF THE INDORSEMENT AND TRANSFER OF BILLS, &c.

THOUGH Inland Bills are frequently accepted before they are indorsed, yet as all bills may be transferred before acceptance, we will consider the points relative to the transfer of bills and notes in this chapter.

It has been already observed,[a] that it is the transferrable quality of bills and notes which principally distinquishes them from other contracts, and that on account of this property, and of their utility in mercantile transactions, they have been pecularly favoured by our courts. The following points relating to the *transfer* of bills are to be considered. *First,* What bills are transferrable. *Secondly,* By and to whom. *Thirdly,* At what time. *Fourthly,* The mode of transfer. *Fifthly,* Its nature, operation, and obligation, and how that obligation may be released or discharged. And *Lastly,* Of the consequences of the loss of a bill, note, or check, and what conduct the holder should thereupon pursue.

I. *What bills, &c. are transferrable.* With respect to bills payable to a certain person *or order,* or to the order of a certain person, no doubt seems ever to have been entertained respecting their negotiability; and though bills payable to *bearer,* or to a certain person or bearer, were formerly thought not to be negotiable, and considered as mere *choses in action,* upon a supposition that such instruments contained no authority to assign them, so as to enable the assignee to *demand* payment of the drawee;[b] yet it is now completely settled,[c] that the decisions tending to support this doctrine, and the reasoning on which they were founded, were equally erroneous. In short, it is now well established that bills, whether payable to *order,* or to *bearer,* are equally negotiable from hand to hand *ad infinitum;* and that the transfer vests in the assignee a right of action on the instrument assigned; sustainable in his own name.[c]

[109] But in general, unless the words "or order," "or bearer," or some other words authorizing the payee of a bill, or note, to assign it, be inserted therein, it cannot be transferred so as to give the assignee a

---

[a] Ante, 5, 6. 8.

[b] Horton *v.* Coggs, 3 Lev. 299. Hodges *v,* Steward, 1 Salk. 125. Nicholson *v.* Sedgwick, 1 Ld. Raym. 180. Mod. Ent. 313. Bills and notes are valid, though they do not contain any words, rendering them negotiable. Smith *v.* Kendall, 6 T. R. 124. Ante, 65, 6.

[c] Grant *v* Vaughan, 3 Burr. 1516.— 1 Bla. Rep. 485. S. C. Hinton's case, 2 Show. 235. Vaughan gave Bicknell a draft upon his banker, payable to ship Fortune *or bearer;* the draft came to the hands of Grant, who sued Vaughan upon it. The defendant contended, that the draft was a mere authority to receive the money, and not negotiable; and that point and another being left to the jury, they found for the defendant, but upon application for a new trial, the court held that it was negotiable, and a new trial was granted, in which the plaintiff recovered. Se also Miller *v.* Race, Burr. 452.

right of action against any of the parties except the indorser himself,[d] unless the negotiable words were omitted by mistake, and in which case they may be supplied.[e] (141) It may, however, be collected from the cases relative to bills payable to fictitious persons,[f] that any words in the bill, or extraneous facts, from whence it can be inferred that the person making it, or any other party to it, intended it to be negotiable, will give it a transferrable quality against that person. And in all cases, though no words authorizing a transfer be inserted in a bill or note, yet it will always have the same operation against the party making the transfer, as if he had power to assign ;[g] (141) for the act of indorsing a bill is equivalent to that of a new drawing;[h] and a transfer by mere delivery, unless where it is otherwise agreed or understood from the nature of the transaction, imposes on the person making it an obligation to his immediate assignee, similar to that created by indorsement. East India certificates are not indorseable, so as to transfer the legal interest;[i] and it was held, that East India bonds were not transferrable so as to pass the legal interest to the purchaser, but this has been altered by a late statute.[k] But an Exchequer bill, the blank in which has not been filled up with any person's name, is transferrable by delivery.[l] A doubt was once suggested, whether a check or draft on a banker were negotiable out of the bills of mortality;[m] but it is now settled, that this instrument is as negotiable as a bill of exchange ;[n] and it seems, that a bill or note payable to bearer, may be transferred and declared on as indorsed.[o] (142)

The law having in general already determined when a bill is assignable, and the mode by which the transfer is to be effected, it is the pro- [110]

---

[d] Hill v. Lewis, 1 Salk. 132, 3. Ante, 66.

[e] Kershaw v. Cox, 3 Esp. Rep. 246.—Ante, 101, 2.

[f] Minet v. Gibson, 2 T. R. 481. 1 Hen. Bla. 569. S. C. Vide ante, 64, in notes.

[g] Hill v. Lewis, 1 Salk. 132. Moor drew one note payable to the defendant, or his order, and another payable to him generally without any words to make it assignable: the defendant indorsed them to Zouch, and Zouch to the plaintiff ; the first objection was, that the plaintiff had been guilty of laches, but the jury thought he had not, and it was then urged, that the second note was not assignable; and Holt, C. J. agreed, that the indorsement of this note did not make him that drew it chargeable to the indorsee; for the words "or to his order," gave authority to assign it by indorsement, but the indorsement of a note which has

not these words is good, so as to make the indorser chargeable to the indorsee.

[h] Id. ibid. Smallwood v. Vernon, Stra. 478. Balingnalls v. Gloster, 8 East, 482.

[i] Williamson v. Thomson, 16 Ves. 450.

[k] Glynn v. Baker, 13 East, 509.—51 Geo. 3. cap. 64. As to a navy bill, see M'Lieshe v. Ekins, Say. 73. cited 13 East, 515, n.(a.)

[l] Wookey v. Pole, 4 B. & A. 1.

[m] Grant v. Vaughan, 3 Burr 1517.

[n] Boehm v. Stirling, 7 T. R. 430.

[o] Waynan v. Bend, 1 Campb. N. P. 175. In an action against the maker of a promissory note, payable to T. L. or bearer, the defendant averred an indorsement by T. L. and Lord Ellenborough held, that the plaintiff having stated such indorsement, though unnecessarily, was bound to prove it; and that the plaintiff could not recover on the money counts, as he was not an original party to the bill.

---

(141) The same point was decided in actions brought in Pennsylvania by the indorsee of a note and bill, not negotiable, against the acceptor of the latter and the maker of the former. Gerard v. La Coste, 1 Dall. 194. Barriere v. Nairac, 2 Dall. 249.

(142) The indorsement of a bill or note is not merely a transfer of the paper; but it is a new and substantive contract. Slacum v. Pomeroy, 6 Cranch, 222. It is in fact the same as a new bill drawn by the indorser on the acceptor, in favour of the indorsee. Van Staphorst v. Pearse, 4 Mass. Rep. 258. See Lennox v. Prout, 3 Wheaton, 520. Bank of N. America v. Barriere, 1 Yeates' Rep. 360.

If the payee of a note, payable to bearer, indorse his name on the note, he will be liable on the note in the same manner as if it were payable to order. Brush v. Reeves's adm. 3 John. Rep. 439.

vince of a court,[p] and not that of a jury, to decide on the negotiability of these instruments, unless in new cases where the law merchant is doubtful, when evidence of the custom may be received.[q]

When a bill or note has been unduly obtained, the negotiation of it may be restrained by a court of equity:[r] which has a peculiar jurisdiction to prevent a party from being sued at law upon a security which has been improperly obtained, and to order it to be delivered up to be cancelled.[s] But at law, except in the instance of a warrant of attorney, there is no jurisdiction to order the security to be vacated, and the contracting party must, at the risk of losing the evidence which might establish his defence, wait till the party who holds the security thinks fit to try the validity of the instrument in an action; and should he be nonsuited, he will still be at liberty to proceed *de novo* upon his security; but a court of equity will often decree instruments to be delivered up to be cancelled, although the objection to their validity might be taken advantage of at law, for fear that the evidence to impeach them may be lost, or a vexatious use made of them.[t] But as the party applying for relief seeks equity, he must observe it, and therefore the court, in affording relief, will compel him to pay what may be justly due, and will impose on him such equitable terms as the justice of the case may require.[u]

[111]

II. Who may transfer. With respect to the persons who may transfer a bill or note, whoever has the absolute property may assign it if payable to order.[x](1) In general a valid transfer can only be made by the payee or the person who is *legally* interested in the instrument, or by his agent, and consequently an indorsement by a person of the same name is inoperative (except against the party making it, and the subsequent indorsers,) although

---

[p] Edie *v.* East India Company, 2 Burr. 1224. Grant *v.* Vaughan, 3 Burr. 1523, 1528.

[q] Stone *v.* Rawlinson, Willes, 561.— Edie *v.* East India Company, 2 Burr. 1216. 1 Bla. Rep. 295. S. C. Carvick *v.* Vickery, Dougl. 653.

[r] Bromley *v.* Holland, 7 Ves. 20. Jervis *v.* White, id. 413. Newman *v.* Milner, 2 Ves. jun. 483. Hammersley *v.* Purling, 3 Ves. 757. Berkeley *v.* Brymer, 9 Ves. 355.

[s] Newland *v.* Milner, 2 Ves. jun. 488. Plaintiff prayed a discovery, injunction, and delivery of a bill of exchange; upon the answers and evidence, the right being clear, the court refused an opportunity of trying it at law, and decreed an immediate delivery. See also Jervis *v.* White, 7 Ves. 413. Sir Edward Smith *v.* Haytwell, Ambl. 66. Bill to be relieved against a promissory note given upon a marriage brokage agreement; on motion the defendant was restrained from parting with or assigning the note, till answer or further order. See also 3 Bro. C. C. 477. Prac. Reg. Ch. 233.
—— *v.* Blackwood, 3 Anst. 851. An

injunction was granted to prevent the negotiating a note obtained at play, upon affidavit before service of the subpœna. See also Newman *v.* Franco, 2 Anst. 519. Andrews *v.* Berry, 3 Anst 624. Newland on Contracts, 491, 2, 3, 4.
Burrows *v.* Jemino, 2 Eq Ca. Abr. 525, pl. 7. Where the acceptance of a bill of exchange became void, by the law of a foreign country, and was vacated by a competent court there, a perpetual injunction was granted against proceedings here.
Berkeley *v* Brymer, 9 Ves. 355. Affidavits cannot be read in support of an injunction to restrain the negotiation of a bill; and from Iveson *n* Harris, 7 Ves. 257, it appears that an injunction is not binding upon a person not party in the cause.

[t] Id. ibid. and see other cases in Newland on Contracts, 493, 4.

[u] Byne *v.* Vivian, 5 Ves. 604. Newland on Contracts, 494, 5. Fitzroy *v.* Gyllim, 1 T. R. 153. Hindle *v.* O'Brien, 1 Taunt. 413. Benfield *v.* Solomon, 9 Ves. 84.

[x] *Per curiam,* in Stone *v.* Rawlinson, Barnes, 165. Willes, 560. S. C.

---

(1) It seems that the maker of a note can never dispute the authority of the payee to indorse it. *Drayton* v. *Dale,* 2 Barn. & Cress. 293. 9 Serg. & Lowb. Ab. 91.

the person entitled to transfer the instrument was not particularly described in it.[y] And we have seen, than an indorsement by an *infant* payee will not pass any interest in the bill against himself, though the acceptor and subsequent indorsers will in general be liable.[z] The same rule applies to the right of transferring a bill made payable to bearer or to order, and indorsed in blank, if the person to whom it is assigned or pledged, knew, at the time he became the holder, that the person making the transfer had no right to make it.[a] If, however, the holder had no knowledge of that circumstance, and took the bill *bona fide*, either absolutely or as a pledge, such transfer will be as operative, and will convey the same rights as if it had been made by a person authorized to make it; for it would be a great clog on the negotiability of bills and checks, if the holder were bound in every instance where there are no suspicious circumstances, to inquire into the right of the person making the transfer.[b] Therefore if indorsed bills be delivered to a person for a particular purpose, and he negotiate them to a third person

II. *Who may transfer.*

[112]

[y] Mead *v.* Young, 4 T. R. 28. Gibson *v.* Minet, 1 Hen. Bla. 607. A bill, payable to Henry Davis, or order, was sent by the post, and got into the hands of a wrong Henry Davis, who indorsed it to the plaintiff; there was no description of Henry Davis on the bill, in addition to his name, nor was any fraud imputable to the plaintiff. This was an action against the acceptor, and on his offering evidence to show that the Henry Davis who indorsed the bill was not the person in whose favour it was drawn, Lord Kenyon was of opinion that the evidence was inadmissible, and he retained that opinion after cause shown against an application for a new trial, but Ashhurst, Buller, and Grose, Justices, held, that unless the indorsement was made by the person to whom the bill was really payable, it was a forgery, and could confer no title, and that therefore it was competent for the defendant to show, that the person who indorsed the bill was not the person in whose favour it was made, and a new trial was accordingly granted.

[z] Ante, 20.—Taylor *v.* Croker, 4 Esp. Ni. Pri. Ca. 187. In an action against the acceptor of a bill, drawn by Eversfield and Jones, on the defendant, and payable to their own order, and indorsed by them to one S. and by him to the plaintiff; it appeared that both the drawers were infants at the time of drawing the bill, but Lord Ellenborough held, that though that might have been a good defence, had the action been brought against the drawers themselves, it was no defence in the present action. Verdict for the plaintiff, but quære if the infant afterwards dissent to his indorsement, whether such defective transfer of his interest in the bill would not defeat the plaintiff's claim.

[a] Roberts and others *v.* Eden, 1 Bos. & Pul. 398. The plaintiffs were assignees of the indorsee of a promissory note, made by the defendant, payable to one Hunt or order, on demand for money

borrowed, and who indorsed it over to the bankrupt. Hunt and the defendant afterwards settled accounts, but the promissory note was not mentioned, it was given in evidence that the note had passed several times between Hunt and the bankrupt, but upon one occasion, Hunt told him, that it must not be negotiated, as he should want it when he settled accounts with defendant. The jury upon the trial, found a verdict for the defendant, and upon a motion for a new trial, the court held, that the verdict was right, and that the evidence was decisive to show that the note was not negotiated to the bankrupt, but only deposited with him as a pledge, and that it must remain in his hands subject to the same equity as if it were in the hands of the original payee. S. P. Treuttel *v.* Barandon, 8 Taunt. 100.

[b] Grant *v.* Vaughan, Burr. 1516. The defendant gave a cash note upon his banker, to one Bicknell, payable to Ship Fortune, or bearer. Bicknell lost it, and the plaintiff afterwards took it *bona fide* in the course of trade, and paid a valuable consideration for it. The banker (in consequence of an order from the defendant) refused to pay it, upon which the plaintiff brought this action. Lord Mansfield left it to the jury to consider, first, whether the plaintiff came to the possession of the bill fairly and *bona fide;* and secondly, whether such draft was in fact and practice negotiable, and the jury found for the defendant; but upon an application for a new trial, and cause shown, the court were of opinion, that the second point ought not to have been left to the jury, because it was clear that such drafts were negotiable, and if the jury thought the plaintiff took the note fairly and *bona fide*, of which there appeared to be no doubt, he was entitled to recover. A new trial was accordingly granted, in which the plaintiff recovered. S. P. Treuttel *v.* Barandon, 8 Taunt. 103.

CHITTY ON BILLS.   P

II. *Who* who does not know the trust, the latter will become beneficially entitled
may trans-to the bills, however fraudulent the conduct of the agent;[c] and if A.
fer.
[113] deposit bills indorsed in blank with B., his banker, to be received when
due, and the latter raise money upon them by pledging them with C., another banker, and afterwards become bankrupt, A. cannot maintain trover
against C. for the bills;[d] and the same doctrine extends to navy bills,[e]
and exchequer bills;[f] and though in general a factor cannot *pledge*

[c] Bolton *v.* Puller, 1 Bos. & Pul. 539.
Forbes and Gregory, traders in London,
were also partners in the house of Caldwell and Co. in Liverpool; Bolton dealt
with Caldwell and Co., and they prevailed
with the house in London to let him make
his bills payable there; Bolton kept no
account but with the house in Liverpool,
and they kept the account with the house
in London, and the payments on Bolton's
bills, when made, were carried by the
house in London to their account with
the house in Liverpool, and by the house
in Liverpool, to *their* account with Bolton.
In February, 1793, he accepted bills payable at the house in London, to the
amount of 19,702*l.*, and to enable the
Liverpool house to provide for their payment, he indorsed to them, (amongst
other bills) a bill for 4000*l.*, and another
for 396*l.*; these two bills they remitted
generally with many others to Forbes and
Gregory, to whom they were considerably
indebted, but before the latter bill arrived, both houses became bankrupt. The
acceptances were payable before the indorsed bills; Bolton was obliged to pay
all his own acceptances, and the assignees
of Forbes and Gregory having refused to
deliver up these bills, he brought trover
for them. A special verdict was found,
and after two arguments, the court were
unanimously of opinion, that the assignees
were entitled to keep the bills; they admitted, that as Forbes and Gregory were
partners in the Liverpool house, they
were to be considered as privy to the fact
that the bills had been indorsed to that
house, to enable it to provide for Bolton's
acceptances; but they held, that the application which had been made of these
bills, was the very thing which Bolton intended, and that therefore the privity of
the London house, in the agreement made
between him and the house at Liverpool,
could have no effect on the transaction
which, *as between the two houses had undoubtedly changed the property in the bills,*
that for the purposes of providing for
Bolton's acceptances, the house at Liverpool was entitled to deal with the acceptances as it thought fit, and they had therefore a right to remit them to Forbes and
Gregory; and as they were indebted to
Forbes and Gregory, in more than the
amount, the assignees of Forbes and Gregory were entitled to keep them. Judgment
for the defendants. Ramsbottom *v.* Cater,
1 Stark. 228. See also Payley on Prin. and
Ag. 154, 5.

[d] Collins *v.* Martin, 1 Bos. & Pul. 648.
2 Esp. 520. S. C.; cited and approved of in
Treuttel *v.* Barandon, 8 Taunt. 100. Wookey *v.* Pole, 4 B. & A. 1. The plaintiffs
sent bills indorsed in blank to Messrs.
Nightingales, to receive the money upon
them; they borrowed money of the defendants, and pledged these bills as a security;
they afterwards became bankrupt, and the
plaintiff brought trover for the bills, there
being no evidence that the defendants
knew under what circumstances the bills
had been left with Messrs. N., or how the
plaintiff's account (he being in cash) stood
with them. Eyre, C. J. thought the action
would not lie, and nonsuited the plaintiff.
On a rule *nisi* to set aside the nonsuit, it
was urged, that though the Messrs. N. might
have negotiated the bills, they could not
pledge them; but after consideration, the
court was unanimous, that they had the
power of binding the plaintiff as well by
pledging as negotiating the bills, of which
they were enabled to hold themselves out
to the world as the absolute owners.
See also Bolton *v.* Puller, 1 Bos. & Pul.
546, in which Eyre, C. J. said, "It is
clear, that if indorsed bills are deposited
with a banker, and they are by him negotiated to a third person, though the
purpose for which they were deposited
should be ever so cruelly disappointed,
the original owner can have no claim to
recover them in trover, against such third
person."
Ex parte Pease and another, in the matter of Boldero and Co. 1 Rose, 238, in
which the Lord Chancellor states the law
to the same effect. See also Payley on
Prin. and Ag. 154, 5.
[e] Goldsmyd and another *v.* Gaden and
another, in Chan. 13th June, 1796, cited
in Collins *v.* Martin, 1 Bos. & Pul. 649.
The plaintiffs, who were brokers, advanced money on three navy bills, and a
deposit of scrip, and though it afterwards
appeared, that both navy bills and scrip
were left by the defendant in the hands of
the party depositing for a particular purpose, and were not his property, but the
property of the defendants; yet, on a bill
filed in equity, it was referred to the Master, to take an account of what was due to
the plaintiffs, and an issue at law was refused by the Chancellor, who thought the
question too clear to be disputed. See also
as to navy bills, Jones *v.* Ryde, 1 Marsh.
157.
[f] Wookey *v.* Pole and others, 4 B. & A.
1.; and see Clayton's case, 1 Meriv. 572 to

the goods of his principal,[g] it is otherwise in the case of a bill. How- **II.** *Who*
ever, it has been decided, that trover lies for bills of exchange indorsed *may trans-*
to an agent for the plaintiffs " for their account," and deposited by him *fer.*
with the defendant, as a security for past and future advances made to
him by the defendants.[h](147)

The fraudulent misapplication by bankers, brokers, and other agents, [114]
in pledging and misapplying the bills and other negotiable securities of
their employers, not being cognizable by the criminal law,[i] the statute
52 Geo. 3. c. 63, was passed to prevent such embezzlement, by which
it is enacted, " That if any person, with whom as banker, merchant,
broker, attorney, or agent, of any description whatsoever, with whom
any ordnance, debenture, exchequer, navy, victualling, or transport bill,
or *other bill*, warrant, or *order for the payment of money*, state lottery
ticket, or certificate, seaman's ticket, bank receipt for payment of any
loan, India bond, or other bond, or any deed, *note*, or other security for
money, or for any share or interest in any national stock or fund, of this
or any other country, or in the stock or fund of any corporation, company,
or society, established by act of parliament or royal charter, or any power
of attorney, for the sale or transfer of any such stock or fund, or any
share or interest therein, or any plate, jewels, or other personal effects
shall have been deposited, or shall be or remain for safe custody, or upon
or for any special purpose, without any authority, either general, special, conditional, or discretionary, to sell, pledge, or transfer such debenture, &c. shall sell, negotiate, transfer, assign, pledge, embezzle,
secrete, or in any manner apply to his own use or benefit, any such
debenture, &c. in violation of good faith, and contrary to the special
purpose for which the things hereinbefore-mentioned, or any or either of
them shall have been deposited, or shall have been or remained with, or
in the hands of such person, with intent to defraud the owner of any
such instrument or security, or the person depositing the same, or the
owner of the stock or fund, share or interest to which such security or
power of attorney shall relate, he shall be deemed guilty of a misdemeanor, and punished with transportation, for any term, not exceeding fourteen years, or undergo any other punishment, as the court in misdemeanors
in general have discretion to inflict."[k]

Where a bill or note has been made payable to, or indorsed to a *feme
sole* who afterwards *marries*, or where it is made during the coverture,
the right of transfer vests in her husband, he being by the marriage
entitled to all her personal property,[l] and he thereby becomes virtually

585, from which it also appears, that if one
of several partners, bankers, improperly
dispose of such bills, the firm will be liable
for the amount.
  [g] Newnome v. Thornton, 6 East, 21; but
see Roberts v. Eden, 1 Bos. & Pul. 398.
This is now clearly settled in Martin v.
Coles, 1 M. & S. 140, and Solly v. Rathbone, 2 M. & S. 298. Guichard v. Morgan,
4 Moore, 36. See the distinctions in Payley
on Prin. and Ag. 154, 5.
  [h] Treuttel v. Barandon, 8 Taunt. 100.
  [i] Walsh's case, 4 Taunt. 258. 284.—

2 Leach, 1054. S. C.; see also Clayton's
case, 1 Meriv. 579.
  [k] See this statute, post, Appendix.—3
Chitty on Crim. Law, 922, 3. and 985, 6.
  [l] Ante, 19. Conner v. Martin, 1 Stra.
516. Sel. Ca. 96. S. C. Rawlinson v.
Stone, 3 Wils. 5. Miles v. Williams, 10
Mod 245. Hatchett v. Baddely, 2 Bla.
Rep. 1081. Caudell v. Shaw, 4 T. R. 361.
Lavie v. Phillips, 3 Bur. 1776.
  Conner v. Martin, 1 Stra. 516. cited
3 Wils. 5. A bill was made payable to
Susan Conner or order, while she was sole.

(147) See *Putnam* v. *Sullivan*, 4 Mass. Rep. 46.

II. *Who* indorsee, so that he may sue thereon in his own name, without alleging *may trans-* or proving any indorsement. * If a bill or note be made payable to a *feme covert*, it is in legal operation payable to the husband, and an effectual indorsement must in general be in his name. * But we have seen, that if the husband permit his wife to act as his agent, or to carry on a trade as a *feme sole*, his authority to indorse may be presumed; and if a promissory note is made payable to a married woman, and she indorse it for value in her own name; and the maker afterwards promises to pay it, in an action against him by the indorsee it will be presumed that the nominal payee had authority from her husband to indorse the note in that form, and the indorsement will be considered as vesting a legal title to the note in the plaintiff. *

If a man become a *bankrupt*, all his property in which he is *beneficially* interested, is vested by the assignment of the commissioners in the assignees, by relation to the act of bankruptcy, so as to defeat all intermediate acts done by him to dispose of his property, and consequently the right of transfer of a bill or note, is in general vested in them from the time of the act of bankruptcy;*(1) and the defect of title in the indorsee may be taken advantage of under the plea of non-assumpsi.;* and after a secret act of bankruptcy committed by one of two co-partners, he cannot by an indorsement in the name of the firm, transfer negotiable securities which existed before the act of bankruptcy, unless under the circumstances presently mentioned;* and it has been doubted, whether the solvent partner can in such case, without the concurrence of the assignees of the bankrupt, indorse the bill;* and at least a de-

She married, and during her coverture indorsed it to the plaintiff, and upon demurrer and argument, the court of Common Pleas held, that the *feme covert* could not assign the note, became by the marriage, it became the sole property of her husband.

Miles *v.* Williams, 10 Mod. 245. Per Parker, C. J. If a note be payable to a *feme sole* or order, and she marries, her husband is the proper person to indorse it.

ᵐ M'Neilayge *v.* Holloway, 1 B. & A. 218. Arnold *v.* Revolt, 1 Brod. & B. 446.

ⁿ Barlow *v.* Bishop, 1 East, 432. 3 Esp. Rep. 266. S. C. Ante, 19, n.; or he may declare on it as payable to himself. Per Richardson, J. in Arnold *v.* Revolt, 1 Brod. & B. 446.

° Coates *v.* Davis, 1 Campb. 485. Ante, 19, note.

ᵖ Pinkerton *v.* Marshall, 2 Hen. Bla. 335. Thomason *v.* Frere, 10 East, 418. Ramsbottom *v.* Lewis, 1 Camp. 279.— Ante, 35, and notes.

ᑫ Pinkerton *v.* Adams, 2 Esp. Rep. 611, admitted in Arden *v.* Watkins, 3 East, 322.

ʳ Ante, 35. Thomason *v.* Frere, 10 East, 418.

ˢ Abel *v.* Sutton, 3 Esp. 107, 8. Ramsbottom *v.* Lewis, 1 Campb. 299. Ramsbottom *v.* Cator, 1 Stark. 288. From Abel *v.* Sutton, it should seem, that after the act of bankruptcy of one of several partners, and the commission issued against him, the property in a bill can only be transferred by the respective indorsements of the assignees, and the solvent partner. Lord Kenyon there says, If a fair bill existed at the time of the partnership, but is not put into circulation till after the dissolution, all the partners must join to make it negotiable; the moment the partnership ceases, the partners are tenants in common of the partnership property undisposed of from that period; and if they send any securities which belonged to the partnership, into the world after such dissolution, all must join in doing so. See observations. 1 Campb. 281. n. (b.)

In Ramsbottom *v.* Lewis, 1 Camb. 289, the declaration stated, that both partners drew and indorsed the bill, although one of the partners was then a bankrupt, and Lord Ellenborough held, that under such declaration, the indorsee could not recover. His Lordship said the declaration states that both parties drew and indorsed the bill, but upon this last supposition at the time of the indorsement, one

(1) But if the assignees do not interfere, an uncertificated bankrupt to whom a note is made payable, may indorse it so as to enable the indorsee to recover. *Drayton* v. *Dale*, 2 Barn. & Cressw. 293, 9 Serg. & Lowb. ab. 91.

c'aration upon such an indorsement, should not state that the bankrupt joined in the indorsement.[t] But it has been adjudged, that if a trader deliver a bill for a valuable consideration to another, previously to an act of bankruptcy, and forget to indorse, he may indorse it after his bankruptcy;[u] and if he and his assignees refuse, they may be compelled to do so by petition to the Chancellor, who will, in such case, order the costs of the petition to be paid out of the estate of the bankrupt.[x] And as in general property, in which a bankrupt has no beneficial interest, does not pass to his assignees under the assignment, therefore where a bill has been accepted by another for his accommodation, he may, after an act of bankruptcy, indorse it, so as to convey a right of action thereon to a third person, against the accommodation acceptor.[y] (151) But if there were an exchange of acceptances or securities between the bankrupt and the accommodation acceptor, then the bill would be considered as accepted for value, and the indorsement after the act of bankruptcy would be invalid.[z] And where a trader having securities in

II. *Who may transfer.*

[117]

partner had no longer any interest in it, and was incapable of exercising any act of ownership over it; the partnership had in fact then ceased to exist, and the solvent partner was to be considered as tenant in common of the bill along with the assignees of the other. However, in general, a transfer of partnership property made by the solvent member of a firm, after an act of bankruptcy committed by his partner, cannot be invalidated. 12 Mod. 246. Fox v. Hanbury, Cowp. 448. Smith v. Oriel, 1 East, 369. Smith v. Stokes, 1 East, 364. 1 Mont. on Part. 154.

[t] Ramsbottom v. Lewis, 1 Campb. 279. 281, note, supra.

[u] Smith v. Pickering, Peake's Cases, 50. Anon. 1 Campb. 492. Rolleston v. Herbert, 3 T. R. 411; and see also 1 Rose, 14, note (a.)

Smith v. Pickering, Peake's Cases, 50. Richardson and Hill drew a bill upon the defendant, payable to their own order, which the defendant accepted; the drawers delivered this bill to the plaintiffs for a valuable consideration, but forgot to indorse it; they afterwards became bankrupts, and then indorsed it. The plaintiffs, as indorsees, now sued the defendant as acceptor; Lord Kenyon was clearly of opinion that the indorsement was good, and the plaintiffs had a verdict.

Anon. 1 Campb. 492, in notes. The bill was delivered to the indorsee, with the intent of transferring the property in it to him more than two months before the commission, but the indorsement was not

in effect written upon it till within two months. Lord Ellenborough held, that the writing of the indorsement had reference to the delivery of the bill, and that the case was clearly within the statute.

[x] Ex parte Greening, 13 Ves. 206. Cullen, 190; but see Ex parte Hall, 1 Rose, 13, 14.

[y] Arden v. Watkins, 3 East, 317. Wallace v Harkacre, 1 Campb. 46 and 47; and Ramsbottom v. Cater, 1 Stark. 288.

Arden v. Watkins, 3 East, 317. On the 5th October, 1801, Lewis Jones committed an act of bankruptcy, on which a commission issued on the 31st December, 1801. On the 4th December, 1801, he drew a bill on Watkins for 100l. payable to his own order, and indorsed it to the plaintiff, who paid him full value; Watkins owed Jones nothing, but accepted the bill to enable him to raise money upon it, and Jones deposited a lease with him, as an indemnity; the assignees insisted upon a restoration of the lease, and Watkins refused to pay the bill; action on the bill and reference. The arbitrator awarded against Watkins, but stated the facts specially to enable him to take the opinion of the court. After a rule *nisi*, to set aside the award, cause shown, and time taken to consider the court were clear that the defendant was liable; that as Jones has no effects in Watkins's hands, no right to indorse devolved upon the assignees, and therefore his indorsement was effectual, and transferred the property to the plaintiff. Rule discharged.

[z] 1 Campb. 179, in notes. Buckler v. Buttivant, 3 East, 72.

---

(151) The payee of a negotiable note, holding it in trust for another person, may by indorsement convey the note for the benefit of the *cestui que trust*, notwithstanding his bankruptcy. *Wilson* v. *Codman*, 3 Cranch, 193.

A transfer of a note by a debtor to his creditor in contemplation of bankruptcy, as collateral security for the payment of the debt, is void as a fraud upon the bankrupt law. *Locke* v. *Winning*, 3 Mass. Rep. 325.

II. *Who may transfer.* his banker's hands to a certain amount, after a secret act of bankruptcy, drew on them a bill for a larger amount for his accommodation, payable to his own order, which, after acceptance, he indorsed to the plaintiff, (who knew of his partial insolvency, but not of the act of bankruptcy) and a commission of bankrupt having been afterwards taken out, it was held that the plaintiff, who was to make title through the bankrupt's indorsement, after his bankruptcy, though he were entitled to sue the acceptors upon the bill, yet could only recover on it the amount of the sum accepted for the accommodation of the bankrupt, over and above the amount of the bankrupt's effects in the hands of the acceptors at the time of the bankruptcy; for which latter amount alone they were liable to account.[a]

This rule of law invalidating transfers by a bankrupt after a secret act of bankruptcy, having been found extremely inconvenient to commerce, it was enacted by the 19 Geo. 2. c. 32, " That no person who is or shall be really and *bona fide* a creditor of any bankrupt, or for or in respect of *goods* really and *bona fide sold* to such bankrupt, or for or in respect of any bill or *bills of exchange*, really and *bona fide* drawn, negotiated, or accepted, by such bankrupt, *in the usual or ordinary course of trade and dealing*, shall be liable to *refund or repay* to the assignee or assignees of such bankrupt's estate, any *money* which, *before the suing forth of such commission*, was really and *bona fide*, and in the *usual and ordinary course of trade and dealing*, received by such person of any such bankrupt, before such time as the person receiving the same shall know, understand, or have notice, that he is become a bankrupt, or that he is in insolvent circumstances."

It does not appear to be settled, whether promissory notes are within this statute.[b] The act only protects *payments* of two descriptions of debts, viz. for *goods sold, and bills of exchange;* and it also requires, that this payment shall be made in the *usual and ordinary* course of trade.[c] With respect to the term " payment," it has been decided,

[118]

[a] Willis v. Freeman, and another, 12 East, 656. In an action by the indorsee, of the drawer of a bill against the acceptor, a verdict was found for the plaintiff, subject to the opinion of the court, upon a case, stating that Anderson, the drawer, being indebted to the plaintiff in more than 2000l., and being insolvent, proposed to pay the plaintiff a composition of 15s. 6d. in the pound, together with the costs of an action which had been brought by the plaintiff against him, by a bill upon the defendants. This proposal being acceded to, Anderson applied to the defendants to accept a bill for 1400l. *for his accommodation.* The defendants accepted the bill, drawn on the 5th of July, and payable on the 10th November, 1809, having in their hands effects of Anderson, to the amount of 888l. 16s. 8d. Anderson, had committed a secret act of bankruptcy on the 7th of March; 1809, upon which a commission issued on the 25th of July. The court of King's Bench held, that to the extent of 888l. 16s. 8d. the defendants had a right to resist payment, on the ground of their being answerable for that amount to the assignees, to whom these funds devolved upon the act of bankruptcy; and that therefore the indorsement by Anderson to that extent, was inoperative; but as to the surplus (511l. 3s. 8d.) for which the acceptance was accommodation, the case of Arden v. Watkins was in point, to show that the indorsement was valid. And they held that the law in this respect had not been altered by the 49 Geo. 3. c. 121. s. 8. And they therefore ordered the verdict to be entered for this reduced sum of 571l. 3s. 4d.

[b] See Harwood v. Lomas, 11 East, 127.

[c] Pinkerton v. Marshall, 2 Hen. Bla. 334. Southey v. Butler, 3 Bos. & Pul. 287. Vernon v. Hall, 2 T. R. 648. Harwood v. Lomas, 11 East, 127. Bayly v. Schofield, 1 M. & S. 338.

Pinkerton v. Marshall, 2 Hen. Bla. 334. A. having recovered a verdict for a certain sum of money against B., B. commits an act of bankruptcy; afterwards A. having had no notice of the bankruptcy, gives time to B., and instead of entering up judgment and suing out execution, takes a

that if a trader, after he has committed a secret act of bankruptcy, indorse a bill of exchange to a creditor, who received the money due
upon the bill, before a commission issues against the trader, such payment is protected by this statute.[d] And if a bill of exchange were
indorsed by a trader after a secret act of bankruptcy, in payment of a
debt for *goods sold*, it should seem that such transfer would be valid

bill drawn by B. on C. at a distant period,
for the amount of the sum recovered. This
is not a payment protected by the stat. 19
Geo. 2. c. 32. A. therefore is liable to refund the money received on the bill to the
assignees of B.

Southey *v.* Butler, 3 Bos. & Pul. 287.
A. trader, subsequent to an act of bankruptcy, being arrested and detained in
prison at the suit of several creditors,
sent for all his creditors but one, and
paid their debts in full ; but no other circumstance occurred from which it could
be presumed that they knew of his bankruptcy or insolvency. Held, that such
payments were not protected by the stat.
19 Geo. 2. c. 32.

Vernon and another *v.* Hall, 2 T. R. 648.
If the payee of a bill of exchange, received from a third person as the price of
an estate, give time to the drawee, on
condition that he shall allow interest,
and afterwards the drawee discharge the
bill, having in the mean time committed
an act of bankruptcy, this is not such a
payment in the ordinary course of trade
as is protected by the 19 Geo. 2. c. 32, and
the assignees may recover the money from
the payee.

Harwood and another *v.* Lomas, 11 East,
127. Odell being indebted to the defendant in 400l., gave him, in August, 1805,
his note for that sum, payable at twelve
months, with interest half-yearly.   Part
only of the money being paid, the defendant, in 1806, arrested Odell for the residue ; and in Hilary Term, 1807, obtained
judgment, which was affirmed on error
the 5th of February, 1808 ; and the next
day of (the 6th of February) Odell paid the
amount of the damage, interest, and costs.
Odell had committed an act of bankruptcy
on the 27th of January, 1808, on which a
commission issued, dated the 19th of February, 1808. In an action by his assignees
to recover this money, the only question
was, whether the payment by the bankrupt was protected by the 19 Geo. 2. c. 32.
The court inclined to think that it was incumbent on the party receiving the money,
to show that the payment was protected
by the statute: but it being admitted that
the note had been given for the balance of
an account stated, consisting (*inter alia*)
of money lent to the bankrupt, the court,
without expressing any opinion as to whether the statute could be construed to extend to notes, held, that this note could
not be said to have been given in the ordinary course of trade and dealing. Postea
to the plaintiffs.

Bayly and others, assignees of Luckraft, bankrupt, against Schofield and another, 1 M. & S. 338. It was held, that
a creditor of the bankrupt, who had sued
out a writ against him, and, without proceeding upon it, afterwards received from
him a bill of exchange in part payment of
his debt, after being apprized that there
had been a meeting of his creditors, and
that the bankrupt's affairs at that time
were only capable of paying the demands
of his creditor by instalments, although
he was assured by the bankrupt's agent,
that they would come round, was liable
to refund the proceeds of such bill to the
assignees of the bankrupt, as a payment
not in the usual course of trade and before notice of his insolvency ; and per
Lord Ellenborough, "the next question
and most important one is, whether the
payment by Luckraft was a payment *bona
fide*, and in the usual and ordinary course
of trade, within the 19 Geo. 2, before such
time as the defendants had notice that he
was become bankrupt, or was in insolvent
circumstances. It may be admitted that
they did not know that he was a bankrupt;
but how does the case stand with respect
to their knowledge of his being in insolvent
circumstances. By insolvent circumstances,
is meant that a person is not in a condition
to pay his debts in the ordinary course, as
persons carrying on trade usually do. Looking at the letter of the 11th of October,
which enclosed the bill, it emphatically
shows him to have been in insolvent circumstances; it speaks of his being unable
to muster a sufficient sum, and of his having
been obliged to pay every one a little as it
came to hand, can that payment then be
said to be in the ordinary course when a
man confesses he is obliged to pay by minute portions to each of his creditors; it is
more like a distribution under a deed of
composition than a payment by a trader
appearing openly at his counter? I should
say, this was not the mode in which a solvent man proceeds."

See the cases upon this part of the provision in the act, 1 Mont. 313, &c.

[d] Hawkins *v.* Penfold, 2 Ves. sen. 550.
Per Lord Chancellor. There is no difference between an actual payment of money
in satisfaction of a debt and indorsing bills
of exchange, provided the money was received on them before the commission of
bankruptcy issued, for I should take that
only as a medium of payment and no more;
and otherwise it would be very hard. See
also 1 Mont. 311, n. h.

II. *Who* with reference to the construction on the stat. 1 Jac. 1. c. 15. s. 14.
may trans-although the bill be not paid until after the issuing of the commission,
fer. because the indorsement of a bill of exchange is deemed *a payment* in
satisfaction, provided the bill be paid when due ;[e] and therefore it
should seem, that although in general a partner who has committed a
secret act of bankruptcy, cannot indorse a bill so as to affect the firm,[f]
yet if he were *bona fide*, and in the ordinary course of trade to indorse
[120] the bill in payment of a debt for goods sold, such indorsement would
be valid under this statute.

It has been recently decided, that the term *insolvent circumstances*,
means that a person is not in condition to pay his debts, in the ordinary
course, as persons carrying on trade usually do, for the object of the
statute was to protect those persons only who receive money under circumstances not calculated to raise suspicion ; but if any such circumstances occur, then they receive the money or bills at their peril, and
are liable to refund ; as where a bankrupt, before his transfer of bills,
proposed to pay his creditors by instalments.[g] But the insolvency
mentioned in this and the stat. 46 Geo. 3. c. 135, means *a general* inability in the bankrupt to answer his engagements, and which is not to
be inferred merely from his renewing bills of exchange in a particular
instance.[h]

The 46 Geo. 3. c. 135. s. 1, contains a provision, giving effect to *all
payments and contracts bona fide* entered into with the bankrupt, more

[e] Wilkins *v.* Casey, 7 T. R. 711. A factor was indebted to his principal in 228*l.*
18*s.*, the principal committed an act of
bankruptcy, and drew on his factor for
222*l.* 18*s.*, the factor did not know of the
act of bankruptcy, and accepted the bills;
before they came due a commission issued,
notwithstanding which the factor paid
them; then the assignees sued the factor
for 222*l.* 18*s.*, and on a case reserved, insisted that though the stat. (1 Jac. 1. c. 15.)
would protect a *payment* before notice of
bankruptcy, it would not a mere acceptance. *Sed per* Lord Kenyon, C. J, the
statute ought to receive a liberal construction: giving goods in exchange would have
been a payment, though not in money, and
so is giving an acceptance, if the bill be
paid when due. The other Judges concurred, and the defendant received judgment.

It appears from the case of Bayly *v.*
Schofield, 1 M. & S. 338, and ante, 118,
note, that as the bill was given in payment
for goods sold, the party might have retained the amount, although the transfer of the
bill was made to him after the act of bankruptcy, if such transfer had been made in
the ordinary course of trade and dealing.
[f] Ante, 85. 115. In Thomason *v.* Frere,
10 East, 418, and in Willis *v.* Freeman,
12 East, 656, the bills were not indorsed
for *goods sold*, and in the last case Lord
Ellenborough expressly alluded to the exceptions introduced by the statutes.

[g] Per Lord Ellenborough, Le Blanc, J.
and Bayley, J. in Bayly *v.* Schofield, 1 M.

& S. 350. 353, 354. See this case, ante,
118, note.
[h] Anon. 4 Campb. 492. in notes. Sittings
in Trin. Vac. 1808. Plaintiff declared as
indorsee of a bill of exchange drawn by
J. S., payable to his own order; the defence was, that J. S. had committed an
act of bankruptcy before the indorsement;
in answer to this the plaintiff relied upon
Sir Samuel Romilly's act, 46 Geo. 3. c.
135, whereby it is enacted, "that all contracts and transactions by and with any
bankrupt *bona fide*, made or entered into
more than two calendar months before
the date of the commission shall, notwithstanding any prior act of bankruptcy committed by such bankruptcy committed by
such bankrupt, be good, provided the person so dealing with such bankrupt, had not
at the time notice of any prior act of bankruptcy having been committed by such
bankrupt, or that he was insolvent, or had
stopped payment." It was contended on
the part of the defendant, that the plaintiff,
at the time when the indorsement was
made, had notice that J. S. was insolvent.
The fact was, that before then J. S. had
renewed his bills with the plaintiff, and
that the bill in question was given in exchange for others which J. S. could not satisfy when due. But Lord Ellenborough
held, that the insolvency mentioned in the
statute, must mean a *general* inability in
the bankrupt to answer his engagements,
which was not to be inferred from his renewing bills of exchange in a particular instance; and the plaintiff had a verdict. See
ante, 118, 119, in notes.

than *two calendar months* before the date of the commission, though made after a secret act of bankruptcy, provided the party had not notice of the prior act of bankruptcy, or that the bankrupt was insolvent or had stopped payment. Under this statute it is clear, that any indorsement or transfer of a bill or note, made after a secret act of bankruptcy, upwards of two months before the date of the commission, will be valid, provided the party in whose favour it were made had no notice of such act of bankruptcy or general insolvency.

If a bill be indorsed by a bankrupt to a particular creditor, by way of *fraudulent preference*, even before an act of bankruptcy, it will be invalid. The rule upon this subject is, that if the preference is not the mere voluntary act of the party, but only consequential, as it is called, as where the act is done in the ordinary course of business, and upon the application of the creditor, or in pursuance of some prior agreement, which was not made in contemplation of bankruptcy, or were done to deliver the party from legal process, or from the threat and apprehension of it, or even from the pressure or importunity of the creditor, then it will not be void, though made the very moment before an act of bankruptcy committed. And where the preference is consequential merely, the creditor's or bankrupt's own knowledge or apprehension of his insolvency, is immaterial, that being frequently the very reason of the creditor's taking such measures against the bankrupt as are precisely the ground of justifying the act done by the bankrupt, in consequence of it.[i] A trader cannot, in contemplation of bankruptcy, indorse a bill or note to his creditor, of his own accord, and without any application. But it is not sufficient to avoid the transaction, that the indorsement was made voluntarily, and that an act of bankruptcy ensues, it must also appear that he had the act of bankruptcy in contemplation at the time when the indorsement was made. Nor has it ever been held, that if a creditor press for payment of his debt, and thereby obtain a transfer of a bill or note to him, that the intention of the bankrupt shall be called in aid to set it aside. If it were transferred through the urgency of the demand, or through the fear of prosecution, whatever may have been in the contemplation of the bankrupt, this will not vitiate the proceeding. Nor will the transaction, if *bona fide*, and not colourable, be impeached by the secrecy adopted in the transaction by the trader, to save his own credit in the view of the world.[k] And where a trader, in contemplation of bankruptcy, and without solicitation, put three checks into the hands of his clerk, to be delivered to a creditor at the counting-house of the latter, but before they were delivered, the creditor called at the trader's, and demanded payment of his debt, upon which the checks were delivered to him, it was held that the intention to give a voluntary preference not being consummated, the delivery of the checks was valid.[l]

So where a creditor obtained a preference in contemplation of an intended deed of composition, and which preference would have been void as against the creditors under that deed, yet as the composition went off, it was decided, that the creditor might hold his securities against the assignees under a commission of bankrupt subsequently issued, but not contemplated at the time of the preference.[m]

[121]

[i] See the rule and cases upon this subject in Smith v. Payne, 6 T. R. 152.—Hartshorn v. Slodder, 2 Bos. & Pul. 589. Crosby v. Crouch, 11 East, 256. Cullen, 280, 1.

[k] Crosby v. Crouch, 11 East, 256.
[l] Bayley v. Ballard, 1 Campb. 416.
[m] Wheelright v. Jackson, 5 Taunt. 109. 633. S. C.

II. *Who may transfer.* So there are cases in which a trader in insolvent circumstances may return bills of exchange to the party from whom he has received them[a] though they would otherwise become the property of his assignees.[a]

If a promissory note be given to an uncertificated bankrupt, *after the commission issued,* and the assignees require the maker to pay them, the right to the note is thereby vested in the assignees, and an action cannot be supported by the bankrupt,[o] unless indeed he acquired the note in respect of a contract made in his favour by the assignees or with their concurrence.[p]

In case of the bankruptcy of a banker, bills deposited with him as agent, to obtain payment, do not pass to the assignees, unless the banker has discounted them, or advanced money upon the credit of them, in which case the assignees acquire the entire property in them if discounted, or have a lien on them *pro tanto* in case of a partial advance.[q] But the effect of bankruptcy upon the property in bills, in the hands of the trader, will be more fully considered in the chapter relating to bankruptcy.

On the *death* of the holder, the right of transfer is vested in his *executor* or *administrator.*[r] (1) If thee xecutor or administrator indorse [123] the bill or note, without qualification, he would be personally liable in

[a] Graff and others, assignees, &c. v. Greffulke, 1 Campb. 89. If a trader, on receiving bills of exchange from one of his creditors abroad, to whom he is indebted beyond the amount of them, after becoming insolvent, but before commiting an act of bankruptcy deliver these bills with the consent of his other creditors, to an agent of the person who had remitted them for the use of the latter, if he should be ultimately entitled to them; this is a legal and valid transaction, and if a commission of bankruptcy afterwards issue against the trader, his assignees cannot maintain an action against the trustee to recover the produce of the bills. Gladstone v. Hadwen, 1 M. & S. 517. Where S. obtained bills of exchange from the defendant upon a fraudulent representation, that a security given by him to the defendant (which was void) was an ample security, and on the next day, having resolved to stop payment, informed the defendant that he had repented of what he had done, and had sent express to stop the bills and would return them, and three days afterwards committed an act of bankruptcy, after which he returned to the defendant all the bills, (except one which had been discounted) and also two bank notes, part of the proceeds of such discount; and the defendant delivered back the security, and afterwards a commission of bankruptcy issued against S., and the assignees under such commission brought trover against the defendant for the bills and bank notes. Held, that the defendant was entitled to retain them.

[o] Kitchen v. Bartsch, 7 East 53.—Smith's Rep. 58. S. C.

[p] Coles v. Barrow, 4 Taunt. 754. Holt C. N. P. 174.

[q] Per Lord Ellenborough, in Giles v. Perkins, 9 East, 14. Carstairs v. Bates, 3 Campb. 301; and see Parr v. Eliason, 1 East, 544, and cases there cited; and see 1 Bos. & Pul. 83, n. a; and see 1 Mont. 354, 5, &c. Ex parte Waring and others, 19 Ves. 345.

[r] Rawlinson v. Stone, 3 Wils. 1. 2 Stra. 1260. Barnes, 164. S. C. A note was payable to A. B. or order; A. B. died intestate, and his administrator indorsed it to the plaintiff. These facts appearing upon the declaration, the defendant demurred, and contended that the personal representative of the payee had no power to indorse a note, but the court of Common Pleas, after three arguments, and the Court of King's Bench, upon error brought, were unanimously of opinion that he had, and each court said it was every day's practice, and the constant usage for executors and administrators to indorse bills and notes payable to the order of their testators or intestates.

(1) If an administrator to whom a bill of exchange, indorsed generally, is delivered for debt due to the intestate, die after it is due, and before it is paid, the administrator de bonis non of such intestate has the right to sue on it. *Catherwood* v. *Chabaud*, 1 Barn. & Cress. 150.

case the bill should be dishonoured.[s] Executors are not personally II. *Who may transfer.* liable in case of the failure of a banker, in whose hands they have deposited bills, part of the estate.[t] (159)

If a bill has been made or transferred to several persons not in *partnership*, the right of transfer is in all collectively, and not in any individually;[u] but where several persons are in partnership, the transfer may be made by the indorsement of one partner only, in which case the transfer is considered as made by all the persons entitled to make it.[x] (159) And it has been held, that though such persons may not be in partnership, and only one has indorsed, yet that if the drawee accepted after the indorsement, he cannot dispute the regularity of the latter.[y] In general we have seen that one partner may, without the express concurrence of the other parties, make a valid transfer of a bill, even in fraud of his co-partners.[z] In the case of a bill payable to A. *for the use of* B., the right of transfer is only in A. because B. has only an equitable and not a legal interest.[a]

[s] King *v.* Thom, 1 T. R. 487. Gibson *v.* Minet, 1 Hen. Bla. 622. Bayl. 62. The court held, that upon a bill payable to several as executors, they might sue as executors; and per Buller, J. no inconvenience can arise from their indorsing the bill; for if they indorse, they are liable personally, and not as executors; for their indorsement would not give an action against the effects of the testator.

[t] Rowth *v.* Howell, 3 Ves. 565, 6. Ante, 25, 28.

[u] Bayl. 55. Carvick *v.* Vickery, Dougl. 653, (n.) ante, 88. and Jones *v.* Radford, 1 Campb. 83. and see Williams *v.* Thomas, 6 Esp. Rep. 18. Ante, 35. Sel. Ni. Pri. 4th ed. 237.

[x] Ante, 33, 4.

[y] Jones and another *v.* Radford, 1 Campb. 83. cited in notes. Indorsee against acceptor of a bill of exchange, payable to two persons. The bill had been indorsed by one in the name of both, and the defendant had accepted it with the indorsement upon it. The defence was, that the payees not being partners, the bill ought to have been indorsed by both. Lord Ellenborough held, that the defendant having accepted the bill so in-

dorsed, could not now dispute the regularity of the indosement. Sed *vide* Smith *v.* Hunter, 1 T. R. 654.

[z] Swann *v.* Steele, 7 East, 210. Ante, 29, n. Ridley *v.* Taylor, 13 East, 175. Ante, 33. n.

[a] Evans *v.* Cramlington, Carth. 5. 2 Vent. 307, Skin. 264. Company of Felt-makers *v.* Dovis, 1 Bos. & Pul. 101. note c. Smith *v.* Kendall, 6 T. R. 124. Selw. Ni. Pri. 4th ed. 337. A bill was payable " to Price or order, for the use of Calvert." Price indorsed it to Evans, after which an extent issued against Calvert, and the money due upon it was seized to the use of the king. These facts appearing upon the pleadings, two points were make upon demurrer; the one whether Calvert had such an interest in the money as might be extended, the other whether Price had power to indorse the bill, or whether he had only a bare authority to receive the money for the use of Calvert; and the Court of King's Bench, and afterwards the Exchequer Chamber, held that Calvert had not such an interest as could be extended, and that Price had power to indorse the bill, and judgment was given for the plaintiff.

---

(159) If a negotiable note be made payable to two executors as such, it cannot be transferred by the indorsement of one of them; both must indorse the note to pass the property by assignment. *Smith* v. *Whiting*, 4 Mass. Rep. 334.

(159) One partner may by an indorsement made by himself in the name of the partnership, entitle himself to sue as indorsee upon a negotiable note given to the partnership. *Kirby* v. *Caswell*, 1 Caines, Rep. 305. And an indorsement to a third person of such a note by one partner by writing the name of the firm on the back of the note, is a valid transfer. *Kane* v. *Scofield*, 2 Caines' Rep. 368.

If one of the partners of a firm has been in the habit of indorsing the name of the firm on bills of exchange as security it is a fact from which the jury may legally infer that he had authority from the other partners; and the *bona fide* holder of such bill may recover against all the partners notwithstanding the indorsement of the name of the firm was expressly prohibited in the articles of partnership. *Bank of Kentucky* v. *Brooking*, 2 Litt. 45.

III. The Indorsements of bills are most usually made after acceptance, and
time when before payment; but though the term "transfer," like the term "ac-
a transfer ceptance," supposes a pre-existing bill, a transfer may be made pre-
may be viously to the bill being completed. Thus it has been adjudged, that
made. if a man indorse his name on a blank stamped piece of paper, such an
indorsement will operate as a *carte blanche*, or letter of credit, for an
indefinite sum, consistent with the stamp, and will bind the indorser
for any sum to be paid at any time, which the person to whom he intrusts the instrument chooses to insert in it,[b] (160) and such paper shall
be considered a bill by relation from the time of signing and indorsing.[c]
So when in an action brought by the indorsee of a post-dated bill, drawn
by the defendant and indorsed by the payee before the day on which it
bore date, and the payee died before such date, the defendant contended
that the bill did not acquire the character of a negotiable bill, within
the custom of merchants, till the time it bore date, and that the payee
who indorsed it, having died before that time, such indorsement conveyed no title to the plaintiff, and that the defendant as drawer, was not
liable; upon a special case reserved; the Court of King's Bench were
of opinion, that such indorsement before the date of the bill, was
legal and valid, and notwithstanding such death of the indorser, the
plaintiff was entitled to recover.[d] But there is an express provision in

[b] Russell *v.* Langstaff, Dougl. 514. Newsome *v.* Thornton, 6 East, 21, 22. Collis
v. Emett, 1 Hen. Bla. 313 316. 319. Ante,
24, in notes.
  [c] *Per curiam*, in Snaith *v.* Mingay, 1
M. & S. 87. Crutchley *v.* Clarence, 2 M.
& S. 90. 1 Marsh. 29. and Usher *v.* Dauncey and others, 4 Campb. 98. See these
cases in notes, ante, 54.
  [d] Pasmore *v.* North, 13 East, 517. The
defendant, on the 4th of May, 1810, drew
a bill for 200*l.* on Brook and Co. dated
the 11th of may, 1810, payable to Totty
or order, 65 days after date. On the 5th
of May, Totty indorsed this bill to the
plaintiff for a valuable consideration, and
on the same day died. After the 4th, and
before the 11th of May, the defendant

received effects of Totty's to the amount
of about 130*l.* to answer this bill. On
the 12th of May, the defendant advised
the drawees of the bill having been drawn,
and of Totty's death, and desired them
not to accept or pay the bill. Acceptance
and payment were accordingly refused:
and this action was brought against the
drawer. A verdict was found for the
plaintiff, subject to the opinion of the
Court of King's Bench, on a case reserved. The court after adverting to the
17 Geo. 3. c. 30 as to bills for less than
5*l*, and to the 48 Geo. 3. c. 149. as to post-
dating drafts upon bankers, held clearly
that the plaintiff was entitled to recover
for the whole amount of the bill, and he
had judgment accordingly.

(160) The same doctrine has been asserted in the United States. *Violet* v. *Patton*,
5 Cranch, 142. *Putnam* v. *Sullivan*, 4 Mass. Rep. 45. So where A. made a note
with a blank for the sum, and sent it to the payee, and requested him to fill it up, it
was held that the payee might lawfully fill up the blank and recover upon the note.
Jordan v. *Neilson*, 2 Wash. Rep. 164. See ante, 36.
  A. wrote his name on a blank paper and gave it to B. who made a note on the other
side payable to C. or order, with interest, and signed it as promissor; C. afterwards received part payment of the note from B., and indorsed the amount on the note, and afterwards brought an action on non-payment of the residue against A., and wrote over
his name " in consideration of the subsisting connexion between me and my son-in-law
B., I promise and engage to guarantee the payment of the contents of the within note
on demand." It was held that C. had a right to fill up the indorsement so as to make A.
responsible as a common indorser, or as a guarantor, warrantor or surety, liable in the
first instance, and in all events as a joint and several promissor would be. S. J. Court
of Massachusetts, Prec. Declar. 113 note. S. C. cited 3 Mass. Rep. 275. See and consult *Herrick* v. *Carman*, 12 John. Rep. 159.
  So the holder of a bill of exchange, with several indorsements *in blank*, has a right
to strike out the names of the indorsers subsequent to the first, and to write over the
name of the first indorser an assignment to himself; or the bill without such assignment
will be considered as his property by his having it in his power to make it. *Ritchie &*
Wales v. *Moore*, 5 Munf. Rep. 388.

17 Geo. S. c. 30. s. 1. that bills and notes for the payment of a less III. *Time* sum than five pounds, shall not be indorsed before the date thereof.[e] of transfer.

Although if a bill of exchange, payable at a certain time after date, be presented for acceptance and refused, and the holder thereof neglect to give due notice of such dishonour to the drawer or indorsers, they are discharged from liability to such holder, yet if before the specified time of payment he indorse the bill to a party, ignorant of the laches, for valuable consideration, such indorsee will not be thereby affected, [125] and may enforce payment from the drawer or prior indorsee.[f] But if such indorsee, at the *time he received the bill, knew of the dishonour*, or took the bill after it was due, he will be affected by such laches and will not be entitled to recover.[g] So where the holder of a bill, before

[e] See observations on this statute, in Passmore *v.* North, 13 East, 517.

[f] O'Keefe *v.* Dunn, 1 Marsh, 643. 6 Taunt. 305, S. C. per Gibbs, C. J. Heath and Dallas, Js. dissentiente Chambre, J. The payee of a bill of exchange presented it for acceptance which was refused, but no notice of such dishonour was given to the drawer, and the payee afterwards indorsed over the bill, without notice to the indorsee of such refusal to accept, and the latter again presented the bill for acceptance, which was again refused. Held, that the indorsee might recover on the bill against the drawer, notwithstanding the laches of the payee, by three, against Chambre, J.—Per Gibbs, C. J., he who takes a bill after it has arrived at maturity, takes it subject to all the defences which could have been made by any previous holder, for the bill being unpaid its date is notice to him sufficient to put him on inquiry, but if he takes the bill before it is due, he takes it not subject to the same infirmity of title, because he then takes it without notice of any suspicious circumstances that may break in upon his remedy against any former holder. This is the general law, but there may be circumstances that may make it otherwise. A holder is not bound to present a bill for acceptance, there is nothing therefore on the face of an unaccepted bill to awaken a suspicion that it has been presented for acceptance and refused. But it is said, the general law is, that where notice is requisite, if notice be not given the drawer, and all persons claiming to be entitled to have notice of the dishonour, are discharged. I think that is a begging of the question; if a holder comes to the question that the drawee will not accept, or will not pay the bill when it becomes due, and omits to give notice, he shall never sue the drawer, because his neglect prevents the drawer from using diligence in withdrawing from the drawee the effects which were destined to satisfy the bill. But I am of opinion, that if the bill is passed for a valuable consideration, without notice of that defect of title, he who so in-

nocently takes the bill is not guilty of any breach of duty towards the drawer, and is therefore not affected by the omission ; Roscoe *v.* Hardy, 12 East, 434, is mainly distinguishable from the present case, in respect that the bill there continued up to the time of its maturity in the hands of a holder who had neglected to give that notice at the time when the bill was first refused acceptance ; and the holder, I agree, had thereby, as to his own claim, discharged the drawer, I am of opinion that the circumstance of the bill continuing in the same hand, materially differs that case from the present. I therefore think that the present plaintiff not having had notice that the bill had been presented for acceptance and dishonoured, before she took it is entitled to recover.

[g] Crossly *v.* Ham, 13 East, 498. The defendant, for the accommodation of Clark, indorsed two bills drawn by Clark, in America, upon Dickenson and Co. in London, for 450*l.* each, in favour of the defendant, dated 10th of February, 1804, and payable 60 days after sight ; these bills were paid over by Clark to Parry, in February, 1804. The defendants Perry and Clark, then, and until after the 14th of April, 1808. resided in America. On the 1st of March, Parry indorsed and remitted the bills to his agents in London, with directions to make a payment to the plaintiff, to whom he then and still was indebted. On the 26th April, the bills were presented for acceptance, dishonoured, and protested for non-acceptance, and notice thereof was given to the defendant. The plaintiff having been advised of the remittance by a letter from Parry, dated on the 12th of April, applied to Parry's agent for 450*l.* ; and on the 6th of June they delivered one of the bills to the plaintiff, *apprising him of its dishonour*, and that therefore he took the bill subject to all its infirmities. The bill became due on the 28th of June, and payment being refused, this action was brought. The defendant, however, produced at the trial an instrument signed by Parry, dated 14th April, 1804, by which he agreed that the defen-

III. *Time* it was due, having téndered it for acceptance, which was refused, kept of transfer. it till due, when it was presented for payment and refused, and then returned to an indorser, who not knowing of the laches paid it; it was held that his ignorance of such laches when he paid the bill did not entitle him to recover, either against the drawer or prior indorsers, who had thus been discharged by the laches of the holder.[h]

There is no legal objection to the validity of a transfer of a bill made after the time appointed for the payment of it.[i] In this case it is said, that the indorsement is equivalent to the act of drawing a bill payable at sight.[k] But bills under five pounds cannot be indorsed after they are due.[l]

There is a material distinction between a transfer made before a bill is due, and one made after that time; in the first case, the transfer carries no suspicion on the face of it, and the assignee receives it on its own intrinsic credit, nor is he bound to inquire into any circumstances existing between the assignor and any of the previous parties to the bill, as he will not be affected by them.[m] But when a transfer of a bill is [127] made *after it is due*, whether by indorsement or mere delivery, it is settled,[n] that at least it is to be left to the jury upon the slightest circum-

dant, on paying one of the bills in London, should be exonerated from paying the other ; and the defendant proved his having, on the 2d of July, paid one of the bills, which then remained in the hands of Parry's agents, who delivered it upon payment. This agreement was until the 2d of July unknown to the plaintiff and Parry's agents. A verdict was found for the plaintiff, and a case reserved for the opinion of the court. The court (Le Blanc, J. absente) held, that the plaintiff having taken this bill after its dishonour, had taken it with all its infirmities, and subject therefore to the agreement between Parry and the defendant. Postea to the defendant. See observations on this in the preceding note.

[h] Roscoe *v.* Hardy, 12 East, 434. 2 Campb. 460. S. C. Acceptance of a bill was refused ; of this, however, the holders gave no notice, but when the bill became due, again presented it for payment, and that being refused they called upon the plaintiff, an indorser, for payment, and he being ignorant of their laches paid it. He now sued the defendant as his indorser, who set up the laches of the said holders as a defence, and the plaintiff was nonsuited. On motion to set aside this nonsuit, it was urged that the plaintiff ought not to be prejudiced by the laches of subsequent holders, of which he was ignorant, without the means of information. But the court held that his ignorance, which had prevented his availing himself of this laches as a defence, could not alter or revive the liability of the defendant, who had been discharged by the same laches. See the observations on this case by Gibbs, C. J. in O'Keefe *v.*

Dunn, 1 Marsh. 622. and 6 Taunt. 305. Ante, 125. note.
[i] Mutford *v.* Walcot, 1 Ld. Raym. 575. Dehers *v.* Harriot, 1 Show. 163. Boehm *v.* Sterling, 7 T. R. 430. Dehers *v.* Harriot, 1 Show. 163. A bill was indorsed to the plaintiff after it was due, and he had judgment without any objection on this ground.
Mutford *v.* Walcot, 1 Ld. Raym. 575. Holt, C. J. said, he remembered a case where a bill was negotiated after the day of payment, and he had all the eminent merchants in London with him at his chambers, and they all held it to be very common and usual, and a very good practice.
[k] Dehers *v.* Harriot, 1 Show. 164.
[l] 17 Geo. 3. c. 30. s 1. Bayl. 62.
[m] Per Buller, J. in Brown *v.* Davis, 3 T. R. 82. Per Gibbs, C. J. in O'Keefe *v.* Dunn, 1 Marsh. 621, 2. 6 Taunt. 305. Ante, 125, note.
[n] Brown *v.* Davis, 3 T. R. 80. Roberts *v.* Eden, 1 Bos. & Pul. 399. Tinson *v.* Francis, 1 Campb. Ni. Pri. 19. Brown *v.* Davis, 3 T. R. 80. Davis drew a note payable to Sandall or order; Sandall indorsed it to Taddy, and he had it presented and noted for non-payment. Davis then paid the money to Sandall, and he took up the note from Taddy, but instead of returning the note to Davis, indorsed it to Brown. Brown thereupon sued Davis, and on Davis' offering to prove these facts, Lord Kenyon thought they would not amount to a defence, unless it could be proved that Brown knew them when he took the note, and he rejected the evidence; but upon a rule *nisi* for a new trial, and cause shown, Lord Kenyon said, he thought there ought

stance, to presume that the indorsee was acquainted with the fraud, or had notice of the circumstances which would have affected the validity of the bill, had it been in the hands of the person who was holder thereof, at the time it became due; and though the indorsee may have been ignorant of the fraud, yet any objection which might have been taken against the bill when in the hands of the indorser, may be taken against him, if the bill or note when he took it, appeared upon the face of it to have been dishonoured;* and though Lord Kenyon, C. J. in this case, appears to have been of opinion, that the mere circumstance of a bill being over due, is not sufficient to affect the indorsee; and though in Columbies *v.* Slim,ᴾ the Court of K. B. held, that an indorsement, after action brought on a note over due, would nevertheless give the indorsee a right of action, unless he had notice of the action; yet Buller, J. and Ashurst, J. were of opinion, in the first-mentioned case, that when a note is over due, its being out of the common course of dealing, is alone such a suspicious circumstance, as makes it incumbent on the party receiving it, to satisfy himself that it is a good one, and that if he omit to do so, he takes it on the credit of the indorser, and must stand in the situation of the person who was holder at the time it was due; and the latter opinion appears now to prevail;ᑫ and therefore where the

---

to be further inquiry, it did not strike him at the trial that the note had been noted before Brown took it, and that that circumstance ought to have awakened Brown's suspicion. Ashurst and Buller, Js. thought that the party taking a note after it was due, was to be considered as taking it on the credit of the person from whom he received it, and that whatever would be a defence against the giver, would be a defence against the receiver; upon which Lord Kenyon said, he agreed with that, if the note appeared on the face of it to have been dishonoured, or if knowledge could be brought home to the indorsee, that it had been so, but otherwise he was not prepared to go that length. Grose, J. said, if collusion could be proved between the defendant and Sandell, the defendant would not be entitled to insist on the objection, but as the cause then stood, he thought there ought to be a new trial. Rule absolute.

* Id. ibid.

ᴾ Trin. 12 Geo. 3. 16 Vol. MS. paper books, page 62.

ᑫ Banks *s.* Colwell, cited 3 T. R. 81. Brown *v.* Turner, 7 T. R. 630. Tinson *v.* Francis, 1 Campb. 19. Boehm *v.* Sterling, 7 T. R. 427. Good *v.* Coe, cited 7 T. R. 427. 429. Bayl. 68.

Banks *v.* Colwell, cited 3 T. R. 81. Indorsee of a note payable *on demand* against the maker. The notes were given for smuggled goods, part of it was paid, and it was not indorsed to the plaintiff till a year and a half after it was given, no privity was brought home to the plaintiff, but Buller, J. was clearly of opinion he ought to be nonsuited, and said it had been repeatedly ruled at Guildhall, that if a bill or note was indorsed over after it was due, the indorsee took it on the credit of the indorser, and stood in his situation. Sed vide Morris *v.* Lee, Bayl. 288. n. b.

Brown *v.* Turner, 7 T. R. 630. Pritchard paid some stock-jobbing differences for the defendant, and drew on him for the amount; defendant accepted the bill, and after it became due, Pritchard indorsed it to the plaintiff, for a prior debt. A question was made, whether the illegality of the original transaction vitiated the bill; the plaintiff having taken it after it became due, and consequently not being entitled to recover on it, if Pritchard could not. Lord Kenyon being of opinion, that Pritchard could not have recovered on the bill, directed a verdict for the defendant, and the court being of opinion that the direction was right, refused a rule *nisi* for a new trial.

Tinson *v.* Francis, 1 Campb. 19. Indorsee against the maker of a promissory note; the defendant proved that it was given for the accommodation of one T. the payee, and dishonoured, and that the plaintiff had received it from a Mr. Stevens, to whom it was given to be returned to the defendant; plaintiff offered to prove that he had given a valuable consideration for the note. Lord Ellenborough said, " after a bill or note is due, it comes disgraced to the indorsee, and it is his duty to make inquiries concerning it, if he takes it, though he give a full consideration for it, be takes it on the credit of the indorser, and subject to all the equities with which it may be incumbered."

Boehm *v.* Sterling, 7 T. R. 428. Muilman lent the defendant his acceptance for 2444l. 14s. at three months, and the defendant gave Muilman a check upon his banker for the amount, dated 17th February, 1796, the year was, perhaps, intended for 1797. On the 20th of January, Muilman gave this check to the plaintiff in payment of an old debt; Muilman died before his acceptance became due, and the defendant was

III. *Time* drawer of a bill payable to his own order after the bill became due,
of transfer. settled with the acceptor, and gave him a receipt in full of all demands,
and the drawer being afterwards in possession of such bill indorsed the
same to the plaintiff, it was held that he could not sue the acceptor.'
This rule equally applies to the case of a banker's check transferred
long after it was first issued.'

A party, however, to whom an over due bill has been indorsed, is
clothed with all the advantages of the party from whom he received it,
and therefore it has been decided, that in an action by the second in-
[129] dorsee against the acceptor of a bill of exchange, if the person who
indorsed it to the plaintiff, could himself have maintained an action
upon it, the defendant cannot give in evidence, that it was accepted for
a debt contracted in smuggling, although it was indorsed to the plaintiff
after it had become due.'(167)   And it is reported to have been decided,
that it is not of itself a defence to an action by the indorsee of a bill,
that it was accepted for the accommodation of the drawer, without
consideration, and that he indorsed it to the plaintiff after it was due,
unless it be also shown, that the plaintiff gave no value for the bill.'

obliged to take it up. In an action upon
the check, the defendant urged, that Muilman could not have sued him upon this
check, and that therefore the plaintiff
could not, because he took it so many
months after it was dated. Lord Kenyon
left it to the jury, whether the plaintiff
took it *bona fide*, and without knowing
the circumstances under which Muilman
held it; they found for the plaintiff, and
on a rule *nisi* for a new trial, and cause
shown, Lord Kenyon admitted, that it was
to be considered as a rule, that the person
who takes a bill after it is due, is subject
to the same equity as the party from whom
he took it, though the bill did not appear
upon the face of it to have been dishonoured, and he thought there was no distinction
in this respect, between checks upon bankers and bills of exchange; but as the defendant had not issued this check until nine
months after it was dated, he thought it
was not competent to him to object to the
time when the plaintiff took it. The other
Judges agreed, that the rule mentioned by
Lord Kenyon was to be considered as settled, but for the reasons given by Lord
Kenyon, that it did not bear upon this
case.   Rule discharged.
' Thorogood *v.* Clark, 2 Stark. 251.
' Boehm *v.* Sterling, 7 T. R. 428. see
the last note but one. Banks *v.* Colwell,
ante 127. *Sed vide* Morris *v.* Lee, Bayl.
283.
' Chalmers *v.* Lanion, 1 Campb. 383.
To an action by the indorsees against the
acceptor of a bill, one ground of defence

was, that the bill had been accepted for
a debt contracted in a smuggling transaction, and that though it had been indorsed for value before it became due, to
a *bona fide* holder ; yet that it had been
indorsed by him to the plaintiffs, after it
was due, and it was contended, that
having been so indorsed to the plaintiffs,
it was competent to the defendant to set
up the illegality of the consideration as a
defence, in like manner as if the action
had been brought by the payee; but
Lord Ellenborough held, that if the
plaintiff's indorser might have maintained
an action upon the bill, the circumstance
of the indorsement to them having been
made after the bill had become due, was
insufficient to let in the proposed defence,
and the court of King's Bench concurred
in opinion with his Lordship.
' Charles *v.* Marsden, 1 Taunt 224.—
Indorsee of a drawer of a bill against the
acceptor. The defendant pleaded that
he had accepted the bill for the accommodation of the drawer, and without any
consideration ; and that it was indorsed
to the plaintiff after it was due, and that
plaintiff knew the circumstance.   On
special demurrer to the replication, the
argument turned on the validity of the
plea ; the court held, that as there was
no averment of fraud in the plea ; nor
that the plaintiff had not given a valuable
consideration for the bill, the plea was
bad, and gave judgment for plaintiff. *Sed*
vide Tinson *v.* Francis, 1 Campb. 19.
Ante, 128.

---

(167) An indorser of a note for the accommodation of the maker, and without consideration is liable to the indorsee, notwithstanding the facts were known to the latter, when
he took the bill. *Brown* v. *Mott*, 7 Johns. Rep. 361. And the same rule is said to apply, even if the indorsee took the note after it was due. Ibid.

A party to a bill or check, who has himself transferred it to another **III. Time** after it was due, or long after the date of the check, will not be at **of transfer.** liberty to object, on the ground of fraud, to the payment of it, when in the hands of a third person, who must necessarily have also received it after it was due; for it is obvious payment could not have been demanded when the bill was due, as it was not then issued; and the difficulty was occasioned by the party himself, who so gave to it an improper circulation.[x] Where it has been improperly indorsed after due, a party interested in having it delivered up, may file a bill in equity, or sometimes support an action of trover, though, in truth, the bill is of no value.[y](168)

[x] Boehm v. Sterling, 7 T. R. 423.— [y] Goggerly v. Cuthbert, 2 New Rep. Ante, 128, n.   178. Ante, 110.

---

(168) Where a note is negotiated after it becomes due, the indorsee takes it, subject to every defence that existed in favour of the maker of the note before it was indorsed. *Johnson* v. *Bloodgood*, 1 John. Cas. 51. S. C. 2 Caines' Cas. in Err. 302. *M'Cullough* v. *Houston*, 1 Dall. Rep. 441. *Humphreys* v. *Blight's* assignees, 4 Dall. 370. *Sebring* v. *Rathbun*, 1 John. Cas. 331. *Prior* v. *Jacocks*, 1 John. Cas. 169. *Jones* v. *Caswell*, 3 Johs. Cas. 29. *Furman* v. *Haskin*, 2 Caines' Rep. 369. *Payne* v. *Eden*, 3 Caines' Rep. 213. *Hendrick* v. *Judah*, 1 John. Rep. 319. *Lansing* v. *Gaine*, 2 John. Rep. 300. *O'Callaghan* v *Sawyer*, 5 John. Rep. 118. *Losee* v. *Dunkin*, 7 John. Rep. 70. *Lansing* v. *Lansing*, 8 John. Rep. 454. *Gold* v. *Eddy*, 1 Mass. Rep. 1. *Wilson* v. *Clements*, 3 Mass. Rep. 1. *Thurston* v. *M'Kown*, 6 Mass. Rep. 428. *Ayer* v. *Hutchins*, 4 Mass. Rep. 370. And where a bill is not taken in the usual course of trade, it is subject to all the equities that subsisted between the original parties. *Evans* v. *Smith*, 4 Binney's Rep. 366. And where a party to a bill cannot maintain an action against another party to the bill, no person claiming subsequently, by a derivative title under the former, and having knowledge of all the facts, can recover against the latter. *Herrick* v. *Carman*, 12 John. Rep. So where a note is indorsed over in trust for the indorser, it is open to the same equities as if the suit was in favour of the indorser himself. *Payne* v. *Eden*.

And a note purchased after it has become due, and after an assignment under a statute upon the maker's insolvency, cannot be set off against a debt due to the insolvent's estate in an action brought by his assignees for the recovery of it. *Johnson* v. *Bloodgood*, 1 John. Cas. 51. 2 Caines' Cas. Err. 303. and see *Anderson* v. *Van Alen*, 12 John. Rep. 343. So a note purchased after knowledge of the issuing of a commission of bankruptcy, although not then due, is subject to all the equities between the original parties; and therefore if proved under the commission, it is liable to the right to set off of the bankrupt against the original payee. *Humphreys* v. *Blight's assignees*, 4 Dall. 370.

But the court will not set aside a judgment on confession to let in an equitable defence, especially where the parties are in *pari delicto*. *Sebring* v. *Rathbun*, 1 John. Cas. 331.

Where a negotiable note is paid *before it becomes due*, and is afterwards indorsed by the payee with notice to the indorsee of such payment, the latter takes the note subject to that defence, and therefore cannot recover against the maker. *White* v. *Kibling*, 11 John. Rep. 128.

If the maker of a note when sued by an indorsee, relies upon payment before indorsement or any other legal defence as against the payee, the burthen of proof of the time of the indorsement rests upon him. *Webster* v. *Lee*, 5 Mass. Rep. 334. See *Stewart* v. *Greenleaf*, 3 Day's Rep. 311.

Where a note is payable on demand, it must be presented within a reasonable time for payment, or it will be considered as out of time and dishonoured; and if it be afterwards negotiated, it will in the hands of the indorsee be liable to all the equities which subsisted between the original parties. *Furman* v. *Haskins*, 2 Caines, 369. Such a note, negotiated eighteen months or two years after its date, will be considered as out of time. Ibid. *Loomis* v. *Pulver*, 9 John. Rep. 224. There is no precise time in which a note payable on demand is to be deemed dishonoured; but it must depend upon the circumstances of the case. *Loose* v *Duncan*, 7 John. Rep. 70. And if no peculiar circumstances are disclosed, and a transfer be made two months and a half after the date, it will be deemed out of season, and let in the defence of payment by the maker. Ibid. See also, *Hendricks* v. *Judah*, 1 John. Rep. 319. *Sandford* v. *Mickles*, 4 John. Rep. 224. *Thurston* v. *M'Kown*, 6 Mass. Rep. 428.

Wherever the holder of a negotiable note has notice either constructively or positively at the time of the transfer to him of any equity subsisting between the original parties,

CHITTY ON BILLS.   R

III. *Time of transfer.* If out of the usual course of business, a bill or note be paid before it is due, by any other party than the acceptor or the maker, and be re-issued before it is at maturity, even in fraud of some of the parties, yet an innocent indorsee may recover upon it.[a] And a bill of exchange [130] is negotiable, *ad infinitum*, until it has been paid by the acceptor, and therefore if the drawer pay it after it is due, he may indorse it to a fresh party, who may sue the acceptor thereon,[a] but when a bill has been once paid by the acceptor, it is *functus officio* at common law, and by the express legislative provision in the stamp laws, no longer re-issuable ;[b] and a bill or note cannot be negotiated after it has been once paid, if such negotiation would make any of the parties liable, who would otherwise be discharged.[c] The stamp laws contain an exception in favour of promissory notes payable to bearer on demand of a sum not exceeding £100, which, if duly stamped for that purpose, may be re-issued after payment by the maker.[d]

A person not originally party to a bill, by paying it for the honour of the parties to it, acquires a right of action against all those parties.[e] And after a payment of a part, a bill may be indorsed over for the residue.[f] If the holder of a bill be indebted to a prior party, and be doubtful as to his solvency, it is not advisable to transfer the bill, be-

---

[a] Burbridge *v.* Manners, 3 Campb. 194.

[a] Per Lord Ellenborough, in Callow *v.* Lawrence, 3 M. & S. 97. Gomeserra *v.* Berkley, 1 Wils. 46.

[b] Id. ibid. Holroyd *v.* Whitehead, 1 Marsh. 130. and 55 Geo. 3. c. 184. s. 19. Thoroughgood *v.* Clark, 2 Stark. 251.

[c] Beck *v.* Robley, cited 1 Hen. Bla. 59 (n.) Brown drew a bill upon Robley, which Robley accepted, payable to Hodgson or order ; Robley did not pay it when it was presented, upon which Brown took it up ; Brown afterwards indorsed it to Beck, and Beck brought an action upon it against Robley, but the jury thought, that when Brown took up the bill, its negotiability ceased, and found

for the defendant ; and on a rule *nisi*, for a new trial, the court thought the jury right, and Lord Mansfield said, "when a draft is given, payable to A. or order, the purpose is, that it shall be paid to A. or order, and when it comes back unpaid, and is taken up by the drawer, it ceases to be a bill; if it were negotiable here, Hodgson would be liable, for which there is no colour." See observations on this case, Callow *v.* Lawrence, 3 M. & S. 97, 8. and Bayl. 66. The King *v.* Burn, 5 Price, 174.

[d] 55 Geo. 3. c. 184. s. 14, &c.

[e] Mertens *v.* Winnington, 1 Esp. Rep. 112. et post.

[f] Hawkins *v.* Cardy, Lord Raym. 360 Carth. 466. 1 Salk. 65. S. C. Hawkins

---

he takes it subject to trial and equity. *Humphreys* v. *Blight's assignees*, 4. Dall. Rep. 371. *White* v. *Kibling*, 11 John. Rep. 128. *Wilson* v. *Holmes*, 5 Mass. Rep. 543. But the mere knowledge that the note was made and indorsed for the accommodation of the maker, will not entitle the indorser to set up that defence against a *bona fide* holder. *Brown* v. *Mott*, 7 John. Rep. 361. ante, 143, note. And if the consideration for a note be specially indorsed on the back of it, it operates as notice to all subsequent holders. *Saunders* v. *Bacon*, 8 John. Rep. 485. And if there be a memorandum on the back of the note, stating its actual execution to have been on an anterior day to the date, it is sufficient notice to put the party upon inquiry into the circumstances. *Wiggin* v. *Bush*, 12 John. Rep. 306.

Where a note not negotiable is assigned, explicit notice must be given to the maker, or he will be justified in paying the amount to the payee. *Meghan* v. *Mills*, 9. John. Rep. 92.

Notice of nonpayment must be given as well to one who indorses a note after it becomes due, as to an indorser of a note before it becomes due. *Stockman* v. *Riley*, 2 M'Cord, 398.

Where a promissory note payable on demand was indorsed eight months after its date, it was held that in order to charge the indorser, a demand on the drawer and notice to the indorser must be proved. *M'Kenney* v. *Crawford*, 3 Serg. & Rawle 351. See also *Poole* v. *Tolleson* 1 M'Cord, 199, S. P.

cause, if he holds it, he may treat it as a mutual credit, and set off the
amount against his own debt; but if he transfers it, and after the act of
bankruptcy is obliged to take it up, he can only prove under the commission, and receive a dividend, and must pay the whole of his own debt. e **III. *Time* of transfer.**

If a party, whether before or after a bill or note be due, become the indorsee or holder by delivery, with notice that the party from whom he receives it, had no right to make the transfer, he will acquire no better right than such party, and a person who discounts a bill for the full value, after he knows that it has been lost by the owner, will not only be precluded from recovering thereon, but will be liable to an action of trover, even without any previous demand;h nor can a person who receives a bill with notice that an action has been commenced thereon, and still depending, sustain another action against the same party.i (196) **[131]**

With respect to the *modes* by which transfers of a bill or note may be made, they depend on the terms of the instrument, as whether it be payable to the bearer, or to the order of the drawer or payee; in the former case it is transferrable by delivery, and in the latter by indorsement, which may be made either in blank, in full, conditional, or restrictive.k   In all cases in order to complete the legal transfer, a de- **IV. *Modes* of transfer.**

---

e. Gardner, 12 Mod. 213.   Johnson v. Kennion, 2 Wils. 262.

f Ex parte Hale, 3 Ves. 304. 3 T. R. 509. 6 T. R. 57. 1 Mont. 543. See post, tit. *Bankruptcy*.

h Lovell v. Martin, 4 Taunt. 799.

i Marsh and another v. Newell, 1 Taunt. 109. This was a rule *nisi*, to cancel the bail bond given herein under the following circumstances:—Plaintiff had arrested defendant on a promissory note payable to plaintiff or bearer; plaintiff afterwards paid the note to one Frost, who likewise arrested the defendant upon the same instrument. The court held, that as the transfer of the note to Frost was accompanied with a no-

tice of the action which was pending, Frost could not, after such notice, be permitted to bring a second action against the defendant.

k Per Eyre, C. J. in Gibson v. Minet, 1 Hen. Bla. 605. "Bills of exchange being of several kinds, the title to sue upon any one bill of exchange in particular, will depend upon what kind of bill it is, and whether the holder claims title to it as the original payee, or as deriving from the original payee or from the drawer; in the case of a bill drawn payable to the drawer's own order, who is in the nature of an original payee, the title of an original payee is immediate and apparent on the face of the bill. The derivative title is a title by assignment, a

---

(196) A note once paid, ceases to be negotiable, and remedies lie only between the then existing parties. Therefore, if an indorsee pay a note on its being dishonoured by the maker, he cannot by a subsequent transfer enable a subsequent indorsee to maintain an action on it against a prior indorser. *Blake* v. *Sewall*, 3 Mass. Rep. 556. *Boylton* v. *Greene*, 8 Mass. Rep. 465. But such assignee may maintain an action upon it in the name of the indorsee who transferred the note to him. *Boylton* v. *Greene*. See *Robertson & Co.* v. *Williams*, 5 Munf. Rep. 381.

A bill of exchange does not lose its negotiable character by being protested; but after protest, may be assigned, or transferred without assignment. 5 Munf. Rep. 388.

And where A. and B. indorsed a promissory note for the accommodation of the defendant, and on its being dishonoured by the defendant, paid, and took it up, and then delivered the note to B. alone, with the original indorsement thereon; it was held, that B. might maintain an action in his own name alone, as indorsee. *Havens* v. *Huntington*, 1 Cowen, 387.

A. purchased a note of B., who indorsed it in blank before it became due. A. sold it to C. before due, who charged the indorser by demand and notice, &c., and after it was due, A. re-purchased it, and sold it to D. Held, that D. might maintain an action on the note against the indorser in his own name. *Williams* v. *Matthews*, 3 Cowen, 252.

And the case of *Boyston* v. *Greene*, was afterwards overruled in Massachusetts, and it was held, that when a promissory note has been paid, or taken up by the *last* indorser, its negotiability is not destroyed, but it may be transferred by him to another, and the new indorsee may maintain an action in his own name against any of the prior parties. *Guild* v. *Eager*, 17 Mass. 615.

IV. *Modes* livery of the instrument to the person for whose benefit it is transferred' of transfer. or some person on his behalf, is essential.[1]

When a bill or note is, by the terms of it, payable to a certain person or bearer, it is transferrable by mere delivery;[m] and where a bill is payable to the order of a fictitious person, it will operate against all parties aware of the circumstance, as a bill payable to bearer, and will be transferrable by delivery.[n]

A bill payable to the order of a certain person, or to that person or order, or to assigns, or to the drawer's order, is transferrable in the first instance only by indorsement.[o]

[132]   No particular form of words is essential to an *indorsement*, the mere signature of the party making it is in general sufficient.[p] An indorsement which mentions the name of the person in whose favour it is made, is called an indorsement in full, and an indorsement which does not, is called an indorsement in blank. After an indorsement in full, the indorsee can only transfer his interest in the bill or note by indorsement in writing, but after an indorsement in blank, he may transfer by delivery only, and so long as the indorsement continues in blank, it makes the bill or note payable to bearer;[q] and if the first indorsement on a bill or note be made in blank, it will, as against the payee, drawer, or acceptor, be assignable afterwards by mere delivery, notwithstanding subsequent indorsements in full having been made thereon.[r] (1)

title which the common law does not acknowledge, but which exists only by the custom of merchants, as it is by force of the custom of merchants, that a bill of exchange is assignable at all, of necessity, the custom must direct how it shall be assigned, and in respect of bills payable to order, the custom has directed that the assignment should be made by a writing on the bill, called an indorsement, appointing the contents of that bill to be paid to some third person, and in respect of bills drawn payable to bearer, that the assignment should be constituted by delivery only."

[1] The King *v.* Lampton and other, 5 Price, 428. Therefore if after the indorsement and before delivery to a partner or other agent for the indorsee, the bill be taken under an extent against the indorser, the Crown are entitled to the same. Id. ibid.

[m] See the last note but one.

[n] Gibson *v.* Minet, 1 Hen. Bla. 600.—Ex parte Royal Burgh of Scotland, 19 Ves. 311. Ante, 64.

[o] Supra, n.[c]

[p] Hill *v.* Lewis, Holt, 117. Pinkney *v.* Hall, Lord Raym. 176.

[q] Peacock *v.* Rhodes, Dougl. 611. 633. A bill was drawn by the defendant, payable to Ingham or order. Ingham indorsed it in blank, after which it was stolen; the plaintiff took it *bona fide*, and paid a valu-

able consideration for it, and acceptance and payment being refused, gave notice to the defendant, and brought this action. A case was reserved for the opinion of the court, and it was contended, that this bill was not to be considered as payable to the bearer, and the plaintiff had no better right upon it than the person of whom he took it; but the court said, there was no difference between a note indorsed in blank, and one payable to bearer, and the plaintiff had judgment. Francis *v.* Mott, at N. P. before Lord Mansfield, cited Dougl. 612, was a similar case, and the Attorney-General, who was for the defendant, after attempting unsuccessfully to show that the plaintiff knew the bill was obtained unfairly, gave up the cause.

[r] Smith *v.* Clark, Peake, 225. A bill was indorsed in blank by the payee, and after some other indorsements was specially indorsed in full to Jackson, or order; Jackson sent it to Muir and Atkinson, but did not indorse it, and Muir and Atkinson discounted it with the plaintiffs. The plaintiffs struck out all the indorsements except the first, which continued in blank. This was an action against the acceptor, and was objected that the plaintiffs could not recover without an indorsement by Jackson, but Lord Kenyon held otherwise, and the plaintiff recovered. The plaintiffs afterwards

(1) An action for contribution cannot be maintained by the first indorser of an accommodation note against the second indorser on the ground of the first indorser having paid the whole to the bank and the maker being insolvent. *Herron v. Weed*, 2 Ldt. 171. See ante 87, note 1.

When a bill or note is payable to the order of the drawer, or of a third person as payee therein named, the name of such drawer or payee must appear in the first indorsement, whether such indorsement be intended to convey to the indorsee the absolute property in the bill or note, or merely to enable him to receive payment thereof, as agent of such indorser; and although such indorsement is usually made by the drawer or payee writing on the back of the bill, yet it may be made by writing on the face of it, for the writing on the face of a note is of the same effect as an indorsement, and is always accepted and taken as such by the courts of law.[t]

IV. *Modes of transfer.*

An indorsement made upon a bill or note thus, " I give this note to A." may be proved as testamentary, and is sufficient to transfer the property therein by the party making it ;[u] but the mere circumstance of the payee putting a number or any private mark on a bill or note will not be equivalent to an indorsement.[x] So where a party promised to indorse a bill, and upon the faith of such promise, a stranger wrote an indorsement in the name of the party, it was considered that such indorsement was invalid.[y]

[133]

We have already seen that a bill of exchange may be drawn by an agent, so also it may be indorsed by a person acting in that capacity ; in which case he must expressly indorse as agent, as, " E. F. *per proc.* A. B." or he may write the name of his principal, otherwise the indorsement would be inoperative.[z](172)

In the negotiation of bills, it frequently happens that parties who are employed merely as agents are obliged to indorse them for the purpose of transmitting them to their principal, and if such indorsement be written conditionally, the agent (though he have no interest whatever in the transaction[a]) will be liable to pay the amount of the bill ; and therefore to exempt themselves from responsibility, it is necessary in such case to specify in the indorsement, that he makes it without intending to incur personal responsibility for the payment, which may be effected by adding the words " *sans recours* " which operates as a special indorsement, and is a notice to subsequent parties taking the bill, that such persons are acting only as agents.[b]

In the case of bills under five pounds, the indorsement must be at-

proved that Jackson desired Muir and Atkinson to discount this bill, but Lord Kenyon thought the plaintiff's case made out without this evidence.

[s] Barlow v. Bishop, 1 East, 432. 3 Esp. 266. S. C.

[t] *Per cur.* Yarborough v. Bank of England, 16 East, 12.

[u] Per Lord Chancellor, in Chatworth v. Leach, 4 Ves. 565.

[x] Fenn v. Harrison, 3 T. R. 757. Ex parte Shuttleworth, 3 Ves. 368.

[y] Moxon and another v. Pulling and another, 4 Campb. 51.

[z] Barlow v. Bishop, 1 East, 432.—3 Esp. 266. S. C. Ante, 27, 8.

[a] Le Feuvre v. Lloyd, 5 Taunt. 749.—Ante, 27, note.

[b] Goupy v. Harden, 7 Taunt. 159. 162. 163. Ante, 27, note, see forms, post, 139, note.

(172) The directors of a bank have power to authorize one of their number to transfer any notes given to the bank ; and a blank indorsement by the person so authorized, signed with his name as attorney, will be a good transfer of such notes. *Northampton Bank* v. *Pepoon*, 11 Mass. Rep. 288.

IV. Modes of transfer. tested by a subscribing witness, and must mention the name and place of abode of the indorsee, and bear date at or before the making thereof; in short, it must be made in the form prescribed in the schedule to the statute 17 Geo. 3. c. 30. s. 1., which regulates these indorsements.[c] Where the residence of the indorser of a bill is not well known in the commercial world, it would be advisable for him in all cases to mention in his indorsement the name of the place where he resides.[d]

In blank.   An indorsement in *blank* is by far the most common, and it is made by the mere writing of the indorser's name on the back of the bill, with-
[134] out any mention of the name of the person in whose favour the indorse-
ment is made, and is sufficient to transfer the right of action to any *bona fide* holder, and so long as it continues in blank, makes the bill or note payable to bearer;[e] but the holder may write over it what he pleases, and a blank indorsement on a bill of exchange, conveys a joint right of action to as many as agree in suing on the bill, though such persons be not in partnership.[f]

It has been said, that such an indorsement does not transfer the pro-
perty and interest in the bill to the indorsee, without some farther act;[g] but that it gives him, as well as any other person to whom it is after-
wards transferred, the power of constituting himself assignee of the beneficial interest in the bill, by filling it up payable to himself (as by writing over the indorser's name " pay the contents,") which he may do at the time of trial;[h] it is now however considered, that a blank in-
dorsement is sufficient of itself to transfer the right of action to any *bona fide* holder. A blank indorsement may be converted into a special one, by the holder's inserting above it the words " pay the contents to A. B." but such holder by writing those words, and transferring the bill to the party named in the indorsement, without writing his own name as an indorser, will not be liable on the bill.[i] If the indorsee fill up the blank indorsement, and make it payable to himself, it is said the

[c] See provision in France, Pothier Traité du Contrat de Change, part 1. chap. 3. num. 130. And see Pardessus, 1 tom. 364 to 379.

[d] Bul. Ni. Pri. 276.

[e] Bayl. 46 Peacock v. Rhodes, Dougl. 633 Ante, 132. Newsome v. Thornton, 6 East, 21, 2.

[f] Per Lord Ellenborough, in Ord v. Portal, 3 Campb. 240.

[g] Clark v Pigot, 1 Salk. 126. 12 Mod. 192. S. C. Lambert v. Pack, 1 Salk. 128. Lucas v. Haynes, id. 130. Lambert v. Oakes, 12 Mod. 244. Ld. Raym. 443. S. C. Vin. Abr. tit. Bills of Exchange, H 6. Bul. Ni. Pri. 275.

[h] Theed v. Lovell. 2 Stra. 1103. Lambert v. Oakes, 12 Mod. 244. Ld. Raym. 443. S. C. Lambert v. Pack, 1 Salk. 127. Lucas v. Haynes, id 130. Dehers v. Harriot, 1 Show. 163. Moore v. Manning, Comyns, 311. Lucas v. Marsh, Barnes, 453. Vin. Abr. tit. Bills of Exchange, H. 8. Bul. Ni. Pri. 275, 8.

[i] Vincent and others v. Horlock and others, 1 Campb. 442. Action against defendants as indorsers of a bill of exchange; the declaration stated the bill to have been drawn by Jacks, payable to his own order, indorsed by him to defen-
dants, and by them to plaintiffs. The fact was, that Jacks, the drawer and payee of the bill, indorsed it in blank to Horlock and Co., and that Caleb Jones, one of the partners in that house, wrote over Jack's signature " pay the contents to Vincent and Co." without signing his own name or that of his firm. Lord Ellenborough.—I am clearly of opinion, that this is not an indorsement by the defen-
dants, for such a purpose the name of the party must appear written, with intent to indorse. We see these words, " pay the contents to such a one," written over a blank indorsement every day, without any thought of contracting an obligation, and no obligation is thereby contracted. When a bill is indorsed by the payee in blank, a power is given to the indorsee of specially appointing the payment to be made to a particular individual; and what he does in the exercise of this power is only *expressio eorum quæ tacite insunt.* This is a sufficient indorsement to the plaintiffs, but not by the defendants. Plaintiff nonsuited. See also Ex parte Isbester, 1 Rose, 20. S. P.

action cannot be brought in the name of the indorser, which otherwise IV. *Modes* it may be.[k] *of transfer.*

A blank indorsement makes a bill transferrable by the indorsee and every subsequent holder by mere delivery;[l] and when the first indorsement has been in blank, the bill or note, as against the payee, the drawer, and acceptor, is afterwards assignable by mere delivery, notwithstanding it may have upon it subsequent indorsements in full, because a holder by delivery, may declare and recover as the indorsee of the payee, and strike out all the subsequent indorsements, whether special or not.[m] (175)

[l] A full or special indorsement contains in itself a transfer of the interest in the bill to the person named in such indorsement, Poth. Traité du contrat du Change, part 1. chap. 2. s. 23, 4. But a bare indorsement, without other words purporting an assignment, does not work an alteration of the property. *Per cur.* Lucas *v.* Haynes, Salk. 130.

Clark *v.* Pigot, 12 Mod. 193. 1 Salk. 126. S. C. Clark having a bill of exchange payable to him or order, put his name upon it, leaving a vacant space above, and sent it to J. S. his friend, who got it accepted; but the money not being paid, Clark brought assumpsit against the acceptor; and it was objected that the action should have been brought by J. S. But per Holt, C. J., J. S. had it in his power to act either as servant or assignee. If he had filled up the blank space, making the bill payable to him, as he might have done if he would, that would have witnessed his election to have received it as indorsee. The property of the bill would have been transferred to him, *and he only could have maintained this action against the acceptor;* but since he has not filled up the blank space, his intention is presumed to act as servant only to Clark, whose name was put there; that on payment thereof, a receipt for the money might be written over his name, and therefore the action is maintainable by Clark.

From the foregoing case it appears, that a blank indorsement is an equivocal act, and that it is in the power of the party to whom the bill is delivered, to make what use he pleases of such an indorsement. He may either use it as an acquittance to discharge the bill, or as an assign-

ment to charge the indorser. Selw. N. P. 4th ed. edit. 331, 2.

Promissory notes and bills of exchange are frequently indorsed in this manner, "pay the money to my use," in order to prevent their being filled up with such an indorsement as passes the interest. Per Lord Hardwicke, Ch. in Snee *v.* Prescott, 1 Atk. 249.

"A bill, though once negotiable, is certainly capable of being restrained. I remember this being determined on argument. A blank indorsement makes the bill payable to bearer; but by a special indorsement, the holder may stop the negotiability" Per Lord Mansfield, C. J. Archer *v.* Bank of England, Dougl. 659.

[l] Peaceck *v.* Rhodes, Dougl. 611. 633. Bayl. 48, 9. A bill was drawn by the defendant payable to Ingram or order; Ingram indorsed it in blank, after which it was stolen; the plaintiff took it *bona fide,* and paid a valuable consideration for it, and acceptance and payment being refused, gave notice to the defendant and brought this action. A case was reserved for the opinion of the court, and it was contended, that this bill was not to be considered as payable to bearer, and that the plaintiff had no better right upon it than the person of whom he took it; but the court said, that there was no difference between a note indorsed in blank and one payable to bearer, and the plaintiff had judgment.

[m] Smith *v.* Clarke, Peake Rep. 235.— 1 Esp. Rep. 180. S. C. Anonymous, 12 Mod. 345. S. P. A bill was indorsed in blank by the payee, and after some other indorsements was indorsed to Jackson or order. Jackson sent it to Muir and Atkinson, but did not indorse it, and Muir and Atkinson discounted it with

(175) A blank indorsement of a bill passes all the interest therein to the indorsees in succession, discharged of all obligations which do not appear on the face of the bill. *Wilkinson* v. *Nicklin,* 2 Dall. Rep. 296. Where a negotiable note is indorsed in blank, the holder may fill it up with any name he pleases, and the person whose name is inserted will be deemed rightfully entitled to sue. *Tyler* v. *Binney,* 7 Mass. Rep. 479. *Lovell* v. *Everton,* 11 John. Rep. 52. And if in fact the indorsee has no interest, he will be deemed a trustee for the benefit of parties having the legal interest. Ibid. And where a person fairly and without fraud becomes possessed of a negotiable note indorsed in blank, it has been held that he may maintain an action thereon, *although it has not been legally transferred to him. Little* v. *O'Brien,* 9 Mass. 423. *Bowman* v. *Wood* 15 Mass. Rep. 534.

IV. *Modes of transfer.* Such being the effect of a first indorsement in blank, it has been observed, that it is advisable for the indorsee in some cases to fill it up so as to make it an indorsement in full, in order to avoid the risk which he may run, in case the bill be lost, of its getting into the hands of a *bona fide* holder.[·] When bills, &c. are deposited in a banker's hands, and entered short in his books, or are in his possession, in case he becomes bankrupt, his assignees will not be entitled thereto, though such deposit enables the banker to pass the interest to a third person taking it *bona fide* for a valuable consideration.[·]

Special or in full. An indorsement in *full*, or special indorsement, is so called, because the indorser not only writes his name or that of his firm, but expresses therein in whose favour the indorsement is made, as, " pay the contents to Mr. A. B. or order." This indorsement, it is said, contains in itself a transfer of the interest in the bill to the person named in the indorsement,[·] and makes the bill transferrable in the first indorsement of A. B. only; though afterwards, if A. B. make a blank indorsement, it is transferrable by delivery as well as by indorsement. In this case, however, a delivery of the bill to the indorsee, or some person on his behalf, is essential to the transfer.[·] As the negotiability of a bill, originally transferrable, can only be restrained by express restrictive words, the words " or order" need not be inserted in a full indorsement to give the bill a subsequent negotiable quality.[·] (176)

the plaintiffs; the plaintiff struck out all the indorsements except the first, which continued in blank This was an action against the acceptor, and it was objected that the plaintiffs could not recover, without an indorsement by Jackson, but Lord Kenyon held otherwise, and the plaintiffs recovered. The plaintiffs afterwards proved that Jackson desired Muir and Atkinson to discount this bill, but Lord Kenyon thought the plaintiff's case made out without this evidence.

Chaters *v.* Bell, 4 Esp. Rep. 120. The declaration stated that a bill was drawn payable to Curry, by him indorsed to defendant, and by the defendant to the plaintiff. There were in fact several intermediate indorsements between Curry and the defendant, which were omitted in the declaration, and it was contended, that the plaintiff should have either declared

as the immediate indorsee of the payee, or have stated all the indorsements. But Lord Ellenborough over-ruled the objection. See also Waynam *v.* Bend, and Critchlow *v.* Parry, 1 Campb. 175.

[·] Beawes, pl. 172.

[·] Zinck *v.* Walker, 2 Bla. Rep. 1156. Bolton *v.* Puller, 1 Bos. & Pul. 547. Haille *v.* Smith, id. 566 Collins *v.* Marrin, id 618. Giles *v* Perkins, 9 East. 12 Carstairs *v.* Bates, 3 Campb. 301. Treuttel *v.* Barandon, 8 Taunt. 100, and see post. tit. *Bankruptcy.*

[·] Poth. pl, 22, 23, 24.

[·] Potts *v.* Reed, 6 Esp Rep. 57. Post, 138, note. Mead *v.* Young, 4 T. R 28, and see the cases in the next note but one

[·] The King *v.* Lambton, 5 Price, 428.

[·] Moore *v.* Manning, Com. Rep. 311. 1 Selw. 332. 4th ed. n. 46. A note was

---

And the right to strike out a special as well as a general indorsement on a note has been recognized in Pennsylvania. *Morris* v. *Foreman,* 1 Dall. Rep. 193. and see *Thompson* v. *Robertson,* 4 John. Rep. 27.

Where a bill is indorsed and sent to an agent to collect, although the indorsement be general, yet the principal may at any time countermand the authority, and thereby prevent the agent from a recovery against the acceptor. *Barker* v. *Prentiss,* 6 Mass. Rep. 430. But it will be otherwise if the agent has a lien. Ibid.

Where the holder of a note indorsed in blank fills up the blank by directing payment to be made to another merely for collection, and the agent returns the note unpaid to the holder, he may strike out the transfer and make the note payable to himself. *bank of Utica* v. *Smith.* 18 Johns. 230.

(176) The same doctrines have been recognized in the United States. A negotiable note indorsed in blank, or by a direction to pay the contents to A., omitting the words " or order," is further negotiable by the holder under such indorsement, but an indorsement " pay the contents to my use," or " to the use of a third person," or " carry this this bill to the credit of a third person," is not an assignment of the security, but is only an authority to pay the money agreeably to the direction of the indorsement. But as to an indorsement " pay the contents to A. B. *only,*" whether it is only an authority to A. B. to receive

The payee or indorsee having the absolute property in the bill, and the right of disposing thereof, has the power of limiting the payment to whom he pleases ;[t] and consequently he may make a *restrictive* indorsement ;

drawn by the defendant, payable to Statham or order, Statham indorsed it to Witherhead, but did not add " or to his order." Witherhead indorsed it to the plaintiff. The defendant contended that there were no express words to authorize Witherhead to assign it, he had no such power; but the whole court resolved, that as the bill was at first assignable by Statham, as being payable to him or order, and all Statham's interest was transferred to Witherhead, and the right of assigning it was transferred also, and the plaintiff had judgment.

Acheson v. Fountain, 1 Stra. 557. Select Cases, 126, S. C. Upon a case made at *nisi prius, coram* Pratt. C. J. it appeared that the plaintiff had declared on an indorsement made by A. whereby he appointed the payment to be to B. or order, and upon producing the bill in evidence, it appeared to be payable to A. or order, but the indorsement was in these words, "Pay the contents to B." and therefore it was objected that the indorsement not being to order, did not agree with the plaintiff's declaration; but, upon consideration, the whole court were of opinion that it was well enough, that being the legal import of the indorsement, and that the plaintiff might, upon this, have indorsed it over to another, who would be the proper order of the first indorser.

Edie v. East India Company, 2 Burr. 1216. and 1 Bla. Rep. 295. S. C. Where a foreign bill of exchange was drawn by A. on B. payable to C. or order, and ac-cepted by B. and C. indorsed it to D. without adding the words, " or order," and D. afterwards indorsed it to E. who brought an action against B. the acceptor, for non-payment, evidence having been adduced at the trial, of the usage of merchants with respect to indorsements of bills payable to order, where the words, " or order," were omitted in the indorsement, which evidence was contradictory, some merchants declaring, that the omission did not make any difference, others that it restrained the negotiability of the bill, and made it payable to the indorsee only, the jury found a verdict for the defendant. On a motion for a new trial, on the ground that evidence of the usage ought not to have been allowed, that the custom of merchants was part of the law of England, and that the law of England was fully settled on this point, the court were unanimous that a new trial ought to be granted, and Lord Mansfield, C. J. said, he was clear, the evidence ought not to have been omitted, for the law was fully settled in the cases of Moore v. Manning, and Acheson v. Fountain. (ante, 186.) The other Judges concurred, and Dennison, J. said, that there was not any instance of a restrictive limitation, where a bill was originally made payable to A. or order; that he had never heard of an indorsement to A. only, and that in general the indorsement followed the nature of the thing indorsed.

[t] Edie v. East India Company, Burr. 1218. Bayl. 49. supra.

---

the money for the use of the indorser or for his own use, if made for value received, or whether in this last case the restriction is not void, and A. B. may further negotiate it, seems not to be settled. If the property be vested in A. B. perhaps he will hold it with its negotiable quality notwithstanding the restriction. Per curiam. *Rice* v. *Stearns.* 8 Mass. Rep. 225. *Wilson* v. *Holmes,* 5 Mass. Rep. 543. But an indorsement "to pay to A. or order at his own risk," does not restrain the negotiability of the note. Ibid. *Russell* v. *Ball*, 2 John. Rep. 50. Nor an indorsement "We assign this note to A. B. without recourse." *Wilson* v. *Codman's* Executors, 3 Cranch, 193. *Barker* v. *Prentiss*, 6 Mass. Rep. 430.

Where the payee of a bill indorsed on it "should the within exchange not be accepted and paid agreeably to its contents, I hereby engage to pay the holder in addition to the principal 20 per cent damages," it was held that a *bona fide* holder might insert above such stipulation, a direction to pay the contents to his order for the value received, for the indorsement was to be considered as general. *Blakeley* v. *Grant*, 6 Mass. Rep. 386. But where the payee of a negotiable note payable in six months, indorsed on it "I guarantee the payment of the within note in 18 months, if it cannot be collected of the promissor before that time;" it was held that no person could entitle himself as holder to maintain an action on the guaranty, except the original party to the guaranty, or a person claiming with the subsequent privity and assent of the payee. It seems to have been the opinion of the court that even admitting that the indorsement was a transfer of the note, yet it did not make the guaranty negotiable. *Tyler* v. *Binney*, 7 Mass. Rep. 479. See also *Williams* v. *Granger*, 4 Day's Rep. 444.

The indorsement of a promissory note to *A. B. or order, for value received,* transfers the legal title in the note to the indorsee, which cannot be divested, except by cancelling the indorsement, or indorsing it again. *Burdick* v. *Green*, 15 Johns. Rep. 247.

IV. *Modes* thus he may stop the currency of the bill, by giving a bare authority to
of transfer. receive the money, as by an indorsement requesting the drawee to "pay
to A. for my use," or to I. S. only," or "the within must be credited
to A. B." which modes prevent a blank indorsement from being filled
up by the indorsee, so as to convey any interest in the bill to himself,[a]
[138] and from making a transfer of the bill, &c.; and, when made for the use
of the indorser, is revocable in its nature like a power of attorney.[x]
But an indorsement of a bill of exchange in these words, " Pay the
contents on the bill to A. B., being part of the consideration in a certain deed of assignment executed by the said A. B. to the indorsers and
others," is not a limited indorsement.[y]

It was once thought, that although the indorser might make a restrictive indorsement, when he intended only to give a bare authority to his
agent to receive payment, yet that he could not when the indorsement
was intended to transfer the interest in the bill to the indorsee, by any
act preclude him from assigning it over to another person, because, as
it was said, the assignee purchases it for a valuable consideration, and
therefore takes it with all its privileges qualities, and advantages, the
chief of which is its negotiability.[s] It has, however, long been settled on
the above principle, that any indorser may restrain the negotiability of
a bill, by using express words to that effect, as by indorsing it, "payable to J. S. only;" or by indorsing it, " the within must be credited to
J. S."[a] or by any other words clearly demonstrating his intention to

[a] Per Wilmot, J. in Edie v. East India
Company, Burr. 1227. Bla. Rep. 299.
S. C. and per Lord Hardwicke, in Snee v.
Prescott, 1 Atk. 249. Bills and notes are
frequently indorsed in this manner, " pray
pay the money to my use," in order to prevent their being filled up with such an indorsement as passes the interest; and see
Poth. pl. 89, 90.

Archer v. Bank of England, Dougl. 615,
687. A bill was drawn by the plaintiffs
upon Claus Heide and Co. payable to Jens
Maestue or order. Maestue indorsed it to
this effect, " *the within must be credited
to captain M. L. Dahl, in account, Chris-
tiana, 17th Jan. 1778. Jens. Mastue,*" and
sent it to Claus Heide and Co. who credited Dahl for the amount, and gave notice
to Dahl and the plaintiffs, that they had
done so; an indorsement by Dahl was afterwards forged upon the bill, and the bank
discounted it. Claus Heide and Co. having become insolvent, Fulgberg paid it, for
the honour of the plaintiffs, and upon the
ground that the indorsement had restrained
the negotiability of the bill, they brought
an action for money had and received
against the bank; Lord Mansfield directed
a nonsuit, but upon a rule to show cause
why there should not be a new trial, and
cause shown, Lord Mansfield, Willes, and
Ashhurst, Justices, thought the indorsement restrictive, and that Dahl himself
could not have indorsed it, and that plaintiffs were entitled to recover, but Buller, J.
thought otherwise, upon which Lord Mansfield said, the whole turned on the question, whether the bill continued negotiable?

and if they altered their opinion, they
would mention the case again; but it never
was mentioned afterwards, and upon a new
trial, Lord Mansfield directed the jury to
find for the plaintiffs, which they did.

[x] Poth. pl. 168. Mar. 72. *acc.* Beawes,
pl. 219. *contra.* Post.

[y] Potts v. Reed, 6 Esp. Rep. 57. Per
Lord Ellenborough, this is not a restrictive
indorsement, and as to the other words,
they are surplusage, and could not affect
the subsequent negotiability of the bill. If
the bill was payable out of a particular
fund, it would affect the negotiability of
the bill, but what was here mentioned, was
not the fund out of which the bill was to be
paid, but the consideration for which the
holder had nothing to do with. Mr. Gamon,
the defendant, was here personally liable,
though the liability might have been created by the fund mentioned in the indorsement, as arising from the fund so designated
by the indorsement; and whenever a party
is personally liable, a bill is negotiable. It
is, however, necessary to prove Pugh's indorsement, as his name is mentioned, in
the indorsement, but though so made payable to him by name, there is nothing to
restrain its future negotiability; in the case
cited, the bill was to be credited to Dahl's
account, no such restriction or direction
was here. See also Haussoulier v. Hartsink, 7 T. R. 733.

[s] Edie v. East India Company, Burr.
1226.

[a] Archer v. Bank of England, Dougl.
637. ante, 137, in note.

make a restrictive and limited indorsement; but a mere omission in the IV. *Modes* indorsement, as leaving out the words "or order," will not in any case of transfer. prevent a bill being negotiable *ad infinitum*.[b]

It is competent also to an indorser, to make only a *conditional* transfer of the bill, and therefore if the payee of a bill, annexes a condition to his indorsement before acceptance, the drawee, who afterwards accepts it, is bound by that condition; and if the terms of it be not performed, the property in the bill reverts to the payee, and he [139] may recover the sum payable in an action against the acceptor.[c]

A payee or indorsee of a bill, may also make a *qualified* indorsement, so as to transfer the interest in the bill to the indorsee, and enable him to sue thereon, without rendering the indorser personally responsible for the payment of the bill; and this is the proper mode of indorsing a bill, where an agent indorses a bill on behalf of his principal, and it is not intended that he shall be personally liable.[d]

Although an indorsement may be made in blank, in full, or restrictive, yet it cannot, after acceptance, be made for less than the full sum appearing to be due upon the bill, &c. transferred,[e] because a personal contract cannot be apportioned, and it would be making the acceptor liable to two actions, when by the contract raised by his acceptance, he intended to subject himself only to one; but when a bill has been indorsed, before acceptance, for part of the sum for which it is drawn, it has been said that the acceptor may, by his acceptance after this indorsement, become liable to two actions;[f] and when the drawer of a [140] bill has paid part, it may be indorsed over for the residue.[g]

---

[b] See ante, 136, note.

[c] Robertson *v.* Kensington and others, 4 Taunt. 30. Payee against the acceptors of a bill of exchange; when the bill was presented for acceptance it had the following indorsement upon it, "Edinburgh, 19th November, 1808, pay the within sum to Messrs. Clarke and Ross, or order, *upon my name appearing in the Gazette as ensign in any regiment of the line, between the 1st and 64th, if within two months from this date;* P. Robertson." The bill had several subsequent indorsements, and when due, was paid by the acceptors to the holder; the plaintiff's name had never appeared in the Gazette as ensign in any regiment of the line; the plaintiff had a verdict, subject to a case reserved for the opinion of the court. The case was afterwards argued, and for the plaintiff it was contended, that it was competent for him, by this special indorsement, to make only a conditional transfer of the absolute interest in the bill, and the defendants, by subsequently accepting the bill, became parties to that conditional transfer; that as the condition was not performed, the transfer was defeated, and they became liable, at the expiration of two months, to pay the plaintiff, to whom the property reverted, the contents of the bill, of which none of the indorsers could enforce payment against the acceptors, because they had all received the bill, subject to the condition, and were

bound thereby. The court gave judgment for the plaintiff.

[d] Goupy and another *v.* Harden and others, 7 Taunt. 150, 1. Evidence was given, that when agents indorse foreign bills, for the mere purpose of transmitting them, without intending to incur responsibility for the payment, it is their practice to add to the indorsement the words, "*sans recours.*" Dallas, J observed, the defendants might have specially indorsed this bill, *sans recours,* if they had thought fit so to do, but they have not done it, and therefore they are personally liable; see also ante, 27, n.

The mode of making a *qualified* indorsement, may be thus: "I hereby indorse, assign, and transfer, my right and interest in this bill to C D. or order, but with this express condition, that I shall not be liable to the said C. D. or any holder, for the acceptance or payment of such bill, A. B." or the form may be, as adopted in France, by the indorser writing his name, and subscribing, "without recourse to me." See ante, 183, n.

[e] Hawkins *v.* Cardy, Ld. Raym. 360. Carth. 466. 12 Mod. 213. 1 Salk. 65. S. C.

[f] Beawes, pl. 236. *Sed quare supra,* last note.

[g] Johnson *v.* Kennion, 2 Wils. 262. Hawkins *v.* Cardy, 1 Salk. 65. Ld. Raym

IV. *Modes of transfer.*   Upon a transfer, whether by indorsement or bare delivery, the bill should be *delivered* to the assignee; and in all cases of a transfer of a bill drawn in sets, each part should be delivered to the person in whose favour the transfer is made, otherwise, the same inconveniencies may follow, which we have seen may arise upon a neglect to deliver each of them to the payee.[h]   A delivery, however, is not essential to vest the legal right in the payee or indorsee, and it need not be alleged in pleading; and if, after acceptance, the acceptor should improperly detain the bill in his hands, the drawer might nevertheless sue him on it, and give him notice to produce the bill, and in default of production, give parol evidence of its contents.[i]   It is not necessary for the holder to give any notice to the acceptor of the indorsements, nor need such notice be averred in pleading.[k]

V. The *effect of a transfer;* & the *right which it vests in the assignee; and the obligation which it imposes on the person making it; and how that obligation may be discharged.*   The nature of a transfer of a bill, note, or check, the right which it vests in the assignee, and the obligation which it imposes on the person making it, may, in a great measure, be collected from what has been previously said.

With respect to the *right* of such assignee, whether by indorsement or delivery, he has such an interest in the bill or note that he may effect a policy of insurance to secure the due payment;[l] and though he has no direct legal or equitable lien upon property deposited by the drawer with the acceptor to cover the liability of the latter, in respect of his acceptance; yet, on the bankruptcy of the drawer and acceptor, the arrangement of the property between the two estates, may indirectly render such an equity available.[m]   If the holder is a debtor to either of the parties to a bill, who he expects will become a bankrupt, it is most

[141]   advisable for him not to negotiate such bill, because if he be the holder at the time of the bankruptcy, he may set off the amount of the bill against the claim of the assignees upon him for the amount of his debt, whereas, if he be not the holder at the time of the act of bankruptcy, he cannot set off the amount, but must pay the whole of his own debt to the assignees, and when the bill has been returned to him, can only prove and receive a dividend upon the same.[n]   We have already seen, that a person who receives a bill, with notice that it is to be negotiated only upon certain terms, holds the bill subject to such terms, and therefore where A., a creditor of B., having deeds in his possession as a security for the debt, received a bill indorsed by B. for the purpose of

---

360. Carth. 466. 12 Mod. 213. & C. Callow *v.* Lawrence, 3 M. & S. 95.

Hawkins *v.* Cardy, Ld. Raym. 360. Carth. 466. 12 Mod. 213. Salk. 65. In an action upon a bill drawn by the defendant for 46*l.* 19*s.* payable to Blackman or order, the declaration stated that Blackman indorsed 43*l.* 4*s.* of it to the plaintiff; the defendant pleaded an insufficient plea, upon which the plaintiff demurred, but the whole court held the declaration bad, because the bill could not be indorsed for less than all the money due thereon, and the plaintiff discontinued his action; and per Gould, J. in Johnson *v.* Kennison, 2 Wils. 262. where the drawer of a bill has paid part, you may indorse it over for the residue, otherwise not, because it would subject him to a variety of actions.

[k] Ante, 106, 7. Bayl 68.

[l] Churchill *v.* Gardner, 7 T. R. 596. Smith *v.* M'Clure, 5 East, 476 2 Smith's Rep. 448, S. C.; but see ante, 131, a.

Churchill *v.* Gardner, 6 T. R. 596. In an action by the payee of a bill, against the acceptor, the declaration stated, that the drawer made his certain bill of exchange, but there was no allegation that he delivered it to the plaintiff and the defendant demurred specially for that cause; but the court was clearly of opinion, that there was no foundation for the objection; the delivery of the bill to the plaintiff being sufficiently implied in the allegation, that the drawer "made" the bill.

[h] Reynolds *v.* Davis, 1 Bos. & Pul. 625.

[i] Tasker *v.* Scott, 6 Taunt. 234.

[m] Ex parte Waring, 2 Rose, 182.

[n] Post tit. *Bankruptcy.*

getting it discounted, but neglects to do so, he cannot appropriate the bill to his own use, and maintain an action upon it against the acceptor;[o] but if a bill be transmitted to a holder, in order that he may get the same discounted and take up another bill which is falling due, and to which he was a party, if he do not succeed in getting such bill discounted, but pays the other, he may retain the transmitted bill and sue the parties thereto, in order to reimburse himself the amount of the bill which he took up.[p] V. *Effects of transfer, &c.*

With respect to the *liability* of the party transferring a bill, it is said that a transfer by *indorsement*, is equivalent in its effect to the drawing of a bill, the indorser being in almost every respect considered as a new drawer on the original drawee;[q](1) on which principle it is said to have been decided, that a promissory note indorsed may be declared on as a bill of exchange;[r] and if the drawee refuse to accept, the indorser is immediately liable to be sued.[s] A transfer by indorsement, vests in the indorsee a right of action against all the precedent parties whose names are on the bill; and after the bill has been duly indorsed by the payee in blank, it is transferrable by mere delivery, and the holder may sue all parties to the bill; but unless the payee, or the drawer, when the bill was payable to his order, has first indorsed it, a party who becomes possessed of it, can only sue the person from whom he obtained it.[t] As the act of indorsing is similiar to that of drawing, the *obligation which it imposes* on the indorser to the indorsee, and the mode in which that obligation may be extinguished, by the holder's laches or otherwise, is in all cases exactly similar to that which a drawer of a bill is under to the payee;[u] for, as observed by Lord Ellenborough, C. J., when it is laid down, that an indorser stands in all respects in the same situation as a drawer, all the consequences follow [142]

[o] Delaney *v.* Mitchell, 1 Stark. 439.

[p] Walsh *v.* Tyler, Sittings at Guildhall, in K. B. *corum* Lord Ellenborough, after Michaelmas Term, 1817. Declaration on a bill of exchange, dated 18th March, 1817, for 50*l.*, payable three months after date, drawn by John Shaw on the defendant Tyler, and indorsed by him to the plaintiff. The defence was, that Shaw the drawer, sent the bill to the plaintiff to be discounted, and with a request to send up the amount to Shaw, in order that he might take up a bill for 77*l.* 10*s.* then falling due and that the plaintiff did not send up the money; and afterwards the bill for 77*l.* 10*s.* having been returned to and paid by him, he proved the amount under Shaw's commission. Per Lord Ellenborough, This affords no defence. If the produce of the bill was to have been applied for another purpose, then the plaintiff had no right to retain the bill or sustain this action; but the plaintiff being unable to discount the bill, and having been compelled to pay that to which he was a party, he had a right to protect himself by applying the bill in question to cover his own advance. Mr. Scarlett for the plaintiff.

[q] Smallwood *v.* Vernon, 1 Stra. 479.—Hill *v.* Lewis, 1 Salk. 133. Williams *v.* Field, 3 Salk. 68. Claxton *v.* Swift, 2 Show. 441. S. C. id. 495. 501. Heylyn *v.* Adamson, 2 Burr. 674. Anon. Holt, 115. Claxton *v.* Swift, Skin. 255. Anon. id. 343. Hill *v.* Lewis; id. 411. Luke *v.* Hayes, 1 Atk. 282. Haly *v.* Lane, 2 Atk. 182. Gibson *v.* Minet, 1 Hen. Bla. 587. Houle *v.* Baxter, 3 East, 182. Ballingalls *v.* Gloster, id. 482.

[r] Brown *v.* Harraden, 4 T. R. 149, cites Buller *v.* Crips, 6 Mod. 29, 30.

[s] Ballingalls *v.* Gloster, 3 East, 481. Starey *v.* Barnes, 7 East, 438.

[t] Anon. Ld. Raym. 738. Miller *v.* Race, Burr. 452. Grant *v.* Vaughan, id. 1516. Peacock *v.* Rhodes, Dougl. 633.

[u] Ibid. Lambert *v.* Oakes, Holt, 117. Ante, 106, 7.

(1) The indorsement of a note to the maker is an extinguishment of it, and it cannot be recovered by his indorsing it to a third person or to the original payee, but such indorsement might create a new obligation in the indorser. *Long* v. *Bank of Cinthiana*, 1 Litt. 290.

V. *Effect* which are attached to the situation of the latter.[x]   The indorser, how-
of transfer, ever, is not under any liability in any instance to the acceptor, unless
&c.   indeed in the case of an acceptance for his honour.[y]   An indorsement
also imposes the same obligation on the person making it, although the
bill contain no words rendering it assignable.[z]   And we have seen, that
if an agent indorse in his own name without qualifying his indorsement,
he will be personally liable even to his principal.[a]

A transfer by *delivery*, without any indorsement, when made on account of a pre-existing debt, or for a valuable consideration passing to
the assignor at the time of the assignment, (and not merely by way of
exchange of paper[b]) as where goods are sold to him,[c] imposes an
[143] obligation on the person making it to the person in whose favour it is
made, similar to that of a transfer by indorsement ;[d] a distinction was
indeed once taken between the transfer of a bill or check for a precedent debt, and for a debt arising at the time of the transfer, and it was
held, that if A. bought goods of B., and at the same time gave him a
draft on a banker, which B. took without any objection, it would
amount to payment by A., and B. could not resort to him in the event
of the failure of the banker.[e]   But it is now settled, that in such case,
unless it was expressly agreed at the time of the transfer, that the assignee should take the instrument assigned, as payment, and run the
risk of its being paid, he may, in case of default of payment by the
drawee, maintain an action against the assignor, on the consideration of
the transfer.[f]   And, where a debtor in payment of goods gives an
order to pay the bearer the amount in bills on London, and the party
takes bills for the amount, he will not, unless guilty of laches, discharge
the original debtor.[g]   And where a person gets a bank note, navy bill,

[x] Bellingalls *v.* Gloster, 3 East, 483.—
Starey *v* Barnes, 7 East, 485.
[y] Poth. pl. 111, 112.
[z] Hill *v.* Lewis 1 Salk. 132. Edie *v.*
East India Company, Burr. 1226. Lambert, *v.* Oakes, Holt, 117. Cooke's Bank.
Law, 173.
Hill *v.* Lewis, 1 Salk. 132. Moore drew
one note payable to the defendant or his
order, and another payable to him generally, without any words to make it assignable ; the defendant indorsed them to
Zouch, and Zouch to the plaintiff ; the
first objection was, that the plaintiff had
been guilty of laches, but the jury thought
he had not, and it was then urged that
the second note was not assignable. And
Holt, C. J. agreed that the indorsement
of this note did not make him that drew
it chargeable to the indorsee, for the
words " or to his order," give authority to
assign it by indorsement, but the indorsement of a note which has not these words,
is good so as to make the indorser chargeable to the indorsee.
[a] Ante, 27.
[b] Hornblower *v.* Proud, 2 B. & A. 327.
[c] Owenson *v.* Morse, 7 T R. 64. Ward
v. Evans, Ld. Raym. 928. Lambert *v.*
Oakes, 12 Mod. 244. Anon. id. 408.
Puckford *v.* Maxwell 6 T. R. 52.
[d] Ward *v.* Evans, Ld. Raym. 928.—
Anon. 12 Mod. 408. Ward *v.* Sir Peter

Evans, id. 521. Moor *v.* Warren, and
Holme *v.* Barry, 1 Stra. 415. Turner *v.*
Mead, id. 416. *semb. contra.* Anon. 12
Mod: 517.
[e] Clerk *v* Mundall, 12 Mod 293. 1 Salk.
124. 3 Salk. 68. S. C. Anon. id. 408.
Anon. id. 517. Anon. Holt, 298, 9. *et
post.* Vin. Abr. tit. Payment, A. Cooke's
Bank. Law, 173.
[f] Owenson *v.* Morse, 7 T. R. 65, 66.—
Popley *v.* Ashley, Holt, 122, ante, 97 to
100.
[g] Ex parte Dixon, cited in 6 T. R. 142,
3; and ante, 96, 7, &c. Ex parte Blackburne, 10 Ves. 204. 1 Mont. 142, 149,
150. *acc.* Vernon *v.* Roverie, 2 Show. 296.
Bolton *v.* Reichard, 1 Esp. Rep. 106.
contra.
Owenson *v.* Morse, 7 T. R. 64. The
plaintiff bought some plate of the defendant, and gave him some country bank-
notes in payment; the notes were dishonoured, on which the defendant refused to
deliver the plate. The plaintiff brought
trover and insisted that the notes were payment, but on a case reserved, the court
held that they were no payment unless the
defendant had agreed to take them as payment, and run the risk of their being paid.
Nonsuit entered. See also Tapley *v.* Martens, 8 T. R. 451.
Ex parte Blackburne, 10 Ves. 204.—
Goods sold, to be paid for by bills at three

or other bill or note discounted, without indorsing it, and it turns out **V. Effect** to be forged, he is liable to refund the money to the party from whom **of transfer,** he received it.[b] And though a party do not indorse a bill or note, **&c.** yet he may by a collateral guarantee or undertaking, become personally liable.[d]

months. The drawers and acceptors becoming bankrupts before the bills were due, the vendors having received dividends under their commissions, entitled to prove under a commission against the vendees who had not indorsed the bills, the deficiency as a debt: till that shall be ascertained a claim and dividend reserved for the whole. The Lord Chancellor said, I take it to be now clearly settled, that if there is an antecedent debt, and a bill is taken without taking an indorsement, which bill turns out to be bad, the demand for the antecedent debt may be resorted to. It has been held, that if there is no antecedent debt, and A. carries a bill to B. to be discounted, and B. does not take A's name upon the bill, if it is dishonoured there is no demand, for there was no relation between the parties except that transaction, and the circumstance of not taking the name upon the bill, is evidence of a purchase of the bill. In a sale of goods the law implies a contract that those goods shall be paid for. It is competent to the party to agree that the payment shall be by a particular bill. In this instance it would be extremely difficult to persuade a jury, under the direction of a judge to say an agreement to pay by bills, was satisfied by giving bills, whether good or bad. The bills were only a mode of paying the debt of 3000l. If they are not paid, the original debt, arising out of the contract for goods sold and delivered, remains. It is clear, the creditor still holding the bills, cannot resort to that original contract. In general cases, where the bill is not paid, if there is no bankruptcy, the creditor must come immediately upon the bill dishonoured, saying, he cannot procure payment, and desiring to have payment; and then he might maintain an action for goods sold and delivered. There may be cases in which he may have received part of the money without involving the difficulty from giving time as to the rest of it; as, if part was paid before it was due; in that case, if no time was given for payment of the residue, an action for goods sold and delivered would lie for the residue.

[b] Jones and another v. Ryde and another, 1 Marsh. 157, 9. 5 Taunt. 488. S. C. Assumpsit for 1000l. for money had and received; at the trial the plaintiffs had a verdict, subject to the opinion of the court, on the following case: The defendants, bill brokers, were possessed of a navy bill, purporting to be for 1884l. 16s 10d. which the plaintiffs, also bill brokers, discounted for them at their request. The plaintiffs afterwards discounted it with Mr. Williams,

who presented it for payment. The date and sum in the bill had been altered since it was issued, and before it came to the hands of the defendants, the bill being originally issued for 884l. 16s. 10d. only. Williams received 884l. 16s. 10d. from the transport-office, and the plaintiffs repaid him the 1000l., and brought the present action. The court, after argument, held, that the plaintiffs were entitled to recover, and although the defendants could not be sued as indorsers (the instrument being transferrable by delivery) they were not released from the responsibility they incurred by passing an instrument which purported to be of greater value than it really was. And per Gibbs, C J. The ground of resisting this claim is, that it was a negotiable security, without indorsement; and that when the holder of a negotiable security passes it away without indorsing it, he means not to be responsible upon it. This doctrine was fully discussed in the case of Fenn v. Harrison, 3 T. R. 757, and the proposition is true, but only to a certain extent. If a man pass an instrument of this kind without indorsing it, he cannot be sued as indorser, but he is not released from the responsibility which he incurs, by passing an instrument which purports to be of greater value than it really is. This question must often have occurred in the case of *bank notes:* I believe it is not disputed, but that if a man take a forged note, he is entitled to recover the amount of it from the person of whom he received it; and I cannot distinguish this from the case of a promissory note; for though one should not be answerable on the note as party to it, one should be liable for the money which had been paid on the supposition of its being worth so much. Mr. Justice Chambre. There can be no doubt in this case: the general principle is perfectly clear, that where money has been paid without a consideration, it is to be recovered back. It would be very mischievous if the doctrine contended for by the defendants could be supported, as it would very materially affect the credit of these instruments The person who takes them, gives credit to the person who passes them to him for the amount, and if they fail, the money must be refunded. In this case, the plaintiffs, or at least Williams, who stood in their place, have done nothing but what was for the advantage of the defendants.

[d] Morris v. Stacey, Holt C. N. P. 153. A., an agent for some manufactures, sells to B., who likewise acted as an agent, a quantity of shoes, and receives certain bills of exchange in payment. B., being press-

V. *Effect* of transfer, &c.   But, as on transfer by delivery, the assignor's name is not on the instrument, there is no privity of contract between him and any assignee, becoming such after the assignment by himself, and consequently no person but his immediate assignee can maintain an action against him, and that only on the original consideration, and not on the bill itself.[k] And if only one of several partners indorse his name on a bill, and get it discounted with a banker, the latter cannot sue the firm, though the proceeds of the bill were carried to the partnership account.[l]

When a transfer by delivery without indorsement, is made merely by way of *sale* of the bill, as sometimes occurs;[m] or exchange of it for other bill,[n] or by way of discount and not as a security for money lent,[o] or where the assignee expressly agrees to take it in payment, and to run all risks;[p] he has in general no right of action whatever against the

[146]

ed to indorse them, refuses, but writes a letter to A., in which he encloses the bills, and adds, "that should they not be honoured when due, he (B.) would see them paid." Held, that this was a sufficient agreement within the 4th section of the statute against frauds to bind B. to pay for the goods in default of his principal.

[k] Ward *v.* Evans, Ld Raym 928. In the matter of Barrington, 2 Sch. & Lef. 112.

In the matter of Barrington and Burton, bankrupts, 2 Sch. & Lef. Rep. 112. B. hands over a negotiable note for valuable consideration to G., not indorsing it, but giving a written acknowledgment on a separate paper, to be accountable for the note to G. G. indorses the note, which, together with the written acknowledgment, comes into the hands of M. for a valuable consideration, and B. and the several parties to the note, become bankrupts; M. cannot prove the note against the estate of B., the written acknowledgment not being assignable: but is entitled to have the amount made an item in the account between B. and G., and to stand in the place of the latter. The Lord Chancellor. This undertaking, though for valuable consideration, was not assignable with the note, nor can it give the holder of the note, to whom it was transferred, a right to prove under it against the estate of Barrington and Burton; the note does not make them debtors. They are indeed chargeable on the ground of their undertaking in account with Gray and Son, but you can make yourselves creditors to the bankrupt's estate, only by your equitable right to stand in the place of Gray and Son. To this end an account must first of all be taken, to see whether the bankrupt's estate is debtor to Gray and Son; and the most proper course would have been to petition that the assignees of Gray and Son might prove for your benefit on the estate of Barrington and Burton; if there shall appear to be a sufficient balance due by them to Gray and Son, you will be entitled to be paid 300*l.* out of that balance. But this under-

taking does not make you creditors on the estate of Burton and Barrington. It only gives you a right to have it made an item in the account between them and Gray and Son.

[l] Emly *v.* Lye, 15 East, 7.

[m] Fenn *v.* Harrison, 3 T. R. 757 Fydell *v.* Clark, 1 Esp Rep. 447. Bank *v.* Newman, 1 Ld. Raym. 422. 12 Mod. 241; and Comyns, 57, S. C. 1 Mont. 142. 149, 150. Ex parte Shuttleworth, 8 Ves. 368. Cullen, 100, 1.

[n] Hornblower *v.* Proud, 2 B. & A. 327.

[o] Fenn *v.* Harrison, 3 T. R. 759. Ex parte Shuttleworth, 8 Ves. 368. Fydell *v.* Clark and another, 1 Esp. Rep. 447.

In Fenn *v.* Harrison, 3 T. R. 759, Lord Kenyon said, It is extremely clear, that if the holder of a bill send it to market without indorsing, his name upon it, neither morality, nor the laws of this country, will compel him to refund the money for which he sold it, if he did not know at the time that it was not a good bill. If he knew the bill to be bad, it would be like sending out a counter into circulation to impose upon the world, instead of the current coin. In this case, if the defendant had known the bill to be bad, there is no doubt that they would have been obliged to refund the money.

Ex parte Shuttleworth, 8 Ves. 368.—Newton gave the bankrupt before his bankruptcy cash for a bill, but refused to allow the bankrupt to indorse it, thinking the bill better without his name. He now proved the amount under the commission, and on a petition to have the bill expunged, the Chancellor granted the petition, observing, that this was a sale of the bill.

Fydell *v.* Clark and another, 1 Esp. 447. Where bankers, in discounting a bill, give their customers bills or notes without indorsing them, which turn out to be bad, the bankers are not liable. S. P. Bank of England *v.* Newman, 1 Lord Raym. 442. Emly *v.* Lye, 15 East, 7. 12.

[p] Owenson *v.* Morse, 7 T. R. 65, 6; ante, 148. Cooke's Bank. Law, 120. Ex parte Shuttleworth, 8 Ves. 368. Ex parte Black-

assignor, in case the bill turns out to be of no value. But there can be **V. *Effect* of transfer, &c.** no doubt, that if a man assign a bill for any sufficient consideration, knowing it to be of no value, and the assignee be not aware of the fact, the former would, in all cases, be compellable to repay the money he had received.q

The *obligation* of the assignor, though it is in general irrevocable, may, as has been already observed, be discharged or released by the act of the holder, in the same manner as the obligation of the drawer;r it may also be discharged by payment of the bill by any prior party;s but the merely taking another party in execution, will only discharge that person, and will not operate in favour of any other."t(189)

If a party indorse a bill for the accommodation of the drawer, which **Indemnity** is also accepted by a third person for the like accommodation, such **of indorser.** indorser may, after he has been compelled to pay the bill, support an action thereon against the acceptor, or may prove under his commission, in case of his bankruptcy.u And such an accommodation indorser, in case there be reasonable ground to apprehend the insolvency of his **[147]** principal, has an equitable right to withhold the payment of any money which we owe to him, until he has been indemnified against any liability on account of his indorsement, though such liability would be no defence at law to an action by the principal.x

burne, 19 Ves. 206. 15 East, 13. 1 Mont. 142. 149, 150.

Ealy v. Lye, 15 East, 13. Per Bayley, J. If a person buy goods of another, who agrees to receive a certain bill in payment, the buyer's name not being on it, and that bill be afterwards dishonoured, the person who took it cannot recover the price of his goods from the buyer, for the bill is considered as a satisfaction. It has been so held, and I can see no difference where money, instead of goods, is given for the bill; and per Kenyon, C J. In Owenson v. Morse, 7 T. R. 66. See the cases, ante, 143 to 144, in notes.

s Anon. 12 Mod. 517. Fenn v. Harrison, 3 T. R. 759. Popley v. Ashley, Holt, 121. Bayl. 167, 3.

t Synderbottom v. Smith, Stra. 649.—Gee v. Brown, id. 792. Ante, 107.

u Hull v. Pitfield, 1 Wils. 46.

x Hayling v. Mulhall, 2 Bla. Rep. 1235. Macdonald v. Bovington, 4 T. R. 825. Claxton v. Swift, 2 Show. 481. et post.

u Houle v. Baxter, 3 East, 177. The defendant, a retail silversmith, procured

goods of Capper, a working silversmith, and to enable him to obtain the silver for the order, accepted a bill, drawn on him by Capper; and to increase the credit of the bill Capper prevailed on the plaintiff to lend his indorsement. Capper then passed the bill to one Abud, who supplied the silver of which the goods were made, and delivered it to the defendant. Before the bill became due, the defendant became a bankrupt, and obtained his certificate. Plaintiff took up the bill, and brought this action, and upon the trial the plaintiff had a verdict, subject to the opinion of the court; and the court held that the bankruptcy of the defendant was a bar in the action, because the plaintiff might have proved under the commission. In Brown and others v. Massey, 15 East, 220, it appears to have been questioned, whether an accommodation indorser could sue an accommodation acceptor, if at the time he so indorsed, he knew that the acceptor had received no value.

x Wilkins v. Casey, 7 T. R. 711. as observed upon by Lord Ellenborough, Ch. J.

(189) If the indorsee after taking the maker in execution, take of him a bond or warrant of attorney to confess judgment, in satisfaction of the execution, this discharges all the other parties. M'Fadden v. Parker, 4 Dall. Rep. 275.

The discharge of one joint promisor under an insolvent act will not operate as a release of the other. Tooke v. Bennett, 3 Caines' Rep. 4.

The holder's proceedings under a commission of bankruptcy against the acceptor of a bill, will not discharge the responsibility of the antecedent parties. Kenworthy v. Hopkins, 1 John. Cas. 107. Post. 362.

A suit may lie by an indorser against his indorsee upon a special guaranty. 4 Yeates' Rep. 436.

VI. Consequences of the loss of a bill, &c. and what conduct the holder should thereupon pursue.

[148]

If the holder of a foreign or inland bill of exchange, check, or note, transferrable by *mere delivery*, (which we have seen may be when the bill was originally payable to bearer, or when the first indorsement has been in blank,[y]) *lose* or be *robbed* of it while in his possession, and it get into the hands of a person who was not aware of the loss, for a sufficient consideration,[z] *previously to its being due*,[a] such person notwithstanding he derived his interest in the instrument, from the person who found or stole it, may maintain an action against the acceptor, or other parties;[b] the original holder, who lost it, will consequently forfeit all right of action; for it may be laid down as a general principle, that whenever one or two innocent persons must suffer by the act of a third, he who has enabled such third person to occasion the loss, must sustain it.[c] And if a person who has not given a consideration for a loss or stolen bill transferrable by mere delivery, present it to the drawee at the time it is due, and he pay it before he has notice of the loss or robbery, such drawee will not in general be liable to pay it over again to the real owner.[d]

But where it is proved on the trial that the bill or note has been lost by the real proprietor, and reasonable notice has been given to the plaintiff to prove the time and circumstances under which he received it, and the consideration which he gave for it, it will be incumbent on

in Willes *v.* Freeman, 12 East, 659. Ex parte Metcalf, 11 Ves. 407. Madden *v.* Kempster, 1 Campb. 12.

[y] Ante, 147.

[z] Solomons *v.* The Bank of England, 13 East, 135. Paterson *v.* Hardacre, 4 Taunt. 114.

[a] Good *v.* Coe, cited in Boehm *v.* Sterling, 7 T. R. 427. Et ante, 126, as to *time* of transfer.

[b] Sir John Lawson *v.* Weston, 4 Esp Rep. 56. Anon., Lord Raym. 738. Anon., 1 Salk. 126. Anon., 3 Salk. 71. Exors, Devallar *v.* Herring, 9 Mod. 47. Miller *v.* Race, Burr. 452. Grant *v.* Vaughan, Burr. 1516. Peacock *v.* Rhodes, Dougl. 633. Hinton's case, 2 Show. 235.

Anon., Lord Raym. 738. Salk. 126. 3 Salk. 71. B. lost a bank bill payable to A. or bearer; C. found it, and assigned it for a valuable consideration to D., who got a new bill for it from the bank. Trover was then brought against D. for the first bill; but by Holt, C. J. " the action will not lie against *him*, because he took it for a valuable consideration, though it would against C. as he had no title; but payment to C. would have indemnified the bank."

Miller *v.* Race, 1 Burr. 452. A bank note, payable to William Tinney or bearer, was stolen out of the mail, in the night of the 11th of December, 1756, and on the 12th came to the hands of the plaintiff for a full and valuable consideration, in the usual course of his business, and without any knowledge that it had been taken out of the mail; he afterwards presented it to

the bank for payment, and the defendant, being one of the clerks, stopped it, upon which an action of trover was brought; and upon a case reserved upon the point, whether the plaintiff had a sufficient property in the note to entitle him to recover, the court was clear in opinion that he had, and that the action was well brought. (*Vide* Lawson and others *v.* Wreston and others, 4 Esp. 56.)

Grant *v.* Vaughan, 3 Burr. 1516. Vaughan gave Bicknell a draft upon his banker, payable to Ship Fortune or bearer; Bicknell lost it, and the plaintiff afterwards took it, *bona fide*, in the course of trade, and paid a valuable consideration for it. The banker refused to pay it, upon which the plaintiff brought this action against Vaughan; Lord Mansfield left it to the Jury to consider, first, whether the plaintiff came to the possession of the bill fairly, and *bona fide*; and, secondly, whether such draft was, in fact and practice, negotiable, and the jury found for the defendant: but upon an application for a new trial, and cause shown against it, the court was clear that the second point ought not to have been left to the jury, because it was clear that such drafts were negotiable, and if the jury thought the plaintiff took the note fairly, and *bona fide*, of which there appeared to be no doubt, he was entitled to recover. A new trial was accordingly granted, in which the plaintiff recovered the money. Peacock *v.* Rhodes, Dougl. 611, 633.

[c] Per Ashurst, J. in Lickbarrow *v.* Mason, 2 T. R. 70.

[d] Post. Poth. pl. 168, 169.

him to prove that he came to the possession of the instrument, *bona fide,* VI. of the
and for a sufficient consideration.[e]   And where a banker paid a check loss of bills,
the day before it bore date, which had been lost by the payee, it was &c.
held that he was liable to repay the amount to the loser, it being proved
to be contrary to the usual course of business to pay drafts before the day
on which they are dated.[f](192) So where a banker after notice discounted a bill drawn on a customer, and by the acceptance made payable at his bank after it had been lost by the holder, and afterwards debited his customer with the amount of the bill, wrote a discharge on it, and
delivered it up to the customer as the banker's vouchee of his account, [149]
it was held that the banker was thereby guilty of a conversion, for
which the loser might sue him in trover.[g]

When a bill is assignable only by *indorsement,* as no interest can be
conveyed otherwise than by that act, any person getting possession of it
by a forged indorsement will not acquire any interest in it, although he
was not aware of the forgery; and consequently the original holder in
such case may, when he has regained possession of the bill, recover
against the acceptor and drawer, although the acceptor may have paid the
bill, and if the person attempting to derive an interest under such indorsement, sue the acceptor, he will be admitted to prove that the indorsement
was not made by the person entitled to make it.[h] It is settled, that

[e] Paterson *v.* Hardacre, 4 Taunt. 114.
Where a bill has been lost, or fraudulently
or feloniously obtained from the defendant,
the holder who sues must prove that he
came to the bill upon good consideration.
But the defendant will not be permitted to
object to the want of such proof unless he
has given the plaintiff reasonable previous
notice, that he may come to trial prepared
to prove his consideration.

Solomons *v.* Bank of England, 13 East,
135. 1 Rose, 99 S. C. The holder of a
bank note is *primâ facie* entitled to prompt
payment of it, and cannot be affected by
the previous fraud of any former holder
in obtaining it, unless evidence be given
to bring it home to his privity. But where
a bank note for 500*l.*, had been fraudulently obtained by some person unknown,
and on its being presented for payment
sometime afterwards by an agent of a
foreign principal, information was given
of the fraud, and the principal was desired to inform the bank how he came
by it; but the only account he would give
of it was, that he had received it in payment of goods from a man dressed in
such a way, of whom he knew nothing ;
and it was further proved, that bank notes
of so large a value were not usually circulated in that foreign country ; this was
held to be sufficient evidence to be left to

a jury, of a principal's privity to the original fraud, in an action of trover brought
by his agent, to recover it from the bank,
who had detained it under the original
owner, to whom it properly belonged.
And the question was not altered by the
agent, who received it on account, having, after notice, made payment for his
principal, which turned the balance in favour of such agent.

[f] Da Silva *v.* Fuller, Sittings at London, Easter 1776, Sel. Ca. 288. MSS.
Post, as to whom 'payment may be made.

[g] Lovell *v.* Martin, 4 Taunt. 799.

[h] Smith *v.* Chester, 1 T. R. 654. Cheap
v. Hanley, cited in Allen *v.* Dundas, 3 T.
R. 127. Mead *v.* Young, 4 T. R. 28.
Ante, 111, note. Gibson *v.* Minet, 1 Hen.
Bla. 607.

Cheap and another *v.* Harley and
Drummond, cited 3 T. R. 127. In this
case, tried before Buller, J. it appeared
that the defendants, who had a house in
America as well as in London, drew two
bills of exchange there, the first and
second of the same tenor and date, on
their house here, payable to the plaintiffs;
one of them being lost, came into the
hands of a third person, who forged an
indorsement of the payees, and received
the amount of it from the defendants
here, and afterwards the real payees

(192) And if a bank pay to a *bona fide* holder a forged check, it cannot recall the
payment. *Levy* v. *Bank of the United States,* 4 Dall, Rep. 234. S. C. 1 Binn.
Rep. 27.

There is an implied warranty in the transfer of every negotiable instrument that it is
not forged. *Herrick* v. *Whitney, et al.* 15 John. Rep. 240.

VI. Of the loss of bills, &c. no action can be supported against the post-master-general, for the loss of bills or bank notes stolen out of letters put into the post-office.[i]

brought their action upon the other bill and recovered.

Aaron Smith and another, assignees of Bagnall and Hand v. Shepperd, London, post, Hil. Term, 16 Geo. 3. The defendant was indebted to Bagnall and Hand, the bankrupts, in thirty pounds, for goods sold and delivered, October, 1774. Comberstall, the bankrupt's servant, brought a bill of parcels in the same hand-writing that all their former bills had been, and fraudulently said his master was in want of cash, and desired he would accept a bill of exchange, which C. immediately drew, signed with his own name, payable to Bagnall and Hand, or order, and gave a receipt on the bill of parcels. The defendant accepted the bill, and C. afterwards carried it away. The bill was brought to the defendant by Spencer, who had it in payment for goods. The names of Bagnall and Hand were indorsed on the bill, and defendant paid it; but that indorsement was a forgery. It was the bankrupt's practice to deliver in their bills at Christmas; but at Christmas, after this transaction, no bill was delivered to defendant. No evidence appeared in whose hand-writing the indorsement was, but it did not appear to be like the bankrupts' or Comberstall's. Lord Mansfield said, "Each party is innocent: the question is, on whom the loss must fall? it should be on him who is most in fault. It is admitted that Comberstall used to receive money, but not draw bills. Here is a bill that does not trust Comberstall at all, for it is to pay to the order of the bankrupts; in this case, if he had been used to draw bills, that would not vary the case, because it is not pretended that the indorsement was by Comberstall; then he that takes a forged bill must abide by the consequence; for the man whose name is forged knows nothing of it. If a bill payable to bearer be lost, and found by another person in the street, who carries it to a banker who drew it, and he pays, it is a good payment, for it is the owner's fault that he lost it. In this case, the name of Bagnall and Hand is forged; it could not be paid without their hand, and the defendant has been negligent in inquiries whether it was their hand or not. The ground which defendant relies on is, that the bill was not delivered at Christmas, as usual, but that is of no weight, because it had been delivered before in October."—Verdict for plaintiff. MSS. of Mr. Serjt. Bond, in Sel. Ca. 248.

[i] Lane v. Cotton, 1 Salk. 17. Whitfield v. Lord Le Despencer, Cowp. 754.— Lane v. Cotton, 1. Salk. 17. Case against the post-master general to recover some exchequer bills taken out of a letter delivered at the post-office, in London,

Turton, Gould, and Powys, Justices, (Holt, C. J. diss.) held that the action would not lie. See also Whitfield v. Lord Le Despencer, Cowp. 754, in which it was held, that case does not lie against the post-master general, for a bank note stolen by one of the sorters out of a letter delivered into the post-office; and Lord Mansfield said, "As to an action on the case lying against the party really offending, there can be no doubt of it; for whoever does an act by which another person receives an injury, is liable in an action for the injury sustained. If the man who receives a penny to carry the letters to the post-office, loses any of them, he is answerable, so is the sorter in the business of his department. So is the post-master for any default of his own. Here, no personal neglect is imputed to the defendants, nor is the action brought on that ground; but for a constructive negligence only by the act of their servants. In order to succeed therefore it must be shown, that it is a loss to be supported by the post-master, which it certainly is not. As to the argument that has been drawn from the salary which the defendants enjoy, in a matter of revenue and police, under the authority of an act of parliament, the salary annexed to the office, is for no other consideration than the trouble of executing it. The case of the post-master, therefore, is in no circumstance whatever, similar to that of a common carrier; but he is like all other public officers, such as the lord's commissioners of the treasury, the commissioners of the customs and excise, the auditors of the exchequer, &c. who were never thought liable for any negligence or misconduct of the inferior officers in their several departments.

Thus, then, the question stood in the year 1619. In that year a solemn judgment was given, that an action on the case would not lie against the post-master-general, for a loss in the office by the negligence or fault of his servant. The nation understood it to be a judgment; and therefore it makes no difference, if what has been thrown out were true, and the writ of error was stopped in the way that has been mentioned. For the bar have taken notice of it as a judgment; the parliament and the people have taken notice of it; every man who has sent a letter since has taken notice of it; many acts of parliament for the regulation and improvement of the post-office, and other purposes relative to it, have passed since, which by their silence have recognized it. The mail has been robbed a hundred times since, and no action whatever has been brought. What have merchants done since, and continue to do at this day, as a

but a deputy post-master may be sued for neglect in not delivering
letters in due time.[k]

Hence it is obvious that the holder of a bill, particularly when transferrable by mere delivery, should, in case of loss, immediately give
notice thereof to the acceptor, and all the antecedent parties:[l] and
when the bill is transferrable by mere delivery, should also give public
notice of the loss, in order to prevent any person from taking it;[m] and [151]
which indeed will not be available unless it be brought home to the
knowledge of the party taking it.[n] It is incumbent also on the party
who has thus lost the bill, even though it has been destroyed, to make
application at the time it is due, for payment, and to give notice to all
the parties of the refusal of the drawee to pay the same, for otherwise
he will lose his remedy against the drawer and indorsers.[o]

It is said by Marius,[p] that the holder of a bill which has been lost,
should, in the presence of a notary and two witnesses, acquaint the acceptor with the loss, and signify to him that at his peril he pay it to
none but himself or his order; and the same writer says, that no person
should refuse to pay a bill which he has accepted, to the loser, on the
ground of its having been lost, if he have sufficient security and indemnification offered to him; and that if he do, he will be liable to make
good all loss, re-exchange, and charges.[q]

We have already seen, that the fraudulent misapplication by agents
of bills and notes entrusted to their care, is punishable by a recent
statute.[r] Other statutes have provided, that to steal or take by robbery
any bills, bank notes, or promissory notes, shall be felony.[s]

In France, as long ago as the beginning of the last century, the
drawer of a bill was compellable to give the holder of it another of the
same tenor, in case he lost the original bill; but in this country no such
general rule prevails in the case of *inland* bills. There is, however, a
proviso in the stat. 9 & 10 W. S. c. 17. s. 3, by which it is enacted,
"That in case any *such* inland bill shall happen to be lost or miscarried
"*within the time before limited for the payment of the same*, then the
"drawer of the said bill is and shall be obliged to give another bill of
"the same tenor with that first given; the person to whom they are
"delivered, giving security, if demanded, to the drawer, to indemnify
"him against all persons whatsoever, in case the said bills so alleged to
"be lost or miscarried shall be found again."[t] It should seem, that

caution and security against a loss? They cut their bills and notes into two or three parts, and send them at different times: one, by this day's post, the other by the next. This shows the sense of mankind as to their remedy. If there could have been any doubt therefore before the de-termination of Lane v. Cotton, the solemn judgment in that case having stood un-controverted ever since, puts the matter beyond dispute. Therefore, we are all clearly of opinion the action will not lie. Per cur. Judgment for the defendant.

[k] Rowning v. Goodchild, 3 Wils. 443. 2 Bla. Rep. 906. 5 Burr. 2711.
[l] Poth. pl. 132.
[m] Beawes, pl. 179.

[n] Sir John Lawson v. Weston, 4 Esp. Rep. 56. Ante, 26, 38.
[o] Thackray v. Blackett, 3 Campb. 164.
[p] Page 77.
[q] Mar. 10. Beawes, pl. 182. 185. Ter-cese v. Geray, Finch's Rep. 301. Vin. Ab. tit. Bills, R.
[r] Ante, 114.
[s] See stat. 2 Geo. 2. c. 25. s. 3. 9 Geo. 2. c. 18; and see the cases and precedents relative to this offence, 3 Chitty's Crim. Law, 928, 929. 967 to 970. 3 M. & S. 539. 2 Leach, 1103.
[t] It is not unusual to declare specially in assumpsit, for not giving a fresh bill; sed quare as to the remedy at law, post.

VI. Of the from the word "*such*," the statute does not extend to *all* bills of ex-
loss of bills, change, but only to the particular bills therein mentioned; namely, such
&c.   as are expressed to be for value received, and payable after date ;* but
it has been observed, that the equity of the statute would comprehend
indorsements also, and that the 3 & 4 Ann. c. 9. which gives the like
remedies upon notes, as were then in use on inland bills, would extend
the statute of William to notes.*

It is perfectly clear, that in case of the loss of a bill, &c. whether
before or after it was due, or when it is payable on demand, and might
by possibility be in the hands of a *bona fide* holder, a *Court of Equity*
has jurisdiction to enforce payment of the amount upon a sufficient
indemnity being given, but not if it were not negotiable ;* and if such
indemnity has been tendered, the defendant will in general have to pay
the costs in equity. In a late case, proof was allowed under a commission of bankrupt in respect of a bill alleged to be lost ; but the most
extensive indemnity was required to be given, and to be settled by the
commissioners, though the loss took place after the bill had been
protested.*

When the defendant himself wrongfully withholds the bill or note, it
is clear he may be sued at law.*

But in general no action at law can be supported against a party to a
bill of exchange, note, or check, indorsed in blank, so as to be transferrable to a *bona fide* holder, and lost *before or on the day it is due*,
although a bond of indemnity has been tendered to the defendant ;* and

" *Sed quære* see Walmsley *v* Child, 1
Ves. sen. 346, 7. Leftly *v.* Mills, 4 T. R.
170. 2 Campb. 215.
    * Bayl. 52. Powell *v.* Monnier, 1 Atk.
613. Kyd, 152. Walmsley *v.* Child, 1 Ves.
sen. 346, 7, where these acts are observed upon. 2 Campb. 215, in notes.
    y Walmsley *v.* Child, 1 Ves. sen. 338.
344. Toulmin *v.* Price, 5 Ves. 238. Ter-
ccse *v.* Geray, Finch's Rep. 301. Vin.
Ab. tit. Bills, R. Ex parte Greenway,
6 Ves. 812. Mossop *v.* Eadon, 16 Ves.
430. As to the mode of proceeding in
equity, 1 Ves. 341. 5 Ves. 338. 9 Ves.
812.
    * Ex parte Greenway, 6 Ves. 812.
    * Smith *v.* M'Clure, 5 East, 477. Pier-
son *v.* Hutchinson, 2 Campb. 212. Infra,
next note. 6 Esp. 126. S. C.
    b Pierson *v.* Hutchinson, 2 Gampb. 211,
6 Esp. Rep. 126. S. C. Powell *v.* Roach.
6 Esp. Rep. 76. Bayl. 169. Selw. Ni.
Pri. 4th edit. 328.
    Pierson *v.* Hutchinson, 2 Campb. 211.
6 Esp. Rep. 126. S. C. This was an action by the indorsee against the acceptor
of a bill of exchange. The Attorney-
General, in opening the plaintiff's case,
stated that he should not be able to produce the bill, as it had been lost; but he
should prove, that before the action was
brought, the defendant had been regularly called upon for payment, and had
been offered an unexceptionable indemnity. According to the usage of mer-

chants, he was thereupon bound to honour his acceptance in the same manner
as if the bill had still remained in the
plaintiff's hands, and had been actually
presented to him in the usual form. It
is laid down by Marius, (p. 19. fol. ed.)
that when an accepted bill is lost, the
party to whom it is payable should notify
this to the acceptor; "and when the bill
"falls due, and the time is come for him
"to go for the money, the party which
"had accepted the bill is not freed from
"present payment of the money, because
"the bill is lost; for though the accepted
"bill be lost, yet he that accepted it is
"not: Neither must the acceptor think
"this to be a sufficient answer for him to
"say, *show me my accepted bill and I will
"pay you*, and such like flams, merely to
"make use of the money a little longer
"time. He may, in case of obstinacy, be
"sued at law for the money, without the
"accepted bill, and be forced to the pay-
"ment thereof with costs and damages:
"and therefore merely by reason of the
"loss of the accepted bill, he can have no
"just cause or plea to detain the money
"beyond the just time from the right party
"who should receive the same." Marius
then goes on to say, that for this purpose
the party entitled to payment, has only to
give bond or other reasonable writing to
the content and good liking of the party
that did accept the bill, and such as in
reason he cannot refuse, engaging to save

if the bill be transferrable by delivery, it should seem, that even if it were lost after it became due, and after action brought, the same rule prevails;[c] nor is the defendant liable to be sued on the consideration of the bill;[d] and even an express promise, without any new consideration,

him harmless from the accepted bill which is lost, and to discharge him from the sum therein mentioned, against the drawer and all others in due form. Therefore, if it should appear in the present case, that the indemnity offered was such as in reason the defendant could not refuse, the production of the bill would be dispensed with, and the acceptance being proved by secondary evidence, the plaintiff would be entitled to a verdict. Lord Ellenborough. If the bill were proved to be destroyed, I should feel no difficulty in receiving evidence of its contents, and directing the jury to find for the plaintiff. Even on a trial for forgery, the destruction of the instrument charged by the indictment to be forged, is no bar to the proceedings. I remember a case before Mr. Justice Buller, where the prisoner had destroyed a bank note he was accused of having forged, by swallowing it. He was acquitted on the merits: but the learned Judge who presided held, that he might have been convicted without the production of the bank note, and this doctrine was approved of by the whole profession. Here, however, the instrument is not destroyed. It is lost after being indorsed by the payee. It may now be in the hands of a bona fide indorsee for value, who might maintain an action upon it against the defendant. This brings it to the indemnity. But whether an indemnity be sufficient or insufficient, is a question of which a court of law cannot judge. There are dicta to be sure, that upon the offer of an indemnity the indorsee of a lost bill may recover at law; but these are so contrary to the principles on which our judicial system rests, that I cannot venture to proceed upon them. Since the plaintiff can neither produce the bill, nor prove that it is destroyed, he must resort to a court of equity for relief. The Attorney-General said, they could shew that the bill had been discounted for the defendant's accommodation, and that the money had come into his hands; but Lord Ellenborough observed, that would not alter the case; for if the plaintiff were allowed to recover on the money counts, the defendant might still be compelled to pay the same sum a second time as a bona fide holder of the bill. Plaintiff nonsuited.

Mayor and others v. Johnson and another, 3 Campb. 324. A traveller received a country bank note payable to bearer, in a provincial town, which he cut in two, and sent the halves on different days by the post, addressed to his employers in London, one of these was stolen from the mail coach, and they received the other. It was held, that under these circum-

stances they could not maintain an action against the makers of the note, on producing that half of it which reached them safely. Lord Ellenborough said, I am of opinion, that this action cannot be maintained. It is usual and proper to pay upon an indemnity, but payment can be enforced at law, only by the production of an entire note, or by proof that the instrument, or the part of it which is wanting, has been actually destroyed; the half of this note, taken from the Leeds mails, may have immediately got into the hands of a bona fide holder for value, and he would have as good a right of suit upon that, as the plaintiffs upon the other half which reached them; but the maker of a promissory note cannot be liable in respect of it to two parties at the same time. Plaintiffs nonsuited.

N. B. This case is distinguishable from that of Mossop v. Eadon, 16 Ves, 430, post, 156, because, in that case, the notes were not payable to order or negotiable, whereas, in the above case, they were payable to bearer.

[r] Poole v. Smith, Holt's C. N. P. 144. In an action by the indorsee of a bill of exchange, against the acceptor; it appeared, that after action brought, and notice of trial, the bill, which was indorsed in blank, had been lost, and it was held, that although the bill had been drawn more than six years, the plaintiff was not entitled to recover, without producing it at the trial; and per Gibbs, C. J. upon the ground of non-production of the bill, I think I am called upon to nonsuit the plaintiff; the rule is an extremely salutary one, and ought not to be relaxed. See also Powell v. Roach and others, 6 Esp. Rep 76. S. P.

But in Brown and others v. Messiter, 3 M. & S. 281, after judgment by default, the court referred it to the Master to see what was due for principal and interest upon a bill of exchange, upon the production of a copy of the bill verified by affidavit of the plaintiff's attorney, the original having been stolen out of his pocket, and no tidings of it gained.

[d] Bevan v. Hill, 2 Campb. 381. A check given for stock sold, was lost by the vendor in going home from the stock exchange; the purchaser was immediately informed of this fact, but refused to pay without an indemnity; four months after, the bankers, on whom the check was drawn, stopped payment, with sufficient money to answer it of the drawer's in their hands; held, that under these circumstances, an action would not lie for the price of the stock. Lord Ellenborough said, it is certainly possible, that this check may get into the

VI. Of the cannot be enforced at law;* though if there be a new consideration for *loss of bills,* the promise, as the executing of a bond of indemnity to the defendant, &c. [155] he may be sued thereon.*

If, however, it can be proved that the bill has been *destroyed,* the party who was the holder may recover at law;* so if the bill was not negotiable,* or has *not* been indorsed, or if it was only *specially indor-*

hands of a person who might maintain an action upon it. The very day it was lost, it might have been passed for value to a *bona fide* holder without notice : I therefore think the defendant was entitled to an indemnity ; he could not, without this, have safely withdrawn the money from Walpole and Co. before their bankruptcy ; he then ceased to be liable upon the check, but the money was gone ; besides, the bankruptcy of Walpole and Co. may not be sustainable, and the defendant is not to be exposed to the risk of the commission being superseded. Plaintiff nonsuited.

Dangerfield *v.* Wilby, 4 Esp. Rep. 159. Where a promissory note has been given for money due by the defendant to the plaintiff, who declares on it, together with the money counts, be must prove the note lost or destroyed before he can have recourse to the money counts, if it appears that the money so claimed was that for which the note was given. Lord Ellenborough said, he was of opinion the plaintiff was not entitled to go into the consideration of the note, for, as the note for any thing that appeared in evidence was in existence, it might be still in circulation, and the defendant be liable to be called upon to pay it, so that he might be subjected twice to the payment of the same demand ; it was therefore incumbent on him to show it to be lost, so that the defendant should not be again subjected to the payment of it.(199) As to any demand therefore, on account of the note, he thought the plaintiff not entitled to recover. The plaintiff was nonsuited ; and see Pierson *v.* Hutchinson, ante, 152, n.

* Davis *v.* Dodd, 4 Taunt. 602. The plaintiff declared upon a bill of exchange for 96*l.* 9*s.* drawn by Allen, to his own order, and accepted by the defendant, and indorsed by Allen to the plaintiff. There were also the usual money counts. Upon the trial, at Maidstone, Summer Assizes, 1812, before Lord Ellenborough, C.J it was proved that the witness had lost the bill out of his pocket, whereupon, when the bill became due, he applied to the defendant, stating the circumstance, and requesting him to

pay the bill, which, until the time of action, had never been presented for payment by any other person; and *defendant repeatedly and expressly promised to pay it.* Lord Ellenborough was of opinion, that as the plaintiff had not presented the bill for payment to the defendant, and as the bill was not produced at the trial, the plaintiff could not recover in this action, and directed a nonsuit. Best, Serjeant, now moved to set aside the nonsuit, and have a new trial; he contended that the express promise to pay the bill was upheld by the consideration of the moral obligation to which the defendant was subject to pay the sum due on his acceptance. The court denied that there was any moral obligation on the defendant to pay this sum to the plaintiff, who, by his negligence, had exposed the defendant to the danger of being compelled to pay the bill when produced in the hands of another holder. It was quite clear that the plaintiff could not recover in this action, if he could recover at all upon this promise, which they much doubted, it must be in an action upon the special undertaking ; the party might have proceeded to enforce the giving of a new bill under the statute, and that seemed to be his only course. The promise contained in the bill is the equivalent given for the consideration paid for the bill, and no new consideration had been subsequently paid to sustain this new promise, which was therefore *nudum pactum,* and could not be enforced. Rule refused.

* Williams *v.* Clements, 1 Taunt. 523. Special assumpsit, alleging that the defendant was indebted on a bill of exchange, and the plaintiff having lost the same, had, at the request of the defendant, given him a bond acknowledging payment and conditioned to indemnify him against the bill, in consideration whereof, defendant undertook to pay the money on request. On motion in arrest of judgment it was held, that such count, stating such new consideration of executing the bond, was sufficient.

* Pierson *v.* Hutchinson, 2 Campb. 212. 6 Esp Rep. 126. S. C. Ante, 152, n. Bayl. 169.

* Mossop *v.* Eadon, 16 Ves. 430, post, 156.

---

(199) The same point was ruled in the same manner in *Holmes* v. *De Camp,* 1 John. Rep. 84. *Angel* v. *Felton,* 9 John. Rep. 149. *Cumming* v. *Hackley,* 8 John. Rep. 202. *Pintard* v. *Tackington,* 10 John. Rep. 104.

ered, the party who lost it may proceed by action on such bill, and secondary evidence of the contents may be admitted.[1] (200)

In Walmsley v. Child,[2] it seems to have been considered, that a party who had lost a bill payable on demand might proceed at law; and in Hart v. King,[3] where a bill of exchange was protested, and afterwards lost, the plaintiff recovered, but it does not appear in what character the plaintiff sued, and it is probable that the bill had never been indorsed. In Ex parte Greenway,[4] Lord Chancellor Eldon said, " that when he was Chief Justice he tried an action in the Common " Pleas, upon a bill alleged to be lost which had been previously " indorsed by the payee, an indemnity was offered by bond, but that " he nonsuited the plaintiff; that the counsel objected strongly upon [156] " the offer of indemnity, and it came before the court on a motion for " a new trial, and there was a long discussion on the nature of these " indemnities in a court of law; that the court had not come to a deci- " sion upon it when he left them, and he did not know the result. But " that he never could understand by what authority courts of law com- " pelled parties to take the indemnity."[5]

But in the case of Mossop v. Eadon,[6] where a bill was filed in equity for payment of a promissory note which had been cut in two parts, one of which was produced and the other alleged to be lost, and offering an indemnity, the bill was dismissed on two grounds; the first, that only half the bill was lost, and secondly, that it was not payable to order, and consequently an action at law was sustainable; and it being urged that the jurisdiction of the court of equity is not destroyed by the courts

[1] Long v. Bailie, 2 Campb. 214, in note, Mossop v. Eadon, 16 Ves. 430. 431. post, 156. Bayl. 163. Selw. Ni. Pri. 4th edit. 323.

Long v. Bailie, Guildhall, 12th December, 1805, coram Lord Ellenborough, 2 Campb. 214. This was an action against the acceptor of a bill of exchange, payable to the order of the drawer, and by him specially indorsed to the plaintiff. It was proved that a person took the bill to have it compared with the affidavit to hold to bail; that a copy was then taken, and the bill was afterwards stolen from such person. The correctness of this copy and the spe-

cial indorsement was proved, and the plaintiff had a verdict.

[2] Walmsley v. Child, 1 Ves. sen. 344, &c.
[3] Hart v. King, 12 Mod. 310. Holt, 112. S. C. Dehers v. Harriot, 1 Show. 163.

[4] Ex parte Greenway, 6 Ves. 812.

[5] See also Toulmin v. Price, 5 Ves. 235. Bromley v. Holland, 7 Ves. 19, 20. 242.

[6] 16 Ves. 430. Note, in that case the bill of exchange was not payable to order, and consequently not negotiable, which makes this case distinguishable from that of Mayor v. Johnson, 3 Campb. 325.

(200) Where a note payable on demand had been lost or destroyed, and it did not appear that it was negotiable, or if negotiable, that it had been negotiated, the payee was allowed to recover on the note. Pintard v. Tackington, 10 John. Rep. 104. But a recovery cannot be had upon a note merely lost and not destroyed, if it had been indorsed before it was lost—Ibid. See also Freeman v. Boynton, 7 Mass. Rep. 483, and Anderson v. Robson, 2 Bay's Rep. 495.

There may be a recovery against the acceptor on a bill of exchange, indorsed to the plaintiff, and lost or mislaid; and the existence of the bill being once established, the plaintiff may prove the loss of it by his own oath. Atwater et al. v. Andrews, 3 Peters' Rep. 412. See, as to the evidence in the case of lost note, Peabody v. Denton, 2 Gallis. Rep. 351.

Defendant being indebted to plaintiff for goods sold gave him a bill of exchange not due (drawn and accepted by two other persons) to a greater amount than the price of his goods, and plaintiff gave defendant the difference in money. Defendant indorsed the bill in blank and plaintiff lost the bill before it was paid; it was held that plaintiff could not sue the defendant for the price of the goods, or on the lost bill. Champion v. Terry, 3 Barn. & Ald. 671.

VI. Of the of law assuming a jurisdiction in such cases, the Master of the Rolls
loss of bills, said, " It is very clear that an action would have laid upon the note
&c. had the loss been proved. The single question is, whether the indemnity you offer is not a ground for coming here ? The court of law could not take notice of it and give a conditional judgment but equity gives that relief at the same time that it orders payment of the money. The other half of the note may be in your possession ; therefore it is fit that you should indemnify them against the possibility, that the two parts may be brought together and passed into another hand." Upon a further hearing the counsel for the plaintiff insisted, that the mere loss of the instrument gives the court of equity jurisdiction, and that it does not depend on the right to require an indemnity, observing that there was no distinction whether a note was negotiable or not. But the Master of the Rolls said, " This argument is in direct contradiction to that of Lord Hardwicke, who, in the case of Walmsley *v.* Child, assumes that this court has no jurisdiction, except for the purpose of ordering an indemnity where indemnity is necessary. I am unwilling to turn the plaintiff round, thinking the merits are with him ; but at the same time I am afraid of breaking in upon the rules established as to the jurisdiction of the courts, that where a party can recover at law, he ought not to come into equity." (1)

When a bill, &c. has been lost *before it was due,* unless the party proceed under the statute 9 & 10 W. 3. c. 17. s. 3, it may be proper that he should be confined to a Court of Equity for relief ; for as a transfer before a bill is due, though made by a person not entitled thereto, may give a *bona fide* holder a right of action thereon ; it is but just that the parties called upon to pay should be previously sufficiently indemnified, and the sufficiency of an indemnity can be more correctly ascertained in a Court of Equity than at Law ;[p] but where a bill has been lost *after* it became due, and that fact be clearly proved, there seems to be no reason why the party who lost it should not be permitted to proceed at law, and indeed without offering an indemnity, inasmuch as the law itself would in such case indemnify all the parties to the bill from any liability to a person who became holder of it after it was due ; for, as we have already seen,[q] a person taking a bill by transfer after it becomes due, holds it subject to all the objections which affected it in the hands of the party who first became wrongfully possessed of it, or who tortiously transferred it, consequently he could not sustain an action thereon against any of the parties to the bill ; and there is an additional reason why this should apply as to the drawer and indorsers of a bill, and the indorsers of a note, namely, that they must have been discharged from liability to any subsequent holder, by the want of notice from such holder of the default in payment by the drawer.[r]

[157]

[p] Ex parte Greenway, 6 Ves. 812. Pierson *v* Hutchinson, 2 Campb. 212. 6 Esp. Rep. 126. S. C. Ante, 152, n.

[q] See Tinson *v.* Francis, 1 Campb. 19. Ante, 138.

[r] Post, as to notice of non-payment.

(1) The *bona fide* owner of a bank note who has transmitted one half thereof by the mail, cannot, on the loss of that half demand payment from the bank of any part of its amount in consequence of holding the retained half merely; but he is entitled to demand the whole amount of said note on satisfying the bank of the truth of the facts, or establishing them by the judgment of a court of Equity, and giving in either case a satisfactory indemnity to secure the bank against a future loss from the appearance of the other half. *Bank of Virginia v. Ward,* 6 Munf. 169.

It is said,[a] that if one part of a *foreign* bill of exchange, drawn in VI. of the loss of bills, &c. sets, be lost by the *drawee*, or be by his mistake given to a wrong person, or if by any other means the holder cannot have a return of the bill, either accepted or not accepted, the drawee must give to the holder or to his order a promissory note for payment of the amount of the bill on the day it becomes due, on delivery of the second part if it arrive in time, if not, upon the note, and if the acceptor refuse to give the note, the holder must immediately protest for non-acceptance, and when due, must demand the money, though he have neither note nor bill, and if payment be refused, a protest must be regularly made for non-payment. In all cases if a bill of exchange be lost, and a new bill cannot be had of the drawer, a protest may be made on a copy.[t]

Where a creditor directs his debtor to remit him, by post, the money due to him by a bill of exchange, cash, note, &c. or where it is the usual way of paying such debt, if the bill be lost the debtor will be discharged;[w] but where the defendant, in discharge of a debt which he owed to the plaintiff, delivered a letter, containing the bills which were lost, to a bellman in the street, it was decided that he was not discharged from liability to pay the debt, because it was incumbent on him to have delivered the letter at the General Post-office, or at least at a receiving-house appointed by that office.[x]

[a] Beawes, pl. 188. Mar. 121. Bul. Ni. Pri. 271.

[t] Dehers v. Harriot, 1 Show. 163, post.

[w] Warwick v. Noakes, Peake, 67.

[x] Hawkins v. Rutt, Peake, 186 ; and see Parker v. Gordon, 7 East, 385.

CHAPTER V.[*]

OF PRESENTMENT OF A BILL FOR ACCEPTANCE—ACCEPTANCE—NON-ACCEPTANCE CONDUCT WHICH THE HOLDER SHOULD THEREUPON PURSUE; AND OF ACCEPTANCE SUPRA PROTEST.

ON delivery of a bill of exchange to the payee, or any other person who becomes holder by transfer, it is in some cases necessary, and in all advisable, to present it for acceptance. On such presentment, the drawee either complies with the drawer's request by accepting the bill, or refuses to do so : in which latter case it is in general incumbent on the holder to give notice to the various other persons who became parties to the bill antecedently to himself; after which any person not originally a party, may accept it *supra protest* for the honour of the drawer or indorsers ; and in some cases the holder may protest a bill for better security. In treating of each of these matters in their natural order, it will be necessary to consider, *First*, when a presentment for acceptance is necessary, and at what time, and in what manner it must be made : *Secondly*, by whom, at what time, and in what manner, an acceptance may be made, and the obligation it imposes on the acceptor : *Thirdly*, the conduct which the holder must pursue, in case of a refusal to accept: *Fourthly*, the protest for better security, and *Lastly*, of acceptances *supra protest*.

Sect. 1.—Of presentment for acceptance ; and 1st, when necessary.
[159]

When a bill is drawn payable within a specified time *after sight*, it is necessary, in order to fix the period when it is to be paid, to *present* it to the drawee *for acceptance ;*[a] but in other cases it is not incumbent on the holder to present the bill before it is due ;[b] and in Bristol, it is said, that the practice is not to present for acceptance or to accept.[c] It is, however, certainly most advisable in all cases to endeavour to get the bill accepted,[d] as by that means the holder obtains the additional security of the drawee, and the bill consequently becomes more ne-

---

[*] As checks, promissory notes, and bills, when payable on demand, are never presented for acceptance, or accepted, the observations in this chapter in regard to presentment for acceptance, will, in general, be inapplicable in these instruments.

[a] Per Eyre, C. J. in Muilman *v.* D'Eguino, 2 Hen. Bla. 565. but if a bill be on an insufficient stamp, no presentment seems necessary, ante, 58.

[b] Per Gibbs, C. S. in O'Keefe *v.* Dunn, 1 Marsh. 616 671. 6 Taunt. 305. S. C. and ante; 125, n. Bayl. 100. 1 Selw. 4th ed. 310, 311. Goodall *v.* Dolley, 1 T. R. 713. Blesard *v.* Hirst, Burr. 2670.— Per Lord Ellenborough, in Orr *v.* Magennis, 7 East, 362. *Acc.* Mar. 46. Com. Dig. tit. Merchant, F. 6. *semb. contra.*

The 7th section of the 3d & 4th Anne, c. 9. enacts, that if the holder do not take his *due course* to obtain *payment* by en-deavouring to get the bill *accepted* and paid, and make his protest for *non-acceptance* or non-payment, the taking the bill shall be considered a payment; but the statute does not appear to require a presentment for acceptance, when it would be unnecessary at common law.

Molloy, b. 2. c. 10. s. 16. If a bill is drawn upon a merchant in London, payable to J. S. at double usance, J. S. is not bound, in strictness of law, to procure an acceptance, but only to tender the bill when the money is due.

Beawes, pl. 266, p. 453. There is no obligation to procure acceptance of a bill payable at a day certain, as the time goes on, whether accepted or not ; but it is otherwise with bills payable at so many days sight. See also Marius, 12, 13.

[c] Johnson *v.* Collins, 1 East, 99.

[d] Mar. 48. Poth. pl. 148.

gotiable :[e] and if the drawee refuse to accept, the drawer and in- 1st, When
dorser may immediately be sued.[f] And it it said, that it is incumbent *present-*
on the bearer of a bill, when he is but the mere agent of the person *ment for*
entitled to it, and on the payee, when he is directed by the drawer to *is necessa-*
do so, to present it for acceptance as soon as possible, because it is only *ry.*
by acceptance that the person on whom the bill is drawn becomes
debtor, and responsible to the holder; and if the affairs of the drawer
should be deranged, an agent who has neglected to present the bill for
acceptance, might be answerable in damages and interest to the person
who employed him.[g] If a person be holder of a bill which is not addressed to any particular individual, but is accompanied with a letter of
advice, mentioning the person on whom the bill is drawn, it is said that
the bill should be presented to the person mentioned in the letter of
advice, who may thereupon accept the bill, and that if he refuse to do
so, it may be protested for non-acceptance.[h]

In cases where it would otherwise be necessary to present a bill for
acceptance, the holder may, as will be seen hereafter, excuse his neglect to do so, by proving that the drawer or other person insisting on
the want of it as a defence, had no effects in the hands of the drawee,
or had given no consideration for the bill.[i]

With respect to the *time* when bills payable *after sight* should be pre- 2dly, At
sented for acceptance, it has been observed, that the only rule which *what time*
can be applied to all cases of bills of exchange, whether foreign or *present-*
inland, and whether payable at sight, or at so many days after sight, or *ment should*
in any other manner, is, that due diligence must be used ;[k] and, as the *be made for*
drawer may sustain a loss by the holder's keeping it any great length of *acceptance.*
time, it is advisable in all cases to present it as soon as possible.[l] [160]

In the case of a *foreign* bill payable after sight, it has been decided,
that it is no laches to put it into circulation before acceptance, and to
keep it in circulation without acceptance, as long as the convenience of
the successive holders requires ; and it has even been laid down, that if
a bill drawn at three days sight were kept out in that way for a year,
this would not be laches ; and if a bill is payable in India sixty days
after sight, it is not necesssarily laches to omit presenting it for acceptance for twenty six days after its arrival. But if, instead of putting it
into circulation, the holder were to lock it up for any length of time,
this would be deemed laches.[m]

[e] Mar. 4th ed. 12. Beawes, pl. 266.—
Claxton *v.* Swift, 2 Show. 496. Selw.
Ni. Pri. 4th ed. 811.
[f] Ballingalls *v.* Glooter, 3 East, 181.—
Allan *v.* Morson, 4 Campb. 115, post.
[g] Poth. pl. 128. Mar. 46.
[h] Mar. 142, 3.
[i] De Berdt *v.* Atkinson, 2 Hen. Bla.
336. *et post*
[k] Per Buller, J. in Muilman *v.* D'Eguino, 2 Hen. Bla. 569. See also Selw.
Ni. Pri. 4th ed. 310. Bayl. 100, 1, 2.
[l] Poth. pl. 143.
[m] In Muilman *v.* D'Eguino, 2 Hen. Bla.
565. In debt on bond conditioned to pay
certain bills drawn on India at sixty days
after sight, in case they should be returned protested, defendant pleaded that they
were not presented for acceptance within

a reasonable time after the drawing. It
appeared that they were drawn the 5th
of March, 1793; that they were indorsed
on that day by defendant to plaintiffs,
who procured them for a house at Paris;
that plaintiffs sent immediate advice to
the house at Paris, and, on receiving
their directions, on the 30th of April, sent
them to India, where they arrived on the
3d of October. On the 5th of October,
the holder wrote to the drawee, who was
from home, desiring him to accept the
bills, and on the 17th of October he sent
an answer of refusal; some of the bills
were thereupon protested the 29th of October, and the rest the 18th of November.
Eyre, C. J. left the case to the jury, but
told them that he thought the bills had
been sent to India in time, as they were

2dly, At what *time* presentment should be made for acceptance

The holder of an *inland* bill payable after sight is not bound instantly to transmit the bill for acceptance, he may put into circula-

put up here for negotiation, and were therefore liable to be delayed, and that they were presented in India in time after their arrival. The jury found for the plaintiff, and on a rule to show cause why there should not be a new trial and cause shown, the court was satisfied with the verdict, and plaintiff had judgment. Eyre, C. J. said, "it is not necessary to lay down any new rule as to bills of exchange, payable at sight, or within a given time afterwards; if it were, I should feel great anxiety not to clog the negotiation of bills circumstanced like these. It would be a very serious and difficult thing to say, that a person buying a foreign bill, in the way these were bought, should be obliged to transmit it by the first opportunity to the place of its destination. There would also be a great difficulty in saying at what time such a bill should be presented for acceptance; the courts have been very cautious in fixing any time for presenting for acceptance an inland bill, payable at a certain period after sight, and it seems to me more necessary to be cautious with respect to a foreign bill payable in that manner. I think, indeed, the holder is bound to present the bill in a reasonable time, in order that the period may commence from which the payment is to take place, but the question what is reasonable time, must depend on the particular circumstances of the case; *and it must always be for the jury to determine,* whether any laches are imputable to the plaintiff. Per Buller, J. the only rule I know of, which can be applied to the case of bills of exchange is, that due diligence must be used. Due diligence is the only thing to be looked at, whether the bill be foreign or inland; and whether it be payable at sight, or at so many days after, or any other manner. But I think a rule may be thus far laid down as to laches with regard to bills payable at sight or a certain time after sight, namely, that they ought to be put in circulation; and if a bill drawn at three days sight were kept out in that way for a year, I cannot say that there would be laches; but if, instead of putting it in circulation, the holder were to lock it up for any length of time, I should say that he would be guilty of laches, but further than this no rule can be laid down. Per Heath, J. no rule can be laid down as to the time for presenting bills payable at sight, or at a given time afterwards. In the French ordinances of 1673, in Postlethwaite and Marius, it is said, that a bill payable at sight or at will is the same thing. See also Bayl. 100, 1, 2.

Goupy and another *v.* Harden and others, 7 Taunt. 159. 2 Marsh. 454.—

1 Holt C. N. P. 342. S. C. Indorsee of two bills of exchange drawn in London, 12th of May, 1815, upon Gould and Co. of Lisbon, at thirty days after sight, payable to defendants, and by them indorsed in London, and transmitted by them to the plaintiffs in Paris, and afterwards indorsed by the plaintiffs to Ricci and Sons, who further negotiated them. It was proved that the drawees paid their bills to the 30th June, 1815, but the bills were not presented to them for acceptance until the 22d August in the same year, when they were refused, and protested for non-acceptance. In this action against the defendants as such indorsers, it was objected that there had been laches in not presenting the bills for acceptance; that the bills were payable at thirty days sight. If they had been sent to Gould and Co. with due diligence, and he had refused to accept upon notice of the dishonour to the defendants, they might have recovered against the house of De Franca and Co. the drawers, who continued solvent more than two months from the date of the bills, but instead of transmitting the bills in the ordinary way to Lisbon, they are sent in general circulation, and the defendants hear nothing of the transaction till five months after the indorsement. Per Gibbs, C. J. on the trial, "The distinction is between bills payable at a certain number of days after date, and bills payable at a certain number of days after sight. In the former, the holder is bound to use all due diligence, and to present such bill at its maturity; but in the latter case, he has a right to put the bill into circulation before he presents it, and then of course it is uncertain when it will be presented to the drawee. It is to the prejudice of the holder if he delays to do it, and he loses his money and his interest. There are dicta that it ought to be done in a reasonable time." Verdict for the plaintiffs.

Goupy *v.* Harden, 7 Taunt. 162. Same case on a motion by defendant to set aside the verdict. Per Gibbs, C. J. "If these bills had been locked up, and not sent into circulation, the case would have been widely different. I know dicta may be found, that a bill payable at sight, must be presented within a reasonable time; but this very question occurred in this court in the case of Muilman *v.* D'Eguino, 2 Hen. Bla. 565. Bills were sent out to India, and one question was, whether they were presented for acceptance within a reasonable time in India, and it was held that they were; but the main question was, whether they were delayed too long in Europe before they were sent out." Upon the last point, Eyre, C. J.

tion, and if he do not circulate it, he may take a reasonable time to present it for acceptance, and a delay to present until the fourth day a bill on London, given twenty miles thereof, is not unreasonable.ᵃ

2dly, At what *time* present-ment should be made for acceptance

says, "There would be great difficulty in saying at what time such a bill should be presented for acceptance. The courts have been very cautious in fixing any time for an inland bill payable at a certain period after sight, to be presented for acceptance; and it seems to me more necessary to be cautious with respect to a foreign bill payable in that manner. I do not see how the courts can lay down any precise rule on the subject." Heath, J. says, "No rule can be laid down as to the time for presenting bills payable at sight or a given time after." The jury have found that these bills were presented in a reasonable time, but the law prescribes only that they must be presented at some time. Buller, J. is still stronger, and lays down the rule only, that the bill must be put into circulation. In the present instance these bills were put into circulation, and they passed through Paris and Genoa. He proceeds to say, "If they are circulated, the parties are known to the world, and their credit is looked to; and if a bill, drawn at three days sight, were kept out in that way for a year, I cannot say that there would be laches. But if, instead of putting it into circulation, the holder were to lock it up for any length of time, I should say that he was guilty of laches, I am therefore clearly of opinion that the parties were not guilty of laches, in putting this bill into circulation before it was presented for acceptance."

ᵃ Fry v. Hill, 7 Taunt. 397. This was an action for goods sold and delivered, and upon the trial before Parke, J. at the Sittings after Michaelmas Term, 1817, it appeared that the defendant having occasion to pay the plaintiff 134l. 18s. for goods, early on Friday the 9th of the month the defendant's bankers on his account as to 134l. 18s. (parcel) and receiving from the plaintiff the difference in cash, delivered at Windsor to the plaintiff's servant, a bill, to which the defendant was no party, drawn by themselves upon their corresponding banker in London, at one month after sight for 140l. The bill was presented for acceptance on the 13th of the same month, and the country bankers having failed on that same day, acceptance was refused. Shepherd, Solicitor-General, contended, that as well by this course of dealing which the plaintiff himself had elected, as by his laches in presenting the bill, he had made the bill his own, and was paid for the goods. The jury, however, under the direction of Pake, J. who relied on Goupy v. Harden, ante, 161, found a verdict for the plaintiff. The Solicitor-General now moved to set it aside, and

enter a nonsuit, renewing the same objections. He insisted that it was the duty of the plaintiff, receiving a bill payable at a certain time after sight, to present it for acceptance, as soon as he conveniently could: If the plaintiff had forwarded this bill for acceptance on the Friday, Saturday, Sunday, or Monday, he would thereby have enabled the defendant to withdraw his funds form his banker's hands. The necessity is more urgent to present for acceptance a bill payable after sight, than a bill payable after date, because, by deferring it, the holder protracts the period of that payment, whereby the drawer proposes to withdraw his effects from the hands of the drawee. Secondly, it was for the plaintiff's own convenience of remittance, that, instead of taking a check for the sum which the defendant proposed to pay, he had commuted it for a bill, and this was strongly evinced by his taking a bill not for 134l. 18s. but for 140l., paying the difference, and therein in blending his own property with this payment, whereby he had rendered the bill completely his own, and was paid for his goods.

Gibbs, C. J. The defendant's argument on the first point, would go to the extent, that the holder of a bill payable after sight is bound to transmit it for acceptance, without putting it into circulation at all. But even if it were a case in which it was required to give instant notice, it has been repeatedly determined that the holder of a bill is not bound to send it on the same day that he receives it; and there was no post to London on the Saturday. He might have sent it on the Sunday. But I do not go upon that ground. The holder must present a bill payable after sight in a reasonable time; but it is in the power of the holder to postpone the day of payment by postponing the day of the presentment for acceptance, and he certainly may put the bill into circulation if he will. In the recent case of Goupy v. Harden, the bills were put into circulation; here it does not appear what was done with the bill in the interval. The question on these bills drawn at sight certainly is left very loose by the cases. The result of the cases undoubtedly is, that which I have stated, and Eyre, C. J. says, in Muilman v. D'Eguino, 2 Hen. Bla. 565, that it is, under all circumstances, a question for the jury to determine whether such a bill was presented in a reasonable time. Buller, J. in the same case, rather narrows that doctrine, and though he agrees, that if it were in circulation a twelvemonth, there would not be laches; yet he says, that if instead of putting it into circulation, the

2dly, At what time presentment should be made for acceptance. It has been said, that the question what is a reasonable time, must depend on the particular circumstances of the case; and that it must always be for the *jury* to determine, whether any laches are imputable to the plaintiff;[o] and this rule appears to have been adopted in the more recent cases applicable to this subject,[p] but from other cases it should seem that reasonable time is to be taken as a question of law dependant upon the facts.[q] It was said by Lord Mansfield,[r] that what is reasonable time for giving notice of the dishonour of a bill, is partly a question of fact and partly of law; it may depend in some measure on facts, such as the distance at which the parties live, the course of the post, &c.; but that whenever a rule can be laid down with respect to this reasonable time, it should be decided by the court, and adhered to for the sake of certainty.[s] Presentment should in all cases be made during the usual hours of business;[t] but a neglect to make a presentment at a proper time may be excused by illness, or by the circumstance of war having been declared, or by other reasonable cause or accident not attributable to misconduct of the holder.[u]

3dly, *Mode of presenting for acceptance.*
[164]
The presentment should be to the drawee himself, or to his authorized agent, for otherwise the drawer or indorsers will not be chargeable.[x] It has been said that *ex rigore*, the drawee ought to accept the bill immediately on presentment, or refuse to do so, and he is not allowed three days for deliberation by the custom of merchants;[y] as, however, it is but reasonable that the drawee should have an opportunity, before he determines whether he will accept or not, of seeing whether he has effects of the drawer in his hands, the payee or holder usually may leave the bill with him twenty-four hours, or until the next day after the presentment, unless in the interim he accept or declare a determination not to accept;[z]

---

holder were to lock it up for any length of time, he would be guilty of laches. Is this, therefore, a case in which the plaintiff can be said to lock up this bill for any length of time? If we were to grant a new trial, the result would come at the last to this: *it would be a question for the jury, whether there has been a default to present a bill within a reasonable time.* That question has already been left to the jury, and they have found that the bill was presented in a reasonable time. We think, as the matter stands, it is perfectly right.—Rule refused.

[o] Per Eyre, C. J. in Muilman v. D'Eguino, 2 Hen. Bla. 609. Boehm v. Sterling, 7 T. R. 425.

[p] Muilman v. D'Eguino, 2 Hen. Bla. 565. ante, 160, note, and Fry v. Hill, 7 Taunt. 397. ante, 162. n.

[q] Darbishire v. Parker, 6 East, 12, 18. Bayl. 109.

[r] In Tindal v. Brown, 1. R 167.

[s] Appleton v. Sweetapple, Bayl. 65. n c. et post. See also Darbishire v. Parker, 6 East, 12, 13. Parker v. Gordon, 7 East, 385.

[t] Mar. 112. Parker v. Gordon, 7 East, 385.

[u] Vide post, as to what will excuse the want of giving notice of non-acceptance, or not presenting for payment; and

see Patience v. Townley, 2 Smith's Rep. 223, 4.

[x] Check v. Roper, 5 Esp. Rep. 175. Declaration against drawer of a bill for default of acceptance. To prove the fact of the bill having been presented to Hammond for acceptance, the plaintiff proved that the bill was sent by the witness, who was called, who carried it to the house which was described to him as Hammond's house; he offered it to some person in a tan-yard, who refused to accept it; but he did not know Hammond's person, nor could he swear that the person to whom he offered the bill was him, or represented himself to be so. Lord Ellenborough said, that the allegation respecting the bill was a material one, as the drawer could only become liable on the acceptor's default, which default must be proved. That the evidence here offered proved no demand on Hammond, and was therefore insufficient, so that the plaintiff could not recover on the bill. Some evidence must be given of an application to the party first liable.

[y] Com. Dig. tit Merchant, F. 6. Marius, 15, 16. and see Hamburg Ordinance.

[z] Ingram v. Forster, 2 Smith's Rep. 243, 4. Bellasis v. Hester, 1 Ld. Raym. 281. Mar. 62. Beawes, pl. 17. Mol-

But it is said that this must not be done if the post go out in the interim.[a] 3dly. *Mode of presenting for acceptance.*

If the drawee of a bill cannot be found at the place where the bill states him to reside, and it appear that he never lived there, or has absconded, the bill is to be considered as dishonoured;[b] but if he have only removed, it is incumbent on the holder to endeavour to find out to what place he has removed, and to make the presentment there;[c] [165] and he should in all cases make every possible inquiry after the drawee, and if it be in his power, present the bill to him; (214) though it will be unnecessary to attempt to make such a presentment, if the drawee has left the kingdom, in which case it will be sufficient to present the bill at his house,[d] unless he have a known agent when it should be present-

b. 3. c. 5. s. 1. Com. Dig. Merchant, F. 6. Molloy, b. 2. c. 10. pl 16.

Bellasis *v.* Hester, Ld. Raym. 281. Per Treby, C. J. The party may have the whole day to view the bill, and that is allowed him by the law.

Marius, 15. No three days for acceptance—twenty-four hours for acceptance. But if the party to whom the bill of exchange is directed, be a merchant well known unto you, and when the bill is presented to him to accept he shall desire time to consider on it, and so shall intreat you to leave the bill of exchange with him, and to come to him the next day, (provided the post do not go away in the interim) and that then he will give you answer whether he will accept or not, herein he doth demand nothing of you but what is usually allowed between merchants known one to another; for, according to custom of merchants, the party on whom the bill is drawn, may have four-and-twenty hours time to consider whether he will accept the bill or not; but that time being expired, you may, in civility, demand of the party on whom your bill is drawn, the bill of exchange you left with him to be accepted, if so he pleased, if he then say that he hath not as yet accepted it, and that he would desire you to call for it some other time, or the like; the four-and-twenty hours being expired, it is at your choice to stay any longer or not, and you may then desire a notary to go to the dwelling-house of the party that hath the bill, and demand the bill of exchange of him, accepted or not accepted, and in default of present delivery thereof, you may cause protest to be made in due form. But though this may be lawfully done, yet, notwithstanding, amongst merchants which do know one another, they do not usually proceed so strictly for acceptance, but do leave their bills with the parties, to whom they are directed to be accepted, some times two or three days, if it be not to their prejudice, as namely, if the post do not depart in the interim; but if the post is to depart within two or three days, then it is a very reasonable thing, and which men, that know the custom of merchants, will not omit to demand their bills, accepted or not accepted, so that they may give advice thereof, by the first post after the receipt of their letters, unto their friend, who sent them the bill, or who delivered the value thereof: for it is to be noted by the way."

In Ingram *v.* Forster, 2 Smith's Rep. 242. Upon the question whether more than twenty-four hours may be allowed to the drawee to determine whether he will accept, the court appear to have considered that if more than that time be given, the holder ought to inform the indorsers thereof.

[a] Mar. 62. Com. Dig. tit. *Merchant*, F. 6.

[b] Anon. Lord Raym. 743.

[c] Collins *v.* Butler, Stra. 1087. The maker of a note shut up his house before the note became due, and in an action against the indorser, one question was, whether the plaintiff had shown sufficient in proving that the house was shut up? and Lee, C. J. thought not; but that he should have given in evidence that he had inquired after the drawer, or attempted to find him out. See also Bateman *v.* Joseph, 12 East, 433, in which Lord Ellenborough left it to the jury, whether the plaintiff had used due diligence to find the party's residence, that being a question of fact. See Beveridge *v.* Burgiss, 3 Campb. 262. Browning *v.* Kinnear, 1 Gow. 81.

[d] Cromwell *v.* Hynson, 2 Esp. Rep. 211. Indorsee against the indorser of a foreign bill. When the indorsement was made, Hynson (a master of a ship) was in Jamaica, where the bill was drawn, but his residence *was at Stepney*. The bill was pre-

(214) The holder of a check must present it for payment at the bank before he can charge the drawer. *Cruger* v. *Armstrong*, 3 John. Cas. 5. and it must be presented within a reasonable time; but if the drawer sustains no injury by the want of a demand within a reasonable time, as if he has withdrawn all his funds, he will still be liable. *Conroy* v. *Warren*, 3 John. Cas. 259. *Cruger* v. *Armstrong*.

3dly. *Mode* ed to him.ʳ If on presentment, it appear that the drawee is dead, the
of present- holder should inquire after his personal representative, and if he live
ing for ac-
ceptance. within a reasonable distance, should present the bill to him.ʳ When a
bill is left for acceptance, and the drawee, after its remaining in his
possession twenty-four hours, requires time to consider of it, and the
holder grants him that time, it is at least advisable, if not necessary,
to give immediate notice to the indorsers and drawer, of the particular
circumstances.ᵍ

Sect. 2. Of   ACCEPTANCE may be defined to be the act by which the drawee evin-
acceptance; ces his consent and intention to comply with, and to be bound by, the
and 1st, by
whom it request contained in a bill of exchange directed to him, or, in other
may   be words, it is an engagement to pay the bill when due.ʰ This engage-
made.   ment is made by the drawee of the bill, or by some other person, *supra*
[166] *protest*, to the drawer or some of the other parties, either before the bill
is drawn, or afterwards, and it may be verbal or in writing; and is either
absolute, partial, or conditional, and when made after the drawing of
the bill, is according to or varying from its tenor. We will consider
these points in their natural order.

1st. By   When the holder of a foreign or inland bill presents it for accept-
whom to be ance, he is entitled to insist on such an acceptance by the drawee as will
accepted. subject him at all events to the payment of the bill according to the
tenor of it ;ⁱ and consequently such drawee must have capacity to contract, and to bind himself to pay the amount of the bill, or it may be
treated as dishonoured. An acceptance may, as has been already observed in a preceding chapter,ᵏ be made by an agent; but in such case,
it will be incumbent on the agent, if required, to produce his authority
to the holder, as, if he do not, the holder may consider the bill as dishonoured, and act accordingly.ˡ And it may perhaps be doubtful, whether the holder is in any case bound to acquiesce in an acceptance by agent,
as it multiplies the proof which he will be obliged to adduce, in case he
should be compelled to bring an action on the bill. ᵐ

There cannot be a series of acceptors of the same bill; it must be

sented for acceptance, dishonoured, and
protested, and then sent to Hynson's house
for payment, with notice of non-acceptance.
Hynson was not then in England, but the
bill was shown to his wife, and the circumstances stated to her. It was urged, 1st.
that notice should have been sent to Jamaica. 2dly. that the demand was not sufficient. But Lord Kenyon over-ruled all
the objections, and the plaintiff had a verdict.

The King *v.* The Inhabitants of Merton,
4 M. & S. 48. affords information upon this
subject. In order to establish a settlement
by apprenticeship, it was proved, that the
indenture was only of one part, and that
upon application to the pauper, who was
then ill and soon afterwards died, to know
what had become of it, he declared, that
when the indenture was given to him he
burnt it; and it was also proved, that inquiry was made of the executrix of the mas-

ter, who said she knew nothing about it
and it was held that this proof was sufficient to let in proof of parol evidence of
the contents of the indenture. Lord Ellenborough, C. J. The making search and
using due diligence are terms applicable to
some known or probable place or person.
in respect of which the diligence may be
be used. See also Carth. 509.

ᵉ Id. ibid. Phillips *v.* Astling and an
other, 2 Taunt. 206.

ᶠ Molloy, b. 2. c. 10. s. 34. Poth. pl.
146

ᵍ Ingram *v.* Forster, 2 Smith's Rep. 243,
4. ante, 164. Molloy, b. 2. c. 10. pl. 16.

ʰ Per Lawrence, J. in Clark *v.* Cock. 4
East, 72.

ⁱ Mar. 2d edit. 22.

ᵏ Ante, 23 to 29.

ˡ Beawes, pl. 87.

ᵐ Coore *v.* Callaway, 1 Esp. Rep. 116
Richards *v.* Barton, id. 269.

accepted by the drawee, or, failing him, by some one for the honour of the drawer, &c.; and therefore, if a bill of exchange be accepted by the drawee, another person who, for the purpose of guaranteeing his credit, likewise accepts the bill in the usual form; is not liable as an acceptor;[n] and unless the consideration of his engagement be expressed on the face of the instrument, it is questionable whether he would be liable in any form of action.[o]

1st By *whom* to be accepted.

The act of one partner, as has been before shown,[p] being considered as the act of both, acceptance by one for himself and partner, or in the name of the firm, will in general be a compliance with the request of the drawer; but if the bill be drawn on two, not being partners, and it be only accepted by one, it should be protested.[q] The competency of the contracting parties in general having been already stated,[r] it will be unnecessary here to make any observations relative to the capacity of the acceptor: it may however, be observed, that if the holder find that the drawee is an infant, *feme covert*, or otherwise incapable of contracting, he may treat the bill as dishonoured.

[167]

A bill, on presentment for acceptance, must be accepted by the drawee within twenty-four hours, or in default thereof, it is liable to be, and indeed, should be treated as dishonoured.[s] This space of time we have seen is allowed the drawee to give him an opportunity of examining into the accounts between himself and the drawer; if, however, the drawee refuse to accept within the twenty-four hours, 'it is not incumbent on the holder to wait till the expiration of them, but he may instantly consider the bill as dishonoured.[u]

2dly. At what *time* it may be made.

Since the late act[x] the acceptance of an *inland* bill made after the 1st of August, 1821, must be in writing on the bill itself. The very term *acceptance* seems to suppose a pre-existing bill, and independently of the act alluded to, it appears to be questionable, *whether in any case an acceptance can be made before the bill is drawn*, and at most the engagement can only be available in favour of a party who has, on the faith of it, given credit on the bill;[y] for, though in Pillans *v.* Van Mierop,[z] it was held, that a promise by the defendant, " to accept such bills

---

[n] Jackson *v.* Hudson, 2 Campb. 447. This was an action on a bill drawn by the plaintiff on I. Irving, and accepted by him, and under his acceptance, the defendant wrote " accepted, Jos. Hudson," payable at, &c. The defendant was sued as acceptor. The plaintiff offered to prove that he had had dealings with Irving, and had refused to trust him further, unless the defendant would become his surety; and the defendant, in order to guarantee Irving's credit, wrote this acceptance on the bill. Lord Ellenborough said, that this was neither an acceptance by the drawee or by any person for the honour of the drawer; that the defendant's undertaking was collateral, and ought to have been declared on as such. See also Clark *v.* Blackstock, 1 Holt, C. N. P. 474. See observations on this point, Manning's Index, 63.

[o] Id. ibid. Wain *v.* Walters, 5 East, 10. Manning's Index, 63. Sed vide Ex parte Gardom, 15 Ves. 286. Morris *v.* Stacey, Holt, C. N. P. 153.

[p] Ante, 29 to 40.

[q] Dupays *v.* Shepherd, Holt, 297. Bul. Ni. Pri. 279. In the case of two joint traders, an acceptance by one will bind the other, but if ten merchants employ one factor, and he draw a bill upon them all, and one accept it, this shall only bind him and not the rest. Vide also Marius, 2d edit. 16. Beawes, pl. 228. Molloy, b. 2. c. 10. s. 18. Bayl. 74.

[r] Ante, 13 to 20.

[s] Ante, 163, in notes. Ingram *v.* Forster, 2 Smith's Rep. 243, 4.

[t] Ante, 163, 4.

[u] Ante, 163, 4.

[x] 1 & 2 Geo. 4. c. 78.

[y] Johnson *v.* Colling, 1 East, 105. Milne *v.* Prest, 4 Campb. 393. 1 Holt, C. N. P. 181. Bayl. 79, 80.

[z] Pillans *v.* Van Mierop, Burr. 1663. See this case observed upon in Pierson *v.* Dunlop, Cowp. 572. Johnson *v.* Collings, 1 East, 105. Clarke *v.* Cock, 4 East, 70. Billans and another *v.* Van Mierop,

2dly. At " as the plaintiff should, in about a month's time, draw upon the defen-
what *time* " dant, upon the credit of a third person," (for whose accommodation
it may be the plaintiff had already accepted bills,) amounted to an acceptance; yet
made. Lord Mansfield afterwards, in the case of Pierson v. Dunlop,[a] qualified
the doctrine laid down in the above case, and observed, that " a promise
" to accept such a bill, did not amount to an acceptance, unless accom-
" panied with circumstances which might induce a third person to take
" the bill by indorsement ;" and Lord Kenyon, C. J. in Johnson v.
Collings,[b] observed, that " he thought that *the admitting a promise*
" *to accept, before the existence of the bill, to operate as an actual ac-*
" *ceptance of it afterwards, even with the qualification last mentioned,*
" *was carrying the doctrine of implied acceptances to the utmost verge*
" *of the law; and he doubted, whether it did not even go beyond the*
" *proper boundary.*" And in the last case it was established, that a
mere promise, by a debtor to his creditor, that if he would draw a bill
upon him for the amount of his demand, he should then have the
money, and would pay it, does not amount in law to an acceptance of
the bills when drawn, and that an indorsee for a valuable consideration,
between whom and the drawee no communication passed at the time of
his taking the bill, can neither recover upon a count in the declaration
upon the bill as accepted, nor on the general count for money had
and received.[c] In a more recent case at *nisi prius* it was decided by
Gibbs, C. J., that a promise to accept a bill of exchange, in a letter
written before the bill is drawn, can only be taken advantage of as an
acceptance by a person to whom the letter was communicated, and who
took the bill upon the credit of it.[d]   Therefore, where a person has,

Burr. 1663.   White drew on the plaintiffs at Rotterdam for 800*l.*, and proposed
to give them credit upon the defendants'
house in London ; the plaintiffs paid
White's bill, and wrote to the defendants
to know, " whether they would accept
such bills as they (the plaintiffs') should
draw in about a month upon them for
800*l.*, on White's credit." The defendants answered that they would ; but
White having failed before the month
elapsed, the defendants wrote to the
plaintiffs not to draw. The plaintiffs did,
however, draw, and on the defendants'
refusal to pay the bills, brought this action.   The jury found a verdict for the
defendants ; but, upon an application for
a new trial, as upon a verdict against
evidence, and two arguments upon it, the
court was unanimous that the defendants'
letter was a virtual acceptance of such
bills as the plaintiff should draw, to the
amount of 800*l.* ; and the rule was made
absolute. See also Mason v. Hunt, Dougl.
297.
    [a] Pierson v. Dunlop, Cowp. 573. John-
son v. Collings, 1 East, 106, n. a. S. P.
Clarke v. Cock, 4 East, 70.
    [b] Johnson v. Collings, 1 East, 98. Col-
lings owed Ruff 23*l.* 10*s.* 6*d.* Ruff applied for payment, and Collings said, that
if he would draw for it at two months he
would pay it.   Ruff drew accordingly,
and indorsed the bill to the plaintiff, but
did not mention to him Collings' promise. The plaintiff now sued Collings, on

the ground that his promise to Ruff was
virtually an acceptance.   But Le Blanc,
J. thought, that as it was not made to a
third person, nor with circumstances
which might induce a third person to
take the bill, it was no acceptance, and
nonsuited the plaintiff. On a rule *nisi* for
a new trial, and cause shown, the whole
court thought it no acceptance ; and Ld.
Kenyon thought, that the admitting a
promise to accept, made before the existence of the bill, to operate as an actual
acceptance of it afterwards, even though
a third person was thereby induced to take
the bill, was carrying the doctrine of implied acceptances to the utmost verge of
the law, and he doubted, whether it did
not go beyond the proper boundary. Rule
discharged.
    [c] Johnson v. Collings, 1 East, 98. Clarke
v. Cock, 4 East, 70. Wynne v. Raikes.
5 East, 514. S. P.
    [d] Milne v. Prest, 4 Campb. 393. 1 Holt,
C. N. P. 181.   It was insisted that the
following letter, written by the defendant
before the bill was drawn, amounted to
an acceptance :—" We acquit you of buying wheat instead of oats ; we will however accept the bills for the wheat when
we receive notice of its being shipped.'
The case of Johnson v. Collings was cited,
for the defendant, to show that a promise
to accept a bill not in existence, was not
binding.   Per Gibbs, C. J.   You are
within that case, unless they show that
the letter was communicated to the plain-

for a sufficient consideration, engaged in writing or in some cases even verbally, to accept a bill, *thereafter* to be drawn, such promise will not be negotiable; and the action for the breach thereof must be brought in the name of the person to whom the promise was made, and the declaration should be special, founded on the agreement.(219.) Although it has never been expressly decided, that the mere writing a name at the bottom of a blank piece of paper will have the operation of an acceptance, yet it may be inferred that it will have the same effect; it having been decided[e] that an indorsement written on a blank stamp, will afterwards bind the indorser for any sum and time of payment which the stamp will admit, and which the person to whom he intrusts it chooseth to insert; and that a person signing his name to a blank paper, and delivering it to another person, for the purpose of drawing a bill in such manner as he should choose, was bound by such signature as a drawer.[f]

2dly. At what time it may be made.

An acceptance being an absolute undertaking to pay, may be made even *after* the time appointed by the bill for payment,[g] and even after

uff, and that he received the bill with a knowledge. A promise to accept not communicated to the person who takes the bill, does not amount to an acceptance; but if the person be thereby induced to take a bill, he gains a right, equivalent to an actual acceptance, against the party who has given the promise to accept.

[e] Russell *v* Langstaff, Dougl. 514. Powell *v.* Duff, 3 Campb. 182.
[f] Collis *v.* Emmett, 1 Hen. Bla. 313.
[g] Per Ld. Ellenborough, C. J. in Wynne *v.* Raikes, 5 East, 521. Jackson *v.* Pigot, Ld. Raym. 364. Salk. 127. Carth. 450. 12 Mod. 212. In an action against the acceptor of a bill, the declaration stated, that it was dated 25th March, 1696, payable one month after date, and that in April, 1697, it was shown to the defendant, and he promised to pay it according to its tenour and effect. After verdict for the plaintiff, it was moved in arrest of judgment, that the promise was void, because, as the day of payment was past at the time of acceptance, it was impossible to pay the bill according to its tenour and effect; but it was answered for the plaintiff, that it amounted to a promise to pay generally, and the court being of that opinion, gave judgment for the

(219) In *Mason* v. *Hunt*, Doug. Rep. 296. Lord Mansfield said, "there is no doubt that an agreement to accept may amount to an acceptance, and it may be couched in such words as to put a third person in a better condition than the drawer. If one man to give credit to another make an absolute promise to accept his bill, the drawer or any other person may show such promise upon the exchange to get credit, and a third person who should advance his money upon it, would have nothing to do with the equitable circumstances between the drawer and the acceptor. But an agreement to accept is still but an agreement, and if it is conditional, and a third person takes the bill, knowing of the conditions annexed to the agreement, he takes it subject to these conditions." These observations were made in a case, where the bill was drawn after the supposed promise of acceptance was made; and therefore are entitled to be deemed something more than mere obiterdicta. The doctrine here stated has been recognized and enforced in respect to a promise to accept a bill not *in esse* in *Maryland.* (*McKim* v. *Smith*, 1 Hall's Law Journal, 485.) and in the Circuit Court of the United States in *Massachusetts* District. *Payson* v. *Coolidge.* See also *Van Reimsdyke* v. *Kane*, 1 Gall. Rep. 680. and *McEvers* v. *Mason*, 10 John. Rep. 207. *Mayhew* v. *Prince*, 11 Mass. Rep. 54. *Banorgee* v. *Hovey*, 5 Mass. Rep. 11. And an agreemant to accept a bill when drawn, if shown to a third person within a reasonable time after the agreement was made, and he take a draft on the credit of it, has been held in *Massachusetts* to be an acceptance. *Wilson* v. *Clements*, 3 Mass. Rep. 1. But although it be clear that a verbal acceptance or an acceptance by a collateral paper is good in law; (*McEvers* v. *Mason*, 10 John. Rep. 207.) yet an agreement to accept a non-existing bill, when drawn, will not operate as an acceptance, unless it be *in writing*, and shown to a third person who takes a draft on its credit, within a reasonable time. Therefore if a person in writing authorize a draft and agree to accept it, a draft drawn two years afterwards, in favour of a person who took it on the faith of the agreement to accept, will not bind the drawee. *Wilson* v. *Clements*, *Payson* v. *Coolidge*, 2 Gallis. Rep. 233. S. C. 2 Wheaton 66. *Goodrich & Deforest* v. *Gordon*, 15 John. Rep. 6.

2dly. At **a** prior refusal to accept,[h] so as to bind the acceptor, though it would what *time* it may be discharge the drawer and indorsers, unless due notice of the prior non-made. acceptance, or of non-payment at the time the bill became due, were given;[i] and in such case, the acceptor would be liable to pay the bill on demand;[k] though in pleading his liability may be stated to have been to pay according to the tenor and effect of the bill.[l] It has been observed,[m] that the drawee, although he have effects of the drawer's, [170] ought not to accept bills, after he is aware of the failure of the drawer, because after that event, one creditor of the drawer ought not to be paid in preference to another. But, payments made to a bankrupt without knowledge of his being so, are protected by the 1st Jac. 1. c. 15. s. 14; and as an acceptance of a bill for a precedent debt, has always been deemed a payment in satisfaction, provided the bill be honoured when due, there is no doubt, and indeed it has been so decided, that if a person not having notice of the bankruptcy of the drawer, accept a bill drawn on him after such bankruptcy, he will be justified in paying his acceptance, although he has afterwards heard of the bankruptcy;[n] but where a trader, after a secret act of bankruptcy, consigned goods to a factor who agreed to advance money thereon, and accordingly accepted and paid bills drawn on him by the trader, and a commission afterwards issued against such trader on such prior act of bankruptcy, after which the factor sold the goods and received the money, it was held that he was answerable to the assignees for the value of the goods.[o] If a person draw a bill of exchange on another, and deliver it to the payee for a sufficient consideration, and the drawer then die, this being an appropriation of a particular fund for the benefit of the payee, it seems that the death would be no revocation of the request to accept, and that the drawee may accept and pay.[p](221)

3dly. *Form* An acceptance may be considered with reference, 1st. to its *form*, and *effect* and 2dly, to its *extent* or *effect*. In point of *form*, before the late act of the diffe-it might be verbal, or written. But by the statute 1 & 2 Geo. 4. c. 78, rent accep-it was enacted, "that from and after the 1st day of August, 1821, no tances whe-acceptance of any *inland* bill of exchange shall be sufficient to charge ther in wri-*any* person, unless such acceptance be in *in writing on such bill*, or if ting or ver-bal, or abso-there be more than one part of such bill, on one of the said parts." In lute, condi-point of *extent* or *effect*, an acceptance is either absolute, conditional. tional, par-partial, or varying from the tenor of the bill. The holder may in all tial or va-cases insist on an absolute acceptance, in writing, on the face of the rying.

---

plaintiff. Milfor v. Walcot, Ld. Raym. 574. Salk. 129. 12 Mod. 410. Gregory v. Walcup, Com. Rep. 75, to the same effect. Beawes, pl. 224. Bayl. 76, Selw. Ni. Pri 4th edit, 312, n. 21.
    [h] Wynne v. Raikes, 5 East, 314. The defendants having previously refused to accept, afterwards wrote to the drawers a letter, stating " our prospect of security is so much improved, that we shall accept or certainly pay all the bills which have hitherto appeared," was held to amount to an acceptance. See post.
    [i] Mitford v. Walcot, 12 Mod. 410.
    [k] See the cases in note, supra.

[l] Id. ibid.
    [m] Poth. pl. 96, *et vide* Pinkerton v. Marshall, 2 Hen. Bla. 334, and cases there cited.
    [n] Wilkins v. Casey, 7 T. B. 711. Ante. 119, note; and see observations in Copland v. Stein, 8 T. R 208.
    [o] Copland v. Stein, 8 T. R. 208. This is altered as to transactions upwards of two months before the date of the commission, see 46 Geo. 3. c. 135.. 49 Geo. 3. c. 121; see also ante, 115 to 120.
    [p] Tate v. Hiblert, 2 Ves. jun. 115, 6. Hammonds v. Barclay, 2 East, 227.235, 236, post, tit. *Payment, sed quære.*

---

(221) And see *Peyson* v. *Hallett*, 1 Caines' Rep. 379. and *Cutts* v. *Perkins*. 12 Mass. Rep. 206. to the same effect.

bill, according to the terms of the bill, and in default thereof, may consider the bill as dishonoured.⁹ 3dly. *Form and effect* of acceptances.

And, therefore, in a late case,ʳ in an action on a bill, against the drawer of a bill drawn on Lisbon, payable in *effective* and *not in val vals*," and the drawee had offered to accept it, payable in *val denaros*, another sort of currency, it was held that the holder might have refused such acceptance, and protested the bill as dishonoured; and Lord Ellenborough said, " The plaintiff had a right to refuse this acceptance. The drawee of a bill has no right to vary the acceptance from the terms of the bill, unless they be unambiguously and unequivocally the same. Therefore, without considering whether a payment in ' *denarbs*' might have satisfied the term ' *effective*,' an acceptance in ' *dcnaros*' was not a sufficient acceptance of a bill, drawn payable in ' *effective*.' The drawee ought to have accepted generally, and an action being brought against them on the general acceptance, the question would properly have risen as to the meaning of the term." So in Parker v. Gordon,ˢ Mr. Justice Lawrence said, " The holder of a bill may refuse to take a special acceptance payable at a banker's, but if he choose to take it, he must comply with the terms of it, and present it there in the usual banking hours, or he will discharge the drawer and indorsers." If, however, he be satisfied with any of these acceptances, each will be obligatory on the acceptor, and if due notice thereof be given to the other parties to the bill, they will also be liable. Premising, as a general rule, that what amounts to an acceptance is a question of law, and not of fact,' the nature of these several acceptances will be considered in their proper order. [171]

Before the recent act,ⁿ it was established that a valid acceptance may be in *writing*, on the *bill itself*, or on *another paper*, as by a letter undertaking to accept bills already drawn,ˣ or that it may be *verbal*; (223) and as that act only relates to *inland* bills, it it still necessary to con- 1st *Form.*   [172]

---

⁹ Poth. pl. 47   3 & 4 Anne, c. 9. s. 5. Parker v. Gordon, 7 East, 387. Gammon v. Scanoll, 5 Taunt. 344. 1 Marsh. 80. S. C.
ʳ Boehm v. Garcias, 1 Campb. 425.
ˢ 7 East, 385.
ᵗ Sproat v. Matthews, 1 T. R. 182. 186.
ᵘ Geo. 4 c. 78. Ante, 170.
ˣ Clarke v. Cock, 4 East, 71. Ex parte Dyer. 6 Ves. 9. Holt, C. N. P. 83, 4. Selw. Ni. Pri. 4th edit. 311. In Crutchey v. Mann, 1 Marsh. 29. it seems to have been doubted, whether an engagement on another paper to accept a foreign bill must not be stamped, but this, it should seem, cannot be necessary.
ˣ Clarke v. Cock, 4 East, 67. Ex parte Dyer, 6 Ves. 9. Lumley v. Palmer, Rep. temp. Hardw. 74. Stra. 1000. S. C. Clarey v. Dolbin, Rep. temp. Hardw. 278. Dupays v. Shepherd, Holt, 297. Mar. 65. See 3 & 4 Anne, c 9. s. 5. Bayl. 70, n. e.

Cox v. Coleman, M. 6 Geo. 2. cited *arguendo*, Ann. 75. A foreign bill drawn on defendant was protested for non-acceptance, and returned, and afterwards de- fendant told the plaintiff, " if the bill comes back I will pay it," and this was held a good acceptance.

Lumley v. Palmer, Str. 1000. Rep. temp. Hardw. 74. In an action against the defendant as acceptor of a bill, the acceptance appeared to be parol only; which Lord Hardwicke, C. J. ruled to be sufficient, that being good at common law, and the stat. 3 & 4 Anne, c. 9. sec. 5 & 8. which requires an acceptance to be in writing, in order to charge the drawer with damages and costs, having a proviso that it shall not extend to discharge any remedy that any person may have against the acceptor. But Eyre, C. J. of the Common Pleas, having ruled it otherwise in Rex v. Maggot 7 Geo. 2. an application was made for a new trial, and the court, to settle the point, ordered it to be argued; upon the argument the court held Lord Hardwicke's direction right, and Eyre, C. J. waived his opinion and agreed with the court of King's Bench, and this determination is referred

---

(223) The same doctrine was recognised in M'Evers v. Mason, 10 Johns. Rep. 207. Wilson v. Clement, 3 Mass. Rep. 1.

3dly. *Form and effect of acceptances.* sider the decisions as they still effect *foreign* bills, and also inland bills drawn before the 1st August, 1821. In Johnson v. Collings,[a] Lord Kenyon, C. J. observed, "that it is much to be lamented, that any thing has been deemed to be an acceptance of a bill of exchange, besides an express acceptance in writing; but he admitted, that the cases had gone beyond that lien, and had determined that there might be a parol acceptance." And in Clarke v. Cock,[a] Lord Ellenborough, C. J. observed, "That if the law in this respect were to be framed *de novo*, it might perhaps be desirable to have nothing else taken as an acceptance, than an acceptance in writing on the bill itself, that every one to whom it passed, might see on the face of the instrument itself, whether or not it were accepted ; but that it is now much too late to recur back to that, after the various decisions in the times of Lord Hardwicke and Lord Mansfield ;" and he also observed,[b] "That it might be for the convenience of mercantile affairs, that a bill might be accepted by a collateral writing, without the bill itself coming to the actual touch of the acceptor, which would sometimes create great delay." And therefore in Clarke and others v. Cock,[c] where A. in consideration of having commissioned B. to receive certain African bills payable to him, drew a bill upon B. for the amount, payable to his own order, and B. acknowledged, by letter, the receipt of the list of the African bills, and that A. had drawn for the amount, and assured him that it would meet with due honour from him ; this was holden an acceptance of the bill by B.; and the purport of such letter, having been communicated by A. to third persons, who, on the credit of it, advanced money on the bill to A., and who indorsed it to them, it was also holden, that B. was liable, as acceptor, to an action by such indorsees, although after the indorsement, in consequence of the African bills having been attached in B's. hands, who was ignorant of his letter having been shown, A. wrote to B., advising him not to accept the bill when tendered to him, which, as between A. and B., would have been a discharge of B's. acceptance, if the bill had still remained in A's. hands. And in Wynne and another v. Raikes and others,[d] it was holden, that a letter from the drawees of a bill in England, to the drawer in America, stating, that " their prospect of security being so much improved, they should accept or certainly pay the bill," is an acceptance in law, although the drawees had before refused to accept the bill, when presented for acceptance by the holder who resided in England, and

[173] again, after the writing such letter, refused payment of it when presented for payment, and although such letter, written before, was not received by the drawer in America until *after the bill* became due.

It is necessary, however, to observe, that an inland bill cannot be protested for non-payment, unless it has been accepted in writing.[e] If a party to a bill, on being asked if it be his own hand-writing, answer that it is, and will be duly paid, or if he has paid several other bills accepted in the same hand-writing, he cannot afterwards set up, as a defence, forgery of his name ; for he has accredited the bill, and induced another to take it.[f]

to and approved of in Julian v. Scholbrooke, 2 Wils. 9. Powel v. Mounier, 1 Atk. 612, and in Pillans v. Van Mierop, Burr. 1662. Lord Mansfield says, a verbal acceptance is binding, and in Sproat v. Matthews, 1 T. R. 182, it was taken for granted by the court and bar, that a parol acceptance was good. See also Stra. 817.

[a] Johnson v. Collings, 1 East, 103
[a] Clarke v. Cock, 4 East, 67.
[b] Id. ibid. 4 East, 71. S. C.
[c] Id. ibid. 4 East, 57.
[d] Wynne v. Raikes, 5 East, 514.
[e] 9 & 10 Wm. 3. c. 17. s. 1.
[f] Leach v. Buchanan, 4 Esp. Rep. 226. Butler v. Gingell, 3 Esp. Rep. 60. Jones

As already observed, an acceptance, in regard to *extent* or *effect*, may 2dly *Extent* or *effect*. be either absolute, conditional, or partial, or varying from the tenor of the bill.   In regard to these, many of the points in the pages immediately preceding, are applicable.

An *absolute* acceptance is an engagement to pay the bill according to *Absolute.* its tenor.   At present, the usual mode of making such an acceptance is either by writing on the bill the word "*accepted*" and subscribing the *drawee's name ;* or by writing the word "*accepted*," only; or it may be by merely writing the *name*, either at the bottom, or across the bill. Where a bill payable after sight is accepted, it is usual and proper also to write the day on which the acceptance is made.[c]   And if on production of such a bill an acceptance appears to have been written by the defendant, under a date which is not in his hand-writing, the date is evidence of the time of acceptance, because it is the usual course of business in such cases for a clerk to write the date, and for the party to write his acceptance under the date.[h]   On a written acceptance by any other person than the drawee, it should seem essential that his name should appear.[i]   By the practice of the London bankers, if one banker who holds a check drawn on another banker, presents it after four o'clock, it is not then paid, but a mark is put on it to show that the drawee has effects, and that it will be paid, and this marking amounts to an acceptance, payable next day at the clearing house.[k]   When an acceptance is made by one partner only, on the partnership account, he should [174] regularly subscribe the name of the firm, or express that he accepts for himself and partner;[l] but any mode which indicates an intention to be bound by the terms of the request in the bill, will bind the firm.[m] And when by an agent for his principal, he must subscribe the name of such principal, or specify that he does it as agent, as otherwise it may, if he be named or described in the direction of the bill, make him personally responsible.[n]   It has been adjudged, that if a bill be made payable in a city or large town generally, it must, by the acceptance, be made payable at some particular house or place there, and if not, that the holder may protest it, which seems reasonable, as otherwise it would be difficult in many cases for the holder to find out the residence of the drawee.[o] (226) Much discussion has of late taken place upon the

[c] Ryde, 1 Marsh. 159, 160 ; and Price v. Neal, there cited.
Leach v. Buchanan, 4. Esp. Rep. 226. Indorser against the acceptor of a bill of exchange ; the only evidence as to the acceptance was, that the defendant had acknowledged to witness that this acceptance was his hand-writing, and that it would be duly paid. The defendant offered to prove that the acceptance had been forged by the drawer, but Lord Ellenborough held, that when the evidence given by the plaintiff was wholly discredited, it could not entitle the defendant to a verdict; and as he so accredited the bill, and induced a person to take it, he should hold him liable for the payment; and the plaintiff had a verdict.
[f] Beawes, pl. 266.
[h] Glossop v. Jacob, 4 Campb. 227. 1 Stark. 69. S. C.
[i] Bayl. 78.
[k] Robson v. Bennett, 2 Taunt. 388.
[l] Ante, 39.
[m] Ante, 39.   Mason v. Rumsey; 1 Campb. 384.
[n] Poth. pl. 118.   Thomas v. Bishop, 2 Stra. 955.   Macbeath v. Haldimand, 1 T. R. 172.
[o] Gregory v. Walcup, Comyns, 75. Mutford v. Walcot, Ld. Raym. 574.

(226) Where a foreign bill is drawn on persons residing in A., payable in B., without any particular place in the latter city being designated where payment is to be made, the holder may demand acceptance and payment of the drawees, at A , and a protest for non-acceptance or non-payment will be good if made there; or the holder may at his election, if payment is not made at B. at the maturity of the bill, protest the bill there for non-payment. For as no place in B. is pointed out to which the holder might resort, and

3dly. *Form and effect of acceptances.* eflect of an acceptance payable at a particular place, and which we will consider when we examine the presentment for payment. If the drawee determine that the bill shall be payable only at a particular place, the statute 1 & 2 Geo. 4. c. 78, enacts. that he must, in his acceptance, express that he accepts the bill "payable at a banker's house, or other place only, and not otherwise or elsewhere."

In general, as no formal act is required to constitute a simple contract, and any mode which demonstrates an intention to become bound by it, will have an obligatory force on the contracting party; any act of the drawee which evinces a consent to comply with the request of the drawer, will constitute an acceptance. Thus the word "accepted," "seen,"[p] "presented,"[q] the day of the month,[r] or a direction to a third person to pay the bill,[s] written thereon, or any other paper, relating to the transaction,[t] will amount to an acceptance; and though the bill be not addressed to any person, yet if defendant write across it, "accepted, C. M." he will be liable as acceptor;[u] nor, indeed, as we have just seen, was it necessary before the late act, that the acceptance should be in writing.[x]

[175]

An acceptance may also as to foreign bills and inland bills drawn before 1st August, 1821, be *implied* as well as expressed; and it is said

[p] Poth. pl. 45.

[q] Anon. Comb. 401. Per Holt, C. J. If the drawee underwrites a bill " presented such a day, or only the day of the month," it is such an acknowledgment of the bill as amounts to an acceptance, and this was declared by the jury to be the common practice; and see Vin. Abr. tit. Bills of Exchange, L. 4. Bayl. 77.

[r] Id. ibid.

[s] Moor *v.* Whitby, Bull. Ni. Pri. 270. A bill, drawn by Newton on the defendant was presented for acceptance ; the defendant wrote upon it, " Mr. Jackson, please to pay this note, and charge it to Mr. Newton's account. R. Withby." It was insisted that this was no acceptance, but only a direction to Jackson to pay it out of a particular fund, and if there were no such fund the money was not to be paid. *Per cur.* This is a direction to Jackson to pay the money, and it signifies not to what account it is to be placed, when paid; that is a transaction between them only, and this is clearly a sufficient acceptance. Bayl. 77, 8. Selw. Ni. Pri. 4th edit. 314.

[t] Wilkinson *v.* Lutwidge, Stra. 648.

Drawer against the acceptor of a bill of exchange. The question was as to the validity of the acceptance. The bill was drawn in New England, and remitted to the plaintiff's correspondent in London, together with another bill drawn upon the same account, both which were sent to the defendant for his acceptance, who. in his letter acknowledging the receipt of them, wrote thus, " the two bills of exchange which you sent me, I will pay them, in case the owners of the Queen Anne do not, and they living in Dublin. must first apply to them. I hope to have their answer in a week or ten days. I do not expect they will pay them, but I judge it proper to take their answer before I do. which I request you will acquaint Mr. Wilkinson with, and that he may rest satisfied with the payment." The defendant insisted that this was only a conditional acceptance, to pay in case the owners of the Queen Anne did not. But Raymond, C. J. held the acceptance an absolute one. See also, Pillans *v.* Van Mierop, 3 Burr. 1663.

[u] 3 Moore, 91.

[x] Ante, 170, 171.

the drawees reside at A. an attempt to search for them at B. would be without object or effect; and the holder is not bound to go elsewhere, as the bill has directed payment at B.; and he may conform his conduct to the tenor of the bill. And on the other hand it is a sound rule that where no particular place of payment is fixed, a demand upon the drawees *personally* is good; and a general refusal to pay is a refusal according to the tenor of the bill, and is equivalent to a refusal to pay in B. *Mason* v. *Franklin,* 3 John. Rep. 202. *Bort* v. *Franklin,* 3 John. Rep. 207.

Where a note is not payable at any particular place, and the maker has a known and permanent residence within the state, the holder is bound to make a demand of payment, there, in order to charge the indorser; but where a note was dated at *Albany,* and the maker had removed to *Canada,* a demand of payment at *Albany* was held sufficient *Anderson* v. *Drake.* 14 John. Rep. 114.

that it **may be inferred from** the drawee's keeping the bill a great length of time, or by any other act, which gives credit to the bill, and induces the holder not to protest it; or is intended as a surprise upon him, and to induce him to consider the bill as accepted.ʲ But it should seem that the mere detention of a bill for an unreasonable time by the drawee [176] will not amount to an acceptance, although the drawee destroy the bill.ᵃ And by the usage of trade in London, a check may be retained by a banker, on whom it was drawn, till five o'clock in the afternoon of the day on which it is presented for payment, and then returned, though it has been previously cancelled by mistake.ᵇ And constructive acceptances ought to be watched with the utmost care, for when a party puts his name on a bill, he knows what he does, and that he thereby enters into a contract; but it is laying down a very loose and dangerous rule when any degree of latitude is given to these cases of constructive acceptances. The cases which have been determined in favour of these constructive acceptances have all been decided upon very special circumstances.ᶜ As far as it respects inland bills drawn after the 1st August, 1821, these constructive acceptances have been

ʲ Clavey *v.* Dolbin, Rep. Temp. Hardw. 278. Peach *v.* Kay, post, 178, n. Harvey *v.* Martin, 1 Campb. 425. Fernandez *v.* Glynn, 1 Campb 426. Poth. pl. 46.

Harvey *v.* Martin, 1 Campb 425. Bayl. 51, n. 2. In an action by the payee and holder of a bill against the defendant as acceptor, it appeared that the bill was drawn in Guernsey, where the drawer and the plaintiff resided, on the defendant, who lived in Cornwall, dated 13th of March, 1805, at three months; that within a fort-night after it was drawn, the plaintiff sent it to the defendant, desiring him to accept it, and remit to S. Dobree, the plaintiff's correspondent in London. On 15th April, 1805, the plaintiff, finding that the bill had not been sent to S. Dobree, wrote to the defendant, requesting him to accept and send it, stating, that though he considered the keeping of the bill as tantamount to an acceptance, yet that it was not the same to him, as S. Dobree would not give him credit for it until he received it accepted. The defendant, however, did not accept the bill, or remit it, or give any notice of his refusal so to do. On 1st of June, the defendant signed a letter, admitting that he had kept the bill, though told by the plaintiff that he considered his doing so as tantamount to an acceptance, as he intend-ed to have paid it, but having no effects of the drawer's, refused to pay; and on 4th of July, when the bill was protested for non-payment, he said he had neglected to write an acceptance upon it, thinking it of no consequence, as he meant to pay it. Lord Ellenborough referred to a MS. case of Trimmer *v.* Oddie, in which Lord Kenyon expressed an opinion, that a mere keeping of a bill was an acceptance, and said he inclined to entertain the same opinion, but should leave that question to the jury, on the custom. Gibbs, however, for the de-fendant. admitting that he could not an-

swer the case, a verdict was found for the plaintiff. And on an application to Lord Ellenborough to certify for a special jury, his Lordship refused, saying, that this was a clear case, but that it it had not been attended with such strong admissions on the part of the defendant, but had been a mere case of a bill kept by the drawee, he should have thought it a fit case for a special jury to decide whether such de-tention of the bill amounted to an accept-ance.

See Scaccia de Commerciis et Cambio, folio 383. num. 335. who, in enumerating the different acceptances, mentions, that which is made *tacite per receptionem et detentionem litterarum.* See also Poth. Contrat de Change, part 1, chap. 3d. page 39, who observes, that the ordonnance having directed that an acceptance should be in writing, had rendered inadmissible the acceptation *tacite* resulting from the drawees having received and retained the bill.

ᵃ Mason *v.* Barff, 2 B. & A. 26.

ᵃ Jeune *v.* Ward, 1 B. & A. 653.

ᵇ Fernandez *v.* Glynn, 1 Campb. 426, in notes; plaintiff paid into the house of Vere and Co. a check on the defendant's house. Vere's clerk took it to the clearing house to be paid, and put it into the defendant's drawer. Vere's clerk received it back be-fore five, cancelled, with a memorandum written under it, *"cancelled by mistake"* The course was proved to be for the clerks to take the checks from the drawers, and send them to the respective bankers, and those which they will not pay are returned before five o'clock. Lord Ellenborough held, that notwithstanding the cancelling, the defendant had till five o'clock to re-turn the bill; and having so returned it, it amounted to a refusal to pay. See also Turner *v.* Mead, 1 Stra. 416.

ᶜ Mason *v.* Barff, 2 B. & A. 35, 6.

3dly. Form and effect of acceptances. put an end to by the late act, requiring the acceptance to be *in writing on the bill itself.*[d]

A verbal or written *promise* to accept, at a future period, a bill *already* drawn, or that a bill then drawn, shall meet due honour,[e] or shall be accepted, or certainly paid when due,[f] amounts to an absolute acceptance; and a promise of the same nature, as for instance, "leave the bill and I will accept it,"[g] and it be proved that the bill was

[177] sent or left accordingly,[h] will also amount to a complete and absolute acceptance, in the hands of a *bona fide* holder, although the drawee had no consideration for the promise.[i] So a letter promising that a bill already drawn shall be paid, will operate as an acceptance, although the letter be not received until after the bill has become due, and although no person has been induced by such promise to take the bill.[k] So a verbal promise to accept, though the party expressly defer a written acceptance, yet where he says, "leave the bill and I will accept it," is a complete acceptance,[l] and a verbal promise to accept a returned bill when it shall come back, is binding if it be returned.[m] But as we have already seen, a promise to accept a non-existing bill is not an acceptance, although the party may be sued specially for the breach of his engagement.[o]

A promise to accept in future, made on an *executory* consideration, will not bind, while the consideration remains *executory*, unless it influence some person to take or to retain the bill ;[p] and in all cases, if the promise to accept in future be obtained from the drawee, by any

[d] 1 & 2 Geo. 4. c. 78. Ante, 170.
[e] Clarke v. Cock, 4 East, 69, 70.
[f] Wynne v. Raikes, 3 East, 514. Ex parte Dyer, 6 Ves. 9.
[g] Bul. Ni. Pri. 270. Molloy, b. 2. c. 10. s. 20. Mar. 17 Bayl. 81. *acc.* Pierson v. Dunlop, Cowp. 573. *Semb. contra,* and *quære* if this answer would amount to an acceptance, if given within the twenty-four hours which the drawee usually has to accept the bill.
Bul. Ni. Pri. 270. A small matter amounts to an acceptance, as saying, "leave the bill with me and I will accept it," for it is giving a credit to the bill, and hindering the protest.
Lord Ellenborough, in Clarke v. Cock, 4 East, 69, said, "It has been laid down in so many cases, that a promise *that a bill when due shall meet with due honour*, amounts to an acceptance, and that without sending it for a formal acceptance in writing. that it would be wasting words to refer to books on the subject."
Lord Ellenborough, in delivering judgment in Wynne v. Raikes, 5 East, 521, said, "A promise to pay an existing bill, is an acceptance. A promise to pay it is also an acceptance. A promise therefore to do the one or the other, *i. e.* to accept or certainly pay, cannot be less than an acceptance."
[h] Anderson v. Hick, 8 Campb. 179 A bill drawn upon the defendants was returned unaccepted, but one of the defendants afterwards told the plaintiff, "if

he would send it (the bill) to the counting-house again, he would give directions for its being accepted." The plaintiff contended that this promise amounted to an acceptance ; but could not prove that the bill was sent back to the defendant's counting-house. Lord Ellenborough said. "This was only a conditional promise to accept, and could not operate as an acceptance till the bill was sent back to the counting-house ;" plaintiff nonsuited. See also Cox v. Coleman, cited Rep. Temp Hardw. 74.
[i] Pillans v. Van Mierop, 3 Burr. 1669.
[k] Wynne v. Raikes, 5 East, 514. ante, 169, note.
[l] Molloy, b. 2. c. 10. s. 20.
[m] Cox v. Coleman, ante, 171, and Anderson v. Hick, 3 Campb. 179. supra, note.
[n] Ante, 167, 168.
[o] Smith v. Brown, 2 Marsh. 41.
[p] Bayl. 78, 79. cites Pillans v. Van Mierop, 3 Burr. 1669. and see Clarke v. Cock, 4 East, 70. Wynne v. Raikes, 5 East, 521. Holt, C. N. P. 183. In Pillans, v. Van Mierop, 3 Burr. 1669, Ld. Mansfield says, it was argued at the trial that this imported to be a credit given to Pillans and Rose, in prospect of a future credit to be given by them to White, and that this credit might well be countermanded before the advancement of any money, and this is so.

fraud or misrepresentation, it will not bind him, unless it be in the ^{3dly. _Form_} hands of a _bona fide_ holder.ᑫ

and *effect* of accept-ances.

To constitute an acceptance there must be some circumstance from whence it may be inferred that the drawee imagined he had induced the holder to consider the bill as accepted,ʳ and the whole of the circumstances must be taken together, and there must be evidence of a contract to charge a party as acceptor.ˢ Therefore an express refusal to accept, as, " I will not accept the bill ;"ᵗ or an answer given by the drawee when the bill is called for, "there is your bill, it is all right ;"ᵘ cannot be construed into an acceptance, unless intended to deceive the holder, and to induce him to consider it as an acceptance.ˣ And where the drawee after a refusal to accept, on the ground that he had no effects, promised to attempt to procure payment for the holder, because he had just received some effects; on which the bill was presented to him, and he desired the holder to leave it, and said, that he would examine into it ; whereupon the bill was left with him eight or ten days, and was then called for, on which the drawee offered to let the holder sell some of the effects, and pay himself ; this conduct was holden not to amount to an acceptance.ʸ So it has been determined, that if the drawee of a bill say he cannot accept it without further direction from I. S., and I. S. afterwards desire him to accept and draw upon A. B. for the amount, the mere drawing a bill upon A. B. will not amount to an absolute acceptance, nor can become such before the bill on A. B. is accepted.ᶻ And where the drawee of a bill, on presentment for payment, said, "this bill will be paid, but we cannot allow you for a duplicate protest," and the holder refused to receive payment without the charges of such protest, this was held not to

[178]

ᑫ Pillans v. Van Mierop, 3 Burr. 1669.
ʳ Ante, 174. Bentinck v. Dorrien, 6 East, 201.
ˢ Per Lord Hardwicke, in Clavey v. Dolbin, Rep Temp. Hardw. 278. Action upon an inland bill of exchange against the acceptor, and the evidence of an acceptance was this ; the bill having been presented for acceptance, and refused by the drawee, because he had no effects, was returned into the country, and a little while afterwards, the bill being hazardous, plaintiff's agent met the drawee and asked him if he could not help to secure him his debt, and he said he would if he could, for he had now some effects in his hands ; whereupon the agent immediately wrote for the bill, and presented it to the drawee, who bid him leave the bill and he would examine into it, and it was left with him eight or ten days, and then the agent called again, and the drawee offered to let him sell some of the effects and pay himself, which the agent refused, and thereupon this action was brought ; and per Lord Hardwicke, indeed, it has been adjudged, that a parol acceptance will be good, and possibly leaving the bill ten days with the drawee might of itself be such a consent as to amount to an acceptance. But this is not so, for you must take the whole together, and there must be evidence of a contract

to charge the acceptor, whereas it is otherwise upon this evidence. Rees v. Warwick, 2 B. & A. 113.
ᵗ Peach v. Kay, Bayl. 78. *acc.* Lumley v. Palmer, Rep. Temp. Hardw. 75, in notes, (where a written refusal is said to amount to an acceptance) *contra.*
In Lumley v. Palmer, Rep. Temp. Hardw. 75, there is this note : "Underwriting or indorsing a bill thus, *I will not accept this bill*, is held by the custom of merchants to be a good acceptance," but in Bayley on Bills, 78, it is stated that Lord Mansfield, in Peach v. Kay, Sittings after Trinity Term, 1781, said, "It was held by all the Judges, that an express refusal to accept, written on the bill, where the drawee apprized the party who took it away, what he had written, was no acceptance ; but if the drawee had intended it as a surprise upon the party, and to make him consider it as an acceptance, they seemed to think it might have been otherwise."
ᵘ Powell v. Jones, 1 Esp. Rep. 17.
ˣ Id. Ibid.
ʸ Clavey v. Dolbin, Rep. Temp. Hardw. 278, ante, 178, note, but see Harvey v. Martin, 1 Campb. 425, 6. ante, 175, in notes.
ᶻ Smith v. Nissen, 1 T. R. 269.

3dly. *Form and effect of acceptances.* amount to an acceptance.[a] So where the drawer of a bill wrote to the drawee, stating, that he valued on him for the amount, and added, "which please to honour;" to which the drawee answered, "the bill shall have attention;" it was held, that these words were ambiguous, and did not amount to an acceptance of the bill, inasmuch, as although an acceptance may be made by a letter to a drawer, still that can only be so where the terms of the letter do not admit of doubt.[b] And in all case when the undertaking is doubtful, the drawee will be at liberty to rebut the presumption in favour of an acceptance; as, where a bill was sent by post to the drawee for acceptance, and he entered it in his bill-book, wrote upon it to the number of the entry, and kept it ten days, and on the tenth day minuted the day of the month on it, and returned it, saying he could not accept, it was adjudged that these circumstances did not constitute an acceptance, it being proved that it was the drawee's practice to enter all his bills, whether he meant to accept them or not.[c]

[180] If the drawee of a bill be desirous not entirely to dishonour it, he may make such an acceptance as will subject him to the payment of the money only on a contingency, in which case the acceptance is called *conditional.*[d] This is permitted, though we have seen that the bill cannot be *drawn* payable on a contingency.[e] The holder *is not bound* to receive such an acceptance, but if he do receive it, he must observe its

[a] Anderson and others v. Heath and others, 4 M. & S. 303. Where the holders of a foreign bill of exchange, payable sixty days after sight, presented it to the drawees for acceptance, which being refused, they protested it for non-acceptance, and afterwards, on the day it became due, presented it to the drawees for payment, making a charge for the expenses of protesting it; to which the drawees said, "this bill will be paid, but we cannot allow you for a duplicate protest." And the holders refused to receive payment, without the charges; and afterwards the drawees revoked their offer to pay; held, that they might well do so, for this did not amount to an acceptance of the bill by the drawees. Lord Ellenborough said, that is this case the defendants had, as it were, commenced the work of discharging the bill, and were upon the very brink of paying it, when the subject of the charge for the duplicate protest was started, which caused them to hold their hand. But at this time neither of the parties were treating about *accepting* the bill, nor was it ever mentioned or contemplated by them; all that was thought of was the payment of the bill. If therefore this could enure as an acceptance, it would enure against the plain intent of the parties. It is undoubtedly true, that if a merchant, upon being applied to for his acceptance, uses words which import a promise to pay the bill, this will amount to an acceptance; but it is not so where the words are used upon a different occasion, and with a different intent. Now in this case all that was ever contemplated was payment, and

as to that the defendant says, if you will take the amount of the bill it shall be paid, but if you choose to insist on having the seventeen shillings, I will not pay it. Not one word passes about acceptance; and the party unfortunately elected to stand upon his claim to the seventeen shillings, but for which he would have been paid. And Le Blanc, J. added, that to hold this an acceptance, would be to hold it something never intended by the parties. And *per curiam,* judgment of nonsuit.
[b] Rees v. Warwick, 2 B. & A. 113.
[c] Powell v. Monnier, 1 Atk. 611. A bill was sent by the post to the drawee for acceptance; he entered it in his bill book (which was his practice with all bills he received, whether he intended to accept them or not) wrote upon it in the number of this entry, and kept it ten days; on the tenth he wrote upon it the day of the month, and returned it, saying he could not accept it. And per Lord Hardwicke, "It has been said to be the custom of merchants, that if a man underwrites any thing, be it what it may, it amounts to an acceptance; but if there were nothing more than this in the case, I should think it of little avail to charge the defendant;" but he decided that a letter, the drawer had written, amounted to an acceptance. and see Mason v. Barff, 2 B. & A. 20.
[d] Bayl. 83, 4, 5. Selw. N. P. 4th edit. 316, 7. Milne v. Prest, Holt, C. N. P. 182. 4 Campb. 393. Anderson v. Hick, 3 Campb. 179. Langston v. Corney, Campb. 176. Gammon v. Schmoll, 5 Taunt. 344. Swan v. Cox, 1 Marsh. 176.
[e] Colehan v. Cooke, Willes, 398. nc'e d. ante. 42 to 50.

terms.[f] He should give immediate notice to the other parties to the bill, of the nature of the acceptance offered;[g] by which means they will not be discharged from liability to pay the bill, in case it should be returned.

Any act which evinces an intention not to be bound, unless upon a certain event, is a conditional acceptance. Thus an acceptance by the drawee of a bill, to pay, "as remitted for;"[h] or "on account of the ship Thetis, when in cash, for the said vessel's cargo;"[i] or a promise to accept a returned bill, "when it shall come back"[k] or to accept "as soon as he should sell such goods;"[l] or an answer "that the bill would not be accepted till a navy bill was paid;"[m] or "that the drawer had consigned a ship and cargo to him (the drawee) and another [181] person at Bristol, but that as he could not then tell whether the ship would arrive at London or at Bristol, he could not accept at that time;"[n] or to pay if a certain house should be given up to the drawee before a named day;[o] have respectively been holden to be conditional acceptances, and not to render the acceptor liable to the payment of the bill until the contingency has taken place.[p] But an answer by the drawee, that he would pay if another person would not, was construed to amount to an absolute acceptance, it appearing that the drawee held himself liable at all events, and that from other circumstances, it was not intended as a conditional acceptance.[q] And until the late decision and statute it was not settled whether the drawee, by accepting the bill, payable at a particular place, qualifies his general liability, so as to render it necessary to present the bill for payment at that place.[r] A conditional acceptance becomes as binding as an absolute one, when the event has happened on which the drawee undertook to pay the bill.[s]

[f] Per Bayley, J. in Sebags v. Abitbol, 4 M. & S. 466. and in Boehm v. Garcias, 1 Campb. 425. Per Lord Ellenborough. The plaintiff had a right to refuse this acceptance. The drawee of a bill has no right to vary the acceptance from the terms of the bill, unless they he unambiguously and unequivocally the same.

Gammon v. Schmoll, 5 Taunt. 353. *Per curiam.* A man is not bound to receive a limited and qualified acceptance; he may refuse it and resort to the drawer; but if he does receive it, he must conform to the terms of it. See also Parker v. Gordon, 7 East, 387. S. P.

[g] Per Bayley, J. in Sebags v. Abitbol, 4 M. & S. 466.

[h] Banbury v. Lisset, Stra. 1212. The drawee accepted a bill "*for Lisset and Galley, of Leghorn, to pay as remitted for thence, at Usance;*" and it was objected in an action against him, that there was no evidence to show he had a remittance and that his acceptance was conditional only. Lee, C. J. declared he so understood it; but he left it to the jury, and they found for the defendant upon another point, and gave no opinion upon this.

[i] Julian v. Shobrooke, 2 Wils. 9. The defendant accepted a bill to pay, *when in cash, for the cargo of the ship, Thetis;* and on being sued, moved in arrest of judgment, that a conditional acceptance was

not good, but the court held otherwise, and over-ruled the objection.

[k] Cox v. Coleman, cited in Lumley v. Palmer, Rep. Temp. Hardw. 74. ante, 171, n.

[l] Smith v. Abbott, Stra. 1152. Anon. 12 Mod. 477.

Smith v. Abbott, Stra. 1152. The defendant accepted a bill, "*to pay when goods consigned to him were sold.*" He sold the goods, and on being sued upon his acceptance, in arrest of judgment, that it was not binding, because it was conditional; but the court, on consideration, held, that though the plaintiff might have refused to take it and have protested the bill, yet as he did take it, it was binding on the defendant.

[m] Pierson v. Dunlap, Cowp. 571. ante, 168, n. An answer "that the bill would not be accepted till a navy bill was paid," was held a conditional acceptance, to pay when the navy bill should be discharged.

[n] Sproat v. Matthews, 1 T. R. 182. post, 182, 3.

[o] Swan v. Cox, 1 Marsh. 177.

[p] Id. ibid. Clark v. Cock, 4 East, 73.

[q] Wilkinson v. Lutwidge, Stra. 648.

[r] Gammon v. Schmoll, 5 Taunt. 344. Sebags v. Abitbol. 4 M. & S. 462. See post, as to presentment for payment.

[s] Banbury v. Lisset, Stra. 1212. Lumley v. Palmer, Rep. Temp. Hardw. 74. Pierson v. Dunlop, Cowp. 571. Sproat v.

3dly. *Form and effect of acceptances.* But it must nevertheless be declared on specially, with an avermen.' that the conditon has been performed.[t]

With respect to the mode of annexing the condition, it is observed, that if a man intend to make a conditional acceptance, and accept in writing, he should be careful to express in such written acceptance the condition he may think proper to annex; for if the acceptance be in writing, but the condition be not, he will not be at liberty to avail himself of it against any subsequent party, if either such party, or any intermediate one between him and the person to whom the acceptance was given, took the bill without notice of the condition, and gave a valuable consideration for it; and at all events, the *onus* of proving such condition will lie upon the acceptor.[u] If, however, the terms of the acceptance be ambiguous, parol evidence may be resorted to in order to explain them.[x] And where an executrix gave an acceptance for a debt due from her testator, and at the same time took a written engagement on another paper from the drawer to renew the bill from time to time until sufficient effects were received from the estate: this was held a sufficient qualification of the acceptance.[y]

Partial or varying.
[182] A *partial* acceptance *varies* from the tenor of the bill, as where it is made to pay part of the sum for which the bill is drawn,[z] or to pay at a different time,[a] or place.[b] An acceptance may also vary from the tenor, in the manner in which the acceptor undertakes to pay the bill;[c] as for instance, part in money, and part in bills, or payable at a banker's, &c.;

Matthews, 1 T. R. 182. supra, n. Lewis v. Orde, 1 Gilb. Evid. by Loft, 179.
[t] Langston v. Corney, 4 Campb. 176. Swan v. Cox, 1 Marsh. 176.
[u] Clarke v. Cock, 4 East, 73. Kains v. Sir Robert Knightly, Skin. 54. Thomas v. Bishop, Rep. Temp. Hardw. 1, 2, 3. cites Mason v. Hunt, Dougl. 296. Bowerbank v. Monteiro, 4 Taunt. 846. Bayl. 84.
[x] Swan v. Cox, 1 Marsh. 179.
[y] Bowerbank v. Monteiro, 4 Taunt. 844.
[z] Wegersloffe v. Keene, 1 Stra. 214. Petit v. Benson, Comb. 452. Molloy pl. 26. Mar. 68. 85. Poth. pl. 48. Wegersloffe v. Keene, 1 Stra. 214. A foreign bill for 127l. 18s. 4d. was drawn on the defendant and he accepted it, to pay 100l. part thereof; he was sued upon this acceptance, and on demurrer to the replication, insisted that a partial acceptance was not good within the custom of merchants, but the court held otherwise, and judgment was given for the plaintiff.
[a] Molloy, 283. In Price v. Shute, as mentioned in Molloy, lib. 2 c. 10. s. 20, a bill drawn payable on the 1st January, was accepted to be paid the 1st of March, the holder struck out the 1st March, and put in 1st January, and when it was due, according to that date, he presented it for payment, which the acceptor refused, whereupon the payee struck out the 1st January, and restored 1st March, and recovered in an action brought on that acceptance, as the case is understood by Buller, J.; see also Bayl. 87, n. b. but in Paton v. Winter,

1 Taunt. 423. Lawrence, J. observed, that Master v. Miller, three Judges against Buller, thought there must have been some mistake in Molloy's account of that decision, or that the case was not law; and that Lord Kenyon held the case not to conflict with Master v. Miller, because there the acceptance only was altered, and there was no alteration of the bill itself. Bayl 87.
Walker v. Atwood, 11 Mod. 190. A bill was drawn on the defendant 8th April, and no time fixed for its payment, it was presented to the defendant 18th April, and he accepted it to pay the 8th September, this being stated in the declaration. the defendant demurred, and insisted, that as no time was prescribed for the payment the bill was payable at sight, and then a promise to pay two or three months after sight was not an acceptance within the custom of merchants, but the court held it was an acceptance within the custom, and the demurrer was overruled.
[b] See the cases of Sebag v. Abithol, 4 M. & S. 462. Gammon v. Schmoll, 5 Taunt. 344. post. Per Abbott, J. Cowie v. Halsall, 1 B. & A. 198, 9.
[c] Petit v. Benson, Comb. 452. A bill was accepted to be paid half in money and half in bills, and the question was, whether there could be a qualification of an acceptance, and it was proved by divers merchants that there might, for that he might refuse the bill totally and accept it in part, but that the holder was not bound to acquiesce in such acceptance.

this also differs from a bill in its original formation, which we have seen must be for the payment of money only.[d]

In case of an acceptance varying in a material respect from the tenor of the bill, the holder, if he intend to resort to the other parties to the bill in default of payment, should immediately give notice to them of such conditional or partial acceptance,[e] and should if he meant to avail himself of the acceptance, express in his notice, the nature of it; for any act from whence it may be collected that the holder does not acquiesce in the acceptance, such as a general notice of non-acceptance, will be a waiver of it.[f]

The liability which an acceptance imposes on the drawee, may be collected from the preceding part of this chapter, in which it has been shown, that an absolute acceptance in an engagement to pay according to the tenor of the bill,[g] and a conditional or partial one, to pay according to the tenor of the acceptance,[h] and a drawee having accepted a bill after a condition annexed thereto by the indorser, is bound thereby, and should not pay the bill until the condition be performed.[i] He is *primarily* liable to pay the bill, and the drawer and indorsers are liable on his default.[k] But he is not liable to pay re-exchange.[l] If he accepted the bill without value, and for the accommodation of the plaintiff, he may resist the payment altogether, and he is at liberty to show that the acceptance was partly only for value, and as to residue, for the accommodation of the plaintiff.[m] It has been already observed, that as the interests of third persons are in general involved in the efficacy of a bill, an acceptance will, when the bill is in the hands of a third person who has given value for it, and who became the holder before it was due, be obligatory on the acceptor, though he received no consideration, and although the holder knew that circumstance;[n] for the very object of an accommodation acceptance, is to enable the party accommodated to obtain money or credit from a third person, and therefore the want of consideration furnishes no defence to one who had advanced money on the credit of the acceptor, though he may have been de-

[183]

[d] Ante, 45.

[e] Mar. 68. 85. Paton *v.* Winter, 1 Taunt. 422, 3. Per Bayley, J. in Sebag *v.* Abitbol, 4 M. & S. 466, Bayl. 115, 6.

[f] Sproat *v.* Matthews, 1 T. R. 182. Bentinck *v.* Dorrien, 6 East, 200. Bayl. 116

Sproat *v.* Matthews, 1 T. R. 182. The drawee of a bill of exchange, when a bill was presented to him for acceptance, said, that a ship was consigned to him and a person in Bristol, and that till he should know to which port the ship would come, he could not accept; but afterwards said that the bill would be paid though the ship should be lost; the plaintiff noted the bill for non-acceptance. The ship did afterwards arrive, and the defendant disposed of the cargo, and in an action against the defendant as acceptor, Buller, J. held, that the acceptance was conditional only, and that the noting showed that the plaintiff did not choose to take it, and directed a nonsuit, and upon a rule to show cause why there

CHITTY ON BILLS.

should not be a new trial, the court discharged the rule.

[g] Poth. pl. 164. Leftley *v.* Mills, 4 T. R. 174.

[h] Poth. pl. 115. 6, 7.

[i] Robertson *v.* Kensington, 4 Taunt. 30. Ante, 139, note.

[k] Laxton *v.* Peat, 2 Campb. 187. n.

[l] Woolsly *v.* Crawford, 2 Campb. 445. Napier *v.* Crawford, 12 East, 420.

[m] Darnell *v.* Williams, 2 Stark. 166.— Ante, 69, &c.

[n] Ante, 69. Simmonds *v.* Parminter, 1 Wils. 187, 8. Vere *v.* Lewis, 3 T. R. 183. Master *v.* Miller, 4 T. R. 339. Poth. pl. 119. 121. Molloy, pl. 28. and Mallet *v.* Thompson, 5 Esp. Rep. 178. Knox *v.* Smith, 3 Esp. 46. per Lord Eldon, C. J. In an action against the acceptor of a bill by an indorsee, for a valuable consideration, it is no defence that the bill was accepted merely for the accommodation of the drawer, and that this was known to the plaintiff; *secus* where the indorsee has notice that the bill

4thly. Of frauded by the drawer.[o] The judgment of Lord Eldon in Smith *v.* the *liabili-* Knox,[p] states the law very clearly upon this subject. He said, "If a *ty* of the person gives a bill of exchange for a particular purpose, and that is *acceptor.* known to the party who takes the bill; as if for example, to answer a particular demand, there the party taking the bill cannot apply it to a different purpose; but where a bill is given under no such restriction, but merely for the accommodation of the drawer or payee, and that is sent into the world; it is no answer to an action on that bill, that the defendant accepted it for the accommodation of the drawer, and that that fact was known to the holder; in such case, if the holder gave a *bona fide* consideration for it, he is entitled to recover the amount though he had full knowledge of the transaction. And though the holder of a bill may have received it with full notice of its having been accepted for the accommodation of the party dealing with him, yet he may retain the same as a security for a subsequent balance, unless the accommodation acceptor withdraw such bill;[q] but if a bill be accepted for the accommodation of the drawer for a particular purpose, which is afterwards satisfied, and the holder have notice thereof, he cannot afterwards apply the bill as a security upon another transaction; and therefore if A. accept a bill for the accommodation of B., which B. delivers over to C., his creditor, to provide for a bill about to become due, and C., before A's. acceptance becomes due, returns it to B. as useless, in order that it may be forwarded to A., and abandons all claim on the bill, he cannot, by subsequently obtaining possession of the bill, acquire a right of action against A.;[r] and where the drawer of a bill, accepted for his accommodation, indorsed it for value to his bankers, and before the bill became due became bankrupt, it was held, that the bankers, who knew that the bill was accepted for the accommodation of the drawer, could not recover from the acceptor more than the amount of their balance, as between them and the drawer at the time of his bankruptcy;[s] and where it can be shown that the plaintiffs are agents for a third person, who ought not in justice to recover the amount of the bill, such proof will defeat the action.[t](1)

[185]   An acceptance by an executor on account of debts due from his tes-

was drawn for a particular purpose, and has not been applied to it.
[o] Id. ibid. Ex parte Marshall, 1 Atk. 231. Arden *v.* Watkins, 3 East, 325.— Smith *v.* Knox, 3 Esp. Rep. 46. Haley *v.* Lane, 2 Atk. 182. Darnell *v.* Williams, 2 Stark. 166.
[p] 3 Esp. Rep. 46. and see the observations of the court as to the liability of an accommodation acceptor, in Fentum *v.* Pocock, Marsh. 16, 17.
[q] Atwood and another *v.* Crowdie and another, 1 Stark. 483. A. and Co. bankers in the country, being pressed by B. and Co. bankers in town, to whom they are indebted, to send up any bills that they can procure, transmit for account an accommodation bill accepted by D. and Co. When the bill becomes due, the balance is in favour of B. and Co. but the

bills are not withdrawn, and afterwards the balance between the houses turns considerably in favour of A. and Co. and is so when B. and Co become bankrupts. It was held that A. and Co. were entitled to recover against the acceptor. Upon a motion for a new trial it was contended, that the bill had not been sent for the purpose of securing a fluctuating balance, but on account of a then existing debt. Lord Ellenborough. Upon what terms D. and Co. originally accepted the bill does not appear, but the circumstances indicate what the nature of the transaction was; their not withdrawing their bills or demanding them back, showed that they considered themselves to be sureties.
[r] Cartwright *v.* Williams, 2 Stark. 340.
[s] Jones *v.* Hubbert, 2 Stark. 304.
[t] Lee *v.* Zagary, 8 Taunt. 114.

---

(1) An accommodation bill is not issued, until it is in the hands of some person who is entitled to treat it as a security available in law. *Downes* v. *Richardson*, 5 Barn. & Ald 674. Ante, 106.

tator, is an admission of assests, and will therefore make him personally responsible in case there be no effects of the testator in his hands ;[n] and it is no defence for an acceptor to an action by a *bona fide* holder, that the drawer's name has been forged ;[x] and if the drawee, on being asked if the acceptance be his hand-writing, answers that it is, and that it will be duly paid, he cannot afterward set up as a defence, forgery of his name, for he has accredited the bill, and induced another to take it.[y](242) If the holder of a bill, the acceptance of which turns out to have been forged by an indorser, delivers it up to him and receives a fresh bill, he may recover upon the latter, unless there was an agreement between him and such indorser to stifle a prosecution for the forgery.[z]

4thly. Of the *liability* of the acceptor.

[n] King v. Thom, 1 T. R. 487.
[x] Price v. Neal, 3 Burr. 1354. 1 Bla. Rep. 390. S. C. Two forged bills were drawn upon the plaintiff, which he accepted and paid ; on discovering the forgery, he brought this action for money had and received, to recover back the money. At the trial, the jury found a verdict for the plaintiff ; and on a case reserved, Lord Mansfield said, it was incumbent on the plaintiff to be satisfied that the bills drawn upon him were the drawer's hand-writing, before he accepted and paid them ; but it was not incumbent on the defendant to inquire into it. See also Smith and another v. Mercer, 1 Marsh. 453. S. P. and Jones v. Ryde, id. 160. Barber v. Gingel, 3 Esp. Rep. 60. Ante, 173.

Wilkinson v. Lutwidge, Stra. 648. In an action against the acceptor of a bill, Raymond, C. J. allowed the plaintiff to read the bill, without proving the drawer's hand, because he thought the acceptance a sufficient acknowledgment on the part of the defendant ; but he said it would not be conclusive ; and if the defendant could show to the contrary, the reading of the bill should not preclude him.

Jenys v. Fawler, 2 Stra. 946. In an action against the acceptor of a bill, Raymond, C. J. held it was not necessary for the plaintiff to prove the drawer's hand, and on the defendant's calling witnesses to swear that they believed it was not the drawer's hand, the Chief Justice would not admit the evidence, and inclined strongly that actual proof of forgery would not exonerate the defendant.

In Smith v. Chester, 1 T. R. 655, Baller, J. said, that when a bill is presented for acceptance, the acceptor looks to the hand-writing of the drawer, which he is afterwards precluded from disputing, and it is on that account he is liable, even though the bill is forged.

Per Dampier, J. in Bass v. Clive, 4 M. & S. 15. Suppose the drawer's name is forged, yet if the drawee accept the bill, he is precluded from averring, as against strangers, that it is a forgery.

[y] Leach v. Buchanan, 4 Esp. N. P. C. 226. The plaintiff, before he took a bill, sent a person with it to the defendant, to inquire whether the acceptance upon it were his hand-writing ; the defendant said that it was, and that it would be duly paid. He now offered evidence of the actual forgery of the acceptance ; but Lord Ellenborough held, that that proof would not discharge the defendant ; that after having so accredited the bill, and induced a person to take it, he was bound to take it. Verdict for the plaintiff.

Cooper v. Le Blanc, 2 Stra. 1051. The plaintiff, on discounting a note, sent to the defendant to know whether an indorsement on it was his, and the defendant said it was, and the note would be paid when due; he would notwithstanding have given evidence by similitude of hands, that the indorsement was a forgery, but Lord Hardwicke would not allow it ; he seemed inclined however to admit proof of actual forgery, but the defendant could not adduce it, and the plaintiff had a verdict. See Wilkinson v. Lutwidge, Stra. 648. supra.

[z] Wallace v. Hardacre, 1 Campb. 45.

(242) It seems that if the drawee accept a forged bill in the hands of a *bona fide* holder, he is bound by it ; for he is presumed to know the hand-writing of the drawer, and by his acceptance to take this knowledge upon himself. *Levy* v. *Bank of the United States*, 4 Dall. 234. S. C. 1 Binn. 27. At all events if he pay the bill, he cannot recover the money back. Ibid. And if a bank once pay a forged check, or carry it to the credit of the holder, it is conclusive upon the bank. Ibid.

4thly. Of the *liability* of the acceptor.

This obligation of the acceptor, it is said, is. *irrevocable.*[a] Thus in

[a] Mar. 88. Molloy, book 2. chap. x. pl. 28. page 103. Laws of Hamburgh, article 7. Bayl. 88.

In Trimmer *v.* Oddy and others, tried before Lord Kenyon, July 12th, 1800, Guildhall, London, Gibbs for plaintiff, Erskine for defendant ; (MS. and cited in Bentinck *v.* Dorrien, 6 East, 200. See also Bayl. 88, in notes. Note, the declarations contained counts against the drawee for having mutilated the bill.) Lord Kenyon said, " If the drawee deface the bill, he is liable as acceptor. About forty years ago it was thought, that if a man wrote any thing upon a bill, he was to be bound as an acceptor ; so that if a man had set down some sums of money, and cast them up on the back of the bill, that would amount to an acceptance. But this is a doctrine to which I cannot subscribe ; but if a party put upon a bill that which essentially injures and defaces it, that makes him liable *as acceptor.* When the defendants had written an acceptance on the bill, they could not be allowed to strike it out again, or that gives no time to the party to change his mind, but if accepted by *mistake,* it might then be otherwise ;" and Lord Kenyon said, he " inclined to think that in such case the drawee would not be liable." It is observed in Bayl. 88, n. 2. that this case was cited in Bentinck *v.* Dorrien, 6 East, 200. and the Hamburgh Ordinances was referred to, as having been recognised by Lord Kenyon to be the law of merchants here ; and Lord Ellenborough said, " the rule is certainly laid down in the Hamburgh Ordinance, as stated that an acceptance once made cannot be revoked, though to be sure that leaves the question open as to what is an acceptance, whether it be perfected before the delivery of the bill." And Lawrence, J. in the last-mentioned case, 6 East, 201. said " when the general question shall arise, it will be worth considering how that which is not communicated to the holder, can be considered as an acceptance, while it is yet in the hands of the drawee, and where he obliterates it before any communication made to the holder." From this it would appear that Mr. J. Lawrence had taken the same view of this question as Pothier, who cites from La Serra, C. 10. a case where the holder of a bill having left it for acceptance, the drawee, before he returned it, cancelled the acceptance which he had written and signed upon it, and it was adjudged that this acceptance was annulled, and observes " *La raison est, que le concours de volontés qui forme un contrat, est* ?*ni concours de volontés que les parties se*

sont réciproquement déclarées ; sans cela, la volenté d'une partié ne peut acquérir de droit a l'autre partie, ni par conséquent être irrevocable. Suivant ces principes, pour que le contrat entre le propriétaire de la lettre et celui sur qui elle est tirée, soit parfait, il ne suffit pas que celui-ci ait en pendant quelque temps la volonté d'accepter la lettre, et qu'il ait écrit au bas qu'il l'acceptoit ; tant qu'il n'a pas déclaré cette volonteé au porteur, le contrat n'est par parfait ; il peut changer de volonté et rayer son acceptation." Traité du Contrat de Change, part 1. ch. 3. s. 3. pl. 44. See also Emerigon Traité des Assurances, ch. 2. s. 4. p. 45. who observes that La Serra, " *Pose en maxime, que tant que l'acceptant est maître de sa signature. c'est à dire, qu'il n'a pas déliveré la lettre de change il peut rayer son acceptation.*" See also Stevenson on Bills, p. 162. 164.

Thornton *v.* Dick and others, 4 Esp. Rep. 270. A bill drawn on the defendants payable three months after sight. was, on the 1st of October, left with them by the plaintiffs for acceptance. It was not called for until the 11th, when it appeared that the words " accepted 1st October, 1799, Q. Dick and Co." had been written upon the bill, and afterwards nearly obliterated. by ink, the words, however, were still legible ; at the time of drawing the bill, the defendants were in advance to the drawer. The plaintiffs, as indorsees, sued the defendants as acceptors, the acceptance and subsequent cancellation were admitted. and the only question was, whether the cancellation having been made before the re-delivery of the bill, had discharged the acceptor. But Lord Ellenborough said. that if a party once accepted a bill he had done the act, and could not retract, and that there was no difference in point of legal effect, whether the bill were payable after sight or after date. Verdict for the plaintiffs.

Roper and others *v.* Birbeck and others. 15 East, 17. A bill of exchange having been accepted payable at Ledbrooke's with a direction in writing on it, " in case of need to apply at Boldero's" and having been dishonoured when due at Ledbrooke's, and thereupon brought to Boldero, who thinking that it had been made payable at his house, under that mistake cancelled the acceptance; but presently observing the mistake, wrote under it, " cancelled by mistake," and signed his initials to it; yet, nevertheless, paid the bill for the honour of the plaintiffs, whose indorsement was on it; it was held, that the plaintiffs, on the proof of such cancellation by mistake, might re

Trimmer v. Oddy and others,[b] and in Thornton and others v. Dick and others,[c] it was holden, that if the drawee of a bill put his name on it as acceptor, he cannot afterwards, even before it has been delivered to the payee, discharge his acceptance by erasing his name; and in a subsequent case,[d] under similar circumstances Lord Ellenborough, C. J. observed, " that the rule is certainly laid down in the Hamburgh Ordi-" nance, that an acceptance once made cannot be revoked; though, to " be sure, that leaves the question open as to what is an acceptance, " whether it be perfected before the delivery of the bill;" and Mr. J. Lawrence observed, " that when the general question shall arise it " will be worth considering, *how that which is not communicated to the* " *holder can be considered as an acceptance while it is yet in the hands* " *of the drawee, and where he obliterates it before any communication* "*made to the holder.*" According to the observations on Price and Shute in Paton v. Winter,[e] it should seem that an acceptance may be altered though the bill itself cannot be; and from the case of Fernandez v. Glynn,[f] it appears, that by the usage of trade in London, a check may be retained by the banker on whom it is drawn till five in the afternoon of the day on which it is presented for payment and then returned, although it has previously been cancelled by mistake. But it is reported, that Lord Ellenborough in that case said, "that had it " been a bill sent for acceptance and accepted, no change of circum-" stances could have altered that fact." It seems, therefore, that this point, as to the cancelling an acceptance, is not completely settled.[g] There appears no reason why the drawee, before he has induced the holder to take or hold the bill on the credit of the acceptance, should not be at liberty to cancel his acceptance; the circumstance of the bill being thereby defaced cannot constitute any sufficient reason why he should be liable as acceptor, for the holder is not prejudiced by the erasure, but may immediately resort to all the antecedent parties on the bill, and which also ought not to be put in circulation after the drawee has determined not to pay it.[h] If a bill has been accepted by mistake, it seems that the drawee is at liberty, before he has delivered it to a third person, to cancel his acceptance.[i] At all events, if the holder

[188]

---

over upon the bill against prior indorsers. Upon a motion for a new trial; Lord Ellenborough, C. J. said, I should have felt considerable pressure in the argument used on the behalf of the defendants, if the fact had borne them out. Undoubtedly the indorsees, generally speaking, are bound to return the bill to the indorsers in the same plight as they received ', and unchanged by any act of theirs; but I cannot consider the act of Boldero as the act of the indorsees, for he had no authority either express or implied from them to do the act, and the whole originated in his mistake. The case then comes to the instances put in argument at the trial, of a blot having fallen upon, or a child having torn or destroyed the instrument. In such cases the law is not so strict as to require the precise formal proof which is ordinarily required, for that would be at once to deprive the party of his remedy. I remember Pothier, in his Treatise on Bills of Exchange, (2 vol. 114, partie 1 ch. 3. s. 3.) speaking of an acceptor who put his signature

to a bill, but had not parted with it, says, that before he does part with it, " *il peut changer de volonté et rayer son accepta-tion.*" *A fortiori,* then, a third person who cancels an acceptance by mistake, having no authority so to do, shall not be held thereby to make void the bill, but shall be at liberty to correct that mistake, in furtherance of the rights of the parties to the bill. *Per curiam.* Rule discharged.

[b] Trimmer v. Oddy and others, ante, 186, note.

[c] Thornton v. Dick, 4 Esp. Rep. 270, Ante, 186.

[d] Bentinck v. Dorrien, 6 East, 199.— 2 Smith's Rep. 337. S. C. See post, 188.

[e] Paton v. Winter, 1 Taunt. 423.

[f] 1 Campb. 426. cited in Roper v. Birkbeck, 15 East, 19.

[g] Bayl. 88, 9.

[h] As to this point of circulating a bill after it has been dishonoured, see Roscow v. Hardy, 12 East, 434. 2 Campb. 458. S. C. Ante, 126.

[i] Trimmer v. Oddy, ante, 186, note.

4thly. Of of the bill, the acceptance of which has been cancelled, cause it to be
the liabili- noted for non-acceptance, he will afterwards be precluded from insist-
ty of the ing that the bill was accepted. [k](1)
acceptor.

How this li-   The liability of the acceptor cannot in general be *released* or *dis-*
ability may charged, otherwise than by payment or by express release or waiver.[l]
be dischar- If, however, by the laws of a foreign country, where the acceptance
ged. was made, and where it was to be performed, the obligation is by any
act vacated, it will no longer have any obligatory force in this country;[m]
[189] and by the consent of the holder, it may in all cases be waived or released, and the waiver may be either expressed or implied.[n] With respect to the mode by which it may be waived or discharged, it may be
observed, that the general rule of law is, that although a simple contract, *previously* to the breach of it, may be discharged by parol, yet,
if it has once been *broken*, then it cannot be discharged without payment or a release in writing;[o] but in the case of a bill, it is otherwise;

[k] Bentinck *v.* Dorrien and another, 6 East, 199. 2 Smith's Rep. 377, S. C. This action, which was by the indorsee against the defendants as acceptors of a bill, was referred, and the arbitrator, after reciting in his award, that the plaintiff, on the 31st May, left the bill with the defendants for acceptance, and they signed an acceptance thereon; but that on the 1st of June, *before the bill was called for*, they cancelled that acceptance; and that the plaintiff thereupon noted the bill for non-acceptance, declared himself to be of opinion that by such noting the plaintiff had precluded himself from insisting that the defendants had bound themselves to pay the bill, and therefore awarded in favour of the defendants. A rule *nisi* was obtained for setting aside this award, on the ground that the acceptance was irrevocable. But after cause shown, the court held, that whether such acceptance could or could not be revoked, the plaintiff had, at all events, by noting the bill for non-acceptance, precluded himself from contending that the acceptance was valid. Rule discharged. Sproat *v.* Matthews, 1. T. R. 182. Ante, 182.

[l] Poth. pl. 76. 118. Mar. 83. 545, 6. Bacon *v.* Searles, 1 Hen. Bla. 88. Fentum *v.* Pocock, 1 Marsh. 14. 5 Taunt. 192. S. C.

[m] Robertson *v.* French, 4 East, 130. Burrows *v.* Jemino, Stra. 732. Sel. Ca. 144. S. C. *et ante*, 93.
Burrows *v.* Jemino, 2 Stra. 732. The plaintiff accepted a bill at Leghorn, and by the law there, if the drawer fails, and the acceptor hath not sufficient effects of the drawer in his hands at the time of the acceptance, the acceptance becomes void. And this being the plaintiff's case, he instituted a suit at Leghorn, and his acceptance was thereupon vacated by the sentence of that court. The plaintiff, on his return to England, was sued as acceptor, and now filed his bill for an injunction and relief. King, Lord Chancellor, held, that the plaintiff's acceptance of the bill having been vacated and declared void by a competent jurisdiction, that sentence was conclusive, and bound the court of Chancery here, and granted a perpetual injunction to enjoin the defendant from suing upon this bill.

[n] Bayl. 90.

[o] Fitch *v.* Sutton, 5 East, 230. Rosal *v.* Lampen, 2 Mod. 43. Edwards *v.* Weeks, id. 259. Langden *v.* Stokes, Cro. Car. 383. May *v.* King, Cases K. B. 538. Vin. Ab. tit. Release. Com. Dig. tit. Pleader, 2 G. 13. et tit. Action on the Case in Assumpsit, G. Heathcote *v.* Crookshanks, 2 T. R. 24. Kearslake *v.* Morgan, 5 T. R. 514.

(1) It is now settled that when a defendant having once written his acceptance with the intention of accepting a bill afterwards changes his mind, and before it is communicated to the holder, or the bill delivered back to him, obliterates his acceptance, he is not bound as acceptor. *Cox* v. *Troy*, 5 Barn. & Ald. 474.
A. having accepted two bills of exchange for nearly the same amount on the same day, sent his clerk to the person in whose hands they both were as agent of two different holders to take up one of them, but the clerk took up the other and brought it to A. who struck out his name as acceptor. In about five minutes from the time he received it, he wrote his name again under the acceptance and sent it back to the agent who received it and gave up the other bill. Held, that the bill first taken up was paid and the indorsers discharged. *Bogart* v. *Nevins*, 6 Serg. & Rawle, 361.

and the courts have gone so far as to decide, that what amounts to an **4thly. _Lia-_** assent to discharge the acceptor, is a question for the jury, arising out **_bility_ of ac-** of the circumstances of the case ;[p] from which it might be inferred, that **ceptor; and how _dis-_** an act indicating an intention to relinquish the right of action, will be **_charged._** sufficient : but that decision appears in some measure to be contradicted **[190]** by the case of Dingwall *v.* Dunster,[q] where the court decided, that no-thing but an *express* consent, or the statute of Limitation, would dis-charge the acceptor; and that no indulgence to him or to the drawer would have that operation ; and in a late case it was decided, that though the holder of a bill may discharge the liability of the acceptor by parol, yet for this purpose, the words must amount to an absolute renunciation of all claim upon him in respect of the bill ;[r] and an ac-ceptor cannot avail himself of a renunciation on the part of a holder of his claim on him, unless it be not only express but founded on some con-

[p] Ellis *v.* Galindo, cited in Dingwall *v.* Dunster, Dougl. 247. James Galindo drew upon his brother for 30*l.*, in favour of the plaintiff. When the bill became due, James paid the plaintiff 8*l.* 15*s.* 4*d.* and indorsed a promise to pay the remainder in three months. Three years elapsed, and then plaintiff sued the drawee upon his accep-'ance. Lord Mansfield thought the defen-dant discharged, and nonsuited the plaintiff. An application was made for a new trial, when Lord Mansfield said, he thought the case did not interfere with Dingwall and Dunster, but a rule to show cause was grant-ed; after cause was shown, Lord Mansfield said, the doubt is, whether the question should not have been left to the jury, it be-ing a question of intention arising out of the circumstances. Willes, J. I thought it should have been left to the jury; and per Buller, J. I rather think the case should have gone to the jury; but I am not there-fore of opinion, that there ought to be a new trial, the indorsement could not have been meant as an additional security, for the drawer was equally liable before, I should have left the question to the jury, but with very strong observations, and as the de-mand is so small, I do not think there ought to be a new trial. Rule discharged.

[q] Dingwall *v.* Dunster, Dougl. 247. *et vide* Anderson *v.* Cleveland, 1 Esp. Rep. 46. Byrn *v.* Godfrey, 4 Ves. 8. Anderson *v.* Cleveland, 13 East, 430.

Dingwall *v.* Dunster, Dougl. 235. 247. Dunster lent Wheate his acceptance, which became due the 13th December, 1774. It was then in the hands of Dingwall; but he finding that Wheate was the real debtor, wrote to his attorney in February and No-vember 1775, for payment, received inter-est upon the bill from Wheate, and suffer-ed several years to elapse, without calling on Dunster. On 13th February, 1775, Dunster wrote to thank Dingwall for not proceeding against him, and said, he had been informed by a person Dingwall had sent, that Wheate had taken up the bill ; but Dingwall took no notice of this letter; he afterwards sued Dunster, for whom the jury found; but upon a rule to show cause

why there should not be a new trial, the whole court held, that there was nothing in the plaintiff 's conduct to discharge Dun-ster; that it meant nothing more than an indulgence to him, and that he would try to recover from the drawer if he could; but by Lord Mansfield, no use has been made of the defendant's letter; probably the fact did not warrant him in asserting that a per-son the plaintiff sent had told him Wheate had taken up the bill ; had the plaintiff by any thing in his conduct confirmed him in such a belief, it might have altered the case. Bayl. 92.

Anderson *v.* Cleveland, 13 East, 430. 1 Esp. Rep. 46. In an action by an indor-see against the acceptor of a bill, no de-mand was proved till three months after the bill was due, and when the drawer had be-come insolvent ; but per Lord Mansfield, the acceptor of a bill or the maker of a note always remains liable. The accept-ance is a proof of having assets in his hands, and he ought never to part with them un-less he be sure that the bill is paid by the drawer. Bayl. 93.

[r] Whatley *v.* Tricker, 1 Camp. 32. The indorsees of a bill knowing that it had been accepted for the accommodation of the drawer, and possessing goods of the draw-er's, from the produce of which they ex-pected payment, said (at a meeting of the acceptor's creditors,) that "they looked to the drawer, and should not come upon the acceptors." In consequence of which the latter assigned their property for the bene-fit of their creditors, and paid them 15*s.* in the pound. The drawer's goods however proved to be of little value, and he became insolvent, upon which the indorsees sued the acceptors. Lord Ellenborough said, that if the plaintiff's language amounted to an unconditional renunciation of all claim upon the acceptors, whereby the latter had entered into an arrangement with their cre-ditors, the acceptors were discharged, if only to a conditional promise not to resort to the acceptors if satisfied, elsewhere they were not. The jury found for the plaintiff. Bayl. 90. Parker *v.* Leigh, 2 Stark. 229.

4thly. *Lia-* sideration.[a] It has also been adjudged, that a release by the holder to *bility of ac-* the drawee, after the bill is drawn, and before acceptance, will not dis-*ceptor; and* charge him from the obligation raised by a subsequent acceptance, be-*how dis-* cause he was not chargeable at the time of the release.[c] And where the *charged.* drawer of a bill of exchange, accepted by defendant, agreed with him and the rest of his creditors to take a composition of eight shillings in the pound, to be secured by promissory notes, to be given by defendant payable on days certain, and that defendant should assign to the credi-tors certain debts upon which they should execute a general release, and the assignment was executed, and all the creditors except the plain-tiff received their composition and executed the release, and plaintiff might have received his promissory notes if he had applied for them; but it did not appear that defendant had ever tendered them to plain-tiff, or that he had ever applied for them, and the plaintiff afterwards, and after the days of payment of the promissory notes had expired, sued the defendant on the bill of exchange, it was held, that he was not pre-cluded by the agreement from recovering.[u] But a general release by the drawer of a bill to the acceptor will, as between them, discharge the acceptor; though the drawer is not the holder, nor has then paid the bill.[x]

[191]   What amounts to a waiver, and discharge of the acceptor's liability, must depend on the circumstances of each particular case. An agree-ment to consider an acceptance as at an end ;[y] or a message by the holder to the acceptor of an accommodation bill, that the business has been settled with the drawer, and that he need not give himself any further trouble ;[z] have been holden to amount to a waiver of an accept-ance. But it should seem, that the holder's receiving a part of the mo-ney due on a bill from the drawer, and taking a promise from him upon the back of it for the payment of the residue at an enlarged time, will not of itself amount to a discharge of the acceptor.[a] It has been de-cided, that if the holder of a bill of exchange agree not to sue the ac-ceptor, upon his making affidavit that the acceptance is a forgery, and such affidavit be accordingly made and sworn, he cannot afterwards bring an action on the bill, though the affidavit be false.[b]

When a bill is accepted in consideration of the future consignment of goods to the acceptor, and the prospect of the profit of the commis-sion on the sale thereof, and the holder of the bill, aware of the na-ture of the acceptance, agrees to take, and receives the bill of lading,

---

[a] Parker *v.* Leigh, 2 Stark. 228; and see Badnall *v.* Samuel, 3 Price 521.

[c] Drage *v.* Netter, Ld. Raym. 65.

[u] Cranley *v.* Hillary, 2 M. & S. 120.

[x] Scott *v.* Lifford, 1 Campb. 250.

[y] Walpole *v.* Pulteney, cited Dougl. 236, 7. 248, 9. Walpole held a bill ac-cepted by Pulteney, but agreed to con-sider his acceptance at an end, and wrote in his bill book, opposite to the entry of this bill, "Mr. Pulteney's acceptance is at an end." Walpole kept the bill from 1772 to 1775, without calling upon Pulte-ney, and then brought this action. The jury found a verdict for the plaintiff; but the court of exchequer thought the ver-dict wrong, and granted a new trial, upon which the jury found for the defendant. Bayl. 90,

[z] Black *v.* Peele, cited, Dougl. 236, 7. 248, 9. Black arrested Peele as acceptor of a bill drawn by Dallas, but on finding that the acceptance was an accommoda-tion one, his attorney took a security from Dallas, and sent word to Peele, that be had settled with Dallas, and that he need not give himself any further trouble. Dal-las afterwards became bankrupt, upon which Black again sued Peele ; but it was held, that as Black had, in express words, discharged Peele, the action could not be maintained. Bayl. 90

[a] Ellis *v.* Galindo, ante, 189, note.

[b] Stephens *v.* Thacker, Peake, 117.— Lloyd *v.* Willan, 1 Esp. Rep. 178.

&c. from the acceptor, which were the consideration of the acceptance, the acceptor is by this act of the holder discharged from the liability imposed on him by his acceptance.[c] He is also discharged when, as has been before observed, the holder, upon an offer by the drawee of a conditional or partial acceptance, gives a general notice of non-accept-ance to any of the antecedent parties, omitting to mention in such notice the nature of the acceptance offered.[d]

But the drawee will not be discharged from liability in the case of an acceptance payable at a banker's, by the holder's neglect to prevent it there although he can prove that he has sustained damages in consequence of such neglect,[e] and though it is reported to have been decided at Nisi Prius, that an accommodation acceptor will be discharged by the holder's giving time to the drawer after having notice that the bill was accepted for his accommodation :[f] yet it has been since decided, that the holder's giving such time or taking a cognovit from the drawer, though he have notice that the bill was accepted for the accommodation of such drawer, will not discharge the acceptor.[g] If, however, an acceptor, in satisfaction of his liability, indorse another bill, and

---

[c] Mason *v.* Hunt, Dougl. 284, 297.— Rowland Hunt agreed that his partner, Thomas Hunt should, on consignment of a cargo, and an order for its insurance, accept bills for 3,600*l.* The cargo was consigned, the order for insurance given, and Thomas Hunt effected the insurance, but be refused to accept the bills. After some negotiation, the plaintiff, being the holder, signed a memorandum, by which after stating that the consignment had been made on account of the bills, and that the Hunts being apprehensive that the neat proceeds might not be sufficient to discharge them, had refused to accept, he accepted the bill of lading and policy, and undertook to apply the neat proceeds, when in cash, as far as they would go, to the credit of the payee, in part payment of the bills. The plaintiff afterwards sued the Hunts, and insisted that Rowland Hunt's agreement was an acceptance; but after a verdict for the defendant, and time taken to consider, upon a rule to show cause why there should not be a new trial, the whole court was clear, that by the memorandum the plaintiff had waived all right to insist upon Rowland Hunt's agreement, for it was obvious, that the whole consideration of the acceptance was the consignment, upon which there would be a commission, and the policy of these the plaintiff had taken to himself.,

[d] Sproat *v.* Matthews, 1 T. R. 182.— Bentinck *v.* Dorrein, 6 East, 199. Ante, 187, 188.

[e] Sebag *v.* Abitbol, 4 M. & S. 462 ; and see post, as to presentment. But since the case of Rowe *v* Young, 2 Brod. & Bing. 165, though qualified by stat 2 Geo. 4. c. 78. if a bill be accepted, payable only at a named place, the want of a due presentment there might be considered as discharging the acceptor.

CHITTY ON BILLS.

[f] Paxton *v.* Peat, 2 Campb. 185.

[g] Fentum *v.* Pocock, 1 Marsh. 14.— 5 Taunt. 192. S. C. This was an action against the acceptor of a bill of exchange, and at the trial the plaintiff had a verdict with liberty for the defendant to move to enter a nonsuit, on the ground, that he was discharged by the plaintiff having taken a cognovit from the drawer ;' and upon motion accordingly, and cause shown, the court held, that the acceptor binds himself at all times to pay the holder (though not perhaps the drawer) until discharged by payment or release, and that though it were an accommodation bill, that would not alter the circumstances and discharge the rule.

Mallet *v.* Thompson, 5 Esp. Rep. 178. The plaintiff, holder of an accommodation note, who took it with full notice that the maker had received *no value* from the indorsee, for whose accommodation the defendant made it, and received a composition, and covenanted not to sue such indorsee, may, notwithstanding, sue the maker, though, on payment of it, he will have a right of action against the indorsee.

Harrison *v.* Cooke, 3 Campb. 362 — Where upon an accommodation bill becoming due, it was presented for payment to the acceptor, and he promised to pay it, it was held that he was not discharged, by time being afterwards given without his consent to the drawer by the indorsee, who knew that it had been accepted for the drawer's accommodation.

In Carstairs *v.* Rolleston, 5 Taunt. 551. 1 Marsh. 207. S. C. it was discussed, but not determined, whether a release to the indorser of an accommodation note, discharged the maker, if the holder was aware at the time of all the circumstances.

A a

4thly. *Liability of acceptor; and how discharged.*

[193]

the holder be guilty of laches, with respect to the latter, in not giving notice to such acceptor of the non-payment of the latter bill, he will thereby discharge such acceptor;[h] but if the latter merely handed over the second bill as a collateral security, without indorsing it, he would not be discharged from liability on the first bill, by any laches of the holder of the second.[i]

We have seen that the *alteration* of the bill, or of the acceptance, without the concurrence of the acceptor, and even in some cases with his assent, will discharge him from liability.[k] And where the drawer of a bill accepted, payable at B. and Co., after keeping it three or four years, indorsed it to the plaintiffs, erasing the name of B. and Co. without the knowledge of the acceptor; B. and Co. having failed since the acceptance, it was held, that the acceptor was thereby discharged.[l] And though there is a case in which it has been supposed to have been decided, that if the holder strike out an acceptance, which varies from the tenor of the bill, and substitute an acceptance according to the tenor, he may afterwards restore the acceptance he struck out, and that such acceptance will continue binding;[m] yet it has been doubted whether the determination went further than to decide that the alteration in the acceptance, (though it annulled the acceptance, and discharged the acceptor) did not destroy the bill as to the other parties.[n]

Liability of a party promising to pay a bill.

[194]

Besides the *liability to pay* a bill of exchange incurred by the act of accepting it, the drawee or another person may subject himself to liability to pay the amount out of the money then in his hands, or which he may afterwards receive, and this, although the bill itself may be invalid; as where it has been drawn on an agent requesting him to pay a sum of money out of a particular fund, though we have seen that such instrument will be wholly void as a bill of exchange, because the payment of it depends upon a contingency.[o] Yet if the drawee promise to pay the amount when he shall receive funds, and the

[h] Bridges v. Berry, 3 Taunt. 130.
[i] Bishop v. Rowe, 3 M. & S. 362.— Hickling v. Hardy, 7 Taunt. 312.
[k] Ante, 100 to 106. Long v. Moore, 3 Esp. Rep. 155, n. A bill of exchange, after acceptance, had been altered by inserting the word " date" in the place of " sight." The plaintiff wanted to go on the common counts, and offered in evidence another bill drawn upon the defendant for the same amount, but not accepted. Lord Kenyon held, that the plaintiff could not recover against the defendant, for he was liable only by virtue of the instrument, which being vitiated, his liability was at an end.
[l] Tidmarst v. Grover, 1 M. & S. 735. Ante, 103.
[m] Price v. Shute, Beawes, s. 222. 1st edit. p. 444. Moll. b. 2. c. 10. s. 28. A bill was drawn, payable 1st of January, and the drawee accepted it to pay, the 1st of March : the holder struck out the 1st of March, and substituted the 1st of January, and sent the bill for payment on that day, which the acceptor refused; the holder then struck out the 1st of Ja-

nuary, and restored the 1st of March. And in an action on this bill, the question was, whether these alterations did not destroy the bill, and Pemberton, C. J. ruled that they did not. And see observations in Paton v. Winter, 1 Taunt. 423. Bayl. 87
[m] Master v. Miller, 4 T. R. 330. Lord Kenyon, in commenting on the case of Price v. Shute, observes, that the books do not say against whom the action was brought, and it could not have been against the acceptor, because his acceptance was struck out by the party himself who brought the action ; and he concludes, " that on the person, to whom the bill was directed, refusing to accept the bill, as it was originally drawn, the holder resorted to the drawer;" however, Buller, J. 4 T. R. 336, says, " that he cannot consider this case in any other light than as an action against the acceptor, because the books only state what passed between the holder and the acceptor." And see Paton v. Winter. 1 Taunt. 428. Bayl. 87.
[o] Ante. 43.

holder, in consequence, retains the bill, the amount, when received, *Liability* will be recoverable from the drawee under the common count for *of a party* money had and received.[p] So a draft on the executor of a debtor, *promising* which the executor promised to discharge on his receiving assets is an *to pay a* equitable assignment of the debt, available against assignees in bank- *bill.* ruptcy.[q] But as a *chose in action* is not assignable so as to enable the assignee to sue the original debtor merely by virtue of such as- [195] signment, it follows, that unless the third person who has funds in hand, expressly promises to pay, and such promise be accepted, the holder of the bill cannot sue him;[r] and if before the party offer to

[p] Stevens *v.* Hill, 5 Esp. Rep. 247. This was an action of assumpsit; the first count was against the defendant as the acceptor of a bill of exchange drawn by Admiral Smith on the defendant his agent; the others were the money counts. The bill had been burnt by accident, and the plaintiff gave parol evidence of it. The defendant was a navy-agent, and the bill was drawn by Admiral Smith, in this form, " out of my half-pay which will become due on the 1st of January, pay to Stevens 15*l.*" This was brought to Hill, who said he had then no money of Admiral Smith's in his hands, but that he would pay it out of the admiral's money when he received it. Admiral Smith was called, he produced an account furnished by Hill as his agent, containing an account of the money received at different times on the admiral's account, and also of the bills drawn by him on Hill, on which there was a balance of 41*l.* due to Hill. It was objected by Garrow, first, that the plaintiff could not recover on the count on the bill, as it appeared to be not a bill of exchange, it being drawn on a particular fund, and not payable generally, which was necessary to constitute a legal bill of exchange. This count was abandoned by the Solicitor-General, who said, that he should go on the count for money had and received. To this it was answered, that the engagement of Hill was to pay the bill when he had money of Admiral Smith's in his hands, and that it appeared by the count which was produced by Admiral Smith, that the admiral was the debtor of Hill, and of course that Hill had no funds in his hands out of which only the bill was to be paid. Lord Ellenborough having taken the papers produced, in which the receipts of money and entries of bills were put under their respective dates, observed, that though on the general balance, a sum of 40*l.* was due to the defendant, yet by referring to dates it would appear that Hill, after the day the bill was brought to him for acceptance, and after his declaration as proved, and before he had been called upon to make any payment, had received money of Admiral Smith's more than sufficient to answer the bill, it was therefore his duty to have reserved for that bill, and not to

have paid other drafts subsequently drawn; he was not therefore protected by subsequent payments. His Lordship added, that a similar case of an army-agent occurred before Lord Kenyon, in which the agent had promised to pay the draft of a person on him, and having neglected to do so, an action was brought; that he was of counsel for the defendant in that cause, and argued that this promise of the agent was *nudum pactum*, but Lord Kenyon over-ruled the objection, and held, that it was an appropriation of so much to the use of the holder of the draft, and made him liable on the receipt of any money upon the credit of which it was drawn. De Bernales *v.* Fuller, cited in 14 East, 590. n. a. 598. S. P.

[q] Ex parte Alderson and another, 1 Madd. 53. 55. 2 Rose, 13. App. Jane Row became indebted to the petitioners in 525*l.*, and being a creditor of the estate of John Fish, deceased, gave them a draft on the executors as follow :— Please to pay Messrs. G. and T. Alderson, or order, four hundred and seventeen pounds, six shillings, as part of the amount due to me for plumber's work done for the late John Fish, Esq. Jane Row." The petitioners presented the draft to the executor, but he, not being prepared with assets, did not accept it, but retained it, to be paid when there should be funds. The Vice-Chancellor. This is a good equitable assignment; the executor bound himself to pay when in possession of assets.

[r] Grant *v.* Austen, 3 Price, 58. Williams *v.* Everett and others, 14 East's Rep. 582. Kelly residing abroad, having remitted bills on England to the defendants, his bankers, in London, with directions in the letters enclosing such bills, to pay the amount in certain specified proportions to the plaintiff and other creditors of Kelly, who would produce their letters of advice from him on the subject, and desiring the amount paid to each person to be put on their respective bills, and that every bill paid off, should be cancelled; and the plaintiff having, before the bills became due, given notice to the defendants that he had received a letter from Kelly, ordering payment of his debt out of that remittance, and having offered them an indemnity if they

Liability of a party &c. pay the bill it has been returned for non-acceptance,[a] the holder has ro remedy against such party.

Indemnity to acceptor & his right   In the case of an acceptance for the accommodation of the drawer, it is usual to take from the drawer a *written* undertaking to indemnify him, which, when it is for a sum above £20, should be stamped as an agreement; but where there is any risk of bankruptcy, it is advisable to take a counter bill or note, so as to enable the acceptor to prove under the commission against the drawer.[b] In the absence of any express contract, the law implies a contract to indemnify.[c] And it should seem, that if an agent has accepted bills for the accommodation of his employer, he may in some cases retain money in his hands to discharge it, unless the bill be delivered up to him, or he be otherwise sufficiently indemnified.[d] And where a sum of money has been lodged with a party to indemnify him against bills of exchange he has accepted for the accommodation of another, an action will not lie against him to recover the money while the bills are outstanding, although the statute of limitations has run upon them.[e] And where a person who has funds in his hands belonging to another, or is otherwise indebted to him, accepts a bill for his accommodation, and the drawer afterwards commits an act of bankruptcy, or becomes insolvent, such acceptor may retain the funds or debt until the bill becomes due, as an indemnity against his liability as acceptor.[f] And since the 49 Geo. 3. c. 121. s. 8. an accommodation acceptor, being in the nature of a surety to the drawer, may prove under the commission against him, although he has been obliged to pay the bill after the act of bankruptcy.[g]

Sect. 3.—Of *non-accept-ance*, and the conduct which the holder must thereupon pursue.   THE inquiry into the conduct which the holder of a bill of exchange should pursue on a neglect or refusal to accept at all, or on the offer of a condition or partial acceptance, may be made under the following heads:

would hand over one of the bills to him, but the defendants having refused to indorse the bill away, or to act upon the letter, admitting, however, that they had received the directions to apply the money, and the defendants having in fact afterwards received the money on the bills when due, held, that they did not by the mere act of receiving the bills and afterwards the produce of them, with such directions, and without any assent on their part to the purport of the letter, and still more against their express dissent, bind themselves to the plaintiff so to apply the money in discharge of his debt due to him from Kelly, and consequently that the plaintiff, between whom and the defendants there was no privity of contract, express or implied, but on the contrary, it was repudiated, could not maintain his action against the defendants as for money had and received by them to his own use, but that the property in the bills and their produce still continued in the remitter. And see Assignees of Holland v. ———, 1 Salk. 143. Williamson v. Thompson, 16 Ves. 442.

[a] Stewart and another v. Fry and another, 1 Moore's Rep. 74. Where persons have received money for the express purpose of taking up a bill of exchange two days after it became due, and upon tendering it to the holders and demanding the bill, find that they have sent it back protested for non-acceptance to the persons who indorsed it to them : Held, that such persons having received fresh orders not to pay the bill, were not liable to an action by the holders for money had and received, when, upon the bills being reprocured and tendered to them, they refused to pay the money.

[b] See post, as to the proof of a bill by surety, and as to cross paper.

[c] Young v. Hockley, Wils. 346. and 262. Sparkes v. Martindale, 8 East. 593. As to what damages the sureties may recover, even cost in error, see 3 Wils. 13. 1 Atk. 262.

[d] Madden v. Kempster, 1 Campb. 12. Ex parte Metcalfe, 11 Ves. 407.

[e] Morse v. Williams, 3 Campb. 418.

[f] Wilkins v. Casey, 7 T. R. 711. as observed upon in Willis v. Freeman, 12 East, 658. 11 Ves. 407. 1 Campb. 12.

[g] See post, Chap. on Bankruptcy. Ex parte Yonge, 3 Ves. & Bea. 46. Stedman v. Mortimer, 13 East, 247.

First, *When notice is requisite.*
Secondly, *The mode of giving notice.*
Thirdly, *The time when it must be given.*
Fourthly, *By whom it must be given.*
Fifthly, *To whom it should be given.*
Sixthly, *Of the liability of the parties on receiving notice.*
Lastly, *Of the consequences of the holder's neglect to give notice, and how waived, &c.*

1st. When notice of non-accept-ance is necessary.

It has already been observed, that a presentment for acceptance is only necessary when a bill is made payable within a certain period *after sight.*[b] If, however, in that or any other case, a bill be presented, and an acceptance be refused, or only a conditional or partial [197] acceptance be offered, notice should immediately be given to the persons to whom the holder means to resort for payment, or they will in general be totally discharged from *their respective liabilities,* not only on the bill·of exchange, but the original consideration of it ;[c] and it is not sufficient for the holder to wait till the time mentioned in the bill for payment has elapsed, and then to give notice of non-acceptance as well as of non-payment.[d] (1) But we have seen that a *bona fide* holder, to whom a bill has been transferred after refusal to accept, is not affected by the neglect of any previous holder in giving notice of that fact.[e] And if the bill were given on a wrong stamp, the neglect to present it for acceptance or give notice of the refusal may not prejudice;[f] and if the bill were given only as a collateral security, and the party delivering it were no party to it, he will not in such case be discharged from his original liability by the laches of the holder.[g] And, as no laches can be imputed to the crown, if a bill be seized under an extent before it is due, the neglect of the officer of the crown to give notice of the dishonour, will not discharge the drawer or indorsers.[h] The reason why the law requires the holder to give due notice of non-acceptance by the drawee is, that the drawer may withdraw forthwith out of the hands of the drawee such effects as he may happen to have, or may stop those which he is in a course of a putting into his hands, and that the indorsers may respectively take the necessary measures to obtain payment from the parties respectively liable to them, and if notice be not given it is a presumption

[b] Ante, 256.
[c] Ante, 97, 98. Bridges v. Berry, 3 Taunt 130. Rucker v Hiller, 16 East, 43. Bayl. 167.
[d] Roscow v. Hardy, 2 Campb. 458. 12 East, 434. S. C. Blesard v. Hirst, 5 Burr. 2670. Goodall v. Dolley, 1 T. R. 712. Anon. 1 Ventr. 45. Poth. pl. 133. Dagglish v. Weatherby, 2 Bla. Rep. 747. per

Lord Ellenborough, in Orr v. Mageanis, 7 East, 362. 3 & 4 Ann. c. 9. s. 7.
[e] Ante, 124, 5. Selw. Ni. Pri. 4th ed. 319.
[f] Ante, 58. Wilson v. Vysar, 4 Taunt. 288.
[g] Ante, 98. Warrington v. Furbor, 8 East, 242.
[h] West on Extents, 28, 9.

(1) The holder of a bill ought to present it for acceptance within a reasonable time, whether such bill was payable at sight or in any other manner; what is reasonable time, depends on the particular circumstances of the case, and it is for the jury to determine whether laches is imputable to the holder. *Fernandez v. Lewis,* 1 M'Cord, 322.

If a bill be payable *after sight* it must be presented within a reasonable time for acceptance, and immediate notice of non-acceptance given to the drawer: it is not sufficient to give notice of the non-acceptance and non-payment together after the day of payment has passed. *Austin* v. *Rodman,* 1 Hawks, 195.

In Pennsylvania it is held, that in an action by an indorsee against the indorser of a foreign bill of exchange which has been protested for non-acceptance, it is not necessary to prove notice of the non-acceptance of the bill. *Read* v. *Adams,* 6 Serg. & Rawle. 356.

1st. When
notice of
non-accept-
ance is ne-
cessary; &
what excu-
ses omis-
sion.

[198]

1st. When of law, that the drawer and indorsers are prejudiced by the omission; and it is on this principle that notice of non-acceptance and non-payment are required.[i]

From some cases to be found in the books[k] it appears to have been formerly holden, that it was incumbent on the person insisting on the want of notice, to prove that he had really sustained damage by the laches of the holder; but it has been settled by later decisions, that such damage is to be presumed, and that the only excuse for the omission is the proof of the want of effects in the hands of the drawee;[l] and it is always presumed, till the contrary appears, that the drawer of a bill has effects in the drawee's hands, and that the indorser or assigno; has given value for it, and consequently that each may have sustained a loss by the holder's neglect to give notice,[m] by which the chance of obtaining satisfaction from the parties liable to them, must necessarily be rendered more precarious.

But if the drawer of a bill, from the time of making it to the time when it was due, had *no effects* in the hands of the drawee or acceptor, and had no right upon any other ground to expect that the bill would be paid, and the bill was drawn for the accommodation of such drawer, he is *prima facie* not entitled to notice of the dishonour of the bill;[n]

[i] Whitfield v. Savage, 2 Bos. & Pul. 280, 1. Orr v. Magennis, 7 East, 362. Claridge v. Dalton, 4 M. & S. 226. Cory v. Scott, 3 B. & A. 621.

[k] Mogadara v. Holt, 1 Show. 318. 12 Mod. 15. S. C. Butler v. Play, 1 Mod 27. Sarsfield v. Weatherby, Comb. 152. Bickerdike v. Bollman, 1 T. R. 406. Vin. Ab. tit. Bills of Exchange, M. Poth. pl. 157, 8. Postlethw. tit. Bills of Exchange, 16, 17. Whitfield v. Savage, 2 Bos. &. Pul. 280, 1.

[l] Bayl. 133, n. 1. Dennis v. Morrice, 3 Esp. Rep. 158. In an action on a bill brought by an indorsee against the drawer, it appeared, that no notice had been given to the defendant of non-payment by the acceptor, to excuse which, the plaintiff offered to prove, that in fact, the defendant had not been prejudiced by the want of such notice. But Lord Kenyon said, the only case in which notice is dispensed with is, where the drawer has no effects in the hands of the drawee. This would be extending the rule still further than ever has been done, and opening new sources of litigation, in investigating whether in fact the drawer did receive a prejudice from the want of notice or not. He rejected the evidence, and nonsuited the plaintiff. Sed. vide Pothier Traite du Contrat de Change, part 1. chap. 5. num. 157, 8.

[m] Per Buller, J. in Bickerdike v. Bollman, 1 T. R. 406, 409. Tatlock v. Harris, 3 T. R. 182. Anon. Ventr. 45. Nicholson v. Gouthit, 2 Hen. Bla. 612. Mogadara v. Holt, 1 Show. 317.

[n] Cory v. Scott, 3 Bar. & Ald. 619. Claridge v. Dalton, 4 M. & S. 229. Legge v. Thorpe, 2 Campb. 310. 12 East, 171. S. C. where the rule, principle, and inconveniences are stated; and see Walwyn v.

St. Quintin, 1 Bos. & Pul. 654, 5. Clegg v. Cotton, 3 Bos. & Pul. 241, 2. Gale v. Walsh, 5 T. R. 239. Poth. pl. 157. Bickerdike v. Bollman, 1 T. R. 405. Goodall v. Dolley, id. 712. Rogers v. Stephens, 2 T. R. 713. Nicholson v. Gouthit, 2 Hen. Bla. 610. Staples v. Okines, 1 Esp. Rep. 333. Wilkies v. Jacks, Peake's Ca. N. P. 202. The progress of the cases on this subject is also stated in Brown v. Maffey, 15 East, 216. See also Bayl. 181, 2, 137.

Bickerdike and another, assignees of Reichard v. Bollman, 1 T. R. 405. The only question upon a case reserved was, whether the bill the bankrupt had drawn in favour of the petitioning creditor, upon a man, who then, and from that time, till the bill became due, was one of the bankrupt's creditors, had discharged so much of the petitioning creditor's debts, no notice having been given of its dishonour to the bankrupt; and the court, after argument, were of opinion it had not, because the reason why notice is in general necessary is, that the drawer may without delay, withdraw his effects from the drawee, and that no injury may happen to him from want of notice; but where the drawer has no effects in the hands of the drawee, he cannot be injured, and is not entitled to any notice. In Brown v. Maffey, 15 East, 221. Lord Ellenborough, C. J. observed, that the doctrine of dispensing with notice of the dishonour of a bill, had grown almost entirely out of this case, and that though there might have been previous decisions to the same effect at Nisi Prius, yet none had been brought in revision before the court till this case; that decision dispensed with notice to the drawer, where he knew

nor can he object, in such case, that a foreign bill should have been 1st. When protested.[o] In this case, the drawer, being himself the real debtor, *notice* of acquires no right of action against the acceptor by paying the bill, and *non-accept-ance is ne-* suffers no injury from want of notice of non-acceptance or non-pay- *cessary; &* ment, and therefore the laches of the holder affords him no defence. [p] *what exec-u-* And therefore where the drawer had supplied the drawee with goods *see omis-* on credit, which did not elapse until after the bill would fall due, and *sion.* the drawer had no right to draw the bill, it was held that he was not discharged by the want of notice of non-payment.[q]

But it is no excuse for not giving notice to the *indorser* of a bill, that the *acceptor had no effects of the drawer.*[r] And although no con-sideration passed between the payee and drawer of a bill of exchange, it is not to be considered an accommodation bill as to the latter, if [200] there was a valuable consideration as between the payee and the ac-ceptor.[s] So a person, who, without consideration, but without fraud,

---

before-hand he had no effects in the hands of the drawee, and had no reason to expect that the bill would be paid when it became due.

Goodall *v.* Dolley, 1 T. R. 712. In this case, upon the application for a new trial, the plaintiff's counsel offered an affidavit that the drawer had no effects in the hands of the drawee; but the court thought that made no difference, the action being brought against the payee; but by Buller, J. had the action been against the drawer I should have been willing to let in the affidavit, that would be like the case of Bickerdike *v.* Bollman. If the drawer has no effects in the hands of the drawee, he cannot be injured by want of notice.

Legge *v.* Thorpe, 12 East's Rep. 171. 2 Campb. 310. S. C. This was an action by an indorsee against the drawer of a foreign bill, drawn upon C. B. Wyatt, payable one month after sight, of which acceptance had been refused. The decla-ration negatived effects in the hands of the drawee, or any consideration for the bill. It appeared, at the trial, that the defendant had no effects in Wyatt's hands, and that the latter had therefore refused accept-ance: but that Wyatt was one of the execu-tors of Weeks, and that Weeks' executors had desired the defendant to employ the payee of this bill to do some carpenter's work on Weeks' property, and the defen-dant drew this bill on Wyatt for the pay-ment of the payee, Wyatt denied that he had assets to pay the bill. The only ques-tion was, whether a protest for non-accept-ance were necessary; Lord Ellenborough thought not; and a verdict was given for the plaintiff, but the point was reserved, and on a rule *nisi* for nonsuit, and cause shown, the whole court held, that this case was governed by those of Bickerdike *v.* Bollman, 1 T. R. 405. and Rogers *v.* Stevens, 2 T. R. 713. and discharged the rule.

[o] Legge *v.* Thorpe, 2 Campb. 310. 12 East, 171. S. C. see the preceding note.

[p] Per Chambre, J. in Leach *v.* Hewitt, 4 Taunt. 733.

[q] Claridge *v.* Dalton, 4 M. & S. 226. post, 208.

[r] Wilks *v* Jacks, Peake Rep. 202. In an action against the defendant, as indorser of a bill, drawn by Vaughan on Eustace and Holland, it appeared, that notice had not been given to the defendant, upon which the plaintiff offered to show, that Vaughan had no effects in the hands of Eustace and Holland. *Sed per* Lord Ken-yon, C. J. "That circumstance will not avail the plaintiff, the rule extends only to actions brought against the drawer; the indorser is in all cases entitled to notice, for he has no concern with the accounts between the drawer and the drawee." The plaintiff then proved a letter from the defendant, acknowledging the debt, and promising to pay, and upon *that* he had a verdict.

[s] Scott *v.* Lifford, 1 Campb. 246. Payee against the drawer of a bill of exchange; the defence was, that the bill was drawn without consideration, and that the plaintiffs had received satisfaction. Agar having an acceptance due to the plaintiffs, requested it renewed, to which they consented, pro-vided that the defendant would draw a bill upon Agar for the amount which he was to accept, and which was accordingly done. Agar also lodged policies of ensu-rance to a large amount with the plaintiffs, by way of collateral security, upon which a certain per centage had since been awarded, due upon them. Lord Ellenbo-rough held, that the bill was an accommo-dation bill, there having been a consideration between the payees and acceptor, and that if it had been proved that the plaintiffs had received any thing upon the policies, that would *pro tanto* be a satisfaction, that the plaintiffs were entitled to recover the whole sum mentioned in the bill, and must deliver up the policies or refund the money received under them.

1st. When indorsed a bill, the drawer and acceptor of which proved to be ficti-
notice of tious persons, is entitled to due notice of the dishonour, or he will be
non-accept- discharged.[t]
ance is *ne-*
cessary; &
what excu-   It has been decided, that where a bill has been drawn for the
ses omis- accommodation of the payee, and the drawer had no effects in the
sion. hands of the drawee, though the payee had, such drawer is not
entitled to notice of non-payment;[u] but this decision seems questionable, for whenever a party to a bill is entitled to his remedy over
[201] against another party, he may be prejudiced by the delay in giving him
notice of the dishonour.[x]

          It has also been holden, that if the payee of a note lend his name
merely to give it credit, and to enable the maker to raise money upon
it, and knows at the time, that the maker is insolvent, he is not entitled to notice, and that it is no defence for him that the note was not
properly presented for payment.[y] But as the payee would in that

[t] Leach v. Hewitt, 4 Taunt. 731. This
was an action against the defendant, as indorser of a bill of exchange, purporting to
be drawn by Rogers, Crooke, and Co. and
dated from the Northampton Bank, and
purporting to be accepted by Rogers and
Co. Lombard Street, in favour of the defendant. It appeared, at the trial, that the
defendant had indorsed the bill at the request of one Cattle, and that it had come
to the hands of the plaintiff for a valuable
consideration. When the bill became due,
no such persons as Rogers and Co. were
to be found in Lombard Street, nor the
drawers at Northampton. After four days,
the plaintiff found the defendant, who lived
in Clerkenwell. The defence was, that he
had not had due notice of the dishonour of
the bill. There was no evidence that the
defendant was party to the fraud. Mansfield, C. J. directed the jury, that if the
conduct of the defendant was not fraudulent, he was entitled to notice, and the jury
finding that the defendant was not privy to
the fraud, the plaintiff was nonsuited; and
upon a rule to set aside the nonsuit, and for
a new trial, the court held, that the defendant was entitled to notice, and discharged
the rule.
[u] Walwyn v. St. Quintin, 1 Bos. & Pul.
652. 2 Esp. 515. S. C. In an action by
the indorsee against the drawer of a bill,
it appeared to have been drawn to accommodate the payee, who had placed securities, on which he wished to raise money,
in the hands of the acceptor, the defendant
had no effects in the hands of the drawee,
and no notice having been given to him of
the dishonour of the bill, the question was,
whether that were made necessary by the
payee's having effects in the hands of the
drawee. Eyre, C. J. directed a verdict for
the defendant, with liberty for the plaintiff
to move to enter a verdict for him. After
a rule *nisi* accordingly, and cause shown,
the court held, that the defendant was not
entitled to notice. Postea to the plaintiff
on another ground.

[x] See Smith v. Beckett, 13 East, 187.
infra, note, and Brown v. Maffey, 15 East,
216. post, 202, note. Bayl. 136, 7. Cory
v. Scott, 3 B. & A. 619.
[y] De Berdt v. Atkinson, 2 Hen. Bls.
336. In an action against the payee of a
note, it appeared that the note was not
presented for payment till the day after it
became due, and that no notice was given
to the defendant till five days after such
presentment, but it also appearing that the
defendant gave no value for the note; that
he lent his name merely to give it credit, and
that he knew at the time the maker was
insolvent. Eyre, C. J. directed the jury
to find for the plaintiff, which they did. A
rule to show cause why a new trial should
not be granted, and upon cause shown,
Eyre, C. J. said, if the maker is not known
to be insolvent, insolvency will not excuse
the want of an early demand, but knowledge excludes all presumption which
would otherwise arise ; here the money
was to be raised upon the defendant's credit; he meant to guarantee the payment,
and no loss could happen to him from the
want of notice And per Buller, J. "The
general rule is only applicable to fair transactions where the bill on note has been given for value, in the ordinary course of
trade. It is said, insolvency does not take
away the necessity of notice; that is true,
where a value has been given, but no further ; here the defendant lent his name
merely to give credit to the note, and was
not an indorser in the common course of
business." Heath and Rooke, Justices,
concurring, the rule was discharged. But
in Bayley on Bills, 3d ed. 136. it is observed, that the court appear to have proceeded on a misapplication of the rule,
which obtains as to accommodation acceptances; in those cases, the drawer being
himself the real debtor, acquires no right
of action against the acceptor by paying
the bill, and suffers no injury from want of
notice of non-payment by the acceptor.
But in this case the maker was the real

case, upon paying the note, have a clear right of action against the maker, it should seem that he is entitled to notice of the dishonour. And where a bill was drawn for the accommodation of a remote indorsee, and the names of all the prior parties were lent to him, it was holden in action against one of those parties, an indorser, that the latter was entitled to notice of the dishonour of the bill, because upon paying it he would be entitled to sue such indorsee for repayment. And the same point was determined in an action against

debtor, and the payee the mere surety, having a clear right of action against the maker, upon paying the note, and therefore entitled to notice to enable him to exert that right.

In Sisson v. Tomlinson, London Sittings, 17th December, 1805. Selw. Ni. Pri. 4th ed. 324, n. 31. and observed upon in Brown v. Maffey, 15 East, 222. Lord Ellenborough, C. J. ruled, on the authority of the preceding case, that where the indorser has not given any consideration for a bill, and knows at the time the drawer has not any effects in the hands of the drawee, he (the indorser) is not entitled to notice of non-payment as a *bona fide* holder for a valuable consideration would be. But see Smith v. Beckett, 13 East, 187, and next note, and Brown v. Maffey, B. R. Hil. 52 Geo. 3. 15 East, 216, in which last case it was holden, that an indorser is entitled to notice of dishonour although he has not received any value for his indorsement if he did not know that the bill was an accommodation bill in its inception.

Smith v. Beckett, 13 East, 187. Bayl. 136. In an action against the payee and indorser of a note drawn by Canning, dated 28th October, 1809, and payable on demand, it appeared that the defendant had lent his name to this and other notes merely to enable Canning to obtain credit with the plaintiffs, his bankers, he having then lately stopped payment, which was well known to all the parties. The plaintiffs made advances for six months on these notes, which advances they afterwards renewed without any communication with the defendant. On the 28th May, 1810, Canning became bankrupt, and payment was afterwards demanded and refused, but no notice of this dishonour was given to the defendant. Lord Ellenborough thought a notice necessary, and nonsuited the plaintiffs; and on a motion to set aside the nonsuit, De Berdt v. Atkinson was cited, but the court held clearly, that a notice was necessary, especially as the advances had been renewed without the plaintiff's knowledge, and see Free v. Hawkins, 8 Taunt. 92. Holt C. N. P. 550.

Brown and others v. Maffey, 15 East, 216. where a bill was drawn, accepted, and indorsed by several indorsers, for the accommodation of the last indorser, and the acceptor had no effects of the drawer in his hands, but that fact was not known

to the defendant, one of the prior indorsers; it was held, that the defendant was entitled to notice of the dishonour before the holder could maintain an action against him, in order to enable him (even if he had no remedy upon the bill) to call immediately upon the last indorser to whom he had lent the security of his indorsement, without value received, and who had received the money upon that security. Lord Ellenborough, after observing on the case of Bickerdike v. Bollman, as ante, 198, said, that decision dispensed with notice to the drawer, where he knew before-hand, that he had no effects in the hands of the drawee, and had no reason to expect that the bill would be paid when it became due. But that exception must be taken with some restrictions, which, since I have sat here, I have often had occasion to put upon it, as where a drawer, though he might not have effects at the time of the drawing of the bill, in the drawer's hands, has a running account with him, and there is a fluctuating balance between them, and the drawer has reasonable ground to expect that he shall have effects in the drawee's hands when the bill became due: in such cases I have always held the drawer to be entitled to notice, because he draws the bill upon a reasonable presumption that it will be honoured, (vide Orr v. Magennis, 7 East, 359. Legge v. Thorpe, 12 East, 171.) when indeed it is a mere accommodation bill, without assets in hand or any expected, no notice to the drawer is necessary according to the established authorities: but I should be sorry to extend the doctrine further. It is said, however, that I extended it to the case of an indorser, in Sisson v. Tomlinson. But without surrendering that case, the circumstances of which were different from the present, and may make it at least more questionable: here it is clear that the defendant had no knowledge of the acceptor's having no assets of the drawer in his hands, and that the drawer put his name to it merely as a co-surety for Woods, and therefore when it was dishonoured, it became most material to the defendant that he should have had notice in order to enable him to proceed against Woods, for whom he was, in substance, though not in form, a surety; for, if he had no notice, he might lose his benefit of reimbursement against Woods, who had received the money upon the security of the defendant. I therefore

CHITTY ON BILLS.

B b

1st. When the drawer.[b] But if the payee of a note lends his name to secure a *notice of non-acceptance is necessary; & what excuses omission.* composition from the drawer to a creditor, and takes effects of the drawers to answer it, he is not entitled to notice, because it would be a fraud in him to call upon the maker who had thus deposited effects in his hands to answer the amount of his indorsement.[c]

It has, however, been held, that it is no excuse for not having presented a note in time for payment, that the defendant indorsed it to guarantee a debt due from the maker, or that the defendant knew before it was due, that the maker could not pay it, and had desired a banker, at whose house it was made payable, to send it to him and he would

[204] pay it,[d] nor can evidence of a parol agreement not to require payment at the appointed time, be received to excuse the neglect to give due notice.[e] And it has been decided that a person who has guaranteed the payment of money to be paid by a bill, is entitled (though no party to the bill) to insist on the neglect, to make a proper presentment or to give due notice of the dishonour of such bill.[f] But in a subsequent

think that the nonsuit was proper for want of such notice. And Grose, J., concurring, Bayley, J., said, he was of the same opinion, and that the foundation of Mr. J. Buller's opinion in Bickerdike *v.* Bollman, was this, that the drawer having no assets in the drawee's hands, could not be injured by the non-payment of the bill, or the want of notice that it had been dishonoured: and that is true, as against the drawer, but as against an indorser who is not the party to provide for taking up the bill in the first instance, and who has a remedy over, the want of notice is an injury to him. In Corney *v.* Mendez Da Costa, 1 Esp. Rep. 302. it would have been a fraud in the indorser to call upon the maker of the note, because, before it became due, the maker had deposited effects in his hands to answer the amount of his indorsement, and therefore he had no right to complain of the want of notice. But in this case, if the defendant had had notice of the non-payment at the time, he would have been enabled to call upon Woods immediately. The case of Smith *v.* Beckett has established, that a party does not waive his right to notice by lending his indorsement as a security to enable the drawer to raise money on it. Rule discharged.

[b] Cory *v.* Scott, 3 B. & A. 619.

[c] Corney *v.* Da Costa, 1 Esp. Rep. 303. Da Costa and Co. compounded with their creditors, and to secure the composition, drew notes in favour of the defendant, which he indorsed to the creditors. The defendant took effects of Da Costa and Co. at the time to the amount of the composition, and an action being brought against him upon one of these indorsements, he insisted that he had no notice of the non-payment of the note until five weeks after it was due, but Buller, J. held, that he was not entitled to notice, and the plaintiff had a verdict. See obser-

vations on this case in Brown *v.* Maffey, 5 East, 222, 3. Ante, 202, in notes.

[d] Nicholson *v.* Gouthit, 2 Hen Bla. 509. Gouthit and Burton undertook to guarantee an instalment on the debt of Green's, and for that purpose Green drew notes payable to Gouthit at Drury and Co's. which Gouthit and Burton indorsed, after which they were delivered to the creditors. Before they became due, Gouthit inquired at Drury and Co's. if they had any effects, and on their saying they had not, he desired them to send the notes to him and he would pay them. Many notes were accordingly presented and paid, but the note in question not being presented till three days after it was due, Gouthit refused to pay it. Burton had supplied him with money to take up all the notes, but as this was not presented when due, he had returned the money destined to pay it. An action was brought against Gouthit, and upon the trial, Eyre, C. J. thought, as he knew the note would not be paid at Drury and Co's. and had provided money for it, and as his indorsement was by way of guarantee, he was not injured by the delay, and that the request to send the notes to him was either a waiver of notice or notice by anticipation; but on a rule *nisi* to enter a nonsuit, and cause shown, though he thought the justice was clearly with the plaintiff, he thought he could not recover; for though the indorsement was by way of guarantee, it was liable to all the legal consequences of an indorsement; and Gouthit's promise to pay was only to pay such as should be duly presented at Drury's. Heath and Rooke, Justices, were of the same opinion, and the rule was made absolute.

[e] Free *v.* Hawkins, 8 Taunt. 92.

[f] Phillips *v.* Astling, 2 Taunt. 206. The declaration stated, that in consideration that the plaintiffs would sell and deliver to Davenport and Finney, certain goods, to be paid for by a bill, to be drawn by D. and F. upon Houghton, at six months; the

case, where the defendant being indebted to the plaintiff for goods sold, and C. being indebted to the defendant, the plaintiff, with the consent of defendant, drew a bill on C. payable at two months, which C. accepted, but afterwards dishonoured it; was held that defendant was not entitled to notice of the dishonour, his name not being on the bill, and that the bill was not to be esteemed a complete payment of the debt under the statute of Ann.ᵍ And it has been held, that proof that before the bill became due the parties liable upon it were bankrupt or insolvent, will be *prima facie* evidence that a demand upon them would have been of no avail, and will dispense with the necessity of making such presentment or giving notice, because the same strictness of proof is not necessary to charge a guarantee, as is necessary to support an action upon the bill itself, and the circumstances created a presumption that the guarantee was not prejudiced by the want of notice.ᵇ(1)

1st. When notice of non-acceptance is necessary; & what excuses omission.

It is no excuse for not giving notice to the drawer, that on an apprehension that the bill would be dishonoured, he lodged other money [203]

defendant undertook to guarantee the payment of such bill. It then averred delivery of the goods, acceptance of the bill, its presentment for payment, and dishonour, At the trial it appeared, that Houghton was at sea when the bill became due, which was on the 14th July, 1808, but that he had an agent residing in London, authorized to accept bills, and who had accepted this. That no presentment for payment was made to this agent when the bill became due; and that on the 16th July, the plaintiff gave D. and F. notice that the bill remained unpaid, but no notice was given to the defendants. In February, 1809, Davenport and Finney became insolvent, and Houghton was declared bankrupt in 1809, after which payment was demanded of the defendants. A verdict was found for the plaintiff, but upon a rule *nisi* for entering a nonsuit, after referring to Warrington *v.* Furbor, (8 East, 242. and infra, note.) said, that here the insolvency of the drawers, and the bankruptcy of the acceptor did not happen until long after the bill became due, and that for any thing that appeared, if the money had been demanded either of the drawer or acceptor, the bill might have been paid, but that the necessary steps not having been taken to obtain payment from the parties who were liable upon the bill and solvent, the guarantee must be discharged, and therefore they made the rule absolute. See also Bridges *v.* Berry, 3 Taunt. 130. Bishop *v.* Rowe, 3 M. & S. 362. Bayl, 138, 9. Cory *v.* Scott, 3 B. & A. 619.

ᵍ Swinyard *v.* Bowes, 5 M. & S. 62.
ᵇ Warrington *v.* Furbor, 8 East, 242. The defendant applied to one Martin, to purchase some goods to the amount of 1000*l.*, the price of which the plaintiffs undertook to guarantee at a credit of six months. The goods were furnished, and the defendant accepted a bill at six months for the amount. This bill became due 3d December, 1801, but on the 21st November preceding, the defendants became bankrupts, and the plaintiffs were obliged to pay Martin 1000*l.* on their guarantee, and now brought this action to be reimbursed; one of the objections made by the defendant at the trial was, that the plaintiffs had not proved a presentment of the bill to the defendant for payment, without which it was insisted, that Martin could not have recovered against the plaintiffs on their guarantee, and therefore, that the latter had paid the money in their own wrong. Lord Ellenborough held the proof unnecessary, this not being an action on the bill, and it being obvious that notice would have been unavailable, the defendants having been then recently stripped of all their property, and the plaintiffs had a verdict; and on a rule *nisi* to set it aside, and cause shown, the court held the verdict right, and Lawrence, J. said, the guarantees were not prevented from showing that they ought not to have been called upon at all, for that the principal debtors could have paid the bill if demanded of them. Rule discharged. See Bayl. 138, 9.

(1) If a guarantor of a bill be informed before it is due of the insolvency of the acceptors, and that the plaintiff looked to him for payment, it is not necessary to prove presentment and notice of non-payment. *Holbrow* v *Wilkins,* 1 Barn. & Cressw. 10.

On a guaranty of a promissory note drawn and indorsed by others, if the drawer and indorser are insolvent when the note becomes due, this would *primâ facie* be evidence that the guarantor was not prejudiced and therefore the giving him notice of non-payment is in such case dispensed with. *Gibbs* v. *Cannon,* 9 Serg. & Rawle, 198.

1st, When which he had of the drawee's, in the hands of the indorser, on an
notice of undertaking by the indorser, that he would return it whenever it
non-accept-should appear that he was exonerated from the bill, for his having
ance is *ne*-other money of the drawee's does not entitle him to apply it to the
cessary; & dishonoured bill, unless he had notice of the dishonour.[i] Nor is it
what *excu*-any excuse for not giving notice to the drawer of a bill if he had
ses omis-effects in the hands of the drawee, that the drawee represented to
sion.
the drawer, when the bill was drawn, that he should not be able to
provide for it, and that the drawer thereby understood that he should
have to provide for it.[k]

[206] If at any time between the drawing of the bill and its presentment
and dishonour, the drawee had *some effects* of the drawer in his hands,
though insufficient to pay the amount, or though the drawer has
afterwards withdrawn such effects, he will nevertheless be entitled to
notice of the dishonour, and the laches of the holder will discharge
him from liability; for this case differs from that where there are no
effects whatever of the drawer in the hands of the drawee at the
time, because the drawer must then know that he is drawing upon
accommodation, and without any reasonable expectation that the bill
will be honoured; but if he have effects at the time, it would be dangerous and inconvenient merely on account of the shifting of a balance, to hold notice not to be necessary; it would be introducing a
number of collateral issues upon every case upon a bill of exchange,
to examine how the accounts stood between the drawer and the
drawee, from the time the bill was drawn, down to the time when
it was dishonoured.[l] For the same reason, if the drawer of a bill

---

[i] Clegg *v.* Cotton. 3 Bos. &. Pul.
259. Indorsees against the drawer of
a bill. The bill was drawn in America, on Cullen, of Liverpool, in favour
of Miller and Robertson, and by them
indorsed to Booth and Co. and it afterwards came to the plaintiff's hands. It
was dated in 1794, and drawn at ninety
days sight. In 1800, the defendant
having other effects of Cullen's in his
hands, deposited them with Miller and
Robertson, and Booth and Co. on an undertaking from them, that they would return these effects whenever it should appear that they were exonerated from
this bill. Cullen afterwards became
bankrupt. The defendant was arrested,
and then said he should apply to Cullen's
assignees to bail him, for he had lodged
property in America to answer the bill,
and if he was discharged for want of
notice, he should pay it over to them.
Acceptance and payment were both refused, but no notice was even given of it
to the defendant. Chambre, J. nonsuited
the plaintiff, on the ground that the defendant was discharged for want of
notice ; and on a rule *nisi* to set aside
the nonsuit, and cause shown, the court
held, that the special circumstances did
not excuse the want of notice ; that there
was no fraud in the defendant, which
was the ground of the rule for dispensing
with notice, and that when Miller and
Bobertson, and Booth and Co. were exonerated, which they were by want of
notice, the money deposited with them
belonged to Cullen's assignees. Rule discharged.
Note.—It did not appear that the defendant had got back the property which
he deposited, but that circumstance was
not relied on.
[k] Staples *v.* Okines, 1 Esp. Rep. 332.
In an action against the drawer of a bill,
the defence was want of notice. The
plaintiff thereupon called the acceptor,
who proved, that when the bill was
drawn, he was indebted to the defendant in more than the amount of the bill,
but that he then represented to the defendant that it would not be in his power
to provide for the bill when it should become due, and that it was therefore then
understood between them that the defendant should provide for it ; and it was contended that this superseded the necessity
of giving the defendant notice. But Lord
Kenyon held, that it did not, and nonsuited the plaintiff.
[l] Orr *v.* Megennis, 7 East, 359.—
3 Smith, 328. S. C. In an action by the
payees against the drawer of a foreign
bill, payable at ninety-days after sight,
the declaration averred presentment for
acceptance and refusal, presentment for
payment and refusal, and protest for
non-payment ; it then averred, that at
the time of making the bill, and from
thence until the presentment for payment,

of exchange, when it is presented for acceptance, has effects in the hands of the drawees, though he is indebted to them in a much larger amount, and they, without his privity, have appropriated the effects in their hands, to the satisfaction of their debt, he is entitled to notice of the dishonour.[m] Nor is actual value in the hands of the

1st. When *notice* of non-acceptance is *necessary;* & what *excuses* omission.

the defendant had no effects in the hands of the drawees. At the trial it appeared, that at the time of drawing the bill, the defendant had effects in the hands of the drawees, but to what amount did not appear; but that when the bill was presented for acceptance, and thence until presentment for payment, he had not any. The bill was only noted for non-acceptance, but was protested for non-payment, no notice of non-acceptance was given to the defendant. The plaintiffs had paid the amount to an indorsee. They were nonsuited for want of proving protest for, and notice of non-acceptance. On motion to set aside the nonsuit, Rickerdike v. Bollman and other cases were cited, to show that no notice and therefore no protest was necessary. But Lord Ellenborough said, that that case went on the ground that there were no effects in the hands of the drawee at the time when the bill was drawn, and the other cases followed on the same ground, but that no case had extended the exemption to cases where the drawee had effects of the drawer's in his hands at the time when the bill was drawn, though the balance might vary afterwards, and be turned into the opposite scale. Rule refused.

Hammond v. Dufrene, 3 Campb. 145. This was an action on a bill of exchange for 301l. 17s. 10d. dated the 25th of April, 1811, drawn by the defendant upon, and accepted by Messrs. Dufrene and Penny, payable at three months after date. To excuse the proof of notice to the defendant of the dishonour of the bill, one of the acceptors was called, who stated, that when the bill was drawn and accepted, they had no effects of the drawee in their hands, but that before the bill became due, he paid a sum of 400l. on their account. Parke, for the plaintiff, insisted, that this was an accommodation bill, and that the drawer, therefore was not entitled to notice of its dishonour. Lord Ellenborough said, I think the drawer has a right to notice of the dishonour of a bill, if *he has effects in the hands of the acceptor at any time before it becomes due.* In that case he may reasonably expect that the bill will be regularly paid, and he may be prejudiced by receiving no notice that it is dishonoured. I am aware that the inquiry has generally been as to the state of accounts between the drawer and the drawee when the bill was drawn or accepted; but I conceive the whole period must be looked to, from the drawing of the bill till it becomes due,

and that notice is requisite if the drawer has effects in the hands of the drawee at any time during that interval: therefore, if the defendant in this case paid a sum of money for Messrs. Dufrene and Penny, before the 28th of July, you must prove that he had due notice it was not paid on that day by the acceptors. The case was afterwards brought before the court, but the direction of the Judge at Nisi Prius upon this point was not questioned.

Thackray v. Blackett, 3 Campb. 164.—The drawer of two bills of exchange, before they became due, received notice that they were accidentally destroyed, and was called upon to give others in their stead, according to the statute of 9 & 10 W. 3. c. 17. When the bills were drawn he had no effects in the hands of the acceptors, but before either was due, they were indebted to him to an amount less than one of the bills, and became bankrupt: Held, that he was nevertheless entitled to notice of the dishonour of both bills. Lord Ellenborough said, the excuse of want of effects in their hands, I think is unavailing as to both bills: I cannot make any distinction between the two. If there was an open account between the parties, and the acceptors were indebted in any sum to the drawer before the bills became due, I cannot say that he must necessarily have been aware before-hand that either of them would be dishonoured. Judges of the greatest authority have doubted of the propriety of the rule laid down in Bickerdike v. Bollman, and I certainly will not give it any extension. Plaintiff nonsuited.

[m] Blackham v. Doren, 2 Campb. 503. This was an action against the drawer of a bill for 250l., payable after sight; of which acceptance had been refused; and to excuse the want of notice of non-acceptance, it was proved, that when the bill was presented, though the drawer had effects in the hands of the drawee to the amount of 1500l., yet that he owed them 10,000l. or 11,000l., and that they had appropriated the effects to go in satisfaction of this debt; this appropriation, however, was without the defendant's privity. Lord Ellenborough said, "If a man draws upon a house, with whom he has no account, he knows that the bill will not be accepted; he can suffer no injury from want of notice of its dishonour, and therefore he is not entitled to such notice; but the case is quite otherwise where the drawer has a fluctuating balance in the hands of the drawee; there notice is peculiarly requisite. Without this, how can the drawer know that credit has been refused to him, and that

1st. When drawee at the time of drawing, essentially necessary to entitle the
notice of drawer to notice of dishonour of the bill, for circumstances may exist
non-accept- which would give a drawer good ground to consider he had a right to
ance is ne-
cessary; & draw a bill upon his correspondent; as where he had consigned effects
what excu- to him, to answer the bill, though they may not have come to him at
ses omis- the time when the bill was presented for acceptance, to which may be
sion.
added the case of bills drawn in respect of other fair mercantile agree-
ments.ᵃ And therefore where the drawer had sold and shipped goods
to the drawee, and drew the bill before they had arrived, and the
drawee not having received the bill of lading, refused to accept the
goods because they were damaged, and also refused to accept the
bill, it was decided, that the drawer was discharged for want of
notice.ᵒ But if the vendor of goods sold upon credit, draws upon
the purchaser a bill, which would be due long before the expiration of
the stipulated credit, he is not entitled to notice of the dishonour, because he had no right to expect that the drawee would honour the
bill.ᴾ It should seem, that although the drawer or other party may

his bill has been dishonoured? It is
said here, that the effects in the hands
of the drawees were all appropriated to
discharge their own debt; but that appropriation should appear by writing,
and the defendant should be a party to
it. I wish that notice had never been dispensed with, then we should not have been
troubled with investigating accounts between drawer and drawee. I certainly will
not relax the rule still farther, which I
should do if I were to hold that notice was
unnecessary in the present case. Plaintiff
nonsuited.
ᵃ Per Lord Ellenborough, in Legge *v.*
Thorpe, 12 East, 175. Per Eyre, C. J.
in Walwyn *v.* St. Quintin, 1 Bos. & Pul.
654. Ex parte Wilson, 11 Ves. 411.
ᵒ Rucker and others *v.* Hiller, 16 East,
43. 3 Campb. 217. 334. S. C. Where
one draws a bill of exchange, with a *bona
fide* reasonable expectation of having assets in the hands of the drawee, as by having shipped goods on his account, which
were on their way to the drawee, but
without the bill of lading or invoice, the
drawer is entitled to notice of the dishonour, though in fact the goods had not
come to the hands of the drawee at the
time where the bill was presented for
acceptance, or he had rejected them, and
he returned it marked "no effects." Lord
Ellenborough, C. J. said, "When the
drawer draws his bill on the *bona fide* expectation of assets in the hands of the
drawee to answer it, it would be carrying
the case of Bickerdike *v.* Bollman further
than has ever been done, if he were not
at all events entitled to notice of the dishonour. And I know the opinion of my
Lord Chancellor to be, that the doctrine of
that case ought not to be pushed further.
The case is very different where the party
knows that he has no right to draw the
bill. There are many occasions where
a drawee may be justified in refusing,
from motives of prudence, to accept a

bill, on which notice ought nevertheless
to be given to the drawer; and if we
were to extend the expression further, it
would come at last to a general dispensa-
tion, with notice of the dishonour, in all
cases where the drawee had no assets in
hand at the very time of presenting the
bill; and thus get rid of the general rule
requiring notice, than which nothing is
more convenient in the commercial world.
A *bona fide* reasonable expectation of assets in the hands of the drawee has been
several times held to be sufficient to entitle the drawer to notice of the dishonour.
though such expectation may ultimately
have failed to be realized.
ᴾ Claridge *v.* Dalton, 4 M. & S. 226.—
The drawer of a bill of exchange, who
has no effects in the hands of the drawee,
except that he has supplied him with
goods upon credit, which credit does not
expire till long after the bill would become due, is not discharged by want of
notice of the dishonour. Time given by
indorsee to the payee does not discharge
the drawee. Lord Ellenborough, C. J.
said, I accede to the proposition, that
where there are any funds in the hands
of the drawee, so that the drawer has a
right to expect, or even where there are
not any funds, if the bill be drawn under
such circumstances, as may induce the
drawer to entertain a reasonable expectation that the bill will be accepted and
paid, the person so drawing it is entitled
to notice; but this bill was drawn in anticipation of the credit, and without any
assurance of accommodation; and Bayley, J. said, the case of Bickerdike *v.*
Bollman has established, and I am disposed to think rightly, that a party who
cannot be prejudiced by want of notice,
shall not be entitled to require it; but
this rule extends only to cases where the
party has no effects, or is not likely to
have effects, or has no expectation that
he will have any. In all other cases, the

not have advanced money or goods to the drawee, yet if he has deposited short bills or policies, or even title-deeds in his hands, or has accepted cross bills, and had reasonable ground to expect that the drawee would accept or pay in respect thereof, he is entitled to notice of the dishonour.[q]

The death,[r] bankruptcy, or known insolvency[s] of the drawee, or

1st. When notice of non-acceptance is *necessary; & what excuses omission.*

drawer is entitled to notice, and this is required in order that he may withdraw forthwith out of the hands of the drawee such effects as he may happen to have, or may stop those which he is in a course of putting into his hands. But at the period when the bill was refused payment, the defendant was not in a condition to have taken any steps against Pickford, the drawee, so as to derive any benefit from a notice; therefore he was not entitled to notice.

[q] In Walwyn v. St. Quintin, 2 Esp. Rep. 515, Eyre, C. J. left it to the jury to say, whether title-deeds were effects or not, and they found in the affirmative. See 1 Bos. & Pul. 652. S. C. Ante, 200.

Ex parte Heath, 2 Ves. & Bea. 240. 2 Rose, 141. S. C. In this case a distinction was taken as to the necessity of notice to the drawer of a dishonoured bill, depending on the fact whether the acceptor has effects, or whether it arose out of a single transaction, or out of various dealings. In the latter case it was held, that notice is equally necessary without effects. And it seems, that securities as title-deeds, and short bills, are effects for this purpose. The Lord Chancellor said, I have often lamented the consequences of distinction, introduced 'n modern times, as to the necessity of giving notice of the non-payment or non-acceptance of a bill of exchange, whether the acceptor had or had not effects, and I have the satisfaction of finding, that my opinion has been adopted by the courts of law. According to the old rule, a bill of exchange, purporting upon the face of it to be for value received, the implication of law from the acceptance was, that the acceptor had effects. Then they came to this general doctrine, that it is not necessary for the holder to give notice, if he can show that the acceptor had no effects. The first objection is, who is to decide whether there are effects or not? in the simple case, where there is nothing but the particular bill, and no other dealing between them, there is no difficulty; but if there are complicated engagements and various accommodation transactions, no one can say whether there are effects or not, and there cannot be a stronger instance than that in the case of Walwyn v. St. Quintin, (2 Esp. Rep. 515. ante, 200,) referred to; Lord Chief Justice Eyre, a very good lawyer, left to the jury to decide, without any solution of the question, whether title-deeds are effects; but a rule that

securities cannot be effects in any case, would be quite destructive of all commercial dealing. Are not short bills, for instance, effects? Is it of no importance to the holder to have notice that he may withdraw them from the possession of the acceptor? The courts were obliged necessarily to decide, that if bills were accepted for the accommodation of the drawer, and there was nothing but that paper between them, notice was not necessary, the drawer being, as between him and the acceptor, first liable; but if bills were drawn for the accommodation of the acceptor, the transaction being for his benefit, there must be notice without effects, and if in result of various dealings, the surplus of accommodation is on the side of the acceptor, he is, with regard to the drawer, exactly in the same situation of an acceptor having effects, and the failure to give notice may be equally detrimental, I will in this instance give an inquiry. It is upon the petitioner to prove, that in all this complication, there is nothing which the law calls effects, he may therefore have liberty to call a meeting, and must pay the costs of this application.

[r] Poth. pl. 146.
[s] Russell v. Langstaffe, Dougl. 497. 515. Esdaile v. Sowerby, 11 East, 114. Ex parte Wilson, 11 Ves. 412. Whitfield v. Savage, 2 Bos. & Pul. 279. Thackray v. Blackett, 3 Campb. 165. Bayl. 115. acc. Ex parte Smith, 3 Bro. C. C. 1. contra.

In Russell v. Langstaffe, Dougl. 497. 515. Lee, said, *arguendo*, that it had frequently been ruled by Lord Mansfield at Guildhall, that it is not an excuse for not making a demand on a note or bill, or for not giving notice of non-payment, that the drawer or acceptor has become a bankrupt, as many means may remain of obtaining payment by the assistance of friends or otherwise; and Lord Mansfield, who was in court, did not deny the assertion. This dictum was also referred to, *arguendo*, in Bickerdike v. Bollman, 1 T. R. 408.

Esdaile v. Sowerby, 11 East, 114. In an action by the indorsees of a bill of exchange, drawn by Cheetham upon Hill, in favour of the defendants, and by them indorsed to the plaintiffs, a verdict was found for the plaintiff, subject to a case for the opinion of the court. The bill, which was payable in London, became due on Saturday, 20th February, and then dishonoured. By a mistake, the no-

1st. When *his* being in prison,[t] constitute no excuses, either at law or in equity,
notice of for the neglect to give due notice of non-acceptance or non-payment;
non-accept-
ance is ne- because many means may remain of obtaining payment by the assist-
cessary; & ance of friends or otherwise, of which it is reasonable that the drawer
what excu- and indorsers should have the opportunity of availing themselves, and
ses omis- it is not competent to the holders to show that the delay in giving notice
sion. has not in fact been prejudicial;[u] nor will the circumstance of the

[211.] drawee's having informed the drawer, before the bill was presented for
acceptance or became due, that he could not honour it, be a sufficient
excuse for not giving notice;[x] and therefore where A. to accommodate
B. lent him a bill drawn by himself upon and accepted by C. who had
effects of his in his hands, and B. indorsed it to D. who indorsed
it over; and the day before the bill became due, B. paid the amount to
A. who, on hearing that C. had failed, gave B. a check for the amount
of the bill, and sent him with it to D. to enable him to pay the bill when
due: and four days after that time A. learning that payment had not
been demanded, desired D. not to pay the bill, as no notice of non-
payment had been given by the holder, and offered to indemnify him,
notwithstanding which D. afterwards paid the bill; it was holden first,
that D. paid the bill in his on wrong, and secondly, that A. was entitled to recover back the money paid into the hands of D. by B. in an
action for money had and received.[y] Again, in Esdaile *v.* Sowerby[z] it
was held, that, though the indorsers of a bill of exchange had full knowledge of the bankruptcy of the drawer, and of the insolvency of the
acceptor before the bill became due, and that it was impossible it could
be paid, yet that they were discharged by the holders not giving them

tice of non-payment was not given to
the defendants till the 27th, whereas it
ought to have been given on the 24th, and
payment was refused, on the ground of
these laches; before the bill became due the
drawer had stopped payment and become
bankrupt, and the acceptor was insolvent.
The drawer had himself apprized the defendant of his situation at the time of his
stopping payment, and that this bill
would not be paid, and they knew that
the acceptor had no funds but such as the
drawer furnished him with, and on the
25th February, they admitted to the
plaintiff's agent, that they knew of the
insolvency of the drawer and acceptor.
It was contended that notice of the dishonour was unnecessary. But the court
was clear that the insolvency of the
drawer and acceptor, and the knowledge
of it, did not dispense with the necessity
of giving notice of the dishonour of the
bill to the defendants. And Lord Ellenborough said, " It is too late now to con-
tend, that the insolvency of the drawer
or acceptor dispenses with the necessity
of a demand of payment or of notice of
the dishonour." Boultbee *v.* Stubbs,
28 Ves. 21. The Lord Chancellor, after
deciding that indulgence to the principal,
by taking a mortgage and giving time,
discharges the surety, though such conduct may be for the benefit of the surety,
said, " It is in most cases for the advantage of the surety, but the law takes so
little notice of that circumstance, that if

the acceptor of a bill becomes bankrupt,
the holder must give notice to the drawer,
as another person has no right to judge
what are his remedies, and the original
implied contract being, that as far as the
nature of the original security will admit,
the security, paying the debt, shall stand in
the place of the creditor."

[t] Per Ld. Alvanly, C. J. in Haynes *v.*
Birks, 3 Bos & Pul. 601.

[u] Esdaile *v.* Sowerby, 11 East, 114.
Russell *v.* Langstaffe, Dougl. 515. Bickerdike *v.* Bollman, 1 T. R. 408. De Berdt
v. Atkinson, 2 Hen. Bla. 336. Nicholson
v. Gouthit, id. 612; and admitted by the
court in Warrington *v.* Furbor, 8 East,
245, 6, 7. Cory *v.* Scott, 3 B. & A. 623.

[x] Nicholson *v.* Gouthit, 2 Hen. Bla. 612.
Staples *v.* Okines, 1 Esp. Rep. 332. In
Esdaile *v.* Sowerby, 11 East, 117, Lord
Ellenborough observed, that as to the
knowledge of the dishonour being equivalent to due notice of it given to him by the
holder, the case of Nicholson *v.* Gouthit, is
so decisive an authority against that doctrine that we cannot enter even into the
discussion of it. Free *v.* Hawkins, 8 Taunt.
92.

[y] Whitfield *v* Savage, 2 Bos. & Pul. 277.
Clegg *v.* Cotton, 3 Bos. & Pul. 239; but
see Brett *v.* Levett, 13 East, 213, 14. as to
an acknowledgment by a drawer before
the bill became due that he knew it would
not be paid, infra.

[z] 11 East, 114. ante, 210; but see Brett
v. Levett, 13 East, 213, 14.

due notice, on account of a mistake by mis-directing a letter containing such notice. But where the drawer of a bill, a few days before it became due, stated to the holder, that he had no regular residence, and that he would call and see if the bill had been paid by the acceptor, it was held that he was not entitled to notice of its dishonour, he having thus dispensed with it ;[a] and if the drawer, on being applied to by the holder before a bill is due, to know if it will be paid, answer, that it will not, he is not entitled to notice of non-payment ;[b] and where one of several drawers of a bill was also the acceptor, it was held, in an action against the drawers, that proof of these circumstances dispensed with the necessity for proving that notice of non-payment was in fact given, because notice to one of several joint drawers of a bill is sufficient, and the acceptor being himself a drawer, he had notice of his own default.[c] (274)

margin note: 1st. When notice of non-acceptance is necessary; & what excuses omission.

[212]

[a] Phipson v. Kneller, 4 Campb. 285. 1 Stark. 116. S. C.
[b] Brett v. Levett, 13 East, 214.
[c] Porthouse v. Parker and others, 1 Campb. 82. in which Ld. Ellenborough held, that the plaintiff was not bound to prove that the defendants had received express notice of the dishonour of the bill which must necessarily have been known to one of them, and the knowledge of one was the knowledge of all. But if there was any fraud in the transaction, a different rule would prevail, Per Lord Ellenborough, in Bignold v. Waterhouse, 1 M. & S. 259.

(274) The doctrines in some of the cases cited in this section, do not seem easily reconcileable; it will be necessary for the judicious reader carefully to weigh and consider them. Many decisions have occurred in the United States on the same questions. It seems to be generally acknowledged that the want of effects in the hands of the drawee will be a sufficient excuse *as against the drawer* for not giving him notice of the non-acceptance or non-payment of a bill. *Hoffman* v. *Smith*, 1 Caines' Rep. 157. *Tunno* v. *Lague*, 2 John. Cas. 1. *Frothingham* v. *Price's Ex.* 1 Bay's Rep. 291. *Warder* v. *Tucker*, 7 Mass. Rep. 449. But if the drawer have a right to draw in consequence of engagements between himself and the drawee, or in consequence of engagements made to the drawee, or from any other cause, he ought to be considered as drawing upon funds in the hands of the drawee, and as therefore entitled to strict notice. *French* v. *Bank of Columbia*, 4 Cranch, 141. The court of King's Bench have also recently declared that a *bona fide* reasonable expectation of assets in the hands of the drawee had been several times held to be sufficient to entitle the drawer to notice of the dishonour, though such expectation may have ultimately failed of being realized. *Reukier* v. *Hiller*, 16 East's Rep. 43. And if a note be made for the accommodation of the indorser, and the money raised on it by a discount in the market, is in fact received by him, he may be considered as a drawer without funds in the hands of an acceptor, and not entitled to notice of non-payment by the maker, 4 Cranch, 141. *Agan* v. *M'Manus*, 11 John. Rep. 180. But the same reasons do not appear to exist where the note has been made and discounted for the accommodation of the maker; and the indorser is in such case therefore entitled to strict notice, 4 Cranch, 141. And an indorser of a bill for the accommodation of the drawer is in all cases entitled to strict notice, although the drawee had no effects of the drawer in his hands. *Warder* v. *Tucker*, 7 Mass. Rep. 449. *Scarborough* v. *Harris*, 1 Bay's Rep. 177 *Frothingham* v. *Price's Ex.* 1 Bay's Rep. 291. *May* v. *Coffin*, 4 Mass. Rep. 341. *Brown* v. *Maffey*, 15 East's Rep. 216. *Hussey* v. *Freeman*, 10 Mass. Rep. 86.
And although some doubt once existed upon the subject, it seemes now to be settled in the United States that the bankruptcy or insolvency of the drawer of a bill or maker of a note, at the time when the note or bill was given or was payable, is no excuse for not giving notice of the non-payment to the indorser, even though the indorsement should have been for the mere accommodation of the drawer or maker. *May* v. *Coffin*, 4 Mass. Rep. 341. *Farnum* v. *Fowle*, 12 Mass. Rep. 89. *Crossen* v. *Hutchinson*, 9 Mass. Rep. 205. *Sanford* v. *Dillaway*, 10 Mass. Rep. 52. *Jackson* v. *Richards*, 2 Caines' Rep. 343. *Bank of America* v. *Varden*, 2 Dal. Rep. 78. *Mallory* v. *Kirwan*, 2 Dall. Rep. 192. *Warder* v. *Carson's* Executors, 2 Dall. Rep. 233. *Bank of America* v. *Petit*, 4 Dall. Rep. 127. *Ball* v. *Dennis*, 4 Dall. Rep. 168. and see *Agan* v. *M'Manus*, 11 John. Rep. 189. *Hussey* v. *Freeman*, 10 Mass. Rep. 84. *Stothart* v. *Parker*, Overt. Rep. 261. *contra.*
And in England it has been recently held, where a person lent his indorsement on a note to the drawer, who was the bankrupt, payable on demand, for the purpose of ena-

CHITTY ON BILLS. C c

1st. When
notice of
non-accept-
ance is ne-
cessary; &
what excu-
ses omis-
sion.
In general, the drawer will, as already observed, be at liberty to rebut the presumption that he could not have been damnified, raised by
the proof of his having no effects in the hands of the drawee, by proving that he has really sustained damage;[d] and a surety for the acceptor, who has been obliged to pay the amount of the bill in consequence
of the acceptor's bankruptcy, need not in an action against him for money paid, prove the due presentment of the bill, &c.[e]

A neglect to give *immediate* notice may however be excused by
some other circumstances besides the want of effects. Thus, the
absconding or absence of the drawer or indorser may excuse the neglect
to advise him;[f] and the sudden illness or death of the holder, or his
agent, or other accident,[g] may constitute an excuse for the want of a

[d] Ante, 207, 8, but see Rogers v. Stephens, 2 T. R. 713.
[e] Warrington v. Furbor, 8 East, 242.
[f] Walwyn v. St. Quintin, 2 Esp. Rep.
516. 1 Bos. & Pul. 652. S. C. Bul. Ni.
Pri. 273, 4. and see Crosse v. Smith,

1 M. & S. 545. Bewes v. Howe, 5 Taunt.
30.
[g] There is no reported case deciding
whether accident will excuse a delay in
giving notice of non-acceptance or non-
payment. In Hilton v. Shepherd, 6 East,

---

bling him to raise money on that security by a deposit thereof with his banker, that a demand and notice was necessary to charge the indorser, especially as in that case there
had been a renewal of the credit for a second term, without the consent or knowledge of
the indorser. *Smith* v. *Becket*, 13 East's Rep. 187.

Where a bill was drawn, accepted and indorsed, by several indorsers, for the accommodation of the *last indorser*, and the drawee had no effects in his hands, but this fact
was not known to the defendant, who was a prior indorser, it was held that the defendant could not be charged without strict notice of the dishonour of the bill, because
he would on payment have been entitled to call upon the last indorser, for whom he
was, in fact, security. *Brown* v. *Maffry*, 15 East, 216.

And a person, who, without consideration, but without fraud, indorses a bill, in which
both drawer and acceptor are fictitious persons, is entitled to strict notice, for he has
only placed himself in the situation of a common indorser. *Leach* v. *Hewitt*, 4 Taunt.
Rep. 731.

When upon a bill payable at so many *after sight*, the holder presents the bill for acceptance, and elects to consider what passes on such presentment as a non-acceptance,
(though in strictness he might have otherwise acted,) and protests the bill for non-acceptance, he is bound by such election, as to all the other parties to the bill, and must give
due notice to them of the dishonour accordingly, otherwise they will be discharged.
Mitchell v. *Degrand*, 1 Mason's Rep. 176.

It lies on the holder of a bill to prove that the drawer had no effects in the hands of
the drawee in order to excuse the want of notice. *Baxter* v. *Graves*, 2 Marsh. 152.

The drawer of a bill is entitled to notice of its dishonour though the drawee be not
indebted to him either when the bill was drawn or fell due provided the drawer had reasonable ground to believe that it would be honoured, and a written authority from the
drawee to the drawer for the latter to draw is sufficient ground. *Austin* v. *Rodman*, 1
Hawks, 194.

Where the drawer of a bill is a partner of the house or firm on which it is drawn it is
not necessary for the holder to prove that notice of its dishonour was given to the drawer. *Gowan* v. *Jackson*, 20 Johns. 176.

Where a demand cannot be made on the drawer, notice must nevertheless be given to
the indorser, and that within as short a period after having ascertained that the demand
could not be made as if the demand had been made. *Price* v. *Young*, 1 M'Cord, 399.

Where there are any funds of the drawer in the hands of the drawee, or if at the
time the bill is drawn there are circumstances sufficient to induce a reasonable expectation that the bill will be accepted or paid, the drawer is entitled to notice of its dishonour, and to due diligence in the presentment of it. *Robinson* v. *Ames*, 20 Johns. 146.
Thus where there were dealings and an open account between the drawer and drawee
and the latter had received considerable shipments of cotton from the drawer, and accepted previous bills, but on account of a fall in the price of the cotton its value was
not equal to the amount of the accepted bills and the last bill drawn was therefore protested for want of funds, it was held that the drawer was entitled to notice. Ibid.

regular notice to any of the parties, provided it be given as soon as pos- 1st. When sible after the impediment is removed.[h] And the holder of a bill[i] of *notice of* exchange is excused for not giving regular notice of its being dis- *non-accept-* honoured to an indorser, of whose place of residence he is *ignorant,*[j] if *cessary,*[ne-] he use reasonable diligence to discover where the indorser may be *what excu-* found.[k] And Lord Ellenborough observed, " When the holder of a *ses omis-* bill of exchange does not know where the indorser is to be found, it *sion.* would be very hard if he lost his remedy by not communicating imme- mediate notice of the dishonour of the bill; and I think the law lays down no such rigid rule. The holder must not allow himself to remain in a state of passive and contented ignorance; but if he uses reasonable diligence to discover the residence of the indorser, I conceive that notice given as soon as this is discovered is due notice of the dishonour of the bill, within the usage and custom of merchants."[l] And it has been considered to be sufficient, when a promissory note has been dishonoured, to make inquiries at the drawer's for the residence of the payee.[m] But in a subsequent case it was held, that, to excuse the not giving of regular notice of the dishonour of a bill, it is not enough to

15, in notes, Garrow and Russell conten- ded, that whether due notice has been giv- en in reasonable time, must, from the neces- sity of the thing, be a question of fact for the consideration of the jury. That it de- pended upon a thousand combinations of circumstances which could not be reduced to rule; if the party were taken ill, if he lost his senses, if he were under duress, &c. how could laches be imputed to him? suppose he were prevented from giving no- tice within the time named by a physical impossibility. Such a rule of law must de- pend upon the distance, upon the course of the post, upon the state of the roads, upon accidents, all which it is absurd to imagine. Lord Kenyon, C. J. I cannot conceive how this can be a matter of law. I can un- derstand that the law should require that due diligence shall be used, but that it should be laid down that the notice must be given that day or the next, or at any pre- cise time, under whatever circumstan- ces, is, I own, beyond my comprehen- sion. I should rather have conceived that whether due diligence had or had not been used was a question for the jury to consi- der, under all the circumstances of the *ac- cident, necessity, and the like.* This, how- ever, is a question very fit to be considered, and when it goes down to trial again I shall advise the jury to find a special verdict. I find invincible objections in my own mind to consider that the rule of law requiring due diligence, is tied down to the next day. In Darbishire v. Parker, 6 East, 3. it was held, that reasonable time is a matter of law for the court.

[h] Turner v. Leach, Sittings at Guildhall, post, Hilary Term, 1818, *cor.* Lord Ellen- borough. Assumpsit by the eleventh in- dorser of a bill of exchange, against the eighth indorser, for default of payment. It appeared, that in due time on the 4th September, 1817, the returned bill, with notice of the dishonour, was left at the

house of Richard Bennett, the tenth in- dorser, enclosed in a letter addressed to him. That in consequence of the danger- ous illness of his wife at a distant place, he had on the 1st September left his house in care of a lad, who had no authority to open letters, intending to return on the 3d Sep- tember, but that in consequence of the in- creasing dangerous illness of his wife, he did not return till after the 8th September, on which day his brother opened the let- ter, and immediately gave notice of the dishonour of the bill to the plaintiff who paid it, and then called upon the defen- dant, who insisted that he was discharged for want of earlier notice. It was urged for the plaintiff, that the dangerous illness of Richard Bennett's wife, excused his absence from home, and the delay in gi- ving notice of the dishonour, and that as the dishonour of a bill is contrary to the contract and expectation of the parties, there is no reason for requiring an indorser to be in the way, or to appoint an agent in his absence to provide for such an event. But Lord Ellenborough ruled that these circumstances constituted no excuse for the delay in giving notice. A case was reser- ved upon another point. See 4 B. & A. 451.

[i] Poth. pl. 144; but a mistake in directing a letter is no excuse. Esdaile v. Sowerby, 11 East, 114, ante, 210.

[k] Bateman v. Joseph, 2 Campb. 461. 12 East, 433. S. C. Browning v. Kinnear, 1 Gow's Rep. 81. What is due diligence, see Harrison v. Fitzhenry, 3 Esp. Rep. 240. Quære, whether reasonable diligence is in this case a question of fact or law? 1 Wightw. 76. 12 East, 433. 2 Campb. 461. 3 Campb. 262. 6 East, 3. as to what is reasonable diligence, see 4 M. & S. 49.

[l] In Bateman v. Joseph, 2 Campb. 462. and see Browning v. Kinnear, 1 Gow's Rep. 81.

[m] Sturges v. Derrick, Wightw. 76.

1st. When **show that the holder, being ignorant of his residence, made inquiries**
notice of **upon the subject at the place where the bill was payable.**[a] **However,**
non-accept- **sending verbal notice to a merchant's counting-house is sufficient, and if**
ance is ne- **no person be there in the ordinary hours of business, it is not necessary**
cessary; & **to leave or send a written one, nor is it necessary to make inquiries after**
what *excu-* **the party; so as to give him notice elsewhere."**[o](1)
ses omis-
sion.

[a] Beveridge *v.* Burgis, 8 Campb. 262. This was an action by the indorsee against the indorser of a bill of exchange. The plaintiff had given the defendant no notice of its dishonour till several months after it became due; the excuse alleged for this omission was, that the plaintiff was ignorant of the defendant's address, which did not appear upon the bill, but the only evidence adduced to show that he had used any diligence to discover this, was, that he had made inquiries upon the subject at a house in the Old Bailey, where the bill was made payable by the acceptor. Lord Ellenborough. Ignorance of the indorser's residence may excuse the want of due notice, but the party must show that he has used reasonable diligence to find it out. Has he done so here? How should it be expected that the requisite information should be obtained where the bill was payable? Inquiries might have been made of the other persons whose names appeared upon the bill, and application might have been made to persons of the same name with the defendant, whose addresses are set down in the directory. Plaintiff nonsuited.

[o] Goldsmith and others *v.* Bland and others, *cor.* Lord Eldon, 1st March, 1800. Bayl. 127, note 1. The plaintiffs sued the defendants as indorsers of two foreign bills, and to prove notice, the plaintiffs showed that they sent a clerk to the defendant's counting-house near the Exchange, between four and five o'clock in the afternoon, nobody was in the counting-house; the clerk saw a servant girl at the house, who said that nobody was in the way, and he returned, having left no message with her. Lord Eldon told the jury, that if they thought the defendants ought to have had somebody in the counting-house at the time, he was of opinion that the plaintiffs had done all that was necessary by sending their clerk; that the notice was in law sufficient, if the time was regular, whether the defendants were solvent at the time or not. The jury thought the defendants ought to have had somebody in the counting-house at the time, and that the plaintiffs had done all that was necessary. Verdict for the plaintiffs for 1633*l.* Post, 220.

Cross and others *v.* Smith and others, 1 M. & S. 545. Notice to the drawers of non-payment of a bill of exchange by sending it to their counting-house during hours of business on two successive days, knocking there; and making noise sufficient to be heard by persons within, and waiting there several minutes; the inner door of the counting-house being locked, is sufficient, without leaving a notice in writing, or sending by the post, though some of the drawers lived at a small distance from the place. See also Bowes *v.* Howe, 5 Taunt. 80. Post, 220.

---

(1) Where the holder, who was ignorant of the indorser's residence, sent the notice to A., who was acquainted with it, requesting him to add to the direction the indorser's place of residence, it was held, that reasonable diligence had been used. *Hartford Bank v. Stedman,* 3 Conn. Rep. 489.

It is not incumbent on the indorser of a promissory note to show the holder where the maker is to be found, so that he may make a demand on the maker, where no application is made to him by the holder. *Duncan v. M'Cullough,* 4 Serg. & Rawle, 480.

If the maker of a promissory note is not to be found when the note becomes due, a demand on him of payment is not necessary in order to charge the indorser. But it is necessary to prove either a demand, or due diligence in endeavouring to make a demand. *Duncan v. M'Cullough,* 4 Serg. & Rawle, 480.

When the holder of a bill was ignorant of the drawer's place of residence, but it appeared that he had not used due diligence to make inquiry, a notice put into the post office directed to a place other than that in which the drawer lived, was held to be insufficient. *Barnwell v. Mitchell,* 3 Conn. Rep. 101.

Where the traveller of A., a tradesman, received in the course of business a promissory note, which he delivered to his master, without indorsing it, and the note having been returned to A. dishonoured, the latter not knowing the address of the next preceding indorser, wrote to his traveller, who was then absent from home, to inquire respecting it; it was held, that A. was not guilty of laches, though several days elapsed before he received an answer, and gave notice to the next party, as he used due diligence in ascertaining his address. *Baldwin v. Richardson,* 1 Barn. & Cressw. 245.

A notice of protest need not state who was the holder of the bill. *Shreive v. Duckham,* 1 Litt. 194.

The holder of a bill of exchange is also excused for not giving notice 1st. When in the usual time, by the day on which he should regularly have given *notice* of notice, being a public festival, on which he is strictly forbidden by his non-accept-religion to attend to any secular affairs.[p] But the loss or destruction of *cessary; &* an accepted bill affords no excuse for the delay in giving notice of non-*what excu-*payment.[q] Nor would the bankruptcy of a drawer or indorser of a bill, *ses omis-*or indorser of a note, excuse the neglect to give notice of the default *sion.* of the drawee, to the bankrupt or his assignee.[r]

It has already been observed,[s] that if the drawee offer a conditional or partial acceptance, the holder must, provided he means to resort to the drawer and indorsers, give notice of such acceptance; it is said, however,[t] that where the drawee refuses to accept absolutely, and makes a conditional acceptance, the terms of which are complied with, no notice of the manner in which the bill has been accepted is necessary ; and that where the drawee undertakes by his acceptance to pay only part of the bill, the parties to the bill are bound to the extent of his acceptance, and an omission to give notice of such partial acceptance, does not discharge them from the obligation to that amount.

The conduct which the holder must adopt on the *dishonour* of a 2dly. [The *foreign* bill, differs materially from that which he must pursue in the *protest* and case of an *inland* bill. Whenever notice of non-acceptance of a *fo-* *form* of no-*reigh bill* is necessary, a *protest*[u] must also be made, which, though *acceptance* mere matter of form, is, by the custom of merchants, indispensibly necessary, and cannot be supplied by witnesses or oath of the party, or in any other way,[x] and as it is said, is part of the constitution of a foreign bill of exchange ; and the mere production of this protest attested by a notary public, without proof of the signature or affixing of the seal

[p] Lindo v. Unsworth, 2 Campb. 602. Notice of the dishonour of a bill was sent to the plaintiff in London, the 6th of October, but he being a Jew, and the 8th of October being the day of the greatest Jewish festival throughout the year, on which all Jews are prohibited from attending to any secular affairs, gave no notice by the post of that day to the defendant who lived at Lancaster, but sent it to him by the post of the 9th. Lord Ellenborough held, that the plaintiff was excused from giving notice on the 8th on the ground of his religion, and the notice sent off on the 9th was sufficient. The plaintiff had a verdict.

[q] Poth. pl. 125. Thackray v. Blackett, 3 Campb. 164. Manning's Ind. 69, ante, 157.

[r] Cooke's Bank. Law, 168. Cullen's Band. Law, 100. Montague's Bank. Law, 143, note (x.) sec. Ex parte Smith, 3 Bro. C. C. 1, contra.

[s] Ante, 182.

[t] Bayl. 115, 26.

[u] See the form post, of a protest for non-payment, which, with the alteration of the words in italics, will suffice in the case of a foreign bill.

[x] Rogers v. Stephens, 2 T. R. 713. Gale v Walsh, 5 T. R. 239. Orr v. Magennis,

7 East, 459. 360. Brough v. Perkins, Ld. Raym. 993. 6 Mod. 80. 1 Salk. 131. 8. C. Bul. Ni. Pri. 271. Bayl. 117, 18.

Rogers v. Stephens, 2 T. R. 713. In an action against the drawer of a foreign bill of exchange, it appeared that the bill had been noted for non-acceptance, but there was no protest, and this was pressed as a ground for nonsuit. Lord Kenyon admitted the objection, but upon the other circumstances thought this a case in which a protest was not necessary.

Gale v. Walsh, 5 T. R. 239. In an action against the drawer of a foreign bill it was reserved as a point, whether it was necessary to prove a protest, and the court thought it so clear, upon motion to enter a nonsuit, that they suggested to the plaintiff's counsel the expediency of making the rule absolute in the first instance, and upon their acquiescence, it was accordingly done; they afterwards, however, wished to have it opened, upon an idea that the drawer had no effects in the hands of the drawee; but it appearing upon the report that the idea was not well founded, the rule stood. And in Brough v. Perkins, Ld. Raym. 993. 6 Mod. 80. Salk. 131, Holt, C. J. says, a protest on a foreign bill is a part of the custom.

2dly. Of (though not so if payable here[y]) will, in the case of a bill payable and
the *protest* protested out of this country, be evidence of the dishonour of the bill,[z]
and *mode* and to it all foreign courts give credit;[a] and it cannot be supplied by
of giving mere proof of noting for non-acceptance, and a subsequent protest for
notice non payment. But proof that the drawer had no effects in the hands
non-accept-of the drawee at the time of drawing the bill, or at any time afterwards,
ance. will in this country excuse the want of a protest, and prevent the drawer being discharged.[b] So a subsequent promise by the drawer to pay
the bill may preclude him from availing himself of the want of a protest.[c] But it is not advisable to omit protesting a foreign bill, because
in foreign courts they would probably not be governed by the exception
introduced by our courts.[d]

If therefore the drawee refuse to accept, the holder or some other
person, if he be ill or absent,[e] should cause it to be protested; for
which purpose he should carry the bill to a *notary*,[f] who is to present
it again to the drawee, and demand acceptance; which should, in case
the bill was drawn on or accepted payable at a banker's, be, during
the usual hours of business, and in London not later than five o'clock;[g]
and if the drawee again refuse to accept, the notary is thereupon to
make a minute on the bill itself, consisting of his initials, the month,
the day and year, and the reason, if assigned, for non-acceptance, together with his charge. The next step which the notary is to adopt is
to draw up the protest,[h] which is a formal declaration on the bill
itself, if it can be obtained, or otherwise on a copy,[i] that it has been
presented for acceptance, which was refused, and why, and that the
holder intends to recover all damages, expenses, &c. which he, or his
principal, or any other party to the bill, may sustain on account of non-
acceptance.[k] The minute above-mentioned is usually termed noting
the bill, but this, it has been said, is unknown in the law, as dis-
tinguished from the protest, and is merely a preliminary step to the
protest, and though it has grown into practice within these few years,
[217] it will not in any case supply the want of a protest;[l] the demand is the
material thing, and must, it is said, in the case of a foreign bill, be
made by a notary public himself, to whom credit is given because he is
a public officer, and it cannot be made by his clerk.[m] This doctrine
was sanctioned in a late case, in which the court observed, that the
rule requiring the attestation of a notary public ought to be strictly
observed.[n] In case, however, there be not any public notary at the
place where the bill is dishonoured, it may be protested by any substantial person of that place in the presence of two or more witnesses,[o]

[y] Chesmer v. Noyes, 4 Campb. 129.
[z] Anon. 12 Mod. 345. Dupays v. Shepherd, Holt, 297. Chesmer v Noyes, 4
Campb. 129. 2 Roll. Rep. 846. 10 Mod.
66. Peake's Law of Evid. 4th edit. 80.
74, in notes.
[a] Molloy, 281. Da Costa v. Cole, Skin.
272, pl. 1.
[b] Orr v. Magennis, 7 East, 359. Legge
v. Thorpe, 2 Campb. 310. 12 East, 171.
As to this point, see ante, 196 to 209.
[c] Gibbon v. Coggon, 2 Campb. 188.
[d] Per Lord Ellenborough, Legge v.
Thorpe, 12 East, 177, 8.
[e] Molloy, b. 2. c. 10. s. 17.
[f] See the nature of his office explained in Burn's Ecc. L. tit. Notary Public;

and see regulations in 41 Geo. 3. c.
79.
[g] Parker v. Gordon, 7 East, 315. Ante,
163.
[h] Per Holt, C. J. in Buller v. Crips,
6 Mod. 29. Selw. Ni. Pri. 307, and note 33.
[i] Dehers v. Harriot, 1 Show. 164.
[k] Poth. pl. 84. Mall. 264. Mar. 16.
[l] Per Buller, J. in Leftley v. Mills, 4 T.
R. 175. Rogers v. Stephens, 2 T. R. 713.
Gale v. Walsh, 5 T. R. 239. Bul. Ni. Pri.
271. Bayl. 72, n. a; and see Orr v. Magennis, 7 East, 359.
[m] Per Puller, J. in Leftley v. Mills, 4
T. R. 175, *sed quære.*
[n] Ex parte Worsley, 2 Hen. Bla. 275.
[o] Bayl. 148.

and it is said it should be made between sun-rise and sun-set. It should in general be made in the place where acceptance is refused; but when a bill is drawn abroad, directed to the drawee at South-ampton, or any other place, requesting him to pay the bill in London, the protest for non-acceptance may be made either at Southampton or in London.ᵖ(281) The form of the protest should always he conformable to the custom of the country where it is made.ᑫ If a conditional or partial acceptance be offered, the protest should not be general, as otherwise it will release the acceptor from the effects of such accept-ance.ʳ A copy of the bill should; it is said, be prefixed to all protests, with the indorsements transcribed verbatim, and with an account of the reason given by the party why he does not honour the bill.ˢ Protests made in this country, must, in order to their being received in evidence, be written on paper stamped with a proportionate stamp.ᵗ

2dly. Of the *protest* and *mode* of giving notice of non-accept-ance.

It has been said, that the making the protest alone is not sufficient, and that a copy of it, or some other memorial, must, within a reason-able time, be sent with a letter of advice to the persons on whom the holder means to call for payment;ᵘ but it has been recently decided, that it is not necessary that a copy of the protest should accompany the notice of non-acceptance,ˣ(282) nor is it necessary to send the protested bill,ʸ but a notice of the dishonour of the bill should in all cases be immediately given.ᶻ It has been even held, that the protest for non-acceptance or non-payment of an inland bill may be drawn up at any time before the trial, provided the bill be noted in due time.ᵃ (282)

[218]

ᵖ Mar. 107.

ᑫ Poth. pl. 155.

ʳ Bayl. 89. Bentinck *v.* Dorrien, East, 119. ante, 182, and see Sproat *v.* Matthews, ? T. R. 182.

ˢ Poth. pl. 135.

ᵗ See 55 Geo. 3. 184. which repeals 44 Geo. 3. c. 98. 48 Geo. 3. c. 149.

ᵘ Bayl. 118. Poth. pl. 841. and see Orr *v.* Magennis, 7 East, 359.

ˣ Bayl. 122. Robins *v.* Gibson, 3 Campb. 334. Cromwell *v.* Hynson, 2 Esp. Rep. 511, 12. Pothier Traite du Contrat de Change, part 1. c. 5. s. 150. Chaters *v.* Bell, 4 Esp. Rep. 48. Manning's Ind. 66. *Acc.* Goostrey *v.* Mead, Bull. N. P. 271. Gibl. Ev. 79. Loveless on Bills, 99. Selw N. P. 307. *semb. contra.* Robins *v.* Gibson, 3 Campb. 334. 1 M. & S. 288. S. C. In an action against the drawer of a foreign bill of exchange the plaintiff proved, that a protest was regularly drawn up, and also that the

drawer had arrived in England before the bill became due, and that a letter was sent to his house, stating that the bill was dishonoured, but not communicating the protest or a copy of it, the defendant contended : that the protest should have accompanied the notice. Lord Ellen-borough was of opinion, that, under the circumstances of the case, enough had been done, and the plaintiff had a verdict; and upon motion for a new trial, the court being of opinion, it was sufficient that the bill was protested, and that the defendant had notice of the fact of its dishonour, although the protest was not communicated to him, and refused the rule.

ʸ Mar. 68. 86. 7. 120. Loveless on Bills, 100.

ᶻ Id. ibid. Hart *v.* King, 12. Mod. 309. Anon. 1 Vent. 45. Orr *v.* Magennis, 7 East, 359.

ᵃ Chaters *v.* Bell, 4 Esp. Rep. 48. Bayl. 122, n. 2. Selw. Ni. Pri. 307. S. C.

---

(281) The same doctrine seems established in *Mason* v. *Franklin*, 3 John. Rep. 202. *Boot* v. *Franklin*, 3 John. Rep. 207. And it was there held that a protest for non-ac-ceptance " that the bill not being paid, and the holders not knowing where to present " the same for payment in London, (the place where payable) caused the same to be " protested," was a good and sufficient protest. Ibid.

(282) It seems however to have been held in *Massachusetts*, that a copy of the pro-test should be given or offered to the drawer, or due diligence used to furnish him with such notice before he can be charged. *Blakeley* v. *Grant*, 6 Mass. Rep. 386.

(282) A notary, on protesting a note for non-payment, is not bound to give notice to the indorsers, it is no part of his duty ; and if he specially undertake with the holder to give notice so as to charge all the indorsers, and the holder recover against one, the no-tary is not liable to the indorser who is so charged for laches in neglecting to give notice to a prior indorser. *Morgan* v. *Van Ingen*, 2 John. Rep. 204.

2dly. Of the *protest* and *mode* of *giving notice of* non-accept-ance. At common law, no *inland bill* could be protested for non-accept-ance; but by the statute 3 & 4 Anne, c. 9. s. 4,[b] which will be observed upon more fully hereafter, a protest was given in case of refusal to accept in writing any inland bill amounting to the sum of five pounds, expressed to be given for value received, and payable at days, weeks, or months after date, in the same manner as in the case of foreign bills of exchange. It has been considered that this protest must be made in order to entitle the holder to demand of the drawer or indorsers, costs, damages, and interest;[c] but in practice the plaintiff recovers interest against a drawer or indorser of an inland bill on proof of due notice without proving a protest; and it has recently been decided, that a protest is not essential to the recovery of in-terest.[d] If the bill be of the above description, and under the amount of twenty pounds, the holder is certainly entitled to the above accumulative remedy, though no protest were made.[e] This protest is directed to be made by such persons as are appointed by 9 & 10 Wil-

[219] liam 3, c. 17, to protest inland bills for non-payment,[f] namely, by a notary public, and, in default of him, by any other substantial person of the city, town, or place, in the presence of two or more credible witnesses. Within fourteen days of the making of this protest, the same must be sent, or other notice thereof must be given to, or left in writing at the usual place of abode of the party from whom the bill was received.[g] The *protest* for non-acceptance in the case of an *inland* bill is by no means necessary, and the want of it does not affect the holder's right to the principal sum, as it would in the case of a foreign bill ;[h] and it is in practice seldom made; an inland bill is in general only *noted* for non-acceptance, which noting, as already observed, is of no avail ;[i] and if not paid when due, it is then noted; and sometimes, though not very often, protested for non-payment,[k](283) and a protest for non-acceptance made in the country must be proved by the notary

Goostrey v. Mead, Bul. Ni. Pri. 272. ob-served on in Orr v. Magennis, 7 East, 361. Roger v. Stephens, 2 T. R. R. 714. Bayl. 122. Manning's Ind. 66.
  Chaters v. Bell, 4 Esp. Rep. 48. In an action by an indorsee against the in-dorser of a foreign bill, it appeared that the bill became due on the 24th of April, when payment was demanded and refused, and the bill was noted for non-payment. Regular notice of the dishonour was given to the defendant, but he refused payment be-cause there was no protest. On the 14th May the protest was formally drawn up, and this action was afterwards brought. Lord Kenyon said, " he was of opinion, that if the bill was regularly noted at the time, the protest might be made at a future period." A verdict was found for the plaintiff, but the point was reserved ; and on the coming on to be tried on a *venire de novo*, before Lord Ellenborough, his Lord-ship expressed his concurrence with the opinion of Lord Kenyon.

[b] See the construction on this statute, Kyd, 149. Bayl. 118. 2 Stra. 910, note 1.
[c] Harris v. Benson, 2 Stra. 910. Lumley v. Palmer, Rep. temp. Hardw. 77. Brough v. Parkins, 2 Ld. Raym. 993. 1 Salk. 131. 6 Mod. 80. S. C. Boulager v. Talleyrand, 2 Esp. Rep. 550. Powell v. Monnier, 1 Atk. 613. Bridgman's Ind. 2 vol. 599, pl. 123. 2d edit. tit. *Trade* vi. Bayl. 158, 9 Manning's Ind. 66.
[d] Windle v. Andrews, 2 B. & A. 696.
[e] Stat. 9 & 10 Will. 3. c. 17. s. 6. Bayl 158, 9. Kyd, 149.
[f] Stat. 3 & 4 Anne, c. 9. s. 6.
[g] Id. section 5.
[h] Boroughs v. Perkins, Holt, 121. Har-ris v. Benson, 2 Stra. 910. Boulager v. Talleyrand, 2 Esp. Rep. 550. Brough v. Perkins, 6 Mod 80. 1 Salk. 131. 3 Salk. 69. Ld. Raym, 992, S. C.
[i] Ante, 216.
[k] 4 & 4 Anne, c. 9. s. 5. Kyd, 150.

(283) In case of an inland bill of exchange, no protest for non-acceptance or non-pay-ment is necessary to entitle the holder to a recovery against the parties to the bill. *Mil-ler v. Hackley,* 5 John. Rep. 375. A bill drawn in the United States upon any part of the United States, is in law an inland bill. *Ibid.* But see *ante,* 12. n.

who made it, and it will not, as in case of a protest made abroad, prove itself.[1]

Notice, however, must be given of the non-acceptance, otherwise, for the reasons above stated,[m] the holder in general discharges the drawer and indorsers from all liability. Any act of the holder, signifying the refusal of the drawee, will be a sufficient notice; though we have seen that in the case of a foreign bill there must also be a protest.[a](284) It has indeed been said in the course of argument, that it is not enough to state in the notice, that the drawee refuses to honour, but that it must go farther, and express that the holder does not intend to give credit to the drawee;[o] but it should seem, that as the only reason why notice is required, is, that the drawer or indorsers may have the earliest opportunity of resorting to the parties liable to them, it is not necessary that they should be informed of their liability, because that is a legal consequence of the default of acceptance of which they must necessarily be apprized by mere notice of non-acceptance.[p]

With respect to the *mode of giving the notice* personal service is not necessary, nor is it requisite to leave *a written* notice at the residence of the party; but it is sufficient to send to or convey verbal notice at the counting-house or place of abode of the party without leaving notice in writing.[q](1) And it is sufficient, both in the case of a foreign

---

[1] Chesmer *v.* Noyes, 4 Campb. 129, ante, 215. In an action against the acceptor of a foreign bill of exchange, it became material to prove the presentment of the bill for payment, and for this purpose the plaintiff's counsel produced a notarial protest under seal. Lord Ellenborough said, the protest may be sufficient to prove a presentment which took place in a foreign country: but I am quite clear that the presentment of a foreign bill in England must be proved in the same manner as if it were an inland bill or promissory note.

[m] Ante, 197.
[a] Ante, 216.
[o] In Tindall *v.* Brown, 1 T. R. 169.
[p] Shaw *v.* Croft, *coram* Lord Kenyon, Sittings after Trin. Term, 1798, MSS. and other cases post, and Selw. 4th edit. 320, n. 25.

[q] Crosse *v.* Smith, 1 M. & S. 545. Goldsmith *v.* Bland, Bayl. 127. et post, and when personal service is not necessary; see 4 T. R. 456. 1 Bos. & Pul. 394.
Goldsmith and others *v.* Bland and others, at Guildhall, *coram* Lord Eldon, 1st March, 1800. The plaintiffs sued the defendants as indorsers of two foreign bills, and to prove notice, the plaintiffs showed that they sent a clerk to the defendant's counting-house near the Exchange, between four and five o'clock in the afternoon, nobody was in the counting-house, the clerk saw a servant girl at the house, who said that nobody was in the way, and he returned, having left no message with her. Lord Eldon told the jury, that if they thought the defendants ought to have had somebody in the counting-house at the time, he was of opinion that the plaintiffs

---

(284) The law does not prescribe any form of notice to an indorser; all that is necessary is, that it should be sufficient to put the party upon inquiry, and to prepare him to pay it or to defend himself. If, therefore, there be some uncertainty in the description of the note in the notice, if it does not tend to mislead the party, it will be good. *Reedy* v. *Seixas*, 2 John. Cas. 337. So where a note was payable at a bank, and notice was given on the day when it became due, but in the notice, the note was stated to be due three days before, and the name of the promisor was mistaken, it was held sufficient notice to charge the indorser, it being in evidence that he was liable on no other note payable to the bank. *Smith* v. *Whiting*, 12 Mass. Rep. 6.

It is not necessary that the notice of dishonour of a bill should contain a notification that the holder looks to the party notified, for payment. *Cowles* v. *Harts*, 3 Conn. Rep. 516.

A notice to an indorser was held sufficient, although it did not state at whose request it was given, nor who was the owner of the note. *Shed* v. *Bret*, 401.

(1) Going to the place of business of the maker of a promissory note, during business hours, to demand payment, and finding it shut, no person being left to answer any inquiries, is due diligence. *Shed* v. *Bret*, 1 Pick. 401.

2dly. Of
the *protest*
and *mode*
of giving
notice of
non-accept-
ance.

[221]

and an inland bill, to send notice by the post, even though the letter should miscarry; for it would be very unreasonable to make it incumbent on the holder to send a person with the notice, where perhaps the distance may be very great;[r] and indeed there is considerable risk in sending notice by a private hand, where there is a regular post, for if the notice arrive later by the former than by the latter, the parties may be discharged,[s] but it is reported to have been decided, that the holder of a dishonoured bill is not bound to send notice to the drawer by the mail or first conveyance that sets out from the place where such holder resides, and that it is sufficient, provided there be no essential delay, if he send notice by a private hand, and although such notice should thereby reach the drawer later in the same day than if it had been sent by the mail, he will not, on that account, be discharged.[t] The safer course however is to send by the post.

had done all that was necessary by sending their clerk; that the notice was in law sufficient, if the time was regular, whether the defendants were solvent at the time or not. The jury thought that the defendants ought to have had somebody in the counting-house at the time, and that the plaintiffs had done all that was necessary. Verdict for the plaintiffs for 1633*l.*

Crosse and others, assignees, &c *v.* Smith and others, 1 M. & S. 545. Notice to the drawers of non-payment of a bill of exchange, by sending to their counting-house, during the hours of business, on two successive days, knocking there, and making noise sufficient to be heard by persons within, and waiting there several minutes, the inner door of the counting-house being locked is sufficient, without leaving a notice in writing, or sending by the post, though some of the drawers live at a small distance from the place. Per Lord Ellenborough. The counting-house is a place where all appointments respecting the business and all notices should be addressed, and it is the duty of the merchant to take care that a proper person be in attendance. It has, however, been argued, that notice in writing, left at the counting-house, or put into the post was necessary, but the law does not require it, and with whom was it to be left? Putting a letter into the post is only one mode of giving notice, but where both parties are residing in the same town, sending a clerk is a more regular, and less exceptionable mode.

[r] Saunderson *v.* Judge, 2 Hen. Bla. 509. Kufh *v.* Weston, 3 Esp. Rep. 54. Haynes *v.* Birks, 3 Bos. & Pul. 602. Parker *v.* Gordon, 7 East, 385, 6. Pearson *v.* Cranlan, 2 Smith's Rep. 404. Langdon *v.* Mills, 6 Esp. Rep. 157. Bayl. 128. 226. *acr.* Dale *v.* Lubbock, 4 Barnard, B. R. 199. Poth. Traite du Contrat de Change, part 1. chap. 5. sect. 2. art. 1. 3, 4. *semb. contra.*

Kufh *v.* Weston, 3 Esp. Rep. 54. Notice of the non-acceptance or non-payment of a bill of exchange is sufficiently given by proving that a letter was regularly put

into the post informing the party of the fact. Assumpsit on a foreign bill of exchange drawn by Garde, at Exeter, on Messrs. Guetano and Co. at Genoa: the defendants indorsed the bill to the plaintiffs. The bill was presented for acceptance at Genoa, and the acceptance refused, the defence was, that it had not been presented in a reasonable time, nor the protest for non-acceptance sent to this country as soon as it ought to have been, and that therefore the defendants had not had due notice of its being dishonoured. In answer to this, it was proved, that the bill had been put into the post-office at London, the third day after it was received from the defendants, which was the first Italian post-day after it had been so received. It was further proved, that from the disturbed state of Italy, for some time before, the regular post had been interrupted, and the bill had not arrived at Genoa till a month after it became due, that it was immediately presented for acceptance, which being refused it was protested, and the protest sent off immediately by the post to England. Lord Kenyon said, that the defendants grounded their defence on the supposed laches of the plaintiff, but he was of opinion, that if the plaintiffs had sent the bill by the ordinary course of the post they had done all they were called upon to do; that they could not foresee that the post would be interrupted, and it could not be expected that they should send the bill by a special messenger, or any extraordinary mode of conveyance. His Lordship said, he therefore thought the plaintiffs had been guilty of no laches, and were entitled to recover, and they accordingly had verdict.

Saunderson *v.* Judge, 2 Hen. Bla. 509. The holder of a note wrote to the defendant, who was one of the indorsers, to say it was dishonoured, and put the letter in the post, but there was no evidence that it ever reached the defendant, and the court held, that sending the letter by the post was quite sufficient.

[s] Darbishire *v.* Parker, 6 East, 8, 9.

[t] Bancroft *v.* Hall, Holt, Ca. Ni. Pri.

2dly. Of the *protest* and *mode* of giving *notice* of non-accept-ance.

Notice of the dishonour of a bill sent by the twopenny post is sufficient, where the parties live within its limits, whether near or at a distance from each other, but it must be proved that the letter, conveying the notice, was put into the receiving-house at such an hour, that according to the course of the post, it would be delivered the day on which the party to whom it is addressed, was entitled to receive notice of the dishonour.[w]

Where notice is to be sent from London by the general post, it has been held, that the letter containing it should be put into the post-office in Lombard Street, or at a receiving-house, and that the delivery to a bellman in the street will not be sufficient;[x] and it is obvious, that the notice should in all cases be given by some person who will afterwards be competent to prove it.

Where there is no post, it is sufficient to send notice by the ordinary mode of conveyance, though notice by a special messenger might arrive earlier ; and therefore in the case of a foreign bill it is sufficient to send it by the first regular ship bound for the place to which it is to be sent, and it is no objection, that if sent by a ship bound elsewhere it would probably have arrived sooner, though the holder wrote other letters by that ship to the place to which the notice was to be sent.[y] It has been

---

476. This was an action against the drawer of a bill of exchange, who resided at Liverpool, the bill was accepted by one Hind, payable in London, and indorsed by the defendant to the plaintiff. The bill being dishonoured, notice was given to the plaintiff, who lived at Manchester, on the 24th of May. On that day he sent a letter by a private hand to his agent at Liverpool, directing him to give Hall notice of the acceptor's default. On the 25th in the afternoon the agent received the letter, and went about six or seven in the evening to the counting-house of Hall, but after knocking at the door, and ringing a bell, no one came to receive a message. The merchants counting-houses at Liverpool do not shut up till eight or nine. The 26th was a Sunday, and notice was not in fact given till the morning of the 27th. It was objected for the defendant, that the notice was not in time after the London letter reached Manchester, a mail set out next morning to Liverpool. The plaintiff should have sent the notice by the mail, which reached Liverpool by ten o'clock, if he prefers a private conveyance, or if he attempts to give notice earlier than by law he is bound to do, and fails in giving an effectual notice, he is not therefore exempt from giving proper legal notice.

Bayley, J. Notice must be given in time, but all a man's other business is not to be suspended for the sake of giving the most expeditious notice. He is not bound to write by post as the only conveyance, or to send a letter by the very first channel which offers. He may write to a friend and send by a private conveyance. Here the notice reaches Liverpool on the 25th No expedition could have brought

it earlier. Between six and seven in the evening in that day, the witness goes to the defendant's counting-house, and it is shut up. A merchant's counting-house or residence of trade is not like a banker's shop, which closes universally at a known hour. It was the defendant's fault that he did not receive notice on the 25th, which he might have done if he had kept his counting-house open till eight or nine, which are the customary hours of closing them at Liverpool. Verdict for the plaintiff.

[w] Scott v. Lifford, 1 Campb. 246. 9 East, 347. Smith v. Mullett, 2 Camp. 208. Hilton v. Fairclough, 2 Campb. 633. 2 Phil. on Evid. 19, 35.

[x] Ante, 157. Hawkins v. Rutt, Peake's Rep. 186. *sed quære* if the latter would not be sufficient.

[y] Muilman v. D'Eguino, 2 Hen. Bla. 565. To debt on bond conditioned to pay certain bills drawn on India at sixty days sight, in case they should be returned protested. Defendant pleaded, that he had not notice so soon as he should have had, it appeared that notice was sent by the first English ships, but that by the accidental conveyance of a foreign ship, not bound for England, and by which the holder wrote to England upon other matters, notice might have been sent sooner, and would have arrived sooner, but Eyre, C. J. told the jury, that notice by the first regular ships bound for England was sufficient, and that it was not necessary to send notice by the chance conveyance of a foreign ship. The jury found for the plaintiff, and the court was satisfied with the verdict, and refused a new trial. See also Darbishire v. Parker. 6 East, 7. Bayl. 128.

2dly. .Of the *protest* and *mode* of giving.notice of non-accept-ance.

recently decided, that where it is necessary or more convenient for the holder to send notice by other conveyance than the post, he may send a special messenger, and he may recover the reasonable expenses incurred by that mode of giving notice.* (288)

* Pearson v, Crallan, 2 Smith's Rep. 404. Assumpsit on a bill of exchange for 30l., indorsed by the defendant to the plaintiff. The plaintiff demanded the amount of the bill and 2l. 12s. 9d. costs. The defendant tendered 31l. 11s. 9d. the expense incurred was on account of a messenger employed in giving the notice. The defendant objected that the holder of a bill was not entitled to give notice by a special messenger, but only by the ordinary course of the post. It was agreed, that if a special messenger should be allowed it was not an unreasonable charge. The 31l. 11s. 9d. having been tendered, and that fact pleaded, and this objection being made to the legality of the charge, the defendant's counsel contended that the plaintiff should be nonsuited, but the learned Judge over-ruled the objection, and ex-

pressly left it to the jury to say, whether the sending by a special messenger was done wantonly or not; and it appeared that the letter possibly would not have reached the defendant for a fortnight, as he lived out of the usual course of the post, and upon this the jury found a verdict for the plaintiff for the amount of the bill, and the full charge for the expenses; and Lawrence, J. said, " In some parts of Yorkshire, where the manufacturers .live at a distance from the post towns, the letters may lie for a long time before they are called for, and it may be necessary to send notice by a special messenger," and Lord Ellenborough, C. J. observed, " That it was rightly left to the jury if it was left for them to say whether the special messenger was necessary, and also whether the charge was reasonable." Rule Nisi refused

(288) The holder is bound to use due diligence to give notice of the non-acceptance, as well as non-payment of a bill to the drawer and indorser, whom he intends to charge *Tunno* v. *Lague*, 2 John. Cas. 1. *Berry* v. *Robinson*, 9 John. Rep. 121. *Hussey* v *Freeman*, 10 Mass. Rep. 84. The agent of the holder is not bound to give notice of the dishonour of a bill to the drawer or indorsers, but is only bound to give notice to his principal, and to transmit to him the requisite protests, in order that the holder may give notice to the drawer and indorsers of the dishonour of the bill. *Tunno* v. *Lague*. *Colt* v. *Noble*, 5 Mass. Rep. 167. And if the agent undertakes to give notice, it will be good, if given as early as it could have been received from the holder. *Tunno* v. *Lague*.

Where the parties reside in the same town or city, the notice of non-acceptance or non-payment must be personal, or left at the dwelling-house or place of business of the party to be charged by the notice. *Ireland* v. *Kip*, 10 John. Rep. 490. S. C. 11 John. Rep. 281. And where the parties lived in *New York*, and notice of non-payment of a note was put into the post-office in the city, directed to the indorser, who resided at *Kip's Bay*, (about three miles and a half from the post office, and within the city,) but the letter carriers did not carry letters to that distance, it was held, that the notice was insufficient. Ibid. In case of a temporary removal of the indorser from the place where payment is to be made, notice, at his last place of residence there, will be sufficient. *Stewart* v. *Eden*, 2 Caines' Rep. 121. But see *Blakeley* v. *Grant*, 6 Mass. Rep. 386. If the agent of the holder call at the indorser's house, and finding it shut up, and that he had gone out of town, put a letter into the post-office addressed to him, informing him of the non-payment or non-acceptance, it will be sufficient notice. *Ogden* v. *Cowley*, 2 John. Rep. 274. A bill was drawn and dated at *New York*, on persons residing there. who accepted it; but the drawers in fact resided at *Petersburgh* in *Virginia.* The bill being protested for non-payment, on the same day or the next day, two letters were put into the post-office, giving notice to the drawers, one directed to *New York*, and the other to *Norfolk*, the supposed place of their residence. It was held, that as it did not appear that the holder knew where the drawers lived, he had used due diligence and the notice was good. *Chapman* v. *Lipscombe*, 1 John. Rep. 294.

A citizen of the United States drew a bill in the *East Indies*, payable in *London* which was transmitted by the holder to his agent in *London*, and being there dishonoured, was returned to the holder in the *East Indies*, with the protest; it was held, that notice of the dishonour of the bill sent to the United States, to the drawer by the holder after the receiving the protests in the *East Indies*, was good, and that the holder was not bound to have sent notice through his agent direct from *London* to the United States. although he knew the domicil of the drawer in the United States. *Colt* v. *Noble*, 5 Mass. Rep 167.

If due diligence be used to give notice to the party to be charged, and he cannot be found, this is equivalent to due notice, *Ogden* v. *Cowley*, 2 John. Rep. 274. *Blakeley*

There does not appear to be any express decision with respect to the time when a *foreign* bill must be protested for non-acceptance, but

v *Grant*, 6 Mass. Rep. 386. But a written notice in such case, left at a former dwelling-house of the party, in which neither he nor his family then resided, is no proof to support an allegation of notice *in fact* even though it should elsewhere be received by the wife of the party, unless she was constituted his agent. *Blakeley* v. *Grant*. But see *Stewart* v. *Eden*, 2 Caines' Rep. 121.

The putting of a letter into the post-office, giving notice of the dishonour of a note or bill, is sufficient notice, although no proof is given of its having been actually received. *Munn* v. *Baldwin*, 6 Mass. Rep. 316. *Miller* v. *Hackley*, 5 John. Rep. 375. And it is a general rule, that if the party to be affected by a notice reside in a different city or place from the holder, the notice may be sent through the post-office to the post-office nearest to the party entitled to such notice. *Ireland* v. *Kip*, 11 John. Rep. 231. See also *Freeman* v. *Boynton*, 7 Mass. Rep. 483.

And if an indorser receives notice of the dishonour of a bill or note, he must immediately give notice to all the prior parties whom he intends to charge. *Morgan* v. *Woodworth*, 3 John. Cas. 89.

But if business be suspended in a city during two months, by a contagious disorder, it will excuse the want of notice during that period. *Tunno* v. *Lague*, 2 John. Cas. 1.

The holder of a bill must use reasonable diligence to ascertain the residence of the drawer for the purpose of giving him notice of its dishonour. It is not sufficient to look for the drawer at the place where the bill is dated, if his residence be elsewhere. *Fisher* v. *Evans*, 5 Binney's Rep. 541. *Freeman* v. *Boynton*. But notice left with the family of a sea-faring man during his absence, is sufficient. *Fisher* v. *Evans*. *Blakeley* v. *Grant*, 6 Mass. Rep. 386. *Freeman* v. *Boynton*.

In general, if at the time when a note or bill falls due, the indorser or drawer is absent from the state, and has left no known agent to receive notice, there is no necessity to prove a notice in order to charge him upon non-acceptance or non-payment by the maker or drawee. *Blakeley* v. *Grant*, 6 Mass. Rep. 388. And when at the maturity of a note, the maker was out of the state, and the holder left a written demand of payment at his dwelling-house, not knowing of his absence, and on the same day gave notice to the indorsers, it was held sufficient to bind the latter. *Sanger* v. *Stimpson*, 8 Mass. Rep. 260. And if the maker has absconded before a note becomes due, and this fact is known to the indorser, it has been held that no demand of payment on him is necessary to charge the indorser. *Putnam* v. *Sullivan*, 4 Mass. Rep. 45.

Where the holder and indorser of a foreign bill of exchange both reside in the same city, proof of notice to the indorser *within three days* after advice of the dishonour of the bill is insufficient. *Bryden* v. *Bryden*, 11 John. Rep. 187. So the neglect to notify to an indorser of the default of payment of a note by the maker, for eight days after its dishonour, the parties living at the time within four miles of each other, is such laches as discharges the indorser. *Hussey* v. *Freeman*, 10 Mass. 84.

Where the indorser lives in the same town with the maker notice ought to be given to him upon the same day on which the demand is made upon the maker. *Woodbridge* v. *Brigham*, 12 Mass. Rep. 403. Where the maker of a note appointed a place to notify to him the note's falling due, a notice and demand at such place is sufficient to charge the indorser. *State Bank* v. *Hurd*, 12 Mass. Rep. 172.

A demand of payment should be made on the last day of grace, and notice of the default of the maker be put into the post-office early enough to be sent by the mail of the succeeding day, where the indorser resides in a different place. *Lenox et al.* v. *Roberts*, 2 Wheaton, 377.

Notice to the indorser is in time if put into the post-office on the next day, and if there be two mails a day it is not necessary that it should be put in in time for the first mail. *Whitwell* v. *Johnson*, 17 Mass. 449.

The holder of an inland bill or note is not obliged to send notice of non-payment until the next day after its dishonour. *Hartford Bank* v. *Stedman*, 3 Conn. Rep. 489.

Where the parties to a note or bill reside in different towns notice may be sent by mail. *Hartford Bank* v. *Stedman*, 3 Conn. Rep. 489.

When the third day of grace falls on *Saturday* the notice of non-payment need not be given until the next *Monday*. *Williams* v. *Matthews*, 3 Conn. 252.

Where the indorser lives in another town notice put into the post-office is sufficient, although never received. *Shed* v. *Bret*, 1 Pick. 401. And if the indorser does not live in a post town, sending the notice to the nearest post town is *perhaps* sufficient. Ibid. *Bussard* v. *Levering*, 6 Wheat. 102.

Where notice to the indorser of a promissory note of which a bank is holder, is given according to the usage of the bank, it is sufficient to charge the indorser. *Bank of United States* v. *Norwood*, C. C. U. S. 1 Harr. & Johns. 423.

3dly. The from analogy to the time .when a protest must be made for non-pay-
time when ment, it should seem that in this country, it, or at least the noting,
protest
must be should be made within the usual hours of business,[a] on the day when
made and the acceptance is refused,[b] and that the neglect to make it at the time
notice giv- will only be excused by inevitable accident, such as sudden illness of
en. the holder, robbery, or other circumstances.[c] It has been considered,
that it is sufficient to note a foreign bill for non-acceptance on the day
of refusal, and that the protest may be drawn any day after by the notary, and be dated of the day the noting was made ; but as this point
is not settled, it is advisable to complete the protest for non-acceptance
on the day it is made.[d](1) We have seen, that when the drawee, after

[224] the bill's remaining in his hands twenty-four hours for acceptance,
requests further time to consider of it, the holder should give imme-

---

[a] Mar. 112.

[b] Leftley v. Mills, 4 T. R. 175.

[c] Poth. pl. 144.

[d] Goostrey v. Mead, Bul. Ni. Pri. 271.
Chaters v. Bell, 4 Esp. Rep. 48.   Rogers
v. Stephens, 2 T. R. 714.   Orr v. Magennis, 7 East, 361.   Robins v. Gibson, 1 M.
& S. 288.   Bayl. 122, 3.   Selw. 4th edit.
345, 6.

Chaters v. Bell, 4 Esp. Rep. 48.   In an
action by an indorsee against an indorser
of a foreign bill, it appeared that the bill
became due on the 24th of April, when
payment was demanded and refused, and
the bill noted for non-payment, Regular
notice of the dishonour was given to the defendant, but he refused payment, because
there was no protest. On the 14th of May
the protest was formally drawn up, and
this action was afterwards brought. Lord

Kenyon said, he was of opinion, that if t··
bill was regularly presented, and noted ?·
the time, the protest might be made at any
future period. A verdict was found for
the plaintiff, but the point was reserved,
and on the case coming on to be tried again
on a venire facias de novo before Lord E'
lenborough, his Lordshsp expressed hi
concurrence with the opinion of Lord Kenyon. But in Selw. Ni. Pri. 4th edit. 345.
6., it is stated, that a case was reserved 1·
Chaters v. Bell, for the opinion of the court
and that the court after argument, conceiving the question to be of great importance, directed it to be turned into a
special verdict; but that the sum in dispute
being small, and the parties unwilling to
incur the expense of a special verdict, th·
recommendation of the court was not attended to, and the case was not mentione t ·
again. See also Bayl. 122.

Notice of dishonour sent by mail is sufficient and proper between places where post-
offices are established, but where the indorser lives in the country and not on a post road,
a special messenger ought to be employed or other means used to convey the notice w.··
the same certainty and despatch. Bank of Logan v. Butler, 3 Litt. 493.   Notice sent
by a notary public and by mail to the indorser is sufficient. Crisson v. Williams, 1
Marsh. 456.

Notice of the non-acceptance of a foreign bill must be given to the indorser in due and
convenient time of which the court are to judge. Phillips v. M'Curdy, 1 Harr &
Johns. 187.

The law does not require of the holder of a note or bill that he shall give the earliest
possible notice of its dishonour. It is sufficient if he uses an ordinary and reasonable diligence. Bank of Utica v. Smith, 18 Johns. 230.

Where the makers of a negotiable note resided in New York the holders at Elizabeth-
town, and the indorser in the neighbourhood of Rahway, and the notary who protested the
note in New York transmitted notice of protest by the next mail to the holder at Elizabeth-
town who sent the notice by the next mail to the indorser, it was held that the notice to
the indorser was in time. State Bank v. Ayres, 2 Hals. 130.

A promissory note was made negotiable and payable at the Newbern branch of
State Bank of North Carolina, and fell due on the 11th December, the indorser lived
Newbern near to the bank. Notice of non-payment was not given to him until the 1
of December. Held that he was discharged by this laches. State Bank v. Smith
Munf. 70.

Notice of protest must go by the first mail after the protest. Dodge v. Bank of K
tuckey, 2 Marsh. 615.

(1) After a refusal by the maker of a promissory note to pay, on demand, made o
the day when the note fell due, the note is dishonoured and notice may be immediate
given to the indorser. Shed v. Bret, 1 Pick. 401.

diate notice to the drawer and indorsers of such request, and of the 3dly. The
time granted.[e]   *time* when
protest
must be
Where a foreign bill has been refused acceptance, and the party to made and
whom notice is to be given is resident abroad, it seems that notice of notice giv-
the protest should be communicated to him, and it is advisable to send en.
a copy of such protest ; but where such party is resident in England, it
suffices to give notice to him of the dishonour, without informing him
of the protest, because he may inquire into the fact.[f] But in all cases
notice of the non-acceptance must be sent or given to the parties to
whom the holder means to resort within a reasonable time after the dishonour of the bill ;[g] and the holder must not delay giving notice till
the bill is protested also for non-payment.[h] It has been much disputed, whether it is the province of the court or of the jury, to decide
what is a reasonable time for this purpose ;[i] it should seem that the
better opinion is, that what is a reasonable time for giving notice is a
question partly of fact and partly of law ; the jury are to find the facts,
such as the distance at which the persons live from each other, the
course of the post, &c. but when those facts are established, the reasonableness of the time becomes a question of law, and consequently [225]
to be determined by the court, and not by the jury.[k](290)

[e] Ingram v. Foster, 2 Smith's Rep. 243.
Ante, 164, 5.

[f] Robins v. Gibson, 1 M. & S. 288.—3
Campb. 334. S. C.   Cromwell v. Hynson,
2 Esp. Rep. 511.   Goostrey v. Mead, Bul.
Ni. Pri. 271, 2.   Gilb. Evid. 79—Pothier
Traite du Contrat de Change, part 1 ch. 5.
s. 150.   Manning's Index, 66.
   Robins v. Gibson, 1 M. & S. 288.—3
Campb. 334. S. C.   This was an action by
the plaintiff as indorsee against the defendant as drawer of a foreign bill of exchange. It appeared at the trial that the
defendant drew the bill at Buenos Ayres,
and previously to the time of its becoming
due, returned to this country. When the
bill became due it was dishonoured and
duly protested, and notice of the dishonour, but not of the bill's having been protested, was left at the defendant's house.
Lord Ellenborough held the notice sufficient, and the plaintiff had a verdict ; and
on a motion for a new trial, his Lordship
said, it did not appear that the defendant
requested to have the protest, and it would
be hazarding too much to leave it without
some request. He had due notice of the
fact of the dishonour of the bill; and as the
circumstances of parties alter, the rule respecting notice also changes according to
the convenience of the case If the party
is abroad, he cannot know of the fact of
the bill's having been protested, except by
having notice of the protest itself : but if,
he be at home, it is easy for him, by making inquiry, to ascertain that fact. Rule
refused.

[g] Darbishire v. Parker, 6 East, 3. 14.
16.   Haynes v. Birks, 3 Bos. & Pul. 601,
602.

[h] Goostrey v. Mead, Bul. Ni. Pri. 271.
Roscoe v. Hardy, 12 East, 434.

[i] Tindal v. Brown, 1 T. R. 168. See the
cases, Bayl. 123, n. 3.

[k] Per Ld. Mansfield, C. J. and Buller, J.
in Tindal v. Brown, 1 T. R. 168. Darbishire v. Parker, 6 East, 3. 9. 10. 12.—
Haynes v. Birks, 3 Bos. & Pul. 599.—
Bayl. 123.   Browning v. Kinnear, 1 Gow.
N. P. Rep. 81. acc. Russell. v. Langstaffe,
Dougl. 514. contra.
   Bateman v. Joseph, 12 East, 433.—
2 Campb. 461. In this case it was held,
that the want of due notice of the dishonour of a bill is answered by showing
the holder's ignorance of the place of residence of the prior indorser whom he
sues, and whether he used due diligence
to find out the place of residence is a
question of fact to be left to the jury.
The court all agreed, that this was a
question proper to be left to the jury,
and they had decided it. Whether due
notice has been given of the dishonour of
a bill, all the circumstances necessary
for the giving of such notice being known,
is a question of law ; but whether the
holder have used due diligence to discover the place of residence of the person to whom the notice is to be given, is
a question of fact for the jury. See also
Per Grose, J. in Scott v. Lifford, 9 East,
347.   Sturges v. Derrick, 1 Wightw.
76.

(290) In some early cases in the United States, it seems to have been held that what
was reasonable notice, was a mere question of fact to be left to the jury. Robertson v.
Ogle. 1 Dall. Rep. 252. Steinmetz v. Currie, 1 Dall. Rep. 270. Bank of North

3dly. The time when protest must be made and notice given. It was once thought, that it would be sufficient to charge the drawer, if notice of the dishonour of a bill were given to him even at the end of two months, provided he had not in the interim sustained any particular damage by the delay ;[l] but it is now settled, that in the case of a foreign bill, notice should be given on the day of the refusal to accept, if any post or ordinary conveyance sets out that day ;[m] and if not, by the next earliest ordinary conveyance.[n]

With respect to inland bills not protested for non-acceptance, notice of the refusal to accept should in all cases be given within a reasonable time ; it should be given at least on the following day.[o](2) With reference to the rule which prevails in giving notice of non-payment, it seems, that each party is entitled to a day, to notify the dishonour to his immediate indorser, but that if the notice is to be given by the post, it must be sent off by the next convenient (not the next possible) post, where the parties do not reside in the same place, and when they do, then by the post, so as to be received on the day after that on which the party giving notice was first informed of the dishonour of the bill.[p] When an inland bill is protested for non-acceptance, if the protest or notice thereof be not sent within fourteen days after it is made, the drawer or indorser will not be liable to damages, &c. under the 3 & 4 Anne, c. 9. s. 5.[q]

4thly. By whom notice must be given. [226] We have already seen, that the notoriety of the insolvency of the drawee, as in the case of bankruptcy, constitutes no excuse for the neglect of the holder to give notice of non-acceptance and non-payment to the drawer and indorsers ;[r] and it appears to have been considered that such notice must come from the holder,[s] and that it will not

---

[l] Butler v. Play, 1 Mod. 27. Sarsfield v. Witherley, Comb. 152. Mogadara v. Holt, 1 Show. 318. 12 Mod. 15. S. C.

[m] Leftly v. Millis, 4 T. R. 174. Anon. Lord Raym. 743. Coleman v. Sayer, 2 Stra. 829. Mar. 97.

[n] Muilman v. D'Eguino, 2 Hen. Bla. 565. Williams v. Smith, 2 B. & A. 496.

[o] Leftley v. Mills 4 T. R. 170. See post, as to notice of non-payment, and Haynes v. Birks, 3 Bos. & Pul. 601.— Darbishire v. Parker, 6 East, 3. and post, as to presentment of checks for payment.

[p] Darbishire v. Parker, 6 East, 3.— Smith v. Mullet, 2 Campb. 208.

[q] See this section, post, Appendix.

[r] Ante, 210. Esdaile v. Sowerby. 11 East, 117.

[s] Bayl. 116, 7. Tindal v. Brown, 1 T. R. 170. Ex parte Barclay, 7 Ves. 507, S. Staples v. Okines, 1 Esp. Rep. 333.— Ante, 205. Kyd, 125.
Tindal v. Brown, 1 T. R. 167. 186. Per Ashurst, J. Notice means something more than knowledge, because it is competent to the holder to give credit to the maker. It is not enough to say that the maker of a note does not intend to pay, but that the holder does not intend to give credit to such maker ; the party ought to know whether the holder

---

America v. *M'Knight*, 2 Dall. Rep. 158. *Scott* v. *Alexander*, 1 Wash. Rep. 335 *Reedy* v. *Seixas*, 2 John. Cas. 337. But it may be collected from the more recent cases, that when the facts are ascertained, then whether the notice be reasonable or not, is purely a question of law. *Taylor* v. *Bryden*, 8 John. Rep. 173. *Bryden* v. *Bryden*, 11 John. Rep. 231. *Ireland* v. *Kip*, 11 John. Rep 231. *Hussey* v. *Freeman*, 10 Mass Rep. 84. See *Ferris* v. *Saxton*, 1 Southard's Rep. 1.

What constitutes reasonable diligence in giving notice of protest, is matter of law, to be decided by the court ; but the speed used, and whether the nearest roads are travelled, &c. are facts for the jury. *Dodge* v. *Bank of Kentucky*, 2 Marsh. 616. *White* v. *Bank of Kentucky*, 3 Marsh. 264. The utmost possible despatch is not necessary.

The reasonableness of notice to an indorser of the non-payment of a promissory note, is a question of fact, to be submitted to the jury, no general rule can be laid down by the court on the subject. *Gurly* v. *The Gettysburg Bank*, 7 Serg. & Rawle, 324.

(2) Notice of the protest of a note, negotiated in bank, is good, if given on the day after the protest, although the parties may reside in the same town where the bank is. *Frankford Bank* v. *Markley*, 3 Marsh. 505.

suffice if it come from any other party, because merely that the parties 4thly. *By* may immediately call on those who are liable to them for an indemnity, *whom* no- but it must import that the holder intends to stand on his legal rights be given. and to resort to them for payment ;[t] and therefore, where the drawer having notice before the bill was due that the acceptor had failed, gave another person money to pay the bill, and the holder neglected to give notice of the dishonour, in was holden that the drawer was discharged.[u] And in a subsequent case, it was held, that notice of the dishonour of a bill of exchange must be given to the drawer and indorsers by the holder himself, or some person authorized by him, or at least not by a mere stranger.[x] And where a few days *before a bill became due*, the acceptor informed the drawer he would be unable to pay, and [227] told such drawer that he must take it up and gave him part of the amount to assist him in so doing, and the latter promised to take up the bill accordingly; it was held, that in an action by the indorsee against the drawer, the latter might nevertheless set up as a defence that the bill was not duly presented for payment, and that he had not regular notice of the dishonour, but that the sum paid him by the acceptor was money had and received to the plaintiff's use.[y] (1)

However, according to the more recent decisions, it is not absolutely necessary that the notice should come from the person who holds the bill when it has been dishonoured, and it suffices if it be given after

intends to give credit to the maker, or to resort to him. Per Buller, J. The notice ought to purport that the holder looks to the party for payment, and a notice from another person cannot be sufficient, it must come from the holder.

Ex parte Barclay, 7 Ves. 597. Barclay was indorsee and holder of two bills drawn by Kemp upon Dearlow, and indorsed by Clay to Barclay. These bills were dishonoured, of which Clay gave notice to Kemp, and on petition by Barclay to be allowed to prove these bills, under a commission of bankrupt issued against Kemp ; one question was, whether this notice from Clay and not from Barclay the holder, was sufficient. And Lord Eldon, after referring to Tindal *v.* Brown, held, that the notice ought to have come from the holder, and dismissed the petition. And he said, "The settled doctrine is according to the language of Mr. Justice Buller, in Tindal *v.* Brown, and there is great reason in it, for the ground of discharging the drawee is, that the holder gives credit to some persons liable as between him and the drawee. Notice from any other person that the bill is not paid, is not notice that the holder does not give credit to a third person. The doctrine has been acted upon very often since." In Selw. Ni. Pri. 4th ed. 320, note 25, it is observed, that in this case the attention of

the court was not directed to Lord Kenyon's opinion in Shaw *v.* Croft, post, 227.

[t] Id. ibid.
[u] Nicholson *v.* Gouthit, 2 Hen. Bla. 612. ante, 211. Whitfield *v.* Savage, 2 Bos. & Pul. 277. and see Esdaile *v.* Sowerby, 11 East, 114. 117.

[x] Stewart *v.* Kennett, 2 Campb. 177. The notice of non-payment had been given by Cutler, who had been employed by the original parties to the bill to get it discounted, but it did not appear that he had any authority or direction from any party to the bill to give notice of the dishonour. Per Lord Ellenborough, If you could make Cutler the agent of the holder of the bill, the notice would be sufficient, but in reality he was a mere stranger. The bill when dishonoured lay at the bankers of Abbott, with whom Cutler had no sort of connexion. But the notice must come from the person who can give the drawer or indorser his immediate remedy upon the bill, otherwise it is merely a historical fact. In this case Cutler was not possessed of the bill, and had no control over it. The defendant, therefore, is not proved to have had any legal notice of the dishonour of the bill, and is discharged from the liability he contracted by indorsing it. Plaintiff nonsuited.

[y] Baker *v.* Birch, 3 Campb. 107.

(1) If there has been such a demand on the maker as the latter is bound by, so that he had no right to refuse payment, the indorser cannot object that the legal forms of a demand were not complied with. *Whitwell* v. *Johnson*, 17 Mass. Rep. 449.

4thly, *By* the bill was dishonoured by any person who is a party to the bill, and *whom no-* who would, on the same being returned to him, have a right of action *tice must* thereon, and such notice will in general enure to the benefit of all the *be given.* antecedent parties, and render a further notice from any of those parties unnecessary, because it makes no difference who gives the information, since the object of the notice is, that the parties may have recourse to the acceptor :[a] and therefore it has been held, that if the drawer or

[228] indorser of a bill of exchange receive due notice of its dishonour from any person who is a party to it, he is directly liable upon it to a subsequent indorser, from whom he had no notice of the dishonour.[a] And it has been recently decided in an action by the indorsee against the drawer, that it is sufficient if the drawer had notice of the dishonour from the acceptor.[b] It is, however, advisable for each party, immediately upon receipt of notice, to give a *fresh* notice to such of those parties who are liable over to him, and against whom he must

[a] Bayl. 141. Kyd, 126. Selw. N. P. 4th edit. 320, n. 25. Shaw *v.* Croft.—Jameson *v.* Swinton, 2 Campb. 373. Wilson *v.* Swabey, 1 Stark. 34.

Shaw *v.* Croft, *cor.* Lord Kenyon, Sittings after Trin. Term, 1798, MS. and see Selw. N. P. 4th ed. 320, n. 25. Assumpsit by the holder of a bill against the drawer. Defence no regular notice of dishonour, but it being proved that a message had been left at the drawer's house by the acceptor, stating that the bill had been dishonoured, Lord Kenyon, said, that it made no difference who apprized the drawer, since the object of the notice was, that the drawer might have recourse to the acceptor.

Jameson & others *v.* Swinton, 2 Campb. 373. Action by the second indorsee of a bill of exchange, drawn by the defendant payable to his own order, and indorsed by him to G. Elsom. The bill became due on Saturday, the 8th of July, when it was in the hands of the plaintiff's bankers. On Monday the 10th, they returned it dishonoured to the plaintiffs, who in the evening of that day, gave notice of the dishonour to Elsom their indorser. Elsom, between eight and nine o'clock in the evening of the following day, gave a like notice to the defendant. The plaintiffs and Elsom resided in London, the defendant at Islington. The question was, whether there was sufficient evidence of the dishonour of the bill to maintain the present action? Best, Serjeant, for the defendant, insisted, that the plaintiffs were bound to give notice themselves to the drawer, and all the indorsers, against whom they meant to have any remedy. They could not avail themselves of a notice given by a third person. Per Lawrence, J. "I do not remember to have heard the first point made before, but I am of opinion that the drawer or indorser is liable to all subsequent indorsees, if he had due notice of the dishonour of the bill from any person who is a party to it. Such a notice must serve all the purposes for which

the giving of notice is required. The drawer or indorser is authoritatively informed that the bill is dishonoured; he is enabled to take it up if he pleases, and he may immediately proceed against the acceptor or prior indorser, and it does seem to me that the defendant in this case had due notice of the dishonour of the bill from Elsom. This is allowing only one day to each party, which, when the parties all reside in the same town, seems now to be the established rule" Verdict for the plaintiff.

Wilson *v.* Swabey, 1 Stark. 34. Assumpsit by the indorsee against the drawer of a bill of exchange. The bill became due on Thursday the 2d of March; notice of the dishonour was communicated to Lewis, an indorser, on the Friday, and by him to the defendant on the Saturday. For the defendant it was objected, that the notice had not been given by the party who sued upon the bill, but Lord Ellenborough was of opinion that notice from any person who was a party to the bill was sufficient. Verdict for the plaintiff.

[a] Jameson *v.* Swinton, 2 Campb. 273. Ante, 227.

[b] Rosher & another *v* Kieran, 4 Campb. 87. This was an action by the plaintiffs as indorsees, against the defendant as drawer of a bill of exchange for 1000*l.* dated Dundalk, 28th of February, 1814, payable to the order of the drawer at ninety days after date, and accepted by Thomas Rowcroft, at Smith, Payne, and Smith's, bankers, in London. The question was, whether the defendant had received due notice of the dishonour of the bill. The bill became due on the 30th of May, when it was presented for payment and dishonoured. *On the same day the acceptor wrote a letter to the drawer*, stating that he had not been able to pay it, and that it was then in the hands of the plaintiffs. Lord Ellenborough held this notice from the acceptor sufficient, and the plaintiffs had a verdict; and see Shaw *v* Croft, ante, 226.

prove notice.[c](292 As already observed, the notice should be given by some agent or servant who will be competent to prove it, and not by the holder in person.

4thly. By whom notice must be given.

The notice of non-acceptance, when necessary, must be given *to all the parties* to whom the holder of the bill means to resort for payment, and though proof that the drawer had no effects in the hands of the acceptor will be an excuse for want of notice with respect so him, it will not have that operation with respect to any of the indorsers ; for they have nothing to do with the accounts between the drawer and the drawee ;[d] and an indorser is entitled to notice although the drawer and acceptor were fictitious.[e] If the party entitled to notice be a bank- [229] rupt, notice should be given to him and his assignees ;[f] if the party be dead, notice should be given to his executor or administrator, and notice should in general be given to a person who has guaranteed the payment of the bill.[g] When the party entitled to notice is abroad at the time of the dishonour, if he have a place of residence in England, it will be sufficient to leave notice of non-acceptance at that place, and a demand of acceptance or payment from his wife or servant would in such case be regular.[h](1)

5thly. To whom notice must be given.

It was once thought, that notice of non-acceptance must in all cases be given to the drawer of the bill, and demand of payment made of him, or that in default thereof, the indorsers would be discharged, notwithstanding they had regular notice. This opinion, however, so far as it related to foreign bills, was over-ruled in the case of Bromley v. Frazier ;[i] and in its relation to inland bills, in the case of Heylin and others against Adamson,[k] and as to checks on bankers in Richford v. Ridge,[l] on the principle, that to require a demand of the drawer,

---

[c] Bayl. 142. Kyd, 126.
[d] See Brown v. Maffet, 15 East, 216. Gendall v. Doliey, 1 T. R. 712. Wilkes v. Jacks, Peake's Rep. 202. Walwyn v. St. Quintin, 1 Bos. & Pul. 216. Ante, 20¹, 2.
[e] Ante, 200.
[f] Ante, 215.
[g] Ante, 224. Bayl. 138, 9. When notice need not be given of a substituted bill, see 3 M. & S. 362. 7 Taunt. 312.

[h] Cromwell v. Hynson, 2 Esp. Rep. 511, 512. Walwyn v. St. Quintin, 1 Bos. & Pul. 652; but see 5 Esp. Rep. 175.
[i] Bromley v. Frazier, 1 Stra. 441.—Selw. N. P. 4th ed. 324.
[k] Heylin v. Adamson, 2 Burr. 669.— Pardo v. Fuller, Com. Rep. 579. Bromley v. Frazier, 1 Stra. 441. Selw. N. P. 4th ed. 324.
[l] 2 Campb. 539, per Lord Ellenborough. The holder of a check is not bound to

---

(295) If an indorser receive notice of the dishonour of a bill or note, he must immediately take it up and give notice to all the antecedent parties, whom he means to charge, otherwise they will not be holden. *Morgan* v. *Woodworth*, 3 John. Cas. 89.

A bill was drawn by the defendant, at New Orleans, on Philadelphia, in favour of the plaintiff, and was by him indorsed, in full, to a third person, and regularly protested for non-acceptance, and non-payment ; but no notice of the dishonour of the bill was proved to have been given to the drawer. The indorsement being in full, cannot be stricken out at the time of trial ; the want of notice destroys the plaintiff's right to recover from the defendant. *Craig* v *Brown*, 1 Peters' Rep. 171.

In an action against the first indorser of a note by a subsequent indorser, it is sufficient if it appear that notice of non-payment was given to the defendant by the holder, and the right of action of the plaintiff is not affected by a delay for more than a year to take up the note and bring his action against the defendant. *Stafford* v. *Yates*, 18 John. 328.

(1) Where previous to a note falling due, the indorser had died at sea, but the fact was not known to the holder, and no administration was granted for several months after the note fell due, it was held, that notice left at the last place of residence of the indorser in *New York*, and another sent to the residence of his family in the country, through the post-office, was sufficient, although no notice had been given to the defendants, the executors of the indorser. *Merchant's Bank* v. *Birch*, 17 Johns. 25.

5thly. To whom notice must be given. would be laying such a clog upon bills, as would deter every person from taking them, since the drawer may perhaps live abroad ; besides, the acceptor is primarily liable, and as the act of indorsing a bill is equivalent to making a new bill, the indorser thereby undertakes as well as the drawer, that the drawee shall honour the bill, and the holder may consequently immediately resort to him, without calling on any of the other parties.

With respect to inland bills protested for non-acceptance, the 3 & 4 Anne, c. 9, directs the protest or notice thereof to be given to the person from whom the bill was received. The preceding observation relative to notice from the holder enuring to the benefit of the antecedent parties here applies. Notice to one of the several [230] partners, joint indorsers, is notice to all,(1) and if one of several drawers be also the acceptor, and there be no fraud in the transaction, no notice in fact is necessary to the other drawers ; and a mere guarantee, whose name is not on the bill or note, is not entitled to notice. Nor is it necessary to give notice to a party who has by his conduct dispensed with it, as by engaging to call on the holder, and ascertain whether the acceptor has paid the bill ; and where a bill has been accepted

give notice of its dishonour to the drawer for the purpose of charging the person from whom he received it. He does enough if he presents it with due diligence to the banker on whom it is drawn, and gives due notice of its dishonour to those only against whom he seeks his remedy.

Et vide Heylin v. Adamson, Burr.

a Ante, 227.
o Porthouse v. Parker and others, 1 Campb. 82. Alderson v. Pope, Id. 404; and see Jacand v. French, 12 East, 317, 322, 3. and per Lord Ellenborough, in Bignold v. Waterhouse, 1 M. & S. 259. Bayl. 142.

Porthouse v. Parker and others, 1 Campb. 82. This was an action against the drawees of a bill of exchange for 461l. 8s. at the suit of the payee. The bill purported to be drawn by one Wood, as the agent of George, James, and John Parker. There was no proof that Wood had authority from the defendants to draw the bill, but a witness swore that he, as the agent of John Parker, the drawee, and one of the defendants, had accepted it on his account. Lord Ellenborough held, that the bill having been accepted by order of one of the defendants, this was sufficient evidence of its having been regularly drawn; and further, that the acceptor being likewise a drawer, there would be no occasion for the plaintiff to prove that the defendants had received express notice of the dishonour of the bill, as this must necessarily have been known to one

of them, and the knowledge of the one was the knowledge of all. Verdict for the plaintiff.

In Bignold v. Waterhouse, 1 M. & S. 259. Lord Ellenborough said, " It is a general rule indeed, that where several are concerned together in partnership, notice to one is equivalent to notice to all, but that rule presumes that the transaction is *bona fide.* Here, however, the case is different, the agreement is made with one of the defendants for his individual benefit alone, and the others are not parties concerned, not being made privy to the agreement. It was incumbent, therefore, on the plaintiffs to show, that notice was given to the other partners."

p Ante, 204; and Swingard v. Bowes, 5 M. & S. 62.

q Phipson v. Kneller, 4 Campb. 285. This was an action against the drawer of a bill of exchange, and the question was, whether the plaintiff was excused for not having given him notice of the dishonour of the bill. It was proved that a few days before the bill became due, the defendant called at the counting-house of the plaintiff, whom he knew to be the holder; and being asked the place of his residence, he said he had no regular residence; he was living among his friends and he would call and see if the bill was paid by the acceptor. Per Lord Ellenborough, this dispensed with notice, and threw upon the defendant himself the duty of inquiring if the bill was paid. Verdict for the plaintiff.

---

(1) If reasonable notice of dishonour is given to one of several joint indorsers, all are bound by it. *Dodge* v. *Bank of Kentucky*, 2 Marsh. 616.

payable at a particular place, it is no defence in an action against
the drawer, that notice of the non-payment was not given to the
acceptor.[r]

5thly, To whom notice must be given.

The liablity of the various parties to a bill, on the dishonour of it
by the drawee, may be collected from the previous pages. If the
drawee on presentment for acceptance, dishonour the bill, either wholly
or partially, the holder may insist on immediate payment by the parties
liable to him, as well from the drawer,[s] as from the prior indorsers,[t] or
in default thereof, may, *instantly* commence actions against each of them;
and though the instrument may be somewhat like a note, yet if it also
resemble a bill, and acceptance be refused, an action is immediately
sustainable.[u](298)   On the same principle it was decided, that if a man
draw a bill, and commit an act of bankruptcy, and afterwards the bill
be returned for non-acceptance, the debt is contracted before the act of
bankruptcy, and may be proved under the commission, which could not
have been the case, if the time when notice of non-acceptance was
given had been considered as the period when the debt was contracted.[x]
So where the defendant, having been arrested, gave the plaintiff a draft
for part of the money due, on which he was discharged out of custody,
but the draft having been dishonoured, he was retaken upon the same
writ, it was decided that the proceedings were regular and justifiable;
and Lord Kenyon said, that in cases of this kind, if the bill which is
given in payment do not turn out to be productive, it is not that which
it purported to be, and that which the party receiving it expected, and
therefore he may consider it as a nullity, and act as if no such bill had
been given :[y] and in a recent case where a bill given in payment for
goods sold was refused acceptance, it was held that the payee having
declared against the drawer on the bill, and joined counts for goods sold,
may treat the bill as a nullity, and recover his demand on the latter
counts, although the credit on the bill be not expired, and that it is
sufficient in such an action to prove a presentment to the drawee for
acceptance, without showing that the bill was protested for non-accept-

6thly. Of the liability of the parties to a bill on non-acceptance   [231]

---

[r] Edwards v. Dick, 4 B. & A. 212.

[s] Ante, 107. Bayl. 149, 150. Bright v. Purrier, Bul. N. P. 269, ante, 107. Milford v. Mayor, Dougl. 56, ante, 107. But Pothier considers the drawer as merely liable to indemnify the holder against the probable non-payment at maturity. Traite du Contrat de Change, part 1. ch. 4, num. 70.

[t] Ballingalls v. Gloster, 3 East, 481. 4 Esp. Rep. 468. S. C. Bishop v. Young, 2 Bos. & Pul. 83, n. a.

Ballingalls v. Gloster, 3 East, 481. John Gloster drew a bill on Jackson, payable to Anthony Gloster's order, and the latter indorsed it to the plaintiffs. Jackson refused acceptance, on which the plaintiffs immediately sued Anthony Gloster, without waiting till the bill, which was drawn at ninety days sight, would have been due.

The plaintiffs had a verdict, with liberty to the defendant to move for a nonsuit. On a rule *nisi* accordingly, it was urged, that an indorser stood in a situation different from that of a drawer, and that although a drawer might be sued immediately on non-acceptance, an indorser could not, until the expiration of the time limited for the payment of the bill. But the court was clear that the case of an indorser was not distinguishable from that of a drawer, and that every indorser was a new drawer. Rule discharged.

[u] Allen v. Mawras, 4 Campb. 115, ante, 21.

[x] Macarty v. Barrow, 2 Stra. 949. 7 East, 437. S. C. Chilton v. Whiffin, 7 Wils. 16.

[y] Puckford v. Maxwell, 6 T. R. 52, ante, 99.

---

(298) The same doctrine has been repeatedly recognised in the United States. *Mason* v. *Franklin*, 3 John. Rep. 202. *Miller* v. *Hackley*, 5 John. Rep. 375. *Sterry* v. *Robinson*, 1 Day's Rep. 11. *Watson* v. *Loring*, 3 Mass. Rep. 557. *Winthrop* v. *Pipoon*, 1 Bay Rep. 468. *Lenox* v. *Cook*, 8 Mass. Rep. 460. *Welden* v. *Buck*, 4 John. Rep. 144.

6thly. Of **ance, or that the drawer had notice of the dishonour.**[a] And if a buyer
the *liabil-* pays for goods by a bill which the drawee refuses to accept, and after-
ity of the wards desires it may be again presented, and it will be honoured, the
parties to a holder is not bound again to present it, nor to return the bill.[a]
bill on non-
acceptance

It seems, however, that the drawer and indorser have a reasonable
time allowed them to pay the bill, after notice of the dishonour, and that
the circumstance of their not paying the amount immediately when they
received such notice, will not preclude them from pleading a tender,
provided they offer to pay the amount on the same day, and before a
writ has been issued, though the acceptor must pay the bill on presentment, and cannot plead a subsequent tender.[b]

When due notice of the non-acceptance has been given to the
drawers and indorsers, it is not necessary afterwards to present the bill
for payment, or if such presentment be made, to give notice of the
dishonour.[c]

With respect to the amount of the sum which the drawer and
indorsers are bound to pay, they are liable, where a bill has been protested, not only to the payment of the principal sum, but to damages,
interest, &c.[d] Where A. deposited a sum of money at the banking-
house of B. in Paris, for which B. gave him his note "payable
in Paris;" "or at the choice of the bearer, at the Union Bank, in
"Dover, or at B's. usual residence in London, according to the course
"of exchange upon Paris;" and after this note was given, the direct
[233] course of exchange between London and Paris ceased altogether,
having been previously to its total cessation, extremely low; the note
was at a subsequent period presented for acceptance and payment at
the residence of B. in London, at which time there was a circuitous
course of exchange upon Paris by way of Hamburgh, and it was
holden, that A. was entitled to recover upon the note according to
such circuitous course of exchange upon Paris, at the time when the
note was presented.[e] Where, however, acceptance or payment have
been rendered illegal by an act of this country, the drawer, &c. may
not be liable to be sued on the bill ;[f] and we have already seen, that
if a person draw a bill in a foreign country upon another in England,

[a] Hickling v. Hardey, 1 Moore Rep. 61.
3 Taunt. 312 S. C.
[a] Hickling v. Hardy, 7 Taunt. 312.
[b] Walker v. Barnes, 1 Marsh. 36.
5 Taunt. 246, S. C. Hume v. Peploe,
8 East, 168.
Walker v. Barnes, 1 Marsh. 36. The
drawer of a bill is only bound to pay
within reasonable time after receiving notice of its being dishonoured, therefore
where he received notice the day after the
bill became due, a tender on the following
day was held to be in time. Per Mansfield,
C. J. This is an action by the indorsee of
a bill of exchange against the drawer,
whose undertaking is to pay the holder on
failure by the acceptor. When the bill is
dishonoured the drawer cannot find out by
inspection who is the holder, and therefore
cannot pay it till he has notice of the dishonour. When he has received notice, he
is bound to pay within reasonable time,
and if he do not, he will be answerable for
damages. The bill became due on the 11th,
on the 12th he received a note from the
plaintiff's attorney, informing him of the
dishonour, and on the 13th he tenders. Is
not this a reasonable compliance with his
undertaking? No jury could give even a
farthing damages. Rule discharged.

[c] Price v. Dardell, Sittings at Guildhall,
London, 11th December, 1794, cor. Lord
Kenyon, his Lordship said, It is in no case
necessary to give notice when it is a second
dishonour; and in De La Torre v. Barclay,
and another, 1 Stark. Ni. Pri. 7, Lord Ellenborough said, that as the bill had been
protested for non-acceptance, a second
protest was perfectly gratuitous and unnecessary. See also Forster v. Jardine,
16 East, 105.

[d] 8 & 9 Wm. 3. c. 17. and 3 & 4 Anne,
c. 9. et post, of the verdict and damages.
[e] Pollard v. Herries, 3 Bos. & Pul. 335.
[f] Pollard v. Herries, ibid. 340.

and it be protested for non-acceptance, the drawer will be discharged from liability to be sued in this country, by his having obtained a certificate of discharge, according to the law of the country where he drew the bill.[g] In De Tastet v. Baring,[h] a verdict having passed for the defendants, in an action to recover the amount of the re-exchange upon the dishonour of a bill drawn in London on Lisbon, upon evidence that the enemy were in possession of Portugal when the bill became due, and Lisbon was then blockaded by a British squadron, and there was in fact no direct exchange between London and Lisbon, though bills had in some few instances been negotiated between them through Hamburgh and America about that period, the court refused to grant a new trial, on the presumption that the jury had found their verdict on the fact that no re-exchange was proved to their satisfaction to have existed between Lisbon and London at the time; the question having been properly left to them to allow damages in the name of re-exchange, if the plaintiff, who had indorsed the dishonoured bill to the holder, had either paid or was liable to pay re-exchange, and saving the question of law, whether any re-exchange could be allowed between this and an enemy's country.

6thly. Of the liability of the parties to a bill on non-acceptance

If the holder of a bill neglect to present it for acceptance when necessary, or to give notice of non-acceptance to those persons entitled to object to the want of it, such conduct, we have seen, discharges them from their respective liabilities.[i]

The consequences however, of a neglect to give notice of non-acceptance, or to protest a foreign bill, may be waived by the person entitled to take advantage of them. Thus it has been decided, that a payment even of part,[k] or a promise to pay,[l] or to "see it

7thly. How the consequences of a neglect to give notice may be waived, or otherwise done away.

g Ante, 92, 3. Potter v. Brown, 5 East, 124.
h 11 East, 265.
i Ante. 196.
k Bayl. 130, 1. 220, 1. Vaughan v. Fuller, 2 Stra. 1246, was an action against the indorser of a note, and it being proved that the defendant had paid part, Lee, C. J. held that that made the proof of demand upon the maker unnecessary.
Horford v. Wilson, 2 Taunt. 12. In an action by the indorsee against the drawer of a bill, which had been dishonoured by the acceptor, it appeared that the defendant had paid part of the money due upon the bill without making objection for want of notice of the dishonour, and the court held upon a motion for a new trial, that from this the jury were warranted in presuming that due notice had been given.
l Bayl. 130, 1. 220, 1. Selw. Ni. Pri. 4th edit. 823. Haddock v. Bury, Mich. Term, 3 Geo. 2. MS. Burnet, J. 7 East, 236, n. a. Per Ld. Raym. C. J. "if an indorsee has neglected to demand of the maker of the note in due time, a subsequent promise to pay by the indorser will cure this laches."
Whitaker v. Morris, Worcester, Lent Ass. 1756. MS. 1 Esp. Rep. 58. Select Ca. 171, S. C. The plaintiff received a note of Yardley, payable to the defend-

ant. When it was due the plaintiff sent the note to demand the money, but not finding Yardley, he kept the note for seventeen or eighteen days, during which time it was proved that he used due diligence to find him; he then wrote to his agent to inform the defendant, who returned no answer. About ten days after the agent went to the defendant, who acknowledged the receipt of the letter, and said, the reason why he had not sent an answer was, that Yardley had promised to order payment in London, and as it was not paid "that he would certainly pay it the day after." The defendant's witnesses proved that Yardley was solvent when the note became due, and for some time after, but then was insolvent. Per Wilmot, J. Holding the note for so long a time was unreasonable, and would have discharged the defendant, if, when he received the first notice, he had disclaimed the having any thing to do with it, but by his conduct, he had waived the neglect and acquitted the plaintiff, however, he left it to the jury, who found for the defendant.
Lundie v. Robertson, 7 East, 231. 3 Smith Rep. 225. S. C. Indorsee against an indorser of a bill, no evidence was given of presentment or notice, but it was proved, that upon being called upon by the plaintiff's clerk some months after the bill was due, the defendant said "he had

7thly. How
the conse-
quences of
a neglect to
give notice
may be
waived, or
otherwise
done away.

paid,"ᵐ or an acknowledgment that "it must be paid,"ⁿ or a promise that "he will set the matter to rights;"° made by the person insisting on the want of notice, after he was aware of the laches, amounts to a waiver of the consequence of the laches of the holder, and admits his right of action. So where an indorsee three months after a bill became due, demanded payment of the indorser, who first promised to pay it if he would call again with the account, and afterwards said that he had not had regular notice, but as the debt was justy due he would pay it, it was held that the first conversation being an absolute promise to pay the bill, was *prima facie* an admission that the bill had been presented to the acceptor for payment in due time, and had been dishonoured,

not the cash by him, but if the clerk would call in a day or two and bring the account, (meaning of the expenses) he would pay it." The bill was shown to him at the time ; on a second application he offered a bill on London for the debt and expenses, which was refused ; he then said, that "he had not regular notice, but as the bill was justly due he would pay it." Chambre, J. thought this sufficient, and verdict for the plaintiff. On a rule *nisi* for a new trial, and cause shown, Lord Ellenborough said, the case admits of no doubt ; it was to be presumed *prima facie* from the promise to pay, that the bill had been presented in time, and that due notice had been given, that no objection could be made to payment, and that every thing had been rightly done ; this superseded the necessity of the ordinary proof, the other conversation does not vary the case, for though the defendant said, he had not had notice, he waived that objection. See Gibbon *v.* Coggon, 2 Campb. 188, where, from the drawers promising to pay a bill, Lord Ellenborough directed the jury to presume that it had been duly protested. See also Taylor *v.* Jones, 2 Campb. 105.

Wood *v.* Brown, 1 Stark. 117. Proof of a letter from the drawer and indorser of an accommodation bill, that the bill will be satisfied before the next term, supercedes the necessity of proving the dishonour of the bill and notice.

ᵐ Hopes *v.* Alder, 6 East, 16. Action against drawer to whom no notice of non-payment had been given. It was proved that upon a meeting some time after, but before the action brought between the plaintiff and defendant, the latter said, "I will see it paid." It was urged for the plaintiff, that this subsequent promise for which there was certainly an equitable consideration, subjected the defendant to liability. This was admitted by the defendant's counsel, and Lord Kenyon, C. J. said, "This subsequent promise was decisive."

ⁿ Rogers *v.* Stephens, 2 T. R. 713. In an action against the drawer of a foreign bill, an objection was taken that there was no protest, but appearing that the defendant had no effects in the hands of the

drawees when the bills were drawn, or afterwards, and that on being pressed for payment by the plaintiff's agent after the bill was dishonoured, he had said, "*it must be paid.*" Lord Kenyon thought a protest or notice unnecessary, and directed the jury to find for the plaintiff, which they did. A rule was afterwards granted to show cause why there should not be a new trial, and it was stated then, and upon showing cause, that the defendant had really been prejudiced by want of notice to the amount of the bill, that he had advanced money to one Calvert to the amount before the bill was drawn; that Calvert desired him to draw on the drawees as Calvert's agents; that he did so on a a supposition that Calvert had effects in their hands; that he afterwards settled with Calvert, and upon a reliance that the bill was paid, delivered him up effects to more than the value of the bill, and that Calvert was since insolvent; that the defendant was prepared with evidence to this effect, but that Lord Kenyon delivered it as his opinion, that it did not make a protest or notice necessary. Lord Kenyon did not recollect that this evidence was offered, but he and all the court thought it answered by the defendant's admission, that "the bill must be paid," because that was an admission that the plaintiff had a right to resort to him upon the bill, and that he had received no damage by the want of notice, and was a promise to pay.

° Anson *v.* Bailey, Bul. N. P. 286. The indorsee of a note presented it for payment, but the maker pretended that the payee had promised not to indorse it over without acquainting him, and so put off the indorsee from time to time for three weeks ; at the end of that period the indorsee wrote twice to the payee, stating what he had done, and the maker's excuse ; the payee answered, that "when he came to town he would set the matter right ;" and upon an action by the indorser against the payee, the jury found for the plaintiff, though the maker became bankrupt before the second letter was written, and though he continued solvent for three weeks after the note was due. See also Wilkes *v.* Jacks, Peake, 202.

and that due notice had been given of it to the indorser, and super-seded the necessity of other proof to satisfy those averments in the declaration, and that the second conversation only limited the inference from the former, so far as the want of regular notice of the dishonour to the defendant went, which objection he waived.[p] So where the drawer of a foreign bill, upon being applied to for payment, said, "my affairs are at this moment deranged, but I shall be glad to pay it as soon as my accounts with my agent are cleared," it was decided that it was unnecessary to prove the protest of the bill.[q](304)

7thly. How the consequences of a neglect to give notice may be waived, or otherwise done away.

It seems to have been once considered, that a misapprehension of the *legal* liability would prevent a subsequent promise to pay from being obligatory;[r] but from the case of Bilbie *v.* Lumley and others,[s] it appears that money paid by one knowing (or having the means of such knowledge in his power) all the circumstances cannot, unless there has been deceit or fraud on the part of the holder, be recovered back again on account of such payment having been made under an ignorance of the law, although the party paying expressly declared that he paid without prejudice;[t] and as an objection made by a drawer or indorser to pay the bill, on the ground of the want of notice, is *stricti juris,*

---

[p] Landie *v.* Robertson, 7 East, 231.—Gibbon *v.* Coggen, 2 Campb. 188. Ante, 284

[q] Gibbon *v.* Coggon, 2 Campb 188.

[r] Chatfield *v.* Paxton and Co. Sittings after Trin. Term, 38 Geo. 3. K. B. MSS. The plaintiff gave a bill to the defendants on Luard and Co. The defendants gave time to the acceptors, and they afterwards became insolvent, of both which circumstances the defendants gave the plaintiff notice, and he at their request, in a letter, accepted another bill, which he afterwards paid; and this action was brought to recover back the money paid. Lord Kenyon.—"My opinion is against the defendants; it is not only necessary that the plaintiff should know all the facts, but that he should know the legal consequences of them; it seems to me that the plaintiff did not know the legal consequences of them, and that he paid this money under an idea that he might be compelled to pay it. When the defendants granted this indulgence of two months to Luard and Co. they gave it at their own risk. Where a

man, knowing all the facts explicitly, and being under no misapprehension with regard to any of them, nor of the law acting upon them, chooses to pay a sum of money, *volenti not fit injuria,* he shall not recover it back again; but the letters of the plaintiff in this case prove directly the contrary, for they are written in a complaining style. Verdict for the plaintiff 2000*l.* and interest from the time of payment. Erskine and Giles for the plaintiff.—Gibbs for the defendants;—See this case observed upon in Bilbie *v.* Lumley, 2 East, 471, and Williams 5. Bartholemew, 1 Bos. & Pul. 326. In Stevens *v.* Lynch, 12 East, 38, the court said, this case proceeded on the ground that the party was ignorant of the *facts.*

[s] Bilbie *v.* Lumley, 2 East, 469. Brisbane *v.* Dacres, 5 Taunt. 143. Williams *v.* Bartholemew, 1 Bos. & Pul. 326.—Stevens *v.* Lynch, 12 East, 38.

[t] See also Brown *v.* M'Kinnally, 1 Esp. Rep. 279. Marriott *v.* Hampton, 2 Esp. Rep. 546. Cartwright *v.* Rowley, id. 723.

---

(304) To the same effect are decisions made in the United States. A promise by an indorser to pay a note or bill dispenses with the necessity of proving a demand on the maker or drawee, on notice to himself. *Pierson* v. *Hooker,* 3 John. Rep. 68. *Hopkins* v. *Liswell,* 12 Mass. Rep. 52.

Where the drawer of a protested bill, on being applied to for payment on behalf of the holder acknowledged the debt to be due, and promised to pay it; saying nothing about notice; it was held, that the holder was not bound to prove notice, on the trial. *Walker* v. *Laverty,* 6 Munf. 487.

If the drawer of a bill of exchange, after the bill becomes due, make an agreement with a prior indorser, reciting that he had drawn the bill in question, that it was over due and ought to be in the hands of the prior indorser; and it was agreed that the latter should take the money due to him upon the bill by instalments, such agreement is evidence in an action by the indorsee against the drawer, that the drawer was then liable to pay the bill, and dispenses with other proof of notice of dishonour. *Genson v. Metz,* 1 Barn. & Cresw. 193.

7thly. How and frequently does not meet the justice of the case, it may be inferred the conse- from this case, and it is indeed now clearly established, that even a mere quences of a neglect to promise to pay, made after notice of the laches of the holder, would give notice be binding, though the party making it misapprehended the law.[a] So may be where the drawer of a bill of exchange, knowing that time had been waived, or given by the holder to the acceptor, but apprehending that he was still otherwise liable upon the bill in default of the acceptor, three months after it was done away. due, said, "I know I am liable, and if the acceptor does not pay it, I will," it was adjudged that he was bound by such promise.[x] And such a promise will dispense with the necessity for a protest of a foreign bill.[y](1)

A promise to pay made after a declaration filed, not only precludes the party from availing himself of the laches of the holder, but also dispenses with evidence in proof of the allegations in such declaration; and if the promise be made to any party to the bill, another person who has afterwards taken it up, may avail himself of such promise, and sue the party making it.[a]

[a] Cooper v. Wall, Guildhall, K. B. 1820, before Abbott, C. J. Scarlett and Chitty for the plaintiff, and Marryatt for defendant. Action against drawer. No evidence of presentment to acceptor, to notice of non-payment to drawer. The bill was due Saturday, 7th August, 1819. On 12th August, witness called with bill on defendant, and informed him that at request of plaintiff, the holder, he called for payment. Defendant said he was sorry the acceptor had not paid the money, that he had promised to advance the money, but that he had deceived him, and that he, defendant, would see the acceptor upon the business, and he would call on the holder; and per Abbott, C. J. this is sufficient to waive laches of holder (though Marryatt considered that there ought to be an express waiver,) and said, that if the drawer deal with the bill after it has been dishonoured, that suffices to charge him.
[x] Stevens v. Lynch, 12 East, 38.— 2 Campb. 322. S. C. and see Taylor v. Jones, 2 Campb. 105.
[y] Gibbon v. Coggon, 2 Campb. 188, 9. Stevens v. Lynch, 2 Campb. 332, 333. Greenway v. Hindley, 4 Campb. 52.
[z] Hopley v. Dufresne, 15 East, 275. Action against indorser of a bill accepted, payable at a banker's. Defence, no regular presentment during banking hours. The declaration alleged a due presentment for payment, and after such declaration filed, the defendant applied to the plaintiff for the indulgence of a further extension of time to pay the bill, which was insisted on as a waiver of the defective presentation. For the defendant it was contended, that there could be no waiver of the defective

presentation, without showing that the defendant, knew, in fact, of the defect at the time, which, though attempted to be, was not shown in this case. For this was cited Bleasard v. Hirst (post, 288,) where a subsequent promise by an indorser to pay the bill having been made under the ignorance of the prior laches of the holder, by which he was discharged, was held to be no waiver of the objection. For the plaintiff, the counsel relied principally on the waiver which took place, after declaration, containing the allegation that the bill was duly presented for payment, was filed; and therefore after the defendant's attention was called to the fact, and he referred to Lundie v. Robertson, (7 East, 231, ante, 234,) where a promise by an indorser to pay the bill three months after it became due, was held to be primâ facie evidence of his admission that the bill had been presented to the acceptor for payment in due time, and dishonoured, and due notice of it given to him. Lord Ellenborough, C. J. stopping the argument, said, that the court thought that it should have been left to the jury to say whether, under the circumstances of the case, the defendant had notice at the time of his application for indulgence, that there had been no due presentation, and therefore made the rule absolute.
[a] Bayl, 221, 2. Potter v. Rayworth, 13 East, 417. Indorsee of a note against the payee and indorser. It appeared that the note which had been negotiated in the country, had been indorsed by the defendant to Fulford, by him to the plaintiff, by the plaintiff to Kirton, and by him to others before it became due; a fortnight after it had

(1) Where there has been laches in not giving notice to the indorser of the non-acceptance of a foreign bill, a promise by the indorser to pay, is not binding on him. *Philips v. M'Curdy*, 1 Harr. & Johns. 187.

If, however, a promise to pay be made without a knowledge of the 7thly. How the conse-quences of a neglect to give notice may be waived, or otherwise done away. [239] fact of non-acceptance, or of the laches of the holder, it will not be binding;[b] and even a payment under such circumstances might, if the party making it were prejudiced by the conduct of the holder, and there were any wilful concealment on his part, be recovered back.[c] The promise also should amount to an admission of the holder's right to receive payment, and therefore where a foreigner said, "I am not acquainted with your laws, if I am bound to pay it I will," such promise was not considered as a waiver of the objection of want of notice :[d] and it has been considered, that if the promise were made on the arrest, it shall not prejudice; but this doctrine seems questionable.[e] If an indorser propose to the holder to pay the bill by instalments, and such offer be rejected, he is at liberty afterwards to avail himself of the want of notice.[f] So it was decided in a late case, that if the drawer or indorser after being arrested, without acknowledging his

---

became due, Kirton, who had taken it up, called on the defendant, who, until then, had received no notice of its dishonour, *the defendant then promised Kirton to pay him the next day;* having failed in this, Kirton resorted to the plaintiff, who paid the amount, and the defence now being the want of notice, the question was, whether the plaintiff could avail himself of this promise so made to Kirton. Graham, B. directed a verdict for the plaintiff, and on motion to set it aside, the court held, that this promise was an acknowledgment by the defendant either with notice or that without notice, he was the proper person to pay the note, and refused a rule. Lord Ellenborough, C. J. said, that whether the promise to pay were made to the plaintiff or any other party who held the note at the time, it was equally evidence that the defendant was conscious of his liability to pay the note which must be because he had had due notice of the dishonour. Bayley, J. considered the promise by the defendant either as an acknowledgment that he had had due notice of the dishonour, or that without such notice he was the proper person to pay the note as for the party for whose use it was drawn. Rule absolute.

[b] Blessard *v.* Hirst, 5 Burr. 2672. Goodall *v.* Dolley, 1 T. R. 712. Williams *v.* Bartholemew, 1 Bos. & Ful. 326. Bayl. 79. Stevens *v.* Lynch, 2 Campb. 333, admitted in 12 East, 89 S. C. Hopley *v.* Dufresne, 15 East, 276, 7, ante, 237, note.

Blessard *v.* Hirst and another, 5 Burr. 2670. The defendant indorsed a bill to the plaintiff, and he indorsed it over; his indorsee presented it for acceptance a month before it became due, and acceptance was refused; it was afterwards presented for payment, and payment was refused, of which notice was given to the defendants, but they had notice of the refusal to accept. The drawer was a bankrupt before the bill became due, but he continued in credit three weeks after the presentment for acceptance. Three days after the notice, one of the defendants

called on the plaintiff at Bradford, on his way to Leeds, and *he said he would take up the bill as he returned*, but on his return he said he was advised he was not bound to do it, upon which this action was brought; and on a case reserved, the court held, that though the holder might not have been obliged to present the bill for acceptance, yet as he did, he ought to have given notice of the refusal, and that by not so doing, he had taken the risk upon himself, and notwithstanding the promise of one of them, the defendants had judgment.

Goodall *v.* Dolley, 1 T. R. 712. A bill drawn in favour of the defendant, payable the 11th January, 1787, was presented for acceptance by the plaintiffs, the 8th November, 1786, when acceptance was refused; they gave no notice to the defendant till the 6th January, and then did not say when the bill was presented, upon which the defendant proposed paying it by instalments, but the plaintiff rejected that offer, and brought this action. Heath, J. thought the defendant discharged for want of notice, and that his offer to pay being made under ignorance of the circumstances, was not binding, and the jury under his direction, found a verdict for the defendant. Upon cause shown against the rule for a new trial, the court thought the verdict and direction right, and discharged the rule.

[c] Chatfield *v.* Paxton, ante, 236, note. Martin *v.* Morgan, 3 Moore, 635. 1 Gow. Rep. 123. S. C. Williams *v.* Bartholemew, 1 Bos. & Pul. 326. Bible *v.* Lumley, 2 East, 469. Malcomb *v.* Fullarton, 2 T. R. 645. *Quære* if not prejudiced could he sustain such action? Farmer *v.* Arundel, 2 Bla. Rep. 824. Price *v.* Neal, 1 Bla. Rep. 390. 3 Burr. 1355. S. C. Ancher *v.* Bank of England, Doug. 637. Bize *v.* Dickason, 1 T. R. 285.

[d] Dennis *v.* Morris, 3 Esp. Rep. 158.

[e] Rouse *v.* Redwood, 1 Esp. Rep. 155.

[f] Goodall *v.* Dolley, 1 T. R. 714, ante, 238.

7thly. How liability, merely offers to give a bill; by way of compromise, for the
the conse- sum demanded, this does not obviate the necessity of proving notice;
quences of
a neglect to and Lord Ellenborough in that case observed, "This offer is neither
give notice an acknowledgment nor a waiver to obviate the necessity of expressly
may be proving notice of the dishonour of the bill. He might have offered to
waived, or give his acceptance at one or two months, although, being entitled to
otherwise
done away. notice of the dishonour of the former bill, he had received none, and
although upon this compromise being refused, he meant to rely upon
this objection. If the plaintiff accepted the offer, good and well, if not,
things were to remain on the same footing as before it was made.;"ᶜ (308)

ᶜ Cuming v French, 2 Campb. 106.

(308) There are many circumstances which in point of law amount to a waiver of
notice. And the doctrines respecting waiver of notice equally apply to the non-acceptance, and non-payment of bills, and non-payment of notes, the cases on this subject
which have been decided in the United States, will be here collected together. If the
maker of a note abscond, and the indorser before it becomes due, informs the holder of
the fact, and requests delay, and agrees to give a new note for the amount, it is a waiver
of demand and notice of non-payment. *Leffingwell* v. *White*, 1 John. Cas. 99. So if
the indorser, before the note becomes due, takes an assignment of *all* the property of the
maker as security for his indorsements. *Bond* v. *Farnham*, 5 Mass. Rep. 170. But it
will be otherwise if he take an assignment of property only to secure him against his
indorsement of other specified notes. Ibid.
And a waiver of notice or an agreement to be bound by a notice different from that
which the law requires, may be inferred from the conduct of the parties. Upon this
ground it has been decided in *Massachusetts*, that if the parties do their business at a
particular bank at which a note is made payable, they will be presumed to agree to be
bound by the usage of that bank as to demand and notice, although such usage may be
entirely at variance with the general rules of law; as for instance, if the usage of the
bank be to make a demand on the maker before the note becomes due, or to give notice
to the indorser before or after the time required by law; or by putting letters into a
post-office, or by any other mode or conveyance varying from the rules of law. *Jones*
v. *Fales*, 4 Mass. Rep. 245. *Widgery* v. *Munroe*, 6 Mass. Rep. 449. *President, Directors & Co. of the Lincoln and Kennebeck Bank* v. *Hammett*, 9 Mass. Rep. 159. *The
same* v. *Page*, 9 Mass. 155. These decisions do not seem to have been recognised in
any other state; and may perhaps be thought to deserve further consideration.
A promise to pay a dishonoured note or bill made with a full knowledge of all the
circumstances, will also be deemed a waiver of a due demand and notice. *Donaldson*
v. *Means*, 4 Dall. Rep. 109. *Pierson* v. *Hooker*, 3 John. Rep. 68. *Duryee* v. *Dennison*, 5 John. Rep. 248. *Miller* v. *Hackley*, 5 John. Rep. 375. *Copp* v. *M'Dugall*, 9
Mass. Rep. 1. *Hopkins* v. *Liswell*, 12 Mass. Rep. 52. But the promise must be explicit and made out by the most clear and unequivocal evidence. Therefore where the
indorser speaking of several bills on different places, and under different circumstances,
said " he would take care of them ;" or " he would see them paid ;" it was held not sufficient evidence of a promise to pay one of the bills on which no notice of non-acceptance
had been given. *Miller* v. *Hackley*, 5 John. Rep. 375. and see *Griffin* v. *Goff*, 12
John. Rep. 423. And what a man says under the surprise of a sudden and unexpected
demand ought to be construed with a good deal of strictness. *May* v. *Coffin*, 4 Mass.
Rep. 341. Indeed it seems to have been held that under such circumstances a promise
to pay a bill which had been protested for non-acceptance, and of which due notice had
not been given to the indorser, did not bind him, as it was wholly without consideration.
and especially as he retracted his promise within a few days afterwards. *May* v. *Coffin*. And it has been repeatedly decided in *Massachusetts*, that if an indorser under
ignorance of the law, or through mistake of the law, promise to pay a dishonoured bill
or note, he is not bound by such promise. *Warder* v. *Tucker*, 7 Mass. Rep. 449.
Freeman v. *Boynton*, 7 Mass. Rep. 483. *May* v. *Coffin*. And it seems generally
agreed that a promise to pay, or an actual payment under a mistake of the facts, is
not binding. *Donaldson* v. *Means*. *Garland* v. *The Salem Bank*, 9 Mass. Rep. 408.
Crain v. *Colwell*, 8 John. Rep. 384. *Tower* v. *Durell*, 9 Mass. Rep. 332. *Fothering-
ham* v. *Price's Ex.* 1 Bay's Rep. 291. *Griffin* v. *Goff*, 12 John. Rep. 423. *Trimble*
v. *Thorne*, 16 John. 152.
But a waiver of a right to notice made by the indorser of a note, does not in general
excuse the holder from demanding payment of the maker at the maturity of the note, for
it may be done in the confidence that the maker will punctually pay it. *Berkshire Bank*
v. *Jones*, 6 Mass. Rep. 524. And a qualified or conditional promise of the indorser to

and it has recently been considered, that admitting that a drawer of a bill may by circumstances *impliedly* waive his right of defence founded on the laches of the holder; yet an indorser can only do so by an *express* waiver, there being a material distinction in this respect between the situation of a drawer and indorser.[h] Where the plaintiff relies on a statement by the indorser after the bill was due, that he knew he was discharged, but that the plaintiff had behaved so well to him in money matters, that he should take no advantage of it, but would pay the money; he must, it is said, also prove a demand on the acceptor.[i]

7thly. How the consequences of a neglect to give notice may be waived, or otherwise done away.

A person who has been once discharged by laches from his liability, is always discharged; and therefore where two or more parties to a bill have been so discharged, but one of them not knowing of the laches, pays it, such payment is in his own wrong, and he cannot recover the money from another of such parties.[k]

[240]

THE custom of merchants is stated to be, that if the *drawee* of a bill of exchange abscond before the day when the bill is due, the holder may protest it, in order to have better security for the payment, and should give notice to the drawer and indorsers of the absconding of the drawee;[l] and if the acceptor of a foreign bill become bankrupt before it is due, it seems that the holder may also in such case protest for better security;[m] but the acceptor is not, on account of the bankruptcy

Sect. 4. Of protest for better security.

---

[h] Borradaile *v.* Lowe, 4 Taunt. 93. and see Shepherd, Serjeant's, argument, id. 96, 7. The defendant, who was an indorser, wrote the following letter, in answer to one from the then holder:— '

" Sir,

"I cannot think of remitting until I receive the draft, therefore if you think proper, you may return it to Trevor and Co. Whitchurch Old Bank, if you consider me unsafe.

28th January, 1811.
Signed J. LOWE, Whitchurch."
"To Mr. John Wilkins."

This letter was held not to amount to a waiver of the laches in not giving due notice of non-payment.

[i] Brown *v.* M'Dermot, 5 Esp. Rep. 265.

[k] Bayl. 442. Roscoe *v.* Hardy, 12 East, 434. Turner *v.* Leech, 4 Barn. & Ald. 451.

[l] Anon. Ld. Raym. 743. Mar. 27. 111, 112. Beawes, pl. 22. 24. 26. 27. 29. Kyd, 139. See Bayl. 69, n. (e.) 72, 73. 75.

The following is an extract from the code of laws at Antwerp, relating to bills of exchange:—" In the case of failure (*de faillité*) of the acceptor before the usage (*l'écheance*) the holder may cause it to be protested, and put in force his recourse (*exercer son récours*.")

[m] Id. ibid. Ex parte Wackerbarth, 5 Ves. 574. Kyd, 139.

---

pay, which is rejected by the holder, is not a waiver of notice. *Agan* v. *M'Manus*, 11 John. Rep. 180. *Crain* v. *Colwell*, 8 John. Rep. 180.

It seems that if an indorsee of a note cannot recover upon it against the maker, by reason of usury between the maker and his indorser, of which usury the indorsee was ignorant at the time of the purchase, he may recover against such indorser, without having given him due notice of the dishonour of the note. *Copp* v. *M'Dugall*, 9 Mass. Rep. 1.

If the drawer of a promissory note be known by the indorser to have been insolvent when the note was made, and when it became due, the indorser is, nevertheless, entitled to due notice of non payment by the drawer. But if the indorser has accepted from the drawer, a general assignment of his estate and effects, notice is not necessary. *Barton* v. *Baker*. 1 Serg. & Rawle, 334.

When the drawer of a note is known to be a bankrupt or insolvent demand and notice are not necessary. *Clark* v. *Minton*, 2 Const. Rep. 682. But it must be an utter and declared insolvency of record and known as such to the indorser. *Kiddell* v. *Ford*. Ibid. 678.

Sect. 4. Of of the *drawer*, compellable to give this security.[a] The neglect to make
protest for this protest will not affect the holder's remedy aga·nst the drawer and
better secu- indorsers,[o] and its principal use appears to be, ¹hat by giving notice
rity. to the drawer and indorsers of the situation of the acceptor, by which
it is become improbable that payment will be made, they are enabled
by other means to provide for the payment of the bill when due, and
thereby prevent the loss of re-exchange, &c. occa-ioned by the return
of the bill.[p] It may be collected, that though the drawer or indorsers
refuse to give better security, the holder must nevertheless wait till the
bill be due, before he can sue either of those parties.[q]

Sect. 5. Of ANY person may, without the consent of the drawer or indorsers,
acceptance accept the bill, *supra protest*, for better security.[r] This security, it
supra pro- is said, is usually given by making another subscription under the pro-
test. test, that the person who becomes new security, will be bound as prin-
[241] cipal for the payment of the sum mentioned in the bill, upon which the
protest is made.[s]

When a foreign bill is protested for non-acceptance, or for better
security,[t] the drawee or any other person may *accept* it *supra protest*,
which acceptance is so called, from the manner in which it is made.
This description of acceptance is frequently made upon a foreign bill,
for the purpose either of promoting the negotiation of the bill when the
drawee's credit is suspected, or to save the reputation, and prevent the
prosecution of some of the parties, where the drawee either cannot be
found, is not capable of making a contract, or refuses to accept; and
such acceptance is called an acceptance for the *honour* of the person on
whose behalf it is made, and it enures to the benefit of all who become parties subsequently to that person.[u]

1st. By The *drawee*, though he may not choose to accept on account of him
whom made in whose favour he is advised the bill is drawn, may nevertheless accept
for the account and honour of the drawer, or in case he do not choose
to accept on account of the drawer, he may accept for the honour of
the indorser ; in which latter case he should immediately send the protest on which he made the acceptance to the indorser.[x] It is said, that
if the holder be dissatisfied with the acceptance *supra protest*, and
insist on a simple acceptance, and protest the bill for want of it, the
acceptor should renounce the acceptance he had made, and should
insist that it be cancelled.[y]

When the drawee will not accept the bill, *any other person may*,
after refusal by him,[z] and after protest, accept it for the honour of the
bill, or of the drawer,[a] or of any particular indorser ;[b] and even a

[a] Beawes, pl. 22.
[o] Ibid. pl. 23.
[p] Ibid. pl. 24.
[q] Ibid. pl. 26.
[r] Ex parte Wackerbarth, 5 Ves. 574.
et infra. See the observations on acceptances *supra protest* in Hoare v. Cazenove, 16 East, 391.
[s] Com. Dig. Merchant, F. 8. cites Mar. 28.
[t] Ex parte Wackerbarth, 5 Ves. 574.
Bayl. 74.
[u] Hussey v. Jacob, Ld. Raym. 88.—

Lewin v. Brunetti, Lutw. 899. Beawes.
pl. 34. Poth. pl. 112, 13, 14. Bayl. 45.
[x] Beawes, pl. 33, 4. see ante, 224.
[y] Id. pl. 37.
[z] Beawes, pl. 38. Hussey v. Jacob,
Lord Raym. 88.
[a] Mar. 125, 6, 7, 8. Lewin v. Brunetti, Lutw. 896. 899. Carth. 129. S. C.
observed upon in Hoare v. Cazenove, 16
East, 391.
[b] Beawes, pl. 38. 42. Jackson v. Hudson, 2 Campb. 448,

bill previously accepted *supra protest*, may be accepted by another person, *supra protest*, in honour of some particular person.[c] No one, however, should accept a bill under protest for non-acceptance for the honour of the drawer. before he has ascertained from the drawee his reason for suffering the bill to be protested ; but if the acceptance be in honour of the indorser, such inquiry is unnecessary.[d]

It is said, that the holder of a bill must receive an acceptance *supra protest*, if offered by a responsible person, it being of no importance to him, whether it be accepted simply, or under a protest, as the acceptor pays the charges, unless he had orders from the remitter not to admit of such an acceptance.[e] But this *dictum* seems to be erroneous, for it has been adjudged that the holder need not acquiesce in any case.[f] There cannot be a series of acceptors of the same bill ; it must either be accepted by the drawee, or failing him, by some one for the honour of the drawer.[g]

The *method of excepting supra protest* is said to be as follows : the acceptor must personally appear before a notary public with witnesses, and declare that he accepts such protested bill in honour of the drawer or indorser, and that he will satisfy the same at the appointed time; and then he must subscribe the bill with his own hand, thus—" accepted *supra protest*, in honour of J. B.,"[h] or, as is more usual, " accepts S. P." A general acceptance *supra protest* is considered as made for the honour of the drawer, unless otherwise expressed. Such acceptance, however, may be so worded, that though it be intended for the honour of the drawer, yet it may equally bind the indorser ; but in this case, notice of such acceptance must be sent to the latter.[i] The holder should always take care to have the bill protested for non-acceptance before the acceptance for honour is made, as otherwise, it is said, the drawer might allege that he did not draw on the person making the acceptance.[k]

An acceptance *supra protest* is as *obligatory* on the acceptor, as if no protest had intervened, it being immaterial to the holder of a bill, on whose account it is accepted.[l] If the acceptance were for the honour of the bill, or of the drawer, the acceptor is liable to all the indorsees, as well as the holder : if in honour of a particular indorser, then to all subsequent indorsees. The acceptance *supra protest*, however, is only a conditional engagement, and to render such acceptor absolutely liable, the bill must be duly presented for payment to the drawee, and protested in case of refusal.[m] (313)

Sect. 5. Of acceptance *supra protest*.

[242]

2dly. Of the mode of accepting *supra protest*.

3dly. Of the *liability* of the acceptor *supra protest*.

[243]

[c] Beawes, pl. 42.
[d] Beawes, pl. 46.
[e] Ibid. pl. 27. 36.
[f] Mitford v. Walcot, 12 Mod. 410. Ld. Raym. 575. S. C. *et vide* Beawes, pl. 87. Gregory v. Walcot, Com. 76. Pillans v. Van Mierope, 3 Burr. 1672. 4.
[g] Jackson v. Hudson, 2 Campb. 447. Ante, 166.
[h] Beawes, pl. 38.
[i] Ibid. pl. 39.

[k] Marius, 88. 125, 6, 7.
[l] Beawes, pl. 35. 45. Mitford v. Walcot, Ld. Raym. 575. 12 Mod. 410. S. C. Gregory v. Walcot, Com. 76. Pillans v. Van Mierop, Burr. 1672. 4. Bayl. 42, n. b.
[m] Hoare and another v. Cazenove and another, 16 East, 391. This was an action on a set of foreign bills of exchange drawn at Hambro', on Pen and Hanbury in London, at one hundred and thirty days after

(313) When a bill of exchange is protested for non-acceptance, and afterwards is taken up and paid for the honour of an indorser, it has been held that the holder is still

4thly. Of the *right* of such acceptor.   A person accepting a bill *supra protest,* either for the honour of a drawer or of an indorser, although without his order or knowledge, has. as it is said, his redress and remedy against such person, and to all other persons who are liable to that person, who must indemnify him from any damage he may have sustained, the same as if he had acted entirely by his direction.[a] He who accepts a bill in honour of the drawer only, has no remedy against any of the indorsers, because he accepts merely on the behalf of the drawer ; but the acceptor for the honour of the drawer of a bill already accepted by the drawee, but protested by the holder for better security, may, when he has paid the bill, sue the drawer or drawee, though in the case of a bankruptcy of these parties, if the first acceptance were for the accommodation of the drawer, a court of equity will compel the acceptor *supra protest* first to resort to the drawer's estate.[c]

[244]   An acceptor, for the honour of an indorser, has no claim upon any party to the bill subsequent to him for whose honour he accepted : but the indorser, for whose honour he accepted, and all the prior parties. the drawer included, are obliged to make satisfaction to the acceptor.[r]

date; the bills were presented to Messrs. P. and H. for acceptance, and refused, and protest duly made for non-acceptance; the bills were afterwards accepted by the defendent under protest for the honour of the first indorsers. When the bill became due, it was not presented to the drawees for payment nor protested for non-payment. The defendants refused to pay the bill, in consequence of orders from the first indorsers. At the trial the plaintiff had a verdict subject to the opinion of the court on the above case; and after two arguments, and time taken to consider, the court were of opinion, that a presentment to the original drawees for payment, and a protest for non-payment by them, was essential as a previous requisite to maintaining an action against an acceptor, for the honour of a first indorser, and ordered the postea to the defendants. Lord Ellenborough said, "the reason of the thing, as well as the strict law of the case, seems to render a second resort to the drawee proper, when the unaccepted bill still remains with the holder, for effects often reach the drawee, who has refused acceptance in the first instance, out of which the bill may and would be satisfied, if presented to him again, when the period of payment had arrived ; and the drawer is entitled to the chance of the

benefit to arise from such second demand, or at any rate, to the benefit of that evidence which the protest affords ; that the demand has been made duly without effect. as far as such evidence may be available to him for purposes of ulterior resort."

[a] Beawes, pl. 47. Smith *v.* Nissen. T. R. 269. Bayl. 73, 4. *et vide post,* of payment *supra protest.*

[c] Ex parte Wackerbarth, 5 Ves. 574 The acceptor of a bill having become bankrupt, and the holders having protested it for better security, Christian and Bowen accepted it for the honour of the drawers. and having paid it, now claimed to be entitled to dividends under the bankrupt's estate. The Chancellor said, he had spoke to persons in trade upon the subject, and the result was, that the person accepting for the honour of the drawer, had a right to come upon the acceptor. He said, however, that the justice of the case require that they should go in the first place against the drawer, if the acceptor had no effects and directed an inquiry to be made, whether the original acceptor, or Christian and Bowen, had effects of the drawer's in hand.

[r] Beawes, pl, 49. 83. 44. Poth. pl 112 Molloy, B. 2. c. 10 s. 24.

bound to cause the bill to be protested for non-acceptance and non-payment, and to regular notice to the antecedent parties in the same manner as if the bill had not been taken up. It is material however to observe that this doctrine was delivered in a case where the action was brought by the indorser for whose honour the bill had been drawn against a prior indorser, and that the neglect to make the protest and give notice was on the part of the persons who had taken up the bill for his honour. *Lenox v. Lenox* 10 Mass. Rep. 1.

CHAPTER V.

OF PRESENTMENT OF A BILL, &c. FOR PAYMENT—OF PAYMENT—OF THE CONDUCT WHICH THE HOLDER MUST PURSUE ON NON-PAYMENT; AND OF PAYMENT SUPRA PROTEST.

IT would be extremely prejudicial to commerce, if the holder of a bill or note, were suffered to give longer credit to the drawee than the instrument directs, and afterwards, in default of payment by the drawee, to resort to the drawer or indorsers, at a time when perhaps the accounts between them and the persons liable to them may have been adjusted, or those persons may have become insolvent;[a] and the common law detests negligence and laches.[b] On this principle, it is settled, that the holder of a bill must present it to the drawee for payment at the time when due, when a time of payment is specified; and when no time is expressed, within a reasonable period after receipt of the bill;[c] and that if he neglect to do so, he shall not afterwards resort to the drawer or indorsers, whose implied contracts are only to pay in default of the drawee, and not immediate or absolute, and who are always presumed to have sustained damage by the holder's laches.[d](315)

Sect. 1. Of presentment for payment; and 1st, When present-sentiment is necessary.

[a] Allen v. Dockwra, 1 Salk. 127. Collins v. Butler, Stra. 1807. Bul. Ni. Pri. 470. 2 Bla. Com. 470.

[b] Per Curiam, in Chamberlyn v. Delarive, 2 Wils. 354.

[c] Poth. pl. 129. Cowley v. Dunlop, 7 T. R. 581, 2.

[d] Heylin v. Adamson, 2 Burr. 669.— Cowley v. Dunlop, 7 T. R 581, 2. acc. Cooper v. Le Blanc, Rep. Temp. Hardw. 295. *semb. contra.*

---

(315) The drawer of a bill, and the indorser of a note, are responsible only after a default of the acceptor or maker; and the holder must first demand payment of him, or use due diligence to demand it before he can resort to the drawer or indorser. *Munroe v. Easton,* 2 John. Cas. 75. *Berry v. Robinson,* 9 John. Rep. 121. *Griffin v. Goff,* 12 John. Rep. 423. *May v. Coffin,* 4 Mass. Rep. 341. And if an indorser of a bill on its becoming due pay the amount to the indorsee, the latter never having demanded payment of the acceptor, he cannot recover the amount from the drawer. *Munroe v. Easton,* 2 John. Cas. 75. It is no excuse for not demanding payment of the drawee, that the drawer has no funds in the hands of the drawee. *Cruger v. Armstrong,* 3 John. Cas. 5. Notice to an indorser prior to a demand upon the acceptor of a bill, or maker of a note, is a mere nullity. *Jackson v. Richards,* 2 Caine's Rep. 343. *Griffin v. Goff.* And in respect to the necessity of a demand, there is no difference whether the note or bill be indorsed before, or after, it became due. *Berry v. Robinson.*

But the want of a demand will be excused when the acceptor has absconded, or cannot be found. *Putnam v. Sullivan,* 4 Mass. Rep. 45. *Widgery v. Monroe,* 6 Mass. Rep. 449. *Stewart v. Eden,* 2 Caine's Rep. 121. And such fact may be given in evidence under the common averment that the note was duly presented, and refused payment. *Stewart v. Eden,* 2 Caine's Rep. 121. *Saunderson v. Judge,* 2 H. Bl. 510. *contra Blakely v. Grant,* 6 Mass. Rep. 386. But an averment in such case that the holder had used due diligence, but could not find the acceptor, would seem to be more correct. *Blakely v. Grant.*

Note If a notary go to the maker's house to demand payment, and find it shut up, and that he is out of town, this is a sufficient demand. *Ogden v. Cowley,* 2 John. Rep 270.

Not only must a demand be made upon the drawee, but it must be made within a reasonable time, otherwise the drawer will be discharged, especially if prejudiced by the neglect. Therefore where a creditor received an order from his debtor on a third per-

CHITTY ON BILLS. G g

1st, When presentment is necessary. An acceptor *supra protest*, we have seen, is also within this rule;[e] and if a bill be accepted, or note made payable a certain time after sight, a presentment is obviously essential, in order to complete the right to payment.[f] And whenever it is incumbent on the holder to present a bill or note for payment at a precise time, and he neglects to do so, he will lose his remedy as well on the bill as upon the consideration or debt, in respect of which it was given or transferred. It appears that a distinction was formerly taken between a bill of exchange given in payment of a precedent debt, and one given for a debt contracted at the time the bill was given;[g] in the latter case, it was always holden, that the person who received it must have used due diligence to obtain

[246] the money from the drawee, and that in default of his so doing, he could not support any action against the party from whom he received it; but in the former case, the bill was not considered as payment, unless the money were actually paid by the drawee, although the holder might have neglected to present it for payment, or to give notice of non-payment; and the holder, though he cold not sue on the bill, might maintain an action for the consideration on which it was given.[h] This distinction, founded, it is presumed, on the principle that a bill, delivered in consideration of a precedent debt, could only be understood as a collateral security, which the assignee might waive, does not any longer exist.[i]

It has been holden that even the bankruptcy,[k] insolvency,[l] or death of the acceptor of a bill, or maker of a note, however notorious, will

---

[e] Ante, 243.

[f] Holmes *v.* Kerrison, 2 Taunt. 323.

[g] Ante, 143.

[h] Clerk *v.* Mundall, 12 Mod. 203.—1 Salk. 124. S. C. Anon. 12 Mod. 408. Anon. Holt, 299. Trials per Pais, 499. Kyd, 171.

[i] Ante, 94, 5, 6. 143. Bul. Ni. Pri. 182. Smith *v.* Wilson, Andr. 187. It seems to be the opinion of a modern writer on bills (Kyd, 172,) that the statute 3 & 4 Anne, c. 9. s. 7. put an end to this distinction; but with deference it is submitted that the clause referred to in support of that opinion, relates only to *such* bills as are alluded to in the 4th section of the act, namely, bills made payable after date, and

expressed to have been given for value received; and the 7th clause also only takes away the accumulative remedy given by the statute 9 & 10 Wil. 3. c. 17. and 3 & 4 Anne, c 9. It is therefore probable that this alteration is rather to be ascribed to the change of opinion in our courts of justice.

[k] Russell *v.* Langstaffe, Dougl. 515. Per Lord Mansfield, because many means may remain of obtaining payment by the assistance of friends or otherwise. Per Lord Ellenborough, in Warrington *v.* Furbor. 8 East, 245. Ante, 210. Bayl. 115.

[l] Per Lord Ellenborough, in Esdaile *r.* Sowerby, 12 East, 117. Ante, 210. Bowet *v.* Howe, 5 Taunt. 30. 16 East, 115. S. C. Bayl. 115.

---

son, on the 9th of December, which the drawee agreed to pay in ten or fifteen days, and the order was not presented until the March following, or afterwards, when the drawee had become insolvent, and the drawer was held discharged. *Brower* v. *Jones,* 3 John Rep. 280.; and see *Cruger* v. *Armstrong,* 3 John. Cas. 5. and *Conroy* v. *Warren,* 3 John Cas. 259. *Stothart* v. *Lewis,* Overt. Rep. 215. If at the time of the note's falling due, the holder is at a place distant from the place of abode of the maker, a reasonable time will be allowed to make the demand. Thus, where at the maturity of the bill, the holder was at 200 miles distance from the maker's place of abode, a demand six days after was held to be within reasonable time; but a demand thirty days after was held unreasonable. *Freeman* v. *Boynton,* 7 Mass Rep. 483.

In order to make a demand good, it is necessary that the party making it should have a written or verbal authority from the holder; and should have with him *the note itself,* for the debtor has a right, upon payment, to receive and cancel it. *Freeman* v. *Boynton.*

If the maker of a note be alive at the time of its falling due, his insolvency does not absolve the holder from showing that he has used due diligence to obtain the amount due *Clair* v *Barr,* 2 March. 256

not excuse the neglect to make due presentment; and in the last case it should be made to his personal representative, and in case there be no executor or administrator, then at the house of the deceased,[m] or the drawer or indorsers will be discharged. If the maker of a note has shut up his house, it will not suffice merely to present it there, for the holder ought to inquire after him, and endeavour to find him out.[n] At all events, although the drawee of a bill, or maker of a note, being bankers, may have shut up and abandoned their shop, yet a presentment there, or to them in person, must be made, and it will not suffice to allege in a declaration, that they became insolvent, and ceased and wholly declined and refused to pay at their bank any notes then payable.[o]

If the holder of a bill at the time it becomes due, be dead, it is said [247] that his executor, although he have not proved the will, must present it to the drawee.[p] If the drawee goes abroad, leaving an agent in England, with power to accept bills, who accepts one for him, the bill when due, must be presented to the agent for payment, if the drawee continue absent.[q] When a bill, transferrable only by indorsement, is delivered to a person without being indorsed, he should nevertheless present the bill for payment to the acceptor, and offer an indemnity to him; and if the acceptor then refuse to pay, the bill should be protested for non-payment.[r] It has been holden, that if a draft be given,

---

[m] Molloy, b. 2. c. 10. s. 34. If a bill be accepted, and the party dies, yet there must be a demand made on his executors or administrators, and in default of payment, a protest must be made. See also Bayl 93, and ante, 211, 212.

[n] Collins *v*. Butler, 2 Stra. 1087. Bayl. 95. Ante, 164; but see Goldsmith *v*. Bland, and Crosse *v*. Smith, 1 M. & S. 545. Ante, 213.

[o] Howe *v*. Bowes and others, 16 East, 112. 1 M. & S. 555. judgment of K. B. reversed on error in Exchequer Chamber, 3 Taunt. 30. The plaintiff declared as holder of a promissory note, made by the defendants on the 2d January, 1809, at Workington Bank, that is, at Penrith, in the county of Cumberland, whereby the defendants then and there promised on demand, to pay one R. W. or bearer there, that is to say at Workington Bank aforesaid, five guineas, value received. The declaration afterwards averred, that after the making of the note, the defendants became insolvent, and then and from thenceforth until and at the time of exhibiting of the bill aforesaid, ceased and wholly declined and refused to pay at the Workington Bank aforesaid, the sum or sums of money specified in any note or notes issued by them from such bank, to wit, at Penrith aforesaid, &c. Lord Ellenborough, C J observed that the mere allegation of insolvency, as an excuse for not presenting the notes for payment at the place, would be impertinent; but in this case, the allegation, the truth of which as reported by the learned Judge, was left to the jury, and found by them, went further, that the defendants had ceased and wholly declined

and refused payment of any of their notes at the place; how then can the question arise? the shutting up of the house might be considered as a refusal to pay the notes there; and as it is not disputed that the banking shop was shut up, and that any demand of payment which could have been made there, would have been wholly inaudible, that is substantially a refusal to pay their notes to all the world. Afterwards upon a writ of error in the Exchequer Chamber, the judgment of the K. B was over-ruled, and Macdonald, C. B. said, " this is extremely simple, it depends entirely on the force and effect of an allegation in the declaration, which, it is said, dispenses with the necessity of presenting the notes in question It is clear that a demand at the place is necessary, unless it is dispensed with The question then is, whether this allegation that the plaintiffs in error ceased and wholly declined and refused to pay at the Workington Bank, any notes issued by them from such bank, carries the matter further than a mere allegation of insolvency; and as it is not alleged that this declaration, they would pay none of their notes, was made to the plaintiff below, it is merely this, that they generally declared, they neither could or would pay any of their notes; this allegation does not appear to the Judges to be sufficient to enable the plaintiff below to maintain his action, therefore judgment must be for the plaintiffs in error."

[p] Poth. pl. 146. Molly, b. 2. c. 10. pl. 24. Mar. 134, 135.

[q] Phillips *v*. Astling, 2 Taunt. 206.

[r] Supra, note.

1st. When presentment is necessary. which ought to be, but is not, stamped, it is not necessary to present it for payment;[a] but the insufficiency of the bill in other respects will constitute no excuse for the non-presentment.[t]

The neglect to make a proper presentment may, however, as far as respects the *drawer's* liability, be excused by the drawee's not having had effects of the drawer in his hands from the time of drawing the bill to the time when it became due ;[u] and where a bill drawn on Leghorn was not presented in due time, owing to the political state of the country at that time, which rendered it impossible to present it, it was holden, that it being afterwards presented for payment as soon as practicable, and refused, the holder might recover, and evidence of this impossibility of presenting the bill at the time of maturity might be given, under the usual averment that the bill was duly presented.[x]

And if a bill be taken under an extent, before it is due, and the party holding it on behalf of the Crown neglect to present it for payment in due time, the drawer and indorsers will continue liable, because no laches are imputable to the Crown.[y]

So the consequences of the neglect to present may be *waived* by a payment of part,[z] or a promise to pay after full notice of the default,[a] are indeed by the same circumstances, which will do away the effect of a neglect to present for acceptance, or to give notice of the refusal.[b](319)

But the circumstance of the drawer having notice before the bill is due, that it will probably not be paid, and promising the holder that he will endeavour to provide effects, and see him again, will not excuse the neglect to present the bill for payment to the drawee on the day the bill is due.[c]

<hr/>

[a] Ante, 58. Wilson *v.* Vysar, 4 Taunt. 288. Ruff *v.* Webb, 1 Esp. Rep. 129. acc. sed vide Swears *v.* Wells, *id.* 317, and Chamberlyn *v.* Delarive, 2 Wils. 353. The reason is, 'that the unstamped instrument cannot be given in evidence.
[t] Chamberlyn *v.* Delarive, 2 Wils. 353. See *quære.*
[u] Ante, 198.
[x] Patience *v.* Townly, 2 Smith's Rep. 223, 4. Ante, 163.
[y] West on Extents, 1st edit. 29, 30.
[z] Vaughan *v.* Fuller, Stra. 1246. Ante, 234.

[a] Ante, 234 to 239. Hopes *v.* Alder, 6 East, 16.
[b] Ante, 238 to 239.
[c] Prideaux *v.* Collier, 2 Stark. 57. This, was an action by the plaintiff as the indorsee of a bill of exchange, dated March 20th 1816, drawn by the defendant upon Wood and Co. payable to his own order, and indorsed by him to the plaintiff Upon the 22d of May, the day before the bill became due; application was made by the plaintiff to Wood and Co. and the answer was, that Collier had no effects in their hands ; but the clerk of Wood and Co. remarked, that the bill would not be

<hr/>

(319) The prevalence of a contagious malignant fever in the place of residence of the parties, which occasioned a stoppage of all business, has been held to be a sufficient excuse for not giving notice until November, of a protest for non-payment made in the preceding September. *Tunno* v. *Lague,* 2 John. Cas. 1.

Payment of part of a check by the drawer after it becomes due, dispenses with the necessity of proving a demand on the bank, in a suit against him. *Levy* v. *Peters,* 9 Serg. & Rawle, 125. And so it seems would a part payment before the check became due. Ibid. But the plaintiff cannot by voluntarily giving credit for part payment, evade the necessity of proving a demand on the drawee, if the defendant disclaims such credit, and insists on the want of a demand. But if the defendant acquiesces in such credit, and insists that the whole has been paid, and relies on length of time and other circumstances to discharge him, he thereby admits a part payment. *Ibid.*

We have next to consider in what cases the *acceptor* of a bill, or maker 1st. When present-ment is ne-cessary. of a note, **may resist an action on account of neglect of the holder to present the instrument for payment. (320) It is a general rule of law, that where it is a precedent debt or duty, the creditor need not allege or prove any demand of payment before the action brought, it being the duty of the debtor to find out his creditor, and tender him the money, and, as it is technically said, the bringing of the action is a sufficient request.** [d] (320)

It might not perhaps be unreasonable, if the law required present-ment to the acceptor of a bill, or maker of a note, before an action be commenced against him, because otherwise he might, or account of the negotiable quality of the instrument, and the consequent difficulty to find out the holder of it on the day of payment, in order to make a ten-der to him, be subjected to an action without any default whatever: and the engagement of the acceptor of a bill, or maker of a note, is to pay the money when due to the holder, who shall for that purpose make pre-sentment. [e]

It is, however, a settled rule of law, that when no particular place is named, in a bill or note, for payment, the acceptor or maker of the note cannot resist an action on account of neglect to present the instrument at the precise time when due, or of an indulgence to any of the other parties. [f] And on the above-mentioned principle, that an action is of

due until the next day, and that it was probable that Collier would be in before that time, and provide effects. On the next day, the 23d, when the bill became due, the defendant said to the plaintiff, that he understood that he the plaintiff was the holder of the bill, which he hoped would be paid; that he would see what he could do, and would endeavour to provide effects, and would see him again The bill was not presented to the drawees on the 23d, but was pre-sented on the 24th. Lord Ellenborough held, that this did not supersede the ne-

cessity of a presentment on the day. See Phipson *v.* Kneller, 4 Campb. 285, ante, 230.

[d] Birks *v.* Trippet, 1 Saund. 33. Carte-*v.* Ring, 3 Campb 459. Capp *v.* Lancas-ter, Cro. Eliz. 548. Co. Litt. 210. b. note 1. Com. Dig. Condition, G. 9.

[e] See the argument in Wegersloff *v.* Keene, 1 Stra. 222. Callaghan v. Aylett, 2 Campb. 549. Lancashire *v.* Killingworth, Ld Raym. 687. Salk. 623. 12 Mod. 530. Com. Dig. Condition, G. 9.

[f] Dingwall *v.* Dunster, Dougl. 247. An-derson *v.* Cleveland, 1 Esp. Rep. 47.

---

(320) An order drawn by a debtor on a person having funds in his hands, is, after pre-sentment to the drawee, an assignment of such funds to the extent of the order, and the drawee cannot afterwards legally part with such funds to the drawer or any other person. *Clayton v. Hallett*, 1 Caines' Rep. 379. And where a bill is drawn upon special funds, the authority in the drawee to pay it, is not revoked by the death of the drawer before presentment of the bill. And it seems that such a bill is to be deemed an assignment of such funds. *Cutts* v. *Perkins*, 12 Mass. Rep. 206.

(320) It has been held no bar to an action on a note payable a day and place certain, that the holder was not present at the time and place to receive payment, and did not there demand payment. It was the duty of the debtor to be there ready to pay. *Rug-g'es v. Patten*, 8 Mass. Rep. 480. When payment of a note drawn payable at a par-ticular place, is demanded personally of the maker elsewhere, and no objection is made by him. it is sufficient to bind the maker. *Herring* v. *Sangen*, 8 John. Cas. 71. But see *Woodbridg-* v. *Brigham*, 12 Mass. Rep. 403.

If a note be payable at a particular bank no demand or attempt to demand payment of the maker is necessary to charge the indorser. It is sufficient if the holder of the note be at the bank on the prescribed day, ready to receive payment, if the maker be not there ready to make it. And by the indorsement of such a note, the indorser guarantees that on the day of payment the maker would be at the bank and pay the note, and that if he did not pay it there, he would be answerable for the amount upon notice. *Berk-shire Bank* v. *Jones*, 6 Mass. Rep. 524. *Woodbridge* v. *Brigham*. But see a report of this case. 13 Mass. Rep. 556

1st.* When itself a sufficient demand of payment, it is settled, that the acceptor or present-maker of a note payable generally, and not at a particularly place, cannot ment is ne-set up as a defence, the want of a presentment to him even before the cessary. commencement of the action, and although the instrument be payable on demand.*

[250]　Before the recent decision in the House of Lords in Rowe v. Young,[f] there had been much discussion and difference of opinion in the courts upon the effect of a direction upon the bill or note, that the same shall be payable at a particular place, and whether the acceptor of the bill. or maker of the note, can resist an action on account of that direction not having been complied with. Both the Courts of King's Bench and Common Pleas agreed, that where a particular place of payment was introduced into the body of a bill or note, and not as a mere memorandum at the foot of the instrument, whether the action were against the drawer or acceptor of the bill, or the maker or indorser of the note, the instrument must be presented at that particular place, and a demand be made there, in order to give the holder a cause of action.[i]　And that in

Anderson v. Cleveland, Sittings after Easter, 1779. MS. 1 Esp. Rep. 47. The indorsee of a bill of exchange brought an action against the acceptor, and it appeared that there was no demand of payment until three months after the bill became due, and the drawer was then insolvent ; it was ruled by Lord Mansfield, that this was no defence, for the acceptor of a bill of exchange, or maker of a promissory note, remains always liable; acceptance is proof of having effects in his hands, and he ought never to part with them, unless it appears that the drawer had provided another fund by paying the bill himself.
　e Rumball v. Ball, 10 Mod. 38. Frampton v. Coulson, 1 Wils C. B 33. Capp v. Lancaster, Cro Eliz. 518. Prac. Reg 538. Reynolds v. Davies, 1 Bos. & Pul. 625.
　h 2 Brod. & Bing. 165.
　i Sanderson v. Bowes, 14 East, 500. Dickenson v. Bowes, 16 East, 110. Roche v. Campbell, 3 Campb. 247. Trecothick v. Edwin, 1 Strak. 468; but see Nicholls v. Bowes, 2 Campb. 498.
　Sanderson v. Bowes and others, 14 East, 500. A promissory note of the defendant's, promising in the body of it, to pay so much at their banking-house at Workington, in Cumberland, requires a demand of payment there, in order to give the holder a cause of action if it be not paid. Per Lord Ellenborough, C. J. This is a duty created by the instrument itself, with certain limits and qualifications: the duty did not arise anterior to the instrument. This case is very materially different from that of Fenton v. Goundry, (13 East, 459,) lately decided by this court, which was the case of a bill drawn generally, but accepted payable at a particular place, which special acceptance we considered merely as importing the intention of the party, that he would be found when the bill became due, at that place, as his house of business, where he should be prepared to pay it ;

there the acceptance payable at the place was no part of the original conformation of the bill itself ; but here the words restrictive of payment at the place named, are incorporated in the original form of the instrument, which alone creates the contract and duty of the party. This action upon the note will not lie, unless the plaintiff has demanded payment at the appointed place; and I cannot but say it is very convenient that such a condition should be incorporated in the note itself ; for it would be very inconvenient, that the makers of notes of this description should be liable to answer them every where, when it is notorious that they have made provision for them at a particular place, where only they engage to pay them; then if the request at the place be a condition precedent, it should have been averred, and for want of such an averment, the declaration is bad ; but I still think this is distinguishable from the case of Fenton v. Goundry.
　Dickenson v. Bowes and others, 16 East. 110. Payment of a promissory note made payable at a certain place named in it. must be demanded there before the makers can be sued on it. Lord Ellenborough, C. J. said, that it had already been decided upon demurrer, that if the particular place of payment be embodied in the note, it was part of the condition on which it was made payable ; that it should be presented for payment at that place. See also Howe v Bowes, 16 East, 112, and 5 Taunt. 130 S. P.
　Bowes v. Howe, 5 Taunt. 30. Error in Exchequer Chamber from King's Bench (16 East, 112.) A note, promising in th. body of it, to pay, on demand, at a particular place, must be presented, and a demand of payment made at that place unless the maker discharge the holders from the presentment and demand; and the presentment and demand must be alleged, unless a discharge is shown.

...en case, at least as respects a promissory note, the presentment and demand must be alleged in the declaration.[k] And if the stipulation at the bottom of a note, for payment at a particular place, be *printed* before the note is complete, it has been holden in the King's Bench, that in such case, a presentment there is necessary.[l] So if the body of the bill, or the address at the foot of it, contains a request to the drawee to pay the bill in London, an acceptance payable at a particular place in the metropolis, requires a presentment there.[m] But still it was said, that there is no necessity to allege or prove notice of the dishonour to the acceptor or maker ;[n] and provided a presentment, and re-

---

[k] Same cases and Roche *v.* Campbell, 3 Campb. 247. Indorsee against indorser of a promissory note, describing the note as payable generally, but in the body it was made payable at a particular place. *Per* Lord Ellenborough. I think there is a fatal variance between them ; the declaration represents the promissory note as containing an absolute and unqualified promise to pay the money; but by the instrument produced, the maker only promises to pay, upon the specific condition that the payment is demanded at a particular place. We have lately held, that where the place of payment is mentioned in the body of the note, it forms a material part of the instrument. There seems to be no doubt, therefore, that it could be set out in the declaration. Plaintiff nonsuited.

[l] Trecothick *v.* Edwin, 1 Stark. 468. The whole of a promissory note being printed, except the names, dates, and sum, and a place of payment inserted at the bottom of the note being also printed, it was held, that a special presentment there is necessary. This was an action on a promissory note made by the defendant. The note was in the usual form, " I promise to pay, &c. at Barclay, Tritton, and Co." The whole of the note was printed, except the names of the parties, the sum, and the date ; the words " at Barclay, Tritton, and Co." were at the bottom of the note, and were also printed. It was contended for the defendant, that since the note was made payable at a particular place specified in printed characters, it was incumbent on the plaintiff to prove a special presentment. Lord Ellenborough held, that it was necessary to prove a special presentment, since the stipulation for payment at a particular place, being printed, was to be considered as a part of the note, having been made at the same time. A special presentment was afterwards proved. Verdict for the plaintiff.

[m] Garnett *v.* Woodcock and others, 1 Stark. 475. A bill is drawn, payable in London, and is accepted payable at a particular banker's in London (semble,) a presentment at that banker's must be proved in an action against the acceptor.

Hodge *v.* Fillis and another, 3 Campb. 463. This was an action by the indorsee against the acceptors of a bill of exchange,

drawn in the following form:—Cork, 12th April, 1813,—2314*l.* 15*s.* 11*d.* at two months' date of this our first of exchange, second and third of the same tenor and date, not paid, pay to our order 2314*l.* 15*s.* 11*d.* and charge the same to account as advised.—W. & A. Maxwell.—To Messrs. Filils and Co. Plymouth.—Payable in London. The bill was accepted by the defendants, " payable at Sir John Perring's and Co. Bankers, London." The first count of the declaration did not state that the bill was made payable at any particular place, either by the drawers or acceptors. The second count stated that it was drawn payable in London, and accepted payable at Perring's and Co's., and contained an averment, that when due, it was presented there for payment. The plaintiff having proved the partnership of the defendants, their hand-writing as acceptors, and the indorsement of W. & A. Maxwell, closed his case. ——— Gifford, for the defendants, contended, that upon this evidence, the plaintiff was not entitled to a verdict. He could not recover on the first count, for that did not properly describe the bill of exchange ; the circumstance of the bill being made payable in London was an essential part of the original contract. The second count described the bill properly, but contained a material averment which had not been proved, viz. that the bill was presented when due at the banker's in London, where it was made payable by the acceptors; without at all considering the effect of an acceptance making the bill payable at a particular place, where it was drawn without any mention of a place of payment, there could be no doubt, that where a particular place of payment is denoted both by the drawers and acceptors, that becomes a term of the contract between the parties, and an averment that the bill was presented for payment there, cannot possibly be rejected as irrelevant. Lord Ellenborough expressed himself to be of this opinion.

[n] Pearce *v.* Pemberly and others, 3 Campb. 261. In an action against the maker of a promissory note, payable at a banking-house, it is not necessary to prove that he had notice of its dishonour. This was an action against the makers of a promissory note, " payable at Vere, Bruce

quest to pay at the particular place, be averred in the declaration,
with the general refusal to pay at the end of the declaration, that wa-
holden to be sufficient without alleging a special refusal at the particular place.°

[253]   On the other hand both the courts agreed that if a promissory note
were payable generally in the body of it, and there was a memorandum
only at the foot denoting that payment should be made at a particular
place, such memorandum would not qualify the contract, and it was not
necessary for the holder to allege or prove any presentment at the particular place,ᵖ and if it be alleged in the declaration that the defen-

and Co's.," being presented there for payment when due, the answer was, "not
sufficient effects." The only point made
for the defendant was, that they were entitled to notice of its dishonour; the place
where it was made payable being, according to recent decisions, a material part of
the instrument; it exactly resembled a bill
of exchange, the bankers standing in the
place of the drawees. Had it been a bill
of exchange, the defendants were clearly
entitled to notice, for they had some effects
in the hands of Vere, Bruce, and Co. and
there was the same reason for their receiving notice, although the form of the instrument was different. They might suppose that the bankers would pay the note;
and they ought, as early as possible, to
have had information that it would be necessary for them to provide for it themselves, and that their balance at the banking-house remained unappropriated. The
necessity of notice to the maker of a
promissory note of its dishonour, results
from the determination, that his liability
does not attach, till payment has been
demanded at the place where it is expressed to be payable. But Lord Ellenborough clearly held, that notice was
unnecessary; and the plaintiff had a verdict.
   ° Butterworth v. Lord Le Despencer, 3
M. & S. 150. Benson v. White, 4 Dow's
Rep. 334. S. P. Declaration against the
maker of a promissory note payable at a
particular place, and avers a presentment
at the place, and that the defendant licet
sæpius requisitus hath hitherto refused,
and still doth refuse to pay. Held well
upon demurrer, and that a refusal at the
particular place need not be averred. Lord
Ellenborough, C. J. said, a presentment of
the note at the house was a request there
to pay the note, and the non-payment of it
is a refusal at the house; if it were necessary that there should be a specific refusal
in a given form, or by some positive act,
it might be argued, that this general refusal would not be good, but a refusal need
not be by an affirmative act; the not paying, which is only a negative act, or shutting the door, is a refusal; all therefore that
is necessary is, that there should be a
special request, and here a special request

is averred. In Saunderson v. Bowes, w·
held, that we could not infer a special
presentment from the allegation of a
general refusal; all we say here is, that
negation of payment every where is a
negation of payment at the place. Dampier, J. The question is, whether the
general averment at the end of the declaration does not in effect allege, that the
defendant did not pay the note at the
place where it was made payable. Presentment at the house must be averred,
but it has never been decided that a special refusal must appear upon the record,
and to determine that it must, would be
to impose a grievous burthen on the plaintiff. Judgment for the plaintiff.
   ᵖ Saunderson v. Judge, 2 Hen. Bla. 509
Bayl. 96. A note made payable at the foot
of it, at the plaintiff's banking-house, was
indorsed to them, and when it became due
the maker having no effects in their hands,
they wrote to one of the indorsers to say
it was not honoured, and afterwards brought
an action against him, but it appearing that
they had made no demand on the maker
they were nonsuited. On showing cause
however, against a rule for a new trial, the
court held, that it was no part of the contract in this case that the note should be
paid at the house of Saunderson and Co.,
and therefore that was not necessary to be
stated in the declaration, and that it was
sufficient to present the note where the
maker made it payable, and as the persons
at whose house it was made payable were
themselves the holders, it was sufficient for
them to refer to their books and see whether they had effects in hands, and a new
trial was granted.
   Wild v. Rennard, 1 Campb. 425, note.
In this case Bayley, J. held, that if a
promissory note be made payable at a
particular place, there is no necessity of
proving, in an action against the maker,
that it has been presented there for payment. And upon this case being cited in
Sanderson v. Bowes, 14 East, 500. Bayley, J. said, that as far as he could i
collect, the place was not incorporated
with the body of the note ; it was only
mentioned in a memorandum at the
bottom. And in Callaghan v. Ayle
2 Campb. 551, and Saunderson v. Judge

fiant made the note payable at the particular place, and that direction **1st. When** were not on the instrument itself, but merely at the foot, this even **present-** would be a fatal misdescription of the instrument.⁋ But the courts, **ment is ne-** or at least some of the Judges, differed as to the effect of an accept- **cessary.** ance payable at a particular place, or a memorandum at the foot of the instrument, that it should be there payable. The Court of King's

2 Hen. Bla. 509. the same distinction is taken.

In Price v. Mitchell, 4 Campb. 200. Gibbs, C. J. ruled accordingly ; he said, I am of opinion that the words at the foot of this promissory note are only a memorandum where payment may be demanded ; had they been inserted in the body of the note, they certainly would have formed a part of the contract and evidence of a presentment for payment at Vere's, Smart, and Co's. would have been necessary to charge the defendant. I find this distinction taken in Bayley on Bills, last edition, p. 96. If a note be made payable at a particular place, and that place be mentioned in the body of the note, presentment for payment must be made at that place, but where the place is mentioned in the margin, it does not appear that such presentment is necessary ; several cases are referred to, which seem to sanction the distinction. Indeed, where the direction to the place of payment is mentioned in the margin or at the foot of the note (as here) the inspection and perusal of the instrument, I think, show that this was not intended to be any condition to the absolute promise to pay contained in the body of the note. His Lordship refused to save the point, and the plaintiff had a verdict.

Richards v. Lord Milsingtown, Holt C. N. P. 364, in notes. This was an action by the indorsee against the maker of a promissory note. The note was in the common form ; but in the margin, and underneath the name of the maker was written, "payable at Bruce and Co's." The declaration did not state that the bill had been presented at Bruce and Co's. ; and no evidence of that fact was tendered by the plaintiff's counsel.— Gibb, C. J. the words "payable at Bruce and Co's." are not introduced in the body of the bill ; they are only inserted in the margin. It is a mere memorandum, not coupled with or qualifying the promise. Look at this instrument ; and the promissory note is perfect without it. I say nothing as to any other case, I find I had already determined the point in Price v. Mitchell, and I feel disposed to preserve my own consistency ; it would be difficult to say in most cases, that what is law as regards bills of exchange, should not be law as respects promissory notes.

1 Exon v. Russell, 4 M. & S. 505.— Where the indorsee declared against the maker of a promissory note, and alleged,

CHITTY ON BILLS.

that he promised to pay, &c. and *made the same payable,* and to be paid *according to the tenor and effect at the house of Messrs. B. and Co.* London, and upon production of the note at the trial, it appeared that the address at the house of Messrs. B. and Co. was not a part of the note, but only a memorandum at the foot of the note. Held, that this was a variance. Lord Ellenborough, C. J. the plaintiff has taken upon himself to aver that such is the import of the note ; he has therefore not truly stated the note, for he has stated that it was made payable at a particular place. Therefore he ought to have been nonsuited upon the ground that he has misdescribed the note as payable at a particular place, which it is not, the address being no part of the contract, but a memorandum. Bayley, J. the plaintiff takes on him to aver it to be part of the note, that it is made payable at a particular place. It is a misdescription of the instrument declared upon.

But in Pannell v. Woodroffe, Sittings after Hilary Term, 1819, at Westminster, before Abbott, J., payee against maker of a note. The declaration stated that the defendant made his promissory note bearing date, &c. by which said note the defendant three months after the date thereof, promised to pay to the said plaintiff or order the sum of 100l. value received, *and made the said note payable at 82, Castle Street, Holborn.* And then and there delivered the said note to the said plaintiff, by means, &c. (stating the liability and promise to pay according to the tenor and effect of the note, but not averring any presentment for payment.) The place of payment was not mentioned in the body of the note, but only by way of memorandum at the bottom ; whereupon E. Lawes, on the authority of the above case of Exon v. Russell, contended, that the first count was open to the objection of variance, but Abbott, J. overruled the objection.

Lawes, in Easter Term, moved for a rule for a new trial or in arrest of judgment, on the ground that the note given in evidence varied from the special statement of it in the declaration, and that that statement importing a special place of payment, the count was bad for want of an averment of presentment. But the court held that the declaration did not import any special or limited promise to pay at a particular place, and that this case was distinguishable from that of Exon v. Russell.

H h

1st. When
present-
ment is ne-
cessary.

Bench held that such direction does not qualify the contract of the acceptor, and that consequently it is not necessary to allege or prove compliance with such direction.[r] And it was decided, that if a person accept a bill, payable at his bankers, and the holder neglected to present it, and eight months after it was due, the bankers having

[r] Fenton v. Goundry, 13 East, 459.—2 Campb. 656, 7. Bayl. 97. Drawer against acceptor of a bill, the declaration stated that the defendant accepted the bill payable at Sykes and Co's., and thereby became liable and promised to pay according to the tenor and effect of the bill, and of his acceptance. There was no averment of the presentment for payment to Sykes and Co., nor of any demand upon the defendant other than the common allegation, that defendant, "although often requested," had not paid the bill. The defendant demurred specially, and assigned for cause the want of an averment of a due presentment for payment, and after argument the court (Le Blanc, J. absente,) held, that the place mentioned in the acceptance was only an intimation to the holder where the acceptor was to be found, that it formed no part of the contract that the bill should be presented there, and that the acceptance, though stated to be payable at a particular place, bound the party to pay the bill generally and universally; the court, however, being desirous of looking into the case of Callaghan v. Aylett, which was cited, gave judgment nisi for the plaintiff, but they did not mention the case again in the course of the term, and the judgment therefore stood for the plaintiff.

Lyon v. Sundries and another, 1 Campb. 423. Indorsee against acceptor declared on generally, but it appeared in evidence that the bill was accepted payable at a particular place, objection on this account; per Lord Ellenborough. How can you make the words, "at Hankey and Co's." more than a mere memorandum? The acceptor of a bill of exchange is liable universally. This very point was brought before the court some time ago, when the judges were all of opinion, that such words formed no part of the contract, and did not require to be set out in the declaration.

Head and another v. Sewell, Holt C. N. P. 368. In an action against the acceptor of a bill of exchange made payable at a particular place by a memorandum at the foot of the bill, it is not necessary to prove a presentment or a demand at that place, but the acceptor is generally and universally liable. Gibbs, C. J., after thirty-five years, in which I have never known this objection to prevail, I cannot admit the necessity of this proof in an action against the acceptor, where the bill is accepted "payable at a particular place," as in the present case it is not necessary to prove a demand at that place. He is generally and universally liable upon such acceptance; it

has often been so determined. I know there are conflicting cases, but I shall not require this proof.

Huffam v. Ellis, 3 Taunt. 415, in the House of Lords, 10th April, 1810. Bayl. 96. An averment that a bill accepted payable at a banker's was when due presented to the bankers for payment, according to the tenor and effect of the bill, and of the acceptors acceptance thereof, and that as well the bankers as the acceptors refused payment, shall be supported after judgment on a sham plea. And it shall be intended that the bill was presented for payment to the acceptor himself, at the house of those persons, semble. For evidence of those facts would be admissible under such an allegation, and not repugnant to it.

Rowe v. Williams, Holt C. N. P. 366, in Trinity Term, 1816. This came before the King's Bench upon a special demurrer to a declaration upon a bill of exchange. That case was precisely the same as Fenton v. Goundry, ante, 254. It was an action against the acceptor of a bill accepted "payable at Sir John Perring and Co's," and there was an averment of the presentment when it became due at Sir John Perring and Co's. The counsel, in support of the demurrer, cited Gammon v. Schmoll, (post, 257,) but the court of King's Bench refused to hear the case argued; saying, that they considered the point as having been determined in their judgment in Fenton v. Goundry. Mr. J. Holroyd read a MS. note of the case of Smith v. De la Fontaine, (Bayl. 128,) tried before Lord Chief Justice Mansfield, in 1785; in which his Lordship held, that words accompanying an acceptance "payable at a particular place," or the words, "accepted, payable at, &c." were not words restricting or qualifying the acceptor's liability, but rendering him generally and universally liable, and that it was not necessary to prove a demand at the particular place in an action against such acceptor. Lord Ellenborough added, "that whatever cases might be adduced in favour of or against the doctrine laid down by K. B. in Fenton v. Goundry, an invincible argument with him for the opinion there given was, the constant and undeviating usage of merchants; who never considered such an acceptance to be a restrictive acceptance; that it was a mere matter of convenient arrangement, and did not raise any obligation on the part of the holder, to demand payment at the particular place." Upon this judgment a writ of error was brought in the house of Lords; see Holt C. N. P. 366, 7. and 2 Brod. & Bing. 165.

funds of the acceptors in their hands, became bankrupt, the acceptor was nevertheless not discharged from liability by such neglect of the holder.* Some of the Judges of the court of Common Pleas on the contrary held, that such a memorandum qualifies the contract of the acceptor, and that in an action against him as well as any other party, a presentment at the particular place must be alleged and proved.†

1st. When presentment is necessary.

[257]

* Sebag v. Abitbol, 4 M. & S. 462.—1 Stark. 79. S. C. A bill of exchange payable at a bankers in London, which by reason of being mislaid was not presented for payment, but the acceptor was some months afterwards informed of its being mislaid, was held not to be discharged, but that the drawer might set off in an action brought against him by the acceptor, although the bankers at whose house the bill was payable failed in the interval, and the acceptor had at all times up to the failure of the bankers a balance in their hands sufficient to cover the acceptance. Lord Ellenborough, C. J. Laches is a neglect to do something which by law a man is obliged to do, whether any neglect to call at a house where a man informs me that I may get the money amounts to laches, depends upon whether I am obliged to call there. This acceptance, though it might be an authority to the bankers to pay the bill, being made payable at their house, is not in express terms an order upon them to pay, as was the case of Bishop v. Chitty, (2 Stra. 1194. Bayl. 129.) where the language of the acceptance was immediately that of a check upon the bankers. I confess I am unable to see any laches in the defendant upon either ground. The plaintiff is informed that the bill is not to be found, after which there surely was not any occasion for him to keep a fund at the house where it was made payable. How can it be said that the plaintiff, after notice that his bill no longer existed, was bound to keep money at his bankers to answer the bill in perpetuum? It seems to me that after such a notice he was at liberty to withdraw his funds, and therefore whatever loss may happen to him by keeping them there must be his loss, and not the loss of the defendant. Bayley, J. As to other points on which there has been some difference of opinion in the two courts, I shall be very ready to change my opinion if ultimately I should see occasion, but I cannot help feeling considerable difficulty upon that point. If this is to be considered as a qualified acceptance, it follows that the holder would have a right to refuse it, he being entitled to have an unconditional acceptance; and indeed, as I rather think, being bound to require it. And if he take such an acceptance as this, payable at a particular place, it may be a question whether he ought not to give notice to all the parties to the bill, and whether by omitting to do so he does not discharge them. In this view of the question, it becomes an important one, and deserves to be well considered; it is true that the holder is not bound to present the bill for acceptance, but I have always understood, that if he does present it, and a qualified acceptance is given, he is bound to give notice. If then the circumstance of the bill's being accepted, payable at a bankers, is to throw on the holder the obligation to present at the particular place, the consequence will be, that any intermediate indorser who may be called on to pay, and does pay the bill, will in his action, over against another party to the bill, be saddled with the proof of an additional fact, beyond what he would have to prove if the acceptance were a general acceptance. This is a point of view which seems to me to be very important, and I rather think that it has not been presented in this view to the minds of those learned persons from whom we are said to differ. Rule absolute.

† Callaghan v. Aglett, C. P. 51 Geo. 3. 3 Taunt. 397, 2 Campb. 549. Bayl. 97. In an action against the acceptor of a bill, it appeared that the bill was accepted, payable at Messrs. Ramsbottoms, bankers, London; and two objections were taken to the plaintiff's right to recover; first, that there was a variance between the acceptance proved, which was a special one, and that averred in the declaration, which was a general one; and secondly, that there was no proof of a presentment for payment at the place where the bill by acceptance had been made payable; a verdict was found for the plaintiff, subject to the opinion of the court upon these points, which were reserved; a rule nisi to set aside this verdict and enter non-suit was obtained; and after cause shown, the court (Mansfield, C. J. absente) held, that a place where a bill is made payable must be considered as part of the contract between the acceptor and the holder. That this was a special and qualified acceptance, binding the acceptor to pay at Ramsbottoms, and not universally. They said it seemed fair, that when a party had provided funds at his bankers for the due satisfaction of a bill, he should be allowed to protect himself from the risk of being arrested upon it by a malicious creditor. They referred to Parker v. Gordon, 7 East, 385, and said it could make no difference (for this purpose) whether the action were against the drawer or acceptor. Rule absolute.

Gammon and another v. Schmoll, 5

1st. When presentment is necessary.

The different reasons in support of each side of these opinions will be found in the cases in the notes.[u] It was observed that the acceptance of a bill seems to be as much the original contract of the acceptor, as a note in the original contract of the maker;[x] and as it was admitted that the drawee may make a qualified or conditional acceptance, and thus narrow the liability which a general acceptance would create, it was difficult to say that he might not qualify his contract and liability as to the place of payment,[y] and whether this be done in the

Taunt. 344. 1 Marsh. 83. C. P. Hil. Term, 1814. In this case it was held, that if a person to whom a bill is directed generally accepts it payable at a particular place, the holder needs not receive such a qualified acceptance, but may resort to the drawer as for non-acceptance. But that such an acceptance is equivalent to an acceptance payable at the particular place and so where else, and narrows the general liability of the acceptor to a liability to pay at that place only. And that if the holder consents to receive such an acceptance, it interposes in the contract a condition precedent, that the holder shall present the bill to the acceptor for payment at the place specified: and therefore declaring on the bill the plaintiffs must aver performance of this like other conditions precedent, by showing a presentment to the acceptor at the place specified, and that whether the action be against the drawer or against the acceptor. Vaughan, Serjeant, argued, that a simple acceptance subjects the acceptor to the largest responsibility that words can create; no presentment any where is necessary, the acceptor is bound to follow the bill and pay the holder if he is within the four seas; he can add nothing which will enlarge his obligation. There is very good reason why the restriction should prevail; suppose the acceptor possessed funds at Bath or in Paris, he is perfectly safe in giving a qualified acceptance if the necessity exists of presenting the bill there, otherwise he cannot venture the bill at all; and if while his funds are stationary he cannot prevent his liability from being ubiquitary, that doctrine will greatly circumscribe the issuing of similar bills. But it is unnecessary to consider the reason of the condition, if a condition be annexed to an acceptance, the condition must be complied with however arbitrary or absurd. The holder is not bound to receive the acceptance with new qualifications thus engrafted on it. But if he does receive the bill thus qualified, he must abide by the qualifications. Chambre, J. I think the case is clear upon rules of plain common sense and understanding, without going through all the cases; a man is not bound to receive a limited and qualified acceptance, he may refuse it and resort to the drawer, but if he does receive it he must conform to the terms of it. The reason given by the court of King's Bench, in Fenton v.

Goundry, shows that they were themselves very doubtful of the grounds of their judgment. It is there said that the meaning was only to point out where the acceptor transacts his business, few people receive an acceptance without previously knowing where the acceptor transacts his business, but if he meant only to point out where he lived, it would be sufficient to write on the bill his name and place of abode; but what is the meaning of these words "accepted payable at?" they have a meaning, they impose a condition, and the person receiving such an acceptance must comply with the condition, and in pleading must show his compliance. It would greatly circumscribe the negotiation of bills of exchange if this were not so, for they would, instead of being of general accommodation, be restrained in their use to such persons in trade as have a fixed place of business, where clerks and servants are always in attendance to pay the bills. Dallas, J. The argument had proceeded on the foundation that the acceptor is always a debtor to the drawer, but that is by no means universally the case, on the contrary, the case is frequently otherwise. In one of the largest branches of our commerce, that with the West India islands, the acceptor is universally in advance. I put the question if the acceptance had contained the words (and not elsewhere,) whether the acceptor would be liable any where else, and the counsel did not deny the limitation; if so, the question is, whether the words "accepted payable at," do not constitute a contract, and whether they are not equivalent to express words of exclusion; and I think they are. The party need not have received from the acceptor living at Bath a limited contract of acceptance, but he has thought fit so to do, and he must perform his condition. Judgment for the defendant. But Gibbs, C. J. appears in other cases to have decided otherwise; see note, 253, and Richards v. Lord Milsington, Holt, C. N. P. 364, and ante. 253, note.

[u] And see the cases and arguments in Rowe v. Young, 2 Brod. & B. 165.
[x] Bayl. 185, n. 1.
[y] In Mitford v. Walcot, Ld. Raym. 575 Holt, C. J. said, "if a bill be payable at London, and the person on whom it is drawn accepts it, but name no house where he will pay it, the party that has

body of the bill or by memorandum at the foot, yet if it were intended 1st. When presentment is necessary. to qualify the contract it should have that operation without regard to the arrangement of the words. In practice it is the invariable course amongst bankers and merchants to present bills accepted payable at a particular place, at such place.

This question was finally discussed and decided in the House of Lords, in the case of Rowe v. Young,[a] in which it was held, that if a bill of exchange be accepted payable at a particular place, (as thus, "accepted payable at Sir John Perring and Co. bankers, London,") the declaration in an action on such bill against the acceptor must aver presentment at that place, and the averment must be proved. This decision occasioned the passing of the statute 2 Geo. 4. c. 78, which, after referring to the above decision, and reciting the resulting inconvenience in practice, and that drawees may, it they think fit, qualify their acceptance by a more precise form of acceptance, enacts, "That after the 1st "of August, 1821, if any person shall accept a bill of exchange paya-"ble at the house of a banker or other place, without further expres-"sions in his acceptance, such acceptance shall be deemed and taken "to be, *to all intents and purposes,* a general acceptance of such bill; "but if the acceptor shall in his acceptance express that he accepts the "bill payable at a banker's house or other place *only, and not otherwise* "*or elsewhere,* such acceptance shall be deemed and taken to be, to all "intents and purposes, a qualified acceptance of such bill, and the ac-"ceptor shall not be liable to pay the said bill, except on default of "payment when such payment shall have been first duly demanded at "such banker's house or other place." (321)

In a case of foreign bill, where the course of exchange has altered, the acceptor will only be liable to pay according to the rate of it, when the bill became due;[a] and if the acceptor undertook by his acceptance to pay within a certain period after demand, he may insist on the want

[259]

---

the bill is not bound to be satisfied with this acceptance." See also Bayl. 86. It should seem therefore that there is no objertion to the holder's receiving a special acceptance stating the place of payment. But in Head v. Sewell, Holt, C. N. P. 335, Gibbs, C. J. seems to have been of opinion, that a special acceptance payable at a particular place, does not render it necessary to prove a presentment there.

[a] 2 Brod. & Bing. 165.

[a] Poth. pl. 174.

---

(321) In *New York* it has been held in an action against an acceptor that the holder need not prove any demand of payment at the place where the bill was accepted to be paid, but it is the business of the acceptor to prove that he was ready at the day and place appointed, and that no one came to receive the money, and that he was always ready to pay. *Foden v. Sharp,* 4 Johns. Rep. 183. See also *Lang v. Brailsford,* 1 Bay's Rep. 222.

Where the cashier of a bank indorses a promissory note, the property of the bank, for the purpose of causing demand and notice to be given, the authority of the bank for the purpose may be implied. *Hartford Bank v. Parry,* 17 Mass. 95.

It is not necessary that the demand or notice should be made by the party to the note or bill: it is sufficient if done by a notary. *Hartford Bank v. Stedman,* 3 Conn. Rep. 489.

A parol authority is sufficient to constitute a person agent for the purpose of making a demand on the drawer of a promissory note. *Shed v. Bret,* 1 Pick. 401.

A demand of payment of a note by an agent having any parol authority as a notary or the mere possession of the paper is sufficient; and such agent is competent to give notice of non-payment. *Bank of Utica v. Smith,* 18 Johns 230.

2dly. By If at the time of presentment, the drawee be *dead*, the holder should
& to whom inquire after his personal representative, and present the bill to him;[t]
and where and in case there be no representative, should demand payment at the
the pre- house of the deceased. [u](335)
sentment
should be
made.

It is sufficient to require payment of the person on whom the bill is
drawn, and it is unnecessary, in case of default of payment, to make
any demand on the drawer, previously to an action against the
indorser.[x]

3dly. Time The time when a bill or note, &c. ought to be presented for pay-
when a bill. ment, when it is payable at a certain time after it is drawn, as in the
&c. should case of a bill payable after date, or after sight, or at usance, depends
be present- on the terms of the instrument itself;[y] and when no time of payment
ed for pay-
ment. is expressed, as in the case of bills payable at sight, or on demand, the
time when presentment for payment should be made, depends on the
local situation of the parties, and other circumstances, necessarily
varying in every particular case. It was once thought, that the propriety of a presentment for payment with respect to the time when it
should be made, was, in all cases, a question for the determination of
a jury; but the decisions of juries having been found to be very much
at variance from each other,[z] and consequently to have rendered the
commercial law in that respect very uncertain, and the usage of merchants having been long since established, it is now settled to be the
province of the *court* to determine the time when a presentment ought
to be made.[a]

The circumstance of the holder having received a bill very near the
time of its becoming due, constitutes no excuse for a neglect to
present it for payment on maturity, for he might renounce it if he did
not choose to undertake the duty, and send the bill back to the party
from whom he received it; but if he keep it he is bound to use
reasonable and due diligence in presenting it: and therefore where the
[263] plaintiff in Yorkshire, on the 26th of December, renewed a bill of exchange, payable in London, which became due on the 28th, and kept it
in his own hands until the 29th, when he sent it by post to his bankers
in Lincoln, who duly forwarded it to London for the presentment, and

not, see Cheek v. Roper, 5 Esp. Rep. 175.   155. Phillips v. Phillips, 2 Freem. 247.
Bayl. 95, 6.   Crawley v. Crowther, id. 257. Tindall r.
[t] Ante, 165. Molloy, b. 2. c. 10. s. 34.   Brown, 1 T. R. 168, 9.
Poth. pl, 146. Bayl. 95.   [a] Bayl. 103, 4. 123, ante, 224, 5. Darb.-
[u] Poth. pl. 146. Mar. 134. Bayl. 95.   shire v. Parker, 6 East, 11, 12. Parker
[x] Heylin v. Adamson, 2 Burr. 669. Ha-   v. Gordon, 7 East, 886. Tindall v. Brown.
milton v. Mackrell, Rep. Temp. Hardw.   1 T. R. 168, 9. 170. Brown v. Collinson,
332.   Beawes, pl. 229. Brown v. Harraden.
[y] Bayl. 102, 3.   4 T. R. 148. Kyd, 45. Molloy, b. 2.
[z] Allen v. Dockwra, 1 Salk. 127. Main-   c. 10. acc. Russell v. Langstaffe, Dougl.
waring v. Harrison, Stra. 506. Coleman v.   515. Muilman v. D'Eugino, 2 H. B. 565,
Sayer, id. 829. Darrach v. Savage, 1 Show.   569. contra.

(835) It has been decided in *Massachusetts*, that if the maker of a note die, and
an administrator be appointed before it becomes due, no demand on the administrator is necessary to charge the indorser, so that notice of the death and non-payment be
duly given to the indorser, unless the maturity of the note happens more than a year after the maker's death. This decision is grounded upon some supposed material difference
between the situation of an administrator in *Massachusetts* and that of one in *England*
Hall v. *Burr*, 12 Mass. Rep. 86.

the bill was dishonoured, it was held that the plaintiff had by his laches lost his remedy against the drawer and indorsers.[b]

When a bill, &c. is payable at *usance*, or at a certain time *after* date or sight, or *after* demand, it is not payable at the precise time mentioned in the bill, *days of grace* being allowed ;[c] but in the case of bills, &c. payable *on demand*, no such days are allowed.

Before we enter into a particular inquiry when bills, &c. payable at usance after date, after sight, after a particular event, at sight, or on demand, ought to be presented for payment, it may not be improper to make a few observations relative to *the mode of computing time* in the case of bills in general, and some remarks with respect to the *days of grace*, and as to *usances.*

When a bill is drawn at a place using one style, and payable on a day certain at a place using another, the time when the bill becomes due must be calculated according to the *style*[d] of the place where it is payable ; because the contract created by the making a bill of exchange is understood to have been made at that place, and consequently should be construed according to the laws of it.[e] In other works it is laid down, that upon a bill drawn at a place using one style and payable at a place using another, if the time is to be reckoned from the date it shall be computed according to the style of the place at which it was drawn, otherwise according to the style of the place where it is payable ; and in the former case the date must be reduced or carried forward to the style of the place where the bill is payable, and the time reckoned from thence.[f] Thus, on a bill dated the 1st of March, old style, and payable here one month after date, the time must be computed from the 19th February new style ; and on a bill dated the 19th February new style, and payable at St. Petersburgh one month after date, from the 1st of March old style.[g] And although in some cases it has been considered, that when computation is to be made *from* an act done, the day in which the act is done is to be included,[h] the law relating to bills of exchange is different ; for the custom of merchants is settled, that where a bill is payable at usance, or at so many days after sight, or from the date, the day of the date, or of the acceptance, must be *excluded* ;[i] and therefore, if a bill drawn payable

[264]

[b] Anderton *v.* Beck, 16 East, 248.
[c] Brown *v.* Harraden, 4 T. R. 141. Leftley *v.* Mills, 4 T. R. 170. Poth. pl. 14, 15 Mar. 76.
[d] As to the old and new style, see Kyd, on Bills, 7, &c. All places where we, in Great Britain, are in the habit of negotiating bills, compute their time as we do, (except that Russia adheres to the old style) by years reckoned in sextiles, from the birth of our Saviour, and divided each into 12 months, and 365 (or in every fourth year 366) days. Bayl. 112.
[e] Poth. pl. 155. Beawes, pl. 251. Mar. 102, ante, 93. acc. Kyd. 8. contra. Old style, it is said ; still prevails in Muscovey, Denmark, Holstein, Hamburgh, Utrecht, Gueldres, East Friesland, Geneva, and in all the protestant principalities in Germany, and the cantons of Switzerland. Beawes, pl. 253. Kyd,

7, 8. Mar. 56. Bayl. 112; see the preceding note.
[f] Bayl. 102, 3.
[g] Bayl. 113.
[h] Glassington *v.* Rawlins, 3 East, 407. Cramlington *v.* Evans, 2 Ventr. 308, 310. Castle *v* Burditt, 3 T. R. 623. Kyd, 6; but see observations of Lord Ellenborough in Watson *v.* Pears, 2 Campb. 296, from which it appears that in many cases the day is to be excluded; see also Pugh *v.* Duke of Leeds, Cowp. 714. Glassington *v.* Rawlins, 3 East, 407. Lester *v.* Garland, 15 Ves. 454.
[i] Bellasis *v.* Hester, Ld. Raym. 280. Lutw. 1591. S. C. Coleman *v.* Sayer, 1 Barn. B. R. 303. Poth. pl. 13, 15. Campbell *v.* French, 6 T. R. 212. Beawes, pl. 252. Bayl. 113. Kyd, 6. Lester *v.* Garland, 15 Ves. 254. acc. May *v.* Cooper, Fort. 376, contra.

3dly. *Time* when the presentment should be made. ten days after sight, be presented on the 1st day of a month, the ten days expire on the 11th, and the bill, by the addition of the days of grace when they are three in number, becomes due on the 14th.[k] When a bill, &c. is drawn payable at usance, or at a certain time after date, and it is not dated, the time when it is payable must be computed from the day it issued, exclusively thereof.[l](338)

Days of grace. The *days* of *grace* which are allowed to the drawee, are so called because they were formerly merely gratuitous, and not to be claimed as a *right* by the person on whom it was incumbent to pay the bill, and were dependent on the inclination of the holder; they still retain the name of grace, though the custom of merchants, recognised by law, has long reduced them to a certainty, and established a *right* in the acceptor to claim them, in all cases of bills or notes payable at usance, or after date, after sight, or after a certain event.[m](338) The number of these days varies according to the custom of the different countries.[n] [265] The following is a list of the days of grace established by the Law Merchant in different countries.[o]

England, Scotland, Wales, Ireland, Bergamo, and Vienna,	3 days.
Frankfort, out of the fair time, - - - - -	4 do.
Leipsick, Naumberg, and Augsburgh, - - - -	5 do.
Venice, Amsterdam, Rotterdam, Middleburgh, Antwerp, Cologn, Breslau, Nurembugh, Lisbon, and Portugal,	6 do.
Naples, - - - - - - - - -	8 do.
Dantzick, Koningsburg, and France, - - - -	10 do.[p]
Hamburgh and Stockholm, - - - - - -	12 do.[q]
Spain, - - - - - - - - -	14 do.

[k] Kyd, 6, 7.
[l] Hague v. French, 3 Bos. & Pul. 173, Armitt v. Breame, Ld. Raym. 1076. Kyd, 7, ante, 59.
[m] Brown v. Harraden, 4 T. R. 151, 2. *Terme de grace, n'est terme de grace que de nom, parce que c'est* humanitatis ratione *qu'elle la accorde, et pour le distinguer de celui porte par la lettre; il est reellement terme* de droit *puisque c'est la loi qui le donne.* Poth. pl. 187. See Coleman v. Sayer, Barnard Rep. B. R. 303. Vin. Ab. tit. *Bills of Exchange;* b. 9. Brown

v. Harraden, 4 T. R. 151, where it is said to have been once decided, that days of grace are not allowable on inland bills.
[n] Beawes, 260. 1st edit. 449. Bayl. 110.
[o] Beawes, pl. 260. Mar. 94. Kyd, 9. Bayl. 110.
[p] Poth. pl. 189.
[q] Kyd, 9. Bayl. 110 ; but see Hamburgh ordinance, art. 16, 17, and quære if not eleven days ; see the next cases.

(338) The same rule is recognised in the United States. *Henry* v. *Jones,* 8 Mass. Rep. 453. *Woodbridge* v. *Brigham,* 12 Mass. Rep. 403. *Jackson* v. *Richards,* 2 Caines' Rep. 343.
By the custom of banks in a particular place, payment of a promissory note may be demandable on the *fourth* day after the time of payment. *Renner* v. *Bank of Columbia,* 9 Wheat. 581.
(338) The days of grace as allowed in England, are generally allowed in the United States. At least no traces can be found of a contrary decision, except in the state of *Massachusetts,* where it is, held, that no days of grace are allowable unless stipulated in the contract itself. *Jones* v. *Fales,* 4 Mass. Rep. 245. In *New York* and in *Pennsylvania,* the days of grace are certainly allowed. *Corp* v. *M'Comb,* 1 John. Cas. 328. *Jackson* v. *Richards,* 2 Caine's Rep. 343. *Lewis* v. *Burr,* 2 Caine's Ca. in Err. 195. *Bank of North America* v. *Petit,* 4 Dal. Rep. 127. 5 Binn. Rep. 541.
A bill drawn payable at five days *after sight,* and accepted on the *first* day of a month, is payable on the *ninth* of the same month, the day of the acceptance being excluded, and the three days of grace allowed, a demand on the *eighth,* and protest for non-payment is too early, and therefore void. *Mitchell* v. *Degrand,* 1 Mason's Rep. 176

Rome, - - - - - - - - - - - 15 days.
Genoa, - - - - - - - - - - 30 do.
Leghorn and Milan, and some other places in Italy, no fixed time.

In a late case, however, it was proved, that at Hamburgh the holder of a bill is not bound to present the bill for payment until the 11th day after the time limited for its payment, where the eleventh is a post-day, but that if the eleventh be not a post-day he must present it by the next preceding post-day.[r] And in another case it was held, that where a bill is drawn on a person resident at a place near Hamburgh, the holder need not present it until the eleventh day, although the eleventh be not a post-day.[s]

On bank post bills payable after sight, it has been said, that no days [266] of grace are claimed:[t] and whenever a bill is drawn payable to the excise, it is also said they usually allow six days beyond the three days of grace, if required by the acceptor, on payment of one shilling to the clerk at the expiration of the six days, for his trouble; and in a case where the commissioners of excise, being the payees of such a bill, gave the drawee the above time, Lord Mansfield decided, that as this custom was a general one, engrafted on such bills, and known universally, the drawer was not discharged by the above indulgence to the drawee.[u]

The days of grace which are allowed on a bill of exchange must always be computed according to the law of the place where it is due.[x] At Hamburg, and in France the day on which the bill falls due makes one of the days of grace; but it is not so elsewhere.[y] In Great Britain, Ireland, France,[z] Amsterdam, Rotterdam, Antwerp, Mid-

[r] Goldsmith and another v. Shee, C. P. cor. Lord Eldon, 20th Dec. 1799. Bayl. 110, n. 1. A bill for 500l., drawn on Katter at Hamburgh, at three usances, was dated the 25th June, 1799; it was presented for payment on the 4th of October, which was a post-day. In an action by the indorsees against the payee, the defence was that the presentment was improper; but it was proved in evidence as a settled usage at Hamburgh, that although it is usual to pay bills on the day they become due, the holder may, if he pleases, keep them a certain number of days, called respite days, and that the number of respite days is eleven, where the eleventh is a post-day; but where the eleventh is not a post-day, the respite days extend to the preceding post-day only, the holder being obliged, at his peril, to protest, and send off the protest by the eleventh day. Verdict for the plaintiffs. But it is observed (Bayl. 111) that this is not consistent with the Hamburgh ordinance, art. 17, in which it is stated, that the holders may postpone the protest until the twelfth day, if it be not a Sunday or a holiday.

[s] Goldsmith and another v. Bland and another, C. P. cor. Lord Eldon, 1st of March, 1800. A bill for 909l. 9s. 9d. drawn on Trevtramus, of Bremen, but payable in Hamburgh, at three months,

was dated the 15th June 1799; it was not presented or protested until the 26th of September, which was not a post-day; another bill for 261l. 7s. 2d. addressed to Voeg, in Lubeck, payable in Hamburgh at three months, was dated the 26th of June, 1799; it was not presented or protested until the 7th of October, which was not a post-day. In an action on these bills against the defendants, as indorsers, it was proved that it was optional in the holder of a bill at Hamburgh whether he would present and protest it on the post-day, before the eleventh day after the day limited for its payment, the eleventh not being a post-day; or whether he would keep it until the eleventh: and one witness proved, that where the drawee lived at Lubeck or Bremen, it was the constant usage to keep the bill until the eleventh, whether it was post-day or not, there being posts from Lubeck and Bremen to Hamburgh every day. Bayl. 111.

[t] Lovl. 227.

[u] Welford v. Hankin, at Guildhall, Sittings after Hillary Term, 1763, 1 Esp. Rep. 59.

[x] Kyd, 3.

[y] Beawes, pl. 260. Selw. N. P. 4th ed. 338, n. 52.

[z] 39 & 40 Geo. 3. c. 39.

3dly. Time when the presentment should be made. dleburg, Dantzick, and Koningsburg, Sundays and holidays are always included in the days of grace; but not so at Venice, Cologn, Breslau, and Nuremburg. In this country, if the third day of grace happen to be a Sunday, Christmas-day, or Good Friday, upon which no money ought to be paid, the holder ought to present for payment upon the second day of grace, and in case it be not then paid, must treat the bill as dishonoured.[a] (341) In other cases, a presentment before the third day of grace, being premature would be a mere nullity.[b]

Of usances. Foreign bills, as have been already observed, are usually drawn payable at one, two or more *usances*. The term *usance* is French, and signified the time which it is the *usage* of the countries between which bills are drawn, to appoint for payment of them.[c] The length of the usance, or time which it includes, varies in different countries, from fourteen days to one, two, or even three months after the date of the bill. Double or treble usance is double or treble the usual time, and half usance is half that time; when it is necessary to divide a month [267] upon a half usance, the division, notwithstanding the difference in the length of the month contains fifteen days.[d]

A *usance* between London[e] and } Amsterdam is 1 *calendar* month after date.

Aleppo	{ sometimes accounted as treble usance }	do.
Altona	is 1 *calendar* month after date.
Antwerp	1 do.	-	do.
Brabant	1 do.	-	do.
Bilboa	2 do.	-	do.
Bruges	1 do.	-	do.
Cadiz	2 do.	-	do.
Flanders	1 do.	-	do.
France	30 days	-	do.
Florence	{ sometimes accounted as treble usance }	do.
Genoa	is 3 *calendar* months after date.
Hamburgh	1 do.	-	do.
Holland	1 do.	-	do.
Leghorn	3 do.	-	do.
Lisbon	2 do.	-	do.
Lucca sometimes 3			do.

[a] Tassel v. Lewis, Ld. Raym. 743. Haynes v. Birks; 3 Bos. & Pul. 599. Kyd, 2. Bayl. 109, 110. Mar. 95, 96.
[b] Wiffen v. Roberts, 1 Esp. Rep. 262. Bayl. 112.
[c] Poth. pl. 15. Haynes v. Birks, 3 Bos.
& Bul. 338. Selw. N. P. 4th ed. 338, n. 50. Bayl. 114.
[d] Mar. 93. Bayl. 114.
[e] Molloy, tit. Bills of Exchange, 2d vol. 2d book, c. 10. Bayl. 114.

(341) So in the United States, wherever days of grace are allowed, if the third day be a Sunday, or a holiday, as the fourth of July, the bill is due on the second day of grace. *Jackson* v. *Richards*, 2 Caines' Rep. 343. *Lewis* v. *Burr*, 3 Caines' Ca. in Err. 195. *Griffin* v. *Goff*, 2 John. Rep. 423. *Farnum* v. *Fowle*, 12 Mass. Rep. 89. But in this last case the court expressed a doubt, if in *Massachusetts*, the principle applied to any other day except Sunday, as there are no fixed and established holidays, on which all business is suspended. See *Jones* v. *Fales*, 4 Mass. Rep. 245. See also *Johnson* v. *Haight & Matthews*, 16 John. Rep. 470, and *Griffin* v. *Coff*, 12 John. Rep. 423.
That if the third day of grace fall on Sunday presentment for payment should be made on Saturday, see *Bussard* v. *Levering*, 6 Wheat. 102. *Furnan* v. *Harman*, 2 M'Cord, 436.

Lisle	is 1 *calendar* month after date.		
Madrid and all Spain	2 do.	-	do.
Middleburgh	1 do.	-	do.
Milan	3 do.	-	do.
Portugal	2 do.	-	do.
Paris	1 do.	-	do.
Rotterdam	1 do.	-	do.
Rome	3 do.	-	do.
Roan	1 do.	-	do.
Spain	2 do.	-	do.
Venice	3 do.	-	do.
Zant	3 do.	-	do.
Zealand	1 do.	-	do.

3dly. Time when the presentment should be made.

Usance between Amsterdam and { Brabant, France, Flanders, and Holland, or Zealand, is 1 calendar month.

Usance between Amsterdam and { Italy, Spain, and Portugal, is 2 calendar months.

Usance between Amsterdam and { Frankfort, Nuremburgh, Vienna, and other places in Germany, on Hamburgh and Breslau, 14 days after sight, 2 usances, 28 days, and half usance 7 days.

These usances are calculated *exclusively* of the day of the date of the bill. At the expiration of the appointed usance the bill would be apparently due, but the custom of merchants has allowed the drawee further time, called days of grace, which are in general calculated as before mentioned, exclusively of the last day of usance; and on the last of these three days the bill should, in this country, be presented for payment.

When bills, &c. are payable at one, two, or more *months after date, or sight,* the mode of computing the time when they become due, differs from the mode of computation in other cases. In general, when a deed or act of parliament mentions a *month,* it is construed to mean a *lunar* month, or twenty-eight days, unless otherwise expressed; but in the case of bills and notes, the rule is otherwise, and when a bill is made payable at a month or months after date, the computation must in all cases be by *calendar,* and not by lunar months;(348) thus when a bill is dated the 1st of January, and payable at one month after date, the month expires on the 1st of February, and with the addition of the days of

[268]

Bills payable after date, &c. when due.

f Poth. 15. Bayl. 144. *acc.* Molloy, 84, *contra.*
g Lutw. 885. Bayl. 114.
h Molloy, 84. Kyd, 4, 5.
i Mutford v. Walcot, 12 Mod. 410.—Bayl. 114.
k Ante, 264.
l 2 Bla. Com. 141. Lacon v. Hooper,

6 T. R. 225. Castle v. Burditt, 3 T. R. 623. The King v. Adderley, Dougl. 464. As to lunar and calendar months, and how they are calculated, see Lang v. Gale, 1 M. & S. 111. Watson v. Pears, 2 Campb. 294. Cathcart v. Hardy, 2 M. & S. 536.
m Beawes, pl. 253. Mar. 74. 90. 2d ed. p. 19. 24. Bayl. 113.

(348) The same rule is recognised in the United States. *Leffingwell* v. *White,* 1 John. Cas. 99. See *Loring* v. *Halling,* 15 John. Rep. 120. And a bill payable at so many days after sight, means so many days after *legal* sight, that is, so many days after the acceptance, for that is the sight to which the bill refers. *Mitchell* v. *Begrand,* 9 Mason's Rep. 176.

Bills payable after date, &c. when due. grace, the bill is payable on the 4th of February, unless that day be a Sunday, and then on the 3d. When one month is longer than the succeeding one, it is said to be a rule not to go, into the computation, into a third month; thus, on a bill dated the 28th, 29th, 30th, or 31st January, and payable one month after date, the time expires on the 28th of February in common years, and in the three latter cases in leap year on the 29th.[x] When the time is computed by days, the day on which the event happens to be excluded.[o]

When a bill purports to be payable so many days *after sight*, the days are computed from the day the bill was accepted, exclusively thereof, and not from the date of the bill, or the day the same came to hand, or was presented for acceptance; for the *sight* must appear in a legal way, which is either by the parties accepting the bill, or by protest for non-acceptance.[p]

Bills at sight when due. With respect to a bill payable *at sight*, though from the very language of the instrument it should seem that payment ought to be made immediately on presentment, this does not appear to be so settled. The decisions and the treatises differ on the question, whether or not **[269]** days of grace are allowable. Pothier,[q] enumerating the various kinds of bills, states that a bill payable at sight is payable as soon as the bearer presents it to the drawee; but in another part of this work,[r] it appears that this opinion is founded on the words of a particular French ordinance, which cannot extend to bills payable in this country; however, he assigns as a reason that it would be inconvenient if a person who took a bill at sight, payable in a town through which he meant to travel, and the payment of which he stands in need of for the purpose of continuing his journey, should be obliged to wait till the expiration of the days of grace after he presented the bill; a reason obviously as applicable to the case of a bill drawn payable *at* sight in this as in any other country. Beawes, in his Lex Mercatoria,[s] says, that bills made payable here *at* sight, have no days of grace allowed, although it would be otherwise in the case of a bill made payable one day *after* sight. Mr. Kyd, in his Treatises,[t] expresses the same opinion. But it seems, that the rule is *unsettled*.[u] In Dehers *v.* Harriot,[x] it was taken for granted that days of grace were allowable on a bill payable at sight. The same point was decided in Coleman *v.* Sayer.[y] And in another case,[z] where the question was, whether a bill payable at sight was included under an exception in the stamp act, 23 Geo. 3. c. 49. s. 4. in favour of bills payable *on demand*, the court held, that it was not; and Buller, J. mentioned a case before Willes, C. J. in London, in which a jury of merchants were of opinion, that the usual days of grace were to be allowed on bills payable at sight. And Mr. Selwyn, in his Nisi Prius, observes, that the weight of authority is in favour of such allowance.[a]

[a] Mar. 75. Kyd, 6.
[o] Bellasis *v.* Hester, Lord Raym. 280. Bayl. 113.
[p] Campbell *v.* French, 6 T. R. 212.— Com. Dig. tit. Merchant, F. 7. Bayl. 112. See Anonymous, Lutw. 1591.
[q] Pl. 12. 172. 196.
[r] Ll. pl. 172.
[s] Pl 256.
[t] Page 10.

[u] Bayl. 62. 66. 2d edit. Bayl. 3d edit. p 42. 109. 110.
[x] Dehers *v.* Harriot, 1 Show. 163.— Mod. Ent. 316.
[y] Coleman *v.* Sayer, Barnard's Rep. B. R. 303. Vin. Abr. tit. Bills of Exchange.
[z] l'Anson *v.* Thomas, B. R. Trin. 24 Geo. 3.
[a] Selw. 4th edit. 339; and see Bayl. 42. 109. 110.

When a check or bill or banker's note is expressed to be payable *on demand*, or when *no time of payment is expressed*, it is payable instantly on presentment, without any allowance of days of grace, and the presentment for payment of such a check or bill must be made *within a reasonable time* after the receipt of it.[b] (345)

When checks, &c. payable on demand should be presented for payment.

It has been frequently disputed, whether it is the province of the court, or of a jury, to determine upon the reasonableness of the time within which a check, &c. payable on demand, should be presented for payment. Formerly it was thought that it was a question for the jury; but the decisions, even of mercantile juries, were found so much at variance from each other, that for the sake of certainty on the subject, it is now settled, that the reasonableness of the time for presentment *is partly a question of fact*, and partly of law; the jury are to find the facts, such as the distance at which the parties are from each other, the course of the post, &c.; but when those facts are established, the reasonableness of the time is a question of law, upon which the judge is to direct the jury,[c] though judges may take the opinion of a jury as to what is convenient with reference to mercantile transactions.[d] This doctrine though formerly by no means universally as-

[270]

[b] Bayl. 103, 4, 5.
[c] Ante, 262. Bayl. 103. 2 Taunt. 394. Tindal v. Brown, 1 T. R. 168.—Darbishire v. Parker, 6 East, 3. 9. 10. 11. 14. 16. Parker v. Gordon, 7 East, 385. Haynes v. Birks, 3 Bos. & Pul. 599. Appleton v. Sweetapple, 1 Esp. Rep. 58. Bayl. 106, note c. The King

v. The Dean of St. Asaph, 3 T. R. 428, note a. In Fry v. Hill, 7 Taunt. 397, it was held, that what is reasonable time for presenting a bill payable after sight for acceptance, is always a question of fact to be determined by a jury.
[d] Per Grose, J. in Scott v. Lifford, 9 East, 847.

(345) The same rules have been recognised in the United States. A note which expresses no time of payment, is by law payable immediately. *Herrick* v. *Bennett*, 8 John. Rep. 374. *Thompson* v. *Ketcham*, 8 John. Rep. 189. *Field* v. *Nickerson*, 13 Mass. Rep. 131. And checks and notes payable on demand, must be demanded within a reasonable time. *Freeman* v. *Haskins*, 2 Caines' Rep. 369. *Cruger* v. *Armstrong*, 3 John. Cas. 5. *Conroy* v. *Warren*, 3 John. Cas. 359. But if the drawer of the check sustain no injury by the delay, as where the bank has always remained in good credit, and the drawer has defeated the payment of the check by withdrawing his funds from the bank, he cannot object to a delay in presenting it. Ibid. If a creditor receive an order on a third person for his debt, and neglect to present it for payment in a reasonable time, the drawer will be discharged. *Brower* v. *Jones*, 3 John. Rep. 203. and see *Tucker* v. *Manwell*, 11 Mass. Rep. 143.

A note payable on demand is not entitled to any days of grace, but an action may be brought on it immediately without any other demand. *Cammer* v. *Harrison*, 2 M'Cord 264.

Where a bill is drawn payable at sight or a certain number of days after sight, there is no fixed rule for its presentment, but the holder is bound to use due diligence and put the note into circulation. *Robertson* v. *Ames*, 20 Johns 146. Where a promissory note is payable on demand with interest, demand and notice must be made and given within a reasonable time after date. *Sice* v. *Cunningham* 1 Cowen. 397. *Martin* v. *Winslow*, 2 Mason. 241. And where such note is made and negotiated in the ordinary way without any agreement or understanding among the parties as to the time when it is to be paid, and all the parties reside in the same city, *five months* is not a reasonable time. Ibid. But such agreement between the original parties, not communicated to the indorser will not bind him. Ibid. And any offer by the indorser to give his own note in satisfaction of the indorsed note, is not a waiver of notice, unless the offer is accepted at the time by the holder. Ibid. In *Winslow* v. *Martin*, 2 Mason 141, a neglect to demand payment of a note payable on demand, for *seven months*, was held an unreasonable delay, and discharged the indorser: and that a promise to pay with a full knowledge of all the facts was binding on the indorser, although otherwise discharged: if he promised in ignorance of material facts affecting his rights, it was not a waiver of those rights.

When sented to;[e] is founded upon the strongest principles of law;[f] it is
justified also in point of expediency, for we find the most contradictory decisions of juries, when the point was left to them. Thus,
in some cases, the keeping of a check or bill, payable on demand,
should be three, four, or five days was holden not too long;[g] and in another case
it was holden, that the presentment must be made within two days,[h]
and in subsequent cases, that it should be made the day the bill is received, and that even an hour is an unreasonable time;[i] and the opinion of juries of merchants has been, that a check on a banker, or a cash
note, payable on demand, ought, if given in the place where it is payable, to be presented for payment the same day it is received, if the
distance, or other circumstances will possibly allow.[k]

margin: When checks, bills, &c. payable on demand should be presented for payment.

Considering it then to be settled, that the time when the presentment
for payment must be made is in general a question of law, we have
now to examine what is the rule of law upon the subject. Upon this
question it has been observed, that there is no other settled rule than
that the presentment must be made *within a reasonable time*, which
must be accommodated to other business and affairs of life, and the
party is not bound to neglect every other transaction in order to present
[271] the bill, note, or check, payable on demand, the same day it is issued.[l]
And, as observed by Lord Mansfield, it would be unreasonable to suppose, that a tradesman should be compelled to run about the town with
a dozen drafts, from Charing Cross to Lombard Street, on the same day;
and he directed the jury to consider, that twenty-four hours was the
usual time allowed for the presentment for payment.[m]

It is laid down, that upon a *bill* or *note*, payable on demand, or at
sight, and given for ease by a person who makes the profit by the money on such bills or notes a source of his livelihood, such as a country
banker, it is difficult to say what length of time such person shall be entitled to consider unreasonable; but upon such bills or notes given by
way of payment, or paid into a banker's, any time beyond that which
the common course of business warrants, is unreasonable.[n]

Upon a bill or note of this kind given by way of payment, the course
of business seemed formerly to allow the party to keep it, if it was payable in the place where it was given, until the morning of the next day
of business after its receipt,[o] and according to more recent decisions, it

[e] Russell v. Langstaffe, Dougl. 515.—
Muilman v. D'Eguino, 2 Hen. Bla. 568, 9.
Hankey v. Trotman, 1 Bla. Rep. 1.—
Bayl. 107. Kyd, 41. Poth. pl. 140.
[f] Darbishire v. Parker, 6 East 10.
[g] Phillips v Phillips, 2 Freeman. 247.
Crawley v. Crowther, id. 257.
[h] Mainwaring v. Harrison, 1 Stra. 508.
[i] Per Lord Mansfield in Tindal v.
Brown, 1 T. R. 168. 9. Hankey v.
Trotman, 1 Bla. Rep. 1. Beawes, 229.
Kyd, 45. Appleton v. Sweetapple, 1 Esp.
Rep. 58. Bayl. 106. Post, 272. Pock-
lington v. Silvester, post.
[k] Appleton v. Sweetapple, 1 Esp. Rep.
58. Bayl. 106. Post, 272. Russell v.
Langstaffe, Dougl. 515, n. b. 110.—
Brown v. Collinson, Beawes, pl. 259.

Kyd, 43. 45. Hankey v. Trotman, 1 Bla
Rep. 1.
[l] Darbishire v. Parker, 6 East, 4. 8. 9
Kyd, 129.
[m] Beawes, pl. 229. Kyd, 45. 127, 128
Ward v. Evans, 2 Salk. 442. S. P. Scott
v. Lifford, 9 East, 347.
[n] Bayl. 104.
[o] Bayl. 104. Ward v. Evans, 2 Lord
Raym. 928. A banker's note was paid to
the plaintiff's servant at noon, and presented for payment the next morning, at which
time the banker stopped payment. On a
case reserved, the court held it was presented in time, and judgment was given
for the plaintiff.
Moore v. Warren, 1 Stra. 415. The de-

should seem that if such a bill or note were payable by or at a banker's, it would suffice to present it for payment at any time during banking hours of the day after it is received.[p] Thus where a note of this kind, payable in London, was given there in the morning, a presentment the next morning was held by the court sufficiently early, though juries have endeavoured to establish a contrary rule, and to find that the instrument must be presented the day it is received;[q] and though it has been supposed that the presentment must be in the forenoon of the next day;[r]

When checks, bills, &c. payable on demand should be presented for payment.

---

fendant gave the plaintiff a banker's note at two o'clock in the afternoon, and he tendered it for payment the next morning at nine: the banker stopped a quarter of an hour before; and Pratt, C. J. told the jury the loss should fall on the defendant, there being no laches in the plaintiff, who had demanded the money as soon as was usual in the course of dealing, and that keeping the note till next morning could not be construed giving a new credit to the banker, and the jury found for the plaintiff. In Holmes v. Barry, Stra. 415, the circumstances were the same, and King, C. J. of the Common Pleas, gave similar directions, and the jury found accordingly.

Fletcher v. Sandys, 2 Stra. 1248.—A banker's note was paid to the plaintiff after dinner, and he sent it for payment the next morning, but the banker had stopped payment; and Lee, C. J. ruled, that there were no laches in the plaintiff, and that in all these cases there must be a reasonable time allowed consistent with the nature of circulating paper credit.

Turner and others v. Mead, 1 Stra. 416. The defendants paid the Sword-Blade Company, the plaintiffs, two bankers notes at three o'clock in the afternoon, and the next morning their servant left them at the bankers in order to call for the money in the evening, it then being the custom with the plaintiffs and the bank, to send out their notes in the morning, and to call for the money in the afternoon. The plaintiffs' servant called for the money between four and five in the afternoon, and the banker had just stopped payment, and because the plaintiffs had done nothing more than was usual in leaving the notes in the morning without taking the money, Pratt, C. J. directed the jury to find for them, which they did.

Hoar v. Da Costa, 2 Stra. 910. The defendant paid the plaintiff a banker's note at twelve; he put it into the bank at one, and at ten the next morning, the runner from the bank carried it with other notes, and left them, as was then usual, to call again for the money: he called at eleven, and was told the banker's servant was gone to the bank; he called again at two, when the banker said he was going to stop, and refused payment, but he paid small notes till four o'clock. The defendant gave notice to the plaintiff the next morning; the question was, whether this note was payment to the plaintiff. It was insisted for the defen-

dant, that if the note had been tendered by itself, it would have been paid; and for the plaintiff, that if there had been no demand there would have been no laches, being within a day after the receipt. Raymond, C. J. said there was no standing rule, and left it to the jury, who found for the plaintiff.

[p] Robson v. Bennett, 2 Taunt. 388.—Post, 275; and Pocklington v. Silvester, post, 274.

[q] Bayl. 106, 7. Beawes, pl. 229. Kyd, 45. 127. See Ward v. Evans, and other cases in notes, ante, 271.

Appleton v. Sweetapple, K. B. Mich. 23 Geo. 3. 1 Esp. Rep. 58. Bayl. 106, note c. & C. 2 Taunt. 394. The case was, that plaintiff received from the defendant a banker's note at one o'clock in the day, but did not call for payment the whole of that day, and in the evening of it the banker failed. A verdict was found for the defendant, on the ground that it was the custom of the City that bills should be brought for payment the day they are received; but on a motion for a new trial, it appearing that there were many exceptions to this custom, as in the case of factors at Bear Key, the salesmen at Smithfield, and others, the court held that it was not sufficiently proved, and even if the decision had been on that ground, it must appear that the custom was reasonable, or the court would control it, and therefore granted a new trial. The jury found again for the defendant, but against the judge's direction: a second new trial was granted, and the jury again found for the defendant, and then the court refused to interfere.

[r] East India Company v. Chitty, 2 Stra. 1175. Bayl. 104, 5. Mainwaring v. Harrison, 1 Stra. 508. On Saturday the 17th of September, about two o'clock, Harrison gave Mainwaring a banker's note, dated the 5th of September, and payable to Harrison or order on demand; Mainwaring paid it away the same afternoon to J. S. and he presented it for payment on Tuesday morning as soon as the shop was open, but the banker stopped payment at that time. Mainwaring paid the money to J. S. and brought this action to recover it from Harrison. Pratt, C. J. left it to the jury whether there had been any neglect, and observed, that as Harrison had kept it eleven days, he probably would not have demanded payment sooner than J. S. did. The jury wished to leave it to the court, whether

When yet the party has twenty-four hours,[s] or according to a more recent decision, he has the whole of the banking hours, or hours of business of the next day to make the presentment.[t]

When checks, bills, &c. payable on demand should be presented for payment.

It has been held, that a bill or note of this kind given by way of payment to a banker, must be presented by him as soon as if it had been paid into his hands by a customer,[u] and that if such a bill or note be paid into a banker's, and be payable at the place where the banker lives, it must be presented the next time the banker's clerk goes his rounds, but it should seem that in all cases it suffices for a banker to present such check the day after he receives it.[x]

If a bill or note, payable on demand, be payable elsewhere than in the place where it was given, it is laid down that the party receiving it must forward it for payment by the post of the next day after he received it,[y] although that post may go out on the same day. But from other cases it should seem, that it would suffice if such bill or note were forwarded for payment by the regular post on the day after it is received.[z] It is certain, however, that the holder's not forwarding such bill or note for payment, by the post, or some conveyance of the day after it was received, would be deemed laches.[a] In a recent case

there had been reasonable time, but the Chief Justice told them they were judges of that, upon which they found for the defendant, and gave it as their opinion, that a person who did not demand a banker's note in two days, took the credit on himself.

East India Company v. Chitty, 2 Stra. 1175. At half past eleven in the morning of the 18th of January, the defendant paid the East India Company's cashier, a banker's note, and they did not send it for payment till the next day at two, at which time the banker stopped payment. The question was, who should bear the loss? and upon examining the merchants, it was held that the company had made it their own by not sending it out the afternoon they received it, or at furthest, the next morning, and the jury found accordingly for the defendant.

[s] Per Lord Mansfield; see Beawes, pl. 229. Kyd, 45.
[t] Pocklington v. Silvester, post, 274.
[u] Bayl. 107. Hankey v. Trotman, 1 Bla. Rep. 1. The plaintiff was a banker, and had a bill on the defendant, for which the defendant paid him a draft upon another bank at twelve at noon, and the plaintiff got it marked for acceptance that night; before the next morning the banker on whom it was drawn stopped. The question was, whether the plaintiff or defendant should bear the loss? The jury found a verdict for the defendant, and upon a rule to show cause why there should not be a new trial, and cause shown, the court (Wright, J. dubitante) held that it was a question of fact, whether the plaintiff had sufficient time for receiving the money, of which the jury

were the proper judges, and the verdict stood.

But see the cases of Rickford v. Ridge. 2 Campb. 537; and Robson v. Bennett, 2 Taunt. 388, and post, 275.

In the last-mentioned case, Mansfield, C. J. said, that Hankey v. Trotman had been over-ruled by Appleton v. Sweetapple. See 2 Taunt. 394.

[x] Rickford v. Ridge, 2 Campb. 537. Post, 275; and Robson v. Bennett, 2 Taunt. 388. Post, 275.
[y] Bayl. 104, 5.
[z] Rickford v. Ridge, 2 Campb. 537.— Post, 275. Darbishire v. Parker, 6 East, 3.
[a] Bayl. 105, 5. and note to Beeching and others, v. Gower, 1 Holt, 315, 316.

Action for money had and received. The defendant paid the plaintiff a check of 20l., drawn on the Maidstone Bank, on the 5th of April. It was given to the plaintiffs at the time of Tunbridge market, and they gave their own notes in exchange. It was given sometime before the post set out on the 5th. The plaintiffs kept it all the 5th and 6th, but sent it to Maidstone by the carrier on the morning of the 7th; the carrier reached Maidstone at nine o'clock on the 7th, but the Maidstone bank did not open that morning. If it had been sent by the post of the 6th, it would have reached Maidstone at an hour earlier, viz. at eight o'clock in the morning of the 7th. Best, Serjt. for the defendant, contended, that the plaintiffs had been guilty of laches. Blosset. Serjeant, for the plaintiffs, contra, relied on Rickford v. Ridge, 2 Campb. 537. Gibbs, C. J. The plaintiff cannot recover, they have been guilty of laches; I will

where the defendant being indebted to the plaintiff, paid to him the debt in country bank notes, (payable in the country, and also in London) on a Friday, several hours before the post went out, and the plaintiff transmitted halves of the notes by a coach on Saturday, and the other halves by Sunday night's post, and all the halves arrived in London on Monday, and were presented for payment and dishonoured on the Tuesday, it was held that the plaintiff had not been guilty of laches, and that he might recover from the defendant his original debt.[b]

When checks, bills, &c. payable on demand should be presented for payment.

With respect to a *check on a banker*, it is now settled that it suffices to present it for payment to the banker at any time during banking hours on the day after it is received, and that no laches can be imputed to the holder in not presenting it for payment in the morning of the second day, although the bankers paid drafts on them until the afternoon, and then stopped payment.[c] And where a person in London received a check upon a London banker, between one and two o'clock, and lodged it soon after four with his banker, and the latter presented it between five and six, and got it marked as a good check, and the next day at noon, presented for payment at the clearing-house, the court held that there had been no unreasonable delay either by the holder in not presenting it for payment on the first day, which he might have done, or by his banker in presenting it at the clearing-house only on the following day at noon; it being proved to be the usage among such bankers, not to pay checks presented by one banker to another after four o'clock, but only to mark them if good, and to pay them the next day at the clearing-house.[d] And it has been holden

[275]

not say that it was not their duty to have sent the check off by the post of the 5th, but the extreme time up to which they were justified in keeping it was till the post of the 6th. They do not send it till the 7th. It does not matter when the carrier arrived, they must suffer for their negligence. Plaintiffs nonsuited.

[b] Williams v. Smith, 2 Barn. & Ald. 496.

[c] Pocklington v. Silvester, Sittings at Guildhall, after Trin. Term, 57 Geo. 3. This was an action brought by the plaintiffs for the amount of a check given by the defendants to the plaintiffs. The defendants drew the check on their bankers, Messrs. Mainwaring and Co. which was paid to the plaintiffs at eleven o'clock in the morning on the 16th of November, 1817, which was not presented till near five o'clock on the 17th. The bankers stopped payment at four o'clock on the 17th of November, and the defendants had notice thereof that evening. At the trial before Gibbs, C. J. at Guildhall, he directed a verdict for the plaintiff, on the ground that the plaintiff had the whole of the banking hours of the next day to present the check for payment. The jury, however, contrary to the direction of the judge, found for the defendants. In the ensuing term the plaintiff obtained a rule for a new trial, and upon the second trial before Burroughs, J. at Guildhall. 10th of

December, 1817, he directed a verdict for the plaintiff, saying, that whatever doubts had been formerly entertained, it was now established as a rule of law, that the party receiving a check on a banker has the whole of the banking-hours of the next day to present it for payment. The jury found accordingly. See also Robson and another v. Bennett and another, 2 Taunt. 388. Rickford v. Ridge, 2 Campb. 937.

[d] Robson v. Bennett, 2 Taunt. 388. On the 11th of September, between one and two o'clock, the defendants gave the plaintiffs a check upon Bloxam and Co. their bankers, in payment for goods. The plaintiffs lodged the check with Messrs. Harrison, their bankers, a few minutes after four, and they presented it between five and six to Bloxam and Co. who marked it as good: it was proved to be the usage amongst London bankers not to pay any check, presented by or on behalf of another banker, after four o'clock, but merely to mark it if good, and pay it the next day at the clearing-house. On the 12th at noon, Harrison's clerk took the check to the clearing-house, but no person attended for Bloxam and Co. who stopped payment at nine on that morning; and the check therefore was treated as dishonoured. The plaintiffs in going with the check to Harrison's passed Bloxam's house. On a

When that a London banker who receives a check by the general post, is not bound to present it for payment until the following day. •

When checks, bills, &c. payable on demand should be presented for payment.

case stating these facts the court held, that there had been no laches in the plaintiffs in not presenting the check to Bloxam and Co. on the 11th for payment, or in his bankers in not presenting it at the banking-house, but merely at the clearing-house, and therefore gave judgment for the plaintiffs.

Per Lord Mansfield, C. J. The whole question amounts merely to this ; a man who has bought goods, and given a draft on a banker, contends, that he has paid for those goods, though he never received the money. A draft was drawn on the 11th of September ; on that day it was carried to the house of the drawee, and in the language of those persons was marked ; the effect of that marking is similar to the accepting of a bill ; for he admits thereby assets, and makes himself liable to pay. It is the practice of the bankers not to pay bills of this description, which are presented after four o'clock but to mark them ; and it is usual that bills marked on one day are carried to the clearing-house, where their clerks meet and pay them on the next day. Therefore it is the same thing as if a banker had written on a check, " we pay this to-morrow at the clearing-house." On the next day, after marking the check, the banker stops payment ; the holder's clerk goes to the clearing-house, where no clerk attends from Messrs. Bloxoms, and the bill is not paid, and the first question is, whether there is any laches as to the time of presentment? As to that the case of Appleton v. Sweetapple decides, that a check need not be presented on the day on which it was drawn ; now this bill was in fact presented and accepted on the very day on which it was drawn. The reason of that haste probably was in order to fix the banker, lest the drawer should be insolvent before the next day, bankers being usually persons of great substance, whereas the drawer may be of less credit ; the mark on the check is an engagement to pay at a particular place ; is not then the presenting it at that place equivalent to presenting at the banking-house ? It seems that it is ; and that it therefore is no laches ; consequently the surplus of the money for the coals remains due, and judgment must be entered for the plaintiff. See also Reynolds v. Chettle, 2 Campb. 596. Selw. Ni. Pri. 4th ed. 341.

• Rickford and others v. Ridge, 2 Campb. 537. The plaintiffs, bankers at Aylesbury, gave the defendant cash for the check upon Smith and Co. bankers in London ; and in an action to recover this money, it appeared that they took the check on the 18th June ; but, instead of sending it to London by the post of that day, which they might have done, they sent it by a morning coach on the 14th, and their bankers, to whom it was directed, received it between three and four o'clock on the same day, and presented it at Smith's house at noon on the 15th, when payment was refused. It was proved that bankers to the west of St. Paul's, where the plaintiff's bankers resided, sent out checks and bills for payment only once in the day, and that generally before the arrival of the post ; and therefore such as arrived by the post on one day generally remained with them until the following morning : so that had this check arrived by the post on the 14th, it would not have been presented until the 15th. The question therefore was, whether such practice were reasonable ? It was admitted that a different practice prevailed to the east of St. Paul's. Lord Ellenborough said, the holder of a check is not bound to give notice of its dishonour to the drawer for the purpose of charging the person from whom he received it. He does enough if he presents it with due diligence to the bankers on whom it is drawn, and gives due notice of its dishonour to those only against whom he seeks his remedy. The question here is, whether if the check had arrived by post on the 14th, the bankers were bound to present it for payment the same day ? This must be decided by the Law-merchant. I cannot hear of any arbitrary distinction between one part of the city and another. It is not competent to bankers to lay down one rule for the eastward of St. Paul's, and another for the westward. They may as well fix upon St. Peter's at Rome. It is always to be considered whether, under the circumstances of the case, the check has been presented with reasonable diligence. This is what the Law-merchant requires. The rule that the moment a check is received by the post, it should invariably be sent out for payment, would be most inconvenient and unreasonable. In Liverpool and other great towns different posts arrive at different hours ; but it would be impossible to have clerks constantly ready to carry out all the bills and checks that may arrive in the course of the day ; nor if it were possible, is it requisite that all other business being laid aside parties should devote themselves to the presenting of checks. The rule to be adopted must be a rule of convenience ; and it seems to me to be convenient and reasonable, that checks received in the course of one day should be presented the next. Is this practice consistent with the Law-merchant ? It cannot alter it. Bankers would be kept in a continual fever if they were obliged to send out a check the

It will be observed that this rule allowing the party receiving a bill, note, or check, payable on demand, until the next day to present it for payment, will not enable a succession of persons to keep such instrument long in circulation, so as to retain the liability of *all* the parties, in case the same should ultimately be dishonoured by the maker of the note, or drawer of the check.[f]   •

When checks, &c. payable on demand should be presented for payment

A presentment for payment of a bill, payable on a day certain, should in all cases be made within a reasonable time before the expiration of the day when it is due; and if by the known custom of any particular place, bills are only payable within limited hours, a presentment there, out of those hours, would be improper.[g] This rule extends also to a presentment out of the hours of business to a person of a particular description, where, by the known custom of the place, all such persons begin and leave off business at stated hours;[h] and therefore when a bill is accepted, payable at a banker's, it must be presented there before five o'clock, or the usual hour of shutting up their shop, and presentment afterwards will not entitle the notary to protest it.[i] And it has been recently determined, that no inference is to be drawn from the circumstance of the bill being presented by a notary in the evening that it had before been duly presented within the banking-hours.[k] However, a presentment of a bill at a bankers, where it is payable, is sufficient, although it be made after banking hours, provided a person be stationed there by the banker to return an answer, and refuses to pay the bill.[l] And when the party to pay the bill or note is not a

Time of the day when the presentment should be made.

[277]

moment it is paid in. The arrangement mentioned by the plaintiffs' witnesses appears subservient to general convenience, and not contrary to the Law-merchant, which merely requires checks to be presented with reasonable diligence."

[f] Admitted in Boehm v. Sterling, 7 R. R. 425.

[g] Bayl. 99. 110. Per Lord Ellenborough, in Parker v. Gordon, 6 Esp. Rep. 42. 7 East, 385; and in Elford v. Teed, 1 M. & S. 28, cited in Marius, 2d ed. 197.

[h] Bayl. 99. Leftley v. Mills, 4 T. R. 170.

[i] Parker v. Gordon, 7 East, 385. 3 Smith, 358. 6 Esp. Rep. 41. S. C. Elford v. Teed, 1 M. & S. 28. Jameson v. Swinson, 2 Taunt. 224. 2 Campb. 874. Selw. Ni. Pri. 4th edit. 312.

Parker v. Gordon. The drawee accepted the bill, payable at Davison and Co. his bankers ; at the part of the town where Davison and Co. lived, bankers shut up at six o'clock. The bill was not presented for payment until after six, when the shop was shut up, and the clerks gone. In an action against the drawer, Lord Ellenborough held, that this was not a good presentment, and nonsuited the plaintiff ; and on a motion for a new trial, the court held, that if a party took an acceptance, payable at a banker's, he bound himself to present the bill during the banking hours ; and therefore rule refused. N. Lawrence and Le Blanc, Justices, said the holder was not bound to take such an acceptance.

[k] Elford v. Teed, 1 M. & S. 28.

[l] Garnett v. Woodcock, 1 Stark. 475. Indorsee of bill against acceptor. The bill in question was drawn by Hodson and Co. in Lancashire, upon the defendants in London, for the sum of 670l., payable to the order of the drawers, and indorsed by the drawers to the plaintiff. The defendants had accepted the bill, payable at Denison's and Co. bankers, London. The bill had been presented at Denison's and Co. between seven and eight in the evening of the day when it became due, and a boy returned for answer no orders. Campbell, for the defendants, contended, that since the bill was drawn in London, the place of payment being in the body of the bill, and had been accepted, payable at Denison's and Co. a presentment there was necessary; and that this was not a sufficient presentment, and cited Parker v. Gordon, 7 East, 385. Elford v. Teed, 1 M. & S. 28. There the court held, that the presentment at a banker's, after banking hours, was a nullity, although the presentment in that case had been made by a notary. He admitted, that when the bill had been made payable at a merchant's, a presentment, after banking hours, where a negative answer had been returned on presentment of the bill, had been deemed to be sufficient; but this was the case of a presentment at a banker's.

Lord Ellenborough. Bankers do not usually pay at so late an hour; but if a person be left there who gives a negative answer, there is no difference between that case and that of a presentment at a mer-

Time of the banker, a presentment at any time, even late in the evening, will in *day* when general suffice. ▪
the present-
ment should
be made.

On presentment for payment, the bill, unless paid, must not be left,
Mode and if it be, the presentment is not considered as made until the money
of present- is called for;▫ and though it has been holden, that bankers are not
ment.
[279] guilty of neglect by giving up the bill to the acceptor, upon his delivery to them of his check on another banker ;▫ this doctrine may now
be questionable.▫

Circum-   If at any instant before the actual payment of a bill or check, given
stances ari- upon a condition, the drawer discover that the condition has not been
sing be-   performed, he may stop the payment thereof to the party who has thus
tween pre-
sentment   eluded the condition;▫ and a banker who, upon presentment of a bill
and actual
payment.

chants. I think, it is perfectly clear, that
if a banker appoint a person to attend, in
order to give an answer, a presentment
would be sufficient if it were made before
twelve at night. Verdict for the plaintiff.
In the ensuing term Campbell moved for
a rule to show cause why there should not
be a new trial; and he cited the words of
Lawrence, J. in *Parker v. Gordon*, 7 East,
385, where he says, "the party might"
have refused to take this special acceptance; but if he chose to take the acceptance payable in that manner, payable at
the bankers, does he not agree to take it
payable at the usual banking hours.
Lord Ellenborough. In that case no
answer was given upon the presentment of
the bill. Upon the trial, I laid down nothing but that, if a servant was stationed
for the purpose of giving an answer, it was
sufficient. In general, there are two presentments, one in the morning, and the
other in the evening; but if there be a presentment in the evening, and the party is
ready to give an answer, he does all that
is necessary. The banker returned an answer by the mouth of his servant, and *non
constat*, but that he was stationed there for
the express purpose. Rule refused.
    ▫ *Barclay v. Bailey*, 2 Campb. 527. The
presentment of a bill of exchange for payment at the house of a merchant, residing
in London, at eight o'clock in the evening
of the day it becomes due, is sufficient to
charge the drawer. Action against the
drawer of a bill of exchange, accepted by
one David Hardy. At eight in the evening of the day the bill became due, it was
presented at the house mentioned on the
face of it, as the drawee's place of residence, when the answer given by a person
who came to the door was, that Mr. Hardy
had become bankrupt, and removed into
another quarter of the town. On the part
of the defendant it was proved, that he
had a person stationed at this house for the
purpose of taking up the bill, from nine in
the morning till four in the afternoon, but
that no one presented it during that time;
and the point was strenuously argued, that
a presentment so late as eight in the even-

ing was insufficient to charge the drawer.
Lord Ellenborough. I think this presentment sufficient; a common trader is different from bankers, and has not any peculiar
hours for paying or receiving money; if the
presentment had been during the hours of
rest, it would have been altogether unavailing; but eight in the evening cannot be
considered an unseasonable hour for demanding payment at the house of a private
merchant, who has accepted a bill. The
plaintiff had a verdict.
    S. P. *Jameson v. Swinton*, 2 Taunt. 224.
2 Campb. 374. S. C. *Bancroft v. Hall*,
Holt, C. N. P. 476.
    Morgan v. Davison, 1 Stark. 114. As-
sumpsit by the indorsee of a bill of exchange against the drawer. The bill was
made payable at Herring and Richardson's, Copthal Court, London. The plaintiff
proved presentment at Herring and Richardson's, who were not bankers, in Copthal
Court, on the day when the bill became due,
between six and seven in the evening, when
no one was there but a girl left to take care
of the counting house. Lord Ellenborough
held, that this was a sufficient presentment;
the hour was not an improper one, and the
holder might reasonably expect to find the
party in his counting-house at that time.
    ▪ *Hayward v. Bank of England*, 1 Stra.
550. Bayl. 102. *Russell v. Hankey*, 6 T.
R. 13.

    Hayward kept cash at the Bank, and
paid in a banker's note; the runner to the
Bank of England left it the next morning,
and called for the money in the afternoon,
but in the interval the banker had stopped;
and though this appeared to be the usual
practice at the Bank, King, C. J. said, it
was dangerous to suffer persons to deal with
notes in that manner, and that the Common
Pleas were of that opinion in the like case,
and he directed the jury to find for the
plaintiff, which they did. Sed vide *Turner
v. Mead*, 1 Stra. 416. and *Hoar v. Da Costa*,
2 Stra. 910.

    ▫ *Russel v. Hankey*, 6 T. R. 13.
    ▫ See post, 287.
    ▫ *Wienholt v. Spitta*, 3 Campb. 376.

or check for payment, cancels the acceptance or drawer's name by mistake, may yet, upon discovering his error, before actual payment, effectually resist such payment as if he had not so cancelled the draft, and where the drawee of a bill, on presentment for payment, said this bill will be paid, but we cannot allow you for a duplicate protest, and the holder refused to receive payment without the charges of such protest, it was held, that the drawee was not bound to pay the bill. So where bankers, at whose house by the terms of the acceptance the bill was payable, had received money for the express purpose of taking up the bill two days after it became due, and upon tendering it to the holders, and demanding the bill, found that it had been sent back protested for non-payment, to the persons who indorsed it to the holders, it was decided, that such bankers, having received fresh orders not to pay the bill, were not liable to an action by the holders for money had and received, when, upon the bill's being got back and tendered to them, they refused to pay the money. But we have seen, that if one banker present for payment to another banker a check on him in the usual course, and the latter marks is as approved, importing that it shall be paid the next day, at the clearing-house, this is binding on the latter, and is equivalent to an acceptance, and he must at all events pay it.

(margin: Circumstances arising between presentment & actual payment.)

If the maker of a promissory note pay money into the hands of an agent to retire it, and the agent tenders the money to the holder, on condition of having it delivered up, and the note being mislaid, this condition is not complied with, and the agent afterwards becomes bankrupt, with the money in his hands, it has been decided, that the maker is still responsible on the note.

(margin: [280])

PAYMENT of a bill may not only be made by the acceptor, but also by any other party to it, and even by a total stranger, as in the case of a payment supra protest, which will be spoken of hereafter; and that of payment by the bail or either of the parties.

(margin: Sect. 2. Of payment; & to whom it may be made.)

Payment should always be made to the real proprietor of the bill, or to one of several partners, or to some person authorized by him to receive it, as a factor, &c.; (358) and payment to the payee will, con-

Raper v. Birbeck, 15 East, 17. Fernandez v. Glynn, 1 Campb. 426. Ante, 176.
Anderson v. Heath, 4 M. & S. 303. Ante, 178, note.
Stewart and another v. Fry and another, 1 Moore, Rep. 74. Holt, C. N. P. 372. S. C. Ante, 195. When money is to be considered as particularly appropriated to payment of a bill, see 14 East, 582. 590.

Robson v. Bennett, 2 Taunt. 388.—Ante, 275.
Dent v. Dunn. 3 Campb. 299.
Poth. pl. 170.
Hull v. Pitfield, 1 Wils. 46.
Poth. pl. 142, 3. Bayl. 142.
Duff v. East India Company, 15 Ves. 213.
Favenc v. Bennett, 11 East, 40.

(358) On presenting a note or bill for payment, the holder must have the bill with him, otherwise the demand will not be deemed effectual so as to charge the other parties. Freeman v. Boynton, 7 Mass. Rep. 483. And as the whole of a set of exchange constitute but one bill, payment to the holder is good, whichsoever of the set he may happen to have in his possession. Durkin v. Cranston, 7 John. Rep. 442. Payment to the general indorsee of a bill is good, and cannot be affected by any transactions between

Sect. 2. Of
payment;&
1st, by and
to whom it
may   be
made.

sequently, be inoperative, if he have ceased to be the proprietor of it,
by having indorsed it to another person, and the drawee has notice of
the fact.[d]   And if a bill be payable to A. B. only, and not negotiable,
it is said that A. B. in person must appear to demand payment.[e] If
the holder of a bill die, payment should not be made to his personal
representative, unless he has a power of administering his effects.[f]
But payment to a person having obtained probate of a forged will of
a deceased party will be valid.[g] On a bill payable to A. or order, to
the use of B. payment should be made to A. or his indorsee, and not
to B.[h] If a bill be beneficial to a minor, payment to him would be
valid ;[i] but a payment to a married woman, after knowledge of that
fact, would not discharge the person making it.[k] When a bill is indorsed to a person merely for the purpose of receiving payment for
the indorser, and the authority given to the indorsee is afterwards
revoked, either by the party himself or by operation of law, as by his
death, it is said that payment to the indorsee will not discharge the
person making it, if he had notice of the revocation;[l] this doctrine,

[281] however, is objected to by Beawes, in his *Lex Mercatoria*,[m] and it
must certainly be confined to the single case of an indorsement to an
agent, for the purpose of his receiving payment for his principal.
Payment of debts should not in general be made to the agent of an attorney.[n] But in ordinary cases, the mere production of a bill of exchange, note, or check, is in general sufficient to warrant the payment
to the person who produces it,[o] and this without reference to the circumstance of his being the habitual agent of the same party.[p]

We have seen,[q] that in general when the holder of a bill or note indorsed in blank or payable to bearer, loses or is robbed of it, and the
person finding or stealing it, presents it to the drawee at the time it is
due, and he pays it without knowing of the loss or robbery, such payment will discharge him ; and although he had notice of such fact, yet
if the person presenting the bill to him was a *bona fide* holder, such notice would not invalidate the payment.(359) But a payment before a
bill or check is due, will not discharge the drawee, unless made to the

[d] Poth. pl. 164.
[e] Marius, 4th ed. 34.
[f] Poth. pl. 166. Bayl. 143.
[g] Allen v. Dundas, 3 T. R. 125.
[h] Cramlington v. Evans, 2 Vent. 310.
Carth. 5. S. C. Marchington v. Vernon, 1
Bos. & Pul. 101, n. c. Smith v. Kendall, 6
T. R. 123, 4. ante, 123.
[i] Poth. pl. 166. Bayl. 143.
[k] Id. 167. Barlow v. Bishop, 1 East,
117. Bayl. 143. Ante, 18, 19.

[l] Poth. 168. et Mar. 72, 3. sed quære.
Tate v. Hilbert, 2 Ves. jun. 114, 5. 118,
121. 16 Ves. 450. 2 Bos. & Pul. 277.
[m] Pl. 229.
[n] Yates v. Frecklington, Dougl. 622.
[o] Owen v. Barrow, New Rep. 103. Per
Ld. Mansfield, C. J. Anon. 12 Mod. 564.
Pal. P. & A. 481.
[p] Anon. 12 Mod. 554. 2 Ld. Raym.
930. Pal. P. & A. 151.
[q] Ante, 147.

him and the person by whom it was remitted; and if the bill has been protested for non-
payment, he may waive the default and accept payment. *Dirkin* v. *Cranston.* But
where a note was indorsed by the defendant for the accommodation of the makers, who
were then in good credit, and *before negotiating*, they became insolvent, and the defendant then directed them not to part with the note, which they promised, but afterwards
passed it to the plaintiffs with full notice of all the circumstances, in satisfaction of a debt,
held that the plaintiffs could not support an action on the note. *Skelding et al.* v. *Warren*, 15 Johns. Rep. 270.

(359) But if he have notice before payment that the bill has been lost, he pays it
his own peril, and if it turns out that the party had no title, he will be liable to the re
owner. *Lovci.* v. *Martin*, 4 Taunt. Rep. 799. See *Gorgerat* v. *M'Carty*, 1 Yeate
Rep. 94.

real proprietor of it ; and therefore, where a banker paid a check the day before it bore date, which had been lost by the payee, it was ad-judged that he was liable to repay the amount to the person losing it[r] and it is perhaps advisable that an acceptor should in no case pay a bill before it is due,[s] or after notice from the drawer or indorser not to pay it.[t] And if bankers pay a check, under circumstances which ought to have excited their suspicion, and induced them to make inquiries be-fore paying it, they cannot take credit for the amount in their account with their customer ;[u] and where a person pays a sum of money into a banker's for a special pupose, viz. to pay a particular bill, and the banker's clerk, by mistake, pays the money to the holder of another bill, he may sue the bankers for the amount, but not the party to whom the payment was made.[x] Where a bill, transferrable only by indorse-ment, and not indorsed, is lost by the person entitled to indorse, no other person can transfer the interest in the bill ; and consequently a payment by the drawee, even to a *bona fide* holder, will not in such case be protected.[y]

Payment *to* a person or his order, after the knowledge of his having [282] committed an act of *bankruptcy*, would be ineffectual.[z] Thus it has been holden, that if a banker pay the draft of a trader keeping cash with him, after notice of an act of bankruptcy, the assignees may recover the money paid, either from the banker,[a] or from the payee of the check, if such payee had notice of the bankruptcy,[b] unless the, payment were by compulsion of law,[c] but still until a commission has issued against the holder, there is no defence to an action at his suit ;[d] and after action *bona fide* brought by such party, it should seem that the defendant might safely put the money into court, in order to pre-vent further costs.[e]

So a payment made to a bankrupt, or his order, without notice of his being so, will, in all cases, discharge the person making it :[f] and it has been holden, that if a debtor, not having notice of the bankruptcy of

[r] Ante, 147.

[s] Com, Dig. tit. *Merchant*, F. 7. Mar. 29. 130.

[t] Bacon v. Searles, 1 Hen. Bla. 89. Mar. 129. Com. Dig. tit. *Merchant*, F. 7. Ante, 148, 9.

[u] Scholey v. Ramsbottom, 2 Campb. 485. Ante, 148, 9.

[x] Rogers v. Kelly, 2 Campb. 123.

[y] Mead v. Young, 4 T. R. 28. Archer v. The Governor and Company of the Bank of England, Dougl. 337. et ante, 148, 9.

[z] Kitchen v. Bartsch, 7 East, 53. ante, 115, 6, 7, &c. Cooke's Bankrupt Laws, 274, 5.

[a] Id. Ibid. Vernon v. Hankey, 2 T. R. 113. 3 Bro. 313.

[b] Vernon v. Hanson, 2 T. 287.

[c] 11 Ves. 557. 1 Mont. 316 ; but see Clegg v. Phillips, 2 Campb. 129.

[d] Prichell and others v. Down and others, 3 Campb. 131. Held, that where two partners have stopped payment, and a commission of bankrupt is taken out against one of them, a debtor to the firm,

CHITTY ON BILLS.

who knows of the stoppage, cannot re-fuse to pay money due to them, on the ground that the other may have commit-ted an act of bankruptcy, in which case his assignees might call upon the debtor to pay a moiety of the money a second time. Per Lord Ellenborough, C. J. The defendants are not under the protec-tion of the act 46 Geo. 3. c. 135. s. 1. but before it was passed they could not have justified refusing to pay the balance in their hands, under similar circumstances, to whatever subsequent inconvenience the payment might have exposed them. *Till the party has actually become a bank-rupt, and a commission has been taken out against him, he may sue his debtors.* There may be peril in paying a man who is known to have stopped payment, but that affords no defence to an action for a debt justly due to him. Verdict for the plaintiffs.

[e] Foster v. Allanson, 2 T. R. 479. 14 East, 588. 2 Ves. jun. 104, 5, 6.

[f] 1 Jac. 1. c. 15. s. 14; and see 46. Geo. 3. c. 135. s. 1. and post. Bayl 143, 4. Cole v. Robins, 3 Campb. 186.

Sect. 2. Of *payment; & 1st, by and to whom it may be made;* his creditor, give him his acceptance in discharge of the debt, he may afterwards pay such acceptance to the holder of the bill, although between the time when he accepted and the time, when the bill became due, he heard of the bankruptcy; the giving, indorsing, or accepting a bill of exchange, being considered as an immediate payment within the meaning of the statute of James, which protects *bona fide payments* made *to* a bankrupt, provided the bill be honoured when due.[s]

[283] So also a payment made *by a bankrupt* to a person not *having notice of the bankruptcy or insolvency*, and being a *bona fide* creditor for goods sold, or by the bankrupt's having drawn, negotiated, or accepted *a bill of exchange* in the *usual or ordinary course of trade and dealing*, is protected by the statute 19 Geo. 2. c. 32.[h] . We have already considered some of the decisions upon this act.[i] It has been doubted whether promissory notes,[k] or checks on bankers, are within this act.[l] It has been held, that payment of a bill to a creditor by a bankrupt under an arrest, after a secret act of bankruptcy, is a payment in the course of trade;[m] but if the payment be intended as a fraudulent preference it will not be valid.[n] If the holder of a bill give time to the acceptor, upon condition that he should allow interest, and he afterwards pay the bill, having previously committed a secret act of bankruptcy, this is not a payment in the usual course of trade within the meaning of the statute.[o] So where A. having recovered a verdict against B., who afterwards committed an act of bankruptcy, and A. not having had notice thereof, took a bill drawn by B. on C. for the amount of the sum recovered, payable at a distant period, which bill was afterwards paid: it was determined that this payment was not protected by the statute, and consequently that A. was liable to refund the money received by him to the assignees of B.[p] And where bankers having accepted a bill for the accommodation of a trader, he, after committing an act of bankruptcy, but before a commission is sued out, lodged money with them to take up the bills, which do not become due till after a commission is sued out, and are then regularly paid by the acceptors,[q] it was held, that they were bound to refund the money to the assignees, [284] and that they neither had a right of set-off under 5 Geo. 2. c. 30., nor could protect themselves under 19 Geo. 2. c. 32. as having received the

---

[s] Wilkins *v.* Casey, 7 T. R. 711. Ante, 119. Bayl. 148; and see Foxcraft *v.* Devonshire, 1 Bla. Rep. 193. 3 Campb. 186.

[h] By this statute it is enacted, "that no person who is or shall be really and *bona fide* a creditor of any bankrupt, for or in respect of goods, really and *bona fide* sold to such bankrupt, or for or in respect of any bill or bills of exchange really and *bona fide* drawn, negotiated, or accepted by such bankrupt, in the usual or ordinary course of trade and dealing, shall be liable to refund or repay to the assignee or assignees of such bankrupt's estate, any money which before the suing forth of such commission was really and *bona fide*, and in the usual and ordinary course of trade and dealing, received by such person of any such bankrupt before such time as the person receiving the same shall know, understand, or have notice, that he is become a bankrupt, or that he is in insolvent circumstances."

See also 46 Geo. 3. c. 135, post, 284. In Harwood *v.* Lomas, 11 East, 131, it was doubted whether payments of promissory notes are within this act.

[i] Ante, 117 to 120.

[k] Harwood *v.* Lomas, 11 East, 131.

[l] Holroyd *v.* Whitehead, 5 Taunt. 444. 1 Marsh. 128.

[m] Cox *v.* Morgan, 2 Bos. & Pul. 398. Ex parte Farr, 9 Ves. 515. Sed vide Southey *v.* Butler, 3 Bos. & Pul. 237; but see Blogg *v.* Phillips, 2 Campb. 129. Cullen, 238, 239. Bayly *v.* Schofield, 1 M. & S. 338.

[n] Singleton *v.* Butler, 2 Bos. & Pul. 283. Southey *v.* Butler, 3 Bos. & Pul. 237.

[o] Vernon *v.* Hall, 2 T. R. 648.; and see 1 Montg. 311, 312, 313. 2 Ves. 560. Cullen, 234.

[p] Pinkerton *v.* Marshall, 2 Hen. Bla. 384.

[q] Tamplin and others assignees of Visich, a bankrupt *v.* Diggins and others, 2 Campb. 312.

money in payment of bills of exchange in the ordinary course of trade. And where bankers, after a secret act of bankruptcy of the acceptor, paid a bill for him, accepted payable at their house, and he afterwards remitted the money to them, it was decided that they were liable to refund; because the bankrupt was not liable to them on the bill, and his re-payment to them was only in satisfaction of a loan, which is not a payment protected by the statute.' So if bankers pay a check drawn upon them by a trader after a secret act of bankruptcy, they cannot retain money received to cover such check.*

So it has been decided, that the assignees of a bankrupt are entitled to recover back money paid by the bankrupt to the defendant after a secret act of bankruptcy, (though before the date of the commission,) which the defendant had before recovered by judgment against the bankrupt in an action on a promissory note, reserving interest half yearly given for the balance of an account among other things consisting of *money lent*, such note not being given in the usual and ordinary course of dealing, so as to be protected by 19 Geo. 2. c. 32., even supposing a promissory note to be within that statute, which only mentions bills of exchange.'

However, by the 46 Geo. 3. c. 135. s. 1, 2., it was enacted, that, "in all cases of commissions of bankrupt thereafter to be issued, all conveyances by, *all payments by and to, and all contracts and other dealings and transactions by and with any bankrupt bona fide made or entered into more than two calendar months before the date of such commission*, shall, notwithstanding any prior act of bankruptcy committed by such bankrupt, be good and effectual to all intents and purposes whatsoever, in like manner as if no such prior act of bankruptcy had been committed, provided the person or persons so dealing with such bankrupt had not at the time of such conveyance, payment, contract, dealing, or transaction, any notice of any prior act of bankruptcy by such bankrupt committed, *or that he was insolvent or had stopped payment,*" and that all and every person and persons with whom the bankrupt shall have really and *bona fide* contracted any debt or debts *before the date and suing forth of such commission, which if contracted before any act of bankruptcy committed, might have been proved under such commission*, shall, notwithstanding any prior act of bankruptcy may have been committed by the bankrupt, be admitted to prove such debt or debts, and to stand and be a creditor under such commission to all intents and purposes whatever, in like manner as if no such prior act of bankruptcy had been committed by such bankrupt, provided such creditor or creditors had not, at the time of such debt or debts being contracted, any notice of any prior act of bankruptcy committed." Since this act, the statute 19 Geo. 2. c. 32, can only come in question where the payment is made within two months before the suing out of the commission.*

[285]

We have already seen that a bill or check should not be prematurely paid ;' Marius gives particular directions on this point.* The general

---

' Holroyd v. Whitehead, 9 Campb. 530. 533. 2 Rose, 145. 5 Taunt. 444. 1 Marsh. 123. S. C.
* Id. ibid.
' Harwood v. Lomas, 11 East, 127. Ante, 283.

* As to the construction of these words, see ante, 120.
* 2 Campb. 315, in note.
' Ante, 148. Bayl. 145, 6.
* Marius, 4th edit. 31.

2dly. With-rule with respect to the time allowed for the payment of money, when
in what a day certain is appointed, is, that the party bound has till the last
time pay-moment of the day to pay it; [a] but it is otherwise with respect to
ment must *foreign* bills, for as the protest for non-payment of them should be
be made. made on the last day of grace, [b] so as to be sent if possible by the post
on that day, it follows that the holder may insist on payment on demand, or at least before the hours of business are expired. [c]

With respect to *inland* bills it has been much discussed whether the
acceptor has not the whole day for payment. On the one hand a bill
of exchange has been assimilated to other contracts, in which the party
has till the last instant of the day to pay the same : but on the other
hand, it has been urged, that the contract of an acceptor of a bill, or
maker of a note, is to pay on demand on the appointed day, and that
if payment be not made on such demand, the contract is broken : and
the holder may treat the bill or note as dishonoured. [d] The latter doctrine appears now to be established ; and, therefore, where the acceptor
having said at eleven o'clock in the day that he would not pay the bill,
it was decided that the holder might immediately resort to the drawer,
so that notice of the dishonour may be given on the same day. [e] It is
[286] not usual or necessary to give notice of non-payment before the following morning, and therefore there can be no objection to the allowance
of the whole day on which the bill becomes due, to pay it in. [f] At all
events, if the holder make a second presentment on the last day of
grace, the acceptor may insist on paying it when such presentment is
made, without paying the fees of noting or protesting, notwithstanding
such presentment he made after banking-hours, and expressly for the
purpose of noting and protesting. [g] But in a late case it was decided,
that a plea of a tender made *after the day of payment* of a bill of ex-

[a] Hudson *v.* Barton, 1 Rol. Rep. 189.
1 Saund. 288, n. 17. Leftley *v.* Mills,
4 T. R. 173.

[b] Tassel *v.* Lee, 1 Ld. Raym, 743, *et
post, sed quære*, see Vin. Abr. tit. Time,
A. 2. pl. 3. Anon. Lutw. 1593.

[c] Colkett *v.* Freeman, 2 T. R. 61. Parker *v.* Gordon, 7 East, 885. 8 Smith's
Rep. 358. S. C.

[d] Leftley *v.* Mills, 4 T. R. 170. arguments of Kenyon, C. J. and Buller, J. disputed by Lord Alvanley, C. J. in Haynes
v. Birks, 3 Bos. & Pul. 602.

[e] Ex parte Moline, 1 Rose, 303. Burbridge *v.* Manners, 3 Campb. 193. Hume
v. Peploe, 8 East, 169.

Ex parte Moline, 1 Rose, 308. In this
case the point was, the acceptor having
said at eleven o'clock in the day that he
would not pay the bill, whether the
holder could immediately resort to the
drawer? The Lord Chancellor was of
opinion that he could. Sir Samuel Romilly mentioned Burbridge *v.* Manners, 3
Campb. 194, S. P.

Burbridge *v.* Manners, 3 Campb. 193.
This was an action on a promissory note
for 101*l.* 15*s.* 5*d.* dated 11th October,
1810, drawn by J. Finney, payable three
months after date, at Fraser and Co's.
to the defendant, indorsed by him to one
Tinson, and by Tinson to the plaintiff.
The note was regularly presented for pay-

ment in the forenoon of the day it became
due, when payment was refused, and in
the afternoon of the same day the plaintiff
caused notice of its dishonour to be sent
to the defendant. Park, for the defendant, objected that this was not sufficient
notice of the dishonour. Finney, the maker
of the note, had the whole of the day it
became due to pay it, and till the last
minute of that day it could not be considered as dishonoured. The notice therefore stated what was untrue, and was
evidently premature. Per Lord Ellenborough. I think the note was dishonoured as soon as the maker had refused payment on the day when it became due, and
the notice sent to the defendant must have
answered all the purposes for which notice in such cases in required. The holder
of a bill or note gives notice of its dishonour in reasonable time the day after it
is due, but he may give such notice as
soon as it has been dishonoured, the day it
becomes due ; and the other party cannot complain of the extraordinary diligence used to give him information. Verdict for the plaintiff.

[f] Leftley *v.* Mills, 4 T. R. 170. Vin. Ab.
tit. Time, A. 2. pl. 3. Haynes *v.* Birks,
3 Bos. & Pul. 599.

[g] Leftley *v.* Mills, 4 T. R. 170. Poth.
pl. 140. 174 ; see post, as to protest for
non-payment.

change, and before action brought, is insufficient, although the plea 2dly. With-
averred that the defendant was always ready to pay from the time of in *time* pay-
the tender, and that the sum tendered was the whole money then due, ment must
owing, or payable to the plaintiff in respect of the bill, with interest be made.
from the time of the default, for the damages sustained by the plaintiff
by reason of the non-performance of the promise.[h] However, a drawer
or indorser may tender within a reasonable time after notice, as it is
not to be expected that he is to be ready at the instant he receives notice to pay the amount.[i] If a promissory note of twenty years date be
unaccounted for, it affords a presumption of payment.[k]

When a bill is drawn here, and payable in a foreign country in 3dly. Pay-
foreign coin, the value of which is reduced by the government of that ment *how*
country, it is said that the bill shall be payable according to the value of *made, and*
the money at the time it was drawn.[i] But though a war between this *what a-*
and a foreign country may in some cases excuse the obligation on a *mounts to it.*
British subject to pay a bill in such foreign country,[m] yet we have seen, [287]
that where a note was made payable in Paris, or at the choice of the
bearer in England, according to the course of exchange upon Paris, it
was holden, that as the direct course of exchange between London
and Paris had ceased, the holder was entitled to recover upon the note,
according to the circuitous course of exchange by Hamburgh at the
time the note was presented.[n] The effect of payment by a remittance of
bills by post, which are lost, has also already been stated.[o] Payment
is frequently made by a draft on a banker, in which case, if the person
receiving the draft, do not use due diligence to get it paid, the person
from whom he received it, and every other party to the bill will be discharged, but not otherwise, unless the holder expressly agreed to run
all risks ;[p] and it has been holden, that the act of writing a receipt in
full will not be evidence of such agreement.q(367)

When payment is made by the drawee giving a draft on a banker,
Marius advises the holder *not to give up the bill until the draft be paid.*[r]
Till lately, the usage in London was otherwise when the drawee was a
respectable person in trade; and in one case, it was decided, that a
banker having a bill remitted to him to present for payment, is not
guilty of negligence in giving it up upon receiving from the acceptor a
check upon another banker for the amount payable the same day,
although such check be afterwards dishonoured;[s] but in a late case at
Nisi Prius, it was considered, that the drawer and indorsers of a bill
would be discharged by the holder's taking a check from and delivering
up the bill to the acceptor, in case the check be not paid; because the

[h] Hume v. Peploe, 8 East, 168.
[i] Walker v. Baines, 5 Taunt. 240. 1 Marsh. 36. S. C.
[k] Duffield v. Creed, 5 Esp. Rep. 52.
[i] Dacosta v. Cole, Skin. 272.
[m] Pollard v. Herries, 3 Bos. & Pul. 340.
[n] Ante, 233. Pollard v. Herries, 3 Bos. & Pul. 335.
[o] Ante, 157.
[p] Vernon v. Boverie, 2 Show. 296. Ward v. Evans, 2 Ld. Raym. 930. 12 Mod. 521.

S. C. Vin. Ab. tit. Payment, A. Dent v. Dunn, 3 Campb. 296. Ante, 94, &c.
[q] Ante, 94 to 100.
[r] Mar. 21. Ward v. Evans, 12 Mod. 521. Vernon v. Boverie, 2 Show. 395.
[s] Russell v. Hankey, 6 T. R. 12. Paley P. & A. 8. 37. 144. 186, 7. and see Turner v. Mead, 1 Stra. 416. Haward and the Bank of England, id. 550. Kyd, 43. Mar. 121. See Haynes v. Birks, 3 Bos. & P. 601. as to sanctioning usage.

(367) So it has been held in *New York*, that a receipt for a note as cash, is not evidence that it is received as an absolute payment. *Tobey v. Barber*, 5 John Rep. 68.
Putnam y. Lewis, 8 John. Rep. 389.

3dly. Pay-
ment *how*
made, and
what a-
mounts to
it.

[288]

drawer and indorsers have a right to insist on the production of the bill, and to have it delivered up on payment by them.[t] If, however, the holder of a draft on a banker receive payment thereof in the banker's notes instead of cash, and the banker fail, the drawer of the check will be discharged.[u] But if a creditor, on any other account than a bill of exchange is offered cash in payment of his debt, or a check upon a banker from an agent of his debtor, and prefer the latter, this does not discharge the debtor, if the check is dishonoured, although the agent fails with a balance of his principal in his hands to a much greater amount.[x] When twenty years have elapsed since the date of a note, &c. payment will be presumed unless the contrary appear.[y] And when bills are taken in payment of a debt, and the party sues upon the original consideration, payment of the bills will be presumed till the contrary appear.[z] And it has been holden, that the production of a check drawn by the defendant payable to the plaintiff and indorsed by him, is evidence of the payment, but the mere insertion of the parties name in the draft would not not have that effect ;[a] and it should seem that in the first place the indorsement on the check would not be evidence unless stamped as a receipt, such indorsement not being within the exception of the 44 Geo. 3. c. 98. schedule A. or 55 Geo. 3. c, 184, in favour of a receipt, discharge, or acquittance written on the back of a bill or note, draft, or order for payment of money, duly stamped, or on the back of a foreign bill payable in Great Britain. And in a recent case it was held that proof of the delivery and payment of a check to the plaintiff is not sufficient evidence of a debt, in order to support a set-off, unless it be shown upon what consideration and under what circumstances the check was given,[b] and it was even held, that the mere circumstance of a check being made payable to A. and of A's. having recovered payment of it, is not evidence that the maker gave it to him.[c]

As bills of exchange differ from other debts in respect of their assignable quality, it has been decided that a negotiable bill of exchange is not to be considered as paid or satisfied by the drawer's bequeathing a larger legacy to the party in whose favour it was drawn, although such party continued to be holder at the time of the testator's death.[d]

If money be paid into a banking-house to be placed to the credit of another upon a condition, the money in the mean time to stand in the bankers books in the name of the party paying it in ; it is at his risk and the loss is his, if the bankers fail before the condition is complied with, though the other party had written to desire it to be paid in generally.[e]

[289]

[t] Powell *v.* Roche, Sittings at Guildhall, before Lord Ellenborough, A. D. 1806 ; Shaw, Clement's Inn, attorney for plaintiff : Neeld & Fladgate, attorneys for defendant ; and see Mar. 22, *et ante*, 578, 9. as to recovering at law, and without producing a bill, &c. and post, as to sending a protested bill.

[u] Vernon *v.* Boverie, 2 Show. 296.

[x] Everett *v.* Collins, 2 Campb. 515; and see Dent *v.* Dunn, 3 Campb. 296. Marsh *v.* Peddar, Holt, C. N. P. 72. Tapley *v.* Masters, 8 T. R. 451 Wyatt *v.* Marquiss of Hartford, 3 East, 147.

[y] Duffield *v.* Creed, 5 Esp. Rep. 52.

[z] Hebden *v.* Hartsink, 4 Esp. Rep. 46.

[a] Egg *v.* Barnett, 3 Esp. Rep. 196 ; see Pfiel *v.* Van Battenberg, 2 Campb. 439 ; but see Aubert *v.* Walsh, 4 Taunt. 293.

[b] Aubert *v.* Walsh, 4 Taunt. 298. See also Cary *v.* Gerrish, 4 Esp. Rep. 9.

[c] Lloyd *v.* Sandilands, 1 Gow. Ca. Ni. Pri. 15.

[d] Carr *v.* Eastabrook, 3 Ves. 561. 2 Roper, 20.

[e] Culley *v.* Short, 1 Cooper Eq. Ca. 148.

In general where a party owes several debts, and pays money gen- 3dly. Payerally to the creditor without directing that it shall be applied in satis- made, and faction of one of the debts in particular, the creditor may apply it in what adischarge of any one of the debts as he may think fit, and this even to mounts to the prejudice of a party who was surety for one of the debts;[f] but in an it. account with bankers the payments, advances, and receipts on each side are to be considered as applicable in reduction of the earliest part of the account;[g] and where bankers discounted for the drawer a bill accepted for his accommodation, and after it was dishonoured were informed of that fact, and requested by the drawer not to apply to the acceptor, and afterwards the drawee's account with them was in his favour, it was decided that the balance being thus once turned in his favour, the bill was to be considered as satisfied, although afterwards the drawer became insolvent, and was much indebted to them in consequence of subsequent advances.[h]

If when a bill or note becomes due, the holder renews the same, or Of the effor valuable consideration agrees with the drawee of the bill, or maker fect of givof the note, to give him time for payment, without the concurrence ing time to of the other parties entitled to sue such drawee or maker on the bill the acceptor note, they will thereby in general be discharged from all liability, or, &c. although the holder may have given due notice of the non-payment.[i] [290]

[f] Goddard v. Cox. 2 Stra. 1194. Bosanquet v. Wray, 6 Taunt. 597. Kirby v Duke of Marlborough, 2 M. & S. 18. Plomer v. Long, 1 Stark. 153.

[g] Clayton's case, cited 1 Meriv. 585. 608; see other cases 2 Bridgm. Ind. 586, 7. 2d edit. tit. Trade.

[h] Marsh and another v. Houlditch, Sittings at Westminster after Easter Term, 1818, before Mr. Justice Abbott. Assumpsit on a bill for 500l., dated 28th June, 1811, payable three months after date, drawn by Joel George Young, upon and accepted by the defendant for the accommodation of the drawer, and indorsed by him to the plaintiffs. The drawer, on being released, swore as follows:—In June 1811, I re-opened my account with the plaintiff, when the bill for 500l. was discounted. I had other bills with them, they were discounted together, I had credit for that sum in my account; no other bills were discounted for me during this account. Defendant had no consideration whatever for this bill; I was aware of the time of its becoming due. On that day I called at defendant's house, he was not at home, I think I found a banker's ticket there. That day or the next, I saw Mr. Fauntleroy, (one of the plaintiffs) I told him the bill was an accommodation from defendant to me; that I should take it up, and requested him not to apply to defendant. He said, very well, and requested me to take it up as soon as I could; he did not like defendant's bills, he had had trouble enough with him. I said he might depend upon me; he said, he should look to me and not mind him. The bill was due the 1st of October, I paid in 104l. at the time of the conversation; shortly afterwards the balance was in my favour. In the

course of the month I paid in 1000l. and did not draw out above 200l. Some months afterwards, for the first time, I heard again of this bill; I failed in October 1812, heard of application to defendant, from him, and went to plaintiffs upon it. In May the bill was at rest completely ; 20th and 23d of May I paid moneys, but cannot recollect on what particular account. I went to plaintiffs on my general accounts, after defendant had had a letter from the plaintiffs; I had an interview with them, and they agreed I should clear up my account as soon as I could; they wanted security or would make me no more advances ; they had a security from me in January, but could make no use of it Mr. Justice Abbott, to plaintiffs' counsel, unless you can alter the fact of the conversation, it is an answer to the action. The banking account of the drawer with the plaintiffs having, at one time after the bill was due, been in his favour to a larger amount than the bill, the plaintiffs were bound to apply the balance in discharge of that bill, and could not keep it as a security for a fluctuating balance, which might ultimately become due to them. Plaintiffs nonsuited. See Hammersly v. Knowlys, 2 Esp. Rep. 665. 1 Meriv. 589. S. P. but see Atwood v. Crowdie, 1 Stark. 488.

[i] Anderson v. George, London, Sittings after Trin. Term, 1757. cor. Lord Mansfield. Selw. N. P. 4th edit. 372. Action by indorsee against indorser of a promissory note. The note was presented for payment when due. The maker desired two or three days time to pay it in, and so from time to time, which was given to him by the then holders. Lord Mansfield said, here is an actual credit given for eight days,

OF PAYMENT

Of the effect of giving time to or releasing the acceptor, &c. There is no obligation of *active diligence* on the part of the holder to sue the acceptor or any other party, and he may forbear to sue as long

and the loss must fall on the plaintiff; and therefore there was a verdict for the defendant.

In Tindal *v.* Brown, 1 T. R. 169. Per Buller, J. As to giving time, the holder does it at his peril; and that circumstance alone would be sufficient to decide this case. For in no case has it been determined, that the indorser is liable after the holder of the note has given time to the maker.

English *v.* Darley, 3 Bos. & Pul. 61. The holder of a bill sued the indorser and acceptor, and took out execution against the acceptor, and received 100*l.* from him, and took his bond and warrant of attorney for payment of the remainder by instalments, with interest and costs, excepting only a nominal sum to enable him to support actions against the other parties. He then brought on to trial this action against the indorser. Lord Eldon thought that the bargain to give indulgence to the acceptor was a bar, and non-suited the plaintiff; and on motion for a new trial, the court was clear that the nonsuit was right; because giving time to the acceptor was a pledge that he should have time from all the other parties, and the holder had no right to give such pledge, and yet hold the other parties liable. Per Lord Eldon, C. J. It is very clear that the holder of a bill may, at his election, sue any or all of the parties to it; and that if they all become bankrupt, he may prove against the estates of all, unless he receive part of the debt from any one; and although the debt be reduced from time to time by dividends, no part of the proof shall be expunged under any of the commissions till 20*s.* in the pound have been received. As long as the holder is passive, all his remedies remain; and if any of the parties be discharged by the act of law, as by an insolvent debtor's act, that operation of law shall not prejudice the holder. With respect to Malin *v.* Mulhall, it may be observed, that the marginal abstract of that case is incorrect; for it appears from the report, that the person first sued was a subsequent indorser: had the plaintiff first sued the prior indorser, and discharged him from execution, it would have afforded sufficient objection to an action against a subsequent indorser. If a holder enter into an agreement with a prior indorser in the morning not to sue him for a certain period of time, and then oblige a subsequent indorser in the evening to pay the debt, the latter must immediately resort to the very person for payment to whom the holder has pledged his faith that he shall not be sued. In the case Ex parte Smith, Lord Thurlow, after consulting with all the Judges, was of opinion that the holder of a bill, by entering into a composition with the acceptor, discharged the indorser; and ac-

cordingly ordered the proof against the estate of the latter, to be expunged, proceeding on the ground of the acceptor's liability being varied by the act of the holder. We all remember the case where Mr. Richard Burke being co-surety for an annuity, the grantee gave time to the principal, and yet argued that Mr. Burke was not released thereby, though the principal was: but it was answered, that the grantee could make no demand on the co-surety, because he must by so doing enforce a payment from the principal contrary to the agreement. Here the plaintiff having taken a new security from the acceptor, has discharged the defendant.

Clark *v.* Develin, 3 Bos. & Pul. 365.— Per Lord Alvanley, C. J. "If the holder of a bill without the knowledge of the other parties, give time to the acceptor, he cannot afterwards call on the other parties without an injury to the person to whom he has given time. In such case, therefore, those parties will be discharged. But a man is not bound to seek his remedy against the acceptor; if he sign judgment against him, he will not be bound to prosecute that judgment. Per Chambre, J. the acceptor of a bill is to be considered as the principal debtor, and the other parties as sureties only; the holder therefore who is the creditor ought not so to negotiate with the acceptor as to prejudice the remaining parties to the bill. On this ground English *v.* Darley proceeded. If a creditor give time to the principal debtor, the collateral securities are discharged, both in law and equity. But in this case defendant having assented to the payment by instalments, cannot now complain of being prejudiced by the conduct of the holder. Rule discharged.

Gould *v.* Robson, 8 East, 576. The holder of a bill upon its becoming due received part-payment of the acceptor, and took a bill from him at a future short date for the remainder, and agreed to keep the original bill in his hands in the interim as a security. He now sued the defendant as indorser, and this was relied upon as a defence. Lord Ellenborough thought at the trial, that it did not amount to giving time to the acceptor, and the plaintiff had a verdict; but upon a motion for a new trial, he and the court were satisfied that it did, and a nonsuit was entered. Lord Ellenborough said, "How can a man be said not to be injured, if his means of suing be abridged by the act of another?" If the plaintiffs holders of the bill had called immediately upon the defendant for payment, as soon as the bill was dishonoured, they might immediately have sued the acceptor and the other parties on the bill. I had some doubts on the trial, but am in-

as he chooses ; but he must not so agree to give time to the acceptor, so as to preclude himself from suing him, and suspend his remedy against him in prejudice of the drawer and indorsers.ᵏ This rule is founded on the principle that the holder by entering into a binding engagement to give time to the acceptor, renders him less active in endeavouring to satisfy the bill than he probably could otherwise be, if he continued liable to an immediate action at the suit of the holder ; besides, if a holder agree to give indulgence for a certain period of time to any one of the parties to a bill, this takes away his right to call on that party for payment before the period expires, and not only to call upon him, but on all the intermediate parties ; for otherwise if he were to oblige them to pay the bill, they could immediately resort against the very person whom the holder has indulged, which would be inconsistent with his agreement.¹ This is a rule of law not confined to bills of exchange ; for if the obligee of a bond with a surety, without communication with the surety, take notes from the principal, and give further time, the surety is discharged.ᵐ(374) The acceptor of a

Of the effect of giving time to or releasing the acceptor, &c.

clined to think now that time was given: The holder has the dominion of the bill at the time: he may make what arrangements he pleases with the acceptor, but he does that at his peril ; and if he thereby alter the situation of any other person on the bill, to the prejudice of that person, he cannot afterwards proceed against him. As to the taking part payment, no person can object to it, because it is in aid of all the others who are liable upon the bill; but here the holder did something more, he took a new bill from the acceptor, and was to keep the original bill till the other was paid. That is an agreement that in the mean time the original bill should not be enforced; such is at least the effect of the agreement, and therefore I think time was given.

Smith and others v. Beckett, 13 East, 187 Where the defendant lent his indorsement on a promissory note to the drawer, which note was payable on demand, for the purpose of enabling him to raise the money on that security from the plaintiffs, his bankers, who agreed to make advances thereon for six months, held, that the bankers, who had renewed their advances at the end of the six months without the knowledge or consent of the defendant, could not recover upon the note thus indorsed by him, without proof of demand on the drawer, and a regular notice of the dishonour to the defendant.

ᵏ Per Lord Eldon, in Wright v. Simpson, 6 Ves. 734. See also Trent Navigation Company v. Harley, 10 East, 40.
¹ Per Bayley, J. in Claridge v. Dalton, 4 M. & S. 232.
ᵐ Rees v. Berrington, 2 Ves. jun. 540. 6 Ves. 905. Selp. v Stacy, 3 Atk 91.— Bac. Abr. Obligation; and Id. 7th vol tit. Obligation, 506. English v. Darley, 2 Bos. & Pul. 62. Ante, 290.

Rees v. Berrington, 2 Ves. jun. 540.— Rees became surety in a joint and several bond, conditioned for the payment to the obligee of a certain sum, with interest, by two instalments; the first on the 31st December, 1789, and the second on the 31st December, 1790. In September, 1790, the whole sum being unpaid, the obligee took promissory notes from the principal obligor for payment of the debt by instalments at extended periods, which notes were afterwards exchanged for others, payable at more distant days. This agreement was without the knowledge of Rees. The principal obligor afterwards became bankrupt, and the executor of the obligee sued Rees the surety ; and on a bill filed for an injunction, the Chancellor held, that the surety was discharged by this indulgence having been given without his consent to the principal. Vide 2 Bos. & Pul. 62.

See also Willison v. Whitaker, 2 Marsh. Rep. 383. Brickwood v. Anniss, 5 Taunt. 614. The plaintiff, after final judgment,

(374) To the same effect are several cases decided in the United States. The people v. Janson, 7 John. Rep. 332. Hunt v. The U. States, 1 Gallis Rep. 32. See Dempsey v. Norton, Kirby's Rep. 397. Ludlow v. Limond, 1 Caines' Ca. 1. Walsh v. Baillie, 10 John. Rep. 180. Rathbone v. Warren, 10 John Rep. 587. Comm. of Berks Co. v. Ross, 3 Binn. 523. King v. Baldwin, 2 John Cha. Rep. 554. Burn v. Poaage Adm. 3 Dessaus. Cha. Rep. 604. Butler v. Hamilton, 2 Dessaus. Cha. Rep. 230. Rutledge v. Greenwood, 2 Dessaus. Cha. Rep. 589.

Taking a collateral security is not giving time to the acceptor. Pring v. Clarkson, 1 Barn. & Cress. 14.

Of the ef-bill is primarily liable ; and the drawer and indorsers may be considered
feet of giv-in the nature of sureties for the performance of his act.ᵃ Therefore
ing time to the taking of a bond, or any security, payable at a future day, from
or releasing the accept-the acceptor of a bill, or maker of a note, without the assent of the
or, &c. other parties thereto, would discharge them from liability ;ᵇ and where
[293] the indorsee of a bill, having sued the acceptor to judgment, and taken
out execution, received of him a sum of money in part payment, and
took his security for the residue, with the exception of only a nominal
sum, it was holden, that he was thereby precluded from afterwards
suing the indorser ;ᵉ and the letting such acceptor out of custody on a
ca. sa. would have the same effect;ᵈ and in a late case it was held, that
if the holder of a bill of exchange when due, after taking part payment from the acceptor, agree to take a new acceptance from him for
the remainder, payable at a future day, and that in the mean time the
holder should keep the original bill in his hands as a security ; such
agreement amounts to giving time and a new credit to the acceptor,
and discharges the indorser, who was no party to such agreement,
though the drawer might have had no effects in the hands of the ac-
ceptor.ʳ Similar indulgence to a drawer or a prior indorser, would
also discharge all subsequent parties.ˢ(375) And where the defendant

having taken bills payable at a future day,
in satisfaction of the debt, the court directed an *exoneretur* to be entered on the bail-
piece; because the principle is, that where
the plaintiff has disarmed himself from
proceeding against the principal, the bail
are discharged; but where he has not, by
taking a security payable at a future day,
precluded himself from proceeding, he may,
although he has agreed without consideration to give time to the principal, proceed
against the bail. See also Thomas *v.* Young,
15 East, 617. and Willison *v.* Whitaker, 7
Taunt. 54, 5.
 ᵃ Clark *v.* Develin, 3 Bos. & Pul. 366.
Ante, 291.
 ᵇ Claxton *v.* Swift, 3 Mod. 87.
 ᵉ English *v.* Darley, 2 Bos. & Pul. 61.
3 Esp. Rep. 49. S. C. Infra, note. Clark
v. Deville, 3 Bos. & Pul. 363. Post, 294.
Walwyn *v.* St. Quintin, 1 Bos. & Pul. 652.
Post, 295. Ex parte Wilson, 11 Ves. 411.
Post.
 ᵈ Id. ibid.

 ʳ Gould *v.* Robson, 8 East, 576. Ante,
291.
 ˢ Id. ibid.
Per Bayley, J. in Claridge *e.* Dalton,
4 M. & S. 232, 3.
Smith *v.* Knox, 4 Esp. Rep. 46. Per
Lord Eldon. " It is said that the holder
may discharge any of the indorsers after
taking them in execution, and yet have
recourse to the others. I doubt the law as
stated so generally. I am disposed to be of
opinion, that if the holder discharge a prior
indorser, he will find it difficult to recover
against a subsequent one.
So also in English *v.* Darley, 2 Bos. &
Pul. 62, Lord Eldon, after adverting to the
inaccuracy of the marginal abstract of the
case of Hayling *v.* Mulhall, said, " Had the
plaintiff first sued a prior indorser, and discharged him from execution, it would have
afforded a sufficient objection to an action
against a subsequent indorser." See Hayling *v.* Mulhall, 2 Bl. Rep. 1235. Post.
298.

(375) In various cases decided in the United States, the same principles have been recognised. *Scarborough* v. *Harris*, 1 Bay's Rep. 177. *Robertson* v. *Vogle*, 1 Dall. Rep.
252. *James* v. *Badger*, 1 John. Cas. 131. *Kenworthy* v. *Hopkins*, 1 John. Cas. 107. If
the holder receive part payment from the maker when a note becomes due, and before
giving notice to the indorser, allows further credit to him, the indorser is discharged.
Cain v. *Colwell*, 8 John. Rep. 384. See *Lynch* v. *Reynolds*, 16 John. Rep. 42. But if
the holder receive part payment and give due notice to the indorser, the latter will be
holden for the payment of the residue. *James* v. *Badger*, 1 John. Cas. 131. And it has
been declared that any credit given by the holder of a bill to the drawer, acceptor, indorser, or promissor, is a consent to hold the demand upon their responsibility, and that
the holder has no remedy afterwards but against them, where the circumstances of the
transaction have rendered them liable absolutely, and at all events. *Shaw* v. *Griffith*,
7 Mass. Rep. 494. But it is admitted that this rule does not hold where the acceptor is
discharged by the holder, and the drawer is sued, having in his hands funds of the acceptor, which have been retained for the express purpose of paying the bill. *Sargent* v.
Appleton, 6 Mass. Rep. 85. And there seem to be other cases in which the rule has received qualifications. See *Hubbly* v. *Brown*, 16 John. Rep. 70.

lent his indorsement on a promissory note to the drawer, which note was payable on demand, to enable him to raise money on that security from the plaintiff, his banker, who agreed to make advances thereon for six months, it was held, that the bankers, who had renewed their advances at the end of the six months without the knowledge of the defendant, could not recover upon the note thus indorsed by him, without proof of the demand on the drawer, and a regular notice of the dishonour to the defendant; and the taking a *cognovit*, payable by instalments at a distant time, might discharge the drawer.[t] But the giving time or taking security from one of several acceptors of a bill or makers of a note will not discharge the other acceptors or makers from liability.

But if there be any evidence of the assent of the drawer or indorser to the security being taken from the acceptor, or if, after notice of the time having been given, the drawer or indorser promise to pay, he is precluded from taking advantage of the indulgence to the acceptor.[x]   [294]

[t] Smith *v.* Becket, 13 East, 187. The King *v.* Sheriff of Surrey, 1 Taunt. 161. Smith *v.* Knox, 3 Esp. Rep. 46. Bayl. 155 and Willison *v.* Whitaker, 2 Marsh. Rep. 383. Ante, 292.
[u] Bedford *v.* Deakin and others, 2 B. & A. 210, where one of three partners, after a dissolution of partnership, undertook, by *deed*, to pay a particular partnership debt on two bills of exchange, and that was communicated to the holder, who consented to take the separate notes of the one partner for the amount, strictly reserving his right against all three, and retained possession of the original bills; and it was held, that the separate notes having proved unproductive, he might still resort to his remedy against the other partners, and that the taking under these circumstances the separate notes, and even afterwards renewing them several times successively, did not amount to satisfaction of the joint debt.

[x] Bayl. 153, 4. Clark *v.* Devlin, 3 Bos. & Pul 363. Atkinson, the acceptor of a bill, having been arrested by the holder, offered him a warrant of attorney for the amount of the bill, payable by instalments. This offer the holder mentioned to the defendant the drawer, proposing to accept of it, who said, " you may do as you like, for I have had no notice of the non-payment " in fact he had had notice. The court held, that this amounted to an assent on the part

---

The holder having protested a bill for non-acceptance, and given due notice to the other parties to the bill, took collateral security from the drawer, and afterwards upon learning that it was probable that the drawee would pay the bill at maturity, relinquished the security. The greater part of the bill was paid at maturity, and it was regularly protested for non-payment of the residue. It was held, that as the holder had not given time to the drawer, but had merely taken security without giving new credit, the indorser was not discharged. It was in effect no more than if the holder of a bill or note had taken part payment from one of the parties. *Hurd* v. *Little*, 12 Mass. Rep. 502.

If the holder of a note release one of the joint makers, excepting from such liability as he may be under to the indorsers, the latter cannot in an action by the holder against them, set up such release as a discharge. *Stewart* v. *Eden*, 2 Caines' Rep. 121.

A part payment by one joint promissor is no discharge of the others from payment of the residue, nor can it be averred as a sufficient consideration for such discharge. *Ruggles* v. *Patten*, 8 Mass. Rep. 480.

A several suit and judgment against one joint promissor of a note, is no bar to a joint action against both, upon the same note. *Sheehy* v. *Mandeville*, 6 Cranch, 253. But see contra *Black* v. *Smith*, 9 Serg. & Rawle, 142. *Robertson* v. *Smith*, 18 Johns. Rep. 459. *Ward* v. *Johnson*, 13 Mass. Rep. 148.

The holder of a negotiable note, who gives further time to, or enters into a new contract with the drawer, does not thereby discharge the indorser. *Bennet* v. *Maule*, Gilmer, 305.

It seems, that if the holder of a note who has sued the maker obtain a judgment, and agree in consideration thereof, not to issue execution before a certain day, before which day he could not, by the practice of the court, have otherwise obtained a judgment; this is not such an indulgence to the maker as will discharge the indorser. *Hallett* v. *Holmes*, 18 Johns. 28.

Where the indorser was also a party to the instrument, by which the maker was released, and joined in the release as a creditor of the maker, it was held under the circumstances, that the indorser was not discharged by the release of the maker. *Bruen* v. *Marquand*, 17 Johns. 58.

Of the ef-
fect of giv-
ing time to
or releasing
the accept-
or, &c.
Thus where the holder of a bill of exchange, of which payment had been refused, informed the drawer of his intention to take security from the acceptor, and the drawer answered, " you may do as you like, for I am discharged for want of notice ;" and it appeared that due notice had been given, it was held that this amounted to an assent on the part of the drawer, and that the holder might still sue him, after taking security from the acceptor.ᶨ But in a subsequent case,ᶻ where the holder of a bill of exchange, on its becoming due, allowed the acceptor to renew it without consulting the indorser, but the indorser afterwards said to the acceptor, "it was the best thing that could be done," it was held, that the indorser was nevertheless discharged, because this was not a recognition of the terms granted by the holder to the acceptor, but such approbation must be considered as referring to the acceptor of the bill, to whom the arrangement was obviously advantageous.

[295]
In the instances before stated,ᵃ where the laches of the holder, in not giving notice of the non-acceptance of a bill, will be excused by the circumstance of the drawer, indorser, &c. not having effects in the hands of the drawee, such parties would also not be discharged by the holder's giving time to or taking security from the acceptor.ᵇ Therefore the holder for a valuable consideration of a bill accepted for the accommodation of the drawer, may prove the bill under a commission against the drawer, notwithstanding he has taken security from the acceptor, and given him time for payment.ᶜ So if the acceptor of a bill be merely an agent for the drawer, who is the purchaser of goods, the holder's renewing the bill without the consent of the drawer, will not discharge him.ᵈ

of the defendant to the security being taken; and therefore that the defendant was not discharged by this indulgence to the acceptor. Selw. 4th edit. 348.

Stevens v. Lynch, 12 East, 38. The defence in this action, which was by an indorsee against the drawer of a bill, was that the plaintiff had given time to the acceptor, in answer to which it was proved, that the defendant knew of such time having been given; but that conceiving himself to be still liable, three months after the bill became due, he said to the plaintiff, " I know I am liable, and if Jones (the acceptor) does not pay it, I will." Upon this Lord Ellenborough directed a verdict to be found for the plaintiff; and upon a motion for a new trial, the court held the direction right, and refused a rule.

ᵧ Id. ibid.
ᶻ Withall v. Masterman, 2 Campb. 179. Selw. 4th edit. 348.
ᵃ Ante, 198 to 209. 233 to 240.
ᵇ Walwyn v. St. Quintin, 1 Bos. & Pul. 652. 2 Esp. Rep 516, 17. S. C. Gould v. Robson, 8 East, 576. Ante, 291. Ex parte Holden, Cooke's B. L. 167.

Collott v. Haigh, 3 Campb. 281. This was an action on a bill of exchange drawn by the defendant upon J. Dufton, accepted by him, and indorsed to the plaintiffs. It appeared that when the bill became due, the plaintiffs gave time for

some weeks to Dufton, upon his lodging some security in their hands, which did not turn out to be available; but it was likewise proved, that Dufton had accepted the bill merely for the defendant's accommodation, without any consideration whatsoever. Lord Ellenborough ruled, that under these circumstances the defendant was not discharged by the time given to the acceptor. The drawer of an accommodation bill must be considered as the principal debtor, and the acceptor only in the light of a surety. The reason why notice of the dishonour of a bill must in general be given to the drawer, is, that he may recoup himself by withdrawing his effects from the hands of the acceptor, and he is discharged by time given to the acceptor without his consent, because his remedy over against the acceptor may thus be materially affected. But where the bill is accepted merely for the accommodation of the drawer, he has no effects to withdraw, and no remedy to pursue, when compelled to pay. He therefore suffers no injury either by want of notice, or by time being given to the acceptor; and in an action on the bill, he cannot defend himself upon either of these grounds. Verdict for plaintiff.

Id. ibid. Ex parte Holden, Cooke's B. L. 167. 1 Mont. 155. Cullen, 100.
ᵈ Clark and another v. Noel, 3 Campb.

After regular notice of the non-payment of a bill, the holder may tacitly *forbear* to sue the acceptor, provided he do not *agree* for sufficient consideration to give a precise time,[e] and may receive *proposals* for a security without prejudicing the claims on the other parties,[f] and it has even been holden, that agreeing (after a bill has become due and been regularly protested for non payment, and notice thereof given) *not to press the acceptor*, will not discharge the drawer.[g] And when the holders of a bill of exchange which had been refused payment by the acceptor, gave notice thereof to the drawers, but informed them that they had reason to believe it would be taken up in a few days, and offered to retain the bill till the end of the week unless they received their instructions to the contrary, it was held that such conduct did not discharge the drawer, although no further notice of non-payment was given;[h] and even an express agreement not to sue, made after giving notice of non-payment, but without sufficient consideration, and without taking any new security, being *nudum pactum*, will not discharge

411. Held that the purchaser of goods to be paid for by bill upon his agent, is not discharged by the seller taking a renewal of the bill, without giving him notice, if the agent had not funds in the hands to pay the bill when it became due. Lord Ellenborough was of opinion that Aaron was only in the nature of the surety, and remarked, that as he was not in cash to pay the bill when it became due, it was rather in favour of the defendant to allow it to be renewed. The debt was originally due from the defendant, and the security taken from his agent could be no extinction of it. It was impossible to say the purchaser of goods could be discharged under these circumstances by want of notice like the drawer of a bill of exchange. The plaintiffs had a verdict, which, in the ensuing term, upon a motion for a new trial, was approved of by the court.

[e] Second resolution in Walwyn v. St. Quintin, 1 Bos. & Pul. 652. Selw. N. P. 4th ed. 347. Wright v. Simpson, 6 Ves. 734.

[f] Walwyn v. St. Quintin, 1 Bos. & Pul. 652. In an action by indorsees against the drawer of a bill, it appeared that after the bill had become due and been protested for non-payment, though no notice thereof had been given to the defendant, he having no effects in the hands of the acceptor. The plaintiffs received part of the money on account from the indorser, and that to an application from the acceptor, stating that it was probable he should be able to pay at a future period, they returned for answer, that they would not press him. It was urged, that either of these facts discharged the drawer. But the court, after argument and time taken to consider, held that they did not, and awarded the *postea* to the plaintiffs. Eyre, C. J. said, that had this forbearance to sue the acceptor taken place before noting and protesting for non-payment, or that the bill

had not been demanded when it was due, it is clear that the drawer would have been discharged; it would have been giving a new credit to the acceptor. But that after protest for non-payment, and notice to the drawer, or an equivalent to a notice, a right to sue the drawer had attached, another holder was not bound to sue the acceptor, he might therefore forbear to sue him. See 2 Esp. Rep. 515. S. C. Manning's Index, 72

[g] Walwyn v. St. Quintin, 1 Bos. & Pul. 652. supra. Bayl. 154.

[h] Forster and another v. Jurdison and another, 16 East, 105. The plaintiffs were indorsees of a bill of exchange drawn by the defendants on J. L. and accepted by him. The bill was duly presented for payment and dishonoured, but the acceptor requested the plaintiffs to keep the bill a week and he should be able to pay it. The plaintiffs gave the defendants notice o the dishonour, and of the acceptor's request. and added they would keep the bill till the end of the week, unless they heard from them to the contrary. It was contended for the defendants, that the plaintiffs should have given them notice at the end of the week of the bill not having been paid, by which laches they were discharged. Wood, B. before whom the cause was tried, was of that opinion, and a verdict was found for the defendants. A rule for a new trial was afterwards obtained, and on cause shown, the court were of opinion, that the plaintiffs had done every thing which was incumbent upon them, to give themselves a title under the bill, and that by their letter, they at most took upon themselves an agency on the part of the defendants to get payment of the bill, and in that character they continued to hold it for the defendants, and that after the notice received by the defendants, the latter were bound to look after the acceptor, and the rule was made absolute.

Of the ef-
fect of giv-
ing time to
or releasing
the accept-
or, &c.

the other parties;[1] and it has been decided, that where all parties have had due notice of the dishonour of a bill, a subsequent indorser is not discharged by a treaty between the attorney of the holder and the drawer and acceptor, that the holder should wait a given time for the payment of the balance in consideration of receiving from the acceptor, or prior indorser, by a certain time, a stipulated proportion of the account, a part only of which proportion was afterwards paid, although the subsequent indorser had no notice of such treaty or the result, nor was informed of the payment of any part of the money due on the bill, or of the ultimate non-payment of the balance till some months after the original dishonour of the bill.[k] And though we have just seen, that taking a *cognovit* payable at a distant time, might discharge the drawer and indorsers;[l] it would be otherwise if a *cognovit* or warrant of attorney be taken without giving time.[m]

Of receiv-
ing part-
payment of
the accept-
or, &c.

It appears to have been holden, that if on presentment for payment, the holder *take less* than the whole sum due thereon of the acceptor, or indorser, in part satisfaction, without the assent to the other parties to the bill, he thereby discharges them, because, as it was said, it is an election to receive payment from the acceptor.[n] But it is now settled, that the holder may receive part payment from the acceptor, or indorser, and may sue the other parties for the residue, provided he do not also give time to the acceptor for the payment of such residue;[o] and if the holder of a joint and several promissory note, enter up judgment by *cognovit* against one of the makers, and levy part under a *fi. fa.* this is no discharge of the other.[p]

[298]   It is said, that if the drawee have on presentment for acceptance, engaged to pay only a part, and the holder has given notice of such partial acceptance to the other parties, he should, when the bill becomes due, receive of the drawee the sum for which he accepted, and cause a protest again to be made for non-payment of the remaining sum.[q]

Effect of
indulgence
as to prior
parties.

Though the giving time to an acceptor, or indorser, will thus in

[i] Semble Walwyn v. St. Quintin, 1 Bos. & Pul. 655. Dean v. Newhall, 8 T. R. 168. Fitch v. Sutton, 5 East, 230.

Arundle Bank v. Goble, K. B. 1817. Action by indorsee against drawer of a bill. The plaintiffs were the holders when the bill became due, and duly presented the same to the acceptor for payment, and wrote a letter to the defendant in due time, informing him of the dishonour, but that from the promise of the acceptor they expected the same would be shortly paid. Afterwards the acceptor applied to them for indulgence for some months. They in reply wrote to the acceptor, that they would give him the time, but that they should expect interest. The cause was tried on the home circuit, before Burroughs, J. when it was contended by Nolan and Comyn for the defendant, that this indulgence to the acceptor discharged the drawer; but the jury found a verdict for the plaintiffs. On motion to the court of K. B. for a new trial, the court held, that as no fresh security was taken from the acceptor, the

agreement of the plaintiffs to wait without consideration did not discharge the drawer, because the acceptor might, notwithstanding such agreement, be sued at the next instant, and that the understanding that interest should be paid by the acceptor, made no difference. Rule refused. See also Willison v. Whitaker, 2 Marsh. 383; and Brickwood v. Anniss, 5 Taunt. 614. Ante, 292; and Bayl. 154.

[k] Badnall v. Samuel, 3 Price, 521.

[l] Ante, 293.

[m] Ayrey v. Davenport, 2 New Rep. 474.

[n] Tassel v. Lewis, 2 Lord Raym. 744. Kellock v. Robinson, 2 Stra. 745. Sel. Ca. 147. S. C. Bul. Ni. Pri. 273. Hull v. Pitfield, 1 Wils. 48.

[o] Gould v. Robson, 8 East, 580, ante, 291. Walwyn v. St Quintin, 1 Bos. & Bal. 652, ante, 296. Bul. Ni. Pri. 271. 271, 275. Mar. 86. Bayl 154.

[p] Ayrey v. Davenport, 2 New Rep. 474. supra, note. Ex parte Gifford, 6 Ves. 805.

[q] Mar. 69, 85, 86.

general discharge all subsequent indorsers, who would be entitled to resort to the party indulged, the giving time to a subsequent indorser will not discharge a prior indorser,[r] and therefore the holder of a bill may sue a prior indorser after having let a subsequent indorser whom he had taken in execution, out of jail, on a letter of license, without paying the debt.[s] And it has been decided, that the holder of an accommodation note, who has received a composition from, and who has covenanted not to sue the payee, for whose accommodation the note was made, may notwithstanding, sue the maker, though on payment of it he will have a right of action against the payee;[t] and if the holder release to the payee all claims in respect of the note, not knowing that he is a surety, this will not discharge the maker.[u] And it has long been settled, that if the holder of an accommodation bill receive a part from the drawer, and takes a promise from him upon the back of the bill, for the payment of the residue at an enlarged time, it is clear that such act will not discharge the acceptor.[x] And though in one case it was held, that if the indorsee of a bill of exchange having notice that it was accepted without consideration, receive part payment from the drawer and give him time to pay the residue, he

[299]

[r] Claridge v. Dalton, 4 M. & S. 232. Hayling v. Mullhall, 2 Bla. Rep. 1235. English v. Darley, 2 Bos. & Pul. 61. Smith v. Knox, 3 Esp. Rep. 47. Nadin v. Battie, 5 East, 147; and see Ex parte Barclay, 7 Ves. 597. Bayl. 151. Selw. 4th ed. 348.

Claridge v. Dalton, 4 M. & S. 232, 3. Per Bayley, J. "If the holder gave time to the payee he cannot call on the indorsers; but this rule does not apply to a party lower down on the bill, as if the fifth indorsee were to give time to the last indorser for six months, proposing in the mean while to endeavour to get payment for the indorsers lower down on the bill: this might well be done."

Hayling v. Mullhall, 2 Bla. Rep. 1235. A bill was indorsed by Sheridan to Boon, and by him to the plaintiff: he sued Boon and took him in execution, but discharged him upon a letter of license. He then sued Sheridan, for whom the defendant became bail, and upon an action against the defendant, he contended that the debt was satisfied by the imprisonment of Boon, but the court was clear it was not, and Mullhall was obliged to pay the money. See the observations on the error in the margin, analysis of this case, in English v. Darley, 2 Bos. & Pul. 62. Supra.

[s] Hayling v. Mullhall, 2 Bla. Rep. 1285, supra.

[t] Mallet v. Thompson, 5 Esp. Rep. 178.

[u] Carstairs and others, assignees, &c. v. Rolleston and others, 5 Taunt. 551.— 1 Marsh. 207. To an action by the indorsees of a promissory note against the drawers, the defendant pleaded, that he drew the note as surety only for the payee, and that the plaintiff had released the payee from all claims in respect of

the said note, without alleging that the plaintiff had notice of the want of consideration between the defendant and payee: Held, that the release did not operate as an extinguishment of the consideration which the plaintiff has given to the payee for notice, so as to make it a note without consideration between himself and the defendant, and therefore that the plea was bad on general demurrer. Gibbs, C. J. This case has been argued on the only ground on which it could be supported for a moment, and ingenuity has furnished an argument which I had not discovered. The object of the defendant was to accommodate the payee, and I admit that the payee could not have sued the makers of the note, nor could an indorsee have done so, unless he had given consideration for it. But it is insisted, that the release which has been given by the bankrupts, who were indorsees to the original payee, operates as an extinguishment of the consideration which they gave for it, and therefore puts them in the condition of indorsees without consideration. I am not of that opinion; the indorsement was for a valuable consideration, and the indorsees had the security of the defendants as makers of the note for their debt, and though they released the original payee, they still retain their remedy against the drawers. Whatever might have been the case, if the bankrupts had had notice, that the instrument was given originally without consideration, as to which I give no opinion, I am decided, that, as the matter now stands, the plaintiffs right of action remains against the defendants. The rest of the court concurred in the opinion of the C. J. Judgment for the plaintiffs.

[x] Ellis v. Gallindo, cited in Dingwall v. Dunster, Dougl. 259.

Effect of thereby discharges the acceptor ; yet in subsequent cases a different

indulgence as to prior parties. doctrine has been established.[a] We have seen, however, that the

[y] Laxton v. Peat, 2 Campb. 185. Bayl. 158.

Laxton v. Peat, 2 Campb. 185. Indorsee of a bill against the acceptor. It appeared that the bill had been accepted for the accommodation of the drawer, which circumstance was known to the plaintiff, who gave value for the bill. When the bill became due the plaintiff received part payment from the drawer ; and gave him time to pay the remainder, without the concurrence of the defendant. Lord Ellenborough. This being an accommodation bill within the knowledge of all the parties, the acceptor can only be considered a surety for the drawer, and in the case of simple contracts, the surety is discharged by time being given without his concurrence to the principal. The defendant's remedy over is materially affected by the new agreement, into which the plaintiff entered with the drawer after the bill was due. The case is exactly the same as if the bill had been drawn by the defendant, and accepted by Hunt, in consideration of a debt due. According to many authorities, the defendant upon that supposition would have been discharged by the time given to Hunt; and the principle of these authorities applies with equal strength to the facts actually given in evidence. Plaintiff nonsuited. But this doctrine seems to have been disputed by Mr. J. Gibbs, in the case of Kerrison v. Cooke, 3 Campb. 362, and he denied the distinction which has been made between an acceptor in the ordinary course of business, and an accommodation acceptor. And Lord Eldon (in 11 Ves. 411) also objected to any such distinction, and in the case of Anderson v. Cleveland, 13 East, 430 (notes,) Lord Mansfield seems to have been of opinion, that a neglect to call upon the acceptor affords no defence, saying that the maker of a note, and the acceptor of a bill remain liable; the acceptance is proof of the acceptor's having effects in hand, and he ought never to part with them unless he is sure that the bill has been paid by the drawer. The same doctrine has been maintained in the case of Dingwall v. Dunster, Dougl. 235, 247. The same doctrine was entertained by Lord Ellenborough in Mallet v. Thompson, 5 Esp. Rep. 178. Where the holder of a note, knowing that it had been made for the accommodation of Dwigg, signed a composition deed releasing Dwigg, without the maker's concurrence. Also in the case of The Trent Navigation Company v. Harley, 10 East, 34, the court appeared to have considered that the neglect of the obligee of a bond to compel the principal to account, did not release the surety from his liability.

[z] Kerrison v. Cooke, 3 Campb. 362. Ragget v. Axmore, 4 Taunt. 730. Fentam, v. Pocock, 5 Taunt. 192. 1 Marsh. 14. S. C. Carstairs v. Rolleston, 2 Taunt. 551. Marsh. 507. S. C. Mallet v. Thompson, 5 Esp. Rep. 178.

Kerrison v. Cooke, 3 Campb. 362. Indorsee against acceptor. The plaintiff after notice that the bill was accepted for the accommodation of the drawer, gave time to the drawee, without concurrence of the defendant, and yet it was held, the plaintiff was entitled to recover. Per Gibbs, J. admitting Laxton v. Peat to be law, of which grave doubts have been entertained, the present case may be distinguished from it. Lord Ellenborough's decision there proceeded upon the ground that the drawer, according to the understanding of the different parties to the bill, was considered as primarily liable, and was in the first instance looked to for payment. But here payment is demanded of the acceptor, when the bill becomes due, and he then promises to pay it. This shows that he was held liable, as in the common case of the acceptor of a bill of exchange, and I am of opinion that he was not discharged by time given, under these circumstances, to the drawer. I am sorry the term "accommodation bill" ever found its way into the law, or that parties were allowed to get rid of the obligations they profess to contract, by putting their names to negotiable securities.

Fentum v. Pocock and another, 5 Taunt. 192. 1 Marsh. S. C. Indorsee against acceptor. When the bill became due, it was duly presented for payment and refused, and the plaintiff was then informed that it was an accommodation bill, and that defendant had no effects of the drawer. The plaintiff received from the drawer 65l., in part discharge of the bill, and afterwards, without the concurrence of the acceptor, took a *cognovit* from the drawer, payable by instalments, and it was held that this did not discharge the acceptor. Per Ld Mansfield's C. J. No doubt if the defendant can succeed in establishing the principle that we must so subvert and pervert the situation of the parties, as to make the acceptor merely a surety, and the drawer the principal, the consequence contended for must follow. This case of Laxton v. Peat, certainly is the first in which it was ever supposed that the acceptor of a bill of exchange was not the first person, and the last person compellable to pay that bill to the holder of it, and that any thing could discharge the acceptor except payment or a release; and I never before knew there was any difference between an acceptance given for an accommodation and an acceptance for value. When I first

acceptor of an accommodation bill may be discharged by the holders, who were bankers of the drawer, receiving more than sufficient to cover it.[a]

Effect of indulgence as to *prior* parties.

If, when the bill becomes due, the acceptor be a *bankrupt*, the holder may, without the assent of the other parties, *prove* the bill under the commission, and receive a dividend or dividends, and such conduct will not discharge the other parties to the bill from their respective liabilities to him, if he have given regular notice of non-payment:[b] (383) so the circumstance of one of the parties to a bill having been charged in execution, and discharged as an insolvent, does not preclude the holder from proceeding against the other parties.[c]

Of *proving* under a *commission*, or against an insolvent debtor, and of *compounding* with the acceptor.

But if the holder of a bill *compound* with the acceptor or other party, without the assent of the drawer, or other subsequent parties,

saw that case in Campbell, I was in the same state as Mr. Justice Gibbs, and doubted a great deal whether it could be law. The case of Collet v. Haigh must be considered not as a separate decision, but as resting on the authority of the former. It is utterly impossible for any Judge, whatever his learning and abilities may be, to decide at once rightly upon every point that comes before him, at Nisi Prius, and whoever looks through Campbell's Reports, will be greatly surprised to see amongst such an immense number of questions, many of them of the most important kind, which came before that noble and learned Judge, not that there are mistakes, but that he is, in by far the most of the causes, so wonderfully right, beyond the proportion of any other Judges. But in this case we think that we are bound to differ from him, and to hold that it is impossible for us to consider the acceptor of an accommodation bill in the light of the surety for the payment of the drawer, and that we cannot therefore say that he is discharged by the indulgence shown to the drawer; certainly the paying the respect to accommodation bills is not what one would wish to do, seeing the mischiefs arising from them. One might find here a very important distinction between this case and the case decided by Lord Ellenborough, namely, that here the person taking the bill did not, at the time when he took it, know that it was an accommodation bill, and that if he did not then know it, what does it signify what came to his knowledge afterwards if he took the bill for a valuable consideration; but it is better not to rest this case upon that foundation; for as it appears to me, if the holder had known in the clearest manner at the time of his taking the bill, that it was merely an accommodation bill, it would make no man-

ner of difference, for he who accepts a bill whether for value or to serve a friend, makes himself in all events liable as the acceptor, and nothing can discharge him but payment or a release. The case before Gibbs, J. has shaken this decision in Laxton v. Peat, and we think rightly; the case cited English v. Darley, is not applicable, where the giving time to an acceptor was held to be a discharge of an indorser, who stands only in the situation of a surety for the first. The rule therefore which has been obtained for setting aside the verdict and entering a nonsuit must be discharged. (1)

[a] Ante, 289, note.

[b] See observations in English v. Darley, ante, 290, 291. Ex parte Wilson, 11 Ves. 412. Stock v. Mawson, 1 Bos. & Pul. 286.

[c] Macdonald v Bovington, 4 T. R. 825. A bill drawn by Macdonald on Bovington, was indorsed to Thompson, who charged Bovington in execution on it. Bovington was discharged as an insolvent, then Thompson sued Macdonald and recovered. Macdonald paid the bill, sued Bovington, and charged him in execution, and on a rule *nisi* to discharge him and cause shown, it was urged that Bovington had satisfied the bill by being charged in execution at the suit of Thompson. Sed per Lord Kenyon, nothing can be clearer than that he has not, it was a mere formal satisfaction as to Thompson, not like actual payment, and when Macdonald was obliged to pay the bill, a new cause of action arose against the defendant by the payment, without regard to what passed in the former action. And per Buller, J. the consequence would be, that because the drawer was obliged to pay the holder, the acceptor would be discharged without paying either. Rule discharged. See also Bayl. 152.

(383) So it has been held in New York, that the proceeding under a commission of bankruptcy in London, against the acceptor, was no discharge of the indorser of a bill drawn here. *Kenworthy* v. *Hopkins*, 1 John Cas. 107.

(1) See on this subject, *Bank of Montgomery* v. *Walker*, 9 Serg. & Rawle, 228.

Of *proving* he thereby releases them from their liabilities, if they had effects in
under   the hands of the acceptor or prior indorser; for there is a material
commis-   distinction between taking a sum of money in part satisfaction of a
sion, or a-   debt, as in the case of a dividend, and taking a sum in satisfaction of
gainst   an   such debt, where the party has an option to refuse less than the whole,
insolvent,   as where he compounds with the acceptor, and thereby deprives all
and of *com-*   other parties to the bill of the right of resorting to him.[d]   And
pounding   though the agent of the holder by mistake signed a composition deed
with   the   in favour of the acceptor, thinking that the proceedings were a bank-
acceptor,   ruptcy, yet it was decided that the drawer was discharged.[e]   And
&c.

[d] Ex parte Wilson, 11 Ves. 410. infra,
note. Cooke's Bank. Law, 168. Cullen,
158, 9. and cases there cited. Ex parte
Smith, 3 Bro. C. C. 1; see observations on
English *v.* Darley, ante, 290, and post,
Chapter on Bankruptcy. 1 Mont. 546.

Ex parte Smith, 3 Bro. C. C. 1. Lewis
and Potter indorsed certain bills and notes
to Esdaile, and became bankrupt. Esdaile
proved the amount of the bills and notes
under their commission, and afterwards received a composition from the acceptors
of the bills, and the makers of the notes,
and gave them a full discharge without the
knowledge of the assignees of Lewis and
Potter. On petition by the assignees to
have the debt in respect of the bills and
notes expunged, the Chancellor held, that
by discharging the acceptors and makers
without the consent of the indorser, the
latter was discharged also. To the same
effect is the case of Ex parte Wilson, 11
Ves. 410. See also Smith *v.* Knox, 3 Esp.
Rep. 46.

In a case where an action was brought
by several partners, as indorsees of a promissory note against the defendant as indorser, and it appeared in evidence that one
of the partners had discharged a *prior* indorser by a deed of composition, it was
holden, that such deed operated as a release
to the defendant. Ellison and others *v.*
Dezell, Bristol Summer Assizes, 1811,
Selw. N. P. 4th ed. 348.

[e] Ex parte Wilson, 11 Ves. 410. In
July, 1799, Andrew Paul Pourtales and
Andrew George Pourtales, drew two bills
of exchange upon Claessan, Kieckhoefer,
and Co. of Hamburgh, at three months after date, for 350*l.* and 250*l.*, payable to
the order of the petitioner, for a valuable
consideration. The bills were accepted:
but before they were due, the acceptors
stopped payment; and the bills were returned protested. The drawers afterwards
became bankrupt. The petitioner's proof
in respect of the bills was objected to, until he should have had recourse to the estate of the acceptors, and have received
such dividend as should be payable from
their estate. The petitioner sent the bills
to his agent at Hamburgh for that purpose;
who received a dividend from the estate of
the acceptors; and was afterwards admitted to prove the residue of his debt under
the commission against the drawers: but be-

fore any dividend was received under
that proof, it appeared that no proceeding
in nature of a commission of bankruptcy
had issued against the acceptors, but their
affairs were settled by a deed of composition, which the petitioner's agent had signed upon receiving the dividend in full discharge of the estate of the acceptors. The
petition prayed, that the dividends under
the commission should be paid to the petitioner. It was admitted there was no fraud;
but the deed of composition was signed,
and the dividend received by his agent
without inquiry. The petition stated, that
the assignees and the solicitor under the
commission pressed the petitioner to apply
and receive what might be obtained from
the estate of the acceptors, representing,
that he should prove for the residue; but
upon the affidavits there was no special undertaking; and the transaction appeared to
originate in a mistake of all parties; supposing the proceeding at Hamburgh was in
the nature of bankruptcy. The Lord Chancellor. The law is not disputed: it was
very well settled by Lord Thurlow upon
great deliberation, that, if a person, having
the security of drawer and acceptor, with
effects, (a distinction much to be regretted,
having given very mischievous authenticity
to accommodation paper) gives the accept-
or time, and much more if the holder fully
discharges the acceptor by composition,
the holder can no longer make a demand
upon the drawer, whether solvent or not;
for this reason, that if the drawer could
come upon the acceptor afterwards, the
acceptor does not receive any benefit by
the composition. The nature of the contract must therefore be, that the holder
shall so deal with the bill that no third
person shall come upon the acceptor in
consequence of his act. I remember Lord
Thurlow said, he had consulted the Judges
upon that case. The decision is therefore
of very high authority. Lord Rosslyn was
struck with this consideration, that if the
holder did all he could substantially do for
the benefit of the persons whose names
were upon the bill, that was all that could
be expected, and held that he should if he
really acted for the benefit of the other
parties by taking a composition from the
acceptor, go on against the drawer. But
the misfortune of that is, that the other
parties have a right by law to consider

where the indorser of a bill of exchange becomes bankrupt, and the holder proves the amount of the bill under his commission, and afterwards compounds with and discharges the acceptor without the consent of the assignees of the indorser, he thereby also discharges the indorser's estate, and the proof of his debt *must be expunged.*[f] Of proving under a commission, &c.

On payment of the amount of a bill or note, it has been considered doubtful whether a person paying can insist on a *receipt* being given;[g] but now the party it should seem is entitled to demand a receipt.[h] It is usual to give a receipt on the back of the bill, and it has been said, that it is the duty of bankers to make some memorandum on bills and notes paid by them.[i] Such receipt need not, like other receipts, be stamped.[k] Where a part is paid, the person paying should take care to have the partial receipt marked on the bill, or he may, as it is said, be liable to pay the amount again to a *bona fide* indorsee.[l] Where an action was brought by the indorser of a bill (who had paid it to an indorsee) against the acceptor, he was nonsuited, although he produced the bill and protest, because he could not produce a receipt for the money paid by him to the indorsee upon the protest, according to the custom of merchants; though Holt, C. J. seemed to be of opinion, that if the plaintiff could have proved payment by any evidence, it would have been sufficient.[m] As it has been held, that a general receipt on the back of a bill of exchange is *prima facie* evidence of its having been paid by the acceptor,[n] it would perhaps be advisable, in

4thly. Of the receipt for payment. [304]

[margin annotation]

what is for their benefit, and are the judges of that; and that has been carried so far, that the actual bankruptcy of the acceptor does not dispense with the necessity of notice to the drawer. That being the law, I felt a wish to find that part of the petition sustained, which represents, that the assignees and the solicitor pressed the petitioner to get what benefit he could in the affairs at Hamburgh, intimating that he should afterwards prove under the commission. But the affidavits amount only to this, that the assignees and the solicitor, being persuaded that there was a bankruptcy at Hamburgh, and a dividend actually set apart, so that in bankruptcy it was to be considered as received in diminution of the proof, do make that representation; and that the petitioner shall receive dividends under that bankruptcy, before he comes to prove under the commission in this country, and the future dividends after proof. The petitioner accordingly sent to his agent at Hamburgh, not inquiring whether the proceedings there was a bankruptcy or a composition, and the agent signed the deed of composition, which, in respect of payments under it, actually discharges the acceptor. The question whether the petitioner was by fraud drawn in, or required to sign the deed of composition, is a mere question of fact. The whole was a common mistake, under the apprehension of all, that it was a bankruptcy; but, that being misapprehension, the consequence from not knowing what the act was, must fall upon the person who did the act, who therefore having, by himself or his agent, accepted a composition in full of the whole

demand, is unfortunately, but effectually, under circumstances, that exclude any demand by him against the drawer's estate.

[f] Ex parte Smith, 3 Bro. C. C. 1. ante, 302, note. Cooke's Bank. Law, 168, 9. Cullen, 158, 9. 1 Montague, 546.; and Ex parte Wilson, 11 Ves. 410. ante, 302, note.

[g] Cole v. Blake, Peake Ni. Pri. 179, 180. See Green v. Croft, 2 Hen. Bla. 30, 31, 32.

[h] 43 Geo. 3. c. 126. s. 5.

[i] Burbridge v. Manners, 3 Campb. 193. ante, 286.

[k] 44 G. 3. c. 98. Schedule A. 23 G. 3. c. 49. s. 4 and 7. In 55 G. 3. c. 184, Schedule, part 1, tit. *Receipts*, the exemptions are as follows:

"Receipts or discharges given for any principal money due on exchequer bills.

"Receipts or discharges written upon promissory notes, bills of exchange, or drafts or orders for payment of money, duly stamped according to the laws in force at the date thereof, or upon bills of exchange drawn out of, but payable in, Great Britain.

"Receipts or discharges given upon bills or notes of the Governor and Company of the Bank of England.

"Letters by the General Post, acknowledging the safe arrival of any bills of exchange, promissory notes, or any other securities for money."

[l] Cooper v. Davies, 1 Esp. 463.

[m] Mendez v. Carreroon, Ld. Raym. 742.

[n] Scholey v. Walsby, Peake Rep. 25.; but see Pfiel v. Van Battenberg, 2 Campb. 439.

5thly. Of
the   effect
of payment,
and of pay-
ment   by
mistake.

[307]

And it appears to have been considered, that if the holder of a check, immediately after the death of the drawer, and before the banker is apprized of it, receive the amount, he will not be liable to refund, though in general the death of the drawer of the check is a countermand of the banker's authority to pay.[a](391)

If bankers pay a cancelled check, drawn by a customer, under circumstances which ought to have excited their suspicion, and induced them to make inquiries before paying it, [f] or if they pay a check after notice from their customer not to do so,[g] they cannot take credit for the amount in their accounts.

Where an action having been brought against the acceptor of a bill of exchange, it was agreed between the parties that the defendant should pay the costs, renew the bill, and give a warrant of attorney to secure the debt, and the defendant gave the warrant of attorney and renewed the bill, but did not pay the costs, it was held that the plaintiff might bring a fresh action on the first bill while the second was outstanding in the hands of an indorsee.[h]

Though a bequest by a debtor to his creditor of a legacy greater than the amount of the debt, will in general be deemed a satisfaction for such debt, it has been held, that a negotiable bill of exchange or note is not satisfied by a legacy ;[i] (392) but in another case it was held, that a debt on a note was discharged by an entry in the testator's hand, that the debtor should pay no interest, nor should he, the testator, take the principal, unless greatly distressed, it being proved that the testator died in affluent circumstances.[k]   It has been recently de-

---

[a] Tate v. Hilbert, 2 Ves. jun. 118.
[f] Scholey v. Ramsbottom, 2 Campb. 485. Et Pothier Traite du Contrat de Change, part 1. c. 4. s. 99. et seq.
Scholey v. Ramsbottom and others, 2 Campb. 485. The defendants were bankers, with whom the plaintiff kept cash. This was an action to recover the balance of his account, and the only question was, whether they were entitled to take credit for a sum of 366l. On Wednesday, the 20th September, 1809, the plaintiff being indebted to Messrs. Miller and Co. drew a check in their favour, in the following form :

"London, Sept. 20, 1809.
"Messrs. Ramsbottom, Newman, Ramsbottom, and Co. pay Messrs. Miller and Co. or bearer, three hundred and sixty-six pounds.
366l.   "ROBERT SCHOLEY."

But finding that the sum was incorrect, he tore the check into four pieces, which he threw from him, and drew another in the same form for 360l. The latter was

presented for payment, and paid by the defendants the same day. On Monday, the 25th of September, the first check was likewise presented for payment by a person unknown. The four pieces into which it had been torn, were then neatly pasted together upon another slip of paper, but the rents were quite visible, and the face of the check was soiled and dirty. The defendants' clerk paid it however without making any inquiries. Lord Ellenborough was of opinion, that, under these circumstances, bankers were not justified in paying a check, and the jury found a verdict for the plaintiff for 366l.

[g] Ante, 148, 9, 281.
[h] Norris v. Aylett, 2 Campb. 329.
[i] Carr v. Eastabrook, 3 Ves. 561.
[k] Aston and others, executors, v. Pye, Common Pleas, Easter Term, 28 Geo. 3. cited in Eldon v. Smyth, 5 Ves. 850. Judgment for defendant, action for 300l., upon a note of hand given by defendant to his uncle, payable twelve months after date. The cause

---

(391) See as to this point, *Cutts* v. *Perkins*, 12 Mass. Rep. 206.
(392) See on this point *Strong* v. *Williams*, 12 Mass. Rep. 391, where it was held, that *prima facie* as a legacy is to be deemed a bounty, and not a payment of a debt due ; though this presumption might be rebutted by circumstances.

The effect of payment may in a great measure be collected from the immediately preceding paragraphs, and from what has been said with respect to a transfer of a bill of exchange after it has been paid.[y] If a person, under a misapprehension of facts, pay a bill which he was under no legal obligation to discharge, as where the person whom he paid had been guilty of laches, which, had the bill not been paid, might, in an action brought upon it, have been a sufficient ground of defence, he may, if prejudiced, perhaps, recover back the money, as had and received to his use;[z](390) and a party knowing a check to be post dated, and that the drawers were insolvent, presented it for payment to the plaintiffs who were bankers, and who, without knowledge of these facts, paid its amount, although they had no funds of the drawers in their hands at the time, but expected some in the course of the day, it was held, that the plaintiffs were entitled to recover it back in an action for money had and received;[a] but a *bona fide* holder, not guilty of laches, cannot in general be compelled to refund; and where the drawee of two forged bills accepted one and paid the other, it was decided, that he could not recover back the amount from the *bona fide* holder.[b] But where the Victualling-Office paid a forged victualling bill, and on discovery of the fraud called on the Bank of England, whom they had paid, and they called on the plaintiff, and he on the defendant, through whose hands it had passed, it was held, that the plaintiff was entitled to recover from him.[c]

Where A. paid a sum of money into his bankers for a specific purpose, and the bankers clerk, by mistake, paid this money to B. who had no right to it, it was held, that A. could not maintain an action against B. to recover it back, but must sue the bankers, and they sue B.[d](391)

[y] See also Hull v. Pitfield, 1 Wils. 46. Bacon v. Searles, 1 Hen. Bla. 88. See the beginning of chap. 5, of the 2d part, post.
[z] Ante, 236.
[a] Martin v. Morgan, 3 Moore, 635.—1 Gow. 123. S. C.
[b] Ante, 236. Price v. Neal, 1 Bla. Rep. 390. 3 Burr. 1354, observed on in Jones v. Ryde, 1 Marsh. 160. Price v. Neale, 3 Burr. 1345. 1 Bla. Rep. 390. S. C. Two forged bills were drawn upon the plaintiff, which he accepted and paid. On discovering the forgery, he brought this action for money had and received, to recover back the money; but on a case reserved, the court held, that it would not lie; and Lord Mansfield said, it was incumbent on him to have been satisfied, before he accepted or paid them, that the bills were the drawer's hand. And in Smith v. Chester, 1 T. R. 655, Buller, J. says, when a bill is presented for acceptance, the acceptor looks to the hand-writing of the drawer, which he is afterwards precluded from disputing, and it is on that account that he is liable even though the bill is forged.
Smith and others v. Mercer, 6 Taunt. 76. 1 Marsh. 453. S. C. A bill of exchange, with a forged acceptance, purporting to be payable at the house of A and Co. bankers, in London, with whom the supposed acceptor keeps cash, is indorsed to B. for a valuable consideration; B. indorses it to his agent in London, who presents it on the 23d of April, at the house of A. and Co. for payment; A. and Co. pay it, and send it on the 30th of April to the supposed acceptor, who disavows it; A. and Co. immediately give notice of the forgery to B., and demand re-payment, which, B. refuses; all parties are ignorant of the fraud: Held, that A. and Co by paying the bill, without ascertaining that the acceptance was genuine, were precluded from recovering the amount from B. Chambre, J. *dissentiente.*
[c] Bruce v. Bruce, 1 Marsh. 165. 5 Taunt. 495, in notis.
[d] Rogers v. Kelly, 2 Campb. 123.

(390) See *Garland* v. *Salem Bank*, 9 Mass. Rep. 408. S. P.
(391) So where money remitted to pay one bill was applied to the payment of another bill, it was held that no action lay against the holder of the latter in favour of the party remitting the money, but he must look to the other parties to rectify the mistake, if any was made. *Dey* v. *Murray*, 9 John. Rep. 171.

Sect. 3. Of the conduct which the holder should pursue on non-payment.

Fourthly, By whom notice should be given. Ante, 226 to 228.
Fifthly, To whom the notice should be given. Ante, 228 to 230.
Sixthly, Of the liability of the parties to the bill on receiving notice. Ante, 230 to 233.
Seventhly, How the consequences of a neglect to give notice may be waived. Ante, 233 to 240.

We will concisely consider in the same order the applicability of the rules already mentioned to the case of non-payment.

1st. When notice of non-payment is necessary.

The *necessity of giving notice of non-payment* is governed by nearly of the same rules as prevail in the case of non-acceptance.[r] Notice, we have seen, ought in general to be given ; or the drawer and indorsers will be discharged from all liability.[s] The want of effects of the drawer in the hands of the drawee, will, we have seen, in general excuse the neglect to give due notice to him ;[t] but few other circumstances will have that effect.[u] When the bill has been already protested for non-acceptance, and due notice thereof has been given, though usual it is not necessary to protest for non-payment, or to give notice thereof ;[x] and after a regular notice of non-payment to the drawer, the engagement of the holder to present the bill again, and his doing so, but omitting to give notice of the second dishonour, will not prejudice his remedy against the drawer on the bill.[y] And persons who are bankers, both for the drawer and acceptor of a bill, and have received it from the drawer and given credit for it in an account between them, if, before it becomes due, they receive directions from the acceptor to stop the payment of it at the place of payment, and do so accordingly, are not bound to give notice of this circumstance to the drawer, the communication of the acceptor being confidential, and it sufficing to give a general notice of non-payment to the drawer.[z] We have seen, that if a note be made payable at a bankers, it is not necessary to give the maker notice of non-payment;[a] and it has been decided, that in an action against the

[310] acceptor of a bill payable at a bankers, it is not necessary to prove that notice of the non-payment was given to the acceptor.[b] But an agreement between all the parties to a bill or note, that it should not be put in suit till certain estates were sold, will constitute no excuse for the want of notice of non-payment, for as such an understanding could not have been given in evidence to prevent the holder from suing on the note, so it ought not to be received to excuse the want of due notice.[c] *The other points respecting the necessity for notice of non-payment, and the excuses for the omission will be found, ante,* 196 *to* 215, *and* 233 *to* 240.

2dly. *Form and mode* of giving and giving notice.

With respect to the *form of the notice of non-payment, and the mode of giving it,* the rules relating to non-acceptance here also in general prevail.[d] In the case of a *foreign* bill, *a protest for non-payment* is as

[r] Ante, 196 to 215, and 233 to 240.
[s] Ante, 196.
[t] Ante, 196 to 209.
[u] Ante, 210 to 215.

[x] Price v. Dardel, *coram* Lord Kenyon, Sittings at Guildhall, London, 11th December, 1794. De La Toore v. Barclay, 1 Stark. 7 and 8. Ante, 232, note.

[y] Forster v. Jurdison, 16 East, 105. Ante, 296.

[z] Croase v. Smith, 1 M. & S. 454.

[a] Pearse v. Pemberlty and others, 3 Campb. 261. Ante, 296.

[b] Treacher v. Hinton, 4 Barn. & Ald. 413. Smith v. Thatcher, id. 200. Edwards v. Dick, id. 212.

[c] Free v. Hawkins, Holt C. N. P. 550. Ante, 47.

[d] Ante, 215 to 222.

essential as a protest for non-acceptance,[a] and can, in general, only be 2dly. *Form* dispensed with by the want of effects of the drawer, in the hands of *and mode* the drawee.[f] And on non-payment, as well of a foreign as an inland *of protest-* bill, notice of non-payment must be given.[g] (395) In case of an inland *ing and giv-* bill, the sending a verbal notice to a merchant's counting-house is suf- *ing notice.* ficient, and if no person be there in the ordinary hours of business, it is not necessary to leave or send a written notice.[h]

The *protest* for non-payment of a *foreign* bill; which is made by a no-tary public, varies in point of form, according to the country in which it is made: in England the form of it is as follows:

ON THIS DAY, the first of November, in the year of our Lord one thousand eight hundred and six, at the request of A. B. bearer of the *original* bill of exchange, whereof a true copy is on the other side writ-ten, I, Y. Z., of London, notary public, by royal authority duly admit-ted and sworn, did exhibit the said bill.

[*Here the presentment is stated, and to whom made, and the reason, if assigned, for non-payment.*]

Wherefore I, the said notary, at the request aforesaid, have protested, and by these presents do solemnly protest as well against the drawer, ac-ceptor, and indorsers of the said bill of exchange, as against all others whom it may concern, for exchange, re-exchange, and all costs, charges, damages, and interest suffered, and to be suffered, for want of *payment* of the said *original* bill. Thus done and protested in London aforesaid, in the presence of E. F.

[*The expenses of noting and protest are then subscribed, for the amount of which, see the Appendix.*]

By the former regulation of the 44 Geo. 3. c. 98. Schedule A. a [**311**] stamp duty of five shillings was imposed on the protest without refer-ence to the amount of the bill, but by the subsequent acts 48 Geo. 3. c. 149, and 55 Geo. 3. c. 184. Schedule A. part 1, title *Protest*, the duties are as follows:

Protest of any bill of exchange or promissory note for any sum of money

	s.	d.
Not amounting to £20.	2	0
Amounting to £20, and not amounting to £100.	3	0
Amounting to £100, and not amounting to £500.	5	0
Amounting to £500, or upwards	10	0

[a] Ante, 215. Selw. Ni. Pri. 4th edit. 345.
[f] Gale v. Walsh, 5 T. R. 239. Chaters
[v] Bell, 4 Esp. Rep. 49. Ante, 198, 9.
[g] Ante, 219, 220.
[h] Ante, 220, 221. Bayl. 127.

(395) This is true only where there has been a previous acceptance of the bill; for if the bill has been dishonoured on presentment for acceptance, and due notice thereof given to the other parties, no presentment for payment, or notice and protest for non-payment, is in general necessary.

2dly. *Form and mode of protesting and giving notice.* The protest should not bear date before the bill is due,[1] but as it must, in the case of a foreign bill, be made on the last day of grace,[k] it must bear date generally on that day; but an inland bill is not to be protested till the day after the third day of grace.[1] When an accepted bill is protested for non-payment, Marius recommends the protest to be sent to the drawer or indorser, and the accepted bill to be kept, unless express orders be given by those parties to the contrary, because the protest for non-payment, with the second accepted bill, will be sufficient proof against the drawer, though not against the acceptor.[m](397) But according to another writer,[n] the drawer or indorser would not be obliged to pay without having the accepted bill delivered up to him, as he would otherwise perhaps have no evidence of the acceptance against the acceptor. Where payment of a non-accepted bill is refused, it is agreed on all hands that there is no risk in sending back the bill with the protest.[o] Where only part of the money for which the bill is payable is tendered, that part may be taken, and the bill must be protested for non-payment of the residue.[p]

Previously to the statute 9 & 10 Will. 3. c. 17. *no inland bill* could be *protested for non-payment;* but by this statute it is enacted, that all bills of exchange drawn in, or dated at any place in England, for the sum of *five pounds* or upwards, upon any person in London, or elsewhere in England, in which bills of exchange shall be expressed *value received,* and payable at a certain number of *days, weeks,* or *months* after the *date* thereof, after presentation and written acceptance, and after the expiration of the days of grace, the holder, or his

[312] agent, may cause the bill to be protested by a notary public, and in default of such notary public, by any other substantial person in the place, in the presence of two witnesses; refusal or neglect being first made of due payment of the same : which protest shall be made and written under a copy of the bill of exchange, in the words or form following:—

"Know all men, that I, A. B., on the   day of   at "the usual place of abode of the said .   have demanded "payment of the bill, of the which the above is a copy, which the "said   did not pay, wherefore I, the said A. B., do hereby "protest the said bill. Dated this   day of ."

The act directs that this protest shall, within fourteen days after it is made, *be sent, or notice of it given,* to the party from whom the bill was received, who is, upon producing such protest, to repay

[1] Mar. 103. Campbell v. French, 6 T. R. 212.

[k] Leftley v. Mills, 4 T. R. 170. Ante, 223 to 225; et post, 313. Selw. Ni. Pri. 4th edit. 345.

[1] Leftley v. Mills, 4 T. R. 170. post, 313.

[m] Mar. 120.

[n] Beawes, pl. 220. Loveless on Bills, 100.

[o] Mar. 121.

[p] Mar. 68. 85, 86, 87. Walwyn v. St. Quintin, 1 Bos. & Pul. 652.

(397) Where one of a set of exchange has been accepted, and protested for non-payment, presenting the protest of the accepted bill together with one of the set, which has neither been accepted nor protested, to the indorser, and a demand of payment will be a sufficient notice to charge him. *Kenworth* v. *Hopkins,* 1 John. Ca. 107. And in such case it is not necessary to produce the protested bill at the time of the notice and demand on the indorser. Ibid. And see *Lenox* v. *Leuret.* 10 Mass. Rep. 1.

the bill, together with all interests and charges from the day such bill *2dly. Form and mode of protesting and giving notice.* was protested ; for which protest shall be paid a sum not exceeding the sum of *sixpence;* and in default or neglect of such protest, or due notice given, the party forfeits his right of action.

Some observations have already been made on this statute.^q It has been decided, that the holder of a bill payable after *sight*, is not entitled to the accumulative remedy given to this statute,^r and that a bill within the meaning of the act, cannot be noted or protested until the day after the last day of grace.^s It has also been decided, that as the directions are positive that no sum exceeding sixpence shall be taken for the protest, no larger sum can legally be demanded, notwithstanding it is customary to charge more.^t It is doubtful, whether the clerk of a notary can, under this statute, make the demand of payment.^u The act only gives an additional remedy, and does not take away the common law one, and therefore it is not necessary to protest, it being in all cases sufficient to give notice of non-payment,^x and the holder is entitled to claim interest from the drawer, although there is no protest.^y A protest must also be made on the non-payment of *coal notes* given pursuant to 3 Geo. 2. c. 26. s. 187.^z

The remaining points relative to the form and mode of protesting and [313] *giving notice, will be found, ante 215 to 222.*

A *protest* for the non-payment of a *foreign* bill, or at least the minute *3dly. The time when protest must be made and notice given.* of it, must be *made on the day of refusal;*^a and it seems not to be settled whether it suffice that a foreign bill be noted by a notary on the day of payment, and the protest drawn up at any time afterwards.^b Notice of the dishonour should be sent to the parties, to whom the holder means to resort, by the earliest ordinary conveyance;^c but it is not necessary to send a copy of the protest.^d

In the case of an *inland* bill, *no protest* for non-payment can be made until the day *after* it is due.^e If a bill be payable at a banker's, and the

^q Ante, 213, 219. Leftley v. Mills, 4 T. R. 170.

^r Id. ibid. post, 313, note.

^s Id. ibid. post, 313, note.

^t Id. ibid. See the list of notary's fees in the Appendix.

^u Ante, 216, 17.

^x Brough v. Parking, 2 Ld. Raym. 992. Harrison v. Benson, 2 Stra. 910. ante, 218, 19. 3 & 4 Ante, c. 9. s. 5. 2 Bla. Com. 469.

^y Windle v. Andrew, 2 Bar. & Ald. 696. 2 Stark. 425. S. C. and, 218.

^z Smith v. Wilson, Andr. 187. see post.

^a Leftley v. Mills, 4 T. R. 170. Tassel v. Lewis, Ld. Raym. 743. ante, 228, note.

^b Ante, 217, 18. 223. Chaters v. Bell, 4 Esp. Rep. 49. ante, 223. Bayl, 122, 3. Selw. 4th ed. 345, 6.

^c Ante, 224. Darbishire v. Parker, 6 East, 7.

^d Ante, 217. Robins v. Gibson, 1 M. & S. 288. 3 Campb. 334. S. C.

^e The words of the statute 9 & 10 Will. 3 c. 17. s. 1. which enable holders to make

protest of bills are " after the expiration of three days," and see Leftley v. Mills, 4 T. R. 170. An inland bill for 20l. 7s. payable fourteen days after sight, became due the 24th of April, 1790. A banker's clerk called with it for payment in the morning, and the acceptor not being at home, left word where it lay. After six, another of the clerks, who was a notary, noted it, and between seven and eight the first clerk went with it again; the acceptor tendered him the amount of the bill and sixpence over, but he insisted on 2s. 6d. for the noting, and that sum not being paid, an action was brought against the acceptor, who pleaded the tender. Lord Kenyon thought the tender of the amount of the bill at any time of the day it was payable was sufficient, upon which the jury found a verdict for the defendant. A rule to show cause why there should not be a new trial was afterwards granted, and upon cause shown, Lord Kenyon thought the acceptor had till the last minute of the day of grace to pay the bill, and that it could

3dly. The notary do not present it there, until after five o'clock, he will not be a
time when competent witness to prove the non-payment of the bill, which should
protest be have been presented before that hour.[f]
must
made and
notice gi-   With respect to the *time* when the notice of non-payment must be
ven.   given, and the *mode* of giving such notice, it might suffice here to
             refer to that part of the work in which the giving notice of non-
[314] acceptance has been considered. But as the rules upon this point are
of such practical importance, we will again consider them in their
more immediate application to this part of our subject, at the same
time requesting the attention of the reader to the preceding observations.[g]

It is incumbent on the holder to prove that notice of the non-payment
was given in due time to the party he sues, and it cannot be left to inference without positive proof, and therefore this is one of the most
important branches of the law respecting bills.[h]

It has been doubted, whether in the case of an inland bill, payable
after date or sight, or on a particular event, the drawee has not *the
whole* of the day when the bill is due to pay it in, without reference
to banking-hours,[i] and consequently, whether notice of non-payment
can be given until after that day.[k] But we have seen, that according
to the more recent decision, notice of non-payment may be given on
the last day of grace.[l] The usual practice is, to present such a bill
for payment in the course of the morning, and if refused in London,
for a *notary* to present it again in the evening, and if payment be
then also refused, the notary notes it, and it should be returned to the
party from whom the holder received it, if resident in the same place,
early in the next morning, (usually by ten o'clock, but depending on
distance) and if residing elsewhere, by the post of that day; and this
course is certainly regular; as *it is in no case necessary to give notice*

not be noted or protested till the following
day. Buller, J. thought they were payable
at any time of the last day of grace upon
demand, so as such demand was made
within reasonable hours, and that they
might be protested on that day. Grose, J.
declined giving any opinion upon these
points, but the whole court concurred that
the bill in question could not be noted because it was payable within a limited time
after sight, and the statute authorizes the noting of such inland bills only as are payable
after date. Lord Kenyon also thought the
sixpence tendered was sufficient for the
noting, and the rule was discharged.
    [i] Parker *v.* Gordon, 7 East, 385. 3 Smith
Rep. 358. S. C. ante, 277, note. Sed vide
ante, 277, notes.
    [g] See the observations, ante, 223 to 225.
    [h] Lawson and another, assignees of
Schiffner *v.* Sherwood, 1 Stark. 314. In an
action by the indorsee against an indorser
of a bill, a witness states that either two
or three days after the dishonour of the
bill, notice was given by letter to the defendant, notice in two days being in time,
but notice on the third too late, it cannot
be left as a question for the jury whether

notice was given in time, although the defendant has had notice to produce the letter
which would ascertain the time. Per Lord
Ellenborough. The witness says two or
three days, but the third day would be too
late. It lies upon the plaintiff to show that
notice was given in due time, and I cannot
go upon probable evidence without positive proof of the fact, nor can I infer due
notice from the non-production of the letter, the only consequence is, that you may
give parol evidence of it. The *onus probandi* lies upon the plaintiff, and since he
has not proved due notice he must be called. Plaintiffs nonsuited.
    [i] Leftley *v.* Mills, 4 T. R. 170, ante, 285.
Haynes *v.* Birks, 3 Bos. & Pul. 602. Colket
v. Freeman, 2 T. R. 59.
    [k] Id. ibid.
    [l] Ante, 285.

    [m] But it is in no case necessary to have
an inland bill presented for payment by a
notary Leftley *v.* Mills, 4 T. R. 170.
unless to subject the drawer and indorsers
to payment of interest, damages, &c. Boulager *v.* Talleyrand, 2 Esp. Rep. 550. ante,
219.

of non-payment of an inland bill on the day of refusal.[a](401) On the 3dly. The day after that on which the bill becomes due, and when it was pre- *time when protest* sented for payment and refused, the then holder must give notice of the *must be* non-payment to the next preceding party; and it seems now to be es- *made and* tablished, that where the parties live in London, or in an adjacent *notice gi-* village within the limits of the two-penny post, each party has an *ven.* entire day, after that on which he was informed of the dishonour, to give notice to the immediate indorser, and that the notice may be given by letter put into the post-office, however near the residence of the different parties may be, sufficiently early to be received on the day on which he is entitled to notice ;[o] and where the parties do not reside in London, it will be sufficient if the party gives notice to his immediate indorser by the next practical post after he has himself received notice ;[p] or he may send notice by a private hand, provided it be delivered on the same day that it would have arrived by the post.[q] And with reference to the principles of the decisions on the first branch of this rule, and for the sake of certainty, it may be considered in all cases sufficient, whether the parties reside in London,[r] or elsewhere, if each forward notice on the day after that on which he received information of the dishonour of the bill.[s] If a party receive notice by a letter delivered on a Sunday he need not open it till Monday, and then it suffices for him to send off notice to the preceding party on Tuesday.[t] The following recent decisions will establish these rules.

According to the cases collected in Darbishire *v.* Parker,[a] the notice of non-payment must be given within a *reasonable* time, which is a

---

[a] Id. ibid. Darbishire *v.* Parker, 6 East, 8, 9, 10. Tindall *v.* Brown, 1 T. R. 168, 9. Russell *v.* Langstaffe, Dougl. 515. Muilman *v.* D'Eguino, 2 Hen. Bla. 565. Burbridge *v.* Manners, 3 Campb. 193. ante, 285, 6.

[o] Scott *v.* Lifford, 9 East 347. 1 Campb. 249. S. C. Smith *v.* Mullet, 2 Campb. 208. March *v.* Maxwell, 2 Campb. 210. Jameson *v.* Swinton, 2 Campb 374. Kilton *v.* Fairclough, 2 Campb. 533. Haynes *v.* Birks, 3 Bos. & Pul. 599. Williams *v.* Smith, 2 Barn & Ald. 500.

[p] Darbishire *v.* Parker, 6 East, 3. ante, 219 to 221, as to the insufficiency of notice by the post.

[q] Bancroft *v.* Hall, 1 Holt, C. N. P. 476. ante, 220, 1.

[r] Jameson *v.* Swinton, 2 Campb. 374. 2 Taunt. 224. S. C.

[s] Per Abbott, C. J. The time within which notice of the dishonour of a bill must be given I have always understood to be the departure of the post on the day following that in which the party receives the intelligence of the dishonour. See Williams *v.* Smith, 2 Barn. & Ald. 500. and Bray *v.* Hadwen, 5 Maule & Sel 68.

[t] Wright *v.* Showcross, 2 Barn. & Ald. 501, note a.

[a] 6 East, 3 & 9 to 12.

---

(401) But it has been held in *Massachusetts* that where the indorser lives in the same town with the promisor, he ought to have notice on the same day on which there is a demand and refusal of payment. *Woodbright* v. *Brigham*, 12 Mass. Rep. 403. But see *Langdale* v *Trimmer*, 15 East, 291. *Bennet* v. *Raugh*, 2 Taunt. Rep. 387. And it is certain that if default be made in the payment of a note the day on which it becomes due, a notice to, and demand on, the indorser afterwards on the same day is not too early. *Widgery* v. *Munroe*, 6 Mass. Rep. 449. *Corp* v. *M'Comb*, 1 John. Ca. 328.

Where a dishonoured note was left with the indorser, who was an attorney, to collect the same, this was held not to be a sufficient notice to charge him as indorser. *Agan* v. *M'Manus*, 11 John. Rep. 180.

The holder of an inland bill or note is not obliged to send notice of non-payment until the next day after its dishonour. *Hartford Bank* v. *Stedman*, 3 Conn. Rep. 489.; but if demand has been made on the maker of a note on the third day of grace, notice to the indorser may be given on that day, and is sufficient. *Lindenberger* v. *Beall*, 6 Wheat. 104.

3dly. The
time when
protest·
must be
made and
notice giv-
en.

But in the recent case of Smith v. Mullet,[1] which was an action by the *fourth* against the *first* indorsee. all the parties to which resided in London, it appeared, that the plaintiff received notice of the dishonour of the bill from his indorsee on the 20th of the month, and gave notice to his immediate indorser. by a letter put into the two-penny post-office on the evening of the 21st, *but so late that it was not delivered out till the morning of the* 22d, it was held that by this neglect the plaintiff had discharged all the prior indorsers, although, in the course of the 22d, notice of the dishonour was given both to the *second* indorsee and to the defendant. And Lord Ellenborough in this case said, "It is of great importance that there should be an " established rule upon this subject; and I think there can be none " more convenient, than that, where the parties reside in London, each " party should have a *day* to give notice. I have before said, the " holder of a bill of exchange is not, *omissis omnibus aliis negotiis*, to " devote himself to give notice of its dishonour. It is enough if this " be done with reasonable expedition. If you limit a man to the " fractional part of a day, it will come to a question, how swiftly the " notice can be conveyed? A man and a horse must be employed, and " you will have a race against time. But here *a day has been lost.* " The plaintiff had notice himself on Monday, and does not give " notice to his indorser till Wednesday. If a party has an entire day " he must send off his letter conveying the notice within post time of " that day. The plaintiff only wrote the letter to Aylett on the Tues-" day; it might as well have continued in his writing desk on the " Tuesday night as lie at the post-office. He has clearly been guilty " of laches, by which the defendant is discharged." And in Marsh v. Maxwell,[k] Lord Ellenborough ruled, that upon the dishonour of a bill, it is not enough that the drawer or indorser receives notice in as many days as there are subsequent indorsers, unless it is shown that each indorsee gave notice within a day after receiving it; and that if any one has been beyond the day the drawer and prior indorsers are discharged; and in a recent case this doctrine was confirmed.[l](407)

[319]

From the above-mentioned case of Smith v. Mullett,[m] it appears, that though the holder is not bound to send a special messenger, and may give notice by the post, he must take care to put the letter in the

[1] Smith v. Mullett, 2 Campb. 208 ; and see id. 374.
[k] Marsh v. Maxwell, 2 Campb. 210.
[l] Turner v. Leach, 4 Barn. & Ald. 451. The indorser of a bill which had been dishonoured, and which a subsequent indorser had made his own by *laches*, paid the bill, and immediately gave notice of dishonour to the defendant and prior indorser; and it was held, that the plaintiff could not recover the amount, although it appeared

that the defendant, in case successive notices had been given by all the parties on the bill, could not have received notice of dishonour at an earlier period. In action against drawer of a bill accepted. payable at a particular place, it is no defence that notice of the dishonour was not given to the acceptor. Edwards v. Dick, 4 Barn. & Ald. 212.
[m] See also Hilton v. Fairclough, 2 Campb. 638.

(407) It is a settled rule that a notice is necessary from the last indorser to every prior indorser, whom he means to charge, immediately after he himself receives notice of the dishonour. *Morgan* v. *Woodworth*, 3 John. Ca. 89. And it is said that the last indorser ought in such case immediately to take up the note, and become himself the real holder. Ibid. And see *Morgan* v. *Van Ingen*, 2 John. Rep. 204. And notice to an indorser before a demand on the maker is a nullity. *Griffin* v. *Goff*, 12 John. Rep. 423. The first indorser in point of *time* is not of course, *first responsible.* *Chalmers et al·* v. *M'Murdo*, 5 Munf. 252.

post sufficiently early on the day after he has himself received notice, that the party to whom it is addressed, may receive the letter on that day.

We have seen that the holder will be excused in the delay of giving notice to the usual time, by the day on which he should regularly have given notice being a day on which he is strictly forbidden by his religion to attend to any secular affairs,[a] or by the absconding of the drawer or indorser.[c]

Where it may be necessary to give notice of non-payment to a banker, it may be proper to give it in the usual hours of business, but to other persons the particular hour of the day is not in general.[p]

The remaining points relative to the time of giving notice, will be found, ante, 223 *to* 225.

In respect to the *person by,*[q] and *to whom,*[r] notice of non-payment should be given, and the *liability* of the different parties to the bill on notice of the non-payment,[s] and how the *consequences* of the laches of the holder may be *waived,* or otherwise done away,[t] the rules already stated, as to the conduct of the holder in the case of non-acceptance, are so applicable, that it would be repetition here to make any observation on these points ; the reader is therefore referred to the preceding part of the work.[u]

3dly. The *time when* protest must be made and notice given.

The *remaining points.* [320]

———————

We have already considered the nature of the protest for better security, and of an acceptance *supra protest.*[x] The nature of a *payment supra protest* remains to be considered.

Sect. 4, Of payment supra protest.

Payment of a bill, whether foreign or inland,[z] being refused, any third person, not party to the bill, as he might have accepted, so he may after protest pay it, *for the honour* of the drawer, or any of the indorsers ;[y] which payment, as it is always made after protest, is called payment *supra protest ;*[z] but the acceptor, if he have previously made a simple acceptance, cannot pay in honour of an indorser, because, as acceptor, he is already bound in that capacity ;[a] he may, however, when he has accepted a bill without having effects of the drawer in his hands, and no provision has been made by the drawer for payment, suffer the bill to be protested, and then pay *supra protest ;*[b] in which case he will have a remedy on the bill against the drawer.[c] A party paying a bill *supra protest,* which has already been accepted by another, may sue such first acceptor ;[d] but if a person take up a bill for the honour of the drawer, he has no right of action

[a] Ante, 214.
[c] Sturges *v.* Derrish, Wightw. 76.
[p] Jameson *v.* Swinton, 2 Taunt. 224. Barclay *v.* Bayley, 2 Campb. 527.— Cross *v.* Smith, 1 M. & S. 545. Bancroft *v.* Hall, Holt, C. N. P. 476. Ante, 277. Bayl. 127.
[q] Ante, 226 to 228.
[r] Ante, 228 to 230.
[s] Ante, 230 to 232.
[t] Ante, 233 to 240.

CHITTY ON BILLS.

[u] Ante, 226 to 246.
[x] Ante, 240. Smith *v.* Nissen, 1 T. R. 269.
[y] Fairley *v.* Roch, Lutw. 621, 892.— Marius, 128. Bayl. 146.
[z] Beawes, pl. 50. Mar. 128.
[a] Beawes, pl. 51.
[b] Id. pl. 52.
[c] Id. Ibid.; and Roper *v.* Birbeck, 15 East, 17. Bayl. 146.
[d] Ex parte Wackerbath, 5 Ves. 574.

P p

Sect. 4. Of against the acceptor, if he accepted it for the accommodation of the
payment drawer.[e]
supra pro-
test.

In general, no person should pay in honour of another, before the
bill has been protested for non-payment ; and it is said that he should
not even then make such payment, before he has declared to a notary
[321] public for whose honour he intends making it, of which declaration the
notary must give an account to the parties concerned, either in the protest itself, or in a separate instrument.[f] If, however, the acceptor *supra
protest* for the honour of the drawer or indorser, receive his approbation of the acceptance, he may pay the bill without any protest for non-
payment.[g]

Although, with respect to other debts, a stranger, who has no interest in them, does not, by paying them, entitle himself to the rights
of a creditor, unless he have the consent of the debtor to such payment,[h] yet, with regard to bills of exchange, a stranger, who pays them
in case of protest, acquires all the same rights that the holder of a bill
had, although no regular transfer of the bill were made to him;[i] and he
may maintain an action against the person for whose honour he discharged the bill, either on the bill itself,[k] or on a count for money paid
to the defendant's use.[l] And in an action upon a bill with several indorsements by a plaintiff, who had paid the bill under protest for the
honour of one of the indorsers, it is sufficient even on a special demurrer to state that he paid the bill according to the usage and custom of
merchants, without stating that he had paid it to the last indorsee.[m] A
person taking up a bill for the honour of the drawer has, however, no
right against the acceptor without effects.[n] The reason of the above
exception to the general rule, precluding a party from constituting himself the creditor of another, without his concurrence, it has been observed, is, that it induces the friends of the drawer or indorsers to render
them this service, it tends to prevent the great expense attending the
return of a bill, and preserves the credit of the trader,[o] &c.

[e] Ex parte Lambert, 13 Ves. 179.—Bayl.
146, 148.
[f] Beawes, pl. 53. Mar. 128.
[g] Beawes, pl. 48.
[h] Exall v. Partridge, 8 T. R. 310. 1 Rol.
Ab. 11. Lampleigh v. Buthwait, Hob. 105.
Stokes v. Lewit, 1 T. R. 20. In Williams
v. Millington, 1 Hen. Bla. 83. Jenkins v.
Tucker, Id. 91.

[i] Mertens v. Winnington, 1 Esp. Rep.
112. Poth. pl. 171. Ex parte Wackerbarth, 5 Ves. 574. Manning's Index, 70.
[k] Fairley v. Roch, Lutw. 891. See
Manning's Index, 70.
[l] Smith v. Nissen, 1 T. R. 239.
[m] Cox v. Earle, 3 Barn. & Ald. 430.
[n] Ex parte Lambert, 13 Ves. 179. Bayl.
148, but see 5 Ves. 574.
[o] Beawes, pl. 54. Poth. pl. 171.

CHAPTER VII.

OF CHECKS ON BANKERS.

A CHECK, or draft, on a banker, is a written order or request, addressed to persons carrying on the business of bankers, and drawn upon them by a party having money in their hands, requesting them to pay, on presentment, to a person therein named, or to bearer, a named sum of money. The form of a check has already been given.[a] It nearly resembles a bill of exchange, but it is uniformly made payable to bearer, and must be drawn upon a regular banker. On account of the daily and immediate use of checks, the legislature has exempted them from stamp duties, provided they be for the payment of money to the bearer on demand, and drawn upon a banker, or person acting as such, residing, or transacting the business of a banker, within ten miles of the place where such draft or order shall be issued, and provided also that such place be specified in such draft or order, and that the same bear date on or before the day the same shall be issued, and do not direct the payment to be made by bills or promissory notes.[b] We have before considered the decisions upon this enactment.[c] If these requisites be not strictly observed, an unstamped check cannot be read in evidence for any purpose.[d]

It was once thought, that a check or draft on a banker is not negotiable generally, but only so within the bills of mortality.[e] But it is now settled, that they are as negotiable as bills of exchange, though, strictly speaking, they are not due before payment is demanded, in which respect they differ from bills of exchange or promissory notes, payable on a particular day.[f] In practice, they are taken in payment as cash, and it has been decided, that a banker in London, receiving bills from his correspondent in the country, to whom they had been indorsed to present for payment, is not guilty of negligence in giving up such bills to the acceptor upon receiving a check on a banker for the amount, although it turn out that such check is dishonoured.[g](1) They [323] must however, be described as checks, and not as cash in an annuity transaction.[h] And in action for usury, the forbearance should be laid from the time when the check was actually received, and not from the

[a] Ante, 51.
[b] 55 Geo. 3. c. 184. Ante, 53.
[c] Ante, 55.
[d] Borradaile v. Middleton, 2 Campb. 53.
[e] Grant v. Vaughan, 3 Burr. 1517.
[f] Per Lord Kenyon in Boehm v. Stirling, 7 T. R. 430
[g] Russell v. Hankey, 7 T. R. 12. Ante, 287.
[h] Poole v. Cabanes, 8 T. R. 328.—Duff v. Atkinson, 8 Ves. 577, 580.

(1) If a person receives a check drawn by another, and passes it in payment, he stands in the situation of an indorser of a bill; and unless he knew that the drawer had not money in bank, is not liable, except on due notice and diligence. *Humphries v. Bicknell*, 2 Litt. 299.

time when it was given.[1] It is said that checks are not protestable;[k] and this doctrine seems to be correct, because checks are payable on presentment, and the statute 9 & 10 W. 3. c. 17, applies only to bills of exchange payable after the date.

In the ordinary course of business, a check cannot be circulated or negotiated so as to affect the drawer, who has funds in the hands of the bankers, after banking hours of the day after he first issues it.[1] But where the drawers of a banker's check issued it nine months after it bore date, upon a consideration which afterwards failed, as between them and the persons to whom they delivered it, it was held that they could not be permitted to object to this circumstance in an action brought by a subsequent holder for a valuable consideration, and without notice, though by the general rule, any person receiving a negotiable instrument after it is due, is deemed to have taken it upon the credit of the person from whom he received it, and subject to the same equities as existed between him and the party sued on such instrument.[m]

With respect to the time when checks should be presented for payment, the general rule seems to be, that it suffices to present it at any time during banking hours of the day after it was issued.[n] If the banker on whom the check is drawn has reason to suspect that the drawer has committed an act of bankruptcy, he cannot safely pay the draft, because the payment of a check on a banker is not protected by the statute 19 Geo. 2. c. 32. s. 1. which mentions only bills of exchange and debts for goods sold.[o] Most of the rules respecting bills of exchange affect checks on bankers, and therefore it may suffice to refer to the preceding part of the work, and to the Index, tit. *Check*.

[1] Borradaile v. Middleton, 2 Campb. 53.

[k] Grant v. Vaughan, 3 Burr. 1519.

[1] Ante, 274, 5.

[m] Boehm v. Stirling, 7 T. R. 423.— Ante, 128, in notes.

[n] Ante, 274, 5.

[o] Holroyd v. Whitehead, 1 Marsh. 128. 5 Taunt. 444.

CHAPTER VIII.

OF PROMISSORY NOTES—BANKER'S NOTES, AND BANK OF ENGLAND NOTES.

THE law respecting bills of exchange, having been pointed out in the preceding chapters, it remains, in the present, to make a few observations relative to promissory notes, banker's notes, and bank of England notes.

A *promissory note* is defined to be a promise or engagement in writing, to pay a specified sum at a time therein limited, or on demand, or at sight, to a person therein named, or his order, or to the bearer.[a] The person who makes the note is called the maker, and the person to whom it is payable the payee, and the person to whom he transfers the interest by indorsement, the indorsee.

Sect. 1. Of promissory notes.

The usual form of the instrument is thus :—

£50   London, 1st January, 1818.
(Stamp) The months after date (or "on demand",) I promise to pay to Mr. A. B. or order, fifty pounds, for value received.

              C. D.

[*Sometimes are here subscribed, "Payable at Messrs. G. H. and Co. bankers, London." But those words are immaterial, ante*, 325,]

Observing on the origin and nature of promissory notes, it has been well remarked, by a modern writer,[b] that, as commerce advanced in its progress, the multiplicity of its concerns required, in many instances, a less complicated mode of payment, and of obtaining credit, than through the medium of bills of exchange, to which there are, in general, three parties. A trader, whose situation and circumstances, rendered credit from the merchant or manufacturer, who supplied him with goods, absolutely necessary, might have so limited a connexion with the commercial world at large, that he could not easily furnish his creditor with a bill of exchange on another, but his own responsibility might be such, that his engagement to pay, reduced into writing, might be accepted with the same confidence as a bill on another.

The validity of these instruments, though favoured by many judges, met with a strenuous opponent in Lord Holt, who, as it has been observed,[c] most pertinaciously adhered to his opinion, that no action could be maintained on a promissory note, as an instrument, but that it was only to be considered as evidence of a debt. He was of opinion, that actions upon notes, as such, were innovations upon the rules of the common law; and that the declarations upon them amounted to

[325]

---

[a] Bla. Com. 467. Bayl. 1. Kyd, 18.   [b] Kyd, 18.
Selw. N. P. 4th ed. 361.   [c] Brown v. Harraden, 4 T. R. 151.

325

OF PROMISSORY NOTES, &c.

Sect. 1. Of the setting up a new sort of specialty unknown in Westminster-hall.[d] promissory The learned Judge appears to have retained this opinion in a case[e] notes. where judgment for the plaintiff, in an action on a promissory note, was reversed, on the ground that the custom alleged in the declaration was void, since it tended to bind a man to pay money without any consideration. As observed by Lord Kenyon, C. J. this question exercised the judgments of the most able lawyers of the last century; but the authority and weight which Lord Holt's opinion had in West-minster-hall, made others yield to him; and it was thought necessary to resort to the legislature,[f] and the 3 & 4 Ann. c. 9, made perpetual

[326] by 7 Ann. c. 25. s. 3. was passed:[g] by which after reciting "that it "had been held, that notes in writing, signed by the party who made "the same, whereby such party promised to pay unto any other per- "son, or his order, any sum of money therein mentioned, were not "assignable or indorsable over, within the custom of merchants, to any "other person; and that such person to whom the sum of money "mentioned in such note was payable, could not maintain an action,

---

[d] Clerke v. Martin, 2 Ld. Raym. 758. Story v. Atkins, id. 1430. Trier v. Bridgman, 2 East, 359. Walmsley v. Child, 1 Ves. 346.

[e] Clerke v. Martin, 2 Ld. Raym. 759. Buller v. Crips, 6 Mod. 29, 30. Grant v. Vaughan, 3 Burr. 1520.

[f] Brown v. Harraden, 4 T. R. 151.

Before the statute of Queen Anne many attempts were made to put promissory notes on the footing of bills of exchange, but without success, vide Pearson v. Garrett, 4 Mod. 242. Clerke v. Martin, Ld. Raym 757. Salk. 129. Burton v. Souter, Ld. Raym. 774, and Williams v. Cutting, Ld. Raym. 825. Salk. 24. 7 Mod. 154. 11 Mod. 24, and see 4 T. R. 151, 152.

"By the 3 and 4 Anne, c. 9. s. 1. Whereas it hath been held, that notes in writing, signed by the party who makes the same, whereby such party promises to pay unto any other person, or his order, any sum of money therein mentioned, are not assignable or indorsable over, within the custom of merchants, to any other person; and that such person to whom the sum of money mentioned in such note is payable, cannot maintain an action by the custom of merchants against the person who first made and signed the same; and that any person to whom such note should be assigned, indorsed, or made payable, could not within the said custom of merchants, maintain any action upon such note against the person who first drew and signed the same;" therefore, to the intent to encourage trade and commerce, which will be much advanced, if such notes shall have the same effect as inland bills of exchange, and shall be negotiated in like manner; be it enacted, that all notes in writing, that after the 1st day of May, in the year of our Lord 1705, shall be made and signed by any person, or persons, body politic or corporate, or by the servant or agent of any corporation, banker, goldsmith, merchant, or trader, who is usually instructed by him, her, or them, to sign such promissory notes for him, her or them, whereby such person or persons, body politic and corporate, his, her, or their servant or agent as aforesaid, doth or shall promise to pay to any other person or persons, body politic and corporate, his, her, or their order, or unto bearer, any sum of money mentioned in such note, shall be taken and construed to be, by virtue thereof, due and payable to any such person or persons, body politic and corporate, to whom the same is made payable, and also every such note payable to any person or persons, body politic and corporate, his, her, or their order, shall be assignable or indorsable over, in the same manner as inland bills of exchange are or may be, according to the custom of merchants; and that the person and persons, body politic or corporate, to whom such sum of money is or shall be by such note made payable, shall and may maintain an action for the same, in such manner as he, she, or they might do, upon any inland bill of exchange, made or drawn according to the custom of merchants, against the person or persons, body politic and corporate, who, or whose servant or agent as aforesaid, signed the same; and that any person or persons, body politic and corporate, to whom such note, that is payable to any person or persons, body, politic and corporate, his, her, or their order, is indorsed or assigned, or the money therein mentioned ordered to be paid by indorsement thereon, shall and may maintain his, her, or their action for such sum of money, either against the person or persons, body politic and corporate, who, or whose, servant or agent as aforesaid signed such note, or against any of the persons who indorsed the same, in like manner as in cases of inland bills of exchange. Bayl. 1, 2.

[g] See observations on this statute. Coleman, v. Cooke, Willes, 395. Bayl 1.

"by the custom of merchants. against the person who first made and Sect. 1. Of
"signed the same ; and that any person to whom such note had been promissory
"assigned, indorsed, or made payable, could not, within the custom notes.
"of merchants, maintain any action upon such note against the person
"who first drew and signed the same, it was to the intent to encourage
"trade and commerce, which would be much advanced if such notes
"*should have the same effect as inland bills of exchange,* and should be
"*negotiated in like manner,* enacted, that *all notes* in writing, made and
"signed by any person or persons, body politic or corporate, or by
"the servant or agent of any corporation, banker, goldsmith, merchant,
"or trader, who is usually intrusted by him, her, or them, to sign
"such promissory notes for him, her, or them, whereby such person or
"persons, body politic and corporate, his, her, or their servant or
"agent as aforesaid, both or shall promise to pay to any other person
"or persons, body politic, and corporate, his, her, or their order, or
"unto bearer, any sum of money mentioned in such note, shall be
"taken and construed to be, by virtue thereof, due and payable to any
"such person or persons, body politic and corporate, to whom the
"same is made payable ; and also every such note payable to any per-
"son or persons, body politic and corporate, his, her, or their order,
"shall be assignable or indorsable over, *in the same manner as inland
"bills of exchange* are or may be, according to the custom of mer-
"chants ; and that the person or persons, body politic and corporate,
"to whom such sum of money is or shall be by such note made paya- [327]
"ble, shall and may maintain an action for the same, *in such manner
"as he,* she, or they, *might do, upon any inland bills of exchange,* made
"or drawn according to the custom of merchants, against the person or
"persons, body politic and corporate, who, or whose servant or agent as
"aforesaid, signed the same ; and that any person or persons, body poli-
"tic and corporate, to whom such note that is payable to any person or
"persons, body politic and corporate. his, her, or their order, is indorsed
"or assigned, or the money therein mentioned, ordered to be paid by
"indorsement thereon, shall and may maintain his, her, or their action,
"for such sum of money, either against the person or persons, body
"politic and corporate, who, or whose servant or agent as aforesaid,
"signed such note, or against any of the persons that indorsed the same,
"*in like manner as in cases of inland bills* of exchange."

It has been considered that this statute of the 3 & 4 Anne, c. 9 giving the like remedy upon promissory notes as upon bills of exchange (though made perpetual by the statute 7 Anne, c. 25, passed after the union with Scotland,) does not extend to promissory notes made in Scotland, because such subsequent statute only made the former act, which was a temporary law of England to have perpetual force *there,* [h] but subsequent statutes appear to recognise notes made in Scotland as valid.[i] And although the statute of Anne may not apply to notes made in England,[k] yet it should seem that notes made in a foreign country would now be held valid at common law,[l] though it would be

[h] King v. Esdale, 6th Dec. 1711. Forbes on Bills, 174.
[i] 39 Geo. 3. c. 107.   12 Geo. 3. c. 72.
[k] Bayl. 18. Carr v. Shaw, infra, note.
[l] In Pollard v Herries, 3 Bos. & Pul. 335, a promissory note was made in Paris, payable there or in England, and no objection was taken on that account. In Hewitt v. Morris, 3 Campb. 303, a declaration, on

a note made at Paris, stated, that it was made in London, and Lord Ellenborough held, that this was no variance, because the contract evidenced by a promissory note is transitory, and the place where it purports to be made is immaterial, and the plaintiff recovered. In Roche v. Campbell, 3 Campb. 247, the plaintiff declared on a note made in Ireland, and no objection was

Sect. 1 Of promissory notes.

improper to declare upon them as made in pursuance of the statute.[m] But it has been held, that the forging a Scotch bank note was not an offence within the English statute 2 Geo. 2. c. 25, against forgery, the [328] note being made payable locally, where it was drawn.[n] The statute 48 Geo. 3. c. 149. s. 21, directs, that all promissory notes made out of Great Britain, or purporting to have been so made, shall not be negotiable, circulated, or paid in Great Britain, unless duly stamped as a promissory note made in Great Britain, and subjects the party offending to £20 penalty, with an exemption in favour of notes made payable only in Ireland. The more recent enactment in the statute 55 Geo. 3. c. 184. s. 29, seems only to apply a similar enactment to promissory notes, payable to bearer on demand.

Although the statute 3 & 4 Anne, enacts, that all notes in writing, made and *signed* by the party making it, shall be valid and assignable in like manner as an inland bill, yet it suffices if his name be written in any part of the note. And it has been held, that if a party write his promissory note thus:—"I, John Dobbins, promise to pay," &c. this is as good as a note, "I promise to pay," and subscribed "J. Dobbins."[o]

The above statute being a remedial law, and made for the encouragement of trade and commerce, the courts have construed it liberally.[p] The statute places promissory notes on the same footing as bills of exchange, and consequently the decisions and rules relating to the one are in general applicable to the other.[q] Thus it has been decided, with

taken on that account. In Spilgerber v. Kolm, 1 Stark. 125, the plaintiff declared on a promissory note, drawn in Prussia, against the maker, and no objection was taken.

[m] Carr v. Shaw, B. R. Hil. 39 Geo. 3. Bayl. 18, n. 1. In an action on a promissory note made at Philadelphia, the first count of the declaration stated, that the defendant at Philadelphia, in parts beyond the seas, to wit, at London, &c. *according to the form of the statute*, &c. made his note in writing, &c. There were also the common money counts. The defendant demurred *specially* to the first count, and pleaded the general issue to the others. On the demurrer the court intimated a strong opinion that the statute did not apply to foreign notes, and advised the plaintiff to amend, but on the general issue Lord Kenyon said the note, though not within the statute, is evidence to support any of the money counts, and the plaintiff had a verdict, at Guildhall, 1st May, 1799. N. B. The pleadings are entered as of Michaelmas Term, 39 G. 3. Roll, 1238.

[n] The King v. Dick, 1 Leach, C. L. 4th ed. 68. 2 East, 925. S. C.

[o] Taylor v. Dobbins, 1 Stra. 399. In case upon a promissory note, the declaration ran, that the defendant made a note *et manu sua propria scripsit*. Exception was taken that since the statute he should have said that the defendant signed the note, but the court held it well enough, because laid to be wrote with his own hand, and there needs no subscription in that case, for it is sufficient if his name is in any part of it. I, J. S. promise to pay, is as good as I promise to pay, subscribed J. S. See also Elliott v. Comper, 1 Stra. 609. 2 Ld. Raym. 1376. and Vin. Abr. tit. Bills of Exchange, 11.

[p] Selw. Ni. Pri. 4th edit. 363.

[q] Bishop v. Young, 2 Bos. & Pul. 80, 4. Hill v. Halford, ibid. 413. Colehan v. Cooke, Willes, 394. 399, note b. Brown v. Harraden, 4 T. R. 152. Carlos v. Fancourt, 5 T. R. 486. Heylin v. Adamson, 2 Burr. 669. Bayl. 3, note a.; and see Smith v. Kendal, 6 T. R. 123.

In Heylin v. Adamson, 2 Burr. 669, the question was, whether the indorsee of a bill was bound to make a demand upon the drawer, as the indorsee of a note must upon the maker; and *per* Lord Mansfield, while a note continues in its original shape of a promise from one man to another, it bears no similitude to a bill; but when it is indorsed, the resemblance begins, for then it is an order by the indorser upon the maker to pay the indorsee, which is the very definition of a bill. The indorser is the drawer, the maker of the note the acceptor, and the indorsee the person to whom it is made payable; and all the authorities, and particularly Lord Hardwicke, in a case of Hamerton v. Mackarell, Mich. 10 Geo. 2. put promissory notes on the same footing with bills of exchange.

In Brown v. Harraden, 4 T. R. 148,

respect to the time when a note is payable, that there is no difference between bills and promissory notes; and the latter when payable at a stated time, are also entitled to three days of *grace* when payable to bearer or order.[r] And in Carlos *v.* Fancourt, where the question was, whether or not a note, payable out of a particular fund, could be declared on as a promissory note, it was decided in the negative, "be-"cause promissory notes must stand or fall on the same rules by which "bills of exchange are governed."[s] In Heylin *v.* Adamson,[t] Lord Mansfield, declared, that though, while a promissory note continues in its original shape of a promise from one man to pay to another, it bears no similitude to a bill of exchange, yet when it is indorsed, the resemblance begins; for then it is an order by the indorser upon the maker of the note to pay to the indorsee; the indorser becomes, as it were the drawer, the maker of the note the acceptor; and the indorsee the payee.[u] This point of resemblance once fixed, the law relative to [330] bills becomes applicable to promissory notes. Hence it is only necessary to refer the reader to the prior parts of the work.

With respect to a particular description of notes in the *coal trade,* there are some peculiar provisions, it having been enacted, that all lightermen, and other buyers or contractors of coal aboard ship, in the port of London, shall, at the time of delivery of such coals, either pay for the same in ready money, or give their *promissory note* for payment, expressing therein the words, *value received in coals,* and that such notes may be protested and noted as inland bills; and that, in default of such protest or noting, and notice thereof given to the indorsers within twenty days after non-payment, they shall be discharged from liability; and it is enacted, that such buyer of coals, and the

where the court decided, that three days grace should be allowed on promissory notes, Lord Kenyon observed, that the effect of the statute was, that notes were wholly to assume the shape of bills; and Buller J. added, that the cases cited in the argument showed clearly, that the courts of Westminster had thought the analogy between bills and notes so strong, that the rules established with respect to the one, ought also to prevail as to the other; that the language of the preamble of the act was express; that it was the object of the legislature to put notes exactly on the same footing with bills; and that the enacting part pursued that intention. The same doctrine is to be found in Carlos *v.* Fancourt, 5 T. R. 482. Edie *v.* East India Company, Burr. 1224.

In 2 Bla. Com. 470, and Bayley on Bills, 69, it is said, that a note may be considered on comparison with a bill as accepted when it issues.

[r] Brown *v.* Harraden, 4 T. R. 152. See the preceding note, and cases, Manning's Index, 65.

Smith *v.* Kendall, 6 T. R. 123. Three days grace are allowed on a promissory note payable to A., without adding, "or to his order," "or to bearer." Lord Kenyon, C. J. said, "If this were *res integra*, and there were no decision upon the subject, there would be a great deal of weight in the defendant's objection;

CHITTY ON BILLS.

but it was decided, in a case of Lord Raymond (2 Ld. Raym. 1545.) on demurrer, that a note payable to B., without adding, or to his order, or to bearer, was a legal note within the act of parliament. It is also said in Marius, that a note may be made payable either to A. or bearer, A. or order, or to A. only. In addition to these authorities, I have made inquiries among different merchants, respecting the practice in allowing the three days grace, the result of which is, that the bank of England, and the merchants in London, allow the three days grace on notes like the present. The opinion of merchants, indeed, would not govern this court in a question of law, but I am glad to find that the practice of the commercial world coincides with the decision of a court of law. Therefore, I think that it would be dangerous now to shake that practice, which is warranted by a solemn decision of this court, by any speculative reasoning on the subject; and consequently this rule must be made absolute, to enter a verdict for the plaintiff."

[s] Carlos *v.* Fancourt, 5 T. R. 486. Hill *v.* Halford, 2 Bos. & Pul. 413.

[t] Heylin *v.* Adamson, 2 Burr. 676.

[u] In Bishop *v.* Young, 2 Bos. & Pul. 83. the court observed, that this resemblance, so far as regards the remedy by action of *debt*, does not hold.

Q q

master of the vessel, shall, for refusing to insert the words, *value received in coals*, or receiving a note for coals without those words, forfeit
£100.[x] Upon this act it has been decided, that it extends only to contractors for coals, and to cases between an indorser and indorsee;[y] and
that though the act directs, that the instrument shall be drawn in a particular form, under a severe penalty, yet, if drawn in a different form,
[331] it is not void, and that the effect of the act is only to subject the party
to a penalty.[z]

————

BANKER'S CASH NOTES, formerly called goldsmith's notes, are in
effect promissory notes given by bankers, who were originally goldsmiths.[a] From Lord Holt's judgment in the case of Buller *v.* Crips,[b]
it appears that these notes were attempted to be introduced by the
goldsmiths, about thirty years previously to the reign of Queen Anne,
and were generally esteemed by the merchants as negotiable; but Lord
Holt as strenuously opposed their negotiability as he did that of common promissory notes, and they were not generally settled to be negotiable until the statute of Anne was passed, which relates to these as
well as to common promissory notes. They appear originally to have
been given by bankers to their customers, as acknowledgments for
having received money for their use.[c] At present, cash notes are
seldom made except by country bankers, their use having been superseded by the introduction of checks.[d] When formerly issued by London bankers, they were sometimes called shop notes: in point of form

[x] See Bayl. 121, 2. 3 Geo. 2. c. 26.
s. 7. " And be it further enacted, by the
authority aforesaid, That from and after
the 24th day of June, 1730, all lightermen, and other buyers of or contractors
for coals, on board of any ship or vessel
in the port of London, shall, at the time
of the delivery of such coals, either pay
for the same in ready money, or for such
part thereof as shall not be so paid for,
shall give their respective promissory
notes, or notes of their hands, for payment thereof, expressing therein the
words, *value received in coals*, payable at
such day or days, time or times, as shall
for that purpose be agreed upon between
such lighterman, or other buyer of or
contractor for coals, and the master or
owner of such ship or vessel, or his agent
or factor on his behalf; and that all such
notes, in case of non-payment at the respective days and times therein mentioned, shall and may be protested or noted,
in such manner as inland bills of exchange
may now be, and in default of such protesting and noting by any indorsee, and
notice thereof given by such indorsee to
the respective indorser or indorsers, with
in twenty days after such failure of payment, such respective indorser or indorsers, to whom such notice shall not be
given, shall not be chargeable with or
liable to answer or pay such sum of money
as shall be mentioned to be payable in or
by such note or notes, nor any part there-

of; any law, usage, or custom to the contrary thereof notwithstanding."
S. 8. " And be it further enacted,
That all such lightermen, or others, buyers
of or contractors for coals, who shall,
after the 24th day of June, 1730, refuse
to give their note or notes for coals to them
respectively delivered, and shall refuse to
insert the said .words, *value received in
coals*, and every such master who shall take
any such note from any dealer in coals, in
which note the words, *value received in
coals*, are not expressly inserted, such
lighterman, buyers of, or contractors for
coals, and masters, shall, for every such
refusal or acceptance, respectively forfeit and pay the sum of one hundred
pounds."
[y] Smith *v.* Wilson, And. 187.
[z] Per Holroyd, J. in Wigan *v.* Fowler,
1 Stark. 463.
[a] Moor *v.* Warren, 1 Stra. 415. Turner
Mead, id. ibid. Hayward and the Bank
of England, id. 550. Smith's Wealth of
Nations, 1 vol 445, 6, 7, 8. but see Brook
v. Middleton, 1 Campb. 449 , where they
were treated as *checks*. Selw. Ni. Pri. 4th
edit. 368.
[b] Buller *v.* Crips, 6 Mod. 29, 30. Nicholson *v.* Sedgwick, Lord Raym. 180.
Horton *v.* Coggs, 3 Lev. 299.
[c] Ford *v.* Hopkins, Holt, 119. 1 Salk.
283. S. C.
[d] See Selw. Ni. Pri. 4th edit. 368.

Sect. 2. Of banker's notes.

they are similar to common promissory notes, payable to bearer on demand, and are stated in pleading as such. On account of their being payable on demand, they are considered as cash, whether payable to order or bearer,[a] but if presented in due time, and dishonoured, they will not amount to payment.[f] If any part of the consideration of an annuity be paid in country bank-notes, the dates and times of payment must be set forth in the memorial, because they are not considered as cash;[g] and if they are deposited with a stake-holder, they cannot be recovered from him as money had and received, unless he agreed to receive them as money.[h] They, like banker's checks, are generally transferred from one person to another by delivery. They may, however, be negotiated by indorsement, in which case, the act of indorsing will operate as the making of a bill of exchange, and the instrument may be declared on as such against the indorser.[i] In other respects they are affected by the same rules as bills of exchange.[k] The time when these notes should be presented for payment, is governed by the rules relating to checks payable on demand, which have already been stated, and to which part of the work the reader is referred.[l]

[332]

Sect. 3. Bank notes

BANK NOTES owe their origin to the 5 William and Mary, c. 20. s. 19, 20. 29., and the 8 & 9 William 3. c. 20. s. 30., by the first of which statutes, power was given to the king to incorporate the persons subscribing towards the raising and paying into the receipt of the exchequer the sum of £1,200,000, by the name of "The Governor and Company of the Bank of England." These notes are uniformly made payable on demand; Lord Mansfield, in Miller v. Race,[m] observed, "That these notes are not, like bills of exchange, mere securities, or "documents for debts, nor are so esteemed; but are treated as money "in the ordinary course and transactions of business, by the general "consent of mankind; and on payment of them, whenever a receipt

[a] Tassel v. Lewis, 1 Lord Raym. 744. Peacock v. Rhods, Dougl. 625. Owenson v. Morse, 7 T. R. 64.
[f] Owenson v. Morse, 7 T. R. 64. Ante, 143, in notes. Ward v. Evans, Lord Raym. 928. Ante, 99, and see ante, 271, 2.
[g] Morris v. Wall, 1 Bos. & Pul. 208.
[h] Pickard v. Bankes, 13 East, 20. A stake-holder receiving country bank notes as money, and paying them over wrongfully to the original staker, after he had lost the wager, is answerable to the winner, in an action for money had and received to his use. It appeared that the deposit had been made in Hull bank notes, payable to bearer, and not in coin of the realm, and the payment over to the other party was in notes of the same description. The learned Judge who tried the cause, thought that these were to be considered as money, as between those parties, and therefore the plaintiff recovered a verdict for the amount. It was afterwards moved to set aside the verdict, and by leave to enter a nonsuit. Notes of this description, it was contended, were no more than com-

mon promissory notes, or bills of exchange. If these were payable at a future day, they could in no sense be considered as money, but the time of payment cannot alter the nature of the thing. The action should rather have been trover, or upon a special assumpsit; and that Mr. Justice Lawrence, in a similar case at Stafford, held, that money had and received would not lie. Lord Ellenborough, C. J. "Provincial notes are certainly not money; but if the defendant received them as ten guineas in money, and all parties agreed to treat them as such at the time, he shall not now turn round and say that they were only paper, and not money: as against him it is so much money received by him." Rule refused.
[i] Lovelass on Bills, 58. Mendez v. Carreroon, Ld. Raym. 743. Hill v. Lewis, 1 Salk. 132, 3. Brown v. Harraden, 4 T. R. 149.
[k] Hill v. Lewis, 1 Salk. 132.
[l] Ante, 273 to 276.
[m] Miller v. Race, 1 Burr. 457. See 3 Atk. 232.

Sect. 3.   " is required, the receipts are always given as for money, not as for
Bank notes   " securities or notes." They pass by a will which bequeaths all the
testator's money or cash,[a] or all his property in such a house; and they
may pass as a *donatio mortis causâ.*[o] In bankruptcies they cannot be
followed as identical and distinguishable from money. If they be lost,
an action of trover will not lie against the *bona fide* holder by the true
owner.[p] In a case, also, on the annuity act, where the whole consideration was described in the memorial as money, and it appeared
that only a part of it was money, and the residue bank-notes, it was
decided on the above principle, that the consideration was well set
out.[q] It has, however, been adjudged, that an action for money had
and received will not lie against a finder of them, to recover the value,
unless money has actually been received for them,[r] though if not produced on the trial, the receipt of their value will be presumed;[s] nor
can they be taken in execution;[t] nor is a tender of bank-notes sufficient, if objected to at the time of the offer,[a] though, after such a
tender, a creditor cannot arrest his debtor, it having been enacted,[x]
that no person shall be held to bail, unless the affidavit of debt allege
that no offer has been made to pay the debt in bank-notes payable on
demand. The stealing of these notes is felony,[y] and the forgery of
them is also by different statutes declared to be felony.[z] They are
assignable by delivery.[a] A mode of enforcing payment of them was
provided by 8 & 9 William 3. c. 20. s. 30, but now when the right to
receive payment is disputed, the course is to proceed by action against
the bank. Possession is *prima facie* evidence of property in a bank
note. Therefore, in trover for a bank-note, it is not a *prima facie*
case for the plaintiff to prove that the note belonged to him, and that
the defendant afterwards converted it; and the defendant will not be
called upon to show his title to the note, without evidence from the
other side that he got possession of it *mala fide,* or without consideration.[b] And in Lowndes *v.* Anderson[c] it was held, that bank-notes
could not be followed by the legal owners into the hands of *bona fide*
holders for valuable consideration without notice. And in Solomons *v.*
The Bank of England,[d] it was decided, that the holder of a bank-note is
[334] *prima facie* entitled to prompt payment of it, and cannot be affected
by the previous fraud of any former holder in obtaining it, unless
evidence be given to bring it home to his privity. But where a bank-
note for £500 had been fraudulently obtained by some person unknown;
and on its being presented for payment sometime afterwards, by an
agent of a foreign principal, information was given of the fraud; and the
principal was desired to inform the bank how he came by it; but the
only account he would give of it was, that he had received it in pay-

[a] Fleming *v.* Brook, 1 Scho. & Lefr. 318,
19.   11 Ves. 662.

[o] Ante, 2. 1 Roper, 3.

[p] Lowndes *d.* Anderson, 13 East, 130,
135. 1 Campb. 551. ante, 147, 8.

[q] Wright *v.* Rehd, 3 T. R. 554. Cousins
v. Thompson, 6 T. R. 335.

[r] Noyes *v.* Price and another, Sittings,
London, post, Hil. Term, 16 Geo. 3. Select Cases, 242.

[s] Longchamp *v.* Kenney, Dougl. 128.

Francis *v.* Nash, Rep. T. Hardw. 53.
Knight *v.* Criddle, 9 East, 48. 4 East, 510.
Dougl. 236.

[a] Wright *v.* Reed, 3 T. R. 554. Grigby
v. Oakes, 2 Bos. & Pul. 526.

[x] 38 Geo. 3. c. 1 s. 8. 43 Geo. 2 c. 18.
s. 2.

[y] 2 Geo. 2. c. 25. s. 3. 9 Geo. 2. c. 18.

[z] 15 Geo. 2. c. 14. s. 11. 13 Geo. 2.
c. 79, s. 1. 41 Geo. 3. c. 39. 2 East's P.
C. 876, &c.

[a] Francis *v.* Nash, Rep. T. Hardw. 53.
supra, note.

[b] King *v.* Milsom, 2 Campb. 5. Richard
v. Carr, 1 Campb. 551.

[c] Lowndes *v.* Anderson, 13 East, 130.
1 Rose, 99, 102, n. a.

[d] Solomons *v.* The Bank of England.
13 East, 135.

ment of goods from a man dressed in such a way of whom he knew
nothing; and it was further proved, that bank-notes of so large a value
were not usually circulated in that foreign country; this was held to be
sufficient evidence to be left to a jury of the principal's privity to the
original fraud, in an action of trover brought by his agent to recover it
from the bank, who had detained it under the authority of the original
owner, to whom it properly belonged. And the question was not altered by the agent who received it, having, after notice, made payments
for his principal, which turned the balance in favour of such agent.

A formal set of words is in general, no more essential to the validity
of a promissory note, cash note, or bank of England note, than it is
to that of a bill of exchange.[e] It is sufficient if a note amount to an
absolute promise to pay money. And a note promising to account
with another, or his order, for a certain sum, value received, is a valid
promissory note, though it contain no formal promise to pay.[f] So
where the note set forth in the declaration was, "I acknowledge my-
"self to be indebted to A. in £—, *to be paid* on demand, for value
"*received*;" on demurrer to the declaration, the court held that this
was a good note within the statute; the words "*to be paid*," amounting to a promise to pay, observing that the same words in a lease would
amount to a covenant *to pay* rent.[g] So a promissory note payable to
B. (omitting the words "or order,") three months after date, was
holden a good note within the statute.[h] So, where a note was in this
form, "I do acknowledge that Sir A. C. has delivered to me all the
"bonds and notes for which £400 were paid to him on account of
"Colonel S., and that Sir A. delivered to me Major G's. receipt, and
"bill on me for £10, which £10, and £15. 5s., a balance due to
"Sir A., I am still indebted, and do promise to pay;" on demurrer to
the declaration the note was adjudged good.[i] And when the promise [335]
was by A. to pay so much to B. for a debt due from C. to B. it was
holden, that it was within the statute, being an absolute promise, and
as negotiable as if it had been generally for value received.[k]

But the mere acknowledgment of a debt, without some words from
whence a promise to pay money can reasonably be inferred, it is said,
will have no other operation than being evidence of a debt: and therefore the common memorandum, "*I O U* such a sum" has been determined not to amount to a promissory note, and need not be stamped.[l]
Nor is an instrument acknowledging the receipt of a draft for the payment of money, and promising to repay the money, a promissory note,
but only a special agreement for the re-payment, depending on the con-

---

[e] Colehan v. Cooke, Willes, 398; see
the cases, ante, 41, 2, Bopl. 34. Selw.
4th edit. 361, 2, 3.

[f] Morris v. Lee, 8 Mod. 362. 1 Stra.
629. Ld. Raym. 1396. S. C. 2 Atk. 32.
Ante, 41, note.

[g] Casborne v. Dutton, Seacc. M. 1 G. 2.
Selw. 4th edit. 363, note p.

[h] Smith v. Kindal, 6 T. R. 123. Ante,
66, note. Moore v. Pain, Rep. Temp.
Hardw. 28, where Ld. Hardwicke, C. J.
said, this point had been ruled often.

[i] Chadwick v. Allen, Stra. 706. Ante,
41.

[k] Popplewell v. Wilson, 1 Stra. 264, on
error, from C. P.

[l] Israel v. Israel, 1 Campb. 498. Fisher
v. Leslie, 1 Esp. Rep. 426. But in Guy
v. Harris, Sittings after Easter Term,
1900, at Guildhall, in the C. P. before
Lord Eldon, such a note was attempted
to be given in evidence by way of set-off,
but his Lordship ruled that it could not
be given in evidence, not being stamped,
being a promissory note, though not negotiable. Mr. Serjeant Marshall for the
plaintiff, Mr. Serjeant Best for the defendant. See Bayl. 4. Manning's Index,
215.

Sect. 4. tingency of the draft's being honoured.[m]　It is advisable, however, to
Form and insert the words " value received."[n]
qualities of
promissory
notes, &c.　　　Promissory notes, given in pursuance of the Lord's act, 32 Geo. 2.
c. 28. s. 13, in order to prevent the debtor's discharge, must be given
in a particular form, the statute enacting, that the prisoner shall be
discharged, unless the creditor insist that he shall be detained in prison,
and shall agree by writing, signed with his name or mark (or if he be
out of England) under the hand of his attorney, to pay and allow the
prisoner weekly, a sum not exceeding 3s. 6d. (or if more creditors than
one insist on his detention, not exceeding 2s. a week each.)[o] to be
paid on Monday in every week, so long as the prisoner shall continue
in execution ; and in every such case the prisoner shall be remanded.
And the court has no power to moderate the sum to be paid to a prisoner on his being remanded, but a note must be signed for the full
sum directed by the act. And if failure be made in payment of the
said weekly sums, the prisoner, upon application to the court in term
time, or in vacation to a judge, may, by order of the court or judge,
be discharged out of custody, on executing an assignment and conveyance of his estate and effects. The decisions on this clause of the
[336] act have already been so ably collected, that it is not necessary here
to state them.[p]

Requisites　　　Certain requisites are indispensable to the validity of all promissory
of notes.　 notes ;[q] thus they must be made payable at all events,[r] and not out
of a particular fund,[s] which may or may not be productive. But a
statement of the consideration for which a note is made will not vitiate it.[t] Notes must also be for the payment of money only, and
not for the performance of any other act ;[u] on the latter principle it
was adjudged, that a written promise to pay £300 to B. or order, " in
three good East India bonds," was not a promissory note ;[v] and that
an undertaking " to pay money, and deliver up horses and a wharf,"
on a particular day,[x] or an engagement " to pay money on demand, or
surrender the body of A. B."[y] would not operate as a note within the
statute of Anne.

　　　A promise by the defendant to pay to plaintiff £26 within a month
after Michaelmas, if defendant did not pay the £26 for which the
plaintiff stood engaged for his brother T. B. is not a promissory note.[z]
So a promise to pay A. B. £— value received, on the death of C. D.
provided he leaves either of us sufficient to pay the said sum, or if we
shall be otherwise able to pay it ;[a] and a promise to pay money within
so many days after the maker of the note should marry, are not within
the statute. So where the promise was to pay A. F. £— out of the
maker's money that should arise from his reversion of £— when sold,

[m] Williamson v. Bennett, 2 Campb. 417. Ante, 46, 7.
[n] Bishop v. Young, 2 Bos. &. Pul. 31. Ante, 67, 8.
[o] 37 Geo. 3. c. 85. s. 3, 4. Tidd, 6th edit. 381 ; but see Barnes, 377. 389. 390.
[p] Tidd's Prac. 6th edit. 381 to 384.
[q] Ante, 41 to 50. Bayl. 4, 5, 6. and 8 to 16.
[r] Ante, 42.
[s] Ante, 43.
[t] Ante, 89.
[u] Ante, 45.

[v] Bul. Ni. Pri 272. Ante, 45.
[x] Id. Martin v. Chauntry, 2 Stra 1271. Ante, 45, note.
[y] Ante, 45. Jenny v. Herle, 2 Lord Raym. 1362. Smith v. Boehm, Gilb. L of Evid. 93. cited Lord Raym. 1352— Ante, 45, note. Williams v. Lucas, 1 P. W. 431, note 1.
[z] Appleby v. Biddulph, 8 Mod. 363. ante, 43, note.
[a] Roberts v. Peake, 1 Burr. 323. Ante, 43, note. Beardsley v. Baldwin, Stra. 1151. 7 Mod. 417.

and the declaration averred the sale of the reversion, yet it was holden that the note could not be declared on as a negotiable note under the statute, because the money was to be paid only on a contingency.[b] So where the promise was to pay £— on the sale or produce, immediately when sold, of the White Hart, St. Albans, Herts, and the goods therein, although it was averred in the declaration, that the house and goods were sold, yet the note was considered invalid.[c] The same principle was recognised in the following cases, though the notes were held good.

A promissory note was given to an infant, payable when he should [337] come of age, viz. on such a day in such a year, this was holden good; for, per Denison J. here is no condition or uncertainty, but it is to be paid certainly, and at all events, only the time of payment is postponed.[d] So where the plaintiff declared in the first count on a promissory note, dated 27th May, 1732, whereby defendant promised to pay to H. D. or order, 150 guineas, ten days after the death of his father, John Cooke, for value received; which note, after the death of the father (which was laid to be on the 2d April, 1741,) was duly indorsed by D. to plaintiff; and in the second count, on a promissory note, dated 15th July, 1732, whereby defendant promised to pay H. D. or order, six weeks after the death of his father, 50 guineas, for value received, the like indorsement laid after the death of the father as before; after a general verdict for plaintiff on both notes, it was insisted for defendant, in arrest of judgment, that these notes were not within the statute 3 & 4 Anne, c. 9. After three arguments, Willes, Chief Justice, delivered the opinion of the court in favour of the plaintiff; on the ground that the notes did not depend on any contingency: that there was a certain promise to pay at the time of giving the notes, and the money, by virtue thereof, would become due and payable at one time or other, though it was uncertain when that time would come; that there was not any weight in the objection, that the maker might have died before his father, in which case the notes would have been of no value, because the same might be said of any notes payable at a distant time, that the maker might die worth nothing before the note became payable. He added that he thought that the averment of the death of the father before the indorsement, did not make any alteration: because they were of opinion, that if the notes were not within the statute, *ab initio,* they could not be made so by any subsequent contingency.[e]

So where the note was to pay within a certain time after such a ship was paid off, it was holden good; because the ship would certainly be paid off some time or other.[f]

It has been said,[g] that in the application of the rule relative to these instruments being payable at all events, there is a distinction between bills of exchange and promissory notes, and that a note may in certain cases be payable on a contingency;[h] but it will appear, that the cases[i] [338]

[b] Carlos *v.* Fancourt, 5 T. R. 481.— Ante
[c] Hill *v.* Halford, 2 Bos. & Pul. 413. Ante, 44. note.
[d] Goss *v.* Nelson, 1 Burr. 226. Ante, 48.
[e] Coleban *v.* Cooke, Willes, 393, affirmed in error, Stra. 1217. Ante, 48.

[f] Andrews *v.* Franklin, Hil. 3 Geo. 1. B. R. 1 Stra. 24. *Sed quære,* see ante, 49, as to this point.
[g] Kyd, 56.
[h] Dawkes *v.* Delorain, 2 Bla. Rep. 782. Ante, 43, 44.
[i] Cooke *v.* Coleban, 2 Stra. 1217. Andrews *v.* Franklin, 1 Stra. 24. Goss *v.* Nel-

Sect. 4.
Form and
qualities of
promissory
notes, &c.
adduced in support of this distinction, are equally applicable to bills
of exchange; and it is now settled, that in general, if a note be payable on a contingency, it will be as inoperative as a bill payable in the
same manner.[k] It has also been observed,[l] that in the application
of the principle that these instruments must not be payable out of a
particular fund, there is a material distinction between bills of exchange and promissory notes; but the case[m] adduced in support of this
opinion, only shows that the statement in a bill or note, of the consideration for which it was made, will not vitiate it.[n] It is also settled,
that it is not necessary that a note, any more than a bill of exchange,
should contain any words rendering it negotiable.[o] In short, all the
rules relative to the qualities of a bill of exchange, are equally applicable to notes, and it would be an unnecessary repetition to enumerate
them.

When a promissory note is made by several, and expressed "we promise to pay," it is a joint note only; but if a note be signed by several persons, and begin "*I* promise," &c. it is several as well as joint, and
the parties may be sued jointly or severally.[p](453) But if a promissory
[339] note appears on the face of it to be the separate note of A. only, it cannot be declared on as the note of A. and B., though given to secure a
debt for which A. and B. were jointly liable.[q]

In an action by A against B. upon a promissory note, it was stated
in the declaration, that B. and another jointly, *or* severally promised to

son, 1 Burr. 227. Evans *v.* Underwood,
1 Wils. 262.
  [k] Carlos *v.* Fancourt, 5 T. R. 486. Ante,
44. Coleban *v.* Cooke, Willes, 388, 9.
Williamson *v.* Bennett, 2 Campb. 417.
Ante, 46.
  [l] Kyd, 53.
  [m] Burchell *v.* Slocock, Ld. Raym. 1545.
  [n] Hausoullier *v.* Hartsink, 7 T. R. 723.
Anon. Sel. Ca. 39. Et Ante, 50.
  [o] Smith *v.* Kendall, 6 T. R. 23. Ante,
66, note.
  [p] Clerke *v.* Blackstock, Holt C. N. P.
474. March *v.* Ward, Peake's Rep. 130.
Butler *v.* Malissy, 1 Stra. 76. Ovington *v.*
Neale, 2 Stra. 819. Rees *v.* Abbott, Cowp.
832. Rice *v.* Shute, 5 Burr. 2611. Com.
Dig. tit. Obligation, F. G. Cabell *v.* Vaughan, 1 Saund. 291, b. n. 4. Abbot *v.* Smith,
2 Bla. Rep. 947. Holmer *v.* Viner, 1 Esp.
Rep. 134. Bayl. 24. 177, 8. Selw. 4th ed.
368.
  March *v.* Ward, Peake's Rep. 130. Assumpsit on a promissory note, made by the
defendant, and one Bowling, in the following words, viz.—" I promise to pay, three
months after date, to W. March, 3*l.* 5*s.* for
value received in fixtures.
     " ROBERT BOWLING."
     " THOMAS WARD."

It was objected, that this promissory
note was joint only, and not several. Lord
Kenyon. I think this note beginning in the
singular number is several as well as joint.
and that the present action may be maintained on it. I remember a case tried before Mr. Moreton at Chester, exactly
similar to the present, wherein I was
counsel for the defendant. I persuaded
the judge that it was a joint note only, and
the plaintiff was nonsuited; but on an application being afterwards made to this
court, they were of a contrary opinion.
and a new trial was granted; the letter "I"
applies to each severally. Verdict for the
plaintiff
  Roberts *v.* Peake, 1 Burr. 323. A note
signed by the defendant alone, but importing in the body of it to have been
made by the defendant and another person, was declared upon as the several
note of the defendant, and it was agreed
that it might be declared upon according
to its legal operation ; but judgment was
given for the defendant upon another
ground. See Siffkin *v.* Walker, 2 Campb.
308.
  [q] Siffkin *v.* Walker and others, 2
Campb. 308. Emley *v.* Lye, 15 East. 7.
Ante, 39.

(453) The same doctrine was held in *Hunt* v. *Adams*, 5 Mass. Rep. 358. and see *Hem-
menway* v. *Stone*, 7 Mass. Rep. 58. And a promissory note given by one member of a
Commercial Company to another member, for the use of the Company, will maintain an
law by the promisee in his own name against the maker. *Van Ness* v. *Forrest*,
6 Cranch, 30.

pay it; and it was holden, that the declaration was good, for *or* was
synonymous to *and*, that they both promised that they, or one of them,
should pay, consequently both and each were liable *in solidum*.[r]   And
it has been held, that if an action be brought on a joint note, and some
of the persons making the note are not made defendants, advantage
can only be taken of the omission by plea in abatement.[s]   And if one
of several makers of a promissory note be an infant, he should not be
sued, nor should the declaration state that he was a party;[t] and if there
be a joint and several promissory note of two persons, and one of them
was a security only for the other, and the circumstance were known to
the holder, and he accept a composition from the assignees of such
principal, amounting to less than the dividend payable under his
commission, it has been held that this conduct releases the surety from
liability.[u]

The amount of the stamp duties, imposed on notes until the 10th [340]
October, A. D. 1808, was regulated by the 44 Geo. 3. c. 98, schedule
A.   The amount of the duties from that time until the 10th October,
A. D. 1808, were regulated by the statute 48 Geo. 3. c. 149. The
present stamp duties on notes are regulated by the 55 Geo. 3. c. 184,
and these are the same as the stamps on bills, except as to notes *re-issuable* after payment by the maker.

The regulations with respect to the stamps on notes in general, and
in particular to re-issuable notes, and the licensing bankers to draw
and re-issue the same, have already been mentioned,[x] and the statute
itself will be found in the Appendix.

[r] Butler *v.* Mallasy, 1 Stra. 76. In an
action on a note, the declaration stated,
that the defendant and another did jointly
or severally promise to pay, and upon demurrer the court held it bad, and the
plaintiff obtained leave to discontinue.
And in Ovington *v.* Neale, Stra. 819.—
Ld. Raym. 1544, the plaintiff declared
upon a note by which the defendant and
another jointly or severally promised to
pay, and upon error the court of King's
Bench held it bad, because the plaintiff
had not shown a title to bring a separate
action against the defendant, for he only
says he has this or some other cause of
action, and judgment for the plaintiff was
reversed.
    However, in Rees *v.* Abbott, Cowp.
832, the declaration upon a note stated,
that the defendant and another made their
note, by which they jointly or severally
promised to pay, and upon error after
judgment by default, Butler *v.* Mallasy,
and Ovington *v.* Neale, were cited as in
point. *Sed per* Lord Mansfield.—" If
' *or* ' is to be considered in this case as a
disjunctive, the plaintiff is to elect, and
by the action he has made his election to
consider the note as several, but in this
case it is synonymous to ' *and*,' and both
and each promise to pay." Judgment affirmed.
[s] Per Buller, J. in Rees *v.* Abbott,
Cowp. 832. See ante, p. 338, note.—
Selw. 4th ed. 369.
    CHITTY ON BILLS.

[t] Burgess *v.* Merrill, 4 Taunt. 468.—1
Chitty on Plead. 3d ed. 35.

[u] Garrett *v.* Jull, B. R. Mich. 22 G. 3.
MS. Selw. 4th ed. 369. An action was
brought against defendant only, on a joint
and several note, made by defendant and
one Stoddart. Plea, non-assumpsit. Defendant gave in evidence an agreement in
writing, entered into by plaintiff with the
assignees of Stoddart, then a bankrupt, to
receive from them 600*l.* in lieu of 883*l.*,
actually due from the bankrupt on this note
(which was for 100*l.*) and on other transactions; and that defendant was only surety
for Stoddart. Defendant obtained a verdict. On motion to set it aside, it was insisted, on the part of the defendant, on the
ground that the agreement put an end to
the plaintiff's recovery on the note, that
the principal could not be discharged without discharging the surety also. On the
part of the plaintiff it was urged, that it
was not the meaning of the agreement that
the defendant should be discharged. But
per Lord Mansfield, C. J. the plaintiff was
party to the agreement, and we cannot receive parol evidence to explain it. Whatever might be the intention of the parties,
the principal cannot be released without
its operating for the benefit of the surety.
Rule discharged. *As to this point, see
ante*, 301.

[x] Ante, 53.
        R r

Sect. 4.
Form and
qualities of
promissory
notes, &c.

Bank notes are exempted from the stamp duty by the 23 Geo. 3. c. 49. s. 9, and other subsequent statutes, in consideration of the payment of the annual sum of £12,000 into the receipt of his majesty's exchequer. The decisions on the former and present stamp acts already stated, are here applicable.[7]

In all points in which a distinction between bills of exchange and promissory notes, has not been pointed out, the rules relative to the one, equally apply to the other, and therefore it will not be necessary to make any further observations in the present chapter.

[7] Ante, 54 to 58.

PART SECOND.

The REMEDIES *on a Bill, Check, or Note.*

———

IN the preceding part of this work, I have endeavoured to point out the nature of the RIGHT which may be acquired by the instruments which are the subject of this Treatise. The REMEDY which the law affords the parties to enforce payment, forms the remaining head of inquiry. In this part of the work no distinct observations on bills and notes will be necessary, as the same remedies are given by law on both species of instrument except that in some cases debt is not sustainable on a promissory note, which distinction will be pointed out. The means of enforcing payment, are either by *action* of *assumpsit*, or *debt*, or, where the party is a *bankrupt*, by *proof* under the commission. In the consideration of the above-mentioned actions, the pleas and defences, and the evidence to be adduced by each party, will also be considered.

CHAPTER I.

BY, AND AGAINST WHOM, AN ACTION OF ASSUMPSIT ON A BILL, CHECK, OR NOTE, MAY BE SUPPORTED.

THE action of ASSUMPSIT is by far the most usual remedy on bills, checks, and notes; and indeed it appears to be the only remedy where no privity of contract exists between the parties, as between the indorsee and the acceptor of a bill, and a remote indorsee and maker of a note, in which case debt is not maintainable,[a] or when the action is against an executor or administrator, against whom debt or simple contract is not in general sustainable.[b]

With respect to the *persons, by, or against whom*, this action may be brought,[c] it may be observed, in general, that whenever a legal right is created, or liability imposed, through the medium of these instruments, that right may be asserted, and that liability enforced, by this action. (439) Therefore a person may sue on a note payable to him, though in trust for a third party.[d] And the wife may join in an action on a note made payable to her during the coverture.[e] When there are several indorsers, it is not necessary that the action should be brought in the name of the holder, or of the last indorser: they may arrange the matter among themselves, and any one indorser may sue the acceptor or drawer, instead of the preceding indorser, striking out all the names below his own.[f] (439) Where a merchant, carrying on trade on his own separate account, introduces into his firm the name of a clerk, who has no participation in profit or loss, but continues to re-

---

[a] Bishop v. Young, 2 Bos. & Pul. 78.

[b] Barry v. Robinson, 1 New. Rep. 293.

[c] Poth. tit. Contrat de Change, part 1. chap. 5. art. 2. *per totum.*

[d] Smith v. Kendall, 1 Esp. Rep. 231. 6 T. R. 123. S. C. Randall v. Bell, 1 M. & S. 723.

[e] Philliskirk et Ux v. Pluckwell, 2 M. & S. 393. Ante, 19. 1 Chitty on Plead. 3d edit. 20.

[f] Per Eyre, C. J. in Walwyn v. St. Quintin, 1 Bos. & Pul. 658. This doctrine was recognised in Parnell v. Townend, Trin. Term, 58 Geo. 3, on an argument of a demurrer, see post. But if a bill were really the property of another, and put into the hands of a defendant to set off against a claim on him, that might present a different question. Per Lord Ellenborough, in Cornforth v. Revetts, 2 M. & S. 512.

---

(439) The same practice is recognised in the United States. *Livingston* v. *Clinton,* 3 John. Cas. 264. *Baker* v. *Arnold,* 1 Caines' Rep. 269. 271. And where the plaintiff is in possession of the bill, when he commences the action, the simple act of indorsing it may be done afterwards. Ibid. See *Ritchie* v. *Moore,* 5 Munf. 388.

Where an action against an indorser was commenced on the same day that the note became due, but after the notice was put into the post-office, and the writ was served before the notice could be received by the course of the mail, it was held that the action was not commenced too soon. *Shed* v. *Bret,* 1 Pick. 401.

But where notice to an indorser who lived at another place, of non-payment and protest of a promissory note, was put into the post-office on the 13th, and by the course of the mail could not reach him before the 19th, it was held that a suit commenced against him on the 16th was too soon. *Smith* v. *The Bank of Washington,* 5 Serg. & Rawle. 318.

ceive a fixed salary, it was held, that in an action on a bill of exchange
payable to the order of this firm, the clerk must be joined as a plaintiff,[s] unless it be distinctly proved that he had no interest.[h] And if a
party, who has commenced an action on a bill, deposit it afterwards as
a security in the hands of a third person, he may still proceed in the
action, if the latter knew that the action was commenced ; and if such
third person, having had this notice, commence another action against
the same defendant, the court will stay his proceedings.[i](439) And the
drawer of a bill, after taking it up, may sue and arrest a bankrupt acceptor, who has not obtained his certificate, although a previous holder,
has proved under the commission.[k]

The *bona fide* holder of a bill, check, or note, may in general
maintain an action thereon against all the parties to it, whose names
are to it, and who became so *previously* to himself.[l] Thus the *payee*
may, in default of payment, sue the acceptor, whether he accepted as
drawee, or merely for the honour of the drawer, and he may also, in
such case, sue the drawer. And *indorsee* may, in general, not only
sue the acceptor and drawer, but also all the prior indorsers ; and an
assignee, by mere delivery, may sue the acceptor, drawer, and indorsers, but he cannot maintain an action against any person whose
name is not on the bill, except the person who assigned it to him,[m] and
then only when the consideration of the transfer was a precedent debt,
or a debt arising at the time, and not when he became the holder, by
discounting the bill upon a purchase thereof, as sometimes occurs.[n]
However, a person to whom the drawer of a bill which had been
accepted for value, has indorsed it after it was dishonoured, and after it had been paid by the drawer, may sue the acceptor in his own
name.[o]

The *drawer* may maintain an action on the bill against the drawee,
in case of a refusal to pay a bill already accepted, but not on a refusal
to accept, in which latter case the action by him must be on the original
consideration of the bill, or in some cases specially on the contract to
accept ; and any party who has given value for the bill, and has been
obliged to pay in consequence of the default of the acceptor, may
maintain an action thereon against all the parties antecedent to himself,
and in this case he is said to hold the bill in his original capacity;[p] and
[344] the drawer of a bill, payable to the order of a *third* person, may,
when the bill has been returned to him, and he has paid it, sue the
acceptor.[q]

[s] Guidon *v.* Mary Robson, 2 Campb. 302.

[h] 1 Chitty on Pleas. 3d ed. 8.

[i] Marsh *v.* Newell, 1 Taunt. 109. And see the observations of Abbott, J. in Randall *v.* Bell, 1 M. & S. 723.

[k] Mead *a.* Braham, 3 M. S. 91.

[l] Bishop *v.* Hayward, 4 T. R. 471.

[m] Ante, 142, 3, 4.

[n] Ante, 145, 6.

[o] See Callow *v.* Laurence, 3 M. & S.

97, ante, 129, 130, which explains Bacon *v.* Searles, 1 Hen. Bla. 88.

[p] Cowley *v.* Dunlop, 7 T. R. 571. Death *v.* Serwonters, Lutw. 885. 888. Bosanquet *v.* Dudman, 1 Stark. 2, 3.

[q] Symonds *v.* Parminter, 1 Wils. 185. 4 Bro. P. C. 604. The plaintiff drew a bill upon the defendant, to the order of Cleer and Co. which the defendant accepted, but did not pay; the plaintiff paid it and brought this action. The declara-
tion stated, that the plaintiff drew the bill;

(439) An assignment of a note made during the pendency of a suit, operates as a discontinuance of the suit. *Hall* v. *Gentry*, 1 Marsh. 555.

Where the holder of a bill sued the acceptor and charged him in execution, and the latter having obtained his discharge under the Lord's act, the holder then sued the drawer, who after paying the bill sued the acceptor, and charged him in execution, this was held to be regular.[r] In the case of an acceptance for the accommodation of the drawer, such acceptor, if he has been obliged to pay, may sue the drawer on his implied contract to indemnify him, but not on the bill itself,[s] though we have seen that he may retain money in his hands as an indemnity ;[t] and a person not originally party to a bill, having paid it *supra protest*, may maintain an action against all, or any of the parties to it, except the person whom he paid ;[u] but the bail of the *maker* of a promissory note, who have paid it, cannot sue the indorsers ;[x] and a banker who pays the acceptance of a customer, who has made it pay- [345] able at his banking-house, cannot sue thereon, as he does not stand in the situation of a party praying *supra protest*.[y](442)

But unless, under circumstances which must be specially stated on the record, no action can be maintained on a bill against a person who became party to it *subsequently* to the holder or plaintiff, for if it were otherwise, the defendant in such action might, as an indorsee deriving from the plaintiff, be entitled to recover back again, in another action

that the defendant accepted, but did not pay it; that the plaintiff became liable and did pay it, by reason whereof the defendant became liable and promised. The defendant demurred, and afterwards moved in arrest of judgment, and contended that the action could not lie; but the court, after two arguments upon the demurrer, and one on motion in arrest of judgment, were of opinion that it would, and judgment was given for the plaintiff. The defendant brought a writ of error in parliament, but did not appear at the bar to support it, and judgment was affirmed.

Louviere v. Laubray, 10 Mod. 36. The plaintiff drew a bill upon the defendant, which the defendant accepted, but afterwards refused to pay; upon this the bill was indorsed to the plaintiff, and the question was, whether he could maintain an action as indorsee; and per Parker, C. J. upon evidence that he had effects in the hands of the defendant enough to answer the bill, and consequently that the acceptance was not upon the honour of the plaintiff, the action is well brought, but if there were no effects, the action would not lie, and the plaintiff recovered.

[r] Macdonald v. Bovington, 4 T. R. 825, ante, 301; and Mead v. Braham, 3 M. & S. 91.

[s] Young v. Hockley, 3 Wils. 346.

[t] Ante, 196.

[u] Ante, 243.

Mertens v. Winnington, 1 Esp. Rep. 112. A bill was drawn by the defendant, and indorsed by Burton, Forbes, and Gregory. The plaintiff paid it for the honour of Burton, Forbes, and Gregory, and brought this action against the defendant as drawer; the defendant contended that a person who paid for the honour of one of the parties, could only sue that party; but Lord Kenyon said he was to be considered as an indorsee, paying full value for the bill, and he directed the jury to find for the plaintiff.

[x] Hull v. Pitfield, 1 Wils. 46. Bayl. 148.

The indorsee of a note sued the maker, and on payment by his bail, permitted them to sue the indorser in his (the indorsee's) name, but the court held that the payment of the money to the plaintiff by the bail for the drawer, was the same thing as if the drawer himself had paid it, and that the note was thereby absolutely discharged and satisfied; that the indorser of a note is only a warranter thereof ; that the drawer will pay it, and if he does not, that the indorser will, and that it is the same thing whether the drawer himself paid the money, or his friend, as the bail did in this case.

[y] Holroyd v. Whitehead, 5 Taunt. 444. 1 Marsh. 128. 3 Campb. 530. S. C.

(442) The acceptor of a bill of exchange, who, at the time of acceptance, had no funds in his hands belonging to the drawer, although he has not paid the bill, may sue the drawer, if he has done something equivalent to payment; as if he is in confinement under a *ca. sa.* at the suit of the holder. *Parker* v. *The United States*, Peters' Rep. 262. See as to the right of the acceptor of a bill of exchange to sue, ib. 267.

against the plaintiff, the identical sum which he, the plaintiff, had previously recovered from him, which would introduce a circuity of action; and therefore where A. having declared on a promissory note against B. made by C. to A. and indorsed by him to B., and by B. again indorsed to A. and having obtained a verdict, the judgment was arrested.[a]

A plaintiff cannot in general maintain his action against the person from whom he received the bill, unless he gave him a valuable consideration for it.[a]

We have before seen, what objections may be taken in an action at the suit of a person attempting to derive an interest in a bill, by a transfer after it was due or paid;[b] and what *laches*, in the holder of a bill, will operate as a forfeiture of his right of action.[c] If the holder of a bill make the acceptor his executor, and die, the right of action at law against all the parties is extinguished, unless the executor formally renounces.[d]
[346] Where a note or bill made by several, is joint and several, it is advisable to proceed in separate actions, if there be any doubt in proving the joint liability of all.[e]

Whenever the holder of a bill, &c. has a remedy against several parties to it, he may commence and proceed in several actions against each of those parties at the same time; and an action commenced against one, will not preclude any other remedy against the others; but as the different persons liable on the bill are debtors to the holder in respect of the same debt, satisfaction by any one will discharge the others from liability as to the principal sum due on the bill,[f] and if the holder reject an offer by a drawer or indorser of a bill, to pay debts and costs of the ac-

---

[a] Bishop *v.* Hayward, 4 T. R. 470. Mainwaring *v.* Newman, 2 Bos. & Pul. 125.
Bishop *v.* Hayward, 4 T. R. 470. The plaintiff declared upon a note payable to himself or order, indorsed by him to the defendant, and by the defendant indorsed back again to him, and obtained a verdict. A rule was granted to show cause why the judgment should not be arrested, on the ground that according to the statement in the declaration, the plaintiff would be liable upon his indorsement to pay the defendant the sum, for which the verdict was given, and upon cause shown, the court held the objection good, because as the plaintiff had not stated it to be otherwise, his indorsement was to be considered as a legal existing indorsement; had any circumstances existed which exempted the plaintiff from answering upon his indorsement to the defendant, they should have been disclosed upon the record, and the declaration framed specially.
[a] Ante, 68 to 73. Mitchinson *v.* Hewson, 7 T. R. 550. Cowley *v.* Dunlop, id. 571. Death *v.* Serwonters, 1 Lutw. 886. Simmonds *v.* Parminter, 1 Wils. 495. 4 Bro. P. C. 704, *acc.* 2 Bla. Com. 446, *contra;* but see Mr. Christian's note.
[b] Ante, 126 to 131.
[c] Ante, 196 to 240.
[d] Poth. pl. 191. 1 Rol. Abr. 922. Woodward *v.* Lord Darcy, Plowd. 184.

Paramour *v.* Yardley, id. 542. Wankford *v.* Wankford, 1 Salk. 299. 2 Bla. Com. 511, 512. 3 Bla. Com. 18. Mainwaring *v.* Newman, 2 Bos. & Pul. 124, 5.
[e] Gray *v.* Palmer, 1 Esp. Rep. 135, 6.
[f] Windham *v.* Withers, 1 Stra. 515. Poth. pl. 160. Bayl. 151. Burgess *v.* Merrell, 4 Taunt. 468. Ex parte Wildman, 2 Ves. sen. 115. Lord Hardwicke. In cases of bills of exchange, or promissory notes, where there is a drawer and indorser, perhaps there may be more than one judgment against all, but there can be but one satisfaction.
Windham *v.* Withers, 1 Stra. 515. The plaintiff having obtained judgment against the drawer and indorser of a note, the principal in one, and the costs in both, were offered him, which he refused, and the court granted a rule to restrain him from taking out execution, and intimated that they would have punished him, had he taken out execution upon both judgments.
Claxton *v.* Swift, 2 Show. 441. 494. Lutw. 882. To an action against the indorser of a bill, the defendant pleaded that the plaintiff had recovered a judgment against the drawer, and that the judgment was still in force, and upon demurrer the court of King's Bench held the plea good, but the court of Exchequer Chamber held otherwise, and the judgment was reversed.

tion against him, the court will make an order to restrain the holder taking out execution; though if the money be paid pending several actions against other parties to the bill, the plaintiff may, without reserving any part of the principal money, proceed in the actions for the recovery of the costs. [g]

It is settled, that when two persons are *severally*, as well as jointly, bound in a bond, and one of them be taken in execution in a separate action, the other may, nevertheless, be sued, because the taking *another's person* in execution, is but the mere security for the payment of a debt, and not a valuable satisfaction of it. [h] It was made a question in the last century, how far this doctrine was applicable to bills of exchange; but it is now settled, that a judgment, [i] or even an execution, against the *person* of any one of the parties to the bill, will not dis- [347] charge the others, though with respect to him it is a full satisfaction of the debt. [k] It is also settled, that the holder's letting a subsequent indorser in execution out of prison on a letter of license, will not discharge a *prior* indorser from his liability to pay the bill; [l] and that if an acceptor be discharged under an insolvent debtor's act, such discharge will not operate in favour of any other person. [m] But if the holder of a bill accept a bond from the drawer, or any other party, in satisfaction of it, such act will discharge other subsequent parties; [n] and we have before seen, [o] that compromising with the acceptor, without the assent of the drawer or indorsers, will release them from their engagements. Actual payment of what is due, will, of course, discharge the parties; and though the holder of a bill may issue execution against the *person* of all the parties, he cannot, after levying the amount of the debt on the *goods* of one issue a *fieri facias* to affect the goods of another. [p]

[g] Toms *v.* Powell, 7 East, 526. 6 Esp. Rep. 40. S. C. 3 East, 316. 3 Campb. 331. Holt, C. N. P. 6.

[h] Blemfield's case, 5 Co. 86. Bayl. 151. Clerk *v.* Withers, Ld. Raym. 1072. 1 Salk. 522. S. C. Claxton *v.* Swift, 2 Show 494. Foster *v.* Jackson, Hob. 59. Bayl. 151, 2.

[i] Ayrey *v.* Davenport, 2 New. Rep. 474. Claxton *v.* Swift, 3 Mod. 87. 2 Show. 494. Lutw. 878. 882. S. C. Bayl, 151, 2.

[k] Id. ibid. Macdonald *v.* Bovington, 4 T. R. 825.

[l] Ante, 298. Haylin *v.* Mullhall, 2 Bla. Rep. 1235. English *v.* Darley, 2 Bos. & Pul. 61. Clark *v.* Clement, 6 T. R. 525. Bayl. 151.

[m] Macdonald *v.* Bovington, 4 T. R. 825. Nadin *v.* Battie, 5 East, 147.

[n] Ante, 290. Claxton *v.* Swift, 3 Mod. 87. English *v.* Darley, 3 Bos. & Pul. 61.

[o] Ante, 301.

[p] Windham *v.* Withers, 1 Stra. 515.

CHAPTER II.

OF THE AFFIDAVIT TO HOLD TO BAIL, ARREST, BAIL ABOVE, AND DECLARATION IN ASSUMPSIT UPON A BILL, CHECK, OR NOTE.

Affidavit to hold to bail.

IN order to *arrest* a party in an action on a bill of exchange or promissory note, the statute 12 Geo. 1. c. 29, requires that an *affidavit* should be made and filed of the *cause of action*, and by the terms of that act the sum due on the instrument must amount to £10, which regulation is not altered by the 51 Geo. 3. 124. s. 21, which renders it necessary that the debt shall be £15, in other cases. This affidavit must be certain and explicit, and so positive, that in case it were untrue, the party making it would be liable to an indictment for perjury.[a] It has been well observed, that the strictness required in these affidavits is not only to guard defendants against the consequences of perjury, but also those who make the affidavit against any misconception of the law; and that the leaning should always be to great strictness of construction, where one party is to be deprived of his liberty by the act of another.[b] There has been some contradiction in the cases in the King's Bench and Common Pleas.[c] But from the most recent cases it appears, that the practice of both the courts is now uniform.[d]

In an action against the *maker* of a note, or the *acceptor* of a bill, who are primarily liable, it is necessary to state in the affidavit, that it was due, or at least to show the date and when it was payable, for otherwise the party being primarily liable, the affidavit that he was indebted might be true, and yet the note or bill might not be due at the time of swearing the affidavit, because the maker of a promissory note, or the acceptor of a bill, becomes debtor immediately, though the instrument be payable at a future day: it being *debitum in præsenti solvendum in futuro.*[e] And the same point has recently been determined in the court of Common Pleas, in an action against the acceptor of a bill.[f] And though in an action against the *indorser* of a bill or note, who can only be liable in default of the acceptor or maker, and whose liability is only collateral and conditional, it has been decided not to be necessary to show that the bill or note is over due, because this case was distinguishable from the former, on the ground that the party being described as an indorser, and as such only a collateral security, could not be indebted, unless the bill had become due and been dishonoured;[g] yet it is now settled that an affidavit to hold to bail, which states that defendant is indebted to the plaintiff as drawer of a bill is not sufficient, unless it also state that the bill is due.[h]

[349]

---

[a] Tidd, 6th ed. 186.
[b] Per Lord Ellenborough in Taylor v. Forbes, 10 East, 316, and see Bradshaw v. Saddington, 7 East, 95.
[c] 3 Tidd, 6th ed. 186, 7.
[d] And see Machu v. Fraser, 7 Taunt. 178.
[e] Per Bayley, J. in Jackson v. Yate, 2 M. & S. 149, and see Holcombe v.

Lambkin, id. 475. and Edwards v. Dick, 3 Bar. & Ald. 495.
[f] Machu v. Fraser, 7 Taunt. 171.
[g] Per Bayley, J. in Jackson v. Yate, 2 M. & S. 149. Davison v. March, 1 New Rep. 157. Holcombe v. Lambkin, 2 M. & S. 475.
[h] Edwards v. Dick, 3 Bar. & Ald. 495

The affidavit must also show in what character the *defendant* became a party to the bill or note, whether as drawer, acceptor, or indorser, for otherwise he might not be liable on the bill, but merely as a guarantee, in which case the nature of his engagement must be stated, as the statute requires an affidavit of the cause of action, and the distinction is between the omission of the plaintiff's title to sue, and the character in which the defendant stands.[1] And therefore an affidavit, stating that the defendant was indebted to the plaintiff in the sum of £95, as the *indorsee* of a certain bill of exchange, drawn by one T. Winslow, without stating how the defendant became liable, whether as acceptor or indorser, was held insufficient,[k] and the term *indorsee* is descriptive of the relation of the plaintiff to the bill and not of the defendant.[l]

But it is not necessary for the affidavit to specify in what particular character the debt is due to the *plaintiff*, whether he claim as payee or indorsee, for if he had no interest in the bill on which he could sue the defendant, he would be guilty of perjury, and would be liable to an action for maliciously holding the defendant to bail,[m] and though it was once decided otherwise in the court of Common Pleas,[n] yet it has been since observed by that court, that such decision took place without the case of Bradshaw *v.* Saddington having been cited, and in the latest case that court appears to have determined to adopt the practice of the court of King's Bench.[o]

Where a party to a bill has signed his Christian name only with initials, and application has been made to him for his name, and he has refused to disclose it, and all possible inquiries have been made to ascertain it without effect, it has been holden that the affidavit and proceedings may state only his initials, and that the court will not discharge him on common bail, or set aside the proceeding.[p] But in a recent case this doctrine was over-ruled; and it was decided that an arrest of a party described in a *testatum* special *capias*, and in the affidavit by the initials of his Christian name is irregular.[q] In order to hold to bail in trover for a bill of exchange, it should be stated in the affidavit that such bill remains unpaid, as well as the value.[r] The usual forms of affidavits are given in the Appendix.

[350]

When a married woman has been arrested as the *acceptor* of a bill, at the suit of an *indorsee*, the court will not order the bail-bond to be cancelled on an affidavit, that the *drawer* when he drew the bill knew the defendant to be a married woman, because her so accepting a negotiable security, and enabling the drawer to impose upon a third person, is in effect representing herself as a single woman to the injury of a third person, but she must find special bail, and plead her coverture, or bring a writ of error.[s] And where a woman was arrested as the *drawer*

Affidavit to hold to bail.

Of the Arrest.

[1] Humphries *v.* Williams, 2 Mash. 231. 6 Taunt. 531. S. C.

[k] Id. ibid.

[l] Note, in Machu *v.* Fraser, 7 Taunt. 172.

[m] *Per curiam,* in Bradshaw *v.* Saddington, 7 East, 94.

[n] Balb *v.* Batley, 1 Marsh. 424. 6 Taunt. 25. S. C.

[o] Machu *v.* Fraser, 7 Taunt. 171, and see Humphries *v.* Williams, 2 Marsh. 231, in which Gibbs, C. J. adverted to the distinction between the plaintiff's title and the defendant's liability.

[p] Howell *v.* Coleman, 3 Bos. & Pul. 466.

[q] Reynolds *v.* Hankin, 4 Bar. & Ald. 586.

[r] Clark *v.* Cawthrone, 7 T. R. 321.

[s] Pritchard *v.* Cowlan, 2 Marsh. 40. Tidd, 6th edit. 201, 2. Jones *v.* Lewis, 2 Marsh. 385. 7 Taunt. 55. S. C.; but see Holloway *v.* Lee, 2 Moore's Rep. 211, and Tidd, 7th edit. 220. 21.

Of the Arrest. of a bill of exchange, at the suit of an indorser; the court refused to discharge her, on the affidavit of a third person, that she was a married woman; and in all cases it should seem that a *feme covert*, applying to be discharged from arrest, must found her application upon her own personal oath of the fact of coverture, and not upon the affidavit of another. [1]

Bail.   An indorser of a bill of exchange may be bail for the drawer in an action against him upon the same bill, though it be objected that he is inadmissible, inasmuch as the plaintiff's security will not be increased by the recognisance of the indorser, who is already liable to the plaintiff on the bill. [u]   And it has been recently determined, that if a party become bail in two separate actions against different parties, on the same bill, it is sufficient for him to swear that he is worth double the amount of the sum sworn to in one action, and that it is not necessary for the bail to swear to double the amount in both actions. [x]

The declaration.
[351]   In an action on a bill of exchange, check, or promissory note, if between the original parties, it is at the option of the plaintiff to declare either upon the instrument itself, or upon the consideration for which it was given; but in the case of remote parties, as the indorser against the acceptor of a bill, or the maker of a note, and where independently of the bill, there is no privity of contract between the parties, the instrument itself must be declared on, adding such of the common counts as the evidence may probably support; but it is always advisable to declare on the instrument itself, as then in case of a judgment by default, the amount of the damages are referred to the master, to be computed by him; but if the declaration do not state the bill, the plaintiff must execute a writ of inquiry. [y]

Count stating the bill, &c.   The declaration, or *count*, in which the *bill, check, or note, is set forth*, necessarily varies in point of form, according to the parties by, and against whom, the action is brought. In the Appendix will be introduced all the different forms which usually occur in practice, and notes to each will be subjoined, explanatory of the proper mode of forming the declaration in each case.

     With respect to the *venue*, as bills of exchange and promissory notes, like bonds, are *bona notabilia* wherever they happen to be, the plaintiff has a right to lay his venue in any county; and the court will not, at the instance of the defendant, change it upon an affidavit that it was really made in a different county. [z]   And if an action be *bona fide* brought on a promissory note, the plaintiff may retain the venue, though the action be also for other causes; and the court will not restrain the plaintiff from proceeding in the county he has elected, for the other causes. [a]   But it would not suffice to retain the venue, that the plaintiff should introduce a count upon a promissory note, which either did not exist, or in respect of which there was no subsisting cause of action. [b] And as in the case of an action on a bond, if very special grounds for changing the venue be laid before the court by affidavit, as that there are several material and necessary witnesses who reside at a great dis-

[t] Jones v. Lewis, 2 Marsh. 385. 7 Taunt. 55. S. C.

[u] Haines v. Manley, 2 Bos. & Pul. 526; but see Jones v. Ripley, 3 Price's Rep. 261.

[x] Moore's Rep. C. P. 29; and see Tidd's Practice, 267.
[y] Osborne v. Noad, 8 T. R. 648.
[z] Tidd's Practice, 6th edit. 633.
[a] Shepherd v. Green, 5 Taunt. 576.
[b] Id. Ibid.

tance from the county where the venue is laid, the court will change the venue, especially if the defendant admit a particular fact, which, in point of form, exists in the original county.[c] Count stating the bill, &c.

It was formerly usual to commence the declaration on a bill of exchange, with a *statement setting out the custom of merchants* relative to the validity of bills of exchange, and that the parties to it were persons within the custom ; but this mode of declaring has long been disused, and is improper ;[d] and though it is usual to state that the bill was drawn and accepted " according to the usuage and custom of merchants, from time immemorial used and approved of," yet even this reference to the custom in any part of the declaration is unnecessary.[e] In declarations on promissory notes made in England, it is usual to state that the defendant became liable to pay by force of the statute of Anne, which renders these instruments available ;[f] but this is unnecessary. And if the note be made out of England, it would be improper, and perhaps fatal, to state that the note was made according to the statute.[g] [352]

In stating the *cause of action*, there are four points principally to be attended to. *First*, The description of the bill, promissory note or check. *Secondly*, How the defendant became party to it ; and his subsequent contract. *Thirdly*, The mode by which the plaintiff derived his interest in, and right of action on, the instrument ; and *Lastly*, The breach of the defendant's contract.

These will suffice without any statement of a *consideration* which is implied.[h]

And *first*, the bill, promissory note, or check (of which a profert is not to be made,[i]) should, like all other contracts, be stated in the declaration, as it was really made in terms, or according to its legal operation ;[k] and if there be a *variance* in any material point, it will be fatal,[l] though stated under a videlicet.[m] (452) 1st. The statement of the bill, &c.

[c] Tidd's Practice 6th edit. 635.

[d] Soper v. Dible, 1 Ld. Raym. 175.—Bromwich v. Loyd, 2 Lutw. 1585. Co. Lit. 89 a. n. 7.
Soper v. Dible, Ld. Raym. 175. In an action upon a bill, the defendant demurred, because the declaration did not set out the custom, and the court held it unnecessary, and that the better way was to omit it.

[e] Hussey v. Jacob, 1 Ld. Raym. 88. Ereskin v. Murray, Ld. Raym. 1542. Carter Dowrish, Carth. 83. Williams v. Williams, id. 269. Mannin v. Cary, 1 Lutw. 279.
This was determined in Ereskin v. Murray, 2 Ld. Raym. 1542. On error after judgment by default, see Ld. Raym. 88. Carth. 83. Lutw. 279.

[f] Brown v. Harraden, 4 T. R. 155.

[g] Carr v. Shaw, Bayl. 18. Ante, 327, notes.

[h] Ante, 9, 10, &c. Bishop v. Young, 2 Bos. & Pul. 81.

[i] Master v. Miller, 4 T. R. 338. Odams v. The Duke of Grafton, Bunb. 243. Suister v. Coel, 1 Sid. 386. 1 Salk. 215. Com. Dig. tit. Pleader, O. 3. Tidd's 6th edit. 618.

[k] Per Gibbs, C. J. in Waugh v. Russel, 1 Marsh. 217, Heys v. Heseltine, 2 Campb. 604. Selw. 4th edit. 350. 1 Chitty on Plead. 3d edit. 297. 303. 308.

[l] Bristow v. Wright, Dougl. 667. Gordon v. Austin, id. 4 T. R. 611. As to variances in general, see 1 Chitty on Plead. 3d edit. 303, &c.

[m] White v. Wilson, 2 Bos. & Pul. 116. 1 Chitty on Plead. 3d edit. 368.

(452) If a declaration state that the defendant, at Dublin, made a promissory note, and thereby promised to pay the same at Dublin, without alleging it to be at Dublin in Ireland; the promissory note must be taken to have been drawn in England, for English

1st. The statement of the bill, &c.   Thus where in an action on a note made by the firm of Austin, Strobell, and *Shirtliff* in those names, the declaration was against them by
the names of Austin, Strobell, and *Shutliff*, and stated that such defendants made the note, the variance was holden fatal;[a] and if a bill drawn
by the name of Couch be declared upon in an action against a third
person, as drawn by Crouch, such variance is also fatal.[o]   And under
a count for usury, in discounting bills, one of which was described as
drawn on a certain person, to wit, John K., it is a fatal variance, if the
bill produced appear to be drawn on Abraham K.[p]

So where in an action by the indorsee against the acceptor, the declaration described the bill as drawn by one *William* Turner, and indorsed
by the said *William* Turner to the plaintiff, and the bill produced in evidence was drawn by Wingfield Turner, the variance was held fatal.[q]
But where the promissory note was signed "for Bowes, Hodgsons, Key,
and Co." and they were sued, and one of them was declared against by
the name of *Thomas Kay* (but whose real name was *John Key*, commonly pronounced Kay,) the Judge was of opinion, that the misnomer
was no objection, it being proved that the *real* partner had been sued,
and served with the process, though under a mistaken *Christian* name;
and that the variance between Key and Kay was immaterial, they being
idem sonans.[r]   And in another case, where the plaintiff declared in the
name of Edward Boughton upon a bill of exchange, drawn by him, pay-
ble to his own order, and accepted by the defendant, and also upon the
common counts, and it appeared that the plaintiff's real name was *Ed-
mund*, and that in that name he had drawn the bill, yet the plaintiff recovered.[s]   And it has been recently held, that a variance between the
real name of an *indorser*, and that which is alleged in the declaration,
and appears on the bill, is immaterial.[t]

If one of several persons, acceptors of a bill, were an infant, the
holder may declare on it, as accepted by the adult only, in the names
of both; and if the defendant pleads in abatement, that the other
partner ought also to have been sued, the plaintiff may reply his infancy;
and it is no departure, and it is most proper, not to state that the
[354] infant was a party to the instrument.[u] And if a bill of exchange purports
to have been drawn by a firm consisting of several persons (as by "Ellis,
Needham, jun. and Co.") in an action by an indorsee against the acceptor, the declaration may aver in the plural that certain *persons* using

---

[a] Gordon v. Austin, 4 T. R. 611. N. B. There is a singular difference between the folio and octavo editions in the statement of this case, the last does not notice the mistake in the *surname*, which was the material objection.
[o] Whitwell v. Bennett, 3 Bos. & Pul. 558. Selw. 4th edit. 349.
[p] Hutchinson v. Piper, 4 Taunt. 810.
[q] Le Sage v. Johnson, Forrest's Rep. 23.

[r] Dickenson v. Bowes and others, 16 East, 110.

[s] Boughton v. Frere, 3 Campb. 29.; but note, it does not appear from the report whether the plaintiff only recovered upon the common counts.

[t] Forman v. Jacob, 1 Stark. 47.

[u] Burgess v. Merrell, 4 Taunt. 468. 1 Chitty on Plead. 3d edit. 85.

---

money; and proof of a note made payable at Dublin, in Ireland, for the same firm in Irish money, does not support the declaration. *Sprowle* v. *Legge*, 1 Barn. & Cresw. 16.
In a declaration on a promissory note, the omission of the place where it is payable is fatal. *Sebree* v. *Dorr*, 9 Wheat. 558.
It is not necessary, in case of a lost note, that there should be a special count stating such loss. *Renner* v. *Bank of Columbia*, 9 Wheat. 597.

the firm drew and indorsed the bill, although in point of fact the firm **1st. The** consisted only of a single individual, the acceptor being estopped from **statement** disputing the fact.[x] So where a declaration described a bill of exchange **&c.** as directed to the three defendants, and accepted by them, and it was proved to have been directed to, and accepted by a fourth party also, who was dead, this was held no variance;[y] and in an action against one of several makers of a joint or several promissory note, the describing it as the separate note of the defendant, without noticing the other parties, is no variance.[z](454)

If it be alleged in the declaration, that defendant on such a day (without laying it under a videlicet) drew a bill of exchange without alleging that it bore date on that day, a mistake of the day will not be material, but if the words "bearing date the same day and year aforesaid" be inserted, then a variance would be fatal;[a] and the mis-statement of a day in a note payable by instalments is fatal.[b] In general, the date of the bill or note should be stated, and if there be no date, then the day it was made, and if that cannot be ascertained, then the first day it can be proved to have existed.[c] And where, in an action on a foreign bill, payable at double usance from the date thereof, the declaration stated the bill to have been drawn on such a day, but did not state the date, the court held it sufficient, and that they would intend that it was dated at the time of drawing it.[d] And where a second count stated, that afterwards, to wit, on the day and year aforesaid, the defendant drew a certain other bill of exchange, payable two months after the date thereof, without mentioning any express date in either count, the last count was held sufficient, the court intending the date to have been the day on which the bill was alleged to have been made.[e] If a bill or note by mistake has been dated contrary to the intention of the parties, the declaration may run thus, "on, &c. (the time intended) at, &c. made, &c. bearing date by mistake, on, &c. but meant and intended by the said A. B. and C. D. to be dated on the [355] said, &c. and then and there delivered, &c. by which said note he the said C. D. then and there promise to pay, two months after the date thereof, (that is to say, after the said, &c. when the said note was so made and intended to be dated as aforesaid,) to the said A. B." &c. It has been held, that in a declaration upon a bill or note importing to be payable within a limited time after the date, and dated on a particular day, the precise day must be stated, and that if a day upwards of six years before the commencement of the action be stated, and the

---

[x] Bass v. Clive, 4 Campb. 78. 4 M. & S. 12. S. C.

[y] Mountstephen v. Brooke and others, 1 Barn. & Ald. 224.

[z] Id. ibid. and ante, 339.

[a] Coxon v. Lyon, 2 Campb. 307, 8. Selw. 4th edit. 360. Fitzgib. 130.

[b] Wells v. Girling, 1 Gow, C. N. P. 21.

[c] Ante, 59. Bayl. 174, 5.

[d] De la Courier v. Bellamy, 2 Show. 422, approved of in Hague v. French, 3 Bos. & Pul. 173.

[e] Hague v. French, 3 Bos. & Pul. 173.

---

(454) If a bill be addressed to W. S. by mistake, for I. S., and it is presented to the right person, it is sufficient, and in the declaration it may be stated that the bill was drawn on W. S. meaning the said I. S. *Starvy* v. *Robinson*, 1 Day's Rep. 11.

Proof of a note dated the 26th July, does not support a declaration stating a note dated on the 25th. *Stephens* v. *Graham*, 7 Serg. & Rawle, 505.

defendant plead *actio non accrevit*, the plaintiff cannot recover,[f] but this doctrine may be questionable.[g]

It is usual also to state the place at which the bill or note was drawn, as thus, "that the drawer on, &c. at Liverpool, to wit, at London, &c. (the venue.") It has been considered that in a declaration on a *foreign* bill, the place at which it bears date must be stated, and that some place in England or Wales should be subjoined, by way of venue, under a videlicet, thus. "at Venice in Italy, to wit, at London, &c."[h] But where a promissory note, dated and made at Paris, was declared upon in an action by the payee against the maker, as made in London, it was decided to be no variance, because the contract evidenced by a promissory note is transitory, and the place where it purports to have been made is immaterial;[i] and it is laid down, that *inland* bills and notes, though they may bear date at a particular place, may be alleged to have been made any where in England or Wales.[k]

The instrument itself must be stated in terms, or according to the legal effect. If it be in foreign language it may nevertheless be stated as if it were in English, without noticing the foreign language.[l] If
[356] the bill be payable at usances, the length of them should be averred thus, " at two usances, that is to say, at two months after the date thereof," and the omission will be fatal on demurrer.[m] And if by the body of the bill or note, it be made payable at a particular place, that qualification of the contract must be stated.[n]

A bill or note payable to the order of the plaintiff, may be stated in the declaration to be payable to him, and there is no occasion to insert any averment that he made no order;[o] and the omission of the word " *sterling*" is immaterial.[p] Though if the bill be payable in Irish currency, and the bill be described as if it were payable in English sterling money, that would be a fatal variance.[q]

And a bill of exchange expressed on the face of it, to be for " value delivered in leather," may be stated in pleading to have been for value *received* in leather.[r] And it has been considered that when a bill of

[f] Stafford v. Forcer, 10 Mod 511, cited 1 Stra. 22. In an action on a note dated in 1704, defendant pleaded that the cause of action did not accrue within six years, the plaintiff replied a bill filed in 1714 ; and that the cause of action accrued within six years of that time, and after verdict for the plaintiff, the court arrested the judgment, because it was stated that the note was made and dated in 1704, and then the cause of action must have accrued above six years before 1714 ; but see Leaper v. Tutton, 16 East, 420.

[g] In Trinity Term, 1818, K. B., the court held that on a guarantee of the debt of another, the plaintiff might give in evidence a verbal promise to revive the original undertaking in writing, so as to defeat a plea of *actio non accrevit infra*

sex annos. Gibbons v. M'Casland, 1 Bar & Ald. 690.

[h] Bayl. 165. Salk. 679. Cowp. 177, 8. 6 Mod. 228. Com. Did. tit. Action. N. 7.

[i] Per Lord Ellenborough, in Houriet v. Morris, 3 Campb. 804.

[k] Bayl 175.

[l] Attorney General v. Valabreque, Wightw. 9.

[m] Barclay v. Campbell, Salk. 181. Smart v. Dean, 3 Keb. 645. Bayl. 184, 5.

[n] Ante, 250.

[o] Frederick v. Cotton, 2 Show. 8. Fisher v. Pomfret, Carth. 480. Bayl. 189, 190.

[p] Glossop v. Jacob, 1 Stark. 69.

[q] Kearney v. King, 2 Barn. & Ald. 301.

[r] Jones v. Mars, 2 Campb. 307, in note. White v. Ledwick, MS. ante, 67, and Highmore v. Primrose, 5 M. & S. 65.

exchange is in this form, "pay to F. G. B. or order £315, value received, and was subscribed by the drawer, it may be alleged in pleading to be a bill of exchange for value received by the drawer from the payee,[a] and it should seem that it is not necessary to insert in the declaration that part of the bill which relates to the consideration.[t] **1st. The statement of the bill, &c.**

It is not advisable to state more of the bill or note declared on than is necessary to enable the plaintiff to recover,[a] and the formal description of the direction to the drawee, should in general be omitted, at least in one count, for fear of a variance; and where a bill is not addressed to any person by name, but accepted by the defendant, the declaration should merely state that the drawer drew the bill, and thereby required the payment of such a sum, and that the defendant accepted without stating any address.[x] If the bill or note were informal, it may be stated in its terms with an innuendo of its meaning, which seems the safest course.[y]

If the rules of law prevent the instrument declared on from operating according to the words of it, it may *ut res magis valeat quam pereat* be stated to have been made in such a manner as the law will give effect [357] to it, though there may be a verbal variation between that statement and the instrument itself.[z] Therefore in the case before-mentioned of a note by which a man promised *never* to pay a sum of money, it was holden that it might be declared on as a promise *to pay*;[a] and bills payable to the *order* of fictitious persons, may be declared on as payable *to bearer*, against every party aware of the fact.[b]

It is incumbent on the plaintiff, in every declaration founded on a breach of contract, to show the contract for the non-performance of which the action is brought, and consequently it is necessary to state in a declaration on a bill, *how the defendant became party to it*, whether by drawing, accepting, or transferring it, as that he " made," " accepted," " indorsed," or " delivered" it ; which allegations will be sufficient, although the defendant did not in fact do either of these acts himself, provided he authorized the doing of them; though, indeed, it is not unfrequent when the fact is so, to state that those acts were done by the procuration of the agent who was employed :[c] and though it is usual to allege a promise, it has been decided that this is unnecessary, as the law implies a promise where there is a legal liability.[d] In an action against the acceptor of a bill and the maker of a note, at the suit of the payee or indorsee, the defendant's promise is to be stated to have been " according to the *tenor and effect of the bill or note*;" but in an action against a drawer or indorser of a bill, or the indorser of a note, after stating the default of the party primarily liable, the liability and the promise of the defendant are stated to have been to pay *on request*, that being the legal result. **2dly. How the defendant became party to the bill, &c.**

The words " his own proper hand, being thereunto subscribed," sub-

[a] Grant v. Da Costa, 3 M. & S. 351. Ante, 67, note.

[t] Id. ibid. per Lord Ellenborough.

[a] Bristow v. Wright, Dougl. 667.— Dundas v. Lord Weymouth, Cowp. 665. Price v. Fletcher, Cowp. 727.

[x] Gray v. Milner, 3 Moore, 91.

[y] Waugh v. Russel, 1 Marsh. 215.

[z] Rolleston v. Mageaton, 4 T. R. 166.

CHITTY ON BILLS.

[a] Ante, 42.

[b] Ante, 64.

[c] Collis v. Emett, 1 Hen. Bla. 313.— Brucker v. Fromount, 6 T. R. 659. Heys v. Heseltine, 2 Campb. 604.

[d] Starkie v. Cheesman, Carth. 510. Salk. 128. S. C. Sed vide Bac. Ab. tit. Assumpsit, F. and Morris v. Norfolk, 1 Taunt. 217.

T t

2dly. How scribed should be omitted. In an action by the indorsee against the acceptor of a bill of exchange, the declaration stated, that the payee indorsed it, *his own proper hand being thereunto subscribed ;* (458) and it appeared that the payee's name, upon the back of the bill, was written under his authority by his wife, and it was held that the defendant having, after notice of non-payment, promised to pay, was not at liberty to object that the indorsement was. not in the hand-writing of the payee himself ;[e] but had it not been for such promise, the variance would have been fatal.[f] And in an action against the drawers of a bill of exchange, the declaration stated, that the defendants made the bill, " their *own proper hands* being thereto subscribed;" and in fact their firm of A. and Co. was subscribed to the bill, and Lord Ellenborough said, " Had it been 'their own proper *hand,*' I should have clearly held it " sufficient. As it stands, I entertain some doubt; but I will not non-suit."[g]

the defendant became party to the bill, &c.

[358]

It is advisable to state the true date of the acceptance of a bill payable after sight, and in any other case where the acceptance is dated of a day different to the date of the bill, it should be described accordingly;[h] but it seems that a variance is not material.[i] And though it has been considered that if the plaintiff allege in terms, that the acceptance was made before the time limited by the bill for its payment, the plaintiff will be precluded from giving in evidence an acceptance afterwards,[k] this doctrine has been disputed by high authority.[l] And where the plaintiff, as indorsee of a bill, against the defendant as acceptor, stated in his declaration, that the defendant became liable to pay and promised to pay according to the tenor and effect of the bill and his acceptance, it was held that he might, under the plea, that the cause of action did not accrue within six years, give in evidence a promise long after the bill was due.[m]

On the before-mentioned rule that the plaintiff should not state more

[e] Helmsley v. Loader, 2 Campb. 450. Payl. P. & A. App. No. 2. Bayl. 182, 3.
[f] Levy v. Wilson, 5 Esp. Rep. 180. Payl. P. & A. 275, 6. Bayl. 183.
[g] Jones & al. v. Mars & al. 2 Campb. 305.
[h] Bayl. 181.
[i] Forman v. Jacob, 1 Stark. 46; and see Young v. Wright, 1 Campb. 139. Ld. Raym. 364. 12 Mod. 212.
[k] Jackson v. Piggott, Ld. Raym. 364. 12 Mod. 212.
[l] Bayl. 181.
[m] Leaper v. Tutton. 16 East, 420.

(458) The same point was ruled, where the note was signed by procuration, and it was alleged that the promissors " *made their note under their hands.*" Essex November Term, 1805. *Gardner* v *Stocker.* Per *Sedgwick*, J. MSS.

An averment that the partners of a firm made the note, " *the proper name and firm of the partners being thereunto subscribed,*" is proved by showing the note signed by one partner in the partnership name. It is not necessary to state that one of the partners signed in the name of the firm; but if so stated, it is good. *Manhattan Company* v. *Ledyard,* 1 Caines' Rep. 192. So an averment that " *certain persons using the name, stile and firm of W. & W. made the note, the proper handwriting of one of them in their said copartnership name, stile and firm, being thereto subscribed,*" is good. *Kane* v. *Scofield,* 2 Caines' Rep. 368. If in an action against two persons, the declaration does not allege them to be partners, or to act under a firm, and it is averred that they " *made the note in their own proper hands and names thereto subscribed,*" proof that one of the defendants subscribed the note with the joint name or firm, is not sufficient to maintain the declaration. *Pease* v. *Morgan,* 7 John. Rep. 468.

If the plaintiff allege himself in the declaration to be the bearer of a note payable to the bearer, this is sufficient, without an express allegation that the maker promised the plaintiff to pay him. *Dole* v. *Weeks,* 4 Mass. Rep. 451; and see *Gilbert* v. *Nantucket Bank,* 5 Mass. Rep. 97.

of the bill than is essential to his title, it is not necessary or advisable 2dly. How in an action against the drawer or indorser of a bill, to state that the the defendrawee accepted it, but if it be stated, it must, in an action against dant became party the drawer be proved, unless it be shown that he indorsed the bill after to the bill, it was accepted, or that after it was due he promised to pay.[a] &c.

If the engagement of either of the parties were conditional, it must be described accordingly, and therefore a conditional acceptance must be so stated, and if declared upon as an absolute engagement, the variance will be fatal, although the condition has been performed.[o] We have already considered when it is necessary to describe the acceptance as payable at a particular place, and when that statement [359] would be improper.[p]

Thirdly, A *plaintiff*, who sues upon a bill, check, or note, must show 3dly. How in his declaration his right to sue thereon, in the same manner as every the plaintiff other plaintiff must show a sufficient title, to enable him to maintain the became a action which he brings.[q] Thus, in an action by the indorsee or bearer party & entitled thereof a bill, it is necessary to show that it authorized a transfer, and he to. must also state that the transfer was made.[r] In general, whatever forms a constituent part of the plaintiff's title, must be set out correctly.[s] But this rule is liable to similar exceptions to that which makes it necessary to set out the instrument as made; and he may set it out, as in case of a bill payable to the order of a fictitious person, according to the effect given to it by law.[t] It has been decided, that the payee of a bill or note payable to his own order, may state it to have been made payable to himself;[u] and a note payable to a married woman, and indorsed by her husband, may be stated to have been payable to the husband.[x] An indorsee may, it is said, declare against his immediate indorser, as on a bill of exchange made by the defendant, directed to the acceptor, and payable to the plaintiff, the act of indorsing being similar in its operation to that of making a bill, but this is not the practice.[y]

In general, however, the plaintiff's title should be stated according to the facts, and if he claim as a remote indorsee, every indorsement is usually set forth : but where the first indorsement is in blank, and the plaintiff is apprehensive he will not be able to prove all the subsequent indorsements, it is proper to add a count stating the plaintiff to be immediate indorsee of some prior indorser. In such case, however, it is said, that in order to render the evidence correspondent to the declaration, all the subsequent names must be struck out of the bill before or at the time of the trial;[z] which may be done, notwithstanding there has been a subsequent indorsement in full.[a] In this case, in order to avoid unnecessary expense, the indorsement may be described concisely

[a] Jones v. Morgan, 2 Campb. 474. Bayl. 181.
[o] Langston v. Corney, 4 Campb. 176. Swan v. Cox, 1 Marsh, 176, ante, 181.
[p] Ante, 250 to 259.
[q] Bishop v. Hayward, 4 T. R. 471.
[r] Bayl. 180.
[s] Per Lord Kenyon, in Gwinnet v. Philip, 3 T. R. 645. Gibson v Minet, 1 Hen. Bla. 605, 6.
Ante, 64.

[u] Frederick v. Cotton, 2 Show. 8. Smith v. M'Clure, 5 East, 476. 2 Smith's Rep. 43. S. C.
[x] Barlow v. Bishop, 1 East, 432. 3 Esp. Rep. 266. S. C. Ankerstein v. Clarke, 4 T. R. 616. Arnold v. Revoult, 1 Brod. & B. 443.
[y] Brown v. Harraden, 4 T. R. 149.
[z] Anon. 12 Mod. 345. Peacock v. Rhodes, Dougl. 633. Anon. Holt, 296. Kyd. 206.
[a] Ante, 135. Bayl. 184.

3dly. How thus : "And the said A. then and there indorsed and delivered the the plaintiff "said bill of exchange to the said B., and the said B. then and there in- became a dorsed and delivered the said bill of exchange to the said C. &c." In an party, &c. action against a remote indorser, though there be several indorsements between that of the payee and the defendant, the plaintiff may declare, as on an immediate indorsement by the payee to the defendant, and by him to the plaintiff, and need not notice the intermediate indorsements.[b](461)

It has been recently decided, that in an action against the indorser of a bill of exchange, in which the declaration stated several prior indorsements, it is not necessary to prove any indorsements on the bill prior to the defendants, though it is otherwise in an action against the acceptor; consequently, where a remote indorser is sued, there will be no risk in stating all the prior indorsements in the declaration.[c] And in another case it was held, that in an action by the indorsee against the acceptor, where several indorsements had taken place, and which were laid in the declaration, and are consequently necessary to be proved in general, yet if the defendant applies for time to the holder, and offers terms, it is an admission of the holder's title, and a waiver of proof of all the indorsements except the first.[d] On an indorsement, for less than the full sum mentioned in a bill or note, the plaintiff must describe the same accordingly, and show that the residue was paid.[e] In describing the indorsement, it is not advisable to allege that the indorser's handwriting was thereunto subscribed, and if that allegation be inserted, and the bill appear to have been indorsed by an agent, the variance will be fatal.[f]

If a note payable to bearer be declared on as indorsed, the indorsement must be proved;[g](1) but when the declaration states that the indorsement was *after* the making of the bill, and it appeared in evidence to have been before,[h] or that it was *before* the bill was due, and appears in evidence to have been made *afterwards* this is not a material variance.[i] It is not necessary to allege, as part of the plaintiff's title, that the bill, &c. was *delivered* to him, as the allegation, that the bill

[b] Chaters *v* Bell, 4 Esp. Rep. 211. Bayl. 183.

[c] Critchlow *v.* Parry, 2 Campb. 182.

[d] Bosanquet *v.* Anderson, 6 Esp. Rep. 43.

[e] Hawkins *v.* Gardner, 12 Mod. 213. Bayl. 183, n. a.

[f] Levy *v.* Wilson, 4 Esp. Rep. 180. ante, 237, 8.

[g] Waynam *v.* Bend, 1 Campb. 175.; and see Manning's Index, 75.

[h] Smith *v.* Mingay, 1 M. & S. 92.

[i] Young *v.* Wright, 1 Campb. 139.

(461) It is not necessary to state the indorsement to be "for value received;" and it so stated, the averment is surplusage, and need not be proved. *Wilson* v. *Codman's Ex.* 3 Cranch, 193. But see *Welch* v. *Lindo*, 7 Cranch's Rep. 159. An indorsement is *prima facie* evidence of being made for the full value. *Riddle* v. *Mandeville*, 5 Cranch. 32. But it is otherwise if made "without recourse." *Welch* v. *Lindo*. And if the indorsement be restrictive as to a right against the indorser, as if it be "without recourse" to the indorser, it is not necessary, in a declaration against the maker by the indorsee, to state such restriction. *Wilson* v. *Codman's Ex.*

But the words "for value received," in setting forth a promissory note in a declaration are words of description, and not an averment, and therefore, if the words are not in the note, the variance is fatal. *Saxton* v. *Johnson*, 10 John. Rep. 418.

(1) The indorsement of a note, payable to bearer, makes the indorser liable, as upon a new bill to bearer. *Eccles* v. *Ballard*, 2 M'Cord, 388.

was payable to the payee, or "that an indorsement was *made*," includes it;^k nor is it necessary to aver notice of an indorsement.^l

4thly. The necessary averments, and defendant's breach of contract.

It is also necessary to show the defendant's *breach of contract*. If a bill be accepted payable when, or if a certain event shall take place, it must be shown that such event has occurred.^m And if the bill be payable at, or after usances, their duration must be averred.ⁿ If a note be payable on or after demand, it is advisable at least in one count in an action against the maker, to allege a demand.^o In general, in an action against the acceptor of a bill or maker of a note, who is primarily liable, it is not necessary to aver or prove any presentment for payment, the action itself being deemed a sufficient demand, and the common breach at the end of the money counts sufficing;^p and we have seen, that unless the bill be accepted payable at a particular place only and not elsewhere, pursuant to the late act, no averment^q of a presentment there is necessary.^r In all cases where by the terms of the original contract, as when in the *body* of the bill or note, it is made payable at a particular place, a presentment there and refusal, or some discharge dispensing with the presentment, must be averred in an action against the acceptor of the one and the maker of the other, and an allegation that the makers of a note, payable in the body of it at a particular house, became insolvent, and ceased, and wholly declined and refused, then and thenceforth to pay at the place specified, any of their notes, does not show a sufficient discharge or excuse for the want of a presentment of the particular note declared on.'(1)

It is sufficient, however, in these cases, if the declaration allege the presentment to have been made to the persons at whose house the bill was made payable, "according to the tenor and effect of the bill," and "the acceptance thereof.'"^t But if a bill be stated to have been accepted, payable by certain persons, at a particular place, it has been holden, in an action against the drawer, that an averment of a presentment to those persons generally, without saying at what place, is sufficient.^u But it suffices, in an action against an acceptor, to aver a presentment at the particular place, without showing that payment was refused there being sufficient to allege the non-payment at the conclusion of the declaration.^x Nor is it necessary to aver, that the acceptor of the bill, or maker of the note, had notice of non-payment at the particular place.^y An allegation in a declaration that a bill of exchange was presented for payment by I. S. does not render it incumbent on the plain-

[362]

k Churchill v. Gardner, 7 T. R. 596. Smith v. M'Clure, 5 East, 477. ante, 95. Bayl. 180.
l Reynolds v. Davies, 1 Bos. & Pul. 624. Bayl. 184.
m Ante, 151; 358.
n Bayl. 184, 5.
o See post, as to the statute of limitation; but see Cro. Eliz. 548. Rumball v. Ball, 10 Mop. 38. Bayl. 187. Ante, 269.
p Frampton v. Coulson, 1 Wils. 33.
q Ante, 259.
r Ante, 230. Bayl. 185.
s Bowes v. Howe, 5 Taunt. 30. Ante, 250.
t Huffan r. Ellis, 3 Taunt. 415. Ante, 255, note. Bayl. 187.
u Ambrose v. Hopwood, 2 Taunt. 61. Bayl. 186.
x Butterworth v. Lord Despencer, 3 M. & S. 150, and Benson v. White, 4 Dow's Rep. 334. Ante, 252.
y Id. Ibid. Pearse v. Pembertly, 3 Campb. 261. Ante, 309, 310.

(1) In an action against the maker of a note, promising to pay at a particular place, it is not necessary that the declaration should allege a demand at the time and place appointed for payment. *Carley* v. *Vance*, 17 Mass. 389.

4thly. The
necessary
averments,
and defen-
dant's
breach of
contract.

tiff to show that a presentment by I. S. was made, the material allegation being the presentment, and the person by whom it was made is immaterial.[a]

When the declaration is against the *drawer* or *indorser* of a bill, or the indorser of a note, as their contract is only conditional to pay, if the acceptor of the one or maker of the other do not, it is necessary to aver a presentment for payment to the drawee of the bill, or maker of the note, on the day it became due,[a] and that he refused to pay,[b](465) or could not be found upon diligent search ; and such averment should correspond with the facts.[c] If, however, the drawee or maker cannot be found, it is sufficient to aver generally, that he was not found, without stating that any inquiry was made after him, though it is now more usual to aver that diligent search was made, and which must, as we have seen, be proved. When he has merely removed, and not absconded.[d] and when it appears that a bill was payable at a banker's, or particular place, a presentment there must be alleged.[e]

In an action against the drawer or indorser of a bill, or the indorser of a note, it is also a most material averment, that the defendant had notice of the dishonour of the bill, or some excuse must be alleged for the neglect to give such notice, and an error in this respect will be fatal even after verdict.[f] In the case of a foreign bill, a protest also should

---

[a] Boehm v. Campbell, 1 Gow. Rep. 55.
[a] Mercer v. Southwell, 2 Show. 180. Bayl. 185, 6.
[b] Rushton v. Aspinall, Dougl. 679.— Lundie v. Robertson, 7 East, 231. Bayl. 185, 6.
[c] Leeson v. Pigott, Bayl. 187. acc. but

see Boulager v. Talleyrand, 2 Esp. Rep. 550.
[d] Starkie v. Cheesman, Carth. 509— Bayl. 187. Ante, 261.
[e] Parker v. Gordon, 7 East, 385.—Ante. 250.
[f] Rushton v. Aspinall, Dougl. 679.—

---

(465) But where in an action by an indorsee against his immediate indorser, there was in the declaration no averment of a demand on the maker on the day when the note became due, but only an averment, "although often requested," &c. it was held, that after verdict the declaration was sufficient. *Leffingwell* v. *White*, 1 John. Cas. 99. In in an action against the *drawer* by the payee, the declaration allege a demand on the acceptor *after* the expiration of the time of payment, it is bad on demurrer. *Linde* v *Burgos*, 1 Selw. N. P. 317.

Where notice is averred to have been actually given of the dishonour of a bill, it must be proved as laid; and therefore if in fact it has not been given, the declaration should state that due diligence had been used to give notice, and assign the reason why it was not done. *Blakely* v. *Grant*, 6 Mass. Rep. 386. But see *Stewart* v. *Eden*. Caines' Rep. 121. And if no demand is made of the maker, and a sufficient excuse exists, that excuse, and not an averment of due presentment should be stated in the declaration. Semb. *Bond* v. *Farnham*, 5 Mass. Rep. 170.

If notice of non-acceptance be duly averred in an action aginst the drawer, but no protest is averred, after verdict it is sufficient, for the law will presume it to be a regular notice by protest. *Lawes on Assumpsit*, 364, note. And it is not necessary or proper to set forth, in the declaration a presentment or protest for non-payment of a bill, where there is an averment of a previous presentment for acceptance and refusal, and due notice thereof given; and if averred, it will be rejected as surplusage. *Mason* v. *Franklin*, 3 John. Rep. 202, note. If the indorser of a note die before it becomes due, in an action against his executor by the holder, the declaration should allege the promise to pay, to be by the executor, and not by the testator, otherwise it will be a fatal variance. *Stewart* v. *Eden*, 2 Caines' Rep. 121.

Where a declaration by indorsee against indorser, avers demand and notice in the usual form, it is sufficient if the plaintiff proves a state of facts, which dispenses with mutual demand, &c. and shows due diligence, &c. *Williams* v. *Matthews*, 3 Cowen, 252.

Where the indorsee of a bill, in an action against the indorser, relies on the want of funds of the drawer in the hands of the drawee, instead of due notice, it is necessary for him to aver that fact in the declaration. *Frazier* v. *Harris*, 2 Litt. 185.

be stated ;^e and the allegation that the plaintiff protested, or caused to be protested, would be improper ;^b and it was formerly considered, that where the plaintiff proceeds for interest, &c. against the drawer or in-dorser of a bill, a protest must also be stated in the case of an inland bill ;ⁱ but that doctrine has lately been over-ruled.^k And the neglect to state the protest of a foreign bill can only be taken advantage of by special demurrer.¹

4thly. The necessary averments, and defen-dant's breach of contract.

If there are any circumstances in the case dispensing with present-ment or protest, or notice of the dishonour, as if the drawer counter-manded the payment, or had no effects in the hands of the drawee, it is advisable to insert a count stating those circumstances.^m In an ac-tion against a drawer or indorser of a bill, and the indorser of a note, their liabilities and promises are stated to have been to pay *on request*, and not according to *the tenor and effect* of the bill.ⁿ

[363]

When there are several different bills or notes, a count on each may, with propriety, and indeed must be inserted in the declaration, how-ever prolix it may thereby be rendered ;^o but the court will, when there are a great many notes of the same description, grant a rule for striking out all the counts but one, and giving the other notes in evidence under the account stated.^p The other points relative to the declarations on bills, notes, and checks, will be found in the notes to the precedents.

———

WITH respect to the *common counts*, although it is not usual, when there is a bill or note, to rely on them alone in pleading, yet they will in many cases supply the omission or defect of the count on the instru-ment itself ; and the plaintiff will be at liberty to go into evidence of the consideration for which he received it, and may recover on the common counts, if adapted to such consideration, in case he cannot substantiate, in evidence, the facts necessary to support the count on the instrument, or such count should be defective:^q (1) taking care that the particulars of his demand state the consideration of the bill, &c.;^r and perhaps to notice such demand in the counsel's opening of the

Sect. 2. Of the counts on the con-sideration, and of the common counts.

Lundie *v.* Robertson, 7 East, 231. Bayl. 185, 6.

^f Gale *v.* Walsh, 5 T. R, 239. Bayl. 188.

^b Witherley *v.* Sarsfield, 1 Show. 127. Bayl. 189.

ⁱ Boulager *v.* Talleyrand, 2 Esp. Rep. 550.

^k Windle *v.* Andrew, 2 Barn. & Ald. 696.

^l Solomons *v.* Staveley, cited Dougl. 684, n. Bayl. 189.

^m See form in Legg *v.* Thorp, 12 East, 171. Bayl. 189; and see Precedents, post, and 3 Chitty on pleading, 3d edit. 44, 45.

ⁿ Bayl. 190.

^o Lane *v.* Smith, 3 Smith's Rep. 118.

^p Cunnack *v.* Gundry, 1 Chitty's Rep. 709.

^q See the cases, Selw. N. P. 4th edit. 353. 4. Bayl. 163, &c. Manning's Ind. 75, 6. Thompson *v.* Morgan, 3 Campb. 101, 2. Tyte *v.* Jones, 1 East, 58, n. a. Alves *v.* Hodgson, 7 T. R. 241. Tatlock *v.* Harris, 3 T. R. 174. Claxton *v.* Swift, 2 Show. 501. Kyd, 58. 197. Peake's Law of Evid. 219. Bul. Ni. Pri. 139. Payne *v.* Bacomb, Dougl. 651. Brown *v.* Watts, 1 Taunt. 353.

^r Wade *v.* Beasley, 4 Esp. Rep. 7.— Selw. N. P. 4th ed. 354, n. 62.

———

(1) In an action on a promissory note, where, besides the special count, there are the usual money counts and for goods sold, &c. the plaintiff may elect on which count to give the note in evidence. *Burdick* v. *Green* 18 Johns. 14.

Sect. 3. Of case on the trial.[a] Thus, where the plaintiff declared on a promissory
the *counts* note, and on a *quantum meruit* for work and labour, which was the
on the *con-* consideration for which it was given, but the note not being duly
sideration. and of the stamped, and a verdict having been taken generally for the plaintiff,
common the defendant moved to enter a nonsuit—the court said, that although
counts. the note, not being stamped, could not be given in evidence, yet the
plaintiff ought to have an opportunity of recovering on the other

[364] count, and accordingly a new trial was granted;[t] and in Wilson v.
Kennedy,[u] where the same point was determined, Lord Kenyon said,
that a promissory note is not like a bond, which merges the demand.[v]
It has also been decided, that it is not necessary to declare on a promissory note, but that in an action for money lent, the same may be
given in evidence;[y] for the stat. 3 & 4 Anne, c. 9, which enables the
plaintiff to declare upon the note, is only a concurrent remedy: and
where a bill was drawn on an agent and made payable out of a particular fund, and consequently invalid, and the agent said he would
pay it when he got money of the principal, it was held, that this was
binding on him, and that if he got the money at any subsequent time,
he was bound to pay the amount, and that it was recoverable as money
had and received.[z] Where, however, the party is discharged by alteration of the bill, &c. or by the laches of the holder, the plaintiff will
not be allowed to go into evidence on the common counts;[a](1) and
where a promissory note has been given for money due from the defendant
to the plaintiff, who declares thereon, together with the money counts,
he must prove the note to have been destroyed before he can have recourse to the money counts, if it appear that the money so claimed was
that for which the note was given.[b] (467)

[a] Paterson v. Zachariah, 1 Stark. 72. see the cases in Wells v. Girling, 1 Gow. Rep. 22, 3.
[t] Alves v. Hodgson, 7 T. R. 241. Tyte v. Jones, 1 East, 58, n. a. Wade v. Breasley, 4 Esp. Rep. 7.
[u] Wilson v. Kennedy, Esp. Rep. 245. Tyte v. Jones, 1 East, n. a. Selw. N. P. 4th ed. 354.
[x] See also ante, 95.
[y] Bul. N. P. 137, 8. Story v. Atkins, 2 Stra. 719. Ex parte Mills, 2 Ves. jun 303.
[z] Stevens v. Hill, 5 Esp. Rep. 217
[a] Long v. Moore, 3 Esp. Rep. 155.
[b] Dangerfield v. Wilby, 1 Esp. Rep. 159. Ante, 96, 7.

(1) If the drawer has been discharged from liability upon the bill by the laches of the holder, the latter cannot recover on a count for money had and received. *Austin v. Rodman,* 1 Hawks 195.
(467) See *Pintard v. Tackington,* 10 Johns. Rep. 104, and other cases collected in the note to p. 185. But a recovery cannot be had upon a note lost, and not destroyed, if it had been indorsed before it was lost. *Pintard v. Packington.* See *Freeman v. Boynton,* 7 Mass. Rep. 583. *Anderson v. Robson,* 2 Bay's Rep. 495. *Usher's Ex v. Guither,* 2 Harr. & M'Hen. Rep. 457. *Morgan v. Reintzel,* 7 Cranch, 273.
A note not negotiable within the statute, expressed to be for value received, may be given in evidence between the original parties under the money counts, if there be proof of a sufficient consideration. *Smith v. Smith,* 2 John. Rep. 235. But if no consideration appear on the face of the note, it is otherwise. *Saxton v. Johnson,* 10 John Rep. 418. And if such a note be transferred and an express promise be made to pay the as-
signee, he may maintain an action on the money counts. *Surtees v. Hubbard,* 4 Esp. Rep. 204. *Mowry v. Todd,* 12 Mass. Rep. 281. Ante, 61. note. So between the assignor and his immediate assignee, an action on such counts may be maintained; but not by a remote assignee against the assignor, for there is no privity between them. *Mandeville v. Biddle,* 1 Cranch, 290. 298.
A bill of exchange may be given in evidence in an action by the payee against the maker under the money counts. *Cruger v. Armstrong,* 3 John. Cas. 5. *Arnold v. Crane,* 8 John. Rep. 79. A note payable to A. or bearer may be given in evidence in an action by the holder against the maker under the money counts. *Pierce v. Crafts,* 12 John. Rep. 90. So in an action by the indorsee against the maker. Ibid And a

The above rule does not in general apply when there is *no privity*
between the plaintiff and defendant, as between the indorsee and the
acceptor, of a bill, and the indorsee and the maker of a note,[c] between
whom, if the plaintiff cannot succeed on the count on the bill, and
there be no express promise to pay the amount, the common counts are
in general of no avail.[d]

The instrument *itself* will, it is said, when duly stamped, in certain
cases, be evidence in support of the counts for money lent, paid, had,
and received, and that founded on an actual or supposed account
stated; and those counts, when applicable, should therefore always
be inserted in the declaration;[e] but in a late case it was held, that a
promissory note is only evidence under the money counts as between
the *original* parties to it;[f] a decision which appears to accord with
the rule of law as to the assignment of *choses in action*, and may pro- [365]
bably affect the authority of some of the decisions presently noticed.[g]

The court for *money lent*, it is said, is proper in an action at the suit
of the payee of a bill against the drawer, and in an action at the suit
of the payee of a bill against the maker, they being evidence of money
lent by the payee to the drawer of the one, and maker of the other.[h]
It is also proper in an action at the suit of an indorsee against his immediate indorser.[i] So a note in this form:—" 3d December, 1751, then
" received of Mr. Harris, the sum of nineteen pounds, on behalf of my
" grandson, which I promise to be accountable for on demand, witness
" my hand, S. Huntbach,"—the grandson being an infant, was holden to
be evidence in support of the court for money lent.[k]

It has been said, that a bill or note is *prima facie* evidence of *money
paid* by the holder to the use of the drawer of the one, and maker of
the other;[l] and that a bill, when accepted, is evidence of money paid by
the holder to the use of the acceptor;[m] and if an indorser has taken up a
bill, he may, having failed in his first count against the acceptor, on account of a variance, recover under the count for money paid.[n] But in
another case Eyre, Chief Justice, said, that the presumption of evidence

[c] Johnson v. Collings, 1 East, 98. Barlow v. Bishop, id. 434, 5. Whitwell v.
Bennett, 3 Bos. & Pul. 559. Houle v.
Baxter, 3 East, 177.
[d] Waynam v. Bend, 1 Campb. 175.
[e] See Wells v. Girling, 1 Gow. Rep.
22, and cases there cited.
[f] See the last note but one.
[g] See Lord Kenyon's observations in
Johnson v. Collings, 1 East, 103, 4, and in
Barlow v. Bishop, id. 434, 5.
[h] Per Lord Ellenborough, in Marshall
v. Poole, 13 East, 100. Ex parte Mills, 2
Ves. jun. 295. Storey v. Atkins, 2 Stra.

725. Clerke v. Martin, Ld. Raym. 758.
Carter v. Palmer, 12 Mod. 380. Grant v.
Vaughan, 3 Burr. 1516. 1525. Smith v.
Kendall, 6 T. R. 124. Carr v. Shaw,
Ante, 327. Bayl. 18, n. 1. 163. *Sed vide*
Cary v. Gerrish, 4 Esp. Rep. 9.
[i] Kessebower v. Tims, K. B. 22 Geo. 3.
Bayl. 164, n. b.
[k] Harris v. Huntbach, 1 Burr. 373.
[l] Bayl. 164.
[m] Id. 165.
[n] Le Sage v. Johnson, Forr. Rep. 23.
Bayl. 164. S. C.

this last case the court overruled the decision in *Waynam* v, *Bend*, 1 Campb. Rep.
175.
An indorsement " without recourse to the indorser" is not evidence in an action by
the indorsee against the indorser under a count for money had and received. *Welch* v.
Lindo, 7 Cranch, 159. But a general indorsement is.—*State Bank* v. *Hurd*, 12 Mass.
Rep. 172.
A promissory note is legal evidence, in an action for money paid, if nothing appear on
its face to render it void : though it may be void from circumstances *dehors* the note.
Myers v. *Irwin*, 2 Serg. and Rawle, 368.

Sect. 2. Of
the *counts*
on the con-
sideration,
and of the
common
counts.

[366]

which a bill of exchange affords, has no application to the assumpsit for money paid by the payee or holder of it, to the use of the acceptor; and that it must be a very special case which will support such an assumpsit.[o] In the case of Cowley *v.* Dunlop,[p] Lawrence, J. expressed opinion that the drawer of a bill, who is obliged to take it up after having negotiated it, is confined to his action on the bill to recover against the accepter. If the drawee, without having effects of the drawer in his hands, accept and pay the bill without having it protested, he may recover the amount in an action for money paid, laid out, and expended, to the use of the drawer;[q] though it is usual to declare on the express or implied promise to provide for the bill at maturity, or to indemnify.[r] (1)

It has been holden, that a bill, as well as a note,[s] is *prima facie* evidence of *money had and received* by the drawer or maker to the use of the holder;[t] and an acceptance is evidence of money had and received by the acceptor to the use of the drawer.[u] But it is doubtful whether the indorsee or holder can use the bill against the acceptor as evidence under this count.[x] And it seems now settled, that the plaintiff can in no case recover under this count, unless money has actually been received by the party sued, and for the use of the plaintiff.[y] (2) If the indorsee of a bill of exchange, who has received a navy bill as a security to him till the bill of exchange is accepted, deposit such navy bill with the drawee, and the drawee receive the money upon it, he is answerable for the amount in an action for money had and received to the use of the indorsee, though he may have done nothing that amounts to an acceptance of the bill of exchange.[z] In an action for money had and re-

---

[o] Gibson *v.* Minet, 1 Hen. Bla. 602. and see Howle *v.* Baxter, 3 East, 177.

[p] Cowley *v.* Dunlop, 7 T. R. 572. Buckler *v.* Buttevant, 3 East, 72. Simmonds *v.* Parminter, 1 Wils. 186.

[q] Smith *v.* Nissen, 1 T. R. 169. Cowley *v.* Dunlop, 7 T. R. 576. Simmonds *v.* Parminter, 1 Wils. 188.

[r] Simmonds *v.* Parminter, 1 Wils. 188.

[s] Vin. Ab. tit. Evidence, A. b. 36.—Ford *v.* Hopkins, 1 Salk. 283.

[t] Bayl. 163. cites Grant *v.* Vaughan, 3 Burr. 1516. *Sed vide* Wayman *v.* Bend, 1 Campb. 175.

[u] Thompson *v.* Morgan, 3 Campb. 101. Bayl. 163.

[x] Johnson *v.* Collings, 1 East, 104. Dims-

dale *v.* Lanchester, 1 Esp. Rep. 201.—Bayl. 96. Brown *v.* London, Freem. 14 1 Ventr. 153. S. C. Israel *v.* Douglas, 1 Hen. Bla. 239. Eaglechilde's case, Holt. 67. *Vide* Waynam *v.* Bend, Campb. 175 But in Bayl. on Bills, 164, it is laid down that the acceptance is evidence of money had and received by the acceptor to the use of the holder, and of money paid by the holder to the use of the acceptor, and an indorsement of money lent by the indorsee to the indorser.

[y] Barlow *v.* Bishop, 1 East, 434, 5.—Waynam *v.* Bend, 1 Campb. 175.

[z] Pierson *v.* Dunlop, Cowp. 571; and see 5 Esp. Rep. 247. 14 East, 590, ante. 193, 4.

---

(1) A. the payee of a note for 1500 dollars indorsed it to B., who indorsed it to a bank by whom it was protested for non-payment. Due notice was given to A. who afterwards paid the bank 800 dollars in part and promised to pay the residue. The bank sued B as indorser and recovered judgment against him for the balance due on the note after deducting the 800 dollars. B. afterwards paid 380 dollars to the bank who continued in possession of the note which had not been fully paid. *Held,* that though B. could not maintain an action on the note, as it had not been fully paid and was the property of the bank, yet that he might recover, the 380 dollars of A. on a count for money paid, laid out, and expended, &c. *Butler* v. *Wright,* 20 Johns. 367.

(2) A bill or note is *prima facie* evidence under a count for money had and received against the drawer or indorser: but the presumption that the contents of the bill or note have been received by the party sued may be rebutted by circumstances, and a recovery cannot be had if it be proved that the money was actually received by another. *Page's Adm.* v. *Bank of Alexandria,* 7 Wheat. 35.

ceived by the holder of a bill against a person who has received a sum Sect. 2. Of
of money from the acceptor to satisfy it, any defence may be set up the *counts*
which could have been available, if the action had been brought against on the *con-*
the acceptor himself.[a] *sideration,*
                                                                       and of the
                                                                       common
  According to the case of Israel *v.* Douglas,[b] an acceptance is evi- *counts.*
dence of an *account stated* by the acceptor with the holder of the bill,
and if there be a variance in describing the bill in an action by drawer,
against acceptor, the former may recover on this count, although there
be only one bill, and one item of account.[c]

  It is here proper to observe, that whenever the bill or note is not
declared upon, it is not adduced in evidence as an instrument carrying
with it the privileges it is otherwise entitled to in respect of its bearing [367]
internal evidence of a consideration ; but it is merely used as a piece
of paper or writing, to found an inference only, in support of the money
counts, which inference may be rebutted and destroyed by contradictory evidence on the part of the defendant ; in which case the jury must
draw, from the whole of the evidence, the conclusion of fact, that so
much money was lent, paid, or had and received, or that an account
was stated.[d]

[a] Redshaw *v.* Jackson, 1 Campb. 372.   [c] Highmore *v.* Primrose, 5 M. & S.
[b] Israel *v.* Douglas, 1 Hen. Bla. 239.   65.
Sed vide Whitwell *v.* Bennett, 3 Bos. &   [d] Story *v.* Atkins, 2 Stra. 725. Gibson
Pul. 559. Johnson *v.* Collinge, 1 East, 98.   *v.* Minet, 1 Hen. Bla. 602.

CHAPTER III.

OF PAYMENT OF DEBT AND COSTS—JUDGMENT BY DEFAULT—AND THE PLEAS AND DEFENCE IN AN ACTION OF ASSUMPSIT ON A BILL, &c.

WHEN the plaintiff has declared, the defendant, if he have any defence, pleads ; if he have no defence, he settles the action by paying the debt and costs ; or he lets judgment go by default ; or obtains time by dilatory pleading. If the defendant wish to see a copy of the bill or note, the practice is stated to be, for a judge on summons, without an affidavit, to make an order for the delivery of a copy to the defendant or his attorney, and that all proceedings be in the mean time stayed.[a] But the court or a judge will not grant leave to inspect a bill in order to ascertain whether it was duly stamped, or has been altered, as those are considered as unjust defences.[b]

Sect. 1. Of staying proceedings on payment of the debt and costs.
If the defendant be advised to settle the action in the first instance, without incurring further expense, he may move the court, in which the action is brought, for a rule, calling on the plaintiff to show cause why, on payment of the debt and costs, all further proceedings should not be stayed : or he may apply to a judge for a summons to the same effect. But where an indorsement was made upon a note by the payee, that if the interest was paid on stipulated days, during his life, the note should be given up ; default having been made in payment of the interest, the Court of Common Pleas refused to stay the proceedings on payment of it, and costs.[c]

If the holder of a bill bring separate actions against the acceptor, the drawer, and indorsers, at the same time, the court will stay the proceedings in the action against the drawer, or any one of the indorsers, upon payment of the amount of the bill, and the costs of that particular action ; but the action against the acceptor will only be stayed on the terms of his paying the costs in all the actions, he being [369] the original defaulter ;[d] and therefore, where several actions have been brought, it may be the least expensive course for the acceptor to suffer judgment by default, in which case he can only be charged with the costs of the particular action against himself ;[e] and if in an action against the acceptor of a bill, an attachment be obtained against the sheriff for not bringing in the body, the sheriff may be relieved on payment of the costs of that action only.[f]

Sect. 2. Of Judgment by default, &c.
When the defendant has no defence, either on the merits or on the pleadings, and is not able to pay the debt and costs in the first instance, he usually obtains time by pleading, or suffers judgment to go

[a] Tidd, 6th edit. 618.
[b] And see Odams v. Duke of Grafton, Bunb. 243.
[c] Steel v. Bradfield, 4 Taunt. 227.—2 Bla. Rep. 958.
[d] Smith v. Woodcock, 4 T. R. 691.—

Windham v. Wither, Stra. 515. Golding v. Grace, 2 Bla. Rep. 749. Tidd, 6th ed 562. See post, 423.
[e] The King v. Sheriff of London. 2 Bar & Ald. 192.
[f] Id. Ibid.

by default, whereupon the plaintiff must, in an action of assumpsit, before he will be entitled to final judgment and execution, ascertain the
amount of the debt, which is done either by referring it to the master
to compute the principal, interest, and costs,(473) or by suing out a
writ of inquiry. By suffering judgment by default, the defendant is
precluded from making any objection to the validity of the instrument;ᵍ
and from availing himself of its loss as a ground of defence.ʰ

Formerly, a writ of inquiry was the only legal mode of ascertaining
what was due in the case of a judgment by default in an action on a
bill or note; but it has long been the practice of the Courts of King's
Bench and Common Pleas, for the plaintiff, instead of executing a
writ of inquiry, to apply to the court in term time, or to a judge in
vacation, on an affidavit of the nature of the action, for a rule or summons to show cause, why it should not be referred to the master or
prothonotaries, in the Common Pleas, to see what is due for principal
and interest, and why final judgment should not be signed for that
sum, without executing a writ of inquiry, upon which the court or
judge will make the rule absolute, on an affidavit of service, unless
good cause be shown to the contrary.ⁱ And although formerly the
Court of Exchequer did not adopt this practice,ᵏ yet now it is other-
wise.ˡ

In the King's Bench, where interlocutory judgment was signed, and [370]
the plaintiff died on a subsequent day in the term, the court, granted
a rule to compute principal and interest on the bill on which the action
was brought ;ᵐ and in another case, they referred it to the master, to
see what was due for principal and interest upon a bill of exchange,
upon producing a copy of the bill verified by affidavit of the plaintiff's
attorney, the original having been stolen out of his pocket, and no
tidings of it obtained.ⁿ

This practice, however, is confined to cases where the declaration
states the bill or note, and does not apply to cases where the instrument is not specially declared upon.º And it is still necessary to sue
out a writ of inquiry, when the bill is payable in foreign money, the
value of which, it is said, can only be properly ascertained by a
jury.ᵖ(474) And in a recent case, the court would not direct the mas-

ᵍ Shepherd v. Charter; 4 T. R. 275.
ʰ Brown v. Messiter, 3 M. & S. 281.—
Ante, 152, 154.
ⁱ Shepherd v. Charter, 4 T. R. 275.—
Rashleigh v. Salmon, 1 Hen. Bla. 252.
Andrews v. Blake, id. 529. Longman v.
Fenn, id. 511. In Chillton v. Harborn,
1 Anstr. Rep. 249, it is said, that the first
case where the court granted this rule, was
that of Rashleigh v. Salmon, 29 Geo. 3.
1 Hen. Bla. 252. Thellusson v. Fletcher,
Doug. 315, 316.

ᵏ Chilton v. Harbon, 1 Anstr. Rep. 249.
ˡ Biggs v. Stewart, 4 Price Rep. 134.
ᵐ Berger v. Green, 1 M. & S. 229.
ⁿ Brown v. Messiter, 3 M. & S. 281.
Ante, 154, note.
º Osborne v. Node, 8 T. R. 648.
ᵖ Messing v. Lord Massarene, 4 T. R.
493. Maunsel v. Lord Massarene, 5 T. R.
87. Nelson v. Sheridan, 8 T. R. 395. Cro.
Eliz. 586. Cro. Jac. 617. Tidd, 6th edit.
598.

(473) This is the settled practice in the courts of the United States in all cases where
the sum is certain, or may be made certain by composition Renner v. Marshall, 1
Wheaton, 215.
(474) If there be no averment of the value of the foreign money in a bill, the defect
is cured by a verdict. Brown v. Barry, 3 Dall. Rep. 365.

Sect. 2. Of
judgment
by default,
&c.
ter to allow re-exchange, in an action upon a bill drawn in Scotland
upon and accepted by the defendant in England ;⁹ and the court refused a reference to the master in an action of debt on a judgment recovered on a bill of exchange.ʳ Where, however, there was a demurrer to one count on a bill of exchange and judgment for the plaintiff,
and a plea to other counts on which issue was joined, the Court of
King's Bench referred it to the master, to see what was due to the
plaintiff on the former.ˢ But in such case a *nolle prosequi* must be
entered as to the other counts, which may be done any time before final
judgment.ᵗ

The plaintiff may, in the King's Bench, obtain a rule for referring a
bill of exchange to the master, on the day on which interlocutory judgment was signed for want of a plea ;ᵘ but where it is signed upon demurrer, as a day is given to the parties upon the record, it might be
thought incongruous to deprive either of them of the whole of the
day, after he is once possessed of it ; and it has therefore been the
practice not to move for such rule until the following day.ˣ In the
King's Bench, the rule nisi and rule absolute, must both be served ; but
there need not be any notice of taxing ; if the defendant wish it, he
must at his peril take care to get a rule to be present.ʸ In the Common
Pleas, notice must be given to the defendant of the prothonotary's appointment to compute principal and interest on the bill, in order that
the defendant may have an opportunity of bringing forward any facts
which may have occurred to reduce the sum which the plaintiff seeks to
recover.ᶻ

[371]

Though the rule Nisi calls upon the defendant to show cause why the
matter should not be referred to the master, yet it has been held in the
Common Pleas, that no irregularity previous to the judgment can be
shown as cause against the reference.ᵃ And the same practice prevails
in the King's Bench; and in a late case, where the defendant's counsel
opposed a rule Nisi, for referring to the master, on an affidavit, showing that the judgment was irregular, it having been signed without a
plea having been demanded, the court determined that this was no
ground for opposing the motion, and that a cross motion to set aside
the judgment must be made, which was accordingly done, and the rule

⁹ Napier *v.* Shneider, 12 East, 430.—
Goldsmith *v.* Taite, 2 Bos. & Pul. 55.
    ʳ Nelson *v.* Sheridan, 8 T. R. 395.
    ˢ Dussery *v.* Johnson, 7 T. R. 473.
    ᵗ Heald *v.* Johnson, 2 Smith's Rep. 46,
47. 1 Stra. 532. Tidd, 6th edit. 599.
    ᵘ Pocock *v.* Carpenter, 3 M. & S. 109.

ˣ Id. Ibid. 3 Smith's Rep. 179.   Tidd.
6th edit. 597.
    ʸ Sellin *v.* Dufton, Hil. 1813.   Farmer
v. Wood, Easter, T. 1816. MS. of Mr. Le
Blanc.
    ᶻ Braning *v.* Patterson, 4 Taunt. 457
Tidd, 6th edit. 597.
    ᵃ Pell *v.* Brown, 1 Bos. & Pul. 369.

Where there were several counts, one on a promissory note, and others for money
lent, money had and received, and *insimul computassent*, and judgment was taken
generally, with a rule that the clerk assess the damages, without entering a *nolle prosequi* on the money counts, judgment was reversed. *Burr* v. *Waterman*, Court of Errors, 2 Cowen, 36 in note.

And where the general money counts are joined with one on a promissory note, the
defendant cannot compel the plaintiff to enter a *nolle prosequi* on the money counts
and assess the damages through the clerk, on the promissory note. *Beard* v. *Van
Wickle.* 3 Cowen, 385.

for referring to the master was enlarged, till the motion of the defendant had been discussed and determined.[b]

When the plaintiff proceeds to ascertain the damages by executing a writ of inquiry, he need not adduce any evidence, but should produce the bill, which it will not be necessary to prove;[c] for where the action is founded on the instrument itself, letting judgment go by default is an admission of the cause of action, and of the defendant's liability to the amount of the bill;[d] and the only reason why the pro-[372] duction of the bill is required, is, that it may be seen whether or not any part of it has been paid:[e] for the same reason, the defendant will not be suffered to give in evidence any matter in defeasance of the action. [f] (477)

The defences of which the defendant may avail himself in this
action, are founded either on a mis-statement in the declaration of the cause of action, or on some defect in the right of action itself. Those of the first description are taken advantage of by a general or special demurrer; by a general demurrer when the mis-statement is substantially bad, and by a special demurrer when it is only formally so. Defences arising from a defect in the right of action itself, are brought forward either in the shape of a special plea, or are given in evidence under the general issue of non-assumpsit. They consist either of a denial that the plaintiff ever had cause of action, or admitting that he once had, of an assertion, that it is either suspended or extinguished. And a plea to an extent in aid, stating that the defendant had accepted a bill drawn upon him by the original debtor, and which did not become due till the day after the inquisition was taken, is good, although the defendant had refused payment, and the original debtor to the crown had been obliged to take it up.[g]

[b] Marshall v. Van Omeran, K. B. Trin. Term, 1818.

[c] Greene v. Hearne, 3 T. R. 301. Bul. Ni. Pri. 278. Thellusson v. Fletcher, Dougl. 316, n. 2. Golding v. Grace, 2 Bla. Rep. 749.

Bevis v. Lindsell, 2 Stra. 1149. On executing a writ of inquiry in an action on a note, the plaintiff did not produce the subscribing witness, but offered other evidence that it was the defendant's hand, and the court held *that* sufficient. For the note being set out in the declaration is admitted, and the only use of producing it is, to see whether any payment is indorsed upon it. Greene v. Hearne, 4 T. R. 301. Upon a rule *nisi* to set aside an inquisition against the acceptor of a bill of exchange, it was urged that the bill, though *produced* before the jury, was not *proved*, but the court held, that by suffering judgment, the defendant admitted the acceptance of the bill, and was liable to its amount: and Buller, J.

said, the only reason of producing the bill is to see whether any part of it is paid.

Mills v. Lyne, B. R. Hil. 26 Geo. 3. Bayl. 227, note g. On a writ of inquiry in an action upon a note, the sheriff directed the jury to give nominal damages only, because the plaintiff could not prove the note. Lawrence insisted that the plaintiff was bound to produce the note (because a receipt of part might have been indorsed thereon,) and to prove the defendant's signature, but per Buller, J. "If you had paid part, you might have pleaded it, but you have let judgment go for the whole," and the court set aside the inquisition.

[d] Anon. 3 Wils. 155. Shepherd v. Charter, 4 T. R. 275.

[e] Per Buller, J. in Greene v. Hearne, 3 T. R. 301.

[f] East India Company v. Glover, 1 Stra. 612. Shepherd v. Charter, 4 T. R. 275.

[g] The King v. Dawson, 1 Wightw. 32. Ante, 95.

(477) But the note should conform to the allegations of the declaration, otherwise it is not evidence on a writ of inquiry Therefore, where the declaration did not allege when the note was payable, and the note produced was payable at 60 days, the variance was held fatal; for a note, in which no time of payment is mentioned, is payable on demand. *Wheeley* v. *Mandeville*, 7 Cranch. Rep. 208.

Sect.'3. Of   Those of the *first* description are also divisible into two heads,
the pleas & namely, those defences which deny that the instrument declared on wa-
defence.   made, indorsed, or accepted, or that the defendant was party to it:
and those which admit such facts, but allege that the contract, supposed to have been raised by them, was void or voidable, on account
of the incapacity of the defendant to contract, as in the case of infancy or coverture, or on account of the *want of consideration*, or the
illegality of it, or on the ground of an improper presentment for acceptance, or payment, or neglect to give notice of the dishonour of
the bill, or some laches of the holder, or the person from whom he
attempts to derive an interest in the instrument; or, admitting there
once existed a valid contract, insist that it was performed by payment
or otherwise; or if unperformed, that there was some legal excuse for
the non-performance of it, as a release or parol discharge before breach.
But we have seen that the defendant cannot give in evidence, as a
[373] defence, a parol agreement to renew,[i] or a verbal engagement that the
bill should be payable only in case a particular fund should be productive.[k](1)

Defences of the *second* description, namely, those which admit that
the plaintiff once had cause of action, but insist that it no longer exists,
are either such as allege that the plaintiff is under an existing disability
to sue, by his being an outlaw, alien enemy, bankrupt, &c.; or that the
defendant is under a disability to be sued, either by his being an insolvent debtor, bankrupt, &c.; or that the action is discharged by an accord and satisfaction,[l] arbitrament, release, (which we have seen, may,
in the case of bills, be by parol,) former recovery for the same cause,
tender, set-off, or the statute of limitations.[m](2)

The statute of limitations begins to operate only from the time when
the bill, &c. is due, and not in general from the date;[n] and therefore
the plea in an action against an acceptor of a bill, or maker of a note,
when payable after date, should be *actio non accrevit*, and not *non-
assumpsit infra sex annos*.[o]

Where a bill or note is payable a certain time after sight no debt
accrues until it has been presented to the drawee, therefore the statute
of limitations is no bar to such a note unless it has been presented for

h Ante, 188 to 193.

i Hoare v. Graham, 3 Campb. 67. Ante,
47.

k Campbell v. Hodgson, 1 Gow's C. N.
P. 74.

l What is not a satisfaction, see Norris v.
Aylett, 2 Campb. 329, 330. Ante, 96, note,
and 307, note.

m Chievly v. Bond, 4 Mod. 105.

n Whittersheim v. The Countess Dow-
ager of Carlisle, 1 Hen. Bla. 631. Renew
v. Axton, Carth. 3. As to the point where
the statute of limitations begins to run on
a note payable on demand, see Topham
Braddick, 1 Taunt. 575, 6. Sir William
Jones, 194. Godb. 487. 12 Mod. 444.—
15 Ves. 487. and see Savage v. Aldren
2 Stark. 232.

o Josselyn v. Lacier, 10 Mod. 294.

(1) Parol evidence is admissible in a suit by the indorsee against the indorser of a
note indorsed in blank, to show that at the time of the indorsement, the indorsee received
the note under an agreement that he would not have recourse upon it against the indorser.
Hill v. *Ely*, 5 Serg. & Rawle, 363.

(2) A plea to an action on a note for the payment of money on a certain day, at a particular place, that the defendant was, at the day and place appointed, ready with his money to pay the note, but the payee was not ready to receive it, and that the money has
ever since remained there for the payee's use, must conclude with a *profert in curia*.
Curley v. *Vance*, 17 Mass. Rep. 389.

payment six years before the action was commenced.[p] With respect to promissory notes payable on demand, it has been held that the statute runs from the date of the note, and not from the time of the demand.[q] An indorsement on a bill or note by the holder of the payment of interest within six years may be given in evidence to prevent the operation of the statute of limitations if it were *bona fide* made when the six years had not elapsed.[r]

An acknowledgment by one of several drawers of a joint and several [374] promissory note will take the case out of the statute as against any one of the other drawers in a separate action on the note against him.[s](479) And in an action against A. on the joint and several promissory note of himself and B. to take the case out of the statute of limitations, it is enough to give in evidence a letter written by A. to B. within six years, desiring him to settle the debt.[t] But the acknowledgment by one partner to bind the other must, in such case, be clear and explicit, and therefore it is not sufficient, in order to take a case out of the statute of limitations in an action on a promissory note, to show a payment by a joint maker of the note to the payee within six years, so as to throw it upon the defendant to show that the payment was not made on account of the note.[u] Where the acceptor of a bill of exchange acknowledged his acceptance, and that he had been liable, but said that he was not liable then, because it was out of date, and that he would not pay it, and that it was not in his power to pay it, this was deemed sufficient to take the case out of the statute.[x]

It has been held, that where one of two drawers of a joint and several promissory note having become a bankrupt, if the payee receive a dividend under the commission on account of the note, this will prevent the other drawer from availing himself of the statute in an action brought against him for the remainder of the money due on the note, the dividend having been received within six years before the action brought.[y] But in a recent case where one of two joint drawers of a bill of exchange became bankrupt, and under his commission the indorsee proved a debt (beyond the amount of the bill) for goods sold, &c. and they accepted a bill as a security they then held for their debt, and afterwards received a dividend; it was held, that in an action by the indorsees of the bill against the solvent partner, the statute of limitations was a good defence, al-

[p] Holmes v. Harrison, 2 Taunt. 323.
[q] Christie v. Fansick, C. P. London Sittings after Mich. Term, 52 Geo. 3. *cor.* Sir J. Mansfield, 2 Selw. 4th ed. 131. 339. Capp v. Lancaster, Cro. Eliz. 548. Rumball v. Ball, 10 Mod. 38. 3 Salk. 227. Ante, 249. *Sed quære,* see 14 East, 500. 3 Campb. 459. 1 Taunt. 575, 6. Sir W. Jones, 194. Godbolt, 437. 12 Mod. 444. 15 Ves. 487.

[r] Searle v. Lord Barrington, 2 Stra. 820. 2 Ves. sen. 43. 54.
[s] Whitcomb v. Whiting, Doug. 652, 3.
[t] Halliday v. Ward, 3 Campb. 32. and see 11 East, 585. 1 Stark. 81.
[u] Holme v. Green, 1 Stark. 488.
[x] Leaper v. Tutton, 16 East, 420.
[y] Jackson v. Fairbank, 2 Hen. Bla. 340.

(479) The same point has been ruled in the United States, even when the acknowledgment was made after the dissolution of the partnership. *Smith* v. *Ludlow,* 6 John. Rep. 267. See *Clements* v. *Williams,* February Term, 1814. MSS. Sup. Court.

But, where an action was brought against A. and B., and C. his wife, upon a joint promissory note made by A. and C. before her marriage, and the promise was laid by A. and C. before her marriage, and the defendant pleaded the statute of limitations, whereupon issue was joined; it was held, that an acknowledgment of the note by A. within six years, but after the intermarriage of B. and C., was not evidence to support the issue. *Pittam* v. *Foster,* 1 Barn. & Cresw. 248.

Sect. 3. Of though the dividend had been paid by the assignees of the bankrupt
the pleas & partner within six years. [z]
defence.

With respect to the mode of taking advantage of these defences,
those which in effect deny that the bill, &c. was made, or that the
defendant or plaintiff was party to it, such as those which are founded
on some defect in the instrument, apparent on the face of it, or on
the ground that the supposed drawing, acceptance, or indorsement,
do not amount to such act, cannot be pleaded, and can only be taken
[375] advantage of, under the general issue of non-assumpsit to which they
amount. But all defences which admit the existence of a contract but
allege that it was never binding, or that if it were, it was either performed, or discharged before breach, *may* be pleaded specially; [a] though
in general, matters which deny that the plaintiff ever had cause of action, are not pleaded, but are given in evidence under the general issue
of non-assumpsit, which puts the plaintiff on proof of his right of action : where, however, such defences lie more in the knowledge of the
defendant than the plaintiff, as in the case of infancy and coverture,
it is considered fairer practice, to plead them in the first instance, or
give notice of them to the plaintiff, previously to the trial of the cause,
as otherwise the plaintiff may be surprised by them at the trial. Defences of the second description, which admit that the plaintiff once
had right of action, are usually pleaded ; and a tender, set-off, bankruptcy, or insolvency of the defendant, and the statute of limitations,
must in all cases be pleaded. [b]

[z] Brandram v. Wharton, 1 Barn. & Ald.   v. Jacob, 1 Ld. Raym. 88, 9.   Com. Dig.
463.   tit. Pleader, E. 14.
[a] Hatton v. Morse, 1 Salk. 394. Hussey   [b] Draper v. Glassop, 1 Ld. Raym. 153.

CHAPTER IV.

OF THE EVIDENCE IN AN ACTON ON A BILL, NOTE, &c.

THE evidence to be adduced in an action on a bill or note, &c. is to be considered with reference, first, to the *plaintiff's* cause of action and secondly, the *defendant's* answer to the action.

The evidence which the *plaintiff* should adduce in support of his declaration, in which the bill, &c. is set forth, may be considered with reference, *first*, to the *facts*, which must be proved ; and *secondly*, to the *manner* of proving those facts.

With respect to the *facts* which must be proved, the evidence is *What facts* in all cases governed by the pleadings, it being necessary to prove *the plaintiff* every thing put in issue, and no more. When the general issue of *must prove.* *non-assumpsit* is pleaded, the plaintiff must prove every material allegation in his declaration, the requisites of which have been already stated ; but on an issue taken on a special plea, replication, or rejoinder, if there be no plea of *non-assumpsit*, it is only necessary to prove the particular point referred to the jury, for whatever is not expressly denied, is admitted by the pleading ; and on the same principle, where the issue lies only on the defendant, as where it is joined on the plea of infancy, and there is no other plea, it is not incumbent on the plaintiff to adduce any evidence in support of his declaration.

Under the *general issue*, the plaintiff must prove,

1st. That the *bill* or *note*, declared on, was *made* as stated in the declaration, either in words, or that its legal operation was as therein described.

2dly. That the *defendant* became *party* to the bill as alleged in the pleadings.

3dly. The *plaintiff's interest* in the bill, as indorsee, bearer, &c. and sometimes the *consideraion* which he gave for it.

4thly. The *special averments*, and the *breach* of the defendant's con- [377] tract.

We will consider each of these heads in their natural order, and the mode of proof to be adduced in support of them.

1st. The *bill or note and the allegations respecting it* must be proved *1st. Proof* as described in the declaration, in terms, or in substance, whoever may *of the bill* be the defendant, and any material variance will be fatal.ᵃ If there *as described*

ᵃ Ante, 352.

1st. Proof of the bill, as describ- ed. were any mistake in the date, or circumstances of the instrument necessary to be explained, then evidence must be adduced accordingly. And in action by the indorsee against the acceptor of a bill, the date of which appears to have been altered by the acceptor, it lies on the plaintiff to show that the alteration was made previous to the indorsement by the drawer, to whose order it was made payable.[b] And if the plaintiff sue on a promissory note which purports to be payable, to a person of a different name, he should be prepared with evidence, that he was the person intended.[c]

In an action against the acceptor or indorser of a bill,[d] or the indorser of a note,[e] the hand-writing of the drawer of the bill and the maker of the note, are considered as admitted and need not be proved, nor can it be contradicted by the defendant, and the circumstance of its having been forged, constitutes no defence, unless it appear that the bill was accepted before the drawer had sight of the bill, in which case it is said, that the drawer's hand-writing must be proved.[f]

In an action against the drawer or indorser of a bill for default of payment, it is unnecessary to allege that it was accepted, but if it be stated, it must be proved ;[g] though proof of an express promise of [378] payment by the drawer after the bill was due, precludes the necessity of proving such acceptance.[h]

If the bill were in foreign money, it should be proved what was the

[b] Johnson v. Duke of Marlborough, 2 Stark. 313. Bul. Ni. Pri. 255.
[c] Willis v. Barrett, 2 Stark. 29. Ante, 68, note.
[d] Wilkinson v. Lutwedge, 1 Stra. 648. Jenys v. Fowler, 2 Stra. 946. Price v. Neale, Burr. 1351. 1 Bla. Rep. 390. Per Dampier, J. in Bass v. Clive, 4 M. & S. 15. Ante, 185. Bayl. 217.
[e] Free and others v. Hawkins, Holt C. N. P. 550. In an action against the payee of a promissory note, who was likewise the indorser, held, that his indorsement was an admission of the hand-writing of the maker. Action by indorsee against the payee of a promissory note, of which Sir Robert Salisbury was the maker, and the defendant became the payee and indorser as surety for Sir R. S. to the plaintiffs. The only evidence on the making of the note by Sir R. S. was by proving the indorsement of the note by the defendant, which was objected to by Mr. Serjt. Lens. But Gibbs, C. J. ruled, from the analogy of a bill of exchange, where the acceptance is an admission of the hand-writing of the drawer, that the indorsement by the payee is an admission of the hand-writing of the maker.
[f] Id. Ibid. Bayl. 219. Peake Evid. 4th edit. 248. sed quære.
[g] Jones v. Morgan and another, 2 Campb. 474. Bayl. 181. 219, 220. Wayman v. Bend, 1 Campb. 174.
Jones v. Morgan and another, 2 Campb. 474. This was an action on a bill of exchange drawn by the defendants, payable to their own order, and indorsed by them to the plaintiff. The bill was drawn upon one T. Burt, by whom it was dishonoured for non-payment, and the declaration unnecessarily stated that he had accepted it according to the usage and custom of merchants. No evidence could be adduced of his hand-writing, but it appeared that after the bill was due, one of the defendants several times promised the plaintiff to pay it. The plaintiff's counsel contended there was no necessity to prove the acceptance, as it had been stated unnecessarily, the liability of the defendants, at all events attaching, upon the non-payment of the bill, and at any rate, that the acceptance was admitted by the promises to pay after the bill was due, and in the plaintiff's hand. Lord Ellenborough was clearly of opinion that the acceptance being stated in the declaration must be proved, and he was inclined to think at the trial, that the promises to pay did not amount to an admission of an acceptance, he therefore directed a nonsuit. But upon a motion in the ensuing term, to set the nonsuit aside, his Lordship and the rest of the court, thought, upon authority of Lundie v. Robertson, 7 East, 231, that the promises to pay were a sufficient admission of the acceptance, and upon the same evidence at the Sittings after Michaelmas Term last, the plaintiff had a verdict. See also Bosanquet v. Anderson, 6 Esp. Rep. 43. Post.
[h] Id. Ibid.   Bosanquet v. Anderson, 6 Esp. Rep. 43. Post.

rate of exchange, and value of such money at the time the bill became due ; and if the bill were payable at usances, the duration of such usances should be proved.

With respect to the MODE *of proving the bill, and the allegation re-* *specting it,* on the rule that the plaintiff must adduce in support of his action the best evidence in his power, he must in general produce the *instrument* declared on, in proof of the allegations that it was made, and proof of the mere loss of the bill will not in general excuse the non-production of it.[i] Where, however, it can be proved, that the original bill has been destroyed,[k] or that it is withheld by the defen-dant,[l] it will suffice to produce a copy, or to give parol evidence of its contents, and where the defendant tore his own note of hand, a copy was admitted as good evidence.[m](485) But in these cases, the plain-tiff must show sufficient probability to satisfy the court, that the ori-ginal note was genuine.[n] And it has been decided, that when the original note is in the hands of the defendant, the plaintiff must give him notice to produce it, or he will not be allowed to go into evidence of its loss or contents ;[o] and this rule has ever been considered as ap- [379] plying to an action of trover, for a bill of exchange in the possession of the defendant ;[p] but it is now established, that in such action of trover, or in any other proceeding, as on an indictment for stealing a bill, or for forging a note which the defendant swallowed, which ne-cessarily imports that the plaintiff means to charge the defendant with the possession of the instrument, no notice to produce need be served upon him.[q] Where a notice has been given in order to let in the se-condary evidence, the service of such notice, and the destruction or detention by the defendant of the instrument must be proved.[r]

If there was a *subscribing witness* to the bill or note, or to an indorse-ment thereof, then in an action against the drawer of the bill or the maker of the note, it will be necessary to subpœna such witness, and if there be any doubt as to his proving that he saw the defendant write his name, the subscription must be proved by some other evidence, which will in that case be admissible ;[s] and if a person sees a de-

[i] Ante, 152, 3, 4.
[k] Ante, 155.
[l] Ante, 152.
[m] Per Holt, C. J. Anon. Lord Raym. 731.
[n] Gaodier v. Lake, 1 Atk. 446.
[o] Phil. on Evid. 3d edit. 889.
[p] Cowan v. Abrahams, 1 Esp. Rep. 50.
[q] How v. Hall, 14 East, 274. Phil. on Evid. 3d edit. 391.
[r] Phil. on Evid, 3d edit. 390.
[s] Lemon v. Dean, Lancaster Lent As-sizes, 1810, cor. Le Blanc, J. 2 Campb. 636. Action on a promissory note, which appeared to be witnessed by one Bentley. Bentley was called, and swore that he did not see the defendant subscribe the note, but the defendant merely desired him to try to write his name upon the paper, and that he did not observe whe-ther any thing was at that time written on it. Plaintiff's counsel then proposed to call witnesses to prove the defendant's hand-writing. Williams objected, that there being a subscribing witness to the note, who was not incompetent, no other evidence of it could be given. He cited Phipps v. Parker, 1 Campb. 412.—Le Blance, J. " I will make no observation upon that case. It may be distinguish-able, as there the instrument was a deed. But I am quite clear, that if the sub-scribing witness to a note, when called, cannot prove it, by reason of his not having seen it drawn, the plaintiff may proceed to prove by other means." Vide Fasset v. Brown, Peake Rep. 23. Grel-lier v. Neale, id. 146.

(485) Secondary evidence of the contents of a note, is admissible where it appears the original is destroyed or lost. *Renner* v. *Bank of Columbia,* 8 Wheat. 596.

1st. Proof of the bill, as described.

were any mistake in the date, or cessary to be explained, then e' And in action by the indorsee of which appears to have bee. plaintiff to show that the a' . ment by the drawer, to wt ': plaintiff sue on a promi' person of a different n' he was the person in'

In an action ag' dorser of a note;' maker of the n', nor can it be ' its having b' bill was a' it is said

is not desired by the parties t utting his name to it, prove i'

proof of his hand the note was pr f the defend' ere was a ' eld, th' of t' ar'

nentic .nether the m. of the defendant's h. ould have sufficed.' It has .e issue is founded on a plea of *non* . bond, some evidence must be given of the . ecuting the deed, which is not to be assumed from u executed by a person in his name, in the presence of the ng witness, who was unacquainted with him.' The payment of oney into court generally precludes the defendant from disputing the validity of the bill, or showing that it is improperly stamped.' In such case the plaintiff should, on the trial, produce the rule, and it will not suffice to call the attorney to prove that he took the money out of court.'

In pay' st'

[378] r

2dly. Proof that defendant was party to the bill, &c.

Secondly, It must be proved, *that the defendant was a party to the bill or note*. Thus in an action against the acceptor of a bill, it must be proved, that the defendant accepted the bill either verbally or in writing;' and if the acceptance was made by an agent, it must be shown that he was legally authorized by the principal :' and in general the agent himself should be subpœnaed ; but it is not in all cases necessary to subpœna the agent himself: thus in an action on a policy of insurance, the affidavit of a person, stating that he subscribed the policy on the behalf of the defendant, which affidavit the defendant himself had previously used on a motion to put off the trial, was, under the particular circumstances, admitted as proof of the agency : for the defendant having used the affidavit for such a purpose, must be considered as having known and adopted its contents, though the single circumstance that the affidavit purported to have been made by a person

---

r M'Craw v. Gentry, 3 Campb. 232.
n Nelson v Whittall, 1 Selw. & Barn. 19.
x Per Lord Ellenborough, Currie v. Child, 3 Campb. 283, cited in Nelson v. Whittall, 1 Selw. & Barn. 22, n. a. and see Gough v. Cecil, Selw. 4th ed. 516. note.
y Per Bayley, J. in Nelson v. Whittall, 1 Selw. & Barn. 21. " It is laid down, in Mr. Phillips's Treatise on the Law of Evidence, that the proof of the hand-writing of the attesting witness is, in all cases, sufficient. I always felt this difficulty, that that proof alone does not connect the defendant with the note. If the attesting witness himself gave evidence, he would prove, not merely that the instrument was executed, but the identity

of the person so executing it ; but the proof of the hand-writing of the attesting witness, establishes merely that some person assuming the name, which the instrument purports to bear, executed it. and it does not go to establish the identity of that person ; and in that respect the proof seems to me defective. In this case, however, there is evidence sufficient to connect the defendant with the note, for he was present in the room when it was prepared.
z Per Dampier, J. in Middleton v Sandford, 4 Campb. 34.
a Israel v. Benjamin, 3 Campb. 40.
b Id ibid.
c Ante, 170 to 182.
d Johnson v. Mason, 1 Esp. Rep. 90

as agent, would not have b... 'ith that authority;· and wh... whatever A. does or say... of B., is admissible i... 'e makes for B., an... 's the agent's ac...

':ˣ and if an indorsement on a promissory tested by a subscribing witness, such f the defendant pay money into court 'e instrument, the signature and its ·e proved, and the only question to

·n against ·
ng of ea·
d-wri·
d a·

·dant was a party to the bill or '·ˣ one of several acceptors is ·others.ᵇ In an action against ·t be proved by the witness ·h it is insisted, amounted ·ird person, that person ·oof of an answer given ·taken up when due, ·be shown that the ·° If the accept-·gnature proved.

[384]

·efendant·
·nce in the name ·
·e that the defendant· we·
·aration.ⁱ

And this doctrine has been carried so fa·, three persons as drawers of a bill of exchange, · drawn by an agent of the firm upon one of the p· that the acceptance by the drawee was evidence aga··· ners of the bill having been regularly drawn and rendered··

·ote, his signa-·by a witness, by the party

Johnson v. Ward, 6 Esp. Rep. 48. Phil. Evid. 3d edit. 79.

Per Gibbs, J. in Langhorn v. Allnutt, 4 Taunt. 519. Phil. Evid. 3d edit. 78.

Gray v. Palmer and another, 1 Esp. Rep. 135. Per Lawrence, J. in Sheriff v. Wilks, 1 East, 52.

Gray and others v. Palmer and Hodgson, 1 Esp. Rep. 135. Assumpsit by the plaintiffs as indorsees of a promissory note against the defendants as the drawers. The note was a joint and several one, signed by James and John Palmer, and Edward Hodgson. The declaration was against them jointly in the common form, viz. that the said James and John Palmer, and Edward Hodgson, made their certain note in writing, commonly called a promissory note, their proper hands-writing being thereto subscribed, &c. Hodgson, one of the defendants, had pleaded a sham plea of judgment recovered, to which there was the usual replication of nul tiel record, and demurrer, in which state the pleadings then stood as to him; the two other defendants James and John Palmer severally pleaded non-assumpsit, and these were the issues in the cause on the record. The counsel for the plaintiff proved the hands-writing of James and John Palmer, and there rested their case. The counsel for the defendants insisted that this alone was not sufficient; for that it was also necessary to prove the hand-writing of Hodgson the other defendant, inasmuch as the plaintiffs had declared on a joint contract against the three defendants. It was answered, that Hodgson had by his plea admitted the note to be his; and it was therefore only necessary to prove it against those parties who had by their

pleas denied it to be theirs, and u... 'he tes-proved as to them, gave the plainti... note; cient title to recover. Lord Kenyon n··· must that it was necessary to prove the hand··· to writing of all the parties to the note las 'n Lordship said, that between the plaintif and Hodgson it was unnecessary to prove his hand-writing, he having by his plea of judgment recovered not denied it; but that the other defendants had a right to have the declaration proved, which could only be by proving the hands-writing of all the defendants subscribed to the note, as the plaintiffs had averred in the declaration they had done.

York v. Blott, 5 M. & S. 71.

Thwaites v. Richardson, Peake Rep. 16.

Id. ibid. Phil. Evid. 3d ed. 75.— Hodenpyl v. Vingerhoed and another.

Hodenpyl v. Vingerhoed and another, cor. Abbott, J. 2d July, 1818, Guildhall. Assumpsit on a promissory note, dated at Rotterdam, and drawn in Dutch, and for the payment of 900 guilders to the plaintiff, and subscribed by the firm of " Vingerhoed and Christian." The declaration stated several christian names of each defendant. A witness swore that he knew the firm of Vingerhoed and Christian, and that there were two persons of those surnames in the firm, but that he did not know their christian names: and that in a conversation with Vingerhoed, he admitted that the note was subscribed by him in the name of the firm. This was held sufficient to establish the action against both defendants. Blunt and Bowman for plaintiffs. But see post.

Id. ibid.

2dly. Proof to prove the authority of the agent.^m So the admission by one partner of
that defen-his partnership with the co-defendants, who were sued with him, as
dant was
party to the acceptors of a bill of exchange, and who had been outlawed, has been
bill, &c. received as proof against him of a joint promise by all.ⁿ The rule has
even been extended in actions so far as to admit the declarations of one
partner to be evidence against another, concerning joint contracts and
their joint interest, although the person who has made such declarations
is not a party to the suit; as where in an action by a creditor against
some of the partnership firm, the answer of another partner to a bill
filed by other creditors was received in evidence against the defendants, not indeed to prove the partnership, but that being established,
as an admission against those who are as one person with him in
interest.^o And the admission of a partner, though not a party to the
suit, is evidence as to joint contracts against any other partner, as well
after the determination of the partnership as during its continuance.^p
So we have seen that the admission of one of several drawers of a
[383] promissory note is sufficient to take the case out of the Statute of Limitations, in a separate action against the others.^q But in a joint action
against three persons as acceptors of a bill of exchange, as a joint liability must be proved, the circumstance of two of the defendants having
been outlawed will not dispense with proof of their joint liability, although the defendant who alone pleaded to the action was in justice
liable to pay the debt.^r So in an action against two persons, as makers
of a note, if one of them suffer judgment by default, his signature must
nevertheless be proved on the trial against the other.^s A declaration of
an agent can only be evidence against the principal where it accompanies
the transaction about which he is employed, and if made at another time
it is not admissible.^t

In an action against the acceptor of a bill, payable *after sight*, it is in
general necessary to prove the date or time of the acceptance; but if his
signature as acceptor is proved, the date of the acceptance appearing
over it, although in a different hand-writing, will be presumed to have
been written by his authority.^u

In an action against the *drawer* or *indorser* of a bill or note, the *hand-
writing of the defendant*, or a signature by his agent, having power to
bind him, must be established in evidence, in like manner as in an action

---

^m Porthouse *v.* Parker and others, 1
Campb. 82.
  Porthouse *v.* Parker and others, 1
Campb. 82. This was an action by payee
against the drawers of a bill, which purported to be drawn by one Wood, as the
agent of George, James, and John Parker,
upon John Parker. There was no proof
that Wood had authority from the defendants to draw the bill, but a witness swore
that he, as the agent of John Parker, the
drawee, and one of the defendants, had accepted it on his account. Lord Ellenborough held, that the bill having been accepted by order of one of the defendants,
this was sufficient evidence of its having
been regularly drawn; and further, that the
acceptor being likewise a drawer, there
would be no occasion for the plaintiff to
prove that the defendants had received express notice of the dishonour of a bill, as

this must have necessarily been known to
one of them, and the knowledge of one
was the knowledge of all.

ⁿ Per Lord Ellenborough, in Sangster *v.*
Mazarredo and others, 1 Stark. 161. Phil
Evid. 3d edit. 161.

^o Grant *v.* Jackson, Peake, 203. Wood !
v. Braddick, 1 Taunt. 104. Nicholl *v.*
Dowding and Kemp, 1 Stark. 81.

^p Wood and others *v.* Braddick, 1 Taunt.
104.

^q Ante, 374.

^r Sheriff *v.* Wilkes and others, 1 East
48.

^s Gray and others *v.* Palmer, 1 Esp. Rep
135. Ante, 381, note.

^t Retham *v.* Benson, 1 Gow, 48, 9.

^u Glossop *v.* Jacob, 4 Campb. 227 —
1 Stark. 69. S. C.

against the acceptor of a bill;[x] and if an indorsement on a promissory note purports to have been attested by a subscribing witness, such witness must be called;[y] but if the defendant pay money into court generally, or upon the count on the instrument, the signature and its validity is admitted, and need not be proved, and the only question to be tried will then be the *quantum*.[z]

2dly. Proof that defendant was party to the bill, &c.

The mode of proving that the defendant was a party to the bill or note has already been partially considered;[a] one of several acceptors is competent to prove the hand-writing of the others.[b] In an action against the acceptor, his acceptance, if by parol, must be proved by the witness who heard him accept; and if the answer, which it is insisted, amounted to an acceptance, was given by a clerk, or third person, that person must be subpœnaed; and it has been held, that proof of an answer given at the house of the drawee, that the bill would be taken up when due, is not sufficient proof of an acceptance, but it must be shown that the answer was given by the drawee, or by his authority.[c] If the acceptance was in writing, it must be produced, and the signature proved. In an action against the drawer or indorser of a bill or note, his signature must also be proved. The signature may be established by a witness, who can swear to the hand-writing, or to an admission of it by the party sued.

Mode of proof.

[384]

The simplest and most obvious *proof of hand-writing* is the testimony of a witness who saw the defendant subscribe the bill or note; but (unless there was a subscribing witness, who, we have seen, must be subpœnaed,[d]) this evidence is not essential, and it will suffice to call a witness who is acquainted with the defendant, and who, from seeing him write, or from correspondence with him, has acquired a knowledge of his hand-writing, and can swear to his belief, that the subscription is the defendant's; and in an action on a foreign bill to prove the hand-writing of the defendant, it is evidence to go to a jury that a person who saw him write *once*, thinks the hand-writing alike, though he has no belief on the subject.[e] This suffices, because in

[x] Gutteridge v. Smith, 8 Hen. Bla. 374.
[y] Stone v. Metcalf, 1 Stark. 53. Ante, 379.
[z] Gutteridge v. Smith, 2 Hen. Bla. 374. supra, note.
[a] Ante, 378 to 383.
[b] York v. Blott, 5 M. & S. 71.
[c] Sayer v. Kitchen, 1 Esp. Rep. 209. Assumpsit against acceptor of a bill, drawn upon him by one Holland, and also a further sum for goods sold and delivered. The plaintiff was unable to prove the hand-writing of the defendant subscribed to the bill by any witness who was acquainted with it, but offered the following as an admission by him, tantamount to proof of his acceptance. This evidence was, that of a clerk of the banking-house into which the bill in question had been paid, and who had brought the bill to the defendant's house for acceptance. The defendant was not then at home; but the clerk received for answer at the house, that the bill would be taken up when due. Mingay, for the plaintiff, contended, that this answer so received at the house of the defen-

dant to a bill, upon which his name appeared as drawee, was a sufficient acknowledgment of the acceptance, upon which to charge him. Lord Kenyon ruled, that it alone, without some proof of the defendant's hand-writing, or something to show that the acknowledgment came from him, was insufficient; the plaintiff having no further evidence to that point, the count on the note was abandoned.
[d] Ante, 379. 383.
[e] Garellis v. Alexander, 4 Esp. Rep. 37. Assumpsit on a foreign bill of exchange. To prove the hand-writing of the defendant, the plaintiff called the clerk of the defendant's attorney. His evidence was, that he had seen the defendant sign the bail bond in the cause, but had never seen him write on any other occasion. Being asked whether he believed the acceptance to be the hand-writing of the defendant, he said he could form no belief on the subject; it was like the hand-writing in which the bail bond was subscribed, and he was about to compare them together. Lord Kenyon told him, he must form a

2dly. Proof that defen- dant was party to the bill, &c.

every person's manner of writing there is a certain distinct prevailing character, which may be easily discovered by observation, and when once known, may be afterwards applied as a standard to try any other species of writing whose genuineness is disputed. A witness may therefore be called and asked whether he has seen the defendant write, and afterwards whether he believes the signature to the bill or note to be the defendant's hand-writing;[r] but it is reported to have been decided at Nisi Prius, that a person who has only seen a party write his surname, is not competent to prove his hand-writing to the christian as well as surname to an acceptance.[s] The usual course is to subpœna a witness who can swear he knows the defendant, and that he has seen him write frequently, or has frequently addressed letters to him, and receives answers in return ; and that from the knowledge he has thus acquired of his hand-writing, he believes the particular signature to be the defendant's hand-writing. A knowledge of the hand-writing acquired by a witness in the course of correspondence with the defendant, is sufficient to enable him to swear to his belief of the hand-writing;[s] but barely having seen letters, purporting to have been franked, by him, or other .papers, which he has no authentic information are of the defendant's hand-writing, is not sufficient.[i]

In forming this belief it has been observed, that a witness therefore, when called to speak of the identity of the defendant's hand-writing ought to judge solely from the impression which the hand-writing itself makes upon his mind, without taking any extrinsic circumstance into his consideration ;[k] and therefore where a witness said, that looking at the hand-writing he should have thought it to have been that of the

[386] party whose name it bore, but from his knowledge of him, he thought he could not have signed such a paper, it was held that this was *prima facie* evidence of the hand-writing ;[l] and on the same principle where it was contended that the paper produced was the forgery of a third person, evidence that such third person had forged the defendant's name to other instruments of a similar nature, was held to be inadmissible,[m] and even in one case which came before the court, the party who

judgment without such comparison of hands. He then looked on the bill again, and said it was like the hand-writing in which the defendant had subscribed the bail bond, but that he could not speak to any belief further than he had already done. Garrow, for the defendant, objected that there was not sufficient evidence, and that it would be of dangerous consequences to allow such loose evidence of a hand-writing to charge a party with a debt.

Lord Kenyon. This is the case of a foreign bill of exchange, and I think there is evidence to go to the jury, and that I am bound to leave it to them. To be sure mere comparison of hands is not admissible evidence of itself: that was Algernon Sydney's case ; but there the witness had never seen him write ; and the only evidence in the case was mere comparison of hands; but in the present case the witness has seen the defendant write, and he speaks to the likeness which the hand-writing, in which the bill is accepted, bears to that which he has seen the defendant actually

write; I therefore think that it is evidence to go to the jury.

But it has been holden, that a witness who has only seen the drawee write his name, pending the action for the purpose of showing the witness his usual mode of writing his acceptance, is not an admissible witness for such drawer to disprove his hand-writing to the bill, on which he is sued, because the defendant might write differently before the witness purposely to establish a defence. Stranger v. Searle, 1 Esp. Rep. 14, 15.

[r] Peake's Evid. 4th edit. 109, 110.—Phil. Evid. 3d edit. 422.

[s] Powell v. Ford, 2 Stark. 264.

[h] See Phil. Evid. 3d edit. 422, 23, 24, 427, 28. Peake's Evid. 4th edit. 110.

[i] Cary v. Pitt, Peake's Evid 4th. edit 110.

[k] Peake's Evid. 4th edit. 110.

[l] Da Costa v. Pym, Sittings at Guildhall after Trin. Term, 37 Geo. 3. Peake's Evid 4th edit. Appendix, 85.

[m] Balcetti v. Serani, Peake's Ni. P

contended that the hand-writing was a forgery, was only permitted, after a great deal of other evidence, to examine a clerk at the post-office, whose businees it is to inspect franks and detect forgeries, to prove that from the appearance of the hand-writing it was, in his opin-ion, a forgery, and not genuine hand-writing ; and in a subsequent case,[a] Lord Kenyon said, that such evidence was wholly inadmissible, and observed, that though in Revet *v.* Braham it was admitted, yet that in his direction to the jury he had laid no stress at all upon it. *2dly.* Proof that defendant was party to the bill, &c.

It has been observed, that the analogies of law appear strongly to support the admissibility of this evidence, for opinion founded on observation and experience is received in most questions of a similar nature. There is a certain freedom of character in that which is original, which imitation seldom attains, and the want of that freedom is more likely to be detected by one whose attention has been directed to the subject than by another who has never given his mind to such pursuits. It does not therefore seem too much to say that such evidence is in all cases inadmissible, though it certainly ought to be received with great caution, and meet with little attention, unless as corroborating other and stronger evidence.

The true distinction, as to the inadmissibility of such evidence seems to have been taken by Mr. Baron Hotham on the trial of The King *v.* Cator,[o] where the defendant being indicted for publishing a written libel, and a person from the post-office who had never seen him write being called as a witness, that Judge permitted the witness to give general evidence that the writing appeared to be in a feigned hand ; but when the witness was asked whether, on comparing such hand-writing with papers proved by others to be the genuine hand-writing of the defendant, he could say it was the disguised hand of the same person, his Lordship rejected the evidence attempted to be introduced by such examination, because it arose only from comparision of hands. The case of Revet *v.* Braham, may therefore still be considered as an existing authority to show, that for the purpose of proving generally and in the abstract that a hand-writing is *not genuine,* such evidence is admissible, though deserving of little attention for the want of freedom in the hand-writing. And the painting of the letters, as it was called by the witness in that case, may arise from the infirmity of the writer, or his not having formed a fixed character, or many other causes which a person unacquainted with the genuine hand-writing cannot take into his consideration. A tradesman who is daily making entries to his books, will acquire a more free and steady character than an illiterate person who can but just write his name ; and a man whose habits of life lead him to write much oftener and with less care, will still get more of a peculiar character in his hand-writing, all which circumstances should certainly be taken into the consideration of a jury before they give weight to such evidence. [**387**]

It has been well observed, that inasmuch as the mind arrives at the belief of hand-writing merely by recollection of the general character from an acquaintance by frequently seeing it, and not from the formation of particular letters or a single inspection, courts of justice have wisely rejected all evidence from bare comparison of hands unsupport-

112. Graft *v.* Lord Brownlow Bertie, Sittings at Westminster, after Trin. Term, 1777. MS. Peake's Evid. 4th edit. 110.　　a Cary *v.* Pitt, Peake's Evid. 4th edit. 110.　o 4 Esp. Rep. 117,

2dly. Proof that defendant was party to the bill, &c. ed by other circumstances ; they will not therefore permit two papers one of which is proved to be the hand-writing of a party to be delivered to a jury for the purpose of comparing them together, and thence inferring that the other is also of his hand-writing;[p] but where witnesses have been called to prove the similitude of hand-writing, and other witnesses have from the same premises drawn a different conclusion, this rule has been relaxed in favour of a jury whose habits of life have accustomed them to the sight of hand-writing.[q] but this mode of proceeding however seems rather a departure from the strict rules of evidence, and before an illiterate jury would probably not be adopted.[r]

In general the signature of a party to a bill or note may be proved as against him by his *admission;* and if he made such admission before the bill was due, and the holder received the bill on the faith of such representation, the party will be precluded afterwards from disputing the fact, or showing that the hand-writing was a forgery :[s] (496) and in **[388]** an action against a person as acceptor, though the plaintiff fail in proving the defendant's hand-writing, and it appear to be a forgery, yet proof that the defendant had paid several other bills, accepted in like manner, will establish his liability.[t] And an admission of a hand writing, made by the defendant, pending a treaty for compromising the suit. is evidence against him.[u] So in action against an indorser, proof that the defendant had a written letter, stating that he had received a bill, corresponding with that upon which the action was brought, and that after issue joined, he had declared that he came to town to hasten the trial of a cause brought against him, on an indorsement he had made upon a bill, and that he carried the cause down by proviso, was held sufficient.[x] But an admission in general only operates against the party making it, and therefore proof that one of the indorsers had confessed his signature is not admissible evidence in an action by an indorsee against the drawer of a bill:[y] and we have seen, that in an action against

[p] Macferson v. Thoytes. Peake's Rep. 20. Brookhard v. Woodley. id. note a.
[q] Allesbrook v. Roach, Sittings at Westminster after Trinity Term, 1795, MS. 1 Esp. Rep. 351, S. C. Dacosta v. Pym. Ante, 386.
[r] Peake's Evid. 4th edit. 110 to 115.
[s] Leach v. Buchanan, 4 Esp. Rep. 226. Cooper v. Le Blanc, 2 Stra. 1051. Ante, 185. Hart v. King, 12 Mod. 809. Bayl. 223.
[t] Barber v. Gingell, 3 Esp. Rep. 60. Ante, 25, note. Bayl. 224, 5.
[u] Walrige v. Kennison, 1 Esp. Rep. 143.

[x] Dale v. Lubbock, 1 Barn. K. B. 193 Bayl. 224.
[y] Hemmings v. Robinson, Barnes. 31 edit. 436. In an action by the indorsee of a note against the maker, it was reserved as a point whether the acknowledgment of an indorser was sufficient evidence to prove his indorsement, and the court held not. In Western v. Wilmott, tried at Westminster Hall, 5th July, 1820, before Abbott, C. J. plaintiff declared against defendant as acceptor of a bill, drawn by Berne, payable to his own order, indorsed by him to Smith, by him to Cross, and by him to the plaintiff. Plaintiff proved the

(496) But notwithstanding an acknowledgment of the signature to the note, the maker may produce evidence of persons acquainted with his hand-writing, to state their opinion that the signature is not genuine, and also to prove the same by signatures known to be his. Such an acknowledgment is not conclusive, and may be shown to have been made by mistake. *Hall* v. *Huse*, 10 Mass. Rep. 39. The acknowledgment of the maker of his hand-writing on the note does away the necessity of proving it by the subscribing witness. *Hall* v. *Phelps*, 2 John. Rep. 451. If the subscribing witness deny the execution of the note, it may be proved aliunde. Ibid. Where the subscribing witness is out of the state, other evidence is admissible to prove the hand-writing of the maker, and this before proving the hand-writing of the subscribing witness. *Horner* v. *Wallis*, 11 Mass. Rep. 309.

several drawers, indorsers, or acceptors, a mere admission upon *the* 2dly. Proof
pleadings by one of his signature will not exempt the plaintiff from that defendant was
proving it against the others, though an admission *in fact* would be other- party to the
wise.[a] The payment of money into court, generally, on the whole bill, &c.
declaration, precludes the defendant from disputing his signature.[a]

But an offer to pay a part as a compromise is no evidence, because,
as observed by Lord Mansfield, men must be permitted to endeavour
to buy their peace without prejudice to them, if the offer do not [389]
succeed.[b]

A promise by the acceptor or other party to pay the bill after it was
due will preclude the necessity for proof of the defendants, or any
other parties, hand-writing.[c]

Thirdly. It will be incumbent *on the plaintiff to prove his interest* in 3dly. Proof
the bill or note, or, in other words, how he became a party to it. The of the plaintiff's interest, &c.
payee or the *bearer* of a bill or note, originally payable to bearer, has in
general only to produce the instrument; though under suspicious circumstances, the bearer of a note transferrable by delivery, may be required
to prove that he or some person, under whom he makes his title, took it
bona fide, and gave valuable consideration for it.[d] But if in an action
by the indorsee of a note, payable to A. or bearer, the indorsement by
A. be unnecessarily stated, it must be proved.[e] Proof of a promissory
note payable to A.B., generally, is *prima facie* evidence of a promise to
A.B. the father, and not to A. B. the son, the names being the same;
but A. B., the son, bringing the action, and being described as the
younger in the declaration, and being in possession of the note, is entitled to recover upon it.[f]

indorsement by Berne, and by Cross, and
that Smith, on being applied to after the
defendant was shown the bill and indorsements, and admitted the indorsement of
Smith as his hand-writing. It was also
proved, that the defendant, after the bill
became due, was shown the bill, and informed that plaintiff was the holder; whereupon he admitted it was a just debt, and
that he would pay shortly. Chitty, for
plaintiff, submitted, that such acknowledgment by Smith was sufficient in this action,
and that defendant's admission was also
equivalent to an account stated. But Abbott, C. J. said, that such admission by a
third person could not affect the defendant;
and that as there was no original defendant,
or priority between the parties, this was
not an account stated ; therefore plaintiff
was nonsuited. But see post, 396, note.

[1] *Ante, 881, 2.

[a] Gutteridge *v.* Smith, 3 Hen. Bla. 374.
Watkins *v.* Towers, 2 T. R. 275. Guillod
v. Nock, 1 Esp. Rep. 347. Israel *v.* Benjamin, 3 Campb. 40.

[b] Bull. N. P. 236. Gunn *v.* Gulloch,
Westminster, Sittings after Trinity Term,
1775.

[c] Helmsley *v.* Loader, 2 Campb. 450.
Jones *v.* Morgan, id. 474. Ante, 377, note.
Bosanquet *v.* Anderson, 6 Esp. Rep. 43.
Post, 396, note.

[d] Per Lord Mansfield, C. J. in Grant *v.*
Vaughan, 3 Burr. 1627. Ante, 68, note.

[e] Waynam *v.* Bend, 1 Campb. 175. Rex
v. Stevens, 5 East, 244. 1 Smith, 437. S. C.;
and see ante, 377, note.

Waynam *v.* Bend, 1 Campb. 175. Action against the defendant as maker of a
promissory note for 200l., payable to L.
Toader or bearer. The declaration stated,
that L. Toader, to whom the sum of money mentioned in the note was payable,
indorsed it to the plaintiff. No evidence
of this indorsement being given, it was
contended, that the plaintiff's case was im-
perfect, and that he must be *called.* The
counsel on the opposite side answered,
that the averment being unnecessary, might
be rejected; and that at any rate the plaintiff
might recover under the count for money
had and received, the note being for value
received. Lord Ellenborough held, that
as an indorsement was stated, though unnecessarily in the count on the note, it
must be proved; and that the plaintiff could
not recover under any of the money counts,
as he was not an original party to the bill,
and there was no evidence of any value
being received by the defendant from him.
A witness, however, was afterwards found
who proved the hand-writing of L. Toader,
and the plaintiff had a verdict.

[f] Sweeting *v.* Fowler and another,
1 Stark. 106.

3dly. Proof of the plaintiff's interest, &c.

So where the first indorsement was in full, directing the acceptor to pay the bill to a certain person, who has indorsed the same to the plaintiff, he must in an action against the drawee or acceptor, prove the indorsement of that person,[p] and all the indorsements stated, though unnecessarily, in the declaration, must be proved,[q] and therefore, it is usual, where there are several indorsements, to insert two counts, one stating the several indorsements, and the other describing the plaintiff as the immediate indorsee of the first indorser.[r]

But if the first indorsement was in blank, it will be unnecessary even in an action against the drawer or acceptor, to prove any of the subsequent indorsements, although they were in full, but they may be struck out at the time of the trial, unless they be unnecessarily stated in the declaration.[s] And a small mistake in the declaration in the [393] name of the indorser, as describing him as Phillip, when the bill and the evidence prove him to be Phillips, will not be material.[t]

If the bill or note be payable to the order of several persons not in partnership, the hand-writing of each must be proved,[u] and though it is reported to have been held in one case, that an acceptance after an indorsement by one of the payees, admits the regularity of the indorsement;[x] that decision appears to be contrary to former authorities, though, if a bill have several indorsements upon it at the time it is presented for acceptance, and the drawee, when he accepts, expressly promises to pay the bill, it has been decided that the indorsements are admitted.[y]

---

ner; it was not proved that Henry was so empowered. The defendant might say, that he had, by his acceptance, admitted the existence of the firm of Stachen and Co. and that the bill was drawn by Henry as their agent, but he does not thereby admit that the indorsement was on the same terms, and it was, therefore, necessary that such procuration should be proved. Rule discharged.

[p] Ante, 134.

[q] Cooper v. Lindo, B. R. Sittings, London, after Mich. Term, 52 Geo. 3 Selw. 4th edit. 336, n. k. Bosanquet v. Anderson, 6 Esp. Rep. 43, post, 396, note. Sedforth and another v. Chambers, 1 Stark. 326, post, 396, and ante, 377.

[r] Ante, 359. Chaters v. Bell, 4 Esp. Rep. 210.

[s] Ante, 135.

[t] Forman v. Jacob, 1 Stark. Rep. 47. It appeared that the name of the indorser was Phillip Phillips; and it was objected that this varied from the allegation of an indorsement by Phillip Phillip, the person being different. The bill itself was payable to Phillip Phillips, and the name was so indorsed on the bill. Per Lord Ellenborough, whether the name on the bill be the party's false or true name is immaterial, if it be his name of trade, the only question is as to the identity of the person.

[u] Carvick v. Vickery, Dougl. 653.

[x] Jones and another v. Radford, K. B. Sittings after Hilary Term, 46 Geo. 3.

1 Campb. 83, (but see Carvick v. Vickery Dougl. 630, 653. Hankey v. Wilson. Say. 223, contra,) held, that in an action upon a bill drawn, payable to the order of two persons not partners, indorsed by one in the name of both, and afterwards accepted by the defendant, that the regularity of the indorsement could not be disputed. Action by the indorsee against the acceptor of a bill of exchange, payable to two persons of the names of Hopkins and M'Michell. The bill had been indorsed by Hopkins in the name of himself and M'Michell, and defendant had accepted it with the indorsement upon it. The defence was, that the payees were not partners, and that the bill ought therefore to have been indorsed by both. But Lord Ellenborough held, that the defendant having accepted the bill indorsed by one for himself and the other, could not now dispute the regularity of this indorsement, but see Carvick v. Vickery, Dougl. 85. Smith v. Chester, 1 T. R 654. Ante, 390.

[y] Sir Joseph Hankey and Company v. Wilson, Sayer's Rep. 223. Upon a rule to show cause why a new trial should not be had in an action of assumpsit it appeared, that the action was brought by the plaintiffs, as indorsees of a bill of exchange; that the defendant had accepted the bill; that there was no actual proof that the name of one of the indorsers on the bill was of his hand-writing; that the name of that indorser, and the names of

In an action against the drawer or acceptor of a bill payable to the order of several persons in partnership, it is in general necessary to prove the partnership, and the hand-writing of one of them or of an agent in the name of the firm.[a]

Where a bill ash been made payable to the order of a fic itious person, it has been decided, that proof, that the party sued, knew of that circumstance at the time he became a party to the bill, or before he transferred the same, will dispense with proof of the hand-writing of the supposed indorser.[a]

Where several persons sue as indorsees of a bill of exchange, if the bill appears indorsed in blank, there is no necessity for their proving that they were in partnership together, or that the bill was indorsed or delivered to them jointly.[b] But when a bill of exchange is payable or indorsed specially to a firm, it has often been ruled, that in an action by the payees or indorsees strict evidence must be given that the firm consists of the persons who sue as plaintiffs on the record.[c] And where a bill of exchange was, by the direction of the payee, indorsed in blank and delivered to A. B. and Co. who were bankers, on the account of the estate of an insolvent, which was vested in trustees for the benefit of his creditors, it was held that A. and B. two of the members of the firm, and also trustees, could not, conjointly with a third trustee who is not a member of the firm, maintain an action against the indorser without some evidence of the transfer of the bill to them as trustees by the firm, by delivery or otherwise.[d] When it is incumbent

all the other indorsers were upon the bill at the time of its being accepted ; *that at the time of his accepting it, the defendant promised to pay the bill,* and that upon this evidence, which was left by Ryder, Ch. J. to the jury, a verdict was found for the plaintiffs. The question was, whether upon this evidence, the matter ought to have been left to the jury? It was holden that it ought. And by the court.—It is in general necessary to give actual proof that the name of every indorser is of his hand-writing ; but it is not necessary to do this in every case. In the present case, it was a matter proper for the determination of a jury, *whether the acceptance of the bill when all the indorsers names were upon it, together with the promise to pay did not amount to an admission* that the name of every indorser is of his hand writing, inasmuch as such an admission would supercede the necessity of actual proof, that the name of any indorser is of his hand-writing.

[a] Ante, 381, 2.

[a] Ante, 64, note.

[b] Ord and others *v.* Portal, 3 Campb. 239. Rordasnz and another *v.* Leach, 1 Stark. 446. Ord and two others *v.* Portal, 3 Campb. 239. Action by the plaintiffs as indorsees, against the defendant as acceptor of a bill of exchange, drawn by one Sted, payable to his own order, and indorsed by him in blank. The plaintiffs case being closed without showing that the plaintiffs were in partnership, or that the bill had been indorsed to them jointly, Garrow, for the defendant insisted that they ought to be nonsuited. The declaration alleged, that the drawer of the bill indorsed and delivered the bill to the three plaintiffs, and there was no evidence whatsoever in support of his allegation. Per Lord Ellenborough. There is no occasion for any such evidence. The indorsement in blank conveys a joint right of action to as many as agree in suing on the bill. The plaintiffs had a verdict.

Rordasnz and another *v.* Leach, 1 Stark. 446. The two plaintiffs sued as the indorsees of two bills of exchange. The bills had been indorsed in blank, and the only question was, whether it was incumbent on the plaintiffs to prove their joint title to sue on the bill by showing that they were partners, or by proving a transfer to them jointly. Lord Ellenborough held, that it was not. Verdict for the plaintiffs.

[c] Note. in Ord *v.* Portal, 3 Campb. 240.

[d] Machell and others *v.* Kinnear, 1 Stark. 499. This was an action by Machell, Boucher, and Birbeck, as the indorsees of a bill of exchange, against t ie defendant as the indorser. The bill in question was dated on the 21st of August, 1815, and was drawn by Corbett on Goldie, for the payment of 400l. six months after date to his own order, indorsed by Corbett to Kinnear, the defendant, and indor-

3dly. Proof on the plaintiffs to prove the names of the partners of a firm, the coun-
of the plain-
tiff's inter- sel for such plaintiffs may suggest to the witness called to prove the
est, &c. partnership, the names of the component members of the firm.[e]

[396]   It has been decided, that the admission by an indorser of a promissory
note of his hand-writing is sufficient evidence of the indorsement in an
action against the maker, because such admission is in derogation of
the party's own title to the note, and therefore admissible.[f]   But this

sed by the latter in blank. The principal
question was, whether under the circumstances such a right had been transferred to
the plaintiffs as entitled them to sue upon
the bill.   It appeared that Machell and
Boucher were two of the partners of which
the firm of Langton and Co. consisted.
Machell, Boucher, and Birkbeck, the three
plaintiffs, were the trustees of the estate of
Holder, an insolvent, for the benefit of the
creditors; Birkbeck not being a member of
the firm of Langton and Co.   The defendant being indebted to the estate of Holder,
transmitted the bill in question to his clerk
in Liverpool, with directions to deliver it
to Langton and Co. on the account of
Holder's estate, and either to indorse it or
to give them a letter of guarantee to secure
the payment.   The clerk accordingly indorsed it in blank and delivered it to Langton and Co.   Garrow, A. G. for the defendant, objected that it was not competent to
two of the firm of Langton and Co. to as-
sociate with themselves a third person who
was a stranger, for the purpose of bringing
an action on the bill, without showing that
the bill had been transferred by Langton and
Co. to the plaintiffs, thus associated.   Mar-
ryat, for the plaintiffs, contended, that since
the bill had been indorsed in blank, it was
competent to any number of persons to as-
sociate together for the purpose of bringing
an action.   And he cited the case of Ord
and others v. Portal, 3 Campb. 239, where
it was held, that an indorsement in blank
conveyed a joint right of action to as many
as agreed to sue upon the bill ; per Lord
Ellenborough, the bill having been indorsed and delivered to Langton and Co. according to Kinnear's direction, Langton
and Co. had authority to appropriate it.
Since it was paid to them on account of
Holder's estate, if they had received the
amount it would have been money had and
received by them on account of the estate,
but the evidence, as it stands, proves the
interest in the bill to be in Langton and Co.
It would be sufficient to prove that Langton and Co. consented to appropriate the
bill to the three plaintiffs as trustees.   If
Langton and Co. had indorsed it to the
plaintiffs, the right to sue would have been
clear, or they might have transferred the
right by a delivery of the bill, but without
some evidence of this kind, the right to sue
still remains in Langton and Co.   Had it
not been for the evidence of the particular

transfer to Langton and Co. an indorsement
in blank might have entitled the parties,
who bring the action to recover.   Plaintiffs nonsuited.

[e] Acerro and others v. Petroni, 1 Stark.
100.   Assumpsit by the plaintiffs, bankers
at Paris, upon an account stated by the defendant.   The witness called to prove the
partnership of the plaintiff could not recollect the names of the component members
of the firm so as to repeat them without
suggestion, but said he might possibly recognise them, if suggested to him.   Lord
Ellenborough, alluding to a case tried before Lord Mansfield, on which the witness
had been allowed to read a written list of
names, ruled, that there was no objection
to asking the witness whether certain specified persons were members of the firm.
The witness recollected the surnames but
not the christian names, of those mentioned
as members of the firm, and their christian
names being specified in the declaration in
the count upon the account stated, and the
terms of the acknowledgment being g n-
erally to Acerro and Co. the plaintiffs were
nonsuited.   Sed quære as to the christian
names, which are not in general material.
See Hodenpyl v De Vingerhoed and another, ante, 381.   3 Campb. 29.   2 Marsh.
159.

[f] Maddocks v. Hankey, 2 Esp. Rep. 647
Assumpsit by the indorsee of a promissory
note against the maker; the promissory note
was drawn by the defendant payable to one
Sellier, who indorsed to Rymer, by whom
it was indorsed to the plaintiff.   The plaintiff proved the hand writing of the defendant and Rymer, by persons acquainted
with them, and the only doubt in the case
was as to the hand-writing of Sellier   The
evidence to establish that fact was of a person who had gone to Sellier, he then being
in prison, and asked him if that was his
hand-writing.—To whom he acknowledged
that it was.   Gibbs, for the defendant, objected to this evidence, insisting, that such
an admission of a fact was not evidence
against the defendant, as it might be material to ascertain the time when the indorsement had been made.   Lord Kenyon said,
that he thought it was admissible and sufficient evidence, as it went in derogation of
the parties own title to the note, but he offered to reserve the case.   The plaintiff had
a verdict; but see ante, 388. note.

doctrine seems now over-ruled;[g] the indorser himself may be called as a witness to prove his own hand-writing ;[h] and he may be called to prove his indorsement after another witness for the plaintiff has negatived it ;[i] though it has been doubted whether, after the plaintiff has failed in proving the indorsement by one witness, he can call any other person.[k] And a promise to pay,[l] or offer to renew,[m] made to an indorsee after the bill was due, dispenses with the necessity for proof of the indorsement, because it admits the title of the holder. And after a partnership has been established in evidence, the admission of a partner, though not a party to the suit, is evidence as to joint contracts against

3dly. Proof of the plaintiff's interest, &c.

[397]

---

[g] Western v. Wilmott, and Hemmings v. Robinson, ante, 388.

[h] Richardson v. Allan, 2 Stark. 334.

[i] Id. ibid.

[k] Id. ibid.

[l] Hankey v. Wilson, Say. 223. Ante, 392, note.

[m] Bosanquet v. Anderson, 6 Esp. Rep. 44. Sedforth and another v. Chambers, 1 Stark. 326. Bayl. 220.

Bosanquet v. Anderson, 6 Esp. Rep. 43. In an action by the indorsee of a bill of exchange, where several indorsements have taken place, which are laid in the declaration, though necessary to be proved in general, yet if defendant applies for time to the holder, and offer terms, it is an admission of the holder's title, and a waiver of proof of all the indorsements except the first. Assumpsit by the plaintiff as indorsee of a bill of exchange, drawn by Wilson in his own favour on the defendant who accepted it, and indorsed over by Wilson. The declaration stated several indorsements on the bill. The evidence for the plaintiff was only proof of the hand-writing of the first indorser, and that the defendant, when the bill became due came to the plaintiffs, who were bankers, and then holders of the bill, and offered another bill in the place of it, he being then unable to take it up. It was contended for the defendant that it was necessary for the plaintiff to prove all the indorsements on the bill stated in the declaration, for that by the averments so made he had bound himself to prove them, though if he had not done so and declared only on the first indorsement, he might have recovered on that only. It was answered by the plaintiff's counsel that it was sufficient for the plaintiff to prove the hand-writing of the first indorser under the circumstances above stated; that of his offering terms to the plaintiff and thereby admitting the bill to be his; and that there was no necessity for proving the hand-writing of all the indorsers though so laid in the declaration, as by such admission and offer he admitted the plaintiff's title to the bill, and thereby waived the necessity of such proof as would be otherwise necessary. Lord Ellenborough said, that the acceptor by his acceptance admitted the hand-writing of his correspondent, the drawer, but if

payable to the drawer's own order, his hand-writing as such indorser must in every case be proved, as that put the bill into circulation, and though he accepted the bills with many names on it, if they were laid in the declaration they should be proved ; but he was of opinion that the offer here made by the acceptor to pay the bill to the plaintiffs, who then held the bill, with all the names on it, was a sufficient admission of the plaintiff's title, which was derived through the several indorsements, and of the defendant's liability so as to supercede the necessity of proof of each persons hand-writing. Verdict for plaintiff.

Sedforth and another v. Chambers, 1 Stark. 826. This was an action by the indorsees of a bill of exchange against the indorser. The bill was drawn by Fish, on Hill and Co., payable four months after date to the order of Fish, and indorsed by Fish to the defendant, by the defendant to Sheckles, by Sheckles to Niblock and Co., and the latter to the plaintiffs. All the indorsements were stated in the declaration. The plaintiffs proved all the indorsements except that of Sheckles, and in order to supercede the proof of this indorsement they gave in evidence a *letter written by the defendant to the plaintiffs, offering to give them a substituted bill to be approved of by any moderate person*, but stating that he had not money to take it up with ; adding, that he hoped it was not in the hands of Niblock and Co. At the time this letter was written the bill was in the hands of the solicitor for the plaintiffs, and the indorsements were complete. The Attorney-General for the plaintiffs submitted, that this evidence was sufficient without further proof, and cited the case of Bosanquet v. Anderson, 6 Esp. Rep. 43, to show that an application by a defendant for time was an admission of liability. Lord Ellenborough remarking, that the hope expressed by the defendant that the bill was not in the hands of Niblock and Co, who were indorsers subsequent to Sheckles, showed that he knew the channel through which the plaintiffs title had been derived, was of opinion that the evidence amounted to proof of their title through that channel. Verdict for the plaintiffs.

any other partner, as well after the determination of the partnership as during its continuance.[o] But although a bill of exchange has been shown to the drawer, with the name of the payee indorsed upon it, and he merely objects to paying it, that he had drawn it without consideration, in an action against him by the indorsee, this does not dispense with regular proof of the indorsement.[p] The payment of money into court generally, on the whole declaration, amounts to an admission of the indorsement, and dispenses with the necessity of proving it.[p]

In an action against an *indorser* of a bill or note, the hand-writing of the drawer,[q] and all *prior* indorsers[r] being admitted by the [398] defendant's indorsement, they need not be proved.　But if a *subsequent* indorsement be stated in the declaration they must be proved, and therefore it is usual when there are indorsers subsequent to the defendant, whom the plaintiff does not wish to discharge, to insert one count, stating all the indorsements, and another describing the plaintiff as immediate indorsee of the defendant.[s]

In an action at the suit of an executor against the acceptor of a bill on a promise laid to the testator, and plaintiff must prove that the bill was accepted in the testator's life-time ;[t] and, as we shall hereafter see, when a bill or note is attempted to be set off against the claim of the assignees of a bankrupt, the party must prove that the note came to his hands before the bankruptcy.[u] But if the act of bankruptcy were secret, and the bill or note proposed to be set off, were afterwards received by the party two calendar months before the commission was issued, and without notice of the bankruptcy, he may set them off.[x]

When the *drawer* of a bill payable to the order of a third person and *returned to and taken up by him,* sues the acceptor, in order to show that the right of action has become vested in him, he should be prepared to prove such return to him,[y] and it has been considered, that

[o] Wood and others v. Braddick, 1 Taunt. 134. Phil. Ev. 3d ed. 75, 6.
[o] Duncan v. Scott. 1 Campb. 104.
[p] Gutteridge v. Smith, 2 Hen. Bla. 374.
[q] Lambert v. Pack, 1 Salk. 127. 1 Ld. Raym. 443. 12 Mod. 244. Holt, 117. S. C. Free v, Rawlings, Holt C. N. P. 550.
[r] Id. ibid. Critchlow v. Parry, 2 Campb. 182. Chaters v. Bell, 4 Esp. Rep. 210. Ante, 359, 360. Bayl. 220.
Critchlow v. Parry, 2 Campb. 192. Action by the indorsee against the indorser of a bill of exchange. The declaration stated several indorsements prior to that of the defendant, which was immediately to the plaintiff. A question arose whether, upon proof of the defendant's hand-writing it was necessary to prove the hand-writing of any of the prior indorsers. Lord Ellenborough at first doubted whether it was not necessary in this case, as well as in an action against the acceptor, to prove all the indorsements that were mentioned in the declaration, and particularly that of the original

payee. Clark, for the plaintiff, contended, that the defendant's indorsement admitted all antecedent indorsements, that even if they were forged, be would be liable ; that he was to be considered as the drawer of a new bill of exchange, and that his contract was very different from that of the acceptor, who only undertook to pay to the payee, or his order, and against whom, therefore, a title through the payee, must be established. Lord Ellenborough was of this opinion and the plaintiff had a verdict.
[s] Ante, 359. Bosanquet v. Anderson. 6 Esp. Rep. 43. Sedford v. Chambers, 1 Stark. 326. Ante, 396.
[t] Anon. 12 Mod. 447. Sarell v. Wae 3 East, 409.
[u] Dickson v. Evans, 6 T. R. 57. Moor v. Wright, 2 Marsh. 209. 6 Taunt. 417 S. C. Oughterlony v. Easterby, 4 Taunt 888. See post, tit. *Bankruptcy.*
[x] 46 Geo. 3. c. 135. s. 3.
[y] As to such action, see ante, 343, 4: and Simmons v. Parminter, 1 Wils. 185. Bro. P. C. 601.

when a prior indorser, who has been obliged to pay a subsequent indor- 3dly. Proof of the plaintil's interest, &c.
ser, sues the acceptor, he should prove such payment.[a]

In an action by an *accommodation acceptor*, against the drawer for [399]
money paid, or specially for not indemnifying the plaintiff, he should
prove that the bill has been in circulation, and the production of the
bill from the custody of the acceptor, is not *prima facie* evidence of
his having paid it, without proof that it was once in circulation after it
had been accepted, nor is payment to be presumed from a receipt
indorsed on the bill, unless such receipt is shown to be in the hand-
writing of a person entitled to demand payment.[a] It has, however,
been held, that a general receipt on the back of a bill is *prima facie*
evidence of its having been paid by the acceptor, and will not of itself
be evidence of a payment by the drawer, though it is produced
by him.[b]

We have seen, that in some cases, the plaintiff will be called upon Considera-
to prove the consideration, which he gave for the bill or note.[c] In an tion.
action by the indorsee of a bill of exchange, if it appear that a prior [400]
party made it under duress, or was defrauded of it, and the plaintiff
has previous notice to do so, he must be prepared to prove under what
circumstances, and for what value he became the holder.[d]

---

[a] Mendez v. Carreroon, sed quære.

Mendez v, Carreroon, 1 Lord Raym.
742. In case upon a bill of exchange
upon the evidence at the trial before Holt, C. J. at Guildhall, Nov. 23,
Mich. Term, 12 William 3, the case was
this: A. drew a bill of exchange upon B.
payable to C. at Paris; B. accepted the
bill, &c. indorsed it, payable to D., D. to
E., E. to F., F. to G., G. demanded the
bill to be paid by B., and upon non-payment, G. protested it within the time, &c.
and then G. brought an action against D.,
and it was well brought, and he recovered;
afterwards D. brought an action against B.,
and though D produced the bill and the
protest, yet because he could not produce
a receipt for the money paid by him to G.
upon the protest, as the custom is among
merchants, as several merchants on their
oaths affirmed, he was nonsuited. But
Holt, C. J. seemed to be of opinion, that
if he had proved payment by him to G. it
had been well enough.

[a] Pfiel v. Van Battenberg, 2 Campb. 439.
Action for money lent. The plaintiff's
case was, that he had accepted and paid
several bills of exchange for the defendant's accommodation. The bills were
produced by the plaintiff, and proved to
have been drawn by the defendant. They
were likewise receipted in the usual form
of bills paid, but it did not appear by
whom the receipts were written. Richardson contended that the simple production
of the bills by the acceptor, was *prima
facie* evidence of payment. They could
not have got into his hands unless he had
paid them, and the presumption that an instrument in the possession of the person
liable upon it is satisfied, has been invaria-

bly acted upon. But the receipts indorsed
on these bills put the matter beyond all
doubt, as the defendant was guilty of
forgery if the bills had not been paid, and
the law would not presume that a man had
committed a capital offence. Lord Ellenborough. Show that the bills were once
in circulation after being accepted, and I
will presume that they got back to the acceptor's hands by his having paid them.
But when he merely produces them, how
do I know that they were ever in the
hands of the payee; or any indorsee, with
his name upon them as acceptor? it is
very possible, that when they were left for
acceptance, he refused to deliver them
back, and having detained them, now produces them as evidence of a loan of money.
Nor do I think the receipts carry the matter a bit further, unless you show them to
be in the hand-writing of the defendant, or
some other person authorized to receive
payment of the bills. A man cannot be
allowed to manufacture evidence for himself at the risk of being convicted of forgery; and it is possible, that though the bills
are unsatisfied, these receipts may have
been fraudulently indorsed without the
plaintiff's privity. The fact of payment
still hangs in doubt, and you must do something more to turn the balance. Prove the
bills out of the plaintiff's possession accepted, and I will presume that they got back
again by payment. If you do not, the plaintiff must be called. However, a witness
afterwards swore that the defendant had
acknowledged the debt, and the plaintiff
had a verdict.

[b] Scholey v. Walsby, Peake's Rep. 24, 5.
[c] Ante, 68, 69, 70, &c.
[d] Duncan v. Scott, 1 Campb. 100. Ante,

Considera-
tion.

But the defendant will not be allowed to call on the plaintiff to prove the consideration which he gave for the bill, unless he has given him reasonable notice that he will be required to offer such proof, so that the plaintiff may come to the trial prepared to establish his consideration.[d] And the merely giving a notice that the plaintiff will be required to prove what consideration he gave, is not sufficient to throw the burden upon him; some suspicion must first be cast upon his title, by showing that the bill was obtained from the defendant, or some previous holder, by undue means, after which, and not till then, the plaintiff will be required to prove how he became the holder.[e] And though it has been decided, that when the plaintiff has in due time received a notice from the defendant to prove the consideration, he ought to do so in opening his case to the jury; and that after his counsel have closed his case, he shall not be permitted to go into evidence of con-

[401] sideration, in reply to the defendant's case;[g] yet a different practice now prevails, and the plaintiff is allowed, after the defendant has proved that he received no value, and has cast a suspicion on the plaintiff's case, to go into full proof of the circumstances, under which he holds the bill.[h] If, however, the defendant can make out a strong case of fraud or want of consideration against the plaintiff, sufficient to establish a defence, it does not then seem necessary to give the plaintiff any notice to prove the consideration.[i]

68, note. Paterson v. Hardacre, 4 Taunt. 114. Ante, 68, note. Rees v. Marquis of Headfort, 2 Campb. 574.

Rees v. Marquis of Headfort, 2 Campb 574. This was an action against the defendant as acceptor of a bill of exchange, drawn by one Whitton, payable to his own order, indorsed by him to Chamberlain and Co. and by them to the plaintiff. The plaintiff made out a *prima facie* case; but Whitton, the drawer, having been called to prove the hand-writing of the parties, it appeared from his cross examination, that he himself had never received any consideration for the bill, and had been tricked out of it by means of a gross fraud. Lord Ellenborough held, that on this ground the plaintiff was bound to prove what consideration he gave for it; and as he was not prepared to do so, his Lordship directed a nonsuit.

[e] Paterson v. Hardacre, 4 Taunt. 114. Ante, 68, note. Mansfield, C. J. declared the decision of the court to be, that wherever a defendant meant to avail himself, as a defence against an action brought upon a bill of exchange, of the circumstances that the bill had been lost, or fraudulently obtained, and that the plaintiff had no right to the possession thereof, it was necessary that the defendant should distinctly give notice to the plaintiff, that he meant to insist, at the trial, that the plaintiff should prove the consideration upon which he received the bill; and no such notice having been given in this case, the rule must be discharged.

[f] Reynolds v. Chettle, 2 Campb. 596. The defendant had given the plaintiff notice to prove what consideration he gave for the bill, which it was submitted he was bound to prove accordingly. Lord Ellenborough. The notice is insufficient to throw this burthen on the plaintiff, you must first cast some suspicion upon his title, by showing that the bill was obtained from the defendant, or some previous holder, by force or by fraud. The plaintiff had a verdict.

[g] Per Lord Ellenborough, in Delanney v. Mitchell, 1 Stark. 439. This was an action by the plaintiff as the indorsee of a bill of exchange, against the defendant as acceptor. Scarlett, for the plaintiff, having adduced the usual documentary proofs, was inclined to rest his case there, intimating, that if in the course of the cause, it should become necessary, he was prepared to prove the consideration given for the bill. The Attorney-General insisted, that since notice had been given, that one ground of defence was the want of consideration, it would not be competent to the plaintiff, after having closed his case, to go subsequently into such evidence. Lord Ellenborough held, that after such notice he could not.

Humbert v. Ruding, K. B. Westminster, 13th July, 1817, action on a bill of exchange. The defendant had given notice to the plaintiff to prove the consideration of the bill, and Lord Ellenborough said, I think, as this is the case, you must go into proof of the consideration in the first instance. Mr. Jervis for the plaintiff.

[h] Abbott, C. J. has, at Nisi Prius, declared that this is the correct course.

[i] Green v. Deakin and others, 2 Stark 347.

Considera-
tion.

We have already stated, when the want of consideration or the illegality of it will affect the plaintiff's right of action.[k] By a recent statute it is declared, that usury in the consideration shall not affect a *bona fide* holder, who became so after the 10th day of June, 1818.[l] In the case of a bank-note, unless there be a strong presumption of fraud or want of consideration, the plaintiff's interest in the security cannot be disturbed.[m]

4thly. In an action against the acceptor upon a general acceptance to pay the bill according to its tenor, and in an action against the maker of a promissory note, it is not necessary to prove *a presentment for payment*, because such presentment, we have seen, is not essential to the action.[n] So in the Court of King's Bench, where a bill is drawn, payable generally as to place, but has been accepted payable at a banker's or other particular place, it is not the practice in an action against the acceptor to go into proof of a presentment at such place, unless such presentment has been unnecessarily averred.[o] But as in the court of Common Pleas a different doctrine has been entertained by some of the Judges, it is advisable for the plaintiff to be prepared to prove that fact.[p] When in the body of a bill, or in the address at the foot, or in a body of a note, it has been made payable at a particular place, the contract is considered as qualified, and a presentment there must be averred and proved in an action against the acceptor of the bill or maker of the note.[q] In short, whenever a particular presentment is essential to the support of the action, or when it has been averred, it must be proved.[r] In case of a *conditional* acceptance, it is necessary to allege, as well as prove, that the terms of the condition have been performed.[s]

4thly. Evidence of the breach of contract, and other circumstances to sustain the action.

[402]

In an action against the drawer or indorser of a bill, or the indorser of a note, as his contract is only to pay in case the party primarily liable does not, the default of such party must be proved, or some evidence

[k] Ante, 68 to 89.
[l] 58 Geo. 3. c. 93.
[m] Solomon *v.* Bank of England, 13 East, 135. Ante, 148. King *v.* Milson, 2 Campb. 5.
King *v.* Milson, 2 Campb. 5. Possession is *prima facie* evidence of property in negotiable instruments. Therefore, in trover for a bank-note, it is not a *prima facie* case for the plaintiff to prove that the note belonged to him, and that the defendant afterwards converted it, and the defendant will not be called upon to show his title to the note, without evidence from the other side, that he got possession of it *mala fide* or without consideration. Trover for a 50*l.* bank of England note. The plaintiff's case was, that he had lost the note from his pocket in the street, and that the defendant, into whose possession it soon afterwards came, was not the *bona fide* holder of it for a valuable consideration. Lord Ellenborough. "There is a distinction between negotiable instruments and common chattels; with respect to the former, possession is *prima facie* evidence of property. I must presume that the defendant, when possessed of this note, was

a *bona fide* holder for a valuable consideration. It lies upon you to impeach his title. You might have thrown so much suspicion upon his conduct in the transaction, as to have rendered it necessary for him to prove from whom he received the note, and what consideration he gave for it. But I think you have not done so. The suspicious circumstances, detailed by the witnesses, may be accounted for from the defendant's ignorance. It would greatly impair the credit, and impede the circulation of negotiable instruments, if persons holding them could, without strong evidence of fraud, be compelled by any prior holder to disclose the manner in which they received them." Plaintiff nonsuited.
[n] Ante, 249.
[o] Ante, 254, note.
[p] Ante, 257, note.
[q] Ante, 250, 1, 2.
[r] As to the cases when a presentment is necessary, see ante, 249 to 259.
[s] Langston *v.* Corney, 4 Campb. 176. Anderson *v.* Hick, 3 Campb. 179; and see Wynne *v.* Raikes, 5 East, 514. 2 Smith. 98. S. C.

4thly. Evidence of the breach of contract, and other circumstances to sustain the action.

[403] must be adduced to dispense with the necessity for such proof. Thus in an action against the drawer or indorser of a bill, or the indorser of a note, it is necessary to prove a *presentment* to the drawee for payment.[1] Though it is not necessary to prove that the presentment was made by the person named in the declaration.[2] Nor is it necessary in an action against the indorser of a bill, to prove any presentment to, or demand upon the drawer, because the indorser by the act of indorsement, engages that the bill shall be paid, which contract being broken by the dishonour of the bill, the holder is entitled to sue without reference to the drawer's breach of contract.[3] When the action is for

[1] Pardo v. Fuller, 2 Comyns, 579. Heylyn v. Adamson, 2 Burr. 676.

Pardo v. Fuller, 2 Comyns, 579. This was an action on a promissory note against the indorser. At the trial before Chief Justice Willes, at Guildhall, it was doubted whether the plaintiff ought not to prove a demand upon the drawer, before the action was brought ; the matter of proof was left to the jury, whether a demand was made or not. On a motion for a new trial, Judge Fortescue mentioned the case of Davies v. Mason, 1 Geo. 2, in the court of Common Pleas, wherein it was agreed by the court, that there ought to be a demand upon the drawer, for the indorser undertook conditionally only, if the drawer did not pay. Indeed, if a note be forged, Chief Justice Holt held the indorser liable though on demand, and indeed no demand can be, for when a note is forged, there is no drawer. So on a note payable to a man or bearer, no demand need be from him to whom it is made payable. But a new trial was denied, for the evidence of the demand was left to the jury who were proper judges of that fact, and knew best the course of dealing.

[2] Boehm v. Campbell, 1 Gow, C. N. P. 55.

[3] Heylyn v. Adamson, 2 Burr. 669. 675. Bromley v. Frasier, 1 Stra. 441.

It was determined in the case of Heylyn v. Adamson, 2 Burr. 669, which examines and reconciles the authorities upon the subject, that to entitle the indorsee of an inland bill of exchange, to bring an action against the indorser upon failure of payment by the drawee it is not necessary to make any demand of or inquiry after the first drawer. This point had been laid down differently in different books, owing to the drawer of a bill of exchange being confounded with the maker of a promissory note. Vide 1 Ld. Raym. 443. Rap. Temp. Hardw. p. 322. 2 Burr. 677. The distinction subsisting between them is thus clearly and satisfactorily laid down by Lord Mansfield, 2 Burr. 675, by whom the law upon the subject now seems to be settled. " As to foreign bills of exchange, the question was solemnly determined by this court, upon very satisfactory grounds in the case of Bromley v. Frasier, 1 Stra. 441. That

was an action upon the case upon a *foreign* bill of exchange by the indorsee against the indorser, and on general demurrer it was objected that they had not shown a demand upon the drawer, in whose default only it is that the indorser warrants." And because this was a point unsettled, and on which there are contradictory opinions in Salk. 131. and 133 the court took time to consider of it. And on the second argument, they delivered their opinions, that the declaration was well enough for the design of the law of merchants in distinguishing these from all other contracts by making them assignable, was for the convenience of commerce, that they might pass from hand to hand in the way of trade, in the same manner as if they were specie. Now to require a demand upon the drawer will be laying such a clog upon these bills as will deter every body from taking them. The drawer lives abroad, perhaps in the Indies, where the indorsee has no correspondent to whom he can send the bill for a demand, or if he could, yet the delay would be so great, that nobody would meddle with them. Suppose it was the case of several indorsements, must the last indorsee travel round the world before he can fix his action upon the man from whom he received the bill! In common experience, every body knows that the more indorsements a bill has, the greater credit it bears, whereas, if these demands are all necessary to be made, it must naturally diminish the value; by how much the more difficult it renders the calling in the money. And as to the notion that has prevailed, that the indorser warrants only in default of the drawer, there is no colour for it, for every indorser is in the nature of a new drawer, and at Nisi Prius the indorsee is not put to prove the hand of the first drawer, where the action is against an indorser. The requiring a protest for non-acceptance is not because a protest amounts to a demand, for it is no more than giving notice to the drawer to get his effects out of the hands of the drawee, who, by others drawing, is supposed to have sufficient wherewith to satisfy the bill. Upon the whole they declared themselves to be of opinion, that in the case of a *foreign* bill of exchange, a demand upon the

default by the drawee to accept, a due presentment, and a refusal must 4thly. Evi-
also be proved ;[f] and when it was essential from the circumstance of dence of
the bill being payable at a banker's, that a presentment should be of contract,
made there, such presentment must, in an action against the drawer or and other
indorser of a bill be proved to have been made in due time, and proof circumstan-
of a presentment by a notary in the evening, when no person was at the ces to sus-
banking-house to give a proper answer, will not suffice,[a] though if it tain the ac-
appear that upon such presentment in the evening, there was some tion.
person at the bankers' who in pursuance of authority gave an answer to [**405**]
the holder, such evidence would suffice.[a]

In an action against the drawer or indorser of a *foreign* bill (and in
an action on an inland bill when a protest is averred,[b]) it is necessary
to prove a *protest* for non-acceptance,[c] or non-payment,[d] the requisites
and points relating to it which have already been considered. But in
the case of an inland bill, interest or damages may be recovered from
a drawer or indorser without proof of a protest.[e] A protest apparently
under the seal of a notary public, and made abroad, need only be produced, and proves itself without showing by whom it was made.[f] But

drawer is not necessary to make a charge
upon the indorser, but the indorsee has
the liberty to resort to either for the
money, consequently the plaintiff (they
said) must have judgment. Every inconvenience here suggested, holds to a great
degree, and every other argument holds
equally in the case of *inland* bills of exchange. We are therefore all of opinion,
that to entitle the indorsee of an inland
bill of exchange to bring an action
against the indorser upon failure of payment of the drawee, it is not necessary
to make any demand of or inquiry after
the first drawer. The law is exactly the
same, and fully settled upon the analogy
of *promissory notes* to bills of exchange,
which is very clear, when the point of
resemblance is once fixed. While a promissory note continues in its original
shape of a promise, from one man to pay
to another, it bears no similitude to a bill
of exchange. When it is indorsed, the
resemblance begins, for then it is an
order by the indorser upon the maker of
the note (his debtor by the note) to pay
to the indorsee. This is the very definition of a bill of exchange. The indorser
is the drawer, the maker of the note is
the acceptor, and the indorsee is the person to whom it is made payable. The
indorser only undertakes, in case the
maker of the note does not pay. The
indorsee is bound to apply to the maker
of the note, he takes it upon that condition, and therefore must in all cases
know who he is, and where he lives, and
if after the note becomes payable, he is
guilty of a neglect, and the maker becomes insolvent he loses the money, and
he cannot come upon the indorser at all.
Therefore, before the indorsee of a promissory note brings an action against the
indorser, he must show a demand or due

CHITTY ON BILLS.

diligence to get the money from the
maker of the note, just as the person to
whom the bill of exchange is made payable, must show a demand or due diligence to get the money from the acceptor,
before he brings an action against the
drawer. This was determined by the
whole court of Common Pleas, upon great
consideration in Pasch. 4 Geo. 2, as cited
by my Lord Chief Justice Lee, in the case
of Collins *v.* Butler, 2 Stra. 1087. So
that the rule is exactly the same upon
promissory notes as it is upon bills of
exchange, and the confusion has in part
arisen from the maker of a promissory
note being called the drawer, whereas by
comparison to bills of exchange, the indorser is the drawer. All the authorities,
and particularly Lord Hardwicke, in the
case of Hamerton *v.* Mackerell, Mich.
10 Geo. 2. according to my Brother Denison's state of what his Lordship said,
put promissory notes and inland bills of
exchange just upon the same footing,
and the statute expressly refers to inland
bills of exchange. But the same law must
be applied to the same reason to the substantial resemblance between promissory
notes and bills of exchange, and not to
the same sound which is equally used to
describe the makers of both."

[f] Ante, 158, &c.

[a] Ante, 259, 276, 577. Parker *v.* Gordon, 7 East, 385. Ante, 277, note.

[a] Garnell *v.* Woodcock, 1 Stark. 475.
Ante, 277, note.

[b] Boulager *v.* Talleyrand, 2 Esp. Rep,
550. Selw. 4th edit. 358. Ante, 362.

[c] Ante, 215.

[d] Ante, 309.

[e] Ante, 218. 312. Windle *v.* Andrews,
2 Barn. & Ald. 696.

[f] Anon. 12 Mod. 345. 2 Rol. Rep. 348.

3 A

4thly. Evi-
dence of
the breach
of contract,
and other
circumstan-
ces to sus-
tain the ac-
tion.

a protest made in England, must be proved by the notary who made it, and by the subscribing witness, if any.ᵉ(1)

In an action against the drawer or indorser of a bill, or indorser of a note, it is in general necessary to prove that due *notice of the dishonour* was given to the defendant. The requisites and time within which notice of non-acceptanceʰ or non-paymentⁱ must be given, have already been considered. This, we have seen, cannot be left to inference without positive proof, and therefore a witness swearing that he gave notice in two or three days after the dishonour, when three days would be too late, will not be sufficient proof.ᵏ

We have already considered what notice of non-acceptanceˡ and non-paymentᵐ is sufficient. If the notice was given by letter, or in writing, it has been decided, that evidence of the contents of such notice cannot be given without first proving the service of a notice to the

[406] defendant to produce such letter or writing, and it is still advisable to serve such notice to produce.ⁿ But in some recent cases it has since

---

10 Mod. 66. Peake Law of Evid. 4th ed. 80, in notes. Bayl. 226.

ᵍ Chesmer *v.* Noyes, 4 Campb. 129. This was an action on a foreign bill of exchange drawn at St. Croix, upon a person at Bristol. In the course of the trial it became material to show that the bill had been presented to him for payment. For this purpose the plaintiff's counsel offered as evidence a notarial protest under seal, stating the fact of the presentment in the usual form, and contended, that by the usage of merchants, a protest under a notary's seal, is evidence of the dishonour of foreign bills of exchange. Lord Ellenborough.—The protest may be sufficient to prove a presentment which took place in a foreign country, but I am quite clear that the presentment of a foreign bill in England must be proved in the same manner as if it were an inland bill, or a promissory note. The plaintiff had a verdict upon other evidence.

ʰ Ante, 196 to 240.

ⁱ Ante, 308 to 320.

ᵏ Lawson *v.* Sherwood, 1 Stark. 314. Ante, 314, note. Elford *v.* Teed, 1 M. & S. 28.

ˡ Ante, 215 to 230.

ᵐ Ante, 309 to 320.

ⁿ Shaw *v.* Markham, Peake's Rep 163 Langdon *v.* Hulls, 5 Esp. Rep. 156. Peake's Law of Evid. 4th ed. 115. Phil. Evid. 3d edit. 395.

Shaw *v.* Markham, Peake, 165. Assumpsit against the defendant as indorser of two promissory notes drawn by Thomas Thomas. A witness of the name of Osborne swore, that when Thomas dishonoured the note, he wrote three letters to the defendant to inform him of it, and sent one to his living at Chester, another to his living at Yorkshire, and a third to the bookseller's where he usually lodged when in London. No notice had been given the defendant to produce these letters, nor any copy kept. Erskine, for the defendant, objected to the evidence, contending, that no notice having been given to produce these letters the plaintiff could not give parol evidence of their contents. Bower, for the plaintiff, answered, that the letters themselves were nothing more than a notice, and that it was an established rule that no notice need be given to produce a notice. Lord Kenyon said, this objection could not be got over, and no evidence of the contents

---

(1) A protest of an inland bill of exchange or promissory note is not necessary, nor is it evidence. *Young* v. *Bryan*, 6 Wheat. 146. *The Union Bank* v. *Hyde*, 6 Wheat. 572. *Nicholas* v. *Webb*, 8 Wheat. 326.

By an act of the legislature of Pennsylvania, 2d January, 1815, the official acts, protests, and attestations of notaries public certified according to law under their respective hands and seals of office may be received in evidence, provided any party may contradict them by other evidence any such certificate. Under this act, notice to the indorser of the non-payment of a promissory note, is held to be an official act, and the protest is *prima facie* evidence thereof. *Browne* v. *Philadelphia Bank*, 6 Serg. & Rawle, 484. *Stewart* v. *Allison*, Ibid. 324. The certificate of the notary under seal is *prima facie* evidence that such person is a notary public. Ibid. But the notary may be admitted to give evidence to explain or rebut the facts stated by him in the protest, *Craig* v. *Stallcross*. And may even be compelled to appear and give such evidence. *Wright* v. *Almond*, Sup. Court, Pennsylvania, March Term, 1825.

been determined that secondary evidence may be given of a written notice of the dishonour of a bill, without notice to produce such writing.° (519) So a copy of a letter containing notice of the dishonour of a bill, is admissible, without notice to produce the original, and proof that duplicate notices of the dishonour of a bill were written, and that a letter was delivered to the defendant upon the dishonour of a bill, together with proof of notice to produce the letter so delivered, as containing notice of dishonour, is evidence, on default of production, that the defendant had notice;ᵖ and proof of a letter from the defendant, in

4thly. Evidence of the breach of contract, and other circumstances to sustain the action.

of the letter could be received without a notice to produce it. Call it a notice, or by any other name, it was still a letter, and must be proved as any other written paper.

Langdon v. Hulls, 5 Esp. Rep. 156. Assumpsit on a bill of exchange drawn by the defendant in his own favour on one Pugh for 50l., two months after date, accepted by Pugh, and indorsed by the defendant to the plaintiff.˙ The plaintiff having proved the acceptance and handwriting of the defendant to the indorsement, then proved that the bill, when due, was presented for payment at Pugh's house, and that it was not then paid. To prove the notice to the defendant as the drawer of the non-payment by the acceptor, the plaintiff proved, by the notary's clerk who presented the bill, that he had left word at the defendant's house that the bill had not been paid, the plaintiff also proved that his attorney, by his directions, had written a letter to the defendant, informing him of the non-payment of the bill by Pugh. It becoming necessary to prove this notice so given by the plaintiff's attorney by letter to the defendant, the attorney was called. No notice had been given to produce this letter, but he having stated that he had written such a letter, was proceeding to state the notice of the non-payment as mentioned in the letter, of which letter he had a copy, when it was objected that evidence of the contents of the letter could not be given, as no notice had been given to produce it. It was answered, that the letter itself was a notice, and that it had been so decided that notice to produce a notice was not necessary, and the case of Jory v. Orchard, 2 Bos. & Pul. 39, was cited, as in point. It was contended by the defendant, that notice of the non-payment of the bill had not been given in due time, and that the letter had not been written until several days after the time for regular notice had expired, and it therefore became important to ascertain the exact time when it was written. Lord Ellenborough said, that notice of the dishonour of a bill of exchange, by letter, was certainly good evidence, and had been so decided, but that there were other

circumstances besides the mere fact of notice, which were necessary to give effect to it, so as to entitle the plaintiff to recover. These were the date and the time when it was sent, which were material, for notice of the dishonour was not sufficient unless given in the time required in the case of bills of exchange. To ascertain the date of the post-mark might be material, he was therefore of opinion that the plaintiff could not give evidence of the contents of the letter, not having given notice to produce it, and that upon that evidence the plaintiff could not recover. The plaintiff then proved ·a subsequent admission by the defendant that he had notice, and had a verdict.

° Ackland v. Pearce, 2 Campb. 601. Phil. Evid. 3d ed. 395.

Ackland v. Pearce, 2 Campb. 601.— Action against drawer of a bill. The witness called to prove notice of the dishonour of the bill said, that on the day it became due, he left a written notice of its having been dishonoured at the defendant's house. Le Blanc, J. after argument, ruled, that the secondary evidence of the contents of this notice might be given without a notice to produce it, and compared it to a notice to quit.

ᵖ Roberts v. Bradshaw, 1 Stark. 28.— Hetherington v. Kemp, 4 Campb. 194.

Roberts v. Bradshaw, 1 Stark. 28. Action on a bill of exchange by the indorsee against the drawer. In order to prove notice of the dishonour, the counsel for the plaintiff called a clerk of the plaintiff's, who stated, that on the 2d of February, the day on which the bill had been dishonoured, his master gave him two papers to compare with each other, one of which the witness now produced, and purported to be a notice of the dishonour of the bill in question. Topping, for the defendant, objected, that this could not be read without proof of notice to produce that which had been so delivered, but Lord Ellenborough, C. J. was of opinion, that a letter acquainting a party with the dishonour of a bill, was in the nature of a notice, and that it was unnecessary to prove a notice to produce such a letter. Upon further examination the witness stated, that upon the day

4thly. Evi- which he acknowledged the receipt of a letter from the holder of a
dence   of named date (being the proper time for giving notice,) but without refer-
the breach ring to its contents, would afford presumptive evidence of the receipt
of contract, by the party of a regular notice.a
& other cir-
cumstances
to sustain   In general, on proof of notice of the dishonour of a bill or note having
the action. been given, it will suffice to show, that a letter, containing information
of the fact, and properly directed, was put in the proper post-office,r or
left at the defendant's house.s In civil cases, the post-mark upon the
letter seems to be evidence of the time and place when it was put into
the post-office.t

    Proof of having sent a notice or other paper by the post, has gen-
erally been considered in mercantile transactions to be sufficient proof
of notice to the party to whom it was directed, and this on a principle
of general convenience. A question has sometimes arisen as to the
requisite proof of the fact of sending by the post. In one case,u
where it became necessary to prove that a license to trade had been
sent by the plaintiff to A. B., it was proved to be the invariable course
of the plaintiff's office, that the clerk, who copys a license, sends it
off by the post, and writes on the copy a memorandum of his having
done so ; a copy of the license in question was produced from the
plaintiff's letter-book, in the hand-writing of a deceased clerk, who
had written a memorandum, stating, that the original had been sent
to A. B.; and a witness, acquainted with the plaintiff's mode of transacting business, swore, that he had no doubt that the original had been
sent according to the statement in the memorandum ; this evidence was
held to be sufficient. In another case relating to a bill,x where the
question was, whether the defendant had received notice of the dishonour of a bill of exchange, it was proved, that on the day after the
bill became due, the plaintiff wrote a letter, addressed to the defendant, stating that it had been dishonoured ; but this letter was put

after he had compared the two papers, he carried a letter from the plaintiff to the defendant, but did not know the contents. Lord Ellenborough was of opinion that this was not sufficient evidence. The plaintiff then proved the service of a notice on the defendant, calling upon him to produce a letter from the plaintiff, giving him notice of the dishonour of the bill mentioned in the declaration. The Attorney-general contended that this was sufficient evidence to go to a jury, that the original had been sent, and that it lay upon the defendant to show, by producing it, that the letter proved to have been delivered on the 3d of February, was nothing more than an invitation to dinner, or something else equally unconnected with the dishonour of the bill in question. Topping.—No answer has been given to the objection; a notice is of no avail to warrant the reading of a copy, unless the party be proved to have been in possession of the original; on the contrary, the notice itself assumes the fact of possession. Lord Ellenborough, C. J.—I think, certainly, that there is a looseness in this evidence, and you may afterwards move the court upon it. Supposing, however,

that the paper delivered had been a perfect blank, or contained matter wholly uncon-nected with the dishonour of the bill. yet might have produced it, and shown the fact to be so, since it is evident what letter was the object of the plaintiff's notice. This is the first time the indentity of such a letter has been so minutely scrutinized and the proof might, in many instances, be atten-ded with great difficulty, as where letters after being written, are placed upon the ta-ble, it might afterwards be exceedingly difficult to identify them with those after-wards put into the post-office. Verdict for the plaintiff. In the ensuing Term the court refused a rule nisi for a new trial.

q Hetherington v. Kemp, 4 Campb. 194.

r Sanderson v. Judge, 2 Hen. Bla. 509. Ante, 221. Scott v. Lifford, 9 East, 347. Ante, 222. Bayl. 226.

s Stedman v. Gooch, 1 Esp. Rep. 5 Jones v Marsh, 4 T. R. 465.

t Archangel v. Thompson, 2 Campb 625.

u Hagendon v. Reed, 2 Campb. 379.

x Hetherington v. Kemp, 4 Campb. 193 Supra, note. Phil. on Evid. 3d edit 390.

down on a table, where according to the usage of his counting-house, letters for post were always deposited, and that a porter carries them from thence to the post office; but the porter was not called, and there was no evidence as to what had become of the letter after it was put down upon the table. A notice to produce the letter had been served upon the defendant. It was contended for the plaintiff, that this was good *prima facie* evidence that the letter had been sent by the post. Lord Ellenborough held, that some evidence ought to be given [409] that the letter had been taken from the table in the counting-house and put in the post-office. If the porter had been called, and if he had said, that although he had no recollection of this particular letter, he invariably carried to the post-office all the letters found upon the table, this might have been sufficient; but it was not sufficient to give such general evidence of the course of business in the plaintiff's counting-house.(522)

4thly. Evidence of the breach of contract, and other circumstances to sustain the action.

The plaintiff, however, may prove facts to excuse his neglect to make a due presentment on a protest in the case of a foreign bill, or to give notice of non-acceptance or non-payment, as that the defendant when drawer, had no effects in the hands of the drawee, from the time it was drawn until it became due.[y]

So proof of a payment of part, or a *promise to pay* after full notice of the laches of the holder, we have seen, dispenses with the necessity for proof in an action against the drawee of a due presentment, protest, and notice, and has been considered as admitting all these facts, as well the right of the holder to sue;[z] and the same evidence suffices in an action against an indorser;[a] though it has recently been con-

[y] Ante, 198 to 215.

[z] Ante, 233 to 540, where the cases establishing and qualifying this rule are collected; and see Greenway v. Hindley, 4 Campb. 52. Lundie v. Robertson, 7 East, 231. Potter v. Rayworth, 18 East, »17.

[a] Taylor v. Jones, 2 Campb. 105.

Taylor v. Jones, 2 Campb. 105. Action against the defendant as indorser of a promissory note, due May 5th, 1805. The plaintiff proved the defendant's indorsement; and also that in the year 1817, the defendant being requested to pay the note, he promised that he would, but prayed for further time. There was no evidence of the presentment of the note to the maker, or of any notice of its non-payment being given to the defendant; nor did it appear that when the defendant so promised to pay, he knew whether any application for payment had been made to the maker. Gaselee, for the defendant, contended, that the subsequent promise did not dispense with proof of the presentment and notice, unless made with full knowledge of the

(522) Although the protest of a notary public is not evidence in the case of promissory notes and inland bills of exchange, yet the books of a notary public proved to have been regularly kept, are admissible in evidence after his death, to prove a demand of payment. and notice of non-payment, of a promissory note. *Nicholas* v. *Webb*, 8 Wheat. 326.

The protest of a deceased notary and a register of protests kept by him in which the notes and memoranda in his hand writing proved by a witness stated that the notary had made diligent search and inquiries after the maker of a note in the city of New York (where the note was dated,) in order to demand payment of him and that he could not be found, &c. and that notice of non payment was put in the post office: Held, that this was sufficient evidence of due diligence as to the demand of payment of the maker of the note, but not of notice to the indorser, as the note or memorandum of the notary did not state where the indorser resided nor to what place the notice to him was directed: But *it seems* that if the notary had stated that the indorser after diligent search and inquiry could not be found, that would have been sufficient to entitle the plaintiff to recover against the indorser. *Holliday* v. *Martinet*, 20 Johns. 168.

4thly. Evidence of the breach of contract, and other circumstances to sustain the action. sidered, that admitting a *drawer* of a bill may, by circumstances, impliedly waive his right of defence founded on the laches of the holder, yet it must be proved, that an *indorser* has *expressly* waived it.[b] And in these cases it is to be left to the jury to say whether, under the circumstances, the defendant had notice at the time of his promise or application, that there had been no due presentment, or that the holder had otherwise been guilty of negligence,[c]

In an action by the drawer against the acceptor of a bill, payable to the order of a third person, and which the drawer has been obliged to pay, it is necessary, in support of the count, stating the return of the bill, to prove the acceptance, the demand of payment, and refusal or neglect to pay, and the return of the bill to the plaintiff, and the payment by him if averred, but it is not necessary to prove that the acceptor had effects in hand, that fact being *prima facie* admitted by the acceptance.[d]

When the acceptor of an accommodation bill sues the drawer specially, and which he cannot do on the bill, he must prove the handwriting of the defendant as drawer, and the payment by himself, or some special damage, as imprisonment in execution,[e] and which in the latter case will not suffice, unless there is a special count in the declaration for not indemnifying.[f] And as the presumption of law is, that the acceptor had consideration for his acceptance, it will be incumbent on him to prove the contrary.[g] *Prima facie*, a general receipt on the back of a bill, imports a payment by the acceptor.[h] But the production of the bill from the custody of the acceptor will not afford for him *prima facie* evidence of his having paid it, without proof that it was once in circulation after it had been accepted ; nor is payment to be presumed from a receipt indorsed on the bill, unless it be shown to be in the hand-writing of a person entitled to demand payment.[i] So in an action by bankers to recover the amount of a bill of exchange accepted by the defendant, payable at their house, and paid by them after it was indorsed, they are bound to proved the indorsement by the payee and the defendant's acceptance, and their payment.[k]

Evidence for the defendant. WITH respect to the evidence on the part of the *defendant*, it must necessarily depend on the circumstances of each case.

laches of the holder. In the cases hitherto decided upon this subject, something appeared that might be considered a waiver of any irregularity with regard to the bill or note, which could not be inferred from a mere promise to pay, made at a time when the party, without being aware of it, was discharged from his liability. But Bayley, J. held, that where a party to a bill or note, knowing it to be due, and knowing that he was entitled to have it presented when due to the acceptor or maker, and to receive notice of its dishonour, promised to pay it, this is presumptive evidence of the presentment and notice, and he is bound

by the promise so made. Verdict for plaintiff.

[b] Borradaile v. Lowe, 4 Taunt. 93. Ante, 239.

[c] Hopley v. Dufresne, 13 East, 275. Horford v. Wilson, 1 Taunt. 15. Bayl. 220.

[d] Vere v. Lewis, 3 T. R. 183. Simmonds v. Parminter, 1 Wils. 185. Ante, 398.

[e] Chilton v. Wiffen, 3 Wils. 12. 13.

[f] Taylor v. Higgins, 3 East, 169.

[g] Vere v. Lewis. 3 T. R. 183.

[h] Scholey v. Walsby, Peake's Rep. 25.

[i] Pfiel v. Van Battenberg, 2 Campb. 439. Ante, 399.

[k] Foster v. Clements, 2 Campb. 17.

If the defendant would wish to establish that the *stamp* is insufficient, he should be prepared to produce and point to the particular provision of a printed copy of the stamp act on which he relies; and if the objection be, that a bill, purporting to have been made abroad, was made in England, and therefore required a stamp, it will not suffice merely to prove that the drawer was in England at the time the bill bears date, but the fact must be established by more positive evidence.[1]

If the defendant relies on the illegality or insufficiency of the *consideration*, he should, in due time before the trial, serve a notice upon the plaintiff's attorney, to prove the consideration he gave for the bill, and the time when, and person from whom he received the same,[m] and he should prove the due service of such notice, for without such notice we have seen, the defendant cannot call on the plaintiff to enter into those circumstances.[n] The defendant should also be prepared with evidence to prove the circumstances under which the bill was drawn or negotiated.[o] If goods were delivered in part of discount, and accepted voluntarily, then the defendant must, in order to make out a case of usury, prove the excess in the charges.[p] But if the defendant prove that goods were forced upon him or another party, then the plaintiff may be called on to prove that they were fairly charged.[q] If the usury was committed in discounting another bill besides that on which the action is brought, in one undivided transaction, no parol evidence is admissible as to the contents of the other bill, unless notice has been given to produce it, and which notice should be proved.[r]

In an action at the suit of an indorsee against the maker of a promissory note where the defence was usury in its creation, it was held, that letters from the payee to the maker, stating the consideration as between them, if shown to have been contemporaneous with the making of the note, were admissible evidence to prove the usury, without calling the payee himself;[s] but in general the letters of an indorser, or at

[1] Abraham *v.* Du Bois, 4 Campb. 269.

[m] See the form of notice, post, Appendix.

[n] Ante, 408.

[o] As to the consideration, see ante, 68 to 89, and index, title *Consideration*.

[p] Coomb *v.* Miles, 2 Campb. 553. Rich *v.* Topping, 1 Esp. Rep. 176. Post, 416.

[q] Davies *v.* Hardacre, 2 Camb. 374. Ante, 87, 8.

[r] Hallam *v.* Withers, 1 Esp. Rep. 259.

[s] Kent *v.* Lowen, Campb. 177. 180. d. S. P. in Walsh *v.* Stockdale, *coram* Abbott, J. Sitting at Guildhall, post, Trin. Term, 1818.

Kent *v.* Lowen, 1 Campb. 177., and 180. d Assumpsit against the defendant as maker of a promissory note for 153*l.* 15*s.* dated 9th August, 1806, at ninety days after date, payable to Messrs. Coates and Co. indorsed by them to J. Watson, and indorsed by him to the plaintiff. The making of the note, and the several indorsements being proved, the Attorney-General opened, as a defence to the action, that the note had been given under a usurious

agreement between the defendant and Coates and Co. To prove this he offered in evidence certain letters from Coates and Co. to the defendant, wherein they proposed to accommodate him with their acceptance at three months, upon receiving his note for the same sum at ninety days, together with two-and-a-half per cent. commission. Park objected to the admissibility of this evidence. He allowed, that in an action against the acceptor of a bill, the drawer or indorser may be called to prove that there was usury in its original concoction, but there the evidence was given upon oath, and an opportunity was afforded to cross-examine the witnesses. Here these letters of Coates and Co. were not upon oath, and might be collusively written, with a view to defeat the fair claim of the plaintiff. Lord Ellenborough ruled, that it was necessary to prove by the post mark, or otherwise, that the letters were cotemporaneous with the making of the note, and that after that they would be evidence of an act done by Coates and Co. who were the payees of the note, and through whom the plaintiff made title.

Evidence for the defendant.
least those written after he has parted with the bill, are not admissible in evidence to impeach the indorsee's title.[t] In an action against the acceptor of a bill given for the price of a horse warranted sound, the breach of warranty, if the horse were returned forthwith, will afford a complete defence.[u] But it has been recently held that if the consideration has only partially failed, and the exact amount to be deducted is unliquidated, the defendant cannot go into evidence in reduction of damages, but it is driven to his cross action ;[x] and a party who has given his promissory note as the stipulated price of a picture, cannot give the inadequacy of the consideration in evidence, with a view to reduce the damages, though he may give it in evidence as a circumstance indicatory of fraud, in order to defeat the contract altogether.[y] And we have seen, that if a note be payable on demand, parol evidence cannot be given of an agreement to wait for payment till after the death of the testator.[z]

[413]
Though we have seen that it is incumbent on the plaintiff in general to prove a due presentment and notice of the dishonour, in support of his action against the drawer or indorser of the bill, yet in doubtful cases it may be necessary for the defendant to be prepared with evidence to negative the plaintiff's *prima facie* proof; and we have seen, that where the holder of a bill, upon its being dishonoured, received part payment, and for the residue another bill, drawn and accepted *by persons not parties to the original bill*, and such holder afterwards sued the indorser upon such original bill, it suffices for him to prove the presentment and dishonour of the substituted bill, and it is incumbent on the defendant to prove that a loss has been sustained in consequence of the want of notice of non-payment of such substituted bill.[a]

———

Competency of witnesses.
WE have already considered when it is necessary to *subpœna* a subscribing witness.[b] It may here be proper to examine the cases respecting the admissibility of *witnesses* in an action on a bill or note.

The general rule is, that it is no objection to the *competency* of a witness that he is also a party to the same bill or note, unless he be *directly* interested in the event of the suit, and be called in support of such interest, or unless the verdict to obtain which his testimony is offered, would be admissible evidence in his favour in another suit.[c] If the verdict will not *necessarily* affect his own interest, he is a com-

Whether the act was proved by an oral declaration, or by other evidence, his Lordship said, made no difference. The post-mark being examined, did show the letters to have been written just before the date of the note, and they were read in evidence accordingly; and Lord Ellenborough told the jury, that if they believed that the note was made on the terms held out in the letters, they must find for the defendant, who had a verdict accordingly; and on a motion for a new trial, it was contended, that the letters of the payee had been improperly admitted, but the court being of opinion that they were legal evidence to prove the usury as

against the indorser; the verdict for the defendant was confirmed.
  [t] Clipsam v. O'Brien, 1 Esp. Rep. 10.
  [u] Lewis v. Cosgrave, 2 Taunt. 2.
  [x] See the cases, ante, 70; 71, 72.
  [y] Soloman v. Turner, 1 Stark. 51. Ante, 70.
  [z] Woodbridge v. Spooner, 3 Barn. & Ald. 233. Chit. Rep. 661.
  [a] Bishop v. Rowe, 3 M. & S. 362. Ante, 98. See 7 Taunt. 312. 3 Taunt. 130.
  [b] Ante, 379.
  [c] Bent v. Baker, 3 T. R. 27. Jordaine v. Lashbrook, 7 T. R. 601. Smith v. Prager, 7 T. R. 62. Jones v. Brooks, 4 Taunt. 46; Bayl. 241.

petent witness, and though his testimony, by defeating the *present* Competen-
action on the bill or note, will probably deter the holder from pro-cy of wit-
ceeding in another action against the witness, yet that only affords nesses.
matter of observation to the jury, as to the *credit* to be given to his testimony.[d]

Thus, though it was formerly held, that no party should be permitted
to give testimony to invalidate an instrument he had signed,[e] a contrary
rule now prevails.[f](528)

Thus, in an action at the suit of an indorsee against the acceptor, the
drawer, or indorser, is a competent witness for the defendant, to prove
that the bill was originally void, or that it was made in London, though
dated at Hamburgh, and consequently invalid for want of an English [414]
stamp.[g] And Lord Mansfield admitted the maker of a note to prove,
in an action against an indorser, that the date had been altered.[h]

But in an old reporter it is stated to have been decided, that a person,
supposed to be the drawer of a bill, cannot, without a release, be called
to prove that he did not draw.[i]

[d] Id. ibid.
[e] Walton *v.* Shelly, 1 T. R. 300.
[f] Bent *v.* Baker, 3 T. R. 36. Jordaine *v.*
Lashbrook, 7 T. R. 601.
[g] Jordaine *v.* Lashbrook, 7 T. R. 601.
and Smith *v.* Prager, id 62.
[h] Levi *v.* Essex, Mich. Term. 1773.
2 Esp. Rep. 708. The plaintiff declared as
an indorsee of a promissory note, drawn by

Foster Charlton, payable to the defendant,
dated the 13th of June, 1775; the defendant insisted, that the date of the note had
been altered from the 3d to the 13th; and
to prove it, called Foster Charlton. Lord
Mansfield admitted him, as at all events he
was liable to pay the note.
[i] Anon. 12 Mod. 345. Dupays *v.* Shepherd, Holt, 297. Trials per Pais, 502.

---

(528) The decision in *Walton* v. *Shelly* seems to have been adhered to in the United
States. In *Massachusetts* and *New York* it has been decided that a party to a negotiable instrument cannot be admitted as a witness to prove the note originally void. *Churchhill* v. *Suter*, 4 Mass. Rep. 156. *Warren* v. *Merry*, 3 Mass. Rep. 27. *Parker* v. *Lovejoy*,
3 Mass Rep. 565. *Widgery* v. *Munroe*, 6 Mass. Rep. 449. *Jones* v. *Coolridge*, 7 Mass.
Rep. 199 *Winter* v. *Saidler*, 3 John. Cas. 185. *Wilkie* v. *Roosevelt*, 3 John. Cas. 206.
Coleman v. *Wire*, 2 John. Rep. 165. *Skilding* v. *Warren*, 15 John. Rep. 270. But he
is a good witness to prove any facts subsequent to the due execution of the note, which
destroys the title of the holder. *Baker* v. *Arnold*, 1 Caines' Rep 258. *Woodhull* v.
Holmes, 10 John. Rep. 231. *Warren* v. *Merry*, 3 Mass. Rep. 37. *Barker* v. *Prentiss*,
6 Mass. Rep. 430. *Park.* r v. *Hanson*, 7 Mass Rep. 470. *Webb* v. *Danforth*, 1 Day's
Rep. 301. *Mann* v. *Swann*, 14 John. Rep. 270. *Hulby* v. *Brown*, 16 Johns. Rep. 70.
Myers v. *Palmer*, 18 John. Rep. 167. The indorser of a negotiable note is not a competent witness, in an action between the indorsee and maker, to prove usury in the transfer of the note *by him. Manning* v. *Wheatland*, 10 Mass. Rep. 502. And in *Pennsylvania*, it has been decided, that an indorser cannot in a like action be a witness, that
there was no original consideration for the bill. *Still* v. *Lynch*, 2 Dall. Rep. 194. See
also *Allen* v. *Holkins*, 1 Day's. Rep. 17. *Bearing* v. *Reeder*, 1 H. & Munf. Rep. 175.
2 Binney, 154. 2 Desaus Cha. Rep. 224.
But this rule is confined to negotiable instruments. *Pleasants* v. *Pemberton*, 2 Dall.
196. 1 Yeates' 202. *Buying* v. *Shippen*, 2 Binn. 165. 168. *M'Ferran* v. *Powers*,
1 Serg. & Rawle, 102. And they must be such as are actually negotiated in the usual
course of business. *Blagg* v *Phœnix Ins. Co.* Cir Co. U. S. Whart. Dig. 270. *Baird*
v. *Cochran*, 4 Serg & Rawle, 390. *Hepburn* v. *Cassel*, 6 Serg. & Rawle, 113. *Bank
of Montgomery* v. *Walker*, 9 Serg. & Rawle, 236.
The indorser is not a competent witness in Pennsylvania in a suit against the maker of
a promissory note, to prove that the note was originally drawn for the indorser's accommodation, and thereby enable the maker to set up a discharge by the holder's giving time
to the indorser.
For, though a party to negotiable paper may be received to prove subsequent facts to
discharge it, yet he is not competent to show that the instrument was not in truth what
it purported on its face to be. *Bank of Montgomery* v. *Walker*, 9 Serg. & Rawle, 236.

Compe ten-
cy of wit-
nesses.

So if the witness has an interest inclining him as much to one of the parties as the other, so as upon the whole to make him indifferent in point of substantial interest in whose favour the verdict may be given, he will be competent to give evidence for either party.[k] Thus one joint maker of a promissory note is a witness to prove the signature of the other who has been separately sued.[l] And where one partner drew a bill in the partnership firm, and gave it in payment to a separate creditor, in discharge of his own debt, the Court of King's Bench held, that in an action by such creditor against the acceptor, either of the partners might be called on the part of the defendant to prove that the partner who drew the bill had no authority to draw it in the name of the firm, and that the bankruptcy of the partners would not vary the question as to the competency of the witness. In this case the partner who drew the bill would have been liable to the plaintiff for the amount of his debt, if the plaintiff had failed in the action; and if the plaintiff had succeeded, he would have been liable to the defendant, the acceptor, and with respect to the other partner, though he would have been liable to the defendant, if the plaintiff recovered, he would have had his remedy over against the joint partner.[m] And though in another case the court held that a witness who might have a remedy by action, whether the plaintiff or defendant had a verdict, was nevertheless, interested, because under the particular circumstances, he would have a greater difficulty in the one case than in the other, to enforce that remedy,[n] it has been observed, that this appears to be the only case which has been decided on such a ground, and that

[415] from the leading cases on this subject which rest on the broad ground of interest, such a circumstance may now more properly be considered as having a strong influence on the witness, but not as forming any solid objection to his competency.[o]

But if the verdict would necessarily benefit or affect the witness, as if he be liable to the costs of the action, then without a release, which will annul his interest in the event, he will not be a competent witness;[p] and therefore in an action against the acceptor of a bill, accepted by him for the accommodation of the drawer; the latter is not, without a release, a competent witness to prove that the holder came to the bill on usurious consideration, because he does not stand indifferently liable to the holder and the acceptor; for the holder can recover against him only the contents of the bill, but the acceptor would be entitled in an action for not indemnifying to recover against him, as well the amount of the bill as the damages he may have sustained, including the costs of the action against himself, and therefore the drawer has a direct interest in defeating such action.[q] (1) This decision seems to overrule the

[k] Phil. Ev. 3d edit. 54 to 57.
[l] York v. Blott, 5 M & S. 71.
[m] Ridley v. Taylor, 13 East, 175. and see York v. Blott, 5 M. & S. 71. Phil. Ev. 3d edit. 55.
[n] Buckland v. Tankard, 6 T. R. 579.
[o] Phil. Ev. 3d edit. 56, 7.
[p] Jones v. Brooke, 4 Taunt. 464. Hardwick v. Blanchard, 1 Gow. C. N. P. 113. Phil. Evid. 3d edit. 49. 56.

[q] Jones v. Brooke, 4 Taunt. 464. Hardwick v. Blanchard, 1 Gow. C. N. P. 113. and see Phil. Ev. 3d edit. 56.
Jones v. Brooke, 4 Taunt. 464. Per Mansfield, Ch. J. This action is brought against Brooke as acceptor of a bill of exchange; at the trial, the defence made, was, that this bill was given by the drawer to the indorser on a usurious consideration, the latter having taken usurious interest on dis-

(1) This doctrine seems recognised in *Bank of Montgomery* v. *Walker*, 9 Serg. & Rawle, 236.

prior cases of Birt v. Kershaw,[r] and Shuttleworth v. Stephens.[s] But
if such accommodation acceptor release such drawer, the latter will be
rendered competent;[t] and the drawer of a bill who has become bankrupt,
is a good witness in an action against an acceptor, who accepted the bill
for the accommodation of such drawer, on being released by such ac- **[416]**
ceptor, although the latter had not formally released the assignees of
the estate.[u] If a person who has guaranteed the payment of a bill, has
been discharged by his bankruptcy and certificate from liabilty to pay
the amount of the bill, he is a competent witness, because he is also
thereby relieved from liability to costs.[x]

In an action against the acceptor of a bill the drawer is a competent
witness either for the plaintiff to prove the hand-writing of the acceptor,[y] or for the defendant to prove that the plaintiff discounted the
bill upon a usurious consideration,[s] or that it has been paid.[s] And

counting the bill; and that the bill 'was accepted for the accommodation of the drawer. An objection was taken to the witness,
who was the wife of the drawer ; and the
objection was overruled, on the ground that
it is now the practice to receive persons
whose names are on bills of exchange, as
witnesses to impeach such bills. And so
it is; but here the question is, inasmuch as
this was an action against the acceptor,
whether she could be received as against
the acceptor, the drawer, as it was contended, being interested to defeat the action: the doubt was this ; the drawer has
an interest to protect the acceptor; for if
the holder succeeds against the acceptor,
the acceptor will have a right against the
drawer, to make the drawer pay, not only
the money, but also all damages he, the acceptor, might have sustained by being sued
for it; for the drawer of an accommodation-
bill is bound to indemnify the acceptor
against the consequences of an acceptance
made for the accommodation of the drawer; we are therefore of opinion that the
drawer cannot be a witness, and consequently the rule must be made absolute for
entering a verdict for the plaintiff ; and see
Hardwick v. Blanchard, 1 Gow. C. N. P.
113.

[r] Birt v. Kershaw, 2 East, 458.
[s] Shuttleworth v. Stevens, 1 Campb.
407.
[t] Hardwick v. Blanchard, 1 Gow. C. N.
P. 113.
[u] Cartwright v. Williams, 2 Stark. 340.
[x] Brend v. Bacon, 5 Taunt. 183.
[y] Dickenson v. Prentice, 4 Esp. Rep. 32.
Barber v. Gingell, 3 Esp. Rep. 62. Bayl.
242.
Dickenson v. Prentice, 4 Esp. Rep. 32.
This was an action against the defendant
as acceptor of a bill, the defence intended

to be set up was that the acceptance was
a forgery; to prove the defendant's hand-
writing, the plaintiff called the drawer, it
was objected that having drawn the bill,
the forgery of the acceptance could only
be imputable to him, and that as he might
be committed for a capital offence if the
forgety was established, he had such an interest as ought to disqualify him. But Lord
Kenyon said, this was matter of observation as to his credit ; but no objection to
his admissibility. He was admitted and
the plaintiff had a verdict. (331)
[s] Rich v. Topping, Peake's Rep. 224.
1 Esp. Rep. 176. S. C. Brown v. Ackerman, 5 Esp. Rep. 119. Bayl. 242.
Rich v. Topping, Peake's Rep. 224. The
drawer himself had indorsed the bill to the
plaintiff for a usurious consideration, he
had a release from the acceptor, which
Lord Kenyon thought was necessary. The
learned reporter, however, in a note on the
case, considers that the witness stood indifferent, and ought to have been received
even without a release, and in Brown v.
Ackerman, 5 Esp. Rep. 119, the drawer
(under precisely similar circumstances) was
admitted without a release, at least it is not
stated that he had any.
[s] Humphrey v. Moxon, Peake's Rep.
52. Carrington v. Milner, Peake's Rep.
6. Bayl. 242.
Humphrey v. Moxon, Peake's Rep. 52.
Assumpsit on a bill of exchange, indorsee
against acceptor. The defendant's counsel
offered to call the drawer to prove that the
bill was paid by him, and relied on the case
of Gardner and Carter, determined some
time since. Erskine objected to this witness. This case differs from that of Gardner and Carter, there the payee was the
plaintiff ; this action is brought by the indorsee. Lord Kenyon. It makes no differ-

---

(531) It has been held in *Massachusetts*, that in an action by an indorsee against the
drawer, the indorser is not a competent witness to prove the hand-writing of the drawer
without a release, or its equivalent, a discharge from liability on the indorsement.
Barnes v. Ball, 1 Mass. Rep. 73. *Rice v. Starnes*, 8 Mass. Rep. 225.

CHAPTER V.

OF THE SUM RECOVERABLE IN AN ACTION ON A BILL, &c.

THE amount of the DAMAGES which the plaintiff is entitled to recover, necessarily depends on the liability of the parties to the instrument ; the nature of which liability has already been considered in that part of the work which treats of the drawing, acceptance, transfer, and dishonour of bills,[a] and from whence it may be collected, that, in general, the sum for which the bill is payable, may be recovered, and in certain cases, interest, and such expenses, as may have been occasioned by the dishonour of it.

1st. The principal money.

With respect to the *principal money,* or that sum which is payable on the face of the bill or note, many instances occur, in which, although the plaintiff may not have given full value for the bill, &c. he may, nevertheless, recover the whole sum, holding the overplus beyond his own demand as trustee for some other party to the bill, &c. entitled to receive such overplus. Thus, if a bill be drawn in the regular course of business, as for money really due from the drawee to the drawer, in such case, in order to avoid several actions, an indorsee, though he hath not given the full value of the bill, may recover the whole sum payable, and be the holder of the overplus as a trustee for the indorser ;[b] and if the holder receive part-payment of the first indorser, he may, nevertheless, recover the whole against the drawer and acceptor, though, if the acceptor pay a part, then only the residue can be recovered against the drawer.[c] This rule, permitting the holder of a bill, &c. to recover more than is due to himself, only applies where there is some other person entitled to receive from the defendant the overplus of what is due to the plaintiff, and if there be no such person, the plaintiff will be permitted only to recover what is due to himself.[d] But in case of bankruptcy, the holder may prove

[420] the whole amount under a commission against a remote party, and receive a dividend until his debt is satisfied, though he cannot prove for more than the sum actually due on the balance of account against his immediate indorser.[e] We have, in the preceding chapter, seen, that a partial failure of consideration cannot be given in evidence to reduce the damages, though the total failure is an answer to the action.[f]

When a bill or note is payable by instalments, and it contains a clause, that on failure of payment of any one instalment, the whole

---

[a] See Index, tit. Damages and Protest.

[b] Wiffen v. Roberts, Esp. Rep. 261.

[c] Walwyn v. St. Quintin, 1 Bos. & Pul. 658. Johnson v. Kennion, 2 Wils. 262. and see the same rule in proof in bankruptcy, Ex parte De Tastet, 1 Rose, 10.

[d] Pierson v. Dunlop, Cowp. 571.—Steel v. Bradfield, 4 Taunt. 227. Jones v. Hilbert, 2 Stark. 304.

[e] Ex parte Bloxam, 6 Ves. 449. 600. S. C. Acc. 5 Ves. 448. Cullen, 97, n 35. Ex parte Leers, 6 Ves. 644., contra, post.

[f] Ante, 412. quære, ante, 71.

shall become due, the holder is entitled to recover the whole amount of 1st. The
the sum for which it was given : but where the instrument 'does not principal
contain~such a clause, it is doubtful on the authorities, whether the money.
holder can legally take a verdict for more than the instalment due.
According to the case of Beckwith v. Nott,[g] and several other cases
cited by Lord Loughborough, in giving the opinion of the Court in the
case of Rudder v. Price,[h] the plaintiff is entitled to the whole sum for
which the note was given ; but according to other cases, and particularly that of Ashford v. Hand,[i] the plaintiff is only entitled to the instalment due at the time of commencing the action. (537) When at the
time of the trial, nearly all the instalments are due, the jury will frequently, for the sake of avoiding another action, give the whole sum in
damages. If the plaintiff take a verdict for more than he is entitled to
recover, the court will either make him correct the verdict, and pay the
costs occasioned by his misconduct, or grant a new trial.[k]

When interest is made payable by the bill, &c. itself, there is no 2dly. Inte-
doubt of its being recoverable as a debt, in other cases it is recovered rest.
only as damages.[l]   Interest is recoverable from the acceptor of a
bill, and the maker of a promissory note payable at a certain time
after date or sight from the day on which they became due, without
proof of any demand,[m] or if payable on demand from the time of the
demand.[n] If a jury should be of opinion that the delay of payment
has been occasioned by the default of the holder, they may refuse to al- [421]
low any interest.[o] Interest is computed and given at law as well as in
equity upon bills of exchange from the time they became due, in the
nature of damages, not strictly as interest ; and for breach of contract
not in pursuance of it.[p] But in case of bankruptcy, although there be
a surplus, bills do not carry interest unless the previous dealings between
the parties afforded evidence of a contract to pay interest.[q] But the

g Beckwith v. Nott, Cro. Jac. 505. Jenk. 333. S. C.

h Rudder v. Price, 1 Hen. Bla. 551.

i Ashford v. Hand, Andr. 370. Robin-son v. Bland, 2 Burr. 1085.

k Bacon v. Searles, 1 Hen. Bla. 88. Pierson v. Dunlop, Cowp. 571. Bayl. 99. acc. Johnson v. Kennion, 2 Wils. 262. Semb. contra.

l Cameron v. Smith, 2 Barn. & Ald. 305.

m 3 Ves. 134. 5 Ves. 803. Lithgow v. Lyon and others, 1 Cowp. Ch. Ca. 22. Lowndes v. Collens, 17 Ves. 27.

n Upton v. Lord Ferrers 5 Ves. 801.

Farquhar v. Morris, 7 T. R. 124. Blaney v. Hendrick, 2 Bla. Rep. 761. 3 Wils. 205. S. C.   Vernon v. Cholmondeley, Bunb. 119. Frith v. Loroux, 4. T. R. 58. Marins, 13. Cotton v. Horsemanden, Prac. Reg. 337, and see the cases and law in De Haviland v. Bowesbank, 1 Campb. 50 to 53. Porter v. Palsgrave, 2 Campb. 473. 3 Ves. 134, 5.

o Per Bayley, J. in Cameron v. Smith, 2 Barn. & Ald. 308.

p Ex parte Williams, 1 Rose, 399. and Ex parte Cocks, id. 317. Lowdes v. Collins, 17 Ves. 27. Lithgow v. Lyon, 1 Comp. Ch. Ca. 29.

q Id. ibid.

(537) It has been held in *Massachusetts*, that the instalments only which are due at
the commencement of the action can be recovered. *Tucker* v. *Randall*, 2 Mass. Rep.
283. And upon a note payable in a certain number of years with interest, in the mean
time, annually, judgment can be recovered upon default of payment of the interest, for
the interest only. *Hastings* v. *Wiswall*, 8 Mass. Rep. 455. *Greenleaf* v. *Kellogg*, 3
Mass. Rep. 568. *Cooley* v. *Rose*, 3 Mass. Rep. 221. And the interest so recoverable
is simple interest only upon the principal sum, although several years interest be in ar-
rear. *Hastings* v. *Wiswall*, 8 Mass. Rep. 455.
And interest is payable only according to the law of the place where the note is drawn
and is to be paid, though sued elsewhere. *Foden* v. *Sharp*, 4 John. Rep. 183. *Slacum*
v. *Pomery*, 6 Cranch. 221.

2dly. Inte-drawer or indorser of a bill of exchange, or the indorser of a note, is rest. only liable to pay interest from the time he receives notice of the dis-honour :[r] in order to subject him to liability in case of an inland bill, it is not necessary to protest it for non-payment ;[s] and where the maker of a promissory note paid money into the hands of an agent to retire it, and the agent tendered the money to the holder on condition of having it delivered up, and the note being mislaid, that condition was not com-plied with, and the agent afterwards became bankrupt with the money in his hands ; it was held, that though the maker was still responsible for the amount of the note, he was relieved from payment of interest ;[t] and when goods are sold, to be paid for by a bill of exchange, and the purchaser neglects to give the bill, the vendor is entitled to interest from the time when the bill, if given, would have become due ;[u] and the interest may, in that case, be recovered under the common count for goods sold ;[x] and this doctrine applies to any case where there is contract to pay by a bill.[y]

But interest is not recoverable on a debt for goods sold, even on limited credit,[z] or for work and labour done,[a] or for money had and re-ceived, or lent, unless there was a course of dealing allowing it,[b] un-

[422] less it can be proved that the defendant made use of the money, and did not merely withhold it.[c]

In some cases it is said, that interest is payable from the date of the note, as where it appears on the face of it to have been given for money lent ;[d] or is payable with interest.[e] Bankers cannot charge in-terest upon interest without an express contract for that purpose.[f]

Under *particulars of demand*, stating that the action was brought to recover the amount of a note of hand, it was holden, that interest on 'it is recoverable, and that when a note is payable by instalments, and on failure of payment, of any instalment, the whole is to become due, the interest is to be calculated on the whole sum remaining unpaid on default of any instalment, and not on the respective instalments at the respective times when they would become payable.[g]

With respect to *the time when interest stops*, Lord Mansfield de-clared,[h] that the general practice of the associates in taking damages in cases where the debt carried interest, was to stop at the commence-

[r] Walker v. Barnes, 5 Taunt. 240.—1 Marsh. 36 S. C.
[s] Ante, 218. 312. 405. Windle v. An-drews, 2 Barn. & Ald. 696
[t] Dent v. Dunn, 2 Campb. 296.
[u] Middleton v. Gill, 4 Taunt. 298, 9. Lowndes v. Collens, 17 Ves. 27. Porter v. Palgrave, 2 Campb. 472. Royce v. Warburton, 2 Campb. 480. 428, note.
[x] Manhall v. Poole, 13 East, 98 ; but see Slack v. Lowell, 3 Taunt. 157.
[y] 1 Furlonge v. Rucher, 4 Taunt. 250.
[z] Gordon v. Swan, 12 East, 419.—2 Campb. 429 ; but see Mountford v. Willis, 2 Bos & Pul. 337. Blancy v. Henrick, 3 Wils. 205. 2 Bla. Rep 761. S. C. Trelawney v. Thomas, 1 Hen. Bl. 305. Du Haviland v. Bowerbank, 1 Camp. 51.
[a] Trelawney v. Thomas, 1 Hen. Bla.

305. Blaney v. Hendrick, 3 Wils. 205. 2 Bla. Rep. 761. S. C. De Haviland r. Bowerbank, l Campb. 51.
[b] Calton v. Bragg, 15 East, 223. Ex parte Williams, 1 Rose, 399. Denton r. Rodie, 3 Campb. 496. Gwyn v. Godby, 4 Taunt. 346.
[c] Thompson v. Morgan, 3 Campb. 102. Walker v. Constable, 1 Bos. & Pul. 306. De Haviland v. Bowerbank, 1 Campb. 50. Crockford v. Winter, id. 129. De Bernales v. Fuller, 2 Campb. 426.
[d] Cotten v. Horsemanden, Prac. Reg. 357. Bayl. 158.
[e] Kennerly v. Nash, 1 Stark, 452
[f] Dawes v. Pinner, 2 Campb. 486. in note ; and ante, 85. But see Bruce r. Hunter, 3 Campb. 467.
[g] Blake v. Lawrence, 4 Esp. Rep. 147.
[h] In Robinson v. Bland, 2 Burr. 1085.

ment of the action ;[1] which practice was not founded in law, but in 2dly. Interest.
mistake and misapprehension ; and that in point of justice, interest
should be carried down quite to the actual payment of the money : but
as that cannot be, it should be carried down to the time when the
demand is completely liquidated, by the judgment being signed, by
which means complete justice is done to the plaintiff, and the tempta-
tion to a defendant to make use of all the unjust dilatories of chicane,
is taken away : for if interest were to stop at the commencement of
the suit, when the sum is large, the defendant might gain by protract-
ing the cause in the most expensive and vexatious manner. In trover
for bills of exchange, interest from the date of the final judgment upon
all such bills as had been received before the judgment, and upon all
such as had been received afterwards from the time of the receipt, was
allowed in the Exchequer Chamber ;[k] but it has been recently determined, that in trover for bills, interest cannot be recovered after the
time of the demand and refusal to deliver them up.[l] So we have seen
that after a tender and wrongful refusal to deliver a bill, the interest [423]
thereon ceases to run.[m]

The rate of interest allowed in this country is £5 *per cent. per
annum*, as well in courts of equity as at law.[n]

In an action against the drawer of a foreign bill of exchange dishonoured here by non-acceptance, where the plaintiff is allowed a *per
centage* as of £10 *per cent.* in name of damages, he is only entitled
to interest from the day the bill ought to have been paid, but where
there is no such allowance for damages, the plaintiff is entitled to
interest from the day the bill was dishonoured for non-acceptance.[o]
And in a late case, upon a bill drawn in Bermuda, on England, which
ought to have been paid in England, the plaintiff recovered 7½ interest,
being the rate of interest at Bermuda.[p]

The only *expense* which the holder of a bill, at the time it became 3dly. Ex-
due, can be put to by the dishonour of it, is, that of the charge for penses.
noting and protesting, and he cannot demand more of any of the parties
to the bill, than a satisfaction for that expense.(541) But a party who

[1] Randolph v. Raginder, Prac. Reg. 357.
[k] Atkins v. Wheeler, 2 New Rep. 205.
[l] Mercer v. Jones, 8 Campb. 477.
[m] Ante, 421.
[n] Upton v. Lord Ferrers, 5 Ves. 803. Ante, 76.
[o] Gantt v. Mackensie, 8 Campb. 51. This was an action on a bill of exchange for 1000l., drawn at Barbadoes, the 18th of February, 1809, by the defendant on Scott, Idles, and Co. in London, payable to the plaintiff at sixty days sight. The bill was refused acceptance on the 17th April, 1809, and was afterwards pre-sented for payment on the 19th June fol-lowing, and again dishonoured. The only question was, from what period in-terest was to be calculated. Lord Ellen-borough left this upon the custom of mer-chants to the special jury, who said the holder of the bill was entitled to 10l. per cent. as damages, and that interest was to be allowed only from the time when the bill was presented for payment ; and Mr. Waddington, the foreman, observed, that he had known it to be so settled in a case before Mr. Justice Buller. Verdict ac-cordingly.   But in a case of Harrison v. Dickson, tried at the same Sittings, which was an action against the indorser of a bill of exchange, drawn upon England from New South Wales, the plaintiff did not claim any per centage, upon the principal as damages, and was allowed interest from the time the bill was dishonoured for non-acceptance.
[p] Cougan v. Banks, N. P. Sittings after Mich. Term, 57 Geo. 3 Dec. 12. Pocock, attorney.

(541) The maker of a note is liable to the payee for the amount of the note only.
Simpson v. *Griffin*, 9 John. Rep. 131. And he cannot be compelled to pay the costs

3dly. Ex-
change.

has been obliged to pay the holder in consequence of the acceptor's refusal, frequently is put to other expenses by the return of the bill, such as *re-exchange, postage, commission,* and *provision.*[q]

Re-ex-
change.

[424]

Re-exchange is the expense incurred by the bill being dishonoured in a foreign country in which it was payable, and returned to the country in which it was made or indorsed, and there taken up: the amount of it depends on the course of the *exchange* between the countries through which the bill has been negotiated.[r]   It is not necessary for the plaintiff to show that he has paid the re-exchange: it appears not to be decided, whether any exchange or re-exchange can be allowed between this and an enemy's country.[s]   It is said,[t] that the relative abundance, or scarcity, of money in different countries, is what forms the exchange between those countries.   In the drawing of bills on a foreign country, the value of money in that country is the first thing to be inquired into; thus, for instance, supposing 71,000 livres tournois are worth £603. 19s. 10d. English money sterling, and that an English merchant has sold goods of the value of £603. 19s. 10d. to a Frenchman, who wishes to pay him for the same by a bill of exchange payable in France, the bill must of course be drawn for 71,000 livres tournois : if at the time the bill is due, the exchange is in favour of France, and consequently the value of 71,000 livres tournois exceeds that of £603. 19s. 10d. English money, and the bill be returned to this country, and the *drawer* or an *indorser,* be called on to take it up, he may (as in the case of Mellish v. Simeon,[u]) be obliged to pay £309. 4s. 5d. more than the amount of the bill, which sum forms what is called the re-exchange, and is the difference between the draft and re-draft.[x]   It appears that the *drawer* of a bill is liable for the whole amount of the re-exchange, occasioned by the circuitous mode of returning the bill through the various countries in which it has been negotiated, as much as for that occasioned by a direct return, although payment of the bill were expressly prohibited by the laws of the country on which it was drawn.[y]   But the acceptor is not liable for

[q] Auriol v. Thomas 2 T. R. 52.
[r] Cullen, 172. 1 Montague's Bank. Law, 146. For the nature of Exchange, see Mont. Esp. L. b. 2. l. 10, and Smith's Wealth of Nations, 2d vol. 144. 213. 234. and the observations in De Tastet v. Bearing, 11 East, 269. Bayl. 159, 160.
[s] De Tastet v. Bearing, 11 East, 265.
[t] Cullen, 102. 172. 1 Montague, 146. For the nature of Exchange, see Mont.

Esp. L. b. 2. l. 10, and Smith's Wealth of Nations, 2d vol. 144. 234. And see observations in De Tastet v. Baring, 11 East. 269.

[u] Mellish v. Simeon, 2 Hen. Bla. 378. Vide note, ante, 106.

[x] Francis v. Rucker, Amb. 674.— 2 Smith's Wealth of Nations, 229.

[y] Ante, 106.

of a suit brought by an indorsee, to whom the payee indorsed it. Ibid. But where it is the custom to protest notes on non-payment, the costs of the protest are recoverable. *Morgan* v. *Reintzel,* 7 Cranch, 273. Where on the indorsement of a note, the consideration passing between the indorsee and his indorser, is not equal to the amount of the note, the indorsee in an action against the indorser, can only recover the consideration which he has already paid. *Braman* v. *Hess,* 13 John. Rep. 52.

The acceptor of a bill and the maker of a note are not liable to an indorser for the costs which he may have incurred in consequence of default of payment by them. *Steele* v. *Sawyer,* 2 M'Cord. 459.

The drawer of a note is not bound to refund to the indorser any costs which he may have paid in consequence of his indorsement when he paid off the note as soon as it became due. *Richardson* v. *Parnall,* 1 M'Cord. 192.

The indorser of a *sealed* note is not liable as indorser, and if he suffer judgment to go against him he cannot recover the costs incurred from the drawer. *Parks* v. *Drake,* 2 M'Cord. 330.

re-exchange, for his contract cannot be carried farther than to pay the Re-ex-
change. sum specified in the bill, together with legal interest, where interest is due.[a] Where A. deposited a sum of money at the banking-house of B., in Paris, for which B. gave him his note payable in Paris, or at the choice of the bearer, at the Union Bank, in Dover, or at B's. usual residence in London, according to the course of exchange upon Paris, and after this note was given, the direct course of exchange between London and Paris ceased altogether, having been previously to its total cessation extremely low, and the note was at a subsequent period presented for acceptance, and payment at the residence of B., in London, [425] at which time there was a circuitous course of exchange on Paris, by way of Hamburgh, and it was holden, that A. was entitled to recover on the note according to such circuitous course of exchange upon Paris, at the time when the note was presented.[a] Between this country and India, it is not customary to make a distinct charge of re-exchange; but it has been the constant course with respect to bills for payment of pagodas in the East Indies, and returned protested, to allow at the rate of 10s. per pagoda, and five per cent. After the expiration of thirty days from the notice to the defendant of the bill's dishonour, which includes interest, exchange, and all other charges.[b] It appears from the case of Francis v. Rucker,[c] that the drawer and indorsers of bills, drawn in Pennsylvania on any person in Europe, and returned protested for non-payment to that country, are liable to the payment of £20 per cent. advance for the damage thereof. But the liability to pay re-exchange does not extend to the acceptor of a bill accepted in England: he is only liable for the principal sum, together with interest, according to the legal rate of interest where the bill is payable.[d]

In De Tastet v. Baring,[e] a verdict having passed for the defendants in an action to recover the amount of the re-exchange upon the dishonour of a bill drawn from London on Lisbon, upon evidence that the enemy was in possession of Portugal when the bill became due, and Lisbon was then blockaded by a British squadron, and there was in fact no direct exchange between London and Lisbon, though bills had in some few instances been negotiated between them through Hamburgh and America about that period, the court refused to grant a new trial, on the presumption that the jury had found their verdict on the fact that no re-exchange was found to their satisfaction to have existed between Lisbon and London at the time; the question having been properly left to them to allow damages in the name of re-exchange, if the plaintiff, who had indorsed the dishonoured bill to the holder, had had either paid, or was liable to pay, re-exchange; and saving the question of law, whether any exchange or re-exchange could be allowed between this and a country in possession of the enemy.

With respect to provision, it is said by Pothier,[f](544) that it is usual Provision, &c.

[a] Napier v. Schneider, 12 East, 420. Bayl. 160.
[a] Pollard v. Herries, 3 Bos. & Pul. 335. Ante, 287; and see Bayl. 159, 160.
[b] Auriol v. Thomas, 2 T. R. 52. Bayl. 161.
[c] Francis v. Rucker, Amb. 672.
[d] Woolsley v. De Crawford, 2 Campb. 445. Napier v. Schneider, 12 East, 420; but see Pothier, cited in Manning's Index, 64.
[e] 11 East, 265. 2 Campb. 65. S. C.
[f] Pl. 86, 87, 88.

(544) In Massachusetts, in actions on foreign bills against the drawer or indorser, the holder is entitled to recover the money for which the bill was drawn, the charges of protest with interest at six per cent. on these sums from the time when the bill should have been paid, and the further sum of ten per cent. of the money for which the bill was drawn,

Provision, for the holder of a bill to allow his agent, to whom he indorses it for the
&c.   purpose of receiving payment for him, a certain sum of money called
[426] "provision," at the rate of so much *per cent.* to recompense him, not
only for his trouble, but also, if such agent be a banker, for the risk
he runs of losing the money, which he is obliged to deposit with his
correspondents in different places for the purpose of re-paying his principal the amount of the money received on the bills. And it is said,
that one half *per cent.* is not an unreasonable allowance, whether the
agent be a banker or not.

The charges above enumerated, are the only legal ones, nor can any
extraordinary loss not necessarily incidental, which the holder or other
parties may be put to by travelling, or by some advantageous engagement being delayed or defeated by the want of punctual payment, be in
any case legally demanded.*

*t Lovelass, 235. cites Lex Merc. 461. 52. Woolsley v. De Crawford, 2 Campb.
Poth. pl. 55. Auriol v. Thomas, 2 T. R. 445.*

---

with interest from the time when payment of the dishonoured bill was demanded of the
drawer. But nothing is allowed for re-exchange, the ten *per cent.* being by immemorial
usage, a substitute for it. *Grimshaw* v. *Bender*, 6 Mass. Rep. 157. *Barclay* v. *Minchin*,
6 Mass. Rep. 162.
In *Pennsylvania,* twenty *per cent.* is allowed in lieu of damages and charges. *Chapman* v. *Steinmets*, 1 Dall. Rep. 261. *Keppele* v. *Carr*, 4 Dall. Rep. 155. *Hendricks* v.
Franklin, 4 John. Rep. 119. *Statute of Pennsylvania*, 1700. *Purdon's Digest*, 66.
The same rule prevails in *New York*. *Kenworthy* v. *Hopkins*, 1 John. Cas. 107. *Hendricks* v. *Franklin*. *Weldon* v. *Buck*, 4 John. Rep. 144. *Thompson* v. *Robertson*,
4 John. Rep. 27. And the holder can recover no more than the contents of the foreign
bill, and twenty *per cent.* damages, with interest, and charges of protest, *at the par of
exchange;* and nothing is to be allowed for the difference between the price of the bill
at the time it was returned, and at the time it was drawn. *Hendricks* v. *Franklin.* But
in the Court of Errors of *New York*, this decision has been overruled by a bare majority,
and it has been held, that the holder is entitled to recover the contents of the bill *at the
rate of exchange*, or price of bills on the place in which it was drawn, at the time of the
return of the dishonoured bill, and notice thereof to the drawer, together with twenty
per cent. damages and interest. *Graves* v. *Dash*, 12 John. Rep. 17. And the twenty
per cent. damages are payable upon a protest for non-acceptance, as well as for non-payment. *Weldon* v. *Buck*. But not where the bill is remitted to pay an antecedent debt.
Kenworthy v. *Hopkins*, 1 John. Cas. 107. *Thompson* v. *Robertson*, S. P. *Chapman* v.
Steinmets, 1 Dall. Rep. 261.
In *Rhode Island*, the damages on foreign bills are settled at ten *per cent. Brown* v
Van Braam, 3 Dall. Rep. 244. 346. *Statutes of Rhode Island*, p. 444. edit. 1798. In *South
Carolina,* the damages on foreign bills are fifteen *per cent.*, with the difference of exchange. *Winthrop* v. *Pepoon*, 1 Bay's Rep. 468. In *Virginia,* the damages on foreign
bills are fifteen *per cent. Slacum* v. *Pomeroy*, 6 Cranch, 221.
And now in *Pennsylvania,* by an act of assembly passed the 30th March, 1821, the
former act is repealed, and the damages recoverable on foreign bills of exchange, over and
above the principal sum, charges of protest, and interest from the time of notice of protest
and demand of principal and damages, are as follows: if drawn on persons in the United
States, or territories thereof, (excepting the state of Louisiana,) five *per cent.* on the principal sum; on persons in Louisiana, or other place in North America, or the islands thereof, (excepting the north-west coast of Mexico,) or in any of the West India or Bahama
islands, ten *per cent ;* on persons in the island of Madeira, the Canaries, the Azores, the
Cape de Verd islands, the Spanish Main, or Mexico, fifteen *per cent.;* on persons in Europe, or the islands thereof, twenty *per cent.;* on persons in any other part of the world,
twenty-five *per cent.*

CHAPTER VI.

OF THE ACTION OF DEBT ON A BILL, &c.

THE remedy by *action of debt*, to enforce payment of a bill or note, and the *proof* of it *under the commission of bankruptcy*, remain to be considered in this chapter.

The *action of debt* on simple contract was formerly much in use, but was afterwards disused on account of the *wager of law ;*[a] it has lately revived in practice, and is now become a common action for the reco- very of money due on simple contract. The principal advantages arising from adopting this remedy are, *first*, that the plaintiff need not, after judgment by default, execute a writ of inquiry, or refer to the Master to compute principal and interest; and *secondly*, that the defen- dant must, in debt, on a *bill of exchange*, if there be no other count in the declaration on another simple contract, put in special bail on bring- ing *a writ of error ;*[b] but bail in error is not necessary, on a judgment by default in debt, on a *promissory note*, the validity of which instru- ment was not established until after the statute James 1. c. 8.[c] And if a declaration, in debt on a bill of exchange, contain any one count on a contract for which debt would not lie at the time of passing the statute 3 James 1 c. 8, bail in error is not necessary.[d] Debt on sim- ple contract, also, is not sustainable against executors or administrators,[e] except in the Court of Exchequer, where wager of law is not allowed,[f] or by special custom in the city of London.[g]

This action may be supported by the *payee* of a *promissory note* against the *maker*, when expressed to be for *value received*,[h] and by the *payee* of a foreign or inland bill of exchange expressed to be for *value received* against the *drawer*,[i] and by the first indorsee against the first indorser, who was also the drawer of a bill payable to his own order.[k] In Bishop v. Young,[l] (the most recent decision on the sub- [428] ject,) the court said, "We do not say how the case would stand, if the " action were brought by any other person than him to whom the note " was originally given, or against any other person than him by whom " it was signed and made, or if the note itself did not express a con- " sideration upon the face of it." Therefore it is still uncertain, whe- ther in respect of the want of privity between the parties, an *indorsee* can support an action of debt against the drawer of a bill or maker of a note.

(margin note: Sect. 1. Of the action of debt on a bill or note.)

---

[a] Gilb. on the Action of Debt, 363, 4.
[b] Ablet v. Ellis, 1 Bos. & Pul. 249. Trier v. Bridgman, 2 East, 359.
[c] Trier v. Bridgman, 2 East, 359.
[d] Webb v. Geddes, 1 Taunt. 540. Trier v. Bridgman, 2 East, 359.
[e] Barry v. Robinson, 1 New Rep. 293. Norwood v. Read, Plowd. 182. Palmer v. Lawson, 1 Lev. 200. Pinchon's case, 9 Co. 86, 7. 3 Bls. Com. 347.

[f] Id. Ibid.
[g] The City of London's case, 8 Co. 126 a. Bishop v. Young, 2 Bos. & Pul. 78. Bayl. 126. Selw. 4th edit. 363, n. 69.
[i] Bishop v. Young, 2 Bos. & Pul. 82, 83, 84. Hodges v. Steward, Skin. 346.
[k] Stratton v. Hill, 3 Price, 253.
[l] Bishop v. Young, 2 Bos. & Pul. 78. 84.

Sect. 1. Of   Debt is not sustainable on a *collateral* engagement, as on a promise
the action   to pay the debt of another ;^m and it has been holden, that debt cannot
of debt on a
bill or note. be supported on a bill of exchange by the *payee* against the *acceptor ;*
therefore bail in error is not necessary upon a judgment in debt against
the acceptor of a bill ;^o *first,* because no privity of contract exists
between those parties ;^p and *secondly,* because in an action of debt on
simple contract, the consideration ought to be shown, which is not
stated in a declaration on a bill; and an acceptance is only in the
nature of a collateral promise or engagement to pay, which creates no
duty.^q In Rumball *v.* Ball,^r the plaintiff recovered in an action of

[429] debt on a promissory note, and in another reporter it is said, that debt
will lie against the maker of a note, but not against an indorser.^s In
Welsh *v.* Craig,^t it was holden, that debt would not lie upon a note,
but, as it has been observed, it does not appear by, or against, what
particular party that action was brought,^u though from the argument of
counsel it may be inferred, that the action was against an indorser.^x
Debt is not sustainable on a promissory note payable by instalments,
unless the whole be due,^y (547)

^m Anon. Hardr. 486.   Com. Dig. tit.
Debt, B.   Purslow *v.* Baily, 2 Ld. Raym.
1040.   Hodsden *v.* Harridge, 2 Saund.
52 b.
ⁿ Bishop *v.* Young, 2 Bos. & Pul. 80. 82,
83.   Anon Hardr. 485.   Simmonds *v.*
Parminter, 1 Wils. 185.   Browne *v.* London, 1 Mod. 285.   Gilb. tit. Debt, 364.
Com. Dig. tit. Debt, B.   Anon. 12 Mod.
345.   Bayl. 94.   1 Taunt. 540.   2 Campb.
137, n. a.
^o Webb *v.* Geddes, 1 Taunt 540.
^p Rol. Ab. 497, pl. 4. 10.   Core's case,
1 Dyer, 21 a.
^q Bishop *v.* Young, 2 Bos. & Pul. 83.
Hodges *v.* Steward, 1 Salk. 125, pl. 5.
Vin. Ab. tit. Bills, N.   But perhaps, the
action of debt might now be sustainable
by the payee, &c. against the acceptor,
first, because with respect to privity of
contract, it has been holden, that if one
deliver money to another to pay over to
a third person, the *cestuique use* may sustain an action of debt against the bailee
to recover it.   Harris *v.* De Bervoir, Cro.
Jac. 687.   1 Rol. Ab. 441. 597. l. 55.
Whorewood *v.* Shaw, Yelv. 23.   And the
acceptance of a bill amounts to a promise
in law, to pay the amount of it to the
person in whose favour it is drawn.   Hussey *v.* Jacob, 1 Ld. Raym. 88.   And se-

eondly, because an acceptance is not a
collateral engagement, nor is it similar to
a promise by A. to pay the debt of B., if
B. do not, an argument which was adduced in support of the doctrine, but the
acceptor is primarily liable.   Bishop *v.*
Young, 2 Bos. & Pul. 83.   And *lastly,*
because whenever the common law or custom raises a duty, debt lies for it, Anon.
Hardr. 486.   Com. Dig. tit. Debt, A.
Hussey *v.* Jacob, Ld. Raym. 88, on which
ground Twisden, J. held, that *indebitatus
assumpsit* would lie on a bill of exchange
at the suit of the payee against the accept-
or.   Brown *v.* London, 1 Vent. 152.
Anon. Holt, 296.   Anon. 12 Mod. 345.
Hodges *v.* Steward, Skin. 346. acc. Brown
v. London, 1 Freem. 14.   1 Mod. 285.
1 Vent. 152. S. C.   Hodges *v.* Steward,
Comb. 204. *contra.*
^r Rumball *v.* Ball, 10 Mod. 38, ob-
served on in Bishop *v.* Young, 2 Bos. &
Pul. 84.
^s 1 Mod. Ent. 312, pl. 13.
^t Welsh *v.* Craig, 2 Stra. 680.   8 Mod.
173. S. C. observed on in Bishop *v.* Young.
2 Bos. & Pul. 80, 81, 82.
^u Bishop *v.* Young, 2 Bos. & Pul. 81.
Bayl. 94, n. c.
^x Bishop *v.* Young, 2 Bos. & Pul. 80.
^y Rudder *v.* Price, 1 Hen. Bla. 548.

(547) In *Maryland* debt will not lie on a note at the suit of a payee or his administrators against the maker.   *Lindo* v. *Gardner,* 1 Cranch, 343.   In *Virginia* debt will not
lie against an acceptor of a bill, even in a suit by the payee.   *Smith* v. *Sagar,* 3 Hen.
and Munf. Rep. 394.   *Wilson* v. *Crowdhill,* 2 Munf. Rep. 302.   But an action of debt
lies by statute for the holder of a bill against the drawer and indorser in case of a default
in payment.   *Slacum* v. *Pomeroy,* 6 Cranch, 221.
   An action of debt cannot be maintained on a note for the payment of a liquidated sum
in current bank paper.   *Campbell* v. *Neister,* 1 Litt. 30.
   But debt lies by the drawer against the acceptor of a bill of exchange payable to the
drawer or order for value received in goods.   *Pridday* v. *Henbrey,* 1 Barn. & Cresw.
674.

CHAPTER VII.

OF BANKRUPTCY.

IN the preceding chapters, our attention has been principally directed to the consideration of the remedies in cases where the parties to a bill or other negotiable security, may be supposed to be *solvent.* In this chapter the rights and liabilities of the parties, and the course of proceeding in the case of *bankruptcy,* will be treated of. In this inquiry, we shall only consider that part of the law of bankruptcy which peculiarly relates to bills of exchange and other negotiable securities.

The subject is to be considered under the following heads :—

I. What constitutes a *trading* by being a party to bills.
II. The *act of bankruptcy* in relation to bills.
III. The *petitioning creditor's debt* by being holder of bill,
IV. The *proof* of bills, &c.
1st. What bills may be proved.
2d. Who may prove.
3d. Against whom and under what commission.
4th. For what sums or to what extent the proof may be made.
5th. The time of proof and of claims.
6th. The mode and terms of proof, and remedy for the dividend.
7th. The consequences of not proving, and effect of certificate.
V. Of *mutual credit.*
VI. General *effect of bankruptcy* on the property of the bankrupt and of others.

I. WHAT CONSTITUTES A *TRADING* BY BEING A PARTY TO A BILL.

With respect to the *trading;* drawing and redrawing bills of exchange, for the sake of the profit, is a trading sufficient to subject a party to be made a bankrupt, without other circumstances, if it be general and not merely occasional.[a] This is founded on the 13 Eliz. c. 7, and 21 James. 1. c. 19. s. 2, which enact, "That every person [431] "using the trade of merchandize by way of bargaining, exchange, bartering, chevisance, or otherwise, in gross or by retail, may become "bankrupts." Instances of this description do not often occur. In the case of Richardson v. Bradshaw,[b] the bankrupt, Wilson, for several years received money from officers and other persons, and his cashier gave accountable notes for it, and these persons drew from time to time upon Wilson for such sums, payable either to bearer or order, as they thought proper; and this repeated dealing was held to be a trafficking in exchange, and a trading sufficient in itself to subject him to a commission of bankruptcy,[c] upon the principle, that persons of this description

1. The trading.

[a] Richardson v. Bradshaw, 1 Atk. 129. Hankey v. Jones, Cowp. 745. 1 Mont. 22. Cullen, 10. Cook, 52.
[b] 1 Atk. 128. Cook, 61.
[c] Richardson v. Bradshaw, 1 Atk. 129. Ex parte Wilson, 1 Atk. 218.

1. The tra-
ding.

make merchandize of money and bills, and gain an extensive credit upon
the profits of that course of dealing, in the same manner as other merchants and traders do by buying and selling, or using the trade of merchandize in gross, or by retail, with respect to other goods and move-
able chattels.[d] On the same principle, borrowing money abroad for the
purpose of repaying it in England at a certain rate of exchange, and
repaying it by bills upon bankers in London, to whom foreign bills were
remitted to make the payment, was held to be a trading.[e] But an occasional drawing and redrawing bills of exchange, though for the sake
of profit, as where it is done for the purpose of raising money to im-
prove a person's own estate, or for other private occasions, will not render a person liable to the bankrupt laws.[f] And the statutes relating to
Exchequer Bills[g] expressly provide that a party circulating the same
shall not be deemed a trader within the bankrupt laws.

II. THE ACTS OF BANKRUPTCY IN RELATION TO BILLS.

2. Act of
bankrupt-
cy.

With respect to the *act of bankruptcy;* stopping payment, or refusing
payment of, or renewing a bill of exchange, does not amount to an act
of bankruptcy.[h] But a denial by a trader to the holder of a bill of exchange actually due, or to his clerk, at any time of the day, when it became due, constitutes an act of bankruptcy, which cannot be avoided by
afterwards appearing in public and paying the bill before five o'clock

[432]

of that day.[i] So if a commission has been issued against a party to a
bill, and he afterwards compromises with the petitioning creditor by
paying a part of the debt, this will in itself constitute an act of bankruptcy;[k] and though stopping payment is not of itself an act of bankruptcy, the statutes which protect payments and other transactions
taking place after a secret act of bankruptcy, expressly provide that
stopping payment shall be equivalent to notice of the act of bankruptcy;[l] but the mere circumstance of a person's renewing a bill is not deemed stopping payment or notice of insolvency.[m]

III. OF A PETITIONING CREDITOR IN RESPECT OF A
BILL.

3. Petition-
ing credi-
tor's debt.

With respect to the petitioning creditor's debt, when founded in part
or the whole on a bill or note, there must be a debt of £100, or debts
of £150, independently of interest, for interest accruing before the act
of bankruptcy, cannot be added to the principal, so as to constitute a
good petitioning creditor's debt, unless interest be specially made payable on the face of the bill.[n] When the bill or note is completely due
and payable before the act of bankruptcy, his right to strike a docket
stands precisely in the same situation as that of other demands completely due. But with respect to bills and other negotiable securities
not due at the time of the act of bankruptcy, the holder stands in a dif-

[d] 2 Bla. Com. 475.
[e] Inglis *v.* Grant, 5 T. R. 530. 1 Mont.
22.
[f] Hankey *v.* Jones, Cowp. 745. 1 Mont.
26. Cullen, 18. Cook, 60, 61. Harrison *v.* Harrison, 2 Esp. Rep. 555.
[g] See the statute, Cooke, 84.
[h] Cullen, 65. Anon. 1 Campb. 492, (n.)
[i] Colkett *v.* Freeman, 2 T. R. 59, Muck-

low *v.* May, 1 Taunt. 479. Ex parte Levy,
7 Vin. 61, pl. 14.
[k] Ex parte Gedge, 3 Ves. 349. Cullen.
57.
[l] 46 Geo. 3. c. 135. s. 8. 49 Geo. 3.
c. 121.
[m] 1 Campb. 492.
[n] Cameron *v.* Smith, 2 Barn. & Ald. 305.

ferent situation. The date of a promissory note made by a bankrupt, is *prima facie* evidence to show that the note existed before the bankruptcy; but no declaration by the bankrupt, subsequent to his bankruptcy, would be admissible to prove the fact.[o] But if two persons exchange acceptances, and before the bills are mature, one of them commits an act of bankruptcy, there is not such a debt due from him to the other, as will sustain a commission.[p]

[433]

The 7 Geo. 1. c. 31,[q] enables persons, who have given credit on bills, bonds, promissory notes, or other personal securities, not due at the time of the act of bankruptcy, to *prove* the same under a commission, deducting a rebate of interest at £5 *per cent.*; however, the 3d section enacted, "That no such creditor shall be deemed or taken "to be a sufficient creditor for or in respect of such debt, to petition; "or join in any petition, for the obtaining, or suing forth any com-"misston of bankruptcy, until such time as such debt shall become "actually due and payable." But the statute 5 Geo. 2. c. 30. s. 22. reciting that this last restriction has been found to be inconvenient, enacts, "That persons taking bills, bonds, promissory notes, or other "personal security for their money, payable at a future day, may "petition for, or join in petitioning for, any commission of bank-"ruptcy."

Since this statute, if a bill be accepted before the act of bankruptcy, though it be not then payable, the holder may issue a commission against the acceptor:[r] and as a bill, although not due at the time of the bankruptcy of the drawer or indorser, may be proved under a commission against them,[s] it should seem, that since the stat. 5 Geo. 2. c. 32. s. 22, a commission might also be issued against such parties;[t] and though it was doubted, at Nisi Prius, whether a bill of exchange is a good petitioning creditor's debt against the *drawer* before it becomes due, or has been dishonoured by the acceptor;[u] it has since been settled, that such a bill does constitute a sufficient petitioning creditor's debt, and that a commission may be issued against the drawer, although the bill was neither due nor had been presented for acceptance or payment, and though after the issuing of the commission, and when the bill became due, the drawee had duly paid it.[x]

It was recently determined,[y] that a bill of exchange to the precise amount of £100, drawn and issued by a trader, before an act of bankruptcy, but becoming due afterwards, is sufficient, when due, to found a petition for a commission of bankrupt against him, though, allowing a rebate of interest, there was not at the time of the act of bankruptcy a debt of £100.

A creditor, by a bill or note, made by the bankrupt before the act of bankruptcy, but not *indorsed* to the holder till after, is allowed to be a petitioning creditor; for this is a case in which the law allows the as-

---

[o] Taylor v. Kinlock, 1 Stark. 175. 179. 2 Rose, 474.

[p] Sarratt v. Austin, 4 Taunt. 200. 208. 2 Rose, 112.

[q] See the statute in the Appendix; and as to the words "give credit," see Lord Ellenborough's observations in Starey v. Barnes, 7 East, 441.

[r] 1 Mont. 44. Cullen, 74.

[s] Macarty v. Barrow, 2 Stra. 949.— 3 Wils. 16. S. C. Ex parte Adney, Cowp. 460. 1 Mont. 150. Cullen, 98. Bayl. 193, 4.

[t] Starey v. Barnes, 7 East, 435.

[u] Rose v. Rowcroft, 4 Campb. 245.

[x] Ex parte Douthat, 4 B. & A. 67.

[y] Brett v. Levett, 13 East, 213. Bayl. 193, n. 3. 1 Rose, 112.

CHITTY ON BILLS. 3 D

3. Petition-
ing credi-
tor's debt.

[434]

signment of a *chose in action*, and the assignment relates to the original debt, and the assignee stands in the original creditor's place.[a] For the same reason, a creditor may, to a debt due to himself before, take a note of the bankrupt, indorsed to him after the bankruptcy, to make up the sum required by the statute: it being sufficient within the words of the statute, that there is an existing debt (of the requisite amount) in the person of the petitioning creditor at the time he petitions.[a] It must be proved, however, in order to support the commission, that the bill was indorsed by the bankrupt to the petitioning creditor before the suing out of the commission.[b]

The holder of a bill or note to the amount of £100, or upwards, though he may have bought it for less, is a creditor for the full sum, and may issue a commission.[c] But these statutes only enable creditors, upon *written* securities to issue a commission, and do not enable a creditor, for goods sold on credit not elapsed, to strike a docket, although the agreement were, that the goods should be paid for by a present bill payable at a future day.[d] And these statutes do not affect bills of exchange or other securities given or indorsed *after* the act of bankruptcy, on which the *commission is founded*, in respect of which a person cannot in general be a petitioning creditor;[e] and though the 46 Geo. 3. c. 135. s. 2, enables persons to *prove* debts, contracted after a secret act of bankruptcy, and before the commission, yet it does not authorize a creditor to strike a docket in respect of such a debt.[f]

But when a good petitioning creditor's debt, and an act of bankruptcy subsequent to it has been proved, it is not sufficient, in order to invalidate a commission founded on it, to prove a prior act of bankruptcy, without also proving a prior debt, sufficient to sustain a commission: and it is not competent for the bankrupt himself to set up a former act of bankruptcy, in order to invalidate his commission.[g] And if a creditor take a bill after an act of bankruptcy for a debt contracted before, drawn by the bankrupt upon one who had no effects in his hands at the time, or previous to the bill's becoming due, the original debt is not extinguished by want of notice to the drawer, of the bill's having been dishonoured, and is sufficient to

[435]

support a commission. Want of notice, though in general tantamount to payment, is not so in this case, for having no effects in the drawee's hands, he cannot be injured.[h] And it has even been held, that if, after committing a secret act of bankruptcy, a trader gives to his creditor a bond for a debt due on simple contract before the act of bankruptcy, it does not so far extinguish the simple contract debt as to deprive the creditor of his right to petition.[i] Where, however, the

[a] Ex parte Thomas, 1 Atk. 73. Anon. 2 Wils. 135. Bingley *v.* Maddison, Co. Bank. Law, 19. Cullen, 74. 1 Mont. 43. 46. 4 Campb. 246, in notes. Bayl. 194, 5.

[a] Glaister *v.* Hewer, 7 T. R. 498. Cooke, 20. Cullen, 75. 1 Mont. 48.

[b] Rose *v.* Rowcroft, 4 Campb. 245.

[c] Ex parte Lee, 1 P. W. 783. Ex parte Marlar, 1 Atk. 150. 1 Mont. 48.

[d] Hoskins *v.* Duperoy, 9 East, 498. Cothay *v.* Murray, 1 Campb. 335.

[e] Moss *v.* Smith, 1 Campb. 489. 490. Cullen, 73. 1 Mont. 40, 41; but see as to the validity of all contracts entered into after a secret act of bankruptcy, more than two calendar months before the date of the commission, 46 Geo. 3. c. 135. Bayl. 195, 6.

[f] Moss *v.* Smith, 1 Campb. 489.

[g] The King *v.* Bullock, 1 Taunt. 71. Bayl. 195, 6.

[h] Bickerdike *v.* Bollman, 1 T. R. 406. Cullen, 75.

[i] Ambrose *v.* Clendon, 2 Stra. 1042. Daw *v.* Holdsworth, Peake, 64. Cullen 75. 1 Mont. 41 to 44.

BANKRUPTCY. 435

laches, or conduct of the holder have deprived him of his remedy at law against the trader, who has committed an act of bankruptcy, it will be equally incompetent to him to strike a docket. And in general, if the commission be against the *drawer* or *indorser* of a bill, it must be proved that he had due notice of non-payment, the same as in an action, but proof that after an act of bankruptcy he admitted that he knew the bill would not be paid, will suffice.[k]

It was held in the case of Man *v.* Shepherd,[l] that if a creditor, knowing that his debtor has committed an act of bankruptcy, receive part of his debt, the payment is void, and the original debt remains in force, and will support a commission, founded on the petition of such creditor. But a debt which could not be recovered in an action, in consequence of a plea of the Statute of Limitations, nor in equity by analogy to it, will not *be sufficient to support a commission*, or be proveable under it.[m] And in general, whatever objection would preclude the holder of a bill from recovering at law, or in equity, will equally preclude him from issuing a commission of bankruptcy; for, as observed by Lord Chancellor Eldon, in the case Ex parte Dowdney, "The meaning of the legislature in the bankrupt acts, requiring the "Lord Chancellor to give execution to all the creditors was, that this "species of execution should be given to those creditors who, if a "commission had not issued, could by legal or equitable remedies "have compelled payment." Hence, it is necessary in considering when a person may strike a docket, or prove in respect of a bill of exchange, to keep in view the rules which have been stated in the previous part of this work, as well as those more particularly relating to this part of the subject.

When the debt, in respect of which the docket is to be struck, is [436] due to *several persons*, whether as general partners or otherwise, they must all be petitioning creditors, and a commission, founded upon the petition of one of such creditors, could not be supported;[n] the proceedings under a commission being analogous in this respect to an action.[o] But it is not necessary that all the partners should join in the affidavit of the debt. It will suffice, if one of them swear that the debt is due to himself and partners.[p]

The petitioning creditor is considered as having determined his election by taking out a commission, and is not allowed afterwards to proceed at law, though for a demand which is alleged to be distinct from that on which he sued out the commission.[q]

IV. OF THE PROOF OF BILLS UNDER A COMMISSION.

Previously to the statute 7 Geo. 1. c. 31, no debt, unless it were completely due, and payable at the *time of the act* of bankruptcy could

*3. Petition-
ing credi-
tor's debt.*

*4. Proof of
bills.*

[k] Brett *v.* Levett, 18 East, 213,—1 Rose, 103, n. a.
[l] 6 T. B. 79. Cullen, 69. 1 Mont. 35.
[m] Ex parte Dewdney, 13 Ves. 379, 498. *acc.*; but see 1 Cooke, 15, *contra.* 15 Ves. 495. If bankrupt do not object no one else can. See 5 Burr. 2638. 1 Mont. 38. 15 Ves. 491, 3, 4.

[n] Buckland *v.* Newsome, 1 Taunt. 477 1 Campb. 474. S. C.
[o] 1 Saund. 153, n. 1. 291, f. g. 2 Stra 820. 1 Bos. & Pul. 73.
[p] 2 Cooke, 1. 4 Mont. 14, n. B. Vide Form of Affidavit, post, Appendix.
[q] Ex parte Lewis, 1 Atk. 154. Ex parte Callow; 8 Ves. 1. Ex parte Ward, 1 Atk. 153. Cullen, 154. Cooke, 25.

4. Proof of be proved, though it became due before the issuing of the commission.[r]
bills.   This statute contains the following recital and enactments :—

> " Whereas merchants and other traders in goods have been very often
> "obliged, and more especially of late years, to sell or dispose of
> " their goods and merchandizes to such persons as have occasion for
> " the same, upon trust or credit, and to take bills, bonds, promissory
> "notes, or other personal[s] securities for their moneys, payable at the
> " end of three, four, or six months, or other future days of payment;
> " and the buyers of such goods becoming bankrupts, and commissions
> "of bankruptcy being taken out against them, before the money upon
> " such bonds, notes, or other securities became payable, it hath been
> " a question whether such persons, giving such credit on such secu-
> "rities, should be let in to prove their debts, or be admitted to have
> "any dividend, or other benefit by the commission, before such time
> " as such securities became payable, which hath been a great dis-
> " couragement to trade, and great prejudice to credit within this
> " realm ;" for remedy whereof, *it is enacted*, " That all and every
[437] > " person and persons, who have given credit, or at any time or times
> " hereafter, shall *give credit* on such *securities* as aforesaid, to any per-
> " son or persons, who is, are, or shall become bankrupts, upon a good
> " and valuable consideration, *bona fide*, for any sum or sums of mo-
> " ney, *or other matter or thing whatsoever*, which is or shall not
> " be due or payable at or before the time of such person's becoming
> " bankrupt, shall be admitted to prove his, her, and their several and
> " respective bills, bonds, notes, or other securities, promise, or
> " agreements for the same, in like manner as if they were made
> " payable presently, and not at a future day ; and shall be entitled
> " unto, and shall have and receive a proportionable part, share, and
> " dividend of such bankrupt's estate, in proportion to the other credi-
> " tors of such bankrupt, deducting only thereout *a rebate of interest*,
> " and discounting such securities, payable at future times, after the
> " rate of five pounds *per centum per annum*, for what he shall so re-
> " ceive, to be computed from the actual payment thereof, to the time
> " such debt, duty, or sum of money, should or would have become due
> " and payable, in and by such securities as aforesaid." *In the second
> section it is enacted*, " That all and every person or persons, who now
> " are, or shall become bankrupts, shall be discharged of and from all
> " and every such bond, note, or other security as aforesaid, and shall
> " have the benefit of the several statutes now in force against bank-
> " rupts in like manner, to all intents and purposes, as if such sum of
> " money had been due and payable before the time of his becoming a
> " bankrupt."

The subsequent statute, 5 Geo. 2. c. 30. s. 22., is considered as a
legislative construction of the 7 Geo. 1. c. 31. and to confine that
statute to *written* securities.[t]   But it is provided by the 49 Geo. 3.
c. 121. s. 9. " That all persons who have given credit to any person
" who shall become bankrupt, upon good and valuable consideration
" for any money whatever, which shall not be due or payable at or
" before the time of such person's becoming bankrupt, shall be admit-
" ted to prove such their debts, as if the same were payable presently,

---

[r] Barnford *v.* Burrell, 2 Bos. & Pul. I.   [t] Hoskins *v.* Duperoy, 9 East, 563; and
                                                         Parslow *v.* Dearlove, 4 East, 438. These
[s] The statute says, " persons," but this   cases settle the point doubted in *Cullen*,
is a mistake, see 5 Geo. 2. c. 30. s. 22.   74, and 1 Mont. 45.

" or not at a future day ; and shall be entitled to, and shall have and 4. Proof of
" receive proportional dividends, equally with the other creditors, de- bills.
" ducting in England, £5 *per cent.*, and in Ireland, £6 *per cent.* inte-
" rest, to be computed from the actual payment, to the time such debts
" would become payable, according to the terms upon which the same
" were contracted."

Upon these statutes, the proof of a bill of exchange under a commis- [438]
sion, may be considered under the following heads :—

1*st*, *What bill, note, &c. may be proved.*
2*d*, *Who may prove.*
3*d*, *Against whom, or under what commission.*
4*th*, *For what sums, or to what extent, the proof may be made.*
5*th*, *The time of proof, and of claims.*
6*th*, *The mode and terms of proof, and remedy for the dividend.*
7*th*, *The consequence of not proving, and effect of certificate.*

1*st*, *What bills are proveable.*

From the judgment of Lord Eldon, in the case Ex parte Dewdney,[a] 1st. What
it may be collected, that wherever a bill of exchange, or other nego- bills prove-
tiable security, would be valid at law, so as to support an action, it able.
may be proved under a commission ; and, on the other hand, it appears
to be a general rule, that a bill, not available at law or in equity, cannot be proved under a commission.   A bill founded upon a usurious,
gaming, or other *consideration*, rendering it void by some statute, cannot be proved, even by a *bona fide* holder :[b] and whenever the holder
himself has received the bill upon any illegal contract, he cannot,
in general, prove such bill in respect of such consideration ;[y] and
the assignees and creditors have a right to insist, that the whole security is void, and unless they submit to pay what is really due, the
court cannot order it, and frequent applications of that sort have been
refused.[z]

In Ex parte Bulmer,[a] where promissory notes, given by a stock-
broker for the balance of an account of money advanced to him to be
employed in stock-jobbing transactions, contrary to the Stock Jobbing
Act, and part of the consideration consisted of the profits upon those
transactions, and the residue for money received, which he had applied
to his own use, Lord Erskine would not permit the petitioner to prove
the promissory notes as binding obligations, as the consideration for them
was made up, though in a very small part, of the fruit of the illegal
use of the money lodged with the bankrupt, but allowed the petitioner
to prove the sum applied by the bankrupt to his own use, as money had
and received.

Where the consideration of the bill consisted of two parts, one bad [439]
and the other good, and no statute declares that the bill, under such
circumstances, shall be absolutely void, the rule in equity, as well as in

---

[a] Ex parte Dewdney, 15 Ves. 495. Ex
parte Mumford, 15 Ves. 289, and Bayl.
191.

[b] Ex parte Skip, 2 Ves. jun. 489. Ex
parte Mather, 3 Ves. 373. Ex parte Mog-
ridge, Cooke, 233.

[y] Ante, 68 to 89, as to illegality of consideration in general.

[z] Per Ld. Hardwicke, in Ex parte Skip,
2 Ves. jun. 489. Cullen, 89. 9 Ves. 84.

[a] 13 Ves. 313 and 320.

1st What bills proveable.

bankruptcy, is, that the security shall avail as to what was good. And, therefore, where a broker, having been employed to effect some insurances, one of which was illegal, (being on a voyage from Ostend to the East Indies,) the principal, in consideration of the money laid out in effecting them, indorsed to him a bill drawn by himself, and payable to his own order, upon, and accepted by a person, who afterwards became a bankrupt; the broker (the indorsee) was not allowed to prove under the commission issued against the acceptor, in respect of such part of the debt as arose on the illegal insurance; but it was held, he might prove for the rest on the bill itself.[b] Where there has been an antecedent legal debt, and a bill is afterwards taken, but which turns out to be invalid, on account of usury, or otherwise, the demand for the antecedent date may be resorted to and proved.[c]

In regard to the *form* of the bill, or the *mode* of acceptance, or transfer, the same objections which would in general preclude the holder of a bill from suing at law, would equally prevent him from proving under a commission. A bill or note, payable at a certain time, or on demand, is proveable, though the demand be not made till after the act of bankruptcy.[d] Thus, if a bill or note be payable on a contingency, it cannot be proved.[e] So with regard to the acceptance, it must be of such a nature, that the party might have supported an action. We have seen, that in the case of Ex parte Dyer,[f] it was held, that a letter, undertaking to accept bills already drawn, is an acceptance, and that the bills may be proved as accepted. The indorsement also is governed by the same rules in bankruptcy, as in an action, and therefore, in re Barrington *v.* Burton,[g] where B. handed over a negotiated note, for valuable consideration, to G., not indorsing it, but giving a written acknowledgment on a separate paper, to be accountable for the note to G., and G. indorsed the note, which, together with the written acknowledgment, came into the hands of M. for a valuable consideration, and B, and the several parties to the note, became bankrupts, it was held that M. could not prove the note against the estate of B., the written acknowledgment not being assignable, but was entitled to have the amount made an item in the account between B. and G. and to stand in the place of the latter.[h] So a written undertaking, guaranteeing the payment of a note of a third person, not due at the time of the act of bankruptcy, is not a debt proveable.[i]

[440]

Bills made payable to fictitious payees may be proved by the indorsees for a valuable consideration against the acceptor, or any party who knew at the time that the payee was a fictitious person.[k] And where a party, who has become bankrupt, has transferred a bill, but has by mistake omitted to indorse it, he or his assignees may be

[b] Ex parte Mather, 3 Ves. 373. Cullen, 89. 1 Mont. 115.

[c] Ex parte Blackburne, 10 Ves. 206. Farrell *v.* Shaen and others, 1 Saund. 295. 3 Campb, 119. 2 Taunt. 184.

[d] Ex parte Beaufoy, Co. Bank. Law, 159.

[e] Ex parte Adney, Cowp. 460. Ex parte Tootell, 4 Ves. 372. Ex parte Minet, 14 Ves. 189. Ex parte Barker, 9 Ves. 110. In re Barrington, 2 Sch. &

Lef. 112. 1 Mont. 127, n. c. Instances of contingences, see ante, 42 to 50.

[f] 6 Ves. 9. Ante, 176.

[g] 2 Sh. & Lef. 112. And see Ex parte Harrison, 2 Bro. 615. Cook's 209.

[h] Ante, 145. Cullen, 109, 111. 1 Mont. 142, 149, 150.

[i] Ex parte Adney, Cowp. 460.

[k] Bennett *v.* Farnell, 1 Campb. 180 130. Ante, 65, in note. Ex parte Clarke, 3 Bro. 238. and Ex parte Allen, Cooke's B. L. 172. 1 Mont. 145.

compelled to indorse, so as to enable the holder to prove.[1] A bill ^{1st. What} which has been lost before or after it it due, may be proved, upon the ^{bills prove-} parties giving a sufficient indemnity to the satisfaction of the commis- ^{able.} sioners.[m] But wherever the holder of a bill has been guilty of such laches or conduct, as would discharge the party at law, supposing he had continued solvent, they will equally preclude the holder from proving under a commission against him.[n] And where the remedy on the bill may have been extinguished at law or in equity by the Statute of Limitations, the holder will not be allowed to prove under a commission.[o]

Where a bill has been paid or considered as cancelled or settled by another bill, it cannot be proved. But bills in lieu of which other bills are given, if permitted to remain with the holder, may be proved in the event of the latter bills not being paid.[p]

2dly, Who may prove.

With respect to the *person who may prove* a bill, we will consider ^{2d. Who} first, the proof by a person, who being the holder, gave value for it at ^{may prove.} the time it became so : and secondly, the proof by a person who did not originally give value for the bill, but has since been compelled to pay it.

First, The *bona fide* holder of a bill or note, made *originally for a* [441] *valuable consideration,* may prove for the whole sum contained in it, either against the acceptor, the drawer, or indorsers, whether the bill was due or not at the time of the act of bankruptcy ;[q] but he must be holder for his own use, not as trustee for another, indebted to the estate.[r] And when a bill or note is drawn before, but indorsed after the secret act of bankruptcy of the acceptor to another person, the indorsee, though he cannot *set off* the amount of the sum payable to any demand on him by the assignees, because the statute 5 Geo. 2. c. 30. relates only to mutual debts due before the bankruptcy;[s] yet he may be a petitioning creditor for the amount, or prove it under the commission, because he stands in the place of the person from whom he received the instrument ; and the debt is not created by the indorsement, but by the acceptance of the bill, or making of the note;[t] nor will the circumstance of a note being indorsed after it was due make any difference.[u] And if an indorser or drawer of a bill for a valuable consideration, take up and pay the whole bill, after the bankruptcy of the acceptor, or of any

[1] Ex parte Greening, 13 Ves. 206. Ante, 116. Cullen, 100, 111. 1 Mont. 142. Smith v. Pickering, Peake's Rep. 50. 3 Bos. & Pul. 40.

[m] Ex parte Greenway, 6 Ves. 812. See further as to lost bills, ante, 147 to 157.

[n] Ex parte Wilson, 11 Ves. 410. Ante, 196. 435. Cullen, 99, 100. Cooke, 167, 8, 9.

[o] Ex parte Dewdney, 15 Ves. 479. Ante, 435.

[p] Ex parte Barclay, 7 Ves. 597.

[q] 7 Geo. 1. c. 31. Ante, 436. Starey v. Barnes, 7 East, 435.

[r] Fair v. M'Iver, 16 East, 139, 140.

[s] Cooke, 567. Marsh v. Chambers, 2 Stra. 1234. Grove v. Dubois, 1 T. R. 114. Dickson v. Evans, 6 T. R. 57. Ex parte Hale, 3 Ves. 304. Hankey v. Smith, 3 T. R. 507, n. a. Cullen, 205. 74. 1 Mont. 543.

[t] Ex parte Brymer, Cooke, 164. 5.— 1 Mont. 48. Cooke, 19. 164, 5. Cites Ex parte Thomas, 1 Atk. 73. Anon. 2 Wils. 135. Et vide Toms v. Mytton, 2 Stra. 744, n. 1. Glaister v. Hewer, 7 T. R. 499, 500. 3 Bos. & Pul. 395. See 46 Geo. 3 c. 135. s. 5.

[u] Bingley v. Maddison, K. B. Mich. Term, 1783. Cooke, 19. 7 T. R. 570. S. C.

2d. Who other party liable to him on the bill, and the bill has not been proved
may prove. by some previous holder, under the commission against such acceptor
or other party, such indorser or drawer is entitled to prove it under the
commission against the acceptor or such other party;[z] and it has even
been decided, that where the bankrupt had accepted a bill for the accommodation of the drawer, and the indorser had indorsed the bill also
for the accommodation of such drawer, and had paid it after the bankruptcy, he might prove it under the commission against such acceptor.[y]
So, in the case Ex parte Hale,[a] it was decided, that the acceptor becoming bankrupt, and the petitioner, having indorsed it before the bankruptcy, took up the bill, he might prove, though he could not set off a
debt due from him to the estate.   And it has been decided, that if an
[442] acceptor for the honour of the drawer, after the bankruptcy of the original acceptor, pay the bill, he may prove it under the commission
against such original acceptor.[a]   But this doctrine was over-ruled in the
case Ex parte Lambert,[b] in which it was decided, that such acceptor
supra protest, cannot prove under the commission against the original
acceptor, where the latter had received no consideration from the
drawer.

If the holder of a bill prove it, and receive dividends under the commission against the acceptor, and also under a commission against another party, the assignees of the latter cannot prove under the commission
against the acceptor the amount of the dividends so paid by them. Upon
this point all the Judges agreed, in the case of Cowley v. Dunlop,[c] for
the same debt cannot be proved twice under the same commission, and
there is no hardship upon the indorser, whose estate has also been compelled to pay a dividend, because it cannot exceed the deficiency of the
amount of the bill, beyond the dividend paid by the acceptor, and such
deficiency would be the very sum which the indorser would have lost,
had he been the holder of the bill.

With respect to an *accommodation* bill, or a bill where one of the
parties may have subscribed his name without having received any value,
many difficulties very frequently arise as to the right of the parties to
prove. A party who has *bona fide* given a valuable consideration for
such bill, we have seen, is not affected by the want of consideration between other parties,[d] *and consequently may prove under a commission
against such other parties.*[e]   But a party who has not given value for
the bill, but has, since the act of bankruptcy been obliged to take it up,
frequently stands in a different situation, and in many cases has been
considered as unable to prove under the commission, on the ground that
he is not clothed with the rights of the *bona fide* holder, nor can justly
swear that the bankrupt was indebted to him at the time of his bankruptcy. The rules upon this subject may be arranged under the following heads:—

[z] Joseph v. Orme, 2 New Rep. 180.
Buckler v. Buttivant, 8 East, 72. Ex
parte Brymer, Co. B. L. 164. Ex parte
Seddon, cited 7 T. R. 565. Howle v. Baxter, 3 East, 177. And see 1 Mont. 147, n.
k. Cullen, 98, n. 36. Bayl. 197. 1 Rose,
20.

[y] Howle v. Baxter, 3 East, 177.—
1 Mont. 152. but quære. See the cases

post, as to a party to an accommodation
bill.
[a] 3 Ves. 304.
[a] Ex parte Wackerbarth, 5 Ves. 574.
[b] 13 Ves. 179.
[c] 7 T. R. 565. 1 Mont. 158, note o.
[d] Ante, 68 to 73. Ex parte Rushforth,
10 Ves. 416, 417.
[e] Cullen, 97.

I. Where there is cross paper between the parties to the accommo- 2d. Who may prove.
dation.

II. Where the accommodating party has taken a security.

III. Where the accommodating party has no security.

    1st, When he has paid before the bankruptcy. [443]

    2d, When he has not paid.

    3d, When he may compel the holder to prove.

    4th, When he may prove under the Stat. 49 Geo. 3. c. 121. s. 8.

First, If a bill of exchange or promissory note, be given either in 1. Cross bills.
consideration of another bill or note, the consideration is valid, and the
holder may prove it under a commission of bankruptcy;[f] and whether
in an exchange of bills, one bill were transferred in consideration of
the other, it must be determined by the particular circumstances of
each case.[g] The bills need not be payable at the same time,[h] but any
variation in the times of payment of the respective bills, is evidence,
whether the parties did or did not transfer the bills in consideration of
each other; nor need the bills be for the same sums, but any variation,
is evidence, whether the parties did or did not transfer the bills in
consideration of each other.[i] And it seems, that an agreement by
each party to pay his own acceptance, is conclusive evidence that the
bills were given in consideration of each other.[k] The consideration of
the bill, for this purpose, may be an acceptance of the party to whom
it is transferred,[l] or the acceptance of another person,[m] or a promissory note.[n]

There is a *material* difference, however, between the right of such a
party to a bill to prove it, and that of a person who has actually advanced a valuable consideration for a bill. The latter is entitled, without qualification, to prove and receive a dividend immediately in equal
proportion with the other creditors.[o] But the former, though he is entitled to prove the cross bill before he has taken up his own,[p] yet the [444
dividends will be withheld until the account relative to the cross bill is
finally settled and adjusted.[q]

A person, who has accepted a bill in consideration of the drawer's

---

[f] Ex parte Maydwell, and Ex parte Beaufoy, Cooke, 159. Ex parte Clanricarde, Cooke, 162. Rolfe v. Caslon, 2 Hen. Bla. 570. Cowley v. Dunlop; 7 T. R. 565. Buckler v. Buttivant, 3 East, 72. 1 Mont. 138.

[g] Vide judgment of Lord Ellenborough in Buckler v. Buttivant, 3 East, 72. 1 Mont. 138. As to distinction between cross bills and reciprocal accommodation, see Bayl. 201. May prove, but cannot issue commission, Bayl. 203, n. 2. 4 Taunt. 200.

[h] Ex parte Maydwell, Cooke, 159. Buckler v. Buttivant, 3 East, 73.—1 Mont. 138.

[i] Buckler v. Buttivant, 3 East, 72. Ex parte Lee, 1 P. Wms. 782. 1 Mont. 839.

[k] Cowley v. Dunlop, 7 T. R. 565.— Buckler v. Buttivant, 3 East, 72. 1 Mont. 139.

[l] See the observations of Le Blanc, J.

3 East, 84. Cowley v. Dunlop, 7 T. R. 565. 1 Mont. 139. Bayl. 202, 3.

[m] Ex parte Clanricarde, Cooke, 162.— Buckler v. Buttivant, 3 East, 72. 1 Mont. 139.

[n] Ex parte Maydwell, Cooke, 159—1. Mont. 139.

[o] Ex parte Marshall, 1 Atk. 130. Ex parte King, Cooke, 157. Ex parte Crosley, Cooke, 158. Ex parte Brymer, Cooke, 164.

[p] Ex parte Clanricarde, Cooke, 160. Ex parte Curtis, and Ex parte Lee, Cooke, 159. Cullen, 133, 4. 1 Mont. 139, 554.

[q] In Cooke, 5th edit. 162, it is stated, that the surety cannot prove till he has taken upon his own paper; but, in 1 Mont. 139, it is stated to be settled otherwise, though formerly doubted. But the dividends are withheld, see 4 Taunt. 204, 5. Bayl. 204, n. 1. 205. 8 Ves. 531.

CHITTY ON BILLS. 3 E

2d. Who may prove.
1. Cross bills.

accepting a cross bill, and where it is understood that each party shall pay his own acceptances, cannot prove under a commission against such drawer any payment made on his own acceptance, either before or after the bankruptcy of the drawer, there being no implied contract of indemnity in the case of such cross acceptances ; but each party is considered as looking to the liquidation of his claim on the other, *by the bill* which he took in lieu of his own, and his remedy thereon, and to those only ; in which case the law will not raise any implied promise *ultra* the bills.[r] The party as acceptor, has no remedy against the drawer, for payment of his own acceptances, because he did not accept in consideration of a promise of indemnity, but in consideration of an agreement, or rather of an actual and executed delivery of other acceptances to the same, or nearly the same amount.[s] And consequently, in these cases of cross acceptance, the payment made by a party on his own acceptance, cannot be proved under a commission against the other acceptor, although no payment whatever has been made by the latter on his acceptance, the only remedy being on the cross bill.[t] It has been held, that if a person become a bankrupt, and the dealings between the bankrupt and a creditor consists of cross bills, which are respectively dishonoured, and a cash account composed of payments in money, and of payments on bills duly dishonoured, all the dishonoured bills must be struck out on both sides, and only the cash balance be proved under the commission.[u] But if the drawer of a bill, accepted in consideration of his own acceptance, take up and pay the *whole* bill after the bankruptcy of the acceptor, and the bill has not been proved by the holder under the commission, such drawer may prove it.[x] Though if the assignees of the drawer of a bill, accepted in consideration of his own acceptance, pay dividends to the holder, *who also receives dividends under the commission against the acceptor,* the drawer cannot prove the amount of such dividends under such latter commission.[y]

[445]

2. Surety having a security.

Secondly, Besides these cases of *cross* paper, a party to an accommodation bill frequently receives by way of *indemnity* a bill or note. If an accommodation acceptor, or other party, who puts his name to a bill without having received value, take at the same time from the principal, or party accommodated, by way of indemnification, a bill or note for a sum of money payable at a day certain, he will be allowed to prove immediately upon such counter security, though the debtor becomes a bankrupt before such counter security is payable, and before the surety himself has paid or been called upon, or even could, by the terms of his engagement, be called upon to pay to the creditor;[z] and this, notwithstanding the counter security has been negotiated by the party and returned to him after the bankruptcy.[a] It has been observed, that such a construction, however it may appear, to a common apprehension, repugnant to the real truth of the transaction, and the real justice of the case as between the parties, has been founded upon this,

[r] Cowley v. Dunlop, 7 T. R. 565. Buckler v. Buttivant, 3 East, 72.
[s] Per Ld. Ellenborough, C. J. in Buckler v. Buttivant, 3 East, 81.
[t] Cowley v. Dunlop, 7 T. R. 565. Buckler v. Buttivant, 3 East, 72.
[u] Ex parte Walker, 4 Ves. 373. Ex parte Earle, 5 Ves. 833. 1 Mont. 141. 148. See the observations of Lawrence,
J. in Buckler v. Buttivant, 3 East, 83, 84. Cooke, 161, 162. Bayl. 206. n. 2, 207.
[x] Cowley v. Dunlop, 7 T. R. 565,1 Mont. 147. 2 New Rep. 180.
[y] Cowley v. Dunlop, 7 T. R. 565. 1 Mont. 148.
[z] Ex parte Maydwell, Cooke,157. 2 Hen Bla. 570. S. C. Cullen, 133, 134. 1 Mont. 131, 132. 134. 153. 157, 158.
[a] Ex parte Seddon, cited in 7 T. R. 570.

that such a counter security creates an absolute debt at law, for which 2d. Who
the surety's liability is a sufficient consideration, and on which, there- may prove.
fore, he is entitled immediately to come in as a creditor under the 2. Surety
commission. With a view, however, to prevent the injury which might having a se-
be done to *real* creditors by allowing such constructively absolute, but curity.
really contingent creditors, to receive dividends upon debts which may
never exist but in *law*, it has been thought necessary, where there are
cross demands between the surety and the bankrupt upon counter
paper, as it is called, and upon which, till either has actually paid,
they are substantially only sureties, though nominally creditors of each
other, to suspend the dividends till it appear what the surety actually pays,
and how far he exonerates the bankrupt's estate from his own paper.[b]

A security of this nature must be a bill, note, or bond, payable at all
events, and not a mere parol, or written undertaking to indemnify.[c] A
promissory note payable on demand, or a bill payable at all events, are
sufficient securities to enable a surety to prove, though no demand has
been made before the act of bankruptcy.[d] But if the acceptor of a [446]
bill receive from the drawer an undertaking to indemnify, or a receipt
for his acceptance, as for money received, this is not such a counter
security as creates a debt capable of being proved.[e] In Ex parte Metcalfe,[f] where A. and B. became bankrupts, the assignees of B. were
allowed to prove under the commission against A., a cash balance due
from A. to B., but the dividends were ordered to be retained to reimburse the estate of A. what it should be compelled to pay upon a distinct
transaction, viz. a loan of bills from A. to B., some of which had been
dishonoured, so that the money, thus in the hands of A., was in the nature of a cross security and indemnification against the accommodation
paper. So in the case of Willis *v.* Freeman,[g] Lord Ellenborough said,
that the case of Wilkins *v.* Casey,[h] has established, that if a man, who
has funds in his hands belonging to a trader who had committed a secret act of bankruptcy, accept a bill for that trader without knowing of
such act of bankruptcy, he may apply those funds, when the bill becomes due, to the discharge of his own acceptance, though a commission
of bankruptcy may have issued in the interim, and will be protected
against any claims the assignees may afterwards make upon him in respect of the funds so applied.

It is not necessary, in all cases, that the security to the accommodating party should be given expressly as an indemnity. Thus it was
held, in the case Ex parte Bloxham,[i] that bankers, who have accepted
bills for the accommodation of the bankrupt, may prove upon the bills
drawn by him and remitted to them in the course of their banking account, though their acceptances were not due at the time of the bankruptcy; and it being objected, that the acceptance was not such a consideration as gave the bankers a right to prove upon the bills deposited,
but not due till after the bankruptcy, and that when the banker accepted, not having bills, but bills were deposited afterwards, to indemnify him, that is not such a giving credit as falls within the statute

[b] Ex parte Curtis, Cooke, 159. Ex parte
Lee, ibid. Cullen, 134.

[c] Vanderhayden *v.* De Paiba, 3 Wils. 528.
Chilton *v.* Wiffin, 3 Wils. 13. Cullen, 131.
1 Mont. 156.

[d] Ex parte Maydwell, Cooke, 159.—
1 Mont. 158.

[e] Ex parte Beaufoy, Cooke, 159. Smith

v. Gells, 7 T. R. 489. Snaith *v.* Gale, 7 T.
R. 364. Cullen, 138. 1 Mont. 157.

[f] 11 Ves. 404. 1 Campb. 12. 12 East,
659.

[g] 12 East, 659. Hammond *v.* Barclay,
2 East, 227.

[h] 7 T. R. 711.

[i] 3 Ves. 531. Bayl. 205.

2d. Who 7 Geo. 1. c. 31, and that in **Ex parte Maydwell**, the acceptance was
may prove. upon the express credit of the note, and that consequently this case
2. Surety was distinguishable. The Lord Chancellor said, that "in Ex parte
having a se-
curity. "Maydwell, it was held, that the liability by the acceptance was a
"good consideration for the promissory note, and the proof was per-
"mitted. Cases occurred afterwards demonstrating some mischief in
"that doctrine: the party proving, but not taking up his own accept-
[447] "ance; and the Lord Chancellor afterwards put that condition upon
"them, that they should take up their acceptances. Upon this sort of
"transaction, bankers accepting upon the credit of bills remitted from
"the country, they must be entitled to prove, but they should prove
"upon the securities."

Where a person has become a party to a bill or note, for the accommodation of another, and has been obliged to pay it after the bankruptcy, he may set off such payment against a debt due from him to
tho bankrupt at the time of his bankruptcy.[k] But this is a case of
mutual credit under the statute 5 Geo. 2. c. 30, which will be afterwards more fully considered.

3. Where   *Thirdly*, Where a person has become a party to an accommodation
there is no bill, or note, though there is neither cross paper nor a security in his
security. hands to indemnify him, yet, if he has paid the bill *before the act of
bankruptcy* of his principal, it is proveable under the commission:[l]
but if he has paid such bill or note *after* the act of bankruptcy of his
principal, he cannot, in general, prove under a commission, unless he
can avail himself of the provisions in the statute 49 Geo. 3. c. 221. s. 8.
This is perfectly clear in the case of an accommodation *acceptor*, or
maker of a note, who, being the party primarily liable, can have no
remedy upon them. Thus where a person accepted a bill to accommodate the drawer, upon a parol promise by the latter to find money to
take it up when due, and to save the acceptor harmless, but who did
not take it up when it became due, and soon after was a bankrupt, and
the acceptor, *after* the bankruptcy of the drawer, was sued upon the
bill and taken in execution for the debt and costs, it was held, that no
debt accrued to him from the drawer, till he paid the debt and costs,
or (which was the same thing as actual payment) till he rendered his
body in satisfaction thereof, and this not being till after the bankruptcy,
could not be proved under the commission against the drawer.[m] And
it makes no difference if, instead of a parol promise, the surety takes a
promise in writing from the drawer that he will take up the bill when
due.[n] The right of an *indorser* of a bill or note, who has become so
merely for the accommodation of another, and has paid the bill after
[448] the bankruptcy, seems not perfectly settled.[o] It was held in the
case of **Brooks v. Rogers**[p] that, if the payee of a bill of exchange, not

[k] Ex parte Boyle, Cooke, 561. Smith
v. Hodson, 4 T. R. 211. Atkinson v. Elliot, 7 T. R. 378.
[l] Cullen, 129. 1 Mont. 131. 153.—13
East, 427.
[m] Chilton v. Wiffin, 3 Wils. 13. Young
v. Hockley, Bla. Rep. 839. 3 Wils.
346. 1 Mont. 154. Cooke, 203, 4, 5.
2 Rose, 47.
[n] Vanderhayden v. De Paiba, 3 Wils.
528. Heskington v. Woodbridge, Dougl.
166. Cooke, 203, 4, 5. Cullen, 131.—
Ante, 445.

[o] The leading cases upon this point are
Brooks v. Rogers, 1 Hen. Bla. 640. Howe
v. Wiggins, 4 T. R. 714. and Howle v.
Baxter, 8 East, 177. 3 Bos. & Pul. 395.
[p] 1 Hen. Bla. 640. In 1 Mont. 131
note d. there is a question whether this
case in law, and Cowley v. Dunlop, 7 T. R.
565, and Buchler v. Buttivant, 3 East,
72, are referred to; and it is suggested
that the whole question is, whether the
payee and drawer stood in the situation
of principal and surety. In Cowley v.
Dunlop, Lawrence, Justice, speaking of

being a creditor of the *drawer*, indorse and get it discounted merely for the purpose of raising money for him, and hand the money to him, and is afterwards obliged to pay it to the indorsee, but not till after the drawer becomes a bankrupt, he cannot prove it under the drawer's commission; because no debt accrued to him from the *drawer* till the money was actually paid, which was not till after the bankruptcy. In the case of Howis *v.* Wiggins, 4 T. R. 714, where a party became payee, and indorser of a promissory note for the accommodation of the maker, who delivered it to a third person with the payee's indorsement, and afterwards became bankrupt, it was held that the payee and indorser, paying it after the bankruptcy, was not entitled to prove his debt accruing only upon payment of the note.^q In the case of Howle *v.* Baxter, 3 East, 177, the bill had been accepted by the bankrupt for the accommodation of the drawer, and the plaintiff, at the request of the drawer, indorsed the bill, merely to give it additional credit, after which the drawer got it discounted, and the acceptor became bankrupt, and the plaintiff was afterwards obliged to pay the account to a *bona fide* holder, after which the defendant obtained his certificate, and the court said, that the plaintiff contracted no liability at the defendant's request, and that he never became surety for him in this transaction, and that the plaintiff's demand against the defendant, the acceptor, arose solely upon the bill, and that there was nothing to prevent his proving it under the commission, and consequently that the bankrupt was discharged by his certificate. Where the party from being *acceptor* of the bill or *maker* of the note is *primarily* liable, and could not have any claim by virtue of the *instrument itself* upon any party to it, there seems sufficient grounds for his not being allowed to prove under the commission; because, independently of 7 Geo. 1. c. 31, no person can prove, unless he has a subsisting legal demand actually payable at the time of the act of bankruptcy,^r and there is no ground for permit-

---

the case of Brooks *v.* Rogers, says, "I argued that case as being the case of principal and surety, and considered Brooks as lending his name to Rogers to get money on the draft of Rogers, of the Olney bank, and that, in substance, it was an advance of money to Rogers on the credit of Brook's name as surety to the bank; but I doubt if that argument is not fallacious; for on Brooks carrying the bill to the bank, the bank lent him the amount of it on the security of the bill, on which Brooks was entitled to recover when returned to him for non-payment."

^q Mr. Montague, in Vol. i. 155, n. *, observes on this decision "that it is a stronger case of *principal and surety* than the case of Brooks *v.* Rogers, 1 Hen. Bla. 640, above mentioned, because in Howis *v.* Wiggins, no money consideration passed between the payee and maker before the bankruptcy of the latter." And see the argument in Howle *v.* Baxter, 3 East, 177. In Cowley *v.* Dunlop, T. R. 565. Grose, J. says. "the case of Howis *v.* Wiggins came on before this court on a motion for a new trial; and possibly under a misapprehension of it, considered it as a case of indemnity; and the ground on which the rule was refused was, on the supposition that Van-

derhayden and De Paiba was in point. I then considered Howis the plaintiff, and payee of the two promissory notes, as having indorsed them as surety for the defendant, with a view to give credit to the notes, and without any consideration for his so doing. In any other way of considering that case, I think it is not to be supported." It was also observed by Lord Ellenborough, in Buckler *v.* Buttivant, 3 East, 82. "It is unnecessary to say any thing of the cases of Brooks *v.* Rogers, and Howis *v.* Wiggins, though I have a *decided opinion on the subject*: it is sufficient for the present to observe that the noble Lord by whom the former of those cases was determined, afterwards changed his opinion in the case Ex parte Seddon, and that the latter case has since been doubted in this court by some of the judges in Cowley *v.* Dunlop." It is observable, however, that the case Ex parte Seddon, cited in 7 T. R. 570, is distinguishable from Brooks *v.* Rogers, and Howis *v.* Wiggins, for Seddon was not allowed to prove on his own paper, but on the note given to him in exchange for it, which rendered that case an instance of cross paper, or counter security, which (it has never been disputed) may be proved.

^r Parslowe *v.* Dearlove, 4 East, 488. Hoskins *v.* Duperoy, 9 East, 498.

2d. Who
may prove.

3. Where
there is no
security.

ting him to prove under this statute, because he being the person primarily liable to pay such bill or note cannot be considered as a person *giving credit on such securities* within the meaning of that statute. But a person who has *indorsed* a bill at the request of another may fairly be considered as giving credit within the meaning of the statute, which enables " any person *who shall give credit upon such securities* to any " person or persons who shall become bankrupts upon a good and valu- " able consideration for any sum or sums of money, *or other matter* or " *thing whatsoever*, which shall not be due at the time of the bankrupt- " cy," to prove such bill or note. The question is whether such an accommodation indorser can be considered as a person giving credit on such securities for " money or other matter, or thing," within the meaning of the statute. Now we have seen that in the case of cross bills, the acceptance on one side is deemed a sufficient consideration for the acceptance on the other, to enable a party, liable to pay his own acceptance, to prove the acceptance of the other party under the commission of those who have become bankrupt,[a] and that where there has not been an exchange of bills, yet if a bill or note, payable at all events, has been given by way of indemnity it may be proved;[b] and we have seen, that

[450]

when a bill has been taken up by an indorser for valuable consideration, although after the act of bankruptcy, he may prove under the commission.[c] If the acceptance of a cross bill, or the holding of a bill or note, by way of indemnity, is to be deemed a sufficient consideration to enable the party to prove the bill or note in his possession, it must be on the ground that his liability on that paper, which he himself is bound to take up, is a good and valuable consideration for " *other matter or thing*" besides money, within the meaning of the statute 7 Geo. 1. c. 31. The decision in Howle *v*. Baxter, 3 East, 177, is only sustainable upon this ground, for in that case the plaintiff had neither advanced money or credit in the way of trade before the bankruptcy, and was merely an accommodation party, who had afterwards paid the bill. It is true that the words in the preamble of the 7 Geo. 1. c. 32. afford only a presumption of an intention in the legislature to assist those merchants and traders who were obliged to sell their goods on trust or credit, and take bills and notes in payment for them. But the preamble cannot control the express enacting words, " *for money, or for other matter, or thing whatsoever.*[d] There appears to be no substantial difference in this respect between a transaction where in consideration of a party's *indorsing* a bill he receives another bill or note by way of indemnity, which it is admitted he may prove, and a transaction, in which a drawer or indorser hands over a bill or note in his possession to the same party and obtains his indorsement by way of giving credit to the instrument, without giving such cross security. In the latter case, according to the decision in Howle *v*. Baxter, 3 East, 177, the principle of which appears to over-rule the cases of Howis *v*. Wiggins, and Brooks *v*. Rogers, the transaction implies that in consideration of the accommodating party

---

[a] Ante, 443, &c.

[b] Ante, 443, &c.

[c] Ante, 447.

[d] In 1 Co. B. L. 188, it is observed, that there is a legislative construction of this very act in 5 Geo. 2. c. 30. s. 22. which, without conceiving a doubt, takes it for granted that the statute is not merely confined to securities for goods sold and delivered in the course of trade, but that it extends generally to all personal securities is a *valuable consideration*, where the time of payment is certain though postponed to a future day, and several cases are collected to prove this position. But it is observable that the section alluded to, only mentions securities for *their money* payable at a future day, by which they are enabled to prove *their debts*, and consequently the words of the statute are less general than are supposed.

becoming so, the party accommodated gives to him all the beneficial interest which a *bona fide* indorsee can have, and when he has actually been obliged to pay the bill, though after the bankruptcy, he is entitled to prove. This question, however, is of considerable difficulty and cannot be considered as fully settled.[y]

2d. Who may prove.
3. Where there is no security.

Fourthly, We have seen that a surety or party to an accommodation bill, having no absolute counter security, cannot, in some cases, come in as a creditor directly, in his own right, if he has not paid till after the bankruptcy of the principal.[z] Yet if the creditor has proved the *whole* debt before he called upon the surety, the court will direct that he shall stand as a trustee for the surety, and will allow the latter (or, in case he too has become a bankrupt, and his estate has paid dividends on account of the principal, will allow his assignees) to have the benefit of the principal creditor's proof, and to receive dividends upon it, but so as that no more shall be paid than 20s. in the pound upon the whole debt.[b]

[451]
4. Benefit of holder's proof.

And a court of equity on a bill filed for that purpose, and on the surety's bringing the money into court, has ordered the creditor to go before the commissioners, and prove his debt for the benefit of the surety,[c] and stayed his proceeding at law against the surety till he had done so.[d] An accommodation acceptor is entitled to the same benefit of proof.[e] And where the surety, previous to the proof by the creditor under the commission against the principal, had lodged the amount of the debt with a banker in trust for the creditor, the surety has been permitted to retake the money for the purpose of enabling the creditor to prove against the principal.[f] Where, however, a banker having money of the bankrupt's in his hands, paid it after notice of the act of bankruptcy, though to creditors whose debts were antecedent, and who would have been entitled to prove under the commission, yet he will not be permitted to stand in the place of those creditors so paid, and to receive dividends thereon with the other creditors.[g]

In Ex parte Mathews,[h] it was held, that if the drawer of a bill take up and pay the whole bill, after the indorser has proved it under the commission against the acceptor, the drawer has an equitable right

[452]

[y] Cullen, 131, 132. 1 Mont. 154, 155. But see Lord Ellenborough's observations in Buckler v. Buttivant, 3 East, 82.
[z] Ante, 448, &c.
[a] See the observations of Lord Eldon in Ex parte Rushforth, 10 Ves. 420.
[b] Ex parte Ryswiche, 2 P. W. 88. Ex parte Marshall, 1 Atk. 129. Ex parte Atkinson, Cooke, 210. Cullen, 156.—1 Mont. 135. 158, 9.
[c] Waight v. Simpson, 6 Ves. 734. Ex parte Atkinson, Cooke, 210. Beardmore v. Cruttenden, Cooke, 211. Cullen, 156. 1 Mont. 135. 159. Ex parte Rushforth, 10 Ves. 412. 414.
[d] Philips v. Smith, Cooke, 211. Cullen, 156. Mr. Cullen, in his work, p. 156, s. 55, says, " Is this to be considered as established, that sureties, having merely conditional securities, and not paying till after the bankruptcy, may come in place of the creditor, and receive dividends? Are they to be so favoured beyond all

other creditors, and without relief to the bankrupt? For such sureties may still, after receiving under the commission, recover the residue of their debt against the bankrupt afterwards, they not being barred by his " certificate." The statute 49 Geo. 3. c.121. s. 8. precludes a surety who can prove, as there pointed out, from suing the bankrupt when he has obtained his certificate, and in effect, prevents him from receiving a greater dividend than any other creditor, see post, 454. The argument, therefore, in Paley v. Field, 14 Ves. 437, 438, is no longer material.
[e] See Lord Eldon's observations in Ex parte Rushforth, 10 Ves. 417. Ex parte Turner, 3 Ves. 243.
[f] Ex parte Atkinson, Cooke, 219.—1 Mont. 135.
[g] Hankey v. Vernon. 3 Bro. 313. Cullen, 158, 9.
[h] 6 Ves. 285. 734. 1 Mont. 147.

3d. Who
may prove.
4. Benefit
of holder's
proof.

to the benefit of the proof made by the indorser. If the payment by the surety be after the bankruptcy of the principal, and before the creditor has proved the debt, it cannot be proved either by the creditor or by the surety. The creditor cannot, in such case, prove, because he cannot swear to an existing debt, and the surety cannot prove, because his payment is after the bankruptcy.[i] It is therefore in general advisable for an accommodation party to compel the holder of the bill to prove before he pays the amount. When such proof has been made, and in consequence of the party proving, having afterwards received his debt from the surety, such proof has been expunged, it may, in some cases, at the instance of the surety, be reinstated for his benefit.[k] But the creditor cannot be turned into a trustee for the surety, to the prejudice of any right the former may have against the principal debtor's estate, on a future and distinct demand; and in such case, the surety will only be allowed such part of the dividend as will remain, after allowing out of it to the creditor, as much as will make up the proportion which he would have received, upon the residue of the debt proved beyond the debt to the surety, if this debt had been expunged.[l] Thus, in the case of Ex parte Turner,[m] the petitioner had lent his name by acceptance and indorsement for the accommodation of the bankrupt, who discounted the bills so accepted and indorsed with Snaith and Co. After the bankruptcy, upon the application of Snaith and Co., the petitioner paid the full value of those bills, amounting to £815. 15s. to them. They were creditors of the bankrupt to a much larger amount, and they proved their whole demand, including the amount of the bills received from the petitioner. The petitioner prayed that Snaith and Co. might assign to him the dividends due upon the proofs, in respect of the bills which he had paid. The Lord Chancellor observing that Snaith and Co. could not be turned into trustees to the prejudice of any right they might have, made the order, that Snaith and Co. should take out of the dividend upon the £815. 15s. so much as would make up the proportion, which they would have received upon the residue of the debt proved beyond the £815. 15s. if

[453]

that debt of £815. 15s. had been expunged, and the rest of the dividend upon the £815. 15s. belonged to the petitioner; and that the dividend should remain in the hands of the assignees, till it shall appear what proportion Snaith and Co. are entitled to. But in the case of Ex parte Rushforth[n] this doctrine was qualified, and it was held that bankers who had proved their whole demand against the principal beyond the amount of their claim on the surety, who had guaranteed advances to that extent, were bound upon payment to them by the surety of their whole demand on him to give him the whole benefit of their proof to that extent against the principal, on the ground that it was not competent to such bankers to go on giving an enlarged credit to such principal without the concurrence of their surety, so as to prejudice his equitable right to the benefit of their proof. So, in the case of Paley v. Field,[o] it was held that a surety for indemnity to a limited amount, having paid to the extent of his engagement, is entitled to dividends upon proof by the creditor under the bankruptcy of the prin-

[i] Cooke, 152. 1 Mont. 135.
[k] Ex parte Mathews, 6 Ves. 285.
[l] Ex parte Turner, 3 Ves. 243, see the reason in Cullen, 157, n. 56, and observed upon by Ld. Eldon in Ex parte Rushforth, 10 Ves. 415. 418, and in Paley v. Field, 12 Ves. 437. Lord Eldon appears, in Ex parte Rushforth, 10 Ves. 418, not to have

perfectly acceded to the principle of the decision in Ex parte Turner; see also 12 Ves. 437, and it is at least qualified in the subsequent cases.

[m] 3 Ves. 243.
[n] 10 Ves. 409. 422.
[o] 12 Ves. 435.

cipal debtor; subject to a deduction of the proportion of the dividend 2d. Who
upon the residue of the debt proved beyond that for which the surety may prove.
was engaged, supposing that expunged. And the Master of the Rolls 4. Benefit
said, "If, in consequence of those ulterior advances, the bankers are of holder's
" to keep dividends of which they would otherwise be trustees for the proof.
" plaintiff, does not he contribute in effect to indemnify them for a loss,
" against which it is expressly provided that he shall not be called upon
" to indemnify them, viz. a loss occasioned by their advancing more
" than the sum of £1500? It is clear then as between these parties
" that sum is to be considered as the amount of the debt. The law,
" resulting from that view of the facts, is not a subject of controversy
" between the parties; for it is agreed upon that statement, the plain-
" tiff is entitled to the equity he seeks by his bill, to consider them as
" trustees for him of whatever dividends they draw from the bankrupt's
" estate on account of this sum of £1500." It was, however, held in
the same case, that the surety is not entitled to the benefit of the proof
made by the creditor against other estates upon a distinct security, with
which the plaintiff had nothing to do.

Fifthly, Many of the difficulties with respect to the proof by a surety, 5. When a
who has no cross paper or counter security to indemnify him, are re- surety or
moved by the Statute 49 Geo. 3. c. 121. s. 8., which enacts, "That person lia-
" in all cases of commissions of bankruptcy already issued, under ble may
" which no dividend has yet been made, or under which the creditors, der 49 Geo.
" who have not proved, can receive a dividend equally in proportion 3. c. 121.
" to their respective debts without disturbing any dividend already s. 8.P
" made; and in all cases of commissions of bankrupts *hereafter* to be [454]
" issued, where, at the time of issuing the commission, any person shall
" be *surety* for, or be *liable for* any debt of the bankrupt, it shall be
" lawful for such surety or person liable, *if he shall have paid* the debt,
" or any part thereof in discharge of the *whole debt*,r although he may
" have paid the same after the commission shall have issued, and the
" creditor shall have proved his debt under the commission, *to stand*
" *in the place* of the creditor as to dividends upon such proof; and
" when the creditor shall not have proved under the commission, it
" shall be lawful for such surety or person liable, *to prove* his demand
" in respect of such *payment* as a debt under the commission, not
" *disturbing* the dividends,s and to receive a dividend or dividends
" proportionably with the other creditors, taking the benefit of such
" commission, notwithstanding such person may have become surety or
" liable for the debt of the bankrupt after an act of bankruptcy had
" been committed by such bankrupt; provided that such person had
" not, at the time when he became such surety, or when he so became
" liable for the debt of such bankrupt, notice of any act of bankruptcy
" by such bankrupt committed, or that he was *insolvent*,t or had stop-
" ped payment; provided always that the issuing a commission of bank-
" rupt, although such commission shall afterwards be superseded, shall
" be deemed such notice. And every person against whom any such

P See Bayl. 198, n. 1.
q In Laxton v. Peat, 2 Campb. 186,
Lord Ellenborough considered an accommodation acceptor as in the nature of a
surety for the drawer.
r A surety who is not able to pay in time
to avail himself of this clause, may, it is
apprehended, still avail himself of the
right of compelling the holder to prove

for his benefit, see ante, 443. 449, &c. *sed
quære.*
s This means not compelling the creditors to *refund* any part of the dividends
received. A point was made in 12 East,
664, but not determined. 1 Sch. & Lef.
242.
t Means a general insolvency, &c. 1
Campb. 492, in notes.

2d. Who
may prove.
5. When
surety may
prove un-
der 49 Geo
3. c. 121.

" commission of bankrupt has been, or shall be awarded, and who has
" obtained, or shall obtain *his certificate*, shall *be discharged* of all de-
" mands at the suit of every such person having so paid, or being *here-
" by enabled* to prove as aforesaid, or to stand in the place of such cre-
" ditor as aforesaid, in regard to his debt in respect of such suretyship
" or liability *in like manner*, to all intents and purposes," as if such
" person had been a creditor before the bankruptcy of the bankrupt, for
" the whole of the debt in respect of which he was surety, or was so lia-
" ble as aforesaid."

[455]

Upon this statute it has been decided that an accommodation acceptor is a person liable for the debt of the bankrupt drawer, and may
prove under his commission,[x] and if an acceptance for the *accommodation* of the drawer of a bill be given before, and renewed after he has
committed an act of bankruptcy, such renewal is a continuation of the
same suretyship; and therefore if a commission of bankruptcy be issued
against the drawer, and the accommodation acceptor afterwards pay the
bill, he will be entitled to prove the amount under such commission;
though, before the renewal of the acceptance he had notice of such
act of bankruptcy having been committed.[y]   Nor will the case be
varied in principle, by the circumstance of the holder of the first bill
having, before the renewal, given time to the drawer; or by that of an
additional name, as that of an indorser having been lent upon the
second bill.[z]

And it has been decided, that if an accommodation acceptor having
paid the bill, afterwards sues the drawer as for money paid, and having
obtained judgment, assigns the judgment debt to a third person, such
assignee of the debt may prove the original debt under the commission against the drawer, and the judgment debt, though greater than
the original debt, will be barred by a certificate." So where a bill
after proof under a commission against the acceptor, was paid by the

---

" Under these words it has been held
that the bankrupt, if sued, must nevertheless plead his certificate, and cannot give
it in evidence under the general issue. Stedman *v.* Martinnant, 12 East, 664.

[x] Ex parte Yonge, 3 Ves. & Bea. 40,
and see next note.

[y] Stedman *v.* Martinnant, 13 East,
127. 12 East, 664. S. C. On the 5th of
January, 1807, the plaintiff accepted a
bill for the accommodation of the defendant the drawer, which became due on
the 19th March, when it was dishonoured.
On the 18th March, 1807, a docket was
struck against the defendant, and on the
21st, a commission of bankrupt was issued,
which was superseded on the 15th of
April. A meeting of the defendant's creditors was then held when time was given
to him to pay his debts by instalments.
On the 9th of June, 1807, the plaintiff
accepted a second bill for the defendant,
in order to take up the former one, for
the same sum with the addition of interest
and stamp; and the indorsement of a
third person was lent as an additional security, which was required by the holders
of the former bill. On the 6th of August,

1807, a valid commission was issued
against the defendant, founded on an act
of bankruptcy committed in the preceding
March. The second bill became due on
the 12th of September, 1807, when the
plaintiff paid it. The first dividend under
the commission was declared and made on
the 6th of August, 1808. On the 4th of
September, 1809, the defendant obtained
his certificate. In an action for money
paid, and the bankruptcy and certificate
pleaded, a verdict was found for the
plaintiff, subject to the opinion of the
court, as to whether the certificate was a
discharge. The court (Le Blanc, J. absente) held, that the second acceptance
was a continuation of the same suretyship
which was created by the first, and that
as such suretyship commenced before any
act of bankruptcy committed, and consequently before the plaintiff could have
any notice of such act, the plaintiff
might, by 49 Geo. 3. c. 121. s. 8. have
proved his demand under the commission,
and therefore the certificate was a bar.
Postea to the defendant.

" Id. ibid. Bayl. 200.

" Ex parte Lloyd, 1 Rose, 4.

drawer, and he after a dividend arrested the bankrupt for the balance, and was also a surety for him on another bill ; the Chancellor made an order, that the bankrupt should be discharged, and that the plaintiff should be restrained from lodging any detainer under the above statute 49 Geo. 3. c. 121. s. 8. & 14.[b]

A partner is considered as a person *liable* for the joint debt of himself and his co-partners, and if the latter becomes a bankrupt, and the solvent partner be afterwards obliged to pay the whole debt, the certificate of the bankrupt partner will protect him from liability to make contribution to such solvent partner ; and therefore where a partner continuing the business took an assignment of all the stock, &c. and covenanted to indemnify the retiring partner from the debts then owing from the partnership, and the continuing partner became a bankrupt, and obtained his certificate, and subsequently an action was commenced against the retiring partner upon an acceptance of the partnership, and judgment was obtained against him, and he paid the debts and costs ; it was held, that no action would lie against the bankrupt upon the covenant ; since, under the 49 Geo. 3. c. 121. s. 8, the retiring partner might on his liability have resorted to, and proved his debt under the commission, and was therefore barred by the certificate.[c]

But there are not any words in the stat. 49 Geo. 3. c. 121. s. 8, compulsory upon the party to prove, or precluding him from suing the bankrupt, subject to such action being rendered ineffectual by his obtaining his certificate, and therefore the drawer of a bill who has paid the amount to the holder, after a commission of bankruptcy issued against the acceptor, may sue the acceptor before he has obtained his certificate, and arrest him upon the bill, notwithstanding the holder has proved the bill under the commission.[d]

Thirdly, against whom, or under what Commission.

3dly, We have next to inquire *against* whom, or under what commission, proof in respect of a bill may be made. And this may be considered under two heads ; *first* with relation to the *particular situation* of the party who has become bankrupt ; and *secondly,* to the *number* of the parties.

First, A party who is a *bona fide* holder of a bill, drawn regularly for value, is, we have seen, entitled to prove in all cases under a commission against any one of the parties, against whom he could have supported an action on the bill, though such party became bankrupt before the bill was due, and at the time when it was uncertain whether it would be paid by the acceptor.[e] So a bill drawn by way of accommodation, though it cannot be proved, as between the parties to the accommodation, yet it may be proved by a *bona fide* holder against all parties, whether they have received value or not.[f] Wherever the holder could have sustained an action on the bill against the party, had he

2d. Who may prove.
5. When surety may prove under 49 Geo. 3. c. 121.

3dly. Against whom, and under what commission

[457]

---

[b] Ex parte Lobbon, 17 Ves. 334, 5.— 1 Rose, 219.

[c] Wood *v.* Dodgson, 2 M. &. S. 195.— 2 Rose, 47.

[d] Mead *v.* Braham, 3 M. & S. 91.

[e] Ante, 443. Ex parte Marlar, 1 Atk. 150. Cullen, 96.

[f] Ex parte Marshall, 1 Atk. 130. Ex parte King, Cooke, 157. Ex parte, Crossley, Cooke, 158. Ex parte Brymer, Cooke, 164. Cullen, 97. 1 Mont. 152.

3dly. continued solvent, he may prove under his commission, in case he
should become bankrupt. The rights and liabilities of parties at law,
have already been considered, and therefore it is unnecessary here again
to notice the various decisions on the subject. In the case of cross
paper, and of a bill or note given by way of indemnity, we have seen
that a party may frequently prove, before he has advanced money, or
been damnified, though the dividends will be withheld till his own
paper has been paid.g We have already considered the liability at law
of a party transferring a bill, and we have seen, that in the case of a
transfer by mere delivery, without an indorsement, the party is not in
any case liable to be sued by any holder, except the party to whom he
immediately transferred it, and then not upon the instrument itself, but
for the precedent debt or consideration between them; and that in the
case of the sale of a bill, the party transferring is not liable to any
party. So in the event of bankruptcy it appears from the case in Re
Barrington,h that if B. hand over a negotiable note for valuable consideration to G., not indorsing it, but giving a written acknowledgment
on a separate paper, to be accountable for the note to G., G. indorses
the note, which, together with the written acknowledgment, comes into
the hands of M. for valuable consideration, and B. and the several parties to the note become bankrupts, M. could not prove the note against
the estate of B., (the written acknowledgment not being assignable,) but
was entitled to have the amount made an item in the account between
B. and G., and to stand in the place of the latter. So in the case of
Ex parte Harrison,i it was held, that if a person transfer a bill, without
indorsing it, but by a written instrument warrant the payment, in the
same manner as if he had indorsed it, and he become a bankrupt before
the bill is due, the holder cannot prove it under the commission against
him. And if a trader procure cash for a bill, but do not indorse it,
because the person paying the cash thinks that the bill will have as
good credit without his indorsement, the bill cannot be proved under a
commission afterwards issued against the trader.k And where a trader
transferred a bill without indorsing it, and there was a private mark
upon the bill, and it appeared in evidence, that all bills transferred by
him without indorsement, but with this mark, were considered by him
as rendering him liable to pay as if he had indorsed them; it was nevertheless held, that such bill could not be proved under a commission
against him.l So where a bill is transferred by way of sale, without
being being indorsed, it cannot be proved under a commission against
the party transferring, even by the person to whom he transferred it.m
But, if the bill were deposited merely as a pledge, the residue of the
debt for which it was deposited, after a sale of the bill, is proveable
under the commission.n

Secondly, With respect to the *number of parties*, the holder of a bill
or note is entitled to prove it under different commissions, against all
the several parties to the instrument, under their respective commissions,
and to receive dividends upon the whole sum under each, to the extent
of 20s. in the pound;o for it is a creditor's right in bankruptcy to prove

Margin notes:
Against whom, and under what commission

[458]

g Ante, 443, &c.
h 2 Sch. & Lef. 112.
i 2 Bro. 615. Ex parte Shuttleworth,
3 Ves. 368. Cullen, 100, 101.
k Ex parte Shuttleworth, 3 Ves. 368.
Ex parte Blackburn, 10 Ves. 206. Cullen,
100, 101.
l Id. ibid.

m Bank v. Newman, 1 Lord Raym. 442.
Ex parte Smith, Cooke, 120. 1 Mont.
142 Ex parte Witter, Cooke, 173. Ante,
142 to 145.
n Id. ibid.
o Ex parte Wildman, 1 Atk. 109. 2 Ves.
113. Ex parte Lefebre, 2 P. W. 407.
Cowper v. Pepys, 1 Atk. 1071. Ex parte

and avail himself of all collateral securities from third persons to the extent of 20s. in the pound;[p] and the holder of a bill drawn by a firm upon some of their members constituting a distinct firm, has a right to prove it against all the parties according to their liabilities upon the bill, provided he was ignorant of their partnership;[q] or such holder may prove it under one or more commissions against some of the parties, and proceed at law against the parties.[r] In Ex parte Rushforth,[s] Lord Eldon said, " It is clear that where a person has a demand upon a bill or bond against several persons, and no part of that demand has been paid before the bankruptcy by any of them, he may prove against each; and the circumstance that one is a surety and the other the principal, or a co-surety as between themselves, does not give a right to stop the holder from receiving dividends, till he has received 20s. in the pound; that is well settled in Ex parte Marshall, and Ex parte Wildman, and it applies to joint and several demands, either by bill or bond." [**459**]

It has long been settled in bankruptcy, that a creditor cannot prove against the joint estate of two bankrupt partners, and also against the separate estate of one of them, but must elect, though he has distinct securities,[t] unless there is a surplus;[u] and a joint debt cannot be proved under a separate commission, except for the purpose of assenting to or dissenting from the certificate, and recovering a dividend out of the surplus, after satisfaction of the separate creditors ; but if there are no joint effects and no solvent partners, or no separate debts, or the joint creditors will pay the separate creditors 20s. in the pound, they may then vote in the choice of assignees, and go at once against the separate estate.[x] But he must have time to look into the accounts of the respective estates, to see which will be most beneficial to him,[y] and has been allowed to defer his election till a dividend be declared.[z] And in Ex parte Bielby,[a] where creditors had proved under a joint commission, upon a joint and several promissory note, but had not received a dividend, they were not permitted to waive their proof and to prove against the separate estate, on the terms of not disturbing any dividends already made. And even receiving a dividend is no determination of an election, and the holder of a security has been allowed to change, on refunding the dividend.[b]

In Ex parte Bonbonus,[c] Lord Eldon said, "There have been many cases where three or more partners, being also concerned in other trades, the paper of one firm has been given to the creditors of another, and they were permitted to take dividends from both estates;" and in case of joint debts, paid by a bill drawn by one of the debtors and accepted

Bloxham, 6 Ves. 449. 600. 645. See the argument in 12 Ves. 438. Cullen, 96. 1 Mont. 143. Cooke, 170. Bayl. 209. The Royal Bank of Scotland, 19 Ves. 310.
[p] Ex parte Parr, 18 Ves. 65. Davison v. Robertson, 3 Dowe's Rep. 220. 230.
[q] Ex parte Adams, 2 Rose, 36. 1 Ves. & Bea. 495. Ex parte Parr, 18 Ves. 65. Davison v. Robertson, 3 Dow. 220. 230.
[r] Ex parte Wildman, 2 Atk. 109. Wilks v. Jacks, Cooke, 168. 1 Mont. 143.
[s] 10 Ves. 416.
[t] Ex parte Bonbonus, 8 Ves. 542. Ex parte Wensley, 2 Ves. & Bea. 254.
[u] Ex parte Rowlandson, 3 P. W. 405.

Ex parte Bankes, 1 Atk. 106. Ex parte Bond and Hill, 1 Atk. 98.
[x] Ex parte Taitt, 16 Ves. 194. 1 Rose, 21, n. a. Heath v. Hall, 4 Taunt, 328.
[y] Ex parte Rowlandson, 3 P. W. 405. Ex parte Bankes, 1 Atk. 106. Ex parte Bond and Hill, 1 Atk. 98.
[z] Ex parte Clowes, Cooke's Bank. Law, 258.
[a] 13 Ves. 70.
[b] Ex parte Rowlandson, 3 P. W. 405, supra, notes.
[c] 8 Ves. 546. Ex parte Wensley, 2 Ves. & Bea. 254.

3dly, by another, each carrying on distinct trades, there may be proof under their separate commissions upon the bill.[d]

Against whom and under what commission

When the *credit has* been joint, the creditor may be admitted to prove under a commission against the partners, notwithstanding he has taken a separate *security.*[e] And if money be lent on the separate notes or

[460] bills of different partners in the same firm, and be applied to the use of the partnership, and the firm, when solvent, agrees to consolidate the debts, and to consider them as partnership debts, the creditor may be admitted against the joint estate.[f] So, on the other hand, when the credit has been separate, the creditor may be admitted to prove against the separate estate, notwithstanding he has taken a joint security.[g]

Fourthly, to what Extent Proof may be made.

4thly, To what extent proof may be made.

Fourthly, With respect to what sum, or to *what extent* proof may be made, it seems that the discounter of a bill or note is entitled to prove the full amount, without deducting the discount.[h] So a holder, who has purchased the bill for less than the amount of it, may prove for the whole.[i] So if a debtor give to his creditor an accommodation bill or note of a third person, to a larger amount than the debt, the creditor is entitled to prove the whole amount of the bill, under a commission against such accommodation party.[k] And the holder of a bill or note, transferred or pledged to him by his debtor as a collateral security for his debt, may prove the whole amount of the security, under a commission against any of the parties, except the debtor from whom he received it, although he has received part-payment of his debt from such his debtor.[l]

In the case of several parties, we have just seen that the holder of a bill or note is entitled to prove his debt under a commission against the drawer, acceptor, and indorsers and to receive a dividend from each upon his whole debt, provided he does not in the whole receive more than 20s. in the pound.[m] So where A. being an indorsee of B. and Co's. acceptances for £1364, issued a separate commission against B. and at the time of suing out the commission, D. the person for whom A. had discounted the acceptances, had, by payments on account, reduced the debt to £420, it was held, that A. was entitled to prove for the whole amount, and for all that he received above the £420, will be a trustee for D.[n] But under a commission against the

[461] party from whom this holder received the bill, he can only prove to the amount of the actual debt then due.[o] There is a distinction in this case, where the creditor applies to prove his debt, after having received a part, and where he applies to prove *previous* to his having received

[d] Ex parte Wensley, 2 Ves. & Bea. 254.
[e] Ex parte Hunter, 1 Atk. 228. 1 Mont. 619. Cullen, 462.
[f] Ex parte Close, 2 Bro. 595. Ex parte Bonbonus, 8 Ves. 542. See other instances in Cullen, 462, 3. 1 Mont. 620.
[g] In Re Bate, 3 Ves. 400. Ex parte Lobb, 7 Ves. 592. See other instances, 1 Mont. 621.
[h] Ex parte Marler, 1 Atk. 150. Cooke, 174. 1 Mont. 148.

[i] Ex parte Lee, 1 P. W. 782. Cullen, 96, 7. Ante, 434.
[k] Ex parte King, Cooke, 169. Ex parte Crossley, ibid. 158. Ex parte Bloxham, 5 Ves. 449. 600, in which Ex parte Bloxham, 5 Ves. 448, was overruled.
[l] Id. ibid. 1 Mont. 144. Bayl. 210. 211, n. 1.
[m] Ante, 458.
[n] Ex parte De Tastet, 1 Rose, 10.
[o] Ex parte De Tastet, 1 Rose, 14. Bayl. 211.

any payment or composition. If the creditor, *at the time of proving,* has received any part of the bill or note, he can only prove for so much as remains; but if, after having proved for the whole, he receives a part of the bill from any of the persons liable to pay it, he is entitled to a dividend upon the whole, provided it does not exceed 20s. in the pound, upon such part as remains due ;ᵖ and as to any overplus beyond 20s. in the pound, it is to be accounted for to the party next entitled to the benefit.ᑫ In Ex parte Bloxham,ʳ it was decided, that a creditor having securities of third persons, accommodation acceptors, to a greater amount than the debt, may prove and receive dividends upon the full amount of the securities to the extent of 20s, in the pound, upon the actual debt; and Lord Eldon said, "I looked upon it as settled, that a creditor cannot hold the paper of his original debtor, a bankrupt, and prove beyond the actual debt upon it, but that that such creditor may have the paper of third persons, who are debtors to such original debtor in more, and prove to the whole amount under the commission against them, and it is not material whether such third persons were indebted to the original debtor, for you cannot attach equities upon bills of exchange." So in Ex parte Bloxham,ˢ the same point was decided, and Lord Eldon said, "A party wants to have a bill discounted, and the banker refuses to discount upon the credit of that bill only, and then the party says, he has in his hands another bill, and offers that as a security for the former, what is that but a right to prove against both estates, until 20s. in the pound has been obtained?"

We have just seen, that if the holder of a bill or note, at the time of proving, has received any part of it, he can prove only for the remainder.ᵗ So it has been held, that where different parties to a bill or note become bankrupts, and a dividend is *declared,* though not paid, under one of the commissions, under which the holder has proved his debt, he cannot afterwards prove under another commission for more than the residue, after deducting the amount of the dividend declared.ᵘ In Ex parte Lears,ˣ the Chancellor made an order, that the dividends should be deducted from the proof, according to this practice, as stated by Mr. Cooke, still expressing doubt as to the principle of it. Hence it is in general advisable, where there are several parties to a bill to prove under the commission against each, as soon as possible, or at least before any dividend has been received, or even a commission opened against either.

In favour of *friendly societies,* it was enacted by 33 Geo. 3. c. 54. "That if any person appointed to any office by a friendly society, and intrusted with, or having in his hands or possession any moneys or effects belonging to such society, or of any securities relating to the same, become a bankrupt, his assignees must deliver over all things belong-

4thly, To what extent proof may be made.

[462]

Friendly societies.

ᵖ Cooke, 150, 1, 2, 3. Cullen, 96.— The Royal Bank of Scotland, Ex parte, 19 Ves. 310. 3 Rose, 310.
ᑫ Cullen, 96.
ʳ 6 Ves. 449.
ˢ 6 Ves. 600, in which the case in 5 Ves. was over-ruled.
ᵗ Supra. 1 Mont. 143, 4.
ᵘ Cooper v. Pepys, 1 Atk. 106. The Royal Bank of Scotland, Ex parte, 19 Ves. 310. 2 Rose, 197. But see in Ex parte

Wildman, 1 Atk. 109, where the Chancellor takes for granted, that in the case of Cooper v. Pepys, the holder had received the dividend before he attempted to prove his debt against the indorser, 1 Mont. 144. Bayl. 210.

ˣ 6 Ves. 644. Note, the reason there assigned by Mr. Cooke fails, since 49 Geo. 3. c. 121. s. 12. See the Royal Bank of Scotland, 19 Ves. 310, n. b. Ex parte Todd, 2 Rose, 202, n.

4thly, To
what ex-
tent proof
may be
made.

ing to such society, and pay out of the assets or effects all sums of money remaining due, which such person received by virtue of his office, before any of his other debts are paid or satisfied.[y] It seems that this provision of the legislature, in preferring the claim of friendly

Friendly
societies.

societies to the claim of all other creditors, is not favoured.[z] If an attorney is, from the commencement of the establishment of a friendly society, in the habit of receiving from the stewards the money of the society, whenever it amounts to a sum which they consider worth placing out at interest ; and of giving them promissory notes from time to time, carrying interest; and the attorney becomes a bankrupt, and indebted to the stewards upon promissory notes payable on one month's notice, and no person has been appointed tresurer, the society is not entitled to a preference.[a] If no treasurer has been appointed by the society, and the president and steward are chosen annually, and the bankrupt has served the office of president and steward in different years, and in the capacity of steward has received the money of the society, and money is afterwards from time to time paid to him by the stewards and clerks, by order of the society, upon promissory notes bearing interest, given by him in the name of a firm of which he is a member, to the president and stewards, the society is not entitled to a preference.[b] A debt upon money lent by the consent of the society, upon a promissory note carrying interest, seems not to be entitled to a preference.[c] A debt upon money lent to a member of the society, upon his security, after he ceases to be an officer of the

[463]

society, is not entitled to preference.[d] And in Ex parte Stamford Friendly Society,[e] it was held, that the preference given to friendly societies by the statute 33 Geo. 3. c. 54. s. 10, over other creditors, was confined to debts in respect of money in the hands of their *officers, by virtue of their offices,* and independent of contract, and therefore does not extend to money held by the treasurer, upon the security of his promissory note, payable, with interest, on demand.[f]

Interest.

The *interest,* which is recoverable at law, has already been stated.[g] With respect to the *proof of interest* under a commission, the rule appears to be, that whenever, by the express terms of the bill or note, interest is reserved, or where there is a contract or agreement between the parties, that the debt shall carry interest, it is payable.[h] Accordingly it has been held, that even upon notes payable on demand, not reserving interest, the interest might be proved, where it appeared to be the known and established custom of the trade to allow it, and that it had actually been paid by the bankrupt, and accounts settled with him, in which it had been charged, and allowed between the parties.[i] But it is reported to have been decided, that interest is not proveable upon a bill or note, unless it be expressed in the body of the note, or there is a special agreement for the payment of it.[k] In Ex parte Hankey,[l] and Ex parte Mills,[m] it was held, that where by the

[y] 33 Geo. 3. c. 54. s. 10.
[z] Ex parte Ross, 6 Ves. 804.
[a] Ex parte Ashley, 6 Ves. 441. Ex parte Ross, 6 Ves. 804. 1 Mont. 524.
[b] Ex parte Ross, 6 Ves. 804.
[c] Id. ibid.
[d] Ex parte Amicable Society of Lancaster, 6 Ves. 98.
[e] 15 Ves. 280.
[f] Cooke, 254, 5.
[g] Ante, 420 to 423.

[h] Cooke, 174. 188. Cullen, 117. 1 Meat 145. 169. Bayl. 212.
[i] Ex parte Champion, 3 Bro. 436. Ex parte, Hankey, ib. 504. Ex parte Mills. 2 Ves. jun. 295.
[k] Ex parte Marlar, 1 Atk. 150.
[l] 3 Bro. 504.
[m] 2 Ves. jun. 295. 1 Mont. 172. Interest is recoverable at law, where goods have been sold upon the terms that a bill should be given, 13 East, 98.

4thly, To what ex-
tent proof
may be
made.
Interest.

Custom of a trade, interest is payable on a debt, and at the regular
time of stating the accounts, the debtor is *debited* for interest, and
afterwards becomes a bankrupt, the interest is proveable under his
commission, notwithstanding the debt was secured by four promissory
notes, of which only one upon the face of it was payable with interest, and the other three were merely notes payable on demand. It
has been laid down, that if the instrument is not expressed to be payable with interest, no interest is in general proveable;ⁿ it should seem,
however, from the case of Parker *v.* Hutchinson,° that interest is in
general payable upon all bills and notes payable at a day certain, but
not upon those payable upon a day uncertain, or shop notes: and
though that case did not arise in bankruptcy, yet, as affording evidence of the agreement of the parties, it appears to be applicable to
the case of bankruptcy, and seems to render the principle of the practice, excluding the proof of interest on bills payable at a day certain, [464]
questionable. A creditor by bill or note is entitled to prove the whole
interest due, whatever may be the amount, though a specialty creditor
can never have interest-beyond the penalty contained in his security.ᵖ
And we have seen that the creditor may prove the full sum for which
the bill or note was given, notwithstanding he received £5 *per cent.* discount, though the statuteᑫ enacts, that upon bills and notes payable at
future time, a rebate of interest shall be deducted from the actual payment of the dividend, to the time when the security would have been
payable.

When interest is allowed to be proved, it is never, in any case of an
insolvent estate, allowed to be computed lower than the date of the
commission, because it is said, the estate being a dead fund, a salvage
of part to each is all that in such a general loss can be expected.ʳ And
where the act of bankruptcy to which the commission relates, is ascertained, no interest is allowed after that act of bankruptcy.ˢ And in some
cases of mutual credit, when both debts carry interest, the computation
of interest should stop on both sides at the same time.ᵗ But in the case
of an estate which turns out to be solvent, and where a surplus comes
to a bankrupt, creditors have a right to interest, up to the actual time
of payment, without regard to the date of the commission,ᵘ provided
the instrument expressly entitles the holder to interest.ˣ Though the
rule was formerly only to allow £4 *per cent.*, it appears from the decision of Upton *v.* Lord Ferrers,ʸ that £5 *per cent.* is to be allowed.
And this is analogous to the different statutes with regard to the rebate
of interest.

Re-ex-
change.

The difference upon the re-exchange of bills protested, and re-drawn
before the bankruptcy, is proveable under the commission, but if incurred after the bankruptcy, it is not proveable.ᵃ So the costs and
charges of protesting bills incurred before the bankruptcy, may be

ⁿ 1 Mont. 170. Cooke, 174. 183.

° 3 Ves. 135. Upton *v.* Lord Ferrers,
5 Ves. 801. 803.

ᵖ Bromley *v.* Goodere, 1 Atk. 75. Cullen, 119.

ᑫ 7 Geo. 1. c. 31.

ʳ Butcher *v.* Churchill, 14 Ves. 573.
Bromley *v.* Goodere, 1 Atk. 79. Ex parte
Bennett, 2 Atk. 528. Cullen, 118. 1 Mont.
173. Ex parte Williams, 1 Rose, 401.

ˢ Ex parte Moore, 2 Bro. 597. Bayley
on Bills, 94.

ᵗ Bromley *v.* Goodere, 1 Atk. 79. Cullen,
119. 1 Mont. 544. ●

ᵘ Ex parte Goring, 1 Ves. jun. 170. Ex
parte Mills, 2 Ves. jun. 295. Butcher *v.*
Churchill, 14 Ves. 573. 1 Mont. 564, 5.

ˣ Ex parte Cocks, 1 Rose, 817. Ex parte
Williams, id. 401.

ʸ 5 Ves. 801. 3.

ᶻ When recoverable, see ante, 423.

ᵃ Ex parte Hoffham, Cooke, 173. Francis *v.* Rucker, Amb. 672. Cullen, 102. 1
Mont. 146.

4thly. To | proved, but not those incurred after the bankruptcy.[b] But where what ex- | by the particular law of the country from which the bill is drawn, or tent proof | when by express stipulation the re-exchange, or costs and charges, are may be | fixed at a particular rate, they may be proved under the commission, made. | though not incurred till after the act of bankruptcy. Thus, by the law Re-ex- | of Philadelphia, the drawer of a returned bill must pay its contents change. | with £20 *per cent.* advance, as liquidated damages ; in this case, if he become bankrupt, the £20 *per cent.* may be proved under his commission, though the bill was not protested till after his bankruptcy.[c]

Fifthly, The Time of proving and making Claim.

5thly. The | From the preceding observations, it may be collected, that no unne-time of | cessary delay should take place in making the proof, and we have seen proof and | that in some cases if the proof be delayed till after a dividend has making | been declared, though not received, it will prevent the holder from claim. | proving the whole amount of his bill under a commission against another person.[d] Formerly creditors were allowed to come in and prove their debts at any time within four months, and until distribution made, but they were not admitted after distribution actually made of any part of the estate ; but now, except in case of gross laches, creditors are allowed to come in at any time, while any thing remains to be divided.[e] And in Re Wheeler,[f] it was decided, that a creditor coming in to prove his debt after a dividend made (provided the delay was not fraudulent, but owing to accident, or unavoidable circumstances) should be put on a footing with other creditors, before any further dividend was made. A creditor who has neglected to prove before a meeting to declare a *second* dividend, is, in strictness, only entitled to be paid future dividends, *pari passu* with the other creditors ;[g] but it is the practice to permit such creditor to be paid former dividends rateably with those who have been paid, and then to direct a general distribution of the residue.[h] Where a creditor has a reasonable cause for not having proved in time to receive a first dividend, he is, upon proving, entitled first to be placed on an equality with the other creditors who received a first dividend, but not so as to disturb a former dividend, and then to receive the future dividends rateably with the other creditors.[i] The [466] mode of being admitted to receive in respect of former dividends, is by making an affidavit of the cause of delay, and by petition to the Chancellor, upon which an order may be obtained ; and the assignees should not pay without it.[k] We have seen, that in the case of a surety paying the debt of his principal after a commission against him, he may at any time prove under the commission, not disturbing the former dividends, and receive a dividend or dividends proportionably with the other creditors.[l]

Claim. | Where a party may not be able to swear to the precise amount of his debt, secured by a bill or note, it is advisable for him to make a

[b] Ex parte Moore, 2 Bro. 597. Anon. 1 Atk. 140. Cullen, 101. 1 Mont. 145.
[c] Francis *v.* Rucker, Amb. 672. Ex parte Moore, 2 Bro. 599. Cullen, 102.
[d] Ante, 461, 2. Ex parte Lears, 6 Ves. 545.
[e] Ex parte Peachy, 1 Atk. 111. Ex parte Styles, id. 208., and id. 79.
[f] 1 Sch. & Lef. 242.

[g] Ex parte Long, 2 Bro. 56. Ex parte Styles, 1 Atk. 208. Harding *v.* Mars. Ch. Ca. 153.
[h] Cooke, 521. 1 Mont. 556.
[i] Ex parte Long, 2 Bro. 50. Ex parte Styles and Pickart, 2 Atk. 208.
[k] 1 Mont. 556.
[l] Ante, 453, 4. 49 Geo. 3. c. 121 s. ?

claim as a means of securing a dividend, when his proof is afterwards established, without the necessity of applying to the Chancellor; and when a proper claim has been made, the dividend must be apportioned for it, and be withheld, until the validity of the claim has been ascertained.[m]

5thly. The time of proof and making claim.

Claim.

Sixthly, The Mode and Terms of Proof, and Remedy for the Dividend.

The mode of proof of bills of exchange is governed by the general rules affecting proof under a commission in other cases, and consequently it will be here only necessary to consider the peculiarities in the case of bills. The ordinary proof is by oath of the creditor.[n] When it is upon the bill or note, the form of the disposition varies according to the mode in which the creditor obtained the bill or note. Under a commission against the party from whom the creditor immediately received the bill or note, the deposition states, that the bankrupt is indebted to the deponent upon the consideration for the instrument, and alleges that no security has been obtained, except the bill or note; but when the bill or note has not been received from the bankrupt himself by the creditor, the deposition states, that he is indebted on the instrument, and then shows the means and consideration by which the deponent became the holder.[o] And where bills have been deposited by way of pledge, the proof is upon the original debt, and the deposition concludes by stating the delivery of the bills as a security, the particulars of which, if numerous, may be stated in a schedule.[p] Where several persons, whether general partners or otherwise, are the holders of the instrument, they must all be named as creditors in the deposition; but it is sufficient, if the deposition be made by one only of the partners.[q] If a bill has been lost, the proof must be admitted upon an indemnity.[r] A creditor is obliged, at the time of proving his debt, to state in his deposition, whether he has a security or not; and every security must be produced at the time when he proves, and the commissioners will mark it as having been exhibited.[s]

6thly. The mode of proof, and terms on which admitted.

[467]

In general, if a party insist upon proving under a commission, he must deliver up the security for the benefit of the creditors,[t] or must apply to the commissioners to have the pledge sold, and to be admitted a creditor for the residue.[u] And where a debtor, by way of collateral security, delivers a bill of exchange or promissory note, without his name appearing upon the paper, this is to be considered as a pledge, and not as an absolute transfer of the bill; and the creditor will not be allowed to prove under the commission against such debtor, and also to retain the securities, but must either give them up or obtain an order for the sale of them, and then prove for the deficiency.[x] Where a creditor, by a debt partly proveable and partly not, under a commission of bankruptcy, has a general pledge, he may apply it to the debt not

[m] Cooke, 255. 1 Mont. 459. 558.
[n] Cullen, 140, 141.
[o] See the forms; post, Appendix. 2 Cooke, 26, 27. 4 Mont. 91 to 93.
[p] See the forms, post, Appendix. 4 Mont. 93.
[q] 2 Cooke, 25. Post, Appendix. Ante, 436.

[r] Ex parte Greenway, 6 Ves. 812.— Ante, 440.
[s] Ex parte Bennet, 2 Atk. 528.
[t] Id. ibid.
[u] Ex parte Coming, Cooke, 123.
[x] Ex parte Trowton, &c. Cooke, 124. Ex parte Hillier, ibid. 123.—Cullen, 147. 1 Mont. 458.

6thly. The proveable under the commission.^{y} If a security is deposited by a
mode of debtor to indemnify his creditor for a balance then due, together with
proof, and such further sums of money as shall be due to him for money to be
terms on advanced and paid for the debtor, either by bill accepted or to be ac-
which ad- cepted, and the debtor become a bankrupt, and the creditor, after the
mitted. bankruptcy, pay various acceptances, he may apply the security, in the
first place, to reduce the demand not proveable, on account of its not
having been paid till after the bankruptcy.^{z} If a security is deposited
by a drawer to indemnify the acceptor, who pays part of his acceptances before the bankruptcy of the drawer, and part after such bankruptcy, the acceptor may apply the security to reduce the demand paid
after the bankruptcy.^{a}

But where the bankrupt did not merely deposit the bills or notes as
a pledge, but indorsed them to the creditor, he has a right to retain the
security and proceed against the other parties, and also to prove his
whole debt at the same time under the commission,^{b} provided he has
[468] not received part, or no dividend, under a commission against another
estate has been declared, before he comes to prove, so that he do not
receive more than 20s. in the pound upon his whole debt.^{c}

Proceeding   Formerly a creditor, who had proceeded at law, might also prove his
at law, and debt under the commission against the same party, renouncing any
proving al- benefit under the commission so as to afford him an opportunity of
so. preventing, as far as he could, the very remedy he had chosen, from
being defeated by the rest of the creditors, discharging the person of
the bankrupt by signing his certificate without his concurrence or control ; and a party might also make a claim, and still proceed at law.^{d}
By the statute 49 Geo. 3. c. 121. s. 14,^{e} directs that a creditor, who
has brought an action against a bankrupt, shall not be permitted to
prove, or make a claim, without relinquishing such action, and that
the proving, or claiming, a debt under a commission, shall be deemed
an election by such creditor to take the benefit of the commission with
respect to the debt so proved or claimed. This statute, however, does
not affect the right of a person not being the petitioning creditor, to
prove one debt under a commission, and to proceed at law for another.
And in Ex parte Govesnor,^{g} Lord Eldon said, " that if a creditor
has a note for one sum and a bond for another, as the remedies and the
relief under those securities are different, he may prove one debt and
hold the bankrupt in execution for the other. But an entire demand
cannot be split, and if there be a demand upon several notes or securities given in respect of the same transaction, it seems that the creditor
cannot adopt there double remedies.^{h}

Reducing   It sometimes happens, after a creditor has made his proof, that
and expun- either from the disclosure of facts not before known or understood, it
ging proof. appears that it ought not to have been admitted, or at least not to the
extent ; or that, from a change of circumstances, the state of the debt

^{y} Ex parte Haward, Cooke, 120. Ex   *-^{c} Cullen, 146. 1 Atk. 110.
parte Arckley, ibid. 126. Ex parte ^{d} Ex parte Sharp, 11 Ves. 203. Cullen.
Hunter, 6 Ves, 94.   153, 159.
     ^{z} Ex parte Haward, Cooke, 120. Ex ^{e} See the construction of this section in
parte Hunter, 6 Ves. 94.   Atherston v. Huddleston, 2 Taunt. 181
     ^{a} Ex parte Arckley, Cooke, 126. Ex ^{f} Cooke, 135. Cullen, 149. *
parte Hunter, 6 Ves. 94. ^{g} 14 Ves. 588.
     ^{b} Ex parte Bennett, 2 Atk, 528. Ante, ^{h} Id. ibid.
457, 8. 1 Mont. 458. Cullen, 146.

proved is materially altered : and, in such cases, it becomes necessary 6thly. The mode of proof, and terms on which admitted.

Reducing & expunging proof.

[469]
either to *reduce* the proof, or to *expunge* it altogether.[1] Thus if any bills, proved and accepted as securities by a creditor who discounted them for the bankrupt, or took them as a security for a general balance, are afterwards paid in full, or in any way fully satisfied, the amount of each bill must be deducted from the proof, and the future dividends only paid on the residue of the debt.[k] So if the holder of a bill compounded with the *prior* names upon it, without the previous assent of assignees of the subsequent parties, the latter are discharged ; and if he takes such composition after having proved under the commission against the latter, the amount of the bill must be deducted from the proof.[l] But the principle of these decisions, is the same as that which precludes a party from recovering at law, and we have seen that, at law, that the holder does not discharge a prior party to a bill by compounding with a subsequent one, even though the former was known to be an accommodation acceptor,[m] so in the case of bankruptcy, compounding with a subsequent party will not affect the right to the dividends under a commission against a prior one, because the estate of the latter had no claim upon that of the former, and therefore could not be prejudiced by the arrangement. It was on this ground held, in the case of Ex parte Giffard,[n] that if a promissory note be made by one principal and three sureties, two of whom, and the principal, become bankrupts, and the holder of the note prove his whole debt under each commission, and afterwards receive a composition of 4s. in the pound from the remaining surety, the receipt for which is expressed to be for £191, and two notes, which, when duly paid, will be in full of the said debt and all other demands ; and the dividend paid by the estate of the principal is 4s. in the pound, and by the bankrupt sureties is 5s. in the pound; no part of the proof under the commission against the bankrupt sureties must be expunged. The commissioners cannot expunge a debt without an order upon petition.[o]

We have seen that in some cases, where the proof has been expunged, Restoring proof. it may be *restored*, in order that the party himself, or some third person, may have the benefit of the original proof, and receive dividends which would not otherwise be recoverable.[p]

Where, between the time of proving his debt and of applying for a Benefit of another's proof.

[470] dividend under a commission against a principal debtor, as acceptor of a bill, maker of a note, or prior indorser, who ultimately ought to pay it, the holder has received from a surety or subsequent indorser, or of an accommodation acceptor, the whole of his debt, such party, thus standing in the situation of a surety, is entitled to the benefit of the proof made by the creditor; and he must receive the dividends as trustee for the security;[q] provided the creditor be not thereby prejudiced in respect of any other claim upon the estate.[r]

If a person, having a demand upon a country firm, who have dealings

[1] Cullen, 158. 1 Mont. 545.
[k] Ex parte Smith. Ex parte Bloxham.
[l] parte Wallace. Ex parte Cropley, Cooke, 155, 156.
[l] Ex parte Smith, 3 Bro. 1. Cooke, 9; and Ex parte Smith and others, Cooke, 171. Cullen, 159. 1 Mont. 546.
[l] Ante, 301, 2, 3.
[m] Ante, 298 to 300.

[n] 6 Ves. 805; see also Williams v. Walsby, 4 Esp. Rep. 220.
[o] Ex parte Nixon, 4 Mont. 34.
[p] Ex parte Matthews, 6 Ves. 285. Cooke, 154.
[q] Ante, 452, &c. Ex parte Ryswicke, 2 P. Wms. 89. Cooke, 152.
[r] Ante, 469, &c.

6thly. The
mode of
proof, and
terms on
which ad-
mitted.

with a house in London, obtain permission from the country firm for one of his creditors to draw upon the London house, and the country firm and the London house became bankrupts, and the drawer, after proving under the commission against the London house, receive payment from his original debtor, that is, the person having a demand upon

Benefit
of another's
proof.

the country firm, such person is entitled to the benefit of the drawer's proof against the London house, if he have not proved the debt under the commission against the country firm, but if he has, it seems he is not entitled.[*] If a banker pay, after notice of an act of bankruptcy committed by his customer, the drafts of a customer, in favour of a creditor whose debt would have been proveable under the commission, the banker is not entitled to stand in the place in which the creditor would have stood had his debt not been paid, and as so standing to receive a dividend rateably with the other creditors.[t]

Remedy to
recover di-
vidend.

Formerly, when a dividend of the bankrupt's estate had been declared by the commissioners, an action might be maintained against the assignees by a party who had proved a bill, for his share of the dividend: and in such action the proceedings, before the commissioners were conclusive evidence of the debt, nor where assignees suffered to set off any debt from the plaintiff to the bankrupt.[u] But it was enacted, by the 49 Geo. 3. c. 121. s. 12, that " no action shall be brought against the assignee for dividends, but on petition to the Chancellor to pay the same with interest and costs, when the justice of the case shall require it."

Seventhly, The Consequence of not proving, and Effect of Certificate.

7thly. Ef-
fect of cer-
tificate.

[471]

It may be laid down as a clear and established principle, that the discharge of the bankrupt should be commensurate and co-extensive with the relief to the creditor, and consequently that all debts shall be discharged by the certificate that either have been, or that *might have been* proved under the commission;[x] and, on the other hand, the bankrupt's remaining still liable, and the creditor's not being able to prove his debt under the commission, are convertible terms.[y] The various instances in which bills and notes may be proved have been considered. The statutes which enable the holder of a bill to prove in particular cases, contain a clause, that in cases where the holder could avail himself of the proof, the certificate shall protect the bankrupt from a further responsibility ; and the statute 49. Geo. 3. c. 121. s. 8. having enabled sureties to prove in various instances where he has been compelled to pay the bill or note after the issuing of the commission has greatly enlarged the effect of the certificate. There are, however, still some cases relating to bills and notes, in which the certificate will not be a bar to any future action. Thus, if the bill or note were drawn and payable in England, and the cause of action accrue here, a certificate abroad will not be any bar to an action in this country, although at the time of making the contract the bankrupt resided abroad, in the country where he afterwards obtained his certificate.[*] But where the

---

* Ex parte Matthews, 6 Ves. 285.

t Hankey v. Vernon, 3 Bro. 313.

u Brown v. Bullen, Dougl. 407; and Ex parte Leers, 6 Ves. 645.

x Ex parte Groom, 1 Atk. 119.—Chilton v. Wiffin, 3 Wils. 13.

y Per Lord Kenyon, in Cowley v. Dunlop, 7 T. R. 565 ; and see 49 Geo. c. 121. s. 14. and 1 Rose, 204.

* Quin v. Keefe, 2 Hen. Bla. 553.—Pedder v. Macmaster, 8 T. R. 609.—Smith v. Buchanan, 1 East, 6; but Burrows v. Jemmino, 2 Stra. 733

cause of action accrues abroad, a certificate in the country where the cause accrued, is a bar to any action in this country.[a] And if a bill of exchange, drawn in Ireland upon a person resident in Ireland, be accepted, and the acceptor become a bankrupt in Ireland, and there obtain his certificate, and afterwards be proceeded against in this country upon the bill, the court will order an *exoneretur* to be entered on the bail piece, on the ground, that as the debt was contracted in Ireland where the commission issued, it was discharged by the certificate.[b] And if a person draw a bill in America, in favour of a firm in America, who have also a house in London, upon a person residing in London, and the bill be refused acceptance, and notice of refusal is given to the drawer in America, and the drawer afterwards become a bankrupt and obtained his certificate in America, it is a bar in this country to any action against the drawer.[c] The general rule of law is, that *debitum et contractus sunt nullius loci*, and that the payment of a debt, wherever it may have been contracted, may be enforced in any country; and consequently, whenever creditor might prove under a commission abroad, it should seem, on principle, that a certificate should be a bar to every debt wherever it was contracted. But, on the other hand, great inconveniencies might ensue from fraudulent certificates in remote countries being obtained before a creditor here could be apprized of the proceeding, and therefore unless the contract was made, or at least in some measure connected with the foreign country, he should not be [472] prejudiced by such certificate. When a certificate abroad operates as a discharge in this country, it seems that the extent of the discharge will depend upon the law of the country where the certificate is obtained.[d]

Where a bankrupt is discharged by his certificate from a *debt* in one form, he cannot be charged by the creditor from the same debt in another form of action: and therefore, in the case of Foster *v.* Surtees,[e] where, by agreement between the plaintiffs, bankers at Carlisle, and the defendants, bankers at Newcastle, the plaintiffs were weekly to send to the defendants all their own notes and the notes of certain other banking-houses; and the defendants were in exchange to return the plaintiffs their own notes and the notes of certain other bankers, and the deficiency, if any, was to be made up by a bill drawn by the defendants in favour of the plaintiffs at a certain date; it was held, that the notes so sent by the plaintiffs to the defendants constituted a debt against them, which the defendants might pay by a return of notes according to the agreement; but if they made no such return, or a short return, and gave no bill for the balance, such balance remaining as a debt against them, which was proveable by the plaintiffs, under a commission of bankrupt issued against the defendants, on an act of bankruptcy committed after the time when the bill for the balance, if drawn, would have been due and payable; and that the plaintiffs could not maintain an action to recover damages as for a breach of contract against the defendants who had obtained there certificates. But, in some cases a creditor has an election to shape his demand on the bankrupt either as a debt, or as for a tort, and if he adopt the latter, the certificate will be no bar. Thus, if a bankrupt to whom a bill has been delivered to obtain the payment when due, and to remit to his employer, discount it at a loss before it was due, and embezzel the

a Potter *v.* Brown, 5 East, 124.
b Ballantine *v.* Golding, Cooke, 115.
c Potter *v.* Brown, 5 East, 124.
d Ex parte Burton, 1 Atk. 255. 1 Mont. 662.
e 12 East, 605.

7thly. Ef- money, if sued for this tort his certificate would be no bar.[f] So if
fect of cer- bills be deposited merely as a pledge, if the bankrupt pledge them as
tificate.   his own, he will continue liable to a special action for this tort.[g]

New con-   The effect of the certificate as to a debt which might have been
tract, or   proved under the commission, may be avoided by a *fresh contract* en-
promise.   tered into with the bankrupt *bona fide* after an act of bankruptcy, even
            before or after he has obtained his certificate.[h] All the debts of a
[473]   bankrupt continue due in conscience, notwithstanding he has obtained
            his certificate ; and though a security, or a promise, as a consideration
            for signing his certificate is void, any security given *bona fide* without
            fraud or imposition on the bankrupt is valid and binding upon him,
            though there be no new consideration.[i] Thus in the case of Trueman
            v. Fenton,[k] where the bankrupt after the act of bankruptcy, and after
            the issuing of the commission, but *before* he had obtained his certificate,
            gave a promissory note in consideration of two former bills of the bank-
            rupt being cancelled, and of an agreement not to accept a dividend under
            the commission, it was held that the certificate was no bar to an action
            on the note. And if a bankrupt, *after* obtaining his certificate, under-
            take to pay any creditor the residue of his debt, the undertaking if
            made freely, and without fraud, is binding.[l] However, a bankrupt
            having obtained his certificate, is not liable upon a promise to pay
            former debt, unless it be express, distinct, and unequivocal.[m]

                    ——————

                V. OF MUTUAL CREDIT AND SET-OFF.

5. Mutual   WHEN at the time of the act of bankruptcy, there were cross de-
credit[n]   mands subsisting between the bankrupt and a creditor, the latter, by
            setting off his debt against his demand, stands in a better situation than
            other creditors not in that situation, who can only prove under the com-
            mission, and receive dividends. In equity, long anterior to the statute
            permitting a set-off at law, a party might avail himself of any cross
            demand, and preclude his creditor from recovering more than the
            balance that might be due to him on a fair adjustment of accounts.
            And though the spirit of the bankrupt laws is to make an equal dis-
            tribution amongst all the creditors, yet this must in justice be governed
            by the nature of the dealings between the parties, and as it may
            fairly presumed that where mutual transactions have taken place be-
            tween a bankrupt and another trader, they have respectively given
            greater credit to each other than would have taken place in any sepa-
            ex parte dealings; it is therefore just, that in the case of bankrupt
            their mutual demands should be set-off against each other. It is
            therefore enacted by the statute 5 Geo. 2. c. 30. s. 28. "That where
            "it shall appear to the commissioners, or the major part of them,
[474]   "that there hath been *mutual credit* given by the bankrupt and a

[f] Parker v. Norton, 6 T. R. 695.   Cullen, 86 to 388. and in 1 Mont. 541.
[g] Johnson v. Spiller, Dougl. 167. Cul- p. where see other points on this subject
len, 113. 391.   &c.
[h] Cullen, 386. 1 Mont. 586.
[i] Trueman v. Fenton, Cowp. 344. Birch   [m] Fleming v. Hayne, 1 Stark. 370
v. Sharland, 1 T. R. 745.
[k] Cowp. 544.   [n] As to mutual debts and credits between
[l] Ibid. and the several cases collected in a bankrupt and other persons, see B.
                                            212 to 216.

"other person, or mutual debts between the bankrupt and any other
"person, *at any time before such person became a bankrupt*, the said
"commissioners, or the major part of them, or the assignees of such
"bankrupt's estate, shall state the account between them *and one debt*
"*may be set against another*, and what shall appear to be due on either
"side on the balance of such account, and on setting such debts
"against one another, and no more, shall be claimed or paid on either
"side respectively." And by the statute 46 Geo. 3. c. 135. s. 3. it is
enacted, "That in all cases in which, under commissions of bankrupt
"hereafter to be issued, it shall appear that there has been mutual
"credit given by the bankrupt and any other person, or mutual debts
"between the bankrupt and any other person, one debt on demand
"may be set-off against another, *notwithstanding any prior act of*
"*bankruptcy* committed by such bankrupt before the credit was given
"to, or the debt was contracted by such bankrupt, *in the like manner*
"*as if no such prior act of bankruptcy had been committed*, provided
"such credit was given to the bankrupt *two calendar months* before
"the date and suing forth of such commission, and provided the
"person claiming the benefit of such set-off, had not, at the time of
"giving such credit, *any notice* of any prior act of bankruptcy by such
"bankrupt committed, or that he was insolvent or had stopped pay-
"ment."

Upon these statutes it is observable that the word *credit* is more com-
prehensive than the word *debt*, and Lord Mansfield said, in the case of
French v. Fenn,° that the act of parliament was accurately drawn to avoid
the injustice that would be done, if the words were only mutual debts,
and it therefore provides for mutual credit. The subject of mutual credit, as far as it relates to bills of exchange and promissory notes, may be
considered under the three following heads:

1st. *The nature of the debt and consideration upon which it is
   founded.*
2d. *The parties between whom the mutual credit may exist.*
3d. *The time when the debt or credit arose.*

1. The na-
ture of the
debt to be
set-off.

I. With respect to *the debt or demand proposed to be set off*, not
only mutual running accounts are within the statutes, but also other
cross demands subsisting at the time of the act of bankruptcy, and
even such debts have been allowed to be set off as could not have been
brought into any account in equity betwixt the parties, such as debts
arising to one party not by contract, but by reason of a fraud on the [475]
other, and therefore not a mutual credit.ᴾ Even a legacy, which cannot be considered as a demand arising from a contract, has, when assented to by the executor, been considered admissible as a set-off
against a demand on the legatee.�q And the illegality of the consideration will not, in the case of bankruptcy, in all cases preclude a person from setting off what is equitably due. And therefore it has been
decided, that a party to a contract, on which he has taken usurious
interest, may set-off the sum really advanced on the contract.ʳ And a
transaction has been held to be a mutual credit, though its operation
seem contrary to an agreement of all the parties, for a vendor of seve-

° Ex parte Stevens, 11 Ves. 27. Cooke, 554. 1 Mont. 529. Cullen, 192 to 197.
ᴾ Cullen, 198; but this is contrary to the intent of the statute of usury; and see Roberts v. Goff, 4 Barnewall & Alderson, 62.
q Jeffs v. Wood, 2 P. W. 128.
ʳ Ryall v. Rolls, 1 Ves. 375.

8. Mutual credit.

1. The nature of the debt to be set-off.

ral parcels of goods sold to the bankrupt, for which the latter gave his acceptances, payable at different times, having received of the bankrupt at the time one of them became due before the bankruptcy, a bill of exchange for a greater amount, and giving an undertaking to pay over the difference when received, was allowed, though contrary to the agreement, to retain it for the debt due to him upon the other parcels, which were not paid for at the time of the bankruptcy; this constituting a mutual credit, on the one side to the bankrupt upon his acceptances, the obligation to pay which, at all events, at a future day, was not superseded by the agreement; and on the other by giving the bill.[a] The same point was established in Ex parte Wagstaff,[c] in which it was held, that an acceptance not due till after the bankruptcy of the drawer, is capable of being set-off against a distinct debt due from such acceptor to the drawer, within the clause of the act as to mutual credit. And where Lord Cork gave the bankrupt his accommodation notes, upon a written undertaking to indemnify, and his Lordship paid the notes after the bankruptcy, he was allowed to set-off the payment against a demand of the bankrupt for business done.[e] But where A. previous to his bankruptcy, deposited a bill of exchange with B. for the specific purpose of raising money thereon, and B. advanced money on the bill, it was held that the assignees of A. were entitled to recover from B. the amount of the bill in an action of trover, having tendered to B. the money advanced by him, though a general balance remained due from the bankrupt to B. and that this did not form a case of mutual credit.[x] If the assignees of a bankrupt affirm the acts of the bankrupt as a contract, by suing a party in assumpsit, he may have the benefit of a set-off, which he could not have had if

[476] he had been sued as for a *tort.* As where goods had been sold to a party by way of fraudulent preference in satisfaction of a debt due to him from the bankrupt, and the assignees sued him as for goods sold and delivered, thereby affirming the transaction as a contract of sale by the bankrupt; the purchaser was allowed to avail himself of a set-off.[y] But if a banker receive and pay money on account of a bankrupt, after notice of his bankruptcy, he cannot set-off the payments against the receipts.[z] A creditor upon a bill of exchange or promissory note of the bankrupt's indorsed to him, *before* the bankruptcy, may set it off against a debt due from him to the bankrupt for goods bought after the indorsement, and also before the bankruptcy, though the bankrupt did not know that the bill was indorsed to and in the possession of the party at the time, for the sending of a bill into the world is considered as gaining *a credit* to the party with every person who takes the bill.[a] The case Ex parte Metcalf,[b] may be considered as a case of mutual credit; A. and B. had become bankrupts, and proof in respect to a cash balance due from A. to B. was admitted, but the dividends were ordered to be retained to reimburse the estate of B. what it might be liable to pay on account of an advance of bills from A. to B. some of which were dishonoured. Where A. before his bankruptcy, discounted certain bills with B. and C. his bankers, and they gave him immediate credit for the value of the bills in his account minus the discount, and a balance was struck before the bankruptcy, and

[a] Atkinson v. Elliott, 7 T. R. 378.—Cooke, 559; but see Ex parte Flint, 1 Swanst. Rep. Ch. 30.
[c] 13 Ves. 65.
[e] Ex parte Boyle, 1 Cooke, 561.
[x] Key v. Flint, 8 Taunt. 21.
[y] Smith v. Hodgson, 4 T. R. 211: but see Thomason v. Frere, 10 East, 413.—Cooke, 557.
[z] Vernon v. Hankey, 2 T. R. 113.
[a] Hankey v. Smith, 3 T. R. 507.
[b] 11 Ves. 404. Madden v. Kempster. 1 Campb. 12. S. P.

whilst the bills were yet running, in favour of A., when the bankers admitted that they had in their hands £934. 8s. 8d. due to A., giving him credit for the bills then running, and A. became a bankrupt, and the bills were dishonoured, it was held, that in an action against the bankers for the balance admitted to be due to A. before his bankruptcy, they have a right to set-off against such claim the amount of the dishonoured bills, it being a case of *mutual credit.*[c]

5. Mutual credit.

1. The nature of the debt to be set-off.

II. To constitute mutuality of debts or of credits, it is in general necessary, that the sum claimed *was due to the bankrupt, and is due to the creditor in their own rights* respectively. Thus a joint and separate debt cannot be set off against each other ;[d] and in the case of the bankruptcy of one only of several partners, the defendant, in an action by assignees and solvent partners, cannot set-off,[e] and a debt due to a party as trustee for another person, cannot be set-off.[f] The right of set-off in this respect appears to be governed by the same rules as prevail at common law.[g] In the case Ex parte Twogood,[h] under separate commissions of bankruptcy, relief in the nature of set-off against a separate creditor of the bankrupt, indebted to the partnership to a greater amount was refused, and Lord Eldon, after pointing out the inconveniences that might ensue if he allowed the petition, said, that there was a good deal of natural equity in the proposition upon which the petition stood, but that pursuing it through all its consequences, it would so disturb all the habitual arrangement in bankruptcy that he dare not do it. But under particular circumstances where great injustice would otherwise prevail, exceptions to this rule are allowed. Thus where a person gave a note to his bankers on account of a supposed balance due to them, but in which there was a mistake, and the bankers indorsed the note to another firm, consisting of some of the partners in the bankinghouse; the maker of the note may set off the debt due to him from his bankers, to an action commenced against him on the note by the firm who hold it, the knowledge of one of the partners in such firm, being deemed equivalent to notice to all, and consequently they were affected by the state of accounts between the maker of the note and his bankers.[i] And in Ex parte Stevens,[k] an equitable set-off, under circumstances, was allowed when there could be none at law. In that case bankers directed to lay out money in navy annuities, but not having done so, represented that they had, and made entries, and accounted for the dividends accordingly; and they took a joint promissory note from the party under that supposition, and her brother, to secure an advance from them to him, upon which the assignees, under their bankruptcy, sued him alone, and an order was made for proof of the balance, setting off the debt upon the note, and that the note should be delivered to her as if she had paid it.

2. In what right due.

[477]

---

[c] Arbouin *v.* Tritton, Holt, C. N. P. 408.

[d] Ex parte Twogood, 11 Ves. 519. Ex parte Stevens, 11 Ves. 27. 1 Mont. 552. 1 Chitty on Pleading, 3d ed. 554, 5.

[e] Staniforth *v.* Fellows, 1 Marsh. 484.

[f] Fair *v.* M'Iver, 16 East, 130.

[g] Tidd's Prac. 4th edit. 598, 9, and see the set-off of one judgment against another, id. 195, 6, and see 1 Chitty on Pleading, 3d edit. 554. 558 to 560.

[h] 11 Ves. 517; but see the cases at law in Tidd's Prac. 4th edit. 895, 6, where a joint demand has been set-off, with the concurrence of the partners, against a separate demand, and *vice versâ.* It appears *equitable* that where all the partners *agree* to set-off their joint demand against the demand of a separate creditor of one of them, it should be allowed, so as to prevent his entire demand being recoverable. But in case of bankruptcy, creditors might be prejudiced by such an arrangement, and the difficulties in effecting it would be insurmountable. 1 Chitty on Pleading, 3d edit. 549. 558 to 560.

[i] Pulier *v.* Roe, Peake, 197.

[k] 11 Ves. 24.

6. Effect of bankruptcy, &c. and this has been so held, notwithstanding that the banker according to custom enter the bills as cash in his customers' accounts, charging interest for the time they have to run, provided the balance of the cash

2d. The property of others. account at the time of the bankruptcy, be in favour of the customer. In a late case[a] it was held, that a customer paying bills, not due, into his bankers in the country, whose practice it was to credit their customers for the amount of such bills, if approved, as cash (charging interest,) is entitled to recover back such bills in specie from the bank-

[484] ers becoming bankrupt; the balance of his cash account, independent of such bills, being in his favour at the time of the bankruptcy; and if payment be afterwards received upon such bills by the assignees, they are liable to refund it to the customer in an action for money had and received; and Lord Ellenborough observed, that "every man who pays bills not due into the hands of the banker, places them there, as in the hands of his agent, to obtain payment of them when due. If the banker discount the bill, or advance money upon the credit of it, that alters the case; he then acquires the entire property in it, or has a lien on it *pro tanto* for his advance. The only difference between the practice stated of *London* and country bankers in this respect is, that the former, if overdrawn, has a lien on the bill deposited with him, though not indorsed; whereas the country banker, who always takes the bill indorsed, has not only a lien upon it, if his account be overdrawn, but has also his legal remedy upon the bill by the indorsement; but neither of them can have any lien on such bills until their account be overdrawn: and here the balance of the cash account at the time of the bankruptcy was in favour of the plaintiffs.[b]"

15. S. C. Short bills remitted by a country bank, to their banker in London, standing at the bankruptcy of the latter entered short in the usual way, not being due. Ordered, on petition in the bankruptcy, to be delivered up by the assignees to the country bank, who not being creditors when the petition was presented, the cash balance being against them, had since become so, turning it in their favour by taking up the bankrupt's acceptances on their account. The order was made without requiring the petition to be amended by stating that fact; but upon consent of the crown holding an extent for acceptances of the bankrupt, on account of duties reserved and remitted specifically by the country bank.

Ex parte Buchanan, in the matter of Kensington, 1 Rose, 280. An order was made upon the provisional assignee to deliver up short bills in the hands of bankers at the time of their bankruptcy, the estate being indemnified against their outstanding acceptances on account of the petitioner.

Ex parte The Burton Bank, &c. 2 Rose, 162. These were petitions presented in the bankruptcy of Messrs. Whitehead, Howard, and Co. bankers in London, by their correspondents in the country, for the purpose of having certain short bills of the petitioners, which were in the possession of the bankrupts at the time of the bankruptcy, delivered up, indemnifying the bankrupts estate against its liability for the

petitioners. The right was considered so indisputable that the following orders were taken by consent.

Ex parte Harford. The provisional assignee to retain the cash balances, and the cash received, and on the short bills, and also a sufficient number of short unpaid to cover the amount of Whitehead and Co's. acceptances, and he is to deliver over to Harford and Co. the residue of said bills, notes, and securities. It is understood, that the cash and rest retained are to be given up as Harford and Co. produce the acceptances cancelled.

Ex parte The Burton Bank. The provisional assignee consents, that all bills, &c. shall be delivered up upon the petitioner leaving such sum as together with the cash balance, equals the acceptances outstanding.

Note. An extent had been issued on the part of the crown; but there was created to satisfy it without resorting to the bills, nor were they scheduled among the property seized under it. See Ex parte Rowton, 1 Rose, 15.

Ex parte Waring and others, 19 Ves. 345.

[c] Giles v. Perkins, 9 East, 12. Tait P. & A. 71.

[a] Giles v. Perkins, 9 East, 12.

[b] See also Ex parte Pease and others 19 Ves. 25. 45. Ante, 482. Ex parte Waring, 19 Ves. 349. Ex parte Buchanan, id. 201. 1 Rose Bank, C. 252. 245.

So in the case Ex parte Sayers,[c] where A., abroad, commissions B. in London, to send him foreign coin, with particular directions as to the manner and time of sending it ; and remits bills, which B. discounts, and the coin required not being to be had in England, sends two remittances not equal to the amount of A's bills to Lisbon for the purpose of procuring it ; with directions, if it cannot be had, to return the bills. The coin not being to be had, bills nearly to the amount of the remittance to Lisbon, not indorsed by the correspondent there, are returned, and B., in the interval, becoming bankrupt, are received by his assignees ; A. was held to have a right to those bills upon the particular circumstances, the Lord Chancellor expressing much doubt, whether such right would exist in the case of remittance to buy goods in the way of trade.

6. Effect of bankruptcy, &c., 2d. The property of others.

And on the same principle, in Hassall v. Smithers,[d] it was held that a remittance in bills and notes for a specific purpose, viz. to answer acceptances, received by the administrator, in consequence of the death of the party to whom it was remitted, was not general assets, the specific purpose operating as a lien, which would also be the effect upon a bankruptcy.

But if the holder of bills deliver them to a banker, expressly on the terms of discount, or if, by the course of dealing between the customer and banker, bills received by the latter are understood by both parties as cash minus the discount, and the customer is at liberty to draw on account thereof, beyond the amount of cash in the hands of the banker, then, in the event of the bankruptcy of the banker, the assignees are entitled to the bills.[e] So where a person having three bills [485]

---

[c] 5 Ves. 169.
[d] 12 Ves. 119.
[e] Ante, 122.   Carstairs v. Bates, 3 Campb. 301.

Carstairs and others, assignees of Kensington, v. Bates, 3 Campb. 301. Where bankers discount a bill of exchange for a customer, giving him credit for the amount of the bill, and debiting him with the discount, the bill becomes the property of the bankers, and upon their bankruptcy their assignees may maintain an action upon it, although there be no balance due to them from the customer. Per Lord Ellenborough. " Is it meant seriously to contest the right of the assignees to recover in this action? The bankers were the purchasers of this bill. They did not receive it as the agents of Allport. The whole property and interest in the bill vested in themselves, and they stood all risks from the moment of the discount. If the bill had been afterwards stolen or burnt, theirs would have been the loss. In Giles v. Perkins, the bankers were mere depositories, with a lien when the account was overdrawn. The customer there drew on the credit of the bills deposited. Here Allport might have drawn out the amount of the bill, deducting the discount as actual cash, in the same manner as if he had dishonoured the bill with a third person, and then paid in the amount in bank notes. The dis-

count makes the bankers complete purchasers of the bill. The transaction was completed ; they had no lien but the thing itself ; the bills was as much theirs as any chattel they possessed. This very distinction was taken in the case cited ; for it was there said, if the banker discount the bill, or advance money on the credit of it, that alters the case ; he then acquires the entire property in it, or has a lien on it pro tanto for his advance." Verdict for plaintiff.

So in Paley P. & A. 72, it is laid down thus : " But in order to prevent the effect of the bankrupt laws from attaching negotiable securities in the hands of a bankrupt agent, there must be a specific appropriation of them, as by lodging of bill for bill, or by the deposit of several in one entire transaction, to answer a particular purpose ; for if they are paid in from time to time, upon a general running account, they become the effects of the person to whom they are so paid, and are not reclaimable. The doctrine is thus generally stated by Lord Hardwicke : 'If bills are sent by a correspondent to a merchant here to be received, and the money to be applied to a particular use, and the merchant becomes bankrupt before the money is received on the bills, the correspondent has a special lien in respect of those bills, and the money shall not be divided amongst the creditors at

CHITTY ON BILLS.   3 I

6. Effect of exchange, applied to a country banker with whom he had no pre-
of   bank- vious dealings, to give for them a bill on London of the same amount,
ruptcy, &c.
2d. The and the bill given by the banker was afterwards dishonoured, held, that
property of this was a complete exchange of securities, and that trover would not
others. lie for the three bills of exchange ; and it was also held, that if the
exchange had not been complete, still that the banker having become a
bankrupt, and the three bills having come to the possession of his a-
[486] signees, must be considered as goods and chattels in the order and dis-
possession of the bankrupt at the time of his bankruptcy, within the
above-mentioned statute 21 James 1. c. 19.[f]

Insolvent   A party to a bill or note who has become insolvent may be discharged
debtors. from liability by the operation of an insolvent act.[g] In a late case,
where after the 1st day of July, 1809, mentioned in the Insolvent
Debtors Act, 49 Geo. 3. c. 115, a promissory note was given for an
antecedent debt, it was decided that as against the payee, the maker
would have been discharged under this act, but that he was not as
against a person to whom the note was subsequently indorsed.[h]

large. But where bills are sent on a   [f] Hornblower v. Prowd, 2 B. & A
general account between the correspon-   327.
dent and the merchant, and as an item   [g] Sharp v. Iffgrave, 3 Bos. & Pul 39
in the account, it is otherwise.' " Bent Lord Kinniard v. Barrow, 8 T. R 49.
v. Puller, 5 T. R. 494.   [h] Lucas v. Winton, 2 Campb 442.

APPENDIX

.\ *B* Throughout the Forms the *parts in Italics* though usually inserted may and in general should be omitted, as will appear from the notes to each part.

SECTION I.

AFFIDAVITS TO ARREST.*

In the King's Bench, (or " Common Pleas," or " Exchequer.")

A. B. of ——, gentleman, maketh oath and saith, that C. D. is justly and truly indebted to this deponent in the sum of £50.

> On a promissory note, payee against maker.

On a promissory note made by the said C. D. payable to this deponent on demand, (or " at a certain day now past.")

And this deponent further saith, that no tender or offer hath been made to pay the said sum of £50, or any part thereof, in any note or notes of the Governor and Company of the Bank of England, expressed to be payable on demand.
Sworn, &c.

On a promissory note, bearing date the ——. day of ——, A. D.——, made by the said C. D., and whereby the said C. D. promised to pay, two months after the date thereof, to this deponent, or order, the sum of £50, for value received.

> The like in another form.

In the sum of £50, as indorsee of a promissory note made by the said C. D. and for the payment of the sum of £50 to one E. F. or order, at a certain day now past, and by him indorsed to this deponent.

> Indorsee against maker.

To this deponent, as the indorsee of a promissory note, bearing date, &c. made by one E. F. and whereby the said E. F. promised to pay, two months after the date thereof, the sum of £50, to the said C. D. or order, and the said C. D. indorsed the same note to this deponent.

> [488]
> Indorsee against indorser.

On a bill of exchange drawn by one E. F. upon, and accepted by the said C. D. and for the payment of the sum of £50 to this deponent, at a certain day now past.

> On a bill of exchange, payee against acceptor.

* As to the affidavit to hold to bail. see ante. 348 to 350.

APPENDIX.   An indorsee of a bill exchange drawn by one E. F. upon and accepted
⋙⋙⋙⋙⋙⋙ by the said C. D. and for the payment to the said E. F. or his order,
Indorsee of the sum of £50, at a certain day now past, and by him the said
against ac- E. F. indorsed to this deponent.
ceptor.

Payee   On a bill of exchange drawn by the said C. D. upon one E. F. and
against   the payment of the sum of £50 to this deponent, at a certain day now
drawer.   past.

Indorsee   As indorsee of a bill of exchange drawn by the said C. D. on one
against   E. F. and for the payment of £50 to the order of the said C. D. at a
drawer.   certain day now past, and by him the said C. D. indorsed to this deponent.

Indorsee   As indorsee of a bill of exchange drawn by one E. F. on G. H. and
against in- for the payment of the sum of £50 to one I. K. or his order, at a certain
dorser.   day now past, and by the said I. K. indorsed to the said C. D. and by
the said C. D. indorsed to this deponent, and which said bill of exchange
hath been refused payment.

The like   As indorsee of a bill of exchange drawn by the said C. D. on one
where bill E. F. payable to the order of the said C. D. and by him the said C. D.
has been indorsed to this deponent, and which said bill of exchange hath been re-
refused ac- fused acceptance by the said E. F.
ceptance.

SECT. II.

DECLARATIONS ON PROMISSORY NOTES.ᵃ

Ellenborough and Markham.   *Michaelmas Term,*
                                       2d George the Fourth.

——, to wit. A. B. complains of C. D. being in the custody of the 1. By payee Marshal of the Marshalsea of our Lord the now King, before the King against the himself, of a plea of trespass on the case upon promises: For that maker. whereas the said C. D.ᵇ heretofore, to wit, on the first of January, in the year of our Lord 1821,ᶜ to wit, at London, in the parish of St. Mary le Bow, in the ward of Cheap,ᵈ madeᵉ his certain promissory note in [490] writing, *his own proper hand-writing being thereunto subscribed,*ᶠ bear-

ᵃ Only a few of the most common forms are here given: for other precedents and notes, see 3 Chitty on Pleading, p 1 to 27. and as to the mode of declaring in general, ante, 351 to 376.

ᵇ A note made by an agent may be stated to have been made by the principal, because that is its legal operation. 12 Mod. 346. 1 Hen. Bla. 313. 6 T. R. 659. Bayl. 175. Ante, 357. Sometimes the declaration states, that the "said C. D. by one E. F. his agent on that behalf, on, &c. at, &c. made, &c." If several make a note jointly and severally, and one only be sued, the declaration may state either that the two jointly and severally made the note, &c. or which is preferable, that the defendant made it without noticing the other party. Ante, 346. Cowp. 832. 1 Esp. Rep. 185. 7 T. R. 596. See post, 490, note.

ᶜ This should be the date of the note or bill; or if it have no date, the day it is-sued, or if that cannot be ascertained, the first day it can be proved to have existed. 10 Mod. 311. Stra. 22. 2 Show. 422. Bayl. 174. Ante, 354. And where a second count stated, "that afterwards, to wit, on the day and year aforesaid," the defendant drew a certain other bill of exchange, pay-able two months after date, without men-tioning any express date in either count, the last count was held sufficient by refe-rence to the first. 3 B. & P. 173. If a note by mistake be dated contrary to the inten-tion of the parties, the declaration should be as follows, " on, &c. (the time intend-ed) at, &c. made, &c. bearing date by mis-take on, &c. but meant and intended by the said C. D. to be dated on the said, &c. aforesaid, and then and there delivered, &c. by which said note be the said C. D. then and there promised to pay two months

after the date thereof (that is to say, after the said, &c. when the said note was so made, and meant and intended to be dated as aforesaid) to the said A B. &c." Ante, 354, 5. If the declaration state, that de-fendant drew a bill, without alleging that it bore date on that day, the day in the de-claration is not material, though not under a videlicet. Coxon v. Lyon, York Lent Assizes, 1810. cor. Thompson, B. 2 Campb. 307; contra if it had alleged that the bill bore date on that day. Ib. 308. Ante, 354, 5.

ᵈ A note, bill, &c. it is said, should be stated to have been made at the place where it bears date, though the venue may be laid in another place for the purpose of trial. Salk. 669. Cowp. 177, 8. 6 Mod. 228. Com. Dig. tit. Action, N. 7. in which case the declaration runs, "at, &c. (the place where the note was made) to wit, at, &c. (the venue.") But in Bayl. 175, it is said, that *inland* bills, though they bear date at a particular place, may be alleged to have been made in any place in England or Wales. And see 3 Campb. 304. Ante, 855.

ᵉ 1 Hen. Bla. 313. Bayl. 176.

ᶠ This statement is unnecessary. Lord Raym 1376. 1484. 1542. 3 Mod. 307. Stra. 399 512. Bayl. 176; and in Levy v. Wil-son, Sittings after Mich. Term, 1804, the plaintiff was nonsuited, on an allegation that the payee indorsed the bill, *his own proper hand being thereunto subscribed,* it appearing in evidence that the indorse-ment was by an agent: and see Levy v. Wilson, 5 Esp. Rep. 180. Therefore these words should always be erased. Sed vide 2 Campb. 305. 450. Variance, when not material, 2 Campb. 307. Bayl. 182. 3 Ante, 357.

APPENDIX. ing date the day and year aforesaid,[e] *and then and there delivered the said note to the said A. B.,*[h] and thereby then and there promised to pay at, &c.,[i] two months after the date thereof, to the said A. B. (*by the name and addition of A. B. Esq.*[k]) or order,[l] the sum of £50,[m] for value received.[n] By means whereof, *and by the force of the statute in such case made and provided,*[o] the said C. D. then and there became liable to pay the said A. B. the said sum of money in the said note specified, according to the tenor and effect of the said note.[p] And being so liable, he the said C. D. in consideration thereof, afterwards, to wit, on, &c. aforesaid, at, &c. aforesaid, undertook, and then and there faithfully promised[q] the said A. B. to pay him the said sum of money in the said note specified, according to the tenor and effect of the said note.

[491]

N. B. The breach of the defendant's promise to pay, is in all cases of bills and notes included in the common breach at the end of the money counts, the day in which should always be after the bill or note is due.—Add such counts as may be applicable to the particular case.

[e] These words are not absolutely necessary, see 2 Show. 422. 3 B. & P. 173. Ante, note, p. 489, for it shall be intended when the date is material, to have been dated on the day on which it was alleged to have been drawn. See 2 Campb. 307, 8. Bayl. 177. Ante, 354.

[h] The averment of the delivery of the note to the payee is not necessary. 7 T. R. 596. 5 East, 478. Bayl. 180. Ante, page 359.

[i] If a note be payable, in the body of it, at a particular place, it is proper so to describe the contract. 2 Hen. Bla. 540. Ante, 250. 356. In an action against an indorser, in which case a presentment is necesary, it seems proper, in all cases, to aver a presentment at the particular place. In an action against the maker of a note, or acceptor of a bill, an allegation of a presentment for payment is never stated, though when the payment is stipulated to be made at a particular place, an averment of presentment is then to be inserted, ante, 250. 356. In an action by the indorsee of a bill or note, it is necessary to show that the same authorized a transfer, but this is not necessary in an action at the suit of payee. Ante, 358. 5 East, 476. Infra, note.

[k] The statement of the addition is unnecessary, and should in general be omitted to avoid a variance. Ante, 356.

[l] The note, &c. is to be stated according to its legal operation. Burr. 323. 2611. Cowp. 832. Blacks. 947. Ante, 355. Thus where the payee is a fictitious person, the note, &c. may be stated to be payable to the person in whose favour the indorsement was made, or to bearer. 1 Hen. Bla. 313. 569. 3 T. R. 182. 481. Bayl. 179. Ante, 357. And when a note has through mistake been made payable to a wrong person, it may be stated to have been payable to the proper one. 4 T. R. 470. Bayl 179. If the bill be "payable to the order of the payee," it may be so stated in the declaration, and there is no occasion for an averment that he made no order, 5 East. 476; and it may be stated to have been made payable to the plaintiff. Bayl. 179. Ante, 356. 2 Show. 8. Cowp. 76. But N. P. 473. 1 Wils. 192. Bayl 190. And where the note or bill has been returned to the payee, *he* may declare in his own right, without stating that fact, ante, 343; and a joint or several note, or a note importing in the body of it to be made by several persons, but signed only by one, may be stated as a several note. Burr. 323. Stra. 76. Bayl. 103, 4. Ante, 338, 9. Bayl. 177, 8.

[m] Omission of word "sterling" here immaterial. Glossop v. Jacob, 1 Stark. 69. Ante, 356.

[n] Value delivered, instead of value received, not material, 2 Campb. 306.

[o] 3 & 4 Ann, c. 9. this is usually stated, but it seems unnecessary, 4 T. R. 149 Ante, 352 Lord Raym. 88. 175. 1642 Carth. 83. 269, 270. Lutw. 279.

[p] This is the proper allegation against the parties *primarily* liable, as when the action is against the *maker* of a note, or the *acceptor* of a bill. But in an action against the drawer of a bill and the indorser of either a bill or note, as the proper part of the declaration shows a liability to pay *immediately* on the default of acceptance or payment by the party primarily liable, the declaration states the liability and promise to be to pay, *on request*. 3 East. 484. Post. Bayl. 190.

[q] The action being founded on a legal liability, no promise need be stated, but is usually inserted, Carth. 509. Salk. 12 Hardr. 486. 1 Stra. 214. Ante, 357. Bac. Ab. tit. Assumpsit. F. Bayl. 190. 1.

For that whereas· the said C. D. heretofore, to wit, on, &c. at, &c. APPENDIX. made his certain promissory note in writing, bearing date the same day and year aforesaid, and then and there delivered the said note to the said A. B. by which said note he the said C. D. then and there promised to pay to the said A. B. (by the name and addition of Mr. A. B.,) or order, the sum of £15 in manner following; that is to say, the sum of £5 upon the first day of August, then next, the further sum of £5 upon the first day of September, then next, and the further sum of £5 upon the first day of October, then next, *and that in case default should be made in any of the said payments, then the whole of the said sum of £15 then remaining unpaid should become due on demand.* By means whereof, and by force of the statute in such case made and provided, the said C. D. then and there became liable to pay to the said A. B. the said sum of £15 in the said note specified, according to the tenor and effect of the said note. And being so liable he the said C. D. in consideration thereof afterwards, to wit, on the day and year first above-mentioned, at, &c. aforesaid, undertook and then and there faithfully promised the said A. B. to pay him the said sum of £15 in the said note specified, according to the tenor and effect of the said note.* And the said A. B. in fact saith,' that after the making of the said note, to wit, on the 4th" day of August next after the making of the said note, *default was made in payment* of the said first-mentioned sum of £5, to wit, at, &c. aforesaid, whereby and according to the tenor and effect of the said note, he the said C. D. then and there became and was liable to pay to the said A. B. the whole of the said sum of £15 in the said note specified, when he the said C. D. should be thereunto afterwards requested.

2. Payee against maker of a note payable by instalments for the whole sum on one default.[r]

[492]

For that whereas the said C. D. heretofore, to wit, on, &c. at, &c. made his certain promissory note in writing, bearing date, &c.

3. Ditto for one instalment.[s]

Same as in the first count as far as the *asterisk*, omitting the words in italics, and then proceed as follows:

And the said A. B. in fact saith, that after the making of the said note, to wit, on the 4th day of August next after the making of the said note, the said first-mentioned sum of £5, part of the said sum of £15 in the said note specified, became and was due and payable from the said C. D. to the said A. B., upon and by virtue of the said note, and which said last-mentioned sum of £5, he the said C. D. then and there ought to have paid to the said A. B. according to the tenor and effect of the said note, and of his said promise and undertaking, so by him made as aforesaid.

For that whereas the said C. D., heretofore, to wit, on, &c. at, &c. 4. First indorsee against maker.[y]

r As to these notes, and when the whole is recoverable, see ante, 420.

s The notes in the preceding form are applicable to this precedent.

t If all the instalments in the note be due by effluxion of time, no averment of default is necessary.

u Mistake in this day will be fatal. Wells v Girling, 1 Gow. C. N. P. 21.

x The notes in the first form are here in general applicable.

y The notes in the first precedent are applicable to this. When the declaration is at the suit of an indorsee of an administrator, there is no occasion to state the letters of administration. Willes, 359. An indorsement by agent may be stated to have been made by the principal, without noticing the agency, ante, 857.

APPENDIX. made his certain promissory note in writing, bearing date the day and
year aforesaid, *and then and there delivered the said note to one* E. F.
and thereby then and there promised, two months after the date thereof, to pay to the said E. F. (by the name and addition of Mr. E. F.) or

Indorse- order, the sum of £50 for value received. And the said E. F. to whom
ment. or to whose order the payment of the said sum of money, in the said
promissory note specified, was thereby directed to be made, after making of the said promissory note, and before the payment of the said
sum of money therein specified, to wit, on, &c.ᵃ aforesaid, at, &c. aforesaid, indorsed the said promissory note, *his own proper hand-writing
being to such indorsement subscribed,*ᵃ and thereby then and there
ordered and appointed the *said sum of money,* in the said promissory note specified,ᵇ to be paid to the said A. B.,ᶜ *and then and there
delivered the said promissory note so indorsed as aforesaid, to the said*
A. B.ᵈ* *Of which said indorsement so made on the said note as
aforesaid, the said* C. D. *afterwards, to wit, on, &c. aforesaid, had
notice.*ᵉ By means whereof, and by force of the statute in such case
made and provided, the said C. D. then and there became liable to pay
to the said A. B. the said sum of money in the said note specified, according to the tenor and effect thereof, and of the said indorsement so
made thereon as aforesaid; and being so liable, he the said C. D., in
consideration thereof, afterwards, to wit, on, &c. aforesaid, undertook,
and then and there faithfully promised the said A. B. to pay him the

[494] said sum of money in the said note specified, according to the tenor and
effect of the said note, and of the said indorsement so made thereon as
aforesaid.

---

5. State- [When the declaration is at the suit of a second or subsequent
ment of a indorsee, the statement of the second indorsementᶠ is introduced
second and at the asterisk in the last precedent, and runs as follows.) And the
of subse- said G. H. (the first indorsee,) to whom or to whose order the payment
quent in- of the said sum of money in the said promissory note specified, was by
dorsements the said indorsement directed to be made after the making of the said
promissory note, and before the payment of the said sum of money
therein specified, to wit, on, &c. aforesaid, at, &c. aforesaid, indorsed

the said promissory note, and thereby then and there ordered and ap- APPENDIX.
pointed the said sum of money therein specified, to be paid to the said
A. B., and then and there delivered the said promissory note so indorsed as aforesaid, to the said A. B. By means whereof, &c. (stating
the defendant's liability and promise to pay as usual, at the suit of an
indorsee.)

———

In order to save expense when there are several indorsements, and par-   6. Short
ticularly when it may be expedient to add a second count on the same statement
bill or note, the following concise statement of the indorsement may be of an in-
adopted. dorsement.

And the said E. F. then and there indorsed and delivered the said
promissory note to the said G. H. And the said G. H. then and there
indorsed and delivered the said promississory note to the said A. B.

———

For that whereas⁕ one E. F. heretofore, to wit, on, &c. at, &c. made 7. Indorsee
his certain promissory note in writing, bearing date the day and year against in-
aforesaid, and then and there delivered the said note to the said C. D., dorser, the
by which said note the said E. F. then and there promised two months maker hav-
after the date thereof, to pay to the said C. D. (by the name and addi- payment.
tion of Mr. C. D.) or order, the sum of £50, for value received. And [495]
the said C. D. to whom or to whose order the payment of the said sum
of money in the said note specified, was to be made after the making
of the said note, and before the payment of the said sum therein specified, to wit, on, &c. aforesaid, at, &c. aforesaid, indorsed the said note,
by which said indorsement, he the said C. D. then and there ordered
and appointed the said sum of money in the said note specified to be
paid to the said A. B. and then and there delivered the said note to the
said A. B.ᵇ And the said A. B. in fact saith, that afterwards, *when* Averment
the said note became due and payable, according to the tenour and effect of present-
thereof, to wit, *on, &c.*¹ at, &c. aforesaid, (*the place where payable,*) to ment for
wit, at, &c. aforesaid, (*the venue*) the said note so indorsed as afore- payment.
said, was *duly*ᵏ presented and shown to the said E. F.¹ for payment

---

⁕ The greater part of the note in the
preceding precedents are applicable to
this.

ᵇ As to the statement of indorsements,
see ante, 492, 3, in notes.

¹ The third day of grace, 4 T. R. 148,
unless it be a Sunday, Good Friday, or
Christmas-day, in which case, the note or
bill is due the preceding day. This day
is material, Doug. 679, unless there be an
express averment that the presentment was
made when the bill became due as above,
in which case a mistake in the day after
the videlicet, would not be material, Bayley, 188. The better way may perhaps be
merely to allege that afterwards, to wit,
⁕⁕ on, &c. at, &c. the bill was duly presented for payment," omitting the words in ita-
lic, see Patience *v.* Townley, 2 Smith's
Rep 224.

ᵏ If there be any doubt as to the proof

CHITTY ON BILLS.

of a presentment on the day the note was
due, omit this word

¹ Though in an action against the maker
of a note or acceptor of a bill, it is otherwise, yet in an action against the indorser
a presentment for payment must be stated,
or that the maker or acceptor could not be
found, or some excuse for the neglect, or
the omission will be fatal even after verdict, 2 Show. 1010. Doug. 654. 680. Bayl.
188. 2 Esp. Rep. 551. The allegations
should correspond precisely with the facts
and evidence ; for where the declaration
averred in the usual form, a presentment
for acceptance or payment and refusal, the
plaintiff cannot give in evidence that the
drawee or maker could not be found. If
the drawee or maker cannot be found, it is
sufficient to aver generally that he was
not found, without stating that inquiry was
made after him. Carth. 509. Bayl. 109.

3 K

APPENDIX. thereof, *and the said* E. F. *then and there had notice of the said indorse-
~~~~~~~~~~~~~~~ ment so made thereon as aforesaid,*⁻ was then and there requested to
pay the said sum of money in the said note specified, according to the
tenour and effect of the said note, and of the said indorsement so
made thereon as aforesaid ;ᵒ but that the said E. F. did not nor
wouldat the · same time when the said note was so presented and
shown to him for payment ·thereof, as aforesaid, or at any time afterwards, pay the said sum of money therein specified, or any part thereof,
but wholly neglected and refused so to do ; of all which said several
premises the said C. D. afterwards, to wit, on the day and year last
[496] aforesaid, at, &c. aforesaid, had notice.ᵒ· By means whereof and by
force of the statute in such case made and provided, the said C. D. then
and there became liable to pay the said A. B. the said sum of money in
the said note specified, when he the said C. D. should be thereunto afterwards requested.ᵖ · Antl ₑbeing so liable, he the said C. D. in
consideration thereof, afterwards, to wit, on the day and year last
aforesaid, at, &c. aforesaid, undertook, and then and there faithfully
promised the said A. B. to pay him the said sum of money in the said
note specified, when he the said C. D. should be thereunto afterwards
requested.ᑫ

See the precedents, post, 504, on Inland
Bills, as to the form of the averment in
these cases.
    ⁻ Notice of the indorsement need not
be averred, 1 B. & P. 625.
    ᵒ A subsequent promise by the defend-
ant to pay, is evidence of a presentment
to the maker or drawee for payment, and
no special count is necessary, 7 East,
231.
    ᵖ This allegation on an averment, show-

ing that it may be dispensed with, is necessary, and the omission would be fatal after
verdict. Rushton v. Aspinal, Doug. 650.
690. If it be doubtful whether the giving
due notice can be proved, it is expedient
to add a count stating an excuse for the not
giving notice, such as the want of effects,
&c. in the hands of the maker ; see the
form, post, 504. Inland Bills.
    ᵖ Ante, 490, note. Bayl. 190.
    ᑫ Ante, 490, note. 491, note.

SECT. III.

DECLARATIONS ON CHECKS ON BANKERS.

FOR that whereas the said C. D. heretofore, to wit, on,[a] &c. at, &c. *according to the usage and practice of merchants*, made his certain draft or order in writing for the payment of money, commonly called a check on a banker, bearing date the same day and year aforesaid, and then and there directed the said draft or order to certain persons by the names, style, and firm of Messrs. E. F. and G. H. and thereby then and there required the said Messrs. E. F. and G. H. to pay to the said A. B. (*by the name and addition of Mr. A. B.*) or bearer, £50, and then and there delivered the said draft or order to the said A. B. And the said A. B. avers, that after the making of the said (*) draft or order, and before the payment of the said sum of money therein specified, to wit, on, &c. aforesaid, at, &c. aforesaid, the said draft or order was presented and shown to the said Messrs. E. F. and G. H. for payment thereof, according to the said usage and practice of merchants, and the said Messrs. E. F. and G. H. were then and there requested to pay the said sum of money therein specified, according to the tenor and effect thereof; but that the said Messrs. E. F. and G. H. did not nor would at the said time when the said draft or order was so shown and presented to them for payment thereof as aforesaid, or at any time afterwards, pay the said sum of money therein specified, or any part thereof, but then and there wholly neglected and refused so to do, whereof the said C. D. afterwards, to wit, on, &c. aforesaid, at, &c. aforesaid, had notice.[b] By means whereof he the said C. D. then and there became liable to pay to the said A. B. the said sum of money in the said draft or order specified, when he the said C. D. should be thereunto afterwards requested.[c] And being so liable, he the said C. D. in consideration thereof, afterwards, to wit, on, &c. aforesaid, at, &c. aforesaid, undertook, and then and there faithfully promised the said A. B. to pay him the said sum of money in the said draft or order specified, when he the said C. D. should be thereunto afterwards requested.[d]

8. By the payee of a check against the drawer.

[497]

For that whereas[e] the said C. D. heretofore, to wit, on, &c. at, &c. according to the usage and practice of merchants, made his certain draft or order in writing for the payment of money, commonly called a check, bearing date the same day and year aforesaid, and then and there directed the said draft or order to certain persons, by the names,

9. By the bearer against the drawer.

---

[a] As to the date, see ante, 489, note.
[b] As to the necessity for this averment and the expediency in some cases of averring an excuse for the neglect to give notice, ante, 496, note.

[c] Ante, 490, note.

[d] Ante, 490, note.

[e] The notes to the preceding precedent are applicable to this.

APPENDIX. thereof, *and the said* E. F. *then and there had notice of the said indorse-* ~~·❜❜❜❜❜❜❜❜❜❜❜❜❜~~ *ment so made thereon as aforesaid,*= was then and there requested to pay the said sum of money in the said note specified, according to the . tenour and effect of the said note, and of the said indorsement so made thereon as aforesaid ;ᵃ but that the said E. F. did not nor wouldat the · same time when the said note was so presented and shown to him for payment ·thereof, as aforesaid, or at any time after- wards, pay the said sum of money therein specified, or any part thereof, þut wholly neglected and refused so to do ; of all which said several premises the said C. D. afterwards, to wit, on the day and year last

[496] aforesaid, at, &c. aforesaid, had notice.ᵒ· By means whereof and by force of the statute in such case made and provided, the said C. D. then and there became liable to pay the said A. B. the said sum of money in the said note specified, when he the said C. D. should be thereunto af- terwards requested.ᵖ · And ‚being so liable, he the said C. D. in consideration thereof, afterwards, to wit, on the day and year last aforesaid, at, &c. aforesaid, undertook, and then and there faithfully promised the said A. B. to pay him the said sum of money in the said note specified, when he the said C. D. should be thereunto afterwards requested.�𝗊

See the precedents, post, 504, on Inland Bills, as to the form of the averment in these cases.

= Notice of the indorsement need not be averred, 1 B. & P. 625.

ᵒ A subsequent promise by the defend- ant to pay, is evidence of a presentment to the maker or drawee for payment, and no special count is necessary, 7 East, 231.

𝗊 This allegation on an averment, show- ing that it may be dispensed with, is neces- sary, and the omission would be fatal after verdict. Rushton *v.* Aspinal, Doug. 650 680. If it be doubtful whether the giving due notice can be proved, it is expedient to add a count stating an excuse for the not giving notice, such as the want of effect, &c. in the hands of the maker ; see the form, post, 504. Inland Bills.

ᵖ Ante, 490, note. Bayl. 190.

ᵃ Ante, 490, note. 491, note.

SECT. III.

DECLARATIONS ON CHECKS ON BANKERS.

FOR that whereas the said C. D. heretofore, to wit, on,[a] &c. at, &c. according to the usage and practice of merchants, made his certain draft or order in writing for the payment of money, commonly called a check on a banker, bearing date the same day and year aforesaid, and then and there directed the said draft or order to certain persons by the names, style, and firm of Messrs. E. F. and G. H. and thereby then and there required the said Messrs. E. F. and G. H. to pay to the said A. B. (by the name and addition of Mr. A. B.) or bearer, £50, and then and there delivered the said draft or order to the said A. B. And the said A. B. avers, that after the making of the said (*) draft or order, and before the payment of the said sum of money therein specified, to wit, on, &c. aforesaid, at, &c. aforesaid, the said draft or order was presented and shown to the said Messrs. E. F. and G. H. for payment thereof, according to the said usage and practice of merchants, and the said Messrs. E. F. and G. H. were then and there requested to pay the said sum of money therein specified, according to the tenor and ef-[497] fect thereof; but that the said Messrs. E. F. and G. H. did not nor would at the said time when the said draft or order was so shown and presented to them for payment thereof as aforesaid, or at any time afterwards, pay the said sum of money therein specified, or any part thereof, but then and there wholly neglected and refused so to do, whereof the said C. D. afterwards, to wit, on, &c. aforesaid, at, &c. aforesaid, had notice.[b] By means whereof he the said C. D. then and there became liable to pay to the said A. B. the said sum of money in the said draft or order specified, when he the said C. D. should be thereunto afterwards requested.[c] And being so liable, he the said C. D. in consideration thereof, afterwards, to wit, on, &c. aforesaid, at, &c. aforesaid, undertook, and then and there faithfully promised the said A. B. to pay him the said sum of money in the said draft or order specified, when he the said C. D. should be thereunto afterwards requested.[d]

8. By the payee of a check against the drawer.

For that whereas[e] the said C. D. heretofore, to wit, on, &c. at, &c. according to the usage and practice of merchants, made his certain draft or order in writing for the payment of money, commonly called a check, bearing date the same day and year aforesaid, and then and there directed the said draft or order to certain persons, by the names,

9. By the bearer against the drawer.

[a] As to the date, see ante, 489, note.
[b] As to the necessity for this averment and the expediency in some cases of averring an excuse for the neglect to give notice, ante, 496, note.
[c] Ante, 490, note.
[d] Ante, 490, note.
[e] The notes to the preceding precedent are applicable to this.

APPENDIX. style, and firm of Messrs. &c.; and thereby theñ and there requested
the said Messrs. &c. to pay to one E. F. or bearer, £50, and then and
there delivered the said draft or order, to the said E. F. [and the said
E. F. to whom, or to the bearer of the said draft or order, the payment of the said sum of money therein specified, was thereby directed
to be made after the making of the said draft or order, and before the
payment of the said sum of money therein specified, to wit, on, &c.
aforesaid, at, &c. aforesaid, duly transferred, assigned, and delivered
the said draft or order, to the said A. B. who thereby then and there
became and was, and from thence hitherto hath been and still is the
lawful bearer thereof, and entitled to the payment of the said sum
[498] of money therein specified.] And the said A. B. avers, that after the
the making of the said, &c. (*as in the preceding form from the asti-
risk to the end.*)

SECT. IV.

DECLARATIONS ON INLAND BILLS.*

F OR that whereas *one* E. F.,[a] heretofore, to wit, on, &c.,[b] at, &c.[c] | 10. Payee according to the usage and custom of merchants from time immemorial against ac- used and approved of within this kingdom,[d] made his certain bill of ceptor. exchange in writing, *his own proper hand being thereunto subscribed,*[e] bearing date the day and year aforesaid,[f] and then and there directed the said bill of exchange to the said C. D. (by the name and addition of C. D. Esq.[g]) by which said bill of exchange he the said E. F. then and there requested the said C. D. two months after the date thereof, to pay to the said A. B. (*by the name and addition of* A. B. *Esq.,*[h]) or or- der, the sum of £50,[i] value received, *and then and there delivered the same to the said* A. B.[k] Which said bill of exchange' the said C. D. [499] afterwards, to wit, on, &c.[l] aforesaid, at, &c. aforesaid, upon sight there- of accepted, according to the said usage and custom of merchants.(*)[m]

* Only a few precedents are given here; see other forms, 3 Chitty on Pleading, 30 to 52, and as to the mode of declaring in general, ante, 351 to 376.

[a] As to this allegation, see ante, 489, note. If it be drawn in the name of a firm, say, certain persons using the names, style, and "firm of A. B. and Co. on, &c. at, &c." It is not advisable to state the names of the individuals composing the firm, un- less the action be against them, when they must be stated. If drawn by one person in the name of a firm, it may be stated to have been drawn by certain persons using the name, style, and firm, &c. although in truth drawn only by one person. 4 Campb. 78.

[b] As to the statement of the date, ante, 489, note.

[c] As to the statement of the place where made, ante, 489, note.

[d] This allegation is unnecessary, Lord Raym. 88. 175. 1542. Carth. 83. 269. 270. Lutw. 279. Ante, 351.

[e] As to the impropriety of this allegation; ante, 357. Bayl. 176.

[f] As to the statement of the date, ante, 489, note. 2 Campb. 307, in notes.

[g] The statement of directions seems in general unnecessary, ante, 356. If stated, a variance would be fatal. It may be sta- ted according to the legal effect, and in an action against the acceptor, in a bill di- rected to him, or in his absence to J. S. the conditional directions to J. S. need not be stated, 12 Mod. 447; and if a bill be di- rected to two, and accepted only by one, it need only be stated to have been direct- ed to him. Bayl. 177.

[h] In general unnecessary, and some- times occasions a variance, ante, 356. 490, note.

[i] As to the statement of the sum, see ante, 60. 66. If the sum in the superscrip- tion vary from that in the body, it may be advisable to insert two counts varying the statement.

[k] As to this averment, ante, 490, note. If at the suit of the drawer these words should be admitted, but will not prejudice though the acceptor's name be inscrted, 5 East, 476.

[l] The acceptance of a bill after sight, should be stated according to the fact, and when the drawee dates his acceptance on a different day from the date of the bill, the real day of acceptance should be in- serted.

[m] An acceptance need only be stated in an action against the acceptor, or where an accepted bill was payable after sight. When the time of payment depends on the presentment, it should be the day of the presentment; but in other cases, exactness as to the day is not material. It has how- ever, been adjudged, that if the plaintiff declare in terms, that the acceptance was *before the bill became due,* and that the defendant accepted to pay according to the tenor and effect of the bill, and it appear on the evidence, that the acceptance in fact was after the day of payment, the plaintiff cannot recover. Lord Raym. 364. Mod. 212. But it is said, that the propriety

APPENDIX. By means whereof, and according to the said usage and custom of merchants, he the said C. D. then and there became liable to pay to the said A. B. the said sum of money in the said bill of exchange specified, according to the tenor and effect of the said bill of exchange, and of his acceptance thereof. ª   And being so liable, he the said C. D. in consideration thereof afterwards, to wit, on, &c. aforesaid, at, &c. aforesaid, undertook, and then and there faithfully promised the said A. B. to pay him the said sum of money in the said bill of exchange specified, according to the tenor and effect of the said bill of exchange, and of his acceptance thereof. º

[500]   *When the declaration is at the suit of an indorsee, proceed as in*
11. By first *the preceding precedent as far as the asterisk, and then state the*
indorsee a- *indorsement as follows :—*
gainst ac-
ceptor.

        And the said E. F. *(the payee, or the drawer, if payable to his own order,)* to whom or to whose order the payment of the said sum of money in the said bill of exchange specified, was to be made after the making of the said bill of exchange, and before the payment of the said sum of money therein specified, to wit, on, &c.ᵖ aforesaid, at, &c. aforesaid, according to the said usage and custom of merchants, indorsed the said bill of exchange, and thereby then and there ordered and appointed the said sum of money in the said bill of exchange specified to be paid to the said A. B. and then and there delivered the said bill of exchange so indorsed as aforesaid to the said A. B.   By means whereof, &c. (state the liability and promise, as in the last precedent.)

————————

12. The   As to the statement of indorsements in general, and of a second or
like by the subsequent indorsement, and of the mode of stating an indorsement
second or concisely, *vide ante*, 493 and 360.
subsequent
indorsee. of this decision may be doubtful. Bayl. 181. 1 Campb. 139. When the bill is accepted, payable at a particular place, it is thus stated, " accepted, &c. according to the usage and custom of merchants, payable at, &c."   As to this, see ante, 248 to 261. If the defendant accepted the bill by agent, the declaration may state the acceptance to have been made by the principal, 2 Campb. 604. 12 Mod. 564; but it frequently runs as follows ; " which said bill of exchange he the said defendant afterwards, to wit, on, &c. aforesaid, at, &c. aforesaid, by one E. F. his agent in that behalf, upon sight thereof accepted, according, &c." If the acceptance were conditional or qualified, it must be described accordingly. 4 Campb. 176. In an action against an acceptor, a presentment for payment is never stated, unless where he accepted it payable at a different place. An averment that the acceptor's hand-writing was subscribed is not advisable, ante, 357. 490, note.

ª This statement of the liability and consequent promise is not absolutely necessary, see ante 257. 491, note. In an action against the acceptor of a bill or maker of a promissory note not payable on demand,

instead of alleging that the defendant became liable, and promised to pay when he should be thereunto afterwards requested. he is stated to have become liable, and promised to pay according to the tenor and effect of the bill, and acceptance in the one case and of the note in the other. Bayl 190. Ante, 490, note.

º Ante, 490, note.   Bayl. 190. The statement of the promise (which is a legal inference from the liability,) is to correspond with the statement of such liability The acceptor of a bill, and the maker of a note, being the persons primarily liable. are stated to be liable, and to have promised to pay according to the *tenor* and *effect* of their original undertaking; but in a declaration against the drawer or indorser of a bill, or the indorser of a note, as it appears from the prior allegations in the declaration, that by the default of the party primarily liable, the defendant has become liable to pay *immediately on request*, (s.e 3 East, 481. Ante, 230, 1.) the declaration accordingly states his liability as well as his promise, to be to pay *on request*. Ante, 490, note.

ᵖ As to the statement of the time of the indorsement, see ante, 493, note.

For that whereas the said A. B. heretofore, to wit, on, &c. at, &c. according to the usage and custom of merchants from time immemorial, used and approved of within this kingdom, made his certain bill of exchange in writing, bearing date the day and year aforesaid, and then and there directed the said bill of exchange to the said C. D. (by the name and addition of Mr. C. D.) by which said bill of exchange, he the said A. B. then and there requested the said C. D. two months after the date thereof, to pay to one E. F. (by the name and addition of Mr. E. F.) or order, the sum of £50, value received, and then and there delivered the said bill of exchange to the said E. F., which said bill of exchange he the said C. D. afterwards, to wit, on, &c. aforesaid, at, &c. aforesaid, upon sight thereof accepted, according to the said usage and custom of merchants. And the said A. B. avers, that afterwards, *when the said bill of exchange became due and payable according to the tenor and effect thereof, to wit, on,* &c.,ᵠ at, &c.,ʳ aforesaid, and the said bill of exchange so accepted as aforesaid, was *duly*ᵗ presented and shown to the said C. D. for payment thereof, according to the said usage and custom of merchants, and the said C. D. was then and there requested to pay the said sum of money therein specified, according to the tenor and effect of the said bill of exchange, and of his said acceptance thereof, but that the said .C. D. did not, nor would, at the said time when the said bill of exchange was so presented and shown to him for payment thereof as aforesaid, or at any time afterwards, pay the said sum of money therein specified, or any part thereof, but then and there wholly neglected and refused so to do, and thereupon afterwards, to wit, on, &c.,ᵗ at, &c. aforesaid, the said bill of exchange was returned to the said A. B. for non-payment thereof, and he the said A. B. as drawer of the said bill of exchange, was then and there called upon and forced and obliged to pay, and did then and there pay to the said E. F. the said sum of money in the said bill of exchange specified, together with a large sum of money, to wit, the sum of £——ᵘ for interest thereon, whereof the said C. D. afterwards, to wit, on, &c. last aforesaid, at, &c. aforesaid, had notice. By means whereof, and according to the said usage and custom of merchants, he the said C. D. then and there became liable to pay to the said A. B. the said sums of money, when he the said C. D. should be thereunto afterwards requested ; and being so liable, he the said C. D. in consideration thereof, afterwards, to wit, on, &c. last aforesaid, at, &c. aforesaid, undertook, and then and there faithfully promised the said A. B. to pay him the said sums of money, when he the said C. D. should be thereunto afterwards requested.

———

For that whereas the said C. D. heretofore, to wit, on, &c. at, &c. according to the usage and custom of merchants from time immemorial, used and approved of within this kingdom, made his certain bill of exchange in writing, bearing date the day and year aforesaid, and then

APPENDIX.
13. By drawer against acceptor on a bill payable to a third person, and returned to the plaintiff and taken up by him.ᵃ

[501]

14. By payee against drawer, the drawee having refused acceptance.

ᵃ Most of the notes to the prior precedents are applicable. As to this declaration, see ante, 348.

ᵠ Ante, 495, notes, See form, 1 Wils. 135. 4 Bro. P. C. 604.

ʳ If the venue be different from the place where the presentment should be made,

state the latter place and the venue afterwards under a *videlicet.*

ᵗ If the fact be doubtful, omit the word "duly," ante, 495, note.

ᵗ Some day about the real time of payment by the plaintiff.

ᵘ Any sufficient sum to cover the real amount.

APPENDIX. and there directed the said bill of exchange to one E. F., (by the name and addition of Mr. E. F., of, &c.) by which said bill of exchange. he the said C. D. then and there requested the said E. F., two months after the date thereof, to pay the said A. B., (by the name and addition of Mr. A. B. &c.) or order, the sum of £50 value received, and then and there delivered the said bill of exchange to the said A. B.[*x]

And the said A. B. avers, that afterwards, and before the payment of the said sum of money, in the said bill of exchange specified, to wit, on the day and year aforesaid, at, &c. aforesaid, the said bill of exchange was presented and shown to the said E. F. for his acceptance thereof, according to the said usage and custom of merchants,[y] and the said E. F. was then and there requested to accept the same, but that the said E. F. did not, nor would, at the said time when the said bill of exchange was so presented and shown to him for his acceptance thereof as. aforesaid, or at any time afterwards, accept the same, or pay the said sum of money therein specified, or any part thereof, but then and there neglected and refused so to do,[z] of all which said several premises, the said C. D. afterwards, to wit, on, &c. aforesaid, at, &c. aforesaid, had notice.[a]

By means whereof, and according to the said usage and custom of merchants, he the said C. D. then and there became liable to pay the said A. B. the said sum of money in the said bill of exchange specified, when he the said C. D. should be thereunto afterwards requested.[b] And being so liable, he the said C. D. in consideration thereof, afterwards, to wit, on, &c. last aforesaid, at, &c. aforesaid, undertook, and then and there faithfully promised the said A. B. to pay him the said sum of money in the said bill of exchange. specified, when he the said C. D. should be thereunto afterwards requested.

[503]
15. Payee or indorsee against drawer or indorser, acceptor having refused payment.†

For that whereas the said C. D. on, &c. at, &c. according to the usage and custom of merchants from time immemorial, used and approved of within this kingdom, made his certain bill of exchange in writing, bearing date the day and year aforesaid, and then and there directed the said bill of exchange to one E. F. (by the name and addition of Mr. E. F., &c.) by which said bill of exchange by the said C. D. then and there requested the said E. F. two months after the date thereof, to pay to the said A. B. or order, the sum of £50, value received and then and there delivered the said bill of exchange to the said A. B., *which said bill of exchange the said E. F. afterwards, to wit, on, &c. aforesaid, at, &c. aforesaid, upon sight thereof, accepted, according to the said usage and custom of merchants.[c]

---

* The notes in the precedents, ante 498 and 500, are in general applicable to this.
[x] If the declaration be. at the suit of an indorsee against an indorser, here follow the indorsements as in the precedent, ante, 500, and as to which, vide ante, 494.
[y] A subsequent promise by the drawer or indorser to pay, is evidence of this presentment, and no special count is necessary, 7 East, 231.
[z] It is not necessary to allege, that an inland bill has been protested, although the plaintiff seek to recover interest. &c. Windle v. Andrews, 2 Stark. 425, see 2 Esp. Rep. 550. 2 Stra. 910. Bayl. 189.

The statement of the protest for non-acceptance of an inland bill, is similar to that in the case of a foreign bill, see post 509.
[a] As to the averment of notice, see ante 496.
[b] The drawer and indorser are liable to pay immediately on the refusal to accept, 3 East, 481, and therefore the liability the promise are stated to be, to pay on request. Bayl. 190. Ante, 230, 490.
† The notes to the precedents, ante, are here applicable.
[c] When the action is for default of payment, the statement of the acceptance

And the said A. B. avers, that afterwards, *when the said bill of ex-* change *became due and payable, according to the tenour and effect thereof,* to wit, on, &c.[d] aforesaid, at, &c. aforesaid, the said bill of exchange was *duly* presented and shown to the said E. F. for payment thereof, according to the said usage and custom of merchants,[e] and the said E. F. was then and there requested to pay the said sum of money therein specified, according to the tenour and effect of the said bill of exchange, and of his said acceptance thereof, but that the said E. F. did not, nor would, at the said time when the said bill of exchange was so presented and shown to him for payment thereof as aforesaid, or at any time afterwards, pay the said sum of money therein specified, or any part thereof, but wholly neglected and refused so to do, of all which said several premises, the said C. D. afterwards, to wit, on, &c. last aforesaid, at, &c. had notice.[f]

By means whereof, and according to the said usage and custom of merchants, the said C. D. then and there become liable to pay to the said A. B. the said sum of money, in the said bill of exchange specified, when he the said C. D. should be thereunto afterwards requested.[g] And being so liable, he the said C. D. in consideration thereof, after- [504] wards, to wit, on, &c. last aforesaid, at, &c. aforesaid, undertook, and then and there faithfully promised the said A. B. to pay him the said sum of money in the said bill of exchange specified, when he the said C. D. should be thereunto afterwards requested.

First count as usual for non-payment, as ante, 503. The second in the same form, as far as the end of the statement of the delivery of the bill to the payee, ante, 503, and then proceed as follows :

And the said A. B. avers, that afterwards, and before the payment of the said sum of money in the said bill of exchange specified, to wit, on the day and year aforesaid, and on divers other days and times, between that day and the time when the said bill of exchange became due and payable, according to the tenour and effect thereof, and also at the time when the said bill of exchange did become due and payable, to wit, on, &c. diligent search and inquiry was made[i] after the said E. F. at, &c.,[k] to wit, at, &c.,[l] in order that the said last-mentioned bill of exchange might be presented and shown to him the said E. F. for his acceptance and payment thereof, according to the said usage and

16. Payee, &c. against drawer, where the drawee could not be found, either to accept or pay.[h]

---

[n] general unnecessary, unless in the case of bills payable after sight, Bayl. 188. And if there be any doubt as to the proof, it is not advisable to state it, for if it be stated it must be proved, 2 Campb. 474. Ante, 357, 377, note.

[d] See ante, 495, note. Bayl. 181. 188.

[e] See ante, 495, note. Bayl. 188, a subsequent promise by the defendant to pay, is evidence of a presentment, 7 East, 231.

[f] As to this averment, see ante, 496, note. Bayl. 189.

[g] As to this statement of the liability and promise, ante, 496, 502.

[h] The necessity for this count appears on the case of Leeson v. Pigott, Sittings after Trin. 1788. Bayl. 187, in which it

was holden, that under a declaration, stating that the bill was presented, and acceptance or payment refused, the plaintiff could not give in evidence that the drawee could not be found. See ante, 495, note. However, a subsequent promise by the defendant to pay, will be sufficient evidence of a presentment to the drawee, and in such case no special count is necessary, 7 East, 231.

[i] Though this is the usual allegation, it is sufficient to allege generally, that the drawee was not found, without showing that any inquiry was made after him, ante 495, note. Carth. 509.

[k] The place where the bill is payable.

[l] The venue.

CHITTY ON BILLS.

3 L

APPENDIX. custom of merchants, but that the said E. F. could not on such search and inquiry be found, nor hath he, at any time since the making of the said bill of exchange, hitherto accepted the same, or paid the said sum of money therein specified, or any part thereof, of all which said several premises, the said C. D. afterwards, to wit, on, &c. last aforesaid, at, &c. aforesaid, had notice. By means whereof, &c. (the defendant's liability and promise to pay on request are stated, as ante, 502, 3.)

———

[505]
17. Payee, &c. against drawer, &c. on default of payment, where the drawee had for payment, and of the drawee's refusal, (see ante, 503, and see 12 East. effects of 171.) and then as follows : the drawer.

When it is doubtful whether due notice of non-acceptance or non-payment can be proved to have been given to the drawer or indorser, and those parties had no effects in the hands of the drawee, or gave no value for the bill ; it is proper in a declaration against such drawer or indorser, after the usual count stating that notice was given, to add a count = proceeding as usual to the end of the averment of the presentment

And the said A. B. avers, that at the time of the making of the said last-mentioned bill of exchange as aforesaid, and from thence, until, and at the time when the same was so presented and shown to the said E. F. for payment thereof as aforesaid, he the said E. F. had not in his hands any effects of the said C. D. nor had he received any consideration from the said C. D. for the acceptance or payment, by him the said E. F. of the said last-mentioned bill of exchange, nor hath he the said C. D. sustained any damage for or by reason of his not having had notice of the non-payment by the said E. F. of the said sum of money, in the said last-mentioned bill of exchange specified; of all which said several premises he the said C. D. afterwards, to wit, on, &c. last aforesaid, at, &c. aforesaid, had notice, by means, &c. state the liability and promise to pay on request, as ante, 503, 4.

———

Form of averment of demand of a fresh bill, where a bill has been lost.=
[506]

Proceed as usual against drawer of a bill, at the suit of indorser stating the bill, acceptance, and indorsement, to plaintiff, and then as follows :

And the said A. B. in fact saith, that afterwards, and before the said last-mentioned bill of exchange became due and payable, according to the tenor and effect thereof, to wit, on the day and year last aforesaid, at, &c. aforesaid, the said last-mentioned bill of exchange was casually destroyed, (or "lost") and the said persons so using the style and firm of E. F. (the "drawees,") then and there well knew the same, and the said C. D. then and there had notice that the said last-mentioned bill of exchange was so destroyed, (or "lost") as aforesaid, and was thereupon then and there and before the said sum of money, in the said last-men-

---

= The form varies according to the circumstances in each particular case. In an action against an indorser, it must be shown, that the drawer and prior indorsers, as well as the acceptor, had no effects, &c. It should seem that an averment of notice should be strictly proved, and therefore this count is strictly necessary, but in Boulager v. Talleyrand, 2 Esp. Rep. 550, the want of effects was admitted in evidence under the general count.

* This form is sometimes adopted, may assist in framing a count in such case, but quære, if it should not be averred that plaintiff was ready to give sufficient indemnity, &c. according to the statute. See ante, 151, 2.

APPENDIX.

tioned bill of exchange specified, became due and payable, according to the tenor and effect thereof, requested by the said A. B. to give to him the said A. B. another bill of exchange, of the same tenor with the said last-mentioned bill of exchange so destroyed, (or "lost,") as aforesaid; but the said C. D. then and there wholly refused so to do. And the said A. B. avers, that afterwards, and when the said sum of money, in the said last-mentioned bill of exchange specified, became due and payable, according to the tenor and effect thereof, to wit, on, &c. at, &c. at London aforesaid, in the parish and ward aforesaid, payment of the said sum of money, in the said last-mentioned bill of exchange specified, was duly requested of the said persons so using the style and firm of E. F. (the drawees,) and also at the place appointed by the said last-mentioned acceptance for the payment thereof as aforesaid, (that is to say,) at, &c. according to the tenor and effect of the said last-mentioned bill of exchange, and of the said acceptance thereof; and the said indorsement so made thereon as aforesaid. But the said persons so using the style and firm of E. F. did not, nor would, nor did any other person or persons when payment of the said sum of money in the said last-mentioned bill of exchange specified, was requested as afore-said, or any time since, pay the said sum of money in the said last-mentioned bill of exchange specified, or any part thereof, but wholly neglected and refused so to do, of all which said several premises last-mentioned, the said C. D. afterwards, to wit, on the day and year last aforesaid, there had notice.

SECT. V.

DECLARATIONS ON FOREIGN BILLS.[*]

---

18. Payee against acceptor.

FOR that whereas one E. F.[a] on, &c.[b] in parts beyond the seas, to wit, at, &c. that is to say, at, &c.,[c] according to the usage and custom of merchants from time immemorial used and approved of,[d] made his certain bill of exchange, *his own proper hand being thereunto subscribed*,[e] bearing date the day and year aforesaid, and then and there directed the said bill of exchange to the said C. D. (by the name and addition of C. D. Esq.,[f]) by which said bill of exchange, he the said E. F. then and there requested the said C. D.[g] two months after the date, (or "at two usances, that is to say,"[h]) of that his first of exchange, second and third of the same tenor and date not paid,[i] to pay to the said A. B. (by the name and addition of A. B. Esq.) or order,[k] the sum [508] of[l] £50, value received, and then and there delivered the said bill of exchange to the said A. B., which said bill of exchange he the said C. D. &c. (state the acceptance and the liability to pay and promise, as in the preceding precedent.)

---

19. Drawer or indorser against acceptor.

In a declaration at the suit of the drawer, upon a bill payable to his

[*] Only a few common forms are here given; see other precedents, 3 Chitty on Pleading, 52 to 63, and how to declare in general, see ante, 351 to 376.

[a] As to the statement by whom drawn, ante, 481, note.

[b] As to the statement of the time and date, ante, 481, notes.

[c] Statement of the place where made, and the venue, ante, 481, note.

[d] Unnecessary, ante, 498, note.

[e] Unnecessary, and not advisable, ante, 498, note. Bayl. 176.

[f] Not necessary, ante, 498, note.

[g] The statement of the bill is to be according to its legal operation, ante, 352.

[h] If the bill be payable at usance, the length of it should be averred as follows, " at two usances, that is to say, at two months after the date thereof," Salk. 131. 3 Keb. 645.—Bayl. 108. Ante, 356. Bayl. 184, 5 and the omission will be fatal on special demurrer, id. ibid. Bayl. 184. Sometimes the averment of usance is more formal, and is inserted just before the statement of the presentment for payment, thus, " and the said plaintiff in fact says, that an usance mentioned in any bill of exchange drawn in London, and payable at Venice is, and at the several times aforesaid was, three months from the date of the said bill,

and no other time whatever." Pay! 184, 5.

[i] It is said, that in an action on a bill consisting of several parts, if the plaintiff may each part, it may be doubted whether he need take notice of this condition, because all the parts collectively make an unconditional bill, and where he has not each part, it should seem more correct to state that the drawer made his certain bill of exchange in writing in three parts, his proper hand being subscribed to each of said parts, bearing date, &c. and directed, &c. and by one of the said parts requested &c. Bayl. 172. 177. 180. 184.

[k] Ante, 490, note.

[l] When the money in which the bill is payable is foreign, it is usual, though perhaps unnecessary, (1 Wils. 185. 4 Bro. Parl. Cas. 604.) to make an averment at the end of the count on the bill as follows, " and the said A. B. avers, that the 3900 livres tournois in the said bill of exchange mentioned, at the time of making the said bill of exchange, and also at the time the same was so presented and shewn for payment as aforesaid, were and still are of great value, to wit, of the value of £xx of lawful money of Great Britain, t.wit at, &c. aforesaid."

own order, the form is similar to the last precedent, omitting the statement of the delivery to the payee, and also resembles the precedent on an inland bill, ante, 498.

If the declaration be at the suit of a drawer, upon a bill payable to a third person, and returned to the drawer for non-payment, the form runs as in the case of an inland bill, ante, 500.

If it is at the suit of an indorsee, the statement of the indorsement is introduced at the end of the acceptance, as in the precedent, ante, 500, the notes to which apply to this case.

———

For that whereas the said C. D. on, &c. in parts beyond the seas, to wit, at, &c. that is to say, at, &c. according to the usage and custom of merchants from time immemorial used and approved of, made his certain bill of exchange in writing, bearing date the same day and year aforesaid, and then and there directed the said bill of exchange to one E. F. (by the name and addidition of E. F. Esq.) by which said bill of exchange the said C. D. then and there requested the said E. F. two months after the date of that his first of exchange (second and third of the same tenor and date not paid,) to pay to the said A. B. (by the name and addition of Mr. A. B.) or order, the sum of £50, for value received, and then and there delivered the said bill of exchange to the said A. B.

20. Payee against drawer, the drawee having refused acceptance.

And the said A. B. avers, that afterwards, and before the payment of the said sum of money in the said bill of exchange specified, or any part thereof, to wit, on, &c. aforesaid,[m] at, &c.[n] aforesaid, to wit, at, &c. aforesaid,[o] the said bill of exchange was presented and shown to the said E. F. for his acceptance thereof, according to the said usage and custom of merchants, and the said E. F. then and there had sight of the said bill of exchange, and was then and there requested to accept the same, but that the said E. E. did not, nor would, at the said time when the said bill of exchange was so presented and shown to him for his acceptance thereof as aforesaid, or at any time before or afterwards accept the same, or pay the said sum of money therein specified, or any part thereof, but then and there wholly neglected and refused so to do, nor did, nor would he then, or at any other time, accept or pay the said second and third of exchange in the said first bill of exchange mentioned, or either of them,[p] but therein wholly failed and made default, whereupon the said bill of exchange afterwards, to wit, on, &c. last aforesaid,[q] at, &c. aforesaid, was duly protested[r] for non-acceptance thereof, ac-

[509]

m The date of the protest for non-acceptance.

n The place in which the drawee is described in the bill to reside.

o The venue.

p This is not necessary, Carth. 509. Ld. Raym. 810. Salk. 130. Stra. 214. Post, 510, note. Bayl. 188.

q The date of the protest, Bayl. 188.

r Sometimes it is stated, that the *plaintiff* caused the bill to be protested ; but where it has been protested on the behalf of another party and returned to the plaintiff, this would be incorrect, and the above form is preferable in all cases. The plaintiff must, in the case of a foreign bill, either state that the bill was protested, Solomons v. Staveley, Dougl. 684, n. 144. Lil. Ent. 55, or show that it was not incumbent on him to protest it, as that the drawee had no effects of the drawer's in his hands, Rogers v. Stevens, 2 T. R. 713. See the form of the averment of the want of effects, ante, 505. But the omission can only be taken advantage of by special demurrer, 1 Salk. 131. 1 Show. 125. Dougl. 684, n. 144. Lil. Ent 55. But it would. be a defect in substance, if no notice be averred, ante,

APPENDIX. cording to the said usage and custom of merchants, of all which said several premises, the said C. D. afterwards, to wit, on, &c. last aforesaid, at, &c. aforesaid, *had notice.*—By means whereof, &c. (the liability and promise to pay are stated as in the case of an inland bill, ante, 503.)

---

21. Payee against drawer, the acceptor having refused payment.

[510]

For that whereas the said C. D. on, &c. in parts beyond the seas, to wit, at, &c. that is to say, at, &c. according to the usage and custom of merchants from time immemorial used and approved of, made his certain bill of exchange in writing, bearing date the day and year aforesaid, and then and there directed the said bill of exchange to one E. F. (by the name and addition of E. F. Esq. &c.) by which said bill of exchange, he the said C. D. then and there requested the said E.F. at two months after the date of that his first of exchange (second and third of the same tenor and date not paid,) to pay to the said A. B. (by the name and addition of A. B. Esq.) or order, the sum of £50, for value received, and then and there delivered the said bill of exchange to the said A. B.; which said bill of exchange, he the said E. F. afterwards, to wit, on, &c. aforesaid, at, &c. aforesaid, upon sight thereof, accepted, according to the said usage and custom of merchants.

And the said A. B. in fact saith, that afterwards *when the said bill became due and payable according to the tenor and effect thereof,* to wit, on, &c. at, &c. aforesaid, that is to say, at, &c. aforesaid, the said bill of exchange so accepted as aforesaid, was duly presented and shown to the said E. F. for payment thereof, according to the said usage and custom of merchants, and the said E. F. was then and there requested to pay the said sum of money therein specified, according to the tenor and effect of the said bill of exchange, and of his said acceptance thereof. But that the said E. F. did not, nor would, at the said time when the said bill of exchange was so presented and shown to him for payment thereof as aforesaid, or at any time afterwards, pay the said sum of money therein specified, or any part thereof, but then and there wholly neglected and refused so to do, *nor did he pay the said second or third of exchange in the said bill of exchange mentioned, or either of them, but therein wholly failed and made default;* and thereupon afterwards, to wit, on, &c. last aforesaid, at, &c. aforesaid, the said bill of exchange was duly protested for non-payment thereof, according to the said usage and custom of merchants, of all which said several premises the said C. D. afterwards, to wit, on, &c. last aforesaid, at, &c. aforesaid, had notice. By means whereof, &c. (*the liability and promise to pay are stated as in the case of an inland bill, ante,* 503.)

---

22. Payee against drawer, where bill has been protested as well for non-acceptance as for non-payment.

Sometimes when a bill protested for non-acceptance, has also been

496, n. In stating the protest, if the plaintiff allege that he protested the bill, *or* *has caused* it to be protested, the declaration will be bad on special demurrer, but will be aided if the defendant plead to the declaration, 1 Show. 125.

*As to the averment of notice, ante, 496, note. When notice is necessary, this allegation is material, Rushton v. Aspinall, Dougl. 680

*The day the bill became due, allow the proper days of grace, as ante, 201, see ante, 495, note, and 2 Smith's R. 224.

*This averment is unnecessary, the preceding allegation, that the money mentioned in the bill was not paid, being a sufficient negative of payment. Carth. 509 Raym. 810. Salk. 130. Strs. 214. 509. Bayl. 188, 9

protested for non-payment, both the presentments and protests are stated, but this, as it has been observed, is unnecessary, as the liability of the drawer and indorser is complete on the protest for non-acceptance. (See 3 East, 481.) When they are stated, the declaration sets forth the presentment for acceptance, the refusal to accept, the protest for non-acceptance, and the notice to the defendant, as ante, 508, and it then proceeds to state the presentment for payment, the refusal, the protest, and the notice to the defendant, as ante, 508, 9, and then concludes with stating the defendant's liability, and promise to pay on *request.*

In a declaration at the suit of the indorsee against the drawer or indorser, the indorsement is inserted immediately preceding the averment of the presentment for acceptance or payment, in the same form as in the case of an inland bill, ante, 500, and the indorsement may be stated in the short form, ante, 500.

23. Indorsee against drawer or indorser.

[511]

SECT. VI.

DEBT ON PROMISSORY NOTES.

24. Payee proof of note against maker.[a] FOR that whereas the said C. D. on, &c. at, &c. made his certain promissory note in writing, bearing date the day and year aforesaid, and then and there delivered the said note to the said A. B., by which said note, he the said C. D. then and there promised to pay, two months after the date thereof, to the said A. B. or order, the sum of £50, for value received.

By means whereof and by force of the statute in such case made and provided, the said C. D. then and there became liable to pay to the said A. B. the said sum of money in the said note specified, according to the tenor and effect of the note ; and although the said sum of money in the said note specified, hath, according to the tenor and effect of the said note, been long since due and payable, yet the said C. D. (al-[512] though often requested so to do) hath not as yet paid the said sum of money, or any part thereof, but hath hitherto wholly neglected and refused so to do, whereby an action hath accrued to the said A. B. to demand and have of and from the said C. D. the said sum of money in the said note specified, parcel of the said sum above demanded.

N. B. Add the proper common counts in debt in the consideration of the note, and the account stated, and the usual conclusion in debt.

25. By the payee of a bill against the drawer, on default of payment by the acceptor.[b] FOR that whereas the said C. D. on, &c. at, &c. according to the usage and custom of merchants from time immemorial used and approved of within this kingdom, made his certain bill of exchange in writing, bearing date the day and year aforesaid, and then and there directed the said bill of exchange to one E. F. (by the name and addition of Mr. E. F., &c.) by which said bill of exchange he the said C. D. then and there requested the said E. F. two months after the date thereof, to pay to the said A. B. or order, the sum of £50, value received, and then and there delivered the said bill of exchange to the said A. B., which said bill of exchange, the said E. F. afterwards, to wit, on the day and year aforesaid, at, &c. aforesaid, upon sight thereof accepted, according to the said usage and custom of merchants.

And the said A. B. avers, that afterwards, *when the said bill of exchange became due and payable, according to the tenor and effect there;*

---

[a] When debt is sustainable on a note, see ante, 427 to 429. See the forms, Morgan's Precedents, 548.—1 Mod. Ent. 312. See the form, 2 Bos. & Pul. 78, debt lies against indorser, when he is also drawer and payee. Stratton v. Hill, 3 Price.

[b] When debt on bills is sustainable, ante. 427 to 429, and supra.

to wit, on, &c.[e] at, &c. aforesaid, the said bill of exchange so accepted
as aforesaid, was duly presented and shown to the said E. F. for payment thereof, according to the said usage and custom of merchants, and
the said E. F. was then and there requested to pay the said sum of money in the said bill of exchange specified, according to the tenor and effect thereof, and of his said acceptance thereof, but the said E. F. did
not, nor would, when the said bill of exchange was so presented and
shown to him for payment thereof as aforesaid, or at any time afterwards, pay the said sum of money therein specified, or any part thereof but then and there wholly neglected and refused so to do, of all which
said premises, the said C. D. afterwards, to wit, on the day and year
aforesaid, at, &c. aforesaid, had notice.

By means whereof, and according to the said usage and custom of [513]
merchants, he the said C. D. then and there became liable to pay the
said A. B. the said sum of money in the said bill of exchange specified,
when he the said C. D. should be thereunto afterwards requested, and
being so liable, he the said C. D in consideration thereof, afterwards,
to wit, on the day and year last aforesaid, at, &c. aforesaid, agreed to
pay to the said A. B. the said sum of money in the said bill of exchange
specified, when he the said C. D. should be thereunto afterwards requested : whereby and by reason of the said sum of money in the said
bill of exchange specified, being and remaining wholly unpaid, an action hath accrued to the said A. B. to demand and have, of and from
the said C. D. the said sum of money in the said bill of exchange specified, parcel of the said sum above demanded.

———————

In the King's Bench. A. B. Plaintiff. Notice to
                        Between   and   plaintiff to
                                   C. D. Defendant. prove con-
                                                     sideration
I hereby give you notice, that on the trial of this cause the above- given by
named defendant will insist and give in evidence, that the supposed him   for
bill of exchange (or "promissory note,") mentioned in the declaration bill.[d]
in this cause, if any such there be, was obtained from the said defendant (or "from G. H.") without legal or sufficient consideration, and
by undue means, and that the said defendant is not liable to pay the
same : and I do hereby further give you notice, and require you on the
said trial to prove the consideration given by the said plaintiff, and
every other party for the said bill of exchange, and when such consideration was given and paid, and in what manner, and the person and
persons by and from whom the same bill of exchange was obtained by
the said plaintiff or any other person, and the time when the said plaintiff and any other person became the holder thereof: and I do hereby
further give you notice, and require you on the said trial to produce
and give in evidence all letters and copies of letters, and books of account, and vouchers, in any way relating to the said bill of exchange :
and in particular a certain letter bearing date, &c. (*here specify any
particular document material to be produced.*)
Dated, &c.   Yours, &c.   L. M.
                                        Attorney for the said defendant.
To Mr. N. O. the above-named plaintiff, and
      Mr. ——, his attorney or agent.

[e] The day the bill became due.   [d] As to this notice, see ante, 400.
CHITTY ON BILLS.   3 M

SECT. VII.

JUDGMENTS IN ASSUMPSIT ON A BILL, &c.

As yet of Michaelmas Term, in the 2d year of the reign of King George the Fourth, witness Sir Charles Abbott, Knt.

Judgment for plaintiff on demurrer to a replication of *nul tiel* record, to a plea of judgment recovered, to a declaration on bill of exchange, and the money counts; with a *remittitur damna* to the money counts, and judgment for plaintiff on the first count for the principal and interest on the bill, on a reference to master to compute principal & interest.

Middletown, to wit.—A. B. puts in his place ———, his attorney against C. D. in a plea of trespass on the case upon promises.

Middlesex, to wit.—The said C. D. puts in his place ———, his attorney, at the suit of the said A. B. in the plea aforesaid.

Middlesex, to wit.—Be it remembered, that, &c. [here copy the demurrer-book, containing declaration on a bill of exchange and money counts, plea judgment recovered, replication *nul tiel* record demurrer thereto, joinder, and award of *curia advisari vult.*]

At which day, before our said Lord the King at Westminster, come as well as the said A. B. by his attorney aforesaid, as the said C. D. by his attorney aforesaid ; and whereupon all and singular the premises being seen, and by the court of our said Lord the King now here fully understood, and mature deliberation being thereupon had, it appears to the said court here, that the said replication of the said A. B. and the matters therein contained, are sufficient in law for the said A. B. to have and maintain his aforesaid action thereof against the said C. D. Wherefore the said A. B. ought to recover against the said C. D. his damages, by reason of the premises. * And hereupon the said A. B. freely here in court, remits to the said C. D. all damages sustained by reason of the not performing of the said several promises and undertakings in the last *four* counts* of the said declaration mentioned: therefore let the said C. D. be thereof acquitted. And because it is suggested and proved, and manifestly appears to the said court here, that the said A. B. hath sustained damages by reason of the not performing of the said promise and undertaking in the said first count of the said declaration mentioned, to £50, besides the costs and charges of the said suit : Therefore it is considered that the said A. B. do recover against the said C. D. the said sum of £50, for his damages last aforesaid ; and also £20 for his said costs and charges by the said court here adjudge to the said A. B. with his assent, which said damages, costs, and charges, in the whole amount to £70, and the said C. D. in mercy, &c.

[515]

Judgment signed the 17th day of May, 1821.

Mercy.

N. B. Insert the memoranda of the warrants of attorney, as in the precedent, ante, 314, and then proceed as follows :—

* More or less, according to the number of the common counts.

——, To wit.—Be it remembered, that on ————————— next after Appendix.
————————— in this same term, before our Lord the King, at Westmin- ∞∞∞∞∞∞∞∞∞∞∞
ster, comes A. B. by E. F. his attorney, and brings into court of our The like
said Lord the King, before the King himself now here, his certain bill on a judg-
ment by *nil*
against C. D. being in the custody of the Marshal of the Marshalsea of *dicit.*
our Lord the King, before the King himself, of a plea of trespass on the
case upon promises, and there are pledges for the prosecution thereof,
to wit, John Doe and Richard Roe, which said bill follows in those
words, that is to say,—to wit, A. B. complains of C. D. being in the
custody, &c. (here copy the declaration to the end, omitting the pledges,
and proceed in a new line as follows:—

And the said C. D. in his proper person (or by G. H. his attorney,)
comes and defends the wrong and injury when, &c. and says nothing
in bar or preclusion of the said action of the said A. B. whereby the
said A. B. remains therein undefended against the said C. D., wherefore
the said A. B. ought to recover against the said C. D. his damages by
reason of the premises, &c. (proceed as in the first precedent, from the
asterisk to the end, and if the final judgment be of a term subsequent
to the interlocutory judgment, insert the continuances as in the next
precedent.)

———————————

N. B. The same as the two precedents to the end of the interlocutory [516]
judgment at the asterisk, and then proceed as follows:—

But because it is unknown to the court of our said Lord the King The like
now here, what damages the said A. B. hath sustained by means of the when final
premises, the sheriff is commanded, that by the oath of twelve good and judgment is
signed of a
lawful men of his bailiwick, he diligently inquire what damages the said different
A. B. hath sustained, as well by means of the premises, as for his costs term from
and charges by him about his suit in this behalf expended, and that he the interlo-
send the inquisition which he shall thereupon take to our said Lord the cutoryjudg-
ment, with
King, at Westminster, on ————————— next after ————— under his a continu-
seal, and the seals of those by whose oath he shall take that inquisition, ance by
together with the writ of our said Lord the King, to him thereupon di- award of
rected, and the same day is given to the said A. B. at the same place. writ of in-
quiry and
return of

*At which day before our said Lord the King, at Westminster afore- *vicecomes*
said, comes the said A. B. by his attorney aforesaid: And the sheriff *non misit*
hath not sent the writ of our said Lord the King to him in that behalf *breve.*
directed, nor hath he done any thing thereupon. * Therefore, as before
the sheriff is commanded, that by the oath of twelve good and lawful
men, &c. (same as above, to the asterisk, inserting a return day in the
subsequent term, and then proceed as follows:) And hereupon the said
A. B. freely in court, remits to the said C. D. all damages, &c. (as
above, from the asterisk, 514.)

* The omission of the following supposed default is not material, 4 Taunt. 148.

SECT. VIII.

NOTARY'S FEES OF OFFICE, AS SETTLED THE FIRST OF
JULY, 1797.

AT a meeting of several Notaries of the city of London, held at the
George and Vulture Tavern, in London aforesaid, on the 1st July, A.D.
1797, the following resolutions were unanimously agreed to, and since
approved and confirmed by the Governor and Company of the Bank of
England.

[517] *First*—That from and after the fifth day of the present month of
July, the *noting,* for all bills drawn upon, or addressed at the house of
any person or persons residing within the ancient walls of the said city
of London shall be charged one shilling and sixpence; and without the
said walls, and not exceeding the limits hereunder specified, the sum
of two shillings and sixpence.ᵃ

Second—For all bills drawn upon, or addressed at the house of any
person or persons residing beyond Old or New Bond Street, Wimpole
Street, New Cavendish Street, Upper Mary-bone Street, Howland
Street, Lower Gower Street, lower end of Gray's-inn Lane, (and not off
the pavement,) Clerkenwell church, Old Street, Shoreditch church,
Brick Lane, St. George's in the East, Execution-dock, Wapping, Dock-
head, upper end of Bermondsey Street, (as far as the church,) end of
Blackman Street, end of Great Surrey Street, Blackfriars-Road, (as far
as the Circus,) Cuper's Bridge, Bridge Street, Westminster, Arlington
Street, Piccadilly, and the like distances, three shillings and sixpence:
and off the pavement, one shilling and sixpence per mile additional.

Third—For *protesting* a bill drawn upon, or addressed at the house
of any person or persons residing within the ancient walls of the said
city, (including the stamp duty of four shillings, and exclusive of the
charge of noting,) the sum of six shillings and sixpence: and without
the ancient walls of the said city, including the like stamp duty, and
exclusive of the said charge of noting, the sum of eight shillings, agreeably to the second article.

Fourth—That *all acts of honour* within the ancient walls or the said
city of London, shall be charged the sum of one shilling and sixpence
upon each bill; and for all acts of honour without the ancient walls of
the said city, to be regulated agreeable to the charge of noting bills out
of the city; and the like charge for any additional demand that may be
made upon the said bill, or when the same is mentioned and inserted in
the answer in the protest.

Fifth—For every *post demand and act thereof*, within the ancient walls

ᵃ But see ante, 312, and 4 T. R. 179.

of the said city, the sum of two shillings and sixpence : and without the walls of the said city, the sum of three shillings and sixpence (provided the same be only registered in the notary's books,) and so in proportion, according to the distance, to be regulated agreeably to the charge of noting bills.

Sixth—For every *copy of a bill paid in part, and a receipt at foot of such copy,* shall be charged two shillings, and so in proportion for every additional bill so copied, (exclusive of the receipt stamp.)

Seventh—For every *duplicate protest of* one bill (including four shillings for the duty,) shall be charged the sum of seven shillings and sixpence ; and so in like proportion of three shillings and sixpence, (exclusive of the duty) for every additional bill.

Eighth—For every folio of *ninety words, translated* from the French, Dutch, or Flemish, into English, shall be charged one shilling and sixpence, and from English into French, Dutch, or Flemish, two shillings for each such folio ; and from Italian, Spanish, Portuguese, German, Danish, and Swedish, one shilling and nine pence per folio of ninety words ; and from Latin, two shillings and sixpence per folio ; and for *attesting the same* to be a true translation, if necessary, seven shillings and sixpence, exclusive of fees and stamps.

Ninth—That all *attestations to letters of attorney, affidavits,* &c. at the request of any gentlemen in the law, shall be charged seven shillings and sixpence, exclusive of fees, stamps, and attendance.

Tenth—For every *city seal* shall be charged one guinea for one deponent, exclusive of attendance and exemplification ; and if more than one deponent, ten shillings and sixpence for each additional affidavit.

Eleventh—For all *notarial copies* shall be charged sixpence per folio of seventy-two words, exclusive of attestation, stamps, &c.

SECT. IX.

DEPOSITIONS IN BANKRUPTCY.

---

1. Affidavit of one petitioning creditor.   A. B. of, &c. grocer, maketh oath and saith, that C. D. of the city of London, merchant, indebted to this deponent[a] in the sum of £100 and upwards,[b] and that the said C. D. is become bankrupt within the true intent and meaning of some or one of the statues made and now in force concerning bankrupts, as this deponent is informed and believes.   A. B.

      Sworn at the public office in Southampton Buildings,
        the   day of   before me

---

2. Affidavit of several[c] petitioning creditors.   A. B. of, &c. C. D. of, &c. E. F. of, &c. G. H. of, &c. severally make oath and say, and first this deponent A. B. for himself saith, that I. K. of, &c. is justly indebted into him, this deponent, in the sum of £30, for, &c. And this deponent C. D. for himself saith, that, &c. [as before.] And all these deponents say, that they verily believe that the said I. K. is become bankrupt within the true intent and meaning of some or one of the statutes made and now in force concerning bankrupts.

                                     A. B.   E. F.
                                       C. D.   G. H.

    All sworn, &c.

---

3. The affirmation of a Quaker.   A. B. of &c. being one of the people called Quakers, being examined upon his solemn affirmation, saith, &c. [as in affidavit, only that instead of the word "deponent," the word "affirmant" is made use of.]

---

[520] 4. Affidavit to obtain a country commission   (*Same as the first form, ante, 655, to the end, and then proceed as follows.*) And this deponent further saith, That the commission, when obtained, will be executed at ——— (*the country place,*) or within ten miles of the same, and not within forty miles of London.

                                       A. B.

      Sworn at ———, in the county of ———, this
      ——— day of ———in the 2d year of the
      reign of George the Fourth, King of the
      United Kingdom, &c. before me, T. M. Master Extraordinary in Chancery.

      Commissioners names, (*here state them.*)

---

[a] Insert (if in partnership) " and to C. D. E. F. &c. this deponent's partners in trade."

[b] Sometimes the debt is stated, as " for goods sold and delivered by, &c. to &c." or " *upon a bill of exchange*." or " *for money lent, &c.*" *according to the nature of the debt :* but this is not necessary 1 Atk. 135. 1 Mont. 390.

[c] The debt of two petitioning creditors must be £150, or three or more, £20. 5 Geo. 2. c. 30. sect. 23.

At the Rolls Coffee-house, in Chancery-lane, the —— day of ——,
one thousand eight hundred and twenty-one.

        A. B. of the parish of ——, being sworn and examined, the **5. Proof**
W. B. day and year, and at the place above-written, upon his oath **of petition-**
saith, that C. D., the person against whom this commission of **ing credit-**
bankrupt is awarded and issued forth, was, at and before the **or's debt.**
date and suing forth of the said commission, and still is, justly
H. H. and truly indebted unto him this deponent in the sum of ——
for (*the consideration must be stated, see the forms of bills of ex-*
change, infra, 521 *to* 524, *proof of bills in different cases*,) and
that the said sum became due at the time following, that is to
H. R. say (*here the time or times when the debt became due must
appear.*)

Signed.[d]

The time when the debt became due must be stated, or a bill of particulars with dates must be annexed and referred to in the depositions.

———

PROOF OF DEBTS.   [521]

At Guildhall, London, 3d Nov. 1821.

        A. B. of, &c. being sworn and examined, the day and year, **6. Deposi-**
G. H. and at the place above-said, before, &c. upon his oath saith, that **tions for**
C. D. of, &c. the person against whom the commission of **moneylent,**
bankrupt, now in prosecution, is awarded and issued, was, be- **secured by**
fore the date and suing forth of the said commission, and still is, **bankrupt's**
justly and truly indebted unto him this deponent, in the sum of **promissory**
I. K. £100, for money lent and advanced by this deponent to the said **note.**
C. D. for which said sum of £100, or any part thereof, this deponent hath not received any security or satisfaction whatsoever,
save and except a promissory note, dated the —— day of ——, **Exception**
A. D. ——, under the hand of the said C. D. whereby he **of a promis-**
L. M. promised to pay to this deponent, on demand, the said sum of **sory note.**
£100.

———

        A. B. of, &c. being sworn, &c. that the said C. D. the person **7. On a**
O. P. against whom, &c. was, at and before the date and suing forth **promissory**
of the said commission, and still is, justly and truly indebted **note made**
unto this deponent in the sum of —— upon a promissory note **by bank-**
under his hand, dated the ——, given by the said bankrupt to **rupt, and**
one E. F. for ——, payable to him or his order —— after date; **indorsedby**
Q. R. which note the said E. F. indorsed to I. K. who indorsed the **a third per-**
same to this deponent for goods sold and delivered by this depo- **son to the**
nent to the said I. K. and money payed by him on account of the **creditor.**
said note to that amount, and for which said sum of ——,
or any part thereof, this deponent hath not, nor hath any person
G. H. to his use, received any security or satisfaction whatsoever, save
and except the said note.   A. B.

[d] All despositions must be signed by the witnesses.

S. D.

I. B.

W. M.

[**522**]

A. B. of, &c. being sworn, &c. [as usual] and still is justly and truly indebted to this deponent, in the sum of £890 and upwards, for money lent by this deponent to the said C. D., before he became bankrupt, for which said sum of £890, or any part thereof, this deponent hath not received any satisfaction or security whatsoever, save the seven following promissory notes; one dated the 22d of May, 1809, under the hand of the said C. D. whereby he promises to pay to this deponent or order, one year after date, £200 with interest; the other six promissory notes are under the hand of one A. F. and made payable to the said C. D., and by the said C. D. indorsed to this deponent, and are for the several and respective sums following: one dated 19th September, 1809, for £150, payable six months after date; another dated 18th October, 1809, for £90, payable six months after date; another 8th November, 1809, for £100, payable four months after date; another dated 4th December, 1809, for £115, payable five months after date; and the other of the said notes, dated 26th December, 1810, for £125, payable six months after date.

A. B.

8. On notes of hand:— One made by the bankrupt and delivered to the creditor: the others indorsed to the creditor.

---

9. On a bill of exchange drawn and delivered by the bankrupt to the creditor.

J. B.

R. F.

G. H.

A. B. of, &c. being sworn, &c. saith, that C. D. the person, &c. was, at and before the date and suing forth of the said commission, and still is, justly and truly indebted unto this deponent in the sum of, &c. and upwards, for money lent by this deponent to the said C. D. before he became bankrupt, for which said sum, or any part thereof, he this deponent hath not, nor hath any person to his use, received any security or satisfaction whatsoever, save and except a certain bill of exchange, dated the —— and drawn by the said C. D. upon and accepted by I. K. and by the said C. D. indorsed and delivered to this deponent.

A. B.

---

10. On a bill of exchange indorsed to the creditor by a third person.

J. B.

R. F.

G. H

A. B. of ——, in the county of ——, mercer, being sworn, &c. that R. E. and F. E. the persons against whom the commission of bankrupt is awarded and issued, were, at and before the date and issuing forth of the said commission, and still are, justly and truly indebted to this deponent in the sum of ——, upon two bills of exchange, both drawn by the said bankrupts, on H. U. and Co. merchants, of ——, and accepted by them, and both payable —— after date, to M. J. T. and Co. or order; one of them for the sum of ——, and the other for the sum of ——, for value in account, both of which said bills of exchange are dated the —— day of ——, and respectively indorsed by the said M. J. T. and Co. and by them delivered to the deponent, for goods sold and delivered by this deponent to the said M. J. T. and Co. and money paid to them on account of the said bills of exchange, to the full amount of the said bills of exchange, deducting the legal discount, and for which said sum, or any part thereof, this deponent hath not, nor hath any person to his use, received any security or satisfaction whatsoever, except the said bills of exchange.

A. B.

A. B. of ———, merchant, being sworn, &c. That P. H. of
J. B. the person against whom this commission of bankruptcy is awarded and issued forth, as being one of the partners, &c. was, at _{11. For}
and before the date of the issuing forth of the said commission, ^{debt} ^{se-}
R. F. and still is, justly and truly indebted unto this deponent in the ^{cured} ^{by}
sum of ———, for premiums on insurances, for which said sum of ^{forth in a}
———, or any part thereof, he this deponent hath not received any ^{schedule.}
G. H. security or satisfaction whatsoever, save and except the under-
mentioned bills of exchange and promissory notes.

                                                           A. B.

Note or bill.	Date.	Drawer.	Acceptor.	Sum £. s. d.	Payable to	At what date drawn.	Indorsers.

A. B. of, &c. ——— claims a debt of ———, due to ———, ^{12. Form}
from ———, for ———, upon, &c. (*here state the promissory note,* ^{of a claim.}
bill of exchange, &c.)   ^{(The claim-}
                                                                   ^{ant is not}
                                                                   ^{sworn.)}
Memorandum.—That on the day and year, and at the place above-
mentioned, A. B. of, &c. claimed a debt under the commission of bankrupt awarded and issued against C. D. of, &c. of £100, to be due from
the bankrupt to (the person for whom the claim is made,) by note of
hand.

(524)

SECT. X.

Statute 9 & 15 W. 3. c. 17. entitled "An Act for the better Payment of Inland Bills of Exchange."

Bills of exchange drawn in England, &c. of £5. or upwards, payable at a certain number of days, &c.
"WHEREAS great damages and other inconveniences do frequently " happen in the course of trade and commerce, by reason of delays of " payment and other neglects on inland bills of exchange in this king- "dom;" be it therefore enacted by the King's Most Excellent Majesty, by and with the consent of the Lords Spiritual and Temporal, and Commons, in this present Parliament assembled, and by the authority of the same, That from and after the four-and-twentieth day of June next, which shall be in the year one thousand six hundred and ninety- eight, all and every bill or bills of exchange drawn in, or dated at and from, any trading city or town, or any other place in the kingdom of England, dominion of Wales, or town of Berwick-upon-Tweed, of the sum of five pounds sterling or upwards, upon any person or persons or in London, or any other trading city, town, or any other place (in which said bill or bills of exchange shall be acknowledged and express-

After acceptance and three days after it is due, may be protested.
ed the said value to be received,) and is and shall be drawn payable at a certain number of *days, weeks,* or *months,* after *date* thereof, and from and after presentation and acceptance of the said bill or bills of ex- change, (which acceptance shall be by the under writing the same under the party's hand so accepting) and *after* the expiration of three days af- ter the said bill or bills shall become due, the party to whom the said

Further provisions relating hereto, 3 & 4 Ann, c. 9. 4. which is made perpetual by 7 Ann, c.25. 1 Salk. 131. Mod. cases in the law,80.373. 6 Mod. 80. The form of the protest.
bill or bills are made payable, his servant, agent or assigns, may and shall cause the said bill or bills to be *protested* by a notary public, and in default of such notary public, by any other substantial person of the city, town, or place, in the presence of two or more credible witnesses, refusal or neglect being first made of due payment of the same, which protest shall be made and written under a fair written copy of the said bill of exchange, in the words or form following:

'KNOW all men, that I, A. B. on the ———— day of ———— at ' the usual place of abode, of the said ————, have demanded pay- ' ment of the bill, of the which the above is the copy, which the said ' ———— did not pay, wherefore I the said ———— do hereby pro- ' test the said bill. Dated this ———— day of ————.

[525]

Protest or notice thereof to be given in fourteen days after made, &c.
II. Which protest so made as aforesaid, shall, within fourteen days after making thereof, be sent, or otherwise due notice shall be given thereof, to the party from whom the said bill or bills were received, who is, upon producing such protest, to repay the said bill or bills, together with all interest and charges from the day such bill or bills were pro- tested; for which protest shall be paid a sum not exceeding the sum of

---

ᵃ As to protest and constructions on this statute, see ante, 311, 312, &c.

sixpence;^b and in default or neglect of such protest made and sent, or APPENDIX.
due notice given within the days before limited, the person so falling or
neglecting thereof, is and shall be liable to all costs, damages, and interest, which do and shall accrue thereby.

III. Provided nevertheless, that in case any such inland bill or bills **Bill lost or**
of exchange shall happen to be lost* or miscarried *within the time be-* **miscarried,**
fore limited for the payment of the same, then the drawer of the said **drawer to**
bill or bills is and shall be obliged to give another bill or bills of the **ther.**
same tenor with those first given, the person or persons to whom they
are and shall be delivered, giving security, if demanded, to the said
drawer, to indemnify him against all persons whatsoever, in case the
said bill or bills of exchange so alleged to be lost or miscarried, shall
be found again.

Statute 3 & 4 Anne, chap. 9. entitled, "An Act for giving like Reme-
"dy upon Promissory Notes, as is now used upon Bills of Exchange,
"and for the better Payment of Inland Bills of Exchange."—
(Made perpetual by 7 Anne, c. 25. s. 3.)

'WHEREAS it hath been held, That notes in writing, signed by **See 1 Burr.**
'the party who makes the same, whereby such party promises to pay **227. 325.**
'unto any other person, or his order, any sum of money therein men- **This act**
'tioned, are not assignable or indorsable over, within the custom of **the benefit**
'merchants, to any other person; and that such person to whom the **of com-**
'sum of money mentioned in such note is payable, cannot maintain an **merce)is li-**
'action by the custom of merchants, against the person who first made **berally con-**
'and signed the same; and that any person to whom such note should **Wils. 2 †**
'be assigned, indorsed, or made payable, could not, within the said **[526]**
'custom of merchants, maintain any action upon such note against the
'person who first drew and signed the same.' Therefore, to the intent
to encourage trade and commerce, which will be much advanced, if
such notes shall have the same effect as inland bills of exchange, and
shall be negotiated in like manner; Be it enacted by the Queen's Most **Promissory**
Excellent Majesty, by and with the advice and consent of the Lords **note may**
Spiritual and Temporal, and Commons, in this present Parliament as- **be assigned**
sembled, and by the authority of the same, That all notes in writing, **or indorsed,**
that after the first day of May, in the year of our Lord one thousand **maintained**
seven hundred and five, shall be made and signed by any person or per- **thereon, as**
sons, body politic or corporate, or by the servant or agent of any corpo- **on inland**
ration, banker, goldsmith, merchant, or trader, who is usually intrusted **bills of ex-**
by him, her, or them, to sign such promissory notes for him, her, or **change.**
them, whereby such person or persons, body politic and corporate, his,
her, or their servant or agent as aforesaid, doth or shall promise to pay
to any other person or persons, body politic and corporate, his, her, or
their order, or unto bearer, any sum of money mentioned in such
note, shall be taken and construed to be, by virtue thereof, due and
payable to any such person or persons, body politic and corporate, to
whom the same is made payable; and also every such note payable to
any person or persons, body politic and corporate, his, her, or their or-

^b Ante, 312. 4 T. R. 170.   † See constructions on this statute
* As to lost bills and constructions on   as to promissory notes, antee, 824 to
this clause, ante, 151, &c.   331.

APPENDIX. der, shall be assignable or indorsable over, in the same manner as inland bills of exchange are or may be, according to the custom of merchants; and the person or persons, body politic and corporate, to whom such sum of money is or shall be by such note made payable, shall and may maintain an action for the same, in such manner as he, she, or they, might do, upon any inland bill of exchange, made or drawn according to the custom of merchants, against the person or persons, body politic and corporate, who, or whose servant or agent as aforesaid, signed the same: and that any person or persons, body politic and corporate, to whom such note is payable to any person or persons, body politic and corporate, his, her, or their order, is indorsed or assigned, or the money therein mentioned, ordered to be paid by indorsement thereon, shall and may maintain his, her, or their action for such sum of money, either against the person or persons, body politic and corporate, who, or whose servant or agent as aforesaid, signed such note, or against

[527] any of the persons that indorsed the same, in like manner as in cases
Plaintiff or of inland bills of exchange ; and in every such action the plaintiff or
defendant plaintiffs shall recover his, her, or their damages and costs of suit; and
may reco- if such plaintiff or plaintiffs shall be nonsuited, or a verdict be given
ver costs. against him, her, or them, the defendant or defendants shall recover his, her, or their costs against the plaintiff or plaintiffs ; and every such plaintiff or plaintiffs, defendant or defendants, respectively recovering, may sue out execution for such damages and costs by *capias*, *fieri facias*, or *elegit*.

How ac- II. And be it further enacted by the authority aforesaid, that all and
tions shall every such actions shall be commenced, sued and brought within such
be brought, time as is appointed for commencing or suing actions upon the case, by
31 Jac. 1. the statute made in the one-and-twentieth year of the reign of King
c. 16. James the First, entitled, ' *An Act for Limitation of Actions, and for avoiding of Suits in Law.*'

Proviso III. Provided that no body politic or corporate shall have power, by
against giv- virtue of this act, to issue or give out any notes, by themselves or their
ing out servants, other than such as they might have issued, if this act had ne-
notes. ver been made.

9 & 10 W. IV. ' And whereas by an act of parliament made in the ninth year
3. c. 17. ' of the reign of his late Majesty King William the Third, entitled, '
' *Act for the better Payment of Inland Bills of Exchange*, it is amon.
' other things enacted, that from and after presentation and acceptan
' of the said bill or bills of exchange (which acceptance shall be by t
' the underwriting the same under the party's hand so accepting; a
' after the expiration of three days after the said bill or bills shall be
' come due, the party to whom the said bill or bills are made payab.
' his servant, agent, or assigns, may and shall cause the same bi. "
' bills to be protested in manner as in the said act is enacted: A
' whereas by there being no provision made therein for protesting su
' bill or bills, in case the party on whom the same are or shall he draw
' refuse to accept the same by under writing the same under his han.
' all merchants and others do refuse to under write such bill or bills "
' make any other than a promissory acceptance, by which means to
' effect and good intent of the said act in that behalf is wholly evaded,
' and no bill or bills can be protested before, or for want of such ac-
' ceptance by underwriting the same as aforesaid.' For remedy whereof
be it enacted by the authority aforesaid, that from and after the first

day of May, which shall be in the year of our Lord one thousand seven APPENDIX.
hundred and five, in case, upon presenting of any such bill or bills of
exchange, the party or parties, on whom the same shall be drawn, shall Party refu-
refuse to accept the same, by underwriting the same as aforesaid, the underwrite
party to whom the said bill or bills are made payable, his servant, agent bill   of
or assigns, may and shall cause the said bill or bills to be protested for exchange,
non-acceptance as in case of foreign bills of exchange; any thing in such   bill
the said act or any other law to the contrary notwithstanding; for which may be pro-
protest there shall be paid two shillings and no more.   non-accept-
                                                                           ance.

V. Provided always, that from and after the said first day of May, No accept-
no acceptance of any such inland bill of exchange shall be sufficient to ance of in-
charge any person whatsoever, unless the same be underwritten or in- land bills of
dorsed in writing thereupon; and if such bill be not accepted by such be   suffi-
underwriting, or indorsement, in writing, no drawer of any such cient, un-
inland bill shall be liable to pay any costs, damages, or interest there- less   the
upon, unless such protest may be made for non-acceptance thereof; and same be un-
within fourteen days after such protest, the same may be sent or other- derwritten,
wise notice thereof be given to the party from whom such bill was re- nor drawer
ceived, or left in writing at the place of his or her usual abode; and if ble to costs,
such bill be accepted, and not paid before the expiration of three days &c.[c]
after the said bill shall become due and payable, then no drawer of such
bill shall be compellable to pay any costs, damages, or interest thereupon, unless a protest be made and sent, or notice thereupon be given,
in manner and form above-mentioned: Nevertheless, every drawer of
such bill shall be liable to make payment of costs, damages, and interest upon such inland bill, if any one protest be made of non-acceptance,
or non-payment thereof, and notice thereof be sent, given, or left as
aforesaid.

VI. Provided, that no such protest shall be necessary, either for non- No protest
acceptance or non-payment of any inland bill of exchange, unless the necessary
value be acknowledged and expressed in such bill to be received, and bill   be
unless such bill be drawn for the payment of twenty pounds sterling or drawn for
upwards, and that the protest hereby required for non-acceptance, shall £20 or up-
be made by such persons as are appointed by the said recited act to wards.
protest inland bills of exchange for non-payment thereof.

VII. And be it further enacted, that from and after the said first day [529]
of May, if any person doth accept any such bill of exchange, for and in By whom
satisfaction of any former debt, or sum of money formerly due unto protest shall
him, the same shall be accounted and esteemed a full and complete be made.
payment of such debt, if such person accepting of any such bill for his ance of bill
debt, doth not take his due course to obtain payment thereof, by endea- esteemed a
vouring to get the same accepted and paid, and make his protest as full   pay-
aforesaid, either for non-acceptance or non-payment thereof.   ment   of
                                                                    debt.

VIII. Provided, that nothing herein contained shall extend to dis- Proviso.
charge any remedy, that any person may have against the drawer, acceptor, or indorser of such bill.

IX. And be it further enacted by the authority aforesaid, that this act Act to con-
shall continue and be in force for the space of three years, from the first tinue three
day of May, and from thence to the end of the next session of parlia- years.
ment, and no longer.

[Made perpetual by 7 Anne, c. 25. s. 3.]

[c] See Windle v. Andrews, 2 Stark. 425.

SECT IX.

STATUTES RELATIVE TO SMALL NOTES AND BILLS MADE OR NEGOTIATED IN ENGLAND.

---

48 Geo. 3. c. 88. A. D. 1808.

An Act to restrain the Negotiation of Promissory Notes and Inland Bills of Exchange, under a limited Sum in England.

'WHEREAS various notes, bills of exchange, and drafts for money
'for very small sums have for some time past been circulated or nego-
'tiated in lieu of cash, within that part of Great Britain called Eng-
'land, to the great prejudice of trade and public credit, and many of
'such bills and drafts. being payable under certain terms and restric-
'tions which the poorer sort of manufacturers, artificers, labourers, and
[530] 'others cannot comply with, otherwise than by being subject to great
'extortion and abuse: And whereas an act, passed in the fifteenth
15 Geo. 3. 'year of the reign of His present Majesty, intituled, " An Act to res-
c. 51. re- 'train the Negotiation of Promissory Notes and Inland Bills of Ex-
pealed. 'change, under a limited Sum, within that part of Great Britain called
'England, for preventing the circulating such notes and drafts:" And
'whereas doubts have arisen as to the power of justices of the peace to
'hear and determine offences under the said act ; and it is therefore
'expedient that more effectual provisions should be made for enforcing
'the provisions of the said act ;' Be it therefore enacted by the King's
Most Excellent Majesty, by and with the advice and consent of the
Lords Spiritual and Temporal, and Commons, in this present Parliament assembled, and by the authority of the same, That from and after
the passing of this act, the said recited act shall be and the same i-
hereby repealed.

Promissory   II. And be it further enacted, That all promissory or other notes-
notes for bills of exchange or drafts, or undertakings in writing, being negotiable
less than or transferrable for the payment of any sum or sums of money, or any
20s. declar- orders, notes or undertaking in writing, being negotiable or transfer-
ed void. rable for the delivery of any goods, specifying their value in money,
less than the sum of twenty shillings in the whole, heretofore made or
issued, or which shall hereafter be made or issued, shall, from and after
the first day of October, one thousand eight hundred and eight, be and
the same are hereby declared to be absolutely void and of no effect ; any
law, statute, usage or custom, to the contrary thereof in anywise not
withstanding.

Penalty on   III. And be it further enacted, That if any person or persons shall
persons ut- after the first day of July, one thousand eight hundred and eight, by
tering such any art, device, or means whatsoever, publish or utter any such notes
notes, 20s. bills, drafts, or engagements as aforesaid, for a less sum than twenty
to £5.

shillings, or on which less than the sum of twenty shillings shall be APPENDIX.
due, and which shall be in anywise negotiable or transferrable, or shall
negotiate or transfer the same, every such person shall forfeit and pay,
for every such offence, any sum not exceeding twenty pounds, nor less
than five pounds, at the discretion of the justice of the peace who shall
hear and determine such offence.

IV. And be it further enacted, That it shall be lawful for any justice   Justices
or justices of the peace, acting for the county, riding, city, or place with- may deter-
in which any offence against this act shall be committed, to hear and mine   on
determine the same in a summary way, at any time within twenty ces within
days after such offence shall have been committed; and such justice or 20 days.
justices, upon any information exhibited or complaint made upon oath [531]
in that behalf, shall summon the party accused, and also the witnesses
on either side, and shall examine into the matter of fact, and upon due
proof made thereof, either by the voluntary confession of the party or
by the oath of one or more credible witness or witnesses, or otherwise,
(which oath such justice or justices is or are hereby authorized to administer,) shall convict the offender, and adjudge the penalty for such
offence.

V. And be it further enacted, That if any person shall be summoned Penalty on
as a witness to give evidence before such justice or justices, either on witnesses
the part of the prosecutor or the person accused, and shall neglect or ing, 40s.
refuse to appear at the time or place to be for that purpose appointed,
without a reasonable excuse for such his neglect or refusal, to be allowed by such justice or justices, then such person shall forfeit for every
such offence, the sum of forty shillings, to be levied and paid in such
manner and by such means as are directed for recovery of other penalties under this act.

VI. And be it further enacted, That the justice or justices before
whom any offender shall be convicted as aforesaid, shall cause the said
conviction to be made out, in the manner and form following : (that is
say,)

'Be it remembered, That on the   day of   Form of
'in the year of our Lord   conviction.
'A. B. having appeared before me [or, us] one [or more] of His
'Majesty's justices of the peace [as the case may be] for the county,
'riding, city, or place, [as the case may be] and due proof having
'been made upon oath by one or more credible witness or witnesses,
'or by confession of the party [as the case may be] is convicted
'of   [specifying the offence:] Given under
'my hand and seal, [or, our hands and seals] the day and year
'aforesaid.'

Which conviction the said justice or justices shall cause to be returned Returnable
to the then next general quarter sessions of the peace of the county, to the
riding, city, or place where such conviction was made, to be filed by Quarter
the clerk of the peace, to remain and be kept among the records of such Sessions.
county, riding, city, or place.

VII. Provided always, and be it further enacted, That it shall be law- Copies
ful for any clerk of the peace for any county, riding, city, or place, and of convictions.

APPENDIX. he is hereby required, upon application made to him by any person or persons for that purpose, to cause a copy or copies of any conviction or convictions filed by him under the directions of this act, to be forth-with delivered to such person or persons upon payment of one shilling for every such copy.

Recovery and appli-cation of penalties.

VIII. And be it further enacted, That the pecuniary penalties and forfeitures hereby incurred and made payable upon any conviction against this act, shall be forthwith paid by the person convicted as fol-lows : one moiety of the forfeiture to the informer, and the other moiety to the poor of the parish or place where the offence shall be committed: and in case such person shall refuse or neglect to pay the same, or to give sufficient security to the satisfaction of such justice or justices to prosecute any appeal against such conviction, such justice or justices shall, by warrant under his or their hand and seal, or hands and seals, cause the same to be levied by distress and sale of the offender's goods and chattels, together with all costs and charges attending such distress and sale, returning the overplus (if any) to the owner ; and which said warrant of distress the said justice or justices shall cause to be made out in the manner and form following ; (that is to say,)

' To the constable, Headborough, or Tithingman of

Form of the war-rant of dis-tress.

' Whereas A. B. of   in the county
' of   is this day convicted before me [or, us] one [or
' more] of His Majesty's justices of the peace [as the case may be
' for the county of   [or, for the
' Riding of the county of York,] or for the town, liberty, or district
' of   [as the case may be] upon the
' oath of   or   a credi-
' ble witness or witnesses [or, by confession of the party, as the
' case may be] for that the said A. B. hath [here set forth the of
' fence] contrary to the statute in that case made and provided, by
' reason whereof the said A. B. hath forfeited the sum of
' to be distributed as herein is mentioned, which he hath refused to
' pay: These are therefore, in His Majesty's name, to command you
' to levy the said sum of   by distress of the
' goods and chattels of him the said A. B. and if within the space
' of five days next after such distress by you taken, the said sum.
' together with the reasonable charges of taking the same, shall no'
' be paid, then that you do sell the said goods and chattels so by

[533]

' you distrained, and out of the money arising by such sale, that
' you do pay one half of the said sum of
' to   of   who informe
' me [or, us, as the case shall be] of the said offence, and the othe
' half of the said sum of   to the overseer of the poor
' of the parish, township, or place where the offence was committed
' to be employed for the benefit of such poor, returning the overplus
' (if any) upon demand, to the said A. B. the reasonable charges of
' taking, keeping, and selling the said distress being first deduc'
' ed ; and if sufficient distress cannot be found of the goods and
' chattels of the said A. B. whereon to levy the said sum
' of   that then you certify the same to me
' [or, us, as the case shall be] together with this warrant. Given
' under my hand and seal, [or, our hands and seals] the
' day of   - in the year of our Lord

IX. And be it further enacted, That it shall be lawful for such jus- tice or justices to order such offender to be detained in safe custody until return may conveniently be had and made to such warrant of dis- tress, unless the party so convicted shall give sufficient security, to the satisfaction of such justice or justices, for his appearance before the said justice or justices, on such day as shall be appointed by the said justice or justices for the day of the return of the said warrant or dis- tress (such day not exceeding five days from the taking of such securi- ty ;) which security the said justice or justices is and are hereby em- powered to take by way of recognisance or otherwise.

X. And be it further enacted, That if upon such return no sufficient distress can be had, then and in such case the said justice or justices shall and may commit such offender to the common jail or house of cor- rection of the county, riding, division, or place where the offence shall be committed, for the space of three calendar months, unless the money forfeited shall be sooner paid, or unless or until such offender thinking himself or herself aggrieved by such conviction, shall give notice to the informer that he or she intends to appeal to the justices of the peace at the next general quarter sessions of the peace to be holden for the county, riding, or place wherein the offence shall be committed, and shall enter into recognisance before some justice or justices, with two sufficient sureties conditioned to try such appeal, and to abide the or- der of and pay such costs as shall be awarded by the justices at such quarter sessions (which notice of appeal, being not less than eight days before the trial thereof, such person so aggrieved is hereby empowered to give :) and the said justices at such sessions, upon due proof of such notice being given as aforesaid, and of the entering into such recogni- sance, shall hear and finally determine the causes and matters of such appeal in a summary way, and award such costs to the parties appeal- ing or appealed against as they the said justices shall think proper ; and the determination of such quarter sessions shall be final, binding, and conclusive, to all intents and purposes.

XI. And be it further enacted, That no person shall be disabled from being a witness in any prosecution for any offence against the act, by reason of his being an inhabitant of the parish wherein such offence was committed.

XII. Provided always, That no proceedings to be had, touching the conviction or convictions of any offender or offenders against this act, shall be quashed for want of form, or be removed by writ of certiorari or any other writ or process whatsoever, into any of His Majesty's courts of record at Westminster.

XIII. And be it further enacted, That if any action or suit shall be commenced against any person or persons for any thing done or acted in pursuance of this act, then and in every such case such action or suit shall be commenced or prosecuted within three calender months after the fact committed, and not afterwards ;. and the same and every such action or suit shall be brought within the county where the fact was committed, and not elsewhere ; and the defendant or defendants in every such action or suit shall and may plead the general issue, and give this act and the special matter in evidence at any trial to be had thereupon, and that the same was done in pursuance and by the autho- rity of this act ; and if the same shall appear to have been so done, or

APPENDIX if any such action or suit shall be brought after the time limited for bringing the same, or be brought or laid in any other place than as afore-mentioned, then the jury shall find for the defendant or defendants : or if the plaintiff or plaintiffs shall become nonsuit, or discontinue his, her, or their action after the defendant or defendants shall have appeared, or if upon demurrer judgment shall be given against Treble the plaintiff or plaintiffs, the defendant or defendants shall and may costs. recover treble costs, and have the like remedy for the recovery thereof [535] as any defendant or defendants hath or have in any other cases by law.

Statutes as By 17 Geo. 3. c. 30. s. 1, made perpetual by 27 Geo. 3. c. 16. to bills and " Whereas the said act (meaning 15 Geo. 3. c. 51.) hath been attend- notes un- " ed with very salutary effects, and in case the provisions therein con- der £5. " tained were extended to a further sum, (but yet without prejudice to " the convenience arising to the public from the negotiation of promis- " sory notes and inland bills of exchange for the remittance of money, " in discharge of *any balance of account or other debt,*) the good pur- " poses of the said act would be further advanced ;" Be it therefore enacted, That all promissory or other notes, bills of exchange, or drafts, or 'undertakings in writing, being negotiable or transferrable for the payment of *twenty shillings, or any sum of money above that sum,* and *less than five pounds,* or which twenty shillings, or above that sum, and *less than five pounds, shall remain undischarged,* and which shall be issued, within that part of Great Britain called England, at any time after the first of January, 1778, shall specify the names and places of abode of the persons respectively to whom, or to whose order, the same shall be made payable, and shall bear date before or at the time of drawing or issuing thereof, and not on a day subsequent thereto, and shall be made payable within the space of twenty-one days next after the day of the date thereof ; and shall not be transferrable or negotiabl after the time thereby limited for payment thereof ; and that every in- dorsement to be made thereon shall be made before the expiration of that time, and bear date at, or not before the time of making thereof : and shall specify the name and place of abode of the person or person to whom, or to whose order the money contained in every such note. bill, draft, or undertaking is to be paid ; and that the signing of every such note, bill, draft, or undertaking, and also of every such indorse ment, shall be attested by one subscribing witness at the least ; and which said notes, bills of exchange, or drafts, or undertakings in wri ting, may be made or drawn in words to the purport or effect as set out in the schedule hereunto annexed, No. 1 and 2. And that all promissory or other notes, bills of exchange, or drafts, or undertakings in writing being negotiable or transferrable, for the payment of twenty shillings or any sum of money above that sum, or less than five pounds ; or which twenty shillings, or above that sum, and less than five pound [536] shall remain undischarged, and which shall be issued within that part of Great Britain called England, at any time after the said 1st day January, 1778, in any other manner than as aforesaid ; and also every indorsement on any such note, bill, draft, or undertaking, to be ne- tiated under this act, other than as aforesaid, shall, and the same hereby declared to be absolutely void ; and the person publishing. tering or negotiating them, is subject to the penalty of £20.

SCHEDULE.

No. 1.

(*Place*)　(*Day*)　(*Month*)　(*Year*)

"Twenty-one days after date, I promise to pay to A. B. of (*place*) or
"his order the sum of　　　　for value received by
"Witness E. F.　　　　　　　　　"C. D."

And the indorsement, toties quoties.

(*Day*)　(*Month*)　(*Year*)

"Pay the contents to G. G. of (*place*) or his order.
"Witness I. K.　　　　　　　"A. B."

No 2.

(*Place*)　(*Day*)　(*Month*)　(*Year*)

"Twenty-one days after date, pay to A. B. of (*place*) or his order the
"sum of　　　　value received, as advised by
"To E. F. of (*place*)　　　　"C. D."
"Witness G. H.

And the indorsement, toties quoties.

(*Day*)　(*Month*)　(*Year*)

"Pay the contents to I. H. of (*place*) or his order.
"Witness L. M.　　　　　　　"A. B."

By 37 Geo. 3. c. 28, it is enacted, "That all promissory notes, and
"other notes for payment of money, which since the 2d day of March,
"one thousand seven hundred and ninety-seven, have been, or which
"hereafter shall be issued by the Governor and Company of the Bank Exceptions
"of England, payable to bearer, notwithstanding the same shall have in favour
"been, or shall be made and issued for the payment of any sum of mo- of Bank of
"ney under the sum of five pounds, shall be good and valid in the law, England.
"to all intents and purposes, in like manner as if the same had been
"made and issued for the sum of five pounds or upwards; and no per-
"son concerned or who has acted, or who shall or may be concerned [537]
"or act in, the making, uttering, publishing, or negotiating such notes,
"shall be subject or liable to any penalty or forfeiture whatsoever in
"respect thereof."

By 37 Geo. 3.ᵃ c. 32.—Whereas it is expedient that the said acts Exceptions
(15th and 17th Geo. 3.) should be suspended for a certain time, so far in favour of
as the same may relate to any notes, drafts, or undertakings made pay- notes for
able on demand;ᵃ Be it therefore enacted, that the said acts, so far as 20 shillings,
payable on demand.

ᵃ Continued by 37 Geo. 3. c 61. s. 2. and　tinued till two years after the expiration of
120.　38 Geo. 3. c. 7.　39 Geo. 3.　43　the restrictions, upon payments in cash
Geo. 3. c. 1.　44 Geo. 3. c. 1. s. 4.　45　by the Bank of England, by 56 Geo. 3.
Geo. 3. c. 25.　55 Geo. 3. c. 6, and con-　c. 21.

APPENDIX. the same relate to the making void of promissory notes, or drafts, or undertakings in writing, payable on demand to the bearer thereof,[b] for any sum of money less than the sum of five pounds in the whole ; and also to restrain the publishing or uttering and *negotiating* of any such notes, drafts, or undertakings as aforesaid, shall, after the second day of March, one thousand seven hundred and ninety seven, be, and the same are hereby declared to be, to all intents and purposes, suspended until the first day of May next.

Mode of enforcing payment of notes for 20 shillings.

Sect. 3. And be it further enacted, " That if any person liable to the " payment of any such notes, drafts, or undertakings in writing, as " may be issued in pursuance of this act, shall neglect or fail to make " full payment in money of the sum or sums for which such notes, " drafts, or undertakings in writing, shall be respectively given or is- " sued or so much thereof as shall be or remain due thereon respec- " tively, by the space of three[c] days after demand thereof, made by the " holder or holders of such notes, drafts, or undertakings in writing, it " shall and may be lawful for any one or more of His Majesty's justices " of the peace for the county, riding, city, division or place, where the " person or persons respectively refusing so to pay any of such notes, " drafts, or undertakings in writing as last aforesaid, shall or may hap- " pen to be or reside, and such justice or justices is or are hereby re- " quired, upon a complaint made by the holder or holders thereof, to

[538] " summon the person or persons against whom such complaint shall be " made, and after his, her, or their appearances, or in default thereof, " upon due proof upon oath (and which oath such justice or justices is " or are hereby empowered to administer) of such summons or warning " having been given, such justice or justices shall proceed to hear and " determine the said complaint, and award such sum to be paid by the " person or persons respectively liable to the payment of every such " note, draft, or undertaking in writing, to the holder or holders there- " of, as shall appear to such justice or justices to be due thereon, to- " gether with such a sum for costs, not exceeding the sum of twenty " shillings, as to such justice or justices shall seem meet ; and if any " person or persons shall refuse or neglect to pay or satisfy such sum " of money, as upon such complaint as aforesaid shall be adjudged, " upon the same being demanded, such justice or justices shall, by war- " rant under, his or their hand and seal, or hands and seals, cause the " same to be levied by distress and sale of the goods of the party so ne- " glecting or refusing as aforesaid, together with all costs and charges " attending such distress and sale, returning the overplus, (if any, to " the owner."

[b] Therefore notes payable otherwise than on demand to the bearer thereof, are still invalid, unless framed according to the 1[?] and 17th Geo. 3.

[c] Extended to seven days by the 37th Geo. 3. c, 61. s. 2.

STAMP ACT.

55 Geo. 3. c. 184.

An Act for repealing the Stamp Duties on Deeds, Law Proceedings, and other written or printed Instruments, and the Duties on Fire Insurances, and on Legacies and Successions to personal Estate upon Intestacies, now payable in Great Britain; and for granting other Duties in lieu thereof.

N. B. The new duties to commence and take place from and after the 31st August, 1815.

Section X. And be it further enacted, That, from and after the passing of this act, all instruments for or upon which any stamp or stamps shall have been used of an improper denomination or rate of duty, but of equal or greater value in the whole with or than the stamp or stamps which ought regularly to have been used thereon, shall nevertheless be deemed valid and effectual in the law; except in cases where the stamp or stamps used on such instruments shall have been specially appropriated to any other instrument, by having its name on the face thereof.

Instruments having wrong stamps, but of sufficient value, valid.

[539] Exception.

XI. And be it further enacted, That if, any person shall make, sign, or issue, or cause to be made, signed or issued, or shall accept or pay, or cause or permit to be accepted or paid, any bill of exchange, draft or order, or promissory note for the payment of money, liable to any of the duties imposed by this act, without the same being duly stamped for denoting the duty hereby charged thereon, he, she, or they shall, for every such bill, draft, order or note, forfeit the sum of fifty pounds.

Making, &c. bills of exchange, &c. not duly stamped.

Penalty.

XII. And be it further enacted, That if any person or persons shall make and issue, or cause to be made and issued, any bill of exchange, draft or order, or promissory note for the payment of money, at any time after date or sight, which shall bear date subsequent to the day on which it shall be issued, so that it shall not in fact become payable in two months, if made payable after date or in sixty days, if made payable after sight, next after the day on which it shall be issued, unless the same shall be stamped for denoting the duty hereby imposed on a bill of exchange and promissory note for the payment of money at any time exceeding two months after date, or sixty days after sight, he, she or they shall, for every such bill, draft, order or note, forfeit the sum of one hundred pounds.

Post dating bills of exchange,&c.

Penalty.

XIII. And, for the more effectually preventing of frauds and evasions of the duties hereby granted on bills of exchange, drafts or orders for the payment of money, under colour of the exemption in favour of drafts or orders upon bankers or persons acting as bankers, contained in the schedule hereunto annexed, Be it further enacted, That if any person or persons shall, after the thirty-first day of August, one thousand eight hundred and fifteen, make and issue, or cause to be made and issued, any bill, draft or order, for the payment of money to the

Issuing unstamped drafts on bankers, without specifying placewhere issued, or if post dated.

APPENDIX. bearer on demand, upon any banker or bankers, or any person or persons acting as a banker or bankers, which shall be dated on any day subsequent to the day on which it shall be issued, or which shall not truly specify and express the place where it shall be issued, or which

[540] shall not in every respect fall within the said exemption, unless the same shall be duly stamped as a bill of exchange, according to this act, the person or persons so offending shall, for every such bill, draft or

Penalty. order, forfeit the sum of one hundred pounds ; and if any person or per-

Receiving. sons shall knowingly receive or take any such bill, draft, or order, in

&c. such payment of or as a security for the sum therein mentioned, he, she, or

drafts. they shall, for every such bill, draft or order, forfeit the sum of twenty

Penalty. pounds ; and if any banker or bankers, or any person or persons acting

Bankers as a banker, upon whom any such bill, draft or order, shall be drawn,

paying shall pay, or cause or permit to be paid, the sum of money therein ex-

them. pressed, or any part thereof, knowing the same to be post dated, or knowing that the place where it was issued is not truly specified and set forth therein, or knowing that the same does not in any other respect fall within the said exemption, then the banker or bankers, or per-

Penalty. son or persons so offending, shall, for every such bill, draft or order, forfeit the sum of one hundred pounds, and moreover shall not be allowed the money so paid or any part thereof, in account against the person or persons by or for whom such bill, draft, or order shall be drawn, or his, hers or their executors or administrators, or his, her, or their assignees or creditors, in case of bankruptcy or insolvency, or any other person or persons claiming under him, her, or them.

Promissory XIV. And be it further enacted, That, from and after the thirty-first

notes to day of August, one thousand eight hundred and fifteen, it shall be law-

bearer on ful for any banker or bankers, or other person or persons, who shall have

demand, not made and issued any promissory notes for the payment to the bearer on

exceeding demand, of any sum of money not exceeding one hundred pounds each,

£100, re-is- duly stamped according to the directions of this act, to re-issue the same

sued by ori- from time to time, after payment thereof, as often as he, she or they,

nal makers shall think fit, without being liable to pay further duty in respect

without fur- thereof; and that all promissory notes, so as to be re-issued as afore-

ther duty. said, shall be good and valid, and as available in the law, to all intents and purposes, as they were upon the first issuing thereof.

Such notes XV. And be it further enacted, That no promissory note for the pay-

not liable ment to the bearer on demand, of any sum of money not exceeding one

to further hundred pounds, which shall have been made and issued by any banker

duty, tho' or other persons in partnership, and for which the proper stamp duty

re-issued by shall have been once paid according to the provisions of this act, shall

certain per- be deemed liable to the payment of any further duty although the same

sons not shall be re-issued by and as the note of some only of the persons who

strictly the originally made and issued the same, or by and as the note of any one

original ma- or more of the persons who originally made and issued the same, and

kers. any other person or persons in partnership with him or them jointly;

[541] nor although such note if made payable at any other than the place where drawn, shall be re-issued with any alteration therein only of the house or place at which the same shall have been at first made payable.

Notes re- XVI. And be it further enacted, That all promissory notes for the

issuable un- payment to the bearer on demand, of any sum of money, which shall

der 48 Gec- have been actually and *bona fide* issued and in circulation, before or

3. c. 149, or upon the said thirty-first day of August, one thousand eight hundred and

53 G. 3. c. 108, to continue re-issuable till end of three years from date.

fifteen, duly stamped according to the aforesaid act of the forty-eighth APPENDIX.
year of His Majesty's reign, and which shall then be re-issuable within
the intent and meaning of that act, or of an act passed in the fifty-third
year of His Majesty's reign, for altering, explaining and amending the
said former act, with regard to the duties on re-issuable promissory notes,
shall continue to be re-issuable until the expiration of three years from
the date thereof respectively, but not afterwards, without payment of
any further duty for the same ; and if any banker or bankers, or other
person or persons, shall at any time after the said thirty-first day of In what
August, issue or cause to be issued for the first time, any promissory case bank-
note for the payment of money to the bearer on demand, bearing date ers issuing
before or upon that day, he, she, or they shall, for every such promis- promissory
sory note, forfeit the sum of fifty pounds.   notes.

Penalty.

XVII. Provided always, and, in regard that certain bankers in Scot- Notes with
land have issued promissory notes for the payment to the bearer on printed
demand, of a sum not exceeding two pounds and two shillings each, dates prior
with the dates thereof printed therein, and many such notes have been 31st, 1813,
but recently issued for the first time, although they may appear by the re-issuable
date to be of more than three years' standing, Be it further enacted, till August
That all such promissory notes as last mentioned, which shall have been 48 Geo. 3.
actually and *bona fide* issued and in circulation before or upon the said c. 149.
thirty-first day of August, one thousand eight hundred and fifteen, duly
stamped according to the said act of the forty-eighth year of His Majesty's reign, and which shall bear a printed date prior to the thirty-
first day of August, one thousand eight hundred and thirteen, shall
continue to be re-issuable until the thirty-first day of August, one thou- [542]
sand eight hundred and sixteen, but not afterwards, without payment Issuing
of any further duty for the same ; and if any banker or bankers, or notes with
other person or persons, shall at any time after the said thirty-first day printed
of August, one thousand eight hundred and fifteen, issue or cause to be dates for
issued, for the first time, any such promissory note, bearing a printed first time.
date prior to the said thirty-first day of August, one thousand eight
hundred and thirteen, he or they shall, for every promissory note so
issued, forfeit the sum of fifty pounds.   Penalty.

XVIII. And be it further enacted, That from and after the thirty-first Issuing
day of August, one thousand eight hundred and fifteen, it shall not be notes in fu-
lawful for any banker or bankers, or other person or persons, to issue ture with
any promissory note for the payment of money to the bearer on demand, dates.
liable to any of the duties imposed by this act, with the date printed
therein ; and if any banker or bankers, or other person or persons, shall
issue or cause to be issued any such promissory note with the date printed therein, he or they shall, for every promissory note so issued, forfeit the sum of fifty pounds.   Penalty.

XIX. And be it further enacted, That all promissory notes hereby al- Notes re-
lowed to continue re-issuable for a limited period, but not afterwards, issuable for
shall upon the payment thereof at any time after the expiration of such riod can-
period, and all promissory notes, bills of exchange, drafts or orders for celled on
money, not hereby allowed to be re-issued, shall, upon any payment payment af-
thereof, be deemed and taken respectively to be thereupon wholly dis- and notes
charged, vacated and satisfied, and shall be no longer negotiable or not re-issu-
available in any manner whatsoever, but shall be forthwith cancelled able, can-
by the person or persons paying the same ; and if any person or per- celled im-
sons shall re-issue, or cause or permit to be re-issued, any promissory on payment

APPENDIX. note hereby allowed to be re-issued for a limited period as aforesaid, at
any time after the expiration of the term or period allowed for that pur-
Re-issuing pose ; or if any person or persons shall re-issue or cause or permit to be
notes, &c. re-issued any promissory note, bill of exchange, draft or order for money, not hereby allowed to be re-issued at any time after the payment
thereof ; or if any person or persons paying or causing to be paid any
Not can- such note, bill, draft or order as aforesaid, shall refuse or neglect to
celling cancel the same, according to the directions of this act, then and in
notes, &c. either of those cases, the person or persons so offending, shall, for every
Penalty. such note, bill, draft or order as aforesaid, forfeit the sum of fifty pounds;
[543] and in case of any such note, bill, draft, or order, being re-issued contrary
Re-issuing to the intent and meaning of this act, the person or persons re-issuing
contrary to the same, or causing or permtiting the same to be re-issued, shall also
act, further be answerable and accountable to His Majesty, his heirs and successors,
duty. for a further duty in respect of every such note, bill, draft, or order, of
such and the same amount as would have been chargeable thereon, in
case the same had been then issued for the first time, and so from time
to time as often as the same shall be so re-issued ; which further duty
shall and may be sued for and recovered accordingly, as a debt to His
Taking Majesty, his heirs and successors ; and if any person or persons shall
notes, &c. receive or take any such note, bill draft, or order, in payment of or as
re-issued a security for the sum therein expressed, knowing the same to be re-
contrary to issued contrary to the intent and meaning of this act, he, she, or they
act. shall, for every such note, bill, draft, or order, forfeit the sum of twen-
Penalty. ty pounds.

Notes and XX. And be it further enacted, That all promissory notes and Bank
bills of post bills which shall be issued by the Governor and Company of the
Bank of Bank of England, from and after the said thirty-first day of August,
England one thousand eight hundred and fifteen, shall be freed and exempted
exempt from all the duties hereby granted ; and that it shall be lawful for the said
from stamp Governor and Company to re-issue any of their notes after payment
duty. thereof, as often as they shall think fit.

XXI. And be it further enacted, That the composition payable by
the said Governor and Company of the Bank of England for the stamp
duties on their promissory notes and Bank post bills, under the afore-
48 Geo. 3. said act of the forty-eighth year of his Majesty's reign. shall cease from
c. 149. s. the fifth day of April last ; and that the said Governor and Company
15, made to shall deliver to the said commissioners of stamps, within one calend-
cease. month after the passing of this act, and afterwards on the first day of
May in every year whilst the present stamp duties still remain in force,
a just and true account, verified by the oath of their chief accountant,
Account of of the amount or value of all their promissory notes and Bank post bill-
notes, &c. in circulation, or some given day in every week, for the space of three
years preceding the sixth day of April in the year in which the account
shall be delivered, together with the average amount or value thereof
Bank of according to such account; and that the said Governor and Company
England to shall pay into the hands of the Receiver-General of the Stamp Duties
pay compo- in Great Britain, as a composition for the duties which would otherwise
sition for have been payable for their promissory notes and Bank post bills issued
duties on within the year, reckoning from the fifth day of April preceding the de-
bills and livery of the said account, the sum of three thousand five hundred
notes. pounds for every million, and after that rate for half a million, but not
[544] for a less sum than half a million, of the said average amount or value
of their said notes and Bank post bills in circulation: and that one ha-

part of the sum so to be ascertained as aforesaid for each year's com- APPENDIX.
position, shall be paid on the first day of October, and the other half
on the first day of April next after the delivery of such account as
aforesaid.

XXII. Provided always, and be it further enacted, That upon the Composi-
said Governor and Company resuming their payments in cash, a new tion made
arrangement for the composition for the stamp duties, payable on when Bank
their promissory notes and Bank post bills, shall be submitted to Par- resumes cash pay-
liament. ments.

XXIII. And be it further enacted, That from and after the thirty- The Bank
first day of August, one thousand eight hundred and fifteen, it shall be and Royal
lawful for the Governor and Company of the Bank of Scotland, and the Bank of
Royal Bank of Scotland, and the British Linen Company in Scotland Scotland, and British
respectively, to issue their promissory notes for the sums of one pound, Linen Com-
one guinea, two pounds and two guineas, payable to the bearer on de- pany, may
mand, on unstamped paper, in the same manner as they were author- issue small
ized to do by the aforesaid act of the forty-eighth year of His Majesty's notes on
reign; they the said Governor and Company of the Bank of Scotland, unstamped paper, ac-
and the Royal Bank of Scotland, and British Linen Company, respec- counting for
tively giving such security, and keeping and producing true accounts of duties, 48
all the notes so to be issued by them respectively, and accounting for Geo. 3. c.
and paying the several duties payable in respect of such notes, in such 149. s. 16.
and the same manner, in all respects, as is and are prescribed and required by the said last-mentioned act, with regard to the notes thereby
allowed to be issued by them on unstamped paper, and also to re-issue
such promissory notes respectively, from time to time after the payment
thereof, as often as they shall think fit.

XXIV. And be it further enacted, That from and after the tenth day Re-issua-
of October, one thousand eight hundred and fifteen, it shall not be law- ble notes
ful for any banker or bankers, or other person or persons (except the issued by
Governor and Company of the Bank of England,) to issue any promis- bankers or others with-
sory notes for money payable to the bearer on demand, hereby charged out license.
with a duty and allowed to be re-issued as aforesaid, without taking Regula-
out a license yearly for that purpose; which license shall be granted tions re-
by two or more of the said commissioners of stamps for the time being, specting li-
or by some person authorized in that behalf by the said commissioners, censes.
or the major part of them, on payment of the duty charged thereon in [545]
the Schedule hereunto annexed; and a separate and distinct license
shall be taken out, for or in respect of every town or place where any
such promissory notes shall be issued by, or by any agent or agents for
or on account of, any banker or bankers or other person or persons;
and every such license shall specify the proper name or names and
place or places of abode of the person or persons, or the proper name
and description of any body corporate, to whom the same shall be
granted, and also the name of the town or place where, and the name
of the bank, as well as the partnership, or other name, style or firm
under which such notes are to be issued; and where any such license
shall be granted to persons in partnership, the same shall specify and
set forth the names and places of abode of all the persons concerned in
the partnership, whether all their names shall appear on the promissory notes to be issued by them, or not; and in default thereof, such
license shall be absolutely void; and every such license which shall be
granted between the tenth day of October and the eleventh day of No-

APPENDIX. *Inland BILL, &c.—continued.*   £ *s.* *d.*

Inland BILL, Draft, or Order for the payment of any ⎫ *The same duty as*
   sum of money though not made payable to the bearer, ⎪ *on a bill of ex-*
   or to order, if the same shall be delivered to the ⎬ *change for the*
   payee, or some person on his or her behalf - - ⎭ *like sum paya-*
                                                 ble to bearer
                                                 or order.

Inland BILL, Draft, or Order for the payment of any ⎫ *The same duty as*
   sum of money, weekly, monthly, or at any other ⎪ *on a bill paya-*
   stated periods, if made payable to the bearer, or to ⎪ *ble to bearer or*
   order, or if delivered to the payee, or some person on ⎬ *order on de-*
   his or her behalf, where the total amount of the mo- ⎪ *mand for a sum*
   ney thereby made payable shall be specified therein, ⎭ *equal to such*
   or can be ascertained therefrom - - - - *total amount.*

                                                       ⎧ *The same duty as*
And where the total amount of the money thereby ⎫ *on a bill on de-*
   made payable shall be indefinite - - - ⎬ *mand for the*
                                                   ⎩ *sum therein ex-*
                                                      pressed only.

And the following instruments shall be deemed and
   taken to be inland bills, drafts, or orders for the payment of money within the intent and meaning of this
   schedule ; *videlicet,*

All drafts or orders for the payment of any sum of money by a bill or promissory note, or for the delivery
   of any such bill or note in payment or satisfaction of
   any sum of money; where such drafts or orders shall
[549]   require the payment or delivery to be made to the
   bearer, or to order, or shall be delivered to the payee,
   or some person on his or her behalf.

All receipts given by any banker or bankers, or other
   person or persons, for money received, which shall
   entitle, or be intended to entitle, the person or persons paying the money, or the bearer of such receipts, to receive the like sum from any third person
   or persons.

. And all bills, drafts, or orders, for the payment of any
   sum of money out of any particular fund which may
   or may not be available, or upon any condition or
   contingency which may or may not be performed or
   happen, if the same shall be made payable to the
   bearer, or to order, or if the same shall be delivered to the payee or some person on his or her
   behalf.

Foreign BILL of EXCHANGE (or Bill of Exchange ⎧ *The same duty as*
   drawn in but payable out of Great Britain) if drawn ⎨ *on an inland bill*
   singly and not in a set. ⎩ *of the same*
                                                      amount and tenor.

Foreign BILLS of Exchange, drawn in sets according to
   the custom of merchants, for every bill of each set,

BILL—*continued.*

	£	*s.*	*d.* Appendix.
where the sum made payable thereby shall not exceed 100*l.* - - - - - - - - -	0	1	6
And where it shall exceed 100*l.* and not exceed 200*l.* - - - - - - - - -	0	3	0
And where it shall exceed 200*l.* and not exceed 500*l.* - - - - - - - - -	0	4	0
And where it shall exceed 500*l.* and not exceed 1,000*l.* - - - - - - - - -	0	5	0
And where it shall exceed 1,000*l.* and not exceed 2,000*l.* - - - - - - - - -	0	7	6
And where it shall exceed 2,000*l.* and not exceed 3,000*l.* - - - - - - - - -	0	10	0
And where it shall exceed 3,000*l.* - - - - -	0	15	0

Exemptions from the preceding and all other Stamp Duties.   [550]

All bills of exchange, or Bank post bills, issued by the Governor and Company of the Bank of England.

All bills, orders, remittance bills, and remittance certificate, drawn by commissioned officers, masters, and surgeons in the navy, or by any commissioner or commissioners of the navy, under the authority of the act passed in the 35th year of His Majesty's reign, for the more expeditious Payment of the Wages and Pay of certain Officers belonging to the Navy.

35 Geo. 3. c. 94.

All bills drawn pursuant to any former act or acts of Parliament by the commissioners of the navy or by the commissioners for victualling the navy, or by the commissioners for managing the transport service, and for taking care of sick and wounded seamen, upon, and payable by the treasurer of the navy.

All drafts or orders for the payment of any sum of money to the bearer on demand, and drawn upon any banker or bankers, or any person or persons acting as a banker, who shall reside or transact the business of a banker, within ten miles of the place where such drafts or orders shall be issued, provided such place shall be specified in such drafts or orders ; and provided the same shall bear date on or before the day on which the same shall be issued ; and provided the same do not direct the payment to be made by bills or promissory notes.

All bills, for the pay and allowances of His Majesty's land forces, or for other expenditures liable to be charged in the public regimental or district accounts, which shall be drawn according to the forms now prescribed or hereafter to be prescribed by His Majesty's orders, by the paymasters of regiments or corps, or by the chief paymaster, or deputy paymaster, and accountant of the army depot, or by the pay-

[551]

BILL—_continued._   £ _s._

masters of recruiting districts, or by the paymasters
of detachments, or by the officer or officers authorized
to perform the duties of paymastership during a va-
cancy, or the absence, suspension, or incapacity of
any such as aforesaid; save and except such bills as
shall be drawn in favour of contractors or others,
who furnish bread or forage to His Majesty's troops,
and who by their contracts or agreements shall be
liable to pay the stamp duties on the bills given in
payment for the articles supplied by them.

PROMISSORY NOTE for the payment, _to the bearer on
demand,_ of any sum of money.

	£	s.	d.
Not exceeding one pound and one shilling	0	0	5
Exceeding 1l. 1s. and not exceeding 2l. 2s.	0	0	10
Exceeding 2l. 2s. and not exceeding 5l. 5s.	0	1	3
Exceeding 5l. 5s. and not exceeding 10l.	0	1	9
Exceeding 10l. and not exceeding 20l.	0	2	0
Exceeding 20l. and not exceeding 30l.	0	3	0
Exceeding 30l. and not exceeding 50l.	0	5	0
Exceeding 50l. and not exceeding 100l.	0	8	6

Which said _notes may be re-issued after payment
thereof,_ as often as shall be thought fit.

PROMISSORY NOTE for the payment, _in any other
manner than to the bearer on demand, but not exceeding two months after date,_ or sixty days after sight,
of any sum of money,

	£	s.	d.
Amounting to 40s. and not exceeding 5l. 5s.	0	1	0
Exceeding 5l. 5s. and not exceeding 20l.	0	1	6
Exceeding 20l. and not exceeding 30l.	0	2	0
Exceeding 30l. and not exceeding 50l.	0	2	6
Exceeding 50l. and not exceeding 100l.	0	3	6

These notes are _not to be re-issued_ after being
once paid.

[552] **PROMISSORY NOTE** for the payment _either to the
bearer on demand,_ or in any other manner than to the
bearer on demand, but _not exceeding two months after
date,_ or sixty days after sight, of any sum of money,

	£	s.	d.
Exceeding 100l. and not exceeding 200l.	0	4	6
Exceeding 200l. and not exceeding 300l.	0	5	0
Exceeding 300l. and not exceeding 500l.	0	6	0
Exceeding 500l. and not exceeding 1,000l.	0	8	6
Exceeding 1,000l. and not exceeding 2,000l.	0	12	6
Exceeding 2,000l. and not exceeding 3,000l.	0	15	0
Exceeding 3,000l.	1	5	0

These notes are _not to be re-issued_ after being once
paid.

PROMISSORY NOTE for the payment to the bearer or
otherwise, at any time _exceeding two months after date,_
or sixty days after sight, of any sum of money,

	£	s.	d.
Amounting to 40s. and not exceeding 5l. 5s.	0	1	
Exceeding 5l. 5s. and not exceeding 20l.	0	2	0

PROMISSORY NOTE—*continued.*

	£	s.	d.
Exceeding 20*l*. and not exceeding 30*l*. - - -	0	2	6
Exceeding 30*l*. and not exceeding 50*l*. - - -	0	3	6
Exceeding 50*l*. and not exceeding 100*l*. - - -	0	4	6
Exceeding 100*l*. and not exceeding 200*l*. - - -	0	5	0
Exceeding 200*l*. and not exceeding 300*l*. - - -	0	6	0
Exceeding 300*l*. and not exceeding 500*l*. - - -	0	8	6
Exceeding 500*l*. and not exceeding 1,000*l*. - -	0	12	6
Exceeding 1,000*l*. and not exceeding 2,000*l*. - -	0	15	0
Exceeding 2,000*l*. and not exceeding 3,000*l*. - -	1	5	0
Exceeding 3,000*l*. - - - - - - -	1	10	0

These notes are *not to be re-issued* after being once paid

PROMISSORY NOTE for the payment of any sum of money by instalments, or for the payment of several sums of money at different days or times, so that the whole of the money to be paid shall be definite and certain

The same duty as on a promissory note, payable in less than two months after date for a sum equal to the whole amount of the money to be paid.

[553]

And the following instruments shall be deemed and taken to be promissory notes, within the intent and meaning of this Schedule ; viz.

All notes, promising the payment of any sum or sums of money out of any particular fund, which may or may not be available ; or upon any condition or contingency, which may or may not be performed or happen ; if the same shall be made payable to the bearer, or to order, and if the same shall be definite and certain, and not amount in the whole to twenty pounds.

And all receipts for money deposited in any bank, or in the hands of the banker or bankers, which shall contain any agreement or memorandum, importing that interest shall be paid for the money so deposited.

Exemptions from the Duties on Promissory Notes.

All notes, promising the payment of any sum or sums of money out of any particular fund, which may or may not be available ; or upon any condition or contingency, which may or may not be performed or happen ; where the same shall not be made payable to the bearer or to order, and also where the same shall be made payable to the bearer or to order, if the same shall amount to twenty pounds, or be indefinite.

And all other instruments, bearing in any degree the form or style of promissory notes, but which in law

PROMISSORY NOTE—*continued.*

£ s. d.

shall be deemed special agreements, except hereby expressly directed to be deemed promissory notes.

But such of the notes and instruments here exempted from the duty on promissory notes shall nevertheless be liable to the duty which may attach thereon, as agreements or otherwise.

Exemptions from the preceding and all other Stamp Duties.

All promissory notes for the payment of money issued by the Governor and Company of the Bank of England.

PROTEST of any bill of exchange or promissory note, for any sum of money,

	£	s.	d.
Not amounting to 20*l.*	0	2	0
Amounting to 20*l.* and not amounting to 100*l.*	0	3	0
Amounting to 100*l.* and not amounting to 500*l.*	0	5	0
Amounting to 500*l.* or upwards	0	10	0

PROTEST of any kind   0 5 0

And for every sheet or piece of paper, parchment or vellum, upon which the same shall be written, after the first, a further progressive duty of   0 5 0

STATUTE AGAINST USURY.

12 ANN. ST. 2. C. 16.

An Act to reduce the Rate of Interest, without any Prejudice to Parliamentary Securities.

WHEREAS the reducing of interest to ten, and from thence to eight, and thence to six in the hundred, hath from time to time, by experience, been found very beneficial to the advancement of trade, and [555] improvement of lands: and whereas the heavy burden of the late long and expensive war, hath been chiefly borne by the owners of the land of this kingdom, by reason whereof they have been necessitated to contract very large debts. and thereby, and by the abatement in the value of their lands, are become greatly impoverished: and whereas by reason of the great interest and profit which hath been made of money at home, the foreign trade of this nation hath of late years been much neglected, and at this time there is a great abatement in the value of merchandizes, wares, and commodities of this kingdom, both at home and in foreign parts, whither they are transported: and whereas for the redress of these mischiefs, and the preventing the increase of the same, it is absolutely necessary to reduce the high rate of interest of six pounds in the hundred pounds for a year to a nearer proportion with the interest allowed for money in foreign states; Be it therefore enacted by the Queen's Most Excellent Majesty, by and with the advice and consent of the Lords Spiritual and Temporal, and Commons, in this present Parliament assembled, and by the authority of the same, That no person or persons whatsoever, from and after the nine-and-twentieth day of September, in the year of our Lord one thousand seven hundred and fourteen, upon any contract which shall be made from and after the said nine-and-twentieth day of September, take, directly, or indirectly, the loan of any moneys, wares, merchandize, or other commodities whatsoever, above the value of five pounds, for the forbearance of one hundred pounds for a year, and so after that rate for a greater or lesser sum, or for a longer or shorter time ; and that all bonds, contracts, and assurances whatsoever, made after the time aforesaid, for payment of principal, or money to be lent or covenanted to be performed upon or for any usury, whereupon or whereby there shall be reserved or taken above the rate of five pounds in the hundred, as aforesaid, shall be utterly void ; and that all and every person or persons whatsoever, which shall, and after the time aforesaid, upon any contract to be made after the said nine-and-twentieth day of September, take, accept, and receive, by way or means of any corrupt bargain, loan, exchange, chevisance, shift, or interest of any wares, merchandize, or other thing or things whatsoever, or by any deceitful way or means, or by any covin, engine, or deceitful conveyance, for forbearing or giving day of payment for one whole year, of and for their money, or other thing, above the sum of five pounds for the forbearing of one hundred pounds for a year, and so after that rate for a greater or lesser sum, or for longer or shorter term,

APPENDIX. shall forfeit and lose for every such offence the treble value of the moneys, wares, merchandizes, and other things, so lent, bargained, exchanged, or shifted.

II. And be it further enacted by the authority aforesaid, That all and every scrivener and scriveners, broker and brokers, solicitor and solicitors, driver and drivers of bargains for contracts, who shall, after the said nine-and-twentieth day of September, take or receive, directly or indirectly, any sum or sums of money, or other reward or thing for brokage, soliciting, driving, or procuring the loan, or forbearing of any sum or sums of money, over and above the rate or value of five shillings for the loan, or for forbearing of one hundred pounds for a year, and so rateably, or above twelve pence, over and above the stamp-duties, for making or renewing of the bond or bill for loan, or forbearing thereof, or for any counter-bond or bill concerning the same, shall forfeit for every such offence twenty pounds, with costs of suit, and suffer imprisonment for half a year; the one moiety of all which forfeitures to be to the Queen's Most Excellent Majesty, her heirs and successors, and the other moiety to him or them that will sue for the same in the same county where the several offences are committed, and not elsewhere, by action of debt, bill, plaint or information, in which no essoign, wager of law, or protection shall be allowed.

---

58 GEO. 3. c. 93.

An Act to afford Relief to the bona fide *Holders of negotiable Securities, without Notice that they were given for a usurious Consideration.*—[*Passed* 10th *June* 1821.]

WHEREAS by the laws now in force, all contracts and assurances whatsoever, for payment of money, made for a usurious consideration, are utterly void: And whereas in the course of mercantile transactions, negotiable securities often pass into the hands of persons who have discounted the same without any knowledge of the original considerations [557] for which the same were given; and the avoidance of such securities in the hands of such *bona fide* indorsees without notice is attended with great hardship and injustice; For remedy thereof, be it enacted by the King's Most Excellent Majesty, by and with the advice and consent of the Lords Spiritual and Temporal, and Commons, in this present Parliament assembled, and by the authority of the same, That no bill of exchange or promissory note, that shall be drawn or made after the passing of this act, shall, though it may have been given for a usurious consideration, or upon a usurious contract be void in the hands of an indorsee for valuable consideration, unless such indorsee had, at the time of discounting or paying such consideration for the same, actual notice that such bill of exchange or promissory note had been originally given for a usurious consideration, or upon a usurious contract.

Bill of exchange or promissory note given for a usurious consideration not void in the hands of an indorsee if he had no notice thereof.

* In Lowes *v.* Mazzaredo, 1 Stark. page 385, it was held, that if the payee of a bill of exchange, indorses it upon a usurious contract at the time of the contract, a *bona fide* holder cannot afterwards recover upon it against the acceptor, which decision just preceded the act.

1 & 2 GEO. IV. c. 70.

An Act to regulate Acceptances of Bills of Exchange.—[Passed 2d July, 1821.]

WHEREAS according to the law as hath been adjudged, where a bill is accepted payable at a banker's, the acceptance thereof is not a general but a qualified acceptance: And whereas a practice hath very generally prevailed among merchants and traders so to accept bills, and the same have, among such persons, been very generally considered as bills generally accepted, and accepted without qualification: And whereas many persons have been, and may be much prejudiced and misled by such practice and understanding, and persons accepting bills may relieve themselves from all inconvenience, by giving such notice as hereinafter mentioned of their intention to make only a qualified acceptance thereof; Be it therefore enacted by the King's Most Excellent Majesty, by and with the advice and consent of the Lords Spiritual and Temporal, and Commons, in this present Parliament assembled, and by the authority of the same, That from and after the first day of August now next ensuing, if any person shall accept a bill of exchange, payable at the house of a banker or other place, without further expression in his acceptance, such acceptance shall be deemed and taken to be, to all intents and purposes, a general acceptance of such bill; but if the acceptor shall in his acceptance express that he accepts the bill, payable at a banker's house or other place only, and not otherwise or elsewhere, such acceptance shall be deemed and taken to be, to all intents and purposes, a qualified acceptance of such bill, and the acceptor shall not be liable to pay the said bill, except in default of payment when such payment shall have been first duly demanded at such banker's house or other place. *Bills accepted payable at a banker's or otherplace, deemed a general acceptance. Bills accepted payable at a banker's or otherplace, only, deemed a qualified acceptance.*

[558]

II. And be it further enacted, That from and after the said first day of August, no acceptance of any inland bill of exchange shall be sufficient to charge any person, unless such acceptance be in writing on such bill, or if there be more than one part of such bill, on one of the said parts. *Acceptances to be in writing on the bill.*

---

39 GEO. 3. c. 85. A. D. 1799.

An Act to protect Masters against Embezzlements by their Clerks or Servants.

' WHEREAS bankers, merchants, and others, are, in the course of
' their dealings and transactions, frequently obliged to entrust their
' servants, clerks, and persons employed by them in the like capacity,
' with receiving, paying, negotiating, exchanging, or transferring, mo-
' ney, goods, bonds, bills, notes, banker's drafts, and other valuable
' effects and securities: And whereas doubts have been entertained
' whether the embezzling of the same by such servants, clerks, and
' others so employed by their masters, amounts to felony by the law of
' England, and it is expedient that such offences should be punished in
' the same manner in both parts of the United Kingdom;' Be it enacted
and declared by the King's Most Excellent Majesty, by and with the

APPENDIX. advice and consent of the Lords Spiritual and Temporal, and Commons, in this present Parliament assembled, and by the authority of the same,

Servants or clerks receiving any money or other effects on their master's account, and fraudulently embezzling or secreting any part thereof, shall be deemed to have feloniously stolen the same; and such offenders & their abettors shall, on conviction, be liable to be transported for fourteen years.

That if any servant or clerk, or any person employed for the purpose in the capacity of a servant or clerk, to any person or persons whomsoever, or to any body corporate or politic, shall, by virtue of such employment, receive or take into his possession any money, goods, bond, bill, note, banker's draft, or other valuable security, or effects, for or in the name or on the account of his master or masters, or employer or employers, and shall fraudulently embezzle, secret, or make away with the same, or any part thereof, every such offender shall be deemed to have feloniously stolen the same from his master or master, employer or employers, for whose use, or in whose name or names, or on whose account the same was or were delivered to, or taken into the possession of such servant, clerk, or other person so employed, although such money, goods, bond, bill, note, banker's draft, or other valuable security, was or were no otherwise received into the possession of his or their servant, clerk, or other person so employed; and every such offender, his adviser, procurer, aider or abettor, being thereof lawfully convicted or attainted, shall be liable to be transported to such parts beyond the seas as his Majesty, by and with the advice of his Privy Council, shall appoint, for any term, not exceeding fourteen years, in the discretion of the court before whom such offender shall be convicted or adjudged.

[559]

---

52 GEO. 3. c. 63. A. D. 1812.

An Act for more effectually preventing the Embezzlement of Securities for money and other Effects, left or deposited for safe Custody, or other special Purposes, in the Hands of Bankers, Merchants, Brokers, Attorneys, or other Agents.

'Whereas it is expedient that due provision should be made to pre-
'vent the embezzlement of government and other securities for money,
'plate, jewels, and other personal effects, deposited for safe custody,
'or for any special purpose, with bankers, merchants, brokers, attor-
'neys, and other agents, entrusted by their customers and employers;'
Be it therefore enacted by the King's Most Excellent Majesty, by and
with the advice and consent of the Lords Spiritual and Temporal, and
Commons, in this present Parliament assembled, and by the authority

Persons subject to punishment, for embezzlement of any deed, or other security for money entrusted to their care.

of the same, That if any person or persons with whom (as banker or bankers, merchant or merchants, broker or brokers, attorney or attorneys, or agent or agents of any description whatsoever) any ordinance debenture, exchequer bill, navy, victualling or transport bill, or other bill, warrant or order for the payment of money, state lottery ticket or certificate, seaman's ticket, bank receipt for payment of any loan, India bond, or other bond, or any deed, note, or other security for money, or for any share or interest in any national stock or fund of this or any other country, or in the stock or fund of any corporation, company or society established by act of parliament or royal charter, or any power of attorney for the sale or transfer of any such stock or fund, or any share or interest therein, or any plate, jewels, or other personal effects, shall have been deposited, or shall be or remain in safe custody, or upon or for any special purpose, (without any authority, either general, spe-

[560]

Appendix.

cial, conditional, or discretionary, to sell or pledge such debenture, bill,
warrant, order, state lottery ticket or certificate, seaman's ticket, bank
receipt, bond, deed, note, or other security, plate, jewels, or other personal effects, or to sell, transfer or pledge the stock or fund, or share of
interest in the stock or fund to which such security or power of attorney shall relate) shall sell, negotiate, transfer, assign, pledge, embezzle, secrete, or in any manner apply to his or their own use or benefit,
any such debenture, bill, warrant, order, state lottery ticket or certificate, seaman's ticket, bank receipt, bond, deed, note, or other security,
as hereinbefore mentioned, plate, jewels, or other personal effects, or
the stock or fund, or share or interest in the stock or fund to which
such security or power of attorney shall relate, in violation of good faith,
and contrary to the special purpose, for which the things hereinbefore
mentioned, or any or either of them, shall have been deposited, or shall
have been or remained with or in the hands of such person or persons,
with intent to defraud the owner or owners of any such instrument or
security, or the person or persons depositing the same, or the owner or
owners of the stock or fund, share or interest, to which such security or
power of attorney shall relate, every person so offending in any part of
the United Kingdom of Great Britain and Ireland, shall be deemed and
taken to be guilty of a misdemeanor, and being thereof convicted according to law, shall be sentenced to transportation for any term not
exceeding fourteen years, or to receive such other punishment as may
by law be inflicted on a person or persons guilty of a misdemeanor, and
as the court before which such offender or offenders shall be tried and
convicted shall adjudge.

'II. And whereas it is usual for persons having dealings with bankers,
'merchants, brokers, attorneys and other agents, to deposit or place in
'the hands of such bankers, merchants, brokers, attorneys and other
'agents, sums of money, bills, notes, drafts, checks, or orders for the
'payment of money, with directions or orders to invest the moneys so [561]
'paid, or to which such bills, notes, drafts, checks or orders relate, or
'part thereof, in the purchase of stocks or funds, or in or upon govern-
'ment, or other securities for money, or to apply and dispose thereof
'in other ways or for other purposes; and it is expedient to prevent em-
'bezzlement and malversation in such cases also;' Be it therefore enacted by the authority aforesaid, that if any such banker, merchant,
broker, attorney or other agent, in whose hands any sum or sums of
money, bill, note, draft, check, or order for the payment of any sum or
sums of money shall be placed, with any order or orders in writing, and
signed by the party or parties who shall so deposit or place the same, to
invest such sum or sums of money or the money to which such bill, note,
draft, check or order as aforesaid shall relate, in the purchase of any
stock or fund, or in or upon government or other securities, or in any
other way or for any other purpose specified in such order or orders,
shall in any manner apply to his or their own use and benefit, any such
sum or sums of money, or any such bill, note, draft, check or order for
the payment of any such sum or sums of money as hereinbefore mentioned,
in violation of good faith, and contrary to the special purpose specified
in the direction or order in writing hereinbefore mentioned, with intent
to defraud the owner or owners of any sum or sums of money; every
person so offending in any part of the United Kingdom, shall in like
manner be deemed and taken to be guilty of a misdemeanor, and being
convicted thereof according to law, shall incur and suffer such punishment as hereinbefore mentioned.

For pre-
venting
bankers &
others, from
disposing
for their
own use of
property de-
posited with
them.

APPENDIX.   III. Provided always, and be it further enacted by the authority

—————— aforesaid, that nothing herein contained shall extend, or be construed

Act not to extend, to prevent any of the persons, hereinbefore mentioned from
to prevent
persons re- receiving any money which shall be or become actually due and paya-
ceiving mo- ble upon or by virtue of any of the instruments or securities hereinbe-
ney due on fore mentioned, according to the tenor and effect thereof, in such man-
securities. ner as he or they might have done, if this act had not been made.

Not to ex-   IV. Provided also, and be it further enacted by the authority afore-
tend   to said, that the penalty by this act annexed to the commission of any of-
partners
not being fence intended to be guarded against by this act, shall not extend, or
privy to of- be construed to extend, to any partner or partners, or other person or
fence. persons of or belonging to partnership, society or firm, except only such
[562] partner or partners, person or persons, as shall actually commit or be
accessary or privy to the commission of such offence : any thing herein contained to the contrary in anywise notwithstanding.

Not to les-   V. Provided also, and be it further enacted by the authority afore-
sen   any said, that nothing in this act contained, nor any proceeding, conviction
remedy at
law   or or judgment to be had or taken thereupon, shall hinder, prevent, les-
equity, re- sen, or impeach any remedy at law or in equity, which any party or
garding parties aggrieved by any offence against this act might or would have
party   ag- had, or have been entitled to, if this act had not been made, nor any
grieved. proceeding, conviction, or judgment had been had or taken thereupon:
but nevertheless the conviction of any offender against this act shall not
be received in evidence in any action at law, or suit in equity, against
such offender ; and further, that no person shall be liable to be convicted by any evidence whatever, as an offender against this act, in
respect of any act, matter or thing done by him, if he shall, at any time
previously to his being indicted for such offence, having disclosed such
act, matter or thing on oath, under or in consequence of any compulsory process of any court of law or equity, in any action, suit, or proceeding, in or to whom, he shall have been a party, and which shall
have been *bona fide* instituted by the party aggrieved by the act,
matter or thing, which shall have been committed by such offender
aforesaid.

Not to af-   VI. Provided always, and it is hereby expressly enacted and declared
fect   trus- that nothing in this act contained shall extend to or affect any person or
tees   or persons being a trustee or trustees in or under any marriage settlement,
mortgagees will, or other deed or instrument, or being a mortgagee or mortgagees
of any property whatsoever, whether real or personal, in respect of any
act or acts done by any such person or persons in relation to the property comprized in or affected by any such trust or mortgage as aforesaid.

Punish-   VII. Provided always, and be it enacted, that every person who
ment   of shall commit in Scotland any offence against this act, which by the pro-
persons of- visions thereof is constituted a misdemeanor, shall be liable to be pun-
fending in
Scotland. ished by fine and imprisonment, or by either of them, or by transportation for any term not exceeding fourteen years, as the judge or judges
before whom such offender shall be tried and convicted may direct.

Act not to   VIII. Provided always, and it is hereby enacted, that nothing herein
restrain
bankers contained shall extend to restrain any banker, merchant, broker, &c.
from disposing of securities on which they have a lien.

torney, or other agent, from selling, negotiating, transferring, or otherwise disposing of any securities, property or other effects as aforesaid,
in their custody or possession, upon which they shall have any lien,
claim or demand, which by law entitles them to sell or dispose thereof,
unless such sale, transfer or other disposal shall extend to a greater
number or to a greater part of such securities, property, or other effects
as aforesaid than shall be requisite or necessary for the purpose of paying or satisfying such lien, claim or demand ; any thing hereinbefore
contained to the contrary thereof in anywise notwithstanding.

£	1 Day				2 Days				3 Days				4 Days				5 Days				6 Days			
	£	s.	d.	f.	£	s.	d.	f.	£	s.	d.	f.	£	s.	d.	f.	£	s.	d.	f.	£	s.	d.	f.
1	0	0	0	0	0	0	0	0	0	0	0	0	0	0	0	0	0	0	0	0	0	0	0	0
2	0	0	0	0	0	0	0	0	0	0	0	0	0	0	0	0	0	0	0	0	0	0	0	1
3	0	0	0	0	0	0	0	0	0	0	0	1	0	0	0	1	0	0	0	1	0	0	0	2
4	0	0	0	0	0	0	0	1	0	0	0	1	0	0	0	2	0	0	0	2	0	0	0	3
5	0	0	0	0	0	0	0	1	0	0	0	1	0	0	0	2	0	0	0	3	0	0	0	3
6	0	0	0	0	0	0	0	1	0	0	0	2	0	0	0	3	0	0	0	3	0	0	1	0
7	0	0	0	0	0	0	0	1	0	0	0	2	0	0	0	3	0	0	1	0	0	0	1	1
8	0	0	0	1	0	0	0	2	0	0	0	3	0	0	1	0	0	0	1	1	0	0	1	2
9	0	0	0	1	0	0	0	2	0	0	0	3	0	0	1	0	0	0	1	1	0	0	1	3
10	0	0	0	1	0	0	0	2	0	0	0	3	0	0	1	1	0	0	1	2	0	0	1	3
20	0	0	0	2	0	0	1	1	0	0	1	3	0	0	2	2	0	0	3	1	0	0	3	3
30	0	0	0	3	0	0	1	3	0	0	2	3	0	0	3	3	0	0	4	3	0	0	5	3
40	0	0	1	1	0	0	2	2	0	0	3	3	0	0	5	1	0	0	6	2	0	0	7	3
50	0	0	1	2	0	0	3	1	0	0	4	3	0	0	6	2	0	0	8	0	0	0	9	3
60	0	0	1	3	0	0	3	3	0	0	5	3	0	0	7	3	0	0	9	3	0	0	11	3
70	0	0	2	1	0	0	4	2	0	0	6	3	0	0	9	0	0	0	11	2	0	1	1	3
80	0	0	2	2	0	0	5	1	0	0	7	3	0	0	10	2	0	1	1	0	0	1	3	3
90	0	0	2	3	0	0	5	3	0	0	8	3	0	0	11	3	0	1	2	3	0	1	5	3
100	0	0	3	1	0	0	6	2	0	0	9	3	0	1	1	0	0	1	4	1	0	1	7	2
200	0	0	6	2	0	1	1	0	0	1	7	2	0	2	2	1	0	2	8	3	0	3	3	1
300	0	0	9	3	0	1	7	2	0	2	5	2	0	3	3	1	0	4	1	1	0	4	11	0
400	0	1	1	0	0	2	2	1	0	3	3	1	0	4	4	2	0	5	5	3	0	6	6	3
500	0	1	4	1	0	2	8	3	0	4	1	1	0	5	5	3	0	6	10	0	0	5	2	2

* N. B. The interest on a bill or note (except when it carries interest by the term of it from the date) is to be calculated from the time it fell due, until the day when final judgment will be signed. The calculation may be at the rate of one penny for each pound each month, but the above table affords the more precise mode of calculation.

£	7 Days				8 Days				9 Days				10 Days				11 Days				12 Days			
	£	s.	d.	f.	£	s.	d.	f.	£	s.	d.	f.	£	s.	d.	f.	£	s.	d.	f.	£	s.	d.	f.
1	0	0	0	0	0	0	0	1	0	0	0	1	0	0	0	1	0	0	0	1	0	0	0	1
2	0	0	0	1	0	0	0	2	0	0	0	2	0	0	0	2	0	0	0	2	0	0	0	3
3	0	0	0	2	0	0	0	3	0	0	0	3	0	0	0	3	0	0	1	0	0	0	1	0
4	0	0	0	3	0	0	1	0	0	0	1	0	0	0	1	1	0	0	1	1	0	0	1	2
5	0	0	1	0	0	0	1	1	0	0	1	1	0	0	1	2	0	0	1	3	0	0	1	3
6	0	0	1	1	0	0	1	2	0	0	1	3	0	0	1	3	0	0	2	0	0	0	2	1
7	0	0	1	2	0	0	1	3	0	0	2	0	0	0	2	1	0	0	2	2	0	0	2	3
8	0	0	1	3	0	0	2	0	0	0	2	1	0	0	2	2	0	0	2	3	0	0	3	0
9	0	0	2	0	0	0	2	1	0	0	2	2	0	0	2	3	0	0	3	1	0	0	3	2
10	0	0	2	1	0	0	2	2	0	0	2	3	0	0	3	1	0	0	3	2	0	0	3	3
20	0	0	4	2	0	0	5	1	0	0	5	3	0	0	6	2	0	0	7	0	0	0	7	3
30	0	0	6	3	0	0	7	3	0	0	8	3	0	0	9	3	0	0	10	3	0	0	11	3
40	0	0	9	0	0	0	10	2	0	0	11	3	0	1	1	0	0	1	2	1	0	1	3	3
50	0	0	11	2	0	1	1	0	0	1	2	3	0	1	4	1	0	1	6	0	0	1	7	2
60	0	1	1	3	0	1	3	3	0	1	5	3	0	1	7	2	0	1	9	2	0	1	11	2
70	0	1	4	0	0	1	6	1	0	1	8	2	0	1	11	0	0	2	1	0	0	2	3	2
80	0	1	6	1	0	1	9	0	0	1	11	2	0	2	2	1	0	2	4	3	0	2	7	2
90	0	1	8	2	0	1	11	2	0	2	2	2	0	2	5	2	0	2	8	2	0	2	11	2
100	0	1	11	0	0	2	2	1	0	2	5	2	0	2	8	3	0	3	0	0	0	3	3	1
200	0	3	10	0	0	4	4	2	0	4	11	0	0	5	5	3	0	6	0	1	0	6	6	3
300	0	5	9	0	0	6	6	3	0	7	4	3	0	8	2	2	0	9	0	1	0	9	10	1
400	0	7	8	0	0	8	9	0	0	9	10	1	0	10	11	2	0	12	0	2	0	13	1	3
500	0	9	7	0	0	10	11	2	0	12	3	3	0	13	8	1	0	15	0	3	0	16	5	1

£	13 Days				14 Days				15 Days				16 Days				17 Days				18 Days			
	£	s.	d.	f.	£	s.	d.	f.	£	s.	d.	f.	£	s.	d.	f.	£	s.	d.	f.	£	s.	d.	f.
1	0	0	0	1	0	0	0	1	0	0	0	1	0	0	0	2	0	0	0	2	0	0	0	2
2	0	0	0	3	0	0	0	3	0	0	0	3	0	0	1	0	0	0	1	0	0	0	1	0
3	0	0	1	1	0	0	1	1	0	0	1	1	0	0	1	2	0	0	1	2	0	0	1	3
4	0	0	1	2	0	0	1	3	0	0	1	3	0	0	2	0	0	0	2	0	0	0	2	1
5	0	0	2	0	0	0	2	1	0	0	2	1	0	0	2	2	0	0	2	4	0	0	2	3
6	0	0	2	2	0	0	2	3	0	0	2	3	0	0	3	0	0	0	3	1	0	0	3	2
7	0	0	2	3	0	0	3	0	0	0	3	1	0	0	3	2	0	0	3	3	0	0	4	0
8	0	0	3	1	0	0	3	2	0	0	3	3	0	0	4	0	0	0	4	1	0	0	4	2
9	0	0	3	3	0	0	4	0	0	0	4	1	0	0	4	2	0	0	5	0	0	0	5	1
10	0	0	4	1	0	0	4	2	0	0	4	3	0	0	5	1	0	0	5	2	0	0	5	3
20	0	0	8	2	0	0	9	0	0	0	9	3	0	0	10	2	0	0	12	0	0	0	11	3
30	0	1	0	3	0	1	1	3	0	1	2	3	0	1	3	3	0	1	4	2	0	1	5	3
40	0	1	5	0	0	1	6	1	0	1	7	2	0	1	9	1	0	1	10	1	0	1	11	2
50	0	1	9	1	0	1	11	0	0	2	0	2	0	2	2	1	0	2	3	3	0	2	5	2
60	0	2	1	2	0	2	3	2	0	2	5	2	0	2	7	2	0	2	9	2	0	2	11	2
70	0	2	5	3	0	2	8	0	0	2	10	2	0	3	0	3	0	3	3	3	0	3	5	1
80	0	2	10	0	0	3	0	3	0	3	3	1	0	3	6	0	0	3	8	2	0	3	11	0
90	0	3	2	1	0	3	5	1	0	3	8	1	0	3	11	1	0	4	2	1	0	4	5	1
100	0	3	6	2	0	3	10	0	0	4	1	1	0	4	4	2	0	4	7	3	0	4	11	1
200	0	7	1	1	0	7	8	0	0	8	2	2	0	8	9	0	0	9	3	3	0	9	10	1
300	0	10	8	0	0	11	6	0	0	12	3	3	0	13	1	3	0	13	11	2	0	14	9	2
400	0	14	2	3	0	15	4	0	0	16	5	1	0	17	6	1	0	18	7	2	0	19	8	2
500	0	17	9	2	0	19	2	0	1	0	6	2	1	1	11	0	1	3	3	1	1	4	7	3

£	19 Days (£ s. d. f.)	20 Days (£ s. d. f.)	21 Days (£ s. d. f.)	22 Days (£ s. d. f.)	23 Days (£ s. d. f.)	24 Days (£ s. d. f.)
1	0 0 0 2	0 0 0 2	0 0 0 2	0 0 0 2	0 0 0 3	0 0 0 3
2	0 0 1 0	0 0 1 1	0 0 1 1	0 0 1 1	0 0 1 2	0 0 1 2
3	0 0 1 3	0 0 1 3	0 0 2 0	0 0 2 0	0 0 2 1	0 0 2 1
4	0 0 2 1	0 0 2 2	0 0 2 3	0 0 2 3	0 0 3 0	0 0 3 0
5	0 0 3 0	0 0 3 1	0 0 3 1	0 0 3 2	0 0 3 3	0 0 3 3
6	0 0 3 2	0 0 3 3	0 0 4 0	0 0 4 1	0 0 4 2	0 0 4 2
7	0 0 4 1	0 0 4 2	0 0 4 3	0 0 5 0	0 0 5 1	0 0 5 2
8	0 0 4 3	0 0 5 1	0 0 5 2	0 0 5 3	0 0 6 0	0 0 6 1
9	0 0 5 2	0 0 5 3	0 0 6 0	0 0 6 2	0 0 6 3	0 0 7 0
10	0 0 6 0	0 0 6 2	0 0 6 3	0 0 7 0	0 0 7 2	0 0 7 3
20	0 1 0 1	0 1 1 0	0 1 1 3	0 1 2 2	0 1 3 0	0 1 3 3
30	0 1 6 2	0 1 7 2	0 1 8 2	0 1 9 2	0 1 10 2	0 1 11 2
40	0 2 0 3	0 2 2 1	0 2 3 2	0 2 4 3	0 2 6 0	0 2 7 2
50	0 2 7 0	0 2 8 3	0 2 10 2	0 3 0 0	0 3 1 3	0 3 3 1
60	0 3 1 1	0 3 3 1	0 3 5 1	0 3 7 1	0 3 9 1	0 3 11 1
70	0 3 7 2	0 9 10 0	0 4 0 1	0 4 2 2	0 4 5 3	0 4 7 0
80	0 4 1 3	0 4 4 2	0 4 7 0	0 4 9 3	0 5 0 1	0 5 3 0
90	0 4 8 0	0 4 11 0	0 5 2 0	0 5 4 0	0 5 8 0	0 5 11 0
100	0 5 2 1	0 5 5 3	0 5 9 0	0 6 0 1	0 6 3 2	0 6 6 3
200	0 10 4 3	0 10 11 2	0 11 6 0	0 12 0 2	0 12 7 0	0 13 1 3
300	0 15 7 1	0 16 5 1	0 17 3 0	0 18 0 3	0 18 10 3	0 19 8 2
400	1 0 9 3	1 1 11 0	1 3 0 0	1 4 1 1	1 5 2 1	1 6 3 2
500	1 6 0 1	1 7 4 3	1 8 9 0	1 10 1 2	1 11 6 0	1 12 10 2

£	25 Days (£ s. d. f.)	26 Days (£ s. d. f.)	27 Days (£ s. d. f.)	28 Days (£ s. d. f.)	29 Days (£ s. d. f.)	30 Days (£ s. d. f.)
1	0 0 0 3	0 0 0 3	0 0 0 3	0 0 0 3	0 0 0 3	0 0 0 3
2	0 0 1 2	0 0 1 2	0 0 1 3	0 0 1 3	0 0 1 3	0 0 1 3
3	0 0 2 1	0 0 2 2	0 0 2 2	0 0 2 3	0 0 2 3	0 0 2 3
4	0 0 3 1	0 0 3 1	0 0 3 2	0 0 3 2	0 0 3 3	0 0 3 3
5	0 0 4 0	0 0 4 1	0 0 4 1	0 0 4 2	0 0 4 3	0 0 4 3
6	0 0 4 3	0 0 5 0	0 0 5 1	0 0 5 2	0 0 5 2	0 0 5 3
7	0 0 5 3	0 0 5 3	0 0 6 0	0 0 6 1	0 0 6 2	0 0 7 0
8	0 0 6 2	0 0 6 3	0 0 7 0	0 0 7 1	0 0 7 2	0 0 7 1
9	0 0 7 1	0 0 7 2	0 0 7 3	0 0 8 1	0 0 8 2	0 0 8 3
10	0 0 8 0	0 0 8 2	0 0 8 3	0 0 9 0	0 0 9 2	0 0 9 3
20	0 1 4 1	0 1 5 0	0 1 5 3	0 1 6 1	0 1 7 0	0 1 7 3
30	0 2 0 2	0 2 1 2	0 2 2 2	0 2 3 2	0 2 4 2	0 2 5 3
40	0 2 8 3	0 2 10 0	0 2 11 2	0 3 0 3	0 3 2 0	0 3 3 3
50	0 3 5 0	0 3 6 2	0 3 8 1	0 3 10 0	0 3 11 2	0 4 1 1
60	0 4 1 1	0 4 3 1	0 4 5 1	0 4 7 0	0 4 9 0	0 4 11 0
70	0 4 9 2	0 4 11 3	0 5 2 0	0 5 4 1	0 5 6 2	0 5 9 0
80	0 5 5 3	0 5 8 1	0 5 11 0	0 6 1 2	0 6 4 1	0 6 6 3
90	0 6 1 3	0 6 4 3	0 6 7 3	0 6 10 3	0 7 1 3	0 7 4 3
100	0 6 10 0	0 7 1 1	0 7 4 3	0 7 8 0	0 7 11 1	0 8 2 2
200	0 13 8 1	0 14 2 3	0 14 9 2	0 15 4 0	0 15 10 2	0 16 5 1
300	1 0 6 2	1 1 4 1	1 2 2 1	1 3 0 0	1 3 10 0	1 4 7 3
400	1 7 4 3	1 8 5 3	1 9 6 3	1 10 8 0	1 11 9 1	1 12 10 2
500	1 14 2 3	1 15 7 1	1 16 11 3	1 18 4 1	1 19 8 2	2 1 1 0

£	1 Month £	s.	d.	f.	2 Months £	s.	d.	f.	3 Months £	s.	d.	f.	4 Months £	s.	d.	f.	5 Months £	s.	d.	f.	6 Months £	s.	d.	f.
1	0	0	1	0	0	0	2	0	0	0	3	0	0	0	4	0	0	0	5	0	0	0	6	0
2	0	0	2	0	0	0	4	0	0	0	6	0	0	0	8	0	0	0	10	0	0	1	0	0
3	0	0	3	0	0	0	6	0	0	0	9	0	0	1	0	0	0	1	3	0	0	1	6	0
4	0	0	4	0	0	0	8	0	0	1	0	0	0	1	4	0	0	1	8	0	0	2	0	0
5	0	0	5	0	0	0	10	0	0	1	3	0	0	1	8	0	0	2	1	0	0	2	6	0
6	0	0	6	0	0	1	0	0	0	1	6	0	0	2	0	0	0	2	6	0	0	3	0	0
7	0	0	7	0	0	1	2	0	0	1	9	0	0	2	4	0	0	2	11	0	0	3	6	0
8	0	0	8	0	0	1	4	0	0	2	0	0	0	2	8	0	0	3	4	0	0	4	0	0
9	0	0	9	0	0	1	6	0	0	2	3	0	0	3	0	0	0	3	9	0	0	4	6	0
10	0	0	10	0	0	1	8	0	0	2	6	0	0	3	4	0	0	4	2	0	0	5	0	0
20	0	1	8	0	0	3	4	0	0	5	0	0	0	6	8	0	0	8	4	0	0	10	0	0
30	0	2	6	0	0	5	0	0	0	7	6	0	0	10	0	0	0	12	6	0	0	15	0	0
40	0	3	4	0	0	6	8	0	0	10	0	0	0	13	4	0	0	16	8	0	1	0	0	0
50	0	4	2	0	0	8	4	0	0	12	6	0	0	16	8	0	1	0	10	0	1	5	0	0
60	0	5	0	0	0	10	0	0	0	15	0	0	1	0	0	0	1	5	0	0	1	10	0	0
70	0	5	10	0	0	11	8	0	0	17	6	0	1	3	4	0	1	9	2	0	1	15	0	0
80	0	6	8	0	0	13	4	0	1	0	0	0	1	6	8	0	1	13	4	0	2	0	0	0
90	0	7	6	0	0	15	0	0	1	2	6	0	1	10	0	0	1	17	6	0	2	5	0	0
100	0	8	4	0	0	16	8	0	1	5	0	0	1	13	4	0	2	1	8	0	2	10	0	0
200	0	16	8	0	1	13	4	0	2	10	0	0	3	6	8	0	4	3	4	0	5	0	0	0
300	1	5	0	0	2	10	0	0	3	15	0	0	5	0	0	0	6	5	0	0	7	10	0	0
400	1	13	4	0	3	6	8	0	5	0	0	0	6	13	4	0	8	6	8	0	10	0	0	0
500	2	1	8	0	4	3	4	0	6	5	0	0	8	6	8	0	10	8	4	0	12	10	0	0

£	7 Months £	s.	d.	f.	8 Months £	s.	d.	f.	9 Months £	s.	d.	f.	10 Months £	s.	d.	f.	11 Months £	s.	d.	f.	12 Months £	s.	d.	f.
1	0	0	7	0	0	0	8	0	0	0	9	0	0	0	10	0	0	0	11	0	0	1	0	0
2	0	1	2	0	0	1	4	0	0	1	6	0	0	1	8	0	0	1	10	0	0	2	0	0
3	0	1	9	0	0	2	0	0	0	2	3	0	0	2	6	0	0	2	9	0	0	3	0	0
4	0	2	4	0	0	2	8	0	0	3	0	0	0	3	4	0	0	3	8	0	0	4	0	0
5	0	2	11	0	0	3	4	0	0	3	9	0	0	4	2	0	0	4	7	0	0	5	0	0
6	0	3	6	0	0	4	0	0	0	4	6	0	0	5	0	0	0	5	6	0	0	6	0	0
7	0	4	1	0	0	4	8	0	0	5	3	0	0	5	10	0	0	6	5	0	0	7	0	0
8	0	4	8	0	0	5	4	0	0	6	0	0	0	6	8	0	0	7	4	0	0	8	0	0
9	0	5	3	0	0	6	0	0	0	6	9	0	0	7	6	0	0	8	3	0	0	9	0	0
10	0	5	10	0	0	6	8	0	0	7	6	0	0	8	4	0	0	9	2	0	0	10	0	0
20	0	11	8	0	0	13	4	0	0	15	0	0	0	16	8	0	0	18	4	0	1	0	0	0
30	0	17	6	0	1	0	0	0	1	2	6	0	1	5	0	0	1	7	6	0	1	10	0	0
40	1	3	4	0	1	6	8	0	1	10	0	0	1	13	4	0	1	16	8	0	2	0	0	0
50	1	9	2	0	1	13	4	0	1	17	6	0	2	1	8	0	2	5	10	0	2	10	0	0
60	1	15	0	0	2	0	0	0	2	5	0	0	2	10	0	0	2	15	0	0	3	0	0	0
70	2	0	10	0	2	6	8	0	2	12	6	0	2	18	4	0	3	4	2	0	3	10	0	0
80	2	6	8	0	2	13	4	0	3	0	0	0	3	6	8	0	3	13	4	0	4	0	0	0
90	2	12	6	0	3	0	0	0	3	7	6	0	3	15	0	0	4	2	6	0	4	10	0	0
100	2	18	4	0	3	6	8	0	3	15	0	0	4	3	4	0	4	11	8	0	5	0	0	0
200	5	16	8	0	6	13	4	0	7	10	0	0	8	6	8	0	9	3	4	0	10	0	0	0
300	8	15	0	0	10	0	0	0	11	5	0	0	12	10	0	0	13	15	0	0	15	0	0	0
400	11	13	4	0	13	6	8	0	15	0	0	0	16	12	4	0	18	6	8	0	20	0	0	0
500	14	11	8	0	16	13	4	0	18	15	0	0	20	16	8	0	22	18	4	0	25	0	0	0

INDEX.

———◆———

A.

ABATEMENT,

in an action against one of two joint makers of a note, advantage of omissions of the other must be taken by plea in abatement, 339.

if one of several acceptors is an infant, and he is left out of the declaration, plea in abatement is not sustainable, 353.

ABSCONDING.—(See *"Removal."*)

of the drawee.   [164. 261.

effect thereof as to presentment for acceptance or payment, of the protest thereupon for better security, 240.

of drawer or indorser, when an excuse for delay in notice of dishonour, 212. 319.

ABSENCE.—(See *"Absconding," "Removal."*)

ACCEPTANCE,

to what bills necessary, 158.—(See *"Presentment for Acceptance,"*) defined, 165.

By whom to be made, 165, 6, 7.

by an executor or administrator, but he is personally liable, 185.—(See *"Executor."*)   [166. 170.

holder is entitled to insist on acceptance according to tenor, if drawee has not capacity to contract, bill may be treated as dishonoured, 166, 7.

by an agent, 166. 23 to 29.—(See *"Agent."*)

question whether holder bound to acquiesce in receiving acceptance by an agent, 166.

by a partner, 166, 7. 29 to 40.—(See *"Partner."*)

there cannot be a series of acceptors to same bill, 166.

by one person when bill directed to two not in partnership, bill may be considered as dishonoured, 167.

The time when to be made, 167 to 170.

the drawee has twenty-four hours to accept a bill, 167.

promise to accept before bill drawn how far valid, 167, 8, 9.

only considered as to foreign bills and bills drawn before 1st August, 1821, as now by 1 & 2 Geo. 4 c. 78, acceptance of inland bill made after 1st August, 1821, must be in writing on face of bill, 167.

on a blank stamp, 169.

ACCEPTANCE SUPRA PROTEST,

of a bill of exchange, what is, 22,

obligations imposed by an, 22.

cannot be made till after refusal to accept by drawee, 158.

any persons may without drawer's consent or that of indorsers, 240, 1.

for the honour of a particular party to it, 241.

how it is in general made, 241.

for what purpose it is made, 241.

such an acceptance enures to benefit of subsequent parties, 241.

By whom it may be made, 241, 2.

the drawee of a bill may make an acceptance on it, 241.

if drawee so accepts, a protest should first be made, 241.

if holder insists on an absolute acceptance, drawee should cancel
the one he had made, 241.

and a bill having on it one, may be afterwards accepted *supra
protest* again, 241.

no one should accept a bill under protest for honour of drawer,
without ascertaining cause of refusal of drawee, 241, 2. [242.

but if he accepts for honour of indorser, no inquiry necessary,
holder not obliged to receive an acceptance *supra protest,* 242.

Mode of accepting supra protest, 242.

must be made in presence of a notary, 242.

a general acceptance *supra protest* is considered as made for the
honour of the drawer, 242.

when it is made so as to bind drawer and indorser, notice of it
should be given to the indorser, 242.

holder should take care to get bill protested before such acceptance is made, 242.

Liability of the acceptor supra protest, 242, 3.

as obligatory as if no protest had intervened, 242.

extends according for whose honour the acceptance made, 242.

it is only conditional, and presentment for payment must be
made to drawee, and protested in case of refusal, 242, 3.

Right of an acceptor supra protest, 243, 4.

he may claim indemnity from such person for whose honour he
accepts, 243.

or from drawer or acceptor, 243.

when in case of bankruptcy of drawer equity will compel such
acceptor first to resort to drawer's estate, 243.

acceptor for the honour of indorser cannot sue any subsequent
parties, 244.

ACCEPTOR.—(See " *Acceptance," " Drawee," " Acceptance supra pro-*

Defined, who is an acceptor, 1. 20.   [*test.")*

Of the liability of the acceptor, 183 to 188.

liable according to terms of acceptance, 183.—(See " *Ac-*

is primarily liable to pay the bill, 183.   [*ceptance.")*

unless expressly made payable a particular place on the
face of the bill, acceptor cannot insist on presentment,
192. 250 to 259.

when not liable to pay re-exchange, 183.

not liable to pay bill if he accepted it without value given
by plaintiff, 183. 70.

may show acceptance to be partly for value and partly for
plaintiff's accommodation, 163. 71.

ACCEPTOR—*(continued.)*

Miscellaneous points.

release by drawer to acceptor does not affect payee's right of action, 5.

set-off due from drawer to acceptor, does not affect holder's action, 5.

of a bill who was an infant at the time of drawing, but of age when accepted, is liable, 17.

in an action against acceptor infancy of indorser no defence, 20.

acceptor for the honour, who is, 22.—(See *Acceptance supra protest.*")

obligations of an acceptor for the honour, 22.

discounting his own acceptance at a premium exceeding 5 per cent. not usury, 77, 89.

refusing to give acceptance or payment, notice must be given to drawer, 98.

time for payment given to, discharges the other parties to a bill, 98.

alteration of bill in the date after acceptance without consent of acceptor, makes bill void, 100, 1.

exchange of an acceptance by one, with another, is a valuable consideration, 104, 5.

is a negotiation, 104, 116, 151.   [107, 196.

of an accommodation bill, may claim indemnity from drawer, accommodation acceptor may retain money in his hands, 196, 344.   [138.

is bound by a conditional indorsement made before acceptance, the same by a qualified one, 139.

but if an indorsement of part of the money mentioned is made after acceptance, he is not liable, 139.

not entitled to notice of indorsements, 140.

who is also one of several drawers not entitled to notice of dishonour, 211.

cannot in general call on an indorser, 142.—(See " *Holder.*")

of a bill, when no right to refuse payment of it, because it is lost, 151, 2.

may be sued in equity for non-payment of a bill stated to be lost, 152.

there cannot be a series of to same bill, 166. 242.

and if there are two acceptors, one of whom was not a drawee, he is not liable on the bill, 166.

nor to any other form of action, if consideration be not expressed, 166.   [162. 170.

ought not to pay his acceptance if he knows of drawer's failure, otherwise if he does not know of it, 170.—(See " *Bankrupt.*")

if holder make acceptor executer, and die, right of action is extinguished, 345.

discharge of an acceptor by an insolvent act, does not prevent action against other parties, 301. 347. 381.

if a bill purport to be drawn by a firm, and the declaration state, that certain persons drew, &c. acceptor is estopped from disputing the fact, 354.

proceedings will not be stayed in an action against, on a bill, if holder sues him, drawer, and indorser, but on payment of the debt and costs of all the actions, 469.—(See " *Staying Proceedings.*")

what the best course to pursue in this case, 369.

ACCOMMODATION BILL.—(*continued.*)

if third party pays bill for drawer's honour, acceptor not liable to such person, 321.

liable to an indorser for like accommodation, 146.

who, in case of acceptor's bankruptcy, may prove under commission, 146, 7.

want of consideration in action by *bona fide* holder will not discharge acceptor, 68, 9. 183.

not liable, if indorsed to plaintiff, after bill became due without value given, 129.

holder *bona fide* may retain for subsequent balance, 184.

accepted for a particular purpose cannot be applied by a holder with notice to any other use, 184.

where plaintiff is agent for another person who ought not in justice to recover on bill, acceptor not liable, 184.

what a waiver of acceptor's liability, 191.

rights of an accommodation acceptor in general, 195, 6. 344.

may and should claim and take a written indemnification from drawer, 107. 344. 195.   [196. 344.

when no express contract the law implies a contract to indemnify, where sum above £20, a written undertaking should be stamped, 195.

where bankruptcy of drawer apprehended, a counter bill should be taken, 195.

agent accepting an, for employer, may retain money of his principal to indemnify himself, 106. 344.

so may acceptor, 344. 196.

the same when person not an agent does so, sed quære, 344.

and this, though drawer commits an act of bankruptcy, 196.

acceptor of, may prove under commission of bankruptcy against drawer, though he paid the bill after the bankruptcy, 196.

what evidence necessary in action by acceptor of, against drawer, to recover money paid, &c., 399. 410.

what is and is not *prima facie* evidence of payment and circulation, by acceptor, 399. 410.

where drawer is a competent witness for acceptor of, in action against acceptor, 415.

liability and rights of an indorsee of an accommodation bill, 141, 2.

entitled to notice on dishonour of, 199.   [6, 7.

drawn for accommodation of remote indorsee and prior names lent him, indorsee entitled to notice, 202.

may be indorsed by a bankrupt after his bankruptcy, 116.

not so if bill be accepted in consideration of an exchange of acceptances, 116.

bona fide holder of, may prove under drawer's commission, though he has accepted security and given time to the acceptor, 295.

ACKNOWLEDGMENT.—(See "*Admission*," "*Evidence*.")

ACT OF BANKRUPTCY.—(See "*Bankrupt*," "*Bankruptcy*.")

ACTION OF ASSUMPSIT ON A BILL OR NOTE,

most usual remedy in cases of bills and notes, 342.

by or against whom action may be brought, 342 to 347.

where legal right created or liability imposed, they may be enforced, 342.

where there are several indorsers, one of them may sue acceptor or drawer, and strike out all names below his own. 342, 6.

where a merchant joins his clerk's name to his firm, the action must be in joint names, though he receive no profit or bear no loss, 342.

otherwise if distinctly proved he had no interest, 347.

if an action is brought on a bill, and afterwards indorsed over to a third person who knows that fact, the action may still be continued, 341.

such third person cannot recover in another action, 341.

may be sustained by a *bona fide* holder against all parties to a bill, &c. who became so previously to himself, 342, 3. 5.

not on subsequent ones, 345.

assignee by mere delivery, when and who he may sue, 341.—(See "*Assignee.*")

a person receiving a bill from drawer after it was dishonoured by acceptor, and paid by drawer, may sue such acceptor in his own name, 341.

drawer may sue, when, 341.—(See "*Drawer.*")

where he must sue acceptor specially on the contract to accept, 341.

acceptor liable when drawer has taken up and passed the bill, 342.

parties not originally liable on, or not parties to a bill subsequently paying it, when and when not they may sue, 130, 344, 5.—(See " *supra Protest,*" "*Bail,*" "*Bankers.*")

what objections may be taken to an action at suit of a person who became holder after due or paid, 126 to 130.—(See "*Indorsement.*"

what laches in the holder of a bill, will be a forfeiture of his right of action, 196 to 240.—(See "*Laches;*" and "*Notice of Non-acceptance.*")

if holder make acceptor executor, right of action extinguished, 345.

unless the executor formerly renounce, 345.

when bill is joint and several, sometimes advisable to proceed in separate actions, 345, 6.

if several actions are brought by the holder against the different parties to a bill, the commencement of one action is no bar to the others, 346.

but payment of the bill and costs by one will discharge the others, 346.

if the holder reject an offer to pay debt and costs, the court will restrain him from taking out execution, 346.

but if the money is paid pending several other actions, he may proceed for recovery of costs, 346.

against one of two obligors in a joint and several bond, taking such one in execution, no bar to an action against the other, 346.

this rule extends to parties to a bill, 346, 7.

letting a subsequent indorser out of execution, will not discharge a prior indorser, 298. 347.

discharge of an acceptor by virtue of an insolvent act, does not prevent an action against the other parties, 347.

but accepting a bond from one party in satisfaction of it, will discharge the other parties, 347.

the same rule prevails when a composition is entered into without the assent of drawer or indorsers, 301. 347.

actual payment will of course discharge the rest, 347.

ADMISSION—*(continued.)*

of one partner, evidence against another as to joint contracts, 382. 397.

as well after as before the determination of the partnership, 382. 397.

a party's hand-writing may be proved against him by his admission, 387.—(See " *Hand-writing.*")

if he made such admission before bill due, and thereby induced holder to take, he cannot afterwards dispute the fact, 387.

or endeavour to show that bill is a forgery, 387.

made pending a compromise is evidence against defendant, 388.

in general only operates against party making it, 388.

what statement in a letter written by defendant is an admission, 388.

proof that one indorser confessed his signature, no admission in an action of indorsee against drawer, 388.

on face of pleadings by one of several drawers, indorsers, or acceptors, of his signature, will not dispense with evidence against the others, 288.

though if made in fact it would be otherwise, 381, 82, 88.

acceptance is not an admission of drawer's indorsement, 390.

and it is not altered by the fact of the acceptance being made after the indorsement, 390.

the same rules extend to acceptance of a bill drawn and indorsed by procuration, 391.

of bill payable to several not partners, acceptance after indorsement by one is no admission of the regularity, 393.

but if acceptor expressly promise to pay it at the time, it is otherwise, 393.

by an indorser of his indorsement, not evidence against maker, 396.

a promise to pay or offer to renew, made to indorsee after bill due, admits holder's title, 396, 7.

payment of money into court, is an admission of the validity of bill, sufficiency of stamp and holder's title, 380. 383. 388. 397.

what objection on part of drawer, no admission of holder's title, 397.

in an action against a subsequent indorser, this indorsement admits hand-writing of drawer and prior indorsers, 397.

acceptance is a *prima facie* admission of effects, 410.

ADVICE,

words respecting, in a bill, 89.

when an unaccepted bill should not be paid without it, 89.

AFFIDAVIT.—(See " *Bankruptcy,*" " *Proof.*")

requisition of affidavit to hold to bail on a bill or note, 348 to 350.

before arrest made, affidavit must be filed of the cause of action, 348.

the sum due on a bill or note must be £10, 348.

in other cases £15, 348.

it must be certain, explicit, and positive, 348.

the reason for requiring strictness in these affidavits, 348.

practice of K. B. and C. P. uniform on this head, 348.

requisites of affidavit against acceptor of a bill or maker of a note, 348, 9.

what requisite in an affidavit against an indorser, 349.

must show what party defendant was, 349.

not necessary to show in what character debt due to plaintiff, 349.

though party to a bill only gives the initials of his christian name, the affidavit and proceeding must state them in full, 350.

AT SIGHT.—(See *"Sight."*)

when bills payable at sight are payable, 268, 9.—See *"Computation of Time,"* *"Grace, Days of."*)

opinion that three days grace are allowable upon, 259.

statute of limitations does not run on bills payable at, till after presentment made, 372.

in actions on bills payable at, evidence of time of acceptance must be given, 383.

ATTESTATION.—(See *"Witness,"* *"Subscribing Witness."*)

when attesting witness to bill or note must be *subpœnaed*, 379, 380, 4.

the like to an indorsement, 384.

ATTORNEY

does not lose his privilege from arrest, by being party to a bill of exchange, 14.

money should not be paid to agent of, in discharge of a debt, 281.

notes given to a prisoner under lord's act, may be signed by the detaining creditor's attorney, 335.—(See *Prisoner."*)

to prove payment of money into court to call the attorney who took it out, is not sufficient, 380.

ATTORNEY, LETTER OR POWER OF,

gives an authority, general or limited, according to its terms, 24, 5.

what words have been construed as carrying a limited authority, 24.

ATTORNEY, WARRANT OF,

in what case a warrant of attorney, given on a usurious transaction, is valid, 83.

may be vacated by a court of law, 110.

AUTER DROIT,

agent may receive money due to the principal in, 25.

no mutual credit in case of, 466, 7.

AUTHORITY—(See *"Agent,"* *"Partner,"* *"Factor."*)

of an agent.—(See *"Agent."*)

of a partner.—(See *"Partner."*)

of a factor.—(See *"Factor."*)

how far authority of an agent extends, 23.

general, if he is a general agent, 23.

if not, circumscribed accordingly, 23.

general, what is, 24.

> a person giving another a blank stamped piece of paper with his name signed, gives a full authority to such person to insert what sum he pleases, 24. 124.

> letter of attorney gives an authority according to its wording, 24, 5.

> likewise power of attorney, 25.

special, is not necessary to constitute a power to draw, &c. bills in name of a principal, 25.

as to implied authority, which is sometimes general and sometimes limited, according to the acts permitted to be done, 25.

usual employ, evidence of general authority, 25.

when a bill is indorsed by a married woman, with husband's knowledge, it is implied, 19. 26. 115.

if a party promise to pay, it is implied, 115.

AUTHORITY—(*continued.*)

holder of a bill may insist on the production of an agent's authority to accept, 166.

once given, but afterwards revoked, to receive payment of a bill, how far payment of it would be sufficient, 230.

mere production of a bill, &c. is sufficient to receive payment, 231.

if an agent of a firm draw a bill, and one of the partners accepts, agent's authority need not be proved, 382.—(See "*Evidence,*" "*Hand-writing.*"

AVERMENT—(See "*Evidence,*" "*Declaration.*" [420.

in declaration of defendant's breach of contract must be shown, 361,

of bill payable on an event, averment that event has occurred must be shown, 361, 402.

of note, payable on demand, advisable in one count at least to aver a demand, 61.

in an action against acceptor or maker of a note, no averment of presentment for payment necessary, 249, 359, 361, 402.

and it need not be proved unless stated, 359, 364, 402.

and the common breach at the end of money counts suffices, 361.

and unless the bill be accepted payable at a particular place according to late act, no averment of presentment there is necessary, 250 to 259, 361.

when an averment is made in an action against acceptor, what is sufficient, 361.

in all cases when a place is named in the body of a bill or note, averment of presentment, or some excuse for not doing so absolutely necessary, 251, 361, 402.—(See "*Evidence.*")

what allegations as an excuse have been deemed insufficient, 362.

when such presentment averred, what is sufficient, 362.

when bill accepted, payable by certain persons, at a place certain, a general averment of such presentment to those persons when suing drawer, is good, 361. [252, 361.

of notice of non-payment at a particular place unnecessary, 251.

not necessary to be given to acceptor unless he can prove damage thereby, Rhodes v. Gent, MS. [402.

no averment is necessary of the party who made presentment, 362,

but when drawer of a bill, or indorser of a note, is sued, averment of presentment must be made, 362.

or some excuse for not doing so, 362.

when drawee or maker have absconded, what averment is sufficient, 362.—(See "*Absconding.*")

when removed, 362.—(See "*Removal.*")

when bill, payable at a banker's or particular place, presentment there must be averred in such action, 362.

and in such action it must be alleged that notice of dishonour was duly given, 362.

or else some legal excuse for not doing so, 362.

and omission of this averment fatal, even after verdict, 362.

in case of a foreign bill a protest must be stated, or bad on special demurrer, 362, 405.

what allegation of protestation bad, 362.

not necessary to aver protest in proceeding for expenses on inland bills, 218, 312, 362, 405.

in case of a conditional acceptance, averment necessary, 402.

it must also be proved, 405.—(See "*Evidence.*")

BAIL,

a bill may be paid by the bail of either party to it, 280.
but the bail of the maker of a note who have paid it, cannot sue indorser, 344.
indorser may be bail for drawer, 351.
if a party be bail in separate actions on same bill, it suffices to swear he is worth double the amount in one action, 350.
the requisites of the affidavit to hold to bail, 348 to 350.—(See " *Affidavit.*")
in action of debt on a bill, but not on a note, when bail necessary after judgment by default, 497.

BANKERS.—(See " *Commission,*" " *Banker's Cash Notes.*")

originally goldsmiths, 331.
may take 5 *per cent.* discount, and a reasonable sum for commission, 84.
what commission they may take, 85.—(See "*Commission.*")
when may charge interest upon interest, 85.
when they may make usual rests in their accounts, so as to charge interest on prior interest, 85
what stipulation by a, does not amount to usury, 86.—(See " *Usury.*")
may charge commission for paying and accepting bills, 88.
where such a charge would be deemed usury, 88.
may transfer bills indorsed in blank to him, 113.—(See " *indorsement.*")   [112, 113.
consequences of his fraudulently pledging or transferring bills,
indictable for misapplying the bills of their customers, by statute, 114.
bills, &c. deposited with a banker as agent, do not vest in his assignees, should he become a bankrupt, 122, 136, 482.
otherwise if he has discounted any of them, 122, 485.
if a banker fail when an executor or agent, not liable for testator's money placed there, 28, 123.
paying a check before it bears date, which had been lost by payee, is liable to repay same to loser, 148.
liable to an action of trover if he discount a bill drawn on a customer, after notice that it was lost, 148.
the private mark on a bill by a banker, as between himself and another banker, may be an acceptance, 173.
may retain a check till five o'clock, and then return it, even though cancelled, 176.—(See " *Check.*")
maker of a note, who is a banker, and *shuts up* and abandons his shop, how far presentment for payment at such shop valid, 246.
presentment for payment of a bill or check to clerk at clearing house, is sufficient, 275.
presentment for payment of a bill or note, payable on demand by banker, what is a reasonable time, 273, 4, 5.
when a bill, payable at a bankers, a presentment must be made there in the usual hours of business, 276, 7.—(See " *Presentment for Payment.*")
and if not done, holder cannot protest bill for non-payment, 277.
but if such presentment is made, and an answer returned, it is good, 277.
doubtful whether a banker is not guilty of neglect in giving up a bill, and taking acceptor's check on another banker, 279, 287, 322.
may refuse to pay a check or acceptance, even though he has cancelled them, 279.

BANKRUPTCY—(*continued.*)

ANKRUPTCY—*(continued.)*

BANKRUPTCY—(*continued.*)

BANKRUPTCY—(*continued.*)

The property of others—(*continued.*)

in case of the bankruptcy of a factor or banker, or other person, what liens allowed on bills in their hands, 482, 3, 4.

but bills delivered to a banker expressly on terms of discount, assignees entitled to them, 485.

what other cases assignees entitled, 485.

VII. Precedents of dispositions in case of bankruptcy.—(See " *Appendix,*" 519 to 523.)

VIII. Miscellaneous Points.

does not affect obligee's right of action after assignment, 7.

of one partner disables him from using name of firm, so as to render co-partners liable, 35. 115.

on bankruptcy of stock broker's proof under commission of promissory notes given upon a stock-jobbing transaction, how far restrained, 80.

as far as it regards transfers, relates only back to the time of the suing forth of the commission, 117.

a trader cannot, in contemplation of, make a voluntary indorsement, 121.

but it must appear that such indorsement was in contemplation of bankruptcy, 121.—(See " *Fraudulent Preference.*")

if bill transferred through urgency of the demand the contemplation of secrecy in the transaction will not vitiate, 121.

bill returned to indorsers, in contemplation of, is not a fraudulent preference, 121.

of a drawer and acceptor of a bill, &c. gives indorsee a lien on drawer's effects in hands of acceptor, 141.

of the acceptor of an accommodation bill, indorser for like accommodation who pays the bill, may prove under the commission, 146.

of the drawer when it prevents drawee from accepting or paying, 170.—(See " *Bankrupt.*")

after secret act of by trader, consigning goods to a factor, how far such factor is obliged to repay the money to assignees, 170.

accommodation acceptor, holder of a counter bill given as an indemnity by the drawer, may prove under drawer's commission of, 195.

notwithstanding the bankruptcy of the drawer of an accommodation bill, acceptor may retain money of drawer's in his hands till bill be due, 196.

of the drawee of a bill no excuse for omission to give due notice of dishonour, 210.

the same with regard to drawer or indorser of a bill, or indorser of a note, 215. 226.

of drawer, after drawing bill, if acceptance refused, holder may immediately prove under the commission, 231.

on bankruptcy of the drawer or drawee, equity will compel an acceptor *supra protest,* to resort to drawer's estate, 243.—(See " *Acceptance supra protest.*")

of the acceptor of a bill, does not excuse omission of presentment for payment, 246.

BANKRUPTCY—(continued.)

Effect at law of proving under a commission of bankruptcy—(continued.)
  a person released from liability by bankruptcy, and certificate, is a competent witness to an action on a bill, the payment of which he guaranteed, 415, 16.
  what amount of bill may be proved under two commissions in, 419, 20.—(See " *Damages.*")
  case of, where bills, &c. carry interest, 421.

BANKRUPT—(See " *Bankruptcy,*" " *Fraudulent Preference.*")
  who has assigned over a bond before his bankruptcy, may sustain an action on it, 7.
  one partner who has become a bankrupt, is disabled from using name of firm, 35, 115.
  this rule qualified, 117.
  a contract made in consideration of signing certificate void, 80.
  who has obtained his certificate in a foreign country, cannot be sued in England, or an instrument drawn and to be performed there, 94.
  cannot transfer bills, &c. 115.—(See " *Bankruptcy.*")
  after a secret act of bankruptcy, cannot transfer bills, &c. by indorsement, 115. but see. 119.—19 Geo. 2. c. 32.
  doubtful whether the solvent partner without assignees consent can, 115.
  nor should a declaration on such note state the joint indorsement, 116.
  a trader who has become bankrupt, may indorse a bill delivered before his bankruptcy, 116.
  and if he and his assignees refuse to do so, Chancellor will compel them, 116.
  estate liable to the costs of such a proceeding, 116.
  no estate in which he is not beneficially interested, passes to his assignees, 116.
  many transfer an accommodation bill, 116.
  a bill drawn for a sum of money, part of which is for his accommodation, 117.
  but such indorsement is only valid as far as that accommodation sum goes, 117.
  when they transfer bills before the suing forth of commission, by statute 19 Geo. 2. c. 32. 117.
  enactment of that statute, 117. 283.
  decisions on the act, 283, 4.
  doubtful whether promissory notes are within this statute, 118, 284.
  a bill indorsed by, after an act of bankruptcy, but paid before the issuing of a commission, is within this statute, 119.
  by a, for a debt for goods sold and paid, after the issuing thereof, it is valid, 119.
  that such transfer is only valid when there are no suspicious circumstances of insolvency, 120.—(See " *Insolvency.*")
  payments made, and contracts entered into by a bankrupt, two months before the date of commission, when valid, 120.
  indorsement of a bill by, by way of fraudulent preference, invalid, 120.—(See " *Fraudulent Preference.*")
  but a creditor pressing a trader to give such indorsement, the intention of the latter to become bankrupt, cannot be called in to vitiate it, 121.
  uncertificated after the commission issued, receiving a note, legal interests vest in his assignees, 122.
  when it does not, 122.

CHECKS ON BANKERS—*(continued.)*

drawn on the executor of a debtor will make executor liable if he promise to pay it, 194

and such check is an equitable assignment of a debt available against assignees of a bankrupt, 194.

need not be presented for payment if it is not stamped, and one is required, 247.

but insufficiency in other respects no excuse for laches, 247.

presentment for payment at clearing house sufficient, 261.—(See *"Presentment for Payment."*)

presentment of for payment may be made at any time on day after receipt, in the usual hours of business, 274, 5, 6.

when a bill is paid by a check, most prudent not to give up bill, 287.

usage of London bankers in this particular, 287.

banker not guilty of negligence in taking a check on another banker in payment of a bill, 322. 287. 279.

drawer and indorsers discharged if holder take a check from acceptor, and give up bill, 287.

this is otherwise in case of a debtor, upon any thing else than a bill of exchange, 287.

production of a check how far evidence of payment, 288.

delivery of check, 288.

when it is necessary to have a receipt stamp, 288.

death of drawer before payment is a countermand of banker's authority to pay, 306.

but if such payment made to a holder before banker had notice of it, holder is not liable to refund, 306.

declarations on, 497.

CHOSE IN ACTION,

defined, action upon must in general be in name of assignor, 5. 8.

doctrine of considered, 5 to 8.

at first applied only to landed estates, 6.

why not assignable at law so as to pass legal interest, 5.

exception in favour of the king, 6.

assignable in equity with sufficient consideration, 7.

assignment of by parol vests equitable interest in assignees, 5. 7.

sufficient to support an assumpsit, 7.

reason and consequence of this doctrine, 7, 8.

bills and notes, &c. exempted from this doctrine, and why, 8.

CHRISTMAS DAY,

bills become due day before, 266.

CLAIM IN BANKRUPTCY—(See *"Bankruptcy."*)

points relating to it, 466.

form of, 523.

CLEARING HOUSE—(See *"Checks on Bankers."*)

presentment at, when sufficient, 261.

CLERGY,

how far they may be parties to a bill, 13.

CLERK—(See *"Banker," "Notary," "Agent."*)

to a notary cannot, it is said, protest an inland bill, 216.

presentment to banker's clerk at clearing house sufficient, 261.

COAL NOTE,
  given in pursuance of statute 3 Geo. 2. c. 26. s. 7, must be protested on non-payment, 312.
  enactments of that statute, 230.
  how they should be made, 330.
  should express to be for value received in coals, 330.
  not invalid if they do not, though party subject to a penalty of £100, 330.
  observations on the statute, and how far same extends, 330.

COGNOVIT,   [192.
  holder of a bill taking one from drawer does not discharge acceptor, taking one from acceptor when it discharges drawer, 293.
  holder may enter up judgment on a cognovit taken from one of two makers of a joint and several note, and levy on a *fi. fa.* without discharging the other, 297.

COHABITATION,
  past illicit cohabitation is a legal consideration, 75.
  future is not, 75.

COLLATERAL SECURITY,
  may be proved, but not bills given in lieu, 140.

COMMISSION OF BANKRUPTCY—(See "*Bankrupt,*" and "*Bankruptcy.*")

COMMISSION—(See "*Bankers.*")
  when may be taken by a banker or merchant besides 5 *per cent.* discount, 84.
  but the charge must be reasonable, or it is usury, 85.
  what is the usual amount of such, 85.
  at 7*s.* 6*d. per cent.* has been deemed usury, 85.
  an agent may charge, besides legal interest, 88.
  a banker may charge, though he does not discount the bill, 88.
  when the charge would be deemed usurious, 88, 9.

COMPANY CORPORATE,
  any contract or trading against the law of is illegal, 79.

COMPANY INCORPORATE,
  one member cannot accept, so as to bind the rest, on a bill drawn by its factor, 38.

COMPARISON OF HANDS,
  not in general admissible in evidence, 384, note, 387.

COMPETENCY,
  of witnesses, 413 to 418.—(See "*Witness,*" "*Release.*")

COMPOSITION,
  secret stipulation in fraud of other creditors void, 76.
  a note given in consideration thereof void, though other creditors did not enter into composition deed, 76.
  holder of a bill compounding with acceptor of prior party, when he discharges drawer or subsequent party, 301. 347.

CHITTY ON BILLS.   3 Z

CONSIDERATION—*(continued.)*

a subsequent illegal consideration is in general no bar to an action or contract founded originally on a lawful consideration, 82.

on the dishonour of a bill, original consideration revives, 98.

what circumstances do and do not alter this rule, 99, 100.

exchange of acceptances, when a valuable consideration, 105.

giving an indemnity bond is a valuable consideration, 155.

not necesssary to state that part of the bill in pleading which relates to it, 356.

in an action on a bill, when evidence of allowable, 363 to 367. 400,1. (See *"Evidence."*)

when plaintiff may be called on to prove what value he gave for it, 400, 1.—(See *"Evidence."*)

want of, will disturb plaintiff's right in a bank note, 401.

CONSTRUCTION

of bills, &c. 41. 92 to 94.—See ante, 605.

CONTINGENCY.—(See *"Condition," "Bills of Exchange."*)

bill or note must not be payable on any, 42.

but they may be accepted payable on a, 180, 1.

and may be indorsed conditionally, 138.

what such a contingency as to invalidate a bill or note, 42 to 45.

payment out of a particular fund is contingent and invalid, 43.

payment of a bill after marriage is contingent, 43.

verbal agreement qualifying liability to pay, will not vitiate, 45.

the happening of the event will not render bill good, 45.

indorsement qualifying the payment of the bill, when it renders bill void, bill or note payable on a, is only a special agreement, 46. 553.　[46.

an instrument in the form of a bill, but adverting to the receipt of another bill, has been considered as a special agreement, 46.

a written stipulation to renew is not contingent, 47.

wish of payee to indulge maker of a bill or note expressed in such bill, is not, 47.

no parol evidence admissible to vary effect of bill, 47.

bill payable on a contingency that must happen, is good, 48.

payable six weeks after death of another is valid, 48.

after a person comes of age, specifying the day, is valid, 48.

any thing of public notoriety or moral certainty is not a, 48.

bills payable at a certain fair are good, 48.

after a certain ship is paid off, 49.

but this is doubtful, 49.

notes payable on a, for less than £20, subject to a stamp duty, 53. for more, must be stamped as an agreement, 53. 553.

if a bill or check is given on a condition, and drawer, when it is presented for payment, discover that it has not been performed, he may stop payment, 279.

a bill payable on a contingency cannot be proved in bankruptcy, 430.

CONTRACT.—(See *"Consideration," "Bills of Exchange."*)

distinction between contracts as to consideration, and when it is presumed and when not, 8 to 10.

are of three descriptions,

matter of record, 9.

specialty, 9.

parol or simple contract, 9.—(See *"Simple Contract."*)

CONTRACT—(*continued.*)

    the first cannot be impeached, and why, 9.

    the second bind party making them, though no sufficient consideration, and why, 9.

    therefore no consideration need be proved in an action on, 9.

    but defendant may avail himself of its illegality, 9.

    but he must state it in pleading, 9.

    the third do not bind, unless consideration be proved, 9.

by law of England, only two kinds of contract, 9, note.

is made between two parties generally, 13.

parties to a contract, and their capacity, as respects bills of exchange, 13 to 40.

with alien enemy in general void, 13.

when not, 13.

by infants, voidable, 15.

an express promise after he came of age, will render contract made by infant, valid, 17.

by married women absolutely, void, 18.

a *feme covert* may enter into when husband legally dead, 18.

written on separate paper to renew a bill, will qualify, though not vitiate the liability on the bill, 47.

parol evidence of contract inadmissible to defeat action on bill, 47.

when a bill is given as the consideration for the performance of a contract, the non-performance of it will not vitiate the bill, 71.

but if such contract is afterwards rescinded *in toto*, or in part, the rule is otherwise, 70.

all good, if not repugnant to certain laws, 74.

what those laws are, 74.

invalid, if made in restraint of trade, 74.—(See " *Trade.*")

    contrary to custom or excise laws, 74.   [74.

    contrary to public justice, as compounding a crime, in consideration of a recommendation to a public office, 74.

    repugnant to general policy, as wagers, 75.—(See " *Wager,*" &c.)

    in restraint of marriage, 75.—(See " *Marriage.*")

    for procuration of marriage, 75.

    in consideration of future illicit cohabitation, 75.

    if prejudicial to the feelings or interests of a third person without his assent, 75.

    contrary to the benevolent intent of others, 75.

    in secret for benefit of one creditor before composition deed signed, 75.

    though composition not effected, 76.

    otherwise if made freely after signing, 76.

    for a usurious consideration, 77.—(See " *Usury.*")

    not so if in hands of *bona fide* holder, 77.

    for a gaming consideration, how far void, 78.—(See " *Gaming.*")

    stock-jobbing consideration, how far void, 79.—(See " *Stock-jobbing.*")

    on a gaming policy, void, 79.—(See " *Policy on Ships,*" &c.)

in consideration of,   [79.

    trading against laws of East India or Russian Company, bribery at an election, 79.

CONTRACT—*(continued.)*
   in consideration of—*(continued.)* ·
               sale of an office, 79.
               simony, 79.
               ease and favour of a sheriff, 80.
               signing bankrupt's certificate, 80.
               insurance in the lottery, 80.
               ransoming any British Ship, 80.
                   any goods captured by enemy, 80.
               of spirituous liquors sold in quantities of less than 20*s.* value, 80.
               of apprentice fee, if indenture void, when bad, and when not, 80.
   void, if the consideration in part or in whole is against a statute, 80.
   if founded on an illegal consideration, a judgment confessed aids the illegality of, 74.
               a legal consideration at first, no subsequent illegality will avoid the same, 82.
   in what cases usury has been determined as not vacating a contract, 83.
   to be performed in a foreign country, the remedy here will be the same as in such country, 94.—(See "*Arrest.*")
   the words and language of a contract must bear the sense attempted to be put upon them, 94.
   not under seal, cannot be extinguished by another, 95, but see 189.
   but a person taking a bill of exchange in discharge of such contract, cannot waive the bill, and resort to the original contract, 95.

COPY,
   how and when to obtain a copy of a bill or note, 368.
   of letter containing notice of dishonour, when admissible in evidence without notice to produce original, 405, 6, 7, 8.—(See "*Letter*," "*Evidence*," "*Notice to produce*," &c.)

CORPORATION.—(See "*Company Incorporate.*")
   when and how may be party to a bill, 14.
   may be a party to a bill under certain restraints, 15.
   cannot be sued in assumpsit in general, 15.
   if exceeding six, how far may be party to what bill, 15.
   unless established for trading purposes cannot be acceptors, 15.

COSTS.—(See "*Staying Proceedings.*")   [116.
   when recoverable, if bankrupt and his assignees refuse to indorse,
   when defendant will be compelled to pay costs of applying to equity in case of lost bill, 152.
   if holder reject an offer to pay debt and costs, court will restrain execution, 346.
   but if money is paid on such offer, pending other actions, he may proceed for the costs, 346.
   on payment of a debt, when proceedings will be stayed, 368.—(See "*Staying Proceedings.*")
   on payment of debt and costs, defendant may obtain a rule to stay proceedings, 368.
   or it may be done by summons from a judge, 368.

CUSTOM OF MERCHANTS,   [12.

special custom, formerly supposed necessary to support inland bills,
of trade in respect to credit given by an agent, discharges his liability, 28.

of merchants only admissible in evidence when law is silent, 37.

will guide the court where a new case on bills arises, 94. 110.

of London, in respect to payment of bills by drafts, &c. 287, 8.

of Bristol, in regard to acceptances, 158.

in action on bill by party paying *supra protest*, sufficient to state he
paid it according to custom, &c. 321.

formerly usual to set it out in the declaration on a bill, but now improper, 451, 2.

though usual now to refer to, this is in no case necessary, 452.

CUSTOMS, LAWS OF.

contract made in violation of, void, 74.

DAMAGES—(See " *Interest*," " *Re-exchange*," " *Provision*," " *Ex-
penses.*")

Principal money to be recovered in an action on a bill, 419, 420.

plaintiff may recover the whole sum, though he did not give full
value for the bill, 419.

in which case overplus held in trust for party entitled to it, 419.

if holder receive part-payment from first indorser, he may recover
the whole against drawer and acceptor, 319.

but if drawer pay part, then only residue can be recovered against
drawer, 419.

but these rules only extend when there is another person entitled to
receive overplus, 419.

but in case of bankruptcy, holder may prove debt against one or more
parties, and receive a dividend, but he cannot prove for more than
sum actually due against from whom he received bill, 419.

when bill or note payable by instalments, 420.

holder of a bill omitting to give notice of dishonour cannot show
that no actual discharge has been sustained, 210.

acceptor discharged if holder neglected to present it at bankers in
proper time, and he sustained damages, Rhodes v. Gent, MS.

in answer to proof by holder that defendant had no effects in hands
of drawee, defendant may prove actual damage, 212.

drawer and indorser not liable for, if protest made on an inland bill,
and it, or notice of it, is not sent within fourteen days after, 226.

on judgment by default in an action on a bill or note, damages referred
to master for computation, 351. 368.

when action in C. P. they are referred to the prothonotary, 369.

to the master in the Exchequer, 369.

what interest recoverable, 405. 420 to 423.

what expenses recoverable, 423 to 426.

     of special messenger, 222, note.
     re-exchange, 423.
     provision, 425.

not necessary to protest inland bills to one party to recover interest
or damages, 405. 421.—(See "*Evidence*," "*Protest*.")

in an action by accommodation acceptor or drawer, when special
damage must be proved, 410.

when imprisonment in execution is not special damage, 410.—See
"*Accommodation Bills*.")

DEATH—(See " *Extinguishment.* ")

of a party, when it revokes powers given by him, 37.

dissolves a partnership, though for a term of years, unless stipulation to contrary, 37.

what circumstances in case of a partnership have been decided as altering the rule, 37.

of holder of a bill vests the same in executor or administrator, 122.

of an indorser of a bill before it bore date does not discharge the drawer, 124.

of drawer of a bill does not revoke his request for drawee to accept, &c. 170.

of drawee of a bill no excuse for omission of notice of dishonour, 210.

of holder when an excuse for delay, 212.

of a party to a bill, notice of dishonour should be given to his executor or administrator, 229.

of acceptor no excuse for omission of presentment for payment, 246.

of drawer where presentment for payment should be made, 262.

of holder when payment must not be to his personal representative, 280.

of drawer of a check, a revocation of banker's authority to pay, 306.

note payable on the death of a person good, 337.

death of one of four acceptors no variance to state that it was accepted by three, 354.

on death of plaintiff after interlocutory judgment, court granted a rule to compute, 370.

on death of subscribing witness, what proof of maker's hand-writing sufficient, 379.—(See " *Witness,* " " *Evidence,* " " *Hand-writing.* ")

DEBT,

of the effect of taking a bill in payment of, 94 to 100.

a promise to give time for payment of a pre-existing, is not binding, 95.

a person taking a bill or note in payment of, cannot afterwards sue on original contract till bill, &c. is due, 95.—(See " *Bills of Exchange.* ")

and if he does on proof of bill having been given, plaintiff must prove its dishonour, or be nonsuited, 97, 8.   [95.

before bill due extent in aid on behalf of the crown cannot be issued,

otherwise if the terms of the agreement for which the creditor receives such bill, &c. are not strictly complied with, 96.

and if such second bill is void the holder may sue on original liability, 96.

incurred in respect of a covenant by three joint covenantors, and a bill is given, on which judgment is recovered, such recovery does not bar the action of covenant, 96.

security by specialty, taking a bill or note, how far it prejudices, 96.

a person taking a renewed bill for one that was due, the latter, if it remain with him, may be sued on, in case the former is not paid, 96.

revived if the bill or note taken in discharge of, is not honoured, 98.

what circumstances will be deemed as altering this rule, 99, 100.

when a precedent debt is due, no demand need be made or proved if alleged, 249.

payment of a debt should not be to an agent or attorney, 281.

payment of a, to or by a bankrupt, when valid, 282.—(See " *Bankrupt,* " " *Bankruptcy.* ")

of the effect of payment of a debt by a bill or check, 287, 8, 9.

DEBT—*(continued.)*

a man owing several debts to one creditor, and paying money to him generally, such creditor may apply it in discharge of which debt he pleases, even in prejudice of a surety, 289.

otherwise when bankers are concerned, 289.—(See " *Banker.*")

a person paying the debt of another without his request, has no remedy against him, 321.

this rule does not extend to payment of bills of exchange *supra protest*, 321. [*Proceedings.*")

payment of, and costs in action on a bill, 368.—(See " *Staying* in an action of debt on judgment recovered in a bill, no reference to master allowed, 270.

DEBT, ACTION OF.—(See " *Action of Debt.*")

DECLARATIONS.—(See " *Averments*", " *Precedents,*" " *Action of* " *Debt.*")

In assumpsit on bills.

1. *Of the statement of the bill,* 351 to 357.

venue, 351.

not necessary to state or refer to custom of merchants, 351.

nor to statute respecting promissory notes, 352, 327, note.

no profert of a bill or note to be made, 352.

but they should be stated in the terms as made, 352.

if an instrument resembles a bill or note, it may be declared on as either, 41, 2.

variance in a material part, fatal, 352.

instances and examples in misnomers, 353.

when one of several acceptors is an infant, the declaration should be against adults only, 353.

no departure to leave out the infant, 353.

when a bill purports to be drawn by a firm, it may be averred in the plural, that certain persons drew, &c. though the firm consisted of one only, 354.

the date to be stated, 354.—(See " *Date.*")

mis-statement of day on note payable by instalments, fatal, 354.

on a bill payable at double usance after date, stating a date but not the real one, is good, 354.

how to frame declaration on a bill or note, dated on a wrong day, 354.

question whether the date of a bill, payable upwards of six years after date, must be precisely stated, 355.

usual to state place where bill drawn, and the venue, under a videlicet, 355.

but no variance to state that a note was made in London, when in fact it was made at Paris, 355.—(See " *Variance.*")

and it is the same in regard to inland bills, 355.

the instrument must be stated in terms, or according to its legal effect, 355. [English, 355.

if drawn in foreign language, it may be stated in the

if payable at usances the length of them must be stated, 356.

omission of such averment fatal on demurrer, 356.—(See " *Demurrer.*")

and if bill is payable at a particular place in the body, qualification must be stated, 356, 250.

DECLARATIONS—*(continued.)*

In assumpsit on bills—(continued.)

DEMAND—*(continued.)*

no days of grace allowed on such bills, 269.—(See *" Days of Grace."*) [269.

should be presented for payment in a reasonable time after receipt, what is a reasonable time a question of law and fact, 269.

bills, &c. payable on demand need not be presented for payment on day issued, 270.

presentment for payment of a bill, &c. payable on demand, the next day is sufficient, if made in usual hours of business, 270.

this rule prevails when bill given to a banker in payment, 271, 2.

the rule allowing a party to retain a check, &c. payable on demand, till day after receipt, does not extend to a succession of holders, 276.

the statute of Limitations runs from date of note payable on demand, and not from demand made, 373, but see 361.

note payable on demand, dated 20 years before commencement of suit, is presumed to have been paid, 305.

demand of acceptance, when necessary, 158.

demand of payment not necessary to be made of drawer in order to charge indorser of a bill, 262.

demand of payment to charge acceptor of a bill, or maker of note when necessary, 250 to 259.

interest recoverable on a bill payable on demand, 420.—(See *" Interest."*)

DEMAND, PARTICULARS OF.—(See *" Particulars of Demand."*)

what necessary to recover on common counts, 363.

DEMURRER,

omission of averment of length of usance in declaration fatal, 356.

omission of allegation of protest in an action on a foreign bill, bad on special demurrer, 362.

what allegation of this protest is bad, 362.

to the count on a bill, and judgment for plaintiff, reference to master allowed, 370.

but a *nolle prosequi* must be entered to other counts, 370.

after interlocutory judgment signed, plaintiff must wait till following day before he can obtain rule to refer, 370.

when a mis-statement in a declaration is substantially bad, advantage may be taken by a general demurrer, 372.

when only formally so by a special one, 372.

DEPOSIT.

if a navy bill is left as a deposit and security till another is accepted, the produce received may be recovered under the count for money had and received, 366.

DESTRUCTION.—(See *" Loss."*)

DEVASTAVIT.—(See *" Executor."*)

DILIGENCE.—(See *" Search," " Inquiry."*)

what sufficient inquiry after residence of drawer or indorser, 213.

CHITTY ON BILLS. 4 B

DIVIDEND—*(continued.)*
  aliter when debt is not proved on the note, 374.
  mode of recovering same, 470.

DONATIO MORTIS CAUSA.—(See " *Gift.*")
  bill of exchange not capable of being, 2.
  a bond is, 2.
  a bank note is, 2, 332, 3.
  an absolute gift to take effect immediately, is not a, 73.

DRAFT.—(See " *Check.*")

DRAWEE.—(See " *Acceptor,*" " *Acceptance,*" " *Presentment for Acceptance.*")
  of a bill of exchange, who is such, 1. 20.
  where there are two, both must accept, or bill must be protested, 39.
  want of address to, cured by acceptance, 91. 174, 5.
  where a bill is directed to A. or B. an acceptance by A. or B. is
    sufficient, 91.
  where a bill is altered by drawee, it is invalidated, when, 104.—(See
    " *Bill of exchange.*")
  when cannot dispute the validity of an indorsement, if he afterwards
    accept, 124.
  refusing to accept makes drawer and indorser immediately liable, 142.
  if a foreign bill is lost, &c. whilst in hands of drawee, he must give
    a promissory note for the sum, 157.
  if he refuse, holder may immediately protest, 157.—(See " *Protest.*")
  and when due, though he have neither bill or note, if payment is re-
    fused, he may protest, 157.
  no presentment to necessary, if drawee cannot be found, &c. 164. 247.
  having left the kingdom, and no agent, no presentment need be made,
    165. 247.
  when dead, presentment should be made to personal representative,
    165.
  when requires time to accept, and holder grants it, he should give
    notice, 165.
  must have capacity to contract, or holder may treat bill as dishonour-
    ed, 166.
  has 24 hours to accept a bill in, 163. 167.
  ought not to give acceptance if he knows of drawer's failure, 169, 170.
  what amounts to an acceptance by, 170. 176.
  all acceptances by, of inland bills, must now be in writing on bill,
    170.
  otherwise as to foreign bills, and inland bills drawn before 1st Au-
    gust, 1821, 170. 175.
  what will not amount to an acceptance by, 177.
  but when acceptance is doubtful, drawee may rebut the presumption
    in favour of it, 179.
  may make an acceptance payable on a contingency, 180.
  release by drawer before acceptance, does not discharge subsequent
    acceptance, 190.
  death, bankruptcy, or known insolvency of, does not excuse the omis-
    sion of notice of the dishonour of a bill, 210.—(See " *Notice of
    Non-acceptance.*")
  of a bill may make an acceptance *supra protest* on same bill, 241.
    (See " *Acceptance supra protest.*")

DAWEE—*(continued.)*

when acceptor *supra protest* may claim indemnity from drawee, 243.—
(See " *Acceptance supra protest.*")

when presentment for payment should be made to his agent, 247.

not bound by a promise to pay a bill if holder would forego the duplicate protest, and he refused, 279.

when drawer not discharged by payment of a bill before due, 281.

paying a bill by check, holder ought not to give up bill, 287.

DRAWER

of a bill of exchange, who is, 1. 20.

release by to acceptor does not affect payee's right of action, 5. 190.

set-off due from, to acceptor, does not, 5,

in an action against, infancy of indorser no defence, 20.

in an action against, want of consideration between him and third
person, no bar, 70.

except such third person gave no value for it, which must be proved,
70, in notes.

of a bill or check given on a verbal condition, which is broken, may
refuse to pay same, 71.

his name must be inserted in some part of a bill, 89.

must be written by himself, or his authorized agent, 89. 90.

when an agent, the proper manner of signing a bill, 90.

when a partner, and bill drawn in name of firm, how to sign it, 90.

liable to any amount to which his name is affixed, even though the
instrument was drawn in blank, and afterwards filled up without
his knowledge, 24, 90, 107. 124.

of a bill, cannot alter the place of payment without acceptor's consent, 103.—(See " *Bill of Exchange.*")

liability of, complete after delivery of the bill to payee or indorsee,
106.

liable even where the acceptor, by laws of foreign country in which
he resides, is prohibited from paying, 106.

but the rule is otherwise if such prohibition arose from law of this
country, 106.

liable if he drew the bill on his own account, or as an agent, 107.—
(See " *Agent.*")

liable immediately if any acts which he by drawing the bill has warranted, are not fulfilled, 107.   [107. 195.

liable to indemnify acceptor if he accepted for his accommodation.

but such liability of, may be discharged by laches of the holder, 107.
(See " *Laches.*")

what laches of the holder will discharge, 245.

when an annuity granted in consideration of a bill accepted but
which was dishonoured, and then paid by drawer, annuity not vacated, 107.

when a bill is drawn abroad by a person here, he is discharged here
if he is so abroad, 107.

liability, though no words of transfer are inserted in a bill, 109.

liable, though indorsed by a married woman, if he afterwards promise
to pay, 115.

liable on an indorsement made by payee, who died before bill bore
date, 124.

if when bill refused payment by acceptor, takes it up, he may indorse
it again, 130.   [130.

of a note may, under certain circumstances, issue it after payment,

DRAWER—*(continued.)*

a receipt on back of bill only evidence of payment by acceptor, though produced by drawer, 399.—(See *"Evidence."*)

cannot be called to prove that he did not draw, without a release, 414.—(See *"Release," "Witness."*)   [415.

bankrupt drawer a witness if released, though assignees not released.

but in all cases, except accommodation bill, he is admissible either for plaintiff or defendant in an action against acceptor, 415, 416. (See *" Witness."*)

sum recoverable against, 419 to 426.—(See *"Damages."*)

DURESS,

proof that bill was obtained by, puts plaintiff to show how he obtained bill, 68, note.

but notice so to do must be served on plaintiff before the trial, 400.

EASE AND FAVOUR.—(See *"Sheriff."*)

bill made in consideration of to a sheriff, void, 79, 80.

EAST INDIA COMPANY,

may be parties to bills, &c. 15.

ECCLESIASTICS,

in France, may not be parties to a bill, 13.

in England may, 13.

and if he might not, he would be liable as a party to a bill, 13, note.

EFFECTS,

want of, in drawee's hands, excuses omission of protest, 216.

want of, in drawee's hands, excuses omission of notice of dishonour to drawer, 198.

but where payee has, and drawer has not, and bill drawn for accommodation of payee, drawer is not entitled to notice, 200.

want of, at time bill becomes due does not excuse omission of notice if drawee had any effects at any time before bill due, 206.

and this although effects withdrawn by drawer, 206.

this rule extends when drawer owes drawee a larger sum, and drawee retains for his own debt, 207.

in hands of drawee not always essentially necessary, 207, 8.

instances and examples, 208, 9.

bona fide reasonable expectation of having effects in drawee's hands to pay a bill, entitles drawer to notice, 209.

want of, in drawee's hands does not excuse omission of notice to indorser, 228.

as far as regards drawer's liability is an excuse for not making presentment for payment, 248.—(See *"Presentment for Payment."*)

holder of a bill giving time to an acceptor who has no effects of drawer's in his hands discharges the other parties, 293.

want of effects of drawer, in acceptor's hands, at time holder compounds with acceptor, prevents such composition from discharging the drawer, 301, 2.

want of effects in drawee's hands excuses omission of notice of non-payment, 309.

if an acceptor has no effects of drawer in his hands, he may suffer bill to be protested for non-payment, and then pay for honour of drawer, 320.

if an acceptor has no effects he cannot be sued by a party paying a bill *supra protest,* 310.

EFFECS—(*continued.*)
if drawee accept and pay a bill without having them of drawer in his hands, and without protesting it, he may recover under the count for money had and received, 365.
proof of want of effects, what it will excuse, 233 to 240. 409.
acceptance is a *prima facie* admission of, in drawee's hands, 410.

ELECTION,
bill for bribery at election illegal, 79.

EMBEZZLEMENT OF BILLS,
Statutes against, 114, see also the statutes in Appendix, 558, 9.

ENGAGEMENT—(See "*Agreement.*"
col'ateral engagement to pay money, action of debt does not lie on, 428.

ENQUIRY—(See "*Search.*")

EQUITY, COURT OF—(See "*Court of Equity.*")

EQUITABLE INTEREST,
vested in assignee of a chose in action, 7.
how far vested draft of a creditor on his debtor, 195.

ERROR,
bail in error required in an action of debt after verdict or judgment by default, 427.
but not necessary in action of debt on a promissory note, 427.
in all cases unnecessary, if declaration contain a count on a contract for which debt would not lie till after the stat. 3 Jac. 1. c. 8, 427,
not necessary on judgment in debt against acceptor, 428.

ESTOPPEL,
if a bill purports to be drawn by a firm the acceptor estopped from disputing the fact, 353.

EVENT—(See "*Condition,*" "*Contingency.*")
bills may not be payable on an event which is not morally sure to happen, 55 to 64.
in the declaration on such bills an averment of such event happening must be introduced, 361.

EVIDENCE—(See "*Witness,*" "*Admission,*" "*Hand-writing.*")
I. *What evidence plaintiff must adduce in general,* 376 to 377.
governed by the pleadings, 376.
when general issue pleaded, plaintiff must prove every allegation in declaration, 376.
when only a special plea, then only the matter in issue, 376.
what not expressly denied, admitted by the pleadings, 376.
when infancy alone pleaded, plaintiff need not prove any part of his declaration, 376.
what must be proved under the general issue, 376, 7.

EVIDENCE—*(continued,)*

Secondly. Proof that the defendant was party to the bill—*(continued.)*

and one of them is a good witness to prove hand-writing of all, 381.

if a partnership is proved, proof of hand-writing of one partner or an agent suffices, 381.

and if partnership proved, proof of admission of one partner of the hand-writing of one of the others to the acceptance, sufficeth, 381.

not necessary to prove that defendant had the christian names stated in the declaration, 382.

acceptance by drawee of a bill drawn by an agent of his firm upon him was evidence against the other partners of bill being regularly issued, 383.

and in such case the agent's authority need not be proved, 382.

declaration of agent, only evidence against principal when it relates to transactions in which agent was employed, 383.

admission of partnership with co-defendants, proof against such person of a joint promise to pay by all, 382.

declaration of one partner evidence against another, 382.

concerning joint contracts and interest, 382.

as well after as before dissolution of partnership, 382.

and this, though person making such declaration is no party to the suit, 382.

the answer of one partner to a bill filed against him evidence against the others, 382.

in a joint action joint liability must be proved, 383.

Semble, plaintiff's counsel may suggest to witness the names of firm, 395.

outlawry of two defendants out of three will not dispense with proof of the joint liability, 383.

if one of two joint makers of a note suffer judgment by default that will not dispense with proof of his signature on the trial against the other, 383.

time of acceptance must be proved in an action on a bill payable at sight, 383.

but if signature proved, and the date appear over it, that is sufficient proof of the time, 383.

in an action against drawer or indorser, the hand-writing of the defendant or his authorized agent must be proved, 383.

an indorsement attested by a subscribing witness must be proved by him, 383.

Mode of proof how defendant became party, 383 to 389.

one of several acceptors competent to prove hand-writing of others, 383.

when acceptance by parol, it must be proved by the person who heard him accept, 383.

and if answer given by a clerk of third person, they must be subpœnaed, 383.

exceptions to that rule, 384.

must be proved that the answer was given by drawee or by his authority, 384.   [proved, 384.

if acceptance in writing, it must be produced, and signature

in an action against drawer indorser, signature must be proved by a person who can swear to hand-writing, 384.

or to an admission by party sued, 384.

EVIDENCE—*(continued.)*
Thirdly. Proof plaintiff's interest—(continued.)

if bill, payable to order of several, not partners, hand-writing of each must be proved, 393.

and acceptance after indorsement of one is no admission of the regularity of the indorsement, 393.

though if acceptor expressly promise to pay at the time it is otherwise, 393.

in an action against drawer or acceptor of a bill payable to the order of several partners, partnership, and the hand-writing of one of them, or an agent of the firm, must be proved, 381, 394.

when bill payable to a fictitious person, what will dispense with the proof of his hand-writing, 394, 64, note.

if several join in suing on a bill indorsed in blank, no evidence of partnership necessary, 394.

otherwise, if indorsed to a firm by name of Co. when strict evidence must be given that the firm consists of the persons who sue, 394.

after indorsement in blank to a firm for benefit of insolvent's estate, two of which firm are trustees with C. for the estate, these three cannot maintain an action on the bill without evidence of transfer from that firm, 394.

when partnership is to be proved, counsel may suggest the names of the firm to the witness, 394.

admission by indorser of his hand-writing, is not evidence of the indorsement in an action against maker, 396.   [396.

indorser himself may be called to prove his own hand-writing, though before, negatived by another witness, 396.

doubtful if plaintiff fails in proving indorsement by one witness, he can call another, 396.

a promise to pay, or offer to renew, dispenses with evidence of indorsement, if made to indorsee after bill due, 396.

what objection made by drawer, who saw bill after indorsement, will not dispense with evidence of it, 397.

payment of money into court, admits indorsement, 397.

in an action against an indorser, hand-writing of drawer or prior indorser need not be proved, 397.

in an action by an executor against accepter, on a promise laid to testator, plaintiff must prove acceptance in testator's lifetime, 398.

to establish a set-off on a bill against assignees of a bankrupt, there must be evidence that party got it before bankruptcy, 398.—(See " *Bankruptcy.*")

but if the act of bankruptcy were secret, evidence of possession two calendar months before is sufficient, 398.—(See " *Bankruptcy.*")

when drawer of a bill, payable to order of third person, and returned to and paid by him, sues, what evidence necessary, 398.

the same where a prior indorser paid a subsequent one, and sues acceptor, 398.

what evidence should be given in an action by accommodation acceptor against drawer for money paid, or specially for not indemnifying, 398.

production of bill by acceptor is not *prima facie* evidence of his having paid it, or that it was once in circulation, 399.

EVIDENCE—*(continued.)*

  Thirdly.   Proof plaintiff's interest—(continued.)

    same with indorsement, if receipt on back, unless accompanied by evidence of the hand-writing, 399.

    a general receipt on back of a bill is *prima facie* evidence of payment by acceptor, 399, 410.

    but to be available by him, proof of circulation after acceptance must be given, 410.

    and will not, of itself, be evidence of payment by drawer, though produced by him, 410.

  When consideration to be proved, 400, 401.   See also 68, &c.

    if it appear to be made or indorsed under duress or by fraud, and plaintiff has had notice to prove consideration, he must do so, 400.

    but even after notice given, plaintiff will not be called on to prove consideration till evidence has been given that bill was obtained by undue means, 400.

    but if a strong case of fraud can be made out, no notice is necessary to be given, 400.

    evidence of usury will not now affect a *bona fide* holder's action, 401, 78.   Appendix, 556.

    in case of a bank note, strong evidence of fraud, or want of consideration, will alone affect plaintiff's right, 401.

  Fourthly.   Evidence of the breach of contract, and other circumstances, 402 to 410.

    not necessary to prove a presentment for payment, in an action against acceptor of a bill, payable generally, or maker of a note, 402, 249.

    if accepted payable at a banker's, according to the late act necessary to prove presentment there, 259.

    and such presentment must be averred in the declaration, 259.

    this now qualifies doctrine laid down in page 402.

    when made payable at a particular place in body of bill, or in address, or in body of note, presentment there must be proved, 514.

    not necessary to prove presentment was made by person named in declaration, 401, 2.

    nor to prove that notice of dishonour at bankers was given to acceptor, unless he shows damage sustained thereby.   Rhodes *v.* Gent, MS. 309, 362.

    in case of a conditional acceptance, performance must be averred as well as proved, 402.

    in an action against drawer or indorser of a bill, or indorser of a note, default of party primarily liable must be proved, 402.

    in such action, presentment to drawee for payment must be proved, 402.

    but evidence for presentment or demand on drawer, unnecessary, 403.

    when action for non-acceptance, a due presentment must be proved, 404.

    and when bill payable at a banker's presentment there must be proved, in an action against drawer or indorser, 404.

    and a presentment at banker's, by a notary, in the evening, is not sufficient, 404, 261, 277, in notes.

    but if a person was stationed there to answer, then it will be good, 277, 405.

EVIDENCE—*(continued.)*
Evidence of the breach of contract, and other circumstances—(continued.)

in an action against drawer or indorser of a foreign bill, protest must be averred and proved, 405, 308, 215, 362.

if averred in an action on an inland bill, it must be proved, 405, 309, 362, 214, 15.

protest of inland bill not necessary, and does not effect holder's remedy in recovering interest, &c. 219, 312, 405, 362.

protest made abroad under seal of notary, proves itself, 405.

protest made in England must be proved by the notary who made it and the subscribing witness, if any, 405.

in an action against drawer and indorser of a bill, and indorser of note, proof of due notice of dishonour must be given, 405.

such proof cannot be left to inference, but it must be by positive evidence, 405.

if notice given by letter, notice to produce same must be given before plaintiff will be allowed to go into evidence of its contents, 405.—(See "*Letter.*")

but it has lately been determined that secondary evidence may be given of the contents of a written notice without notice to produce it, 406.

and a copy of a letter containing notice of dishonour, is admissible without notice to produce original, 407.

what is evidence in default of production of a letter, after notice to produce was given, that due notice of dishonour was received, 407.—(See "*Notice of Non-Acceptance and Non-Payment.*")

and proof that a letter was received from defendant, acknowledging the receipt of a letter from holder of a named date, but not referring to its contents, is presumptive evidence of due notice of dishonour, 407.

when evidence of notice of dishonour given, it will suffice to show that a letter, containing such notice, was put into the post-office or left at defendant's house, 408.

in civil cases, post-mark evidence of time and place, when and where put into the office, 408.—(See "*Post.*")

proof that notice or other paper was sent by post, always considered sufficient, 408.—(See "*Letter.*")

a question sometimes arises as to what is the requisite proof of the fact of sending by post, 408.

instance and example each way, 408, 9.

plaintiff may prove facts to excuse neglect to present, to give notice, or to protest in case of a foreign bill, 409, 219. [409.

want of effects in hands of drawer sufficient excuse for these, what evidence dispensed with, on proof of a promise to pay, after full notice of laches, 409.

though drawer may impliedly waive, proof is necessary of indorser's express waiver of holder's laches, 409, 239.

the evidence must be left to a jury to say whether at time of promise or application defendant had notice of dishonour, 410.

in an action by drawer against acceptor of a bill payable to a third person, and taken up by drawer, what evidence necessary, 410.

not necessary to prove that acceptor had effects in his hands, acceptance *prima facie* evidence of effects, 410. [410.

when acceptor of accommodation bill sues the drawer specially, what he must prove, 410.

EXCISE LAWS,

contract made in repugnance of, void, 74.

extraordinary days of grace allowed by, on bills payable to the excise, 266.

and such time allowed by the excise to drawee, does not discharge the drawer.

EXCISE OFFICER,

when release given by for penalties incurred, is sufficient consideration for a note, 75.

EXECUTION,

a bill or note cannot be taken in execution, 2. 332.

of effect of giving time, &c. to acceptor, &c. 290.

taking a party in by the holder of a bill, does not discharge the others, 146. 346.

the same rule prevails on joint and several bonds, 346.

suing acceptor to, and taking part payment and security for the rest, with exception of nominal sum, indorser discharged, 293. 297.

the rule is the same when acceptor in custody on a *ca. sa.* and is let out, 293.

may be taken out against, on a joint and several note against one of the parties, and part levied without discharging the other, 297.

a subsequent indorser let out of, on a letter of license, does not prevent holder suing a prior indorser, 347. 298.

a party to a bill charged in, but discharged as an insolvent, does not release the liability of other parties to it, 301. 344. 347.

how notes should be made when a prisoner is declared in under the lord's act 335.—(See *"Prisoner."*)

acceptor of a bill who has been charged in execution by the holder, and discharged by the lord's act, may be charged again by the drawer who has paid it, 344.

if holder of a bill reject an offer to pay debt and costs, court will not allow him to take out execution, 346, 7.

may issue against all parties to a bill, but the levy can only be against one, 347.

when imprisonment in, cannot be proved as special damage in an action, accommodation acceptor against drawer, 410.—(See *"Accommodation Bill," "Evidence."*)

EXECUTOR AND ADMINISTRATOR.—(See *"Administrator," "Legacy."*)

a bill or note is a simple contract in payment of debts, 1.

a bill *bona notabilia* where debtor resides, 1.   [2.

a bank note may pass as *donatio mortis causa,* but not a bill or note,

a bank note may pass under a bequest of property in a house, but not a bill or note, 2.

executor entitled to recover from agent, if testator or intestate assign over an instrument which does not pass legal interest, 8.

bound by act of his agent, authorized to transact all deceased's affairs, 24.

but it has been decided otherwise, 25.

liable on a bill issued by a firm from which he receives his share for benefit of an infant, 29, 30, note.

of a deceased partner liable in equity on a bill or note given in name of a firm, though in fraud of the deceased, 32.

CHITTY ON BILLS.   4 D

EXECUTOR AND ADMINISTRATOR—*(continued.)*

liable where a banker's check is given and paid away for valuable
consideration, 73.

may indorse bills of the testator or intestate, 122.   [223.

but such indorsement must be qualified, otherwise personally liable,
not liable on failure of a banker in whose hands they have placed
part of the estate, 123.

acceptance by an executor, is admission of assets, 185.   [185,
and he is personally liable, though he has no assets in his hands,
liable to pay a draft drawn on him, if he promise so to do, 194.

when a party to a bill is dead, notice of dishonour must be given to,
229.

when presentment for payment must be made to, 246.—(See "*Presentment for Payment.*")   [247.

when holder is dead, presentment for payment must be made by,
payment to a person with a probate of a forged will, is valid, 280.

debt on simple contract, and sustainable, against, 342.

if holder of a bill make acceptor executor, right of action extinguished, 345.

unless he formerly renounce, 344.

in an action by executor against acceptor, he cannot prove acknowledgment since the death, if promise laid to testator, 398.—(See
"*Evidence.*")

EXPENSES—(See "*Damages.*"

of protest, what, 216. 312.

what may be recovered in an action, 423.

of a special messenger giving notice of non-payment when recoverable, 222, note.

what may be proved under a commission of bankrupt, 464.

EXPUNGING,

of expunging proofs, 468.—(See "*Bankruptcy.*")

EXTENT,

in aid cannot be issued where the creditor has taken a bill not
due, 95.

when legal transfer of bill incomplete, extent may issue with effect,
131, note.

bill of exchange not due taken under it, parties to it not discharged,
if no presentment for payment made, 248.

what is a good plea to an extent in aid, 372.—(See "*Pleas.*")

EXTINGUISHMENT—(See "*Bills of Exchange,*" "*Executor.*")

taking a bill, how far an extinguishment of prior debt, 94 to 100.

taking a bill amounts to agreement to give credit, 95 to 100.

of right of action by death, &c. 344.

FACTOR—(See "*Agent.*")

of an incorporate company drawing a bill on such company, acceptance of one member does not bind the rest, 38.

of several individuals, (not partners or a company) the rule is the
same, 38.

consequences of his pledging bills, 113.

trover lies for bills indorsed to for plaintiff's account if parted
with by, 113.

FACTOR—(*continued.*)
indictable if he do so fraudulently, 114. 151.
liable to repay money to assignees of a bankrupt, under what circumstances, 170.

FEES—(See *"Notary."*)

FELONY,
compounding of, no consideration to found a contract on, 74.
to steal bills, &c. 151.

FEME COVERT—(See *"Baron and Feme," "Married Woman."*)
contracts by, in general, absolutely void, 16.
cannot be a party to a bill of exchange, 18.
nor to a promissory note, 18.   [18.
sole trader of London, cannot be sued in courts at Westminster, but sometimes chargeable in equity, 18.
but may contract when her husband is legally dead, 18.
a promise by, after husband's death, to pay a note made in husband's life-time valid, if she had separate property secured to her when note was given, 18.
otherwise if not, 18.
indorsement of a bill or note by, does not pass any interest, 19.
but if after such indorsement, maker promises to pay it, it is valid, 115.
but when indorsed with husband's knowledge, court will infer it was done by his authority, 19. 115. 36.
indorsement of a bill by, invalidates it, as against all the antecedent parties to it, 19.
a bill given by, if indorsed by husband, how far valid, 22.
a bill given to a feme sole on her marriage vests in husband, 19.
husband may indorse such bill, 19. 114.
not necessary to join wife in action by husband on such bill, 19.
may be an agent, 23.
and as an agent may indorse bills, 114.
when demand of acceptance and payment of a bill to, is sufficient, 229.
payment of a bill to, after knowledge of that fact, invalid, 280.
may join her husband in an action on a note made payable to her during coverture, though not necessary, 19. 342.
if arrested as acceptor of a bill by holder, she will not be discharged on common bail, though drawer knew that fact, 350, *sed quære.*
what she should do in such case, 350.
if arrested as drawer, affidavit of coverture must be sworn by herself and not by a third person, 350.
a bill payable to one, if indorsed by husband, may be declared on as payable to him, 359. 22.

FESTIVAL—(See *"Sunday."*)
Jews holy festival, when it excuses delay in notice, 214.

FICTITIOUS NAMES,
to a bill, consequence of making use, 64, 5.
indorsement of a fictitious persons' name on a bill is forgery, 65.
when bill payable to a fictitious person, formality of indorsement when waived, 94.

FORGERY—(*continued.*)

cannot be set up as a defence, if defendant admit his hand-writing before instrument due, and thereby induce holder to take, 387.

if defendant set up forgery as a defence, and plaintiff fail in proving defendant's hand-writing, yet if he can prove that he accepted and paid bills made in like manner, plaintiff will recover, 388.

and this though the forgery appears apparent, 388.

a person in prison on a charge of, when it will not affect his competency to be a witness, 416.

FORMS—(See "*Precedents.*")

of bills of exchange, 51.

of a check, 51.

of a promissory note, 324.

in general no particular forms necessary, 41.

of an indorsement, 132.

of an acceptance, 170.

of notice of non-acceptance, what necessary, 215 to 223.

    of a foreign bill, 215.

    of an inland bill, 218.

of an acceptance *supra protest*, 213.

of notice of non-payment, what necessary, 310.

    of a foreign bill, 310.

    of an inland bill, 312.

concise form of stating indorsement, 359.

FRAUD,

by one partner on co-partners, with knowledge of holder, discharges their liability to him, 30, 1.

what will, and what will not raise a presumption of, 33. [33.

a bill given for an antecedent debt by one of many partners does, taking an instrument from one partner in his own hand-writing does, 33.

but knowledge that partner was using for his own private benefit does not, 33.

subsequent approbation by the partners avoids any previous fraud, 34.

between parties to a bill fraud may be questioned, 70.

if a bill is obtained fraudulently, equity will relieve, 73. [101.

alteration of a bill with intent of, is forgery, and invalidates the same, erasure in a bill or note afford presumption of fraud, 105, 6.

a bill transferred after it is due carries presumption of knowledge of fraud, 127.

bona fide holder of bank note not affected by the fraud of former holder, 333, 4.

but where it was proved that fraud had been used in getting possession of a bank note, which was afterwards forwarded from abroad to an agent in England, what evidence sufficient to be left to a jury of fraud, 333.

and question not altered by agent's after notice, having made payments on principal's account, and turned balance in his favour, 334.

if bill had been obtained from a prior party by, plaintiff may be called on to prove consideration, 400.

but not if he has not had notice before trial so to do, 400.

otherwise if a strong case of fraud can be made out sufficient to establish a defence, 401.—(See "*Evidence.*")

FRAUD—(*continued.*)

in case of a bank, strong evidence of fraud will alone discharge plaintiff's right, 401.

though no evidence of inadequacy of inconsideration admissible, yet it may be proof indicatory of fraud, and defeat the contract altogether, 412.—(See "*Evidence.*")

FRAUDS, STATUTE AGAINST,

requires consideration to be expressed in a formal guarantee, 3.
by means of a bill of exchange this avoided, 3.

FRAUDULENT PREFERENCE—(See "*Bankrupt,*" "*Bankruptcy.*")

when it invalidates transfer of a bill, 120. 481. [121.

must appear to have been made in contemplation of such bankruptcy, but if it is not the voluntary act of the party, the rule is otherwise, what has been decided as being consequential, 121. [121.

when the creditor's or debtor's apprehension of insolvency will not vitiate the act, 121.

the intention of, not completed till after creditor's demand, this will not vitiate, 121.

obtained by a creditor in contemplation of deed of composition afterwards abandoned, he may hold the security, 121.

when it is not fraudulent to return bills to their indorsers, in contemplation of insolvency, 122.

payment, made by bankrupt by way of, invalid, 283, 4.

FREIGHT,

bills, &c. drawn to pay money on account of, when good, 49.

FRIENDLY SOCIETIES—(See "*Bankruptcy.*")

preference and proof in case of bankruptcy, 462.

FUND—(See "*Contingency,*" "*Condition.*")

bills and notes payable out of a particular fund, invalid, 43 to 50. 336.

GAMING,

all securities, bills, notes, &c. for money lost by, void, 78.

but an action will lie for money won at whist, not exceeding £10. 78.

enactment of the stat. Ann. c. 14. on, 78.

when a bill is void, a second security given for what is fairly due to the *bona fide* holder of said bill, is valid, 78.

consideration no defence in action against drawer if drawer indorsed it over for value, 79.

in a lottery is illegal, 79.

in a horse-race is illegal, 79.

stock-jobbing transaction is illegal, 79.

policy of ships and lives illegal, 80.

GENERAL ISSUE—(See "*Pleas,*" "*Defence.*")

what defence may be given in evidence under, 374, 5.—(See "*Defence,*" "*Pleas.*")

when pleaded, plaintiff must prove each allegation in his declaration, 375.—(See "*Evidence.*")

what must be proved under, 375.

GIFT—(See "*Donatio Mortis Causa.*")
  promissory note or checks given as such, whether it can be enforced
    72.

GIVING TIME—(See "*Indulgence*," "*Time*," "*Presentment for Payment.*" [*ment.*"])
  effect of giving time to acceptor in general, 290 to 217.—(See "*Pay-*
    in case of bankruptcy, 440.

GOLDSMITHS' NOTES—(See "*Bankers' Cash Notes.*")

GRACE—(See "*Days of Grace.*")

GUARANTEE,
  consideration must in general be expressed in, 3.
  doubtful whether one partner can give a guarantee, so as to bind his
    co-partners, 30.
  how far a person who gives a guarantee, is liable, 67.
  a person giving a collateral engagement, may make himself liable on
    a bill, though he do not indorse it, 144.
  a person indorsing a note to guarantee debt due from maker, may
    insist on omission to present for payment, 203.
  the same where a person no party to the bill, guarantees the payment
    of it, 204. 259. *sed quære.* see 230.
  where this rule is otherwise, 204. 230.
  if the party to a bill, before it becomes due, is a bankrupt or in-
    solvent, the person making the, is not entitled to notice of dis-
    honour, 204.
  for acceptor in action against him, need not prove presentment of
    the bill, 212.
  a person who has secured payment of a bill, is generally entitled to
    notice, 220.
  if two persons join in the making of a joint and several note, and
    one is surety for the other, and holder knowing it accept com-
    position from the other, the surety is discharged, 339.
  a guarantee of a note not due at a date of commission, is not prove-
    able under such commission, 440.
  after a person made a guarantee to pay a debt, and discharged there-
    from by bankruptcy and certificate, he is competent witness, in
    respect to such debt, 410.

HAND-WRITING—(See "*Evidence*," "*Witness.*")
  of drawer as such considered as admitted in an action against the
    acceptor of a bill and maker of a note, 377.
  and forgery of it, no defence, unless proved that acceptance was
    made before bill drawn, or acceptor saw it, 377.
  in which case the drawer's hand-writing must be proved, 377.
  when it must be proved by the subscribing witness, and when other
    evidence of subscription admissible, 379.
  if note attested by a subscribing witness who is dead, what proof of
    defendant's hand-writing is sufficient, 379.—(See "*Subscribing
    Witness.*")
  the same when subscribing witness had become insane, 379.
  when there are several acceptors or makers, the hand-writing of all
    must be proved, 381. 393.
  one of whom is sufficient for such proof, 381. 383.

HAND-WRITING—(*continued.*)

HAND-WRITING—*(continued.)*

of fictitious payee, what will dispense with evidence of it, 394. 64. n.

admission of indorser of his hand-writing to a note, evidence against the maker, 395.—(See *"Admission."*)

of drawer and prior indorsers not admitted by indorsement of a subsequent indorser, 396.

indorser himself may prove his hand-writing, 396.

so after another witness has negatived it, 496.

of a person entitled to payment must be proved to entitle acceptor of an accommodation bill to recover on production of the bill with receipt indorsed, 399.

hand-writing of drawer must be proved in a special action by accommodation acceptor against drawer, 410.

of person entitled to make, must be proved before a receipt, 410.

HOLDER—(See *"Indorsee," "Payee," "Indorsement," "Transfer."*)

who is the holder, 20, 1.

what conduct he should pursue in case of loss of bill, 147 to 157.—(See *"Loss."*)

on non-acceptance, 196 to 230. 158.—(See *"Notice," "Non-acceptance."*)

on non-payment, 308 to 320.—(See *"Notice," "Non-payment."*)

must prove consideration in an action on a bill or note given by one partner in fraud of the rest, 31.

of a bill of exchange, &c. *bona fide,* when entitled to recover, 70. (See *"Usury," "Consideration," "Gaming."*)

when he has once returned bill as useless, cannot afterwards sue acceptor, 70. 184.

may now recover on bill founded on usury, 77.

a judgment in favour of a *bona fide,* aids the illegal consideration, 78.

bill given for gambling considered void in hands of, 78.

otherwise if bill be renewed, 79.

bona fide may maintain action against the drawer of such bill, 79.

bona fide of a bill when a loser on account of illegal consideration may sustain an action against his indorser on original contract, 81.

same if after agreement to take another bill and do other acts, this agreement is not complied with, or such second bill is void, 96.

of a bill for which another has been given, may sue on the first bill, in case the latter is not paid, 96.

bona fide of a bill cannot recover on it, if it has been altered even without his knowledge, 104.—(See *"Bill of Exchange."*)

holder without notice, may recover, though his indorser had no right to transfer, 112.—(See *"Bankrupt."*)

on death of holder, his executor or administrator may indorse, 122. (See *"Executor."*)

how far the laches of the holder of a bill afterwards indorsed to a *bona fide* indorsee, without notice thereof, affect such indorsee, 124.—(See *"Laches."*)

of a bill transferred to him after it was due, is liable to the same objections, and has the same advantages as if it were in the hands of his immediate indorser, 126.

this rule applies to a banker's check, transferred long after it was first issued, 128.

not prejudiced if such transfer was made by party to it, 129.

what holder should do if he is indebted to a prior party, and suspects his insolvency, 130. 141.—(See *"Set-off."*)

CHITTY ON BILLS. 4 E

HOLDER—*(continued.)*

of a bill by turning a blank into a special indorsement, does not
make himself liable without adding his name, 134.

need not give notice of indorsements to acceptor, 140.

may effect a policy of insurance for due payment 'of bill, 140.

if a banker be a party to a bill, a holder may set-off his claim on
him, against the amount of the bill, 130. 141.—(See " *Set-off.*")

if he received it for a particular purpose, must fulfil it, 141. 184.

what circumstances will alter this rule, 141.

transfer to holder, gives a right of action to him against all parties to
the bill, 142.

but if it is payable to order, and not first indorsed, the holder can only
sue him from whom he received it, 142.

obligations to the assignor of a bill may be discharged by acts of, 146.

what conduct he should pursue in presentment for acceptance, 158
to 165.

not obliged to acquiesce in an acceptance by an agent, 166.

may insist on the production of agent's authority, 166.

of a bill may refuse special acceptance, 166. 180. 182.—(See
" *Acceptance.*")

must give notice of special acceptance if he takes it, 180.

of an accommodation bill, how far allowed to recover on it, 184.

when agent for third party who ought not to recover, he will be disabled, 184.

what promise, &c. to discharge acceptor, will be binding on
him, 190.

of a bill with an acceptance forged by indorser, may recover on another given him by indorsee, when he gave up the first, 105.

otherwise if there is an agreement to stifle prosecution for the
forgery, 485. 74.

of a bill receiving part of the money due on it, and enlarging the
time for payment of residue, is not a waiver of acceptance, 191.

of a bill not entitled to show that defendant has sustained no actual
damage by omission of notice of dishonour, 210.

of a foreign bill, what he should do in case bill is dishonoured, 215.

how he should give notice, 219 to 222.

if more convenient to him, may send notice by a special messenger,
and recover reasonable expenses, 222.

when notice of dishonour should be given by, 223 to 225.

by whom such notice should be given, 226 to 228.

may resort to an indorser after a bill is dishonoured, without calling
on drawer or acceptor, 229.

how the consequences of laches may be removed, 233 to 240.

when he may protest for better security, 240.

not obliged to receive an acceptance *supra protest*, 241.

on non-acceptance of a foreign bill, he should protest bill, before he
lets another accept for the honour, 241.

what he should do in presentment of a bill for payment, 245 to 280.

should in all cases make presentment for payment, 245.—(See " *Presentment for Payment.*")

if holder is dead, when it becomes due, presentment for payment
must be by his executor, or personal representative, 247.

of a bill transferrable only by indorsement, who got it without such
indorsement, should on presentment for payment offer indemnity,
247.

and if payment is then refused he may protest the bill, 247.

INDORSEMENT—*(continued.)*

Of the effect of indorsement and transfer, &c. and liability of transferrer, 140 to 146.—(See " Holder," " Indorsee.")

   a transfer of a note by indorsement is equivalent to drawing a
bill of exchange, 141.

and such note may be declared on as a bill, but this is not
usual, 142.

a transfer of indorsement gives a right of action against all
parties to a bill, 142.

but if bill payable to order is not first indorsed by payee, holder
can only sue the person from whom he got it, 142.

a transfer by delivery, without indorsement, what obligations
it imposes, 142. 6. 7.

                 unless expressly otherwise agreed, in
the event of non-payment, the ori-
ginal cause of action returns, 142,
3, 4, 5, 6.

                 of a bill or note, without indorsement,
a person may make himself liable,
145, 6.——(See " Guarantee,"
" Agreement.")

on transfer of a bill by delivery, without indorsement, the assignor cannot be sued on bill, but his assignee must resort to
original cause, 146.

what circumstances will render this cause unavailing, 146.

by one of several partners, how far partnership liable, 29. 123. 145.

the obligations imposed by, can only be released by act of the
holder, 146.

when a bill transferrable only by, and is delivered to a person
without such indorsement, presentment for payment ought to
be made, 247.

indorsement of a bill to an agent to get it paid, whose authority
is afterwards revoked, but who receives the payment, how far
it is valid, 280, 1.

how to be set out in pleading, sometimes advisable to add a
count stating plaintiff as indorsee of some prior indorser, 359.

form of a concise indorsement, 359.

in an action against acceptor by indorsee, application for time is
a waiver of proof of all indorsements except the first, 360.

for less than due, must be described in pleading accordingly,
360.

and not necessary to state that it was made in indorser's hand-
writing, and if it was not it would be fatal, 360.

if a note payable to bearer is declared on as indorsed, it must
be proved, 360.

if a declaration aver indorsement to have been before, and evidence show that it was made after the bill was due, this is not
a fatal variance, 360.—(See " Variance.")

notice of indorsement is not necessary to be averred, 360.

if unnecesssarily stated in an action by indorsee on a note, &c.
transferrable by delivery, it must be proved, 389.—(See
" Evidence.")

if attested by a subscribing witness, he must be called, 383.
390.—(See " Witness.")

drawer's hand-writing to an indorsement must sometimes be
proved, 390.—(See " Hand-writing.")

INDORSEMENT—*(continued.)*

*Of the effect of indorsement and transfer,.&c. and liability of trans-
ferrer*—*(continued.)*

indorser himself may prove his own indorsement, 396.

identity of payee with a person making indorsement, must be
. proved, 391.

where there are several, usual to insert two counts, 392. 359.

and all but the first may be struck out at the time of trial, if
not stated in declaration, 135. 392.

if in blank, several, not partners, may join in suing on the instrument, 394.

what proof in such case necessary, 393, 4.

when bill payable to a firm, what evidence necessary, 394.

INDORSER.—(See " *Indorsee,*" " *Indorsement,*" " *Transfer.*")

of a bill of exchange, who is, 1. 22.

infancy of, no defence to an action by or against the drawer or acceptor, 17.

alteration of a bill after indorsement, without consent of, invalidates
the same, 100, 1.—(See " *Alteration.*")

liable to any amount if he indorses a blank bill, 124.

how far discharged by laches of a holder,.124, 5. 171.—(See " *Laches.*")

to what extent he may recover money paid in ignorance of such
laches, 125, 6.

when residence of unknown, advisable to state it on the bill, 133.

must be done in case of a bill under five pounds, 133.—(See " *Small
Bills.*")

may make a conditional indorsement, 138.—(See " *Indorsement.*")

a qualified indorsement, 139.

has the same advantages and disadvantages as the drawer, 142.

not liable to the acceptor, 142.—(See " *Holder.*")   [146.

obligation imposed on an, by indorsement, may be discharged, when,
for the accommodation of a party, when may retain money in his
hands, 146.

liable immediately to be sued if drawee refuse to accept, 142. 159.
        if acceptor does not pay, 183.   [198.

when not giving notice to, of the dishonour of a bill discharges him.

when it is not material, 212. 3.   [215.

bankruptcy of indorser no excuse for want of notice of dishonour.

tender may be pleaded by, though made after notice of the dishonour
of bill but before writ issued, 232.   [239.

can only by express waiver, waive his right of defence of laches.

any person may make an acceptance *supra protest,* without his consent, 240.   [262.

may be sued, without making any demand of payment from drawer,

discharged, if holder take a check from acceptor in payment, 287.

of the effect of giving time to, 290 to 296.

of a foreign accepted bill, not obliged to pay without having the bill
delivered up to him, 311.

any one indorser may sue acceptor or drawer, when there are several indorsers, 342.—(See " *Action.*")

cannot be sued by the bail of the maker of a note who have paid it
for him, 344.

may be bail for drawer, 350.

in an action against indorser, not necessary to prove any indorsemen'
prior to his, 359.

INDORSER—*(continued.)*
a small variance between declaration and evidence, in his name, immaterial, 392.
in an action against, hand-writing of drawer and prior indorsers, admitted by his indorsement, 397.
may prove indorsement, 396.
if a subsequent indorsement be stated, it must be proved, 398.
usual to insert two counts, one stating all indorsements, and one stating plaintiff as immediate indorsee, if wished not to discharge subsequent indorsers, 398.
letters written by, in general not admissible in evidence to impeach indorsee's right, 411, 12.
see an exception, 412.
in what cases a competent witness, 417.—(See " *Witness.* "
sum recoverable against, 419 to 426.—(See " *Damages.* ")

INDULGENCE.—(See " *Giving Time,* " " *Payment.* ")
the effect of giving time to prior parties to a bill, 290 to 301.
giving time to acceptor or prior indorser, discharges a subsequent one, 298.
giving time to a subsequent one will not discharge a prior one, 298.
holder of a bill may sue prior indorser after letting a subsequent one out of execution on a letter of license, 298.
of an accommodation note receiving a composition from payee, and agreeing not to sue him, may recover from maker, 298.
and a release to such payee, of all claims in respect to note, not knowing that he is a surety, will not discharge the maker, 298.
holder of an accommodation bill may take part-payment from drawer, and a promise to pay residue, without discharging acceptor, 299.
this doctrine once doubted now fully established, 299.
effect in case of bankruptcy, 440.

INFANCY.—(See " *Infant.* ")
in general specially pleaded, 375.
if pleaded alone, no evidence in support of declaration required, 376. (See " *Evidence.* ")

INFANTS.—(See " *Agent.* ")
contract by, only avoidable, 16.
except in case of necessaries, 16.
what are necessaries, 16.
may not be parties to a bill of exchange, &c. 16.
except in case of necessaries, 16.
cannot be sued on a bill given for necessaries but by original parties, and even then doubtful, 16.
is liable as acceptor, 17.
on an express promise to pay after he attained twenty-one, a bill drawn before, 17.
may sue on a bill in his favour, 17.
but it is said he is bound by a single bill given for necessaries, 16.
may be an agent, 23.
a bill, payable six weeks after he shall come of age, specifying day, is good, 48. 337.
cannot make an indorsement so as to charge himself, 111.
and if he does, acceptor and subsequent indorsers liable, 111.
payment of a bill to an infant, how far valid, 280.

INFANTS—(*continued.*)

if an infant joins in the making of a joint note, he ought not to be sued, 339.

the same where he is an acceptor of a bill, 353.

and in such case holder ought not to sue him, even if he accepts with other adults, 353.

and it is no departure to omit such infant's name, 353.

when a third party is an infant in an action by two others, what form of note holden evidence under the count for money lent, 365.

INFORMAL BILL, &c.

if a bill, &c. is informal in its terms, better to state it in pleading, with innuendoes, 353.

INITIALS,

party to a bill, giving only the initials of his christian name, affidavit and proceedings need state them only, 350,

the court will not discharge him on common bail, nor set aside proceedings, 350.

this doctrine now over-ruled, 350.

INJUNCTION—(See " *Court of Equity.*")

when negotiation of bill restrained by, 110.

INLAND BILLS—(See " *Bills of Exchange.*")

INQUIRY.—(See " *Search.*")

INQUIRY, WRIT OF.—(See " *Practice,*" " *Reference to Master.*")

no occasion to execute inquiry on judgment by default, in an action on a bill or note, 351, 369, &c.

otherwise if bill is not stated in the declaration, 351, 370.

if bill payable in foreign money, this writ must be executed, 370.

in executing a writ of inquiry after judgment by default, what evidence must be adduced, 371.

INSANITY,

of a subscribing witness, what evidence of the defendant's handwriting sufficient, 379.

INSOLVENCY,

a proposal to pay creditors by instalments, is a suspicious circumstance of, 120.

not to be inferred from the renewing of bills in particular instances, 120.

mentioned in the 1 Jac. 1. c. 15, and 46 Geo. 3. c. 135, means a general inability to pay, 120.

enactment of the statute 46 Geo. 3. c. 135—121.

debtors or creditors apprehending same, does not render a transaction a fraudulent preference, 121.—(See " *Fraudulent Preference.*")

of a principal suspected, equity entitles an accommodation indorser to retain money in his hands, 146, 7.

to a party to a bill, which has been guaranteed by a third person no party to it, when excuses omission of notice of dishonour, 204.

JUDGMENT—*(continued.)*

but in such case a *nolle prosequi* must be entered to the other counts, 370.

on motion to refer to master, no irregularity previous to judgment is available, 371.

if there is any it must be the subject of a cross motion to set it aside, 371.

after judgment by default, no matter is admissible in evidence in defeasance of the action, 371, 2.

by default, equivalent to an admission, 371.—(See " *Admission.*")

but if one of two makers of a note suffer judgment by default it must nevertheless be proved on the trial against the other, 388.

after judgment by default in an action of debt, when bail in error is necessary, 427.

Precedents of Judgment on Bills and Notes, 514 to 516.—See " *Precedents.*")

JUDGMENT, FINAL.—(See " *Judgment,*" " *Judgment Interlocutory.*"

cannot be signed in an action on a bill after judgment by default, till after reference to master or inquiry, 368.

after demurrer to count on bill and judgment for plaintiff, may refer to master and enter the *nolle prosequi,* at any time before final judgment signed, 370.

interest carried on till it is signed, 422.

otherwise in trover, 422.

JUDGMENT, INTERLOCUTORY—(See " *Reference to Master.*")

after, and death of plaintiff, court will grant a rule to compute, 370.

after such judgment, and the loss of bill, court granted a rule to refer to master on production of a copy of the bill, verified by affidavit of the loss of the original, 370.

practice confined to cases where bill or note specially declared on, 370.

signed for want of a plea, rule to refer may be moved for the same day, 370.

signed on demurrer, plaintiff must wait till the following day, 370.

JURY,

how far the question of reasonable time in giving notice of dishonour or making presentment is to be determined by, or by court, 224. 270.

time when presentment for payment should be made, is not to be determined by, 262.

judge may take opinion of, as to reasonable time, with reference to mercantile transactions, 270.

jury to determine what is reasonable time for presenting a bill payable after sight, 270, note.

decisions of as to reasonable time have been very contradictory, 270.

due diligence on inquiry after drawer or indorser, whether a question for jury, 213.

evidence left to jury to say whether there was full notice of dishonour, &c. at the time of promise to pay, 410.—(See " *Evidence.*" " *Promise.*")

when a note is payable by instalments, jury will sometimes give whole amount in damages, 410.

may under circumstances refuse giving interest, 420, 1.

LACHES—*(continued.)*

Miscellaneous—*(continued.)*

but if the bill was not indorsed it is otherwise, 192.

in not presenting bill for acceptance, and not giving notice of non-acceptance, does not prejudice if bill on a wrong stamp, 197.

cannot be attributed to the king, or his agents acting for him, 197. 248.

in not giving notice of dishonour, in what cases not material, 198.—(See " *Effects*," " *Notice of Non-acceptance.*")

may be waived by party who may take advantage of them, 233. (See " *Notice of Non-acceptance,*" " *Waiver.*")

promise to pay a dishonoured bill without knowledge of laches, is not binding, 238.—(See " *Promise,*" " *Waiver.*")

a person party to a bill once discharged by, he is always discharged, 240.

in not protesting a foreign bill, when it is not material, 240.—(See " *Effects,*" " *Protest.*")

of a holder in not making presentment for payment, does not discharge acceptor, 256.

in action against acceptor, no notice of dishonour necessary where bill payable at banker's unless acceptor proves damage for want of it, Rhodes *v.* Gent, MS. and see 309.

what has been deemed laches in sending notice of dishonour by the post, or by private hand, 316.

if laches proved, evidence of consideration cannot be received, 98. 196. 364.—(See " *Declaration.*")

LAW MERCHANT—(See " *Custom.*")

governs the legal system of bills of exchange, 8.

founded on the rules of good faith and equity, 8.

when silent, evidence of a custom is admissible, 37. 110.

is part of the law of the land, and need not be stated in pleading, 351.

LEGACY—(See " *Executor.*")

of a larger amount than the bill bequeathed to payee, is not a payment of the bill, even though he be holder of it, 288, 307.

but it has been held that a bill is discharged by an entry in testator's hand, that debtor should pay no interest or principal unless testator was distressed, 288.

LETTER,

acceptance of a bill by, how far valid, 172.—(See " *Acceptance.*")

notice of dishonour given by, how far valid, 211.—(See " *Notice of Non-acceptance,*" " *Post.*")

mistake in directing letter giving notice, no excuse for delay, 211.

letter written by one of the makers of a joint and several note to the other desiring him to settle debt, will take case out of Statute of Limitations, 374.—(See " *Limitations.*")

containing notice of dishonour, notice to produce same should be given, 405.—(See " *Evidence.*")

what is evidence in default of production after notice to produce given, that due notice of dishonour was received, 40, 56.

LETTER.—(*continued.*)

proof that a letter was received from defendant acknowledging the receipt of a letter from holder of a named date, but not referring to its contents, is presumptive evidence of due notice of dishonour, 407.

when evidence of notice of dishonour given, what other evidence in regard to letters will suffice, 408.—(See *"Post Office," "Post."*)

in civil cases post-mark on letter evidence of time and place when and where put in the post, 401.—(See *"Post," "Evidence."*)

in an action by indorsee against maker of note, in order to establish usury, what letters from payee to maker admissible, without calling payee, 411.

LETTER OF LICENSE,

subsequent indorser let out of execution on letter of license, is no bar to an action against a prior one, 298.

LIABILITY

of acceptor, 183 to 188.

how discharged, 188 to 193.

of drawer, 106, 7.

how discharged, 197. 245.

of indorser and transferrer, 140 to 147.

how discharged, 197. 245.

of party promising to pay a bill, 193 to 195.

how to be stated in an action on a bill against acceptor, and on a note against maker, 357.

how to be stated in an action on a bill or note against the drawer or indorser of the one, and the indorser of the other, 363.

person discharged from liability on a bill by bankruptcy and certificate, is a competent witness in an action on same bill, 416.—(See *"Witness."*)

LIEN,

vendor of an estate does not waive it by taking a bill or note, and receiving its amount by discount, 96.

in case of a partial advance by a banker on a bill deposited with him, and such banker becomes bankrupt, his assignees have a lien on it, 122. 482, 3.

when indorsee has no lien on the effects of drawer in the hands of acceptor, 140.

but if the drawer and acceptor become bankrupts, it is otherwise, 140, 1.

accommodation acceptor or indorser what lien they have, 146, 7. 195.

lien in case of bankruptcy in general, 482 to 486.

LIMITATIONS, STATUTE OF,

bills of exchange affected by, 2.

indorsements of partial payments on a bill made by holder will in some cases take case out of, 304. 373.

indorsement of payment of interest within six years will sometimes have same effect, 373.

effect of statute where bill or note dated upwards of six years past, 355.

begins to operate from time bill due, and not from time made, 373.

actio non accrevit the proper plea, 373.—(See *"Plea."*)

LIMITATIONS, STATUTE OF—(continued.)

non assumpsit infra sex annos not proper, 373.

cannot be pleaded to an action on a bill payable after sight, unless bill has been presented, 373.

note payable on demand supposed that statute runs from date of note, 373.

acknowledgment of one of several drawers of a joint and several note, how far evidence to take the case out of the statute, 374.

letter written by one of such drawers to another, desiring him to settle debt, evidence to take case out of the statute, 374.

a payment generally by one maker of a joint and several note to payee, is not sufficient to take case out of the statute against the other, 374.

acknowledgment by one partner to take case of the statute against the other must be clear and explicit, 374.

a receipt of a dividend under the bankruptcy of the joint maker of note within five years, on account of note, will bar the statute in an action against the other, 374.

aliter when the debt proved was not on the note, 374.

must be specially pleaded, 375.

in case of bankruptcy, precludes proof, 440.

LONDON—(See *"Feme Covert."*)

custom of London in respect to payment of bills by drafts, &c. 387, 8.

no wager of law allowed by the custom of London, 427.

LORD'S ACT—(See *"Insolvent Debtors."*)

LOSS OF BILLS AND NOTES,

General points, 147 to 157.

if a bill is transferrable by delivery, and holder loses it, he must bear the loss, if any, 147.

this rule applies if he be robbed of it, 147.

but in an action on it on notice to prove consideration, &c. at the trial, plaintiff must do it, 68. 148. 400.

when a check is lost and paid by banker before it bore date, he is liable to repay same to loser, 148.

when a bill drawn on a customer, and by acceptance made payable at his banker's, who discounts same after notice that it had been lost, how far such banker is liable, 148.

but if a bill transferrable only by indorsement be lost, and afterwards get into hands of *bona fide* holder, he cannot recover, 149.

and this although such indorsement be forged, 149.

bona fide holder without notice cannot recover on it, 149.

bills, &c. lost out of letters put in post-office, postmaster general not liable, 150.

but liable for neglect, &c. 150.

when a bill, &c. is lost, holder should give notice to all the parties to it, and public notice in the newspaper, 151.

loss of a bill, &c. no excuse for not making application for payment, 151.   [151.

and when acceptor has no right to refuse payment to the loser,

MAKER—*(continued.)*

maker of an accommodation note may be sued, though composition taken from payee, &c. 298.

releasing such payee, not knowing that he is a surety, will have same effect, 298.

in an action against, when necessary to aver presentment at particular place, 361.

if maker make note payable at a certain place by memorandum at foot, that does not qualify contract, 361.

MARRIAGE,

a contract made in restraint of, void, 75.

for procuration of, void, 75.

MARRIED WOMAN.—(See "*Feme Covert.*")

MASTER, REFERENCE TO.—(See "*Reference to Master.*")

MEMORANDUM,

effect of it on the back of a note or bill, or separate paper, 46, 7.

at foot of note making it payable at a place certain in an action against maker on it, no averment of presentment there necessary, 361.

MERCHANTS.—(See "*Bills of Exchange.*")

inland bills formerly valid only between merchant and merchant, 12.

what notice of dishonour is sufficient to, and how it should be served, 214.

judges may consult them in new cases, 94. 270.

MISDEMEANOR,

compounding of not a legal consideration, 74.

bankers and agents embezzling bills is, 114.

MISDESCRIPTION—(See "*Misnomer.*")

of payee of a bill, where it will not vitiate, 63. 389.

in address of a letter, no excuse for delay in notice, 211.

MISNOMER—(See "*Misdescription.*")

if the name of a party to a bill is mis-spelt in declaration, when it is fatal, 353.

in a count for usury, 353.

what misnomers have been held as not fatal, 353.   [392, 3.

in respect to indorser between declaration and evidence, immaterial.

MIS-SPELLING

of a name in drawing a bill may be rectified by parol evidence, 65.

a party's name to a bill in a declaration, how far fatal, 353.—(See "*Misnomer.*")

MIS-STATEMENT

in declaration, how taken advantage of, 372.—(See "*Demurrer.*")

MISTAKE

in directing a letter, no excuse for delay in notice, 211.

MONEY COUNTS.—(See " *Declaration.* ")
the utility of, and when applicable in case of bills and notes, 363 to 367.

MONEY HAD AND RECEIVED,
when money recoverable back, 239. 305, 6. 211.

MONEY, PAYMENT OF INTO COURT,
admits validity of bill or note, and sufficiency of stamp, 380, 3, 8.
admits holder's title, 397.

MONTH,
means calendar in case of bills and notes, 268.
how calculated as to time of payment of bills and notes, 264, 9.

MUTUAL CREDIT.—(See " *Set-off,*" " *Bankruptcy.*")
general observations, and 5 Geo. 2. c. 30. s. 28, 473 to 474.
nature of debt to be set-off, 474.
in what right due, 476.
time when the mutual debts or credits arose, 477.

NAME—(See " *Misdescription,*" " *Misnomer,*" " *Mis-spelling.*").
of payee, mistake in, 62 to 64.

NAVY BILL,
consequence of their being misapplied by banker or agent, 113.

NEGLECT.—(See " *Laches,*" " *Release.* ")

NEGOTIABILITY,
not essential to validity of a bill or note, 65. 108.
what words usual and essential to make bill or note negotiable, 66. 108 to 111.

NEGOTIATION,
a bill or note cannot be altered after it was perfected, and complete before such negotiation, 103.
an exchange of acceptances is, 105.
delivery of a bill to drawee by drawer to be accepted is not, 105.
of a bill or note may be restrained by a court of equity, but not by law, 110.

NEW STYLE.—(See " *Style.*")
of old and new style where they prevail, 363, 4.

NOLLE PROSEQUI
must be entered to other counts after demurrer to the one on a bill and judgment for plaintiff upon reference to master to compute, 370.
but this entry may be made any time before final judgment, 370.

NON-ACCEPTANCE.—(See " *Notice of Non-acceptance,*" " *Protest.*")
of non-acceptance, and what holder ought to do thereon, 196 to 240.
notice of should in all cases be immediate, 217. 219.   [to 233.
drawer and indorsers immediately liable to pay and to be sued, 230

NON-ACCEPTANCE—(*continued.*)

and this, though the instrument be somewhat like a note, 231. 21.

bankruptcy of drawer after drawing a bill, on non-acceptance the debt may be proved under the commission, 231.

party arrested, and giving a draft in payment which is dishonoured, may be arrested again on the same writ, 231.

if a person take a bill from drawer in payment of goods sold on non-acceptance, he may recover on the common counts, 231.

and it is sufficient in such action for drawer to prove the present-ment for acceptance, 231.   [231.

without showing that bill was protested, or that drawer had notice.

drawee refusing to accept, but requesting holder to call again, holder not bound to present it or return the bill, 232.

drawer and indorsers may plead a tender any time before action commenced, 232.

but acceptor cannot if he does not pay immediately on present-ment, 232.

when notice of non-acceptance has been given, no presentment for payment need be made, 232.

parties to bill protested for non-acceptance, liable to pay principal, interest, and damages, 232.

when a note is payable according to a course of exchange, what liabilty is incurred, 232, 3.

and if a party to a bill is discharged by foreign laws where bill was drawn, he cannot be proceeded against here, 233.

if holder omits to give notice of when made, the other parties dis-charged, 233.

NON-PAYMENT.—(See "*Notice of Non-payment,*" "*Protest.*")

conduct holder should pursue on non-payment, 308, 9.

bill should, if foreign, be protested, and notice of dishonour given whether foreign or inland, 308.—(See "*Notice of Non-payment.*"

a protest must be made on non-payment of coal notes given under 3 Geo. 2. c. 26. s. 7., 312.

NOTARY PUBLIC,

his office and duty in general, 216.

his duty when protesting a bill for non-acceptance, 216.

must draw up protest on bill itself if possible, otherwise on a copy, 216.

demand of payment must be made by him before protest is completed, 216.

and this demand must be made by the notary himself, and can-not be by his clerk, 217. 312.

acceptance *supra protest* must be made in presence of, 242.

his conduct on protesting for non-payment, 310 to 313.

cannot protest a bill for non-payment by a banker, if present-ment is not made in the usual hours of business, 277. 404.

unless person is stationed there to answer, when presentment is good, 404.

and no inference that bill was presented in due time is to be drawn from presentment made by a notary in the evening, 277.   [312.

doubtful whether clerk of, can protest under 9 & 10 W. 3. c.17.

unsettled whether can note a bill for non-payment on day of re-fusal, and draw up protest afterwards, 313.

NOTARY PUBLIC—*(continued.)*
his office and duty in general—(continued.)

if a bill be presented at a banker's by a notary after five o'clock, when he cannot prove non-payment, 313.

on payment of a bill for honour of another, a declaration should be made before a notary, for whose honour it was done, 320.

his duty on such occasion, 321.

protest under seal of notary made abroad, proves itself, 405.

but if made in England, notary who made it, and the subscribing witness, if any, must be called, 405.

table of fees of office, Appendix, 516 to 518.

NOTES.—(See " *Promissory Notes," " Bankers' Notes," " Cash Notes."*)

NOTICE IN GENERAL,

notice of determining agent's authority, what to be given, 26.—(See " *Agent.*")

express notice to creditor from several partners, disavowing authority of one partner disables him from binding them, 34.

notice of dissolution of partnership, what to be given, 38.

not necessary to be given of indorsements, 140.

should be given of loss of bill or note, 151.—(See " *Loss of Bill.*")

should be given of partial or conditional acceptance, and how, 180, 2.—(See " *Acceptance.*)

should be given when holder protests bill, because drawee has absconded, 240. 243.

of taking in K. B. unnecessary, if defendant wish to obtain a rule he must do it at his own peril, 370.   [371.

of prothonotaries appointment to compute must be given in C. P.

to produce bill on trial when in hands of defendant, when necessary, 378.

but this does not extend to trover for a note, or an indictment for stealing one, 379.

NOTICE OF DISSOLUTION OF PARTNERSHIP.—(See " *Partners.*")

in the Gazette, how far in general sufficient, 26. 36. 38.   [36. 38.

in case of, express notice must be given to a former customer, 26.

in the Gazette, and sent round to customers, and bill drawn by one partner after such notice, the others need not apply for injunction, 36.

alteration in bankers printed checks have been deemed good notice to customers using them, 36.

not necessary where dormant partner withdraws his name, 36.

one partner refusing to sign a notice, the rest may file a bill, 38.

NOTICE TO PRODUCE BILL

should be given when acceptor detains it, and is sued on it, 140. 378,

but not necessary in trover or indictment for stealing bill, 379.

NOTICE TO PRODUCE A LETTER, &c.

containing notice of dishonour, must formerly have been given before plaintiff could be allowed to go into evidence of its contents, 405.

CHITTY ON BILLS.   4 H

NOTICE TO PRODUCE A LETTER, &c.—(*continued.*)

but it has been lately determined that parol evidence of the contents of a written notice may be given, without notice to produce same, 406.

and a copy of a letter, containing notice of dishonour, is admissible without such notice, 407.

on such notice given, what is evidence that notice of dishonour was received in default of production, 407.

in order to establish usury as a defence, in discounting another bill besides one on which action brought, notice to produce same is necessary, 411.

NOTICE TO PROVE CONSIDERATION   [411.

should be given when consideration to be disputed on trial, 68, 148.

'orm of such notice.—Appendix, 513.

but plaintiff will not be called on to prove consideration, even after this notice has been given, till his title has been first prejudiced, 411.—(See "*Evidence.*")

this notice not required, if defendant can make out a strong case of fraud, 411.—(See "*Fraud.*")

NOTICE OF NON-ACCEPTANCE.—(See "*Protest.*")

When necessary and consequence of not giving it, 196 to 215.

if bill be presented for acceptance, although unnecessarily, and refused, notice of dishonour must be immediately given, 197.

the reason why the law requires notice to be given, 197.

should be given if drawee refuse acceptance or payment, 97, 197.

of a bill should be given by an agent, where one employed, 28.

not necessary, when defendant admits drawee's refusal to accept, but requests holder to present again, who does, and is refused, 98.

what should be given, when drawee requires time, 165, 224.

_when drawee gives any other than an absolute acceptance, 180, 197.

but none necessary, if holder is content with the special acceptance, 215.

but where acceptor gives only a partial acceptance, how far notice is required, 215.

but such notice should express the nature of the acceptance, 182.

and if it does not, it will be a waiver of the acceptance, 182, 192.

neglect to give, by the king or his agents, does not prejudice, if bill is on a wrong stamp, notice is not necessary, 197.   [197.

What excuses omission of it, 197 to 215.

no damage sustained, is no excuse for omission of notice, 198.

unless in action against acceptor on bill payable at a particular place, Rhodes *v.* Gent, MS.

want of effects, &c. of drawer in drawee's hands, is an excuse as against drawer, 198.—(See "*Effects.*")

the same where bill accepted for accommodation of drawer, 198.

drawer selling goods to drawee, credit for which did not elapse till after bill of drawee became due, drawer not entitled to, 199.

how far want of consideration excuses the neglect to give notice, 199.

NOTICE OF NON-ACCEPTANCE—(*continued.*)
What excuses omission of it—(*continued.*)

no excuse for not giving notice to the indorser that acceptor had no effects of drawer, 200. 228.

no consideration given for a bill between indorser and another, and no fraud, but the drawer and acceptor, fictitious persons, such indorser must have notice, 200. 228, 9.

but when payee has, and drawer has not effects in drawee's hands, and bill drawn for the accommodation of the payee, how far drawer entitled to notice, 200.

payee of note, lending name to give it credit, is entitled to notice, though he knew maker was insolvent, 201.

but payee lending name, and taking effects of drawer's to answer it, is not entitled, 203.

bill drawn for accommodation of remote indorsee, and prior names lent him, indorser entitled to notice, 202.

indorser of note to guarantee debt due from maker is entitled to notice, 203, *sed quære*, 204. 230.

so in an action against drawer, 202.

evidence of parol agreement not to require payment at appointed time not admissible to excuse it, 203.

a person, though no party to the bill, but who has guaranteed the payment of it, entitled to notice, 204. 259, *sed vide* 230.

when otherwise, 204. 230.

if the party to such bill or note, becomes insolvent or a bankrupt, before they become due, the party guaranteeing is not entitled, 204.

apprehension on the part of the drawer, and certain acts done in furtherance of such fear, that bill would be dishonoured, no excuse for omission of notice, 205.

knowledge on the part of the drawer that bill would be dishonoured, if drawer had effects of drawee's in his hands, is no excuse for want of notice, 205.

when want of effects in drawee's hands, excuses omission of notice, 206 to 209.—(See "*Effects.*")

effects of drawer in drawee's hands, not always essential to entitle drawer to notice, 237, 8.

goods shipped by drawer to drawee, and bill drawn on drawee before they arrived, if drawee dishonour, drawer is entitled to notice, 208.

bona fide reasonable expectation that bill will be honoured, entitles drawer, 209, 198.

if vendor of goods sold upon a credit, draw a bill on vendee, payable before credit expires, he is not entitled to notice, 208.

death, bankruptcy, or known insolvency of drawee, no excuse for omission of notice, 210.

this rule will extend to the drawer or indorser of a bill, and indorser of a note, 215.

the same rule extends if drawee is in prison, 210.

and such omission of notice will defeat plaintiff's claim, either at law or equity, 210.

drawee telling drawer that he could not honour bill, does not excuse omission of notice, 211.

and money paid by a third person to take up a bill, after neglect to give notice, may be recovered back on the count for money had and received, 211.

NOTICE OF NON-ACCEPTANCE—*(continued.)* ·

What excuses omission of it—(continued.)   [211. 220.

given by letter, which was mis-directed, how far it will operate, what has been decided as dispensing with notice, 211.

where one of several drawers is also acceptor, no notice is necessary, 211.

what excuses neglect to give immediate notice, 212 to 215.

when party, ignorant of indorser's residence, if he use reasonable diligence to discover it, want of immediate notice not material, 213.

what that reasonable diligence is, 213.

verbal notice at a counting-house is sufficient, 214.

and if nobody there, not necessary to leave or send a written notice, 214.

immediate notice excused by such day being a public festival,214.

but the loss or destruction of the bill is no excuse for want of notice, 214.

when drawer or indorser of a bill, or indorser of a note, is a bankrupt, notice must be given to his assignee, 215.

want of due notice excused by holder's religion forbidding him to attend to secular affairs, 214. 319.

notice of non-acceptance having been given, no notice of non-payment is requisite, 232.

2. *The protest, and form, and mode of notice of non-acceptance,* 215 to 222.

points relating to protest, 215 to 219,—(See " *Protest.*")

what is sufficient notice, 219.

personal service of notice not requisite, 219.

not to leave a written notice at parties residence, 220.   [220.

a verbal notice at parties residence or counting-house, sufficient,

notice by post sufficient, even though letter miscarries, 220.

and if sent by a private hand, and it arrive after the post, the parties are discharged, 220, 1.

otherwise if sent by a private hand, and no essential delay take place, 221.

when notice sent by twopenny post sufficient, 222.

and all notices, when sent by post, ought to be put into receiving-house, 222.

delivery of notice to bellman in street, not sufficient, 222, *sed quære.*

when there is no post, how notice should be given, 222.

when more convenient to holder he may send notice by a messenger, and recover expenses, 222.

3. *Time when notice may be given,* 223 to 225.

when a foreign bill is dishonoured, and party to whom notice is . given resident abroad, a copy of protest ought to be sent with it, 223, 4.

otherwise if such party be resident in England, 223, 4.

must be given in a reasonable time after dishonour to those to whom holder means to resort, 224, 5.

and holder must not delay giving notice till bill protested for non-payment, 224.

and in case of a foreign bill notice should be given on the day of refusal to accept, or earliest possible conveyance afterwards, 225.

NOTICE OF NON-PAYMENT—*(continued.)*

3. *Of the time when notice must be given—(continued.)*
    drawer discharged if one indorsee has given due notice to his indorser, 319.
    want of due notice is excused by the holder's religion forbidding him to attend to secular affairs, 319.
    or by the drawer or indorser absconding, 319.
    when notice is to be given to a banker, it must be in the usual hours of business, 319.
    to others, time of day not material, 319.

4. *By whom notice should be given,* 320.
    rules the same as in case of non-acceptance, 226 to 228.—
    (See *"Notice of Non-Acceptance."*)

5. *To whom notice should be given,* 320.
    rules the same as in case of non-acceptance, 228 to 230.—
    (See *"Notice of Non-Acceptance."*)

6. *Liabilities of the different parties thereupon,* 320.
    rules the same as in case of non-acceptance, 230 to 233.—
    (See *"Non-Acceptance."*)

7. *How consequences of laches waived,* 320.
    rules the same as in case of non-acceptance, 233 to 240.—
    (See *"Notice of Non-Acceptance."*)

NOTING—(See *"Protest," "Notice," "Notary."*)
of a bill, what it is, 216. 312.
how far supplies place of protest, 216.

OBLIGATION—(See *"Liability."*)

OBLIGEE,
of a bond, when assigned, action must be brought in name of the original obligee, 5.
who has assigned over a bond and then become a bankrupt, may support an action on it, 7.
of a bond, with a surety, giving time for payment of it, without surety's consent, surety discharged, 292.

OBLIGOR,
of a bond, to release to, or set-off due to, from obligee, a bar to any action by an assignee, 5.
action against one of two obligors on a joint and several bond, and taking him in execution, no bar to an action against the other, 346.

OFFICE,
recommendation to a public, no consideration, 75.
purchase of, no consideration, 75.
sale of, illegal, 79.

OLD STYLE—(See *"Style."*)
of old and new style, where they prevail, 363, 4.

"OR ORDER," WORDS OF.—(See *"Indorsement," "Transfer."*)
of bills payable to, 65 to 66.
not essential that they should be, 66.
if the bill is intended to be negotiable, these or other words of transfer ought to be inserted, 66.
if omitted by mistake, they may be inserted afterwards without a fresh stamp, 66.
and such insertion will not invalidate them, 102.
if a bill ·or note is payable to order of plaintiff, it may be stated in declaration to be payable to him, 356. 9.
no necessity to aver that he made no order, 356. 9.
bills payable to the order of a fictitious person may be treated against all aware of the fact as bills payable to bearer, 357. 9.

OUTLAWRY,
of two out of three defendants in a joint action, will not dispense with proof of the joint liability, 389.

OVER DUE BILLS—(See *" Indorsement."*)
of the transfer of a bill after it is due, 125. 129, 130.—(See *"Indorsement."*)

PARDON,
soliciting a pardon is no consideration, 74.

PAROL—(See *" Agreement," " Contract," " Evidence."*)
assignment of a chose in action by, vests equitable interest in assignee, 5. 7.
contracts in action on, consideration must be proved, 9.
includes unsealed written and verbal contracts, but not bills or notes, 9, 10.
an agent may be appointed by, and in general is, 23.
agreement to renew, &c. no evidence as a defence to an action on a bill, 47. 372.

PAROL ACCEPTANCE—(See *" Acceptance."*)
where binding, 171.

PARTIAL
acceptance, law applicable to, 182.—(See *" Acceptance."*)
indorsement, law applicable to, 139.—(See *" Indorsement."*)
payment does not discharge drawer or indorser, 296.
by the drawer when does not discharge acceptor, 299.

PARTICULAR FUND—(See *" Contingency," " Bills of Exchange."*)
bills payable out of, when invalid, 43.
promissory notes payable out of, when invalid, 336.

PARTICULARS OF DEMAND,
must state consideration of the bill, if intended to proceed at trial on common counts, 363.
interest recoverable under them, stating action brought to recover amount of note, 422.

PARTIES—(See *" Bills of Exchange," " Infant," " Feme Covert," "Agent," "Partner."*)

PARTNERS—*(continued.)*

    drawing a bill in name of firm, must state it accordingly, 39.

    otherwise partnership not liable, 39.

    but this rule does not extend to the acceptance or indorsement of a bill, previously drawn on the firm, 39. 173, 4.

    drawing bills in his own name, and applying proceeds to partnership account, co-partners not liable, 39.

    but this has been decided otherwise, 39.

    when a bill is drawn by, in name of firm, how to sign it, 90.

    how to declare on a bill drawn by one, in name of firm, 90.

    how far bankruptcy of one partner restrains the acts of the solvent partner, 35.—(See *" Bankrupt," " Bankruptcy."*)

    may indorse bills in name of firm, 123.—(See *" Indorsement."*)

    notice of dishonour of a bill to one, notice to all, 229, 230.

    payment to one partner, in name of several, good, 286.   [293.

    giving time to one of several acceptors, does not discharge the rest,

    if a merchant joins his clerk's name to his firm as partner, an action must be in their joint names, 342.

    unless distinctly proved that he had no interest, 343.

    acknowledgment by one partner to bind another, to take case out of the Statute of Limitations, must be clear and explicit, 374.

    proof of admission by one partner of the hand-writing of another, to an acceptance, is enough, 381.

    one is competent to prove hand-writing of others, when, 381. 3. 414.

    the declarations of one partner, how far evidence against another, 382.—(See *" Admission," " Evidence."*)

    after partnership established, admission of one partner evidence as to joint contracts against another, as well before as after dissolution, 382. 397.—(See *" Admission," " Evidence."*)

    when one partner may be called to prove that another had no authority to draw bill in name of firm, 414.

    and when bankruptcy of the firm would not affect the competency of witness, 414.

PARTNERSHIP.—(See *" Partners," " Company Incorporate."*)

    after dissolution of, by agreement, notified in Gazette, a partner cannot use the name of firm, 36.

    what is sufficient notice of dissolution of, 36.—(See *" Notice."*)

    a dormant partner may dissolve without notice, 36.

    firm affected by an admission after dissolution of, and previous partnership transaction, 37.

    death of, dissolves partnership though for a term of years, 37.

    unless a stipulation be made to the contrary, 37.

    express authority given to a partner after dissolution to receive debts, does not empower him to draw bills, &c. 38.

    a partner refusing to sign a notice of dissolution, co-partners may file a bill, 38.

    not liable on any bill drawn, &c. by one partner, unless expressly stated, 39

    otherwise when a bill, &c. is drawn on a firm, 39.

    when a bill is indorsed to several general partners, the indorsement of one suffices, 123.

    if established, the proof of the hand-writing of one partner to an acceptance, &c. is enough, 381.—(See *" Hand-writing," " Evidence."*)

    after indorsement in blank, no proof of partnership required, though several join in suing on the bill, &c., 394.

PARTNERSHIP—*(continued.)*

    the names of persons in partnership may be suggested to a witness
    called to prove it by counsel, 395.

    admissions of one partner evidence as in joint contracts against the
    other as well before as after dissolution, 382. 397.—(See " *Admission*," " *Evidence*.")

PARTS OF FOREIGN BILLS, 62.—(See " *Sets*.")

PAYEE,

    of a bill of exchange, who is, 1. 20.

    where two persons, not in partnership, are to bill drawn by them-
    selves, with both their names attached, both must indorse, 37.

    right of action not affected by a release from drawer to acceptor, 5.
    same with regard to set-off, 5.

    the wish of to indulge the maker of a bill or note expressed in such
    note, is not a contingency, 47.

    forgery of an indorsement of, to one part of a foreign bill, no defence
    to an action on the other parts, 62.

    bill must specify to whom it is to be paid, 62.

    payable to " A. or B." bad, 63.

    when bill drawn in blank, holder may fill it up with his name, 63.

    but in an action against acceptor, authority from drawer for so doing
    must be proved, 63.

    where two persons of same name, payee should be described care-
    fully, 63.

    to whom a bill may be made payable in general, 64.

    where a mis-description of will not vitiate a bill, 63.

    of a bill originally founded on a good consideration, indorsing same
    over for a usurious contract, how far such bill is void, 81. 77. see
    Appendix, 556.

    delivery of a bill to is not essential to vest legal interest, 94. 140.

    alteration of a bill by, in what particular, invalidates the same, 104.

    when payee mentioned in a bill, he must indorse to give third per-
    son interest, 131. 142.

    may make a conditional indorsement before acceptance, and this
    bind the acceptor, 137, 8.

    may make a qualified indorsement, 139.

    effect on, when bill drawn as an accommodation one, 199, 200.

    when omission of notice of dishonour to, is material, 200.

    payee of a note lending name to give it credit is entitled to notice of
    dishonour, though he knew maker was insolvent, 201.

    payment of a bill made to, unless he be holder, inoperative, 280.

    payee of a check receiving the money on, after knowledge of the
    bankruptcy of the drawer, when he may be sued, 282.

    payment of a bill to, who is holder of the same by bequeathing a
    larger legacy than amount of bill, is not valid, 288.

    mere circumstance of a check being payable to A., and of his hav-
    ing received payment of it, not evidence that maker gave it him,
    288.

    of a bill may sue acceptor, whether he accepted as drawee, or for
    honour of drawer, and in such case drawer also, 343.

    when his identity with a person making indorsement must be proved,
    390. 1.—(See " *Evidence*," " *Identity*.")

PAYMENT.—(See "*Presentment for Payment*," "*Receipt*.")
General Points.

of a debt, when should not be to an agent or attorney, 281.
till payment of a bill by the acceptor, it may be transferred *ad infinitum*, 129, 130.
payment of by acceptor will discharge all parties to it, 347.
for the honour of a bill gives a right of action to the person making such payment, 130.
and after payment of part, it may be indorsed over for the residue. 130. 140.
a policy of insurance may be effected for securing the payment, 140.
of a bill by a prior party, discharges the subsequent one, 146.
application for, must be made though the bill be lost, 151.
of a bill, if made without knowledge of laches, whether it may be recovered back, 305.
of one bill by giving another, does not prevent holder suing on the first, in case the latter is not paid, 97.
part payment of a bill is a waiver of neglect to make presentment for payment, 248.

1. *By and to whom payment of a bill may be made,* 280 to 285.
may be made by any of the parties, and even by a total stranger, may be made by the bail of either of the parties, 280.　[280.
but not so as to charge a prior party, 344.
should be made to the real proprietor of the bill, 280.
to one of several partners, 280.
or to some person authorized to receive it, 280.
to payee, unless holder, is inoperative, 280.
and if a bill is payable to A. B. and not negotiable, A. B. must demand payment, 280.
if holder dead, when payment must be made to his personal representative, 280.
but such payment to a person who has probate of a forged will, valid, 280.
on a bill payable to A. or order, for the use of B. payment must be to A., 280.
if a bill beneficial to a minor, valid, but to a married woman, after knowledge of that fact, is not, 280.
how far payment to a person who had authority to receive it, but which is afterwards revoked, is valid, 280, 1.
in ordinary cases, mere production of the bill or note is sufficient to authorize the payment, 281.
how far payment of a bill that has been lost, with or without notice of it, it is good, 281.
but payment of a check or bill before due, will not discharge the drawer, unless it be made to the real proprietor, 281.
advisable that an acceptor should not pay his bill before due, or after notice from drawer or indorsee not to do so, 147. 281.
of a check by a banker under suspicious circumstances, makes them liable to repay the money to drawer, 281.—(See "*Banker*.")
how far the payment of a bill transferrable only by indorsement is protected, 281.
to a bankrupt, with notice of the fact, ineffectual, 282.—(See "*Bankrupt*," "*Bankruptcy*.")
payment by a bankrupt, how far valid, 282 to 285.

PAYMENT—*(continued.)*

Of the effect of giving time to, or releasing acceptor—*(continued.)*

similar indulgence to drawer or indorser discharges subsequent parties, 292.

and advances made on a note payable on demand, beyond time agreed upon between plaintiff and the drawer, indorser discharged, 293.

taking a cognovit payable by instalments at a distant time, or one without giving time, how far drawer discharged, 192. 293. 297.

evidence of an assent or a promise to pay after time given, reverses the rule, 294.

giving time to one of several acceptors, does not discharge the rest, 293.

and drawer making assent under a mistake that he was discharged may be sued, 294.

but if assent given by an indorser to the acceptor, he may not, 294.

when the laches of a holder are excused for want of effects, he may give time to acceptor, without discharging such parties, 294, 5.

a holder for a valuable consideration of an accommodation bill may prove it under drawer's commission, though he has taken security from acceptor, 295.

the same rule prevails where the acceptor is merely the drawer's agent, 295.

holder may receive proposals for an arrangement, and forbear to sue, without prejudice to claim on other parties, 295.

how far an agreement "not to press the acceptor," discharges other parties, 295, 6.

how far an offer to retain the bill for a few days, made to drawer, would do so, 296.

what treaty between attorney of holder, and drawer and acceptor will discharge subsequent indorser, 297.

an express agreement not to sue acceptor, made after notice of non-payment, but without consideration, does not, 296.

5. *Of receiving part-payment*, 297.

a holder may receive part-payment from acceptor, and sue other parties, 297.

recovering part-payment from drawer does not discharge accommodation acceptor, 297.

holder of a joint and several note may enter up judgment on a cognovit against one, and levy on a *fi. fa.* without discharging the other, 297.

what conduct holder should pursue on presentment for payment on a partial payment, 298.

6. *Of the effect of indulgence to prior parties*, 298 to 301.—(See "*Indulgence.*")

7. *Of the receipt for payment*, 303 to 305.—(See "*Receipt.*")

8. *Of the effect of payment and payment by mistake*, 305 to 306.

payment of a bill by mistake, when the money may be recovered back, 305.

banker's paying under a mistake, when recoverable back, 306.

on payment of a forged bill, the money cannot be recovered back from a *bona fide* holder, 306.

exceptions to this rule, 306.

PAYMENT—(continued.)

PAYMENT SUPRA PROTEST.

POST—*(continued.)*

what is a reasonable time in regard to sending notice by, 315, 6.

what has been deemed laches in regard thereto, 316 to 319.

the court will not consider whether the time of receipt corresponds with the time when a letter sent by, would arrive, 318.

but if notice is sent by, the letter must be put into at such a time that it may arrive on the morning of the day after the sender received notice, 318, 9.

mode of proving forwarding a letter by post, 408.

post-mark evidence of time and place when and where letter put into the post-office, 402.

proof-notice, or other paper, sent by post in mercantile transactions, always sufficient, 408.—(See *"Evidence."*)

question sometimes arises as to what is the requisite proof of the fact of sending by post, 408.

instance and example each way, 408, 9.

POST-MASTER,

general, not liable, if bills, &c. are lost out of letters put into post-office, 150.

deputy may be sued for neglect in not delivering letters in due time, 150.

POST-OFFICE.—(See *" Post."*)

when a clerk to it, may be called to give evidence as to genuineness of hand-writing, and whether it be feigned, 386.

argument to support this position, 387.

on proof of notice of dishonour given, it will suffice to show that a letter containing such notice, was put in the proper post-office, 408.

post-mark, evidence of time and place when and where letter put into the post-office, 408.

POST-MARK.—(See *" Post-Office."*)

PRACTICE.—(See *" Action," " Affidavit," " Arrest," " Bail," " Declaration," " Defence," " Demurrer," " Error," " Exemptions," " Judgment," " Pleas and Pleading," " Reference to Master," " Staying and Setting aside Proceedings," " Variance," " Venue."*)

PRECEDENTS.—(See *" Affidavits," " Declarations," " Judgments." " Notice to prove."*)

Of affidavits to hold to bail, 487, 8.—(See *" Affidavits."*)

on promissory notes.

payee against maker, 487.

the like in another form, 487.

indorsee against maker, 487.

indorsee against indorser, 488.

on bills of exchange.

payee against acceptor, 488.

indorsee against acceptor, 488.

payee against drawer, default payment, 488.

indorsee against drawer, 488.

the like on default acceptance, 488.

PRECEDENTS—(*continued.*)

PRESENTMENT FOR PAYMENT—(continued.)

PRESENTMENT FOR PAYMENT—*(continued.)*

6. *Circumstances arising between presentment and actual payment—* *(continued.)*

    where drawee promised to pay bill, if holder would forego charge for duplicate protest, and holder would not, the drawer not bound, 279.

    presentment of a check by one banker to another, who marks it as good, such other must pay it at all events, 279.

7. *Pleadings, and Evidence respecting.*

    in action against acceptor of bill or maker of a note, when necessary to aver presentment, 361. 358, 9.

    advisable to do so in one count, 402.

    it must be proved if stated, 402.

    in an action against drawer or indorser of a bill, or indorser of a note, presentment for payment to acceptor must be proved, 402.

    not necessary to prove that presentment was made by person stated in declaration, 402.

    but not necessary to prove presentment or demand on drawer, 403.

PRESUMPTION,

    what is and what not sufficient, to raise, of fraud in respect of bills. &c. given by one only of many partners, 33.

    subsequent approbation raises, of previous authority, 34.

    compelling a party to take goods on the discount of a bill, affords presumption of usury, 87.

    alterations and erasures on a bill or note affords, of fraud, 105, &.

    indorsement of a bill after it is due, when affords presumption of fraud, 127. 129.

    bankruptcy or insolvency of a party to a bill which has been guaranteed by a third person on dishonour of the bill, and notice received, raises an, that part of the guarantee is not injured, 204.

    promissory note, unaccounted for twenty years, is presumption of payment, 286. 305.

    in an action against the finder of Bank notes, if not produced on trial, the presumption is that value has been received, 333.

PRINCIPAL.—(See " *Agent.*")

    how far bound by agent's acts, 23.

    not bound by an act of an agent delegated by an agent, 26.

    unless by express authority, 26.

    if in one absence a person acts for a person, which acts he afterwards approves, he is bound by such person's acts on a second occasion, 25.

    the same where one person usually signs an instrument in another's name, 25, 6.

    may call on an agent to pay a bill indorsed by him without a qualification, 142.

    only bound by agent's admission, when it relates to commerce in which agent is engaged for principal, 383.

    authority to draw does not import authority to indorse, 391.

PRISONER,

notes made for payment of weekly sums to a, under lord's act, must be made according to the form there laid down, 335.

if one creditor insist on his detention, it must be for payment of a sum not exceeding 3s. 6d. per week, 335.

of more than one, not exceeding 2s. per week each, 335.

must be paid on the Monday of every week so long as he shall continue in execution, 335.

the court no power to moderate the sum, 335.

by whom they must be signed, may be so by the creditor's attorney, 335.

if failure is made in payment, he may be discharged on application to a judge in vacation, or to the court in term, 335.

but must execute an assignment and conveyance of his estate, 335.

further decision on this stat. collected in Tidd's Prac. 6th edit. 381 to 384—335.

insolvent debtor, when discharged from liability, 486.

PRIVILEGE.—(See " *Attorney.*")

an attorney does not lose it as acceptor of a bill, 14.

PROBATE.—(See " *Executor.*")

a person having obtained a probate of a forged will, and payment of a bill made to him is valid, 280.

PROCURATION—(See " *Agent.*")

drawing, accepting, and indorsing by.—(See " *Agent.*")

when an act is done by, it ought to be stated on the instruments, otherwise agent is liable personally, 27. 107. 174.

but this does not extend to a government agent, 28.

how to sign a bill drawn by, 90.

how to indorse a bill by, 133.

when any act in relation to a bill is done by, it may be stated in the declaration to be done by the principal, 357.

acceptance of a bill after it has been drawn and indorsed by procuration, what it admits, 391.—(See " *Admission,*" " *Evidence.*")

PROMISE.—(See " *Agreement,*" " *Admission.*")

to give time for payment of pre-existing debt how far valid, 95.

subsequent to pay dishonoured foreign bill, cures want of protest, 216.

to pay a bill by a party discharged from laches, waives such laches, 234, 5.

instances and examples, 235.

how far a, made under misapprehension of law to pay a dishonoured bill, valid, 236.

such a promise would operate in discharge of the proof of protest to a foreign bill, 237.

after declaration filed, operates in holder's favour, 237.

and if such promise was made to any party to bill, and another has taken it up, latter may sue the party making it, 237.

but a promise made without knowledge of non-acceptance or laches, is not valid, 238.

'and a promise ought to be an admission of holder's right to receive payment of the bill, 239.

   2. *Particular proof relative to Promissory Notes*—*(continued.)*
     a note promising to account with another, or his order, for a
       certain sum, is good, 334.
     what forms have been adjudged as being good notes, 334, 5.
     they need not be payable to B. or order, 334.
     a mere acknowledgment of a debt, without words inferring a
       promise to pay, is not a good note, 335.
     I. O. U. such a sum is not a note, and need not be stamped, 335.
     it is evidence of a debt only, 335.
     an instrument acknowledging the receipt of a draft for payment
       of money, and promising to repay it, is not a good note, 335.
     but it is a special agreement, 335.
     advisable to insert in notes the words "value received," 335.
     note given under Lord's act, must be made in the form pre-
       scribed by statute, 335.—(See "*Prisoner.*")
   Requisites of notes, 336 to 340.—(See "*Bills of Exchange.*")
     they must be payable at all events, 336.
     must be for the payment of money only, 336.
     a note promising to pay money in East India bonds bad, 336.
     the same of a note to pay money, and deliver up horses and
               wharf, 336.
                and surrender A. B's. body, 336.
     a promise to pay money in a certain time, made by defendant to
       plaintiff, if defendant did not pay the same for his brother,
       is bad, 336.
     the same where it depends on sufficient being bequeathed by a
       person's will, or he is otherwise able to pay it, 336.
     the same when it is made to pay money after another's mar-
       riage, 336.
     the same out of a fund arising from the sale of a reversion, 336.
     the same arising from the sale of the White Hart inn, St. Al-
       bans, when sold, 336.
     for instances and examples the other way, 336, 7.
     notes payable on the death of a person, are good, 337.
             when a ship is paid off, good, 337.
     need contain no words rendering it negotiable, 337.
     rules relative to bills of exchange, will in all cases apply to
       notes, 337, 8.
   Of notes joint and several, and joint only, 338 to 339.
     when made by several, and expressed, we promise, &c. it is
       joint only, 338.
     but if signed by several, and expressed, I promise, &c. joint
       and several, 338.
     but if it appear on the face to be the sole note of A., it cannot
       be declared on as being the joint note of A. and B., though
       given to secure a joint debt, 339.
     in an action on a joint note, if all the parties to it are not joined,
       advantage can only be taken by plea in abatement, 339.
     but if one be an infant he should not be sued, 339.
     if there be a joint and several note of two persons, one surety
       for the other, and holder knowing it, accept a composition
       from the other, this will discharge the surety, 339.
   Of the stamp.
     stamp duties regulated by the 55 Geo. 3. c. 184., 340. 538.
     List of, Appendix, 547.

REFERENCE TO MASTER—(*continued.*)

court will not direct to allow re-exchange in an action on a bill drawn in Scotland upon, and accepted in England, 370.

reference not allowed in an action of debt on a judgment recovered on a bill, 370.

but it is permitted on judgment for plaintiff, on demurrer to the count on the bill, 370.

but in such case a *nolle prosequi* must be entered, 370.

plaintiff may in K. B. obtain a rule to refer on same day interlocutory judgment is obtained for want of a plea, 370.   [370.

but when signed on demurrer, he must wait till the following day, on motion to refer to master, no irregularity previous to judgment is available, 370.

in K. B. if defendant's attorney wish to be present, he must obtain rule for that purpose, 370.

but in C. P. defendant must have notice of appointment, 370, 1.

REFUSAL.—(See " *Non-acceptance*," " *Non-payment.*")

RE-ISSUABLE NOTES.—(See " *Promissory Notes*," " *Stamps.*")

when re-issuable after payment, and how to be stamped, 52, 3. 129. 130, 340.

statute 55 Geo. 3. c. 184, relating thereto, 540 to 545.

RELEASE.—(See " *Laches*," " *Neglect*," " *Waiver.*")

by drawer of bill to the acceptor, does not affect payee's right of action, 5.

otherwise on a bond, 5.

when by an excise officer, of a person for penalties is a good consideration for a note, 75.

by drawer to drawee before acceptance, will not discharge a subsequent one, 190.

a general by drawer to acceptor, will as between them, discharge acceptor, 190.

the effect of to the acceptor, 290 to 297.—(See " *Payment.*")

the effect of to prior indorsers, 298 to 301.—(See " *Payment.*")

what circumstances release or discharge obligation of acceptor, 188 to 193.

in case of bills, may be by parol, 373.

giving time to acceptor, discharges drawer and indorsers, 290 to 297. (See " *Payment.*")

what discharges drawer and indorser in general, 107.

by neglect to present for acceptance, 158 to 165.

by neglect to give notice of refusal to accept, 196 to 215.

by neglect to present in due time for payment, 245 to 259.

by neglect to give due notice of non-payment, 309.

by giving time to the acceptor, &c. 290 to 297.

by compounding with the acceptor, 301.

by the holder's making the acceptor his executor, 345.

drawer cannot be called to prove that he did not draw without a release. 414.—(See " *Witness.*")

as to effect of, and release as to competency of witnesses, 414 to 418. (See " *Witness.*")

acceptor discharged on neglect to present bill for payment when accepted at a particular place, if acceptor sustain damage therefrom, Rhodes *v.* Gent, MS.

REMEDY,
in case of the infraction of a contract, &c. regulated here according
to the laws of the country in which it is to be performed, 93, 4.
when a bill is to be paid in a country where arrest is allowed, the
only remedy here is by service of process, 93, 4.
on a bill by action, 343.—(See " *Action*.")
by proof under a commission.—(See "*Bankruptcy*.")

REMOVAL.—(See " *Absconding.* ")
of the drawee, effect thereof as to presentment for acceptance &
payment, 164. 261.
of the drawer or indorser, an excuse for delay in notice of dishonour, 212, 319.
in case of drawee or maker, what averment of presentment is necessary, 362.

RENEWAL,
no parol evidence of an agreement to make, is admissible, 47. 57.
an offer of, made to indorsee after bill due, admits the holder's title.
396, 7.—(See " *Admission*.")
renewing bill at request of acceptor, discharges drawer and indorsers, 290.
agreement to renew without consideration, not binding, and does not
discharge, 296.
same if a conditional agreement not performed, 297.

REQUEST,
on bill to pay, 62.

REQUISITES
of a bill of exchange, 41, &c.—(See " *Bills of Exchange*.")
of a promissory note, 324, &c.—(See " *Promissory Note*.")

RESIDENCE,
ignorance of drawer's or indorser's, when excuses delay in notice.
213.

REVOCATION,
by drawer of a bill, when not revocable, 106.
of an indorsement, 146,
whether the acceptance of a bill can be revoked, 186 to 188.

ROBBERY.—(See " *Loss*.")

RULE.—(See " *Judgment*," " *Reference to Master*," " *Staying Proceedings*.")
nisi, to stay proceedings in an action on a bill, &c. may be obtained
on payment of debt and costs, 368.—(See " *Staying Proceedings*.")
how and when to obtain a rule to refer a bill to master, to compute
principal, interest, and costs, 369.—(See " *Reference to Master*.")
to prove payment of money into court the rule must be produced,
380.

SABAOTH,
  or Jewish festival, excuses delay in giving notice, 214.

SALE—(See " *Exchange.*")
  of a bill, when not usurious, 77.

SATISFACTION.—(See " *Payment.*")
  of a bill or prior debt, what amounts thereto, 95 to 100.
  a good plea in bar, 373.
  what is not a satisfaction, 373, note, 96, note, 307, note.

SEARCH,
  what sufficient, after drawee, 164, 5.
  what sufficient search after residence of drawer or indorser, 213.

SECURITY,
  bill of exchange, when a preferable security, 3. 9.
  but there are some disadvantages, and what, 4.   [293. 295.
  when the taking security from acceptor discharges the other parties,
  of protest for better security, 240.
  if a bill is left as security till another is accepted, how it may be
    recovered back, 366.

SERVANT.—(See "*Agent.*")

SET OF BILLS,
  points relating to foreign bills drawn in sets, 62.
  stamps on, when made in England, 54.—Appendix, 549.

SET-OFF AND MUTUAL CREDIT—(See " *Bankruptcy.*")
  due from drawer to acceptor, does not affect payee's right of action on
  otherwise in an action on a bond, 5.   [a bill, 5.
  of a debt due from *cestui que trust,* allowed defendant in an action
    on a bond given to plaintiff as trustee, 7.
  not allowed on an unstamped bill or note, 55, note.
  holder of a bill indebted to a bankrupt, party to the bill, may set his
    debt against amount of it, 130. 141.—(See "*Bankruptcy.*")
  otherwise if he transfer it, and is afterwards obliged to take it up,
    130. 141.—(See "*Bankruptcy.*")
  when must be specially pleaded, 373. 5.
  to establish a, against assignees of bankruptcy, evidence of posses-
    sion two months before a secret act of bankruptcy, is sufficient,
    398.—(See " *Evidence.*")
  but if the act were not secret, evidence of possession before the act
    was committed must be given, 398.—(See " *Bankruptcy.*")
  set-off and mutual credit in bankruptcy, 473 to 480.—(See "*Bank-
    ruptcy.*")

SETTING ASIDE PROCEEDINGS,
  when they will not be set aside for stating only the initials of the
    defendant's Christian name, 350.

SHERIFF,
  a contract made in consideration of ease and favour, void, 80.
  may be relieved on payment of costs of one action, on attachment
    against him, for not bringing in the body, 369,

STAMPS,
    1. *Statutes relating to.*
        formerly no stamp was necessary on a bill of exchange, 52.
        but now duty imposed on them by 22 Geo. 3. c. 33.—52.
        regulating statute now is 55 Geo. 3. c. 184.—52.—(See Statute,
           Appendix, 538, &c.)
    On *Inland* bills.
        amount of, depends on the sum and the time it has to run, 52,
           (See Scale, Appendix, 547 to 549.)
    On *Foreign* bills.
        drawn out of England, not chargeable, 52.
        drawn in, and payable out of Great Britain, and not in a set, the
           same stamp as an inland bill, 52. 542.
        if drawn here in sets, the amount raises according to their value,
           52.—(See Scale Appendix, 549.)
    Exemptions from the duties on bills.
        bank of England, 52.—Appendix, 550.
        certain bills drawn by certain persons in public service, 53.
           550.
        drafts for payment of money on demand, drawn on a banker
           within ten miles of the place where draft is drawn, 53. 550.
    On *Promissory notes.*
        same as inland bills, if not re-issuable, 53.—(See Scale, Appen-
           dix, 551 to 554.)
        amount of, when to be re-issued after payment, 53.—(See Scale,
           Appendix, 551.)   [552.
        amount of, on notes payable by instalments, 53.—Appendix,
        amount of, on instruments resembling the form of a note, for
           less than £20., 53.—Appendix, 553.
    Exemptions from duty on promissory notes.
        bank of England, 53.—Appendix, 553.
        notes payable on a contingency for more that £20, 53.—Appen-
           dix, 553.
        penalty £50, in one case £100, 52, 3.
           how incurred, 53.
    Decisions on the Stamp Acts, 54 to 58.
        stamp only necessary on bills drawn in Great Britain, 54.
        drawn in blank in Ireland, filled up in England, not necessary,
        same when a like bill was drawn in Jamaica, 54.   '[54.
        drawn in England, but dated at a place abroad, must have a
           stamp, 54.
        a bill for £50, with all legal interest, what stamp necessary, 54.
        a bill payable at sight is not a bill payable on demand, so as to
           avoid the duty, 55.
        a check drawn on a person not a banker, must have a stamp, 55.
        bills or notes cannot have a stamp affixed after they are drawn,
           55, 6.
        but if it is, the instrument is available, 55, 6.
        having a wrong stamp cannot be received in evidence, 56, 7.
        a larger stamp valid, provided it be of the proper denomination,
           57.—Appendix, 538.
        when bill paid by a drawer, he may indorse it over to another
           without a fresh stamp, 57.
        a bill, &c. drawn in any part of the king's dominions, where a
           stamp is imposed on bill, as in Jamaica, and not having such
           stamp, is void, 57.

CHITTY ON BILLS.   4 N

STAMPS—*(continued.)*
   Decisions on the Stamp Acts—(continued.)
      otherwise when drawn in a foreign *independent* state, 57.
      when a bill has a wrong stamp, how far neglect to present
        acceptance or payment discharges drawer and indorser,
        197.—(See "*Notice of Non-Acceptance*," "*Laches.*")
      payment of money into court upon a whole declaration, prec
        defendant from objecting to the stamp on a bill or note, 5s.
      a bill or note not having a stamp, is not allowed in evidence
        set-off, 55.
      a fresh stamp not necessary, if words of transfer being omir
        by mistake are afterwards inserted, 66.
      bills when due, paid by acceptor, cannot be re-issued without
        new stamp, 130.
      exception in favour of notes of hand under £100, and par
        on demand, 130.—Appendix, 551, 2.
      a check, when necessary to have the stamp of a receipt, 28.
      what receipt need not have a stamp, 304, note.
      in what cases a check is exempted from stamp duties, 322.
      when defendant objects to insufficiency of stamp, proof b
        printed copy of stamp act not sufficient, 411.—(See "*E*
        dence.")
      may not inspect bill or note to ascertain, 368.
  3. *On protests.*
      Stamps on protests for non-acceptance, what, 217.—Appendi
         for non-payment, 311.—Appendix, 554.

STATUTE OF LIMITATIONS.—(See "*Limitations, Statute of.*")

STATUTES.
  5 Richard 2, st. 1, 2, 11.
  23 Henry 6, ch. 9, relates to ease and favour to sheriff, 80.
  32 Henry 8, ch. 9, disallowing the assignment of choses in actio
  21 ———, ch. 18, relating to clergymen, traders, and farmers,
  5 Edward 6, ch. 16, relates to the sale of offices, 79.
  13 Elizabeth, ch. 7,   to bankrupts, 430, 1.
  31 ———, ch. 6,   to simony, 79.
  1 James 1, ch. 15, s. 14,   to bankrupts, 120. 282. 170.
  3 ———, ch. 8,   to bail in error, 427.
  21 ———, ch. 19. s. 2,   to bankrupts, 431.
  16 Charles 2, ch. 7, avoids all securities for money lost at play, 78.
  29 ———, ch. 3, s. 4, statute against frauds, 3.
  5 William and Mary, ch. 22, relates to bank of England, 14.
  5 ———, ch. 21, exempt bank bills from stamps, 52.
  5 ———, ch. 20, relates to the bank and bank notes, 332.
  8 & 9 ———, ch. 20,   to the bank and bank notes, 332.
  9 & 10 ———, ch. 17, places inland bills on same footing as
    foreign, 12. 67. 151. 6.—Appendix, 525.
  1 Anne, stat. 2, ch. 22, relates to alteration of bills, &c. 105.
  3 & 4 Anne, stat. 2, ch. 9, confirms 9 & 10 William 3, ch. 17.—
    12. 67. 97. 152. 229.—Appendix, 525.
  6 Anne, stat. 2, ch. 12, restrains bills drawn by a corporation, 15.
  7 ———, stat. 2. ch. 25, makes 3 & 4 Anne, c. 9, perpetual, 326. 525.
  8 ———, stat. 2, ch. 9, relates to apprentices, 80.

STATUTES—(*continued.*)

STAYING PROCEEDINGS,

when one action has been brought on a bill, and the bill afterwards
transferred to a third, who commences another, the court wi̎
order the proceedings to be stayed, 343.

on payment of debt and costs, defendant may obtain a rule to stay
proceedings, 368.

when this may be done by summons, 368.

but where an indorsement was made to pay interest for a certain
time, and to give up note, the court of C. P. refused to stay on
payment of it and costs, 368.

if holder bring several actions against acceptor, drawer, and indorser, the court will stay proceedings against drawer or indorser, on payment of the debt and costs of that particular
action, 368.

an attachment against sheriff for not bringing in the body, set aside
on payment of costs of one action only, 369.

but action against acceptor only stayed on payment of debt and
costs of all the actions, 369.

what the best course to pursue in this case, 369.

in an action on a bill court will stay them sometimes till creditor has
proved his debt under a bankrupt's commission, 451.

STEALING

a bank note felony, 333.

STOCK JOBBING,

a transaction in is illegal, 79.

a bill given in respect of such transaction is void in the hands of a
person who got it after it was due, or with notice of it, 79.

under what circumstances proof under bankruptcy was restrained
on promissory notes given for such transactions in, 79.

STOLEN BILL.—(See "*Loss.*")

STOPPING PAYMENT.—(See "*Bankruptcy.*")

stopping payment upon a subsequent transfer of a bill invalid, 120.
                                payment, invalid, 284.

TIME.—(See "*Computation*," "*Reasonable Time*," "*Presentment for Acceptance*," "*Presentment for Payment*.")
   how computed, in case of bills, 93. 262 to 278.
   of payment ought to be stated on the bill, 60, 1, 2.
   of transfer or indorsement, when to be made, 124 to 131.
   of presentment for acceptance, 159 to 163.
   allowed for acceptance, 167.
   of presentment for payment, 262 to 278.
   for making protest, 215 to 219. 213.
   when to give notice of non-acceptance, 219 to 225. 167.
   when to give notice of non-payment, 313 to 319.
   giving time for acceptance or payment, consequences of, 290, &c.
   conditional agreement to give time does not discharge drawer or in-
     dorser, 297.

TRADE,
   any contract made in general restraint of, bad, 74.
   otherwise if such contract is qualified, 74.
   in opposition to the laws of a chartered company illegal, 79.

TRANSFER.—(See "*Indorsement*," "*Assignment*.")
   by indorsement.—(See "*Indorsement*.")
   by delivery.—(See "*Indorsement*," "*Assignment*.")

TROVER,
   cannot be maintained for bills against indorsee of the person to
     whom they had been pledged, 113.
   will lie for bills improperly indorsed over, 129.
   a person discounting a bill which he knows has been lost by the real
     owner, is liable to an action of, 130, 1.
   will lie against a banker for discounting a bill after notice of its
     having been lost, 149.
   will lie for wrongfully withholding bills, &c. 152.
   in trover, for bank notes, what evidence has been deemed sufficient
     to establish right of property, 308. 33.
   an action of, will not lie against a *bona fide* holder by true owner,
     of bank notes lost, 333.
   in order to hold to bail in trover for a bill, affidavit should state that
     such bill is unpaid, and value of it, 350.
   on trial of an action in trover for a note, no notice to produce same
     necessary, 379.—(See "*Evidence*," "*Notice*.")
   for bills, interest ceases after demand and refusal to surrender, 423.

TRUSTEE,
   of bills, payable to one for the use of another, by whom to be
     indorsed, 123.
   to whom payment should be made, 280.

USANCE,
   definition of the term, 266.
   foreign bills in general payable at usances, 266.
   varies according to custom of different countries, from fourteen days
     to three months after date of bill, 266.
   a double, treble, or half a usance, what they are, 266.
   when a month is divided it it always fifteen days, 266.
   the different usances between different places, 267.

USURY—*(continued.)*

an acceptor of a bill is not guilty of, for taking more than five *per cent.* on discount of it, 88.

a broker is not guilty for taking 10 *per cent.* for getting a bill discounted, 89.

in an action for, on a check, forbearance should be stated from time it was given, 324.

in a count for, variance in name, when fatal, 353.—(See "*Misnomer.*")

how it should be proved as a defence, in an action on a bill, 411, 2.—(See "*Evidence.*")

letters from a person, whilst he holds a bill, are evidence against subsequent holder, 411.

VALUE RECEIVED,

words in a bill, when they import value received by drawer, of payee, 67.

when means value received by drawee, 68.

what and how may be stated in a bill or note, 49, 50.

for various instances, 49, 50.

in France, must be expressed in a bill, otherwise in England, 67.

these words need not be stated in a bill, 67.

when an inland bill or note should contain these words, 67.   [67.

a bill or note having these words, who may sustain an action of debt, to aid a variance these words may be inserted at trial, 67.

the usual interpretation of these words, 67, 8.

need not be stated in the declaration, 67, note.

particular statement of the value will not render bill contingent, 49.

unless in an inland bill, cannot be protested for non-acceptance, 218.

    or for non-payment, 311.

statement in declaration of whom value received, 68. 356.

declaration for value "received" in leather, instead of value "delivered," &c. is no variance, 356.

bill or note must express to be for value received, in order to sustain the action of debt, 427.

VARIANCE.—(See "*Declaration.*")

in statement of words "value received," 68.

in stating a material part of a bill or note in a declaration, fatal, 352, though it be stated under a videlicet, 352.—(See "*Videlicet.*")

what is, and what is not, a variance in respect to names, 353.—(See "*Misnomer.*")

in respect to real name of indorser, from that which appears in the declaration and bill, immaterial, 353.

no variance to omit the name of an infant acceptor, 353.

no variance for a declaration to state that bill was accepted by three persons, though proved to have been so by a fourth, but who was dead, 354.

no variance to describe a joint and several note as made by one person only, 354.

when a mis-recital of the date of a bill or note would be a variance, and when not, 354.

mis-statement of day in note payable by instalments, fatal, 354.

no variance to state in a declaration that note was made in London, when, in fact, it bears date at Paris, 355.

and it is the same in regard to inland bills, 355.

VARIANCE—(*continued.*)
omission of word "sterling" immaterial, 356.
no variance to state in the declaration " value received in leather,"
  if bill run, " value delivered in leather," 356.
if a note promise never to pay, no variance to leave out the word
  " never," 357.
no variance to state acceptance different from day on which it was
  in fact made, 358.
it is a fatal variance to omit a statement in a declaration on a bill of
  a conditional engagement, though it be performed, 358.
no variance to state in pleading that bill was payable to plaintiff if
  it was payable to his order, 359. 356.
if bill payable to a married woman, and indorsed by her husband,
  no variance to state it in pleading as payable to him, 359.
it is no variance to state in declaration that indorsement was made
  before due, and evidence show it have been after due, and *vice
  versa*, 360.
it is said the same rule prevails in regard to an acceptance, but it
  seems to be doubtful, 358.
between evidence adduced, and description of bill or note, fatal, 377.
a small variance between declaration and evidence in respect to indorser's name, immaterial, 393.

VENDOR
of an estate does not waive his lien on it by taking a bill or note,
  and receiving its amount by discount, 96.
of goods sold on a credit, if he draw a bill on vendee for amount
  of them, payable before credit has expired, he is not entitled to
  notice of dishonour, 208.
of goods entitled to interest from time bill would have been due, if
  at time of the sale vendee agreed to pay by a bill, 421.—(See " Interest.")
interest is then recoverable on the count for goods sold, 421.

VENUE,
in an action on a bill or note, may be laid in any county, 351.
court will not change it on affidavit of defendant that it was made in
  another, 351.
in an action on a note *bona fide* brought, plaintiff may retain the venue though it be for other causes, 351.
but it will not suffice to retain the venue to introduce a count on a
  non-existing note, 351.
but the court will sometimes on very special circumstances change
  the venue, 351.
what is a special circumstance to induce court to change venue, 351.
in actions on foreign bills it must be so, 355.

VERBAL
acceptance.—(See " *Acceptance.*")
release, the operation of it, 189.—(See " *Release.*")

VERDICT,
if a prior party to a bill sue a subsequent one, and get a verdict,
  judgment will be arrested, 354.
omission of averment of notice of dishonour, fatal even after verdict, 362.

CHITTY ON BILLS.   40

VERDICT—(*continued.*)

verdict to be obtained if it does not necessarily affect the interest of a witness, he is competent, 413.—(See " *Witness.*")

otherwise if it does, 413. 5.—(See " *Witness.*")

if plaintiff take a verdict for more than due, court will make him correct same, and pay costs, or grant a new trial, 420.

VIDELICET,

a variance in stating a bill or note in a declaration is fatal, though it be stated under a videlicet, 352.

when the date of a bill in a declaration is laid under a videlicet, yet a mis-recital would be fatal, 354.

usual to state place where bill drawn or venue under a videlicet, 355.

question whether in actions on foreign bills it can be done so, 355.

if a bill is payable at usances, the length of them must be averred, with a videlicet, 356.

WAGER,

if repugnant to principles of general policy, illegal, 75.

on the event of a war, illegal, 75.

———————— of an election, illegal, 75.

———— produce of a particular branch of the revenue, illegal, 75.

———— event of a game of cricket, a horse-race and foot-race against time, illegal, 75.

———— sex of a third person without his concurrence, 75.

how far legal at common law, 76.

WAIVER.—(See " *Laches,*" " *Neglect,*" " *Release.*")

In general.

of the liability, or obligation

of a drawer, 106.

of an indorser, 146.

of an acceptance, 188 to 193.

of a conditional or qualified acceptance, 180.

of the right to insist on holder's laches   [240.

in omitting to give due notice of non-acceptance, 255 to

in omitting a due presentment for payment or notice of non-payment, 248. 320.

to insist on discharge by indulgence to acceptor, 294.

to whose use the waiver will enure, 237, note.

Particular points.

taking a promissory note in payment for an estate, is not a waiver of vendor's lien, 96.

of an acceptance, what has been deemed such, 183.   [92, 3.

bill payable to a fictitious payee, is a waiver of indorsement,

of an acceptance is a question for the jury, 189.

any act expressive of an intention to relinquish a right of action is a waiver, 189.

but this appears questionable, 189.

to discharge acceptor must be express, and founded on consideration, 190.

what amounts to a, of acceptance, depends on the circumstances of the case, 191.

instances and examples of what have been deemed as a, 191.

holder of a bill taking part of the money due on it, and enlarging time for payment of residue, is not a waiver, 191.

WITNESS SUBSCRIBING.—(See *"Evidence," "Witness."*)

when he must be subpœnaed, 379.

when he must be produced to prove the hand-writing of the maker of a note, 379.

when other evidence admissible to prove the subscription, 379.

a person seeing another sign an instrument, but does not then attest it, cannot put his name to it afterwards, and prove same, 379.

if dead, proof of his hand-writing, and the defendant's presence when note prepared, is sufficient, without proof of defendant's hand-writing, 379.

the same where he had since become insane, 379.

the most prudent course in these cases, 379.

if cannot prove the making of the note, it may be proved by other means, 380, note, and see 2 Campb. 646.

indorsement attested by a, must be proved by him, 389, 390.

to a protest, if any, must be subpœnaed, 405.

WRIT,

a party may be arrested twice on same writ, if on first arrest he give a draft in payment, which is afterwards dishonoured, 231.

issued after tender made by drawer and indorser or acceptor, how far invalidates such tender, 232.

WRIT OF INQUIRY.—(See *"Inquiry, Writ of."*)

THE END.

NEW LAW PUBLICATIONS.

BY MR. CHITTY.

A PRACTICAL TREATISE on the CRIMINAL LAW, with a copious Collection of Precedents of Indictments, Informations, Presentments, and every Description of Practical Forms, in 4 vols. royal 8vo.

A TREATISE on PLEADING, Third Edition, with an extensive Collection of Precedents, in 3 vols. royal 8vo.

A TREATISE ON THE GAME LAWS and on FISHERIES, with Forms of Proceedings before Magistrates, Grants, Conveyances, Appointments, Reservations, &c. &c., in 3 vols. royal 8vo.

NEW ARRANGEMENT OF COKE-LITTLETON.—In Three Volumes, Royal Octavo.—A New and Systematic Arrangement of Lord Coke's First Institute of the Laws of England, on the Plan of Sir Matthew Hale's Analysis, with the Annotations of Mr. Hargrave, Lord Chief Justice Hale, and Lord Chancellor Nottingham; and a New Series of Notes and References, to the present Time; including Tables of Parallel Reference, Analytical Tables of Contents, and a very extensive Index. By J. H. THOMAS, Esq.

WS - #0023 - 191124 - C0 - 229/152/36 [38] - CB - 9780331189377 - Gloss Lamination